First Canadian Edition

Health Assessment and Physical Examination

First Canadian Edition

Health Assessment
— and —
Physical Examination

Mary Ellen Zator Estes

RN, MSN, FNP, APRN-BC, NP-C
Family Nurse Practitioner in Internal Medicine
Fairfax, Virginia
and
Clinical Faculty Nurse Practitioner Track
School of Nursing
Ball State University
Muncie, Indiana

Madeleine Buck

RN, B.Sc.(N), M.Sc. (A)
School of Nursing
McGill University
and
Clinical Associate
McGill University Health Centre
Montreal, Quebec, Canada

THOMSON
NELSON

Australia   Canada   Mexico   Singapore   Spain   United Kingdom   United States

THOMSON

NELSON

Health Assessment and Physical Examination, First Canadian Edition

by Mary Ellen Zator Estes and Madeleine Buck

Associate Vice President, Editorial Director:
Evelyn Veitch

Publisher:
Veronica Visentin

Senior Acquisitions Editor:
Kevin Smulan

Marketing Manager:
William de Villiers

Senior Developmental Editor:
Rebecca Ryoji

Photo Researcher:
Melody Tolson

Permissions Coordinator:
Melody Tolson

Senior Content Production Manager:
Tammy Scherer

Production Service:
International Typesetting and Composition

Copy Editor:
Kathy van Denderen and Karen Rolfe

Proofreader:
Amy Rodriguez

Indexer:
Edwin Durbin

Senior Manufacturing Coordinator:
Charmaine LeeWah

Design Director:
Ken Phipps

Interior Design Modifications:
Dianna Little

Cover Design:
Montage Studio

Cover and Part/Chapter Openers Image:
Antony Nagelmann/Getty Images (nurse)
Lawrence Lawry/Photodisc (stethoscope)

Compositor:
International Typesetting and Composition

Printer:
Quebecor World

Library and Archives Canada Cataloguing-in-Publication Data

Main entry under title:

Estes, Mary Ellen Zator
  Health assessment and physical examination/Mary Ellen Zator Estes, Madeleine Buck.—1st Canadian ed.

Includes bibliographical references and index.
ISBN 978-0-17-610284-5

1. Nursing assessment—Textbooks.
2. Physical diagnosis—Textbooks.
I. Buck, Madeleine,1957- II. Title.

RT48.E88 2007   616.07′5
C2007-900106-8

NOTICE TO THE READER

Publisher does not warrant or guarantee any of the products described herein or perform any independent analysis in connection with any of the product information contained herein. Publisher does not assume, and expressly disclaims, any obligation to obtain and include information other than that provided to it by the manufacturer.

The reader is expressly warned to consider and adopt all safety precautions that might be indicated by the activities described herein and to avoid all potential hazards. By following the instructions contained herein, the reader willingly assumes all risks in connection with such instructions.

The publisher makes no representations or warranties of any kind, including but not limited to, the warranties of fitness for particular purpose or merchantability, nor are any such representations implied with respect to the material set forth herein, and the publisher takes no responsibility with respect to such material. The publisher shall not be liable for any special, consequential, or exemplary damages resulting, in whole or part, from the reader's use of, or reliance upon, this material.

*Dedicated to Betty Liduke, Mary Musoma, Tasilo Mdamu, and
other members of the Nursing team of the Highlands Hope
Consortium for their commitment, courage, creativity, and
perseverance in dealing with the HIV pandemic in Tanzania.*

Madeleine M. Buck

Brief Contents

Contents

Preface

*H*ealth assessment forms the foundation of all nursing care. Assessment is an ongoing process that evaluates the whole person as a physical, psychosocial, and functional being, whether the patient is young or old, well or ill. *Health Assessment and Physical Examination*, First Canadian Edition, provides a well-illustrated approach to the process of holistic assessment, including physical assessment skills, clinical examination techniques, and patient teaching guidelines.

Beginning nurses will welcome the text's clear and systematic presentation as they learn the skills of health assessment. The links between pathophysiology and abnormal findings help to ensure that the health assessment knowledge base is accurate and integrated. Practising nurses and nurse practitioner students will find the book helpful as they perform advanced assessment techniques and update their knowledge of epidemiological trends, emerging assessment issues, and guidelines. From this first Canadian health and physical assessment text of its kind, readers will gain knowledge and skills for comprehensive health assessment in the current Canadian health care delivery system as well as for emerging roles in primary health care and advanced practice.

CONCEPTUAL APPROACH

This text is designed to help readers learn to assess a patient's physical, psychological, social, and spiritual dimensions of health as a foundation of nursing care. The skills of interviewing, documentation, inspection, percussion, palpation, and auscultation are refined to help students make accurate and relevant clinical judgments and promote healthy patient outcomes.

The concept for *Health Assessment and Physical Examination*, First Canadian Edition, arose from a need for up-to-date, evidence-based, comprehensive, and well-organized assessment information that could be easily read and assimilated. The goals that form the foundation of this text are empowering readers as educated clinicians and decision makers, developing their skills of analysis and critical thinking, and encouraging excellent clinical and nursing skills.

Health Assessment and Physical Examination, First Canadian Edition, embraces a dual focus, based on nursing as an art and a science. Strong emphasis on science encompasses all the technical aspects of anatomy, physiology, and assessment, while highlighting clinically relevant information. Emphasis on the art of nursing is displayed through themes of assessment of the whole person: cultural, spiritual, familial, and environmental considerations; patient dignity; and health promotion. Such an approach encourages nurses to be systematic, relevant, and thorough in their assessments while being sensitive and responsive to their patients' unique situations.

Health Assessment and Physical Examination, First Canadian Edition, offers a user-friendly approach that delivers a wealth of information. The consistent, easy-to-follow format with recurring pedagogical features is based on two frameworks:

1. The **IPPA** method of examination (**I**nspection, **P**alpation, **P**ercussion, **A**uscultation) is consistently applied to body systems for a complete, detailed physical assessment.
2. The **ENAP** format (**E**xamination, **N**ormal Findings, **A**bnormal Findings, **P**athophysiology) is followed for every IPPA technique, providing a useful and valuable collection of information. Pathophysiology is included for each abnormal finding, acknowledging that nurses' clinical decisions need to be based on scientific rationale.

Readers of *Health Assessment and Physical Examination*, First Canadian edition, will need an understanding of anatomy and physiology, as well as a familiarity with basic nursing skills and the nursing process.

ORGANIZATION

Health Assessment and Physical Examination, First Canadian Edition, consists of 25 chapters organized into 5 units. **Unit 1, Laying the Foundation,** provides the basis for the entire assessment process by guiding the reader through the nursing process, the critical thinking process, the patient interview, and the health history. Specific review of legal and ethical issues, and documentation processes, as well as tips on professionalism, approaching patients, and discussing sensitive topics, help the reader understand the many important aspects of the nurse–patient partnership in the assessment process.

Unit 2, Special Assessments, highlights developmental, cultural, spiritual, and nutritional areas of assessment, emphasizing the holistic nature of the assessment process. These chapters are key in encouraging the reader to be aware of the scope of factors that influence the patient's global health situation.

Unit 3, Physical Assessment, opens with a description of fundamental assessment techniques, including measuring vital signs and assessing pain, and then details assessment procedures and findings for specific body systems. The format used for all applicable physical assessment chapters in this unit includes:

1. Anatomy and physiology
2. Health history
3. Equipment
4. Physical assessment
   a. Inspection
   b. Palpation
   c. Percussion
   d. Auscultation
5. Gerontological variations
6. Case study

The examination techniques presented are related primarily to adult patients. Gerontological considerations are included for each body system chapter, with a focus on identifying normal age related variations. Because assessment techniques and findings may differ in pregnant women and children, these populations are discussed in separate chapters in **Unit 4, Special Populations.** The chapter on the pregnant patient includes variations in examination techniques and special techniques used only on pregnant patients, as well as normal and abnormal findings related to pregnancy. The chapter on the pediatric patient presents physical differences in the examination and explains special techniques used only with children.

Unit 5, Putting It All Together, helps the reader assimilate and synthesize the wealth of information presented in the text in order to perform a thorough, accurate, and efficient health assessment. A comprehensive and complex case study helps make this unit a complete health assessment resource tool.

NEW TO THIS FIRST CANADIAN EDITION

- All chapters have been updated to reflect Canadian realities in health assessment and clinical care. Health and physical assessment approaches and evaluation procedures have been revised to reflect Canadian standards and guidelines, including provincial and territorial variations.

- Nursing processes that Canadian nurses espouse, including the collaborative partnership, evidence-based practice and decision making, holistic assessment and care, and professionalism, have been integrated.

- Patient profiles (case studies) that illustrate a range of Canadian health issues humanize the material and help students apply critical-thinking concepts that they have learned in the chapters.

- Best practice guidelines, systematic reviews, and evidence-based approaches to a range of health and physical assessment areas have been incorporated throughout the book, including the recommendations of the Canadian Task Force on Preventive Care.

- Canadian epidemiological trends in a range of health and illness issues have been incorporated to help nurses identify and anticipate key health issues in the Canadian population.

- Terminology has been refined to reflect the Canadian context of nurses. For example, "health issue or concern" replaces "chief complaint" as the reason for a nursing encounter; this change reflects the broader range of reasons Canadians may seek nursing assessment. The assessment of "stress" has been expanded from previous editions to include "stress and coping" processes and outcomes—an approach that many Canadian nurses value and integrate into their practice. Sexually transmitted illness (STI) replaces sexually transmitted disease (STD) to reflect Canadian views that "STD" carries a social stigma and because "infection" can include symptomatic and asymptomatic conditions for which Canadians seek care.

- All biochemistry and mathematical units are converted to System International (SI) values.

- In addition to the assessment of religion in the health history identified in previous editions, spirituality is now added as a part of the health assessment. This addition was made because recent findings indicate that Canadians describe themselves as less "religious" yet more "spiritual."

- Assessment in Brief cards show the steps for performing each type of physical examination. These are printed on perforated, heavy paper stock so that readers can use them as a resource while studying or in clinical situations.

- Life 360° boxes present skills that relate to the "art" of nursing, such as making all patients feel comfortable during an examination or dealing with sensitive issues such as partner abuse.

- Canadian web resources and bibliographic materials are added to each chapter to provide readers with a range of professional and patient resources.

- The Instructor's Manual is updated to include case study analyses that address strengths, deficits, and risks in the patient health history analysis. This approach complements the North American Nursing Diagnosis Association (NANDA) classification system "diagnostic" approach.

Selected chapter-specific enhancements are also high-lighted in this new edition:

- **Chapter 1**, *Critical Thinking and the Nursing Process*, explains the concept of evidence-based practice, the underlying principles of the scientific or nursing process, and the elements of critical thinking. The North American Nursing Diagnosis Association (NANDA) classi-fication system remains from previous editions with a dis-cussion of alternate terminology such as "nursing analysis" or "nursing summary" used by Canadian institu-tions that do not embrace a NANDA classification system.
- **Chapter 2**, *The Patient Interview*, now includes the Canadian Nurses Association principles of ethical practice and confidentiality and position statement on violence. The Canadian context for scope of practice and legal expectations are also incorporated, includ-ing the Principles for the Privacy Protection of Personal Health Information. The collaborative part-nership between nurse and patient is added to reflect the nature of the nurse–patient relationship that Canadian nurses embrace.
- **Chapter 3**, *The Complete Health History Including Documentation*, now includes a discussion of the 12 deter-minants of health that form the basis of many health assessment and health promotion programs in Canada. The following content matter was added or revised to reflect Canadian issues or standards of practice: defini-tions related to sexuality issues and Public Health Agency of Canada's STI Risk Assessment Questionnaire; over-the-counter and natural health products legislation; blood transfusion services by Hema-Quebec and the Canadian Blood Services Agency; the alcohol and drug abuse screening tool CAGEAID, which reflects Canadian Medical Association guidelines; trends in tobacco use across the country and smoke cessation resources; Canadian Nurses Association position state-ment on reducing the use of tobacco products and the "Ask, Advise, Assist, Arrange" intervention; domestic vio-lence and spousal abuse incidence information, resources, CNA position statement, RNAO Best Practice Guideline, and sample screening tool; Canadian immu-nization standards and emerging communicable dis-eases in Canada; excerpts from Health Canada module on drug abuse terminology for use when assessing illicit drug history; Canadian Centre for Occupational Health and Safety list of workplace hazards; Canada Fitness Guide and patterns of sedentary activity; and health pro-motion activities to deal with peer pressure or bullying.
- **Chapter 4**, *Developmental Assessment*, addresses the role of changing Canadian demographics and life expectancy in shaping the 'norms' and issues associ-ated with 'traditional' developmental expectations.
- **Chapter 5**, *Cultural Assessment*, presents updated details on the range of cultures in Canada. Concepts of cultural competence and cultural safety are elabo-rated to address emerging health care issues.
- **Chapter 6**, *Spiritual Assessment*, now has information on trends in religiosity versus spirituality in Canadians.

- **Chapter 7**, *Nutritional Assessment*, has been updated to include the recently released Eating Well with Canada's Food Guide and the most recent Canadian recommendations on Daily Required Intake (DRI), omega 3/6 fatty acids, trans fats, obesity in adults and children, and the DASH diet for hypertension. The Pan-Canadian Healthy Living Strategy and Health Canada Vitality programs are presented. The chapter also presents the Canadian Working Group on Hypercholesterolemia and Other Dyslipidemias recom-mendations for lipid laboratory values. All nutritional recommendations made by the Dieticians of Canada, Canadian Pediatrics Society Nutrition Committee, and Health Canada are provided. Use of body mass index (BMI) and waist circumference (WC) as indicators of health or risk are added to the assessment content.
- **Chapters 8 and 9**, *Physical Assessment Techniques*, and *General Survey, Vital Signs, and Pain*, have been updated to include Canadian standards for routine practices and transmission-based precautions. The Canadian Hypertension Screening recommendations, including the Canadian diagnostic algorithm, and an overview of risk factors, epidemiology, and prevention recommendations of the Canadian Hypertension Education Program have been added. The Canadian Pain Coalition Charter of Pain Patient's Rights and the Canadian Emergency Department Triage and Acuity Scale classification of central versus peripheral pain augment the section on pain assessment.
- **Chapter 10**, *Skin, Hair, Nails*, is expanded to include Canadian statistics throughout. The NPUAP classifica-tion system of pressure ulcers and the Braden scale for determining pressure ulcer risk have been added to reflect Canadian best practice guidelines. The Canadian Cancer Society SunSense recommendations and Canadian UV (ultraviolet) Index guidelines aug-ment the health promotion aspect of this chapter.
- **Chapter 11**, *Head, Neck, and Regional Lymphatics*, includes important Canadian statistics on migraines and thryoid cancer as well as Canadian screening recommendations.
- **Chapter 12**, *Eyes*, contains updated photos covering additional diseases of the eye and new photos of the funduscopic examination. Canadian epidemiology of eye pathology, the Canadian Diabetic Association Clinical Practice Guidelines and the Canadian Opthalmological Association updates on screening and eye care issues are provided to enhance the nurse's understanding of relevant assessment issues.
- **Chapter 13**, *Ears, Nose, Mouth, and Throat*, has multiple new photos and discusses hearing-loss risk factors, epistaxis, and oral cancer risk factors. Canadian stan-dards for hearing safety and trends in hearing risks of young Canadians have been added.
- **Chapter 14**, *Breasts and Regional Nodes*, has been updated to include Canadian epidemiology and screening recommendations. A debate overview on the issue of breast self-examination (BSE) is provided to help Canadian nurses keep current with differing

interpretations of systematic reviews on this practice. The bibliography is augmented to include popular books recommended by breast cancer survivor groups.

- **Chapter 15**, *Thorax and Lungs*, includes the Public Health Agency of Canada recommendations on personal protection and screening measures for SARS. The two-step PPD is added as the Canadian standard for tuberculosis screening. Canadian statistics on asthma, tuberculosis, and smoking as well as smoke-cessation initiatives/programs are identified to help Canadian nurses keep current.
- **Chapter 16**, *Heart and Peripheral Vasculature*, includes Canadian epidemiology, "Know the Nine" modifiable myocardial risk factors and Canadian guidelines for hormone replacement therapy.
- **Chapter 17**, *Abdomen*, includes Canadian epidemiology of hepatitis types and stomach cancer. A nursing alert about *H. Pylori* was added due to the clinical significance and recent task force on *H. Pylori* infections in Canadian hospitals.
- **Chapter 18**, *Musculoskeletal System*, has augmented discussion of fall risk assessment and Canadian scoliosis and osteoporosis screening guidelines.
- **Chapter 19**, *Mental Status and Neurological Techniques*, incorporates Canadian Heart and Stroke Foundation statistics, modifiable and non-modifiable risk factors, and recommended terminology (e.g., "brain attack"). Proverbs are "Canadianized" and a table of proverbs from other languages (e.g., Italian, Japanese, Chinese, French) is added (including a link to a website that gives more proverbs to fit cultural backgrounds) to help ensure "cultural accuracy" in this area of assessment. Canadian practice guidelines on screening for depression and delirium in older adults and the Alzheimer Society of Canada's 10 warning signs of Alzheimer's disease have been added. Suicide trends and risk factors reflect Canadian statistics. Because current estimates indicate that up to 40% of Canada's returning peacekeepers will experience some form of PTSD, details on this form of mental health problem have been augmented.

- **Chapter 20**, *Female Genitalia*, has extensive updates on ovarian, uterine, and cervical cancers including Canadian statistics, risk factors, and signs/symptoms of pathology. The Public Health Agency of Canada diagnostic features of vaginal discharge and Health Canada and the Society of Gynecologic Oncologists of Canada guidelines for cervical cancer screening have been added. A nursing alert on Female Genital Mutilation (FGM) is provided, given trends in immigration and refugee patterns from countries where FGM is practised. Canadian reporting guidelines and partner notification recommendations for control of STIs are provided.
- **Chapter 21**, *Male Genitalia*, now includes Canadian epidemiology and risk factors for testicular and bladder cancer, and new photos of sexually transmitted infections.
- **Chapter 22**, *Anus, Rectum, and Prostate*, now has Canadian trends in cancer related to these areas with respective recommendations for digital rectal examination, fecal occult blood testing, and prostate-specific antigen (PSA) testing.
- **Chapter 23**, *Pregnant Patient*, incorporates Canadian statistics and monitoring recommendations. Abuse in pregnancy is addressed. Canadian guidelines for folic acid supplementation, glucose testing, amniocentesis, chorionic villi sampling, ultrasound, and Rh(D) assessment have been added.
- **Chapter 24**, *Pediatric Patient*, provides 3rd and 97th percentile curves as per Canadian recommendations (replacing 5th and 95th percentile curves). Canadian recommendations for vision screening, temperature measurement, fluoride supplementation, age adjustment in prematurity, childhood immunization, sleep position, and bed sharing are provided. The Rourke Baby Record (from the Canadian Paediatric Society) Evidence Based Infant/Child Health Maintenance guide is provided.
- **Chapter 25**, *The Complete Health History and Physical Examination*, has been updated to include a comprehensive case study that illustrates a complete health history and physical examination.

SPECIAL FEATURES

Many successful features from the previous edition of *Health Assessment and Physical Examination* have been retained in this new edition. These features stimulate critical thinking and self-reflection, develop technical expertise, and encourage readers to synthesize and apply information presented in the text.

- **Reflective Thinking** boxes introduce ethical controversies and clinical situations readers are likely to encounter, stimulating critical thinking, effective decision making, and active problem solving. These

boxes also promote self-examination on particular issues so readers can understand the varying viewpoints they may encounter in patients and coworkers. These boxes encourage reflection on issues in a personal context, raise awareness of the diversity of opinions, and foster empowerment.

- **Life 360°** boxes help you examine your feelings and emotional behaviour about learning how to be comfortable with diverse types of patients, as well as learning how to make them comfortable.

continues

- **Nursing Checklists** offer an organizing framework for the assessment of each body system or for approaching a given task. Certain nursing checklists outline specific questions or points to consider when caring for patients with assistive devices.

- **Nursing Tips** help you to apply basic knowledge to real-life situations and offer hints and shortcuts useful to both new and experienced nurses.

- **Nursing Alerts** highlight significant epidemiological trends and risk factors, as well as serious or life-threatening signs or critical assessment findings that merit attention.

- The **ENAP** format (examination, normal findings, abnormal findings, pathophysiology) allows you to study the content that is specifically relevant to your own practice. The **IPPA** format (inspection, percussion, palpation, and auscultation) is applied consistently to each assessment skill.

- **Health Histories** outline all areas of assessment related to each body system. The standard format used throughout the text teaches the importance of consistency and organization when discussing topics with patients during the health history interview.

- **Case Studies** humanize the material and help readers apply critical thinking concepts. Case studies present realistic scenarios, offering readers an opportunity to apply the chapter material, thereby encouraging extrapolation and intuitive thinking. Case studies list normal and abnormal assessment findings in the context of a clinical scenario. Each case study includes a sample patient history, genogram, physical assessment findings, and laboratory data in documentation format, emphasizing the nurse's responsibilities for correct charting. The case studies are written in abbreviated format to simulate real clinical documentation and deliberately have different charting styles to reflect the wide variety of norms in actual clinical practice. Analyses of the case studies, including sample nursing care plans, are included in the *Instructor's Guide* on the Instructor's Resource CD-ROM.

PEDAGOGICAL FEATURES

Health Assessment and Physical Examination, First Canadian Edition, also includes many pedagogical features that promote learning and accessibility of information. This text guides the novice as well as advanced practice nurse in the art and science of conducting a comprehensive health history, health assessment, and physical examination.

- **Outstanding photographs and drawings** highlight assessment techniques and procedures, anatomy and physiology, and normal and abnormal findings. The photo program is expanded and updated, especially in the area of nose pathologies and sexually transmitted infections, providing better images of many diseases.
- **Competencies** open each chapter and introduce the main areas targeted for mastery in each chapter. They also provide a checkpoint for study and tie in to crucial assessment skills.
- **Nursing Checklists** at the end of chapters offer a conceptual framework for chapter review, highlighting main points. Other nursing checklists offer step-by-step approaches to certain problems or situations, and serve as excellent resources for quick review.
- **Review Questions** offer readers an opportunity to assess their understanding of the content and better define areas needing additional study. All chapters include self-quizzes on key information to test knowledge. Many chapters also include short scenarios with related questions.

- **Key Terms** are highlighted and defined in the text the first time they are used.
- **References and a bibliography** document the theoretical basis of each chapter and provide additional resources for continued study.
- **Web Resources** are provided at the end of each chapter to direct the reader to additional learning resources; the accompanying *Student Web site* provides further web-based resources.
- The **Appendices** provide specific resources for dealing with special populations.
- The **Glossary** at the end of the book defines all key terms used in the text and serves as a comprehensive resource for study and review.
- The **Index** facilitates access to material and includes special entries for tables and illustrations.
- A list of **Abbreviations and Symbols** inside the back text cover includes common abbreviations used in charting, along with their definitions, for quick reference.

EXTENSIVE TEACHING AND LEARNING PACKAGE

A complete supplements package was developed to achieve two goals:

1. To assist readers in learning the essential skills and information needed to secure a career in the nursing profession.

2. To assist instructors in planning and implementing their programs for the most efficient use of time and other resources.

Instructor's Resource CD-ROM

ISBN 0-17-644254-5

Free to all instructors who adopt *Health Assessment and Physical Examination*, First Canadian Edition, in their courses, this comprehensive resource includes the following:

Instructor's Guide

- **Key Terms** list provides the key terms for each chapter alphabetically with corresponding definitions.
- **Helpful Hints and Exercises** offer tips for laboratory exercises, clinical skill building, small group work, and classroom discussion.
- **Skills Checklists** outline physical assessment techniques to be evaluated for each body system, pregnant patient and pediatric techniques, and comprehensive head-to-toe assessment outlines.
- Nursing diagnosis (analysis) of case studies presented in the text with corresponding **Care Plans**. You can also download the Instructor's Manual from our password-protected instructor resource centre located at www.healthassessment.nelson.com

Computerized Test Bank

The computerized test bank, which has been completely rewritten for maximum clarity and accuracy, includes multiple-choice questions for each chapter and can be used to generate custom tests.

PowerPoint Presentations

A vital resource for instructors, PowerPoint presentations for each chapter parallel the content in the text, serving as a foundation from which instructors may customize their own presentations. You can also download the Power Point presentations from our password-protected instructor resource centre located at www.healthassessment.nelson.com

Image Library

The Image Library is a software tool that includes an organized digital library of approximately 600 illustrations and photographs from the text. Copy and save any of the images on the CD to facilitate classroom presentations. You can also easily paste images into a Microsoft PowerPoint presentation.

Student Web Site

The *Estes Student Web site* enables users of *Health Assessment and Physical Examination*, First Canadian Edition, to access a wealth of information designed to enhance the book. The Web site includes:

- Expanded glossary
- Additional web links to online resources
- Self-study chapter quizzes
- Pain assessment and management information
- Instructor resources such as additional discussion points.

To access the site for *Health Assessment and Physical Examination*, First Canadian Edition, go to www.healthassessment.nelson.com

ADDITIONAL RESOURCES

Delmar's Heart & Lung Sounds for Nurses CD-ROM

ISBN 0-7668-2416-0

Delmar's Anatomy & Physiology CD-ROM

ISBN 0-7668-2415-2

Delmar's Health Assessment CD-ROM

ISBN 0-7668-2413-6

Delmar's Manual of Laboratory and Diagnostic Tests

ISBN 0-7668-6235-6

Delmar's Guide to Laboratory and Diagnostic Tests Individual Web License

ISBN 1-4018-1167-1

Student Lab Manual

ISBN 1-4018-7208-5

Clinical Companion

ISBN 1-4018-7207-7

How to Use This Text

These pages offer suggestions for how you can
use the features of this text to gain competence
and confidence in your assessment and nursing skills

Posture

E   1. Stand in front of the patient.
   2. Instruct the patient to stand with the feet together.
   3. Observe the structural and spatial relationship of the head, torso, pelvis, and limbs. Assess for symmetry of the shoulders, scapulae, and iliac crests.
   4. Ask the patient to sit; observe posture.
N   In the standing position, the torso and head are upright. The head is midline and perpendicular to the horizontal line of the shoulders and pelvis. The shoulders and hips are level, with symmetry of the scapulae and iliac crests. The arms hang freely from the shoulders. The feet are aligned and the toes point forward. The extremities are proportional to the overall body size and shape, and the limbs are also symmetrical with each other. The knees face forward, with symmetry of the level of the knees. There is usually less than a 5 cm interval between the knees when the patient stands with the feet together, facing forward. When full growth is reached, the arm span is equal to the height. In the sitting position, both feet should be placed firmly on the floor surface, with toes pointing forward.
A   Forward slouching of the shoulders produces a false thoracic kyphosis.
P   These findings can be caused by poor posture habits.

Gait and Mobility

E   1. Instruct the patient to walk normally across the room.
   2. Ask the patient to walk on toes and then on the heels of the feet.
   3. Ask the patient to walk by placing one foot in front of the other, in a "heel-to-toe" fashion (tandem walking).
   4. Instruct the patient to walk forward, then backward.
   5. Ask the patient to side step to the left, then to the right.
   6. Instruct the patient to ambulate forward a few steps with the eyes closed.
   7. Observe the patient during transfer between the standing and sitting position.
N   Walking is started in one smooth, rhythmic fashion. The foot is lifted 2.5 to 5 cm off the floor and then propelled 30 to 45 cm forward in a straight path. As the heel strikes the floor, body weight is then shifted onto the ball of that foot. The heel of the foot is then lifted off the floor before the next step forward. The patient remains erect and balanced during all stages of gait. Step height and length are symmetrical for each foot. The arms swing freely at the side of the torso but in opposite direction to the movement of the legs. The lower limbs are able to bear full body weight during standing and walking. Prior to turning, the head and neck turn toward the intended direction, followed by the rest of the body. The patient should be able to transfer easily to various positions.
A   Indications of gait disturbance include hesitancy or multiple attempts to initiate walking, unsteadiness, staggering, grasping for external support, high stepping, foot scraping due to inability to raise the foot completely off the floor, persistent toe or heel walking, excessive pointing of the toes inward or outward, asymmetry of step height or length, limping, stooping during walking, wavering gait, shuffling gait, waddling gait, excessive swinging of the shoulders or pelvis, and slow or rapid step speed. Table 18-6 provides examples of abnormal gait patterns.

E Examination	**N** Normal Findings	**A** Abnormal Findings	**P** Pathophysiology

---

ENAP format: In order for the assessment process to become "instinctual" for you, we have highlighted each step of the ENAP process:

- **Examination** sequences show you the step-by-step process of performing an assessment.

- **Normal Findings**, highlighted in blue, describe what you will find in a normal assessment.

- **Abnormal Findings** outline the variations from normal you may see in pathological states.

- **Pathophysiology** explains the scientific rationale for abnormal conditions; many are illustrated.

- **ENAP** reminder boxes repeat on assessment pages for easy reference.

Reflective Thinking helps you develop sensitivity to ethical and moral issues and guides you to think critically in clinical situations and become an active problem solver. You may want to read each one and explore the issues *before* reading the chapter. Then as you read the chapter, evaluate your original thoughts. If you read the boxes as you go through the chapter, you may want to write down your thoughts, then go back and look at them later.

Reflective Thinking

Assessing Your Documentation

After completing the health history, reflect on the techniques you used to elicit the history. Did you rush the patient? Did you use too many open-ended or closed questions? Was your documentation concise? What could you have done better?

Life 360°

Assessing Home Safety

Examine the safety of your personal living quarters and the immediate outside environment. Next, re-examine your living quarters for safety as if you had an 85-year-old person living with you. Are there internal or external changes that would need to be made for the safety of the older person?

Life 360° boxes explore situations throughout the life span. Page through and read each one *before* reading the chapter. Then challenge yourself to evaluate your own opinions after reading all the chapter content.

Anatomy and Physiology: Understanding the function of the body systems is an important component of completing an accurate assessment. The information necessary for a complete and accurate assessment is highlighted, and detailed illustrations help you visualize anatomy in the context of an actual patient.

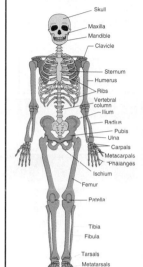

Appendicular skeleton (blue)
Axial skeleton (grey)

Figure 18-1 Adult Skeleton: Anterior View.

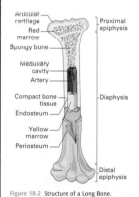

Figure 18-2 Structure of a Long Bone.

*T*he musculoskeletal system provides the ability to maintain and change body position in response to both internal and external stimuli. Muscle tone and bone strength allow an individual to maintain an upright and erect posture position. Muscle contraction and joint movement allow an individual to move toward positive stimuli and away from noxious stimuli. Changes in the musculoskeletal system will affect the individual's ability to complete activities of daily living, occupation, and recreation. The musculoskeletal system functions closely with the neurological system, such that a disturbance in the neurological system can grossly impact the musculoskeletal system.

ANATOMY AND PHYSIOLOGY

The musculoskeletal system consists of an intricate framework of bones, joints, skeletal muscles, and supportive connective tissue (cartilage, tendons, and ligaments). Although the primary purpose of the musculoskeletal system is to support body position and promote mobility, it also protects underlying soft organs and allows for mineral storage. In addition, it produces select blood components (platelets, red blood cells, and white blood cells). Only those aspects of the musculoskeletal system that are responsible for body position and mobility are discussed in this chapter.

Bones

The adult human skeleton comprises 206 bones (Figure 18-1). Bone is ossified connective tissue. The skeleton is divided into the central **axial skeleton** (facial bones, skull, auditory ossicles, hyoid bone, ribs, sternum, and vertebrae) and the peripheral **appendicular skeleton** (limbs, pelvis, scapula, and clavicle). A bone's size and shape are directly related to the mobility and weight-bearing function of that bone. In some cases, bone size and shape are also related to the protection of underlying internal organs and tissues (e.g., the ribs in relation to the lungs, heart, and thoracic aorta).

Shape and Structure

Bones have long, short, flat, rounded, and irregular shapes. The long bone is a shaft (**diaphysis**) with two large ends (**epiphyses**). The two epiphyses each articulate with another bone to form a joint. A 1 to 4 cm layer of cartilage covers each epiphysis in order to minimize stress and friction on the bone ends during movement and weight bearing. The thickness of the cartilage layer varies, depending on the amount of stress placed on that joint. The interior of the diaphysis is the **medullary cavity**, which contains the bone marrow (Figure 18-2).

Short bones are found in the hands (carpals) and feet (tarsals). Flat bones, such as the skull and parts of the pelvic girdle, are associated with the protection of nearby soft body parts. Rounded, or sesamoid, bones are often encased in the fascia or in a tendon near a joint, such as is the patella. Irregular bones include the mandible, vertebrae, and the auditory ossicles of the inner ear.

Muscles

There are over 600 muscles in the human body, and they can be characterized as one of three types. Cardiac and smooth muscles are involuntary, meaning that the individual has no conscious control over the initiation and termination

Nursing Tip

Weakness Rating Scale

A 0–10/10 scale can be used to obtain the patient's subjective rating of the intensity of the weakness. When a 0–10/10 scale is being utilized, 0 represents complete absence of weakness and 10 represents weakness necessitating complete bed rest.

Nursing Tips: The wide variety of helpful hints, tips, and strategies presented here will help you as you work toward professional advancement. Study, share, and discuss them with your colleagues.

Nursing Checklists outline important points for you to consider for an assessment. Checklists also serve as a reference guide to reviewing procedural steps and summarizing the assessment process.

◄ NURSING CHECKLIST ►

General Approach to Musculoskeletal Assessment

1. Assist the patient to a comfortable position.
2. Offer pillows or folded blankets to support a painful body part.
3. If necessary because of a painful body part or limited mobility, provide the patient assistance in disrobing. Allow the patient extra time to remove clothing.
4. To maximize patient comfort during the physical assessment, maintain a warm temperature in the exam room.
5. Be clear in your instructions to the patient if you are asking the patient to perform a certain body movement or to assume a certain position. Demonstrate the desired movement if necessary.
6. Notify the patient before touching or manipulating a painful body part.
7. Inspection, palpation, range of motion, and muscle testing are performed on the major skeletal muscles and joints of the body in a cephalocaudal, proximal-to-distal manner. Always compare paired muscles and joints.

continues

HEALTH HISTORY

The musculoskeletal health history provides insight into the link between a patient's life and lifestyle and musculoskeletal information and pathology.

PATIENT PROFILE *Diseases that are age-, gender-, and race-specific for the musculoskeletal system are listed.*

Age Osteosarcoma (10–20 and 50–60)
Ankylosing spondylitis (20–40)
Bursitis (20–40)
Rheumatoid arthritis (onset 20–40 unless juvenile form of the disease)
Systemic lupus erythematosus (SLE) (25–35)
Low back pain (30–50)
Gout (onset over 30, postmenopausal female)
Type I osteoporosis (menopausal female)
Carpal tunnel syndrome (pregnant or menopausal female)
Degenerative joint disease or osteoarthritis (onset after 55 in the female
   and before 45 in the male)
Type II osteoporosis (onset 50–70)
Multiple myeloma (50–70)
Paget's disease (50–70)

Gender

Female Type I osteoporosis, rheumatoid arthritis, scoliosis, carpal tunnel syndrome,
SLE, postmenopausal gout, polymyalgia rheumatica, scleroderma,
myasthenia gravis, multiple sclerosis (M...

Male Type II osteoporosis, ankylosing spondyliti...
syndrome, Dupuytren's contracture, ps...
dystrophy (MD), amyotrophic lateral sc...

Ethnicity

Caucasian Rheumatoid arthritis, primary osteoarthriti...
osteoporosis, Paget's disease, Dupuytre...
spondylitis

African descent SLE, rheumatoid arthritis

HEALTH ISSUE/CONCERN *Common health issues/concerns for the muscul...
information on the characteristics of each sig...*

Pain The subjective sense of discomfort in the a...

Location Muscle, bone, tendon, ligament, or joint

Quantity Degree of interruption in the patient's usu...
(changes in walking, bathing, dressing,
sitting, transfer to a sitting or standing p...
pushing, and pulling)

Associated Manifestations Inflammation, skin abrasion, laceration, b...
deformity, muscle spasm, paresthesia, d...
of weight bearing and movement, exces...
depression, insomnia, guarding of the p...
facial grimacing, anxiety, social withdra...
diaphoresis, tachycardia, elevated bloo...

Aggravating Factors Muscle contraction, muscle spasm, joint m...
bearing, obesity, dependent position, c...
compliance to physical or occupational...

Health Histories teach you an organized, thoughtful, and consistent approach to patient care, and guide your interview through each body system. This enables you to link health history clues to the patient's history and clinical status.

CASE STUDY **The Patient with Musculoskeletal Pain**

The case study illustrates the application and objective documentation of the musculoskeletal assessment.

Crystal Conway is a physical education teacher at an elementary school who presents to your clinic today in pain.

HEALTH HISTORY

PATIENT PROFILE 28 yo divorced woman, no children

HEALTH ISSUE/CONCERN "My back & neck are so painful. My hands are numb."

HISTORY OF HEALTH ISSUE/CONCERN Pt was in Mexico 2 mos ago on spring break when she was involved in a MVA. Car was stopped when a 2nd vehicle ran into her at 50 kph. Pt wearing seat belt. Experienced cervical neck pain & exacerbation of LBP. Transported to local hospital where spinal X-rays were taken. X-rays neg. Pt discharged on codeine 60 mg c̄ acetaminophen 650 mg q 6 & cyclobenzaprine (skeletal muscle relaxant) 10 mg po tid. Both meds taken for 10 days. Pt had been feeling better until yesterday at 8 AM when she slipped on ice on her way to work. Denies ↓ LOC, lacerations/abrasions, bleeding. Felt ok so continued on to work. Since that time her back & neck pain have returned. Cervical neck pain is throbbing (6/10 intensity), s̄ radiation, aggravated by mvt; took codeine/acetaminophen × 2 doses s̄ relief; denies numbness/tingling in arms/hands, denies △ in mobility/coordination. Exacerbation of longstanding midspinal LBP. Achy sensation c̄ shooting pains down both legs (9/10 intensity). Mild tingling in Ⓡ lateral calf & foot. Denies loss of bowel/bladder control or incoordination of legs. Sitting & lying down make pain worse. Standing, leaning onto a chair is the only tolerable position. Pt also c/o burning pain (4/10 intensity s̄ radiation) in Ⓡ index & middle fingers, unable to maintain good grip on tennis racket; pt is Ⓡ handed. Pt is a new PE teacher (in her probationary period) at local school & needs to get back to work. Concerned that this injury may jeopardize her job as she cannot conduct or demonstrate athletics in accord c̄ her job description.

PAST HEALTH HISTORY

Medical History Asthma dx age 9; minor exacerbation with URTI. LBP started 3 yrs ago p̄ football game when she was tackled; intermittent tx c̄ NSAIDs & heating pad
Genital herpes since age 21; Ø recent outbreaks
Wisdom teeth excision age 19 s̄ sequelae

Surgical History

Medications Ibuprofen 400 mg po 2–3 × qwk
Alesse (Levonorgestrel & estrogen) oral contraception

Communicable Diseases Genital herpes age 21; usually 2–3 outbreaks q̄ yr, especially when stressed

Allergies Perennial allergies to grasses, ragweed, pollen

Injuries and Accidents MVA as per HPI
Back injury sustained in tackle football game age 25

Special Needs Denies

Blood Transfusions Denies

Childhood Illnesses Not sure if she had varicella

Immunizations Hepatitis A for travel to Mexico; usually gets influenza vaccine at work q yr

---

Case Studies in each body system chapter help you practice performing a complete health history and physical assessment with an actual patient. Documentation-style entries teach you correct charting, and the variations in styles reflect real-life situations you will ultimately encounter in practice.

Nursing Alert

Osteoarthritis Risk Factors

- Obesity
- Family history
- Age > 40
- Joint abnormality
- Overuse of joint
- History of joint trauma

Nursing Alerts help you identify and respond efficiently and effectively to critical situations to ensure the health and safety of your patients.

GERONTOLOGICAL VARIATIONS

With age, bone density decreases due to an increased rate of bone reabsorption that exceeds the rate of bone cell replenishment. Bone density loss is accentuated in the elderly female due to the estrogen deficiency that accompanies menopause. Although components of bone tissue become calcified with age, the loss of bone density results in a weaker bone that is more susceptible to fracture. For example, the elderly patient with osteoporosis is at risk for hip or wrist fracture from a minor fall. Other changes seen as a result of bone density loss include thoracic kyphosis and a reduction in height. Thoracic kyphosis will cause a change in the patient's centre of gravity, making the patient more prone to loss of balance and to falls.

With age, muscle fibres deteriorate and are replaced by fibrous connective tissue. Muscle atrophy is accompanied by a reduction in muscle mass, a loss of muscle strength against resistance, and a reduction in overall body mass. The fat content of the body increases, with particular distribution around the waistline.

The elderly patient may be less able to perform heavy physical activity or activities of daily living, especially if these activities are prolonged in duration. The severity of muscle atrophy will be influenced by the patient's activity level and by peak muscle mass. Because muscle atrophy with aging is a gradual process, some elderly patients are able to compensate for the loss in muscle strength, and changes in activities of daily living may be minimal. The ability to maintain an active lifestyle, including physical exercise, will act to prevent disuse muscle atrophy and will maximize muscle strength.

There is a decrease in water content of cartilage, which leads to a narrowing of joint spaces, possibly pain, crepitus, and decreased movement of the affected area. There is also a reduction in the ability of cartilage to repair itself following trauma or surgery. Articulating cartilage will deteriorate slightly due to a lifetime of wear and tear.

A decrease in the water content of the intervertebral discs occurs with age, resulting in a reduction of vertebral flexibility. Thinning of the discs, which results in a decrease in height, makes the elderly patient prone to back pain and injury.

Gerontological Variations in each body system chapter help you learn about the normal physiological changes that occur with aging, so you can offer sensitive and appropriate care to your older patients.

Advanced Technique

Skin Scraping for Scabies

1. Place a drop of mineral oil on a sterile #15 scalpel blade.
2. Scrape the suspected papule or known scabies burrow vigorously in order to excavate the top of the papule or burrow. Flecks of blood will mix with the oil.
3. Place some of the oil and skin scrapings onto a microscope slide and cover with a cover slip.
4. Examine the slide for mites, ova, or feces.

Advanced Techniques help you identify examination sequences that are performed in selected clinical scenarios based on the patient's clinical presentation and history.

REVIEW QUESTIONS

1. Which of the following is used to establish potential strategies to assist patients in reaching their desired health goals?
   a. Critical thinking
   b. Analytical thinking
   c. Clinical reasoning
   d. Strategic planning
   The correct answer is (c).

2. In which phase of the critical-thinking process does the nurse reflect on critical-thinking skills that were used?
   a. Self-regulation
   b. Explanation
   c. Inference
   d. Interpretation
   The correct answer is (a).

3. Which statement about objective data is true?
   a. It usually comes from the health history.
   b. It cannot always be validated.
   c. It is observable and measurable.
   d. It can be obtained from family members.
   The correct answer is (c).

4. Which is the correct sequence of nursing analysis/diagnosis formulation?
   a. Collecting information, clustering information, interpreting information, naming the cluster
   b. Naming the cluster, collecting information, interpreting information, clustering information
   c. Collecting information, interpreting information, clustering information, naming the cluster
   d. Naming the cluster, interpreting information, collecting information, clustering information
   The correct answer is (c).

5. The nursing analysis/diagnosis of "Ineffective airway clearance related to asthma as evidenced by dyspnea, wheezes, and restlessness," is indicative of a:
   a. Strength
   b. Deficit
   c. Risk
   d. Outcome
   The correct answer is (b).

Review Questions at the end of each chapter present questions to assist you with the learning process and help you assimilate the information presented in the text. Many chapters contain short case scenarios with related questions, which help you apply the information you have learned to actual clinical cases.

Assessment in Brief

Effective Interviewing

- Be aware of your personal beliefs and how they were acquired. Avoid imposing your beliefs on those you interview.
- Listen and observe. Attend to verbal and affective content as well as to nonverbal cues.
- Focus your attention on the patient. Do not listen with "half an ear." Do not think about other things when you are interviewing.
- Maintain eye contact with the patient as is appropriate for the patient's culture.
- Notice the patient's speech patterns and any recurring themes. Note any extra emphasis that the patient places on certain words or topics.
- Do not assume that you understand the meaning of all patient communications. Clarify frequently.
- Paraphrase and summarize occasionally to help patients organize their thinking, clarify issues, and begin to explore specific concerns more deeply.
- Allow for periods of silence.
- Remember that attitudes and feelings may be conveyed nonverbally.
- Consistently monitor your reactions to the patient's verbal and nonverbal messages.
- Do not judge, criticize, or preach.
- Avoid the use of nontherapeutic interviewing techniques.

Assessment in Brief

General Approach to the Health History

- Present with a professional appearance. Avoid extremes in dress so that your appearance does not hinder information gathering.
- Ensure an appropriate environment, e.g., adequate privacy, good lighting, comfortable temperature, and ensure there are no noise or distractions.
- Sit facing the patient at eye level, with the patient in a chair or on a bed. Ensure that the patient is as comfortable as possible because obtaining the health history can be a lengthy process.
- Ask the patient whether he or she has any questions about the interview before it is started.
- Avoid the use of medical jargon. Use terms the patient can understand.
- Ask intimate and personal questions only when rapport has been established.
- Remain flexible in obtaining the health history. It does not have to be obtained in the exact order it is presented in this chapter or on institutional forms.
- Remind the patient that all information will be treated confidentially.

Assessment in Brief cards show the steps for performing each type of assessment. These are printed on perforated, heavy paper stock so you can use them as a resource while studying or in clinical situations.

Acknowledgments

*H*aving experienced frustration at the lack of a comprehensive health and physical assessment text that incorporated Canadian standards, guidelines, and approaches, I was thrilled to take on the challenge of the Canadianization of Estes' *Health Assessment and Physical Examination*, Third Edition. In some ways it was a relatively easy process because I had already completed many "updates" to meet the needs of my nursing students—I simply had to transcribe the many inserts and notations that I had made throughout my years of working with previous editions. That said, there was a lot of time and effort required to be comprehensive in the revision of this text; many people had direct and/or indirect involvement in this project. In particular, I would like to thank:

- The reviewers who took the time to reflect on this text, and compare and contrast it with competing and previous editions: Virginia Birnie, Camosun College; Jonathon Bradshaw, George Brown College; Michelle Chisholm, St. Francis Xavier University; Kim English, Sir Sandford Fleming College; Sandra Filice, Humber College; Karon Foster, University of Toronto; Melodie Hicks, Vanier College; Diane Pirner, Ryerson University; Christine Poitras, Saskatchewan Institute of Applied Science and Technology; and Madelene Heffel Ponting, Malaspina University-College.

- Veronica Visentin and Evelyn Veitch from Thomson Nelson who first approached me with the idea of publishing this text; they sensed the need and could provide the means for doing so.
- Other members of the Thomson Nelson team and freelance group, including Kevin Smulan, Rebecca Ryoji, Susan Calvert, Carrie McGregor, Melody Tolson, Kathy van Denderen, Karen Rolfe, and Vastavikta Sharma.
- My students at McGill University who provided many insights from their perspective as learners and users of the text.
- Betty Liduke, RN, from Njombe, Tanzania, for reminding me that hope is important; it is because of a visit to her clinical setting that (unfortunately) certain photos such as marasmus remain in this book.
- Caroline Marchionni who is the most efficient and effective research assistant I have ever worked with.
- My colleague Marcia Beaulieu who is meticulous and diplomatic—and always great in giving balanced feedback.
- My family, in particular Wayne for his emotional and instrumental support; Alice and Julie for taking on many responsibilities; Cupid for keeping me company late at night; my mother Anna Buck who showed concern and interest throughout; my late father, Louis, and mother, Gertrude, whom I wish I had been able to know for longer.

About the Authors

*M*ary Ellen Zator Estes obtained her baccalaureate and master's degrees in nursing and her Family Nurse Practitioner certificate from the University of Virginia. She has taught at the University of Virginia, Marymount University, Northern Virginia Community College, and The George Washington University Medical Center. She has also served as Clinical Faculty for Ball State University.

With over 25 years experience as a clinician and academician, Ms. Estes has taught health assessment and physical examination courses to nurses and nursing students from a variety of backgrounds. Her hands-on approach in the classroom, clinical laboratory, and health care setting has consistently led to positive learning experiences for her students.

Ms Estes's professional development is well demonstrated at the local, regional, and national levels. She has delivered numerous presentations throughout the country. She has been an active member of the Virginia Council of Nurse Practitioners, the American Academy of Nurse Practitioners, Sigma Theta Tau, American Association of Critical Care Nurses, American Nurses Association, and Virginia Nurses Association.

Ms Estes has been listed in *Who's Who in American Nursing* and *Who's Who in American Education*. She is currently a nurse practitioner at an internal medicine practice in Fairfax, Virginia.

*M*adeleine M. Buck obtained her Bachelor of Science (Nursing) and Master of Science in Nursing degrees from McGill University. Her 28-year career has included extensive clinical practice experiences in acute and community care settings as well as a three-year work experience in a First Nations setting. Her work at McGill University as clinical educator, teaching scholar, and administrator as well as her clinical associate position at the McGill University Health Centre have focused on ensuring that nurses at all levels of practice and education are as knowledgeable and skilled as possible. Her main areas of teaching include acute stressors and coping processes, acute and chronic illness management, and symptom management.

Described as a "stickler for detail," she espouses a comprehensive inductive and deductive approach to health assessment that includes gaining an understanding of patients' lived experiences, attention to subtle cues, and analysis of the strengths, deficits, and risks in clinical situations. She advocates the use of critical thinking and clinical judgment in clinical practice as well as a situation-responsive approach to patient assessment and intervention. Her experiences with the McGill Medical Simulation Centre have led to creative and innovative teaching and learning approaches that emphasize safe learning environments for students to gain competence and confidence with clinical skills.

Ms Buck is a member of the Bureau of Accreditation for the Canadian Association of Schools of Nursing. Her international work includes nursing consultation for the Highlands Hope Consortium, a group of three HIV-AIDS treatment centres in Tanzania, and acting as an advocate for the achievement of the Millennium Declaration Goals established by the United Nations.

NEL

UNIT 1

Laying the Foundation

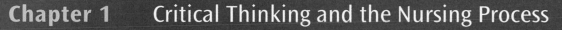

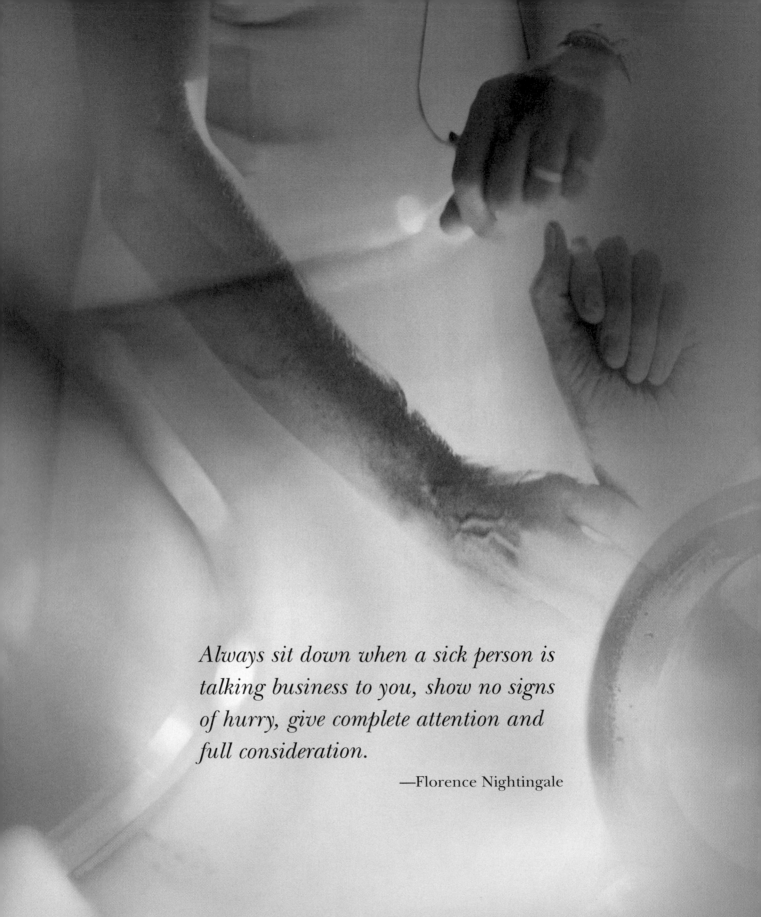

Always sit down when a sick person is talking business to you, show no signs of hurry, give complete attention and full consideration.

—Florence Nightingale

CHAPTER 1

Critical Thinking and the Nursing Process

COMPETENCIES

1. Describe how nursing is both an art and a science.

2. Discuss the components of critical thinking.

3. Apply the Universal Intellectual Standards to the critical-thinking process.

4. Define and describe the nursing process.

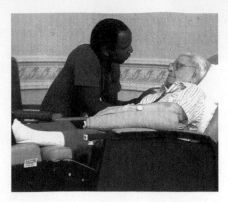

Figure 1-1 Nurses embody a combination of caring attitudes and technical expertise.

*N*ursing is a blend of art and science. The art of nursing allows nurses to incorporate aspects of caring and sharing into their practice. Over time, nurses build repertoires of professional experiences that serve as a clinical portfolio of responses to various patient situations. Experienced nurses make intuitive links that are not made by novice nurses, because experienced nurses can delve into their professional portfolio of experiences and select strategies that have been successful in the past. Professional intuition develops over time, as nurses begin to link certain patterns or events to specific outcomes. Experienced nurses seem to do this with little conscious effort. The novice, on the other hand, may need guidance to perceive links intuitively recognized by the experienced nurse.

For example, a critical care nurse may feel that his or her patient is deteriorating despite the fact that the patient's vital signs are stable. The experienced nurse has a "feel" for the patient and the situation. A few hours later the patient goes into cardiopulmonary arrest. How did the experienced nurse know this? That is part of the art of nursing (Figure 1-1).

The science of nursing involves the use of analytical thinking based on scientific principles and research data. In analytical thinking, the nurse studies the nature of the information, breaks the information into its constituent parts, and identifies any relationships and patterns. Causation, key factors, and possible outcomes to a situation are also identified. For example, with knowledge of lung physiology, pathophysiology of asthma, and environmental triggers, the nurse can analyze why the asthmatic patient is having an acute attack in a room filled with cigarette smokers and a wood-burning fire. Analytical thinking skills can be learned and developed as clinical experience is gained.

Conducting health assessments and physical examinations use both the art and science of nursing. Critical thinking and clinical reasoning are essential elements of this process.

CRITICAL THINKING AND CLINICAL REASONING

Critical thinking is a purposeful, goal-directed thinking process that uses clinical reasoning to resolve patient care issues. It combines logic, intuition, and creativity. **Clinical reasoning** is a disciplined, creative, and reflective

Reflective Thinking

Art and Science

Have you ever met a nurse who has a strong knowledge base but does not demonstrate a caring approach to patients? Have you ever met a nurse who is very caring but has a poor knowledge base? How do you feel about the need for both knowledgeable and caring nurses?

Reflective Thinking

Are you a critical thinker? If you answer yes to the following questions, then you are!

- Do you ask yourself a lot of questions as you try to figure out what is happening in a patient situation?
- Even if you discover what the answers to these questions are, do you still keep wondering if you have missed something?
- Do you go back to books or references to see if there are gaps in what you know about a particular topic so that you can be sure you have not missed anything?
- Are you generally able to see the obvious and even less obvious links in a clinical situation?
- Do you arrive at conclusions and set priorities that, in the end, are validated or confirmed as relevant and accurate? If they were not accurate, do you think back on how you arrived at the conclusion so you can be better at it the next time?
- If someone challenges your thinking, do you remain open to hearing what they have to say and even consider that you have missed something and are glad to learn another opinion or view?

TABLE 1-1

Key Elements of Clinical Reasoning

- All reasoning has a purpose

- All reasoning is an attempt to figure something out, to settle a question, or to solve a problem

- All reasoning is based on assumptions

- All reasoning is done from a particular point of view

- All reasoning is based on data, information, and evidence

- All reasoning is expressed through, and shaped by, concepts and ideas

- All reasoning contains inferences by which we draw conclusions and give meaning to data

- All reasoning leads somewhere or has implications and consequences

Source: From "Helping Students Assess Their Thinking," by R. Paul and L. Elder, 2000. Retrieved April 15, 2005, from http://www.criticalthinking.org/resources/articles/helping-students-assess-their-thinking

approach used together with critical thinking; its purpose is to establish potential strategies to assist patients in reaching their desired health goals. Critical thinking and clinical reasoning skills are essential to every nurse's clinical practice. For example, a patient in the cardiac care unit complained of chest pain after eating dinner and immediately went for a nap. Your critical thinking skills lead you to assess all aspects of the patient's condition in an effort to determine the etiology of the pain and treat it accordingly. You recognize that in addition to the diagnosis of angina, the patient also has a history of gastroesophageal reflux and a hiatal hernia. The patient takes omeprazole 40 mg every morning. You pursue a line of questioning that teases out more information about the patient's pain. You use clinical reasoning skills to determine that the patient's pain is most likely gastrointestinal in nature because the pain is located in the epigastric area, whereas recent chest pain was located in the substernal region. In addition, the patient had no electrocardiogram (ECG) changes with the pain, and the pain was relieved when the patient sat up.

The Foundation for Critical Thinking outlines eight guidelines of reasoning (Table 1-1).[1] Knowing and understanding these guidelines help the novice and experienced nurse master the reasoning process. The time frame in which this mastery occurs differs for every person. As with many skills, the more clinical reasoning is practised, the more natural it becomes.

Components of Critical Thinking

Critical thinking encompasses many skills, including *interpretation, analysis, inference, explanation, evaluation,* and *self-regulation.*[2] These skills will be discussed to show their relationship with health assessment and physical examination.

Interpretation of situations requires the nurse to decode hidden messages, clarify the meaning of the information, and categorize the information. For example, a patient may claim to be seeking health care for a cough and cold, but actually may be concerned about whether the cough is a sign of lung cancer. Accurate interpretation implies that the nurse is clinically competent and professionally capable of obtaining the information.

During *analysis,* the nurse examines the ideas and data that were presented, identifies any discrepancies, and reflects on the reason for the discrepancies. The nurse can begin to frame the main points of the patient's story. For instance, a patient may complain of insomnia but upon questioning might reveal that he sleeps six hours at night and takes a two-hour nap each afternoon. The nurse can often get a clearer picture of the patient's overall situation by noting such discrepancies.

Inference can be a challenging skill for the novice nurse because a certain level of knowledge and experience must be possessed in order to draw conclusions and provide alternatives in any given scenario. *Inference* speculates, derives, or reasons a specific premise based on information and assumptions obtained from the patient. If a patient complains of an exacerbation of asthma every morning, the nurse can inquire about a history of heartburn or gastroesophageal reflux disease (GERD). Only an experienced nurse would make the association between these causative factors.

Explanation requires that the conclusions drawn from the inferences are correct and can be justified. The use of scientific and nursing literature constitutes the basis for clinical justification. To continue with the example in the preceding paragraph, GERD as a contributing factor of asthma is well documented in the literature; there is a documented scientific link between GERD and asthma.

The *evaluation* process examines the validity of the information and hypothesis. For example, a nurse has assessed a five-year-old child with cystic fibrosis who has experienced laboured breathing and wheezing. Based on the findings, the nurse has implemented a nebulizer treatment, postural drainage, and chest physiotherapy. Upon reassessment after treatment, the nurse found no wheezing and the respiratory rate was within normal limits. The nurse undertook an evaluation process that led to a conclusion that could then be implemented.

Self-regulation is a key component to the critical-thinking process. During this process, the nurse reflects on the critical-thinking skills that were employed and then determines which techniques were effective and which were problematic. After interviewing a patient, the nurse reflects on whether leading, biased, or judgmental questions were posed to the patient. The nurse might also reflect on the use of open-ended questions and the effectiveness of using an interpreter. The recognition of both positive and negative outcomes is crucial to developing higher level thinking skills and professional expertise.

Universal Intellectual Standards for Critical Thinking

The quality of critical thinking can be evaluated by applying the seven Universal Intellectual Standards (UIS).[3] These standards are *clarity, accuracy, precision, relevance, depth, breadth,* and *logic.*

Clarity, simply stated, asks if the message or information is clear. For example, a person with alcoholism may report a substance abuse problem. The nurse, using critical-thinking skills, would need to clarify the substance abuse specifically as an alcohol problem versus a problem with other substances.

The second key element of the UIS is *accuracy.* Have the thinking process and information been accurate? For example, thinking that the person with alcoholism drinks to excess every day may be an inaccurate fact. That person may binge or drink heavily only on certain occasions. The nurse has to ask questions to ensure accurate understanding of information.

Precision is the third UIS. To state that a patient "drinks excessively" is judgmental and not precise. How much is excessive? Precision in thinking and data collection is essential. The statement, "The patient reports drinking 500 mL of whisky every day" is precise.

Has the thinking been *relevant*? If the person with alcoholism presented with the need for rehabilitation secondary to alcohol withdrawal and delirium tremens, then the information that the patient's grandfather died at age 82 of renal failure would not be relevant. This latter statement may be a true statement, but it does not connect to the central issue of alcoholic rehabilitation.

The UIS of *depth* can be a challenging standard for novice nurses to achieve because they may not possess the appropriate knowledge base to know when to delve deeper into a given problem for related data. For instance, perhaps the nurse did not ascertain that the patient has four relatives who have a history of alcoholism, or that the patient recently had a child die and was fired from a job, which led to an exacerbation of the drinking.

The sixth UIS is *breadth.* Does the patient's story have more to it than was relayed to the nurse? Does the nurse need to consider the views of another person, such as a close friend or spouse? Does the nurse need to obtain additional data so as to gain an accurate analysis of the person's situation?

Finally, the UIS of *logic* needs to be applied to clinical reasoning. Does the patient's or significant other's story seem logical? If the patient stated that her only child recently died and that caused her to drink heavily, and then later this child came to visit her mother, what does this imply? Another way to think logically is attributing signs and symptoms to disease entities. If the patient has experienced tremors—is this due to alcohol withdrawal or Parkinson's disease? Logical thinking would seem to point to the former etiology.

Consistent application of these standards to critical thinking leads to sophistication of clinically useful skills.

CRITICAL THINKING AND THE NURSING PROCESS

The **nursing process** provides a framework to ensure that the elements of critical thinking are followed. The five interrelated phases (or steps) of the nursing process to be discussed are assessment, diagnosis, planning, implementation, and evaluation. Following these phases helps to ensure that patient care is organized and prioritized as well as relevant and related to the priorities and unique characteristics of the situation. The nursing process also ensures accountability in that patient care is evaluated and modified accordingly throughout. Depending on the nursing philosophy that is used by the individual or institution, some of the steps in the nursing process can be labelled differently. For example, units that use the North American Nursing Diagnosis Association (NANDA) classification system will use the term "Nursing Diagnosis" to formulate and document the results of the assessment phase. Institutions that do not use the NANDA classification system may use the term "nursing analysis," "nursing conclusions," "nursing hypotheses," or "nursing summary" to represent the "diagnosis." Some institutions may only note four phases of the above process, clustering assessment and diagnosis into one phase—generally called assessment—with the assessment encompassing the data collection process and the hypotheses or conclusions that have been made based on the data.

Again, based on philosophical stance and the predominant practice model of nursing that is used to guide the process of nursing, some institutions choose to use the term "scientific process" or "thinking process" rather than "nursing process." Some institutions may view each of these espoused processes as being no different from a cognitive analytical point of view. The proponents of the scientific process over the nursing process argue that while the *content* of nursing is different from other professionals, the *process* of thinking is no different and thus should not be depicted as such.

Regardless of the terminology used, the essence is that nurses must *think* and must act in a way that ensures optimal health of the clients they serve. Regardless of where or with what population nurses work with, nurses must be systematic to ensure quality of care. Nurses must collect data about people (assessment); they must place meaning on that data in order to conclude what in the situation is important (diagnoses); they must set some direction (planning) and act on the situation to achieve health goals (implementation); and they must then determine whether or not what happened was successful in meeting the stated goal or objectives (evaluation).

The primary focus of this text is assessment. The physical, emotional, mental, developmental, spiritual, and cultural assessments provide the foundation for the other steps of the nursing process.

Assessment

Assessment is the first step of the nursing process and involves the orderly collection of information concerning the patient's health status. The assessment process aims to identify the patient's current health status, actual and potential health issues or concerns, and areas for health promotion. The sources of information include the patient's health history, the physical assessment, and diagnostic and laboratory data. Collectively, these data constitute the nursing database from which the nurse will develop a plan of care for the patient; the data also serve as a baseline against which future comparisons can be made (Figure 1-2).

Health History

The health history interview is a means of gathering **subjective data,** usually from the patient. The data collected are subjective in that the information cannot always be verified by an independent observer. In some instances,

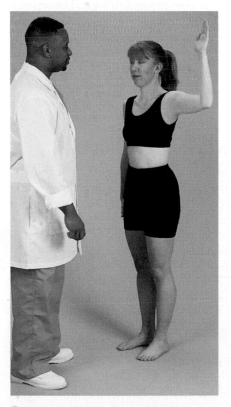

Figure 1-2 Collecting baseline data is an important step in the assessment of a patient's overall health status.

however, this information can be validated during the physical assessment; for instance, the existence of a patient-reported breast lump can be confirmed through palpation.

The health history can also be obtained from sources other than the patient. Relatives, neighbours, and friends of the patient can provide insightful data for the health history. The patient's past charts or medical records are additional sources of information, as are health care colleagues. In some instances, total strangers may be the only source of information, such as in the case of a severe accident where the patient is rendered unconscious. The nurse can and should use every available medium to gather as much information about the patient as possible. The health history is further discussed in Chapter 3.

Physical Assessment Findings

Physical assessment findings constitute a second source of information that is used in the assessment phase of the nursing process. Physical assessment findings constitute **objective data,** or information that is observable and measurable, that can be verified by more than one person. Data are obtained using the senses of smell, touch, vision, and hearing. This text describes the systematic and comprehensive physical assessment techniques that will elicit objective data (see Chapters 8–24).

The physical assessment data can be obtained in a body system (see Table 1-2), or head-to-toe, approach.

Diagnostic and Laboratory Data

The final element that contributes to the information gathering in the assessment phase of the nursing process is diagnostic and laboratory data. Results of blood and urine studies, cultures, X-rays, and diagnostic procedures constitute objective data about the patient's status.

It is imperative that the nurse document all assessment findings. The written record is a legal tool used to chart the patient's current health status but also serves as a means of communicating information to other health care colleagues.

Remember that the assessment phase of the nursing process is dynamic in that the nurse continuously adds to the database, validating the data, and interpreting the data. With these data the nurse can progress to the second phase of the nursing process, the nursing analysis.

Diagnosis (Nursing Analysis, Nursing Conclusions)

The NANDA defines a **nursing diagnosis** as "a clinical judgment about individual, family, or community responses to actual or potential health problems/life processes." A nursing diagnosis is the second step in the nursing process and provides the basis for selection of nursing interventions to achieve outcomes for which the nurse is accountable. Institutions that do not use the NANDA system may use the terms "nursing analysis," "nursing conclusions," or "nursing assessment." Regardless, the diagnosis is formulated after the assessment data are analyzed. The process involves four steps as identified by Gordon: collecting information, interpreting information, clustering information, and naming a cluster or problem formulation.[4] Collecting information refers to the data gathered in the assessment phase of the nursing process, which is a continuous means to gain as much information about the patient as possible.

Next, the data are interpreted. The clinical importance of the information becomes relevant in its interpretation. The data, or cues, are evaluated against the standards for a patient population. Using inferential reasoning, the nurse begins to see patterns or clusters of data and sorts the data into meaningful groups. If the NANDA model is used, then clustering is done based on the "human response patterns." A range of nursing models are used in the education and

TABLE 1-2

Body System Assessment

1. General survey, vital signs, and pain
2. Skin, hair, and nails
3. Head and neck
4. Eyes
5. Ears, nose, mouth, and throat
6. Breasts and regional nodes
7. Thorax and lungs
8. Heart and peripheral vasculature
9. Abdomen
10. Musculoskeletal system
11. Mental status and neurological techniques
12. Female or male genitalia
13. Rectum and prostate

practice setting so the analysis or diagnosis reflects the approach used within the preferred nursing philosophy. Some nurses use a systems approach and cluster data and analyses related to the cardiovascular system, respiratory system, and even the family system. Other frameworks address health and coping as key cluster groups. Nurses can review the various nursing theories that guide their practice, or the practice of their institution, to help them know which cluster themes are relevant within the framework they are using. This text uses a purposeful method of data clustering that is described in detail in Chapter 3.

Finally, the nurse must make conclusions about the various clusters in order to formulate a statement about the essence of the clinical situation. All subsequent priorities will likely evolve from these statements. The final statement should indicate the nature of the strengths (analyses about what is helping the situation), deficits (things that are hindering the situation), and risks (though not a problem now, these are things that could impact negatively on the patient's health situation). For example, a summary of strengths, deficits, and risks related to a patient recovering from surgery might be "overall positive postoperative recovery (strength) but experiencing reduced lung expansion because of poor pain control and immobility (deficit)"; "client at risk for delayed wound healing (risk) because of poor protein intake and poor diabetes control (deficits)"; "patient extremely motivated to do what has to be done to recover properly (strength)." The NANDA framework develops wellness, actual, and risk diagnoses. Each analytical statement should identify the issue at hand as well as any factor that is influencing the situation, because it is likely that the factor relating to the issue has to be addressed within the nursing interventions. So, to follow up on the patient discussed earlier who is at risk of delayed wound healing, it is clear that to avoid the risk becoming a reality (an actual deficit), nursing interventions need to address the control of blood glucose and the nutritional status of the patient—something that will at least be facilitated by the patient's level of motivation.

Some clinical settings require that the defining characteristics of the analysis (diagnosis) be identified in any statements to ensure that others can understand the rationale behind the diagnosis or analytical statement. The words, "as evidenced by" or "as indicated by" precede the "defining characteristics." For example, the following statements include the defining characteristics: patient is experiencing anxiety (a deficit) related to the threat of death as evidenced by expressed concerns due to change in life events, shakiness, and voice quivering (defining characteristics). Because the defining characteristics are noted, others will know what led to the particular nursing analysis; in addition, these characteristics can be monitored as indicators that the situation is improving or worsening. This type of additional statement can also mean that others may provide different ways of analyzing the situation. For example, another health professional might feel that the defining characteristics of expressed concerns, shakiness, and voice quivering could be the result of something other than anxiety because of pending death.

Planning

Planning represents the third step in the nursing process. The nurse prioritizes nursing diagnoses or analyses to formulate a goal and then tests the subsequent nursing interventions aimed toward achieving the goal. Once the nurse has formulated an analysis of the patient's situation, the nurse establishes patient goals, ideally in collaboration with the patient (Figure 1-3). Some institutions cite the goal after the diagnosis and replace planning with "implementation." The essence is that once the analysis of the situation has been outlined, including identification of factors or variables that are influencing the situation, a focus (or goal) to ensure ongoing health must be established. The goal must be identified, along with the strategies to be used to achieve that goal. For example, a goal for the patient at risk of wound infection might be to improve nutritional status.

Figure 1-3 Nurse and patient review outcomes.

Prioritization

The nurse formulates all of the nursing diagnoses that are derived from the clustering of data. When there is more than one nursing diagnosis, the nurse must decide which problem(s) is the most vital to the patient's well-being at that particular time. Generally, the nurse determines the priorities based on the balance between the strengths, deficits, and risks in any given patient situation. Imminent health risks generally take precedence in the priority-setting exercise. Priorities are continually monitored and reassessed if necessary, in light of new data that emerge or as the patient response changes. As much as possible, the patient and the nurse should work collaboratively to establish goals and priorities, each bringing their understanding of the situation to the dialogue. When patients feel a part of the process, the identified goals are more likely to be achieved. There are some patients, however, who do not wish to participate in goal setting because they feel this is the domain of the health care professional.

Intervention Selection

Interventions are planned strategies, based on scientific rationale, devised by the nurse to assist patients in meeting their health outcomes. Whenever possible, the patient, family, and significant others can assist in planning the interventions. As with prioritization, interventions are more likely to be accurate and relevant if they have been tailored to the unique characteristics of the patient and family. Engaging the individual and family in this process generally increases the patient's motivation to follow the proposed interventions because they have been jointly determined.

It is essential that the plan of care be comprehensive to ensure that the identified goal can be achieved. The interventions can be independent nursing actions (those that the nurse implements) or collaborative actions (those that require other members of the health care team). With all interventions, sound nursing judgment is required to ensure that the intervention is appropriate to the particular goals that have been set and that interventions fit with the unique nature of the situation. A growing trend in health care is toward **evidence-based practice.** No longer are health care practices being done "because they have always been done that way," nor are they being done intuitively. Rather, evidence-based practice uses the outcomes of scientific studies to guide clinical decision making and clinical care. For example, a systematic review indicates that the use of a tepid sponge bath in reducing fever in children may provide mild symptom relief; however, the procedure does not lower the hypothalamic set point to achieve a reduction in fever. In fact, there can be an increase in temperature if the child is overcooled and develops shivers during the procedure. As a result, the nursing intervention of providing a tepid sponge bath to reduce a child's fever may not be relevant or accurate. Evidence-based practice also includes the use of clinical expertise and takes into account resources. So, if the nurse assesses that the child enjoys a tepid bath, and the parents feel that they can comfort and prevent the child from shivering, and are made aware that the fever will not be reduced, then providing the bath within these parameters would be considered "evidence-based." Systematic reviews are continually being released that address a range of health issues and the interventions that are used to address them. Best practice guidelines also help the nurse to determine the most relevant nursing interventions for addressing such issues as pain management, smoking cessation, prevention of pressure ulcers, and many other topics. By taking advantage of research findings (many of which are available through online library access), clinical conferences, and expert testimony, nurses can become informed and incorporate evidence into their professional practice.

Implementation

The fourth step in the nursing process is **implementation.** In this phase the nurse executes the interventions that were devised during the planning stage to help the patient meet predetermined outcomes. The time frame of the implementation phase varies from patient to patient and from nursing diagnosis to nursing diagnosis. Remember that the nurse usually simultaneously implements the interventions from multiple nursing diagnoses for a patient at any given time. The patient may achieve the outcome for one priority issue while progressing toward the outcome for another.

Implementation is a dynamic process. The nurse is continually interacting with the patient, the family, and other health care colleagues, obtaining new data and making new judgments. Plans of care can be changed or eliminated altogether based on the continuous flow of information.

Evaluation

Evaluation is the fifth and final phase of the nursing process. During evaluation, the patient's progress in achieving the goal(s) is determined. Even before the time frame for assessing outcomes is reached, the nurse is continually assessing the patient's progress toward the outcomes, making evaluation a continual and dynamic process. Each intervention should be evaluated by the nurse, patient, and family (when appropriate). It is important to know which interventions helped and which ones had either no impact or a negative impact on the overall goal achievement. The outcome can be met, partially met, or not met. If the patient outcome has been met, the nurse documents this information and then periodically re-evaluates the patient's need for knowledge on the health matter. If the outcome was only partially met or not met, this too is documented. In the latter situation, nurses should consider these factors: Was the original analysis accurate? Was the priority accurate and relevant? Was the time frame adequate? Were the interventions accurate and comprehensive? Was the patient outcome accurate? Has the patient's condition changed sufficiently that the outcome is no longer appropriate? After going over the questions, the nurse and the patient may decide to revise the patient outcome and nursing interventions or to eliminate them. Based on the ongoing assessment and evaluation, new nursing diagnoses may be formulated that warrant nursing intervention. These are added to the patient's plan of care.

[handwritten marginal note: when goals not met]

DOCUMENTING THE NURSING PROCESS

Nurses use many methods to document the nursing process, including the progress note and the nursing care plan. The progress note documents the patient's progress toward achieving stated goals using different progress note charting systems, such as:

SOAPIER: Subjective data, objective data, analysis of data stated as a nursing diagnosis, plan, intervention/implementation, evaluation, revision

PIO: Problem, intervention, outcome

CBE: Charting by exception

Focus® charting

DAR: Data, action, response/revision

PIE: Problem, intervention, evaluation

Each charting method has advantages and disadvantages. The nurse should verify institutional policy on charting directives.

The **nursing care plan** combines the elements of the nursing process to document the progress of patient care in a standardized fashion. Nursing care plans serve as a means of communicating patient progress with other health care colleagues and ensuring continuity of care among the nursing staff.

◄NURSING CHECKLIST►

Critical Thinking and Nursing Process Review

1. Incorporate critical thinking and clinical reasoning into all aspects of patient care.
2. Evaluate the quality of critical thinking by applying the seven Universal Intellectual Standards (UIS).
3. Frame critical thinking by using the nursing process.
4. Apply all four phases of the nursing process to address different patient issues.
5. Begin with a thorough assessment of the patient, using a health history, physical assessment, and laboratory data and diagnostic procedures. Document findings.
6. Formulate and prioritize nursing analyses according to the patient's status. Record them on the patient's clinical record.
7. Work with the patient to develop mutually agreeable and achievable goals, each with its own set of interventions and measurable outcomes.
8. Implement actions in conjunction with other members of the health care team.
9. Evaluate the patient's progress toward achieving outcomes.
10. Continually reassess and reprioritize analyses/diagnoses, goals, and established outcomes as the patient's status changes in order to provide the best patient care.
11. Document the patient's progress toward outcomes.

REVIEW QUESTIONS

1. Which of the following is used to establish potential strategies to assist patients in reaching their desired health goals?
   a. Critical thinking
   b. Analytical thinking
   c. Clinical reasoning
   d. Strategic planning
   The correct answer is (c).

2. In which phase of the critical-thinking process does the nurse reflect on critical-thinking skills that were used?
   a. Self-regulation
   b. Explanation
   c. Inference
   d. Interpretation
   The correct answer is (a).

3. Which statement about objective data is true?
   a. It usually comes from the health history.
   b. It cannot always be validated.
   c. It is observable and measurable.
   d. It can be obtained from family members.
   The correct answer is (c).

4. Which is the correct sequence of nursing analysis/diagnosis formulation?
   a. Collecting information, clustering information, interpreting information, naming the cluster
   b. Naming the cluster, collecting information, interpreting information, clustering information
   c. Collecting information, interpreting information, clustering information, naming the cluster
   d. Naming the cluster, interpreting information, collecting information, clustering information
   The correct answer is (c).

5. The nursing analysis/diagnosis of "Ineffective airway clearance related to asthma as evidenced by dyspnea, wheezes, and restlessness," is indicative of a:
   a. Strength
   b. Deficit
   c. Risk
   d. Outcome
   The correct answer is (b).

Visit the Estes online companion resource at
www.healthassessment.nelson.com for additional content
and study aids.

BIBLIOGRAPHY

Alfaro-LeFevre, R. (2003). *Applying nursing process: A tool for critical thinking.* Philadelphia: Lippincott Williams & Wilkins.

Carpenito-Moyet, L. J. (2006). *Nursing diagnosis: Application to clinical practice* (11th ed.). Philadelphia: Lippincott.

Klardie, K. A., Johnson, J., McNaughton, M. A., & Meyers, W. (2004). Integrating the principles of evidence-based practice into clinical practice. *Journal of the American Academy of Nurse Practitioners, 16*(3), 98–105.

Kuiper, R. (2005). Self-regulated learning during a clinical preceptorship: The reflections of senior baccalaureate nursing students. *Nursing Education Perspectives, 26*(6), 351–56.

Nightingale, F. (1859). *Notes on nursing: What it is, and what it is not.* Philadelphia: Lippincott.

Profetto-McGrath, J. (2005). Critical thinking and evidence-based practice. *Journal of Professional Nursing, 21*(6), 364–71.

Profetto-McGrath, J., Hesketh, K., Lang, S., & Estabrooks, C. (2003). A study of critical thinking and research utilization among nurses. *Western Journal of Nursing Research, 25*(3), 322–37.

Ritter, B. J. (2003). An analysis of expert nurse practitioners' diagnostic reasoning. *Journal of the American Academy of Nurse Practitioners, 15*(3), 137–41.

REFERENCES

[1]Paul, R., & Elder, L. (2000, March 1). *Helping students assess their thinking.* Retrieved April 15, 2005, from http://www.critical-thinking.org/resources/articles/helping-students-assess-their-thinking

[2]Pesut, D. J., & Herman, J. (1999). *Clinical reasoning: The art and science of critical and creative thinking.* Clifton Park, NY: Thomson Delmar Learning.

[3]Elder, L., & Paul, R. (2000, March 1). *Universal intellectual standards.* Retrieved July 19, 2004, from http://www.critical-thinking.org/University/univlibrary/unistan.html

[4]Gordon, M. (2002). *Manual of nursing diagnosis* (10th ed.). St. Louis, MO: Mosby.

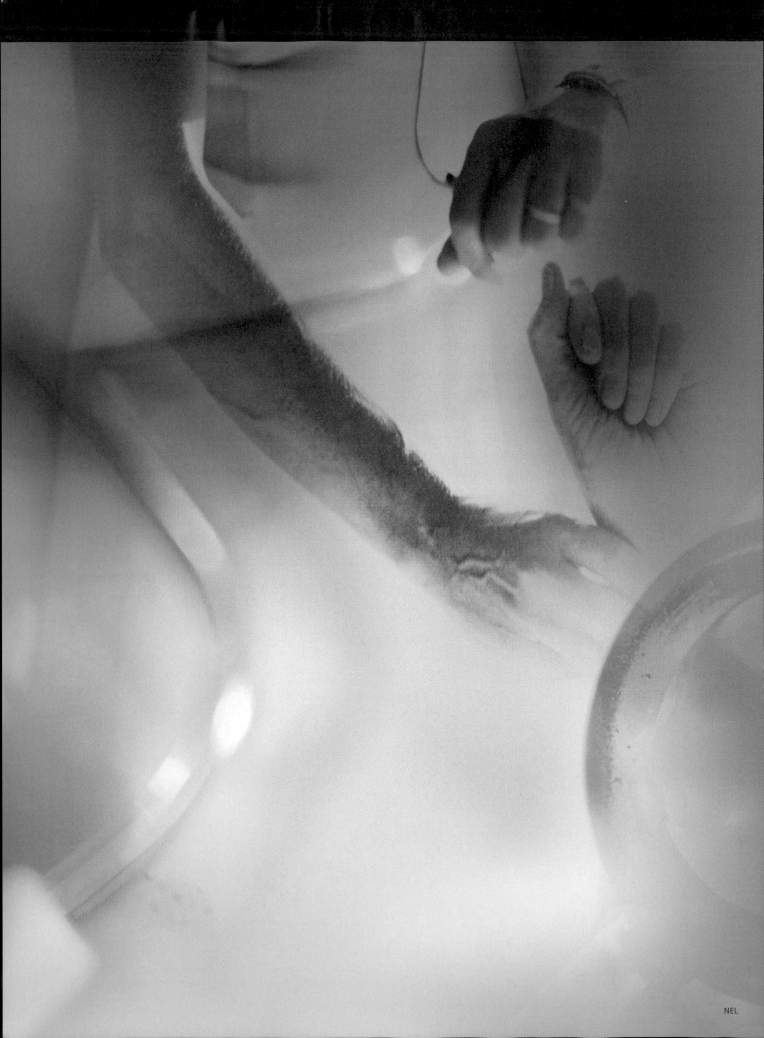

NEL

CHAPTER 2

The Patient Interview

COMPETENCIES

1. Prepare an appropriate setting for the nurse–patient interview.

2. Recognize personal perceptions that facilitate or hinder the interview process.

3. Define effective interviewing techniques.

4. Describe problematic interviewing behaviours.

5. Demonstrate how to transform problematic interviewing behaviours into more effective ones.

6. Adapt the interview process for the patient with special needs.

7. Adapt the interview process for elderly patients.

*T*he nursing health assessment interview is a purposeful, time-limited verbal interaction between the nurse and the patient to collect information regarding the patient's health status. Other purposes of the interview include validating appropriate health and illness information presented by the patient or found in the patient's record, and identifying the patient's knowledge of personal health and illness status. Accurate and complete information about the patient serves as a foundation for subsequent nurse–patient interactions and for medical and nursing interventions. The nurse–patient interaction requires skill in interviewing techniques, which the nurse can learn and refine.

THE PATIENT INTERVIEW

The nursing interview is holistic in nature and gathers information about the total patient. The interview includes an assessment of physical, mental, emotional, developmental, social, cultural, and spiritual aspects of the patient. Data are collected concerning the patient's present and past states of health, including the patient's family status and relationships, cultural background, lifestyle preferences, and developmental level. Other factors considered in data collection are the patient's self-concept, religious affiliation, social supports, sexuality, and reproductive processes.

The Role of the Nurse

The nurse is often the first person from the health care team to interact with the patient and frequently assumes the role of intermediary for the patient to the larger health care system (Figure 2-1). The climate and tone of the initial patient interview can influence all future interactions the patient has in the health care setting. The nurse's attitude and expectations, both positive and negative, set the stage for the interview and can affect its outcome.

First impressions of individuals are important and imprint long-lasting thoughts and feelings. The personal appearances of both the patient and the nurse contribute significantly to the formation of first impressions. Health care providers who present a professional appearance that is appropriate for the particular work setting are more readily accepted by patients.

The nurse is the facilitator of the interview and thus collaborates with the patient in establishing a mutually respectful dialogue. Encouraging the patient to speak freely and expressing concern for the patient are essential. For example, if the patient thinks that no one in the health care setting is attending to what he or she says, the patient will likely say very little. Because accurate data collection is the primary purpose of the interview, the patient must feel comfortable and safe enough to provide information, to ask questions, and to express fears or concerns.

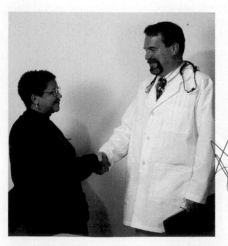

Figure 2-1 Beginning the interview with a friendly introduction will help the patient feel at ease.

◄ NURSING CHECKLIST ►

Preparing for the Interview

1. Gather all available patient information.
2. Seek out an appropriate setting for the interview.
3. Set aside a block of time for the interview.
4. Assess yourself for possible problematic thoughts or feelings.
5. Begin the interview with a friendly introduction.
   - Introduce yourself by name and title.
   - Call the patient by formal name, e.g., Mrs. Adams.

The nurse can foster an atmosphere of safety and comfort by approaching each patient with an accepting, respectful, and nonjudgmental attitude.

The Role of the Patient

The patient is an active and equal participant in the interview process and should feel free to openly communicate thoughts, feelings, perceptions, and factual information. Most patients possess previous knowledge of or experience with the health care system that influences their current perceptions and behaviour. Understanding how patients see their role in the system is vital to the successful completion of any health interview. If patients view themselves as taking an active role in their own health care and in health care decisions, they are more apt to question health care providers, to treat themselves, and to expect a role in decision making. Patients who view health care providers as all-knowing may take on a more passive role, expecting the "experts" to know what to ask them and to make the best decisions on their behalf.

The Collaborative Partnership

The nurse and patient each bring a unique perspective to any health-related situation and, ideally, will enter into a collaborative partnership. Gottlieb and Feeley describe this relationship as "the pursuit of person-centered goals through a dynamic process that requires the active participation and agreement of all parties. The relationship is one of partnership and the way of working together is collaborative."[1] In this partnership, nurses and patients each bring their knowledge, experience, and expertise to the relationship. For example, the nurse may have detailed knowledge about the epidemiology, risk factors, pathophysiology, and treatment plan of cardiac illness; however, it is the patient and his or her family who knows what the lived experience of this illness process is, how it influences their day-to-day life, how easy or difficult it is to manage all of the demands, and how personal and family goals are enhanced or deterred as a result of dealing with the illness. In effect, the partnership allows the nurse and patient to become more than the sum of its parts. Achieving mutually agreed-on health goals is more likely to occur when there is joint communication and decision making. The principles of the collaborative partnership are summarized in Figure 2-2.

---

1. Both person and nurse want to and agree to enter into a collaborative relationship.
2. The collaborative partnership can assume many forms depending on the person's preferences, abilities, and circumstances.
3. The nurse continuously assesses the conditions that influence collaboration and adjusts the form that the collaborative partnership takes to best fit the person's needs and abilities and the situation.
4. The collaborative partnership is purposeful and goal directed.
5. To achieve mutually agreed-on goals, both the nurse and the person need to have as thorough an understanding of the situation as is possible at that point in time. This involves sharing with one another the other's unique perspective.
6. In a collaborative partnership, the person is the essential and primary source of information.
7. Both person and nurse contribute resources that are used collaboratively.
8. Collaboration, in some situations, involves sharing a very different perspective with a person, challenging his view, or inviting him to see something different.
9. The collaborative partnership may change within an encounter and across encounters as the situation changes or as the person's needs or abilities evolve.
10. A collaborative partnership approach requires a varied repertoire of communication and interpersonal skills.

Figure 2-2 Principles of the Collaborative Partnership

Source: From Laurie N. Gottlieb and Nancy Feeley, with Cindy Dalton, *The Collaborative Partnership Approach to Care: A Delicate Balance* (pp. 10–11). Copyright © 2006 Elsevier Canada, a division of Reed Elsevier Canada, Ltd. All rights reserved. Reprinted by permission of Elsevier Canada, 2006.

FACTORS INFLUENCING THE INTERVIEW

Factors that can affect the patient's comfort level, and therefore the effectiveness of the interview, are discussed in the following sections.

Legal Considerations

As health professionals, nurses are accountable to the public to ensure that the highest standards of care are met. In all provinces and territories, nurses have professional and legal obligations to maintain their standard of practice, which is monitored by the regulatory nursing organization that granted the nurse a licence to practise. Nurses must have ongoing competency in their practice by reflecting on their learning needs to maintain and develop their knowledge base in whatever domain of practice they work in. They are expected to be aware of the most recent evidence to support or negate the interventions they use in their daily clinical practice. If nurses do not fulfill such expectations, they can be held liable for acts of commission (doing something that should not have been done) or acts of omission (failure to do something that should have been done).

Nurses are also expected to practice within the legislated boundaries as set out in provincial and territorial government structures. For example, all licensed health professionals in Canada have a "scope of practice" that outlines the parameters or boundaries of what they are legally allowed to do. Although there are many aspects of care that all health professionals are responsible for, some responsibilities are specific to individual professions. For example, all health professionals, including physicians, physical therapists, dentists, and nurses must uphold a high level of moral conduct, but performing invasive techniques, such as insertion of a peripheral central catheter, may be in the domain of only a physician or a nurse. Nurses must know how their scope of practice is defined in whatever region they are working in to ensure they maintain legal expectations.

Other legal expectations for nursing practice that are common across Canada include the requirements that all patient interactions (face to face, telephone, letters, faxes, e-mails) be documented, that privacy and confidentiality be respected, that any communicable disease or infection considered to be a public health concern be reported according to provincial or territorial requirements (see Appendix A and B), that suspected and known cases of child abuse be reported to appropriate health officials, and that a patient's right to informed consent and right to refuse treatment or assessments be respected.

Ethical Considerations

All licensed health professionals across Canada are expected to practise with a high degree of professionalism that includes moral and ethical conduct. Although each nursing regulatory body has its own specific code of ethics or ethic standards, the following ethical principles guide nursing practice across the country:

- Autonomy: a patient's right to self-determination; to respect a patient's thoughts and actions as to what he or she thinks is best for herself or himself
- Beneficence: to do what is "good" for the patient
- Nonmaleficence: to do no harm to the patient
- Justice: to be fair and impartial to the patient
- Fidelity: to be faithful to the patient
- Veracity: to be truthful to the patient
- Utilitarianism: to perform the greatest good for the greatest number of people

The ethical principles are not foolproof nor are they always easy to practise, but being aware of these principles helps to guard the rights of patients. Many

TABLE 2-1 Nursing Values—Canadian Nurses Association Code of Ethics for Registered Nurses

Safe, competent, and ethical care
Nurses value the ability to provide safe, competent and ethical care that allows them to fulfill their ethical and professional obligations to the people they serve.

Health and well-being
Nurses value health promotion and well-being and assisting persons to achieve their optimum level of health in situations of normal health, illness, injury, disability or at the end of life.

Choice
Nurses respect and promote the autonomy of persons and help them to express their health needs and values, and also to obtain desired information and services so they can make informed decisions.

Dignity
Nurses recognize and respect the inherent worth of each person and advocate for respectful treatment of all persons.

Confidentiality
Nurses safeguard information learned in the context of a professional relationship, and ensure it is shared outside the health care team only with the person's informed consent, or as may be legally required, or where the failure to disclose would cause significant harm.

Justice
Nurses uphold principles of equity and fairness to assist persons in receiving a share of health services and resources proportionate to their needs and in promoting social justice.

Accountability
Nurses are answerable for their practice, and they act in a manner consistent with their professional responsibilities and standards of practice.

Quality Practice Environments
Nurses value and advocate for practice environments that have the organizational structures and resources necessary to ensure safety, support and respect for all persons in the work setting.

Source: Canadian Nurses Association Code of Ethics for Registered Nurses (2002), p. 8, http://www.cna-nurses.ca/cna/documents/pdf/publications/CodeofEthics2002_e.pdf. Reprinted with permission from the Canadian Nurses Association

Reflective Thinking

Breaking Confidentiality

A woman in the emergency room reveals that her extensive physical injuries are the result of partner violence rather than the result of a fall as she had initially stated. She also fears for her children because her partner has subjected them to extensive emotional abuse. She asks you not to share this information with anyone because she is fearful of her partner's reaction. What is your response to this disclosure? What is your institution's policy concerning confidentiality? What are your responsibilities as a nurse in this situation? Is a report mandated by law in your province or territory for this action?

institutions have a multidisciplinary ethics committee that may employ an ethicist to help health care providers deal with difficult situations.

The Canadian Nurses Association (CNA) Code of Ethics for Registered Nurses (2002) is based on eight principles that are central to ethical nursing practice (Table 2-1).

Confidentiality

Confidentiality is one of the hallmarks of moral conduct for health professionals. It is essential in developing trust between nurse and patient. The patient's willingness to communicate private and personal health information is predicated on the assumption that the information will be used with discretion and for the benefit of the patient. Patients must be confident that the intimate details they share about their social, physical, emotional, and mental health will be guarded with utmost confidentiality. Verbal assurances of confidentiality often ease the patient's concerns and fosters trust in the relationship, but the nurse's behaviour must also reflect professionalism at all times.

The CNA Code of Ethics for Registered Nurses (2002) provides helpful guidelines for ensuring confidentiality in nursing practice (Table 2-2).

The CNA Code of Ethics limits disclosure without consent to situations where there is a risk of serious harm to the person, or to other persons, or a legal obligation to disclose. "Disclosure without consent has been limited to narrowly defined purposes or situations: emergencies, avoiding or preventing

TABLE 2-2	**Confidentiality**

Nurses safeguard information learned in the context of a professional relationship and ensure it is shared outside the health care team only with the person's informed consent, or as may be legally required, or where the failure to disclose would cause significant harm.

1. Nurses must respect the right of each person to informational privacy, that is, the individual's control over the use, access, disclosure and collection of their information.

2. Nurses must advocate for persons requesting access to their health record subject to legal requirements.

3. Nurses must protect the confidentiality of all information gained in the context of the professional relationship, and practice within relevant laws governing privacy and confidentiality of personal health information.

4. Nurses must intervene if other participants in the health care delivery system fail to maintain their duty of confidentiality.

5. Nurses must disclose a person's health information only as authorized by that person, unless there is substantial risk of serious harm to the person or to other persons or a legal obligation to disclose. Where disclosure is warranted, information provided must be limited to the minimum amount of information necessary to accomplish the purpose for which it has been disclosed. Further, the number of people informed must be restricted to the minimum necessary.

6. Nurses should inform the persons in their care that their health information will be shared with the health care team for the purposes of providing care. In some circumstances nurses are legally required to disclose confidential information without consent. When this occurs nurses should attempt to inform individuals about what information will be disclosed, to whom and for what reason(s).

7. When nurses are required to disclose health information about persons, with or without the person's informed consent, they must do so in ways that do not stigmatize individuals, families or communities. They must provide information in a way that minimizes identification as much as possible.

8. Nurses must advocate for and respect policies and safeguards to protect and preserve the person's privacy.

Source: Canadian Nurses Association Code of Ethics for Registered Nurses, p. 14, from http://www.cna-nurses.ca/cna/documents/pdf/publications/CodeofEthics2002_e.pdf. Reprinted with permission from the Canadian Nurses Association

a serious and imminent harm to a third party (such as a communicable disease or child abuse), public health and safety, the administration of justice and oversight of the professional by a regulatory body."[2] The severe acute respiratory syndrome (SARS) outbreak that occurred in Toronto, Ontario, in 2003 is an example of when public health took precedence over patient confidentiality. At that time, "index cases" (people with the illness) were named in the media to ensure that contacts would come forward for health assessment as well as follow quarantine recommendations to prevent further spread of SARS.

Privacy Protection of Personal Health Information

With the increased use of information technology systems in documenting patient data, the issue of privacy and health information in Canadian institutions has attained a higher priority than ever before. Because of its nature, there is an expectation that health information will be used only for the benefit of the individual who puts his or her trust in the health professional or health care facility. Higher levels of privacy protection must therefore be afforded to health information than other forms of personal information. The Principles for the Privacy Protection of Personal Health Information in Canada were developed jointly by the CNA, the Canadian Dental Association, the Canadian Healthcare Association, the Canadian Medical Association, the Canadian Pharmacists Association, and the Consumers' Association of Canada.[3] Nurses are expected to embrace and enact the principles that advocate:

- Privacy: Individuals have a right of privacy with respect to their personal health information.
- Consent: Individuals have the right to provide or withhold consent with respect to the collection, use, disclosure, or access of their personal health information.

- Knowledge: Individuals have a right of knowledge with respect to their personal health information.
- Individual Access: Individuals have the right to access their own personal health information.
- Accuracy: Individuals have the right to have their personal health information recorded as accurately as possible and to review and amend their health records to ensure accuracy.
- Recourse: Individuals have the right to recourse when they suspect a breach in the privacy of their health information.

Proximal Environment

The interview setting directly influences the amount and quality of information gathered. The time and effort nurses spend in finding an appropriate setting for the interview indicates concern for the patient and for the quality and quantity of information collected. Whenever possible, the interview should be conducted in a private room with controlled lighting and temperature (Figure 2-3). If securing this type of setting is not possible, control the environment by minimizing distractions and interruptions and increasing the comfort level of the patient. Use any physical barriers available in the room to provide as much privacy as possible. If efforts fail to ensure even minimal privacy, shorten the interview and gather only immediately pertinent information; defer the complete interview until privacy can be guaranteed.

Figure 2-3 A private setting for the interview is required when discussing personal or intimate health concerns with patients.

Approach

Before approaching the patient, gather all accessible patient information. Admission data and past medical records are often available and can significantly reduce the time needed for the interview. Be aware that patients may be frustrated by having to repeat information that has already been provided.

Begin the interview with an introduction, stating your name and title. Call the patient by his or her formal name at first, and ask how the patient prefers to be addressed. Simple communication using appropriate names is respectful and helps identify patients as unique persons at a time when they may be feeling quite anxious. Giving recognition also helps to lower patient anxiety and increase patient comfort level.

Examples of approaches you can use:

"Good morning, Mrs. Harris."

"Hello, Mr. Carpenter, it is nice to see you again."

Figure 2-4 Write down important information during the interview, while maintaining your focus on the patient.

Nursing Tip

Note Taking

Taking notes during the interview is useful, but the simple act of writing down what the patient says may cause some patient discomfort. Early in the interview, explain the necessity of jotting down pertinent information and show the patient the form you will be using. Over time, you will become adept in skills that expedite charting information. If the patient leads the interview or discusses sensitive issues, give the patient your full attention and defer the formal recording of information. Instead, jot down short phrases, words, and dates that can be used to complete the formal data recording after the interview (Figure 2-4).

Explain to the patient what is to follow and give an approximate time frame for the interview; this approach helps to establish trust and increases the patient's feeling of control. The more effective you are in establishing trust, the easier it will be to obtain information from the patient; for example, "Hello, Mr. Rappaport, my name is Marielle Pereira. I am a registered nurse and will be asking you some questions about why you are here today."

Time, Length, Duration

To become fully involved with the patient, enough time must be set aside for the interview. When scheduling an interview for the hospitalized patient, look at the patient's daily activities, then select a block of time for the interview that does not conflict with the patient's mealtimes or other planned activities. Ask the patient what interview times would be least disruptive to his or her daily routine and try to accommodate the patient's request.

Biases and Preconceptions

Personal belief and value systems, attitudes, biases, and preconceptions of both nurse and patient influence the sending and receiving of messages. The cultural and family contexts of each serve as a lens for interpreting societal views on ethnicity, gender, and health care. Nurses' and patients' views of themselves as cultured and gendered beings influence greatly how they think and feel about health and illness; such views also have an impact on how they respond to different clinical situations. For example, the nurse may unintentionally treat male and female patients differently, even in something as simple as addressing the patient (e.g., "Mr. Johnson" versus "Rebecca"). The nurse must be sensitive to personal as well as patient contexts in order to treat all patients fairly and respectfully.

The nurse's subjective impressions of the patient may lead to faulty assumptions about patient abilities or illnesses. For example, a patient who appears disheveled may be viewed by the nurse as not caring for his or her appearance or being in financial difficulty when, in fact, this patient has high self-esteem and is financially affluent. To counter faulty assumptions, biases, and preconceptions, nurses must continually validate information and personal impressions by gathering data thoughtfully and using effective interview techniques. Generally, the nurse's subjective feelings during the interview indicate the climate of the interview and can be used to provide additional assessment information. For example, the nurse's feelings of anxiety may be an indication or a reflection of the patient's feelings of fear, anxiety, or anger. Careful attention to these feelings may prompt you to change the interview format (to lower patient anxiety) or to refocus the questions (to gather specific data). It is important to demonstrate a nonjudgmental, accepting attitude. Helpful strategies, especially in situations that may be difficult for the nurse because of discrepancies in values and beliefs, include: (1) avoid displaying surprise, alarm, or shock; (2) avoid pretending not to hear what was said; and (3) avoid criticizing the patient.[4]

STAGES OF THE INTERVIEW PROCESS

The three stages in the interview process are the introduction or joining stage, the working stage, and the termination stage.

Stage I

The **joining stage** is the introduction stage of the interview process during which the nurse and the patient establish trust and get to know one another.

Work with the patient to define the relationship and create goals for this and any subsequent interactions.

Stage II

The **working stage** of the interview process is the time during which the bulk of the patient data is collected. It is the nurse's responsibility to keep the interview goal directed, which includes refocusing the patient and redefining the goals established in the joining stage.

Stage III

The **termination stage** is the last stage of the interview process during which information is summarized and validated, and plans for future interviews are discussed. Give the patient an indication of the amount of time left in the interview and allow the patient the opportunity to supply additional information and make comments or statements. For example, "We have about five minutes more, Mr. Raferty. Is there anything else you would like to add or mention?"

FACTORS AFFECTING COMMUNICATION

Elements that can affect the sending and receiving of messages are discussed in the following sections.

Listening

Active listening, or the act of perceiving what is said both verbally and nonverbally, is a critical factor in conducting a successful health assessment interview. According to Bradley and Edinberg, the primary goal of active listening is to decode patient messages in order to understand the situation or problem as the other person sees it.[5] Pay careful attention to all sensory data to make sense of the patient's message and formulate an appropriate response. Beware of how personal characteristics and choice of communication techniques—and the manner and timing of their use—can affect communication.

Nonverbal Cues

Nonverbal communication is conveying a message without speaking. Nonverbal behaviours effectively supplement the spoken word and provide information about both nurse and patient. Noting these behaviours offers insight into the patient's cultural expectations, current physical and emotional states, and perceived self-image. Nonverbal cues such as body position, repetitive movements of the hands or legs, rapid blinking, lack of eye contact, yawning, fidgeting, excessive smiling or frowning, and frequent clearing of the throat may indicate that the patient is not comfortable discussing their health or feelings verbally.

Health care settings can evoke a great deal of anxiety, uncertainty, or fear in patients. Loss of personal control is a major obstacle confronting patients in health care settings. In an attempt to maintain some control in unfamiliar circumstances and to decrease anxiety, patients frequently look to nurses for cues on how to behave or how to respond to questions. The nurse's nonverbal cues can signify empathy and attention, or indifference and inattention. Such behaviours powerfully influence patient comfort levels, feelings of control, and willingness to share information. Because of this, nurses need to continuously monitor their own nonverbal behaviours.

Reflective Thinking

Encouraging Active Listening

Remember the last time you attempted to talk with someone who didn't appear to be listening. How did that make you feel? What kind of things did you do to get your message across? How many times have you listened to patients with "half an ear"? What might have caused you to do this? Identify a few specific actions that you might take to ensure that your patients feel heard.

Figure 2-5 Appropriate distance between the nurse and the patient during the interview will facilitate the information-gathering process.

Distance

The amount of space a person considers appropriate for interaction is a significant factor in the interview process and is determined in part by cultural influences. In Canada, distances are generally categorized as follows:

- Intimate distance is from the patient to approximately 0.5 metres.
- Personal distance is approximately 1 to 1.5 metres.
- Social distance is approximately 1.5 to 3.5 metres.
- Public distance is approximately 3.5 metres or more.

Intimate distance is the closest and involves some physical contact. Personal distance may also involve physical contact, which can ease communication such as in the case of hearing impairment. In some situations, personal distance may be threatening or invasive to the patient. Social distance is considered appropriate for the interview process because it allows for good eye contact and for ease in hearing and in seeing the patient's nonverbal cues (Figure 2-5). Public distance is usually used in formal settings such as in a classroom where the teacher stands in front of the class; this distance is not considered practical for an interview.

Personal Space

Personal space is the area over which a person claims ownership. In an inpatient health care agency, the patient's room and bathroom are considered the patient's personal space. The patient may be very protective of this space and regard unauthorized use of it as an invasion of privacy.

EFFECTIVE INTERVIEWING TECHNIQUES

Effective interviewing techniques facilitate, support, and foster interactions between the nurse and the patient. The techniques encompass both verbal and nonverbal approaches. The skilled nurse understands the communication process and effectively uses purposeful, goal-directed methods that assist in gathering information and at the same time address the patient's health concerns. Individuals who come to a health care provider are frequently anxious, so the nurse who effectively communicates interest and concern toward patients greatly enhances the interview process.

Certain verbal communication techniques facilitate this interaction but the successful use of these techniques varies from individual to individual. At first, the techniques in the sections that follow may feel awkward, stilted, or forced; it must be kept in mind that communicating effectively is a learned skill (similar to other nursing skills) and, as such, improves with practice.

Using Open-Ended Questions

Open-ended questions encourage the patient to give general rather than more focused information. Beginning the health assessment interview with open-ended questions provides the patient with a sense of control; the patient decides what to say, how much to say, and how to say it. These types of questions indicate respect for the patient's ability to articulate important or pressing health concerns and to help set priorities.

Examples of open-ended questions:

"What are some of your concerns about caring for your mother at home?"
"How do you typically deal with an asthma attack?"

Open-ended questions that begin with the words *how, what, where, when,* and *who* will usually elicit the greatest amount of information than questions that begin with the word *why. Why* questions can make patients defensive, thus setting up an adversarial relationship between nurse and patient. Open-ended questions, though quite helpful in the health assessment interview, can be time-consuming and may not be appropriate in situations requiring quick access to information and a rapid response by health care providers. Overuse of this type of question, especially with a confused patient who is vague in his or her responses, or who may be extremely talkative, may cause the nurse to miss important information.

In certain situations, perhaps because of anxiety or unfamiliarity with the health care system, patients may try to ascertain what answers the nurse wants and what areas the nurse feels are important, rather than focus on areas that are most significant to them. Encourage the patient to define what is important when eliciting the health history and allow the patient to speak uninterrupted. After the patient completes an answer, the nurse can proceed with further questions or clarification.

Using Closed Questions

Closed questions regulate or restrict patient response and are frequently answered with a "yes" or a "no." Closed questions help focus the interview, pinpoint specific areas of concern, and elicit valuable information quickly and efficiently.

Examples of effective closed questions:
"Are you thinking of hurting yourself?"
"Has this type of allergic reaction ever happened to you before?"

However, if used too frequently, closed questions can disrupt communication because they limit patient responses and interaction. Even well-directed closed questions may imply that the nurse is in charge of the interview, often knows the answer to the question asked, and is directing the patient's response.

Examples of ineffective closed questions:
"Do you still feel sad and depressed?"
"Are you afraid to tell your parents that you are sexually active?"

Facilitating

Once the health assessment interview has started, periods may occur when patients stop talking because of anxiety, uncertainty, or embarrassment. Use a variety of verbal and nonverbal means to encourage patients to continue talking. Saying "go on" or "uh-huh," simply repeating key words the patient has spoken, or even nodding your head or touching the patient's hand prompts the patient to resume speaking. These actions also indicate to the patient that the nurse is interested and attentive (Figure 2-6).

Using Silence

If understood and used effectively by the nurse, periods of silence help structure and pace the interview, convey respect and acceptance, and, in many cases, prompt additional patient data. Silence on the part of the patient may indicate feelings of anxiety, confusion, or embarrassment, or simply a lack of understanding about the question asked or an inability to speak the language. Nonverbal data are often lost if the nurse is a persistent talker. Conversely, if overused, silence can create an awkward, disjointed interview, providing minimal structure or direction for the patient and little helpful data for the nurse.

Figure 2-6 The nurse can facilitate the interview by displaying empathy and encouraging the patient to continue talking.

Using silence effectively may appear to be a difficult skill to master. Frequently, silences seem to last longer than they actually are. When silences occur, some nurses feel discomfort and pressure to speak in order to be actually "doing" something therapeutic; instead, nurses can use silence to observe the patient's nonverbal behaviour.

Grouping Communication Techniques

Applying communication techniques often seems mechanical and artificial to the novice nurse; one way to diminish this reaction is to group or cluster the techniques according to their primary purposes. Grouping strategies based on their purpose helps to clarify the intent of each communication response and indicates when in the assessment interview its use might be helpful.[6] One simple method to group interview techniques is to divide them into two groups: listening responses and action responses.

Listening Responses

Listening responses are the nurse's attempts to accurately receive, process, and then respond to patient messages. Listening responses include making observations, restating, reflecting, clarifying, interpreting, sequencing, encouraging comparisons, and summarizing. The responses provide one way for the nurse to communicate empathy, concern, and attentiveness. Patients "need to know that the interviewer has heard what they have been saying, seen their point of view, and felt their world as they experience it."[7] In order to listen to what the patient says, the nurse must not only process the words spoken by the patient but also must understand the context of the patient's experience.

Listening responses enable the nurse to understand the patient's perspective. Patients will realize that they have been heard and that you are working for and with them to elicit and clarify their health concerns.

Making Observations

When making observations, the nurse verbalizes perceptions about the patient's behaviour, then shares them with the patient. Calling attention to behaviour about which the patient might be unaware can prove insightful in that it helps increase the patient's conscious awareness of the behaviour. Sharing observations also validates patient competency and sense of control in an environment or situation where the patient often feels out of control, uncertain, or overwhelmed.

Examples of making observations:

"Talking about these symptoms seems to make you tense. I notice that you are clenching your fists and grimacing." **or**

"I notice that each time you've been confronted with that particular problem, you've known how to handle it appropriately."

Restating

Restating is the act of repeating or rephrasing the main idea expressed by the patient; it informs the patient that you are paying attention. Restating also promotes further dialogue by giving the patient an opportunity to explain or elaborate on an issue or concern.

Examples of restating:

Patient: "I don't sleep well anymore. I find myself waking up frequently at night."

Nurse: "You're having difficulty sleeping?" **or**

"You don't sleep well?"

Reflective Thinking

Maintaining Personal Control

Recall your last experience as a patient in a hospital or other health care facility. Did you feel any sense of control regarding what was happening to you? Did you want any control in the situation? When you feel out of control, how do you behave? When you feel out of control, what do you do to alleviate the feeling? What behaviours do you think patients use to help them feel more in control when they are sick?

Reflecting

Reflection focuses on the content of the patient's message as well as the patient's feelings. In reflecting, the nurse directs the patient's own questions, feelings, and ideas back to the patient, which allows the patient to reconsider or expand on what was just said. The patient's point of view is given value, and the nurse, though showing an interest in what the patient has said, refrains from giving advice, passing judgment, or assuming responsibility for the patient's thoughts or feelings.

Examples of reflecting:

Patient: "Do you think I should tell the doctor I stopped taking my medication?"

Nurse: "What do you think about that?"

Patient: "Well, yes, I think that I probably should. Not taking my medication could be one of the reasons I'm feeling so rundown. But that medication just makes me so teary and agitated."

Nurse: "You sound a bit agitated now. It seems as if you've been thinking about this a lot."

Patient: "I told that young doctor that I had problems with this medication, and he just didn't listen."

Nurse: "Sounds as if you are pretty angry with him."

Clarifying

Clarifying is a communication technique the nurse can use to verify something the patient has said, or to pinpoint the message when the patient's words and nonverbal behaviour do not match. The nurse must be sure to understand exactly what the patient means before continuing, because communication may stop if the patient feels misunderstood or not heard. Distortions or misunderstandings about patient data can occur if the nurse interprets patient statements using only personal experiences and perceptions. Even more crucial is making assumptions that cause the nurse to proceed from a faulty database.

Example of a clarifying response:

Patient: "During certain activities, I have the most awful pain in my back."

Nurse: "Tell me what you mean by awful." **or**

Nurse: "I'm not sure that I follow you—when does this pain occur?"

Example of a problematic response, involving an assumption:

Patient: "We hardly have any time for exercise in our family. We are so busy."

Nurse: "I know what you mean!"

Interpreting

Interpreting means that the nurse shares with the patient the inferences or conclusions gathered from the interview. Although there is always the risk that the interpretation of the facts may be incorrect, the skilled nurse is well poised to link events that perhaps the patient could not piece together.

Examples of interpreting:

Nurse: "Your headaches seem to occur every time you eat nuts and chocolate." **or**

Patient: "My stomach pains seem to occur only from late summer to mid spring."

Nurse: "From what you have just told me, could it be the stress of your teaching job that is causing your pain?"

Sequencing

To effectively assess patient needs, the nurse often requires knowledge of a time frame within which symptoms or problems developed or occurred. Getting at this information involves asking the patient to place a symptom, a problem, or an event in its proper sequence. Sequencing also helps the patient and nurse become aware of any patterns in the patient's behaviour that might indicate recurring themes. The themes can relate to feelings (depression or anxiety), behaviour (refusal to take appropriate medications, consistently putting self in risky situations), or experiences (being beaten, being hurt, or being misunderstood by health care providers). Pattern identification provides the nurse with clues for further focus.

Examples of sequencing:

"Did this sharp pain occur each time you had sexual intercourse or only when you didn't empty your bladder first?" **or**

"What specific events led you to feel overwhelmed and suicidal?"

Encouraging Comparisons

Encouraging comparisons is a technique that enables the nurse and the patient to become more aware of related patterns or themes, or specific symptomatology, in the patient's life. The patient can then comfortably deal with unfamiliar situations by placing the symptoms or problems into a familiar context. Often, an awareness of successful prior dealings with similar situations increases patient confidence levels and self-care potentials.

Examples of encouraging comparisons:

"Have you had similar experiences?" **or**

"In what way was this allergy attack different from or the same as your previous ones?" **or**

"In what way was your reaction to this medication similar to or different from your reaction to other antibiotics you've taken before?"

Summarizing

Summarizations help patients (and the nurse) to organize their thinking. Because of this, summarizing is a communication technique that is especially useful at the end of the health assessment interview. A brief, concise review of the important points covered helps the patient identify anything that has been left out and gives the nurse an opportunity to confirm that what he or she understood the patient to say is actually what was said. In addition, summarizing indicates interest and concern that the patient feels heard as well as is finished.

Nursing Tip

The Use of Humour in the Patient Interview

Humour can be an effective communication technique in the patient interview. It can make an anxious patient feel more at ease, diffuse tension, and make it easier for a patient to discuss sensitive issues. However, ill-timed humour or the use of inappropriate humour can offend individuals and make them distrustful of the nurse.

Example of summarizing:

"During this past hour, you have shared with me several health concerns of which the most worrisome to you is your difficulty in losing weight. Is that correct?"

Summarizing also provides a means of smoothly transitioning to a new topic or section of the health assessment.

Example of transitioning:

"You talked about your past experience with diabetes and what happened to you yesterday; now let's talk about why you came in today."

Action Responses

Action responses are the second group of effective interviewing techniques. These responses stimulate patients to make some change in their thinking and behaviour. Action responses include such communication techniques as focusing, exploring, presenting reality, confronting, informing, limit setting, and normalizing.

Focusing

Focusing allows the nurse to concentrate on or to track a specific point the patient has made. This technique is particularly useful with patients whose heightened anxiety level increases their confusion, alters their concentration, or causes them to jump from topic to topic. With the nurse's assistance in focusing, the patient can proceed with the health history in a clearer, more organized, thoughtful, and thorough manner.

Examples of focusing:

"Tell me more about the chest pain you experience when you begin to exercise." **or**

"You've mentioned several times that your wife is concerned about your smoking. Let's go back to that."

Exploring

In exploring, the nurse attempts to develop, in more detail, a specific topic or patient concern (Figure 2-7). The purpose of exploring is to identify patterns or themes in symptom presentation or in the way patients handle problems or health concerns.

Examples of exploring:

"Tell me more about how you feel when you do not take your medication."

"Could you describe for me how you handle those periods in your life when you feel out of control?"

Presenting Reality

This technique is useful in the health assessment interview when the nurse is confronted with a patient who exaggerates or makes grandiose statements. Presenting reality, when done in a nonargumentative way, encourages the patient to rethink a statement and perhaps modify it.

Example of presenting reality:

Patient: "I can never get an appointment at this clinic."

Nurse: "Mr. Jasper, I've seen you several times in the past four months."

Patient: "Well, yes, but I can never get an appointment at a time that is convenient for me."

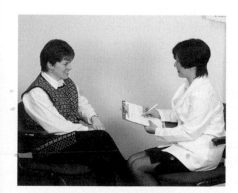

Figure 2-7 Through the technique of exploring, the nurse can help the patient identify patterns or themes regarding health concerns.

Confronting

Confronting is a verbal response the nurse makes to a perceived discrepancy or incongruence between the patient's statements and behaviours. Gently challenging the discrepancy can help the patient reframe a situation in order to see things differently. Confrontation can be used to focus the patient's attention on some aspect of personal perception or behaviour that, if changed, could lead to more effective or adaptive functioning.[8] When confronting is done in a caring, empathetic manner, rather than a critical or accusatory one, patients feel encouraged to see themselves as competent and effective individuals.

Example of confronting:

Patient: "I have been working on lowering my risk for a heart attack. I take my cholesterol pill every day and have been watching my diet."

Nurse: "You say that you are working on reducing your cardiovascular risk; however, I notice that you continue to smoke two packs of cigarettes every day and your triglycerides have doubled in the past three months. Perhaps we can discuss this a bit more?"

Informing

Providing the patient with essential information, such as explaining the nature of or the reasons for specific tests or procedures, is a nursing action that helps build trust and decreases patient anxiety. Information giving also provides the patient with possible choices that the patient can then evaluate correctly.

Example of informing:

Patient: "Dr. Jones told me that I need to have my gallbladder taken out."

Nurse: "Did you understand what she told you about your gallbladder surgery?"

Patient: "No, I didn't understand what she said . . . something about a tube."

Nurse: "There is a relatively new technique where the surgeon inserts a tube in your abdomen to remove the gallbladder rather than making a large incision."

Patient: "Yes, that was it; please tell me more about that."

Limit Setting

During the interview with a seductive, hostile, or talkative patient, the nurse may find it necessary to set specific limits on patient behaviour. For example, if the patient persists in asking personal questions or rambles despite frequent attempts by the nurse to focus, it will be difficult to obtain the required information. Patient behaviour of this kind may be a manifestation of stress produced by the interview situation itself or simply a characteristic specific to that patient. In such situations, patients may require some guidance in how to behave—calmly, clearly, and respectfully tell the patient what behaviour is expected. Limit only the behaviour that is problematic or detrimental to the purpose of the interview; avoid making a "big issue" of the behaviour. When limit-setting, do not argue or make empty threats or promises, but do offer the patient alternatives.

Example of appropriate limit setting:

"When you ask me questions about my sex life it makes me feel uncomfortable and I would like you to stop asking me such questions. You came to the clinic today because of a personal health reason so please tell me about it so that I can know more how we can help you."

Example of ineffective limit setting:

"If you don't start answering my questions, we'll never finish."

Nursing Tip

Answering Personal Questions

A lifetime of experiences and emotions is brought to each patient encounter. It is natural for the patient to be curious about you as the health care provider. Sharing personal experiences makes you a "real" person to the patient and helps develop a respectful nurse–patient interaction. For some patients, focusing on the nurse's dialogue alleviates their tension around the topic under discussion, or it may be a way of measuring the credibility of the nurse. Most nurses sense when the boundary between a professional and a social interaction has been crossed. In these cases, it is important to direct the focus back to the patient by using a simple statement such as "Enough about me, let's get back to your health history."

Figure 2-8 Normalizing allows the nurse to reassure the patient that many other patients with similar health concerns react in the same manner.

Normalizing

Patients faced with unexpected or life-threatening illnesses, or invasive and risky treatment options such as surgery, respond in ways that seem extreme or out of the ordinary (e.g., becoming depressed or overly distressed). Normalizing allows the nurse to offer appropriate reassurance that the patient's response is quite common for the situation. This approach helps to decrease patient anxiety and encourages patients to share thoughts and feelings that were withheld for fear of being judged or misunderstood (Figure 2-8). Be mindful that if used inappropriately or out of context, normalizing can give false reassurance.

Example of normalizing:

"It is no wonder that you've been feeling shocked and overwhelmed since you first found that lump in your breast. Many women who have that experience react in a similar way."

NONTHERAPEUTIC INTERVIEWING TECHNIQUES

Effective communication techniques facilitate dialogue between nurse and patient, but some interviewing techniques can change, distort, or block communication and should be avoided. Verbal and nonverbal behaviours that involve inattentiveness, imposition of values, judgment, lack of interest, or an "I know what's best for you" attitude hinder communication by creating distance rather than connection. Patients on the receiving end of these behaviours may feel angry, defensive, or incompetent and may refuse to actively participate. Ineffective interview techniques include requesting an explanation, probing, offering false reassurance, giving approval or disapproval, defending, and advising.

Requesting an Explanation

Questions that begin with the word *why* are often perceived by the patient as challenging or threatening. *Why* questions imply criticism in that the patient is asked to provide a reason or justification for personal beliefs, feelings, thoughts, and behaviours. If patients are unable to provide answers, either from lack of knowledge or because they do not know the answer (some individuals are unaware of why they do things), they may feel inadequate, defensive, or angry. Instead, ask the patient to *describe* the belief, feeling, or behaviour, which often helps the patient to elaborate. By enlarging the context, the patient's self-awareness is increased, and the nurse is able to gather relevant information.

Example 1 of requesting an explanation:
Patient: "I guess I drink two or three six-packs of beer a weekend."
Nurse: "Why do you drink that much?"
Patient: "That's not very much; my friend drinks the same amount."

A more appropriate response in the preceding example might be:
"It sounds as if you might be concerned about the amount of beer you drink." (reflection)

Example 2 of requesting an explanation:
Patient: "I'm not sure why I came to the clinic today; I just feel miserable. I don't want to see anyone. I just want to stay in bed with the covers pulled over my head."

Nurse: "Why do you feel that way?"

Patient: "I don't know."

A more effective response would be:

"What happened that caused you to feel so miserable?" (clarification) or "It sounds as if you are feeling rather overwhelmed today." (reflection)

Probing

Repeated or persistent questioning about a statement or a behaviour increases patient anxiety and can cause confusion, hostility, and a tendency to withdraw from the interaction. Patient withdrawal can result in longer periods of silence, which can also escalate the nurse's anxiety. Anxious nurses tend to become more active and directive in the interview. The patient's unwillingness or hesitancy to discuss a certain event or health concern may indicate patient misunderstanding, misinformation, or a major problem area that needs further clarification or exploration.

A rule of thumb nurses can use to identify whether they are probing is to pay close attention to their behaviours and feelings. If nurses feel frustrated, irritated, or feel that they are pursuing the patient, or have become involved in a verbal tug of war with the patient, then they are most likely probing. Moving on to the next part of the health assessment, asking the patient's permission to return to the subject later, or just sitting quietly until the patient begins to speak are more appropriate ways for the nurse to gather information.

Example 1 of probing:

Nurse: "What makes you drink a six-pack of beer after dinner each night?"

Patient: "I'm not sure."

Nurse: "Well, are there things going on in your life right now that would cause you to drink that much?"

Patient: "Not really."

Nurse: "I don't really think that you would drink that much if things weren't happening in your life right now."

Example 2 of probing:

Nurse: "What makes you think that you have arthritis?"

Patient: "I'm not sure, I just think I do. It just seems like I have the same health problems as my mother and she had arthritis."

Nurse: "Well, do you have pain?"

Patient: "Yes." (pauses)

Nurse: "Why do you think the pain is arthritis pain?"

Reflective Thinking

False Reassurance

Consider the following example of false reassurance.

Mr. and Mrs. Quinn are awaiting results of diagnostic testing that will confirm or reject a diagnosis of fetal neurological impairment. Mrs. Quinn says to the nurse, "It's taking so long to get the results, I'm sure that there must be something wrong with the baby." The nurse replies, "Oh, no, you don't need to worry. Everything will be just fine!"

- What do you suppose motivated the nurse's response?
- What impact will the nurse's response have on the Quinns?

Offering False Reassurance

False reassurances are vague and simplistic responses that question the patient's judgment, devalue and block the patient's feelings, and communicate a lack of understanding and sensitivity on the nurse's part. The impulse to give false reassurance typically originates from the nurse's own feelings of anxiety and helplessness; it is an attempt by the nurse to take care of herself or himself rather than the patient, which can often increase patient anxiety. A more valuable nursing response would be to first acknowledge personal feelings of anxiety and then to acknowledge the patient's feelings.

Examples of false reassurance:
"Everything will be fine."
"I wouldn't worry about that."

Example of an appropriate response:
"It must be frightening to think about the possibility of surgery."

Giving Approval or Disapproval

During the health assessment interview, nurses may feel pressured to comment on a patient's statement, feeling, or behaviour, especially if the patient's response contradicts the nurse's own beliefs or feelings. Telling a patient what is right or wrong is moralizing and limits the patient's freedom to verbalize or behave in ways that might not please the nurse. Comments such as "What a good idea," "You shouldn't feel that way," or "That is bad" hinder the nurse's attempts to establish rapport, support patient competence, and facilitate communication. When there is concern that the patient's expressed beliefs or behaviours are ill-informed, harmful, or destructive, it is more effective for the nurse to explore the source of the belief or the impact of the patient's behaviour on others.

Examples of effective responses:
"Tell me how you came to that conclusion?"
"What do you think the consequences will be if you continue to keep your illness from your wife?"

Defending

Occasionally, patients who have had previous stressful or unpleasant experiences with health care professionals, hospitals, or other agents of the health care system will criticize or verbally attack the nurse. Defending the attack is not helpful for the nurse; it implies that the patient does not have the right to hold strong opinions or to express hostile feelings. In addition, deflection or criticism of the patient's feelings more often than not blocks expression of these feelings or reinforces them. Defensiveness is not therapeutic, because it requires nurses to speak not only for themselves, but also for others, something that nurses realistically cannot do.

Examples of inappropriate responses:
"This hospital has an excellent reputation. I'm sure that if you were kept waiting as long as you say, there was a good reason."
"No one here would lie to you."

It is more respectful and useful to accept and support patients' rights to express their feelings, whether the nurse agrees with the patient or not. Empathetic responses defuse any antagonism and minimize patient resistance to the continued interaction.

Examples of appropriate responses:

Nurse: "You sound pretty angry about your previous experiences in this hospital."

Patient: "Of course I am. Wouldn't you be upset if no one ever told you what was going on and no one answered your call bell?"

Nurse: "I guess I'd be pretty upset if I thought people were not treating me respectfully or that my needs were being neglected."

Advising

Consistently telling a patient what to do does not foster competence. Advising encourages patients to look to others for answers, deprives them of the opportunity to learn from past mistakes, and discourages independent judgment. Because some patients may resort to dependent, passive behaviour when faced with illness, it is important that the nurse not reinforce the behaviour, but rather support the patient's healthy functioning as much as possible.

Example of ineffective responses:

Patient: "Do you think that I should have an abortion?"

Nurse: "Well, if I were you, I'd certainly think long and hard before I'd have another child. You are having difficulty feeding the one you have now." **or**

"No, I think you should continue the pregnancy. Abortion is never the answer."

The nurse's response should support the patient's own problem-solving ability through the use of therapeutic communication techniques, such as exploring or reflection.

Examples of exploring:

"Tell me more about what made you consider an abortion." **or**

"What other alternatives have you considered?"

Examples of reflection:

"Do you think you should?" **or**

"How would you feel about having the abortion?"

Using Problematic Questioning Techniques

Experienced and novice interviewers alike will find themselves, on occasion, feeling nervous and perhaps unsure of how to proceed during the health assessment interview. Anxiety leads to the use of interview techniques and responses that, while not specifically identified as nontherapeutic, are potentially problematic. Ineffective techniques increase patient anxiety, decrease the flow of needed information, and may garner irrelevant data. The following sections outline several examples of problematic interviewing techniques.

Posing Leading Questions

Leading questions indicate to the patient that the nurse already has a certain answer in mind. Asking these types of questions may intimidate the patient and curtail further communication, especially if the topic is one that the patient perceives as sensitive or is a source of anxiety.

Examples of leading questions:

"You've never had any type of sexually transmitted infections, have you, Miss Jenkins?" **or**

"You are going to be breastfeeding, aren't you?"

Interrupting the Patient

Changing the subject or interrupting the patient prevents completion of a thought or idea and introduces a new focus. Such behaviour may ease the nurse's discomfort, but it shows a lack of respect and often confuses or irritates the patient. Questions should focus on one particular topic until all relevant data have been collected and the patient feels finished.

Neglecting to Ask Pertinent Questions

It is easy for the nurse to become complacent while conducting patient interviews. Do not let a patient's physical appearance, personality, or social standing distract you from ascertaining pertinent information. For example, do not assume that a well-dressed patient who discusses a luxury car is well off. Likewise, do not presume that a poorly dressed or ill-mannered patient is poor or uneducated. All patients deserve to be treated respectfully during the patient interview.

Talkativeness

A nurse who is extremely talkative portrays nervousness and uncertainty. Attempts to maintain control of the interview and to ease personal anxiety may cause the nurse to talk more than necessary. Talkativeness decreases patient spontaneity and increases patient passivity, causing the nurse to work even harder at obtaining necessary information. The patient's interpretation may be that the nurse's thoughts are more important than the patient's.

Using Multiple Questions

Nurses may confuse patients by asking them several questions at once. Too many questions may put patients on the defensive, minimizing patient participation and impeding the flow of necessary information.

Using Medical Jargon

The use of medical jargon or slang can be quite anxiety provoking for the patient. The health care system has its own culture and language, including acronyms or abbreviations. Patients who feel frightened and powerless in this unfamiliar environment are further disadvantaged by any perceived language barrier. The patient may believe that the nurse is not willing to share, or is attempting to hide information when medical jargon is used, or that the nurse feels superior and is unwilling to engage in mutual problem solving. Conduct the interview using language that is common to both participants, and check periodically with the patient to clarify meaning; this indicates to the patient that the nurse is interested and has a desire to work collaboratively.

Being Authoritative

The use of authority by a health care professional can be problematic. It reinforces a patriarchal nurse–patient relationship and limits the establishment of a collaborative relationship.

Example of negative use of authority:
"I've been a nurse for over ten years, and I think I know what is best for you."

However, in a few situations, the use of authority can be an effective communication technique.

Example of positive use of authority:

"As your health care provider, knowing about your previous heart attack, history of high blood pressure, and family history of stroke, I suggest you consider stopping smoking."

Having Hidden Agendas

Frequently, patients seek health care for one problem but actually are concerned about other problems. The patient may believe that the overriding issue is embarrassing, private, or insignificant, but once in the presence of a health care provider the patient may open up and discuss concerns. For example, a patient may seek care for a sore throat, then ask for blood work to test for HIV. The nurse should deal with the patient's concerns in the best way possible, then follow up when indicated.

INTERVIEWING THE PATIENT WITH SPECIAL NEEDS

Patients with special needs offer a particular challenge to the nurse during the interview. Although the goal of the interview and the specific interviewing techniques remain the same, the process differs according to the patient's impairment. Conducting a successful assessment interview with the patient with special needs may require more time and effort than usual and often requires the help of an intermediary, such as a family member or a friend of the patient.

The Patient Who Is Hearing Impaired

Some hearing-impaired patients can read lips, so it is important that the nurse remain within sight of the patient and face the patient while talking. If the patient uses a hearing device, make sure it is in working order and is turned on. Background noise can distract the patient and should therefore be minimized. Even if an **intermediary** (a liaison between the patient and a member of the health care team) assists in the interview, always face the patient and direct all communication to the patient (Figure 2-9). It is common for those speaking to a hearing-impaired person to speak loudly or slowly, both of which detract from the patient's ability to read lips. Although tone and inflection of voice are lost to the hearing-impaired patient, nonverbal cues such as facial expressions and body movements can effectively convey the meaning of what is being said.

Patients who have never had the ability to hear or who have had hearing loss for a long time may have speech that is difficult to understand. Often, the best approach to interviewing these patients is to allow additional time and to use a written form for gathering data. When communicating through writing, always remain with the patient to clarify questions and answers.

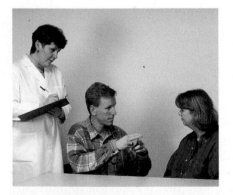

Figure 2-9 When using an interpreter during the interview, always direct your questions and attention to the patient.

The Patient Who Is Visually Impaired

When interviewing a patient with a visual impairment, always look directly at the patient as if the patient were sighted. Because the visually impaired patient cannot rely on visual cues, the nurse's voice intonation, volume, and inflection become more important. It is common for those speaking to a visually impaired patient to speak loudly; this is not necessary and can hinder communication.

Touch is especially important to the visually impaired patient; however, an unanticipated touch can be frightening. Before touching the patient, be certain to inform the patient and ask permission to touch. Let the patient know when you are entering or leaving the room, and orient the patient to the

Nursing Tip

Caring for the Illiterate Patient

The patient who is illiterate is unable to complete or verify written assessment data. Therefore, alternative strategies must be used to ensure that education on treatment and follow-up is simple and clear. Some strategies to use include:

- Illustrated charts that describe procedures and treatments
- A picture of a clock to indicate time
- Colour-coded medications
- Patient recall on instructions to double-check accuracy
- Follow-up with a home health care agency when indicated to ensure appropriate care

◄NURSING CHECKLIST►

How to Use an Interpreter

1. Use a trained medical interpreter whenever possible.
2. When possible, allow the interpreter and patient a few minutes to converse before initiating the interview.
3. Instruct the interpreter to translate the patient's replies sentence by sentence, thus avoiding summarization; this strategy ensures that important information is not omitted.
4. Keep questions brief. Inform the interpreter what information you want to obtain.
5. Maintain eye contact with the patient, not the interpreter, during the questioning and translating.
6. Observe the patient's nonverbal communication, being sensitive to cultural influences.
7. Be patient! Extra time needs to be allotted for this type of interview.
8. When available, use preprinted questions and health care instructions in the patient's native language.

immediate environment; use clock hours to indicate position of items in relation to the patient. Partially sighted patients may cling to the independence that their limited vision allows; offer them assistance and follow their cues or responses.

The Patient Who Is Speech Impaired or Aphasic

When interviewing a patient who has a speech impairment, ask simple questions that require yes or no answers and allow additional time for responses. Convert open-ended questions such as "How are you today?" to closed questions such as "Are you feeling well now?" Repeat or rephrase any questions the patient has not understood. A written interview format, letter board, or yes/no cards are alternate methods of communication. Even when all closed questions have been asked and answered, allow the patient with aphasia to contribute to the information gathering. For example, "I have asked all the questions I have to ask you for now. Would you like to tell me anything related to any of the questions I have asked?" Then continue with, "Would you like to say anything else before we conclude the interview?"

When someone else is speaking for the patient, the nurse should speak and direct questions to the patient, not to the intermediary. If you ask the aphasic patient to complete a written format of the interview, remain with the patient to clarify questions and to explain data requirements.

Dealing with Language Barriers

The assistance of an interpreter may be necessary in situations where there is a language barrier between the health care professional and the patient. Most health care agencies have a register of interpreters available, though sometimes the patient will bring a translator to the agency. The translator may not be able to answer questions for the patient, so it is important that the nurse direct questions to the patient and not to the interpreter.

Often, information that is lost in the translation can be gained through non-verbal cues. Pay special attention to the patient's facial expressions and body movements. The use of signs, such as pointing, can be helpful in an emergency situation; however, a more complete interview should be deferred until an interpreter is present.

The Patient Who Has a Low Level of Understanding

The patient with a low level of intelligence requires time to process the interview questions, to formulate answers, and to clarify the meaning or intent of the interview. Rushing through the process may cause the patient to become confused, lose concentration, or refuse to answer. Request permission from the patient to interview the patient's family or caregiver if supplemental information is required, and respect the patient's right to be present during all phases of the interview. Always direct interview questions to the patient, and allow the patient to request assistance from family members or the caregiver. Observe the interaction between the patient and the family or caregiver, because nonverbal communication can provide valuable information about the patient's present health or illness state as well as about the relationship between the patient and the family member or caregiver.

The Patient Who Is Crying

On some occasions patients can be expected to cry during the interview, such as when parents have related events that led to their child's death. Other times a patient may cry unexpectedly, which affords an opportunity for the nurse to gain information that is important to the patient by gently asking what is causing the emotional response. Show empathy and allow the patient to cry. Offering tissues indicates to the patient that it is okay to cry and conveys a message of thoughtfulness (Figure 2-10).

The Patient Who Is Anxious and Angry

Patients and those who speak for patients in health care settings are frequently emotionally upset. For example, the parent of a sick child may be overwhelmed by events that led to the child's hospitalization. Emotional outbursts and crying are often the result of such stress. Allow the patient, family member, or significant other to express emotions. If it is obvious that the person is holding back tears, give permission to express emotion with a simple statement such as, "I can see that you are upset; it's okay to cry."

When interviewing an obviously angry person, recognize and acknowledge the emotion. A natural instinct is to personalize the anger and become angry in return; instead, recognize the emotion and bring it to the patient's attention. "You appear very angry about something. Before we continue with the interview,

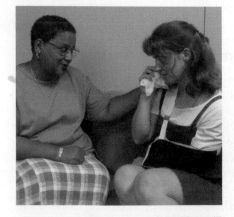

Figure 2-10 Supporting the crying patient will facilitate a trusting nurse–patient relationship.

please tell me about your feelings." Avoid statements such as "Take a moment to get hold of yourself," because this directive implies that the patient's feelings are not appropriate and should not be expressed. Acknowledging patients' emotions and giving them permission to express feelings conveys respect and enhances genuine communication.

The Patient Who Is Hostile

Before beginning the interview, review any documentation that might alert you to people with a past history of violence or poor impulse control. Try to gain an understanding of why such behaviour is being exhibited. It is important to be aware that anger and hostility can be "contagious"; do not reciprocate with a defensive attitude.

The risk of aggression can be minimized through nonthreatening interventions such as limit-setting and refocusing. Exploring the sources of the hostility may help to clarify and allay such feelings; however, if a negative tone continues and hostility increases, the nurse must consider his or her own safety. Positioning yourself near an accessible exit, keeping your face to the patient, leaving the door ajar, and alerting a colleague about a worrisome interview are ways to ensure personal safety. Signs of increasing tension in the patient (e.g., clenched fists, raised- or angry-toned voice) may be an indication to leave a potentially threatening and dangerous situation. Most health agencies have team strategies to deal with such situations.

The Patient Who Is Sexually Aggressive

A sexually aggressive patient may act out during the interview by, for example, standing very close to the nurse and saying, "You have been so nice to me, and I would like the chance to be nice to you." It is important to set limits and to focus on tasks when dealing with sexually aggressive patients. The nurse can achieve this by defining appropriate boundaries, sharing personal reactions, and refocusing the patient; for example, by stating, "It makes me feel very uncomfortable when you stand this close to me. Let's get back to getting information to assist in your health care needs."

The Patient Who Is Under the Influence of Alcohol or Drugs

The patient who is under the influence of alcohol or drugs can present a challenge to the nurse. Depending on the quantity and type of substance ingested, the patient can have central nervous system (CNS) depression or can be disruptive with CNS stimulation. In either case, the patient's judgment may be impaired, which can lead to physical harm to those in the immediate environment. For this reason, when the nurse encounters a violent or agitated patient, appropriate security measures should be taken.

The Patient Who Is Very Ill

Patients who are very sick may not have the strength or ability to complete the entire interview process. Collect pertinent data from the patient and defer the remainder of the interview for a later time. It may be necessary to interview a family member or significant other. Show respect for the patient by asking permission to do this and by allowing the patient to be present during the interview. Allow the patient to participate as much as possible in answering questions and giving information.

Figure 2-11 Family members, such as adult children or spouses, can provide valuable assistance during the interview process.

The Older Adult

Interviewing the older person may require additional time for question interpretation and patient responses. If necessary, schedule more than one interview for older patients who may have multisystem changes or issues, a weakened physical condition, or a cognitive impairment. A family member or caregiver may have to be interviewed in order to assess the patient's past and present health or illness status. As in any interview situation, when the patient is assisted by another individual, include the patient and assess the quality of interaction between the two (Figure 2-11).

◀NURSING CHECKLIST▶

Effective Interviewing

- Be aware of your personal beliefs and how they were acquired. Avoid imposing your beliefs on patients.
- Listen and observe. Attend to verbal and affective content as well as to non-verbal cues.
- Focus your attention on the patient. Do not listen with "half an ear." Do not think about other things when you are interviewing.
- Maintain eye contact with the patient as is appropriate for the patient's culture.
- Notice the patient's speech patterns and any recurring themes. Note any extra emphasis that the patient places on certain words or topics.
- Do not assume that you understand the meaning of all patient communications. Clarify frequently.
- Paraphrase and summarize occasionally to help patients organize their thinking, clarify issues, and begin to explore specific concerns more deeply.
- Allow for periods of silence.
- Remember that attitudes and feelings may be conveyed nonverbally.
- Consistently monitor your reactions to the patient's verbal and nonverbal messages.
- Do not judge, criticize, or preach.
- Avoid the use of nontherapeutic interviewing techniques.

REVIEW QUESTIONS

1. The role of the nurse in the patient interview is to:
   a. Freely communicate thoughts, feelings, and perceptions
   b. Influence the patient's decision-making process
   c. Facilitate the interview process for the patient
   d. Passively observe the patient's use of the health care system
   The correct answer is (c).

2. Which situation depicts an appropriate use of sharing confidential information?
   a. Discussing your patient's postoperative complications with a friend in the hospital elevator

   b. Relating to a 19-year-old patient's parents that she has vaginal bleeding from her recent abortion
   c. Describing your patient's sexual activity to the unit receptionist
   d. Presenting a clinical update on a patient's sickle cell crisis to the nurse manager on rounds
   The correct answer is (d).

3. In which stage of the interview process is information summarized and validated?
   a. Introductory stage
   b. Joining stage
   c. Working stage
   d. Termination stage
   The correct answer is (d).

4. Which distance may be the most appropriate to use when interviewing a patient with a severe hearing impairment?
   a. Intimate
   b. Personal
   c. Social
   d. Public
   The correct answer is (b).

5. The effective interviewing techniques that stimulate patients to make some changes in their thinking and behaviour are called:
   a. Listening responses
   b. Action responses
   c. Verbal communication
   d. Active listening
   The correct answer is (b).

6. You ask your patient if his chest pain started before, during, or after exercise the past two days. This pattern identification exemplifies the communication technique of:
   a. Encouraging comparisons
   b. Sequencing
   c. Interpreting
   d. Summarizing
   The correct answer is (b).

7. The nurse says to the patient, "Let's talk further about what may be keeping you from having a restful sleep each night." This statement reflects the use of which communication technique?
   a. Collaboration
   b. Limit setting
   c. Normalizing
   d. Informing
   The correct answer is (a).

8. The preoperative nurse comforts the anxious patient awaiting surgery. You overhear the nurse tell the patient, "Don't worry. Everything will turn out fine. You're in good hands." This exemplifies which nontherapeutic interviewing technique?
   a. Requesting an explanation
   b. Probing
   c. Offering false reassurance
   d. Advising
   The correct answer is (c).

9. You are interviewing a patient who was injured in a hockey game. You ask him, "Being such a well-conditioned athlete, you likely don't use any illegal substances. Is that right?" This question is an example of:
   a. Posing leading questions
   b. Being authoritative
   c. Having a hidden agenda
   d. Engaging in talkativeness
   The correct answer is (a).

10. Which action would alert the nurse to the possibility that a patient may become hostile?
    a. The patient is speaking in a loud voice with clenched fists.
    b. The patient is crying and suddenly comes over to you and gives you a hug.
    c. The patient is sitting across the room from the nurse, laughing hysterically.
    d. The patient is looking out the window while tapping his foot.
    The correct answer is (a).

> Visit the Estes online companion resource at
> **www.healthassessment.nelson.com** for additional content and study aids.

REFERENCES

[1] Gottlieb, L. N., & Feeley, N & Dalton, C. (2006). *The collaborative partnership approach to care: A delicate balance* (p. 8). Toronto: Elsevier Canada.

[2] Canadian Nurses Association. (2003). *Privacy and health information: Challenges for nurses and for the nursing profession* (p. 5). Ethics in practice, November, 2003. Retrieved May 30, 2006, from http://www.cna-nurses.ca/cna/documents/pdf/publications/ Ethics_Pract_Privacy_Health_Nov_2003_e.pdf

[3] The Privacy Working Group (Canadian Dental Association, Canadian Medical Association, Canadian Pharmacists Association, Canadian Healthcare Association, Canadian Nurses Association, Consumers' Association of Canada). (2000). *Principles for the privacy protection of personal health information in Canada*. Retrieved June 1, 2006, from http://cna-aiic.ca/CNA/documents/pdf/publications/principles_privacy_ protection_e.pdf

[4] Gottlieb, Feeley & Dalton. *The collaborative partnership approach to care: A delicate balance* (p. 84).

[5] Bradley, J. C., & Edinberg, M. A. (1990). *Communication in the nursing context* (3rd ed.). East Norwalk, CT: Appleton & Lange.

[6] Cormier, W. H., & Cormier, L. S. (1991). *Interviewing strategies for helpers: Fundamental skills and cognitive behavioral interventions* (3rd ed.). Pacific Grove, CA: Brooks/Cole.

[7] Ivey, A. (1994). *Intentional interviewing and counseling: Facilitating client development in a multicultural society* (3rd ed.) (p. 99). Pacific Grove, CA: Brooks/Cole.

[8] Cormier & Cormier. *Interviewing strategies for helpers: Fundamental skills and cognitive behavioral interventions.*

[9] Canadian Nurses Association. (2002). *Position statement: Violence*. Retrieved June 1, 2006, from http://www.cna-nurses.ca/CNA/documents/pdf/publications/PS57_ Violence_March_2002_e.pdf

BIBLIOGRAPHY

Buresh, B., & Gordon, S. (2006). *From silence to voice what nurses know and must communicate to the public.* Ithaca: ILR Press/Cornell University Press.

Caldwell, P. (2006). *Finding you finding me: Using intensive interaction to get in touch with people whose severe learning disabilities are combined with autistic spectrum disorder.* Philadelphia: Jessica Kingsley.

Calero, H. H. (2005). *The power of non-verbal communication: What you do is more important than what you say.* Los Angeles, CA: Silver Lake Pub.

Canadian Nurses Association. (2006). Public health nursing practice and ethical challenges. *Ethics in practice, February 2006.* Available at http://www.cna-nurses.ca/cna/documents/pdf/publications/Ethics_in_Practice_Jan_06_e.pdf

Cegala, D. J., Post, D. M., & McClure, L. (2001). Effects of patient communication skills training on the discourse of older patients during the primary care interview. *Journal of the American Geriatric Society, 49*(11), 1505–11.

Charon, R. (2006). *Narrative medicine: Honoring the stories of illness.* New York: Oxford University Press.

Deering, C. G., & Cody, D. J. (2002). Communicating with children and adolescents. *American Journal of Nursing, 102*(3), 34–42.

Frisch, N. C., & Frisch, L. E. (2006). *Psychiatric mental health nursing* (3rd ed.). Clifton Park, NY: Thomson Delmar Learning.

Hughes, J., Louw, S. J., & Sabat, S. R. (2006). *Dementia: Mind, meaning, and the person.* New York: Oxford University Press.

Jeffrey, D. (2006). *Patient-centered ethics and communication at the end of life.* Oxford: Radcliffe.

Koernig Blais, K. (2006). *Professional nursing practice: Concepts and perspectives.* Upper Saddle River, NJ: Pearson/Prentice Hall.

Petronio, S. (2002). *Boundaries of privacy: Dialectics of discussion.* Albany, NY: SUNY Press.

Registered Nurses' Association of Ontario. (2002, revised 2006). *Establishing therapeutic relationships.* Toronto: Registered Nurses' Association of Ontario.

Thomas, R. K. (2006). *Health communication.* New York: Springer.

Sheldon, L. K. (2004). *Communication for nurses.* Clifton Park, NY: Thomson Delmar Learning.

Warner, H. K. (Ed.) (2006). *Meeting the needs of children with disabilities: Families and professionals facing the challenge together.* New York: Routledge.

WEB RESOURCES

Canadian Nurses Association
http://www.cna-nurses.ca/cna/

World Literacy of Canada
http://www.worldlit.ca/

Nursing Regulatory Bodies
- Alberta: College and Association of Registered Nurses of Alberta http://www.nurses.ab.ca/
- British Columbia: College of Registered Nurses of British Columbia http://www.crnbc.ca/
- Manitoba: College of Registered Nurses of Manitoba http://www.crnm.mb.ca/
- New Brunswick: Nurses Association of New Brunswick http://www.nanb.nb.ca/
- Newfoundland: Association of Registered Nurses of Newfoundland and Labrador http://www.arnnl.nf.ca/
- Northwest Territories and Nunavut: Registered Nurses Association of Northwest Territories and Nunavut http://www.rnantnu.ca/
- Nova Scotia: College of Registered Nurses of Nova Scotia http://www.crnns.ca/
- Ontario: College of Nurses of Ontario http://www.cno.org/
- Prince Edward Island: Association of Registered Nurses of Prince Edward Island http://www.anpei.ca/
- Quebec: Ordres des Infirmières et Infirmiers du Québec (Quebec Order of Nurses) http://www.oiiq.org/
- Saskatchewan: Saskatchewan Registered Nurses' Association http://www.srna.org/
- Yukon: Yukon Registered Nurses Association http://www.yrna.ca/

CHAPTER 3

The Complete Health History, Including Documentation

COMPETENCIES

1. Identify the key determinants of health.

2. State the purpose of the four different types of health history and provide an example of when each is used.

3. Identify the components of the complete health history.

4. Describe how to assess the 10 characteristics of a health issue or concern.

5. Diagram a patient's genogram correctly.

6. Demonstrate sensitivity to patients of different ethnic backgrounds, religions, sexual orientations, and socioeconomic status when conducting a health history.

7. Conduct a complete health history on ill patients and on well patients and record the data.

*T*he health history interview is usually the first step of patient assessment. The patient's health status is obtained from the well or ill patient and from other sources. The health history also provides information on a patient's social, emotional, physical, cultural, developmental, and spiritual identities. The patient's subjective information is combined with the physical assessment findings to guide the nurse in analyzing the strengths, deficits, and risks in any patient situation so that the most accurate and relevant plan of care can be developed.

The health history interview is the mutual opportunity for the nurse and patient to become more comfortable with each other as they form a collaborative partnership. The health history typically takes place before the physical assessment, because patients usually feel more at ease with the collection of health data than with the physical assessment. The health history can be broadly or narrowly focused, depending on the patient's needs and physical condition. Analysis of the information obtained in the health history is the basis for planning the health care education needs of the patient and indicates the areas needing attention in the physical assessment.

DETERMINANTS OF HEALTH

For a health history to be relevant, it is important for the nurse to be aware of the multiple factors that influence health, often referred to as the **determinants of health.** Determinants of health represent a wide range of proximal and distal variables that can influence the patient's health. Lifestyle, environment, human biology, and health services each play key roles in determining an individual's level of health. The following excerpt (from *Toward a Healthy Future: Second Report on the Health of Canadians*[1]) illustrates the complexity of what seems to be a fairly straightforward reason for a patient seeking health care.

"Why is Jason in the hospital?

Because he has a bad infection in his leg.

But why does he have an infection?

Because he has a cut on his leg and it got infected.

But why does he have a cut on his leg?

Because he was playing in the junk yard next to his apartment building and there was some sharp, jagged steel there that he fell on.

But why was he playing in a junk yard?

Because his neighbourhood is kind of rundown. A lot of kids play there and there is no one to supervise them.

But why does he live in that neighbourhood?

Because his parents can't afford a nicer place to live.

But why can't his parents afford a nicer place to live?

Because his Dad is unemployed and his Mom is sick.

But why is his Dad unemployed?

Because he doesn't have much education and he can't find a job.

But why . . . ?"

Health Canada has identified 12 determinants of health: income and social status; social support networks; education; employment/working conditions; social environments; physical environments; personal health practices and coping skills; healthy child development; biology and genetic endowment; health services; gender; and culture. The 12 determinants of health from *Toward a Healthy Future* are summarized below:

- *Income and social status:* Although the old adage "money can't buy love" may be true, it does influence the quality of living conditions, food, and necessities that people have access to. Low-income Canadians have, on average, a shorter life span and are more likely to suffer more illnesses than higher income Canadians (regardless of age, sex, race, and place of residence). The National Longitudinal Survey of children and youth found that children who are from immigrant or refugee families actually did better in school than Canadian-born classmates who came from equally low-income homes: "The immigrant context of hope for a brighter future may lessen poverty's blows."

- *Social support networks:* Having emotional and instrumental support from family, friends, and communities helps people manage day-to-day demands and unexpected or crisis situations. Canadians who have social support networks generally feel more in control of their lives, feel that their lives are satisfying, and have higher levels of well-being than Canadians with low levels of support or who are completely isolated.

- *Education and literacy:* Because of its close links with socioeconomic status, education is also an important variable in health status. Education develops knowledge and problem-solving skills, and contributes to a person's sense of mastery—the "I can do it factor." Unfortunately, Canadians with low literacy levels tend to have a shorter life span and have poorer health than Canadians with high levels of literacy.

- *Employment and work conditions:* Having a job where one feels in control, safe, and rewarded generally bodes well for the health of Canadians. Although the stresses of employment can be demanding, the stress of unemployment or being employed in a job over which one has little control of the circumstances can give rise to negative health outcomes, such as having no health or retirement benefits, or reduced levels of well-being.

- *Social environments* that extend beyond the home to the community, region, province, or country also play a role in health. Having a sense of social stability, feeling that one is safe and not a victim of racism, for example, can influence an individual's sense of well-being and that life is manageable and predictable.

- *Physical environments* that ensure clean air, healthy water and food supply, and safe and adequate transportation services, promote health.

- *Personal health practices and coping skills* refer to the choices people make and a belief in the abilities they have in shaping their health. Taking part in health maintenance and health promotion activities are important variables that support health, such as doing physical exercise, or choosing not to smoke or not to drink and drive. Learning how to cope with a range of stressors not only buffers the psychological demands of stress but also lowers the physiological impact that stress can have on the body. "Effective coping skills enable people to be self-reliant, solve problems and make informed choices that enhance health. These skills help people face life's challenges in positive ways without recourse to risky behaviours such as alcohol or drug abuse."

- *Healthy child development,* from a fetus and up to six years of age, can influence an individual's potential for the rest of his or her life. Whether it is the number of synapses the brain forms or the sense of security that an individual develops, it is very important that infants and children be given the best start to life as possible.

- *Biology and genetic endowment* have long been established as fundamental determinants of health.

- *Health services,* particularly those that promote and maintain health, prevent disease, and provide curative and restorative functions, are important in achieving one's health potential. A person's ability to access these services is also vital.

- *Gender* influences the roles, social status, personality traits, and attitudes of individuals, thus affecting each person's health status. Men are more likely to die prematurely than women, mostly because of heart disease, fatal unintentional injuries, and suicide. Although women live on average four or five years longer than men, they tend to have higher levels of depression and chronic conditions such as arthritis and allergies.

- *Culture* can influence health in that it affects whether someone is marginalized, stigmatized, devalued, or whether a person has access to the health care appropriate for his or her particular way of living.

HEALTH STATUS ACROSS CANADA

- Despite important improvements in the health of Aboriginal people in Canada, Aboriginals "continue to endure social, economic, and environmental conditions that are worse, on average, than those experienced by other Canadians."[2]
- Immigrants, refugees, the disabled, the poor, the homeless, people with stigmatizing conditions, the elderly, children and youth in disadvantaged circumstances, people with poor literacy skills, women in precarious circumstances, and Aboriginal people are vulnerable populations who are more likely than others to become ill and less likely to receive appropriate care.[3]
- Owing to Canada's geography and distribution patterns of the population, health human resource manpower and access to health care is an issue for many Canadians who live in rural (includes isolated, northern, remote) settings.
- Regional variations in life expectancy are such that residents of British Columbia have, overall, the longest life expectancy at 80.4 years while the people of Nunavut have the lowest at 68.7 years.[4]

 ## TYPES OF HEALTH HISTORY

The four types of health history to be discussed are complete, episodic, interval or follow-up, and emergency. The **complete health history** is a comprehensive history covering the many facets of the patient's past and present health status. It is usually gathered during a patient's initial visit to a health care facility on a nonemergency basis and upon admission to hospital. The **episodic health history** is short and is specific to the patient's current reason for seeking health care. For example, a patient seeking care for a sore throat would have an episodic health history taken. The **interval** or **follow-up health history** builds on a preceding visit to a health care facility. It documents the patient's recovery from illness, such as a sore throat, or the progress from a prior visit. Finally, the **emergency health history** is elicited from the patient and other sources in an emergency situation. Only information required to treat the emergent need of the patient is gathered; after the life-threatening condition is no longer present, the nurse may elicit a more comprehensive history from the patient.

PREPARING FOR THE HEALTH HISTORY

Conducting a health history interview may require 30 to 60 minutes. Inform the patient prior to the interview of the amount of time that will be required. If the history cannot be completed within the allotted period, continue the interview at another time to avoid patient fatigue. If the patient will be spending some time in the health care facility, additional information can be obtained during routine nursing care. Some health care agencies request that the literate patient complete detailed health history forms prior to the interview; in this instance, the nurse can validate the responses during the health history and save valuable time. Information can also be obtained from past medical records, which can be updated during the interview.

COMPUTERIZED HEALTH HISTORY

Some health care facilities use computerized health histories that are of two types: patient generated and health care provider generated. In patient-generated health histories, the patient inputs answers to various questions on a computer and then reviews the information with the nurse. The computerized health history is beneficial to patients who may be embarrassed to verbally report specific information or who feel anxious when asked detailed information. In the health care provider-generated health history, the nurse inputs information on screen after the patient interview.

Figure 3-1 The Health History Interview.

General Approach to the Health History Interview

1. Present with a professional appearance. Avoid extremes in dress so that your appearance does not hinder information gathering.
2. Ensure an appropriate environment, e.g., adequate privacy, good lighting, comfortable temperature, and a quiet area with no distractions. Refer to Chapter 2 for additional information.
3. Sit facing the patient at eye level, with the patient in a chair or on a bed. The patient should be made as comfortable as possible because obtaining the health history can be a lengthy process. Figure 3-1 illustrates an appropriate setting.
4. Ask the patient whether he or she has any questions about the interview before it is started.
5. Avoid the use of medical jargon; use terms the patient can understand.
6. Ask intimate and personal questions only when rapport has been established.
7. Remain flexible in obtaining the health history. It does not have to be obtained in the exact order it is presented in this chapter or on institutional forms.
8. Remind the patient that all information will be treated confidentially.

IDENTIFYING INFORMATION

The patient usually completes the identifying information prior to the actual physical examination.

Current Date

Record the month, day, year, and time that the health history is recorded. If the health history will not be recorded during the interview, document the time the health history was taken and the time it was recorded.

Biographical Data

The following biographical data are usually requested for the patient record:

Patient name	Occupation
Address	Work address
Phone number	Work phone number
Date of birth	Usual source of health care
Birth place	Source of referral
Health care number	Emergency contact

THE COMPLETE HEALTH HISTORY ASSESSMENT TOOL

All elements of a complete health history are outlined in the following pages. Two examples of the complete health history are provided, one for the well patient and one for the ill patient.

Nursing Tip

Eliciting Information from Reluctant Patients

Some patients may seem reluctant to answer certain questions, particularly if they pertain to their sexual history, use of alcohol and tobacco, or family history when there is presence of abuse or neglect. Establish a therapeutic relationship by explaining to the patient why the information is needed, which may allay anxieties about disclosing personal information. Using the "third person technique" may help provide a context for questions, without implying guilt. For example, if assessing a postpartum mother who is living in a stressful situation, it may be less threatening if the nurse states, "Sometimes new parents can lose patience with their child to the point where they feel like screaming or shaking the baby; is this something that you have experienced or worry about?" rather than simply asking, "Do you ever feel like shaking your baby?"

Source and Reliability of Information

It is usually the adult patient who is the historian. However, in some instances, such as in emergency situations, the historian may be someone other than the patient. Assess the reliability of the historian and note the name of the historian, as well as that person's relationship to the patient. It is also important to consider the mental state of the historian because emotions and certain medical conditions can influence the retelling of events. For example, information provided by a patient with severe Alzheimer's disease may not be accurate. If an interpreter was used, note this in the record and supply the person's name.

Patient Profile

The **patient profile** includes a notation about age, gender, ethnicity, and a brief summary of how the patient appears (e.g., in distress, tired looking, calm).

Health Issue or Concern

The reasons patients seek health care can relate to general health issues that are normative, such as "I need a check up," or are anticipatory, such as, "I am approaching menopause so I want to learn about how to stay healthy." Such concerns involve health maintenance, illness prevention, or health promotion approaches. However, patients also may seek health care because of specific worries or concerns, such as a **sign** (objective finding) or **symptom** (subjective finding). The patient's issue or concern should be recorded as direct quotes in the chart.

When describing a patient's reason for seeking health care, some texts refer to the "Chief Complaint," which implies that a patient only presents with complaints. This text opts for more general terminology (e.g., health issue or concern) that encompasses health maintenance, health promotion, symptomatology, and developmental or situational issues/concerns that may arise across a patient's life span.

Present Health and History of Health Issue or Concern

If a patient seeks health promotion, the nurse should review the present health status. If the patient presents with a particular health issue or concern, then the nurse obtains the **history of the health issue or concern** in order to document the chronological account of the situation and the events surrounding it. The chronology can be taken from the current state of the problem back to its origin (reverse chronology), or can be taken from the origin of the issue or concern leading to the current status (forward chronology). Both approaches are acceptable as long as the one chosen is consistent with subsequent documentation of chronological events. Allow the patient to give the detailed history without interruption, and then ask questions if any information is incomplete.

When a patient presents with a particular sign(s) or symptom(s), a thorough assessment of each health issue or concern must ensue. Each sign or symptom must be assessed as part of the health history to ensure that a comprehensive and relevant assessment occurs. The 10 characteristics of a sign or symptom are:

1. Location
2. Radiation
3. Quality
4. Quantity
5. Associated manifestations
6. Aggravating factors
7. Alleviating factors
8. Setting
9. Timing
10. Meaning and impact

Note that not all signs or symptoms have all 10 characteristics; hoarseness, for example, may not be characterized by quantity; a skin lesion may not "radiate." The symptom of a headache will be used in the next section to demonstrate the use of these 10 characteristics.

Location

Location refers to the primary area where the sign or symptom occurs or originates.
"Where does your head hurt? Can you point to the location of the pain?"
"Is it in one location in your head or spread out (diffuse or localized)?"
"Does this current headache differ from headaches you have had in the past?"

Radiation

Radiation is the spreading of the symptom from its original location to another part of the body. The areas of radiation can be diagnostic for specific pathologies. (Objective signs generally do not radiate; rather, their location may extend, such as when a lesion becomes larger.)
"Does the headache move to another part of your head or body? If so, where?"
"Is the pain presently radiating?"
"Describe how the pain feels in the area to which it radiated."

Quality

The quality of the sign or symptom experience describes the way it feels to the patient. Use the patient's own terms to describe the quality. If the

PQRST MNEMONIC

One way to remember the characteristics of a presenting sign or symptom is to use the PQRST mnemonic.

P   is for what provokes the pain (aggravating factors) and for palliative measures (alleviating factors)
Q   is for the quality
R   is for region (location) and radiation
S   is for severity (quantity) and setting
T   is for timing

The PQRST mnemonic does not include associated manifestations, nor meaning and impact, so remember to ask the patient about these characteristics.

patient is having difficulty describing pain, for example, suggest some quality terms, such as *gnawing, pounding, burning, stabbing, pinching, aching, throbbing,* and *crushing.*

"What does the headache feel like?"

"What word would you use to describe it?"

"Is the pain deep or closer to the skin (superficial)?"

Quantity

Quantity depicts the severity, volume, number, or extent of the presenting sign or symptom. Signs can be objectified, such as by measuring a lesion and noting its diameter or by enumerating the number of lesions present (e.g., three macular lesions of 2 cm each within a 5×5 cm area). The patient may use the terms *minor, moderate,* or *severe,* and *small, medium,* or *large* to describe the sign or symptom. Although this terminology is important, it is subjective and can be difficult to quantify. If the patient consistently uses the same terms, using a relative scale helps to assess whether the issue is improving or becoming worse, as reported by the patient.

A variety of scales are available that measure symptoms, with the most well-known and most used scales relating to the assessment of pain. The quantity of pain is often measured using a **Visual Analog Scale,** a numerical scale that rates pain from 0 (no pain) to 10 (worst pain possible). Refer to Chapter 9 for additional pain-intensity scales.

"Using a scale of 0 to 10, where 0 represents no pain, and 10 is the worst pain that you can imagine, rate the pain that you are having now."

"When was the last time that your headache was at this level?"

"Has the severity of the headache changed? In what way?"

"Has the headache interfered with your normal daily activities? How?"

Associated Manifestations

Associated manifestations are the signs and symptoms that accompany the principle sign or symptom. Frequently, a sign or a symptom is accompanied by other signs or symptoms (e.g., a lesion accompanied by pruritus; chest pain accompanied by diaphoresis). Positive findings are the associated manifestations that the patient has experienced along with the principle symptom. Negative findings, also called **pertinent negatives,** are manifestations expected in the patient with a suspected pathology but which the patient denies. If the patient does not mention specific signs or symptoms associated with the illness, ask the patient whether they are present. Document both positive findings and pertinent negatives; both give clues to the patient's condition. For example, a patient with headaches may have nausea, vomiting, and diaphoresis as positive associated manifestations. Photophobia and nuchal rigidity are pertinent negatives because they might be present in a patient with headaches but absent in this patient at this time; lack of these associated manifestations may lead to a different diagnosis.

"Besides your headache, are you experiencing any additional symptoms? What are they?"

"Have these symptoms occurred before? Do they always occur when you have a headache?"

Aggravating Factors

Factors that worsen the severity of the principal sign or symptom are the **aggravating factors.**

"What, if anything, makes your headache worse?"

"When you stopped this activity, did the pain lessen?"

> ## Nursing Tip
>
> **Variety of Alleviating Factors**
>
> Remember that alleviating factors encompass more than pharmacological interventions. The nurse needs to be aware of the various treatments that patients implement or seek out to relieve their discomfort. Treatments include, but are not limited to, ice, heat, herbal supplements, exercise, magnet therapy, yoga, massage, homeopathy, heat wraps, and other alternative and complementary medicine interventions.

Figure 3-2 Stressful thoughts or events may be the setting in which a principle symptom is experienced.

Alleviating Factors

Alleviating factors are events that decrease the severity of the sign or symptom that is being assessed.

"Have you done anything that decreases the severity of the headache? What?"

"Has this worked in the past?"

"When you stopped this activity, did your headache become more severe?"

Setting

The setting in which the sign or symptom occurs can provide valuable information about its course. The setting can be the actual physical environment of the patient, the mental state of the patient, or can be an activity in which the patient was involved (Figure 3-2). The patient may or may not be aware of any link between the setting and the occurrence of the symptom. For instance, the odour of some chemicals can induce headaches in some individuals.

"What were you doing when the headache started? Where were you?"

"Has this activity precipitated the headache on other occasions?"

"Has the headache occurred before in that setting? How many times?"

"What were you thinking about when the headache occurred?"

"Has the headache occurred before when you were feeling this way?"

Timing

The timing used to describe a sign or symptom experience has three elements: onset, duration, and frequency. Onset refers to the time the experience began and is usually described as gradual or sudden. Duration depicts the amount of time the sign or symptom was present. *Continuous* and *intermittent* are terms that describe the duration of the experience. When possible, the duration of the experience should be stated specifically, using minutes, hours, or days. Frequency describes the number of times the experience occurs and how often it develops (e.g., number of times per day, season of year).

"When did the headache first start? How long did the headache last?"

"Did the headache come on suddenly or gradually?"

"Is the pain continuous or intermittent? If intermittent, how much time elapsed between episodes?"

"When was the last time you experienced a headache? Is the pain different in any way from the first time that you experienced it?"

"Have you ever experienced this type of headache before? When?"

"How often does the headache occur in a week? In a month?"

"Have you detected a pattern to the headache's occurrence?"

Meaning and Impact

The final information required in the assessment of the sign or symptom history is the meaning or significance of the symptom to the patient and the impact of the experience on the patient. For example, the patient having headaches is concerned because her father started having headaches at her age and was diagnosed with a brain tumour.

The impact of the experience on the patient's lifestyle also should be investigated. For example, consider the elderly patient who complains of minor headache but admits to cancelling routine activities; in this case, the condition is presented as mild but its impact is serious.

"What does it mean to you to have these headaches?"

"How do you see the headaches affecting your lifestyle?"

Past Health History

The **past health history** (PHH) or past medical history (PMH) provides information on the patient's health status from birth to the present. Some patients may think you are ignoring their current reason for seeking health care when you ask about their PHH. The following statements can help ease the transition into the PHH or PMH:

"I will get back to the reason for your visit today in a few minutes. Now I would like to ask some questions related to your health in the past."

"Sometimes the reason for an illness is connected with your past health. For this reason, let's discuss your past health."

Medical History

The medical history comprises all medical problems and their **sequelae** (complications) that the patient has experienced during adulthood, including chronic as well as serious episodic illnesses. Forward or reverse chronology can be used to describe the medical history. If the patient denies medical illnesses, rephrase the questions. Some patients may discount "a little high blood pressure" as being insignificant.

Nursing Tip

Obtaining and Recording an Accurate Medication History

- Frequently, the patient discounts the use of over-the-counter medications such as acetaminophen, ibuprofen, vitamins, cathartics, enemas, douches, cold remedies, and antacids. Ask the patient whether such products are used, explaining that they can adversely interact with prescribed medications and with one another. When interviewing women of childbearing age, ask whether they use birth control pills. If contact is made with the patient prior to the health care visit, ask the patient to bring in all current medications.
- **Institute for Safe Medication Practices (ISMP) Do Not Use List.** The ISMP has issued a list of abbreviations, symbols, and dose designations known to contribute to medication errors, thus compromising patient safety (see Appendix E). It is important to follow the ISMP guidelines when the patient's medication list is documented to minimize errors. For example, include the leading zero when writing "0.5 mg of Synthroid"—instead of writing ".50"—keeping in mind that terminal zeros may result in the patient receiving 10 times the prescribed dosage.

"Are you presently under the supervision of a health care provider for any medical illness?" **or**

"Have you ever been diagnosed as having an illness? What was it?"

"When was the illness diagnosed?"

"Who diagnosed this problem?"

"What is the current treatment for this problem?"

"Do you follow the prescribed treatment? Do you have any difficulty following the prescribed treatment?"

"Have you ever been hospitalized for this illness? Where? When? For what period of time? What was the treatment? What was your condition after the treatment?"

"Have you ever experienced any complications from this disease? What were they? How were they treated?"

Surgical History

Record each surgical procedure, both major and minor, including the year performed, the name of the hospital, and any sequelae, if known.

"Have you ever had surgery? What type? When and where was the surgery performed?"

"Were you hospitalized? For what period of time?"

"Were there any complications? How were they treated?"

"Are you currently receiving any treatment related to this surgery?"

"Have you ever had an adverse effect from anesthesia?"

Medications, Over-the-Counter, and Natural Health Products

Past and present consumption of prescribed medications and nonprescriptive over-the-counter (OTC) products, including natural health products (NHPs), can affect the patient's current health status. Ask the patient the following questions regarding medications.

Prescription Medication

"What prescription medications are you currently taking? Who prescribed them?" **and**

"What prescription medications have you taken in the past? Who prescribed them?"

"What is the dose? How often do you take this medication?"

"How do you take this medication (e.g., pills, drops, inhaler, ointment, injection)?"

"How long have you been taking this medication?"

"Have you ever experienced any side effects with this medication?"

"Have you ever had an allergic reaction to this medication? What happened?"

"Tell me the purpose of these medications."

Life 360°

Over-the-Counter and Natural Health Products

A surgical nurse is conducting a preoperative history on a female patient. The patient takes medication for hypertension, diabetes, a seizure disorder, an overactive bladder, and osteoporosis. The patient tells the nurse that she also has purchased four other supplements from a natural food store. The patient cannot recall the names of the products but knows they are supposed to help her mood, her stiff joints, her immune system, and reduce her weight. How should the nurse proceed?

Nursing Tip

Natural Health Products

According to Health Canada, 71% of Canadians regularly take natural health products (NHPs).[5] Health Canada defines NHPs as vitamins and minerals, herbal remedies, homeopathic medicines, traditional Chinese medicines, probiotics, and other products such as amino acids and essential fatty acids. Whether patients use NHPS to improve their health or to combat illness and pain, the nurse must note the reason in the health history. Glucosamine, ephedrine, and St. John's Wort are just a few of the many products that patients may take. Health Canada's Natural Health Products Directorate ensures that "all Canadians have ready access to natural health products that are safe, effective and of high quality, while respecting freedom of choice and philosophical and cultural diversity." However, it is only since 2004, when the Natural Health Products Regulations were enacted, that NHPs have gone through regulatory approvals. A NHP that has been reviewed by Health Canada for claims of safety, quality, and health must have an eight-digit licensed Natural Product Number (NPN) on the label; homeopathic medicines that have been assessed will have an eight-digit DIN-HM (Drug Identification Number-Homeopathic Medicine) number on the label. Because many people consider NHPs to be "natural," patients do not consider them to be harmful, or may not realize that NHPs can interact adversely with one another or with prescription medications. As well, owing to the fairly recent legislation on labelling, people may not be verifying labels to ensure that safety standards have been met. Therefore, patients should be asked at every encounter which NHPs they consume, and the patient should be advised accordingly.

Over-the-Counter and Natural Health Products

"Do you currently take any over-the-counter or natural health products? Which ones?"

"Why do you take these products?"

"Do you take any home remedies? Which ones? For what purpose?"

Repeat all but the first and last questions from the *Prescription Medication* section.

"Do you ever take Aspirin, acetaminophen, ibuprofen, antacids, calcium supplements, nutritional or herbal supplements, vitamins, or laxatives? Do you douche? Administer enemas? Do you take allergy pills or cold medications?" (If yes, repeat all but the first and last questions of the previous section.)

General Questions

"How do you dispose of unused medications?"

"Where do you keep or store your medications?"

"Do you ever share medications with another person? Who? For what reason?"

"Do you have any questions concerning your medications?"

Communicable Diseases

Communicable diseases can have a grave impact on the individual as well as on society. Some communicable diseases generate enough of a concern to the community that they must be reported to the public health department. Polio*, measles, diphtheria, mumps, and rubella have almost been eradicated in Canada since mass immunization programs were established (*there has been no wild polio infection in Canada since 1988; however, there remains an ongoing risk of poliovirus importation from polio-endemic regions). In contrast, other communicable illnesses have been on the rise, such as syphilis (caused by the *Treponema pallidum* bacteria), acquired immune deficiency syndrome (AIDS) (caused by the human immunodeficiency virus—HIV), hepatitis C, and tuberculosis. More recently, severe acute respiratory syndrome (SARS) (caused by the corona virus), West Nile virus, and bovine spongiform encephalopathy (BSE or "mad cow disease") have become public health concerns. Subsequent to the SARS outbreak of 2003, along with concerns about the avian influenza H5N1 virus (bird flu), Canada has been addressing its ability to respond to a possible pandemic (infection of large populations around the world) situation.

Sexually transmitted infections (STIs) are a type of communicable disease. STI risks vary among patients, and exploration of risk factors or illness indicators requires diplomacy to avoid possible embarrassment or stigmatization. Health Canada recommends use of the STI Risk Assessment Questionnaire (see Figure 3-3) when assessing for STIs. There is substantial value in asking the patient about possible remote exposure to communicable diseases because pathology may only manifest itself many years after exposure, such as in the case of AIDS (average incubation period of 10 years with a range of 3 weeks to 20 years) and tuberculosis (incubation period of 2 weeks to 24 months).[6]

Canada's Public Health Agency list of Notifiable Diseases (STI and non-STI illnesses) is found in Appendix A. Specific illnesses must be reported in some sectors and not in others, depending on regional variations. Criteria for notification of partners are outlined in Appendix B. See Figure 3-4 for the STI Help Online, a popular Health Canada resource.

Nursing Alert

Latex Allergy and Latex-Food Syndrome

Natural latex proteins are similar to the proteins found in such foods as bananas, avocados, chestnuts, apples, carrots, kiwis, strawberries, and mangos. People who are allergic to these foods may also be allergic to latex—a phenomenon called latex-food syndrome.

Allergies

Carefully explore all patient allergies, including medications, animals, insect bites, foods, and environmental allergens. Allergies should be written down in red ink in a conspicuous location on the patient's chart as an alert. If the patient is hospitalized, then an armband indicating the allergy(ies) must be worn.

"Are you allergic to any medications? Latex? Animals? Foods? Insect bites? Bee stings? Anything in the environment?"

"Are you allergic to anything that you touch? What symptoms do you get when exposed to this substance? What treatment do you use? Is it effective?"

"Have you experienced any complications from the allergies? Which?"

"Have you ever seen an allergist for this problem? What happened?"

"Do you carry an EpiPen with you?" (for patients with life-threatening allergies)

Category and elements	Important questions to guide your assessment
Relationship	
• Present situation	• Do you have a regular sexual partner?
• Identify concerns	• If yes, how long have you been with this person?
	• Do you have any concerns about your relationship?
	• If yes what are they? (e.g., violence, abuse, coercion)

Figure 3-3 STI Questionnaire.
STI = sexually transmitted infection
Source: http://www.phac-aspc.gc.ca/std-mts/sti_2006/pdf/primary_care-soins_primaires_e%20.pdf. Public Health Agency of Canada (2006). Reproduced with permission of the Minister of Public Works and Government Services Canada, 2006.

Sexual risk behaviour
- Number of partners
- Sexual preference, orientation
- Sexual activities

- Personal risk evaluation

- When was your last sexual contact? Was that contact with your regular partner or with a different partner?
- How many different sexual partners have you had in the past 2 months? In the past year?
- Are your partners, men, women or both?
- Do you perform oral sex (i.e., kiss your partner on the genitals or anus)?
- Do you receive oral sex?
- Do you have intercourse (i.e., Do you penetrate your partners in the vagina or anus [bum]? Or do your partners penetrate your vagina or anus [bum])?
- Have any of your sexual encounters been with people from a country other than Canada? If yes, where and when?
- How do you meet your sexual partners (when travelling, bathhouse, Internet)?
- Do you use condoms, all the time, some of the time, never?
- What influences your choice to use protection or not?
- If you had to rate your risk for STI, would you say that you are at no risk, low risk, medium risk or high risk? Why?

STI history
- Previous STI screening
- Previous STI
- Current concern

- Have you ever been tested for STI/HIV? If yes, what was your last screening date?
- Have you ever had an STI in the past? If yes, what and when?
- When was your sexual contact of concern?
- If symptomatic, how long have you had the symptoms that you are experiencing?

Reproductive health history
- Contraception

- Known reproductive problems
- Pap test
- Pregnancy

- Do you and your partner use contraception? If yes, what? Any problems? If no, is there a reason?
- Have you had any reproductive health problems? If yes, when? What?
- Have you ever had an abnormal Pap test? If yes, when? Result if known.
- Have you ever been pregnant? If yes, how many times? Outcome: number of live births, abortions, miscarriages.

Substance use
- Share equipment for injection

- Sex under influence

- Percutaneous risk other than drug injection

- Do you use alcohol? Drugs? If yes, frequency and type?
- If injection drug use, have you ever shared equipment? If yes, last sharing date.
- Have you had sex while intoxicated? If yes, how often?
- Have you had sex while under the influence of alcohol or other substances? What were the consequences?
- Do you feel that you need help because of your substance use?
- Do you have tattoos or piercings? If yes, were they done using sterile equipment (i.e., professionally)?

Psychosocial history
- Sex trade worker or client

- Abuse

- Housing

- Have you ever traded sex for money, drugs or shelter?
- Have you ever paid for sex? If yes, frequency, duration and last event.
- Have you ever been forced to have sex? If yes, when and by whom?
- Have you ever been sexually abused? Have you ever been physically or mentally abused? If yes, when and by whom?
- Do you have a home? If no, where do you sleep?
- Do you live with anyone?

Figure 3-3 *continued*

Alberta	1-800-772-2437
British Columbia	1-800-994-4337
Manitoba	1-800-782-2437
Newfoundland and Labrador	1-800-563-1575
New Brunswick	1-877-784-1010
Northwest Territories	1-800-661-0844
Nunavut	1-800-661-0795
Eastern Arctic	1-800-661-0795
Nova Scotia	1-800-566-2437
Ontario	
English	1-800-668-2437
Français	1-800-267-7432
Prince Edward Island	1-800-314-2437
Quebec	1-888-855-7432
Saskatchewan	1-800-667-6876
Yukon	1-800-661-0408, x 8323
	1-877-957-8953
Canada	www.aidssida. cpha.ca/english /links_e/index .htm

Figure 3-4 STI Help Online.
Source: http://www.phac-aspc.gc.ca/std-mts/phone_e.html. Reproduced with permission of the Minister of Public Works and Government Services Canada, 2006.

Nursing Tip

Exploring Risks of Sexually Transmitted Infection

- The terms "sexually transmitted disease" (STD) and "venereal disease" (VD) have now been replaced with the term "sexually transmitted infection" (STI). STI has become the term of choice because "infection" can include symptomatic and asymptomatic conditions. As well, "infection" carries less of a social stigma than the term "disease."
- Be aware of the "I have been tested syndrome" when exploring for risks of STIs. People may develop a false sense of security and may feel less vulnerable to STIs after having multiple negative STI results despite ongoing sexually risky behaviour. Some people may also believe that because they have given blood for transfusions that they have been "tested" for STIs, in particular for HIV.
- Be aware of your preconceived biases about who is at risk of a STI. For example, if you believe that the elderly do not have sex or that they do not have multiple sexual partners, then you may not explore an area about their sexual health that is important.
- Chlamydia is the most commonly reported STI in Canada; two-thirds of cases are women, with the majority in the 15–24 year age group. Gonorrhea is the second most commonly reported STI in Canada, the rate of which doubled between 1997 and 2004. The majority of gonorrhea cases (60%) involve men, which may be related to increased transmission among the population of men who have sex with men. Rates of syphilis have increased ninefold overall between 1997 and 2004 and was 15 times higher in men over the same period of time.[7]

Injuries and Accidents

A patient's injury and accident history can reveal a pattern that is amenable to health promotion. For example, an elderly woman who has sustained an injury from slipping on throw rugs in the home would benefit from learning how to maintain a safe home environment. A child not wanting to wear a helmet when cycling or playing hockey would require creative nursing interventions to ensure the child's safety.

"Have you ever been involved in an accident?" **or** "Have you ever been injured in any way?"

"What occurred? Did you require treatment or hospitalization? Were there any complications or long-term effects from this injury/accident? What were they?"

Nursing Tip

Allergies versus Side Effects

Many people report that they are allergic to specific medications. When questioned further on the specific reaction to a medication, patients may frequently report symptoms such as nausea, headache, diarrhea, and vomiting. Although such symptoms should not be discounted, it is vital to keep in mind that the symptoms are not related to drug allergies—they are adverse reactions to the medication. True drug allergies usually manifest as urticaria, breathing difficulties, or anaphylaxis.

Nursing Tip

The SANE Nurse

The sexual assault nurse examiner (SANE) has received extensive training in the handling of victims of sexual assault. Intensive course work combined with clinical training enables the nurse to sit for the SANE certification exam, which is administered by the International Association of Forensic Nurses. The SANE collects evidence (e.g., mouth, vaginal, and anal swabs; head and pubic hair; blood samples) with a physical evidence recovery kit (PERK) that is used in legal proceedings. These nurses provide much-needed sensitivity while gathering the physical evidence and are experts in providing crisis intervention and supporting the patient. In addition, they guide the patient to community resources to help with the healing process.

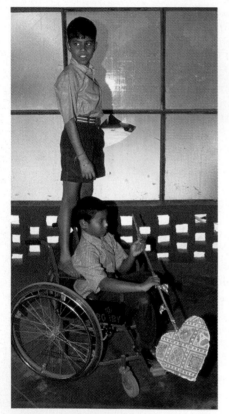

Figure 3-5 The patient with special needs can often fully participate in daily activities. *Courtesy of WHO/P. Virot.*

"Have you ever sustained an injury in a car accident? Describe."

"Have you ever had a broken bone? Stitches? Burns?"

"Have you ever been assaulted? Raped? Shot? Stabbed?"

Special Needs

The awareness of any cognitive, physical, or psychosocial disability is essential to the individualized health care of a patient (Figure 3-5). Patients may receive less than optimal health care if their particular limitations are not identified and considered when planning treatment. For example, the pelvic exam of a woman with schizophrenia or dementia may be deferred, seemingly to avoid undue stress, but can be a risky omission in the event of pathology.

"Do you have any disability or special need(s)? Describe."

"What type of limitations does this disability/special need place on you?"

"What strategies do you use to limit the effect the disability/special need has on your lifestyle?"

"What support systems help you cope with this disability/special need?"

"Does your disability/special need place an extra financial burden on you? How do you handle that?"

Blood Transfusions

The chance of contracting an infectious disease from a blood transfusion is minimal because the Canadian Blood Services Agency and Hema-Quebec continuously update their screening tools and history-taking procedures to protect the blood supply. Here are a few questions about blood transfusion that the nurse can ask the patient.

"Have you ever received a blood transfusion (whole blood or any of its components)? When?"

"Why did you receive this blood product? What quantity did you receive?"

"Did you experience any reaction to this blood product? What was it?"

Childhood Illnesses

Rarely are adults familiar with a complete history of their childhood illnesses, so it is best to ask patients about specific childhood diseases by name. Use of both medical and lay terminology helps to ensure an accurate history is obtained.

"Have you ever had any of the following illnesses: varicella (chickenpox), diphtheria, pertussis (whooping cough), measles, mumps, rubella, rheumatic

Varying Immunization Schedules

Routine vaccinations can vary among different age groups and in different parts of the country. For example, annual influenza immunizations are administered without a fee to all residents in some provinces, whereas other regions only offer free immunizations to certain high-risk groups, such as the very young and the elderly. Some immunizations have been eliminated whereas others have been added to the vaccination schedule as recommended by The National Advisory Committee on Immunization. The smallpox vaccination was discontinued in 1977 (except for the Canadian Forces who continued smallpox immunization up to 1988) because smallpox has been eradicated worldwide. In the 1990s, the Haemophilus Influenzae type b (Hib) and hepatitis B vaccines were added to the recommended immunization schedule. More recently, meningococcal, pneumococcal, and varicella vaccines were added. Local immunization campaigns and routine immunization programs are mounted when public health concerns arise, such as when there is an outbreak of hepatitis A or pertussis (whooping cough). Be alert to changes in immunization schedules when interviewing patients to ensure they have received the appropriate immunizations specific to their history. Also be sensitive to patients from other countries who may present with a different immunization history than patients raised in the Canadian health care system.

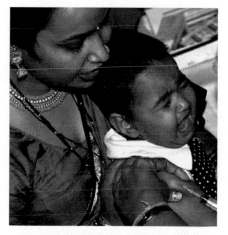

Figure 3-6 Most immunizations are given in childhood. *Courtesy of WHO/P. Virot.*

fever, or scarlet fever?" (Eliminate this question if it was previously asked during the communicable disease section.)

"How old were you when the illness occurred? Was an actual diagnosis made? By whom?"

"Were there any complications? What were they?"

Immunizations

Most immunizations are received in childhood (Figure 3-6), though a few may be given in the adult years. The adult patient may not recall the exact dates when the immunizations were given but may say, "I received everything that I should have." A record of immunizations is often important for school admission and helps to avoid repeat vaccinations as an adult. Table 3-1 lists the National Guidelines for Childhood Immunizations recommended by the National Advisory Committee on Immunization. Table 3-2 outlines the immunization schedule for children younger than 7 years who were not immunized in early infancy. Table 3-3 outlines the immunization schedule for children 7 years and older who were not immunized in early infancy. Table 3-4 outlines the routine immunization requirements for adults. There may be minor variations in the implementation of these schedules among provinces and territories, so it is important to verify local recommendations.

Many parents worry about the risks of immunizations. The Public Health Agency of Canada has prepared a helpful summary for parents to consider when deciding whether or not they should vaccinate their child(ren). Table 3-5 provides a comparison of the effects of a range of diseases relative to the side effect of the vaccines.

TABLE 3-1 National Advisory Committee on Immunization (NACI) Recommended Immunization Schedule for Infants, Children and Youth

Age at vaccination	DTaP-IPV	Hib	MMR	Var	Hep B	Pneu-C	Men-C	dTap	Flu
Birth					Infancy 3 doses ★				
2 months	O	✳				◈	◗		
4 months	O	✳				◈	◗		
6 months	O	✳				◈	◗ or		6-23 months ◈ 1-2 doses
12 months			■	❖	or	◈ 12-15 months	◗ if not yet given		
18 months	O	✳	■ or						
4-6 years	O		■		Pre-teen/ teen 2-3 doses if not yet given				
14-16 years							◗ if not yet given	♦	

- **O DTaP-IPV** Diphtheria, Tetanus, acellular Pertussis, and inactivated Polio virus vaccine
- **✳ Hib** Haemophilus influenzae type b conjugate vaccine
- **■ MMR** Measles, Mumps and Rubella vaccine
- **❖ Var** Varicella vaccine
- **★ Hep B** Hepatitis B vaccine
- **◈ Pneu-C** Pneumococcal conjugate vaccine
- **◗ Men-C** Meningococcal C conjugate vaccine
- **♦ dTap** Diphtheria, Tetanus, acellular Pertussis vaccine (adult formulation)
- **◈ Flu** Influenza Vaccine

Notes:

- **O Diphtheria, Tetanus, acellular Pertussis and inactivated Polio virus vaccine (DTaP-IPV):** DTaP-IPV vaccine is the preferred vaccine for all doses in the vaccination series, including completion of the series in children who have received ≥ 1 dose of DPT (whole cell) vaccine (e.g., recent immigrants).

- **✳ Haemophilus influenzae type b conjugate vaccine (Hib):** Hib schedule shown is for the haemophilus b capsular polysaccharide – PRP conjugated to tetatus toxoid (Act-HIB[TM]) or the Haemophilus b oligosaccharide conjugate – HbOC (HibTITER[TM]) vaccines.

- **■ Measles, Mumps and Rubella vaccine (MMR):** A second dose of MMR is recommended, at least 1 month after the first dose for the purpose of better measles protection. For convenience, options include giving it with the next scheduled vaccination at 18 months of age or at school entry (4-6 years) (depending on the provincial/territorial policy), or at any intervening age that is practical. The need for a second dose of mumps and rubella vaccine is not established but may benefit (given for convenience as MMR). The second dose of MMR should be given at the same visit as DTaP-IPV (± Hib) to ensure high uptake rates.

- **❖ Varicella vaccine (Var):** Children aged 12 months to 12 years should receive one dose of varicella vaccine. Individuals ≥ 13 years of age should receive two doses at least 28 days apart.

- **★ Hepatitis B vaccine (Hep B):** Hepatitis B vaccine can be routinely given to infants or preadolescents, depending on the provincial/territorial policy. For infants born to chronic carrier mothers, the first dose should be given at birth (with Hepatitis B immunoglobulin), otherwise the first dose can be given at 2 months of age to fit more conveniently with other routine infant immunization visits. The second dose should be administered at least 1 month after the first dose, and the third at least 2 months

| TABLE 3-1 | National Advisory Committee on Immunization (NACI) Recommended Immunization Schedule for Infants, Children and Youth *continued* |

after the second dose, but again may fit more conveniently into the 4 and 6 month immunization visits. A two-dose schedule for adolescents is an option (see NACI original document for further details).

❖ **Pneumococcal conjugate vaccine -7-valent (Pneu-C):** Recommended schedule, number of doses and subsequent use of 23 valent polysaccharide pneumococcal vaccine depend on the age of the child when vaccination is begun (see NACI original document for further details).

▶ **Meningococcal C conjugate vaccine (Men-C):** Recommended schedule and number of doses of meningococcal vaccine depends on the age of the child (see NACI original document for further details). If the provincial/territorial policy is to give Men-C after 12 months of age, 1 dose is sufficient.

◆ **Diphtheria, Tetanus, acellular Pertussis vaccine-adult/adolescent formulation (dTap):** a combined adsorbed "adult type" preparation for use in people ≥ 7 years of age, contains less diphtheria toxoid and pertussis antigens than preparations given to younger children and is less likely to cause reactions in older people.

❖ **Influenza vaccine (Flu):** Previously unvaccinated children in the 6-23 month age group require 2 doses with an interval of at least 4 weeks. The second dose is not required if the child has received one or more doses of influenza vaccine during the previous immunization season (see NACI original document for further details).

Source: http://www.phac-aspc.gc.ca/naci-ccni/is-si/recimmsche-icy_e.html. Reproduced with the permission of the Minister of Public Works and Government Services Canada, 2006.

Routine immunizations are also associated with different groups of people. Health care workers frequently receive hepatitis B vaccination. Travellers visiting certain regions in developing areas of the world may receive numerous vaccines prior to departure. Since 2004, the Canadian Task Force on Preventive Health[8] has recommended annual influenza ("flu") vaccination in *all* healthy adults and children, though provincial funding for the flu vaccine may only be provided for certain at-risk populations such as the elderly or people with chronic illness.

"What immunizations have you received since birth? When?"

"Have you received any immunizations as an adult: varicella, hepatitis A, hepatitis B, influenza, tetanus, pneumococcal, meningococcal?"

"Did you experience any allergic reactions to the immunizations? Were there any complications?"

"(If born outside Canada or from Northern Canada) have you received the Bacillus Calmette-Guerin (BCG) vaccine (against TB)?"

"Have you ever received any other immunizations (cholera, typhoid fever, yellow fever), perhaps prior to visiting a specific geographical region?"

| TABLE 3-2 | Routine Immunization Schedule for Children < 7 Years of Age Not Immunized in Early Infancy |

Timing	DTaP[1]	IPV	Hib	MMR	Td[3] or dTap[10]	Hep B[4] (3 doses)	V	P	M
First visit	X	X	X[11]	X[12]		X	X[7]	X[8]	X[9]
2 months later	X	X	X	(X)[6]		X		(X)	(X)
2 months later	X	(X)[5]						(X)	
6-12 months later	X	X	(X)[11]			X			
4-6 years of age[13]	X	X							
14-16 Years of age					X				

P Pneumococcal vaccine
M Meningococcal vaccine

Source: http://www.phac-aspc.gc.ca/publicat/cig-gci/pdf/part2-cdn_immuniz_guide-2002-6.pdf, Table 2. Reproduced with the permission of the Minister of Public Works and Government Services Canada, 2006.

TABLE 3-3 Routine Immunization Schedule for Children ≥ 7 Years of Age Not Immunized in Early Infancy

Timing	dTap[10]	IPV	MMR	Hep B[4] (3 doses)	V	M
First visit	X	X	X	X	X	X[9]
2 months later	X	X	X[6]	X	(X)[7]	
6-12 months later	X	X		X		
10 years later	X					

M Meningococcal vaccine

Notes:

1. DTaP (diphtheria, tetanus, acellular or component pertussis) vaccine is the preferred vaccine for all doses in the vaccination series, including completion of the series in children who have received ≥ 1 dose of DPT (whole cell) vaccine.
2. Hib schedule shown is for PRP-T or HbOC vaccine. If PRP-OMP is used, give at 2, 4 and 12 months of age.
3. Td (tetanus and diphtheria toxoid), a combined adsorbed "adult type" preparation for use in people ≥ 7 years of age, contains less diphtheria toxoid than preparations given to younger children and is less likely to cause reactions in older people.
4. Hepatitis B vaccine can be routinely given to infants or preadolescents, depending on the provincial/territorial policy; three doses at 0,1 and 6 month intervals are preferred. The second dose should be administered at least 1 month after the first dose, and the third at least 2 months after the second dose. A two-dose schedule for adolescents is also possible (see original document for further details).
5. This dose is not needed routinely, but can be included for convenience.
6. A second dose of MMR is recommended, at least 1 month after the first dose for the purpose of better measles protection. For convenience, options include giving it with the next scheduled vaccination at 18 months of age or with school entry (4-6 years) vaccinations (depending on the provincial/territorial policy), or at any intervening age that is practicable. The need for a second dose of mumps and rubella vaccine is not established but may benefit (given for convenience as MMR). The second dose of MMR should be given at the same visit as DTaP IPV (± Hib) to ensure high uptake rates.
7. Children aged 12 months to 12 years should receive one dose of varicella vaccine. Individuals ≥ 13 years of age should receive two doses at least 28 days apart.
8. Recommended schedule, number of doses and subsequent use of 23 valent polysaccharide pneumococcal vaccine depend on the age of the child when vaccination is begun (see original document for specific recommendations).
9. Recommended schedule and number of doses of meningococcal vaccine depends on the age of the child (see original document for specific recommendations).
10. dTap adult formulation with reduced diphtheria toxoid and pertussis component.
11. Recommended schedule and number of doses depend on the product used and age of the child when vaccination is begun (see original document for specific recommendations). Not required past age 5.
12. Delay untill subsequent visit if child is < 12 months of ages.
13. Omit these doses if the previous doses of DTaP and polio were given after the fourth birthday.

Source: http://www.phac-aspc.gc.ca/publicat/cig-gci/pdf/part2-cdn_immuniz_guide-2002-6.pdf, Table 3. Reproduced with the permission of the minister of Public Works and Government Services Canada, 2006,

TABLE 3-4 Routine Immunization of Adults

Vaccine or toxoid	Indication	Further doses
Diphtheria (adult preparation)	All adults	Every 10 years, preferably given with tetanus toxoid (Td)
Tetanus	All adults	Every 10 years, preferably given as Td
Influenza	Adults ≥ 65 years; adults < 65 years at high risk of influenza-related complications and other select groups	Every year using current vaccine formulation
Pneumococcal	Adults ≥ 65 years; conditions with increased risk of pneumococcal diseases	See NACI original document
Measles	All adults born in 1970 or later who are susceptible to measles	May be given as MMR

TABLE 3-4 Routine Immunization of Adults *continued*		
Vaccine or toxoid	**Indication**	**Further doses**
Rubella	Susceptible women of childbearing age and health care workers	May be given as MMR
Mumps	Adults born in 1970 or later with no history of mumps	May be given as MMR

Source: http://www.phac-aspc.gc.ca/publicat/cig-gci/pdf/part2-cdn_immuniz_guide-2002-6.pdf, Table 4. Reproduced with permission of the Minister of Public Works and Government Services Canada, 2006.

TABLE 3-5 Comparison of Effects of Diseases and Vaccines			
Disease		**Effects of Disease**	**Side Effects of Vaccine**
Incidence Before Vaccination	**Incidence After Vaccination**		
Polio			
Spread by feces and saliva. Incubation: 1–2 weeks. Infection may lead to fever, headache, nausea and vomiting, muscle weakness, and paralysis.		1% of infections have clinical symptoms but about 1 in 20 hospitalized patients dies, and 50% of survivors remain paralyzed.	IPV used in Canada so vaccine associated polio, though very rare, is no longer a risk. Local discomfort or inflammation in 5% of recipients. —see side effects of DTaP vaccine below for combination use.
Range 2.5–28.3/100,000 Epidemic years had up to 20,000 cases of paralytic disease.	Indigenous disease eradicated from the Americas. Still endemic in other parts of the world.		
Diphtheria			
Spread by nasal droplets. Incubation: 2–5 days. Infection leads to severe pharyngitis and cervical adenopathy. Patient is infectious for up to 2 weeks.		Case fatality rate 5–10%. Toxin may lead to myocardial and neurological complications.	DTaP vaccine—about 20% have local discomfort or inflammation, 5% have fever. A transient nodule may develop at the injection site, lasting a few weeks. Up to 70% at the 4–6 yr booster develop redness and swelling.
Highest in 1924 with 9,000 cases that year.	Now 2–5 reported cases per year; none reported in 1996.		
Tetanus			
Bacteria present in soil and animal feces. Incubation: 3–21 days. Causes painful muscular contractions and convulsions.		Case fatality about 10%. Risk is greatest for the very young or old.	See above—side effects of DTaP vaccine. Local erythema and swelling not uncommon with adult boosters, and increasing with age. Peripheral neuropathies have been rarely reported.
Average 40–50 deaths per year.	3–5 cases per year reported, only 5 deaths in the last 18 years and none since 1991.		

continues

TABLE 3-5 Comparison of Effects of Diseases and Vaccines *continued*

Disease		Effects of Disease	Side Effects of Vaccine
Incidence Before Vaccination	**Incidence After Vaccination**		
Pertussis			
Spread by cough and nasal droplets. Incubation: 7–10 days. Symptoms include runny nose and irritating cough, which may develop into whooping cough.		About 1% case fatality in patients under 6 months, from pneumonia or fatal encephalopathy (usually hypoxic). Several deaths still occur every year, particularly in unimmunized infants.	See above—side effects of DTaP vaccine. Rate of reactions to acellular pertussis vaccine is less than with whole cell.
Average 153/100,000.	Average 10/100,000.		
Hib			
Spread by nasal droplets. Incubation: 2–4 days. Presents as an acute illness with fever, vomiting, and lethargy (symptoms of meningitis) in 55–65%. In the remainder, it can also cause epiglottitis, pneumonia, bacteremia, and other complications.		Case fatality of meningitis is 5% (10-15% of survivors have permanent neurologic sequelae and 15–20% have deafness).	5% have discomfort or local inflammation, 2% have fever. Usually given in combination with DT (see above—side effects of DTaP vaccine).
Leading cause of bacterial meningitis in infancy. About 2,000 cases per year.	Only anecdotal cases now being reported, less than 60 cases per year in the last few years.		
Measles			
Spread by cough and nasal droplets. Incubation: 1–2 weeks. Symptoms include fever, sore throat, cough, runny nose, itchy eyes, and a red rash that starts on the face and spreads to the rest of the body.		Complications such as bronchopneumoni a and otitis media in about 10%. 1/1,000 encephalitis (case fatality 10%, permanent sequelae 25%). 1/25,000 develops SSPE.	5–10% have discomfort, local inflammation or fever with or without a noninfectious rash. 1/1 million recipients develop encephalitis. About 1/24,000 develop transient thrombocytopenia.
Cyclic, with increasing incidence every 2–3 years. About 300,000 to 400,000 cases per year estimated.	Recent outbreaks with 11,000 cases (1989) and 2,300 (1995). With 2 dose schedule, now fewer than 400 cases per year.		
Mumps			
Spread by saliva. Incubation: 2–3 weeks. Symptoms include fever and parotitis.		1/200 children develop encephalitis. 20–30% of postpubertal males develop orchitis, 5% of females develop oophoritis. Occasionally, mumps causes infertility or deafness.	Fever and a mild skin rash occasionally occurs. 1% of recipients may develop parotitis. 1 in 3 million recipients may develop aseptic meningitis.
Highest in 1942 with 52,344 cases	Average incidence 2.35/100,000, or about 500 cases annually.		
Average incidence 136/100,000			

TABLE 3-5 Comparison of Effects of Diseases and Vaccines *continued*		
Disease	**Effects of Disease**	**Side Effects of Vaccine**
Incidence Before Vaccination / **Incidence After Vaccination**		
Rubella		
Spread by nasal droplets. Incubation: 2–3 weeks. Symptoms include fever, headache, itchy eyes, cervical adenopathy, and rash.	50% develop a rash and adenopathy; 50% of adolescents and adults have acute arthralgias or arthritis; 1/6,000 develops an encephalopathy. Infections in the first 10 weeks of pregnancy have a 85% risk of CRS.	About 10% have discomfort, local inflammation or fever. About 5% have swollen glands, stiff neck or joint pains. About 1% develop a noninfectious rash. Transient arthralgias or arthritis may occur, more in postpubertal females.
Highest in 1936 with 69,401 cases		
Average 149 /100,000	Average of 8.5/100,000. About 2,000 cases reported annually.	

Source: http://www.phac-aspc.gc.ca/publicat/cig-gci/vaccine_e.html. Reproduced with the permission of the Minister of Public Works and Government Services Canada, 2006.

Family Health History

The family health history (FHH) records the health status of the patient as well as the health status of immediate blood relatives. At a minimum, the FHH should contain the age and health status of the patient, spouse/partner, children, siblings, and the patient's parents. Ideally, the patient's grandparents, aunts, and uncles should be incorporated into the history as well. It is helpful to draw the FHH genogram while the patient is describing the family history to you because it can be completed much more quickly than narrative documentation. Documenting this information is done in two parts: the genogram, and a list of familial or genetic diseases, including pertinent negatives (e.g., no history of heart disease or diabetes). The history of family illnesses can cue the nurse to the multiple demands faced by individual members. The nurse can then further explore how the patient copes with these demands. Figure 3-7 demonstrates the appropriate method for constructing the **genogram.**

The burgeoning field of **genomics** (the study of the genetic makeup of the human cell) has meant that nurses increasingly need to be well versed in illnesses with genetic links. New knowledge and technology are evolving that will help

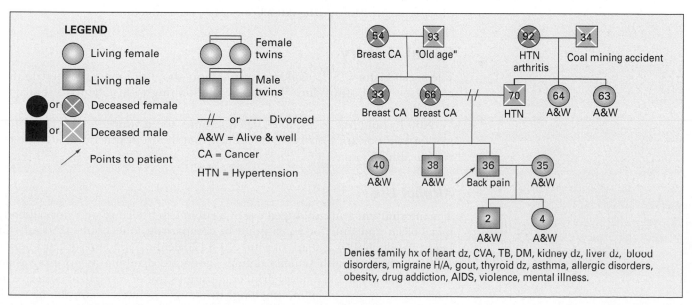

Figure 3-7 Family Health History and Genogram.

Nursing Tip

The CAGE Questionnaire

The CAGE questionnaire is an easily administered alcoholism screening tool that can be used to assess a patient's drinking habits.[9] The four questions in the tool are:

Have you ever felt you should **C**ut down on your alcohol intake (or drug use)?

Have people **A**nnoyed you by criticizing your alcohol intake (or drug use)?

Have you ever felt **G**uilty about your alcohol intake (or drug use)?

Have you ever needed alcohol (or drugs) for an **E**ye-opener (morning consumption)?

Positive responses to two or more of these questions necessitate a more thorough history on alcohol consumption. The parentheses above add drugs to the standard CAGE questionnaire thus generating an **A**dapted to **I**nclude **D**rugs questionnaire called CAGEAID.

---

prevent disease, provide for early disease detection, develop personalized patient interventions for disease, and, ultimately, provide a cure for certain diseases.

The nurse may want to preface the FHH questions with the following statement:

"Different diseases tend to run in families. I would like to ask you about your family and their health to gain a better understanding of your background." Questions about the FHH can then be continued:

"Tell me about the members of your family: spouse/partner, children, siblings, and parents. How old are they?"

"Do any of these individuals have any medical illnesses or diseases? What are they?"

"Have there been any deaths in your immediate family? What was the cause of death? How old was this person at the time of death?"

"What is the current age of each of the following members of your family: maternal and paternal grandparents, aunts, uncles?"

"How old are they?"

"Do any of these individuals have any medical illnesses or diseases? What are they?"

"Has anyone in your family ever had any of the following illnesses: heart disease, sudden cardiac death before age 50, hypertension, stroke (brain attack), tuberculosis, diabetes mellitus, cancer, kidney disease, blood disorders, sickle cell anemia, arthritis, epilepsy, migraine headaches, gout, thyroid disease, liver disease, asthma, allergic disorders, obesity, alcoholism, mental illness (schizophrenia, depression), drug addiction, AIDS, HIV infection?"

Social History

The **social history** (SH) explores information about the patient's lifestyle that can affect health. Introduce this area of questioning with statements similar to the following:

"Now I would like to ask you some questions about your lifestyle. This information is important because of the effects that different practices can have on your health."

Alcohol Use

The intermittent and prolonged use of alcohol can interfere with normal body metabolism and function. As a point of comparison, one bottle (350 mL) of beer (5% alcohol) = 150 mL of wine (10–14% alcohol) = 50 mL of hard liquor (40% alcohol). Health Canada defines moderate drinking as no more than seven drinks per week; a heavy drinker consumes five or more drinks on five or more occasions in a given month; binge drinking is defined as consuming more than four drinks per sitting.

"How much and what type of alcohol do you drink in an average week?"

"How often do you drink?"

"What quantity do you usually consume at one time?"

"Has your drinking pattern changed? In what way?"

"When did you first start to drink?"

"How long have you been drinking the amount that you are currently consuming?"

"Have you ever lost consciousness or blacked out after drinking?"

"Have you ever forgotten what happened when you were drinking?"

"Do you drive after drinking?"

"Did you ever drink during pregnancy? (for women) How much?"

"Do you think you have a drinking problem?"

"Do you ever feel bullied or pressured into drinking? How do you handle this situation?"

Drug Use

The questions about use of drugs in the SH section of the complete health history should not be confused with the medication section under the PHH. The latter includes the use and abuse of prescription medications, OTC, and NHPs, whereas the former refers to the use of illegal substances. Remind the patient that this information will be kept confidential and that such information enables the health care team to understand the range of health care issues the patient is dealing with.

"Do you use or have you ever used marijuana, amphetamines, uppers, downers, cocaine, crack, heroin, PCP, inhalants, or other recreational or street drugs?"

"When did you first start to use drugs?"

"What amount do you use?"

"How often do you use this drug?"

"Has this amount changed? In what way?"

"In what form do you use the drug (pill, needle, snort, other)?"

"Describe how you inject the drug. Do you share needles? Do you clean needles between uses?"

"Have you experienced any health problems from the drug use?"

"Have you ever overdosed? What happened?"

Nursing Tip

Terminology and Drug Abuse[10]

Bang: slang for injecting.

Blackout: alcohol-induced amnesia or memory loss without loss of consciousness.

Booting: a procedure whereby IV heroin users inject the needle into their veins, withdraw some blood, mix it with the heroin, and then complete the injection.

Chasing the dragon: the most common way to smoke heroin is to place it on a small sheet of tin foil, melt the heroin by heating it over a flame, and inhale the smoke as it comes off the melting substances.

Designer drugs: slang for substances derived from fentanyl-type opiates with both stimulant and hallucinogenic properties.

Ecstasy: a popular name for a designer substance, MDMA, that has psychedelic qualities and provides a euphoric "rush" of cocaine-like, mind-expanding effects without scary visual distortions.

Freebasing: the chemical process of changing common white cocaine powder into a purer, more potent, smokeable form of cocaine "base," which the user then smokes in a glass water pipe that is heated by a butane lighter.

Hallucinogen: a substance that induces or produces hallucinations in a substance user.

continues

Hot knives: knives that are used to smoke hash. The knives are heated on the stove or with a blow torch and small pieces of hash are picked up on one knife and pressed against the other to cook the pieces; the smoke is inhaled. A paper or glass tube will protect the lips from burning against the hot knives.

Ice: a highly addictive crystallized form of methamphetamine that produces a euphoric high that lasts for several hours; ingested in pill form, snorted, or injected IV.

Mainlining: a substance administration method in which a drug is injected directly into a vein; intravenous injection.

Methamphetamine: a synthetic amphetamine substance, know as "meth" or "speed," commonly abused by intravenous injection for the rapid, intense euphoria of the "rush" or "flash" effect.

Phencyclidine (PCP): a unique psychoactive drug having psychedelic, stimulant, depressant, hallucinogenic, psychoto-mimetic, analgesic, and anesthetic properties, used legally today only in veterinary medical practice because of its unpleasant side effects in humans.

Roid rage: slang for the tendency of some anabolic steroid users to become unusually aggressive and display sudden bursts of explosive violence.

Shooting gallery: a place where substance users can go to inject substances. Needles and/or other paraphernalia may be available.

Speed: methamphetamine.

Water pipe: considered the healthiest way to smoke pot (and tobacco). The water acts as a filter, removing more of the toxins than a cigarette filter and giving smoke rich in THC (tetra hydro cannabinol).

Withdrawal: occurs when a user discontinues drug administration and may include several symptoms of pain and dysphoria, including vomiting, nausea, diarrhea, headache, depression, irritability, anxiety, cramps, elevation of heart rate and blood pressure, and convulsions.

Reflective Thinking

Nursing Care in Situations of Illicit Drug Use

Fifteen-year-old Barbara tells the school nurse that she was pressured into trying cocaine at a party and since then she has snorted on her own volition 10–12 times. Barbara says that she now craves cocaine and is upset because she does not like this feeling. "I am so worried that I am going to get into trouble and I feel like I am out of control. I am so angry at myself for giving in to the pressure and now look what has happened!"

- How would you respond to Barbara's situation? What resources are available in your town/city/province/territory to help people in Barbara's situation?
- Do you exhibit any biases when working with people who take street drugs? Do these biases interfere with your nursing care? If so, what actions do you take to control your bias?
- Explore the legal ramifications of working with people who take illegal drugs. Are there special provisions if the patient is a minor?

"Have you ever been through a drug rehabilitation program? What was the outcome?"

"Do you think you have a drug problem?"

"Do you ever feel bullied or pressured into using drugs? How do you handle this situation?"

Tobacco Use

Tobacco is the greatest single factor in preventable death and disease in Canada. If tobacco is used, it is the role of the nurse to encourage the patient to quit. The Canadian Nurses Association (CNA) notes that "it is important for nurses to integrate tobacco use assessments, counselling and interventions into their practices."[11] Owing to the addictiveness of nicotine, nurses are aware that simply telling people to quit smoking may not be effective unless smoke cessation strategies are discussed, especially for heavy smokers (those who smoke 25 or more cigarettes a day). Many resources are available to the nurse to assist the patient in the smoking cessation process (see Nursing Tip, Cross-Canada Resources for Smoking Cessation).

Fortunately, Canadians are gradually kicking the habit. In the mid-1960s, close to half of Canadian adults smoked (59% of men and 37% of women over 18); by 2003, 21% of men aged 18 or older and 17% of women were daily smokers. Those who do smoke are smoking fewer cigarettes on a daily basis (in 1985, daily smokers consumed an average of 20.6 cigarettes per day; in 2003, smokers were down to 15.9 cigarettes per day). The continued decline, especially in men, is a positive trend, but the higher incidence of adolescent girls starting to smoke compared to boys is worrisome. In 2003, 20% of teen girls and 17% of boys reported smoking. British Columbia had the lowest rate of current smokers (16%), and Quebec had the highest (25%). Quebecers also reported the highest average number of cigarettes consumed per day by daily smokers (16.8), whereas Albertans reported the lowest average (14.6). Smoking prevalence is higher within the Aboriginal population for every age group.[12, 13]

Nursing Tip

Cross-Canada Resources for Smoking Cessation

Province/Territory	Phone Number	Web Link
Alberta Smokers' Helpline	1-866-332-2322	NA
British Columbia Quit Now By Phone	1-877-455-2233	http://www.bc.quitnet.com/
Manitoba Smokers' Helpline	1-877-513-5333	NA
New Brunswick Smokers' Helpline	1-877-513-5333	NA
Newfoundland and Labrador Smokers' Helpline	1-800-363-5864	http://www.smokershelp.net/
Northwest Territories Quit Now By Phone	Call the public health unit, or 1-800-O-Canada	NA
Nova Scotia Smokers' Helpline	1-877-513-5333	NA
Nunavut Quit Now By Phone	1-866-877-3845	NA
Ontario Smokers' Helpline	1-877-513-5333	http://www.smokershelpline.ca/
Prince Edward Island Smokers' Helpline	1-888-818-6300	NA
Quebec Smokers' Helpline Ligne j'Arrête!	1-866-jarrête (527-7383)	http://www.jarrete.qc.ca/
Saskatchewan Smokers' Helpline	1-877-513-5333	NA
Yukon Quit Now By Phone	1-800-661-0408 (x 8393)	NA

Nursing Tip

The Four A's of Smoking Cessation

Ask: At every patient encounter the nurse *asks* the patient about his or her smoking habits: type, amount, duration.

Advise: The nurse strongly *advises* the patient that quitting smoking is in his or her best health interest.

Assist: The nurse *assists* the patient in selecting an appropriate nicotine withdrawal method (e.g., "cold turkey," patch, gum, nasal spray, prescription medication, acupuncture, or hypnosis). Advantages and disadvantages of each method are discussed to empower the patient to make an informed decision.

Arrange: The nurse *arranges* for a close follow-up with the patient once the smoking cessation is started. Studies demonstrate that patients who have a support mechanism (professional or nonprofessional) and encouragement have greater success in quitting smoking. The follow-up can be a scheduled appointment or successive phone calls during which the nurse inquires how the patient is doing in meeting the smoking cessation goals and if there are any questions about the chosen withdrawal method.

The quantity of cigarettes smoked is usually described in **pack/year history.** To calculate the pack/year history, multiply the number of packs of cigarettes smoked on a daily basis by the number of years that the patient has smoked: A patient who has smoked 2.5 packs a day for 30 years has a pack/year history of 75 ($2.5 \times 30 = 75$). Some health care providers quantify tobacco use in the number of packs per day (PPD) for a specified number of years, for example, 2 PPD $\times$ 15 years.

"Do you use or have you ever used tobacco (filtered or nonfiltered cigarettes, pipes, cigars, chewing tobacco, snuff)?"

"At what age did you start to use tobacco?"

"What quantity do you use on a daily basis? Has this amount changed? In what way?"

"Have you ever tried to quit smoking? What method(s) did you use? What was the outcome?"

"How long ago did you quit?"

"Do you think you have a smoking (tobacco) problem?"

"Do you live with someone who smokes?"

"If you do not smoke, are you being pressured to start? How do you deal with these pressures?"

Reviewing Evidence about Smoke Cessation

Check the following resources for up-to-date information on smoke cessation.

- Hughes, J. R., Stead, L. F., & Lancaster, T. (2004). Antidepressants for smoking cessation. *The Cochrane Database of Systematic Reviews* 2004, Issue 4. Art. No.: CD000031.
- Ussher, M. (2005). Exercise interventions for smoking cessation. *The Cochrane Database of Systematic Reviews* 2005, Issue 1. Art. No.: CD002295.
- Møller, A. & Villebro, N. (2005). Interventions for preoperative smoking cessation. *The Cochrane Database of Systematic Reviews* 2005, Issue 3. Art. No.: CD002294.
- Registered Nurses' Association of Ontario. (2003). *Integrating smoke cessation into daily nursing practice.* Toronto: Registered Nurses' Association of Ontario.

Nursing Tip

HITS Screening Tool

The HITS screening tool assesses for domestic and intimate partner violence.[14] It is easily administered in a short period of time. The patient is asked how many times each incident has occurred in the past month or year.

H   Have you been physically **H**urt?
I   Have you been **I**nsulted or did someone talk down to you?
T   Have you been **T**hreatened with physical harm?
S   Has someone **S**creamed at you or cursed you?.

Domestic and Intimate Partner Violence

Domestic and intimate partner violence occurs within relationships based on kinship, intimacy, dependency, or trust and can include a range of abusive behaviours from psychological, emotional, and sexual, to financial abuse. Domestic violence is a disturbingly commonplace occurrence in the lives of many Canadians. According to the General Social Survey on Victimization (2004), cited in *Family Violence in Canada: A Statistical Profile* (2005),[15] 7% of women and 6% of men in a current or previous spousal relationship encountered spousal violence during the five years up to and including 2004. During the same time span, 24% of Aboriginal women and 18% of Aboriginal men reported spousal violence. The rate of domestic violence in gay or lesbian relationships was double the heterosexual couple rate. (See Nursing Alert, Domestic and Intimate Partner Violence—Unfortunate Realities for more details. Chapter 24 discusses specific details about violence against children.)

The CNA notes that as trusted health care professionals, nurses must become knowledgeable about issues of violence and must provide a full range of interventions, from the promotion of nonviolent interactions to actual support and treatment for victims and survivors of violence.[17] The Registered Nurses' Association of Ontario "Best Practice Guideline" on women abuse recommends implementation of routine universal screening for such abuse in all health care

Nursing Alert

Domestic and Intimate Partner Violence in Canada—Unfortunate Realities[16]

- Rates of spousal violence are highest in the age group 15–24, in relationships of less than three years, and in common-law unions.
- Discontinuing the relationship helps many victims, but violence still continues despite separation in half of female victims and one-third of male victims.
- Although men can be victims, women suffer the most risk with respect to more frequent violent incidents and more emotional sequelae; women are more likely to sustain serious injury as a result of violent forms of abuse.
- Twice as many women than men are stalked by current or previous partners, to the extent that they fear for their life.
- There is a strong correlation between emotional abuse and violence, with 25% of women in emotionally abusive relationships also experiencing physical violence.
- 97% of family homicide-suicides relating to spouses involved the female being killed by her male spouse.
- Rates of violence do not vary with family income or level of education.

settings.[18] It is vital to be familiar with your provincial or territorial statutes regarding reporting actual and suspected violence and abuse, as well as the local resources available to help people in such situations. Intervention requires interprofessional and intersectoral collaboration—nurses cannot deal with these incidents on their own.

Some clues that might alert the nurse to the possibility of domestic and intimate partner violence are:

- Frequent injuries, accidents, or burns
- Previous injuries for which the individual did not seek health care
- Injury is inconsistent with the patient's report of how it occurred
- Refusal of the patient to discuss the injury
- Significant other accompanies the patient to health care encounters, answers questions for patient, and refuses to leave the patient's side
- Significant other has a history of previous violence or substance abuse

Appendix F outlines a sample Woman Abuse Screening Tool (WAST). Using the communication technique of normalizing, the nurse can screen for potential domestic and intimate partner violence. Some appropriate introductory comments might include:

"Many women experience domestic and intimate partner violence. Has this ever happened to you?"

"Domestic and intimate partner violence occur very frequently in our community. Keeping this in mind, I would like to ask you some questions."

A single broad question can also be used to screen for domestic and intimate partner violence:

"In the past year, have you been hit, kicked, punched, or hurt in other ways by someone close to you?"

"Have you been put down, ridiculed, taunted, or forced to engage in sexual acts that you did not feel comfortable engaging in by someone close to you?"

If the patient answers "yes" to any of these questions, you need to inquire whether or not the patient feels safe in his or her current environment or situation. It is imperative to document physical violence assessment findings concisely and accurately. Incorporate drawings of injury locations or use printed anatomical maps on which injuries can be documented. Many agencies photograph the injuries so that physical violence can be validated in the event of legal proceedings.

Reflective Thinking

Assessing for Domestic and Intimate Partner Violence

You note that Tasha has come to the ED three times in the past six months. Six months ago, she reported falling down the steps and hitting her head. Her old chart documents that she was seen for a mild, closed head injury with concussion. Two months ago, she reported falling while ice skating and broke her left arm. Today, she presents with multiple facial and mouth lacerations. She tells you that she fell off her bike. You note multiple ecchymoses on the exposed areas of her skin.

- What questions would you ask Tasha?
- Describe the physical examination that you would conduct.
- Investigate your agency's policy on reporting actual and suspected violence or abuse.
- Investigate the regulations in your community on reporting actual and suspected violence or abuse.
- What resources are available in your community to help someone in Tasha's situation?

Sexual Practice

Sexual practices relate to the transmission of communicable diseases and include various illnesses and medications that can affect sexual function. Data about the patient's sexual practices may not be accurate if obtained in front of the patient's partner, parents, or other family members, so use discretion when assessing this area. Some nurses may feel uneasy or embarrassed in regard to what constitutes "acceptable" sexual practices. Examine your personal feelings on human sexuality and attain a comfort level that allows you explore this area of the health assessment. The health histories in Chapters 20 and 21 offer additional information about female and male reproductive health.

"What term would you use to describe your sexual orientation (heterosexual, homosexual, bisexual)?"

"At what age was your first sexual experience?"

"With how many partners are you currently involved? Has this changed?"

"What method of birth control do you use? Do you have any questions about it?"

"What measures do you use to prevent exchange of body fluids during sexual activity?"

"Do you engage in oral sex or anal intercourse?"

"Have you ever had a sexual partner who had a sexually transmitted disease?"

"Do you take any prescription or over-the-counter medications to help your sexual performance?"

"Do you use any sexual aid devices?"

"Are you satisfied with your sexual performance?"

"Are you being pressured to have sex when you do not want to? How do you deal with this pressure?"

Travel History

Endemic illnesses may be endogenous to specific regions in the world or to a single country. Some patients may present with symptoms that cannot be attributed to routine illnesses. Therefore, a complete travel history is warranted when obtaining a health history.

"Where within Canada have you travelled? Was this a rural or an urban environment? When?"

"Have you ever travelled outside of Canada? Where? When? How long were you away?"

"Did you receive any immunizations before you visited that area?"

"Did you need to take any medications before or while you were gone?"

"Were you ill when you were there? Was a diagnosis made? By whom? What was it?"

"What treatment did you receive? Were there any complications?"

"Since returning from this area, have you been ill or not feeling normal?"

Work Environment

The work environment can give rise to physical, chemical, biological, ergonomic, and psychosocial hazards that can influence health. Failing to inquire about a patient's past and current work environment could result in omission of important data in forming an accurate analysis of a presenting health issue or concern. For example, if a male patient complains of new onset of shortness of breath but is not questioned about his work at a skating rink where nitric oxide is used, an important factor in determining the cause of the respiratory problem could be missed. A soldier returning from military duty in the Middle East who has witnessed a comrade die a violent death must be monitored for post traumatic stress disorder.

"Are you exposed to excessive noise, vibration, radiation, or extremes of heat or cold in your work?"

"Do you work with any chemicals or raw materials?"

"How do you protect yourself from such work hazards?"

"Are material safety data sheets available to you? Do you follow the recommendations?"

"Do you work with any biological hazards such as viruses, insects, plants, animals?"

"Do you spend the majority of your workday sitting, standing, lifting, or doing repetitive work?"

"Do you enjoy your work?"

"Is your work mentally or emotionally demanding?"

"Do you experience any conflict, violence, or harassment in your workplace?"

"Do you feel secure in your work?"

"Have you had any work-related accidents or injuries?"

Home Environment

When assessing the patient's home environment, consider both the physical and psychosocial aspects. The physical assessment encompasses a broad spectrum of topics: physical condition of the house, exposure to toxic substances, and the presence of appliances, furnaces, telephones, and electricity. The discovery of radon gas in some homes also has been a recent health concern.

The psychosocial component of the home environment identifies the relative safety of the neighbourhood.

Physical Environment

"How old are your living quarters (i.e., house or apartment building)?"

"In what condition are your living quarters?"

"Is your home cleaned regularly?"

"Do you have heat, air conditioning, and electricity? What type of heating system do you have?

"What is the temperature on your hot water heater?"

"From what source do you draw your water (e.g., well, reservoir)?"

"Do you have smoke detectors? Where? Are the batteries inspected on a regular basis?"

"Do you have a carbon monoxide detector?"

"Do you have any throw rugs? Are they taped to the floor?"

"Do you use a nightlight when it is dark?"

"Do you think your living space is adequate for the number of people who live with you?"

"Have you ever had your living quarters tested for the presence of radon? What was the result?"

"How often do you have your fireplace or chimney cleaned?"

"How often do you replace the filter in your ventilation system?"

"What pets do you have? Do they live inside or outside?"

"Do you have easy access to a grocery store? Pharmacy? Health care facility?"

"Where do you store your medications, cleaning supplies, and other toxic substances? How are they secured?" (if children live in the living quarters)

"Do you have a gun in the house? Where is it stored? Where are the bullets stored?"

Psychosocial Environment

"Do you feel safe in your neighbourhood?"

"Does your neighbourhood have a crime watch prevention program?"

Hobbies and Leisure Activities

Asking patients about their hobbies and leisure activities is necessary because some activities can pose health risks (Figure 3-8). For example, repeated exposure to the glue used in constructing model cars and planes can lead to respiratory ailments.

"What hobbies do you have?" **or** "What do you like to do in your spare time?"

"Have you ever felt sick during or after any leisure activities? What happened?"

"Have you ever had an injury from your hobby?"

"Are the hobbies and leisure activities relaxing?"

Figure 3-8 Inquiring about a patient's hobbies or leisure activities can sometimes provide clues on a patient's complaint.

Stress

Stress is a physiologically defined response to changes that disrupt the resting equilibrium of an individual. **Distress** is negative stress, or stress that is harmful and unpleasant. **Eustress** is positive stress that challenges the individual, provides motivation, and prevents stagnation.

"What are the current stressors in your life?"

"What is your greatest stress at the present time?"

"Have you ever progressed from the point of being stressed to panic? What were the circumstances? How did you handle it?"

"Are you able to recognize when you become stressed?"

"How do you cope with stress?"

Education

Elicit information on the patient's ability to read and write, and then tailor your questions accordingly.

"What was the highest level of education that you completed?"

"Do you have any plans to continue your education?"

Economic Status

Patients and nurses may be equally uncomfortable discussing financial status. The patient's economic status is needed in order to ascertain how the patient lives on the income. Patients who lack adequate financial resources may need a referral to social service agencies.

"What are the sources of your income?"

"Are you able to meet food, medication, housing, clothing, and personal expenses for your needs?"

"Are you able to save any money?"

Religion and Spirituality

Religion and spirituality can be powerful forces in a patient's life (Figure 3-9). Nurses need to be aware of and sensitive to implications that spirituality or religious beliefs may have on the patient's health care status and practices. Chapter 6 provides a more detailed assessment of religion and spiritual practices.

"Are you affiliated with a specific religion?"

"Do you currently practise this religion?"

"Do your religious/spiritual beliefs affect your health status? In what way?"

Ethnicity

Closely associated with religious practices is the patient's culture, or ethnic background, which can penetrate all areas of a patient's life. Integrate familiarity with various cultures into your knowledge base so you will be sensitive to and more completely understand the patient's ethnic heritage. Chapter 5 discusses the cultural assessment in greater detail.

"With what culture or ethnic group do you identify yourself?"

"What are common practices in your culture that might influence your health?"

Roles and Relationships

Family roles, work roles, and interpersonal relationships provide clues about possible stressors, areas for health promotion, and available support systems.

"Who lives with you?"

"What type of relationship do you have with these individuals?"

"What is your role within your family (e.g., caregiver, breadwinner, child, student)?"

"What responsibilities go along with this role?"

Figure 3-9 Religion can affect many facets of a person's health.

Figure 3-10 The characteristic patterns of daily living for this parent include early morning child care and lunch preparation.

"Do you experience any role strain?"

"Who do you turn to for support?"

"Describe the relationship that you have with your family, friends, and neighbours."

Characteristic Patterns of Daily Living and Functional Health Assessment

Questions about a patient's usual lifestyle, or **characteristic patterns of daily living**, reveal information about the patient's normal daily timetable: meals, work, sleep schedules, and social interactions (Figure 3-10). If the patient is impaired physically, anatomically, or psychologically, you need to perform a functional health assessment (see Appendix D). The **functional health assessment** documents a person's ability to perform instrumental activities of daily living (IADL) and physical self-maintenance activities.

"Describe a typical day for you, starting from the time you wake up to the time you go to bed."

"Do you need assistance with any activities of daily living? (If yes) Is assistance readily available?"

"Do you socialize, meet, or talk with people outside your house on a daily basis?"

"Does your schedule change on certain days or on the weekend? Describe."

Health Maintenance Activities

Health maintenance activities (HMA) are practices a person incorporates into his or her lifestyle to promote healthy living. You can make the transition from the SH to HMA with a statement such as:

"There are many things you can do to promote your health and that of your family. I would like us to discuss some of those practices."

Sleep

Many illnesses have sleep pattern disturbances as a characteristic. Increased or decreased sleep patterns can both occur. For this reason you need to learn about the patient's current and usual sleep habits.

"At what time do you usually go to bed? What time do you usually awake?"

"Is this an adequate amount of sleep for you? How do you feel when you awaken?"

"How long does it take you to fall asleep? Once asleep, do you have difficulty staying asleep? If you awaken, is it easy for you to fall back to sleep?"

"Do you have any leg discomfort or get short of breath (paroxysmal nocturnal dyspnea) when you are asleep?"

"Do you have to get up in the night to urinate (nocturia)?"

"Do you have a bedtime routine? What do you do if you have difficulty falling asleep?"

"What is your usual emotional state or mental condition when you go to bed? When you awaken?"

"Have you ever been told that you snore loudly or excessively?"

"Do you ever have difficulty staying awake?"

"Have you ever been told that you have sleep apnea or narcolepsy?"

"Do you take a nap during the day? For how long?"

"Do you fall asleep unintentionally at times other than night time?"

Diet

Refer to Chapter 7 for a more thorough discussion of nutrition and diet history.

"Are you on any special therapeutic diet (low salt, low cholesterol, low fat, etc.)?"

"Do you follow any particular diet plan (vegetarian, liquid, Atkins diet, etc.)?"

Figure 3-11 The use of safety devices can prevent potentially serious injuries.

Nursing Tip

"FIT" Acronym

An easy way to remember what questions to ask a patient regarding an exercise regimen is the use of the "FIT" acronym.

F **F**requency of the activity
I **I**ntensity of the activity
T **T**iming, or duration, of the activity).

"How many meals a day do you eat? At what times do you eat? Do you snack? When?"

"Has your weight fluctuated in the past year? Explain."

Exercise

Aerobic exercise appropriate to the patient's age and physical condition leads to cardiovascular, respiratory, and musculoskeletal fitness as well as mental alertness. Combining aerobic exercise with weight lifting (increases strength) and calisthenics (enhances flexibility) establishes a complete physical fitness regimen. Nonaerobic activity also has beneficial effects on the body, even though the target heart rate may not be attained. Canada's Physical Activity Guide to Healthy Active Living outlines the benefits and general recommendations for physical activity for all Canadians (Figure 3-12).

"Do you participate in a formal or informal exercise program? (if yes) How long have you been doing this?"

"What type of exercise do you do?"

"How many times per week do you exercise?"

"How long do you exercise (in minutes)?"

"What is your resting heart rate?"

"What is your heart rate at the most intense time of your exercise?"

"For what period of time do you maintain this elevated heart rate?"

"Have you ever experienced any injuries from your exercise regimen? What type?"

"Does your health pose any restrictions on your ability to exercise?"

Stress Management

Knowing how the patient handles stress is vital to the health assessment. Some commonly used stress management techniques are exercise, eating, biofeedback, yoga, progressive muscle relaxation, aromatherapy, imagery, massages, verbalization, praying, humour, pet therapy, music therapy, and support groups. For some people, stress management techniques include smoking, drinking, drugs, and violence.

"What do you do to help alleviate the stress when you become stressed?"

"When do you use this skill? Is it effective for you?"

"How many times per day do you use this technique? Per week?"

"Have you tried other ways to manage stress? How did they work?"

Use of Safety Devices

Knowing whether or not the patient uses safety devices on the job, in the home, and in the environment is an opportunity to teach health promotion skills (Figure 3-11).

"Do you wear a seat belt when you are in an automobile?"

"Do you wear a helmet if playing hockey or riding a bicycle (motorcycle, skate board, etc.)?"

Health Check-ups

Health check-up information demonstrates patterns of health care practices by the patient during illness and health and provides potential sources of health education.

"When was the last time you had the following performed: pulse and blood pressure, complete physical examination, PAP or prostate exam (as indicated by sex), urinalysis, hematocrit, and blood chemistry, including blood glucose and cholesterol? What were the results?"

"How often do you see a dentist, an ophthalmologist? For what reason?

CANADA'S

Physical Activity Guide
to Healthy Active Living

Physical activity improves health.

Every little bit counts, but more is even better – everyone can do it!

Get active your way – build physical activity into your daily life...

• at home
• at school
• at work
• at play
• on the way
...that's active living!

Increase
Endurance
Activities

Increase
Flexibility
Activities

Increase
Strength
Activities

Reduce
Sitting for
long periods

 Health Santé
Canada Canada

 Canadian Society for
Exercise Physiology

Figure 3-12 Canada's Physical Activity Guide to Healthy Active Living
Source: http://www.phac-aspc.gc.ca/pau-uap/fitness/pdf/guideEng.pdf. Reproduced with the permission of the Minister of Public Works and Government Services Canada, 2006.

Choose a variety of activities from these three groups:

Endurance

4-7 days a week
Continuous activities for your heart, lungs and circulatory system.

Flexibility

4-7 days a week
Gentle reaching, bending and stretching activities to keep your muscles relaxed and joints mobile.

Strength

2-4 days a week
Activities against resistance to strengthen muscles and bones and improve posture.

Starting slowly is very safe for most people. Not sure? Consult your health professional.

For a copy of the *Guide Handbook* and more information:
1-888-334-9769, or
www.paguide.com

Eating well is also important. Follow *Canada's Food Guide to Healthy Eating* to make wise food choices.

Get Active Your Way, Every Day—For Life!

Scientists say accumulate 60 minutes of physical activity every day to stay healthy or improve your health. As you progress to moderate activities you can cut down to 30 minutes, 4 days a week. Add-up your activities in periods of at least 10 minutes each. Start slowly... and build up.

Time needed depends on effort

Very Light Effort	Light Effort *60 minutes*	Moderate Effort *30-60 minutes*	Vigorous Effort *20-30 minutes*	Maximum Effort
• Strolling	• Light walking	• Brisk walking	• Aerobics	• Sprinting
• Dusting	• Volleyball	• Biking	• Jogging	• Racing
	• Easy gardening	• Raking leaves	• Hockey	
	• Stretching	• Swimming	• Basketball	
		• Dancing	• Fast swimming	
		• Water aerobics	• Fast dancing	

Range needed to stay healthy

You Can Do It – Getting started is easier than you think

Physical activity doesn't have to be very hard. Build physical activities into your daily routine.

- Walk whenever you can – get off the bus early, use the stairs instead of the elevator.
- Reduce inactivity for long periods, like watching TV.
- Get up from the couch and stretch and bend for a few minutes every hour.
- Play actively with your kids.
- Choose to walk, wheel or cycle for short trips.

- Start with a 10 minute walk – gradually increase the time.
- Find out about walking and cycling paths nearby and use them.
- Observe a physical activity class to see if you want to try it.
- Try one class to start – you don't have to make a long-term commitment.
- Do the activities you are doing now, more often.

Benefits of regular activity:

- better health
- improved fitness
- better posture and balance
- better self-esteem
- weight control
- stronger muscles and bones
- feeling more energetic
- relaxation and reduced stress
- continued independent living in later life

Health risks of inactivity:

- premature death
- heart disease
- obesity
- high blood pressure
- adult-onset diabetes
- osteoporosis
- stroke
- depression
- colon cancer

ACTIVE LIVING

No changes permitted. Permission to photocopy this document in its entirety not required.
Cat. No. H39-429/1998-1E ISBN 0-662-86627-7

CANADA'S
Physical Activity Guide
to Healthy Active Living

"Do you know how to perform breast self-examination? How often do you perform it? Do you have any questions about it? What was the date and the result of your last mammogram?" (for women)

"Do you know how to perform a testicular self-examination? How often do you perform it? Do you have any questions about it?" (for men)

"Do you have any other health care providers (psychiatrist, psychologist, podiatrist, occupational or physical therapist, chiropractor, shaman, etc.)? For what reason? How often do you see this person?"

Review of Systems

The **review of systems** (ROS) is the patient's subjective response to a series of body system–related questions and serves as a check that vital information is not overlooked. The ROS covers a broad base of clinical states, but it is by no means exhaustive. The review follows a head-to-toe or **cephalocaudal** approach and includes two types of questions: sign or symptom related and disease related. Remember to ask the questions in terms that are understood by the patient. The signs or symptoms and diseases are grouped according to physiological body parts and systems. Some of the diseases may have been discussed earlier in the interview.

TABLE 3-6	Review of Systems
General	Patient's perception of general state of health at the present, difference from usual state, vitality and energy levels, body odours, fever, chills, night sweats
Skin	Rashes, itching, changes in skin pigmentation, ecchymoses, change in colour or size of mole, sores, lumps, dry or moist skin, pruritus, change in skin texture, odours, excessive sweating, acne, warts, eczema, psoriasis, amount of time spent in the sun, use of sunscreen, skin cancer
Hair	Alopecia, excessive growth of hair or growth of hair in unusual locations (hirsutism), use of chemicals on hair, dandruff, pediculosis, scalp lesions
Nails	Change in nails, splitting, breaking, thickened, texture change, onychomycosis, use of chemicals, false nails
Eyes	Blurred vision, visual acuity, glasses, contacts, photophobia, excessive tearing, night blindness, diplopia, drainage, bloodshot eyes, pain, blind spots, flashing lights, halos around objects, floaters, glaucoma, cataracts, use of sunglasses, use of protective eyewear
Ears	Cleaning method, hearing deficits, hearing aid, pain, phonophobia, discharge, lightheadedness (vertigo), ringing in the ears (tinnitus), usual noise level, earaches, infection, piercings, use of ear protection, amount of cerumen
Nose and Sinuses	Number of colds per year, discharge, itching, hay fever, postnasal drip, stuffiness, sinus pain, sinusitis, polyps, obstruction, epistaxis, change in sense of smell, allergies, snoring
Mouth	Dental habits (brushing, flossing, mouth rinses), toothache, tooth abscess, dentures, bleeding or swollen gums, difficulty chewing, sore tongue, change in taste, lesions, change in salivation, bad breath, caries, teeth extractions, orthodontics
Throat and Neck	Hoarseness, change in voice, frequent sore throats, dysphagia, pain or stiffness, enlarged thyroid (goiter), lymphadenopathy, tonsillectomy, adenoidectomy
Breasts and Axilla	Pain, tenderness, discharge, lumps, change in size, dimpling, rash, benign breast disease, breast cancer, results of recent mammogram
Respiratory	Dyspnea on exertion, shortness of breath, sputum, cough, sneezing, wheezing, hemoptysis, frequent upper respiratory tract infections, pneumonia, emphysema, asthma, tuberculosis, tuberculosis exposure, result of last chest X-ray or PPD
Cardiovascular and Peripheral Vasculature	Paroxysmal nocturnal dyspnea, chest pain, cyanosis, heart murmur, palpitations, syncope, orthopnea (state number of pillows used), edema, cold or discoloured hands or feet, leg cramps, myocardial infarction, hypertension, valvular disease, intermittent claudication, varicose veins, thrombophlebitis, deep vein thrombosis, use of support hose, anemia, result of last ECG

TABLE 3-6	Review of Systems *continued*
Gastrointestinal	Change in appetite, nausea, vomiting, diarrhea, constipation, usual bowel habits, melena, rectal bleeding, hematemesis, change in stool colour, flatulence, belching, regurgitation, heartburn, dysphagia, abdominal pain, jaundice, ascites, hemorrhoids, hepatitis, peptic ulcers, gallstones, gastroesophageal reflux disease, appendicitis, ulcerative colitis, Crohn's disease, diverticulitis, hernia
Urinary	Change in urine colour, voiding habits, dysuria, hesitancy, urgency, frequency, nocturia, polyuria, dribbling, loss in force of stream, bedwetting, change in urine volume, incontinence, urinary retention, suprapubic pain, flank pain, kidney stones, urinary tract infections
Musculoskeletal	Joint stiffness, muscle pain, cramps, back pain, limitation of movement, redness, swelling, weakness, bony deformity, broken bones, dislocations, sprains, crepitus, gout, arthritis, osteoporosis, herniated disc
Neurological	Headache, change in balance, incoordination, loss of movement, change in sensory perception or feeling in an extremity, change in speech, change in smell, syncope, loss of memory, tremors, involuntary movement, loss of consciousness, seizures, weakness, head injury, vertigo, tic, paralysis, stroke, spasm
Psychological	Irritability, nervousness, tension, increased stress, difficulty concentrating, mood changes, suicidal thoughts, depression, anxiety, sleep disturbances
Female Reproductive	Vaginal discharge, change in libido, infertility, sterility, pelvic pain, pain during intercourse, postcoital bleeding; menses: last menstrual period (LMP), menarche, regularity, duration, amount of bleeding, premenstrual symptoms, intermenstrual bleeding, dysmenorrhea, menorrhagia, fibroids; menopause: age of onset, duration, symptoms, bleeding; obstetrical: number of pregnancies, number of miscarriages or abortions, number of children, type of delivery, complications; type of birth control, hormone replacement therapy
Male Reproductive	Change in libido, infertility, sterility, impotence, pain during intercourse, age at onset of puberty, testicular or penile pain, penile discharge, erections, emissions, hernias, enlarged prostate, type of birth control
Nutrition	Present weight, usual weight, desired weight, food intolerances, food likes and dislikes, where meals are eaten, caffeine intake
Endocrine	Exophthalmos, fatigue, change in size of head, hands, or feet, weight change, heat and cold intolerances, excessive sweating, polydipsia, polyphagia, polyuria, increased hunger, change in body hair distribution, goiter, diabetes mellitus
Lymph Nodes	Enlargement, tenderness
Hematological	Easy bruising or bleeding, anemia, sickle cell anemia, blood type, exposure to radiation

Reflective Thinking

Assessing Your Documentation

After completing the health history, reflect on the techniques you used to elicit the history. Did you rush the patient? Did you use too many open-ended or closed questions? Was your documentation concise? What could you have done better?

Both positive and pertinent negative findings are documented in the ROS. When a response is positive, ask the patient to describe it as completely as possible. Refer to the 10 characteristics of a health issue or concern when gathering more information about positive responses of signs and symptoms. Table 3-6 lists the symptoms and diseases that can be ascertained during the ROS. Many institutions have preprinted ROS sheets that are convenient to use because positive findings are circled and noted; negative responses are not circled. As you become more experienced, you can combine the ROS with the physical examination of the patient, which often shortens the interview time with the patient.

CONCLUDING THE HEALTH HISTORY

After completing the ROS, ask the patient if there is any additional information to discuss. At the conclusion of the interview, thank the patient for the time spent in gathering the health history. Inform the patient what the next step will be; for example, physical assessment, diagnostic tests, and treatment, and when to expect it.

Nursing Alert

Role of Technology

Technology is changing the way we interface with the health care arena. Computers are being used at the bedside to document assessment findings and patient care. Patients can enter their health history on computers, schedule their own appointments, and obtain test results and consultation via e-mail or fax. Health care providers use computers to link directly to pharmacies to prescribe medications; to solicit patients' health histories, signs, and symptoms; to diagnose patients; and to implement treatment plans, all done via e-mail and the Internet. Technology readily puts the patient in direct contact with a health care provider; however, the privacy and legal issues are complex and still evolving.

Become aware of your institutional policies on communication and data collection using advanced forms of technology. Ensure that all measures to guard privacy and confidentiality are upheld. Make sure that alternate forms of technology do not compromise the accuracy and thoroughness of your assessment, such as when assessing a symptom over the telephone or by e-mail—critical thinking will determine if such an assessment can be supported without a face-to-face interview.

DOCUMENTATION

The documentation of the health and physical assessments is the legal record of the patient encounter. The information also serves as the medium among health professionals to communicate about the patient's condition, describing the patient's status and the care delivered to the patient. The patient record may be read by a multitude of professionals: nurses; doctors; dieticians; respiratory, physical, speech, and occupational therapists; risk managers; quality assurance personnel; accreditation organizations; lawyers; and, ultimately, the patient! Because all of these people have access to the patient's chart, documenting in a professional and legally acceptable manner is required. Table 3-7 outlines general principles to guide your documentation. Table 3-8 provides specific assessment-oriented do's and don'ts for documentation. Each institution also has its own documentation system. If you perform computerized charting in your workplace, always safeguard your access code.

Many health care facilities have preprinted health history forms that are checklists and require few narrative notes. Other facilities require the nurse to document the health history in its entirety. The two health histories that follow illustrate how to document the complete health history of an ill patient as well as a well patient.

THE SYSTEM-SPECIFIC HEALTH HISTORY

This text uses a system-specific health history in each body system chapter (see Chapters 10–22). The health history provides detailed information that guides questioning and provides clues of related pathology. Only those sections relevant to the body system being assessed are addressed in the body system history, and each chapter may differ due to the nature of the material.

TABLE 3-7 Assessment-Specific Documentation Guidelines

1. Record all data that contribute directly to the assessment (e.g., positive assessment findings and pertinent negatives).
2. Document any sections of the assessment that were omitted, deferred, or refused by the patient.
3. Avoid using judgmental language such as "good," "poor," "bad," "normal," "abnormal," "decreased," "appears to be," and "seems."
4. Avoid evaluative statements (e.g., "patient is uncooperative," "patient is lazy"); instead, cite specific statements or actions that you observed (e.g., "patient said 'I hate this place' and kicked trash can").
5. Record time intervals precisely (e.g., write "every 4 hours," "bid," instead of "seldom," "occasionally").
6. Provide specific measurements (e.g., "mass is 3 cm × 5 cm"); do not make relative statements about findings (e.g., "mass is the size of an egg").
7. Draw pictures when necessary (e.g., location of scar, masses, lesions, reflexes, etc.).
8. Refer to findings using anatomic landmarks (e.g., left upper quadrant [of abdomen], left lower lobe [of lung], midclavicular line, etc.).
9. Use a clock face to describe findings that have a circular pattern (e.g., 2 cm × 2 cm mass palpated at 03:00 position of right breast; pressure equalizing tube noted at 09:00 in left tympanic membrane).
10. Document any change in the patient's condition during a visit or from previous visits.
11. Describe what you observed, not what you did.

TABLE 3-8 General Documentation Guidelines

1. Ensure that you have the correct patient chart and that the patient's name and identifying information are on every page of the record.
2. Document the time when the patient encounter is concluded to ensure accurate recall of data (follow institution's guidelines on frequency of charting).
3. Avoid distractions while documenting to ensure details are not overlooked and to avoid errors.
4. If interrupted while documenting, reread what you wrote to ensure accuracy.
5. Date and time each entry.
6. Sign each entry with your full legal name and with your professional credentials, or per your institution's policy.
7. Do not sign a note that you did not write.
8. Do not leave space between entries.
9. Do not insert information between lines.
10. Cross out errors using a single line, then date, time, and sign the correction (check institutional policy); avoid erasing, crossing out, or using correction fluid.
11. Never correct another person's entry, even if it is incorrect.
12. Use quotes to indicate direct patient responses (e.g., "I feel lousy").
13. Document in chronological order; if chronological order is not used, state why.
14. Use legible writing.
15. Use a permanent ink pen. (Black ink usually photocopies well.)
16. Document in a complete and concise manner by using phrases and abbreviations as appropriate (see the abbreviation list on the inside back cover of this book). Avoid using abbreviations, acronyms, and symbols that are deemed dangerous by the Institute for Safe Medication Practices (ISMP) (see Appendix E).
17. Insert a zero to the left of the decimal point when writing numbers less than 1; this avoids confusion as to the use of a decimal point.
18. Document telephone calls that relate to the patient's case.
19. Always reread your notes to check their accuracy.
20. Remember, from a legal standpoint, if you didn't document it, it wasn't done.

HEALTH HISTORY

COMPLETE HEALTH HISTORY: WELL PATIENT

Today's Date	May 11, 2007
BIOGRAPHICAL DATA	
Patient's Name	Philip Teoli
Address	3609 22nd Avenue, Montreal, QC
Phone Number	H (514) 834-1234
Date of Birth	March 4, 1989
Birthplace	Montreal, Quebec
Occupation	Student
Usual Source of Health Care	Dr. Stevens, General Practitioner
Source of Referral	Friend of parents
Emergency Contact	Nadia Teoli (mother); Same phone #
Source and Reliability	Self; reliable historian
PATIENT PROFILE	18-year-old man; parents are third generation Italian, single, living at home with parents, looks well.
HEALTH ISSUE/CONCERN	"I am going to university & I need to get a physical; I need my last dose of hepatitis B vaccine."
PRESENT HEALTH	Pt describes himself as a healthy male $\bar{s}$ any significant medical problems.
PAST HEALTH HISTORY	
Medical History	Hepatitis A age 3 from day care outbreak; Ø sequelae; allergic rhinitis since age 16 (grass, mould, ragweed, pollen, cats)
Surgical History	Hernia repair age 6; Ø sequelae
Medications	OTC antihistamine during allergy season; acetaminophen for headache; "I try not to use too many drugs—only when I really need to;" no natural health products or prescription medications
Communicable Diseases	Hepatitis A per above; denies STI; has never had HIV testing
Allergies	PCN: urticaria & wheezing occurred at age 2; rhinitis with exposure to grass, mould, ragweed, pollen, cats
Injuries and Accidents	Fx Ⓛ index finger age 8 playing basketball; splint × 5 wks; Ø sequelae
Special Needs	Denies
Blood Transfusions	Denies
Childhood Illnesses	Varicella age 4; Ø sequelae; impetigo as 1–2 year old

Immunizations	"I'm up-to-date except that I missed the last dose of the hepatitis B series so need to get that."

FAMILY HEALTH HISTORY

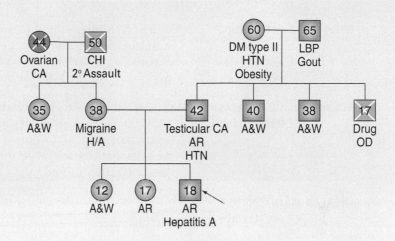

LEGEND

- ⬤ Living female
- ⬛ Living male
- ⊗ Deceased female
- ⊠ Deceased male
- ╱ Points to patient

AR = Allergic rhinitis
A&W = Alive & well
CA = Cancer
CHI = Closed head injury
DM = Diabetes mellitus
H/A = Headache
HTN = Hypertension
LBP = Low back pain
OD = Overdose

Denies family hx of heart dz, CVA, TB, kidney dz, liver dz, blood disorders, thyroid dz, asthma, AIDS, mental illness

SOCIAL HISTORY

Alcohol Use	2–3 beers on wkend at parties; sometimes drives after drinking
Drug Use	Smokes marijuana 2–3 times a month; no other illicit drug use reported
Tobacco Use	Denies
Domestic/Intimate Partner Violence	Denies
Sexual Practice	"I'm heterosexual but I have had sex with men."
Travel History	Visits Italy q 2–3 yrs to visit relatives; goes to the Caribbean every second winter
Work Environment	Lifeguard at swim club this summer
Home Environment	
Physical Environment	Lives in 15 yo house c̄ parents & 2 sisters; has all modern conveniences; parents perform all maintenance
Psychosocial Environment	Describes as "nice"
Hobbies and Leisure Activities	Reading, visiting c̄ friends, online chat rooms
Stress	Getting ready for university; "I'm the first in my family to go to university so there is a lot of pressure."
Education	Recent college grad, top 25% of class

continues

Economic Status	Parents will pay for half of university expenses; has been saving for some time; will have to work every second weekend during the school year.
Religion	"My parents are Catholic but I don't go to church."
Ethnicity	Third generation Italian on father's side; mother is French Canadian
Roles and Relationships	Oldest of 3 children; states parents are proud of him and sisters want to emulate him academically; gets along $\bar{c}$ 2 younger sisters; respects & loves parents; "I don't have a lot of friends but the ones I have are solid and would do anything for me."
Characteristic Patterns of Daily Living	Wakes at 04:30 & eats protein bar; lifeguards early bird swim at club at 06:00; teaches swim lessons from 08–11:00, then gets lunch at snack bar; 12–13:00 rotates chairs at main pool; swims & then lifts weights; eats dinner at 18:00 $\bar{c}$ family; goes out $\bar{c}$ friends from 20–23:00 then to bed

HEALTH MAINTENANCE ACTIVITIES

Sleep	6.5 hrs on wkdays, > 10 on wkends
Diet	3 meals daily, no particular diet; snacks in the evening, usually chips
Exercise	Swims 1 hr daily then lifts weight for 1 hr; would like to try out for university swim team
Stress Management	Swims, reads
Use of Safety Devices	Wears seat belt; uses sunscreen when outside > 1 hr; reapplies q 2–3 hrs
Health Check-ups	Dentist 1×/yr; only seeks medical attention when really sick; does not know how to perform TSE

REVIEW OF SYSTEMS

General	High energy levels, healthy, denies recent illness
Skin	Denies rashes, itching, changes in skin pigmentation, ecchymoses, pruritus, change in moles, sores, lumps, change in skin texture, body odours, acne, has only had 2 sunburns in 3 yrs of life guarding
Hair	Denies alopecia, hirsutism, dandruff, pediculosis, hair chemicals
Nails	Denies change in nails, splitting, breaking, onychomycosis
Eyes	20/25 vision at eye exam 4 yrs ago; wears sunglasses when life guarding; denies blurry vision, photophobia, diplopia, eye drainage, bloodshot eyes, pain, blind spots, floaters, flashing lights, halos around objects, glaucoma, cataracts
Ears	Denies hearing deficits, hearing device, pain, discharge, vertigo, tinnitus, earaches; got "swimmers ear" 3 yrs ago that resolved with topical antibiotic
Nose and Sinuses	Averages 1–2 colds/yr; gets "runny nose" during spring time and was told by family MD that he has allergic rhinitis—it resolves once

	spring pollen season is over; denies current discharge, itching, postnasal drip, sinus pain, polyps, obstruction, epistaxis, change in sense of smell
Mouth	Brushes and flosses teeth 1–2 ×/d; denies toothache, tooth abscess, dentures, bleeding/swollen gums, sore tongue, change in taste, lesions, change in salivation, bad breath, difficulty chewing
Throat and Neck	Denies hoarseness, change in voice, frequent sore throats, difficulty swallowing, pain/stiffness, goiter
Respiratory	Denies sputum, sneezing, wheezing, hemoptysis, pneumonia, emphysema, asthma, TB
Cardiovascular	Denies PND, heart murmur, palpitations, CP, syncope, edema, orthopnea, cold hands/feet, leg cramps, MI, intermittent claudication, varicose veins, thrombophlebitis, anemia, rheumatic heart disease
Breasts and Axilla	Denies change in size, pain, tenderness, discharge, lumps, dimpling, rash
Gastrointestinal	Regular bowel habit: BM q AM, soft & brown; denies vomiting, diarrhea, constipation, melena, change in stool colour, hematemesis; ↑ flatulence, belching, heartburn, regurgitation; dysphagia, abdominal pain, jaundice, peptic ulcers, hemorrhoids, hepatitis, gallstones
Urinary	Denies change in urine colour, voiding habits, hesitancy, urgency, frequency, nocturia, polyuria, dribbling, loss in force of stream, bedwetting, suprapubic pain, kidney stones, incontinence
Musculoskeletal	Denies bony deformity, weakness, ↓ ROM, swelling, sprains, dislocations, gout, arthritis, herniated disc, back pain
Neurological	Denies change in balance, incoordination, loss of movement, change in sensory perception, change in speech, change in smell, tremors, syncope, loss of memory, involuntary movement, loss of consciousness, sz, weakness, vertigo, tremors, tics, CVA
Psychological	Looking forward to starting university in 6 wks; "All of my hard work has paid off—I just hope I will be able to meet the next level of demands!" Has some worries about possibly disappointing his parents if he does not get the grades he is used to; denies nervousness, difficulty concentrating, mood changes, depression, suicidal thoughts
Male Reproductive	Uses condoms c̄ all partners; denies impotence, painful intercourse, testicular/penile pain, penile discharge, hernia
Nutrition	Usual & present weight 82 kg; food preferences: beans/rice; food dislikes: broccoli; drinks 2–3 caffeinated beverages daily
Endocrine	Denies exophthalmos; change in size of head, hands, or feet; cold intolerance; polyuria; polydipsia; polyphagia; change in body hair distribution; goiter
Lymph Nodes	Denies enlargement or tenderness
Hematological	Denies easy bruising/bleeding, anemia, blood type B+

HEALTH HISTORY

COMPLETE HEALTH HISTORY: ILL PATIENT

Today's Date	February 12, 2007
BIOGRAPHICAL DATA	
Patient's Name	Rick Berg
Address	1256 Waverly Street, Winnipeg, MB
Phone Number	H (204) 648-1111
Date of Birth	January 27, 1964
Birthplace	Calgary, Alberta
Occupation	Pharmaceutical sales representative
Usual Source of Health Care	Visits health clinics as needed; no regular GP
Source of Referral	Friend
Emergency Contact	Patricia Berg (wife), cell phone (204) 648-2222
Source and Reliability of Information	Self; reliable historian
PATIENT PROFILE	43-year-old man, presents with his wife; he looks pale and anxious.
HEALTH ISSUE/CONCERN	"I lost the job I had for 12 years and have just started a new job as a sales rep. for a pharmaceutical company. My asthma is acting up so I need to get it under control because I can't be off sick this early into my new job."
HISTORY OF ISSUE/CONCERN	Pt was in usual state of good hl until 1 wk ago; at that time had SOB $\bar{c}$ tightness in the chest & mild wheezing; has been using Ventolin 2 inhalations 3–4 ×/d, usually makes breathing easier; no other meds taken; pt usually runs 2–3 km daily & he has not felt up to running the past wk; describes ⊕ SOB; temp 39.2°C yesterday; ⊕ sore throat, ⊕ myalgias, ⊕ fatigue; denies otalgia, PND, sputum, cough, sinus pressure, tooth pain, nasal discharge, nasal polyps, H/A; noticed that sx started the day $\bar{p}$ he did yard work; reports that he & his wife rescued a stray cat 2 wks ago & the cat now lives in the house & often sleeps on his bed; pt is concerned b/c he has not felt this ill in many yrs
PAST HEALTH HISTORY	
Medical History	1990 dx'd $\bar{c}$ asthma; no overnight hospitalization required but had 2–3 acute attacks requiring emergency intervention; no intubation; 2002 dx'd $\bar{c}$ GERD; placed on Omeprazole; watches diet to minimize effects
Surgical History	Has never had surgery
Medications	
Prescription	Omeprazole 20 mg po daily × 3 yrs; Ventolin i–ii inhalations q4–6 h prn × 15 yrs

OTC	MVI, vitamin C daily (does not know doses), ibuprofen 200–400 mg po 1–3 × daily prn (usually 2–3 ×/month)
Communicable Diseases	Denies; negative HIV test last year; no hy gonorrhea, TB, herpes simplex, syphilis, hepatitis
Allergies	Bee stings cause SOB & flushing; no longer has EpiPen; denies allergies to meds, foods, animals
Injuries and Accidents	Fractured radius as child from playing hockey; no sequelae
Special Needs	States none
Blood Transfusions	Never
Childhood Illnesses	Varicella age 7 s̄ sequelae
Immunization	"I assume I got everything when I was a child."

FAMILY HEALTH HISTORY

LEGEND

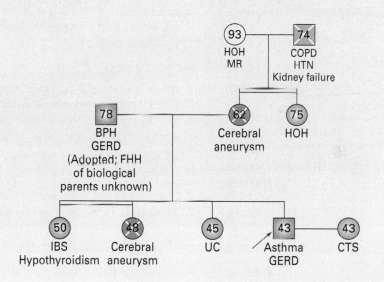

- ⬤ Living female
- ⬛ Living male
- ⊗ Deceased female
- ⊠ Deceased male
- ╱ Points to patient
- ═══ = Twins

BPH = Benign prostatic hypertrophy
COPD = Chronic obstructive pulmonary disease
CTS = Carpal tunnel syndrome
GERD = Gastroesophageal reflux disease
HOH = Hard of hearing
HTN = Hypertension
IBS = Irritable bowel syndrome
MR = Mitral regurgitation
UC = Ulcerative colitis

Denies family hx of CAD, CVA, TB, DM, liver dz, blood disorders, migraine H/A, gout, obesity, drug addiction, AIDS, violence, mental illness

SOCIAL HISTORY

Alcohol Use	"I drink 1 or 2 beer a weekend."
Drug Use	Denies
Tobacco Use	Occasional cigar
Sexual Practice	"I've only ever been c̄ my wife; all is OK in this department."
Domestic and Intimate Partner Violence	Denies
Travel History	Travelled extensively as youth; has not been outside Canada for 15 yrs

continues

Work Environment	Maintains home office; most of day is spent on the road calling on different hl care providers at their offices in the suburbs
Home Environment	
Physical Environment	Lives in 50-yo bungalow c̄ wife; has been working on repairing the house for the past 2 mos; "comfortable"
Psychosocial Environment	Describes as "safe"
Hobbies and Leisure Activities	Yard work, repairing the house; collects coins
Stress	Fixing house, succeeding in new job & new career
Education	Biology degree (undergraduate)
Economic Status	"We are OK as long as I don't miss work."
Religion/Spirituality	Jewish; goes to synagogue & follows Kosher diet.
Ethnicity	"I'm Jewish."
Roles and Relationships	"I'm happy in my marriage—I don't know where I would be if it weren't for my wife. I haven't been included into the team at work yet but I am gradually fitting in."
Characteristic Patterns of Daily Living	Wakes at 05:00 & goes for a run; showers, eats breakfast then works out of home office for 1 hr; at 08:30 starts to make his business calls on various medical practices; usually eats on the road; returns home at 18:00 & checks messages/e-mails for about 1 hr; has dinner c̄ wife at 19:30; works around house until 22:00
HEALTH MAINTENANCE ACTIVITIES	
Sleep	7 hrs on wkdays, 8–9 hrs on wkends; feels this is sufficient
Diet	3 meals daily, avoids fatty & spicy foods
Exercise	Runs 2–3 km a day, 6–7 d/wk; stretches ā & p̄ running
Stress Management	Running, meditation
Use of Safety Devices	Wears seat belt; goggles c̄ woodwork in house
Health Check-ups	Regular checks c̄ GP; complete physical examinations last yr; not sure how to perform TSE
REVIEW OF SYSTEMS	
General	Until 1 wk ago reported high energy levels, healthy; denies recent illness
Skin	Uses sunscreen when outside >2 hr, SPF 30; denies rashes, itching △ in skin pigmentation, ecchymoses, warts, eczema, psoriasis, pruritus, △ in moles, sores, lumps, △ in skin texture, body odours, acne
Hair	Denies alopecia, hirsutism, dandruff, pediculosis, hair chemicals
Nails	Denies △ nails, splitting, breaking, onychomycosis

Eyes	20/25 vision at eye exam last yr c̄ glasses; wears Rx sunglasses on bright days; denies blurry vision, photophobia, ↑ tearing, diplopia, eye drainage, bloodshot eyes, pain, blind spots, floaters, flashing lights, halos around objects, glaucoma, cataracts
Ears	Denies hearing deficits, hearing aid, pain, discharge, vertigo, tinnitus, earaches, infection
Nose and Sinuses	Averages 3–4 colds/yr; denies discharge, itching, hay fever, postnasal drip, snoring, sinus pain, allergies, polyps, obstruction, epistaxis, △ in sense of smell
Mouth	Brushes teeth 3–4 ×/d; flosses q hs; denies toothache, tooth abscess, dentures, bleeding/swollen gums, sore tongue, △ in taste, lesions, △ in salivation, bad breath, difficulty chewing
Throat and Neck	Denies hoarseness, △ in voice, frequent sore throats, difficulty swallowing, pain/stiffness, goiter
Respiratory	Asthma per HPI/PHH; denies sputum, sneezing, wheezing, hemoptysis, pneumonia, emphysema, & TB exposure
Cardiovascular	No PND, heart murmur, palpitations, CP, syncope, edema, orthopnea, cold hands/feet, leg cramps, MI, intermittent claudication, varicose veins, thrombophlebitis, anemia, rheumatic heart disease
Breasts and Axilla	No change in size, pain, tenderness, discharge, lumps, dimpling, rash
Gastrointestinal	Regular bowel habit: BM q AM, soft & brown; heartburn/GERD per PHH; no vomiting, diarrhea, constipation, melena, △ in stool colour, hematemesis; ↑ flatulence, belching, dysphagia, abdominal pain, jaundice, peptic ulcers, hemorrhoids, hepatitis, gallstones
Urinary	Denies △ in urine colour, voiding habits, hesitancy, urgency, frequency, nocturia, polyuria, dribbling, loss in force of stream, bedwetting, suprapubic pain, kidney stones, incontinence
Musculoskeletal	Denies bony deformity, weakness, ↓ ROM, swelling, sprains, dislocations, crepitus, gout, arthritis, herniated disc, back pain
Neurological	No H/A, △ in balance, incoordination, loss of movement, △ in sensory perception, △ in speech, △ in smell, tremors, syncope, loss of memory, involuntary movement, loss of consciousness, sz, weakness, vertigo, spasm, tics, CVA
Psychological	Not nervous, irritable, anxious; no sleep disturbance, difficulty concentrating, mood changes, depression, suicidal thoughts
Male Reproductive	Doesn't use birth control b/c wife had hysterectomy 15 yrs ago; denies impotence, △ in libido, painful intercourse, testicular/penile pain, penile discharge, hernias, BPH
Nutrition	Usual weight 80 kg, present weight 87 kg; food preferences: fruits/vegetables/meats; food dislikes: fried foods/fast foods; eats Kosher
Endocrine	Denies exophthalmos; △ in size of head, hands, or feet; cold intolerance; polyuria; polydipsia; polyphagia; △ in body hair distribution; goiter
Lymph Nodes	Denies enlargement or tenderness
Hematological	Denies easy bruising/bleeding, anemia, blood type A−

REVIEW QUESTIONS

Questions 1–6 refer to the following situation: Asia, a 54-year-old female, was boating two days ago with her husband. She slipped on the deck and hurt her left foot. Since then her left foot has remained painful.

1. Which statement best describes Asia's chief complaint?
   a. "I've had foot pain before."
   b. "I slipped in the boat two days ago and hurt my left foot."
   c. "This pain does not radiate up my leg."
   d. "I've been intending to have my feet examined for some time."
   The correct answer is (b).

2. The patient states that the pain in her left foot is severe. Which characteristic of a chief complaint does this exemplify?
   a. Location
   b. Quality
   c. Quantity
   d. Timing
   The correct answer is (c).

3. Which type of health history would you perform on this patient who has been at your clinic three times in the past year?
   a. Complete health history
   b. Episodic health history
   c. Interval health history
   d. Emergency health history
   The correct answer is (b).

4. You ask the patient if she is experiencing any other symptoms with her foot pain. The patient's reply is an example of which characteristic of a chief complaint?
   a. Associated manifestations
   b. Pertinent negatives
   c. Aggravating factors
   d. Timing
   The correct answer is (a).

5. Which has the highest priority when eliciting the health history of this patient?
   a. Communicable diseases
   b. Education
   c. Childhood illnesses
   d. Allergies
   The correct answer is (d).

6. Which statement about this patient's injury is documented correctly?
   a. Mass the size of an egg on the left medial malleolus
   b. Occasionally takes ibuprofen for the pain
   c. Peripheral circulation seems within normal limits
   d. Left foot with 2+ nonpitting edema
   The correct answer is (d).

7. The patient denies hay fever, postnasal drip, stuffiness, and epistaxis. In which ROS section would this statement appear?
   a. Eyes
   b. Ears
   c. Nose and sinuses
   d. Throat and neck
   The correct answer is (c).

8. You question a patient about alcohol and drug consumption. What screening tool can be used?
   a. FIT
   b. PQRST
   c. CAGEAID
   d. HITS
   The correct answer is (c).

9. In a genogram, a square that is blackened represents a:
   a. Living female
   b. Living male
   c. Deceased female
   d. Deceased male
   The correct answer is (d).

10. The Visual Analog Scale is a tool that is used to measure which characteristic of a chief complaint?
   a. Quality
   b. Quantity
   c. Location
   d. Radiation
   The correct answer is (b).

Visit the Estes online companion resource at www.healthassessment.nelson.com **for additional content and study aids.**

REFERENCES

[1]Federal, Provincial, and Territorial Advisory Committee on Population Health. (1999). *Toward a healthy future: Second report on the health of Canadians.* Retrieved May 25, 2006, from

http://www.phac-aspc.gc.ca/ph-sp/phdd/pdf/ toward/toward _a_healthy_english.PDF. Reproduced with the permission of the Minister of Public Works and Government Services Canada, 2006.

[2]Canadian Population Health Initiative. (2004). *Improving the health of Canadians*. Ottawa: Canadian Institute for Health Information, 153.

[3]Beiser, M. & Stewart, M. (2005). Reducing health disparities: A priority for Canada. *Canadian Journal of Public Health, 96*, S4–8.

[4]Canadian Institute for Health Information. (2005). *Health indicators*. Ottawa: Canadian Institute for Health Information.

[5]IPSOS Reid. (March, 2005). *Baseline natural health products survey among consumers*. Retrieved May 24, 2006, from http://www.hc-sc.gc.ca/dhp-mps/alt_formats/hpfb-dgpsa/pdf/pubs/eng_cons_survey_e.pdf

[6]American Academy of Pediatrics. (2006). *Red Book online*. Retrieved June 11, 2006, from http://aapredbook.aappublications.org/

[7]Public Heath Agency of Canada. (2004). *Canadian sexually transmitted infections surveillance report: Pre-Release*. Retrieved May 28, 2006, from http://www.phac-aspc.gc.ca/std-mts/std-data _pre06_04/index.html

[8]Langley, J. M., Faughnan, M. E., & the Canadian Task Force on Preventive Health Care. (2004). Prevention of influenza in the general population: Recommendation statement from the Canadian Task Force on Preventive Health Care. *Canadian Medical Association Journal, 171*, 1169–70.

[9]Mayfield, J., McLeod, G., & Hall, P. (1974). CAGE questionnaire: Validation of a new alcoholism screening instrument. *American Journal of Psychiatry, 131*(10), 1121–23.

[10]Public Health Agency of Canada. *Sexual health and sexually transmitted infections: Self-learning module; Terry's case*. Retrieved June 10, 2006, from http://www.phac-aspc.gc.ca/slm-maa/terry/in02_e.html

[11]Canadian Nurses Association. *Position statement: Reducing the use of tobacco products*. Retrieved May 27, 2006, from http://www.cna-nurses.ca/CNA/documents/pdf/publications/PS49_Reducing_use_Tobacco_June_2001_e.pdf

[12]Shields, M. (2003). *Healthy today, healthy tomorrow? Findings from the National Population Health Survey: A step forward, a step back: Smoking cessation and relapse*. Statistics Canada. Retrieved May 23, 2006, from http://www.statcan.ca/english/research/82-618-MIE/2004001/pdf/82-618-MIE2004001.pdf

[13]Minister of Health. (2005). *The 2004 progress report on tobacco control*. Ottawa, Canada: Health Canada. Retrieved March 12, 2006, from http://www.hc-sc.gc.ca/hl-vs/pubs/tobac-tabac/prtc-relct-2004/index_e.html

[14]Sherin, K. M., Sinacore, J. M., Li, X. Q., Zitter, R. E., & Shakil, A. (1998). HITS: A short domestic violence screening tool for use in a family practice setting. *Family Medicine, 30*(7), 508–12. Reprinted with permission from the Society of Teachers of Family Medicine.

[15]Statistics Canada—Canadian Centre for Justice Statistics. (2005). *Family violence in Canada: A statistical profile*. Ottawa: Minister of Industry. Retrieved May 23, 2006, from http://www.statcan.ca/ english/freepub/85-224-XIE/85-224-XIE2005000.pdf

[16]Ibid.

[17]Canadian Nurses Association. (2002). *Position statement: Violence*. Retrieved May 23, 2006, from http://www.cna-aiic.ca/CNA/ documents/pdf/publications/PS57_Violence_March_2002_e .pdf

[18]Registered Nurses' Association of Ontario. (2005). *Women abuse*. Toronto: Registered Nurses' Association of Ontario. http://www.rnao.org/bestpractices/PDF/BPG_Women_Abuse. pdf

BIBLIOGRAPHY

Beiser, M. (2005). The health of immigrants and refugees in Canada. *Canadian Journal of Public Health, 96*, S30 (15 pp.).

Kulig, J. C. (2005). Rural health research: Are we beyond the crossroads? *Canadian Journal of Nursing Research, 37*(1), 3–6.

MacLeod, M. L. P., Kulig, J. C., Stewart, N. J., Pitblado, J. R., & Knock, M. (2004). The nature of nursing practice in rural and remote Canada. *Canadian Nurse, 100*(6), 27–31.

Rinfret-Raynor, M., Turgeon, J., & Dube, M. (2002). A systematic screening protocol of domestic violence: Measurement of efficiency. *Canadian Journal of Community Mental Health, 21*, 85–99.

Snyder, M., & Lindquist, R. (Eds.). (2002). *Complementary/alternative therapies in nursing* (4th ed.). New York: Springer.

Stamler, L. & Yiu, L. (Eds.) (2005). *Community health nursing: A Canadian perspective*. Toronto: Pearson Prentice Hall.

Registered Nurses' Association of Ontario. (2003). *Integrating smoking cessation into daily nursing practice*. Toronto: Registered Nurses' Association of Ontario.

WEB RESOURCES

Canadian Guidelines on Sexually Transmitted Infections, 2006 Edition.
http://www.phac-aspc.gc.ca/std-mts/sti_2006/sti_intro2006_e.html

Canadian Immunization Guide, 2002
http://www.phac-aspc.gc.ca/publicat/cig-gci/pdf/cdn_immuniz_guide-2002-6.pdf

Canadian Blood Services
http://www.bloodservices.ca/

Canadian Centre for Occupational Health and Safety
http://www.ccohs.ca/

Child and Family Canada
http://www.cfc-efc.ca

National Clearing House on Family Violence
http://www.phac-aspc.gc.ca/ncfv-cnivf/familyviolence/index.html

Natural Products Directorate—Health Canada
http://www.hc-sc.gc.ca/ahc-asc/branch-dirgen/hpfb-dgpsa/nhpd-dpsn/index_e.html

Provincial/Territorial Health Agency/Department	Web Address
Alberta Health and Wellness	http://www.gov.ab.ca/home/index.cfm?page=50
British Columbia Ministry of Health	http://www.gov.bc.ca/bvprd/bc/channel.do?action=ministry&channelID=-8387&navId=NAV_ID_province
Manitoba Ministry of Health	http://www.gov.mb.ca/health/index.html
New Brunswick Department of Health and Wellness	http://www.gnb.ca/0051/index-e.asp
Newfoundland and Labrador Health and Community Services	http://www.health.gov.nl.ca/health/
Northwest Territories Department of Health	http://www.hlthss.gov.nt.ca/
Nova Scotia Department of Health	http://www.gov.ns.ca/heal/
Nunavut Department of Health and Social Services	http://www.gov.nu.ca/Nunavut/English/departments/HSS/
Ontario Ministry of Health and Long-Term Care	http://www.health.gov.on.ca/
Prince Edward Island Health and Social Services	http://www.gov.pe.ca/infopei/index.php3?number=3279
Quebec Ministry of Health and Social Services	http://www.msss.gouv.qc.ca/en/
Saskatchewan Ministry of Health	http://www.health.gov.sk.ca/
Yukon Department of Health and Social Services	http://www.hss.gov.yk.ca/

UNIT 2

Special Assessments

The power of forming any correct opin-ion as to the result must entirely depend upon an inquiry into all the conditions in which the patient lives.

—Florence Nightingale

NEL

CHAPTER 4

Developmental Assessment

COMPETENCIES

1. Identify the defining concepts and principles of major developmental theories.

2. Assess patients' developmental levels by applying the major developmental theories.

3. Incorporate appropriate developmental tasks associated with each life stage into a patient's assessment.

4. Select appropriate developmental assessment tools for use in screening for developmental difficulties.

Figure 4-1 All individuals pass through identifiable growth and development stages.

*A*ll individuals, from birth to death, pass through identifiable, cyclical stages of growth and development that determine who and what they are and can become (Figure 4-1). **Growth** refers to an increase in body size and function to the point of optimum maturity. **Development** refers to patterned and predictable increases in the physical, cognitive, socioemotional, and moral capacities of individuals that enable them to successfully adapt to their environments.

Assessing the growth and development status of adults and children is an integral part of the patient's health assessment. It must be noted, however, that even though most development is patterned and predictable, general patterns should not to be "imposed" on patients; instead, the nurse should assess and compare the individual's unique development to the general parameters.

DEVELOPMENTAL THEORIES

A variety of theories have been developed that depict and predict growth and development. The traditional theories are the "ages and stages" theories of Jean Piaget, Sigmund Freud, Erik Erickson, and Lawrence Kohlberg. The **ages and stages developmental theories** are based on the premise that individuals experience similar sequential physical, cognitive, socioemotional, and moral changes during the same age periods, each of which is termed a **developmental stage.** During each developmental stage, specific physical and psychosocial skills known as **developmental tasks** must be achieved. An individual's readiness for each new developmental task is dependent on successfully achieving prior developmental tasks in an appropriate environment. If prior developmental tasks have not been achieved or if the appropriate environment was not available, the individual's capacity to successfully adapt to the environment and develop new skills may be reduced. A key nursing role in assessment is to help identify any areas of deficiency and then develop a plan of care that addresses the patient's needs.

Life event or **transitional developmental theories** are based on the premise that development occurs in response to specific life events, such as new roles (e.g., parenthood) and life transitions (e.g., career changes), events that may require individuals to change their life patterns. Life events and transitions, which can occur singly or together and may cause positive or negative stress, are not tied to a specific time or stage in the life span. Each event, however, does have certain tasks associated with it that must be achieved. For example, developmental tasks associated with marriage must be achieved regardless of the individual's age at the time of marriage. A variety of factors affect how an individual responds to life events: biological status, personality, cultural orientation, socioeconomic status, interpersonal support systems, number and intensity of life events, and orientation to life.[1, 2, 3] Although the stress associated with each life event or transition can serve as an impetus for growth, excessive stress can disrupt the individual's equilibrium and lead to physical and psychological health problems.[4, 5] Nurses can play a critical role in identifying the life events and stressors of patients and can help them maintain health and control stress.

Ages and Stages Developmental Theories

The major tenets of Piaget, Freud, Erikson, and Kohlberg are discussed next; these are summarized in Table 4-1.

Piaget's Theory of Cognitive Development

Piaget's theory of cognitive development depicts age-related, sequential stages through which all developing children must progress to learn to think, reason, exercise judgment, and to implement the cognitive skills (e.g., language development, problem solving, decision making, critical thinking, and oral

TABLE 4-1	Summary of Ages and Stages Developmental Theories			
STAGE/AGE	PIAGET'S COGNITIVE STAGES	FREUD'S PSYCHOSEXUAL STAGES	ERIKSON'S PSYCHOSOCIAL STAGES	KOHLBERG'S MORAL JUDGMENT STAGES
1. Infancy Birth to 1 year	**Sensorimotor** (birth to 2 years): begins to acquire language Task: Object permanence	**Oral:** pleasure from exploration with mouth and through sucking Task: Weaning	**Trust vs. Mistrust** Task: Trust Socializing agent: Mothering person Central process: Mutuality Ego quality: Hope	
2. Toddler 1 to 3 years	**Sensorimotor:** continues **Preoperational** (2 to 7 years) begins: use of representational thought Task: Use language and mental images to think and communicate	**Anal:** control of elimination Task: Toilet training	**Autonomy vs. Shame and Doubt** Task: Autonomy Socializing agent: Parents Central process: Imitation Ego quality: Self-control and willpower	**Preconventional Level:** **1. Morality Stage:** Avoid punishment by not breaking rules of authority figures
3. Preschool 3 to 6 years	**Preoperational:** continues	**Phallic:** attracted to opposite-sex parent Task: Resolve Oedipus/Electra complex	**Initiative vs. Guilt** Task: Initiative and moral Socializing agents: Parents Central process: Identification Ego quality: Direction, purpose, and conscience, responsibility	**2. Individualism, Instrumental Purpose, and Exchange Stage:** "Right" is relative, follow rules when in own interest
4. School Age 6 to 12 years	**Preoperational:** continues **Concrete Operations** (7 to 12 years) begins: engage in inductive reasoning and concrete problem solving Task: Learn concepts of conservation and reversibility	**Latency:** identification with same-sex parent Task: Identify with same-sex parent, and test and compare own capabilities with peer norms	**Industry vs. Inferiority** Task: Industry, self-assurance, self-esteem Socializing agents: Teachers and peers Central process: Education Ego quality: Competence	**Conventional Level:** **3. Mutual Expectations, Relationships, and Conformity to Moral Norms Stage:** Need to be "good" in own and others' eyes, believe in rules and regulations
5. Adolescence 12 to 18 years	**Formal Operations** (12 years to adulthood): engage in abstract reasoning and analytical problem solving Task: Develop a workable philosophy of life	**Genital:** develop sexual relationships Task: Establish meaningful relationship for lifelong pairing	**Identity vs. Role Confusion** Task: Self-identity and concept Socializing agents: Society of peers	**4. Social System and Conscience Stage:** Uphold laws because they are fixed social duties Central process: Role experimentation and peer pressure Ego quality: Fidelity and devotion to others, personal and sociocultural values
6. Young Adult 18 to 30 years	**Formal Operations:** continues		**Intimacy vs. Isolation** Task: Intimacy Socializing agent: Close friends, partners, lovers, spouse Central process:	**Postconventional Level:** **5. Social Contract or Utility and Individual Rights Stage:** Uphold laws in the interest of the

continues

TABLE 4-1	Summary of Ages and Stages Developmental Theories *continued*			
STAGE/AGE	PIAGET'S COGNITIVE STAGES	FREUD'S PSYCHOSEXUAL STAGES	ERIKSON'S PSYCHOSOCIAL STAGES	KOHLBERG'S MORAL JUDGMENT STAGES
			Mutuality among peers Ego quality: Intimate affiliation and love	greatest good for the greatest number; uphold laws that protect universal rights
7. Early Middle **Age** 30 to 50 years			**Generativity vs. Stagnation** (30 to 65 years) Task: Generativity Socializing agent: Spouse, partner, children, sociocultural norms Central process: Creativity and person-environment fit Ego quality: Productivity, perseverance, charity, and consideration	
8. Late Middle **Age** 50 to 70 years			**Generativity vs. Stagnation** continues	**6. Universal Ethical Principles Stage:** Support universal moral principles regardless of the price for doing so
9. Late Adult 70 years to death			**Ego Integrity vs. Despair** (65 years to death) Task: Ego integrity Socializing agent: Significant others Central process: Introspection Ego quality: Wisdom	

and written communication) needed to successfully adapt to their environments.[6] Cognitive development is influenced by innate intellectual capacity, maturation of the nervous and endocrine systems, and environmental interactions during which sensory and motor input is experienced and processed. Piaget divides cognitive development into four periods: sensorimotor stage, preoperational stage, concrete operations stage, and formal operational stage.

Sensorimotor Stage

During this stage (birth to 2 years), the developing child perceives the world primarily through sensation and action response. The primary cognitive developmental task is to learn **object permanence;** that is, to form a mental image of an object and to recognize that although the object is removed from view, it still exists. Object permanence is usually achieved by the eighth month of life and facilitates the achievement of the second cognitive task—the development of a sense of self separate from the child's environment. An additional cognitive task involves using language and mental representations to think about events before and after they occur.

Preoperational Stage

The second cognitive development period is the preoperational stage (2 to 7 years), which is characterized by **egocentrism;** that is, viewing the world in terms of self only and interpreting events in terms of the consequences they have for self. Learning usually occurs through imitating others, exploring the environment, and asking numerous questions. Thinking is concrete, and reasoning is intuitive and is based on what is directly seen, heard, or personally experienced. The major cognitive developmental task for this stage is to use language and mental representations to think and communicate about objects and events in the environment.

Concrete Operations Stage

During the third cognitive development period (7 to 12 years), thinking becomes socialized and less self-oriented and others' points of view are given consideration. Thinking becomes increasingly logical and coherent; facts are organized through sorting, ordering, and classifying; the concept of time evolves; different aspects of situations are dealt with simultaneously; reasoning is inductive; problems are solved concretely and systematically; and communication is enhanced through the expansion of oral, reading, and writing skills. The major developmental tasks are mastering the concepts of **conservation** (understanding that altering the physical state of an object does not change the object's basic properties) and **reversibility** (understanding that an action does not need to be experienced before one can anticipate the results or consequences of the action).

Formal Operational Stage

The last cognitive development period is the formal operational stage (12 years to adulthood) in which thinking becomes increasingly abstract, logical, analytical, and creative. Ideas are combined to form concepts, and concepts are combined to form constructs and hypotheses. Theories are developed and tested, and alternate solutions for problems are generated and examined. The antecedents, moderators, and outcomes of ideas, concepts, situations, and actions are recognized and incorporated into the individual's worldview. The primary cognitive developmental task is to develop a workable philosophy of life.

Freud's Psychoanalytic Theory of Personality Development

Sigmund Freud contended that human behaviour is motivated by psychodynamic forces within an individual's unconscious mind.[7] Driven to act by these internal forces, individuals repeatedly interact with the external environment to develop their personality and psychosexual identity.

Personality

Personality, according to Freud, consists of three components with distinctly separate functions: id, ego, and superego. The **id,** evident at birth, is inborn, unconscious, and is driven by biological instincts and urges to seek immediate gratification of needs such as hunger, thirst, and physical comfort. The **ego** is conscious, rational, and emerges during the first year of life as infants begin to test the limits of the world around them. The ego seeks realistic and acceptable ways to meet needs. The **superego,** appearing in early childhood, is the internalization of the moral values formed as children interact with their parents and significant others. The superego blocks unacceptable behaviour, generated by the id, that could threaten the social order—creating feelings of guilt when the moral code is compromised, and generating feelings of pride when the moral code is upheld.

Freud believed individuals experience an ongoing struggle among the id, ego, and superego. Achieving a balance among the three, however, is prerequisite to the development of socially acceptable behaviour and an integrated personality. In order to achieve balance and to protect itself from excess anxiety created by the ongoing struggle, the ego uses unconscious defence mechanisms such as repression, denial, projection, and rationalization.

Psychosexual Stages

Freud perceived the desire to satisfy biological needs, primarily sexual, as the major drive governing human behaviour. At different psychosexual developmental stages, individuals experience tension in a specific body region that prompts them to seek gratification and to resolve associated conflicts. If an individual's needs are met during a given stage and conflicts are resolved, development proceeds to the next stage, and healthy integration of the developing personality will occur. If resolution of the conflict does not occur, however, the individual will become fixated at that stage, and personality and psychosexual identity will be arrested or impaired. Freud identified five psychosexual stages of development: oral, anal, phallic, latency, and genital.

Oral Stage. The oral psychosexual stage (birth to 1 year) is focused on the sensory areas of the mouth, lips, and tongue. Sucking, biting, chewing, swallowing, and vocalizing produce pleasure and reduce tension. The major conflict during this stage centres around weaning. Oral personality traits that begin to emerge are optimism versus pessimism, cockiness versus self-belittlement, admiration versus envy, determinism versus submission, and gullibility versus suspiciousness.

Anal Stage. In the anal psychosexual stage (1 to 3 years), the focus is on the anal and urethral sensory areas. Expulsion and retention of body wastes produce pleasure and reduce tension. The major conflict involves toilet training. Anal personality traits that begin to emerge are orderliness versus messiness, acquiescence versus stubbornness, overgenerosity versus stinginess, rigid punctuality versus tardiness, and expansiveness versus constrictiveness.

Phallic Stage. The phallic psychosexual stage (3 to 6 years) is focused on the sensory areas of the genitals. Pleasure is provided and tension is reduced through penile and clitoral exploration and stimulation. The four major conflicts involve the **Oedipus complex** (young boys' sexual attraction toward their mothers and feelings of rivalry toward their fathers), **Electra complex** (young girls' sexual attraction toward their fathers and rivalry with their mothers for their fathers' attention), **castration anxiety** (young boys' fear of having their penis cut off or mutilated), and **penis envy** (young girls' desire to have a penis). Phallic personality traits are gaiety versus sadness, gregariousness versus isolationism, stylishness versus plainness, blind courage versus timidity, and brashness versus bashfulness.

Latency Stage. During the latency psychosexual stage (6 to 12 years), the focus is on the exploration and discovery of the total body's relatedness, coordination, and uses rather than on a specific body region. Channelling generalized psychic and physical activity into knowledge acquisition and vigorous play provides pleasure and reduces tension. The major conflicts are identifying with the same-sex parent, learning and testing mental and physical capabilities, and comparing one's capabilities with peer norms.

Genital Stage. The genital psychosexual stage (12 years to adulthood) is focused on full sexual maturity and function. The formation of friendships and sexual relationships provide pleasure and reduce tension. Becoming sexually desirable to others and establishing meaningful relationships in preparation for lifelong pairing are the major conflicts during this stage.

Erikson's Epigenetic Theory of Personality

The most frequently used theory of personality development is Erik Erikson's epigenetic theory, which is based on the biological concept that all growing organisms have an inherent plan of development.[8] Each part of a growing entity has a designated time of ascendancy and forms the basis for growth of the next part until the functional whole is fully developed. Erikson's theory was built on Freud's theory of personality but goes beyond it by depicting personality development as a passage through eight sequential stages of ego development from infancy through old age.

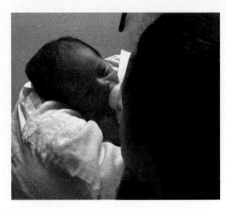

Figure 4-2 Strong parental bonding and attention to needs help the infant develop trust.

According to Erikson, individuals must master and resolve, to some extent, a core conflict/crisis during each stage by integrating their needs and skills with the social and cultural demands and expectations of their environment. Moving on to another stage is dependent on the resolution of the core conflict of the preceding stage. No core conflict is ever completely mastered; rather, a conflict can present itself in a new form, which provides new opportunities to resolve the core conflict. Thus, the potential for further development and refinement always exists. Each of the eight stages discussed below has an associated central process for resolving the conflict, a key socializing agent, and an ego quality that results from the favourable resolution of the core conflict.

Trust versus Mistrust Stage

The core conflict/crisis for the first developmental stage (birth to 1 year) is trust versus mistrust. When infants' basic needs are met by prompt, consistent, predictable, loving parent figures, basic, relative trust evolves (Figure 4-2). If infants' needs are intermittently, inadequately, or perfunctorily met, mistrust results.

Autonomy versus Shame and Doubt Stage

The second developmental stage (1 to 3 years) is focused on the autonomy versus shame and doubt core conflict/crisis. If parental figures overprotect their children, overly criticize and punish their children's attempts to explore and control their environments and body activities, or block their attempts to make independent decisions, then children will have shame, doubt, and uncertainty about their abilities and themselves.

Initiative versus Guilt Stage

During the third developmental stage (3 to 6 years), the core conflict/crisis is initiative versus guilt. When children are encouraged to explore their environments and to plan and work toward goals that do not infringe on the rights of others, they develop initiative and moral responsibility. In contrast, if children are restricted from exploration of their environments or are made to feel that their enterprise and active imaginations are bad, they will experience guilt and lose the courage to conceive of and pursue valued goals.

Industry versus Inferiority Stage

The central conflict/crisis for the fourth developmental stage (6 to 12 years) is industry versus inferiority. Children develop competence when they are encouraged to engage in achievable tasks and activities, to compete and cooperate with others, and to learn the rules and norms of a widening social and cultural environment. If children are not given sufficient opportunities or support to develop their abilities, or fail to achieve when pushed beyond their abilities, they may feel inadequate and inferior, resulting in avoidance of new learning activities.

Identity versus Role Confusion Stage

The fifth stage of development (12 to 18 years) is focused on the core conflict/crisis of identity versus role confusion. Adolescents make the transition from childhood to adulthood by redefining their future roles in society, by exploring life work possibilities, and by integrating their self-concept and values with those of their peers and society. Supportive, understanding interactions with peers and adult role models help clarify self-identity and lead to the ego quality of fidelity and devotion to others as well as personal and sociocultural values and ideologies. Unfavourable interactions or overidentification with popular teen fads and peer culture heroes can result in role confusion and difficulty in clarifying personal identity.

Intimacy versus Isolation Stage

Intimacy versus isolation is the core conflict/crisis associated with the sixth developmental stage (18 to 30 years). The capacity for intimate affiliation with, and the love of, significant others is the favourable resolution of this core conflict. Unsuccessful resolution results in feelings of aloneness and social isolation.

Generativity versus Stagnation Stage

The seventh developmental stage (30 to 65 years) is focused on the core conflict of generativity versus stagnation. Generativity occurs when a person is able to meet the needs of others while being equally concerned with providing for oneself. Qualities of productivity, perseverance, charity, and consideration result from the development of generativity. Generative young and middle-aged adults nurture the products of their creativity at home, at work, and in their communities. Individuals who do not resolve the core conflict become self-absorbed and feel chronically unfulfilled.

Ego Integrity versus Despair Stage

During the eighth and last stage of development (65 years to death), the core conflict/crisis is ego integrity versus despair. If an individual has reviewed his or her life and has accepted what has passed and is satisfied with the present, the individual will have a sense of integrity. In contrast, remorse for the past and what might have been will result in despair.

Kohlberg's Theory of Moral Development

The basic premise of Kohlberg's theory of moral development is that when a conflict occurs among any of several universal values (e.g., punishment, affection, authority, truth, law, life, liberty, and justice), the moral choice that must be made and justified requires cognitive and systematic problem-solving capabilities, which constitute moral reasoning.[9] The individual's moral reasoning and associated behaviours parallels the development of cognitive behaviour primarily. According to Kohlberg, moral development is contingent upon children's ability to learn and internalize parental and societal rules and standards, to develop the ability to empathize with others' responses, and to form their own standards of conduct. Moral development progresses through three levels, with two distinct stages per level for a total of six stages. Keep in mind that Kohlberg's theory of moral development has fallen under heavy criticism because an all-male population was studied.

Preconventional Level

The first level of moral development is divided into two stages. In stage 1, the morality stage, individuals have an egocentric point of view and avoid breaking rules and damaging persons and property in order to prevent punishment by authority figures with superior power. In stage 2—the individualism, instrumental purpose, and exchange stage—individuals have a concrete individualistic perspective and follow rules only when doing so is primarily in their own or sometimes in someone else's immediate interest, and because "right" is relative, or what is "fair," and represents an equal exchange.

Conventional Level

The second level of moral development is divided into two stages. In stage 3 (mutual interpersonal expectations, relationships, and interpersonal conformity), individuals are concerned about and can envision the perspective of others, try to fulfill the expectations of self and others through conformity to moral norms, have "good" motives, believe in rules and regulations, and maintain relationships by being trustworthy, loyal, respectful, and appropriately grateful. In stage 4 (social system and conscience), individuals can differentiate societal points of view from interpersonal agreements and motives, and avoid the breakdown of the social system by recognizing and supporting its roles and laws.

Postconventional Level

This third level of moral development is also divided into two stages. In stage 5 (social contract or utility and individual rights), individuals recognize that moral and legal viewpoints may conflict, that most rules are relative to the group that made them, but also that rules are upheld in the interest of the greatest good for the greatest number. In addition, individuals recognize that as people's needs change, laws may need to be changed by working through the legal system. Nonetheless, laws that protect universal rights such as life and liberty must be upheld regardless of people's changing opinions or desires. In stage 6 (universal ethical principles) some middle-aged or older adults develop a rational, universal moral perspective and a commitment to laws and social agreements based on principles of justice, equal rights, and respect for human dignity. When laws violate these moral principles, the principle rather than the law must be followed regardless of the price to be paid. Kohlberg contends that few people attain, and even fewer maintain, this state of moral development.

DEVELOPMENTAL STAGES, TASKS, AND LIFE EVENTS

Improved nutrition, medical advances, and healthier lifestyles have contributed to the increased longevity of people in Canada and other Western countries. This fact is one reason why the preceding theories of development do not completely agree about the age associated with each developmental stage. In 2005, the life expectancy of Canadian men and women was 77.4 and 82.4 years respectively, compared to 59 and 61 in 1920.[10] By 2017, life expectancy is projected to be 80 years for men and 84 years for women.[11] Other than living longer, the proportion of Canadians who are older has increased significantly. The decline in birth rate and the maturation of the baby boomers (people born between 1946 and 1965) has meant that the median age (the point where exactly one half of the population is older, and the other half is younger) of Canadians has been increasing steadily. In 1966 the median age in Canada was 25.4 years; 30 years later it was 35.3 years, and in 2005 it reached an all time high of 38.5 years.[12] So, as the nation's population is aging, what was once considered to be the beginning of late adulthood (55 to 70 years) is now viewed as a part of middle adulthood, and what was considered to be the latter part of late adulthood (70+ years) is now recognized as the beginning rather than the end of this period. The developmental assessment process presented in this text, therefore, will be presented using the following stages:

Stage 1: Infancy (birth to 1 year)

Stage 2: Toddler (1 to 3 years)

Stage 3: Preschooler (3 to 6 years)

Stage 4: School-age child (6 to 12 years)

Stage 5: Adolescence (12 to 18 years)

Stage 6: Young adulthood (18 to 30 years)

Stage 7: Early middle adulthood (30 to 50 years)

Stage 8: Late middle adulthood (50 to 70 years)

Stage 9: Late adulthood (70 years to death)

The following section gives a composite sketch of the developmental tasks, life events, and transitions for each major theory of development. The list of tasks for each developmental stage are not exhaustive nor do they reflect all the tasks facing the full range of normal human conditions and circumstances. In addition, the life events included in each stage are not restricted

---

Life 360°

Evaluating Developmental Theories

- Do you agree with the major premises of the developmental theories presented in this chapter?

- How do you think changing trends in society influence the achievement or expectations outlined in the various theories? For example, knowing that Canadians tend to form long-term relationships with partners at later ages, would you assess a single 33-year-old woman as not having achieved "intimacy"?

- How does culture influence the expectations outlined in the developmental theories presented in this chapter?

Reflective Thinking

Helping Parents Understand Development

Caregivers are often nervous about their infants and have many questions. Consider how you would respond to each of these questions:

- "My sister's baby was already holding his bottle at six months, but my little boy doesn't seem to be able to do that . . . and he's two weeks older than my sister's baby! Is there something wrong with him?"
- "I want to be sure I buy the right toy for my niece. What do you suggest for her? She will be having her third birthday next week."

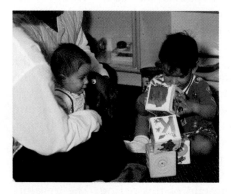

Figure 4-3 Dramatic and rapid growth and development are hallmarks of the first year of life.

to that stage but may occur or reoccur during other developmental stages. Generally, ask yourself if the patient's overall development seems consistent with the tasks usually associated with the person's chronological age; failure to meet tasks in one area does not necessarily indicate abnormal development. It is expected that the following will form a general framework on which you can base your assessment of a patient's growth and development. Remember to consider each individual as a whole entity, not just a collection of tasks met or not met.

Developmental Tasks of Infants (Birth to 1 Year)

Infancy is a period of dramatic and rapid physical, motor, cognitive, emotional, and social growth, which marks it as one of the most critical periods of growth and development. During the first year of life, infants change from totally helpless, dependent newborns to unique individuals who actively interact with their environments and form meaningful relationships with significant others (Figure 4-3). A list of key gross and fine motor, language, and sensory milestones associated with this period can be found in Table 4-2.

One of the major tasks of infancy is weaning. It requires children to give up the breast or bottle, which has been a major source of gratification, and to learn to use a cup. Readiness for weaning usually occurs between 6 months and 12 to 14 months, when the infant has learned that good things also come from a spoon, when more motor control has been developed so a cup can be grasped and brought to the mouth, and when the desire for freedom of movement overtakes the desire to be held while eating.

Conducting a comprehensive assessment of an infant requires evaluation of the degree to which the infant has achieved the developmental tasks of infancy. It is important to remember that although infants experience similar sequential physical, cognitive, socioemotional, and moral changes during the same age periods, there is still a degree of normal variability from one child to another. Developmental tasks that must be achieved during infancy are to develop:

1. A basic, relative sense of trust.
2. A sense of self as dependent but separate from others, particularly the mother.
3. A desire for affection and a response from others, particularly the mother.
4. A preverbal communication system, including emotional expression, to communicate needs and desires.
5. Conceptual abilities and a language system.
6. Fine and gross motor skills, particularly eye-hand coordination and balance.
7. A need to explore and recognize the immediate environment.
8. Object permanence.

Reflective Thinking

Understanding Toilet Training

Parents often have difficulty with "potty training" their child and become frustrated when their first attempts are not successful. What suggestions could you give the caregiver who has been trying unsuccessfully for the past two months with her 15-month-old son? She comments that she had absolutely no problems with her first child, a daughter, at this age and cannot understand what the problem is this time.

TABLE 4-2   Growth and Development During Infancy

AGE	GROSS MOTOR	FINE MOTOR	LANGUAGE	SENSORY
Birth to 1 Month	• Assumes tonic neck posture • When prone lifts and turns head	• Holds hands in fist • Draws arms and legs to body	• Cries	• Comforts with holding and touch • Looks at faces • Follows objects when in line of vision • Alert to high-pitched voices • Smiles
2 to 4 Months	• Can raise head and shoulders when prone to 45°–90°; supports self on forearms • Rolls from back to side	• Hands mostly open • Looks at and plays with fingers • Grasps and tries to reach objects	• Vocalizes when talked to; coos, babbles • Laughs aloud • Squeals	• Smiles • Follows objects 180° • Turns head when hears voices or sounds
4 to 6 Months	• Turns from stomach to back and then back to stomach • When pulled to sitting, almost no head lag • By 6 months can sit on floor with hands forward for support	• Can hold feet and put in mouth • Can hold bottle • Can grasp rattle and other small objects • Puts objects in mouth	• Squeals	• Watches a falling object • Responds to sounds
6 to 8 Months	• Puts full weight on legs when held in standing position • Can sit without support • Bounces when held in a standing position	• Transfers objects from one hand to the other • Can feed self a cookie • Can bang two objects together	• Babbles vowel like sounds, "ooh" or "aah" • Imitation of speech sounds ("mama," "dada") beginning • Laughs aloud	• Responds by looking and smiling • Recognizes own name
8 to 10 Months	• Crawls on all fours or uses arms to pull body along floor • Can pull self to sitting • Can pull self to standing	• Beginning to use thumb-finger grasp • Dominant hand use • Has good hand-mouth coordination	• Responds to verbal commands • May say one word in addition to "mama" and "dada"	• Recognizes sounds
10 to 12 Months	• Can sit down from standing • Walks around room holding onto objects • Can stand alone	• Picks up and drops objects • Can put small objects into toys or containers through holes • Turns many pages in a book at one time • Picks up small objects	• Understands "no" and other simple commands • Learns one or two other words • Imitates speech sounds • Speaks gibberish	• Follows fast-moving objects • Indicates wants • Likes to play imitative games such as patty cake and peek-a-boo

Developmental Tasks of Toddlers (1 to 3 Years)

The toddler period is one of steadily increasing motor development and control, intense activity and discovery, rapid language development, increasingly independent behaviours, and marked personality development (Figure 4-4). Key gross and fine motor, language, and sensory milestones associated with the toddler period can be found in Table 4-3.

TABLE 4-3	Growth and Development During Toddlerhood			
AGE	**GROSS MOTOR**	**FINE MOTOR**	**LANGUAGE**	**SENSORY**
12 to 15 Months	• Can walk alone well • Can crawl up stairs	• Can feed self with cup and spoon • Puts raisins into a bottle • May hold crayon or pencil and scribble • Builds a tower of two cubes	• Says four to six words	• Binocular vision is developed
18 Months	• Runs, falling often • Can jump in place • Can walk up stairs holding on • Plays with push and pull toys	• Can build a tower of three to four cubes • Can use a spoon	• Says 10 or more words • Points to objects or body parts when asked	• Visual acuity 20/40
24 Months	• Can walk up and down stairs • Can kick a ball • Can ride a tricycle	• Can draw a circle • Tries to dress self	• Talks a lot • Approximately 300-word vocabulary • Understands commands • Knows first name, refers to self • Verbalizes toilet needs	
30 Months	• Throws a ball • Jumps with both feet • Can stand on one foot for a few minutes	• Can build a tower of eight blocks • Can use crayons • Learning to use scissors	• Knows first and last name • Knows the name of one colour • Can sing • Expresses needs • Uses pronouns appropriately	

One of the major developmental tasks for toddlers is toilet training. Readiness for toilet training is usually evident by the ages of 18–24 months (girls tend to be ready to toilet train earlier than boys) when the following are present: voluntary control of the anal and urethral sphincters; gross motor skills of sitting, walking, and squatting; fine motor skills needed to remove clothing; cognitive skills of recognizing the urge to defecate or urinate and verbalizing the urge to do so; and willingness and ability to please the parents by sitting on the toilet for 5–10 minutes. Parental recognition of the child's level of readiness to invest the necessary time for toilet training is also essential for the toddler's successful mastery of this task. A variety of life events and transitions may produce stress in the toddler. Among the most stressful are personal injury, illness or death of a parent, or loss of a parent through separation or divorce.

Children who have been successful in accomplishing the developmental tasks of infancy enter the toddler period with the basic relative trust needed to achieve the next tasks. The principal developmental tasks that must be mastered during the toddler stage are to:

1. Interact with others less egocentrically.
2. Acquire socially acceptable behaviours.
3. Differentiate self from others.
4. Tolerate separation from key socializing agents such as the parent(s) or caregiver(s).

Figure 4-4 Refinement of skills and a growing sense of independence are most noted in toddlers.

5. Develop increasing verbal communication skills.
6. Tolerate delayed gratification of wants and desires.
7. Control bodily functions (toilet training) and begin self-care (feed and dress self almost completely).

Figure 4-5 Preschoolers often have very active imaginations and enjoy imitating adult roles.

Reflective Thinking

Preschoolers' Readiness for School

You are performing a physical examination on 5-year-old Jamie for his annual check-up. After the exam, you ask the parents if they have any questions. Jamie's father expresses concern that the other children in his son's preschool class are printing their names, but Jamie is not. How would you respond to this concern?

Developmental Tasks of Preschoolers (3 to 6 Years)

During the preschool period, children are focused on developing initiative and purpose. Play provides the means for physical, mental, and social development and becomes the "work" of children as they begin to understand, adjust to, and work out experiences with their environment. As shown in Figure 4-5, preschoolers have an active imagination and an ability to invent and imitate. They constantly seek to discover the why, what, and how of objects and events around them, are literal in their thinking, are increasingly sociable with other children and adults other than their parents, and are increasingly aware of their places and roles in their families. Key gross and fine motor, language, and sensory milestones associated with the preschool period can be found in Table 4-4.

The preschool stage of development is characterized by the refinement of many of the tasks that were achieved during the toddler stage and also the development of the skills and abilities that prepare children for the significant lifestyle change of starting school. Readiness for school is demonstrated by increased attention span and memory, ability to interact cooperatively, ability to tolerate prolonged periods of separation from family, and independence in performing basic self-care activities. Among the principal developmental tasks that must be mastered during the preschool stage are to:

1. Develop a sense of separateness as an individual.
2. Develop a sense of initiative.
3. Use language for increasing social interaction.
4. Interact in socially acceptable ways with others.
5. Develop a conscience.
6. Identify sex role and function.
7. Develop readiness for school.

Developmental Tasks of School-Age Children (6 to 12 Years)

With a well-developed sense of trust, autonomy, and initiative, school-age children increasingly reduce their dependency on the family as their primary

TABLE 4-4	Growth and Development During Preschool Years			
AGE	**GROSS MOTOR**	**FINE MOTOR**	**LANGUAGE**	**SENSORY**
3 to 6 Years	• Can ride a bike with training wheels • Can throw a ball overhand • Skips and hops on one foot • Can climb well • Can jump rope	• Can draw a six-part person • Can use scissors • Can draw a circle, square, or cross • Likes art projects, likes to paste and string beads • Can button • Learns to tie and buckle shoes • Can brush teeth	• Language skills are well developed with the child able to understand and speak clearly • Vocabulary grows to over 2,000 words • Talks endlessly and asks questions	• Visual acuity is well developed • Focused on learning letters and numbers

Figure 4-6 School-age children have well-developed motor skills and often play games in peer groups.

Figure 4-7 Older children can be active in sharing family responsibilities.

TABLE 4-5	Growth and Development During School-Age Years			
AGE	GROSS MOTOR	FINE MOTOR	LANGUAGE	SENSORY
6 to 12 Years	• Can use in-line skates or ice skates • Able to ride two-wheeler • Plays baseball	• Can put models together • Likes crafts • Enjoys board games, plays cards	• Vocabulary increases • Language abilities continue to develop	• Reading • Able to concentrate on activities for longer periods

socializing agents and move to the broader world of peers (primarily same-sex peers) in their neighbourhoods and schools, as well as to teachers and adult leaders of social, sports, and religious groups. They are increasingly exposed to the views, and seek approval, from people outside the home. School-age children become industrious workers as they develop significant physical, social, and intellectual skills needed to operate in a more diverse environment. They strive to be a part of a peer group and to achieve a variety of skills that are approved by others; in so doing, they become competent and confident in their own eyes (Figure 4-6). Key gross and fine motor, language, and sensory milestones associated with this period can be found in Table 4-5.

The principal developmental tasks that must be mastered during the school-age stage are to:

1. Become a more active, cooperative, and responsible family member (Figure 4-7).
2. Learn the rules and norms of a widening social, religious, and cultural environment.
3. Increase psychomotor and cognitive skills needed for participation in games and working with others.
4. Master concepts of time, conservation, and reversibility, as well as oral and written communication skills.
5. Win approval from peers and adults.
6. Obtain a place in a peer group.
7. Build a sense of industry, accomplishment, self-assurance, and self-esteem.
8. Develop a positive self-concept.
9. Exchange affection with family and friends without seeking an immediate payback.
10. Adopt moral standards for behaviour.

Developmental Tasks of Adolescents (12 to 18 Years)

The adolescent period is one of struggle and sometimes turmoil as the adolescent strives to develop a personal identity and achieve a successful transition from childhood to adulthood. The biological, social, cognitive, and psychological changes associated with adolescence are the most complex and profound of any developmental period. Physical and sexual maturity are reached during adolescence, with girls experiencing puberty and a growth spurt earlier than boys. In addition, adolescents develop increasingly sophisticated cognitive and interpersonal skills, test out adult roles and behaviours (Figure 4-8), and begin to explore educational and occupational opportunities for their future. Key gross and fine motor, language, and sensory milestones associated with this period can be found in Table 4-6.

Adolescents who have the support and trust of their families as they tackle the developmental tasks of this period are more likely to have a smoother and successful transition from childhood to adulthood. If parents have been too controlling, too permissive, or too confrontational during this period, adolescents may

Figure 4-8 Adolescence is a time of developing self-identity, forming close relationships with peers, and rapid physical changes.

TABLE 4-6	Growth and Development During Adolescence			
AGE	GROSS MOTOR	FINE MOTOR	LANGUAGE	SENSORY
12 to 19 Years	• Muscles continue to develop • At times awkward, with some lack of coordination	• Well-developed skills	• Vocabulary is fully developed	• Development is complete

experience difficulty in judging the appropriateness of their behaviour and in forming self-identity as competent, worthwhile individuals. Finding acceptance in a desired peer group or receiving more positive than negative responses from their growing sexual or friendship interests helps adolescents to become self-assured and competent in forming and maintaining adult relationships. The principal developmental tasks that must be mastered during the adolescent stage are to:

1. Develop self-identity and appreciate own achievements and worth.
2. Form close relationships with peers.
3. Gradually grow independent from parents.
4. Evolve own value system and integrate self-concept and values with those of peers and society.
5. Develop academic and vocational skills and related social, work, and civic sensitivities.
6. Develop analytic thinking.
7. Adjust to rapid physical and sexual changes.
8. Develop a sexual identity and role.
9. Develop skill in relating to people from different backgrounds.
10. Consider and possibly choose a career.

Developmental Tasks of Young Adults (18 to 30 Years)

Young adulthood is a time of separation and independence from the family and of new commitments, responsibilities, and accountability in social, work, and home relationships and roles (Figure 4-9). Individuals are exposed to more diverse people, situations, and values and, in recent decades, to a more rapidly changing socioeconomic and technological environment than ever before. The movement, particularly in the Western world, from an industrial to an information era has made extended education and delayed complete emancipation from the family and the commitment to a lifelong partner. Socioeconomic and cultural changes have also legitimized the entry of young women into the workforce.

Figure 4-9 Young adulthood often means separating from the family and embracing new commitments and responsibilities.

Reflective Thinking

Adolescents' Reactions to Physical Changes

As the school nurse, you are presenting sexual education classes to all students in a junior high school. While you are explaining sexually transmitted illnesses, a few of the girls begin to giggle. You overhear one girl saying, "Sophie doesn't have to worry about getting that. She's so flat-chested that no guy will even look at her." How would you handle this situation?

Reflective Thinking

Young Adult Experiencing Conflict Concerning a Developmental Task

Ingrid is a 33-year-old woman having a routine screening gynecological assessment. She tells the nurse that all of her friends are having babies and that her partner wants children soon. "I'm not ready for kids. Maybe I don't ever want kids. My partner is pressuring me, my parents, my friends, everybody!" How would you proceed if you were the nurse in this situation?

When parents and young adult offspring are able to resolve normal generational differences in philosophy and lifestyles, mastery of the young adult developmental tasks is greatly facilitated. Among the developmental tasks that the young adult must achieve are to:

1. Establish friendships and a social group.
2. Grow independent of parental care and home.
3. Set up and manage one's own household.
4. Form an intimate affiliation with another and choose a mate.
5. Learn to love, cooperate with, and commit to a life partner.
6. Develop a personal style of living (e.g., shared or single).
7. Choose and begin to establish a career or vocation.
8. Assume roles and responsibility in professional, political, religious, and civic organizations.
9. Learn to manage life stresses accompanying change.
10. Develop a realistic outlook and acceptance of cultural, religious, social, and political diversity.
11. Form a meaningful philosophy of life and implement it in home, employment, and community settings.
12. Begin a parental role for one's own or life partner's children, or for young people in a broader social framework; for example, teaching, health care, or volunteer work.

Developmental Tasks of Early Middle Adulthood (30 to 50 Years)

Middle age, spanning the ages of 30 to 70 years, is the longest stage of the life cycle and is now often divided into early and late middle adulthood. During early middle adulthood, individuals experience relatively good physical and mental health; settle into their careers, lifestyles, relationships (married, parental, partnered, single), political, civic, social, professional, and religious activities; and achieve maximum influence over themselves and their environments. Individuals also experience a need to contribute to the next generation, such as raising children or producing something socially useful to others.

Many who have chosen to express their generativity through parental roles may have an increase in leisure time and financial resources to pursue enjoyable, nonparental goals and activities once their children leave home. Others, following divorce and remarriage, may see a merging of offspring into new family groupings and the return to previous parental cycles. An increasing number of others may find themselves having to take on the responsibility of chronically ill, aging parents. Each life event or role transition can generate stress and disruption in individuals' lives. Developing effective coping strategies to manage the stress is a developmental task facing individuals in all life stages.

Among the developmental tasks that must be achieved during early middle adulthood are to:

1. Attain a desired level of achievement and status in career.
2. Review, evaluate, refine, and redirect career goals consistent with one's personal value system.
3. Learn and refine competencies in personal and career interests.
4. Manage life stresses accompanying change.
5. Develop mature relationships with life partner and significant others.
6. Participate in social, professional, political, religious, and civic activities.
7. Cope with an empty nest and possibly a refilled nest.
8. Adjust to aging parents and help plan for when they will need assistance.
9. Enjoy hobbies and leisure activities and develop ones for postretirement (Figure 4-10).
10. Plan for personal, financial, and social aspects of retirement.

Figure 4-10 Middle-aged adults often develop new interests, such as crafts or travel.

Figure 4-11 The free time that may accompany the late middle adulthood years can be particularly satisfying and enjoyable.

Developmental Tasks of Late Middle Adulthood (50 to 70 Years)

Many individuals during late middle adulthood may be diagnosed with a chronic health problem, such as arthritis, cardiovascular disease, cancer, diabetes, or asthma. In addition, women generally experience a decrease in estrogen and progesterone production and undergo menopause during their late 40s or early 50s. Changes also occur during late middle adulthood in work, family, social, and civic areas.

A variety of development tasks must be achieved by individuals during late middle adulthood. Among these tasks are to:

1. Manage life stresses accompanying change.
2. Maintain interest in current political, cultural, and scientific advances, trends, and issues.
3. Maintain affiliations with social, religious, professional, civic, or political organizations.
4. Adapt to health status changes that accompany aging.
5. Continue current activities and develop new interests and leisure activities that can be pursued consistent with changing abilities (Figure 4-11).

The Sandwich Generation

People who must provide for the needs of their children as well as those of their aging parents have been termed the "sandwich generation," a metaphor for being "squeezed" between two demands. According to Statistics Canada:[13]

- In 2002, 27% of people aged 45–64 with unmarried children in the home were also caring for a senior. More than 8 in 10 of these individuals worked, causing some to reduce or shift their hours or to lose income.
- Women felt sandwiched more than men, spending an average of 29 hours/month (compared to 13 hours by male counterparts) providing more personal and in-home care such as bathing, feeding, and meal preparation. Men tend to assist with transportation and external household maintenance.
- On a positive note, while sandwiched workers were more likely to feel stressed—about 70% compared with about 61% of workers with no child-care or elder-care responsibilities—almost all (95%) felt satisfied with life in general, almost the same number as those with less caregiving responsibilities.

Reflective Thinking

When an Elderly Parent Needs Special Care

Jean (52) and Don Allen (56) had finally helped the last of their three children move into his own apartment in another city and had been looking forward to having more time together when Jean's mother, 76 years old and recently widowed, was diagnosed with cancer. Because Jean's mother lives alone, will be receiving chemotherapy on an outpatient basis, and will need a great deal of help during this period, Jean and Don have agreed to have her live with them until the chemotherapy is completed.

- What developmental needs would you anticipate that Jean, Don, and Jean's mother might experience?
- What anticipatory counselling would you provide related to these needs?

Figure 4-12 Having free time and independence from job responsibilities are among the benefits of late adulthood.

6. Adjust to increased interaction and time spent with life partner without the presence of children.
7. Develop supportive, interdependent relationships with adult children.
8. Help elderly parents and relatives cope with lifestyle changes (may include providing a home for them).
9. Adjust to possible or actual loss of parents, life partner, elder family members, and friends through death or their decreasing abilities to maintain independent living and self-care.
10. Prepare for and adjust to changes in roles, finances, or lifestyles resulting from retirement.

Developmental Tasks of Late Adulthood (70 Years to Death)

Individuals in late adulthood widely diverge in how they physically and emotionally age and how they confront and adjust to the changes associated with this stage. People who have accomplished the developmental tasks of middle adulthood are comfortable with the achievement of their life goals and the independence from the workplace, and also welcome the time to pursue leisure activities. Although there is an inevitable loss of work-related status and social outlets, and a decrease in income, in physical or cognitive capabilities, in resistance to illness, and in recuperative powers, most individuals adjust to these changes with equanimity. Indeed, a high percentage manage their activities of daily living independently and in their own homes, enjoying new roles and giving advice and moral support to members of younger generations, and sharing leisure activities with friends in their own age group (Figure 4-12).

Life 360°

Self-Reflection on Life Events

Reflect on your own personal history and review how you resolved or accomplished each of the developmental tasks and crises according to each major developmental theory presented in this chapter.
- Were there any developmental crises and tasks that you experienced that did not fit the theories presented?
- Are there any tasks and crises with which you think you need additional experiences to master?

Reflective Thinking

Encouraging a Life Review

As the nurse manager of a senior's residence, you decide to conduct a weekly class for interested patients who want to share their life experiences.
- How would you prepare for the class?
- What agenda would you establish?
- How would you evaluate the usefulness of the class?

Conducting a **life review** is an important developmental task during late adulthood. This task entails reviewing the experiences, relationships, and events of your life as a whole, viewing successes and failures from the perspective of age, and accepting your life choices and their outcomes. Individuals who successful complete the life review task feel that they have been a meaningful part of human history, have integrity, and are able to face death with equanimity. If individuals fail to achieve the life review developmental task, a sense of hopelessness, resentment, futility, despair, fear of death, and clinical depression may result. Among the developmental tasks that must be achieved during late adulthood are to:

1. Accept and adjust to changes in health status.
2. Maintain and develop new activities that contribute to a continuing sense of usefulness and self-worth, enhance self-image, and help retain functional capacities.
3. Develop new roles in family as eldest member.
4. Establish affiliation with own age group.
5. Accept and adjust to social, financial, and lifestyle changes.
6. Adapt to loss of life partner, family members, and friends.
7. Work on life review.
8. Prepare for inevitability of own death.

STAGES OF FAMILY DEVELOPMENT

A review of developmental stages, tasks, and life events is not complete without considering the family context of the person being assessed. Carter and McGoldrick have described six stages in the life cycle of the traditional family as well as the emotional processes of transition and the second-order changes in the family's status that are required in each developmental stage (Table 4-7).[14] The tasks associated with families who have experienced divorce have also been taken into account in Rankin's Changing Life Cycle (Figure 4-13).

TABLE 4-7 The Stages of the Family Life Cycle

FAMILY LIFE CYCLE STAGE	EMOTIONAL PROCESS OF TRANSITION: KEY PRINCIPLES	SECOND-ORDER CHANGES IN FAMILY STATUS REQUIRED TO PROCEED DEVELOPMENTALLY
1. Leaving home: Single young adults	Accepting emotional and financial responsibility for self	1. Differentiation of self in relation to family of origin 2. Development of intimate peer relationships 3. Establishment of self in regard to work and financial independence
2. The joining of families through marriage: The new couple	Commitment to new system	1. Formation of marital system 2. Realignment of relationships with extended families and friends to include spouse

continues

TABLE 4-7	The Stages of the Family Life Cycle *continued*	
FAMILY LIFE CYCLE STAGE	**EMOTIONAL PROCESS OF TRANSITION: KEY PRINCIPLES**	**SECOND-ORDER CHANGES IN FAMILY STATUS REQUIRED TO PROCEED DEVELOPMENTALLY**
3. Families with young children	Accepting new members into system	1. Adjusting marital system to make space for child(ren) 2. Joining in child-rearing, financial, and household tasks 3. Realignment of relationships with extended family to include parenting and grandparenting roles
4. Families with adolescents	Increasing flexibility of family boundaries to include children's independence and grandparents' frailties	1. Shifting of parent–child relationships to permit adolescent to move in and out of system 2. Refocus on midlife marital and career issues 3. Beginning shift toward joint caring for older generation
5. Launching children and moving on	Accepting a multitude of exits from and entries into the family system	1. Renegotiation of marital system as a dyad 2. Development of adult-to-adult relationships between grown children and their parents 3. Realignment of relationships to include in-laws and grandchildren 4. Dealing with disabilities and death of parents (grandparents)
6. Families in later life	Accepting the shifting of generational roles	1. Maintaining own and couple functioning and interests in face of physiological decline; exploration of new familial and social role options 2. Support for a more central role of middle generation 3. Making room in the system for the wisdom and experience of elderly people; supporting the older generation without overfunctioning for them 4. Dealing with loss of spouse, siblings, and other peers; preparing for own death; life review and integration

Source: From Carter, B., & McGoldrick, M. (1999). *The expanded family life cycle* (3rd ed.). Boston: Allyn and Bacon. Copyright © 1999 by Pearson Education. Reprinted with permission of the publisher.

Nursing Tip

Denver Developmental Screening Test (DDST)

The Canadian Task Force on Preventive Health Care recommends that the Denver Developmental Screening Test (Appendix C) be excluded from the periodic health examination of asymptomatic children; however, it is a good resource when delays are suspected.

Family Type	Tasks	Characteristics/Examples	Common Transitions
Emerging	Finding suitable partners	Formalization of marital bond	Change in personal relationships—addition of spouse or significant other. Loss of friends, changes in family relationships
	Constitution of meaningful adult relationships	Decision to live with person of opposite or same sex with nonformalized bond	Changes in roles and status—unmarried to married status, addition of parental role. Possible changes in job, career, related to change in personal relationships
	Decisions related to childbearing and infertility	Traditional or nontraditional family pattern, that is, opposite sex partners obtain in vitro fertilization or same sex partners adopt	Change in familiar environment—moving households
	Decision to remain childless	Opposite or same sex partners	
Solidifying or Reconstituting	Solidification of adult partners' bonds. Childrearing and required interface with schools, health care institutions, and other societal institutions	Stable nondivorcing families. Childrearing tasks involve nurturance, education, socialization, and provision of climate suitable to development of responsible individuals. Characteristics of families with children are similar whether the family is traditional or not	Change in roles and status—loss or change in marital role through divorce and/or remarriage. Continued career changes
			Changes in personal relationships—potential loss of significant other, that is, mate, child. Loss of parents in family of origin
			Changes in physical and mental capacities—major health change
	Reconstitution of family bonds with integration of new family members and loss of old ones	Divorced families and blended families	Changes in possessions—loss or acquisition of loved possessions necessitated by change in income or catastrophic occurrences
Contracting	Launching and release of children to environments separated from family	Traditional nuclear family releases young adult children to armed services, college, marriage, or work	Change in personal relationships—loss of spouse, children, siblings
	Adjusting to loss of adult partner	Death, late-in-life divorce	Change in roles and status—retirement
	Adjusting to loss of work, parental roles	Enforced retirement with consequences of lowered standard of living	Changes in physical and mental capacities—exacerbation of chronic problems, onset of acute episodes
	Integration of leisure time and adjustment to lack of responsibility for children and/or occupation. Development of avocation	Younger, healthy retired couples. Older, healthy workers who choose to continue employment	Changes in familiar environment—moves required by decreased income, loss of spouse, or health problems
	Adaptation to caregiving		

Figure 4-13 Changing Life Cycle.

Source: Rankin, S. (1986). Family traditions, expected and unexpected. In Gillis, C. L., Highley, B.L., Roberts, B., & Martinson, I. (Eds.). *Toward a science of family nursing.* Redwood City, CA: Addison Wesley. p. 180. Table 11-1 Developmental Family Framework and Common Family Traditions

DEVELOPMENTAL ASSESSMENT TOOLS

A variety of developmental assessment tools is available for use by the nurse, though some of the tools require special training. The most commonly used tools assess mental, physical, emotional, and social functional status of individuals and families. Table 4-8 summarizes some of the most frequently used tools.

TABLE 4-8   Developmental Assessment Tools

TOOL	TARGET POPULATION	ASSESSMENT PARAMETERS	SPECIAL CONSIDERATIONS
Brazelton Neonatal Behavioral Assessment Scale (BNBAS)[15]	Newborns	Temperament characteristics: state of arousal, orienting responses to stimuli, ability to deal with disturbing stimuli, social behaviour, motor skills	When results are shared with parents, increased and improved newborn-parent interactions have been noted
Denver II[16] (see Appendix C)	1 month–6 years old	Personal-social, fine motor-adaptive, language, gross motor skills	Standardized for minority populations
Revised Prescreening Developmental Questionnaire (R-PDQ)[17]	1 month–6 years old	Personal-social, fine motor-adaptive, language, gross motor skills	Answered by parents to identify children who need more complete screening
Early Language Milestones Scale (ELM)[18]	1 month–3 years old	Early language development	Tests auditory visual, auditory receptive, expressive language in greater depth than Denver II
Carey Infant and Child Temperament Questionnaires[19, 20, 21]	4 months old–preschoolers	Pattern of temperamental attributes	Influences on child's relationships with parents and other caregivers are assessed
Washington Guide to Promoting Development in the Young Child[22]	Birth–5 years old	Play, motor activities, language, feeding, dressing, toilet training, discipline, sleep	Provides expected tasks for each age group and suggestions about appropriate child-rearing practices
HEADSS (Home, Education, Activities, Drugs, Sex, and Suicide) Adolescent Risk Profile[23]	Adolescents	Home, education, activities, drugs, sex, suicide	Identifies high-risk adolescents, and provides a guide for anticipatory guidance
NGAGED (Now, Growth and Development, Activities of Daily Living, General Health, Environment, and Documentation)[24]	Child with disabilities	Personal, family, social, school	Evaluates degree to which child engages in life activities as function of overall well-being and indicator of areas needing intervention
Stress Scale for Children[25]	Children	Desirable and undesirable life events experienced within last 6 months to 2 years and amount of adjustment that was needed to handle the events	Self-administered; higher scores correlate with increased probability of developing stress-related illness
Recent Life Changes Questionnaire[26]	Adults		
Life Experiences Survey[27]	Young and middle-age adults	Events that have occurred within the past year and the type and extent of impact the events have had	Self-administered; identifies respondents at high risk for high stress and in need of stress and coping counseling
Everyday Hassles Scale (EHS)[28, 29]	Adults	Everyday irritants that contribute to stress, and behaviours and feelings that promote well-being	Studies have suggested that day-to-day hassles are more strongly correlated with physical and psychosocial problems and than outcomes are life events

TABLE 4-8 Developmental Assessment Tools *continued*

TOOL	TARGET POPULATION	ASSESSMENT PARAMETERS	SPECIAL CONSIDERATIONS
Stress Audit[30]	Adults	Experienced and anticipated stressful events, stress symptoms, responses to stress, overall vulnerability to stress	Self-administered; identifies stress profile and provides anticipatory guidance
Sense of Coherence (SOC) Scale[31]	School age–adults	Sense of coherence (comprehensibility, manageability, meaningfulness)	Gender, culturally, and socioeconomically neutral; results can be used for anticipatory guidance
Functional Activities Questionnaire (FAQ)[32]	Older adults	Level of independence demonstrated in the performance of activities of daily living	Can be completed by significant other or caregiver
Folstein Mini-Mental Status Examination (MMSE)[33, 34]	Older adults	Cognitive function	Can be easily administered in any clinical setting. A telephone version is also available. Assists in determining the need for a more definitive neurological examination.
Minimum Data Set (MDS) for Nursing Facility Resident Assessment and Care Screening[35]	Nursing home residents	Cognitive patterns, communication and hearing patterns, vision patterns, physical functioning and structural problems, psychosocial well-being, mood, and behaviour patterns, activity pursuit patterns, bowel and bladder status, disease diagnoses, health conditions, oral nutritional status, oral and dental status, skin condition, medication use, treatments and procedures, customary activities of daily living routines	Required by federal law for all patients residing in nursing homes
Functional Assessment Screening in the Elderly (FASE)[36]	Older adults	Functional disability	Suggests interventions when abnormal results are present
Beck Depression Inventory (BDI)[37]	Adults	Mood, pessimism, sense of failure, dissatisfaction, guilt, sense of disappointment in oneself, punishment, self-accusations, self-punitive wishes, crying spells, irritability, social withdrawal, indecisiveness, body image, function at work, sleep disturbance, fatigue, appetite disturbance, weight loss, preoccupation with health, loss of libido	Score indicating depression warrants referral to a mental health specialist
Calgary Family Assessment Model (CFAM)[38]	Families	Structural, developmental, and functional	Includes emphasis on diversity issues such as race, culture, ethnicity, gender, and sexual orientation
Friedman Family Assessment Model (FFAM)[39]	Families	Developmental stage and history of a family, environmental data, family structure and functions, family stress and coping	Comprehensive and culturally sensitive

CASE STUDY   The Infant with Failure to Thrive

HEALTH HISTORY

Legal Guardian	Ngoc-Diep Cheng (biological mother & primary caregiver) & Trung Cheng (father & occasional caregiver)
Source of Information	Mother
PATIENT PROFILE **HEALTH ISSUE/CONCERN**	11 mos, 3 wk old male, looks pale, irritable (per mother) "Henry isn't growing & he's been a very poor eater since he was about 5 or 6 mos old. At first we thought he was just going to be a small child. My whole family, males as well as females, are small."
HISTORY OF ISSUE/CONCERN	At 12 mo well-baby check-up 2 days ago, pt's physical growth (Wt: 6.8 kg, & length: 86.6 cm) was noted to be below the 3'rd percentile. Admission dx: Nonorganic failure to thrive (NFTT).
BIRTH HISTORY	
Prenatal	GR 3, PARA 1; 2 spontaneous abortions during the first trimester over the 3 yrs prior to pt conception. Denies drug use, smoking, infections, or injuries during any pregnancy. All pregnancies were planned. Began prenatal care immediately post missed period & ⊕ home pregnancy test.
Labour and Delivery	Full term, 3500 gm, length 52 cm, head circumference 34 cm at birth c̄ Apgar score of 9 and a lusty cry at 1 & 5 min.
Postnatal	Child & mother's courses prior to & post discharge were unremarkable.
MEDICAL HISTORY	No illnesses or injuries other than an occasional cold. No exposure to TB, HIV. Up-to-date on all immunizations. For first 4 mos, physical growth (weight & length) remained within the 50th percentile. Able to roll from back to side, grasp & try to reach objects, cooed, babbled, laughed, & smiled in recognition when parents talked to & held him. At 6 mos physical growth was within the 35th percentile & fine motor, gross motor, personal-social, & language skills began to lag. Pt is now a poor eater, does not attempt to feed self c̄ finger food, will not play pat-a-cakes, frequently turns away when name is called, rarely tries to pick anything up x̄ a favoured soft teddy bear, which he rolls or leans against rather than holds; frequently whimpers but rarely vocalizes, cries, or laughs; stands only c̄ support & assistance, & is only intermittently responsive to his environment. Will quietly sit for long stretches of time in the corner of his playpen "just staring into space."
DEVELOPMENTAL ASSESSMENT	Denver II (see Appendix C)—failure in all 4 categories: personal-social, fine motor-adaptive, language, & gross motor. During testing generally appeared disinterested. No fearfulness noted. Frequently slow to respond.

SOCIAL HISTORY

Home Environment

Mother reports no significant physical change in the home environment. Mother works at home. Father's office is 6 blocks from family home. Family lives in a 3 BR home. Parents rarely drink ETOH. Do not use recreational drugs. One pet, a golden Lab, has become more attentive to child's mother over the last 6 mos & now rarely leaves her side.

Economic Status

Financially secure.

Roles and Relationships

Parents married 10 yrs. Waited to start family until careers well established. Mother is a successful children's author & full-time caregiver. Has not been able to write anything since the birth of child. Father is a criminal lawyer & works or is on-call 24/7. Has rarely consistently been available to assist in caregiving.

About 7 mos ago, mother started having trouble c̄ her motor skills (e.g., over time developed an intermittent fine tremor & lost ability to safely hold her infant). "It was like my muscles would just give way when I would first try to pick Henry up or when I would start to put him down & I would just drop him!" Became increasingly forgetful, fearful, & easily fatigued. Primary physician at first suggested she was having "some postpartum depression." When motor skills continued to deteriorate, husband insisted she see a neurologist who confirmed the diagnosis of multiple sclerosis (MS) 2 wks ago.

After the pediatrician's tentative diagnosis of pt's NFTT, mother searched the Internet to obtain information about the etiology, tx, & prognosis of NFTT. Mother is quite distraught; believes her MS symptoms made it impossible for her to provide a safe & loving environment for her son so he couldn't develop a sense of trust. "I was supposed to be his socializing agent & I couldn't be because I got to where I was afraid to pick him up. I was in such denial that I waited too long to get medical help & all the time my baby was becoming more & more developmentally delayed! What if I've permanently damaged him?"

FAMILY HEALTH HISTORY

LEGEND

- ⬤ Living female
- ◼ Living male
- ⊗ Deceased female
- ⊠ Deceased male
- ⟋ Points to patient

A&W = Alive & well
DM = Diabetes mellitus
MS = Multiple sclerosis
NFTT = Nonorganic failure to thrive
OA = Osteoarthritis

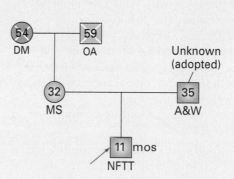

Denies FHH of genetic disorder, congenital anomaly, SIDS, ADHD, and MR.

◀ **NURSING CHECKLIST** ▶

Developmental Assessment

- Note the patient's stated chronological age.
- Tailor your questions to the patient's level of ability according to developmental parameters until you can accurately assess the actual developmental level.
- When assessing small children, verify information with the caregiver.
- If a third party is assisting in the interview (for an elderly or handicapped patient), address all questions to the patient, not the intermediary.

REVIEW QUESTIONS

1. When a nurse is assessing a toddler for Erikson's stage of autonomy versus shame and doubt, which is important to recognize?
   a. The need to toilet train the child
   b. That independence should be encouraged in activities of daily living
   c. The need to name objects for the child and describe their function
   d. That the child needs to be held often
   The correct answer is (b).

2. The nurse is teaching the mother of a teenager what she would note if her child has reached Kohlberg's postconventional stage of development. The teenager would:
   a. Expect to be totally autonomous
   b. Espouse only one moral point of view
   c. Be capable of making decisions after considering differing moral approaches
   d. Make decisions based on whether they please others or not
   The correct answer is (c).

3. The nurse is assessing a 4-month-old infant to determine her gross motor development. Which would be age-appropriate development for this infant?
   a. Ability to sit alone without support
   b. Ability to hold her head up when prone and use forearms for support
   c. Ability to hold her head, chest, and abdomen up by bearing weight on the hands
   d. Bounces when held in a standing position
   The correct answer is (b).

4. When approaching the door of an examining room in which Dan, a school-age child, is waiting, the nurse knocks on the door before entering the room. While assessing Dan's developmental level, the nurse encourages Dan to demonstrate his favourite activity. The nurse is applying the theories of:
   a. Piaget and Kohlberg
   b. Kohlberg and Freud

   c. Piaget and Freud
   d. Freud and Erikson
   The correct answer is (d).

5. A first-time mother asks the nurse when she can expect her 2-month-old to start to crawl. The most appropriate response would be:
   a. 3 months
   b. 6 months
   c. 8 months
   d. 11 months
   The correct answer is (c).

6. While the nurse is assessing a preschool child, the child's father states that his daughter enjoys jumping rope. Which age is his daughter most likely to be?
   a. 18 months old
   b. 2 years old
   c. 30 months old
   d. 5 years old
   The correct answer is (d).

7. A nurse assessing a toddler would expect to see the child:
   a. Building a tower of four blocks, drawing a circle, and jumping in place
   b. Pouring liquids, drawing circles, and throwing a ball overhand
   c. Dressing and undressing self, running, jumping, and riding a bike
   d. Walking up and down stairs, pushing and pulling toys, and buttoning a shirt
   The correct answer is (a).

8. One of the principal developmental tasks of adolescents is to:
   a. Develop self-identity and appreciate own achievements and worth
   b. Exchange affection with family and friends without seeking an immediate payback
   c. Be independent of parental care and home
   d. Manage life stress accompanying change
   The correct answer is (a).

9. When administering a developmental surveillance cxam, the nurse is assessing:
   a. Parenting behaviours of the child's parents
   b. Fine and gross motor skills, language, and psychosocial behaviour
   c. Task resolution across the developmental years
   d. The child's temperament characteristics
   The correct answer is (b).

10. When assessing a preschooler's readiness for school, the nurse would expect to see:
    a. Beginning independence in performing basic self-care activities
    b. Knowing his or her first and last names and expressing needs
    c. Tolerating prolonged periods of separation from family
    d. Differentiating self from others
    The correct answer is (c).

Visit the Estes online companion resource at www.healthassessment.nelson.com for additional content and study aids.

REFERENCES

[1]Lazarus, R. S., & Folkman, S. (1984). *Stress, appraisal and coping.* New York: Springer.

[2]Antonovsky, A. (1987). *Unraveling the mystery of health: How people manage stress and stay well.* San Francisco: Jossey-Bass.

[3]Aldwin, C. M. (1992). Aging, coping, and efficacy: Theoretical framework for examining coping in life-span developmental context. In M. L. Wykle, E. Kahana, & J. Kowal (Eds.), *Stress & health among the elderly.* New York: Springer.

[4]Wong, D. L., Hockenberry, J. J., Wilson, D., Perry, S., & Lowdermilk, D. (2006). *Maternal child nursing care* (3rd ed.). Philadelphia: Mosby.

[5]Grey, M. (1993). Stressors and children's health. *Journal of Pediatric Nursing, 8(2),* 85–91.

[6]Piaget, J. (1952). *The origins of intelligence in children.* New York: International Universities Press.

[7]Freud, S. (1946). *The ego and the mechanism of defense.* New York: International Universities Press.

[8]Erikson, E. (1974). *Dimensions of a new identity.* New York: W. W. Norton.

[9]Kohlberg, L. (1981). *The philosophy of moral development: Moral stages and the idea of justice.* New York: Harper & Row.

[10]Statistics Canada. (2005). *Life expectancy at birth.* Retrieved October 9, 2006, from http://www40.statcan.ca/l01/cst01/health26.htm

[11]Statistics Canada. (2005). *Population projections of visible minority groups, Canada, provinces and regions 2001–2017.* Retrieved May 31, 2006, from http://www.statcan.ca/english/freepub/91-541-XIE/91-541-XIE2005001.pdf

[12]Statistics Canada. (2006). *Annual demographic statistics 2005.* Retrieved May 31, 2006, from http://www.edrs.mcgill.ca/StatCan/Demog/Data/Report/2005/DEMOG_E.PDF

[13]Williams, C. (2004). *The sandwich generation. Statistics Canada: Perspectives on labour and income, 5(9).* Retrieved May 23, 2006, from http://www.statcan.ca/english/freepub/75-001-XIE/10904/art-1.htm

[14]Carter, B., & McGoldrick, M (2005). *The expanded family life cycle: Individual, family and social perspectives* (4th ed.). New York: Pearson.

[15]Brazelton, T. B. (1996). *Neonatal behavioral assessment scale* (3rd ed.). Philadelphia: J. B. Lippincott.

[16]Glascoe, F. P., Foster, E. M., & Wolraich, M. L. (1997). An economic analysis of developmental detection methods. *Pediatrics, 99,* 830–37.

[17]Frankenburg, W. K., Dobbs, J., Archer, P., Shapiro, H., & Brisnick, B. (1996). *The Denver II Technical Manual.* Denver, CO: Denver Developmental Materials, Inc.

[18]Coplan, J. (1983). Evaluation of the child with delayed speech or language. *Pediatric Annals, 14,* 202–08.

[19]Carey, W. B., & McDevitt, S. (1978). Revision of the infant temperament questionnaire. *Pediatrics, 61,* 735–39.

[20]Hegvik, R., McDevitt, S., & Carey, W. (1982). The middle childhood temperament questionnaire. *Journal of Developmental Behavior in Pediatrics, 3,* 197–200.

[21]Fullard, W., McDevitt, S., & Carey, W. (1984). Assessing temperament in one- to three-year-old children. *Journal of Pediatric Psychology, 9,* 205–17.

[22]Powell, M. L. (1981). *Assessment and management of developmental changes and problems in children* (2nd ed.). St. Louis: Mosby.

[23]Neinstein, L. S. (2002). *Adolescent health care: A practical guide* (4th ed.). Baltimore: Lippincott Williams & Wilkins.

[24]Guillett, S. E. (1998). Assessing the child with disabilities. *Home Healthcare Nurse, 16,* 402–09.

[25]Saunders, A., & Remsberg, B. (1984). *The stress-proof child: A loving parent's guide.* New York: Holt, Rinehart, & Winston.

[26]Rahe, R. H. (1975). Epidemiological studies in life change and illness. *International Journal of Psychiatry. 6,* 133–46.

[27]Sarason, J. G., Johnson, J. H., & Siegal, J. M. (1978). Assessing the impact of life changes: Development of life experiences survey. *Journal of Consulting Clinical Psychology, 46,* 932–46.

[28]Lazarus, R. S. (1981). Little hazards can be hazardous to your health. *Psychology Today, 15(7),* 58–62.

[29]Lazarus, R. S., & Folkman, S. (1984). *Stress, appraisal and coping.* New York: Springer.

[30]Miller, L. H., Smith, A. D., & Mehler, B. L. (1991). *The stress audit.* Brookline, MA: Biobehavioral Associates.

[31]Antonovsky, A. (1993). The structure and properties of the sense of coherence scale. *Social Science Medicine, 36(6),* 725–33.

[32]McDowell, I., & Newell, C. (1996). *Functional disability and handicap. Measuring health: A guide to rating scales and questionnaires* (2nd ed.). New York: Oxford University Press.

[33]Folstein, M. F., Folstein, S. E., & McHugh, P. R. (1975). "Mini-Mental State": A practical method for grading the cognitive state of patients for the clinician. *Journal of Psychiatric Research, 12,* 189–98.

[34]Brandt, J., Spencer, M., & Folstein, M. (1988). The telephone instrument for cognitive status. *Neuropsychiatry, Neuropsychology, and Behavioral Neurology, 1,* 11–17.

[35]Carnevali, D. L., & Patrick, M. (1993). *Nursing management for the elderly* (3rd ed.). Philadelphia: J.B. Lippincott.

[36]Resnick, N. M. (1994). Geriatric medicine & the elderly patient. In L. M. Tierney, Jr., S. J. McPhee, & M. A. Papadakis (Eds.), *Current medical diagnosis & treatment* (33rd ed., pp. 41–60). Norwalk, CT: Appleton & Lange.

[37]Gallagher, D. (1986). The Beck depression inventory and older adults: Review of its development and utility. In T. L. Brink (Ed.), *Clinical gerontology: A guide to assessment and intervention* (149–63). New York: Haworth Press.

[38]Wright, L. M., & Leahey, M. (2005). *Nurses and families: A guide to family assessment and intervention* (4th ed.). Philadelphia, PA: F.A. Davis.

[39]Friedman, M. M., Bowden, V.R., & Jones, E.G. (2003). *Family nursing: Research, theory and practice* (5th ed.). Upper Saddle River, NJ: Prentice Hall.

BIBLIOGRAPHY

Carno, M. A., Hoffman, L. A., Carcillo, J. A., & Sanders, M. H. (2003). Developmental stages of sleep from birth to adolescence, common childhood sleep disorders: overview and nursing implications. *Journal of Pediatric Nursing, 18*(4), 274–83.

Carter, A. S., Briggs-Gowan, M. J., & Davis, N. O. (2004). Assessment of young children's social-emotional development and psychopathology: Recent advances and recommendations for practice. *Journal of Clinical Psychology and Psychiatry, 45*(1), 109–34.

Murray, R. B., Zentner, J. P., Pangman, V., & Pangman, C. (2006). *Health promotion strategies through the life span* (Canadian edition). Toronto: Pearson Education Canada.

WEB RESOURCES

Canadian Child Care Federation
http://www.cccf-fcsge.ca/

Child and Family Canada
http://www.cfc-efc.ca/menu/childdev_en.htm

Child Care Canada
http://www.childcarecanada.org/

Child Welfare League of Canada
http://www.cwlc.ca/

Health Canada–Division of Aging and Seniors
http://www.phac-aspc.gc.ca/seniors-aines/

Vanier Institute of the Family
http://www.vifamily.ca/

CHAPTER 5

Cultural Assessment

COMPETENCIES

1. Assess own cultural values, beliefs, and behaviours.

2. Identify potential areas of cultural conflict between the values and customs of patients, their families, and those of health care providers.

3. Conduct a comprehensive cultural assessment.

4. Describe the process for providing culturally competent nursing care.

*C*anada is known around the world as a multicultural society whose ethnocultural makeup has been shaped by years of immigration. In addition to Aboriginal people (First Nations, Inuit, and Métis), waves of new peoples arriving from a range of countries have helped populate this vast country from coast to coast. In fact, immigration accounted for almost 65% of Canada's population growth in 2005 (compared to only 37% in 1972).[1] Nurses working anywhere in Canada will need to be culturally competent and will benefit from the many rewards of working with clients from diverse cultural backgrounds.

CULTURALLY COMPETENT CARE

The Canadian Nurses Association espouses **cultural competence** and defines it as "the application of knowledge, skill, attitudes and personal attributes required by nurses to provide appropriate care and services in relation to cultural characteristics of their clients (individuals, families, groups, and the population at large). Cultural competence includes valuing diversity, knowing about cultural mores and traditions of the population being served and being sensitive to these while caring for the individual."[2] Culture, in fact, is one of the 12 determinants of health (see Chapter 3) in that it plays a role in health by influencing whether someone is marginalized, stigmatized, devalued, or even has access to appropriate health care. Nurses who are culturally competent will deliver care that is characterized by **cultural safety**—care that is based on recognition and respect rather than on power inequities, or individual or institutional discrimination.

The Canadian health care system is one of **cultural diversity,** consisting of patients and health care providers from different combinations of ethnic (e.g., Arabic), racial (e.g., Caucasian), national (e.g., Swiss), religious (e.g., Sikh), generational (e.g., grandparent), marital status (e.g., single), socioeconomic (e.g., middle class), occupational (e.g., accountant), preference in life partner (e.g., heterosexual), health status (e.g., handicapped), and cultural orientations coexisting in a given location. Cultural diversity should be viewed as an opportunity for health care professionals to experience the benefits of exchange and cooperation across cultures.

At the time of the last analyzed census in 2001, Canada had over 34 ethnic groups with at least 100,000 members each, and a record 18.4% of the Canadian population was born outside of Canada.[3] This proportion will continue to increase as a result of Canada's commitment to welcoming new peoples—to rejuvenate our aging society, to provide refugees with needed protection, and to provide skilled and unskilled labour for jobs not being filled by Canadians. The face of immigration has shifted from a predominately European (including the United Kingdom) influx (70% of immigrants) prior to 1970, to an Asian and Pacific influx (52% of immigrants) since 1970. The remaining 30% of immigrants prior to 1970 included Americans (15%), Asians (10%), and émigrés from the Caribbean, Middle East, and Africa (5%). Since 1970, the "traditional" sources of immigration shifted to Asia and Pacific (52% of immigration) followed by Africa and the Middle East (20%), South and Central America (9%), Europe and the United Kingdom (17%), and the United States (2%). Newcomers disperse themselves all across Canada, but over half (52%) are spread almost evenly between Ontario and British Columbia. The next most popular provinces are Alberta (14.9%), Manitoba (12.1%), Yukon (10.6%), and Québec (9.9%).[4] The 2006 Canadian Census currently under study predicts an even higher proportion of Canadian residents born outside our country with origins from an even broader range of homelands.

It is projected that by 2017, 1 in 5 Canadians will be from a visible minority, and 22% of the population will be made up of immigrants. Owing to trends in

Figure 5-1 Respect and interest in cultural background will provide a strong basis for communication. *Photo courtesy of Smithsonian Institution.*

immigration destination, it is expected that one third of residents of British Columbia and one half of residents of metropolitan Toronto will be visible minorities in 2017.[5]

The changes in the demographic and ethnic composition of the population make it imperative that nurses be able to communicate effectively with a culturally diverse group of patients, make accurate cultural assessments, and plan, provide, and evaluate culturally competent health care (Figure 5-1). Nurses must be aware of and make use of the knowledge and theories that help explain the situations and responses of patients within the context of each patient's cultural, ethnic, gender, and sexual orientations.

New residents to Canada may differ in their attitudes toward the health care system, and may have different health behaviour patterns, and types of health problems. Even after new immigrants undergo **acculturation** (an informal process of adaptation through which the beliefs, values, norms, and practices of a dominant culture are learned by new members born into a different culture), many of their beliefs and attitudes may be an amalgam of their original practices and those of the dominant Canadian culture. Nurses must keep in mind health beliefs and behaviours in the context of each patient's culture in order to deliver culturally competent health care.

Culturally competent nursing care is provided by nurses who use research and **cross-cultural nursing care** models (nursing care provided within the cultural context of patients who are members of a culture or subculture different from that of the nurse) to identify patients' health care needs. The process of culturally competent nursing care consists of: (1) eliciting patient statements of cultural values and beliefs so that culturally sensitive approaches to care can be provided; (2) recognizing and understanding the behaviours and responses of different cultural groups to health and illness; (3) obtaining information on ethnic variations and on normal racial growth patterns to assist in identifying abnormal patterns and designing appropriate interventions; and (4) using the ethic of **cultural relativism,** which is the belief that no culture is either inferior or superior to another, that behaviour must be evaluated in relation to the cultural context in which it occurs, and that respect, equality, and justice are basic rights for all racial, ethnic, subcultural, and cultural groups.

To provide culturally competent nursing care, nurses must first be willing and able to confront their own stereotyping and cultural biases, or **ethnocentrism** (a perception that a person's own cultural group, and its values, beliefs, norms, and customs, are superior to all others), and to examine the impact these biases may have on the patient. Nurses must also understand the dynamics and respond to the challenges inherent in **bilingualism** (the habitual use of two different languages, particularly when speaking), **multiculturalism** (when individuals live and function in two or more cultures simultaneously), and their patient's **cultural identity** (the cultural definition or cultural orientation with which an individual self-identifies). In addition, consideration should be given to the potential for **culture shock:** the disorientation, uncertainty, and alienation that can occur during the process of adjusting to a new cultural group.

Assessing a patient's cultural beliefs, values, and customs through observation and interview is an essential part of the health assessment. A balance is needed between the data related to the specific individuals and their families who are being assessed and the data related to the cultural group to which they have been **enculturated** (the informal process through which the beliefs, values, norms, and practices of a culture are learned by members born into the culture). The nurse, therefore, needs to have experience with a range of individuals and families from any given cultural group in order to determine where in this range the patient being assessed fits. In addition, knowledge of the physical and biological norm differences, as well as the health risks, associated with the patient's racial, ethnic, and cultural group must be considered.

During the interview, the nurse should avoid stereotyping the patient or depending too heavily on an "ideal," or normative, racial, ethnic, or cultural characteristic or trait. No single individual or family within a culture or subculture will display all of the characteristics representative of that culture, and normative summaries do not include all of the diversity that may be part of a given culture. An understanding of basic racial, ethnic, and cultural concepts associated with the conduct of culturally competent health assessments, however, can serve as a *guide* for the nurse.

BASIC CONCEPTS ASSOCIATED WITH CULTURALLY COMPETENT ASSESSMENTS

Culture

Culture is a learned and socially transmitted orientation and way of life of a group of people. Culture enables members of a group to find coherence and to survive in the world around them through the development of unique patterns of basic assumptions and shared meanings. The cultural beliefs, values, customs, and norms that result from these assumptions and meanings shape how the group members think, act, and relate to others, as well as how they perceive life in terms of time, space, health, illness, family, and of their roles as spouses, parents, workers, and community members. The beliefs, values, and norms of a cultural group are passed informally from one generation to another, exert a powerful force on all group members, and are very difficult to change (Figure 5-2).

Figure 5-2 Children often adopt the ways of the dominant culture while embracing elements of their parents' culture. © Dewitt Jones/CORBIS

Subculture

Subculture refers to membership in a smaller group within a larger culture. These smaller groups possess many of the values, beliefs, and customs of the larger culture but have unique characteristics in relation to age, education, marital status, preference in life partner, generational placement, occupation, socioeconomic level, health status, or religion. Membership in subcultures is generally involuntary and is not usually constrained by obvious physical characteristics such as skin colour, body build, or mannerisms.

Numerous subcultures exist within each culture. For example, an individual can be simultaneously a member of at least 13 subcultures: 50-year-old (generational), white (race), overweight (health status), Manitoban (regional), conservative (political value system), heterosexual (sexual preference), male (gender), nurse (occupation), father of two teenagers (family status), divorced and recently remarried (marital status), Baptist (religious affiliation), of Irish ancestry (genetic), and currently living in a metropolitan area (lifestyle). Each subculture influences to some degree the behaviour of its members, as does the primary culture.

It is important to recognize that every individual has a combination of cultural influences, derived from membership in the primary culture as well as multiple subcultures, which creates a **multicultural identity.** This unique multicultural identity makes it critical for the nurse to assess each patient in context rather than simply as a normative member of a single culture, subculture, race, ethnic, or minority group.

Racial Groups

Race classifies individuals based on the shared traits of skin tone, facial features, and body build, all of which are inherited from biological ancestors and are usually sufficiently obvious to warrant a member as being part of a specific racial group. The racial characteristics of some patients can have an impact on their health status; for example, the incidence of skin cancer in darkly pigmented individuals, who have a high level of melanin, is much lower than in light-skinned individuals. Nurses should therefore ask about the patient's self-identified racial group when performing a cultural assessment.

Ethnic Groups

Ethnic group members share a unique national or regional origin and social, cultural, and linguistic heritage. The most recent ethnic diversity survey of Canadians 15 years and older, conducted by Statistics Canada, revealed that 46% of Canadians reported only British (includes English, Scottish, Irish, Welsh and other British Isles origins), French, and/or Canadian ethnic origins.[6] Of this group, the majority (21%) cited British ethnicity, 10% French origins (including French Canadian), 8% Canadian only; and 7% were a mixture of British, French, and/or Canadian origins. The next largest stated ethnicity are people of European descent (21% of Canadians over 15), followed by Chinese and East Indian (13%). The remaining 20% cited mixed ethnic heritages. Interestingly, and some would say not surprisingly, many people with ancestry outside of Canada will cite that they are "Canadian" when asked about their ethnicity; for example, "I am Irish Canadian." In addition to identifying themselves as Canadian, people also note other identities, such as Québécois, Acadian, Newfoundlander, Maritimer, Westerner, Haida, Mi'kmaq, or Mohawk, to name a few.

Reflective Thinking

HIV-Positive Patient

You are working on an orthopedic unit and have just finished admitting a 26-year-old homosexual man who is HIV-positive. The patient sustained multiple lacerations and a compound fracture of his left femur when he was struck by a car running a red light. As you approach the nurses' station, you overhear some colleagues making homophobic remarks about the patient.

- What are your thoughts and feelings about working with this patient?
- How would you respond to what you have just overheard?
- How might you help your colleagues increase their cultural sensitivity and ensure the provision of culturally competent care for this patient?

Life 360°

Cultural Norms

Gather a group of colleagues from various cultures and subcultures. Make a composite list of what each believes to be general cultural norms within his or her culture or subculture. Then have each person generate a list of cultural norms from the following topics: breastfeeding in public, law and order, breakfast foods, home remedies for illness, common courtesies, smoking, and holiday celebrations. Compare your lists. What items are similar? What are the differences? Were there any surprises?

Nursing Tip

First generation and *second generation* (and so forth) are terms used to indicate ancestry when referring to a patient's ethnic background: A person who is first generation has at least one parent who was born outside Canada; a second generation family member has parents who were both born in Canada but whose grandparents were born outside Canada. Forty percent of Canadians are either first or second generation.

The importance that individuals place on the adherence to their ethnic or cultural background varies from person to person. Half of Canadians indicate that they have a strong sense of belonging to their ethnic group, particularly first-generation residents; for example, 78% of Filipinos, 65% of East Indians, 65% of Portuguese, 60% of French Canadians, 58% of Chinese, and 56% of Italians reported a strong sense of belonging to their ethnic group. Some ethnic groups who have been in Canada for many generations maintain the customs and traditions from their original homeland, such as 92% of Punjabis, 81% of Greeks, 79% of Filipinos, and 76% of Jamaicans.[7]

Ethnic identity, or self-identification with an ethnic group, is subjective and not always obvious. For example, Egyptians tend to identify with their country of origin, but Armenians born in a country such as Iran, and Palestinians born in countries such as Lebanon or Israel, identify with their respective cultures rather than their countries of origin.[8] When conducting a culturally competent assessment, therefore, it is appropriate to determine the patient's self-identified ethnic group as well as place of birth.

Minority Groups

Minority group members are individuals who are considered by themselves or by others to be members of a minority because they have a different racial, cultural, ethnic, gender, sexual orientation, or different socioeconomic level than do members of the dominant cultural group. Minority group members may receive different or unequal treatment and different degrees of acceptance from members of the dominant group. In Canada, visible minorities are more likely to feel uncomfortable or out of place than those who are Caucasian and "white" in colour. For example, 24% of Canadians of all visible minorities felt uncomfortable or out of place most or some of the time as a result of their visibly different characteristics. Unfortunately, 20% of visible minorities, particularly Blacks, feel they have been discriminated against or unfairly treated sometimes or often.[9]

Although members of a minority may not be a true minority worldwide, or within a given region, it is their membership in a subculture and the difference in the power they have to influence the dominant cultural environment that leads to their designation and subsequent treatment as a minority.

Values, Norms, and Value Orientations

Cultures and subcultures have a fundamental set of principles, known as values, that govern how each group member thinks, acts, and responds to the internal and external environment. **Cultural values** tend to be acquired subconsciously during the process of enculturation and are usually a fundamental, often unchanging, set of principles that serve to build an individual's beliefs, customs, goals, and aspirations.

Cultural norms are the often unwritten but generally understood prescriptions for acceptable behaviour in the various situations that group members encounter in their daily lives. Every group member is bound by these norms and may be criticized, punished, or ostracized by other group members when the norms are violated.

All cultures have a fundamental set of values and concurrent **value orientations;** that is, patterned principles that provide order and direction to individuals' thoughts and behaviours and help solve commonly occurring human problems.[10, 11, 12] Different cultures have five areas of unique value orientations (time, human nature, activity, relational, and people to nature) that have major relevance for culturally competent health assessments and care (Table 5-1).

TABLE 5-1 Basic Cross-Cultural Values, Value Orientations, and Beliefs

VALUE	VALUE ORIENTATION AND BELIEFS
Time What is the time orientation of human beings?	Past focus: Reverence for long-standing traditions Present focus: Live in "here and now," perceive time in a linear fashion. Future focus: Willing to defer gratification to ensure they can meet a future goal; tend to be disciplined in scheduling and using time.
Human Nature What is the basic nature of human beings?	Human beings are basically good. Human beings are evil but have a perfectible nature. Human beings are a combination of good and evil requiring self-control to perfect nature; lapses occasionally occur and are accepted. Human beings are neutral, neither good nor evil.
Activity What is the primary purpose of life?	Being orientation: Human beings' value resides in their inherent existence and spontaneity. Becoming-in-being orientation: Human beings' value is inherent but they must engage in continuous self-development as integrated wholes. Doing orientation: Human beings exist to be active and to achieve.
Relational What is the purpose of human relations?	Linear relationships: Welfare and goals of the hereditary and extended family are emphasized. Goals of the family take precedence over the individual's. Collateral relationships: Welfare and goals of social and family group are emphasized. Group goals take precedence. Individual relationships: Individual goals and accountability for own behaviour emphasized.
People to Nature What is the relationship of human beings to nature?	Human beings dominate nature and have control over their environment. Human beings live in harmony with nature and must maintain that balance. Human beings are subjugated to nature and have no control over their environment.

Source: *Compiled from information in Variations in* Value Orientations, *by K. Kluckhorn and F. Strodtbeck, 1961, Evanston, IL: Row, Peterson; and* Transcultural Nursing: Assessment and Intervention *(4th ed.), by J. N. Giger and R. E. Davidhizar, 2004, Baltimore: Mosby.*

Reflective Thinking

Fundamental Cultural Values

- What is your time orientation?
- What do you believe about the basic nature of human beings? What do you believe is your basic nature?
- What do you believe is your primary purpose in life?
- What do you believe about the purpose of human relations?
- What do you believe your relation is to nature and the supernatural?

Figure 5-3 Values, customs, and beliefs are shared by members of cultural and familial groups.

Beliefs

Cultural beliefs consist of the explanatory ideas and knowledge that members of a culture have about various aspects of the world, based on the group's cultural values and norms (Figure 5-3). Such beliefs influence the meaning individuals attach to health and illness, how they prefer to treat illness, and the health behaviours they engage in. Because health and illness are culturally determined, what is considered to be health or illness in one culture may not be the same in another. In addition, many cultures distinguish between a "**folk illness,**" believed to be caused by disharmony, an imbalance, or as punishment, and a "**scientific illness,**" in which the presence of pathology is the defining characteristic. In the case of a folk illness, a **folk practitioner** (a healer or other individual who is not part of the scientific health care system but is believed to have special knowledge or power to prevent, treat, or provide resources needed to heal folk illnesses) would be consulted because health care practitioners are not believed to be knowledgeable in recognizing or treating such illnesses.

Folk Illnesses

Two major types of folk illnesses are usually delineated: naturalistic and personalistic. **Naturalistic illnesses** are believed to be caused by an imbalance or disequilibrium between essentially impersonal factors. For example, the most common imbalance is between "hot" and "cold" (Table 5-2). Whether an illness and its treatment is classified as hot or cold is culturally determined and does not relate to the actual temperature of the patient or to the substances used to treat the illness. In general, "hot" illnesses are treated with "cold" substances, and vice versa, to restore the balance between the two. These beliefs are held by many Hispanic, Arab, and Asian ethnic groups and cultures. Although most cultures who share these beliefs use the hot and cold terminology, among traditional Chinese, these forces are called *yin* (cold) and *yang* (hot).

Understanding the health belief patterns of patients and the meanings attached to symptoms, illnesses, and treatments can be helpful in understanding those patients who refuse to participate in a given treatment regimen or insist on a specific treatment. For example, patients who believe in hot and cold conditions may insist on being given an antibiotic—considered to be a *caliente* (hot) treatment—for a viral upper respiratory infection (URI), which is considered to be a *frio* (cold) condition. Explanations about the lack of benefit in treating viral URIs with antibiotics and the potential for building a resistance when used unnecessarily may not dissuade patients who insist on its use. Substituting another substance such as vitamins, which are also considered to be hot treatments, shows an acceptance of the patient's beliefs and "does the least harm."

Reflective Thinking

Multicultural Identity

- What are the values and beliefs that most characterize each culture and subculture to which you belong? With which do you agree?
- Do any of your values and beliefs that are derived from membership in one culture or subculture conflict with those from any other?
- If there is any conflict between the values of two or more of the cultures or subcultures with which you identify (e.g., health care professional, religious, socioeconomic, political party), have you resolved these conflicts? If so, how did you do this and what helped you to reconcile these conflicts?

TABLE 5-2 Hot and Cold Conditions, Foods, and Treatments

HOT (Caliente/Yang) CONDITIONS
Constipation
Diarrhea
Fever
Hypertension
Infections
Kidney problems
Liver problems
Pregnancy
Skin rashes, sores
Sore throat
Ulcers

COLD (Frio/Yin) CONDITIONS
Cancer
Colds
Depression
Earache
Infertility
Headache
Joint pain
Lactation
Malaria
Menstruation
Paralysis
Pneumonia
Postpartum psychoses
Rheumatism
Stomach cramps
Teething
Tuberculosis

HOT (Caliente/Yang) FOODS
Aromatic beverages
Beans
Cereal grains
Cheese
Chili peppers
Chocolate
Eggs
Evaporated milk
Fried foods
Goat's milk
Hard liquor
Meats (beef, lamb, waterfowl)
Oils
Onions
Peas
Spicy, hot foods
Temperate-zone fruits (apples, grapes, pears, peaches)
Vinegar
Wine

COLD (Frio/Yin) FOODS
Barley water
Bean curds
Avocados
Bland foods
Bottled whole milk
Cashew nuts
Dairy products
Fresh vegetables (carrots, turnips, squash, eggplant)
Green vegetables
Honey
Meats (chicken, fish, goat)
Tropical fruits (bananas, grapefruits, mangos, oranges, pineapples)
Raisins

HOT (Caliente/Yang) MEDICINES AND HERBS
Anise
Aspirin
Castor oil
Cinnamon
Cod-liver oil
Garlic
Ginger root
Iron preparation
Penicillin
Tobacco
Vitamins

COLD (Frio/Yin) MEDICINES AND HERBS
Bicarbonate of soda
Linden
Milk of magnesia
Orange flower water
Sage

Source: Compiled from data obtained in *Contemporary Psychiatric-Mental Health Nursing,*[13] *Cultural Diversity in Health and Illness,*[14] and *Transcultural Nursing: Assessment and Intervention.*[15]

Personalistic illnesses are believed to occur because an individual has either committed some offense and is being punished, or because of another person's acts of aggression (sometimes unintentional). Witchcraft and the "evil eye" are two sources of personalistic illnesses. More often than not, witchcraft is used to punish individuals for an emotional or a physical injury, an illness, or a death they are thought to have caused, or occasionally because they possess something that is coveted by another. In general, the evil eye is given unintentionally, for example, by complimenting a child unprotected by an amulet, gold cross, or other protective device or by not touching the child while offering the compliment. The fear is that the child unprotected by an amulet will lose her good looks or may develop a severe headache, restlessness, irritability, high fever, diarrhea, weight loss, or sleeplessness if the person complimenting the child was not touching the child at the time.

Self-Care Practices

All cultural groups use a variety of self-care practices that may include the use of "folk medicine" and remedies. Group members may also aid in their own health promotion and maintenance. For example, a person of Vietnamese origins may use *cao gio* (rubbing the skin with a coin) to treat diseases believed to be caused by wind entering the body (e.g., URIs). After applying an ointment on the skin over the affected body area (chest, shoulders, upper back), the edge of the coin is moved along the skin until ecchymotic stripes appear, demonstrating that the treatment is successful. *Cao gio* is rarely painful or injurious, and more often than not the recipient perceives the treatment to be helpful. Finding these areas of ecchymosis, however, can lead to the erroneous diagnosis of abuse if knowledge of this folk remedy is lacking.

Customs and Rituals

Customs and rituals are culturally learned behaviours that are much easier to observe or learn about through interviewing than are the values and beliefs on which the customs and rituals are based. **Customs** are frequent or common practices carried out by tradition and include communication patterns, family and kinship relations, work patterns, dietary and religious practices, and health behaviours. **Cultural rituals** are highly structured and prescribed patterns of behaviour used by a cultural group to respond to or in anticipation of specific life events such as birth, death, illness, healing, marriage, and worship.

Communication Patterns

Communication patterns are the means through which members of a cultural group transmit and preserve the values, beliefs, norms, and practices of their culture. Communication practices reflect, determine, and ultimately mould the culture by using both verbal and nonverbal means of expressing or concealing thoughts and feelings.

In some cultures the expression of thoughts and feelings is open and dramatic with frequent touching and sharing of territorial space, whereas other cultures may regard such open expression as unacceptable. For example, among Southeastern Asians, avoiding confrontation is considered positive and expressing annoyance, anger, or hatred is negative. In addition, many new immigrants from East Africa and Southeast Asia may find the immediate, social pleasantness and friendliness of the Canadian health care provider confusing or offensive when they realize that such behaviours do not reflect the personal intimacy and friendship that such behaviours would signify in their own cultures.

Although the process of communication is universal, the intonation, rhythm, speed, use of silence, facial expressions, eye and head movements, body posture, touch, styles and types of feedback, as well as other "rules" for communication may be culturally unique. For example, unlike people in Western cultures, Bulgarians

> ## Nursing Tip
>
> **Overcoming Language Barriers**
>
> Special approaches for overcoming language barriers:
> - Speak slowly and distinctly in a normal tone.
> - Use gestures or pictures to illustrate meaning.
> - Avoid clichés, jargon, and value-laden terms.
> - Avoid defensive or offensive body language.
> - Obtain feedback to confirm accurate understanding.
> - Provide reading material written in the appropriate language.
> - Use a culturally sensitive interpreter with fluency in health care terminology.
> - Speak to the patient, rather than to the interpreter.
> - Use the same interpreter for each interaction.

nod their head to indicate "no" and move their head back and forth to indicate "yes." In other cultures, a "yes" response may be indicated in some other way, such as among Tongans, who raise their eyebrows to indicate "yes." Sometimes a verbal "yes" may actually mean "no." For example, when Tunisians say "yes *N'sha'llah*" (God willing), it reflects the belief that only God has control over the future, and, therefore, can mean "no."

Many communication variables are culture specific and may include the value placed on eye contact, proximity to others, role of small talk, direct versus nondirect questioning, topic taboos or topics the patient is reluctant to talk about, as well as who makes health decisions for family members in a given culture.

Cultural Meaning of Symptoms

One of the most important techniques when performing a culturally competent health assessment is to make every effort to discover the cultural meaning of the patient's perceptions and to encourage the patient to communicate interpretations of health, illness, and symptoms. When people experience pain or other symptoms associated with illness, they interpret the symptoms and react to them in ways that fit their cultural norms. The nurse should try to discover the cultural meaning the patient gives to symptoms and attempt to elicit statements about symptoms the patient considers to be significant or expects as being part of life.

In addition, each culture has its own system for communicating the distress associated with illness. For example, some cultures value enduring pain stoically and expect this behaviour from both children and adults. In contrast, others use expressive reactions to communicate distress, especially chronic pain, but may not show or describe the pain to their families and closest friends. To discover the cultural meaning that a patient attaches to symptoms, Wenger proposes that nurses use a bidirectional translation process.[16] This method of ascribing cultural meaning involves collecting the patient's symptom statements and analyzing them in the context of meanings and thought patterns that are shared by other members of the patient's culture. As the patient communicates these meanings, link this cultural knowledge to the health care practices and therapeutic regimens that are perceived to be the most culturally congruent and efficacious. Listen to the patient's symptom descriptions, reflect on the meaning the patient seems to attach to the symptoms, and allow the patient time to determine if the reflected inferred-meaning statement accurately reflects the patient's own reality. Then restate and restructure the inferred meaning until the patient validates its accuracy.

Language Barriers

In seeking clarification of the meaning patients attach to their illness experiences, it is important to accurately identify and then remove or overcome any language barriers that may exist. A variety of language barriers can exist even between two people who speak the same language. The barriers may be due to different connotative meanings for words, the use of clichés or value-laden terms, a reliance on jargon specific to an individual's age or background, the complexity of the sentence structure, and the meanings attached to body language.

Family and Kinship Relations

Transculturally, family and kinship patterns are linear, collateral, or individualistic. A linear family pattern usually consists of the nuclear family in addition to hereditary, linearly extended family members such as grandparents, aunts, uncles, and cousins. The welfare, continuity, and goals of the hereditary family take precedence over those of the individual family member. The linear family is typically patriarchal, emphasizes the enculturation of children, and greatly respects elder family members.

Among families in which collateral patterns are the norm, the welfare and goals of the lateral group members, such as the families of siblings and close peers as well as the nuclear family, are important, and an individual's goals are subordinate to those of the social family group. These families tend to socialize primarily within their social family group, are generally open in their expressions of friendship, and highly value their children (Figure 5-4). Although the male is usually the head of the family responsible for activities outside the home, women also play a major role in decision making, particularly in relation to child-rearing and caring.

In cultures in which the individualistic, nuclear family pattern is prevalent, the individual family member's goals take precedence, and self-responsibility and accountability for one's own behaviour are the norm. There is less respect for authority figures and less respect and sense of responsibility for elder family members, though generosity in times of crises is characteristic. Sharing of parental responsibilities between parents is common.

Societal changes, such as increasing rates of divorce and remarriage, increasing numbers of couples choosing to get married but waiting until they become established in their careers before having children, or choosing not to get married or not to have children, increasing numbers of couples who work to pay for the basics, increasing numbers of singles people choosing to have or adopt children, and increasing support for and recognition of same-sex unions and adoption of children, are leading to many different family configurations. These configurations include blended families, single-parent families, intergenerational families, same-sex families, multiracial families, and foster families (Figure 5-5). Understanding the patient's family characteristics and configuration is essential in determining who needs to be involved in health care decisions and taught about providing the health care needed by the patient.

When assessing the family, kinship, and work patterns, it is important to determine the family's actual structure. It may be helpful to draw a genogram (Figure 5-7) and an ecomap (Figure 5-6). An **ecomap** is a diagram depicting a person's relationship with his or her family, friends, peers, neighbours, and work associates, noting those with whom the patient has the most frequent contact and their relative importance to the patient.

Cultural Assessment

To guide your cultural health assessment of patients and families, refer to Table 5-3. The assessment should be tailored to those areas having a direct impact on the patient's immediate health status.

Figure 5-4 Sharing meals together is often an important family function.

Figure 5-5 Families come in many shapes and configurations.

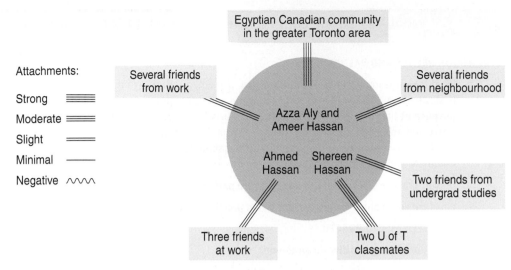

Figure 5-6 Ecomap of Shereen's Friends.

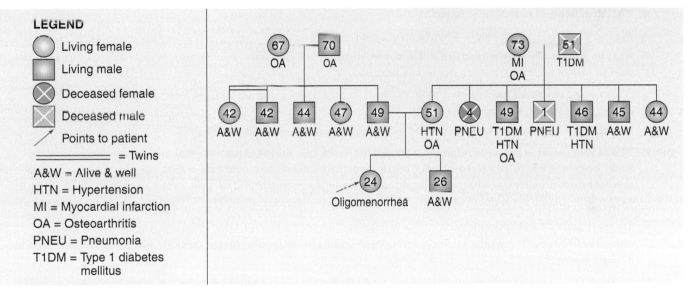

Figure 5-7 Genogram: Hassan Family.

TABLE 5-3   Echols-Armstrong Cultural Assessment Tool (EACAT)

Directions: The questions in bold print are recommended for use during the initial contact with the patient. The remaining items can be used if time permits or if examples are needed to prompt the patient's replies. If a long-term health care relationship or prolonged hospitalization and/or home care is anticipated, it is advisable to complete all remaining questions during subsequent encounters.

1. **ETHNIC GROUP AFFILIATION AND RACIAL BACKGROUND**

   a. **Would you tell me how long you have lived here in _____?**

   b. **Where are you from originally?** (or Where were you born? or Where were your parents or grandparents born and raised?)

   c. **With which particular ethnic group would you say you identify?** (Chinese, Vietnamese, Arab, Black, Filipino, Aboriginal, etc.) **How closely do you identify with this ethnic group or combination of ethnic groups?**

   d. **Where have you lived and when? What health problems did you experience or were you exposed to when you lived in each place? What helped you recover from each of the health problems identified?**

continues

TABLE 5-3   Echols-Armstrong Cultural Assessment Tool (EACAT) *continued*

2. MAJOR BELIEFS AND VALUES

a. What is your primary **time orientation:** past, present, or future? What do you believe is the **basic nature of human beings:** basically good; evil but can be perfected; good and evil requiring self-control; or neither good nor evil? What is the primary **purpose of life:** just to be whatever one is; to be who one is while striving for self-improvement; or to exist to be constantly active and achieving, striving for excellence? What is the **purpose of human relations?** Whose goals should take precedence: the family, the community, or the individual? What should be the **relationship between human beings and nature:** humans dominate and control nature; live in harmony with nature; or be subjugated to nature with no control over it?

b. Do you practise any special activities that are part of your cultural traditions?

c. What are your values, beliefs, customs, and practices related to education, work, and leisure?

3. HEALTH BELIEFS AND PRACTICES

a. **What does being healthy mean to you?**

b. What do you believe promotes being healthy?

c. **What do you do to help you stay healthy?** (hygiene, immunizations, self-care practices such as OTC drugs, herbal drinks, special foods, wearing charms)

d. **What does being ill or sick mean to you?**

e. What do you believe causes illness? What do you believe caused your illness?

f. **What do you usually do when you are sick or not feeling well?** (self-care and home remedies, herbal remedies, healing rituals, wearing medals or charms, prayers, rely on folk healers)

g. When you are sick or not feeling well, who do you go to for help? How helpful are they and for what type of problems?

h. Who determines when you are and when you are not sick? Who cares for you at home when you are sick? **Who do you want to be with when you are sick?** Who do you want to be with you when you are in the hospital?

i. **Who in your family is primarily responsible for making health care decisions** (such as when to go to someone outside the family for help, where to go, who to see, what help to accept), **who should be taught how to deal with your** (or your loved one's) **specific health problems** (or what can be taught about how to prevent problems)?

j. What do you believe about mental illness, chronic disease, handicapping conditions, pain, dying, and death?

k. **Are there any cultural or ethnic sanctions or restrictions** (related to the expression of emotions and feelings, privacy, exposure of body parts, response to illness, certain types of surgery, or certain types of medical treatments) **that you want to or must observe?**

l. **By whom do you prefer to have your health and medical care provided: a nurse, physician, or other health care provider? Do you prefer they have the same cultural background** (or be the same age) **or gender as your own?**

4. LANGUAGE BARRIERS AND COMMUNICATION STYLES

a. What language(s) or dialect(s) do you speak or read? Which one do you speak most frequently? Where? (home, work, with friends) **In which language are you most comfortable communicating?**

b. How well do you understand spoken and written English? French? **Do you need an interpreter when discussing health care information and treatments?** Is there a relative or friend you would prefer to have interpret? Is there anyone you do not want to interpret?

c. **Are there special ways of showing respect or disrespect in your culture?**

d. **Are there any cultural preferences or restrictions related to touching, social distance, making eye contact, or other verbal or nonverbal behaviours when communicating?**

e. Are there culturally appropriate forms of greeting, parting, initiating or terminating an exchange, topic restrictions, or times to visit?

5. ROLE OF THE FAMILY, SPOUSAL RELATIONSHIP, AND PARENTING STYLES

a. **What is the composition of your family? Who is considered to be a member of your family?** (Include a genogram and an ecomap if needed.)

b. **With what ethnic group(s) does your family as a whole** (parents, aunts, uncles, cousins) **identify?** How do their ethnic identity and traditions affect the decision-making processes of your own family? **How does their ethnic identity, and which of their ethnic traditions, do you think most affect their health status?**

TABLE 5-3   Echols-Armstrong Cultural Assessment Tool (EACAT)   *continued*

   c. Which of your relatives live nearby? With which of your family members and relatives do you interact the most often?

   d. How do each of your family members, relatives, and you and your significant other interact in relation to chores, mealtimes, child care, recreation, and other family-oriented responsibilities? Are you satisfied with these interactional patterns?

   e. What are the major events that are most important to your family (marriage, birth, holidays, religious ceremonies), and how are they celebrated?

   f. What are your family's goals for the health and well-being of the family as a group? What dreams do they have for the family's future? Do they work together as a family unit or individually to achieve these goals and dreams? What barriers do they see that might inhibit the accomplishment of these goals and dreams?

   g. In what ways do your family members believe the nurse, physician, and other health care practitioners can help the family members achieve their goals and dreams for health and well-being of the family?

   h. With what social (church, community, work, recreation) groups does your family interact, and what is the nature of their social contact and social support?

   i. Are there special beliefs and customs practised by your family related to marriage, conception, pregnancy, childbirth, breast feeding, baptism, child care (including attitude toward children, discipline, showing affection), puberty, separation, divorce, health, illness, and death?

   j. What are the family members' health and social history, including health habits, recent major stress events, work patterns, participation in religion, community activities, and recreation patterns?

6. RELIGIOUS INFLUENCES OR SPECIAL RITUALS (See original document).

7. DIETARY PRACTICES (See original document).

CASE STUDY   A Young Woman with Oligomenorrhea

This case study illustrates the application and objective documentation of the cultural assessment.

Ms. Shereen Hassan is a 24 yo woman originally from Egypt. She presents for the first time to the women's clinic $\bar{c}$ oligomenorrhea of 4 mos duration. Shereen's menses onset at age 14 yrs was accompanied by primary dysmenorrhea. Treatment $\bar{c}$ NSAIDs such as ibuprofen & naproxen brought some relief. In university she began to use exercise (jogging & swimming) in addition to NSAIDs to successfully minimize her dysmenorrhea. At present Shereen is a competitive long-distance runner as well as a full-time doctoral student. Shereen's mother accompanies her.

CULTURAL ASSESSMENT

1. Ethnic group affiliation and racial background

   a. Would you tell me how long you have lived here in Toronto?
   Pt has lived here since entering her doctoral program in biology at University of Toronto 3 yrs ago.

   b. Where are you and your parents from originally?
   Pt born & raised in Mississauga, Ontario. Her parents, Azza Aly (mother) & Ameer Hassan (father) were born in Egypt & originally came to Canada at the ages of 20 & 22 yrs, respectively, to attend graduate school. Parents met & married $\bar{c}$ agreement of their respective families. Became Canadian citizens 8 yrs later. Both parents work at local university.

continues

c. **With which particular ethnic group would you say you identify and how closely do you identify with this ethnic group or combination of ethnic groups?**
"I see myself as Egyptian Canadian. I embrace both cultures & have walked a very delicate line all my life . . . I believe there is more emphasis on being modest & compliant because of my Egyptian roots compared to my friends whose parents were born in Canada. (Shereen directs a big smile toward her mother.) Her mother states "the biggest challenge facing Egyptian parents in North America is to raise a daughter c̄ Egyptian values while living in the sexually "freer" society. Showing respect (*ihteram*) & deference to the wishes of parents & politeness (*adab*) to all elders & those in authority are expected of our children, especially daughters. Egyptian children, especially daughters, are expected to involve their parents in all decisions, whether large or small, & regardless of topic, but most certainly educational & health matters even when married."

d. **Where have you lived and when? What health problems did you experience or were you exposed to when you lived in each place? What helped you recover from each of these health problems?**
"I have lived in the Toronto region all my life. I was never sick as a child or teenager except for dysmenorrhea that started when I was 14." Pt's primary dysmenorrhea was relieved c̄ NSAIDS in high school & c̄ NSAIDS & exercise in university. 3 yrs ago she was accepted in the doctoral program in biology at University of Toronto. Pt began to train & participate in women's long-distance running races under the coaching of a track & field athletic trainer. When the athletic trainer took a leave 7 mos ago, pt & her friends continued to train, "stepping it up a notch," s̄ getting another coach. When pt acknowledged to her mother last weekend that she had been experiencing some oligomenorrhea over the past 4 mos, her mother insisted she be evaluated medically. Her mother states "I want her to excel at anything she does, but no Egyptian man will consent to marry an infertile woman!"

2. Major beliefs and values

a. **What are some of the traditions, values, and beliefs that are most important in your culture?**
Time orientation: "The Egyptian side of me says that planning ahead is to potentially defy God. But my Canadian side knows the importance of planning for the future & living today in a way that will ensure a happy life ahead of me."

Basic nature of human beings: "As a Muslim I do not believe in 'sins' in the same way some of my friends do. I believe that human beings are born pure & that it is not until we reach adolescence that we are held accountable for sins or bad deeds."

Primary purpose of life: "I believe in continuous self-improvement which is why I am going to school. My parents view is that a 'good daughter' will marry & put her whole heart into raising healthy & successful children."

Purpose of human relations: "We believe strongly in the traditional nuclear family. We value sticking together. The goals & honour of our family always take precedence over the individual."

Relationship between human beings and nature: "Muslim Egyptians believe that whatever happens is by God's will (*Iinshalla*). Humans may share control over nature c̄ God, but God has ultimate control over the universe. He created the earth so human beings could use it & benefit from it to fulfill His plan."

3. Health beliefs and practices

a. **What does being healthy mean to you?**
"For me being healthy means being able to meet all my responsibilities & obligations to my family & school. Muslim women generally view health as a blessing from God. An illnesses or diseases may be considered God's will & a person's fate. I believe illness is a test of a human being's patience. I think people need to stay fit & follow a healthy diet."

b. **What do you do to help you stay healthy?**
In addition to her exercise regimen, pt also tries to eat a wholesome, mostly vegetarian diet, but when she returns to her parents' home at least 2 weekends a mo, she "just lets go & eats everything. No one can cook the best of both worlds like my mother!" Pt is up-to-date on all her immunizations.

c. **What do you usually do when you are sick or not feeling well?**
Pt uses OTC medicines for things like colds, muscle strain, & upset stomach. "If it is something really affecting my life or extremely painful, I see a doctor. When we have an illness, it is expected that the family will relieve us of our responsibilities so that we can focus energy on getting better. Some people have a problem with this idea but we view it as supporting recovery."

d. Who do you want to be with when you are sick and who in your family is primarily responsible for making health care decisions?

"My family insists on knowing how I feel at all times. When I am ill, my mother expects to look after me. My father & mother will make decisions on my behalf if I am not able to."

e. Are there any cultural or ethnic sanctions or restrictions that you want to or must observe?

"I believe most Egyptian Canadian women tend to be modest & private about sexuality. Health providers should explain why they are doing something. Though I do not think this approach would be any different for any other woman regardless of origins! Like most women, I prefer if my body is covered rather than left exposed for everyone to see."

f. By whom do you prefer to have your health and medical care provided and do you prefer they have the same cultural background or gender as your own?

"My parents hold to every word the doctor says; I question much more than they would. They grew up not to challenge authority but I am different—if I want to know something then I will question it. My parents say this is arguing with authority but I say it is what is expected in Canada. I don't mind having a male or female doctor or nurse but my mother will never go to a male doctor."

4. Language barriers and communication styles

a. In which language are you most comfortable communicating?

"I am fluent in English & Egyptian-Arabic & can speak a bit of French."

b. Are there special ways of showing respect or disrespect in your culture or any cultural preferences or restrictions related to touching, social distance, making eye contact, or other verbal or nonverbal behaviours when communicating?

"It is always appropriate among Egyptian Canadians to smile, make direct eye contact, & even touch frequently & warmly when in same sex groups c̄ people they trust. Between genders, communication is different in that restraint, sometimes to the point of a flat affect, is expected between the sexes. It is believed that the truth of a person's words & intent is seen in a person's eyes. 'Showing too much interest' can compromise a woman's reputation & honour &, therefore, her family's honour as well. Direct or intense eye contact in a business or professional situation, however, implies honesty & sincerity."

5. Role of the family, spousal relationship, and parenting styles

a. What is the composition of your family? Who is considered to be a member of your family?

"My brother & I as well as our parents are the only ones in Canada; we keep in close phone or e-mail contact with my aunts & uncles in Egypt. We go back every two years."

b. With what ethnic group(s) does your family as a whole identify? How does their ethnic identity and which of their ethnic traditions do you think most affect their health status?

See above.

c. In what ways do your family members believe the nurse, physician, and other health care practitioners can help your family members achieve their goals and dreams for the health and well-being of the family?

"The main thing is to respect the cultural ways already noted."

d. With what social (church, community, work, recreation) groups does your family interact and what is the nature of their social contact and social support?

"My parents friends are mostly other Egyptian Canadians in this area. I have friends of all nationalities though my family would be upset if I did not marry someone from our religion or background. I'm expected to call home every day to speak with my parents. They expect me to come home at least 2×/mo for the full weekend. My brother, being male, is not expected to talk c̄ my parents but 1 or 2×/wk & visit my parents home 1×/mo. My brother & I talk on the phone maybe 2–3×/wk, but if we get too busy, we try to touch base at least 1×/wk."

e. What are the family members' health and social history, including health habits, recent major stress events, work patterns, participation in religion, community interaction, and recreation patterns?

Family members' health: Maternal grandparents have osteoarthritis; 2 aunts & 3 uncles are alive & well. Paternal grandmother has osteoarthritis & has had a myocardial infarction; 1 aunt is alive & well; 2 paternal

continues

uncles have Type 1 diabetes & hypertension; 1 aunt & 1 uncle died in childhood from pneumonia. Paternal grandfather died at 56 yr from complications of Type 1 diabetes.

Recreation patterns: Pt is, as noted above, a competitive long-distance runner & spends her free time training c̄ 2 friends. Her brother is a skillful tennis player & swimmer who exercises at least 2 ×/wk & on weekends. Pt's parents rarely engage in sports activities, but until now have been supportive of their children's participation.

6. Religious influences or special rituals

"We are Muslim, we live our faith."

7. Dietary practices

Egyptian diet (↑ fruits/vegetables, grains, ↑ sodium)

Note: Compiled using information from Meleis[17] and Swearingen.[18]

REVIEW QUESTIONS

1. When an individual perceives his or her own cultural group and cultural values, beliefs, norms, and customs are superior to all others, it is called:
   a. Acculturation
   b. Cultural relativism
   c. Enculturation
   d. Ethnocentrism
   The correct answer is (d).

2. The belief that illness occurs because an individual comes in contact with polluting agents (bad food, blood, contaminated water) is a:
   a. Folk illness
   b. Naturalistic illness
   c. Metaphysical illness
   d. Scientific illness
   The correct answer is (b).

3. Mrs. Anne Fraizer Hillson is a 35-year-old registered nurse from Manitoba who attends the Anglican Church, votes Conservative, and belongs to a hiking club. When assessing Mrs. Hillson, health professionals should do so within the context of the above-mentioned cultural influences that make up her:
   a. Ethnic identity
   b. Value orientation
   c. Cultural orientation
   d. Multiculturalism
   The correct answer is (d).

4. Value orientations:
   a. Consist of explanatory ideas and knowledge that members of a given culture have about various aspects of their world
   b. Are culturally learned behaviours associated with a specific culture and include communication patterns, family relations, work patterns, and health practices
   c. Consist of the subjective sense of ethnic definition or social orientation with which an individual self-identifies
   d. Are patterned principles about time, human nature, activity, family relations, and nature that provide order and give direction to individuals' thoughts and behaviours
   The correct answer is (d).

5. In collateral families, men are the head of the family but women play a major role in decision making, and an emphasis is placed on the goals of the:
   a. Adults over those of children
   b. Children over those of adults
   c. Group over those of individuals
   d. Individual members over those of the group
   The correct answer is (c).

Visit the Estes online companion resource at www.healthassessment.nelson.com **for additional content and study aids.**

REFERENCES

[1]Statistics Canada. *Annual population statistics 2005.* Retrieved June 13, 2006, from http://www.edrs.mcgill.ca/StatCan/Demog/ Data/Report/2005/DEMOG_E.PDF

[2]Canadian Nurses Association. *Position statement: Promoting culturally competent care.* Retrieved June 11, 2006, from

http://www.cna-nurses.ca/CNA/documents/pdf/publications/PS73_Promoting_Culturally_Competent_Care_March_2004_e.pdf

[3] Statistics Canada. *Proportion of foreign-born, Canada, provinces and territories, 1991, 1996 and 2001.* Retrieved June 14, 2006, from http://www12.statcan.ca/english/census01/products/analytic/companion/etoimm/provs.cfm#diversity_varied

[4] Ibid.

[5] Statistics Canada—Canadian Heritage. (2005). *Population projections of visible minority groups, Canada, provinces, and regions 2001–2017.* Ottawa. Retrieved June 14, 2006, from http://www.statcan.ca/english/freepub/91-541-XIE/91-541-XIE2005001.pdf

[6] Statistics Canada. Housing, Family and Social Statistics. (2003). *Ethnic diversity survey: Portrait of a multicultural society.* Catalogue number 89-593-XIE. Ottawa, ON: Statistics Canada.

[7] Statistics Canada. (2003). *Canada's ethnocultural portrait: The changing mosaic.* Retrieved June 16, 2006, from http://www12.statcan.ca/english/census01/products/analytic/companion/etoimm/pdf/96F0030XIE2001008.pdf

[8] Meleis, A., Lipson, J., & Paul, S. (1992). Ethnicity and health among five Middle Eastern immigrant groups. *Nursing Research, 41*(2), 98–103

[9] Statistics Canada—Canadian Heritage. *Population projections of visible minority groups, Canada, provinces, and regions 2001–2017,*

[10] Giger, J. N., & Davidhizar, R. E. (2004). *Transcultural nursing: Assessment and intervention.* (4th ed.). Baltimore: Mosby.

[11] Kluckhorn, K. & Strodtbeck, F. (1961). *Variations in value orientations.* Evanston, IL: Row, Peterson.

[12] Spector, R. E. (2004). *Cultural diversity in health and illness* (6th ed.). Upper Saddle River, NJ: Prentice Hall Health.

[13] Kneisl, C. R., Wilson, H. S., & Trigoboff. (2003). *Contemporary psychiatric-mental health nursing.* Upper Saddle River, NJ: Prentice Hall.

[14] Spector, *Cultural diversity in health and illness.* (6th ed.). Upper Saddle River, NJ: Prentice Hall Health.

[15] Giger & Davidhizar, *Transcultural nursing: Assessment and intervention.*

[16] Wenger, A. F. Z. (1993). Cultural meaning of symptoms. *Holistic Nursing Practice, 7*(2), 22–35.

[17] Meleis, A. (2003). Egyptians. In P. Hill, J. G. Lipson, & A. I. Meleis, *Caring for women cross-culturally* (pp. 123–41). Philadelphia: F. A. Davis.

[18] Swearingen, P. L. (Ed.). (2004). *All-in-one care planning resource: Medical-surgical, pediatric, maternity, and psychiatric nursing care plans.* Philadelphia: Mosby.

BIBLIOGRAPHY

Anderson, J. M. (2005). The conundrums of binary categories: Critical inquiry through the lens of postcolonial feminist humanism. *Canadian Journal of Nursing Research, 36*(4), 11–16.

Anderson, J., Perry, J., Blue, C., Browne, A., Henderson, A. B., Khan, K., Kirkham, S. R., Lunam, J., Semeniuk, P., & Smye, V. (2003). "Rewriting" cultural safety within the postcolonial and postnational feminist project toward new epistemologies of healing. *Advances in Nursing Science, 26*(3), 196–214.

Andrews, M. M., & Boyle, J. S. (2002). *Transcultural concepts in nursing care* (4th ed.). Philadelphia: J. B. Lippincott.

Leininger, M. M., & McFarland, M.R. (2006). *Culture care diversity and universality: A worldwide nursing theory* (2nd ed.). Sudbury, MA: Jones & Bartlett.

Munoz, C., & Luckmann, J. (2005). *Transcultural communication in nursing* (2nd ed.). Clifton Park, NY: Thomson Delmar Learning.

Shearer, R., & Davidhizar, R. (2003). Using role-play to develop cultural competence. *Journal of Nursing Education, 42*(6), 273–76.

Wu, Z., Penning, M. J., & Schimmele, C. M. (2005). Immigrant status and unmet health care needs. *Canadian Journal of Public Health, 96*(5), 369–73.

WEB RESOURCES

Aboriginal Nurses Association of Canada
http://www.anac.on.ca/

Assembly of First Nations
http://www.afn.ca/

Canadian Council for Refugees
http://www.web.ca/ccr/

International Health Resources
http://www.ih.ualberta.ca/handbook/cultural_organizations.html

Transcultural Nursing Society
http://www.tcns.org/

NEL

CHAPTER 6

Spiritual Assessment

COMPETENCIES

1. Describe how different spiritual beliefs might influence the patient's view of health, growth and development, illness, and death.

2. Conduct a spiritual assessment on the patient.

3. Identify the indicators that might mean the patient is experiencing spiritual distress.

4. Formulate nursing interventions that promote the patient's spiritual well-being.

5. Identify your personal spiritual beliefs and how they affect your nursing care.

*N*ursing assessment of the spiritual aspects of health and illness is an important element of providing care that is accurate and relevant in any patient care situation. There are many proposed links between spirituality and such outcomes as quality of life, general health status, abilities to find meaning and to cope with difficult situations, and dealing with death and dying issues. If nurses are to address all aspects of a patient's health and well-being, often referred to as **holistic** nursing, then spirituality in patient care must be addressed.

SPIRITUALITY AND RELIGION

There is a range of definitions of **spirituality;** however, most involve a relationship to something that is intensely personal and goes beyond the physiological and psychological to the existential search for meaning and purpose of life and all of its complexities. Spirituality generally integrates values and ultimate concern with oneself, one's relationship with a higher power, and the surrounding environment. Spirituality involves the search for the sacred, such as a divine being, or the ultimate reality or truth. For many, health is a concern, but it may not be the primary concern. Factors such as leaving behind a good reputation, passing on morals to the next generation, being in a good relationship with a higher power, and being in harmony with the forces in the universe may be a main concern for the patient and could therefore drive the patient's health care choices.

By contrast, **religion** is an organized system of beliefs usually centred around the worship of a supernatural force or being, which in turn defines the self and the self's purpose in life. Religion exists in group form over time and is a tradition of shared beliefs. Although many variances may exist among believers within any given religion, there are common threads uniting the followers. A religious system of beliefs can be highly organized and include **rituals,** which often are solemn, and ceremonial acts that reinforce faith. **Faith** is the assent to the truth of the beliefs and may also refer to the total orientation of the self's entire life to the belief structure. **Dogma** refers to the beliefs of the religion that are so essential to the identity of the religion that to deny them is to deny the religion itself. Religions also include **codes of ethics,** which are codified beliefs and lists of mandatory or prohibited acts that help define the self's relation to the object of worship.

Although many people might use the terms *spirituality* and *religion* interchangeably, with the changing role of religion in North America, the trend is toward viewing these concepts as distinct. With a steady increase in the numbers of Canadians, especially those under 40, reporting no religious affiliation (16.2% of all Canadians in 2001 compared to 12.3% a decade earlier, and only 1% in 1971[1]), it would be erroneous to state that these people are not "spiritual." Some authors argue that while association with formalized religion may be declining across Canada, spirituality is flourishing.[2] In fact, in the most recent Canadian Community Health Survey, more than 60 to 70% of residents in a range of geographical locations across Canada indicated that spirituality was moderately to very important to them.[3] As nurses embrace spirituality as a universal phenomenon with a range of individual expressions, rather than formalized religion, we "attempt to transcend ideological and theological differences among religious groups, thereby establishing a common ground for discussion."[4]

The relationship between spirituality and religion is illustrated in Figure 6-1. One can be spiritual without being religious. Although spirituality lies at the heart of many religions, a person can be religious without being spiritual. For example, a particular Jewish person may fulfill religious obligations

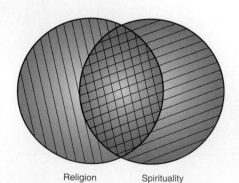

Religion   Spirituality

Figure 6-1 The Relationship between Religion and Spirituality.

to attend temple and participate in required rituals without believing in or worshipping Yahweh, which is the central tenet of the religion. The religion may have no impact on this person's behaviour or outlook on life and may not help define what is important to that person.

In addition, an individual can be both spiritual and religious, by participating in a religion and by holding its spiritual core at the centre of the individual's being, actions, and beliefs. For example, a Catholic who believes in God and worships God in the manner specified by Catholicism, and whose belief in God is manifested in thought, actions, purpose, and identity, may exhibit the properties of both religion and spirituality.

Religions in Canada

The pluralistic nature of Canadian society means that a nurse is likely to meet clients from a range of religious backgrounds who have inherent spiritual beliefs. (Table 6-1) Over 77% of Canadians describe themselves as Christian, with the majority being Catholic, followed by Protestant and then Christian Orthodox. Other predominant religious groups include Muslim (2%), Jewish (1.1%), Buddhist (1%), Hindu (1%), and Sikh (0.9%).[5] Although the majority of Canada's Aboriginal population is Christian, more and more are turning to their heritage for traditional spiritual beliefs and practices.[6] Owing to immigration trends, particularly in large cities across Canada, there is a much wider variety of religions and spiritualities than was encountered even 10 years ago.

The following are some interesting trends in the religious affiliations of Canadians.[7]

- Seven out of 10 Canadians identify themselves as Roman Catholic or Protestant, with a slight drop in Catholics from 1991 to 2001 and a significant drop in Protestants* from 35% to 29% in the same time period. The latter represents a drop of about 8.7 million people. (*Excludes the Baptist, Adventist, and Hutterite dominations that experienced increases.)
- More and more Canadians are referring to themselves as "Christians" rather than specifying a particular religion—possibly indicating an acceptance of the spiritual aspects but not the rituals prescribed by the dominant religions in this group.

TABLE 6-1 Top 10 Religious Denominations, Canada, 2001		
	Number	%
Roman Catholic	12,793,125	43.2
No religion	4,796,325	16.2
United Church	2,839,125	9.6
Anglican	2,035,495	6.9
Christian, not included elsewhere*	780,450	2.6
Baptist	729,475	2.5
Lutheran	606,590	2.0
Muslim	579,640	2.0
Protestant, not included elsewhere**	549,205	1.9
Presbyterian	409,830	1.4

*Includes persons who report "Christian," as well as those who report "Apostolic," "Born-again Christian," and "Evangelical."
**Includes persons who report only "Protestant."

Source: From the Statistics Canada publication "Religions in Canada, 2001 Census," Catalogue 96F0030XIE2001015, released May 13, 2003, URL: http://www12.statcan.ca/english/census01/Products/Analytic/companion/rel/canada.cfm.

- Half of adult Canadians engage in religious activities on their own rather than follow traditional "church going" practices, indicating that attendance at religious services may not be an accurate indicator of religiosity.[8]
- Fewer and fewer Canadians are attending religious services, and those who do are going less often. Between 1986 and 2001, there was a drop of 8% in the number of people (over 15 years of age) who attended weekly religious services. It is expected that the most recent 2006 survey will indicate further reductions once data are analyzed.
- The number of Canadians reporting Greek and Ukrainian Orthodox affiliations has declined, but the affiliation with Serbian and Russian Orthodox religions has more than doubled.
- As a result of immigration trends from Asia and the Middle East, the number of Canadians identifying Islam, Hinduism, Sikhism, or Buddhism as their religious affiliation is increasing steadily. In fact, the number of Muslim Canadians more than doubled between the 1991 and the 2001 census.
- Provincial variations include the following:[9,10]
  - Quebec has the highest number of Catholics (83% of its population), followed by New Brunswick; British Columbia has the lowest number of Catholics.
  - 73% of Canada's Hindu population live in Ontario.
  - Almost half of Canada's Sikh population live in British Columbia; the second largest group is found in Ontario (38%).
  - 81% of Canadians with Buddhist affiliation live in Ontario (42%), British Columbia (28%), and Alberta (11%).
  - 85% of Jewish Canadians live in either Ontario (58%) or Quebec (27%).
  - British Columbians are least likely to have a religious affiliation (36%), and Quebecers are more likely to cite an affiliation.

Religiosity

Statistics Canada measures religiosity, or the condition of being religious, by assessing religious affiliation, attendance at religious service, personal religious practices, and importance of religion. Based on these criteria, a recent report indicates that 40% of Canadians have a low degree of religiosity, 31% are moderately religious, and 29% are highly religious.[11] Older Canadians and women tend to have higher religiosity indexes than younger Canadians and men. Forty-one percent of immigrants who arrived in Canada between 1982 and 2001 report high levels of religiosity, especially those who arrived from South Asia, Southeast Asia, the Caribbean, and Central and South America. Table 6-2 provides an interesting profile of how Canadians in different age ranges view the importance of religion in their life.

RELIGION AND ILLNESS

To nurse people with strong religious affiliations, it is important to understand how various religions view illness. Almost all religions attempt to explain why human beings suffer from illness and death and how higher powers can affect healing. Religion rarely, if ever, describes disease as resulting from a strictly biological cause with a scientific solution.[13] Instead, some religious explanations of disease indicate that it was sent directly by the creator or a lesser god, caused by sin or the poor performance of a ritual act, or resulted from the malevolence of relatives, neighbours, or ancestors. Based on these explanations, the cure for disease is to be found in confessing sin, purification rites, exorcism, or the transmission of power to the patient such as by the sacrament

TABLE 6-2 The Importance of Religion to One's Life, by Age, Canada, 2002					
The importance of religion to one's life, by age, Canada, 2002					
	Importance of religion to you[1]				
	High	Moderate	Low	No religion	Total
	Percentage				
15 to 29	34^2	20^2	22	25^2	100
30 to 44	*39*	*23*	*20*	*19*	*100*
45 to 59	43^2	22	20	15^2	100
60 or older	62^2	16^2	13^2	9^2	100

1. Importance of religion to you is scored from 1 (not important at all) to 5 (very important). High importance is defined as a score of four or five, moderate importance — a score of three and low importance — a score of one or two. Those reporting no religious affiliation were not asked this question.

2. Statistically significant difference from reference group in italics, at the 95% confidence level.

Source: From the Statistics Canada publication "Canadian Social Trends," *Who's Religious?* Catalogue 11-008, June 28, 2006
URL: http://www.statcan.ca/english/freepub/11-008-XIE/11-008-XIE2006001.pdf

---

Reflective Thinking

Self-Evaluation of Spirituality

Are you spiritual? Are you religious? Are you both? Are you neither? What is most important in your life? What are your beliefs? Have your beliefs changed from when you were younger? How do you feel about people whose beliefs differ markedly from yours?

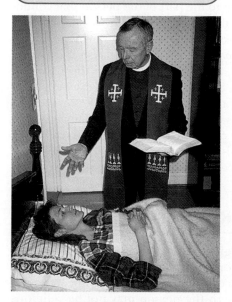

Figure 6-2 Rituals such as the sacrament of the Anointing of the Sick are important expressions of religious belief.

of the Anointing of the Sick (Figure 6-2), plastering, or other rituals. Acts of healing are not performed by physicians and nurses, but by priests, elders, mediums, and others who have access to the higher powers that control disease. Given these beliefs, the patient who has seen a neighbour successfully repel disease with prayers may benefit more from this experience than from taking a prescribed medication.

Being familiar with various religious terms helps nurses to communicate more effectively with patients (Figure 6-3). The concept of **god** may vary from a dispassionate, distant deity to a dynamic, personal, present being. "God" may be called by many names, such as Allah, Yahweh, Jehovah, or Shiva, though Judaism considers the name of God to be so sacred that believers are not supposed to pronounce the name at all. **Prayer** is the means by which some people communicate with their higher power(s). **Monotheistic religions** such as Judaism, Christianity, and Islam believe in only one all-powerful, omnipresent, and omnipotent God (capital *G*) who created the universe. **Polytheistic religions** such as Hinduism recognize many gods (spelled with a lowercase *g*) who may have different levels of power and status. Gods may even compete with each other but are all ultimately manifestations of the one true higher power behind existence.

A patient may claim to be an **atheist** (a-theist; that is, without God), or one who does not believe in God. An **agnostic** (a-gnosis; that is, without knowledge) is one who is unsure if God exists. Atheists or agnostics may be very spiritual

Life 360°

Meaning and Illness

You are nursing a woman who has just been diagnosed with metastatic breast cancer. She is sobbing and states, "It must be God's way of punishing me for all of the bad things I have done in my life." Another patient whose illness situation is deteriorating tells you that "It is the will of God and nothing can be done." What are your ideas about why these patients are reacting this way? Do you think that these reactions are helpful ways of coping with such situations? How would you respond in these situations?

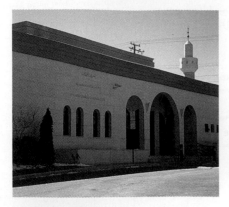

Figure 6-3 All Muslims must face Mecca, Saudi Arabia, to pray. Here, the minaret of a mosque is aligned with Mecca.

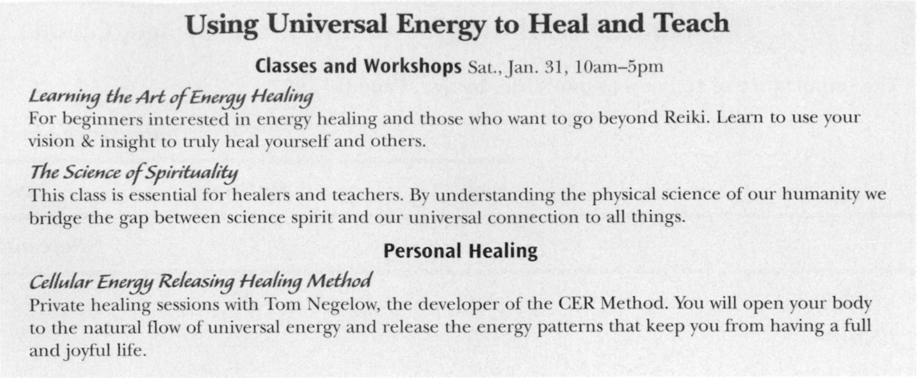

Figure 6-4 This ad displays some of the characteristics of New Age spirituality: "Universal connection to all things," "universal energy," and, by implication, personal transformation.

> **Reflective Thinking**
>
> **Meeting Patients' Spiritual or Religious Needs**
>
> What would you do if a patient requested that you participate in a religious practice that conflicted with your own spiritual, religious, or institutional practices? How would you respond? What do you think the impact of refusing to participate in this practice might be?

if they hold certain beliefs to be of utmost importance to their lives, such as attaining great knowledge, living in harmony with humanity, or showing kindnesses to others. To members of the three major monotheistic religions (Judaism, Christianity, and Islam), a **pagan** is someone who is not monotheistic, or is someone who believes in an animistic, and usually polytheistic, spirit-filled belief system. **Animism** is a belief that all components of the universe, including humans, have some form of life force—a concept contained in many Native American religions. **New Age** religion is a popular, heterogeneous, free-flowing spiritual movement that has no holy book, organization, membership, clergy, geographic centre, dogma, or creed, but includes a cluster of common beliefs that may be grafted onto an existing religion. These beliefs include **pantheism,** in which god is believed to be in everything that exists; reincarnation; auras; energy fields; ecology; personal transformation; and evolution toward a new age where wars and discrimination will not exist, and all will be peace and harmony (Figure 6-4).

A **cult** is the religious devotion to a set of beliefs or to a person. Cults are thought to be fanatical and are societally disapproved, but the difference between a religion and a cult depends on the person who is making the definition. A patient may be insulted if his or her religion is referred to as a cult, so you must show sensitivity to all expressions of spirituality. The concept of the **soul** varies from the essential, spiritual part of a person to the part of the person that continues to exist after physical death. The idea that the soul or body of a person continues to live on in some form after physical death is central to many religions, especially to Christianity. **Spirit** can encompass the same concept as soul, can refer to a disembodied being or supernatural force, or can indicate the Christian Trinitarian concept of God, as in the Holy Spirit. **Reincarnation** is the belief that the person is reborn into another life after death. In Hinduism, a person seeks to obtain release from endless reincarnations by doing good deeds. Many religions describe a peaceful or joyful place, or state one goes to or becomes if the ethics of the religion are followed. Christians call this **heaven,** whereas Buddhists believe in **nirvana,** which is the state of perfect blessedness and peace of the soul.

HOLISTIC HEALTH AND SPIRITUALITY

Nurses meet people from a range of religions, each having their specific spiritual tenets, rites and rituals, and views on health and illness. It is important that nurses know specific details of a particular religion to provide a context for exploring a patient situation. Although the person may not be religious per se, the patient may embrace specific elements of a religion (e.g., the Catholic who states he is not religious may still ask to see a priest if he is dying). Table 6-3 illustrates how certain religions view a range of events from birth to

TABLE 6-3   Religions and Health Care

RELIGION	JUDAISM	ISLAM	ROMAN CATHOLIC/ORTHODOX	PROTESTANT
Description	Judaism is an ancient religion dating to about 2000 BCE. It is a monotheistic religion that believes that God (Yahweh) has chosen the Jewish people and made a covenant with them. The covenant is that the Jews will worship God and follow His laws, and in return God will protect and preserve them. Over its long history, Judaism has developed several traditions, among them Orthodox, which believes in a strict interpretation of the Scriptures; Conservative, which allows for some modern interpretation of the Scriptures; and Reform, which is a blending of tradition with modern-day moral demands. Jews are largely concentrated in the Middle East, Europe, and the United States, but can be found worldwide, including Asia, Africa, and South America.	Islam is a monotheistic religion sharing early Judeo-Christian religious roots. It was established when the Prophet Mohammed (d. 632 CE) preached the word of God as revealed to him by an angel. The essence of Mohammed's prophecies is that God (Allah) is the one, true God and is absolutely sovereign. The central tenet of the faith is "There is no God but Allah and Mohammed is His Prophet." Several versions of Islam have developed, among them Sunni, Sufi, and Shiite. Islam has spread beyond its origins in the Middle East to Europe, Asia, Africa, and the Americas. The five pillars of Islam are regular prayer five times a day facing Mecca, fasting during Ramadan, giving alms to charity, pilgrimage to Mecca if possible, and reciting, at least once in the lifetime, the shahada (creed): "There is no God but Allah, and Mohammed is His Prophet."	A monotheistic religion and an offshoot of Judaism, Christianity dates from the death and resurrection of Jesus, about 30 AD. Christians believe that Jesus is the son of God, that Jesus died on the cross to serve as a sacrifice for the sins of humanity, that Jesus was resurrected from the dead, and that God exists in three forms: God (Father), Jesus (Son), and the Holy Spirit. Roman Catholicism is the oldest and largest of the Christian denominations with about one billion members worldwide. Rejecting the authority of the Pope (and other political and theological issues), the Eastern Orthodox churches separated from the Catholic Church in 1000 AD and developed into a group of independent churches with separate hierarchies along nationalistic lines (e.g., the Greek Orthodox Church, the Russian Orthodox Church). Roman Catholicism and Orthodoxy are sacramental religions in which sacraments, rituals that impart grace and help from God to the believer, are provided to the believer by bishops, priests, and deacons. There are seven sacraments: Baptism, Holy Eucharist, Confirmation, Holy Matrimony, Confession of Sins, Anointing of the Sick, and Holy Orders. The most important is the Holy Eucharist in which bread and wine are transformed into the true body and blood of Jesus Christ through a miracle of God acting through the priest. These are the distinguishing beliefs of Catholics and Orthodox believers.	The Protestant churches began in the 16th-century Reformation, a political and theological break with the Roman Catholic Church. Protestant beliefs are distinguished from Catholic and Orthodox beliefs by: • Rejecting the authority of the Pope and the teaching authority of the church. • De-emphasizing the Eucharist and the central role of the priest. • Rejecting the sacramentalism of the Catholic Church. Protestant churches retain two sacraments only: baptism and the Holy Communion or the Last Supper (in which the bread and wine function as symbols of Jesus only, and not actually as his body and blood). (Lutheran and Episcopal churches retain some sacramentalism and do believe that the bread and wine are more than symbolic of Jesus.) • Emphasizing the Bible and the individual's interpretation of it. Protestant churches have developed widely along diverse lines, and so vary widely in their theological views.

continues

TABLE 6-3 Religions and Health Care *continued*

RELIGION	JUDAISM	ISLAM	ROMAN CATHOLIC/ORTHODOX	PROTESTANT
Religious Leaders	Rabbi: a religious authority of the faith. A rabbi renders decisions interpreting the laws that Jews are required to abide by to preserve their covenant with God. Cantor: a trained person who leads prayer services, performs marriages and funerals, and provides the musical part of prayer services. Mohel: A person trained in the ritual and spiritual aspects of the tradition of circumcision.	Imam: a trained Muslim preacher and teacher.	Bishops: priests who have been promoted to provide leadership over a certain diocese or area. In the Catholic Church, the bishop of Rome (the Pope) has primary authority over the whole church and appoints all other bishops. Priests: preside over the Mass and other sacraments and provide teaching and leadership in the church under the authority of a bishop. Catholic priests must be celibate males, although some married converts have been ordained priests. Orthodox priests may be married but, if married, cannot become bishops. Deacons: men, married or unmarried, who function as assistants to priests. They may perform baptisms and preside over funerals, may visit patients in hospitals, and bring already consecrated Eucharist to patients. They cannot preside over a Mass, hear confessions, or anoint the sick. Monks and nuns: celibate, vowed members of religious orders. Monks may or may not be priests. Monks and nuns function in a wide variety of roles, from cloistered prayer to work as physicians, nurses, hospital chaplains, teachers, and church administrators.	Priests (Episcopal) perform many of the same functions as Catholic priests: anointing the sick, hearing confessions, administering the Eucharist. Usually, but not always, they wear black or coloured clerical shirts and jacket. May be men or women, married, single, or, recently, even noncelibate and homosexual. Ministers (Methodist, Presbyterian, others) and Pastors (Lutherans, Baptists, Pentecostals): lead worship and prayers, preach the Bible, instruct the faithful, pray over the sick. They may be male or female, married or single, homosexual or heterosexual, depending on the denomination. Likely to wear street clothes but may wear clerical suits or dress.
Holy Books and Artifacts	Torah: the first five books of the Bible contained in a scroll. Bible: a collection of divinity inspired writings concerning God's interaction with and revelations to the Jewish people. Talmud: the tradition of interpretation of holy law.	Koran (Qur'an): the collection of the prophecies of Mohammed. The Koran is central to the faith of Muslims. Shari'a: the body of Islamic law. Hadith: the tradition of Islamic law. Islamic women may cover their heads and faces with veils.	The Bible, which includes several Old Testament chapters not seen in the Hebrew or Protestant Bible. The Bible is central to the Christian faith. Priests dress distinctively in black with a white stiff collar. Nuns may or may not wear habits, distinctive dress with headgear. Monks may or may not wear distinctive robes. Church members may wear crucifixes, depicting Jesus being crucified on the cross, and may carry rosary beads, a string of beads that aids prayer. Roman Catholics and Orthodox may	The Bible, without the Apocrypha (the Old Testament chapters used in the Roman Catholic Bible). Protestants may wear crosses, which emphasize the resurrection of Jesus. Episcopal priests and Lutheran pastors may wear clerical black clothes with the distinctive white collar. There is a

TABLE 6-3 Religions and Health Care *continued*

RELIGION	JUDAISM	ISLAM	ROMAN CATHOLIC/ORTHODOX	PROTESTANT
	Observant men may wear a small, round cap for the top of the head called a Kipah (or yarmulke). Men may also wear a prayer shawl called a Tallith.		also use religious medals to remind them of the presence and blessings of God and the saints of God. Devout members may wear scapulars, pieces of cloth embroidered usually with the Virgin Mary or other religious symbol, connected by string, under their clothes. These aid in prayer and also protect the soul after death. It would be important for the devout person to continue to wear these even in the hospital or during surgery.	trend toward combining these with street clothes. Usually, Baptist, Methodist, Presbyterian, and Pentecostal ministers wear street clothes.
Holy Day of the Week	Friday from sundown until Saturday at sundown.	Friday.	Sunday.	Sunday.
Holy Holidays, Festivals, Observances	Rosh Hashana: Jewish new year; it usually occurs in the fall. Yom Kippur: occurs 10 days after Rosh Hashana; a solemn day of atonement and fasting. Sukkot: the feast of tabernacles, a harvest festival; it occurs 5 days after Yom Kippur. Hanukkah: this lesser feast is a 7-day feast of lights. Passover: usually falls in early spring and recalls the exodus of the Jews from enslavement in Egypt. Shavuot: festival occurring 50 days after Passover	Muslims are expected to pray five times a day from before sunup to after sundown. Prayer should be done in a clean place, and the believer should be clean. A person is considered to be unclean if he or she has recently eliminated body wastes, passed flatus, or is asleep. Proper cleansing for prayer includes washing the hands, face, nostrils, ears, arms to the elbows, and feet to the ankles, and moistening the head. After menstruation, childbirth, or sexual intercourse, a complete bath including washing the hair is required before prayer.	Catholics are required to attend Mass every Sunday, and it is considered a sin to miss Mass unless prevented by illness or other circumstances (such as not being able to get to a Mass), or important work (such as providing health care). Other less important work should not be performed on a Sunday, which is considered a day of rest. In addition, there are 6 Holy Days of Obligation in which Mass attendance is also required, and for which it is a serious sin to miss Mass (exceptions the same as above). These days are January 1, the Solemnity of Mary; Ascension Thursday, which occurs 40 days after Easter, though many dioceses have moved this feast to the following Sunday; August 15, the Assumption of the Blessed Virgin Mary; November 1, All Saints Day; December 8, the Immaculate Conception of Mary; and December 25, Christmas. Orthodox Easter is calculated differently and usually falls on a different Sunday than Catholic and Protestant Easter. Other important church observances are: Advent, a 4-week	All Protestant churches observe Christmas and Easter, but some denominations eliminate or de-emphasize other observations.

continues

TABLE 6-3 Religions and Health Care *continued*

RELIGION	JUDAISM	ISLAM	ROMAN CATHOLIC/ORTHODOX	PROTESTANT
	and commemorating the giving of the Torah to Moses on Mt. Sinai.	Muharam 1 Rasal-Sana: the New Year. Ramadan: the 9th month in the Muslim lunar calendar is a time of fasting, meditation, and spiritual purification. Because the Islamic calendar is based on a lunar cycle, the month of Ramadan can fall in any season. Shawwal 1 "Id ad-Fitr": a 3-day celebration following Ramadan. Dhu-al-Hijjah 1–10: this last month of the Muslim calendar is when the journey to Mecca is made. The journey to Mecca is one of the religious pillars of Islam, and Muslims are obligated to go once in their lifetimes if they are able.	period of penance and preparation before Christmas; Lent, a 40-day period of penance before Easter; Holy Thursday, a day to commemorate the institution of the Eucharist and the priesthood 3 days before Easter; Good Friday, a day of fasting and prayer in commemoration of the Crucifixion of Jesus Christ; Easter, the greatest feast day in the Church, in which the resurrection of Jesus Christ is proclaimed; and Pentecost, a Sunday 6 weeks after Easter in which the coming of the Holy Spirit to the church is remembered.	
Dietary Restrictions	Dietary rules are complex and are not kept by all Jews. Kosher food denotes food prepared according to strict dietary laws, which prohibit pork and any other meat of an animal with a cloven hoof that chews a cud, as well as shellfish. Any meat to be eaten must be ritually slaughtered according to strict laws. Meat and dairy products must not be taken together.	Pork and products made from pork, such as gelatin and lard, are forbidden. Alcohol and street drugs are also forbidden. Strictly speaking, all meat should be ritually slaughtered according to religious laws, but in practice, even religious Muslims are relaxed about this requirement.	Catholics are to refrain from meat on Fridays during Lent. Catholics are supposed to practise some form of penance on all Fridays. This may take the form of refraining from meat, or another form such as extra prayer.	None. Some Protestant denominations (Baptist, Pentecostal) forbid the use of alcohol and smoking.

TABLE 6-3   Religions and Health Care   *continued*

RELIGION	JUDAISM	ISLAM	ROMAN CATHOLIC/ORTHODOX	PROTESTANT
Periods of Fasting	Fasting is associated with Yom Kippur and also with some minor holidays. Fasting may be set aside on the advice of a physician.	There is fasting from dawn to sundown during the 28-day month of Ramadan. Pregnant women, menstruating women, and the sick are not required to fast, but they must make up the fast at a later time.	All Catholics who are not ill or children are supposed to fast (that is, eat only one light meal and two smaller meals in one day, and no meat) on Ash Wednesday and Good Friday.	Fasting is de-emphasized in the Protestant tradition.
Medical Treatment	Jews are encouraged to seek medical care and treatment when needed as part of the religious obligation to take care of oneself. Jews hold medicine and physicians in high esteem. Prayers and visitation are proper for the sick.	Healing the sick is considered the highest service to God after religious requirements. Seeking medical treatment for illness is encouraged, and there is no prohibition for doing so. Privacy should be maintained for women and girls during illness and hospitalization. Female bodies should remain covered; gowns should have long sleeves if possible.	Medical treatment is encouraged, even obligated, as part of the obligation to care for oneself. Anointing of the sick with oil and prayers is appropriate at the time of illness. Reception of the Eucharist, if possible, is believed to give special graces to the patient and is considered very important to and for the devout patient.	Same as Roman Catholicism/Ortho-doxy, although some Fundamental and Pentecostal offshoots may emphasize prayer and spiritual healing over medical treatment. Mainline Protestants may practise the anointing of the sick. Prayers and visitation are appropriate for the sick.
Birth Control	Sexual relations are permitted only within marriage. Birth control is allowed within marriage.	Sexual relations are permitted only within marriage. Teachings on birth control are contradictory, but in general, the use of birth control within marriage to control family size or to protect the health of the wife is permitted.	Sexual relations are permitted only within marriage. Procreation is one of the celebrated purposes of marriage. Birth control is forbidden by the Roman Catholic Church. Natural family planning, in which intercourse is timed with the menstrual cycle to prevent conception to limit family size or protect the health of the mother, is permitted.	Sexual relations are permitted only within marriage. Birth control is permitted.

continues

TABLE 6-3 Religions and Health Care   *continued*

RELIGION	JUDAISM	ISLAM	ROMAN CATHOLIC/ORTHODOX	PROTESTANT
Infertility Treatment	A primary purpose of marriage is the procreation of children, and infertility treatments are permitted. Whether to allow the use of gametes (that is, donor egg or donor sperm) from outside the marriage is under discussion.	Procreation is one of the celebrated purposes of marriage, so medical treatment used to treat infertility is acceptable as long as gametes from within the marriage are used and as long as the couple is still married and both husband and wife are alive. Using gametes (donor egg, donor sperm) from outside the marriage would be considered adultery.	Infertility treatment is permitted, with certain important restrictions. Gametes should not leave the body, and only gametes from within the marriage may be used. Thus, medications to stimulate ovulation and surgical treatments to enhance fertility are permitted, but donor egg, donor sperm, in vitro fertilization (IVF), and intracytoplasmic sperm injection (ICSI) are forbidden. The Catholic Church considers all embryos to be human beings and so is against the storage or destruction of, or research on, human embryos.	Infertility treatment is permitted. The use of donor egg or donor sperm is not condemned by most Protestant churches.
Abortion	Judaism has a high respect for life, including prenatal life. However, the fetus is not considered to be fully human until birth. Jewish law does reluctantly permit abortion under some circumstances, such as to preserve the life or welfare of the mother.	Abortion is forbidden after the fetus is "ensouled." There is some controversy as to whether the ensoulment occurs at 40 or 120 days of pregnancy. The father must give permission for the abortion. Abortion after the time of ensoulment is considered murder.	The fetus is considered human from the time of conception. Abortion is therefore prohibited, except when it is done as the effect of another procedure, the purpose of which is not to cause the death of the fetus (for example, a hysterectomy of a pregnant, cancerous uterus is permitted, but the direct abortion of the same fetus is not).	Most Protestant denominations consider fetal life human, but reluctantly allow abortion to preserve the health of the mother. The Southern Baptist Convention recently reversed its pro-choice position and returned to a pro-life position, but it has no authority over its member churches. Many Baptist churches reluctantly allow abortion as a last resort or to save the life of the mother.
Observances at Birth	Circumcision is performed on all males, traditionally at the age of 8 days. Girls may undergo a naming ceremony.	At the time of birth, the baby's father, nearest male relative, or the mother whispers the central tenet of the	Baptism is a very important sacrament that should be performed shortly (within a month or so) after birth. Baptism is considered a necessary step for the person to go to heaven. Thus, an ill child of devout Catholic or	Prayers and blessings are customary at the time of birth. If the child is ill at birth, baptism may be performed by most Protestants except

TABLE 6-3 Religions and Health Care *continued*

RELIGION	JUDAISM	ISLAM	ROMAN CATHOLIC/ORTHODOX	PROTESTANT
		Islamic faith into the baby's ear: "There is no God but Allah, and Mohammed is His Prophet." These are the first words the baby should hear. Some Muslim women may refuse to be attended to by male nurses or physicians. A birth is considered legitimate only if it occurs 6 months after marriage.	Orthodox parents should be baptized immediately and can be baptized by any Christian with water and the words, "I baptize you in the name of the Father, and of the Son, and of the Holy Spirit."	Baptists and Pentecostals.
Rites of Initiation	Boys undergo a bar mitzvah at age 13, a celebration of religious adulthood. In the Reform and Conservative traditions, girls may undergo a parallel ceremony called a bat mitzvah.	Males are routinely circumcised at, or within 7 days after, birth. Female circumcision is a cultural practice found in parts of Asia and Africa not required by Islam, although it is practised by some Muslims and justified by them with passages from the Koran.	Baptism is traditionally performed for children as infants. Children are confirmed at about age 12, when they complete instruction about the church.	Protestant churches vary widely over the issue of baptism. Some churches, such as Episcopal, Lutheran, and some Presbyterian churches, baptize infants shortly after birth. Other churches, such as many Baptist and most Pentecostal churches, only baptize older children and adults who confess that Jesus Christ is their Lord and Saviour. If a child is ill at birth, some churches will and some will not baptize the infant.
Withdrawal of Life Support	Active euthanasia and assisted suicide are forbidden because of the position of the sanctity of human life and the prohibition of murder.	Active euthanasia and assisted suicide are forbidden because of the position of the sanctity of human life and the prohibition of murder. It is permitted to	Suicide and active euthanasia are forbidden because of the principle of the sanctity of life. The withdrawal of life support has been the subject of much controversy in the church, but is permitted if the condition of the patient is hopeless and as long as the purpose of the withdrawal of support is to reduce pain and suffering, and not to kill the patient.	Suicide is forbidden. Some mainline Protestant denominations have expressed some sympathy for assisted suicide and active euthanasia, but in general, suicide and active euthanasia are

continues

TABLE 6-3 Religions and Health Care *continued*

RELIGION	JUDAISM	ISLAM	ROMAN CATHOLIC/ORTHODOX	PROTESTANT
	Hastening death is equivalent to murder. The withdrawal of life support is allowed under the right circumstances, as it is simply the removal of impediments to a natural death.	withdraw life support if the treatment is serving only to prolong the patient's death, or if the patient's condition is medically hopeless.		forbidden, because of the sanctity of life and the prohibition of murder. The withdrawal of life support is appropriate when the patient's condition is hopeless and the treatment is serving only to prolong the patient's death.
Death	Suicide is forbidden. Orthodox Jews may position and wash a dead body. Autopsies are controversial but are permitted if they will serve to provide information that will save other lives in the future. Burial should be done within 24 hr of death, though this may be extended to 48 hr in special circumstances. Cremation is forbidden. There is a 7-day period of mourning called Shiva that begins the day of the funeral. Some Jews customarily may not shave during this time and may cover mirrors.	Suicide is forbidden. Relatives and friends are normally present when a person dies. There may be an expectation for the patient to say, or for a person to whisper, into the ear of the patient, the central tenet of the Islamic faith, "There is no God but Allah, and Mohammed is His Prophet," so that these are the last words the person hears before death. After death the body is washed, usually by a family member. Men wash a man's body, and women wash a woman's body. Autopsies are permitted if they serve to help solve a crime or will provide further medical knowledge. Burial should be commenced without delay, preferably the	Prayers are appropriate at the time of death. Burial or cremation is permitted. Autopsies are permitted, especially if they aid medical knowledge. Devout Catholics and Orthodox at the point of death, or seriously threatened with illness or serious surgery, may request the Last Rites, so called because they involve 3 sacraments: the Rite of Confession, Anointing of the Sick, and Holy Eucharist. A priest must be called to the bedside to perform these rites. Last Rites may be performed more than once, if, for example, the patient recovers and then becomes seriously ill again.	Prayers are appropriate at the time of death. Episcopal priests and Lutheran pastors may administer the Eucharist and anoint the sick. Other pastors and ministers may pray with the family over the sick person, often laying their hands on the sick person as they pray. Bible readings are important to the dying person and the family.

TABLE 6-3 Religions and Health Care *continued*

RELIGION	JUDAISM	ISLAM	ROMAN CATHOLIC/ORTHODOX	PROTESTANT
		same day. There are detailed teachings regarding funerals and burials. Attending funerals is a meritorious act. Funerals may be held in absentia for an important person.		
Organ Donation	Organ donations and receiving transplanted organs are permitted, since the procedure saves life. One exception is Orthodox Jews, who reject the "brain death" definition of death and agree with the cardiac definition of death only.	Organ donations and receiving transplanted organs are permitted, as are blood transfusions.	Organ donation is permitted.	Organ donation is permitted, though some Baptists or Pentecostals may be against organ donation, believing that they should go to heaven with all their body parts.

RELIGION	JEHOVAH'S WITNESSES	BUDDHISM	HINDUISM	NATIVE SPIRITUALITY[14]
Description	"The Watchtower Bible and Tract Society," commonly known as the Jehovah's Witnesses, was founded in the 1870s. Their beliefs are centred on a unique interpretation of the Bible. They differ from traditional Christianity in their belief that Jesus is God's son but inferior in status to God, and their beliefs concerning the	Buddhism was founded in the 6th century BCE by Siddhartha Gautama, who achieved enlightenment at age 35 by purifying his mind and thus achieved the title of "The Buddha," or "Enlightened One." He spent the remainder of his years preaching the Dharma, or "Way," in an effort to help others reach enlightenment. Buddhism centres around the imaged ideal of the Buddha, the transformation of consciousness, and the transformation of	Hinduism is an ancient religion that originated in India around 1500 BCE. It is a complex religion that embraces a variety of gods, practices, and spiritual paths. Hinduism is a polytheistic religion that teaches that ultimately there is only one god, or essence of existence—Brahman. Brahman appears in different forms, most notably in the forms of Krishna, Shiva, and Vishnu. Hinduism teaches that although the universe goes through endless cycles, the divine does not change. Humans are expected to follow the cosmic order (dharma) in life and hope to achieve spiritual liberation (moshka). This occurs through selfless	There are at least 56 distinctive native traditions documented in Canada, including the Inuit. The majority of Native Canadians are Christian, but more of them are incorporating some traditional beliefs and practices into their life, with some turning entirely to their heritage to meet spiritual needs. Although there are specific beliefs across the many Native traditions, certain common

continues

TABLE 6-3 Religions and Health Care *continued*

RELIGION	JEHOVAH'S WITNESSES	BUDDHISM	HINDUISM	NATIVE SPIRITUALITY[14]
	end-time (how and when it will occur and its character) differ as well. Their name for God is Jehovah.	karma (the balance of accumulated sin and merit). The goal in Buddhism is the mind's attainment of Nirvana. The eightfold path to Nirvana includes: right understanding, right thinking, right speech, right conduct, right livelihood, right effort, right mindfulness, and right concentration. There are two forms of Buddhism: Theraveda (found in Burma, Cambodia, Laos, Thailand, Vietnam, Sri Lanka, and is the most common form of Buddhism found in the United States), which emphasizes karma and the worship of Buddha relics; and Mahayana (found in China, Korea, Japan, Tibet, Mongolia, and Russia), which emphasizes ceremony and ritual. Because Buddhism has proved to be so highly adaptable to local cultures and religions, it is difficult to isolate one strict Buddhist Dharma, or way. Buddhism has thus become enmeshed with cultures throughout the world.	acts and good thoughts (karma). The cultural caste system of India was early on incorporated into Hinduism. The castes range from brahmins (priest caste) to untouchables (lowest class). Complex social and religious rules govern these castes.	characteristics may serve to illustrate the spirituality of Native people. Native beliefs are often not religions per se, but are centred around creation and animistic beliefs in the souls and spirits in animals and land surrounding the people. The importance of the community is emphasized. Often, the view of humanity is humble, and the original or supreme creator god is now withdrawn. There are no temples, holy books, or creeds.
Religious Leaders	All baptized persons are considered ordained ministers. Jehovah's Witnesses believe that a clergy class	Monks and Nuns: celibate, vowed members of religious orders, who wear special robes, have shaved heads, and function as teachers and bearers of Buddhist tradition.	Priests: offer sacrifices to the gods and idols; control worship. Guru: a teacher of spiritual ways. Sadhu: a "peaceful man," a sort of Hindu holy man, like a monk, but not in a formal order. May wander from village to village. Yogi: a spiritual teacher.	No organized clergy; however, elders and shamans (angatkuk for the Inuit) play important roles. Elders are wise and have life experiences by virtue of their age; Shamans have

TABLE 6-3 Religions and Health Care *continued*

RELIGION	JEHOVAH'S WITNESSES	BUDDHISM	HINDUISM	NATIVE SPIRITUALITY[14]
	and special titles are improper. Elders or overseers (all male): lead each congregation and lead worship, provide pastoral care, visit the sick, teach, and preach sermons. Ministerial students: young men who assist elders in the functioning of the Kingdom Hall. "Publishers and Pioneers": active Witnesses who go door to door in an attempt to convert the public.	A Guru or Spiritual Guide: a highly respected, important teacher who wears special robes and generally travels with attendants. It is not uncommon for devout Buddhists to have a picture or icon of their Guru with them. Kadam: a lay teacher of Buddhism; may have taken some vows, but can be married and wears street clothes. Buddhist tradition also holds that all followers are leaders.		specialized knowledge of herbs and medicines and act as physical and spiritual healers.
Holy Books and Artifacts	The New World Translation of the Bible, which Jehovah's Witnesses believe to be the most accurate translation of the ancient languages of the Bible. Kingdom Hall is where Jehovah's Witnesses meet and worship. They reject the Christian symbol of the cross, because they believe that Jesus was crucified on a single upright wooden stake with no cross beam.	*The Tibetan Book of the Dead:* intended to be read into the ear of one who is dying or has just died. *The Buddha Dharma:* 100 volumes of the collected words of the Buddha with the commentary of scholars. Statues of the Buddha are common and should be treated with respect, as should photographs of Buddha statues. Any pictures, statues, or religious books must be treated with respect. Many Buddhists wear mala beads, a string of prayer beads, wrapped around their left wrist. If it	The Vedas: 4 ancient (1500 BCE) holy books containing hymns and stories. The hymns are sung to the gods during the presentation of sacrifices. Upanishads: a book dating from 500 BCE, including philosophical stories. Bhagavad Gita: often called the bible of Hinduism. It details the story of Krishna and explores the themes of destiny and salvation. Cows are sacred in Hinduism, symbolizing mother earth, bounty, and Krishna. Feeding a cow is an act of worship. The Ganges River: in India, it is a symbol of life without end, and most Hindus want to bathe in and/or drink its spiritual waters. Other worship artifacts: statues or dolls depicting various gods are common, as well as sandalwood, flat stones, incense, water, candle or oil lamp, flowers, and food offerings.	Usually, there are no holy books, and the religious tradition is passed on orally and through experience with rituals and festivals. Religious artifacts may include feathers, gourds, drums, shells, a medicine pouch worn around the neck with important religious symbols inside, and grasses or other sources for incense.

continues

TABLE 6-3 Religions and Health Care *continued*

RELIGION	JEHOVAH'S WITNESSES	BUDDHISM	HINDUISM	NATIVE SPIRITUALITY[14]
		becomes necessary to remove them, they do so with care and treat them with respect. It is believed to cause bad karma to cut the string of mala beads.		
Holy Day of the Week	No one day is any holier than any other. Most services are held in the evenings during the week or on Sunday.	Buddhist tradition teaches that every day is a holy day. Various cultures and traditions within Buddhism may hold different days as special days (such as the 1st and 15th days of the month).	There is no particular holy day to Hindus. Devotees of particular gods may observe chosen holy days.	None.
Holy Holidays, Festivals, Observances	Memorial of Jesus' death: celebrated annually at the time of the Last Supper of Jesus. Falls in the spring at the time of Passover. Jehovah's Witnesses do not celebrate Christmas or Easter, because there is no command by Jesus to do so. They are forbidden to celebrate "worldly" holidays such as Thanksgiving.	Wesak: the birth of the Buddha is celebrated for 1 to 15 days, usually falling in April or May. There can be many other holidays, depending on the form of Buddhism.	Divali: New Year, Festival of Lights. Holi: spring festival dedicated to Krishna. Dasara: 10 days of celebration in honour of Kali. Tarpan: a time of oblation to forefathers. Makar Sankranji/Pongal: a celebration of spring; homage paid to the sun. Shivaratri: a 24-hour celebration and fasting in honour of Lord Siva. Ram Navami: a celebration of Lord Rama's birth. The story of Rama is chanted for 24 hrs. Janmashtami: Lord Krishna's birthday. Ganesh Chaturthi: day to honour Lord Ganesh. Navaratri: 9-day festival in praise of Lord Rama.	Festivals are often associated with changes in seasons and with harvests. Sundance (celebrated by First Nations in and surrounding the Prairies) is a ceremony held at the time of the full moon in June or July. A mid-winter feast, held around the winter solstice, celebrates the upcoming spring season. Thanksgiving ceremonies may take place at any time of the year. During pipe ceremonies, sweet grass is burned to make a sacred place for spirits to visit. Giveaway or potlatch ceremonies celebrate special events such as a birth or

TABLE 6-3 Religions and Health Care *continued*

RELIGION	JEHOVAH'S WITNESSES	BUDDHISM	HINDUISM	NATIVE SPIRITUALITY[14]
				wedding, and involve giving gifts. The Inuit may pray to Nuliajuk, the spirit of the sea, prior to a hunt for seal or fish.
Dietary Restrictions	No food containing blood (such as blood sausages) is allowed, because Jehovah's Witnesses believe it is forbidden to take in blood. Meat should have all blood drained out of it before cooking; meat approved by the American Dietetic Association meets this criterion.	Some Buddhists, but not all, are vegetarians. Different schools of thought in Buddhism have different views on diet. Strict Buddhists may refuse strong spices.	Because cows are sacred, no beef is eaten, though milk and milk products, particularly yogurt, are staples of a Hindu's diet. Some Hindus are vegetarians, others are not. Nonvegetarians do not eat pork. Roasted meat may be eaten after a sacrificial ceremony. If one has dedicated a specific fruit to God, one is forbidden to eat that fruit for the rest of one's life.	Varies.
Periods of Fasting	None.	Some Buddhists may fast as a path to spiritual enlightenment, presenting an opportunity to think and reflect. Other Buddhists may not support fasting.	At such times, Hindus who eat meat may be vegetarians or may fast altogether.	Fasting may be a special form of prayer, supervised by an elder.
Medical Treatment	Jehovah's Witnesses do seek medical care for all infirmities. The only limitation on their use of health care services is an important religious belief that the Bible forbids the ingestion of blood. This belief prohibits the use of whole blood, packed RBCs, plasma, WBCs, and platelets. Other preparations in which the amount of blood is very minute, such as albumin, immune globulins, and	Medical treatments that may enhance life and the search for enlightenment are approved of. Buddhism has a high regard for the healing nature of the doctor-patient relationship. Doctors and nurses are respected.	Taking care of the body is seen as a good thing. There is no conflict between religion and seeking medical care, as long as a person is not harmed without purpose. The study of medicine has a long and honoured tradition in Hindu culture. Traditional Hindu medicine offers homeopathic, herbal, non-Western care for diseases.	Illness may be related to a sin or an unhappy spirit or god. A specialist in the religion may be consulted to discern the cause of the illness. A healing circle may take place where those present pass a symbolic object, such as a feather, to wish for physical, emotional, and spiritual healing. Rattles may be used to call the spirit of life to assist in

continues

TABLE 6-3 Religions and Health Care *continued*

RELIGION	JEHOVAH'S WITNESSES	BUDDHISM	HINDUISM	NATIVE SPIRITUALITY[14]
	hemophiliac preparations, are up to the conscience of the individual. Autotransfusion is controversial.			healing the sick person. Shamans may prescribe a range of medicinal products.
	Jehovah's Witnesses understand the implications (including possible death) of refusing blood. However, full medical treatment is acceptable as long as no blood is used. They appreciate and seek nonblood treatments for bleeding, such as Hespan, vasopressors, MAST trousers, intraoperative blood salvage, etc. Bone marrow transplants are a matter of conscience.			A sick person may wish to burn sweet grass or other sacred herbs to help with healing.
	Jehovah's Witnesses are encouraged to carry cards indicating refusal of blood as well as general advance directives. It is important for the nurse to understand that Jehovah's Witnesses who accept blood or blood products believe that they are committing a serious sin and may thereby forfeit their eternal life.			
Birth Control	Sex is permitted only within marriage. Birth control is a matter of personal choice. Birth control that prevents implantation (such as some forms of the pill) is prohibited.	Birth control is discouraged because it is unnatural.	The traditional Hindu point of view is against birth control because children are seen as a gift, and many children are an even greater blessing.	Usually not practised. Children are seen as blessings and essential to survival.

TABLE 6-3 **Religions and Health Care** *continued*

RELIGION	JEHOVAH'S WITNESSES	BUDDHISM	HINDUISM	NATIVE SPIRITUALITY[14]
Infertility Treatment	Infertility treatment is up to the individual conscience. No donor gametes from outside of the marriage are permitted.	Infertility may be seen as Buddha's plan. Infertility treatments may be seen as unnatural. This is controversial.	Infertility treatment is permitted, as long as gametes (donor egg, sperm) from outside the marriage are not used. Donor gametes are seen as being against the marriage.	A couple may seek treatment from the tribal elder for infertility, but may be reluctant to seek outside medical assistance.
Abortion	Abortion is prohibited if it is done solely to prevent the birth of an unwanted child. However, abortion is permitted if needed to save the life of the mother.	The morality of abortion depends on the circumstances. Abortion may be supported if the child is suffering in the womb. Nothing is absolute in Buddhism, however, and in general, any form of killing may be seen as adding to bad karma, and thus abortion would be discouraged. Compassion and wisdom must be emphasized.	The traditional Hindu view prohibits abortion, because it is seen as a form of killing that leads to the accumulation of bad karma. In modern practice, however, some Hindus practise abortion.	Usually not practised or tolerated openly.
Observances at Birth	None.	At an early age—from 1 month to 100 days of age—the parents of a new baby give thanks to the Buddha and dedicate the child to Buddha.	On the 10th to 11th day after birth, a priest performs a naming ceremony for the newborn, invoking the blessings of gods and goddesses.	Often, a dedication or thanksgiving ceremony will take place. The child may be given a birth name that identifies him for legal purposes and is also given a traditional name at a naming ceremony. The traditional name reflects the personality and can change within an individual's life as he or she changes.
Rites of Initiation	Baptism by immersion is done when the child (or adult) can and	It depends on the child. A child may be taken to a temple for a	Mundan: the first haircut for a boy. Dvija: for boys of the upper 3 castes, a rite of initiation at age 15. The boy is invested with 3 strands of	Often, a boy reaching puberty or adulthood undergoes an initiation rite that

continues

TABLE 6-3 **Religions and Health Care** *continued*				
RELIGION	**JEHOVAH'S WITNESSES**	**BUDDHISM**	**HINDUISM**	**NATIVE SPIRITUALITY**[14]
	does give consent to be a Jehovah's Witness, usually at puberty.	ceremony of further dedication.	the sacred thread, signifying right thought, right speech, right actions.	includes some shedding of blood, if only a small amount.
Withdrawal of Life Support	Life is sacred and the willful taking of life under any circumstances is wrong. Reasonable and humane effort should be made to sustain and prolong life. However, the Scriptures do not require that extraordinary, complicated, distressing, or costly measures be taken to sustain a person if such measures would merely prolong the dying process and/or leave the patient with no quality of life. Any advance directives of patients that specifically define what is to be done are to be respected.	Buddhism values life but sees death as a natural part of life. Maintenance, comfort care, and withdrawal of life support is acceptable for those patients who are crossing the threshold of death. But good karma results from saving, prolonging, or improving life. The most weighty sin for a Buddhist is to take the life of another living being.	When the body is beyond repair, Hinduism supports the withdrawal of artificial life support in order to allow for a natural death. The point of life is liberation— moshka—from the endless cycles of life and death through good karma.	Life support is seen as unnatural and therefore not necessary.
Death	The soul dies with the body, but resurrection will occur for 144,000 individuals at the end-time, and such will be born again as spiritual sons of God. Euthanasia is forbidden. Suicide is not approved of but understood as the product of mental illness. Autopsies are permitted only if	Death is a natural part of life. The state of mind at the time of death is very important: calm and peaceful is preferred as this will cause a happy rebirth. At death, existence for the Buddhist can take a sudden turn for the better or the worse, depending on the good or evil done in life. Suicide is strongly	The atmosphere around the dying person must be peaceful, a spiritual silence, so the last thoughts are of God. Holy water, such as from the Ganges River, is poured into the mouth of the dying person. Hindus prefer to die at home, as close to mother earth as possible, so many prefer to die on the floor or even on the ground. A married woman's nuptial thread (necklace) or amulets are removed just before death to allow the soul's free journey to infinity. The family washes the body, and the eldest son arranges for a funeral and cremation within 24 hrs of death.	There are complex beliefs about death and the treatment and disposal of the body. Some followers may be forbidden to touch a dead body or be required to undergo a cleansing ritual after touching or being near a dead body. Often, the spirit of the person is believed to live on after death, and ancestor worship is often involved.

TABLE 6-3 Religions and Health Care *continued*

RELIGION	JEHOVAH'S WITNESSES	BUDDHISM	HINDUISM	NATIVE SPIRITUALITY[14]
	legally necessary, so that the body will not be subjected to unnecessary mutilation. Burial and cremation are permitted.	criticized, except for self-sacrifice. Cremation is common. During the entire death process, it is important to keep a calm and serene environment. Touch the patient as little as possible. After death, the body should not be disturbed with movement, talking, or crying.	The body should lie under a white sheet and be disturbed as little as possible. Embalming or beautifying the body is forbidden. Autopsies are discouraged. Children under 2 are buried, and there are no rituals for infants, because the soul from the last life had not yet lived. The names of gods are chanted at the funeral, and the family fasts and wears white for purity. Suicide and active euthanasia are forbidden, because killing accumulates bad karma.	Some specific examples include: • Traditional Algonkians believe the dead person goes to the Land of Souls if the Path of Life has been followed; interment takes place 4 days after death, personal possessions are buried with the body and include a medicine bundle. Mourning takes place for 1 year. • Traditional Iroquoian Peoples follow the Great Law of Peace and the soul is told to go to the Creator. Although some may mourn for 1 year, a feast is generally held after 10 days to release mourners from these responsibilities. • Traditional People of the Interior Plateau may light a sacred fire that is burned for 3 days and nights, with the burial taking place on the 4th day. Families grieve for 1 year and may cut their hair in observance.
Organ Donation	The Jehovah's Witnesses forbade organ transplant in 1967 but reversed this decision in 1980. Organ transplants and organ	This is controversial. Some Buddhists accept the concepts of brain death and organ donation. If the donation of organs	Traditional Hindu thought is against receiving organ donations because organ donation is not natural. Donating organs involves disturbing the body after death, which is discouraged.	Organ donation is discouraged because of death and burial practices.

continues

TABLE 6-3 Religions and Health Care *continued*

RELIGION	JEHOVAH'S WITNESSES	BUDDHISM	HINDUISM	NATIVE SPIRITUALITY[14]
	donations are matters of individual choice. There is no biblical injunction against taking in body tissue or bone as there is against taking in blood.	is able to help others, this may bring good karma and would be approved of.		

death. *These descriptions provide context and are in no way meant to be prescriptive and do not represent the actual practices and beliefs of any particular person.* Nurses must further explore whether or not the individual shares the same values, beliefs, and practices as out lined by the dominant religion.

Spiritual distress is the state in which a patient feels that the belief system, or his or her place within it, is threatened. Commonly, the circumstances in which nurses find themselves providing care—birth, accidents, illness, and the dying process—are the same events that provoke spiritual distress. As Holst notes, "Suffering dispels the illusion that we are infinite without limits. In that regard, suffering can be a great moment of [spiritual] truth for the sufferer."[15]

Any reminder of a person's own mortality can serve to evoke both wonderment about the meaning and purpose of life and disquiet about the answers that spirituality or religion provide. Spiritual distress may manifest as anxiety, withdrawal, distractedness, hopelessness, or crying behaviours. Therefore, nursing interventions directed toward resolving the distress should consider the spiritual status of the patient.

Nursing Tip

Gaining Patient Trust

Many people believe that spiritual issues are very private. Patients may fear that they will be ridiculed for their beliefs. It is important, therefore, to build an atmosphere of trust with the patient before you delve into questions about the patient's spiritual beliefs. Begin the health history interview with questions concerning the patient's health history. As the patient reveals personal or intimate details about his or her physical being, you can build trust with the patient by remaining nonjudgmental and maintaining an attitude of respect, empathy, and understanding. The patient will then gradually feel more comfortable discussing the psychological and spiritual portions of the interview.

Reflective Thinking

Religious Practices Influencing Care Provided to a Young Child

A three-year-old child arrives at the emergency department by ambulance after being involved in a head-on collision. All family members except the father and the child have died on arrival. The young child has sustained extensive trauma to the face as a result of being partially thrown through the windshield. The father accompanied the child in the ambulance and has made it known that the family members are Jehovah's Witnesses and, thus, do not permit blood transfusions. This information is relayed to you on the patient's arrival. The child's blood pressure drops from 80/40 to 50/20, and a hematocrit value of 0.23 comes back from the laboratory. You are asked to call the blood bank for two units of blood.
1. How would you respond to this request?
2. Do your religious beliefs conflict with this family's beliefs?
3. If you feel you cannot assist with the blood resuscitation, would you feel comfortable asking a fellow coworker to step in for you?
4. What is your institution's policy in such situations?

> ◄**NURSING CHECKLIST**►
>
> **General Approach to Spiritual Assessment**
>
> 1. Conduct this assessment as part of the history-taking portion of a general patient assessment once trust has been established, rather than as a stand-alone interview.
> 2. Choose a quiet, private room that will be free from interruptions.
> 3. Ensure that the room's light is sufficiently bright to observe the patient's verbal and nonverbal reactions.
> 4. Greet the patient, introduce yourself, and explain that you will be taking a health history.
> 5. Position yourself at eye level with the patient.
> 6. Portray an interested, nonjudgmental manner throughout the interview. Respect silence and diversity.

ROLE OF THE NURSE IN SPIRITUAL CARE

Nurses have a vital role to play in the spiritual care of patients by:

1. Performing a spiritual assessment. (It is impossible to know if a patient is in a state of spiritual distress or spiritual well-being unless an assessment is done.)
2. Establishing priorities based on the assessment.
3. Planning, implementing, and evaluating appropriate strategies for spiritual care.

Spiritual Assessment

Conducting the Spiritual History

The purpose of a spiritual history is to collect information in order to understand the patient's religious or spiritual beliefs and practices, if any.

1. Begin the interview with the physical history of the patient. Move on to the psychological history and end with the spiritual history. Keep in mind that the physical history may itself raise spiritual or religious issues. For example, patients may reveal a requirement for a vegetarian diet (Hindu), or a history of circumcision (Jews), or the fact that their hair has never been cut (women: Orthodox Jews; men: Sikhs). Use these facts to launch the assessment of the patient by saying, "Are you a vegetarian for religious reasons, or for health reasons, or some other reason?" or, "You mentioned circumcision—was that done for religious reasons?"
2. Ask the patient whether he or she has an **advance directive** (such as a living will or durable medical power of attorney), which states what should be done if the patient is too ill to self-direct medical care. This question opens the door to a discussion about spiritual beliefs. For example, the patient may say, "I don't believe in keeping the body alive when the soul is gone," or, "It's for God to decide when I die, not me." By probing with gentle, interested, open-ended questions, you can delve further into the details of the patient's spiritual beliefs. Attempt to get the patient to elaborate by asking, "Can you tell me more about that?" or by restating the belief, "So, you believe that God should decide" If the patient does not know what an advance directive is, take the opportunity for teaching and try to elicit the same spiritual information.

Figure 6-5 Awareness of cultural and religious norms and customs will help you deliver appropriate nursing care. Islam separates the sexes in many aspects of public life, as illustrated here.

Figure 6-6 Comment on the patient's religious reading materials and use them to ask about the patient's spiritual beliefs.

TABLE 6-4

Questions for Ascertaining a Patient's Spiritual Beliefs

What is the most important thing in your life?

What do you depend on when things go wrong?

Do you pray?

Are you a person of faith?

Do you attend regular worship services?

What do you believe in?

Why do you think you have become ill now?

Is there anything more important to you than regaining your health?

3. Ask the patient whether he or she has signed an organ donor card or given any thought to donating organs or tissue after death. Again, the patient's answers to these questions will probably involve spiritual and/or religious beliefs. If the patient is an organ donor, note this information and ask what led to this decision and if it has been discussed with the family or significant others. If the patient seems reluctant to discuss the issue, ask, "What do you believe about all this?" Try to get the patient to elaborate by asking open-ended questions, such as "Can you tell me more about that?" If the patient does not understand organ donation, use the opportunity to do some teaching. As the issue becomes clear to the patient, you should be able to elicit some information about the patient's spiritual beliefs. Whatever the patient's response, be sure to respect the patient's position on the matter.

4. Ask the patient if there are any spiritual or religious beliefs that will affect the health care received (Figure 6-5). The patient may be unsure of what to expect from medical care, so you may need to probe to seek the answers. You want to know whether the patient needs to be on a special diet (such as a diet without pork), has specific beliefs about certain forms of treatment (such as a refusal of blood products), or if the patient wants to have a certain religious ritual performed at a certain time (such as baptism of a critically ill infant). It is helpful to know the general requirements for various religions so you are aware of what areas to assess (see Table 6-3). However, it is important to remember that not every member of an organized religion adheres to its formal requirements. Do not assume that every Muslim will fast during Ramadan, or that every Jehovah's Witness will refuse blood transfusions.

5. Observe the patient for clues about spiritual or religious beliefs. Does the person make comments about higher powers or meanings that transcends day-to-day life? Does the patient have religious reading material, such as a Koran or religious pamphlets? Are other religious artifacts, such as small statues, shawls, or amulets, on display? Comment on these items and use them to ask about the patient's spiritual beliefs. For example, "I see you have several crystals with you. Are you a spiritual person?" or, "This is interesting—what is it? What does it mean?" or, "I see you're reading a book about philosophy. Are you interested in philosophical and spiritual things?" (See Figure 6-6.)

6. Ask the patient who should be notified in the event that there is a change in his or her condition. After noting this, ask if the patient also wants you to notify a place of worship or a specific religious leader. Ask who will be supportive to the patient, family, and significant others during the illness. The patient may name other relatives, friends, or a religious organization. This is another opportunity to probe gently into the patient's spiritual beliefs.

7. If the patient's affiliation with a specific religion or faithfulness to a particular spiritual belief has not been identified, select from among the questions listed in Table 6-4 to try to ascertain these beliefs. It is helpful to practise these questions to develop some comfort in opening a discussion in this area. These questions offer a gentler approach than asking, "What is your religion?" which implies that everyone belongs to some sort of religion, and may embarrass or insult a patient.

8. If the patient is experiencing any threat to his or her health, such as being newly diagnosed with a chronic illness, being admitted to a hospital because of an acute illness, or is undergoing an assessment after an accident that was frightening or caused an injury, state the obvious and ask whether the patient is thinking spiritually about the change. For example, "You just had a heart attack two days ago. This type of experience can often make people wonder about things spiritual or religious. Is that something that is happening to you?"

9. If the patient is reluctant to talk, or becomes hostile to questions about religion or spirituality, do not push it. This may be an area more private to the patient than his or her own bowel or sexual habits. Record the patient's sensitivity to spiritual issues and move on to another topic.

Nursing Tip

Through the Back Door

A patient may resist answering questions about spiritual beliefs, even during considerable spiritual distress. One key to assessing the patient's spirituality is to inquire about the spiritual and emotional state of the patient's significant other, such as "How is your wife holding up under all this?" or "How are things going at home while you're here in the hospital?" The patient may display considerable worry about the effect the illness is having on significant others, which is often a reflection of the patient's own concern about his or her fate, spiritual and otherwise.

Nursing Tip

Spiritual assessment and support are particularly important during times of change or crisis, including:

1. Birth, accidents, and death
2. Sudden change in condition
3. The imparting of bad news, such as a grim prognosis
4. Serious discussions concerning plans that have to be made for patients with complex needs, such as a conference that focuses on pain control and placement in hospice or home care with a patient with terminal cancer
5. Discussions about withdrawal of life support or about other bioethical dilemmas
6. Enduring a long, chronic illness

Nursing Tip

Signs of Spiritual Distress

Signs of spiritual distress may be subtle or overt, but you should be alert to their deep meanings and not brush them off as the patient's "having a bad day." Such signs may include:

- Crying, sighing, or withdrawn behaviour.
- Verbalization of questions about spiritual beliefs, such as "What does it all mean?" or "An experience like this really makes you put things into perspective," or "I just don't understand why this is happening to me."
- Verbalizations about worthlessness, hopelessness, or death, such as "I'd be better off dead" or "I guess we've all got to go sometime."
- Verbalizations about God and God's purposes, such as "I guess the gods have it in for me," or "It's payback time," or "I wonder what I did to deserve this," or "When God says it's your time to go, you go no matter what, I guess."
- Explicit requests to the nurse or others for spiritual or religious assistance, such as requests for prayers or the special placement of religious artifacts.

Planning and Implementation

Once priorities have been established, you can plan and implement nursing interventions for the patient. The following interventions are appropriate for spiritual nursing care:

1. Listen actively. It is important for patients to verbalize their feelings—either of spiritual distress or of their appreciation of their spiritual beliefs in times of trial. Be alert to times when the patient wants to talk, and avoid waving off the patient's concerns with simple platitudes such as "It'll all look better tomorrow." Take the patient's concerns seriously. Allow the patient to talk and encourage the patient to continue talking by nodding, restating, and asking questions that gently probe for more information. Verbalization of doubts and suffering can be therapeutic; resist the temptation to try to convince the patient that spiritual concerns are not valid.

2. Project an empathetic and warm response to the patient's concerns. Part of the cause of spiritual distress is often the fear that no one really cares about the patient's existence or fate. Show interest in the patient and the patient's ultimate concerns, and not just the patient's physical and technical issues.

3. Display respect for the patient's spiritual beliefs by demonstrating tolerance for the patient's religious and spiritual beliefs. Recognize which practices are religious (see Table 6-4) to the patient by encouraging the patient to participate in those practices that relieve spiritual distress or that enhance the patient's spiritual well-being. Provide privacy for the patient to practise religious or spiritual beliefs, and offer to bring religious items closer to or within view of the patient. Ask the patient what should be done with religious or spiritual artifacts. For example, say, "This looks special. Do you have a particular place you want me to put this?" You also demonstrate respect for the patient's beliefs by waiting to enter a room or not speaking until the patient has finished praying, if possible, and by offering to call someone the patient believes will provide spiritual support, such as a rabbi, spiritual advisor, or church member. Provide privacy when that person is visiting the patient.

4. Ensure patients are able to practise their religion or spirituality as much as possible by providing privacy (Figure 6-7) or meeting the patient's needs to carry out specific rituals or practices. For example, if hospital regulations forbid open flames, suggest a menorah with electric lights.

5. Make appropriate referrals to the hospital chaplain or the patient's own spiritual or religious leader from the community. Hospital chaplains of any religion generally function as spiritual and religious resource people within a health care institution. Take advantage of their expertise, even though the patient may be Buddhist and the chaplain is Jewish, for example. The chaplain will visit a patient to discuss spiritual concerns, without judging the patient or trying to convert the patient to the chaplain's own religion. Nonreligious people may not have need for a chaplain; however, the chaplain who focuses on spirituality rather than religious issues may be of help to such people.

7. There are several interventions you should avoid when working with a patient's spirituality, and these are listed in Table 6-5.

Figure 6-7 Make it possible for patients to practise their religion and spirituality as much as possible.

Evaluation

Evaluate the effect of your nursing interventions by observing the patient. Signs that the patient's spiritual distress has decreased include:

1. Acceptance of spiritual support from the source with which the patient feels most comfortable
2. Decrease in crying, restlessness, and sleeplessness. There may even be a decrease in complaints of pain or the severity of pain

TABLE 6-5 Nursing Actions To Avoid When Intervening in the Patient's Spiritual Condition

It is important to show respect for your patients' religious and spiritual beliefs. These actions are considered disrespectful of such beliefs and should be avoided.

1. Do not proselytize your own spiritual beliefs. Share your beliefs if the topic comes up, but it is never appropriate to try to convert the patient to another set of beliefs. In a worst-case scenario, the patient may fear that you will not provide care unless he or she espouses your beliefs. You may also unwittingly undermine the patient's support system at a time when the patient needs it most.

2. Do not instruct the patient in religious or spiritual doctrine. In a time of spiritual distress, a patient needs support, not instruction. Let the religious or spiritual leader take the lead in any instruction that is required, and follow nursing interventions that will enhance spiritual well-being.

3. Do not respond to the patient with clichés. Clichés such as "No sense crying over spilled milk," or "There's always someone else around who's worse off than you," are inappropriate because they tend to blame or diminish the anguish of the patient. Saying things such as "God helps those who help themselves," or "It was God's will," are just as inappropriate because they patronize and trivialize both the patient's problems and religion. Additionally, most well-known religious clichés are based on Western Judeo-Christian culture and have no bearing on other kinds of religions or spiritual beliefs. Respond instead with real, heartfelt words or, in some cases, with silence or with touch, if appropriate.

3. Decrease in statements of worthlessness and hopelessness
4. Verbalization of satisfaction with spiritual beliefs and the support and comfort they provide. The patient may talk openly about spiritual beliefs and even offer spiritual insights to other patients, to you, or to other health care professionals. These are healthy signs that the patient is admitting acceptance of spiritual beliefs.

Nursing Tip

Arranging for Pastoral Care

Most institutional chaplains have received special training in **pastoral care,** which is the care and response needed when a person is in a spiritual crisis. In their practice of pastoral care, these chaplains can be valuable aids for the patient in spiritual distress. However, some patients, when asked, may refuse a visit with chaplains based on the incorrect belief that they are present only to visit dying patients, to practise their own religious rituals, or to preach their own dogmas. If the patient is in spiritual distress, initiate a chaplaincy referral. The chaplain can provide a satisfying explanation for the visit, such as "I normally visit with all patients before surgery," and the patient will not miss out on a valuable resource for alleviating spiritual distress.

CASE STUDY   The Spiritual Side of the Withdrawal of Life Support

Tim is a 45-year-old patient in a nursing long-term care (LTC) facility. He has been in a persistent vegetative state for 10 years after suffering from an arrhythmia and subsequent lack of oxygen before he was resuscitated. Tim's wife of 20 years stopped visiting him five years ago, except occasionally, and is now pursuing measures to remove his feeding tube and wants no further antibiotics given for his next infection. Tim's parents strongly disagree with her plans and are pursuing guardianship of their son. There have been angry confrontations between Tim's wife and parents, and the ethics committee is in a quandary about what to do.

continues

SPIRITUAL HISTORY

HISTORY OF ISSUE/CONCERN   He was admitted to the LTC facility p̄ a prolonged stay in a local acute care hospital. He collapsed at home & was pulseless & breathless for at least 15 min until the rescue team arrived & began CPR. The pt's heartbeat was restored at the hospital. However, brain damage was severe & it took mos before the patient was weaned from the ventilator & his tracheostomy removed. Neurologists have dx him as being in a persistent vegetative state (PVS). He had an automatic cardioverter defibrillator implanted to treat his underlying ventricular arrhythmia that was the cause of his cardiac arrest. He has sleep & wake cycles, & sometimes seems to respond to his parents & caretakers. He has a urinary catheter & suffers from repeated UTIs, requiring tx c̄ ath. He also has a permanent gastrostomy tube, through which he receives bolus tube feedings, medications & water. He experiences occasional diarrhea & pressure ulcers. He does not need to be restrained. He is able to breathe on his own but has repeated bouts of pneumonia & has required atb & O_2 for tx.

Spiritual Assessment   Tim is a Roman Catholic, though it is not clear if he was a strong adherent of the faith in his adult years. He never shared with his family how he would want to be treated in the event he was in such a situation. Tim's wife is a nonpractising Protestant who attended Mass with Tim occasionally before his illness but no longer attends any church. She states that no God could exist that could allow such a thing to happen to her husband. In the last 5 years, she has begun to date other men and now wants to remarry. Tim's parents are devout Roman Catholics who have become even more devout through the struggle with their son's illness. They are in strong agreement with Church teaching that the withdrawal of tube feeding in a nonterminally ill patient is the same as murder. The family is in a crisis. There have been angry confrontations between the wife and the parents, & the wife has taken steps to bar the parents & local priests from visiting Tim.

REVIEW QUESTIONS

1. What is the belief that all components of the universe, including humans, have some form of life force?
   a. New Age
   b. Paganism
   c. Animism
   d. Pantheism
   The correct answer is (c).

2. The fastest growing religion(s) in Canada is/are:
   a. Non-Judeo-Christian religions
   b. Judaism
   c. Christianity
   d. Protestant
   The correct answer is (a).

3. An appropriate action to provide spiritual support is:
   a. Share your religious views with the patient
   b. Pray with the patient at the onset of your shift
   c. Correct the patient in areas where he or she misunderstands church doctrine
   d. Discuss with the patient what he/she finds helpful in relieving spiritual distress
   The correct answer is (d).

4. The Roman Catholic "Last Rites" include:
   a. The sacrament of the Anointing of the Sick
   b. The sacraments of the Anointing of the Sick and Holy Eucharist
   c. The sacraments of the Anointing of the Sick, Holy Eucharist, and Confession
   d. The sacraments of the Anointing of the Sick, Holy Eucharist, Confession, and Confirmation
   The correct answer is (c).

5. A Jehovah's Witness may refuse life-saving blood or blood products because:
   a. They interpret a passage of the Bible to mean that it is a sin to take blood into the body
   b. They have been brainwashed
   c. They do not understand how blood products work
   d. They interpret the Bible incorrectly
   The correct answer is (a).

6. Some objects a practising Buddhist may have with him or her include:
   a. A set of prayer beads, perhaps wrapped around the left wrist
   b. A statue of Krishna
   c. A picture of Iman
   d. A broken arrow, protective charms, and paper strips
   The correct answer is (a).

7. A Muslim family member may want access to a critically ill patient at the point of death because:
   a. It is important to hold hands with someone who is dying
   b. Family is very important in Muslim culture
   c. Prayer is very important in Muslim culture
   d. The last thing a dying Muslim should hear whispered into his or her ear is, "There is no God but Allah, and Mohammed is His Prophet."
   The correct answer is (d).

8. If a patient becomes hostile or uncomfortable when discussing religion and spirituality during your spiritual assessment, you should:

a. Press the patient for details about why he or she is so hostile

b. Offer to pray for the patient

c. Explain that studies show prayer helps patients get better

d. Record that the patient is uncomfortable with religious and spiritual issues, and move on to another topic

The correct answer is (d).

Visit the Estes online companion resource at **www.healthassessment.nelson.com** for additional content and study aids.

REFERENCES

[1] Statistics Canada. *Population by religion, by province and territory (2001 Census).* Retrieved May 30, 2006, from http://www40.statcan.ca/l01/cst01/demo30b.htm

[2] Bibby, R. W. (1993). *Unknown gods: The ongoing story of religion in Canada.* Toronto: Stoddart.

[3] Statistics Canada. (2000). *Table 105–0073 Importance of spirituality, by age group and sex, household population aged 12 and over, selected provinces, territories and health regions.* Retrieved October 10, 2006, from http://cansim2.statcan.ca/cgi-win/cnsmcgi.exe?Lang=E&RootDir=CII/&ResultTemplate=CII/CII_&Array_Pick=1&ArrayId=1050073

[4] Reimer Kirkham, S., Pesut, B., Meyerhoff, H., & Sawatzky, R. (2004). Spiritual caregiving at the juncture of religion, culture, and state. *Canadian Journal of Nursing Research, 36*(4), 148–69.

[5] Statistics Canada. *Population by religion, by province and territory (2001 Census).*

[6] Government of Canada. *Religions in Canada: Native spirituality.* Retrieved October 10, 2006, from http://www.forces.gc.ca/hr/religions/engraph/religions23_e.asp

[7] Statistics Canada. *Religions of Canada: Canada still predominantly Roman Catholic and Protestant (2001 Census).* Retrieved October 10, 2006, from http://www12.statcan.ca/english/census01/Products/Analytic/companion/rel/canada.cfm

[8] Clark, W., & Schellenberg, S. (2006). *Who's religious? Canadian social trends, May.* Retrieved October 10, 2006, from http://www.statcan.ca/english/freepub/11-008-XIE/2006001/main_religious.htm

[9] Statistics Canada. *Population by religion, by province and territory (2001 Census).*

[10] Statistics Canada. *Table 105–0073 Importance of spirituality, by age group and sex, household population aged 12 and over, selected provinces, territories and health regions.*

[11] Clark & Schellenberg, *Who's religious? Canadian social trends, May.*

[12] Ibid, p. 6.

[13] Government of Canada. *Religions in Canada: Native spirituality.*

[14] Ibid.

[15] Holst, L. (1985). *Hospital ministry: The role of the chaplain today.* p. 11. New York: Crossroad.

BIBLIOGRAPHY

Friesen, J. W. & Friesen, V. L. (2006). *Canadian Aboriginal art and spirituality: A vital link.* Calgary: Detselig Enterprises.

Grant, D. (2004). Spiritual interventions: How, when, and why nurses use them. *Holistic Nursing Practice, 18*(1), 36–41.

Kirkham, S. R., Pesut, B., Meyerhoff, H., & Sawatzky, R. (2004). Spiritual caregiving at the juncture of religion, culture, and state. *Canadian Journal of Nursing Research. 36*(4), 148–69.

Koenig, H. G., & Cohen, H. J. (Eds.). (2002). *The link between religion and health: Psychoneuroimmunology and the Faith Factor.* New York: Oxford University Press.

O'Brien, M. E. (2003). *Parish nursing: Health care ministry with the church.* Mahwah, NJ: Paulist Press.

Sawatzky, R. (2006). A meta-analysis of the relationship between spirituality and quality of life: A thesis proposal. In Wood, M. J., & Ross-Kerr, J. (Eds.), *Basic steps in planning nursing research.* Boston: Jones & Bartlett.

Sawatzky, R. & Pesut, B. (2005). Attributes of spiritual care in nursing practice. *Journal of Holistic Nursing, 23*(1), 19–33.

WEB RESOURCES

BBC World Service: Religions of the World
http://www.bbc.co.uk/religion/religions/

Wikipedia: Major Religious Groups
http://www.en.wikipedia.org/wiki/major_world_religions

NEL

CHAPTER 7

Nutritional Assessment

COMPETENCIES

1. Describe key recommendations of Eating Well with Canada's Food Guide.

2. Devise a teaching plan that you can use to educate patients on the Food Guide.

3. Describe the Dietary Reference Intakes for adequate nutritional intake for all age groups.

4. Identify nutritional requirements for different age groups.

5. Perform a nutritional history and physical assessment.

6. Perform anthropometric measurements.

7. Describe laboratory analyses needed and their clinical significance to the nutritional assessment.

NOTE: Although Canada has adopted the metric system of measurement, many Canadians discuss their weight in pounds rather than kilograms. Therefore, certain parts of this chapter will refer to and use calculations that include pounds as well as kilograms.

*N*utrition, or the processes by which the body metabolizes and utilizes nutrients, affects every system in the body. We must have food and drink to sustain life, but what type and how much are the questions that must be asked when assessing a patient's nutritional health. Health care providers must also understand how the body digests and absorbs nutrients, the importance of meeting daily nutritional requirements, and how to assess the causes and results of an imbalance of nutrients. Psychological, social, environmental, financial, and cultural issues should also be considered during a nutritional assessment.

Most Canadians are aware of the important role nutrition plays in health and well-being across the life span. At the national level, Health Canada's mission is "to help the people of Canada maintain and improve their health," and at the provincial and territorial level, all of the Ministers of Health have agreed upon the importance of the *Integrated Pan-Canadian Healthy Living Strategy* to promote healthy eating and physical activity of Canadians. How these two factors relate to influence the attainment of healthy weights is of key importance to deal with emerging health issues such as heart disease and diabetes in Canadians. The goals of the *Healthy Living Strategy* are:[1]

Healthy Eating

- By 2015, increase by 20% the proportion of Canadians who make healthy food choices according to the Canadian Community Health Survey (CCHS), and Statistics Canada (SC)/Canadian Institute for Health Information (CIHI) health indicators.

Physical Activity

- By 2015, increase by 20% the proportion of Canadians who participate in regular physical activity based on 30 minutes/day of moderate to vigorous activity as measured by the CCHS and the Physical Activity Benchmarks/ Monitoring Program.

Healthy Weights

- By 2015, increase by 20% the proportion of Canadians at a "normal" body weight based on a body mass index (BMI) of 18.5 to 24.9 as measured by the National Population Health Survey, CCHS, and SC/CIHI health indicators.

This chapter addresses key aspects of the *Healthy Living Strategy*, including the promotion of healthy eating and physical activity as a means to achieve a healthy weight. Ultimately, the goal is the health and well-being of all Canadians.

HEALTHY EATING IN CANADA—EATING WELL WITH CANADA'S FOOD GUIDE

Eating Well with Canada's Food Guide (Figure 7-1) provides Canadians with guidelines about the amount and type of food needed to meet nutrient requirements across the lifespan. Released in 2007, the Food Guide recommends a healthy eating pattern to achieve overall health; ensures Canadians get enough vitamins, minerals and essential nutrients; and aims to reduce the risk of obesity and chronic illnesses such as heart disease, type 2 diabetes mellitus, osteoporosis, and certain types of cancer.

Since the first food guide, *Official Food Rules*, was introduced in 1942, there have been several versions of recommendations for healthy eating. While the first guide addressed such issues as wartime food rationing, subsequent revisions of Canada's Food Guide have incorporated the ever growing body of nutritional science knowledge (see Figure 7-2 for examples of the Canada Food Guide throughout the years). The most recent edition has taken into account

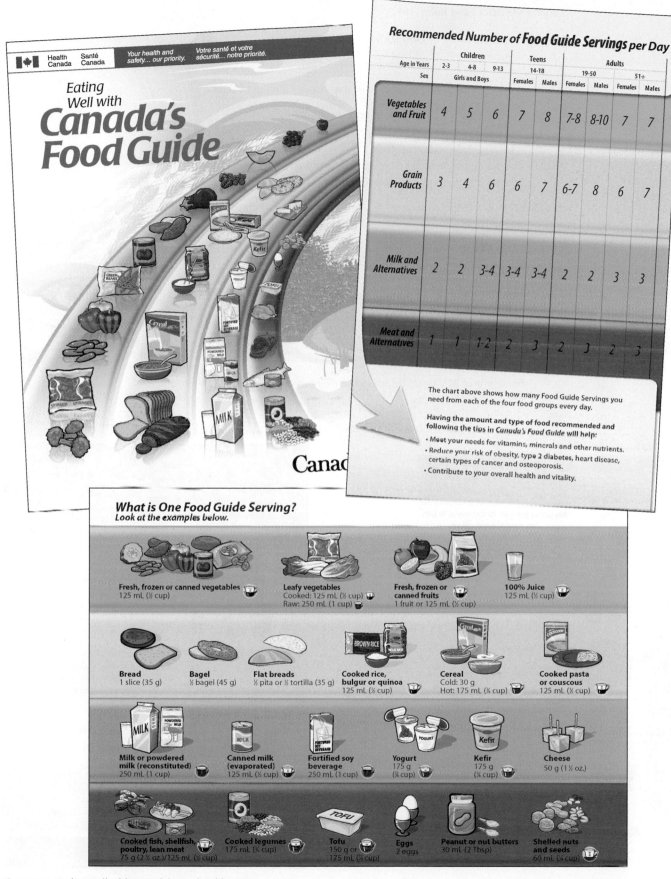

Figure 7-1 Eating Well with Canada's Food Guide, 2007

Source: http://www.hc-sc.gc.ca/fn-an/food-guide-aliment/hist/fg_history-histoire_ga_e.html#food, Health Canada, 2007. Reproduced with the permission of the Minister of Public Works and Government Services Canada, 2007.

Canada's Official Food Rules (1942)

CANADA'S OFFICIAL FOOD RULES

These are the Health-Protective Foods

Be sure you eat them every day in at least these amounts.

(Use more if you can)

MILK–Adults—1 pint, Children—more than 1 pint. And some CHEESE, as available.

FRUITS–One serving of tomatoes daily, or of a citrus fruit, or of tomato or citrus fruit juices, and one serving of other fruits, fresh, canned, or dried.

VEGETABLES (In addition to potatoes of which you need one serving daily)—Two servings daily of vegetables, preferably leafy green, or yellow, and frequently raw.

CEREALS AND BREAD–One serving of a whole-grain cereal and 4 to 6 slices of Canada Approved Bread, brown or white.

MEAT, FISH, etc.–One serving a day of meat, fish, or meat substitutes. Liver, heart or kidney once a week.

EGGS–At least 3 or 4 eggs weekly.

Eat these foods first, then add other foods you wish.

Some source of Vitamin D such as fish liver oils is essential for children, and may be advisable for adults.

Canada's Food Rules (1949)

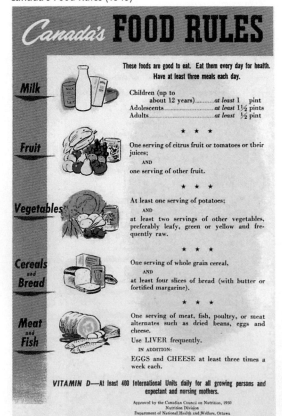

Canada's Food Guide (1961)

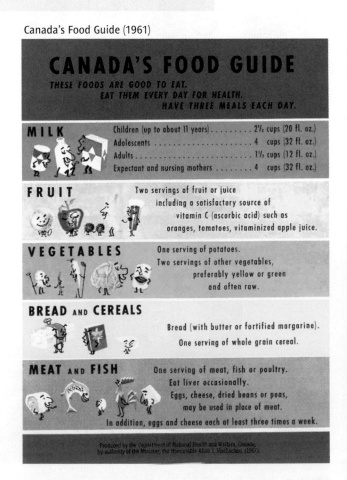

Figure 7-2 Canada Food Guide throughout the Years

Source: http://www.hc-sc.gc.ca/fn-an/food-guide-aliment/hist/fg_history-histoire_ga_e.html#food, Health Canada, 1942, 1949, 1961, 1977, 1992. Reproduced with the permission of the Minister of Public Works and Government Services Canada, 2006.

Canada's Food Guide (1977)

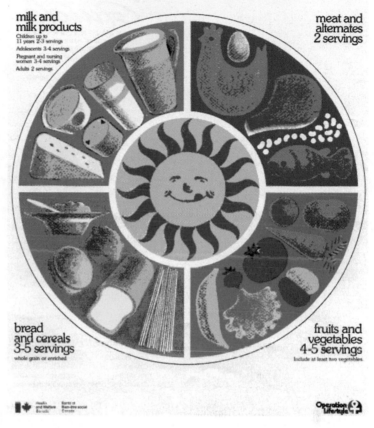

Figure 7-2 *continued*

the patterns of food used by Canadians, including the range of ethnic cuisines being practised across the provinces and territories. It has also considered the epidemiological trends of nutrition related illnesses—especially those associated with obesity. The latest Canada Food Guide—the most detailed of all the previous guides—ensures that Dietary Reference Intakes (DRIs) required for healthy nutrition are met.[2] To address the specific needs of Canada's First Nations, Inuit, and Metis population, Health Canada is developing a different food guide that will take into account traditional local foods.

Canada's Food Guide emphasizes healthy eating "patterns" of food consumption over time rather than food choices made at any given meal. The Food Guide embraces a *total diet approach* to account for a range of energy needs. Whereas previous guidelines outlined simple *foundation diets* that did not meet daily energy requirements, the 2007 edition addresses issues of energy balance, fats, carbohydrates, dietary fibre, and moderation in the use of salt and sugar. Similar to the previous food guide, Canada's Food Guide to Healthy Eating, the Eating Well with Canada's Food Guide (Figure 7-1) takes the form of a food rainbow, depicting types of food from each of the macronutrient food groups. While the nature of the four groups remains relatively the same—vegetables and fruit, grain products, milk and alternatives, and meat and alternatives—the arcs of grain products and vegetables and fruits have been switched. Formerly, grains constituted the most prominent arc; now, vegetables and fruits have moved into the highest intake category with grains moved to the second largest intake group. Note that food with the smallest number of daily servings is on the bottom, the shortest arc

Canada's Food Guide (1992)

Figure 7-2 *continued*

of the rainbow, and that food with the largest number of daily servings is on the top in the broadest arc of the rainbow. The most recent Food Guide provides guidelines for children as young as two years—unlike the former edition that provided specific recommendations for children over the age of 4. Health Canada provides an excellent on-line interactive tool, My Food Guide, so that people can tailor the Eating Well with Canada's Food Guide to individual factors such as age, sex, physical activity level, culture, and even food preferences!

The Eating Well with Canada's Food Guide includes key directional statements—the most detailed than ever before. Some of the guidelines include:

- Have vegetables and fruit more often than juice
- Eat at least one dark green and one orange vegetable every day (such as broccoli and carrots)
- Have at least half of daily grain products intake from whole grain
- Have meat alternatives such as beans, lentils, and tofu often
- Eat at least two food guide servings of fish every week
- Satisfy thirst with water
- Drink skim, 1% or 2% milk each day—drink fortified soy beverages if you do not drink milk
- Reduce the total amount of fat in the diet, especially saturated and trans fats, however, a small amount of unsaturated fat is recommended each day (30–45 ml for an adult)
- Lower salt and sugar intake

- Achieve and maintain a healthy body weight by enjoying regular physical activity—adults should get 30 to 60 minutes of moderate physical activity every day and children should get 90 minutes
- All women who could become pregnant should take 400 µg (0.4 mg) of folic acid a day to avoid neural tube defects in the unborn fetus
- All adults over 50 years of age should, in addition to following the Food Guide, take a daily vitamin D supplement of 10 µg (400 IU) a day

FOOD GROUPS

Vegetables and Fruit

The most prominent arc of the rainbow contains all fresh, frozen, canned, and dried vegetables and fruits, including fruit and vegetable juices. In general, one medium-sized fruit or vegetable, or 125 mL (1/2 cup) of fresh fruit or vegetable juice, accounts for one serving. The recommended number of daily servings of vegetables and fruit ranges from four a day for a two-year-old and up to seven a day for men and women over 50. The guide is very specific in recommending that Canadians of all ages have *at least* one serving *each* of a dark green and an orange vegetable each day. Broccoli, collards, green peas, and spinach are a few examples of green vegetables—all are high in folate. Carotenoids are provided by orange vegetables such as squash, carrots, and sweet potatoes. If people do not find orange vegetables appealing, the Food Guide suggests replacing these with orange-coloured fruits that contain carotenoids such as apricots, cantaloupe, or mango (while oranges provide folate and vitamin C, they are not a good source of carotenoids).

Grain Products

The next arc of the rainbow depicts grain products. Grains are an important source of carbohydrates, which should contribute 45–65% toward an individual's daily energy requirements. The Food Guide recommends that Canadians choose at least half of their daily grain intake from whole grain products, especially those lower in fat, sugar, or salt. Intake of grain products ranges from three a day for a two- or three-year-old up to 8 a day for 19–50 year old men. It is a misconception that foods such as pasta are fattening. It is only when prepared or served with other foods that contain high quantities of fats (such as sauces made with cream) that these foods become a significant source of fat and salt. Whole-grain products should be chosen over refined or enriched breads because they contain more dietary fibre. Select enriched cereals and pastas because they contain more iron and B vitamins than their nonenriched counterparts. Commercial cookies and pies may be considered grain products but can be a considerable source of fat and refined sugars. Many Canadians do not realize that common portions of grain products such as one bagel, a piece of pita, or a bun is actually two servings. In contrast, one slice of whole wheat bread (35 g) is one serving.

Milk and alternatives

Milk products are an important source of calcium and Vitamin D. Children aged 2–8 years and men and women 19–50 years require 2 servings per day; youth 9–18 years should have 3 or 4 servings; adults over 51 require 3 servings a day. One Food Guide serving would be 250 mL of milk (1 cup), 175 gm (3/4 cup) of yogurt, or 50 gm (1 1/2 oz) cheese. In addition, the Food Guide recommends that men and women over 50 take a daily 10µg (400 IU) vitamin D supplement. The emphasis is placed on choosing lower fat milks, cheeses, and ice cream. Although all liquid milk contains an equal amount of vitamins A and D, there are differences in the fat content of whole milk (3.25% milk fat or MF) compared to skim (0.1% MF). Most firm, ripened cheeses contain more than 28% MF. Ice cream, sour cream, and whipping cream can be very high in fat. Yogurt and cheese do not have added vitamin D, and cottage cheese has the lowest amount of calcium of all milk or dairy products.

Meat and Alternatives

Two or three servings of meat and alternatives provide much of an adult's daily protein requirements. Certain cuts of meats are higher in fat, but baking, broiling, roasting, or microwaving can limit fat compared to frying. Trimming visible fat from meat and draining off liquid fat when cooking are other methods to lower the fat content. Other foods in this category include fish, beans, lentils, peas, and tofu. These foods are generally low fat and provide an important source of fibre and protein, which are especially important for vegetarians. Never before has a Food Guide recommended at *least* two servings of fish a week—this recommendation is based on the omega-3 fats, eicosapentaenoic acid and docosahexaenoic acid, that are found in salmon, mackerel, rainbow trout, and sardines. Health Canada warns that fresh tuna, shark, and swordfish should be avoided by pregnant women and young children as they can lead to over-exposure to mercury. One serving of meat and alternatives is: 75 g of cooked fish, chicken, beef, or pork; two eggs; 60 mL of nuts; or 30 mL of peanut butter.

Other Foods

Not all foods fall directly into the four main groups—some of these foods are higher in fat or calories with limited nutritional value and should therefore be used sparingly. However, no food in this category is inherently bad or harmful. This category includes:

- Foods that are mostly fat and oils: butter, margarine, mayonnaise, cooking oils, salad dressing, shortening, lard.
- Foods that are mostly sugar: most jams, jellies, white and brown sugar, honey, syrup, candy, marshmallow, sherbet, Popsicles.
- Beverages: cola, sports drinks, fruit-flavoured drinks, coffee, tea, alcohol, water.
- High fat and/or high salt food: potato chips, nachos, corn chips, pretzels, cheese-flavoured puffs, potato sticks.
- Herbs, spices and condiments: oregano, basil, and other green herbs, salt, pepper, ketchup, mustard, barbecue sauce, horseradish, pickles, relish, soya sauce.

ALCOHOL AND CAFFEINE

Alcohol and beverages containing caffeine should be consumed in moderation. Generally, moderate drinking is defined as no more than seven alcoholic drinks per week. Binge drinking (consuming more than four drinks per sitting) should be avoided. The Canadian Food Guide defines equivalent quantities of alcohol to be: one bottle (350 mL) of beer (5% alcohol) = 150 mL of wine (10–14% alcohol) = 50 mL of hard liquor (40% alcohol). Pregnant women and breast-feeding mothers should not consume any alcohol.[3]

Caffeine is a stimulant that should be consumed in moderation. Generally, individuals can consume up to 450 mg of caffeine per day without an increased risk of hypertension or heart disease. Pregnant women and breast-feeding mothers should limit the amount of caffeine they consume as it may be passed onto the fetus or the baby. An average mug of filtered coffee contains about 200 mg of caffeine.

Salt

Salt is "hidden" in many foods, and the reliance on commercial preparations (such as canned vegetables and processed sandwich meats) means that the average

Canadian consumes far more salt than required. High intakes of sodium have been related to the development of hypertension. People should limit the quantity of high-salt snack foods such as chips, peanuts, and nachos. Other high-salt foods include frozen or ready-to-eat dinners and most condiments. When seasoning foods, nonsodium alternatives should be chosen, such as spices, herbs, lemon juice, salt substitutes and salt-free replacements. Labels on foods should be routinely checked for sodium content and "low salt" or "low sodium" alternatives should be considered.

Portion Size versus Calorie Counting

The Eating Well with Canada's Food Guide does not make specific recommendations about the amount of calories that should be consumed per person per day. This approach is an important difference from the American food guide, MyPyramid, described below. An individual who follows the Canadian Food Guide will consume between 1800 and 3200 calories per day depending on the size and number of food portions eaten.

VITALITY MESSAGE: "ENJOY EATING WELL, BEING ACTIVE AND FEELING GOOD ABOUT YOURSELF. THAT'S VITALITY"

The Vitality message encourages Canadians of all ages to follow the Canada Food Guide to Healthy Eating so they can make wiser choices as part of a commitment to a healthier lifestyle. A focus on active living instead of a rigorous, prescribed exercise regimen, coupled with the message "feel good about yourself," promotes the idea that healthy weight is not necessarily a low weight but one that is right for a variety of body morphologies.

FOOD GUIDES IN THE UNITED STATES

The United States is another country with a strong history of promoting the health of its citizens through the development of food guides. For example, the "Basic Four" food guide, first issued in 1956, divided foods into four groups: milk and dairy, meats, vegetables and fruits, and breads and cereals. The United States Department of Agriculture (USDA) issued several revisions and published recommendations in 1992 using the Food Guide Pyramid, which expanded on the original basic four food groups to include guidelines on proportions and moderation. Six different food groups represented specific nutrients. In 2005, the USDA published MyPyramid, a new food guidance system to replace the original 1992 Food Guide Pyramid. The MyPyramid system (Figure 7-3) offers individuals a more personalized approach to nutrition that combines healthy eating with physical activity.

MyPyramid applies to Americans over age two and was developed to help people make informed and healthy food choices. The colour bands in MyPyramid represent the types of foods that should be consumed. Similar to Canada's Food Guide, the width of the bands denotes the approximate relative quantity of each food that should be consumed. In addition, MyPyramid incorporates the concept of physical activity into its design by depicting a person climbing the stairs. An interesting feature of MyPyramid is that individuals can access the MyPyramid website and enter their age, gender, and physical activity to obtain a personalized guideline. Twelve different pyramids are available on the website using these parameters. The 12 pyramids range from daily intake levels of 1000–3200 calories. By following the appropriate pyramid, an individual should be able to maintain a healthy body weight and decrease the risk of nutrition-related chronic diseases.

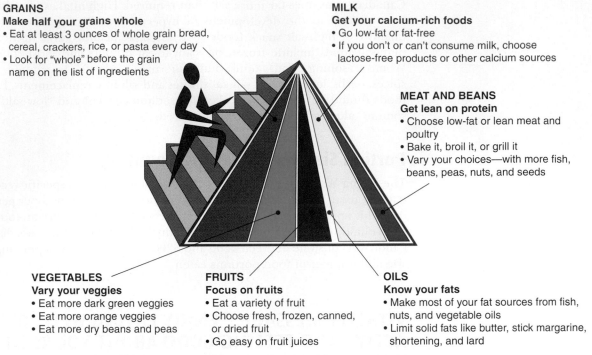

GRAINS
Make half your grains whole
- Eat at least 3 ounces of whole grain bread, cereal, crackers, rice, or pasta every day
- Look for "whole" before the grain name on the list of ingredients

MILK
Get your calcium-rich foods
- Go low-fat or fat-free
- If you don't or can't consume milk, choose lactose-free products or other calcium sources

MEAT AND BEANS
Get lean on protein
- Choose low-fat or lean meat and poultry
- Bake it, broil it, or grill it
- Vary your choices—with more fish, beans, peas, nuts, and seeds

VEGETABLES
Vary your veggies
- Eat more dark green veggies
- Eat more orange veggies
- Eat more dry beans and peas

FRUITS
Focus on fruits
- Eat a variety of fruit
- Choose fresh, frozen, canned, or dried fruit
- Go easy on fruit juices

OILS
Know your fats
- Make most of your fat sources from fish, nuts, and vegetable oils
- Limit solid fats like butter, stick margarine, shortening, and lard

Figure 7-3 Steps to a Healthier You: MyPyramid
Note: From *Inside MyPyramid,* by the U. S. Department of Agriculture, 2005. Retrieved October 11, 2006, from http://www.mypyramid.gov/pyramid.

DIETARY REFERENCE INTAKES

In 1995, Health Canada began collaborating with the Food and Nutrition Board (FNB) of the Institute of Medicine (IOM), National Academy of Sciences in the United States to develop harmonized recommendations for the daily intake of key nutrients. **Dietary Reference Intakes** (DRIs) are used to assess an individual's diet and are the basis on which nutritious, balanced diets are devised (Table 7-1). DRIs replace previously published Recommended Nutrient Intakes (RNIs) in Canada and have three components:

- Adequate Intake (AI): the intake value specific for each sex and various age groups that is estimated to provide adequate nutrition.
- Tolerable Upper Intake Level (UL): the maximum level of daily nutrients that is unlikely to pose health risks for most of the general population.
- Recommended Dietary Allowances (RDA): the recommended amounts of nutrients that individuals should eat daily. Recommendations differ based on sex, age, and whether the patient is pregnant or lactating.*

Nursing Tip

Dietary Reference Intakes for a wide range of foods is available at:

http://www.hc-sc.gc.ca/fn-an/nutrition/reference/table/index_e.html

---

*Recommendations are not requirements, because requirements reflect the amounts needed to prevent deficiencies. Recommendations exceed the required amounts to ensure that the entire population is considered.

TABLE 7-1 Dietary Reference Intakes (DRIs): Recommended Intakes for Individuals, Food and Nutrition Board, National Academy of Sciences, Institute of Medicine

Life Stage Group	Protein (g)	Vitamin A (µg/d) RDA/AI*	Vitamin A UL	Vitamin D (µg/d) RDA/AI*	Vitamin D UL	Vitamin E (mg/d) RDA/AI*	Vitamin E UL	Vitamin K (µg/d) RDA/AI*	Vitamin C (mg/d) RDA/AI*	Vitamin C UL	Thiamin (mg/d) RDA/AI*	Riboflavin (mg/d) RDA/AI*	Niacin (mg/d) RDA/AI*	Niacin UL	Vitamin B6 (mg/d) RDA/AI*	Vitamin B6 UL	Folate (µg/d) RDA/AI*	Folate UL	Vitamin B12 (µg/d) RDA/AI*	Vitamin B12 UL	Calcium (mg/d) RDA/AI*	Calcium UL	Phosphorus (mg/d) RDA/AI*	Phosphorus UL	Magnesium (mg/d) RDA/AI*	Magnesium UL	Iron (mg/d) RDA/AI*	Iron UL	Zinc (mg/d) RDA/AI*	Zinc UL	Iodine (µg/d) RDA/AI*	Iodine UL	Selenium (µg/d) RDA/AI*	Selenium UL
Infants																																		
0.0–0.6 mo	13	400*	600	5*	25	2.0*	ND	2.0*	40*	ND	0.2*	0.3*	2*	ND	0.1*	ND	65*	ND	0.4*	ND	210*	ND	100*	ND	30*	ND	0.27*	40	2*	4	110*	ND	15*	45
0.7–12 mo	14	500*	600	5*	25	2.5*	ND	2.5*	50*	ND	0.3*	0.4*	4*	ND	0.3*	ND	80*	ND	0.5*	ND	270*	ND	275*	ND	75*	ND	11	40	3	5	130*	ND	20*	60
Children																																		
1–3 yrs	16	300	600	5*	50	6	200	30*	15	400	0.5	0.5	6	10	0.5	30	150	300	0.9	ND	500*	2500	460	3000	80	65	7	40	3	7	90	200	20	90
4–8 yrs	24	400	900	5*	50	7	300	55*	25	650	0.6	0.6	8	15	0.6	40	200	400	1.2	ND	800*	2500	500	3000	130	110	10	40	5	12	90	300	30	150
Males																																		
9–13 yrs	45	600	1700	5*	50	11	600	60*	45	1200	0.9	0.9	12	20	1	60	300	600	1.8	ND	1300*	2500	1250	4000	240	350	8	40	8	23	120	600	40	280
14–18 yrs	59	900	2800	5*	50	15	800	75*	75	1800	1.2	1.3	16	30	1.3	80	400	800	2.4	ND	1300*	2500	1250	4000	410	350	11	45	11	34	150	900	55	400
19–30 yrs	58	900	3000	5*	50	15	1000	120*	90	2000	1.2	1.3	16	35	1.3	100	400	1000	2.4	ND	1000*	2500	700	4000	400	350	8	45	11	40	150	1000	55	400
31–50 yrs	63	900	3000	5*	50	15	1000	120*	90	2000	1.2	1.3	16	35	1.3	100	400	1000	2.4	ND	1000*	2500	700	4000	420	350	8	45	11	40	150	1000	55	400
50–70 yrs	63	900	3000	10*	50	15	1000	120*	90	2000	1.2	1.3	16	35	1.7	100	400	1000	2.4	ND	1200*	2500	700	4000	420	350	8	45	11	40	150	1000	55	400
70+ yrs	63	900	3000	15*	50	15	1000	120*	90	2000	1.2	1.3	16	35	1.7	100	400	1000	2.4	ND	1200*	2500	700	3000	420	350	8	45	11	40	150	1000	55	400
Females																																		
9–13 yrs	46	600	1700	5*	50	11	600	60*	45	1200	0.9	0.9	12	20	1	60	300	600	1.8	ND	1300*	2500	1250	4000	240	350	8	40	8	23	120	600	40	280
14–18 yrs	44	700	2800	5*	50	15	800	75*	65	1800	1	1	14	30	1.2	80	400	800	2.4	ND	1300*	2500	1250	4000	360	350	15	45	9	34	150	900	55	400
19–30 yrs	45	700	3000	5*	50	15	1000	90*	75	2000	1.1	1.1	14	35	1.3	100	400	1000	2.4	ND	1000*	2500	700	4000	310	350	18	45	8	40	150	1100	55	400
31–50 yrs	53	700	3000	5*	50	15	1000	90*	75	2000	1.1	1.1	14	35	1.3	100	400	1000	2.4	ND	1000*	2500	700	4000	320	350	18	45	8	40	150	1100	55	400

continues

TABLE 7-1 Dietary Reference Intakes (DRIs): Recommended Intakes for Individuals, Food and Nutrition Board, National Academy of Sciences, Institute of Medicine *continued*

Life Stage Group	Protein (g)	FAT-SOLUBLE VITAMINS Vitamin A (μg/d) RDA/AI*	UL	Vitamin D (μg/d) RDA/AI*	UL	Vitamin E (mg/d) RDA/AI*	UL	Vitamin K (μg/d) RDA/AI*	UL	WATER-SOLUBLE VITAMINS Vitamin C (mg/d) RDA/AI*	UL	Thiamin (mg/d) RDA/AI*	UL	Riboflavin (mg/d) RDA/AI*	UL	Niacin (mg/d) RDA/AI*	UL	Vitamin B6 (mg/d) RDA/AI*	UL	Folate (μg/d) RDA/AI*	UL	Vitamin B12 (μg/d) RDA/AI*	UL	MINERALS Calcium (mg/d) RDA/AI*	UL	Phosphorus (mg/d) RDA/AI*	UL	Magnesium (mg/d) RDA/AI*	UL	Iron (mg/d) RDA/AI*	UL	Zinc (mg/d) RDA/AI*	UL	Iodine (μg/d) RDA/AI*	UL	Selenium (μg/d) RDA/AI*	UL
50–70 yrs	50	700	3000	10*	50	15	1000	90*	ND	75	2000	1.1	ND	1.1	ND	14	35	1.5	100	400	1000	2.4	ND	1200*	2500	700	4000	320	350	8	45	8	40	150	1100	55	400
70+ yrs	50	700	3000	15*	50	15	1000	90*	ND	75	2000	1.1	ND	1.1	ND	14	35	1.5	100	400	1000	2.4	ND	1200*	2500	700	3000	320	350	8	45	8	40	150	1100	55	400
Pregnant	60	770	3000	5*	50	15	1000	90*	ND	85	2000	1.4	ND	1.4	ND	18	35	1.9	100	600	1000	2.6	ND	1000*	2500	700	3500	350	350	27	45	11	40	220	1100	60	400
Lactating	65	1300	3000	5*	50	19	1000	90*	ND	120	2000	1.4	ND	1.6	ND	17	35	2	100	500	1000	2.8	ND	1000*	2500	700	4000	310	350	9	45	12	40	290	1100	70	400

Note: The table is adapted from the DRI reports, see *www.nap.edu*. It represents Recommended Dietary Allowances (RDAs) in bold type, Adequate Intakes (AIs) in ordinary type followed by an asterisk (*), and Upper Limits (ULs). RDAs and AIs may both be used as goals for individual intake. RDAs are set to meet the needs of almost all (97 to 98 percent) individuals in a group. For healthy breastfed infants, the AI is the mean intake. The AI for other life stage and gender groups is believed to cover the needs of all individuals in the group, but lack of data prevent being able to specify with confidence the percentage of individuals covered by this intake.

UL = The maximum level of daily nutrient intake that is likely to pose no risk of adverse effects. Unless otherwise specified, the UL represents total intake from food, water, and supplements. Due to lack of suitable data, ULs could not be established for Vitamin K, thiamin, riboflavin, vitamin B₁₂, pantothenic acid, biotin, or carotenoids. In absence of ULs, extra caution may be warranted in consuming levels above the recommended intakes.

ND = Not determinable due to lack of data of adverse effects in this age group and concern with regard to lack of ability to handle excess amounts. Source of intake should be from food only to prevent high levels of intake.

Source : Reprinted with permission from Dietary Reference Intakes (DRIs): Recommended Intakes for Individuals, Food and Nutrition Board © 2001 by the National Academy of Sciences. Courtesy of the National Academies Press, Washington, D. C.

Life 360°

Natural Health Products and DRIs

A wide variety of vitamins and supplements are available at drug stores, natural product stores, and other locations, including the Internet. Canada differs from other countries, including the United States, in how vitamin and mineral supplements are classified in that they are considered to be natural health products (NHPs). Vitamin and mineral supplements are not viewed as foods so are subject to specific regulations that came into effect in 2004. NHPs include vitamins and minerals, herbal remedies, homeopathic medicines, traditional medicines (e.g., Chinese medicines), probiotics, and other products including amino acids and essential fatty acids. The NHP's regulations require a compulsory premarket product review to ensure that any health claims made by the manufacturers are supported by appropriate evidence. As well, the bottle's contents are assessed to make certain that the label indicates what is in the bottle, along with information about treatment, dosage, and health warnings.[4]

Reflective Thinking

Implementing the Eating Well with Canada's Food Guide

- Review the key recommendations of the Food Guide.
- Perform a personal assessment of how well your diet conforms to each of the recommendations.
- Interview a pregnant woman, a lactating woman, a teenage girl and boy, a man in his 50s, and a woman in her 70s. How does their diet and activity compare with the Eating Well with Canada's Food Guide key recommendations?

FOOD LABELLING

Recent changes to the Food and Drug Act in Canada in 2003 made clear nutrition labelling a requirement for most foods. Nutrition facts (see Figure 7-4) are printed on labels to allow consumers to make informed choices about the foods they eat. Regulations restrict the diet-related health claims that can be made about specific foods, which will apply to all food manufacturers as of December, 2007. Standardized nutrition facts tables appear on most manufactured foods and indicate the nutritional value of the food.

NUTRIENTS

To perform a proper nutritional assessment the nurse must have a clear understanding of the various nutrients needed to provide an adequate diet, the reason nutrients are needed, and the food sources that provide them

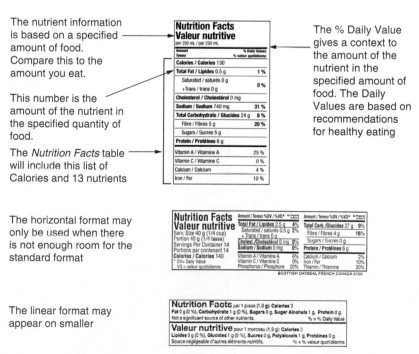

The nutrient information is based on a specified amount of food. Compare this to the amount you eat.

This number is the amount of the nutrient in the specified quantity of food.

The *Nutrition Facts* table will include this list of Calories and 13 nutrients

The % Daily Value gives a context to the amount of the nutrient in the specified amount of food. The Daily Values are based on recommendations for healthy eating

The horizontal format may only be used when there is not enough room for the standard format

The linear format may appear on smaller

Figure 7-4 Nutrition Facts Label.

Source: http://www.hc-sc.gc.ca/ahc-asc/media/nr-cp/2003/2003_01bk1_e.html

Figure 7-5 Accurate nutritional assessment necessitates knowledge of the nutrients within the food. *Courtesy of WHO/P. Virot.*

(Figure 7-5). **Nutrients** are the substances found in food that are nourishing and useful to the body. Carbohydrates, proteins, fats, vitamins, minerals, and water are the nutrients essential for life.

Carbohydrates, proteins, and fats supply the body with energy, which is measured in units called **kilocalories** (kcal), or calories. A calorie is the amount of heat required to raise 1 g of water 1° centigrade. Whereas the USDA has specific recommendations and guidelines for calculating caloric requirements based on activity level and ideal body weight (IBW) multiplied by a specific number of calories per pound, Health Canada does not stipulate daily calorie counts per se, but instead focuses on the portions and portion sizes. *(The table below is provided for reference only.)*

CALORIES/POUND of Ideal Body Weight

ACTIVITY	FEMALES	MALES
Sedentary	14	16
Moderate	18	21
Heavy	22	26

A 130-pound female who performs a moderate amount of exercise should have a daily intake of 2340 calories (18 × 130), and a 165-pound male who performs the same amount of exercise should have an intake of 3465 calories (21 × 165). Compare this to an 1820 calorie intake (14 × 130) for a 130-pound woman who leads a sedentary lifestyle and a 2640 calorie intake (16 × 165) for a 165-pound man who leads a sedentary lifestyle.

Carbohydrates

The major source of energy for the various functions of the body is **carbohydrates.** Each gram of carbohydrates contains four calories. Adults require 45–65% of the daily caloric intake in the form of carbohydrates to prevent ketosis and protein breakdown of muscles.

Carbohydrates help form adenosine triphosphate (ATP), which is needed to transfer energy within the cells. Carbohydrates supply fibre and assist in the utilization of fat. The primary sources of carbohydrates are bread, potatoes, pasta, corn, rice, dried beans, and fruits. Dietary deficiency of carbohydrates can result in electrolyte imbalance, fatigue, and depression. An excess in carbohydrates may produce obesity and tooth decay and may adversely affect those with diabetes mellitus.

Diets high in fibre have been shown to be beneficial in disease prevention by possibly decreasing weight and reducing the risks of colon and rectal cancer, heart disease (decreases serum cholesterol levels), dental caries, constipation, and diverticulosis.

Proteins

There are four calories in every gram of protein, but foods usually are a combination of protein and fat (meats, milk), or protein and carbohydrates (legumes).

Nursing Tip

High-Fibre Diet

- Eat fresh foods instead of processed foods.
- Eat whole-grain flour and breads.
- Increase fibre intake slowly to prevent constipation.
- Increase water intake with fibre; minimum is six to eight glasses per day.
- Obtain fibre from the diet rather than from supplements.

Nursing Alert

Hypervitaminosis

Hypervitaminosis is a toxic amount of vitamins in the body. It occurs with both water-soluble vitamins and fat-soluble vitamins. Vitamins that have been shown to cause serious toxic effects if taken in large amounts include vitamins A, K, C, and B_6.

Encourage patients to obtain proper nutrients through a healthy diet rather than supplements. If your patient insists on taking supplements, the supplements should use the DRIs as a guide. It is important to stress that vitamin supplements should not replace a healthy diet.

Nursing Tip

Omega-3 and Omega-6 Fatty Acids

Omega fatty acids are becoming well publicized in medical literature and in the public media. The two main types of Omega fatty acids are Omega-3 and Omega-6 fatty acids, which are polyunsaturated fats that are cardioprotective in nature. The consumption of Omega-3 fatty acids has been related to a decrease in triglycerides. This fatty acid is found in flax and in fatty fish such as salmon, sardines, trout, and mackerel. Some products such as eggs, yogurt, and milk may have Omega-3 fatty acids added to them. Omega-6 fatty acids are derived from sunflower, safflower, and corn oils. Some nuts such as almonds, pecans, Brazil nuts, sunflower seeds, and sesame seeds also contain Omega-6 fatty acids. The Heart and Stroke Foundation of Canada recommends eating broiled, steamed, or baked fish two or three times per week to capitalize on the heart-healthy benefit of these fatty acids but notes that Omega-6 fat sources should be eaten in moderation because they can increase calorie intake significantly.[6]

Canada's Food Guide recommends that adults obtain 10–35% of their total daily caloric intake from protein. Protein requirements vary depending on the status of the individual. Breast-feeding women, athletes, and people recovering from illness may require up to 2.0 g/kg/day. Most recent guidelines recommend a protein intake of 1.5–2.0 g/kg/day for most patients with moderate to severe stress. In nutritionally depleted patients, protein requirements can exceed 150 g per day if they are ill or have had surgery.[5] Protein is composed of 22 amino acids that can be classified as essential and nonessential. Nine essential amino acids cannot be synthesized, and their availability depends completely on dietary sources. In addition, the body is only capable of synthesizing nonessential amino acids if an adequate supply of protein is available. It is for this reason that an adequate daily intake of protein is necessary. Protein sources that contain all nine essential amino acids are termed *complete proteins*. Proteins that lack one or more of the essential amino acids are called *incomplete proteins*. Amino acids are needed to form the basis of all cell structures in the body. Protein is needed to manufacture and repair body tissue; it helps to maintain osmotic pressure within the cells, is a component of antibodies, and is ultimately a source of energy. The major sources of protein are meat, poultry, fish, eggs, tofu, cheese, and milk. Legumes (dried beans and peas) also are a good source of protein when eaten with corn or wheat. This is helpful information for vegetarians and for people whose incomes will not cover the purchase of meat and milk products.

Fats

Lipids, or fats, contain nine calories per gram. The Heart and Stroke Foundation of Canada recommends that fat consumption be reduced to 20–35% of total calories (about 45–75 g/day for a woman and about 60–105 g/day for a man).[7] **Fats** supply the essential fatty acids that form a part of the structure of all cells and help to lower serum cholesterol. Essential fatty acids must be supplied by the diet. The food sources of fat are animal fat (butter, shortening, lard) and vegetable fat (vegetable oil, margarine, and nuts), all of which influence the texture and taste of food. **Saturated fats,** which have been found to raise cholesterol levels, come from animal sources (butter, lard, fatty meats) and vegetable sources (coconut, palm, and partially hydrogenated oils that occur in some processed foods). **Monounsaturated fats** (olive and canola oils, avocado, nuts) help reduce **low-density lipoproteins** (LDLs) but do not reduce **high-density lipoproteins** (HDLs). **Cholesterol** is a lipid contained only in animal products. It is found in muscles, red blood cells, and cell membranes and is transported in the blood by HDLs and LDLs. HDLs carry cholesterol toward the liver while LDLs carry the cholesterol toward the cells and then deposit it in the tissues.

There is a strong association between high levels of LDLs and coronary artery disease (CAD). High levels of HDLs protect against CAD. Health Canada recommends the consumption of more polyunsaturated fat, especially Omega-3 fatty acids (see Nursing Tip, Omega-3 and Omega-6 Fatty Acids), monounsaturated fat, and lower amounts of saturated and trans fatty acids.

Triglycerides account for most of the lipids stored in the body's tissues. In the bloodstream, triglycerides produce energy for the body. An elevated triglyceride level occurs in hyperlipidemia, a risk factor for CAD.

A deficiency of fat in the diet can cause a decrease in weight, lack of satiety, and skin and hair changes. An excess of fat in the diet contributes to obesity and is linked to CAD. There has also been a correlation between high-fat diets and certain cancers (colon, breast, and prostate, in particular).

Trans Fatty Acids (Trans Fats)

Trans fatty acids raise LDLs and reduce HDLs and are more likely than saturated fats to increase the risk of cardiovascular disease. Trans fats are created when an unsaturated fat is hydrogenated to convert a liquid vegetable oil into a solid such as in the manufacturing of margarine. Trans fats can thus appear in partially hydrogenated margarine, in commercially baked goods such as crackers, cookies, chips, and in deep-fried fast food. Dairy products, beef, and lamb also contain trans fats, but these are not considered to be as dangerous as those obtained from hydrogenated trans fats.

Health Canada has recognized that the consumption of trans fats can increase the risk of heart disease.[8] In fact, Canada was the first country to introduce mandatory labelling of trans fats in packaged food products and instituted this labelling on most prepackaged foods in 2005 to help individuals make healthier choices. Furthermore, the Heart and Stroke Foundation of Canada is working intensely with Health Canada to develop strategies for reducing trans fats in Canadian foods.

Vitamins

Vitamins are organic substances needed to maintain the function of the body. They are not supplied by the body in sufficient amounts and must be obtained from dietary sources. **Fat-soluble vitamins** (vitamins A, D, E, and K) are stored in dietary fat and absorbed in the fat portions of the body's cells. **Water-soluble vitamins** include C, thiamine (B_1), riboflavin (B_2), niacin, pyridoxine (B_6), folacin (folate), cobalamin (B_{12}), pantothenic acid, and biotin. These vitamins are not stored in the body and are excreted in the urine. Various disease conditions occur when a vitamin source is lacking (Table 7-2).

Minerals

Minerals are inorganic elements that help build body tissue and regulate body processes such as fluid and acid-base balance, nerve cell transmission, vitamin absorption, enzyme and hormonal activity, and muscle contractions. Minerals are divided into two classifications. **Macrominerals,** or major minerals, are needed by the body in large amounts (>100 mg/day) (Table 7-3). **Microminerals,** or trace minerals, are needed in smaller amounts by the body (<15 mg/day) (Table 7-4).

The most common mineral deficiency in the world is lack of iron, which can result in iron-deficiency anemia. Lack of iron is particularly prevalent among infants, adolescents, and pregnant or menstruating women.

TABLE 7-2	Fat-Soluble Vitamins and Water-Soluble Vitamins		
NAME	**FOOD AND OTHER SOURCES**	**FUNCTIONS**	**DEFICIENCY/TOXICITY**

Vitamin A (retinol)	Animal
	  Kidney
	  Liver
	  Whole milk
	  Butter
	  Cream
	  Cod liver oil
	Plants
	  Dark green leafy vegetables
	  Deep yellow or orange fruit
	  Fortified margarine
		Dim light
		  vision
		Maintenance
		  of mucous
		  membranes
		Growth and
		  development
		  of bones
			Deficiency
			  Night blindness
			  Xerophthalmia
			  Respiratory infections
			  Bone growth ceases
			Toxicity
			  Cessation of menstruation
			  Joint pain
			  Stunted growth
			  Enlargement of liver

Vitamin D (cholecalciferol)	Animal
	  Eggs
	  Liver
	  Fish liver oils
	  Fortified milk
	Plants
	  None
	Sunlight
		Bone growth
		Teeth
		  development
			Deficiency
			  Rickets
			  Osteomalacia
			  Osteoporosis
			  Poorly developed teeth
			  Muscle spasms
			Toxicity
			  Kidney stones
			  Calcification of soft tissues

Vitamin E (alphatocopherol)	Animal
	  None
	Plants
	  Legumes
	  Whole grains
	  Dark green leafy vegetables
	  Margarines
	  Salad dressing
		Antioxidant	Deficiency
			  Destruction of RBCs
			Toxicity
			  Hypertension

Vitamin K	Animal
	  Egg yolk
	  Liver
	  Milk
	Plants
	  Green leafy vegetables
	  Cabbage
		Blood clotting	Deficiency
			  Prolonged blood clotting
			Toxicity
			  Hemolytic anemia
			  Jaundice

Thiamin (vitamin B$_1$)	Animal
	  Pork
	  Beef
	  Liver
	  Eggs
	  Fish
	Plants
	  Whole and enriched grains
	  Legumes
		Coenzyme in
		  oxidation of
		  glucose
		Normal
		  appetite
		Healthy
		  nervous system
			Deficiency
			  Gastrointestinal tract,
			  nervous, and cardiovascular
			  system problems
			Toxicity
			  None

continues

TABLE 7-2 **Fat-Soluble Vitamins and Water-Soluble Vitamins** *continued*

NAME	FOOD AND OTHER SOURCES	FUNCTIONS	DEFICIENCY/TOXICITY

Riboflavin (vitamin B$_2$)	Animal
	  Liver
	  Kidney
	  Milk
	Plants
	  Green leafy
	  vegetables
	  Cereals
	  Enriched bread
		Aids release of
		  energy from food
		Healthy skin
		Healthy vision
			Deficiency
			  Cheilosis
			  Glossitis
			  Photophobia
			Toxicity
			  None

Pyridoxine (vitamin B$_6$)	Animal
	  Fish
	  Poultry
	  Pork
	  Milk
	  Eggs
	Plants
	  Whole-grain cereals
	  Legumes
		Synthesis of
		  nonessential
		  amino acids
		Conversion of
		  tryptophan
		  to niacin
		Antibody
		  production
			Deficiency
			  Cheilosis
			  Glossitis
			Toxicity
			  Liver disease

Vitamin B$_{12}$	Animal
	  Seafood
	  Meat
	  Eggs
	  Milk
	Plants
	  None
		Synthesis of
		  RBCs
		Maintenance
		  of myelin
		  sheaths
			Deficiency
			  Degeneration of myelin
			  sheaths
			  Pernicious anemia
			Toxicity
			  None

Niacin (nicotinic acid)	Animal
	  Milk
	  Eggs
	  Fish
	  Poultry
		Transfers hydrogen
		  atoms for synthesis
		  of ATP
		Healthy skin
		Healthy
		  nervous system
		Healthy digestion
			Deficiency
			  Pellagra
			  Dermatitis
			  Dementia
			  Diarrhea
			Toxicity
			  Vasodilation of
			  blood vessels

Folacin (folic acid)	Animal
	  Liver
	Plants
	  Green leafy vegetables
	  Spinach
	  Asparagus
	  Broccoli
	  Kidney beans
		Synthesis of
		  RBCs
			Deficiency
			  Glossitis
			  Macrocytic anemia
			  Neural tube defects of fetus
			  in pregnant females
			Toxicity
			  None

Biotin	Animal
	  Milk
	  Liver
		Coenzyme in
		  carbohydrate
		  and amino acid
			Deficiency
			  Dermatitis
			  Loss of hair

TABLE 7-2	Fat-Soluble Vitamins and Water-Soluble Vitamins *continued*		
NAME	**FOOD AND OTHER SOURCES**	**FUNCTIONS**	**DEFICIENCY/TOXICITY**
	Plants	metabolism	Toxicity
	Legumes	Niacin	None
	Mushrooms	synthesis from	
		tryptophan	
Pantothenic acid	Animal	Metabolism of	Deficiency
	Eggs	carbohydrates,	Burning sensation of feet
	Liver	lipids, and	Toxicity
	Salmon	proteins	None
	Yeast	Synthesis of	
	Plants	acetylcholine	
	Mushrooms		
	Cauliflower		
	Peanuts		
Vitamin C	Plants	Prevention of	Deficiency
(ascorbic acid)	All citrus	scurvy	Scurvy
	Broccoli	Formation of	Bruises easily
	Tomatoes	collagen	Muscle cramps
	Brussels sprouts	Healing of	Ulcerated gums
	Potatoes	wounds	Toxicity
		Release of	Raised uric acid level
		stress	Hemolytic anemia
		hormones	Kidney stones
		Absorption of iron	Rebound scurvy

RBC = red blood cell; ATP = adenosine triphosphate.

Water

Water accounts for 50–60% of the body's weight. People cannot survive more than a few days without water. The daily amount needed depends on the size of the person, the climate, and the amount of activity. The average adult needs six to eight 240 mL glasses of water a day; athletes and those living in hot, dry climates require more. Thirst is not always an adequate indicator of water intake needs, especially in infants or very ill individuals who may have a poor thirst mechanism. Those who engage in intense physical activity may have a decreased thirst sensation as well (Figure 7-6).

Figure 7-6 Preventing dehydration is an important element of proper nutrition.

Nursing Tip

Preventing Iron-Deficiency Anemia

- Identify those patients at risk (e.g., children under two years of age, adolescents, women with heavy menstrual flow, pregnant women, individuals with malabsorption syndromes, gastrointestinal bleeding, and gross dietary deficiencies).
- Perform a complete nutritional assessment on high-risk patients.
- Encourage patients to eat food high in iron, such as lean meats, poultry, fish, enriched breads, legumes, leafy green vegetables, dried fruits, and nuts.

TABLE 7-3 Major Minerals

NAME	FOOD SOURCES	FUNCTIONS	DEFICIENCY/TOXICITY

Calcium (Ca^{++})	Milk, cheese
	Sardines
	Salmon
	Green vegetables
		Development of bones and teeth
		Permeability of cell membranes
		Transmission of nerve impulses
		Blood clotting
			Deficiency
			  Osteoporosis
			  Osteomalacia
			  Rickets
			  Poor tooth formation

Phosphorus (P)	Milk, cheese Poultry Lean meat, fish Nuts Legumes	Development of bones and teeth Transfer of energy Component of phospholipids Buffer system	(Same as calcium)

Potassium (K$^+$)	Oranges
	Bananas
	Dried fruits
	Meat
	Cereals
		Contraction of muscles
		Maintaining water balance
		Transmission of nerve impulses
		Carbohydrate and protein metabolism
			Deficiency
			  Muscle cramps, weakness
			  Fatigue
			  Irregular heart rhythm
			  ST segment depression
			Toxicity
			  Diarrhea
			  Irritability
			  Irregular heart rhythm
			  Cardiac standstill

Sodium (Na$^+$)	Table salt
	Beef, eggs, poultry
	Milk, cheese
		Maintaining fluid balance in blood
		Transmission of nerve impulses
			Toxicity
			  Increase in blood pressure
			  Edema
			  Seizure
			  Coma

Magnesium (Mg^{++})	Green vegetables
	Milk, nuts, legumes
	Whole grains
		Synthesis of ATP
		Transmission of nerve impulses
		Activation of metabolic enzymes
		Relaxation of skeletal muscles
			Deficiency
			  Cardiac arrhythmias
			  Seizures
			Toxicity
			  Respiratory and cardiac arrest

Nursing Tip

Daily Fluid Intake

Approximately 2.3–2.8 litres of fluid are consumed by the average adult on a daily basis. If an adult drinks six 240 mL glasses of fluids per day, the total ingested liquid is 1440 mL. Added to this total is approximately 700 mL from the water content of food and 200 mL from water produced as the result of oxidation.[10] All totalled, this adult's daily intake of fluid would be 2.3 litres. If eight 240 mL glasses of fluids are consumed in one day, then the total fluid intake would increase to 2.8 litres.

TABLE 7-4 Trace Minerals

NAME	FOOD SOURCES	FUNCTIONS	DEFICIENCY/TOXICITY
Iron (Fe^+)	Meat, organ meats, fish, poultry Dried fruits, beans Fortified cereals	Transports oxygen and carbon dioxide	Deficiency Iron-deficiency anemia Toxicity Genetic hemochromatosis
Iodine (I^-)	Seafood Iodized salt	Regulates basal metabolic rate	Deficiency Goiter Cretinism Myxedema
Zinc (Zn^+)	Eggs, oysters, liver Legumes Milk	Formation of collagen Component of insulin Component of many vital enzymes Wound healing	Deficiency Growth retardation
Selenium (Se^-)	Liver, seafood Grains	Antioxidant	
Copper (Cu^+)	Oysters, liver Nuts Legumes Whole grains	Oxidation of glucose	Toxicity Wilson's disease
Manganese (Mn^+)	Nuts, peas, beans, fruits	Component of metabolic enzymes	
Fluoride (F^-)	Fluoridated drinking water Seafood	Reduces dental caries	Toxicity Mottled-looking teeth
Chromium (Cr)	Eggs, meats Whole-grain cereal	Binds insulin to cell membranes	

Nursing Alert

Signs and Symptoms of Dehydration

- Health history reveals inadequate intake of fluids.
- Decrease in urine output.
- Urine specific gravity >1.035.
- Weight loss (percent body weight): 3–5% for mild, 6–9% for moderate, and 10–15% for severe dehydration.
- Eyes appear sunken; tongue has increased furrows and fissures.
- Oral mucous membranes are dry.
- Decreased skin turgor.
- Sunken fontanels in infants.
- Changes in neurological status may occur with moderate to severe dehydration.

VEGETARIAN DIETS

More and more Canadians are choosing vegetarian diets for health and ethical considerations. Some vegetarians may include dairy products and eggs in their diets (lacto-ovo-vegetarians) whereas others exclude eggs (lacto-vegetarians). Total vegetarians (vegans) eat only nonanimal products. In fact, approximately 4% of Canadians now follow vegetarian diets. The Dieticians of Canada and the American Dietetics Association state that a well-planned vegetarian diet can provide the essential nutrients required for all stages of the life cycle and can prevent the occurrence of certain chronic diseases associated with higher fat diets.[11, 12] When compared to nonvegetarians, vegetarians have lower blood cholesterol levels and blood pressure, and a reduced occurrence of type 2 diabetes mellitus and some cancers. Furthermore, vegetarians often have a lower body mass index (BMI)—a high BMI is a risk factor for cardiovascular disease. A vegetarian food guide in the form of the familiar Canada Food Guide rainbow was developed by the Dieticians of Canada to guide consumers in making healthy food choices (see Figure 7-7). Note that serving sizes are quite small and that food items may be included in more than one category. Thus, one meal may be made up of several servings from each food group.

Vegetarian food guide rainbow

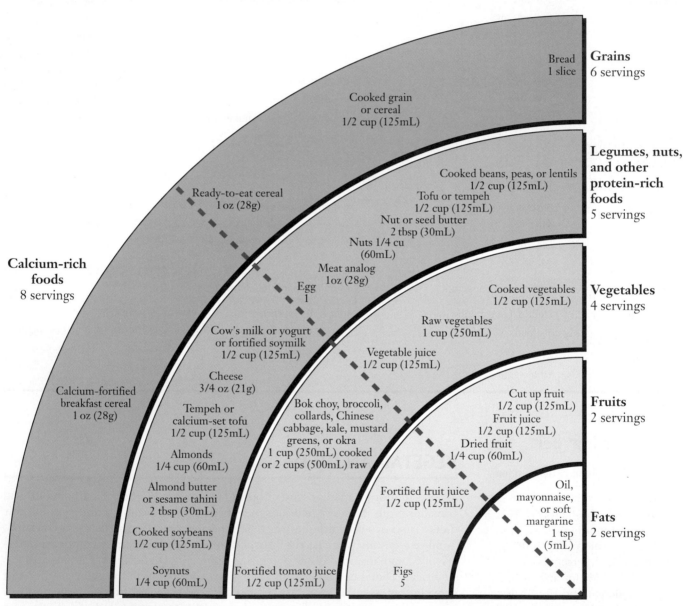

Grains
6 servings

Bread
1 slice

Cooked grain
or cereal
1/2 cup (125mL)

**Legumes, nuts,
and other
protein-rich
foods**
5 servings

Cooked beans, peas, or lentils
1/2 cup (125mL)

Tofu or tempeh
1/2 cup (125mL)

Nut or seed butter
2 tbsp (30mL)

Nuts 1/4 cu
(60mL)

Ready-to-eat cereal
1 oz (28g)

Meat analog
1oz (28g)

Egg
1

Vegetables
4 servings

Cooked vegetables
1/2 cup (125mL)

Raw vegetables
1 cup (250mL)

Vegetable juice
1/2 cup (125mL)

**Calcium-rich
foods**
8 servings

Cow's milk or yogurt
or fortified soymilk
1/2 cup (125mL)

Cheese
3/4 oz (21g)

Calcium-fortified
breakfast cereal
1 oz (28g)

Tempeh or
calcium-set tofu
1/2 cup (125mL)

Almonds
1/4 cup (60mL)

Almond butter
or sesame tahini
2 tbsp (30mL)

Cooked soybeans
1/2 cup (125mL)

Soynuts
1/4 cup (60mL)

Bok choy, broccoli,
collards, Chinese
cabbage, kale, mustard
greens, or okra
1 cup (250mL) cooked
or 2 cups (500mL) raw

Fortified tomato juice
1/2 cup (125mL)

Fruits
2 servings

Cut up fruit
1/2 cup (125mL)

Fruit juice
1/2 cup (125mL)

Dried fruit
1/4 cup (60mL)

Fortified fruit juice
1/2 cup (125mL)

Figs
5

Fats
2 servings

Oil,
mayonnaise,
or soft
margarine
1 tsp
(5mL)

Figure 7-7 Vegetarian Food Guide Rainbow

Source: http://www.dietitians.ca/news/downloads/vege_guide(EN).pdf. Courtesy of Dietitians of Canada.

NUTRITION THROUGH THE LIFE CYCLE

Nutritional needs change throughout the life cycle and are affected by both physical and developmental changes. The nurse must have a clear understanding of these changes and how they affect the patient, and must anticipate what guidance may be indicated when conducting a nutritional assessment. **Anticipatory guidance** covers health promotion, informs at-risk individuals of physical, cognitive, psychological, and social changes that occur, and explains their nutritional needs.

Children

Recommended daily nutritional requirements for children change with each age group. An understanding of development with regard to physical, cognitive, and psychosocial changes is needed to properly assess the nutritional needs of children. Educating the caregiver about these changes before they occur helps families to have more realistic expectations and to understand what is within the normal range and what should be cause for concern.

Infants

Infants grow more during the first 6 to 12 months of life than at any other time. This is also the time when there is rapid neurological development, which indicates a need for proper nutrients. If the infant cannot be breast-fed for the full

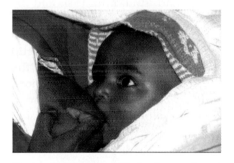

Figure 7-8 Breast milk is the preferred source of an infant's nutrition for the first 12 months. *Courtesy of WHO/P.Virot.*

Figure 7-9 Providing finger foods increases an infant's independence and assists with fine motor development.

Nursing Alert

Preventing Choking

Instruct parents to:
• Avoid use of foods that may cause choking in infants and small children (up to 3 years old), such as corn, nuts, raw peas, carrots and celery, small candies, wieners, popcorn, and any other small, hard foods.
• Stress the importance of having the child sit up while eating; prohibit running with food or objects in the mouth.

◄NURSING CHECKLIST►

Nutritional Assessment of Infants

• If the infant is breast-fed, how often and for how long?
• If the infant is not breast-fed, how much formula does the infant consume at each feeding, and how often does the infant eat? (Estimate how much is consumed in 24 hours.) How is the formula prepared? (The formula must be prepared correctly; this also helps establish how much the infant is eating.) How is the prepared formula stored?
• How does the infant react to eating? Does the infant appear satisfied?
• Does the infant appear to have any respiratory distress or reflux while eating? Are there any problems with constipation or diarrhea? If so, how is it treated? Have any allergies been discovered?
• Is the infant taking any supplemental food?
• Is the infant ever put in bed with a bottle? If yes, instruct the caregivers about infant bottle caries and the importance of not propping the bottle or placing it in the bed.

6-month minimum recommendation, nurses should inform parents that even a few weeks of breast-feeding can be beneficial, except in cases where the mother is HIV-positive (HIV infection can be transmitted via breast milk). Support the caregiver's feeding decision and discuss schedules, habits, and warning signs of inadequate intake or other problems.

Infants' hunger reflexes (sucking, rooting, and swallowing) should be assessed when evaluating their nutritional status. Infants feel hunger and express the need to eat by crying. Between 4 and 6 months, infants can feed themselves a cracker, and at 8 to 12 months they are able to drink from a cup by themselves. Ongoing developmental assessment is also needed to ensure the infant is achieving milestones (see Chapter 24). Foods should be introduced one at a time to observe for possible allergic reactions. The recommended order of new foods starts with the least allergenic, as outlined in the Nursing Tip, Infant Feeding Guidelines.

Fluoride Supplementation

Not all Canadian cities have fluoride added to tap water. See Chapter 24 for recommendations about fluoride supplementation.

Toddlers

Toddlers have their own unique nutritional needs as their physical growth slows. Toddlers' increased independence and control over their bodies is

Nursing Tip

Foods to Avoid in Early Infancy

It is recommended that infants *not* be fed egg whites until they are at least 12 months of age and *not* offered peanuts, nuts, or fish until age three because of the allergenic potential of these foods. Eggs should be thoroughly cooked to prevent salmonella poisoning. Also, infants under 12 months should not have honey because of the possibility of botulism toxicity.

Nursing Tip

Lactose Intolerance

Lactose intolerance is the inability of the body to digest foods that contain the carbohydrate lactose due to an insufficient amount of the enzyme lactase. Lactose intolerance can affect people of all ages, who may experience abdominal pain and cramping, bloating, flatulence, nausea, and diarrhea. Lactose-digesting enzymes and a lactose-free diet can limit the severity of the symptoms. If these measures are strictly followed by the patient and symptoms persist, then another etiology needs to be explored.

Nursing Alert

Obesity Epidemic in Children

A school-age child comes home from school, grabs a soda, chips, and cookies, and sits in front of the TV. After a while this child moves on to chat with friends on the Internet and play computer games. A sedentary lifestyle and dietary practices are some of the reasons for the alarming increase in the rate of childhood obesity in Canada. From 1981 to 1996, there was a dramatic increase in the prevalence of overweight and obese children in Canada. For boys aged 7 to 13 years, the prevalence increased from 10.6% to 32.6%, and for girls, it increased from 13.1% to 26.6%.[16] In 2004, 26% of all boys and girls aged 2 to 18 were overweight or obese.[17] For Aboriginal children, the picture is even more grim. In one Ojibwa-Cree community in Canada, 64% of girls and 60% of boys were overweight.[18]

With this increase in obesity, the number of children diagnosed with diabetes mellitus, hypertension, and hyperlipidemia has also increased. This obesity epidemic demands that nurses be involved in identifying children at risk and intervening with children who are already overweight.

demonstrated in their eating patterns, such as refusing to eat or desiring only certain foods. They may say "no" even to food they desire in order to demonstrate that they are in charge. These behaviours are normal responses at this developmental stage and should not be considered a problem unless they are excessive.

Instruct parents to offer small portions of foods that the toddler can self-feed, and to provide only one new food at a time. Toddlers are very good at imitating and often exhibit food dislikes that are shown at home (particularly if there is an older sibling). Encourage routine mealtimes that are enjoyed with the family together, which provides toddlers with role models for developing good eating habits.

Dental Health

Promote good dental health early on by not giving a bottle to the child who is about to fall asleep; the presence of milk in the mouth can lead to tooth decay. Pacifiers and bottle nipples should never be dipped in sweet solutions such as sugar or honey.[15]

Preschoolers

Preschoolers have food dislikes and may become picky eaters. Giving them choices, serving small amounts of foods they can eat easily (finger foods), and

Nursing Tip

The average rate of anaemia for Canadian children living in urban centres is 4–5%. Iron-deficiency anaemia is eight times more prevalent in infants and toddlers from First Nation communities in northern Ontario and Nunavut than in other children across Canada.[14] The high consumption of cow's milk or evaporated milk (which is low in bioavailable iron and frequently consumed owing to its low cost and availability in remote communities), is thought to be the cause of anaemia. In addition, infants who are breast-fed beyond 6 months of age and who do not receive any other iron supplementation (e.g., iron-rich cereal) are at risk for depletion of their iron stores, and hence anaemia. *Helicobacter pylori* (a bacterium that lives in the stomach) was present in the digestive tracts of 99% of the anaemic children, suggesting that eradicating this bacterium may improve outcomes. Nurses play an important role by encouraging the use of iron-fortified foods after the age of 6 months and by regularly screening all children who are at risk of anaemia

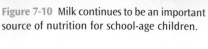

Figure 7-10 Milk continues to be an important source of nutrition for school-age children.

providing a routine and enjoyable eating environment helps to foster good eating habits.

Preschoolers often have smaller appetites compared to toddlers, which can be caused by drinking too many beverages (milk, juice, fruit punch) and by their slower increase in growth. Because preschoolers often resist new foods and may eat only one food at a time, caregivers should be encouraged to offer them other foods. Discuss the need to provide healthy snacks rather than foods that are high in sugar. Preschoolers benefit from helping to prepare food, setting the table, and making some decisions.

School-Age Children

School-age children tend to have erratic growth patterns that are reflected in their equally erratic eating patterns. They also tend to continue having strong likes and dislikes. Encourage families to maintain a balanced diet and to limit foods high in sugar (Figure 7-10). Caregivers should be advised to teach children proper nutrition and to show them how to read nutrition and ingredient labels. Also inform the family that pubescent chubbiness is a normal part of growth that often precedes a rapid increase in height.

Adolescents

Adolescents experience rapid growth and change and their nutritional needs fluctuate accordingly. Adolescents are concerned with body image and often compare their bodies to those of their peers in an attempt to fit into an acceptable identity. A poor body image can lead to eating disorders such as anorexia nervosa, bulimia nervosa, and obesity. Although anorexia nervosa and bulimia nervosa can occur at any age, they are frequently seen in adolescents. Several important elements to look at when assessing for anorexia nervosa or bulimia nervosa are listed in Table 7-5.

Level of physical activity must also be taken into account for a nutritional evaluation. An understanding of different sports and their requirements may help you screen for potential problems. In some sports (e.g., hockey, football), players are encouraged to be large and heavy; this puts them at a risk for possible anabolic steroid use (Figure 7-11). Possible toxic effects of steroid use include cancer of the liver, short stature, behavioural changes, endocrine problems (acne, impotence, testicular atrophy), and hypertension. In sports where

Figure 7-11 Adolescent athletes are at risk for anabolic steroid use.

◀NURSING CHECKLIST▶

Nutritional Assessment of the Toddler, Preschooler, and School-Age Child

- Do you have any problem or concern with your child's eating?
- Is your child a picky eater? If so, how is this handled?
- Does your family eat together?
- Does your child have any food likes or dislikes?
- What does your child eat for snacks? Are healthy lunch and snack options available if in day care or school?
- Is your child involved in sports or any other physical activity?
- What is your child's meal schedule? Where and when does your child eat?
- Does your child eat foods from all the groups in the Canada Food Guide to Healthy Eating?
- Does your child have any food allergies?
- Does your child drink beverages with added sugar (e.g., soda, fruit punch)? If so, how much?

| TABLE 7-5 | **Diagnostic Criteria for Anorexia Nervosa, Bulimia Nervosa, and Eating Disorders Not Otherwise Specified** |

ANOREXIA NERVOSA

A. Refusal to maintain body weight at or above a minimally normal weight for age and height (e.g., weight loss leading to maintenance of body weight less than 85% of that expected; or failure to make expected weight gain during period of growth, leading to body weight less than 85% of that expected).

B. Intense fear of gaining weight or becoming fat, even though underweight.

C. Disturbance in the way in which one's body weight or shape is experienced, undue influence of body weight or shape on self-evaluation, or denial of the seriousness of the current low body weight.

D. In postmenarcheal females, amenorrhea, i.e., the absence of at least three consecutive menstrual cycles.

Specify type:

> **Restricting Type:** during the current episode of anorexia nervosa, the person has not regularly engaged in binge-eating or purging behaviour (i.e., self-induced vomiting or the misuse of laxatives, diuretics, or enemas).

> **Binge-Eating/Purging Type:** during the current episode of anorexia nervosa, the person has regularly engaged in binge-eating or purging behaviour (i.e., self-induced vomiting or the misuse of laxatives, diuretics, or enemas).

BULIMIA NERVOSA

A. Recurrent episodes of binge eating. An episode of binge eating is characterized by both of the following:

(1) eating, in a discrete period of time (e.g., within any two-hour period), an amount of food that is definitely larger than most people would eat during a similar period of time and under similar circumstances

(2) a sense of lack of control over eating during the episode (e.g., a feeling that one cannot stop eating or control what or how much one is eating)

B. Recurrent inappropriate compensatory behaviour in order to prevent weight gain, such as self-induced vomiting; misuse of laxatives, diuretics, enemas, or other medications; fasting; or excessive exercise.

C. The binge eating and inappropriate compensatory behaviours both occur, on average, at least twice a week for three months.

D. Self-evaluation is unduly influenced by body shape and weight.

E. The disturbance does not occur exclusively during episodes of anorexia nervosa.

Specify type:

> **Purging Type:** during the current episode of bulimia nervosa, the person has regularly engaged in self-induced vomiting or the misuse of laxatives, diuretics, or enemas.

> **Nonpurging Type:** during the current episode of bulimia nervosa, the person has used other inappropriate compensatory behaviours, such as fasting or excessive exercise, but has not regularly engaged in self-induced vomiting or the misuse of laxatives, diuretics, or enemas.

EATING DISORDER NOT OTHERWISE SPECIFIED

The Eating Disorder Not Otherwise Specified category is for disorders of eating that do not meet the criteria for any specific eating disorder. Examples include:

1. For females, all of the criteria for anorexia nervosa are met except that the individual has regular menses.

2. All of the criteria for anorexia nervosa are met except that despite significant weight loss, the individual's current weight is in the normal range.

3. All of the criteria for bulimia nervosa are met except that the binge eating and inappropriate compensatory mechanisms occur at a frequency of less than twice a week or for a duration of less than three months.

4. The regular use of inappropriate compensatory behaviour by an individual of normal body weight after eating small amounts of food (e.g., self-induced vomiting after eating two cookies).

5. Repeatedly chewing and spitting out, but not swallowing, large amounts of food.

6. Binge-eating disorder: recurrent episodes of binge eating in the absence of the regular use of inappropriate compensatory behaviours characteristic of bulimia nervosa.

Note. Reprinted with permission from the *Diagnostic and Statistical Manual of Mental Disorders*, Copyright © 2000, American Psychiatric Association.

Reflective Thinking

Childhood Obesity

Nurses are often consulted about health issues that relate to diet and weight.

- How would you deal with a 3-year-old child of average height with a weight of 35 kg who presents for a physical examination? What would you say to the caregiver?
- How would you help an obese teenager deal with taunting and rejection from classmates?
- How would you present nutrition information to a first grade class? Fourth grade? Seventh grade (Secondary I)? Eleventh grade (Secondary V)?

decreased weight is desirable (e.g., wrestling, gymnastics), athletes may try many methods to "make weight." Instruction about proper nutrition to help reduce body fat without compromising health is needed when working with all athletes.

Young and Middle-Aged Adults

Growth and caloric needs usually stabilize in young and middle-aged adults. Eating habits may be altered by changes in activity levels and by the effects of work and life stressors. In Canada, the number of overweight or obese people has increased dramatically in the last 25 years. Health Canada conducted the Canadian Community Health Survey in 2004 and determined that 5.5 million or 23.1% of adult Canadians are obese, and that 8.6 million or 36.1% are overweight. Canadians who are overweight or obese make up more than 59% of the population![19] See Figure 7-12 for a profile of obesity across Canada.

Obesity occurs when calories consumed are greater than calories expended or when there is a decrease in activity level, or both. Obesity can come about at any age but is frequently seen in young and middle-aged adults (Figure 7-13). The Canadian Office of Nutrition Policy and Promotion has adopted the World Health Organization (WHO) guidelines, which use BMI to determine if a person is deemed obese or overweight.[20] (See the section Body Mass Index for a discussion of how to calculate BMI). People with a BMI between 25.0 and 29.9 kg/m^2 are considered to be overweight; those with a BMI >30 kg/m^2 are considered obese.

Obesity places a person at risk for hyperlipidemia, CAD, hypertension, diabetes mellitus, obstructive sleep apnea, gallbladder disease, certain cancers (e.g., breast, endometrial, colon, prostate, and kidney), and impaired fertility, and it challenges activities of daily living. *It is estimated that from 1985 to 2000, more than 57,000 Canadians died from conditions related to obesity.[21]*

Patients who are overweight or obese frequently experience yo-yo dieting, or weight cycling. They may diet for a period of time, achieve their goal weights, and then cease dieting. The majority of people return to their usual eating habits and regain the lost weight, and they may add a few more kilograms as well. Most diets fail because they neither address behaviour modification for eating nor include an exercise regimen. The use of fad diets (i.e., diets that promise results without effectively altering lifestyle or that require extreme limitations in one nutrient group—a very low carbohydrate but high protein diet) and fad exercise regimens (e.g., vibrating machine or sauna) may be harmful to a person's health. However, some fad programs are relatively safe if followed

◀NURSING CHECKLIST▶

Nutritional Assessment of Adolescents

- Are you involved in any sports? If so, are there any requirements regarding weight or food?
- Are you on any specific diet or meal plan?
- Do you skip any meals?
- Do you feel content with your weight? If not, how much do you feel you should weigh? What do you do to control your weight?
- How often do you weigh yourself?
- Have you ever induced vomiting or used laxatives, diuretics, or diet pills to help with weight control?
- Do you eat snacks? What kind? What are your between-meal eating habits?
- Do you exercise regularly? How often, and what kind of exercise?

Reflective Thinking

Adolescent Issues

- Beth, 14-years, tells you that she is "fat." She is an accomplished ballet dancer who was recently rejected for a lead role in a theatre production "because of my weight." Her height is 160 cm and weight 43 kg. What would you say to Beth?
- Jamal, the captain of a high school weight-lifting team, informs you that he takes "roids (sic) to make me stronger and more muscular" and requests that you not tell anyone because "I'll get kicked off the team." How would you address this situation?

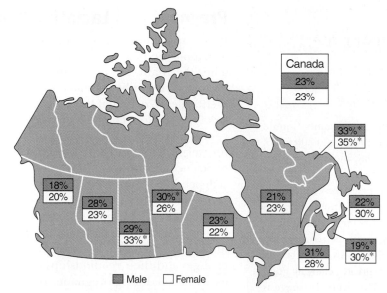

Figure 7-12 OAC Measured Obesity Rates (BMI > 30) Among Adults 18 Years and Over, Canada Excluding the Territories (2004).

Notes: *Significantly different (p < .05) from the Canadian average. E Coefficient of variation between 16.6% and 33.3% (interpret with caution).

Source: From the Statistics Canada publication "Nutrition: Findings from the Canadian Community Health Survey," Catalogue 82–620, released July 6, 2006, URL: http://www.statcan.ca/english/research/82-620-MIE/82-620-MIE2006002.htm.

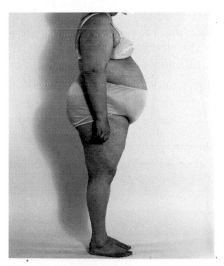

Figure 7-13 Obese Adult. *Courtesy of the Armed Forces Institute of Pathology.*

for a short period of time with adequate professional supervision. Type 2 diabetes mellitus is usually diagnosed after age 40 and is associated with family history and obesity. This type of diabetes is often not diagnosed until complications arise, because the person has few or mild symptoms.

Obesity is also associated with CAD, one of the leading causes of death in Canada. The primary cause of CAD is **atherosclerosis,** which is the development of lipid plaques along the coronary arteries. The risk factors for atherosclerosis are discussed in Chapter 16. The metabolic syndrome, previously termed syndrome X, is increasing in prevalence in Canada. In order to be diagnosed with metabolic syndrome, three of five risk factors need to be present: abdominal obesity, elevated blood pressure, elevated fasting blood glucose, elevated triglycerides, and low HDL. Patients with metabolic syndrome are at an increased risk for diabetes mellitus and CAD.

Osteoporosis is a disease that reduces bone mass. It is more common in women and is often not detected until the person falls and fractures a bone. Anorexia nervosa should be suspected in a young, thin female with osteoporosis. Other health problems associated with undernutrition include infertility and impaired immune function. (See Chapter 18 for additional information.)

Nursing Tip

DASH Diet for Hypertension

The Dietary Approaches to Stop Hypertension (DASH) diet and reduced dietary sodium help hypertensive patients eat a nutritionally sound diet while lowering the effects of their diet on their blood pressure. The DASH diet is low in total fat, cholesterol, saturated fats, red meats, sweets, and sugar-containing beverages, and it is rich in vegetables, fruits, and low-fat dairy products. The DASH diet may not be appropriate for patients with advanced renal disease because it contains too much potassium and protein.

Pregnant and Lactating Women

It is important to assess and counsel the pregnant woman about proper nutrition—to promote a healthy pregnancy and to ensure the development of a healthy infant. If the woman does not gain adequate weight, the infant has an increased risk of being small for gestational age and may be prone to developmental delay, neonatal mortality, and other illnesses. However, the mother is at risk for gestational diabetes, hypertension, prolonged labour, birth trauma, and cesarean section if the weight gain is excessive.[22] In Canada, recommendations for weight gain are taken from guidelines produced by the National Academy of Science, Institute of Medicine in the United States (1990). Target weight gain is dependent on prepregnancy BMI. Women with a low prepregnancy BMI (<20) should gain more weight than those who have a high BMI (>27). A woman with a BMI of <20 should gain 12.5 to 18.0 kg. If her BMI is 20–27, then the gain should be less (11.5 to 16.0 kg). If a woman has a BMI of >27, weight gain should be limited to 7.0 to 11.5 kg. Assessment includes a general knowledge of physical changes and their relationships to nutrition. Some of the common complaints experienced during pregnancy (e.g., heartburn, constipation, nausea, and vomiting) can be alleviated by dietary changes, such as small frequent meals, increased fluid intake, and a well-balanced diet.

Iron supplements and prenatal vitamins are given routinely during pregnancy because diet alone is often not adequate in meeting the body's requirements. There is evidence that folic acid helps to reduce the risk of neural tube defects, especially when instituted three months prior to pregnancy. (See Chapter 23 for a full discussion of folic acid recommendations in pregnancy.) Health Canada recommends an additional 100 calories per day in the first trimester, 300 calories in the second or third trimester, and an increase in milk consumption, which increases both protein and caloric intake. Pregnant women should also be encouraged to drink 6 to 8 glasses of fluid daily (water, fruit juices, and milk); lactating women need additional fluids, ranging from 2 to 3 litres daily.

Pica, or cravings for substances other than food, is a phenomenon documented primarily in pregnant women. It is the practice of eating dirt, clay, starch, or even ice cubes, and may lead to nutritional difficulties such as an increased risk of anemia.

Older Adults

The eating habits of Canadian seniors are quite varied. In one recent study, over 50% of Canadians over 65 self-reported that their eating habits were excellent

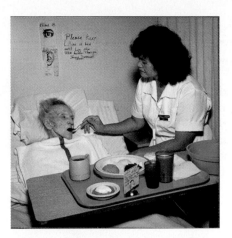

Figure 7-14 Older adults may have health problems that affect their ability to self-feed.

Nursing Tip

Psychosocial Implications of Food

The psychosocial implications of food and eating cannot be stressed enough. Food elicits certain memories and feelings of when we were younger (e.g., the smell of Aunt Millie's turkey roasting or the taste of Gramma's chocolate chip cookies). It is also important to take into account other aspects of the patient's nutritional history. If an older adult lives alone, there may be difficulty in obtaining food or preparing it; loneliness at mealtimes may also be a factor.

or very good, whereas 16% rated their habits as fair or poor. Only slightly more than 40% of seniors ate the daily recommended servings of fruits and vegetables as established by the Canada Food Guide. Alarmingly, 4% reported having lacked food during the year because they were short of money. Canadians over the age of 65 account for 7% of all food bank users.[24]

Good eating habits and nutrition established early in life will benefit adults as they age, whereas poor eating habits may contribute to disease processes (e.g., hypertension, diabetes mellitus, and CAD). Caloric needs decrease as a person ages due to the reduction in basal metabolic rate, so health teaching should focus on modifications in portion size to coincide with reduced activity and decreased caloric requirements.

Assess any problems the elderly may have with difficulty chewing (oral problems) or swallowing (possible stroke or Parkinson's disease), decreased appetite, decreased taste and smell, and decreased ability to self-feed (musculoskeletal diseases, such as osteoarthritis; and degenerative neurological disorders) (Figure 7-14). The older adult should eat in a sitting position to avoid aspiration, which may occur because the emptying time of the esophagus is decreased. Constipation, due to a decrease in gastrointestinal motility, is a common problem that can be alleviated through adequate fluid intake and by eating foods high in fibre.

There are numerous socioeconomic conditions that can affect the nutrition of older adults: income, transportation, and social support. Many older adults have a fixed income, which limits their food choices. Without adequate public or personal transportation, older adults may not have the means to obtain their food. Eating is a social as well as a nutritional ritual; cooking responsibilities are often shared in a family and eating is a bonding, congenial event. Older adults who live alone may not "feel" like eating because of their solitary nature.

Life 360°

Culturally Based Nutritional Practices

• Your Islamic patient has been fasting during Ramadan. He is diabetic and continues to become hypoglycemic. What would be your plan of care? How would you help him balance his religious and nutritional needs?

• LoAn is a pregnant Vietnamese female who is HIV-positive. She incorporates the observance of yin and yang into her daily rituals. LoAn confides that she is looking forward to breast-feeding her child. You realize that pregnancy is a yang condition and lactation is a yin condition, which is in line with LoAn's beliefs. What information would you discuss with LoAn, knowing that a mother who is HIV-positive is advised against breast-feeding?

◄NURSING CHECKLIST►

Nutritional Assessment of Older Adults

• Do you have any physical limitations that affect your eating?
• Do you have any difficulty swallowing? (Is there a history of a cerebrovascular accident or a neuromuscular disorder?)
• Do you have any dental problems that interfere with eating?
• Who buys and prepares your food?
• Do you eat alone or with someone?

CULTURAL DIFFERENCES

It is not possible for the nurse to have knowledge of all cultural differences, but an open and understanding attitude and acceptance of various religious and cultural beliefs is imperative in obtaining an appropriate nutritional assessment and in educating the patient. Certain foods may have special meanings and memories for patients, or food may be traditional among people with the same cultural backgrounds (e.g., turkey for Thanksgiving and tourtière at Christmas). Regional considerations, food preferences, and religious beliefs that restrict consumption of specific foods should also be considered. Understanding these issues is helpful in establishing rapport and individualizing the nutritional plan. Be sure to inquire about various cultural and religious influences on dietary practices during the nutritional assessment.

HEALTH HISTORY

The nutritional history or subjective information gathered is one of the most significant aspects of the nutritional assessment in that it gives an understanding of the patient's dietary habits and practices. The nutritional health history provides insight into the link between a patient's lifestyle and nutritional information and pathology.

PATIENT PROFILE — *Diseases that are age- and gender-specific for nutrition are listed.*

Age — Anorexia nervosa (adolescents)
Bulimia nervosa (adolescents)

Gender

Female — Over 90% of patients with anorexia nervosa are female.

HEALTH ISSUE/CONCERN — *Common health issues or concerns about nutrition are defined, and information on the characteristics of each is provided.*

Anorexia — Lost or decreased interest and desire for food

Quantity — Amount of food consumed in relation to patient's normal intake

Associated Manifestations — Physical weakness, fatigue, nausea, cramps, dietary intolerances, weight loss, abdominal distension, abdominal fullness, anxiety, depression

Aggravating Factors — Smoking, sleeplessness, odours, pain, emotional status, cardiorespiratory distress

Timing — Early morning, afternoon, bedtime, continuous, days, weeks, months, during pregnancy

Dysphagia — Difficulty swallowing; associated with damage to the 9th or 10th cranial nerve, causing paralysis of the swallowing mechanism or disorders of the throat, neck, or esophagus

Associated Manifestations — Weight loss, choking, or difficulty breathing when swallowing

Aggravating Factors — Solid or liquid foods

Alleviating Factors	Position, throat lozenges
Timing	Associated with specific times and meals during the day
Weight Gain	Number of pounds gained above usual weight
Associated Manifestations	Use of medications (corticosteroids), pregnancy, sedentary lifestyle, high-calorie, high-fat diet, increased appetite
Setting	Stress, depression, and negative body image
Timing	Over what period of time
Weight Loss	Number of pounds lost below usual weight
Associated Manifestations	Nausea, vomiting, diarrhea, use of laxatives or diuretics, medication side effects, decreased appetite, increase in exercise, malabsorption diseases, diseases increasing demand of nutrients
Setting	Stress, depression, and negative body image, following a particular diet, participating in a structured weight-loss program (e.g., Weight Watchers)
Timing	Over what period of time
PAST HEALTH HISTORY	*The various components of the past health history are linked with nutrition pathology and nutrition-related information.*
Medical History	
Nutrition-Specific	Obesity, malnutrition, malabsorption diseases, anorexia nervosa, bulimia nervosa, dysphagia, weight cycling
Non-Nutrition-Specific	Diabetes mellitus, coronary artery disease, increased cholesterol level, burns, cerebrovascular accident, hypertension, cancer, diverticulosis, muscular dystrophy, multiple sclerosis, Parkinson's disease, Crohn's disease, ulcerative colitis, gout, pancreatitis, cholelithiasis, dental disease
Surgical History	Gastric reduction (bypass or stapling), jaw wiring to reduce intake of food in morbid obesity, any surgical procedure that alters food intake from postsurgical complications, nausea, or normal recovery
Medications	Review all medications for actual or potential side effects that may affect appetite or growth (antibiotics may cause gastrointestinal disturbances, Ritalin may cause anorexia, and long-term steroid use may affect linear growth), vitamins, supplements
Communicable Diseases	Children with AIDS: failure to thrive; adults with AIDS: wasting syndrome
Allergies	Gastrointestinal disturbances may occur with medication, food, and environmental allergies; infants may manifest allergies as dietary disturbances (lactose intolerance)
Injuries and Accidents	Affect eating or the ability to self-feed, such as facial or mouth trauma; need for nasogastric tube feeding, gastrostomy
Special Needs	Affect ability to cut, handle, chew, or swallow food
FAMILY HEALTH HISTORY	*Nutritional diseases that are familial are listed.* Food allergies and intolerances, eating disorders, obesity, as well as any medical conditions that may contribute to nutritional problems (e.g., diabetes mellitus, hyperlipidemia, hypertension, CAD, celiac disease, cancer)

continues

SOCIAL HISTORY	*The components of the social history are linked to nutritional factors and pathologies.*
Alcohol Use	Alcohol has very little nutrient value and abuse may lead to nutritional deficiencies. These include an inadequate intake of food, decreased sense of taste and smell, altered metabolism of nutrients (decreases storage and increases excretion of nutrients), and decreased absorption through intestinal mucosa. There is also an increased excretion of calcium with alcohol consumption that increases the risk of osteoporosis. In a pregnant woman, chronic alcohol consumption can lead to a low-birth-weight baby.
Drug Use	Drug abuse alters nutrition due to the patient's increased dependence on the substance and decreased intake of proper nutrients. Many drugs alter food intake by causing anorexia (amphetamines) and decreasing sense of smell and taste (cocaine).
Tobacco Use	Smoking is associated with decreased estrogen levels in women, which increases their risk of osteoporosis. Tobacco is also an appetite suppressant that may stimulate weight gain when the person quits smoking. Tobacco may also alter the senses of taste and smell.
Travel History	Recent travel may cause problems with gastrointestinal disturbances. It may also temporarily change the normal dietary habits of the patient.
Hobbies and Leisure Activities	Food-related hobbies or food activities (gourmet cooking), or the amount of physical activity
Education	Education level may not necessarily translate into an adequate knowledge of nutritional needs.
Economic Status	Resources for purchase of adequate food
Religion	See Chapter 6 for religious restrictions on diet.
HEALTH MAINTENANCE ACTIVITIES	*This information provides a bridge between health maintenance activities and nutritional function.*
Sleep	Stress increases when a patient is sleep deprived, which may contribute to nutritional problems.
Diet	See Table 7-7 for questions to be asked during the diet history.
Exercise	Patients with anorexia nervosa may exercise to excess.
Stress Management	Increasing or decreasing food consumption
Health Check-Ups	Lipid profile, last weight, height, and any other laboratory or diagnostic results

EQUIPMENT

- Wall-mounted unit (stadiometer), rod attached to the scale that has a right-angle headboard
- Tape measure
- Scale (preferably a balance-beam scale or electronic scale)
- Skinfold calipers (ideally one with a spring-loaded lever)

NUTRITIONAL ASSESSMENT

Table 7-6 illustrates a comprehensive nutritional assessment that includes the nutritional history, physical assessment, anthropometric measurements, laboratory data, and diagnostic data.

The Nutritional History

The first step in the nutritional assessment is the nutritional history. A comprehensive history is always warranted when the patient has a chronic medical

TABLE 7-6 Comprehensive Nutritional Assesment

NUTRITIONAL HISTORY

PHYSICAL ASSESSMENT	1. General appearance
	2. Skin
	3. Nails
	4. Hair
	5. Eyes
	6. Mouth
	7. Head and neck
	8. Heart and peripheral vasculature
	9. Abdomen
	10. Musculoskeletal system
	11. Neurological system
	12. Female genitalia
ANTHROPOMETRIC MEASURES	Weight: _____ kg
	Height: _____ cm
	BMI: _____
	Waist to hip ratio _____
	% Usual Body Weight: _____
	% Weight Change: _____
	Triceps Skinfold: _____ mm
	Mid-Arm Circumference: _____ cm
	Mid-Arm Muscle Circumference: _____ cm
LABORATORY DATA	Hematocrit (Hct): _____
	Hemoglobin (Hgb): _____ g/L
	Cholesterol: _____ mmol/L
	HDL-C: _____ mmol/L
	LDL-C: _____ mmol/L
	Total cholesterol: _____ HDL-C ratio
	Triglycerides: _____ mmol/L
	Transferrin: _____ g/L
	TIBC: _____ µmol/L
	Iron: _____ µmol/L
	Total Lymphocyte Count: _____ 10^9 cells/L
	Prealbumin: _____ mg/L
	Albumin: _____ g/L
	Glucose: _____ mmol/L
	Antigen Skin Testing _____
	Creatinine Height Index: _____ %
	Nitrogen Balance: _____ g
	Blood Urea Nitrogen: _____ mmol/L
DIAGNOSTIC DATA	DEXA Scan _____
	X-rays _____

condition, or an unexplained weight loss or gain. Specific diet information may be obtained in a variety ways via the Diet History (Table 7-7). The first method is the 24-hour recall, where the patient relates what has been consumed in the past day. Patients may also keep a food diary, recording what foods and drinks were consumed over a specific 72-hour period. These histories can provide essential information; however, they may not truly represent a typical diet for the patient

TABLE 7-7 Diet History

PART 1: GENERAL DIET INFORMATION

Do you follow a particular diet?

What are your food likes and dislikes?

Do you have any especially strong cravings?

How often do you eat fast foods?

How often do you eat at restaurants?

Do you have adequate financial resources to purchase your food?

How do you obtain, store, and prepare your food?

Do you eat alone or with a family member or other person?

In the last 12 months have you

- experienced any change in weight?
- had a change in your appetite?
- had a change in your diet?
- experienced nausea, vomiting, or diarrhea from your diet?
- changed your diet because of difficulty in feeding yourself, eating, chewing, or swallowing?

PART 2: FOOD INTAKE HISTORY
(24-HOUR RECALL, 3-DAY DIARY, DIRECT OBSERVATION)

Time	Food/Drink	Amount	Method of Preparation	Eating Location

because he or she may change usual dietary habits, omit foods that were eaten, or record incorrect entries knowing that the information will be evaluated.

Direct observation and recording of the food and drink consumed by the hospitalized patient is another method the nurse can use to obtain food and caloric intake patterns. Once the food intake history is recorded, the nurse evaluates the diet and food consumption. Health Canada, the Dieticians of Canada, and the Canadian Diabetic Association offer recommendations for dietary assessment.

Physical Assessment

Certain physical signs may indicate poor nutrition. See Table 7-8 for a list of signs and symptoms of poor nutritional status.

◄NURSING CHECKLIST►

General Approach to Nutritional Assessment

1. Explain all procedures to patients and family members.
2. Ask patient to remove shoes prior to height measurement.
3. Have older children or adults remove heavy clothing (an adult may wear a hospital gown).
4. Explain and review results with patient and family.

TABLE 7-8	Physical Signs and Symptoms Of Poor Nutritional Status	
	SUBJECTIVE	**OBJECTIVE**
1. General appearance	Fatigue, poor sleep, change in weight, frequent infections	Dull affect, apathetic, increased weight, decreased weight
2. Skin	Pruritus, swelling, delayed wound healing	Dry, rough, scaling, flaky, edema, lesions, decreased turgor, changes in color (pallor, jaundice), petechiae, ecchymoses, xanthomas (slightly elevated yellow nodules)
3. Nails	Brittle	Dry, splinter hemorrhages, spoon-shaped, pale
4. Hair	Easily falls out, brittle	Less shiny, dry, changes in color pigment
5. Eyes	Vision changes, night blindness, eye discharge	Hardening and scaling of cornea, conjunctiva pale or red
6. Mouth	Mouth sores	Lips: cracked, dry, swollen, fissures around corners Gums: recessed, swollen, bleeding, spongy Tongue: smooth, beefy red, magenta, pale, fissures, sores, increased or decreased in size, increased or decreased papillae Teeth: missing, caries
7. Head and neck	Headaches, decreased hearing	Xanthelasma, irritation and crusting of nares, swollen cheeks (parotid gland enlargement), goiter
8. Heart and peripheral	Palpitations, swelling	Cardiac enlargement, changes in blood pressure, vasculature tachycardia, heart murmur, edema
9. Abdomen	Tender, changes in appetite, nausea, changes in bowel habits	Edema, hepatosplenomegaly, vomiting, diarrhea
10. Musculoskeletal	Weakness, pain, cramping, frequent fractures	Muscle tone is decreased, flabby muscles, muscle system wasting, bowing of lower extremities
11. Neurological system	Irritable, changes in mood, numbness, paresthesia	Slurred speech, unsteady gait, tremors, decreased deep tendon reflexes, loss of position and vibratory sense, paresthesia, decreased coordination
12. Female genitalia	Changes in menstrual pattern	None

Anthropometric Measurements

Anthropometric measurements are the various measurements of the human body, including height, weight, and body proportions. They measure growth patterns in children and changes in nutritional status in adults.

Measurements are easily obtained and can assist in an objective assessment that can be compared over time.

Height

A standing height is obtained for patients 3 years and older (Figure 7-15).

E 1. Have the patient stand erect with back and heels against the wall or measuring device.
2. Place the headboard at a right angle to the wall and along the crown of the patient's head.
3. Record height to the nearest mm.

E Examination	N Normal Findings	A Abnormal Findings	P Pathophysiology

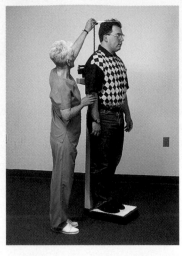

Figure 7-15 Measuring patient height

Nursing Tip

Measuring Height of the Bedridden Patient

When a patient is bedridden or immobile, measure recumbent length with a rod or metre stick.

Figure 7-16 Measuring patient weight

N Compare to standardized charts for patients up to 20 years (see Chapter 24, p. 869 to 871). Bear in mind that patients will reflect familial growth patterns. Also compare to the patient's height and weight at the last visit.

A Insufficient growth is abnormal.

P Chronic malnutrition may result in a decrease in height because the body does not have the nutrients necessary for proper growth.

P A patient with osteoporosis may demonstrate a decrease in height due to thinning of the bones and possible vertebral compression fractures.

A Excessive growth is abnormal.

P Hormone abnormalities may cause excessive growth, as in acromegaly, gigantism, and precocious puberty.

P Genetic and metabolic syndromes that affect growth are Marfan's syndrome and Klinefelter's syndrome.

Weight

1. Have patient stand on scale, facing weights (Figure 7-16).
2. Slide weight until balanced.
3. Read and record to the nearest 100 g (10 g for infants).
4. Calculate percentage of ideal body weight (IBW), using the formula:

$$\% \, IBW = \frac{Current \ Weight}{IBW*} \times 100$$

5. Calculate the percentage of usual body weight, using the formula:

$$\% \, Usual \ Body \ Weight = \frac{Current \ Weight}{Usual \ Body \ Weight} \times 100$$

6. Calculate the percentage of weight change, using the formula:

$$\% \, Weight \ Change = \frac{Usual \ Weight - Current \ Weight}{Usual \ Weight} \times 100$$

Note: In Canada, BMI, waist circumference (WC) and waist-to-hip ratio (see below) are generally used to determine an individual's weight status rather than IBW. However, IBW calculations are provided because some agencies and/or patients may prefer this approach.

N A person's weight is compared to the theoretical ideal for their height. An IBW between 90 and 109 is adequate.

A Obesity is abnormal. Mild obesity occurs when the patient is 20–40% above the IBW; moderate obesity occurs when the patient is 40–100% above the IBW; and morbid obesity occurs when a patient is more than 100% above the IBW.

P Obesity occurs when there is excess body fat because of increased food intake, decreased activity level, or both.

P Some medications may contribute to weight gain (e.g., steroids).

P Some disease processes may contribute to weight gain, such as hypothyroidism because of decreased metabolic rate.

A Genetics may influence weight gain.

P A weight under 90% of IBW is termed undernutrition. A weight between 80 and 90% of the IBW is mild undernutrition; between 70 and 80% is moderate undernutrition; and below 70% is severe undernutrition.

| **E** | **Examination** | **N** | **Normal Findings** | **A** | **Abnormal Findings** | **P** | **Pathophysiology** |

---

*IBW formulae originated in the United States with metric variations that have evolved, as follows:

Males: IBW = 50 kg + 2.3 kg for each inch over 5 feet.

Females: IBW = 45.5 kg + 2.3 kg for each inch over 5 feet.

P Decreased food intake may occur with dental problems, depression, medications, alcoholism, anorexia nervosa, and poverty.

P Inadequate nutrition may occur with impaired absorption, as present in malabsorption diseases (e.g., celiac disease), AIDS, and small bowel disease.

P There may be a loss of nutrients with diarrhea, vomiting, and diabetes mellitus.

P Increased demand for nutrients may be present in malignancies, fever, burns, and hyperthyroidism. This increased demand may account for the weight loss that occurs early in cancer even when calories are not decreased. If this continues, the patient exhibits signs of extreme malnutrition and wasting, which is called **cachexia.**

Body Mass Index

Body Mass Index (BMI) is a measurement that reflects body composition. The degree to which the patient is overweight, obese, or underweight can be determined with this measurement. BMI is related to increased mortality when it is very high or very low. The predictive value of BMI in the development of illness has some limitations in young people who have not reached full growth, very lean individuals, very muscular individuals, and adults older than 65 years as well as for certain ethnic or racial groups of Canadians such as First Nations people, and Canadians of Black and South Asian origins.[25]

BMI is an index of weight-to-height. It does not reflect the actual distribution of fat on the body and, as a result, Health Canada recommends the use of waist circumference (WC) measurements in addition to BMI. The formula to determine BMI is:

$$\text{BMI} - \frac{\text{weight (in kg)}}{\text{m}^2}$$

The BMI can be difficult to calculate because many Canadians continue to report their weight in pounds and their height in feet and inches. Thus, two methods of BMI calculations are provided:

E 1. Determine the BMI measurement by using the BMI nomogram (Figure 7-17) (ideal method),

OR (less ideal method):

1. Multiply the weight in pounds by 703.
2. Multiply the height in inches by the height in inches.
3. Divide the first number in 2 by the second number in 3.
4. The answer is the BMI.

For example: weight = 107 lbs, height = 60 inches

$107 \times 703 = 75221$

$60 \times 60 = 3600$

$75221 / 3600 = 20.9$ or 21

N A BMI of 18.5–24.9 is considered within normal limits.

A A BMI of 25.0–29.9 is considered overweight. A BMI of 30.0–34.9 is considered Obese (Class I), 35–39.9 is moderately obese (Obese Class II), and greater than 40 is extremely obese (Obese Class III).

P A BMI greater than 25 is associated with an increased morbidity and mortality from cardiovascular disease, cancer, and other diseases.

A A BMI less than 18.5 is abnormal.

P A BMI less than 18.5 is underweight and can be associated with possible malnutrition. The malnutrition can be self-induced (e.g., anorexia nervosa, bulimia), caused by illness (e.g., cancer, AIDS), or it can be from a lack of adequate nutrition.

Note: For people over the age of 65 years, the normal range is extended and may begin at levels higher than 18.5 and include BMIs that fall into the overweight classification.[26] The relative risk classifications do not apply to pregnant or breast-feeding women.

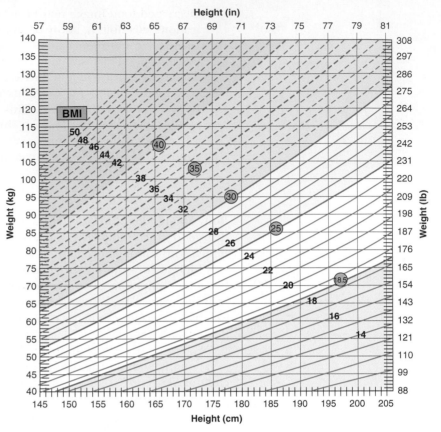

Figure 7-17 Body Mass Index (BMI) Nomogram (Health Canada, 2003)
Source: http://www.hc-sc.gc.ca/home-accueil/important_e.html. Reproduced with the permission of the Minister of Public Works and Government Services Canada, 2006.

Use the Health Canada BMI Nomogram (Figure 7-17) to determine a patient's BMI (kg/m²). Use a ruler to locate the point on the chart where height (in or cm) and weight (lb or kg) intersect. Then read the number on the **dashed line that corresponds to this point.** For example, an individual who is 180 cm in height and who weighs 67 kg has an approximate BMI of 21.

Waist-to-Hip Ratio and Waist Circumference

Body fat distribution is linked to morbidity and mortality. Fat distribution gives rise to two predominant body shapes: gynoid (pear shaped) and android (apple shaped) (see Figure 7-18). Women tend to deposit fat more in their hips and

Nursing Tip

Interpreting Anthropometric Measurements

It is important to interpret anthropometric, laboratory, and diagnostic data collectively. One abnormal result does not provide sufficient evidence to diagnose malnutrition. Deficiencies and toxicities usually occur in more than one assessment area. Monitor the results of the nutritional assessment and observe trends that occur.

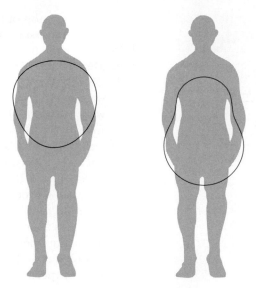

Figure 7-18 Apple shape and pear shape

buttocks, giving them a pear-shaped appearance. Men, on the other hand, tend to deposit fat around the abdominal midline, thus giving them an apple appearance. Abdominal fat includes fat located under the skin (subcutaneous) and fat that surrounds organs (visceral fat). Waist circumference is a good indicator of abdominal fat. Excess abdominal fat (and especially excess visceral fat) has been linked to the development of type 2 diabetes mellitus, CAD, and hypertension. It was found that even among individuals with normal or obese BMIs, those who had a WC above the cut-off were at greater risk than those below the WC cut-off values (See Figure 7-19).[27]

Waist circumference and waist-to-hip ratio are simple methods to determine a person's body fat distribution and are recommended by Health Canada to be used in addition to BMI when assessing health status.[28] For individuals who have a BMI ≥ 35, measuring WC will not provide any additional information about the individual's relative risk.

E 1. Stand beside the person. The patient's feet should be 25–30 cm apart. Measure the waist in centimetres at the part of the trunk located midway between the lower costal margin (bottom of lower rib) and the

		BMI		
		Normal (18.5–24.9)	Overweight (25.0–29.9)	Obese Class 1(30.0–34.9)
	< 102 cm (males)	Least Risk	Increased Risk	High Risk
WC	< 88 cm (females)			
	≥ 102 cm (males)	Increased Risk	High Risk	Very High Risk
	≥ 88 cm (females)			

Figure 7-19 Relative Risk Based on Waist Circumference and BMI
Source: Adapted from: National Institutes of Health (1998). *Clinical guidelines on the identification, evaluation and treatment of overweight and obesity in adults: The evidence report.* Washington, DC: NIH, p. 17. Courtesy of National Institutes of Health.

| E | Examination | N | Normal Findings | A | Abnormal Findings | P | Pathophysiology |

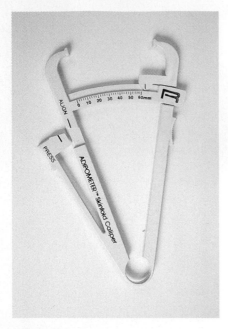

A. Skinfold Calipers

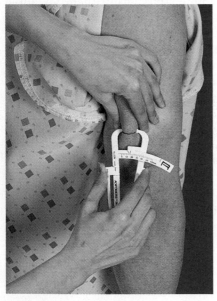

B. Measuring Triceps Skinfold

Figure 7-20 Skinfold thickness

iliac crest (top of the pelvic bone). Fit the measuring tape snugly without compressing abdominal tissue. Measure to the nearest 0.5 cm *at the end of expiration.*

  2. Measure the hips at the widest point.
  3. Divide the waist measurement by the hip measurement to obtain the waist-to-hip ratio. For example:
    waist = 63.5 cm, hips = 88.9 cm   63.5/88.9 = 0.71

N For men, a WC between 80 and 99 cm is normal, and for women, a WC between 70 and 88 is normal. A waist-to-hip ratio ratio <0.8 is normal in women and <1.0 is normal in men.

A A WC for men ≥ 102 cm, for premenopausal woman ≥ 88 cm, and postmenopausal women ≥ 110 cm is associated with an increased risk of developing health problems. A waist-to-hip ratio greater than 0.8 in women and 1.0 in men is abnormal.

P These measurements are associated with the adverse morbidity and mortality of obesity and are associated with increased risk of diabetes mellitus, CAD, and hypertension.

Skinfold Thickness

Skinfold thickness is used to determine body fat stores and nutritional status. It is a more reliable indicator of body fat than is weight, because more than half of the body's total fat is located in the subcutaneous tissue. The most common measurement site is the **triceps skinfold** (TSF). Measurements can also be performed in subscapular and suprailiac skinfolds.

E 1. Place the patient in a sitting or standing position.
  2. Take the measurements on the nondominant arm, with the patient in a relaxed position.
  3. Make a mark on the posterior portion of the upper arm midway between the acromion process and the olecranon process.
  4. Using your nondominant hand, grasp the skin and pull it free from the muscle.
  5. Apply the caliper with your dominant hand and align the markers (Figure 7-20).
  6. Note the measurement to the nearest 0.5 mm.
  7. Release the skin and repeat two or three times.
  8. Average the findings to determine the TSF.

N See Table 7-9. Normal measurements fall between the 5th and 95th percentiles.

A See abnormal findings and pathophysiology under mid-arm and mid-arm muscle circumference.

Mid-Arm and Mid-Arm Muscle Circumferences

The **mid-arm circumference (MAC)** provides information on skeletal muscle mass. This measurement alone is not of great significance but it is used to calculate the **mid-arm muscle circumference (MAMC).**

E 1. Instruct patient to flex the arm at the elbow.
  2. Measure the circumference of the upper arm (MAC) midway between the acromion process and the olecranon process.
  3. Calculate MAMC using the formula:

$$\text{MAMC (cm)} = \text{MAC (cm)} - [3.14 - \text{TSF}^*\text{(cm)}]$$

| E | Examination | N | Normal Findings | A | Abnormal Findings | P | Pathophysiology |

---

*The TSF is measured in mm. You need to convert the TSF from mm to cm in order to calculate the MAMC.

TABLE 7-9 Triceps Skinfold Percentiles*

TRICEPS SKINFOLD PERCENTILES (MM²)

Age (yr)		Males								Females					
	n	5	10	25	50	75	90	95	n	5	10	25	50	75	90	95
1–1.9	228	6	7	8	10	12	14	16	204	6	7	8	10	12	14	16
2–2.9	223	6	7	8	10	12	14	15	208	6	8	9	10	12	15	16
3–3.9	220	6	7	8	10	11	14	15	208	7	8	9	11	12	14	15
4–4.9	230	6	6	8	9	11	12	14	208	7	8	8	10	12	14	16
5–5.9	214	6	6	8	9	11	14	15	219	6	7	8	10	12	15	18
6–6.9	117	5	6	7	8	10	13	16	118	6	6	8	10	12	14	16
7–7.9	122	5	6	7	9	12	15	17	126	6	7	9	11	13	16	18
8–8.9	117	5	6	7	8	10	13	16	118	6	8	9	12	15	18	24
9–9.9	121	6	6	7	10	13	17	18	125	8	8	10	13	16	20	22
10–10.9	146	6	6	8	10	14	18	21	152	7	8	10	12	17	23	27
11–11.9	122	6	6	8	11	16	20	24	117	7	8	10	13	18	24	28
12–12.9	153	6	6	8	11	14	22	28	129	8	9	11	14	18	23	27
13–13.9	134	5	5	7	10	14	22	26	151	8	8	12	15	21	26	30
14–14.9	131	4	5	7	9	14	21	24	141	9	10	13	16	21	26	28
15–15.9	128	4	5	6	8	11	18	24	117	8	10	12	17	21	25	32
16–16.9	131	4	5	6	8	12	16	22	142	10	12	15	18	22	26	31
17–17.9	133	5	5	6	8	12	16	19	114	10	12	13	19	24	30	37
18–18.9	91	4	5	6	9	13	20	24	109	10	12	15	18	22	26	30
19–24.9	531	4	5	7	10	15	20	22	1060	10	11	14	18	24	30	34
25–34.9	971	5	6	8	12	16	20	24	1987	10	12	16	21	27	34	37
35–44.9	806	5	6	8	12	16	20	23	1614	12	14	18	23	29	35	38
45–54.9	898	6	6	8	12	15	20	25	1047	12	16	20	25	30	36	40
55–64.9	734	5	6	8	11	14	19	22	809	12	16	20	25	31	36	38
65–74.9	1503	4	6	8	11	15	19	22	1670	12	14	18	24	29	34	36

*The Lange caliper was used in these studies.

Source: Reprinted with permission from: Frisancho, A. R. (1981). New norms of upper limb fat and muscle areas for assessment of nutrition status. *American Journal of Clinical Nutrition*, 34, p. 2540, American Society for Clinical Nutrition.

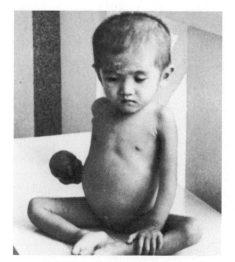

Figure 7-21 Patients with kwashiorkor can have a normal weight as well as TSF and MAC. Edema is common. *Courtesy of the World Health Organization.*

N   See Table 7-10. Normal measurements fall between the 5th and 95th percentiles.

A   Results less than the 3rd percentile on the standard charts are abnormal.

P   **Kwashiorkor,** or protein malnutrition, is a severe deficiency in good-quality protein. This can develop even if the patient is consuming an adequate number of calories. Because of the decrease in visceral proteins (especially albumin), edema may develop, particularly in the abdomen. This can also lead to a decreased immune function. The TSF, MAC, and weight can be within normal limits. Additional physical signs are scaly, flaky skin, depigmentation of the hair, enlarged liver, and mental apathy (Figure 7-21). It can occur with the ingestion of liquid diets that are low in protein, malabsorption diseases, hypermetabolic states, cancer, and AIDS.

P   **Marasmus,** or protein–calorie malnutrition, is a severe nutritional disorder in which there is an inadequate intake of protein and calories. As a result, there is a wasting of skeletal muscle and subcutaneous fat. This disorder can also occur from poor absorption of proteins, such as with burns, anorexia nervosa, tuberculosis, cancer, AIDS, and malabsorption diseases.

Patients with marasmus have symptoms similar to kwashiorkor except that they appear more emaciated and do not have edema (Figure 7-22). If severe enough, these patients can have impaired cell-mediated immunity.

P Mixed marasmus and kwashiorkor is a severe form of protein–calorie malnutrition. It is typically seen in patients who are in a severe hypermetabolic state (such as trauma or burns), as well as a near starvation state. There is a reduction in subcutaneous tissue, visceral proteins, and somatic proteins.

A Results greater than the 97th percentile on the standard charts are abnormal.

P Obesity is suggested.

P If edema is present on the assessed body parts, the measurement may not be a reliable indicator of nutritional status.

TABLE 7-10 MAC and MAMC Percentiles

	MID-ARM CIRCUMFERENCE (MM)							MID-ARM MUSCLE CIRCUMFERENCE (MM)						
Age Group	5	10	25	50	75	90	95	5	10	25	50	75	90	95
Males														
1–1.9	142	146	150	159	170	176	183	110	113	119	127	135	144	147
2–2.9	141	145	153	162	170	178	185	111	114	122	130	140	146	150
3–3.9	150	153	160	167	175	184	190	117	123	131	137	145	148	153
4–4.9	149	154	262	171	180	186	192	123	126	133	141	148	156	159
5–5.9	153	160	167	175	185	195	204	128	133	140	147	154	161	169
6–6.9	155	159	167	179	188	209	228	131	135	142	151	161	170	177
7–7.9	162	167	177	187	201	223	230	137	139	151	160	168	177	190
8–8.9	162	170	177	190	202	220	245	140	145	154	162	170	182	187
9–9.9	175	178	187	200	217	249	257	151	154	161	170	183	196	202
10–10.9	181	184	196	210	231	262	274	156	160	166	180	191	209	221
11–11.9	186	190	202	223	244	261	280	159	165	173	183	195	205	230
12–12.9	193	200	214	232	254	282	303	167	171	182	195	210	223	241
13–13.9	194	211	228	247	263	286	301	172	179	196	211	226	238	245
14–14.9	220	226	237	253	283	303	322	189	199	212	223	240	260	264
15–15.9	222	229	244	264	284	311	320	199	204	218	237	254	266	272
16–16.9	244	248	262	278	303	324	343	213	225	234	249	269	287	296
17–17.9	246	253	267	285	308	336	347	224	231	245	258	273	294	312
18–18.9	245	260	276	297	321	353	379	226	237	252	264	283	298	324
19–19.9	262	272	288	308	331	355	372	238	245	257	273	289	309	321
25–34.9	271	282	300	319	342	362	375	243	250	264	279	298	314	326
35–44.9	278	287	305	326	345	363	374	247	255	269	286	302	318	327
45–54.9	267	281	301	322	342	362	376	239	249	265	281	300	315	326
55–64.9	258	273	296	317	336	355	369	236	245	260	278	295	310	320
65–74.9	248	263	285	307	325	344	355	223	235	251	268	284	298	306
Females														
1–1.9	138	142	148	156	164	172	177	105	111	117	124	132	139	143
2–2.9	142	145	152	160	167	176	184	111	114	119	126	133	142	147
3–3.9	143	150	158	167	175	183	189	113	119	124	132	140	146	152

E	Examination	N	Normal Findings	A	Abnormal Findings	P	Pathophysiology

TABLE 7-10 MAC and MAMC Percentiles *continued*

Age Group	MID-ARM CIRCUMFERENCE (MM)							MID-ARM MUSCLE CIRCUMFERENCE (MM)						
	5	10	25	50	75	90	95	5	10	25	50	75	90	95
4–4.9	149	154	160	169	177	184	191	115	121	128	136	144	152	157
5–5.9	153	157	165	175	185	203	211	125	128	134	142	151	159	165
6–6.9	156	162	170	176	187	204	211	130	133	138	145	154	166	171
7–7.9	164	167	174	183	199	216	231	129	135	142	151	160	171	176
8–8.9	168	172	183	195	214	247	261	138	140	151	160	171	183	194
9–9.9	178	182	194	211	224	251	260	147	150	158	167	180	194	198
10–10.9	174	182	193	210	228	251	263	148	150	159	170	180	190	197
11–11.9	185	194	208	224	248	276	303	150	158	171	181	196	217	223
12–12.9	194	203	216	237	256	282	294	162	166	180	191	201	214	220
13–13.9	202	211	223	243	271	301	328	169	175	183	198	211	226	240
14–14.9	214	223	237	252	272	304	322	174	179	190	201	216	232	247
15–15.9	208	221	239	254	279	300	322	175	178	189	202	215	228	244
16–16.9	218	224	241	258	283	318	334	170	180	190	202	216	234	249
17–17.9	220	227	241	264	295	324	350	175	183	194	205	221	239	257
18–18.9	222	227	241	258	281	312	325	174	179	191	202	215	237	245
19–19.9	221	230	247	265	290	339	345	179	185	195	207	221	236	249
25–34.9	233	240	256	277	304	342	368	183	188	199	212	228	246	264
35–44.9	241	251	267	290	317	356	378	186	192	205	218	236	257	272
45–54.9	242	256	274	299	328	362	384	187	193	206	220	238	260	274
55–64.9	243	257	280	303	335	367	385	187	196	109	225	244	266	280
65–74.9	240	252	274	299	326	356	373	185	195	208	225	244	264	279

Source: Reprinted with permission from: Frisancho, A. R. (1981), New norms of upper limb fat and muscle areas for assessment of nutrition status, *American Journal of Clinical Nutrition*, 34, p. 2540. American Society for Clinical Nutrition.

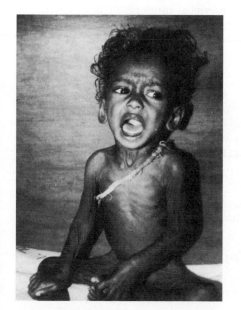

Figure 7-22 Marasmus is characterized by decreased weight, TSF, MAC, and muscle wasting. *Courtesy of the World Health Organization.*

Laboratory Data

Laboratory analysis is used to screen for potential nutritional problems and to assist with diagnosis when problems are suspected after a thorough history and physical are conducted. Caution must be exercised when interpreting these laboratory values because they can be affected by pathophysiological processes. The lab data needs to be considered in context with the patient's history, physical examination, and anthropometric measurements.

Hematocrit and Hemoglobin

Hematocrit is the proportion of red cells to volume of whole blood. **Hemoglobin** is the iron component of the blood that transports oxygen. Both values are obtained from a venous blood sample.

N   Hemoglobin and hematocrit results should fall within expected values as shown in Table 7-11. Increased hematocrit and hemoglobin may normally occur with people living in high altitudes due to the decrease in partial pressure of oxygen in those areas.

A   Decreased hematocrit and hemoglobin are abnormal.

P   Moderate to severe anemia may indicate decreased iron intake, leukemia, cirrhosis, hyperthyroidism, hemorrhage, hemodilution, or hemolytic reactions.

TABLE 7-11

Normal Values for Hematocrit and Hemoglobin

	NORMAL VALUES	
	Hematocrit	Hemoglobin
Age		g/L
1 mo	0.38–0.52	107–171
12 mo	0.37–0.41	113–141
1–2 yr	0.32–0.40	110–140
9–14 yr	0.36–0.42	120–144
18–44 yr		
Female	0.38–0.44	117–155
Male	0.43–0.49	132–173
65–74 yr		
Female	0.38–0.44	117–161
Male	0.37–0.51	126–174

P Increased hematocrit and hemoglobin are abnormal.

P Chronic hypoxia, such as in cyanotic heart defects, can result in polycythemia. Severe dehydration may also result from hemoconcentration.

Lipids

In 2003, the Working Group on Hypercholesterolemia and Other Dyslipidemias published revised guidelines to assist health care providers in assessing and managing hyperlipidemia.[29] Routine lipid screening is recommended for men aged 40 and over, and for women who are post-menopausal or over 50 years. Those with significant risk factors for CAD, such as diabetes mellitus, hypertension, history of smoking, abdominal obesity, and a strong family history of premature cardiovascular disease, should be screened earlier. The Working Group determined target *LDL-C levels and **total cholesterol: HDL-C ratio for patients based on their 10-year risk of coronary artery disease.

*LDL Cholesterol (LDL-C) (mmol/L)

<2.5	Target level for patients at high risk of CAD
<3.5	Target level for patients at moderate risk of CAD
<4.5	Target level for patients at low risk of CAD

HDL Cholesterol (HDL-C) (mmol/L)

<1.04	Very low (undesirable)
1.04–1.29	Low (less desirable)
1.30–1.54	Acceptable
>1.55	Desirable

Total Cholesterol (mmol/L)

<5.19	Desirable
5.2–6.19	Borderline high
>6.20	High
>7.21	Extremely high

**Total Cholesterol: HDL-C ratio

<4.0	Target level for patients at high risk of CAD
<5.0	Target level for patients at moderate risk of CAD
<6.0	Target level for patients at low risk of CAD

Triglycerides (mmol/L)

<1.70	Optimal
1.70–2.25	Borderline high
2.26–5.64	High
>5.65	Very high

A Elevated total cholesterol: HDL-C ratio, LDL-C, and triglycerides above desirable range are abnormal. HDL-C less than 1.04 mmol/L is undesirable in adults.

P Elevated lipid levels (except HDL-C) can be due to increased fat intake, genetics, and some medications (e.g., steroids, estrogens, cyclosporin) and can lead to an increased risk of cardiac disease.

Transferrin, Total Iron-Binding Capacity, and Iron

Transferrin is a protein that regulates iron absorption. Transferrin can be measured by the **total iron-binding capacity (TIBC),** the amount of iron with which

E	Examination	N	Normal Findings	A	Abnormal Findings	P	Pathophysiology

it can bind. **Serum iron** is the amount of transferrin-bound iron. These data are obtained from a venous blood sample. Serum transferrin can be calculated using the following formula: Transferrin = $(0.8 \times$ TIBC$) - 43$.

N   Normal adult levels are:

Transferrin

	Male	2.2–3.6 g/L
	Female	2.5–3.8 g/L

TIBC

45–63 µmol/L

Serum iron

	Male	13.2–31.3 µmol/L
	Female	11.6–29.6 µmol/L

A   An increase in transferrin is abnormal.

P   Increased levels of transferrin are found in inadequate dietary iron, iron-deficiency anemia, hepatitis, and oral contraceptive use.

A   Decreased levels of transferrin are abnormal.

P   Decreased levels of transferrin are found in pernicious anemia, sickle cell anemia, anemia associated with infection or chronic diseases, cancer, and malnutrition.

A   Increases in serum iron levels are abnormal.

P   Increases in serum iron levels are found in hemolytic anemias and lead poisoning.

A   Decreases in serum iron levels are abnormal.

P   Decreases in serum iron levels are found in iron deficiency, chronic diseases, third-trimester pregnancy, and severe physiological stress.

Total Lymphocyte Count

Total lymphocyte count (TLC) is measured in the complete blood count with differential and measures immune function and visceral protein status. When the white blood cell (WBC) count is abnormally high (bacterial infections) or low (AIDS), the TLC is not always a reliable indicator of nutritional status.

N   Normal adult levels are $1.5-1.8 \times 10^9$.

A   A decrease in the TLC of less than 1.5 indicates moderate protein deficiency, whereas a count of less than 0.9 indicates severe protein deficiency.

P   Protein deficiency occurs when the body is malnourished, such as when a patient is immunocompromised.

Antigen Skin Testing

Antigen skin testing is another test of immune function. Intradermal injections of various antigens can be used, such as with PPD tuberculin skin tests, mumps virus, *Candida albicans*, streptokinase, *Streptococcus*, *coccidioidin*, and *Trichophyton*. Results are read at 24 and 48 hours postinjection.

N   **A negative skin reaction (no induration or erythema) after being tested with various antigens is normal. These are antigens to which most people have been exposed and have developed an antibody response.**

A   A positive reaction to antigens placed intradermally is abnormal, which is indicated by a red area or induration 5 mm or more around the test site 24 hours or more after the injection. A negative reaction to only one of the antigens tested or a delayed positive reaction may occur with malnutrition.

P   Poor antibody response occurs in patients who are immunocompromised. They have a decreased ability to fight infection and build antibodies. Protein malnutrition has been shown to decrease immune function. This

Life 360°

Nutritional Assessment of Cardiac Status

You are scheduled to perform a history and physical on a 52-year-old man. He does not drink alcohol, use tobacco, or salt his food. He runs 6.4 km five days a week. His BMI is appropriate for his height. The patient's father and grandfather both died of myocardial infarction in their 40s. You inform the patient that you would like to obtain blood work for his lipid profile since it has not been checked in more than 10 years. The patient tells you that this is unnecessary since he observes a heart-healthy lifestyle. What would you say to the patient? How would you proceed with the rest of the history and physical examination?

TABLE 7-12
Prealbumin and Albumin Values
Albumin
Normal value	38–45 g/L
Mild depletion	30–37 g/L
Moderate depletion	25–29 g/L
Severe depletion	<25 g/L
Prealbumin
Normal value	200 mg/L
Mild depletion	100–150 mg/L
Moderate depletion	50–100 mg/L
Severe depletion	<50 mg/L

diminished reaction to antigens is called **anergy.** Antigen skin testing is often called anergy pas.

Prealbumin

Prealbumin (also called thyroxine-binding prealbumin) is the transport protein for thyroxine and retinol-binding protein. The half-life is 24 to 48 hours so it is an excellent value to monitor the effects of recent nutritional support and changes in nutritional status.

N See Table 7-12, Prealbumin and Albumin Values, for normal values.

A Liver disease, such as cirrhosis and hepatitis, as well as severe stress from infection, burn injury, and sepsis, prolonged surgery, hyperthyroidism, and cystic fibrosis can all lead to decreased prealbumin levels.

P Severe acute conditions where severe catabolism occurs tend to lower the prealbumin level. In the case of liver disease, the levels are lower because of decreased hepatic synthesis of proteins.

Albumin

Albumin is formed in the liver. It transports nutrients, blood, and hormones, and helps maintain osmotic pressure. Albumin must have functioning liver cells and an adequate amount of amino acids to be synthesized. It is an indicator of visceral protein status. Because albumin has a long half-life (about 20 days), it is not an indicator that detects subtle or early changes in nutritional status. It is measured from a venous blood sample.

N See Table 7-12, Prealbumin and Albumin Values, for normal values.

A Less than 38 g/L is abnormal.

P Decreased levels of albumin may indicate malnutrition because of a decrease in visceral protein stores, or a decrease in the amount of protein stored in organs. The decrease may not be seen until the protein deficiency reaches a chronic stage.

P Decreased levels of albumin are also found in massive hemorrhage, burns, and kidney disease.

Glucose

Serum glucose tests the body's ability to metabolize glucose. It is best assessed after a fasting period and from a venous blood sample. The Canadian Diabetes Association recommends that Canadians aged 40 years and over receive a screening for type 2 diabetes mellitus every three years. If the individual has other risk factors such as hyperlipidemia, obesity (BMI >25), or hypertension, then screening should be started earlier than 40 years of age and done more frequently. The tests should include a fasting plasma glucose (FPG) or a two-hour 75 g oral glucose tolerance test (OGTT).[30]

N The normal glucose levels are:

  Adult: FPG (no caloric intake for at least 8 hr) 3.6 – 5.5 mmol/L

A An increase in glucose level is abnormal.

P **Hyperglycemia** occurs when glucose is not being transported into the cells by insulin; it can be found in diabetes mellitus, impaired glucose tolerance, vitamin B_1 deficiency, and convulsive states.

A A decrease in serum glucose level is abnormal.

P **Hypoglycemia** occurs when there is too much insulin and not enough glucose in the blood; it is found in pancreatic disorders, liver disease, and insulin overdose.

E	**Examination**	N	**Normal Findings**	A	**Abnormal Findings**	P	**Pathophysiology**

Nursing Alert

Diagnosis of Diabetes

The prevalence of diabetes mellitus in Canadians is increasing in line with the high incidence of obesity. It is estimated that for every one person diagnosed with diabetes mellitus, there is another person who has not yet been diagnosed. Nurses must be aware of the criteria for diagnosis because they are frequently screening for this metabolic disorder. Any patient with one of the following indicators of diabetes mellitus must be referred to the appropriate health care professional.

$$FPG \geq 7.0 \text{ mmol/L}$$

or

Casual plasma glucose ≥ 11.1 mmol/L + symptoms of diabetes
Casual plasma glucose is taken at any time of the day, without regard to the interval since the last meal. Classic symptoms of diabetes = polyuria, polydipsia, and unexplained weight loss

or

2h plasma glucose with a 75 g OGTT ≥ 11.1 mmol/L.

Creatinine Height Index

Creatinine is a substance normally excreted in the urine; it is dependent on the amount of skeletal muscle mass and measures the amount of protein reserves. Urine creatinine is tested after collecting a 24-hour urine sample. An ideal urine creatinine level by height table is used to establish the denominator in the equation used to calculate Creatinine Height Index (CHI). Use the following equation to calculate CHI:

$$CHI = \frac{\text{actual 24-hour creatinine excretion}}{\text{ideal 24-hour creatinine excretion}} \times 100$$

The CHI is not an accurate indicator of skeletal muscle mass in patients who are dehydrated or have renal dysfunction.

N Normal values for creatinine, collected with a 24-hour urine sample, are 0.13–0.22 mmol/kg/day. For CHI, where values are compared to an ideal urine creatinine by height table, normal CHI values are greater than 90%.

A CHI between 80% and 90% indicates mild protein deficiency.
CHI between 70% and 80% indicates moderate protein deficiency.
CHI of less than 70% indicates severe protein deficiency.

P Protein malnutrition may be indicated by the loss of lean body mass, which can occur in severe trauma, prolonged fever, and stress.

Nitrogen Balance

Nitrogen is one of the compounds of amino acids; it is incorporated into protein from food sources and is excreted in urine and feces. The balance of intake of nitrogen to output of nitrogen is compared, usually with a 24-hour urine sample. The nitrogen balance can be calculated using this formula:

$$\text{Nitrogen Balance} = \frac{\text{grams of protein eaten in 24 hours}}{6.25} - (UUN^* + 4)$$

---

*UUN = 24-hour urine urea nitrogen (in grams).

N   A zero balance is normal. A positive balance indicates tissue formation, found in growing children and in pregnant women.

A   A negative nitrogen balance is abnormal and indicates a catabolic state (the body excretes more nitrogen than is consumed).

P   More nitrogen is excreted than taken in, which means there is destruction or wasting of tissue. This can occur in malnutrition and in catabolic states (burns, severe stress, trauma, surgery).

Diagnostic Data

Radiographic studies are used to determine bone formation and to assess development. Rickets and scurvy are examples of long-term nutritional deficiencies that have radiographic manifestations. Rickets is a deficiency of vitamin D, and scurvy is a deficiency of vitamin C; both are characterized by softening and deformities of the bones. A bone density, or dual-energy X-ray absorptiometry (DEXA), scan is a low-radiation, noninvasive test that assesses the hip, spine, and wrist for osteoporosis. Although osteoporosis can result from many variables, nutrition is one of the leading etiologies in various age groups.

CASE STUDY   The Patient Who Is Obese

Robert is scheduled to have surgery next week for gastric bypass surgery. He presents today for his preoperative work-up.

HEALTH HISTORY

PATIENT PROFILE	33 yo high school teacher who has "tried everything" to lose weight with no success. Visibly obese, slightly short of breath.
HEALTH ISSUE/CONCERN	"I'm way too fat—I feel like all of my students make fun of me and I am a bad example. Nothing I have done so far has helped so I need to do something drastic."
PRESENT HEALTH	Has been overwt for as long as he can remember. Was encouraged to work hard while growing up & started to snack when he was studying in elementary school; never involved in sports; congratulated c̄ food by parents for achieving academic success; mother always told him that "a fat child is a happy child;" in high school decided that he was getting too heavy & went on his 1st diet (eating only one meal a day); lasted 3 days & gained 4.5 kg; in university he started running & lost 10 kg in 5 mos but quickly regained during exam time; ongoing pattern of yo-yo dieting, including eating patterns prescribed by dieticians & multiple fad diets; he always regains more weight than he loses; has tried acupuncture, hypnosis with no success. Links his divorce to his obesity & has gained 15 kg since this event; believes that a radical △ in his lifestyle is the only solution; feels frustrated c̄ his wt & would like to lose at least 45 kg.
PAST HEALTH HISTORY	
Medical History	Wt cycling per health history Depression × 3 yrs; sees counselor 1 × month; well controlled on meds

MVP: sees cardiologist (Dr. Samuels) q 6–12 mos; dental prophylaxis observed
Occasional heartburn, self medicates

Surgical History Cholecystectomy 6 yrs ago s̄ sequelae; severe N & V p̄ anesthesia

Medications Acetaminophen 650 mg po prn; MVI po daily; Ranitidine 150 mg po prn
(takes 1–2 × per wk); Pseudoephedrine 30 mg po q 4 hr prn
(occasional sinus congestion)

Communicable Diseases Denies STIs/hepatitis/HIV

Allergies NKA

Injuries and Accidents Minor cuts; had suturing as child

Special Needs None

Blood Transfusions None

Childhood Illnesses Varicella as toddler

Immunizations Usual childhood immunizations per recollection; had hepatitis B series
10 yrs ago & hepatitis A series 2 yrs ago; last dT 3 yrs ago; receives
annual influenza vaccine

FAMILY HEALTH HISTORY

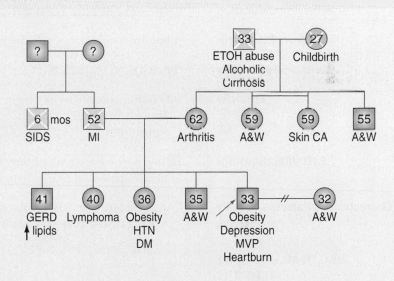

LEGEND
- Living female
- Living male
- Deceased female
- Deceased male
- / Points to patient
- —//— = Divorced
- ══ = Twins

A&W = Alive & well
CA = Cancer
DM = Diabetes mellitus
ETOH = Ethyl alcohol
GERD = Gastroesophageal
  reflux disease
HTN = Hypertension
MI = Myocardial infarction
MVP = Mitral valve prolapse
SIDS = Sudden infant death
  syndrome

Denies FHH of food allergies/intolerances, eating disorders, celiac dz,
malabsorption syndromes

SOCIAL HISTORY

Alcohol Use 5–8 beer a week (spread out)

Drug Use Occasional marijuana

continues

Tobacco Use	Smoked 1.5 PPD × 8 yrs; quit 7 yrs ago
Domestic or Intimate Partner Violence	Was fondled by uncle starting at age 10; refuses to elaborate but says he "is over it"
Sexual Practice	States that his obesity has been a major deterrent in finding dates since his wife left him; no relationships since
Travel History	Mexico q summer × 8 yrs; hoping to go to Israel on school trip next year
Work Environment	Teaches high school in a large urban centre; has to climb 3 flights of stairs to his classroom; lots of support from his colleagues
Home Environment	Lives alone in a small 3rd floor apartment; his ex-wife got the house they had bought together. No elevator—he chose this arrangement on purpose as he felt it would "force" him to exercise on a daily basis.
Hobbies and Leisure Activities	Reads a lot; photography
Stress	Divorce has been stressful: "I never thought she would leave me. It is so hard for me to meet women because of my weight. Some of the high school students make fun of me & I really get down about this; I feel they do not see me as a credible teacher; if only they could look beyond my weight."
Education	Bachelor of Science (Biology) and teaching diploma.
Economic Status	"I have no worries; my wife did not ask for alimony & I make a good salary."
Religion/Spirituality	"I don't go to church but I am very philosophical."
Ethnicity	"My father was of Greek origin & my mother's family came from Iran—what a mix; you can imagine the discussions we had in our household!"
Roles/Relationships	Talks c̄ parents q wk via phone; meets colleagues at work-related dinners & meetings; would like to date but no success.
Characteristic Patterns of Daily Living	"I work, sleep, & eat. Since my divorce I spend more time than ever at work; I rarely do anything else."
HEALTH MAINTENANCE ACTIVITIES	
Sleep	8–10 hrs q night; usually feels rested in AM
Diet	
Diet History	• Does not follow any particular diet at present • Likes all foods, especially sweets • Has strong cravings late at night for chocolate & ice cream • Eats fast food breakfast q AM • Usually has dinner at restaurants 2–3 × per wk c̄ colleagues • At home eats alone & is not motivated to prepare meals so orders in or buys prepared meals • Occasional heartburn, especially p̄ lg, fatty meals c̄ ETOH

Food Intake History

Time	Food/Drink	Amount	Method of Preparation	Eating Location
07:00	Sausage, egg, cheese biscuit	2 sandwiches	Fast food	Restaurant
	Hash browns	4	"	"
	Apple Danish	1	"	"
	Orange juice	360 mL	"	"
	Coffee	2–3 cups	"	"
10:00	Banana	1	Fresh	Office
	Donut	2	Purchased	"
13:00	Ham sub $\bar{c}$ lettuce, tomato, mayonnaise & cheese	30 cm	Deli	Office
	Chips	2 small bags	Bagged	"
	Soft drink	500 mL, nondiet	Bottled	"
16:00	Cookies	4	Store-bought	Office
19:00	Shrimp	6 lg	Broiled	Restaurant
	Steak	454 g	Fried	"
	Baked potato c cheese & sour cream	11g	Baked	"
	Salad	Salad-bowl size	Fresh	"
	Corn	240 mL	Fresh	"
	Cheesecake	1 slice	Baked	"
	Beer	240 mL		"

Exercise   Nothing recently

Stress Management   Eats chips & chocolate; discusses some problems with a colleague at work

Use of Safety Devices   Wears seat belt

Health Check-Ups   Last complete physical examination was 1 yr ago by cardiologist; optometrist prn for contact lens (last visit 2 yrs ago)
Dentist q yr

NUTRITIONAL ASSESSMENT

Physical Assessment

		Subjective	Objective
1.	General appearance	"I am too fat"	Obese
2.	Skin	c/o frequent intertriginous rashes	Intact; Ø rashes
3.	Hair	None	WNL
4.	Nails	None	Fingernails—WNL Toenails $\bar{c}$ onychomycosis
5.	Eyes	Visual acuity	Conjunctiva pink
6.	Mouth	None	Lips/gums/tongue/teeth WNL
7.	Head and neck	None	Gross hearing WNL, nares patent, Ø discharge

continues

8. Heart and peripheral	Palpitations c̄ stairs	BP: 145/92 vasculature HR: 88 & reg
9. Abdomen	Some constipation	Lg rounded abd, ≈ BS Ø mass, Ø HSM
10. Musculoskeletal	None	Flabby muscles system FROM all joints
11. Neurological system	None	Mental status, DTR, cerebellar fx all WNL

ANTHROPOMETRIC MEASUREMENTS

Height: 172.7 cm
Weight: 140.6 kg
% IBW: $310/171 \times 100 = 181\%$
BMI: 47.1
Waist circumference and Waist-to-Hip
    Ratio: Pt refused to be measured
TSF: 300 mm
MAC: 440 mm

LABORATORY DATA

MAMC: $44 - (3.14 \times 3) = 34.58$ cm
Hct: 0.42
Hgb: 102 g/L
Lipids:
    Cholesterol: 8.35 mmol/L
    HDL-C: 1.01 mmol/L
    LDL-C: 4.53 mmol/L
    Total cholesterol: HDL-C ratio: 8.27
    Triglycerides: 4.40 mmol/L
Transferrin/TIBC/Iron: Not performed
Total Lymphocyte Count: 1.75×10^9
Antigen Skin Testing: Ø indicated
Prealbumin: 350 mg/L
Albumin: 49 g/L
Glucose: 8.6 mmol/L (fasting)
Creatinine Height Index: Ø indicated
Nitrogen Balance: Ø indicated

DIAGNOSTIC DATA

X-rays: Ø indicated
DEXA Scan: Ø indicated

◄NURSING CHECKLIST►

Nutritional Assessment

Nutritional History

Physical Assessment

Anthropometric Measurements

- Height
- Weight
- Body mass index
- Waist circumference and waist-to-hip ratio
- Skinfold thickness
- Mid-arm and mid-arm muscle circumference

continues

Laboratory Data

- Hematocrit/hemoglobin
- Cholesterol, HDL-C, LDL-C, total cholesterol: HDL-C ratio, and triglycerides
- Transferrin, total iron-binding capacity, and iron
- Total lymphocyte count
- Antigen skin testing
- Prealbumin
- Albumin
- Glucose
- Creatinine height index
- Nitrogen balance

Diagnostic Data

- X-rays
- DEXA scan

REVIEW QUESTIONS

Questions 1–5 refer to the following situation:

Milka is a 21-year-old college student who is a member of the school's competitive dance team. She is 175.3 cm in height and weighs 47.6 kg. In the past few weeks, she has increased her daily runs from 8 km to 16 km.

1. Milka presents to the student health centre because she has not menstruated in six months. Due to her appearance, which condition do you suspect she may have?
   a. Osteomalacia
   b. Diabetes mellitus
   c. Anorexia nervosa
   d. Dysfunctional uterine bleeding
   The correct answer is (c).

2. You inquire about Milka's dietary habits. She informs you that for the past week she has only eaten three candy bars per day in an attempt to lose weight. If each candy bar contains 60 g of carbohydrates and 25 g of fat, what is her daily caloric intake?
   a. 465 calories
   b. 640 calories
   c. 1360 calories
   d. 1395 calories
   The correct answer is (d).

3. Milka tells you that one month ago she weighed 52.2 kg. What is her percent weight change?
   a. 8.7%
   b. 9.5%
   c. 81.4%
   d. 91.3%
   The correct answer is (a).

4. What is Milka's BMI (using the calculation method)?
   a. 4.4
   b. 15.5
   c. 16.9
   d. 19.8
   The correct answer is (b).

5. If Milka has a TSF of 10 mm and a MAC of 22.1 cm, what is her MAMC?
   a. 16.2 cm
   b. 18.9 cm
   c. 162 cm
   d. 189 cm
   The correct answer is (b).

6. Sophie is having a complete physical examination with blood work. Which laboratory value alerts you that she is at risk for cardiac disease?
   a. Triglycerides 1.64 mmol/L
   b. Cholesterol 4.78 mmol/L
   c. HDL-C 1.34 mmol/L
   d. LDL-C 5.69 mmol/L
   The correct answer is (d).

7. Which laboratory value most accurately reflects recent changes in nutritional status?
   a. Glucose
   b. HDL
   c. Prealbumin
   d. Hematocrit
   The correct answer is (c).

Questions 8 and 9 refer to the following situation:
Angela is a nursing student who elects to participate in a one-week mission to Central America.

8. On Angela's first day at the mission she assesses a child who has an edematous abdomen, scaly skin, and alopecia. Angela suspects that this child may have:
   a. Marasmus
   b. Kwashiorkor
   c. Celiac disease
   d. Lactose intolerance
   The correct answer is (b).

9. Which assessment findings might Angela expect to find in a malnourished patient?
   a. Loss of deep tendon reflexes, xanthelasma, flabby muscles
   b. Splenomegaly, tremors, enlarged gallbladder
   c. Xanthomas, goiter, hepatomegaly
   d. Bowing of the legs, missing teeth, pale conjunctiva
   The correct answer is (d).

10. Neural tube defects are associated with a deficiency of which nutrient in a pregnant woman?
    a. Vitamin D
    b. Folic acid
    c. Niacin
    d. Pantothenic acid
    The correct answer is (b).

Visit the Estes online companion resource at www.healthassessment.nelson.com **for additional content and study aids.**

REFERENCES

[1] Public Health Agency of Canada. (2005). *The integrated pan-Canadian healthy living strategy.* Retrieved May 29, 2006, from http://www.phac-aspc.gc.ca/hl-vs-strat/pdf/hls_e.pdf

[2] Health Canada, Office of Nutrition Policy and Promotion. (2005). *Revision of Canada's food guide to healthy eating.* Retrieved October 12, 2006, from http://www.hc-sc.gc.ca/fn-an/food-guide-aliment/revision/fg_rev_pro_overview-cal_rev_apercu_e.html#5

[3] Health Canada. *Eating Well with Canada's Food Guide: A resource for educators and communicators.* Retrieved February 7, 2007, from http://www.hc-sc.gc.ca/fn-an/alt_formats/hpfb-dgpsa/pdf/pubs/res-educat_e.pdf

[4] Health Canada—Drugs and Health Products. *Natural health products.* Retrieved October 23, 2006, from http://www.hc-sc.gc.ca/dhp-mps/prodnatur/index_e.html

[5] ASPEN Board of Directors. (2002). Guidelines for the use of parenteral and enteral nutrition in adult and pediatric patients: 2001 revision. *Journal of Parenteral and Enteral Nutrition, 26,* (suppl 1): 1SA.

[6] Heart and Stroke Foundation of Canada. *Healthy eating—fish oil.* Retrieved May 29, 2006, from http://ww2.heartandstroke.ca/Page.asp?PageID=1613&ContentID=9069&ContentTypeID=1

[7] Heart and Stroke Foundation of Canada. *Position Statement. Trans fatty acids "trans fats" and heart disease and stroke.* Retrieved October 12, 2006, from http://ww2.heartandstroke.ca/images/English/TransFat-ENGLISH-APR04.pdf

[8] Health Canada—Food and Nutrition. *Trans fats.* Retrieved October 12, 2006, from http://www.hc-sc.gc.ca/fn-an/nutrition/gras-trans-fats/index_e.html

[9] Public Health Agency of Canada. *Suggested clinical approach for detection and management of hypercholesterolemia.* Retrieved October 12, 2006, from http://www.phac-aspc.gc.ca/ccdpc-cpcmc/hhk-tcs/english/guide/pdf_e/book_cholesterol.pdf

[10] Roth, R. A., & Townsend, C. E. (2003). *Nutrition and diet therapy* (8th ed.). Clifton Park, NY: Thomson Delmar Learning.

[11] Dieticians of Canada (2003). A new food guide for North American vegetarians. *Canadian Journal of Dietetic Practice, 64*(2), 81–86.

[12] Dieticians of Canada. (2003). Vegetarian diets: Position of the American Dietetic Association and Dietitians of Canada. *Canadian Journal of Dietetic Practice, 64*(2), 62–81.

[13] Canadian Paediatric Society, Dietitians of Canada, and Health Canada. (2005). *Nutrition for healthy term infants.* Ottawa: Minister of Public Works and Government Services.

[14] Christofides, A., Schauer, C., & Zlotkin, S. H. (2005). Iron deficiency and anemia prevalence and associated risk factors in First Nations and Inuit communities in Northern Ontario and Nunavut. *Canadian Journal of Public Health, 96*(4), 304–07.

[15] Canadian Paediatric Society, Dietitians of Canada, and Health Canada, *Nutrition for healthy term infants.*

[16] Cole, T. J., Bellizzi, M. C., Flegall, K. M., & Dietz, W. H. (2000). Establishing a standard definition for child overweight and obesity worldwide: International survey. *British Medical Journal, 320*(7244), 1240–43.

[17] Sheilds, M. (2004). *Nutrition: Findings from the Canadian health survey. Issue no. 1. Measured obesity: Overweight children and adolescents.* Statistics Canada Cat. No. 82-620-MWE. Ottawa, ON: Statistics Canada. Retrieved May 27, 2006, from http://www.statcan.ca/english/research/82-620-MIE/2005001/pdf/cobesity.pdf

[18] Young, T. K., Dean, H. D., Flett, B., & Wood-Steiman, P. (2000). Childhood obesity in a population at high risk for type 2 diabetes. *Journal of Pediatrics, 136*(3), 365–69.

[19] Tjepkema, M. (2004). *Nutrition: Findings from the Canadian community health survey. Issue no. 1. Measured obesity: Adult obesity in Canada.* Statistics Canada Cat. No. 82-620-MWE2005001. Ottawa, ON: Statistics Canada. Retrieved October 12, 2006, from http://www.statcan.ca/english/research/82-620-MIE/2005001/pdf/aobesity.pdf

[20] Health Canada. (2003). *Canadian guidelines for body weight classification in adults.* Retrieved March 11, 2006, from http://

www.hc-sc.gc.ca/fn-an/alt_formats/hpfb-dgpsa/pdf/nutrition/weight_book-livres_des_poids_e.pdf

[21]Katzmarzyk, P. T., & Ardern, C. I. (2004). Overweight and obesity mortality trends in Canada,1985–2000. *Canadian Journal of Public Health, 95*(1), 16–20.

[22]Health Canada. (1999). *Nutrition for a healthy pregnancy: National guidelines for the childbearing years.* Retrieved April 22, 2006, from http://www.hc-sc.gc.ca/fn-an/nutrition/prenatal/national_guidelines_cp-lignes_directrices_ nationales_pc_e.html

[23]Health Canada. (2005). *Nutrition for a healthy pregnancy: National guidelines for the childbearing years. The prenatal period. Food safety.* Retrieved April 22, 2006, from http://www.hc-sc.gc.ca/fn-an/nutrition/prenatal/national_guidelines-lignes_directrices_nationales-06g_e.html#1

[24]National Institute of Nutrition (NIN). (2002). Tracking nutrition trends IV: An update on Canadians' nutrition-related attitudes, knowledge and actions, 2001. Ottawa: NIN.

[25]Health Canada, *Canadian guidelines for body weight classification in adults.*

[26]Ibid.

[27]Dobbelsteyn, C. J., Joffres, M. R., MacLean, D. R., & Flowerdew, G. (2001). A comparative evaluation of waist circumference, waist-to-hip ratio and body mass index as indicators of cardiovascular risk factors. The Canadian Heart Health Surveys. *International Journal of Obesity, 25*(5), 652–61.

[28]Health Canada, *Canadian guidelines for body weight classification in adults.*

[29]Genest, J., Frohlich, J., Fodor, G., & McPherson, R. (2003). Recommendations for the management of dyslipidemia and the prevention of cardiovascular disease: Summary of the 2003 update. Reprinted from *Canadian Medical Association Journal, 169*(9), 921–24, October 28, 2003. Used with permission of the publisher.

[30]Canadian Diabetes Association. (2003). *Clinical practice guidelines.* Retrieved October 12, 2006, from http://www.diabetes.ca/cpg2003/download.aspx. Used with permission from Can J Diabetes, 2003: 27(Suppl 2): S7.

BIBLIOGRAPHY

Bloch, A. S. (2007). *Issues and choices in clinical nutrition practice.* Philadelphia: Lippincott Williams & Wilkins.

Dudek, S. (2006). *Nutrition essentials for nursing practice* (5th ed.). Philadelphia: Lippincott Williams & Wilkins.

WEB RESOURCES

Canada Council on Food and Nutrition
http://www.ccfn.ca/

Dietitians of Canada
http://www.dietitians.ca

Health Canada—Food and Nutrition
http://www.hc-sc.gc.ca/fn-an/index_e.html

Health Canada: Office of Nutrition Policy and Promotion
http://www.hc-sc.gc.ca/ahc-asc/branch-dirgen/hpfb-dgpsa/onpp-bppn/index_e.html

Institute of Nutrition, Metabolism, and Diabetes (INMD)
Health Canada
http://www.cihr-irsc.gc.ca

National Eating Disorder Information Centre
http://www.nedic.ca/

National Association of Anorexia Nervosa and Associated Disorders
http://www.anad.org/site/anadweb/content.php?type=1&id=10985

UNIT 3

Physical Assessment

She must have a respect for her own calling, because God's precious gift of life is often literally placed in her hands; she must be a sound, and close, and quick observer.

—Florence Nightingale

CHAPTER 8

Physical Assessment Techniques

COMPETENCIES

1. Describe how to maintain routine practices during the physical assessment.

2. Establish an environment suitable for conducting a physical assessment.

3. Describe how to perform inspection, palpation, percussion, and auscultation, and which areas of the body are assessed with each technique.

4. Demonstrate inspection, palpation, percussion, and auscultation in the clinical setting.

*I*nspection, palpation, percussion, and auscultation are the techniques used to assess the patient during a physical examination. This chapter introduces the assessment techniques and equipment used to conduct physical examinations.

ASPECTS OF PHYSICAL ASSESSMENT

Physical assessment can serve many purposes:

1. Screening of general well-being. The findings will serve as baseline information for future assessments.
2. Validation of the health issues or concerns that brought the patient to seek health care.
3. Detection of pathology in situations when the patient does not present with a health issue or concern but variations in health are detected by virtue of the systematic approach of physical assessment.
4. Monitoring of current health problems for amelioration or deterioration and determining appropriate referral if necessary.
5. Formulation of nursing analyses that will help determine care and treatment plans, including education and anticipatory guidance needs of the patient and family.

Role of the Nurse

The nurse plays a vital role in the health and physical assessment of the patient. The knowledge base of nursing is broad and includes an understanding of the many health and illness issues that can arise across the life span, the role of the family in health and illness events, and the nature of coping with normative and non-normative events. Nurses assess the biological, psychological, social, and spiritual nature of patient situations to gain a holistic understanding of the situation. Nurses are trusted members of the health care team and have a significant presence in the health care system. People may disclose health issues or concerns to nurses either formally (such as during a well-baby clinic visit) or informally (such as the teenager who meets the nurse in the school hallway and says "My friend thinks she is pregnant"). Nurses are often the entry point into the health care system—they often play a "triage" role in community and hospital clinics, provide telephone information services to help people determine if a health issue or concern needs further assessment, act as case managers to coordinate care, and may be the only health care professional available in remote settings. Nurses provide care to hospitalized patients as well as those in long-term and palliative care facilities—their round-the-clock presence ensures ongoing assessment for responses to illness situations. By conducting a systematic health and physical assessment, a nurse can determine the relevance of health issues or concerns that patients present with as well as establish the most accurate therapeutic plan to address the uniqueness of the patient situation.

Routine Practices and Transmission-Based Precautions

The transmission of infectious illnesses such as hepatitis and human immunodeficiency virus (HIV), and the increasing prevalence of antibiotic-resistant organisms, such as methicillin-resistant staphylococcus aureus (MRSA) and vancomycin-resistant enterococcus (VRE), among other potential infections, is a primary concern for health care professionals and for patients. On the one hand, health care workers must protect themselves and other patients from transmissible illnesses carried by a particular patient; on the other hand, the

---

Nursing Alert

Latex Allergies

In accordance with routine practices, nurses frequently use gloves when dealing with patients' body fluids. Be alert to the possibility that you, as well as your patients, may have latex allergies. Reactions range from eczematous contact dermatitis to anaphylactic shock. Before touching patients while wearing latex gloves or using other latex products, ask them if they have any known allergy to latex products. Many hospitals and clinics, especially those dealing with the pediatric population and people with chronic illness, are moving toward latex-free environments. See Chapter 3, p. 55 for discussion of latex-food syndrome.

Nursing Alert

Gloves are not a substitute for handwashing; rather, they provide an additional measure of protection, particularly from blood and moist body substances. Hands can become contaminated through gloves or during their removal.

Nursing Alert

Clostridium difficile (C. difficile)

The bacterium *C. difficile* is the most frequent cause of diarrhea in hospitalized patients, particularly those receiving antibiotic therapy. Epidemics caused by a hypervirulent toxinotype III ribotype 027 strain have occurred in certain provinces.[3] The high mortality rate from *C. difficile*–associated disease has led to increased vigilance in infection control procedures to prevent spread. This spore-forming, gram-positive anaerobe is found in fecal matter, and health care workers who do not follow strict infection control procedures can spread the bacteria to other patients or contaminate surfaces through hand contact. Nurses performing health and physical assessment in hospital and community clinics where patients may have *C. difficile* infection must be aware that they should use soap and water for hand hygiene because alcohol-based hand rubs may not be as effective against spore-forming bacteria.[4] Nurses should also use gloves during patient care and wear gowns if soiling of clothes is likely.

patient must be protected from any contamination by health care workers or the environment in which care is delivered.

Routine practices, formerly known as universal precautions, were developed by Health Canada's Laboratory Centre for Disease Control to protect health care professionals and patients. Routine practices should be used with every patient throughout the entire encounter. Figure 8-1 illustrates the routine practices recommended by Health Canada. Complete guidelines for acute care, ambulatory care, home care, and long-term care facilities are also available.[1] Figure 8-2 summarizes the recommended procedure for washing hands.

Another level of precaution called **transmission-based precautions** is to be used in conjunction with routine practices. Routes of transmission of microorganisms have been classified as contact (includes direct contact, indirect contact, and droplet transmission), airborne, common vehicle, and vectorborne. Direct contact transmission occurs when microorganisms are transferred from direct physical contact between an infected or colonized person and a susceptible host, such as in the transmission of impetigo, scabies, and varicella zoster virus. Indirect contact transmission occurs when passive transfer of microorganisms via a contaminated intermediate object such as unwashed hands or contaminated stethoscopes occurs. Droplet transmission is a form of contact transmission and refers to large droplets, ≥5 μm in diameter, that arise from the respiratory tract during coughing, sneezing, or invasive procedures (e.g., suctioning). Pertussis and *Haemophilus influenzae* are examples of this mode of transmission. Droplet transmission occurs at a distance of <1 metre. Airborne transmission spreads microorganisms <5 μm by air currents and inhalation. They can also be passed through ventilation systems. Measles and the varicella virus as well as the tuberculosis bacterium can spread by this mode. Common vehicle transmission refers to a single contaminated source, such as food, medication, intravenous fluid, or an insulin vial. Vectorborne transmission refers to transmission by insect vectors, such as the tsetse fly, spreading malaria in African countries. Vectorborne transmission has not been reported in Canada. Additional information about routine practices and transmission-based precautions can be viewed on the Health Canada website at http://www.phac-aspc.gc.ca/publicat/ccdr-rmtc/99vol25/25s4/index.html.

ASSESSMENT TECHNIQUES

Physical assessment findings, or objective data, are obtained through the use of four specific techniques that are usually performed in this order: inspection, palpation, percussion, and auscultation. An exception is in the assessment of the abdomen, when auscultation is performed prior to percussion and palpation, as the latter two can alter bowel sounds. These four techniques when used systematically can validate information provided by a patient in the health history, can verify a suspected diagnosis, and can ensure comprehensive assessment. In addition, a health issue may be discovered that was not originally identified by the patient as a concern, such as when palpation of the abdomen yields abnormal findings when there were no subjective symptoms of pathology.

Usually, the easiest assessment skills to master are inspection and basic auscultation. Percussion and palpation may take more time and practice to perfect. With time and practice, the physical assessment techniques become second nature. You may decide not to perform all assessment skills in the same order as they are presented in this text, which is acceptable as long as basic guidelines are observed.

Inspection

"A conscientious nurse is not necessarily an observing nurse; and life or death may lie with the good observer." This statement by Florence Nightingale provides

ROUTINE PRACTICES

(for complete recommendations, see Health Canada Infection Control Guidelines[1])

HAND WASHING	Performed before and after any direct hand contact with a patient (including the skin, body fluids, blood, secretions and excretions and wound exudates) or contaminated items (e.g., urinal, wound dressing).
	Plain soap is used for routine hand washing; antiseptic hand rinse is used before performing invasive procedures or when caring for an immunocompromised person.
	Waterless antiseptic hand rinses are an alternative to hand washing, especially when access to sinks is limited. Hand washing with soap and water before using waterless antiseptic hand rinses is necessary when there is visible soiling.
GLOVES	Not required for routine care that is limited to contact with the patient's intact skin.
	Clean, non-sterile gloves are worn for contact with blood, body fluids, secretions and excretions, mucous membranes, draining wounds or non-intact skin.
	Used in addition to, not as a substitute for, hand washing. Wash hands before and *after* wearing gloves.
	Remove gloves immediately after care to avoid environmental contamination.
MASK, EYE PROTECTION, FACE SHIELD	These are worn during patient care activities and procedures that are likely to generate splashes or sprays of blood, body fluids, secretions, or excretions.
GOWNS	Used when soiling of clothing or uncovered skin is a risk such as during procedures or care activities that can generate splashes or sprays of blood, body fluids, secretions, or excretions.
ACCOMODATION	Single patient rooms are not required for routine patient care in the acute care setting; transmission based precautions can call for a single room or negative pressure room for certain airborne or contact transmitted microorganisms.
PATIENT CARE EQUIPMENT	Needles and sharp instruments must be disposed of puncture-resistant containers.
	In acute care settings, reusable equipment that has been in direct contact with the patient must be cleansed before use with another patient.
	In the ambulatory setting, items that are only in contact with intact skin must be cleansed on a routine basis if cleaning between patient use is not feasible. A barrier, such as a sheet or paper, on the examination table will prevent contamination between patients.
ENVIRONMENTAL CONTROL	In the acute care setting, cleaning and disinfection of environmental surfaces and patient furniture must be completed on a routine basis

Figure 8-1 Routine Practices.

Source: Excerpted from Health Canada Infection Control Guidelines.

Procedure	Rationale
Remove jewelry before hand wash procedure.	
Rinse hands under warm running water.	This allows for suspension and washing away of the loosened microorganisms.
Lather with soap and, using friction cover all surfaces of the hands and fingers.	The minimum duration for this step is 10 seconds: more time may be required if hands are visibly soiled.
	For antiseptic agents 3–5 mL are required.
	Frequently missed areas are thumbs, undernails, backs of fingers and hands.
Rinse under warm running water.	To wash off microorganisms and residual hand washing agent.
Dry hands thoroughly with single-use towel or forced air dryer.	Drying achieves a further reduction in number of microorganisms.
	Reusable towels are avoided because of the potential for microbial contamination.
Turn off faucet without recontaminating hands.	To avoid recontaminating hands.
Do not use fingernail polish or artificial nails.	Artificial nails or chipped nail polish may increase bacterial load and impede visualization of soil under nails.

Figure 8-2 How to Wash Hands.
Source: Health Canada Infection Control Guidelines, *How to Wash Hands,* from http://www.phac-aspc.gc.ca/publicat/ccdr-rmtc/98pdf/cdr24s8e.pdf. Reproduced with the permission of the Minister of Public Works and Government Services Canada, 2006.

inspiration and direction for inspection, which is usually the first technique used during the assessment process. **Inspection** is an ongoing process that uses the nurse's senses of vision and smell to consciously observe the patient throughout the entire physical assessment.

Vision

Use of sight can reveal many facts about a patient. Visual inspection of a patient's respiratory status, for example, might reveal a rate of 38 breaths per minute and cyanotic nailbeds. In this case, the patient is tachypneic and possibly hypoxic and would need a more thorough respiratory assessment. The process of visual inspection necessitates full exposure of the body part being inspected, adequate overhead lighting, and, when necessary, **tangential lighting** (light that is shone at an angle on the patient to accentuate shadows and highlight subtle findings).

Smell

The nurse's olfactory sense also provides vital information about a patient's health status. The patient may have a fruity breath odour characteristic of diabetic ketoacidosis; the smell of urine or feces may indicate difficulties with self-care. The classic odour that is emitted by a *Pseudomonas* infection is another well-recognized smell to the experienced nurse.

Reflective Thinking

Testing Accuracy of Observation

Walk into a patient's room with a colleague and observe the patient and the environment for 30 seconds. Leave the room and record your observations. Compare your findings with those of your colleague's. Were your lists similar? Re-enter the patient's room and validate the accuracy of your observations.

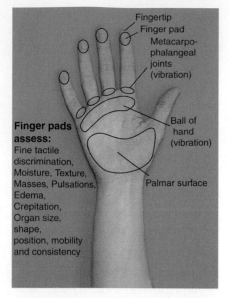

Finger pads assess:
Fine tactile discrimination, Moisture, Texture, Masses, Pulsations, Edema, Crepitation, Organ size, shape, position, mobility and consistency

A. Palmar Surface

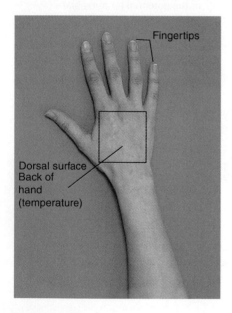

B. Dorsal Surface

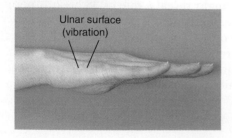

C. Ulnar Surface

Figure 8-3 Parts of the Hand Used in Palpation.

Nursing Tip

Order of Assessment Procedures

A good rule of thumb to follow when sequencing assessment procedures is to progress from the least intrusive to the most intrusive. Assessments that may cause discomfort should be performed last whenever possible in order to prevent patient anxiety, fear, and muscle guarding. For example, palpation of a tender area in the abdomen should be performed last. In the pediatric patient, the assessment of the ears and throat is usually performed last because these are the most uncomfortable for the child and may cause crying.

Palpation

The second assessment technique is **palpation,** which is the act of touching a patient in a therapeutic manner to elicit specific information. Prior to palpating a patient, some basic principles need to be observed. The nurse should have short fingernails to avoid hurting the patient. Hands should be warmed prior to placing them on the patient; cold hands can make a patient's muscles tense, thus distorting assessment findings. Encourage the patient to breathe normally throughout the palpation and discontinue immediately if pain is experienced. Most significantly, the patient needs to be informed where, when, and how the touch will occur, especially when he or she cannot see what is happening. The patient is therefore aware of what to expect in the assessment process.

Different sections of the hands are used for assessing certain areas of the body. The dorsum of the hand is most sensitive to temperature changes in the body. Therefore, placing the dorsum of the hand on a patient's forehead to assess body temperature is more accurate than using the palmar surface of the hand. The palmar surface of the fingers at the metacarpophalangeal joints, the ball of the hand, and the ulnar surface of the hand best discriminate vibrations, such as a cardiac thrill and fremitus. The finger pads of the hand are used most frequently in palpation to assess fine tactile discrimination, skin moisture, and texture; the presence of masses, pulsations, edema, and crepitation, and the shape, size, position, mobility, and consistency of organs (Figure 8-3).

Gloves must be worn when examining any open wounds, skin lesions, a body part with discharge, as well as internal body parts such as the mouth and rectum.

There are two distinct types of palpation techniques: light and deep palpation, each of which is briefly described here and covered in greater detail in chapters describing body systems where palpation is specifically used.

Light Palpation

Light palpation is done more frequently than deep palpation and is always performed before deep palpation. As the name implies, **light palpation** is superficial, delicate, and gentle. The finger pads are used to gain information on the patient's skin surface to a depth of approximately 1 cm below the surface. Light palpation reveals information on skin texture and moisture; overt, large, or superficial masses; and fluid, muscle guarding, and superficial tenderness. To perform light palpation:

1. Keeping the fingers of the dominant hand together, place the finger pads lightly on the skin over the area that is to be palpated. The hand and forearm will be on a plane parallel to the area being assessed.
2. Depress the skin 1 cm in light, gentle, circular motions.

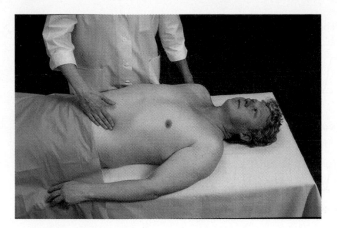

Figure 8-4 Technique of Light Palpation.

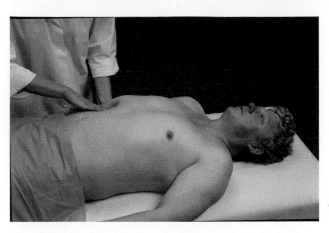

Figure 8-5 Technique of Deep Palpation.

3. Keeping the finger pads on the skin, let the depressed body surface rebound to its natural position.
4. If the patient is ticklish, lift your hand off the skin before moving it to another area.
5. Using a systematic approach, move the fingers to an adjacent area and repeat the process.
6. Continue to move the finger pads until the entire area being examined has been palpated.
7. If the patient has complained of tenderness in any area, palpate this area last. Figure 8-4 shows how light palpation is performed.

Deep Palpation

Deep palpation can reveal information about the position of organs and masses, as well as their size, shape, mobility, consistency, and areas of discomfort. Use your hands to explore the patient's internal structures to a depth of 4 or 5 cm, or more (Figure 8-5). This technique is most often used for the abdominal and male and female reproductive assessments. Variations in this technique are single-handed and bimanual palpation, which are discussed in Chapter 17.

Percussion

Percussion is the technique of striking one object against another to cause vibrations that produce sound. The density of underlying structures produces characteristic sounds that can be indicative of normal and abnormal findings. The presence of air, fluid, and solids can be confirmed, as can organ size, shape, and position. Any part of the body can be percussed, but only limited information can be obtained in specific areas such as the heart. The thorax and abdomen are the most frequently percussed locations.

Percussion sound can be analyzed according to its intensity, duration, pitch (frequency), quality, and location. **Intensity** refers to the relative loudness or softness (also called the amplitude) of the sound. **Duration** of percussed sound describes the time period over which a sound is heard when elicited. **Frequency** describes the concept of pitch and is caused by the sound's vibrations, or the highness or lowness of a sound. More rapidly occurring vibrations have a pitch that is higher than that of slower vibrations (Figure 8-6). The **quality** of a sound is its timbre, or how a person perceives it musically. **Location** of sound refers to the area where the sound is produced and heard.

The process of percussion can produce five distinct sounds in the body: **flatness**, **dullness**, **resonance**, **hyperresonance**, and **tympany**. Therefore, when an unexpected sound is heard in a particular area of the body, the cause must be further investigated.

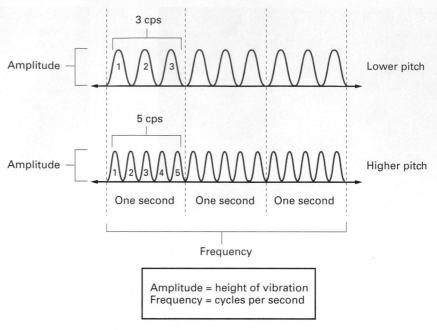

Figure 8-6 Percussion Pitch.

Table 8-1 illustrates each of the five percussion sounds in relation to its respective intensity, duration, pitch, quality, location, and relative density. In addition, examples are provided of normal and abnormal locations of percussed sounds.

Sound waves are better conducted through a solid medium than through an air-filled medium because of the increased concentration of molecules. The basic premises underlying the sounds that are percussed are:

1. The more solid a structure, the higher its pitch, the softer its intensity, and the shorter its duration.
2. The more air-filled a structure, the lower its pitch, the louder its intensity, and the longer its duration.

There are four types of percussion techniques: immediate, mediate, direct fist percussion, and indirect fist percussion. It is important to keep in mind that

TABLE 8-1 Characteristics of Percussion Sounds

SOUND	INTENSITY	DURATION	PITCH	QUALITY	NORMAL LOCATION	ABNORMAL LOCATION	DENSITY
Flatness	Soft	Short	High	Flat	Muscle (thigh) or bone	Lungs (severe pneumonia)	Most dense
Dullness	Moderate	Moderate	High	Thud	Organs (liver)	Lungs (atelectasis)	↓
Resonance	Loud	Moderate-long	Low	Hollow	Normal lungs	No abnormal location	
Hyperresonance	Very loud	Long	Very low	Boom	No normal location in adults; normal lungs in children	Lungs (emphysema)	
Tympany	Loud	Long	High	Drum	Gastric air bubble	Lungs (large pneumothorax)	Least dense

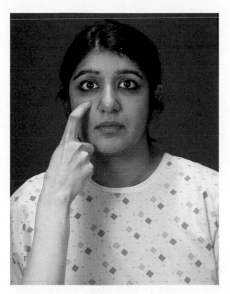

Figure 8-7 Technique of Immediate Percussion.

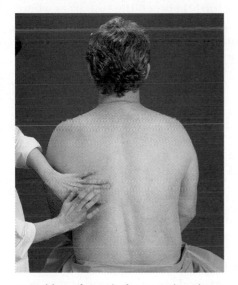

A. Position of Hands for Posterior Thorax Percussion

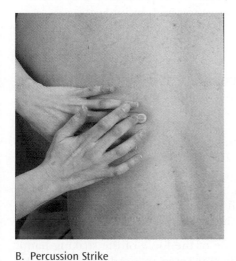

B. Percussion Strike

Figure 8-8 Technique of Mediate Percussion.

the sounds produced from percussion are generated from body tissue up to 5 cm below the surface of the skin. If the abdomen is to be percussed, the patient should have the opportunity to void before the assessment.

Immediate Percussion

Immediate or **direct percussion** is the striking of an area of the body directly. To perform immediate percussion:

1. Spread the index or middle finger of the dominant hand slightly apart from the rest of the fingers.
2. Make a light tapping motion with the finger pad of the index finger against the body part being percussed.
3. Note what sound is produced.

Percussion of the sinuses (Figure 8-7) illustrates the use of immediate percussion in the physical assessment.

Mediate Percussion

Mediate, or **indirect, percussion** is a skill that takes time and practice to develop and to use effectively. Most sounds are produced using mediate percussion. Follow these steps to perform mediate percussion (Figure 8-8):

1. Place the nondominant hand lightly on the surface to be percussed.
2. Extend the middle finger of this hand, known as the **pleximeter,** and press its distal phalanx and distal interphalangeal joint firmly on the location where percussion is to begin. The pleximeter will remain stationary while percussion is performed in this location.
3. Spread the other fingers of the nondominant hand apart and raise them slightly off the surface. This prevents interference and, thus, dampening of vibrations during the actual percussion.
4. Flex the middle finger of the dominant hand, called the **plexor.** The fingernail of the plexor finger should be very short to prevent undue discomfort and injury to the nurse. The other fingers on this hand should be fanned.
5. Flex the wrist of the dominant hand and place the hand directly over the pleximeter finger of the nondominant hand.
6. With a sharp, crisp, rapid movement from the wrist of the dominant hand, strike the pleximeter with the plexor. At this point, the plexor should be perpendicular to the pleximeter. The blow to the pleximeter should be between the distal interphalangeal joint and the fingernail. Use the finger pad rather than the fingertip of the plexor to deliver the blow. Concentrate on the movement to create the striking action from the dominant wrist only.
7. As soon as the plexor strikes the pleximeter, withdraw the plexor to avoid dampening the resulting vibrations. Do not move the pleximeter finger.
8. Note the sound produced from the percussion.
9. Repeat the percussion process one or two times in this location to confirm the sound.
10. Move the pleximeter to a second location, preferably the contralateral location from where the previous percussion was performed. Repeat the percussion process in this manner until the entire body surface area being assessed has been percussed.

Recognizing Percussion Sound

When using mediate and immediate percussion, the change from resonance to dullness is more easily recognized by the human ear than is the change from dullness to resonance. It is often helpful to close your eyes and concentrate

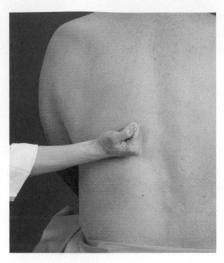

Figure 8-9 Technique of Direct Fist Percussion: Left Kidney.

Nursing Tip

At-Home Practice of Percussion

- Percuss two glasses—one filled with water, the other empty. Compare the sounds.
- Percuss the wall of a room and listen for the change in tones when a studboard is reached.
- Percuss your thigh. Puff your cheeks and percuss them. Compare the sounds.

on the sound in order to distinguish if a change in sounds occurs. This concept has implications for patterns of percussion in areas of the body where known locations have distinct percussible sounds. For example, the techniques of diaphragmatic excursion and liver border percussion can proceed in a more defined pattern because percussion can be performed from an area of resonance to an area of dullness. Another helpful hint is to validate the change in sounds by percussing back and forth between the two areas where a change is noted.

As stated earlier, the percussion technique can take considerable time to develop and perfect. Practicing the technique in the home environment can be a helpful learning experience; see the Nursing Tip, At-Home Practice of Percussion.

Direct Fist Percussion

Direct fist percussion is used to assess the presence of tenderness and pain in internal organs, such as the liver or the kidneys. To perform direct fist percussion (Figure 8-9):

1. Explain this technique thoroughly so the patient does not think you are hitting him or her.
2. Make a fist with your dominant hand.
3. With the ulnar aspect of the closed fist, directly hit the area where the organ is located. The strike should be of moderate force, and it may take some practice to achieve the right intensity.

The presence of pain in conjunction with direct fist percussion may indicate inflammation of that organ or a strike that was too high in intensity.

Indirect Fist Percussion

Indirect fist percussion has the same purpose as the direct method and is preferred over the direct method. It is performed in the following manner (Figure 8-10):

1. Place the palmar side of the nondominant hand on the skin's surface over the organ to be examined. Place the fingers adjacent to one another and in straight alignment with the palm.
2. Make a fist with your dominant hand.
3. With the ulnar aspect of the closed fist, use moderate intensity to hit the outstretched nondominant hand on the dorsum.

The nondominant hand will absorb some of the force of the striking hand. The resulting intensity should be of sufficient force to produce pain in the patient if organ inflammation is present.

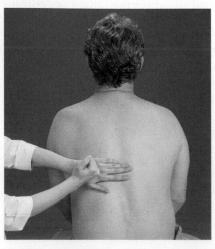

Figure 8-10 Technique of Indirect Fist Percussion: Left Kidney.

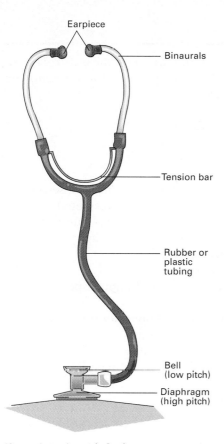

Figure 8-11 Acoustic Stethoscope.

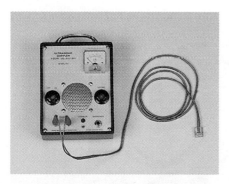

Figure 8-12 Doppler Ultrasonic Stethoscope.

Auscultation

Auscultation is the act of actively listening to body organs, including sounds that are produced voluntarily and involuntarily. A deep inspiration a patient takes during the lung assessment illustrates a voluntary sound; heart sounds are involuntary sounds. Auscultation requires a quiet environment, with sounds analyzed in relation to their relative intensity, pitch, duration, quality, and location. There are two types of auscultation: direct and indirect.

Direct Auscultation

Direct or **immediate auscultation** is the process of listening with the unaided ear. This can be done by listening to the patient from some distance away or by placing your ear directly on the patient's skin surface. An example of immediate auscultation is the wheezing that is audible to the unassisted ear in a person having a severe asthmatic attack.

Indirect Auscultation

Indirect or **mediate auscultation** is the process of listening with an amplification or mechanical device. The nurse most often performs mediate auscultation with an acoustic stethoscope (Figure 8-11), which does not amplify the body sounds, but instead the earpieces block out environmental sounds. The earpieces come in various sizes; choose an earpiece that fits snugly in the ear canal without causing pain. Angling the earpieces and binaurals toward the nose permits the natural direction of the ear canal to be accessed. In this manner, sounds will be directed toward the adult tympanic membrane. The length of the rubber or plastic tubing should be between 30.5 and 40 cm. Stethoscopes with longer tubing will diminish the body sounds that are auscultated.

The acoustic stethoscope has two listening heads: the bell and the diaphragm. The bell is a concave cup that transmits low-pitched sounds; the diaphragm is flat and transmits high-pitched sounds. Breath sounds and normal heart sounds are examples of high-pitched sounds. Bruits and some heart murmurs are examples of low-pitched sounds. Another commonly used stethoscope has a single-sided, dual-frequency listening head with a single chest piece. The nurse applies different pressures on the chest piece to auscultate high- and low-pitched sounds.

Prior to auscultation, any dangling necklaces or bracelets must be removed as they can cause false noises. Warm the headpieces of the stethoscope in your hands before use, because shivering and movement can obscure assessment findings. When using the diaphragm, place it firmly against the skin surface to be auscultated. If the patient has a large quantity of hair in an area, it may be necessary to wet the hair to prevent it from interfering with the auscultated sounds. Otherwise, a grating sound may be heard. The bell is placed lightly on the skin surface that is to be auscultated. The bell will stretch the skin and act like a diaphragm and transmit high-pitched sounds if it is pressed too firmly on the skin. Auscultation requires a great deal of concentration so closing your eyes during the auscultation process may help to isolate the sound. Sometimes more than one sound is heard in a given location. If this occurs, each sound must be assessed separately. The stethoscope can act as a vector in the transmission of pathogens and therefore must be cleaned after each patient. Auscultation is a skill that requires practice and patience so do not expect to become an expert overnight.

Amplification of body sounds can also be achieved with the use of a Doppler ultrasonic stethoscope (Figure 8-12). Water-soluble gel is placed on the body part being assessed, and the stethoscope is placed directly on the patient. Fetal heart tones and unpalpable peripheral pulses are frequently assessed via the Doppler ultrasonic stethoscope.

Nursing Tip

Headpiece Mnemonic

The word *bellow* can be used to remember which frequency is transmitted by the headpiece of the stethoscope: The "bell" transmits "low" sounds

EQUIPMENT

Gathering necessary equipment beforehand is important for the physical assessment to proceed efficiently. The equipment needed to perform a complete physical examination of the adult patient includes:

- Pen and paper
- Marking pen
- Tape measure
- Clean gloves
- Penlight or flashlight
- Scale (the patient will need to walk to a central location if a scale cannot be brought to the patient's room.)
- Thermometer
- Sphygmomanometer
- Gooseneck lamp
- Tongue depressor
- Stethoscope
- Otoscope
- Nasal speculum
- Ophthalmoscope
- Transilluminator
- Visual acuity charts
- Tuning fork
- Reflex hammer
- Sterile needle
- Cotton balls
- Odours for cranial nerve assessment (coffee, lemon, flowers, etc.)
- Small objects for neurological assessment (paper clip, key, cotton ball, pen, etc.)
- Lubricant
- Various sizes of vaginal speculums
- Cervical brush
- Cotton-tip applicator
- Cervical spatula
- Slide and fixative
- Occult blood test material
- Specimen cup
- Goniometer

The use of these items is discussed in the chapters describing the assessments for which they are used. Figure 8-13 illustrates some of the equipment used in the physical assessment.

1. Tuning Fork
2. Visual Occluder
3. Ruler
4. Visual Acuity Chart
5. Reflex Hammer (brush at bottom)
6. Reflex Hammer
7. Pen and Marking Pen
8. Penlight
9. Thermometer
10. Sphygmomanometer
11. Slide and Fixative
12. Specimen Cup
13. Vaginal Speculum
14. Lubricant
15. Goniometer
16. Clean Gloves
17. Cervical Spatula
18. Cervical Brush
19. Cotton-tip Applicator
20. Tongue Depressor
21. Occult Blood-Testing Material
22. Tape Measure
23. Acoustic Stethoscope
24. Ophthalmoscope
25. Otoscope with Speculum
26. Objects for Neurological Examination (key and cotton ball)
27. Sterile Needle

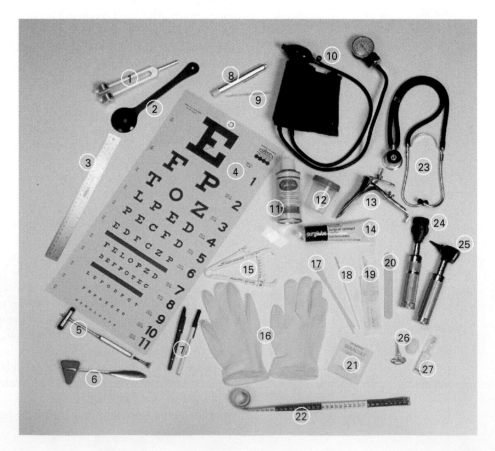

Figure 8-13 Equipment Used in Physical Assessment.

◄NURSING CHECKLIST►

Preparing for a Physical Assessment

- Always dress in a clean, professional manner; ensure that your name pin or workplace identification is visible.
- Remove all bracelets, necklaces, or earrings that can interfere with the physical assessment.
- Fingernails must be short and hands warmed for maximum patient comfort.
- Hair must not fall forward and obstruct vision or touch the patient.
- The room should be well lit, warm, and provide privacy.
- Necessary equipment should be ready for use and within reach.
- Introduce yourself to the patient: "My name is Veronica Rojas. I am the nurse who is caring for you today and will be performing your physical assessment."
- Clarify with the patient how he or she wishes to be addressed: Miss Jones, José, Mr. Casy, Rev. Grimes, etc.
- Explain what you plan to do and how long it will take; allow the patient to ask questions.
- Instruct the patient to undress (the undergarments can be left on until the end of the assessment); provide a gown and drape for the patient and explain how to use them.
- Allow the patient to undress privately; inform the patient when you will return to start the assessment.
- Have the patient void prior to the assessment.
- Wash your hands in front of the patient to show your concern for cleanliness.
- Observe routine practices and transmission-based precautions, as indicated.
- Ensure that the patient is accessible from both sides of the examining bed or table.
- If a bed is used, raise the height so that you do not have to bend over to perform the assessment.
- Position the patient as dictated by the body system being assessed; see Figure 8-14 for positioning and draping techniques.
- Enlist the patient's cooperation by explaining what is to be done, where it will be done, and how it may feel.
- Warm all instruments prior to their use (use your hands or warm water).
- Examine the unaffected body part or side first if a patient's complaint is unilateral.
- Explain to the patient why you may be spending a long time performing one particular skill: "Listening to the heart requires concentration and time."
- If the patient complains of fatigue, continue the assessment later (if possible).
- Be cognizant of your facial expression when dealing with patients who are unkempt or with disturbing findings (infected wounds, disfigurement, etc.).
- Conduct the assessment in a systematic fashion every time to avoid forgetting a particular assessment.
- Thank the patient when the physical assessment is concluded and inform the patient what will happen next.
- Document assessment findings in the appropriate section of the patient record.

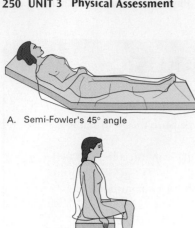

A. Semi-Fowler's 45° angle

Skin, head, and neck; eyes, ears, nose, mouth, and throat; thorax and lungs; heart and peripheral vasculature; musculoskeletal; neurological; patients who cannot tolerate sitting up at a 90° angle

B. Sitting (High Fowler's) 90° angle

Skin, head, and neck; eyes, ears, nose, mouth, and throat; back; posterior thorax and lungs; anterior thorax and lungs; breast; axillae; heart; peripheral vasculature; musculoskeletal; neurological

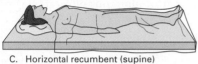

C. Horizontal recumbent (supine)

Breasts; heart and peripheral vasculature; abdomen; musculoskeletal

D. Dorsal recumbent

Female genitalia; patients who cannot tolerate knee flexion

E. Side Lying

Skin; thorax and lungs; bedridden patients who cannot sit up

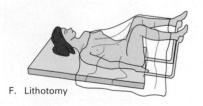

F. Lithotomy

Female genitalia and rectum

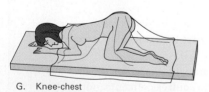

G. Knee-chest

Rectum and prostate

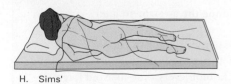

H. Sims'

Rectum and female genitalia

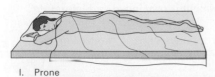

I. Prone

Skin; posterior thorax and lungs; hips

Figure 8-14 Positioning and Draping Techniques.

◄**NURSING CHECKLIST**►

Physical Assessment Techniques

Inspection
- Vision
- Smell

Palpation
- Light palpation
- Deep palpation

Percussion
- Immediate, or direct, percussion
- Mediate, or indirect, percussion
- Direct fist percussion
- Indirect fist percussion

Auscultation
- Immediate, or direct, auscultation
- Mediate, or indirect, auscultation

Nursing Tip

Golden Rules for Physical Assessment

- Stand on the right side of the patient; establishing a dominant side for assessment will decrease movement around the patient.
- Perform the assessment in a head-to-toe approach.
- Always compare the right- and left-hand sides of the body for symmetry.
- Proceed from the least invasive to the most invasive procedures for each body system.
- Always perform the physical assessment using a systematic approach; if it is performed the same way each time, you are less likely to forget some part of the assessment.

REVIEW QUESTIONS

1. A physical assessment is best conducted:
   a. In a toe-to-head approach
   b. When comparing right- and left-hand sides of the patient's body
   c. While standing at the foot of the patient's bed or examination table
   d. Proceeding from the most invasive to the least invasive procedures
   The correct answer is (b).

2. The Health Canada routine practices were developed to:
   a. Protect the patient and health care professional
   b. Prevent litigious action against HIV transmission
   c. Provide health care workers with a cleaner environment
   d. Reduce the number of annual needle-stick contaminations
   The correct answer is (a).

Questions 3 and 4 refer to the following situation:

A 59-year-old woman with emphysema is admitted to your unit.

3. In what order would you conduct the physical assessment of the thorax and lungs?
   a. Inspection, palpation, percussion, auscultation
   b. Inspection, auscultation, palpation, percussion
   c. Auscultation, palpation, percussion, inspection
   d. Palpation, percussion, inspection, auscultation
   The correct answer is (a).

4. What position best facilitates this assessment?
   a. Sims'
   b. Lithotomy
   c. Dorsal recumbent
   d. High Fowler's
   The correct answer is (d).

5. Vibration is best palpated with which section of the hand?
   a. Fingertips
   b. Finger pads
   c. Ulnar surface
   d. Dorsal surface
   The correct answer is (c).

6. Which percussion sound is loud in intensity, moderate-long in duration, low in pitch, and has a hollow quality?
   a. Flatness
   b. Dullness
   c. Resonance
   d. Tympany
   The correct answer is (c).

7. Which percussion technique is usually used to assess the maxillary sinuses?
   a. Immediate percussion
   b. Mediate percussion
   c. Direct fist percussion
   d. Indirect fist percussion
   The correct answer is (a).

8. Which characteristics best describe tympany?
   a. Soft intensity, short duration, high pitch
   b. Moderate intensity, moderate duration, high pitch
   c. Loud intensity, long duration, high pitch
   d. Very loud intensity, long duration, very low pitch
   The correct answer is (c).

9. The bell of the stethoscope is used to assess what characteristic?
   a. High-pitched sounds
   b. High-amplitude sounds
   c. Low-pitched sounds
   d. Low-amplitude sounds
   The correct answer is (c).

10. Which of these positions is best for assessing the rectum?
    a. Semi-Fowler's
    b. Horizontal recumbent
    c. Side lying
    d. Prone
    The correct answer is (c).

Visit the Estes online companion resource at
www.healthassessment.nelson.com **for additional content and study aids.**

emerging strain of *Clostridium difficile* associated with outbreaks of severe disease in North America and Europe. *Lancet. 366*(9491), 1079–84, Sep 24-30.

[4]Public Health Agency of Canada. *Clostridium difficile (C. difficile): Questions and answers.* Retrieved October 16, 2006, from http://www.phac-aspc.gc.ca//c-difficile/index.html

REFERENCES

[1]Health Canada. (1999). Infection control guidelines: Routine practices and additional precautions for preventing the transmission of infection in health care. *Canada Communicable Disease Report 1999, 25S4*, 1–155. Retrieved October 15, 2006, from http://www.phac-aspc.gc.ca/publicat/ccdr-rmtc/99pdf/cdr25s4e.pdf.

[2]Health Canada. (1998). Infection control guidelines: Hand washing, cleaning, disinfection and sterilization in health care. *Canada Communicable Disease Report 1998, 24S8*, 1–55.

[3]Warny, M., Pepin, J., Fang, A., Killgore, G., Thompson, A., Brazier, J., Frost, E., & McDonald, L. C. (2005). Toxin production by an

BIBLIOGRAPHY

Chinnes, L. F. (2005). Gain new perspectives in improved guidelines and practices. *Nursing Management, 36*(12), 29–31.

Ehiri, J. E. & Ejere, H. O. D. (2003). Hand washing for preventing diarrhoea. *The Cochrane Database of Systematic Reviews 2003*, Issue 2, Art. No.: CD004265.

Pittet, D. & Donaldson, L. (2005). Clean care is safer care: The first global challenge of the WHO World Alliance for Patient Safety. *American Journal of Infection Control, 33*(8), 476–79.

CHAPTER 9

General Survey, Vital Signs, and Pain

COMPETENCIES

1. Describe general assessment observations.

2. Discuss factors affecting respiratory rate and heart rate.

3. Describe the characteristics that are included in an assessment of pulse.

4. Discuss factors influencing body temperature.

5. Describe factors influencing blood pressure and blood pressure measurement.

6. Obtain a patient's vital signs.

7. Conduct an assessment on a patient experiencing pain.

A complete physical assessment is initiated by performing general observations of the patient, obtaining the patient's **vital signs,** and assessing the patient for pain. Initial observations can provide data about the patient's general state of health. Vital signs include the patient's respirations, pulse, temperature, blood pressure (BP), and level of pain. These measurements provide information about the patient's basic physiological status. The presence of pain can affect a patient's physical, emotional, and mental health.

EQUIPMENT

- Stethoscope
- Watch with a second hand
- Thermometer (gloves and lubricant if using a rectal thermometer)
- Sphygmomanometer

Nursing Tip

Environmental Cues

In addition to observing the patient, look around the room for clues about the patient's health status. For example, an inhaler, nasal spray, a hearing aid, or used tissues may all provide information about the patient's health.

GENERAL SURVEY

Initial observations include collecting information about the patient's physical and psychological presence, and signs and symptoms of distress.

Physical Presence

Observe the patient's:

1. Stated age versus apparent age
2. General appearance
3. Body fat
4. Stature
5. Motor activity
6. Body and breath odours

Stated Age versus Apparent Age

N The patient's stated chronological age should be congruent with the apparent age.

A It is significant for a patient to appear older or younger than the chronological age.

P Endocrine deficiencies of growth hormone associated with dwarfism can manifest in a younger-than-chronological-age appearance in younger life and premature aging later in life.

P Genetic syndromes (e.g., Turner's) manifest in an "old-person" facial appearance.

| E | Examination | N | Normal Findings | A | Abnormal Findings | P | Pathophysiology |

P   Chronic disease, severe illness, and prolonged sun exposure that causes facial wrinkling can lead to a patient looking older than the chronological age.

General Appearance

E   Observe body symmetry, any obvious anomaly, and the patient's apparent level of wellness.

N   The patient should exhibit body symmetry, no obvious deformity, and a well appearance.

A   Asymmetry is seen when a paired body part does not look the same on the contralateral side.

P   The unilateral facial drooping of Bell's palsy, a limb appearing at an abnormal angle, and unilateral paralysis are examples of body asymmetry.

A   A missing limb, cleft lip, and burned facial skin are examples of obvious anomalies.

P   The pathophysiology of each of these examples is varied and needs to be investigated further via history and physical assessments.

A   The patient who appears ill is abnormal.

P   A patient who appears ill usually is ill and needs to be carefully assessed via the history and physical examination.

Body Fat

N   Body fat should be evenly distributed. Body fat composition is difficult to estimate accurately without the use of immersion tanks or calipers. Research has indicated that body fat content, rather than actual body weight, is most closely linked to pathology (e.g., a person can be within normal limits on height and weight charts but have a high proportion of body fat to lean body mass.)

A   Obesity occurs when there are large amounts of body fat. It poses health risks to the patient that warrants a comprehensive nutritional assessment (see Chapter 7).

P   Excess caloric intake and decreased energy expenditure are the most common causes of obesity.

P   Some disease processes, such as hypothyroidism, which slows the basic metabolic rate, may result in obesity.

A   Cushing's syndrome manifests in a rounded moonlike face, truncal obesity, fat pads on the neck, and relatively thin limbs.

P   Excessive production of cortisol resulting from an anterior pituitary tumour or large doses of prolonged steroid therapy produces Cushing's syndrome.

P   A thin or frail appearance occurs when there are limited body fat stores. Severely limited fat stores can be a life-threatening condition.

P   Energy expenditures that exceed caloric intake will result in decreased fat stores. This may be caused by several conditions, including:

   • Anorexia nervosa, which results in inadequate intake of calories from food and overexpenditure of energy by means of exercise.
   • Hyperkinetic states in which the body's metabolic needs are greater than the ability to ingest calories.
   • Many chronic disease processes may be due to hyperkinetic states or a result of malabsorption diseases.

Stature

N   Limbs and trunk should appear proportional to body height; posture should be erect.

A   A slumped or humpbacked appearance is abnormal.

P Osteoporosis, especially in postmenopausal women, may cause a slumped or humpbacked appearance.

P Patients experiencing depression may also present with a slumped posture.

A Long limbs relative to trunk length are abnormal.

P Marfan's syndrome, an inherited disease, can result in the development of long limbs, a tall, thin appearance, and poorly developed muscles due to a defect in the elastic fibres of connective tissues.

Motor Activity

N Gait as well as other body movements should be smooth and effortless. All body parts should have controlled, purposeful movement.

A An unsteady gait or movements that are slow, absent, or require great effort are abnormal. Tremors or movements that seem uncontrollable by the patient are also abnormal.

P Arthritis can result in slow and difficult movement because joint movement is painful. See Chapter 18 for additional information.

P Neurological disturbances can result in tics, paralysis, or ataxia, and can cause difficulty with the smoothness of movement. See Chapter 19 for additional information.

Body and Breath Odours

N Normally, there is no apparent odour from patients. It is normal for some people to have bad breath related to the types of foods ingested or due to individual digestive processes.

A Severe body or breath odour is abnormal.

P Poor hygiene can cause body odours due to perspiration and bacteria left on the skin.

P An alcohol smell on the breath can result from alcohol ingestion or from ketoacidosis in a diabetic patient.

P Bad breath can result from poor oral hygiene, allergic rhinitis, or from infections such as tonsillitis, sinusitis, or pneumonia.

P Liver disease can give rise to hepatic fetor as a result of volatile aromatic substances.

P Severe vaginal infections can result in an offensive body odour.

Psychological Presence

Observe the patient's:

E 1. Dress, grooming, and personal hygiene
2. Mood and manner
3. Speech
4. Facial expressions

Dress, Grooming, and Personal Hygiene

N Generally, patients should appear clean and neatly dressed. Clothing choice should be appropriate for the weather. Norms and standards for dress and cleanliness may vary among cultures, age groups, and fashion trends.

A A disheveled, unkempt appearance or clothing that is inappropriate for the weather (such as a wool coat in hot weather) is abnormal.

P Psychological or psychiatric disorders such as depression (characterized in part by lethargy, mood swings, anhedonia [or lack of pleasure in activities],

| E | Examination | N | Normal Findings | A | Abnormal Findings | P | Pathophysiology |

fatigue, etc.), psychotic disorders (characterized by a distortion in thinking), and dementia (processes that alter perceptions of reality) may be reflected in inappropriate appearance (hair, makeup) or clothing selection.

P   Poor self-esteem or a homeless lifestyle may be reflected by general neglect of personal hygiene, grooming, and dress.

P   An unclean appearance may reflect neglect of the patient by the caretaker(s).

Mood and Manner

P   Generally, a patient should be cooperative and pleasant.

A   An uncooperative, hostile, or tearful adult, or an adult who seems unusually elated or who has a flat affect, needs further assessment.

P   Bipolar, paranoid, and psychotic disorders and depression produce a distortion in reality (unclear thinking and perceptions), resulting in abnormal behaviours. Dementia or confusion in the elderly can also result in disturbances of mood and manner (see Chapter 19).

Speech

N   The patient should respond to questions and commands easily. Speech should be clear and understandable. Pitch, rate, and volume should be appropriate to the situation.

A   Speech that is slow, slurred, mumbled, very loud, or rapid needs to be assessed further.

P   Hyperthyroidism can cause rapid speech because of hormones that are stimulatory in nature and result in hypermetabolism and hyperactivity.

P   Alcohol ingestion can cause slow, mumbled, or slurred speech because alcohol affects the central nervous system, causing transient brain dysfunction.

P   Loud speech may be associated with hearing difficulties because individuals with decreased ability to hear may not be able to hear themselves at normal conversational decibels.

P   Strokes (brain attacks) can result in aphasia if the speech centre is affected.

Facial Expressions

N   The patient should appear awake and alert. Facial expressions should be appropriate for what is happening in the environment and should change naturally.

A   Unchanging or flat facial expression, inappropriate facial expression, tremors, or tics are abnormal.

P   Apathy or depression may cause lack of facial expression due to feelings of lethargy or sadness.

P   Dementia may cause inappropriate facial expression because the patient's perception of reality is distorted.

P   Bell's palsy, a condition resulting in paralysis of the muscles in the face, may cause the mouth to droop and the affected side of the face to appear flaccid, with the inability to completely close the eye on the affected side.

Distress

Observe for:

E   1. Laboured breathing, wheezing or coughing, or laboured speech.

2. Painful facial expression, sweating, or physical protection of painful area.

3. Serious or life-threatening occurrences, such as seizure activity, active and severe bleeding, gaping wounds, and open fractures.

4. Signs of emotional distress or anxiety that may include but are not limited to tearfulness; nervous tics or laughter; avoidance of eye contact;

Life 360°

Assessing for Distress

Think of the last patient you cared for who was in distress. Recall the physical, physiological, and emotional signs and symptoms that the patient exhibited. How were the signs and symptoms different from a patient who has not experienced distress?

Nursing Tip

Assessing Vital Signs

Vital signs should be assessed at the beginning of each patient visit. A hospitalized patient should be assessed as often as prescribed or as often as the patient's condition requires.

◄NURSING CHECKLIST►

General Approach to Vital Sign Assessment

- Gather equipment.
- Explain the procedure to the patient.
- Select equipment according to the patient's age, size, and developmental level, and the site being assessed. Specific decision-making criteria are discussed under each section of the assessment.
- Warm the stethoscope headpiece before touching the patient with it.
- Assess vital signs and record findings.

cold, clammy hands; excessive nail biting; inability to pay attention; autonomic responses such as diaphoresis; or changes in breathing patterns.

N   Breathing should be effortless, without coughing or wheezing. Speech should not leave a patient breathless. Face should be relaxed and the patient should be willing to move all body parts freely. There should be no serious or life-threatening conditions. The patient should not perspire excessively or show signs of emotional distress such as nail biting or avoidance of eye contact.

P   Shortness of breath with laboured speech, wheezing, or coughing is abnormal.

P   Pulmonary disease may be present (see Chapter 15).

A   Pain as evidenced by facial grimacing, crying, moaning, sweating, or protection of a body part is an abnormal finding.

P   Tissue damage results in pain and needs further investigation into the character, location, intensity, and occurrence of the pain as well as factors associated with increased and decreased pain.

A   Excessive nail biting, avoidance of eye contact, nervous laughter, tearfulness, or lack of interest may be indicators of emotional distress or emotional pain.

P   Nervous habits are often displayed when a person is in an uncomfortable or new situation. A tearful or sad affect can result from emotional pain related to situations the patient may be experiencing or has experienced.

VITAL SIGNS

Vital sign measurements include respiration, pulse, temperature, and blood pressure, and level of pain.

Respiration

Respiration is the act of breathing, which supplies oxygen to the body and occurs in response to changes in the concentration of oxygen (O_2), carbon dioxide (CO_2), and hydrogen (H^+) in arterial blood. Inhalation, or inspiration, occurs when air is taken into the lungs. The diaphragm and the intercostal muscles contract and can be observed by the movement of the abdomen outward, and movement of the chest upward and outward, resulting in the lungs filling with air. Exhalation, or expiration, refers to the airflow out of the lungs. The external intercostal muscles and the diaphragm relax; the abdomen and the chest return to a resting position.

Nursing Tip

Respiration Assessment

Most frequently, respirations can be measured while measuring the radial or apical pulse. If respirations are shallow and the patient is supine, put the patient's arm across his or her chest, take a radial pulse, and feel the chest rise while you observe respirations.

| E | Examination | N | Normal Findings | A | Abnormal Findings | P | Pathophysiology |

TABLE 9-1	Respiratory Rate	
AGE	RESTING RESPIRATORY RATE (Breaths/Minute)	AVERAGE
Newborn	30–50	40
1 year	20–40	30
3 years	20–30	25
6 years	16–22	19
10 years	16–20	18
14 years	14–20	17
Adult	12–20	18

Respiratory rate is measured in breaths per minute. One respiratory cycle consists of one inhalation and one expiration.
To assess respiratory rate:

E 1. Stand in front of or to the side of the patient.
   2. Discreetly observe the patient's breathing (rise and fall of the chest)—the breathing pattern may be altered if the patient is being "watched."
   3. Count the number of respiratory cycles that occur in one minute.

N Table 9-1 lists the normal respiratory rates for different ages. Respiratory rates decrease with age and can vary with excitement, anxiety, fever, exercise, medications, and altitude.

A **Tachypnea** is a respiratory rate greater than 20 breaths per minute in an adult.

P Hypoxia and metabolic acidosis are common causes of tachypnea. The increased respiratory rate is a compensatory mechanism that provides the body with more oxygen and eliminates excess hydrogen ions when the body's metabolism is increased.

P Stress and anxiety cause the release of catecholamines, which can elevate the respiratory rate.

A **Bradypnea** is a respiratory rate less than 12 breaths per minute in an adult at rest.

P Head injury resulting in increased intracranial pressure in the respiratory centre of the brain can cause bradypnea.

P Medications or chemicals such as opioids, barbiturates, or alcohol depress the respiratory centre of the brain and can cause bradypnea.

P A lower metabolic rate that occurs during normal sleep can result in bradypnea.

A **Apnea** is the absence of spontaneous breathing for 10 or more seconds.

P Many causes of apnea are unknown.

P Traumatic injury to the brain stem may lead to apnea. Death ensues in the absence of respirations and pulse.

Pulse

As the heart contracts, blood is ejected from the left ventricle (stroke volume) into the aorta. A pressure wave is created as the blood is carried to the peripheral vasculature. This palpable pressure is the **pulse.** Pulse assessment can determine heart rate, rhythm, and the estimated volume of blood being pumped by the heart.

Rate

Pulse rate is the number of pulse beats counted in one minute. Several factors influence heart rate or pulse rate. These include:

- The sinoatrial (SA) node, which fires automatically at a rate of 60–100 times per minute and is the primary controller of pulse rate and heart rate.
- Parasympathetic or vagal stimulation of the autonomic nervous system, which can result in decreased heart rate.
- Sympathetic stimulation of the autonomic nervous system, which results in increased heart rate.
- Baroreceptor sensors, which can detect changes in BP and influence heart rate. Elevated BP can decrease heart rate, whereas decreased BP can increase heart rate.

Other factors influencing heart rate include:

- Age: Heart rate generally decreases with age.
- Gender: The average female's pulse is higher than a male's pulse.

TABLE 9-2

Scales for Measuring Pulse Volume

3-POINT SCALE

Scale	Description of Pulse
0	Absent
1+	Thready/weak
2+	Normal
3+	Bounding

4-POINT SCALE

Scale	Description of Pulse
0	Absent
1+	Thready/weak
2+	Normal
3+	Increased
4+	Bounding

- Activity: Heart rate increases with activity. Athletes will have a lower resting heart rate than the average person because of their increased cardiac strength and efficiency.
- Emotional status: Heart rate increases with anxiety.
- Pain: Heart rate increases.
- Environmental factors: Temperature and noise level can alter heart rate.
- Stimulants: Caffeinated beverages and tobacco elevate heart rate.
- Medications: Digoxin decreases heart rate; amphetamines increase heart rate.
- Disease state: Abnormal clinical conditions can affect the heart rate (e.g., increased heart rate in hyperthyroidism, fever).

Rhythm

Pulse rhythm refers to the pattern of pulses and the intervals between pulses. A regular pulse occurs at regular intervals with even intervals between each beat. Normal sinus rhythm is an example of a regular pulse.

An irregular pulse can be regularly irregular or irregularly irregular. A regular irregular rhythm is one in which an abnormal conduction occurs in the heart, but at regular intervals. Ventricular bigeminy is an example of a regularly irregular rhythm. In ventricular bigeminy, the irregular conduction, called a premature ventricular complex (PVC), occurs prior to the expected QRS complex. This PVC will occur at a regular rhythm (every other beat). An irregularly irregular rhythm has no predictable pattern, such as in atrial fibrillation.

Volume

Pulse volume (also called pulse strength or amplitude) reflects the stroke volume and the **peripheral vasculature resistance** (afterload). It can range from absent to bounding. Table 9-2 displays the two most commonly used scales: a 3-point and a 4-point scale. When reporting pulse volume, 2+/4+ indicates a normal pulse (2+) on a 4-point scale, whereas 2+/3+ indicates a normal pulse (2+) on a 3-point scale. Refer to the Nursing Tip, Documenting Pulses. If a pulse is not palpable, then attempt to ascertain its presence with a Doppler ultrasonic stethoscope. The letter "D" in a pulse chart or stick figure represents the pulse that was detected by using this stethoscope.

Site

Peripheral pulses can be palpated where the large arteries are close to the skin surface. There are nine common sites for assessment of pulse (Figure 9-1). When routine vital signs are assessed, the pulse is generally measured at one of two sites: radial or apical.

Measuring the apical pulse is indicated for patients with irregular pulses or known cardiac or pulmonary disease. The assessment of apical pulse can be accomplished through palpation but is most commonly accomplished through auscultation.

Radial Pulse

To palpate the radial pulse:

E 1. Place the pad of your first, second, or third finger on the site of the radial pulse, which is along the radial bone on the thumb side of the inner wrist.
   2. Press your finger gently against the artery with enough pressure so that you can feel the pulse. Pressing too hard will obliterate the pulse.

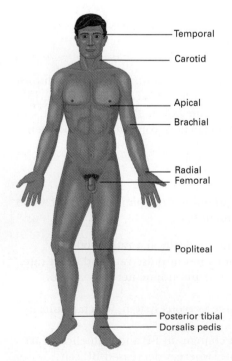

Temporal
Carotid
Apical
Brachial
Radial
Femoral
Popliteal
Posterior tibial
Dorsalis pedis

Figure 9-1 Peripheral Pulse Sites.

E	**Examination**	N	**Normal Findings**	A	**Abnormal Findings**	P	**Pathophysiology**

TABLE 9-3

Pulse Rate: Normal Range According to Age

AGE	RESTING PULSE RATE (Beats/Minute)	AVERAGE
Newborn	100–170	140
1 year	80–160	120
3 years	80–120	110
6 years	70–115	100
10 years	70–110	90
14 years	60–110	85–90
Adult	60–100	72

3. Count the pulse rate using the secondhand of a watch. If the pulse is regular, count for 30 seconds and multiply by 2 to obtain the pulse rate per minute. If the pulse is irregular, count for 60 seconds.
4. Identify the pulse rhythm (regular or irregular) as you palpate.
5. Identify the pulse volume as you palpate (use scales from Table 9-2).

N/A/P   Refer to the section on Rate.

Apical Pulse

To assess the apical pulse:

E   1. Place the diaphragm of the stethoscope on the apical pulse site.
   2. Count the pulse rate for 30 seconds if regular, 60 seconds if irregular.
   3. Identify the pulse rhythm and volume.
   4. Identify a **pulse deficit** (apical pulse rate greater than the radial pulse rate) by listening to the apical pulse and palpating the radial pulse simultaneously.

N/A/P   Refer to the section on Rate.

Rate

N   Normal pulse rates vary with age (Table 9-3). The heart rate normally increases during periods of exertion. Athletes commonly have resting heart rates below 60 because of the increased strength and efficiency of the cardiac muscle.

A   **Tachycardia** refers to a pulse rate faster than 100 beats per minute in an adult.

P   Psychophysiological stressors such as trauma, blood volume loss, anemia, infection, fear, fever, pain, hyperthyroidism, shock, and anxiety can increase pulse rate because of increased metabolic demands placed on the body.

P   Some tachycardia may not have clinical significance; however, in patients with myocardial disease, tachycardia can be a sign of decreased cardiac output, congestive heart failure, myocardial ischemia, or dysrhythmia.

A   **Bradycardia** refers to slow pulse rates. Pulse rates that fall below 60 in adults are considered to be bradycardic.

P   Medications such as cardiotonics (digoxin) and beta blockers decrease the heart rate.

P   Bradycardia usually occurs with excessive vagal stimulation or decreased sympathetic tone. Conditions that may cause bradycardia are eye surgery, increased intracranial pressure, myocardial infarction, hypothyroidism, and prolonged vomiting.

A   **Asystole** refers to the absence of a pulse. Palpate or auscultate for a pulse for 10–15 seconds to establish asystole.

P   Cardiac arrest resulting from biological or clinical death can result in asystole.

P   Pulseless electrical activity (electromechanical dissociation) can be caused by hypovolemia, pneumothorax, cardiac tamponade, or acidosis and results in the absence of a pulse despite the presence of electrical activity in the heart muscle.

A   A pulse deficit occurs when the apical pulse rate is greater than the radial pulse rate.

P   Dysrhythmias (such as atrial fibrillation, premature ventricular contractions, second or third degree heart block) and heart failure can cause pulse deficits because some heart contractions are too weak to produce a pulse pressure to the peripheral site. Severe vascular disease can also cause pulse deficits.

Rhythm

N   Normal pulse rhythm is regular with equal intervals between each beat.

A   **Dysrhythmias,** or **arrhythmias,** refer to pulse rhythms that are not regular. Rhythms may consist of irregular beats that are random or that present in a regular pattern.

Nursing Tip

Documenting Pulses

Document the amplitude of a patient's pulses by drawing a small stick figure and labelling the pulses accordingly (Figure 9-2A), or by recording the pulses in tabular format (Figure 9-2B).

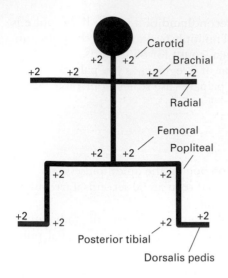

Scale = 3+

A. Stick Figure Peripheral Pulse Documentation

Figure 9-2 Methods to Document Peripheral Pulses.

	CAROTID	BRACHIAL	RADIAL	FEMORAL	POPLITEAL	PT	DP
R	2+	2+	2+	1+	1+	D	D
L	2+	2+	2+	2+	1+	1+	1+
Scale = 4+							
D = Doppler Ultrasonic Stethoscope							

B. Tabular Peripheral Pulse Documentation.

P Cardiac dysrhythmias that are atrial and ventricular in origin cause abnormal rhythms, such as atrial flutter and ventricular fibrillation.

Volume

N The pulse volume is normally the same with each beat. A normal pulse volume can be felt with a moderate amount of pressure of the fingers and obliterated with greater pressure.

A Small, weak pulses are referred to as weak or thready pulses, or pulses easily obliterated with light pressure.

P Decreased cardiac stroke volume caused by heart failure, hypovolemic shock, and cardiogenic shock can result in weak pulses.

P A low pulse amplitude occurs in states of increased peripheral vascular resistance, such as in aortic stenosis and constrictive pericarditis.

P Weak pulses occur in conditions when ventricular filling time is decreased, such as in dysrhythmias.

A Bounding pulses are full, forceful pulses that are difficult to obliterate with pressure.

P Hyperkinetic states such as exercise, fever, anemia, anxiety, and hyperthyroidism can cause bounding pulses.

P Early stages of septic shock are characterized by bounding pulses because of decreased peripheral vascular resistance.

Temperature

Scales, variables, routes, and measurement methods for assessing temperature are outlined.

Temperature Scales

The Celsius scale is the official Canadian scale for measuring **temperature,** but many patients, especially the elderly, will report temperature in Fahrenheit degrees. Medical facilities use the Celsius scale. Figure 9-3 summarizes the temperature conversion formula.

Variables Affecting Body Temperature

Core body temperature is established by the temperature of blood perfusing the area of the hypothalamus (the body's temperature control centre), which triggers the body's physiological response to temperature. An ideal thermometer would accurately measure central brain stem temperature at the hypothalamus. Invasive procedures that provide temperatures of the arterial blood, esophagus, or bladder are reliable indicators of core temperature, but are impractical. More practical methods for measurement of body temperature are

Celsius		Fahrenheit
42		107.6
41		105.8
40		104.0
39		102.2
38		100.4
37		98.6
36		96.8
35		95.0
34		93.2

To convert:
(9/5 x temperature in Celsius) + 32 = temperature in Fahrenheit

5/9 x (temperature in Fahrenheit – 32) = temperature in Celsius

Figure 9-3 Correlation between Celsius and Fahrenheit Scales.

E	Examination	N	Normal Findings	A	Abnormal Findings	P	Pathophysiology

less reliable and can result in variations in body temperature readings. In addition, there are physiological variables that affect body temperature:

- **Circadian rhythm** patterns: Normal body temperature (as well as pulse and BP) fluctuates with a patient's activity level and the time of day. Core body temperature is lower during sleep (lowest in the early morning just before awakening) than during waking activities (highest in the afternoon or early evening). A 0.5°C to 1.0°C fluctuation in body temperature throughout the day is considered within the normal range.
- Hormones: In women, increased production of progesterone at the time of ovulation raises the basal body temperature about 0.35°C.
- Age: Infants and young children are affected by the environmental temperature to a much greater extent than adults because their thermoregulation mechanisms are not fully developed. The elderly are more sensitive to extremes of environmental temperature due to a decrease in thermoregulatory controls.
- Exercise: Body temperature rises due to increased metabolic activity.
- Stress: Stimulation of the sympathetic nervous system increases the production of epinephrine, resulting in increased metabolic activity and higher body temperature.
- Environmental extremes of hot or cold.

Measurement Routes

There are four basic routes by which temperature can be measured: oral, rectal, axillary, and tympanic, each of which has advantages and disadvantages (Table 9-4).

Measurement

Oral Method

E
1. Place the thermometer at the base of the tongue and to the right or left of the frenulum, and instruct the patient to close the lips around the thermometer and to avoid biting the thermometer (Figure 9-4A). Ensure that 15 minutes have passed if the patient has consumed a hot or cold beverage or food.
2. Leave the thermometer in the mouth for the time recommended by your agency or institution (usually 3–10 minutes).
3. Read the thermometer and record the temperature.

Rectal Method

E
1. Position patient with the buttocks exposed. Adults may be more comfortable lying on the side (with the knees slightly flexed), facing away from you, or prone.
2. Put on clean gloves.
3. Lubricate the tip of the thermometer with a water-soluble lubricant.
4. Ask the patient to take a deep breath; insert the thermometer into the anus 1.25 to 3.50 cm, depending on the patient's age.
5. Do not force the insertion of the thermometer or insert into feces.
6. Hold the thermometer in place for 3–5 minutes or for the time recommended by your institution.

Axillary Method

E
1. Place the thermometer into the middle of the axilla and fold the patient's arm across the chest to keep the thermometer in place.
2. Leave the thermometer in place 5–10 minutes, depending on your institution's protocol.

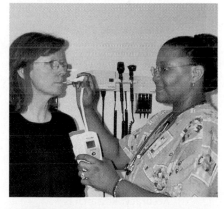

A. Oral Temperature

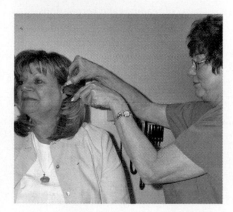

B. Tympanic Temperature

Figure 9-4 Measuring a Patient's Temperature.

TABLE 9-4   **Advantages and Disadvantages of Four Routes for Body Temperature Measurement**

ROUTE	NORMAL RANGE	ADVANTAGES	DISADVANTAGES
Oral Average 37.0°C (slightly lower in the morning; slightly higher in late afternoon)	36.0°–38.0°C	Convenient; accessible	**Safety:** Glass thermometers are not recommended by the Canadian Paediatric Society. **Physical abilities:** Patients need to be able to breathe through the nose and be without oral pathology or recent oral surgery; route not applicable for comatose or confused patients. **Accuracy:** Oxygen therapy by mask, as well as ingestion of hot or cold drinks immediately before oral temperature measurement, affects accuracy of the reading.
Rectal Average 0.4°C higher than oral	36.7°–38.0°C	Considered most accurate	**Safety:** Contraindicated following rectal surgery. Risk of rectal perforation in children less than 2 years of age. Risk of stimulating Valsalva maneuver in cardiac patients. Possible source of infection in patients with mucositis or who are neutropenic. **Physical aspects:** Invasive and uncomfortable.
Axillary Average 0.6°C lower than oral	35.4°–37.4°C	Safe; noninvasive	**Accuracy:** Thermometer must be left in place for at least 5 minutes to obtain accurate measurement.
Tympanic Calibrated to oral or rectal scales	See oral or rectal	Convenient; fast; safe; noninvasive; does not require contact with any mucous membrane	**Accuracy:** Research is inconclusive as to accuracy of readings and correlations with other body temperature measurements. Technique affects reading. Tympanic membrane is thought to reflect the core body temperature.

Electronic Thermometer

E   1. Remove electronic thermometer from the charging unit.
    2. Attach a disposable cover to the probe.
    3. Using a method described (oral, rectal, or axillary), measure the temperature.

4. Listen for the sound or look for the symbol that indicates maximum body temperature has been reached.
5. Observe and record the reading.
6. Remove and discard the probe cover.
7. Return the electronic thermometer to the charging unit.

Tympanic Thermometer

E 1. Attach the probe cover to the nose of the thermometer.
2. Gently place the probe of the thermometer over the entrance to the ear canal. If the patient is under 3 years old, pull the pinna down, aiming the probe toward the opposite eye. If the patient is over 3 years old, grasp the pinna and pull gently up and back, aiming the probe toward the opposite ear (see Figure 9-4B). Make sure there is a tight seal.
3. Press the start button on the thermometer handle.
4. Wait for the beep, remove the probe from the ear, and read and record the temperature.
5. Discard the probe cover.
6. Return the thermometer to the charger unit.

N Normal body temperatures are described in Table 9-4.

A **Hyperthermia,** pyrexia, or fever are conditions in which body temperatures exceed 38.5°C. Clinical signs of hyperthermia include increased respiratory rate and pulse, shivering, pallor, and thirst. There can be many causes of hyperthermia (including infection), which results from an increased basal metabolic rate.

A **Hypothermia** occurs when the body temperature is below 34°C.

P Clinical signs of hypothermia include decreased body temperature and initial shivering that ceases as drowsiness and coma ensue. Hypotension, decreased urinary output, lack of muscle coordination, and disorientation also occur as hypothermia progresses.

A Hypothermia can be caused by prolonged exposure to cold, such as immersion in cold water or administration of large volumes of unwarmed blood products.

P Hypothermia can be induced to decrease the tissues' need for oxygen, such as during cardiac surgery.

Blood Pressure

Blood pressure (BP) measures (in millimeters of mercury [mm Hg]) the force exerted by the flow of blood pumped into the large arteries. Arterial BP is determined by blood flow and the resistance to blood flow as indicated in the following formula:

$$MAP = CO \times TPR$$

mean arterial pressure (MAP) = cardiac output (CO) × total peripheral resistance (TPR)

Changes in BP can be used to monitor changes in cardiac output. Ineffective pumping, decreased circulating volume, as well as changes in the characteristics of the blood vessels can affect BP. There is a diurnal variation in BP as characterized by a high point in the early evening and a low point during the early deep stage of sleep.

It is important to assess BP at every opportunity, in particular as a means of screening for hypertension–known as the "silent killer"–which, even if severe, has

E	Examination	N	Normal Findings	A	Abnormal Findings	P	Pathophysiology

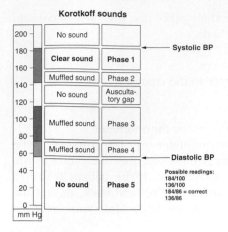

Korotkoff sounds

200	No sound	
180	Clear sound	Phase 1	← Systolic BP
160	Muffled sound	Phase 2
140	No sound	Ausculta-tory gap
120		
100	Muffled sound	Phase 3
80		
60	Muffled sound	Phase 4	← Diastolic BP
40	No sound	Phase 5
20		
0		

mm Hg

Possible readings:
184/100
136/100
184/86 = correct
136/86

Figure 9-5 Korotkoff Sounds.
Source: Reprinted from www.hypertension.ca with permission of the Canadian Hypertension Education Program.

no symptoms. The Heart and Stroke Foundation and the Canadian Hypertension Education Program (CHEP) indicate that the health of millions of Canadians is being placed at risk because of avoidable delays in diagnosis and treatment of hypertension.[3]

Korotkoff Sounds

Korotkoff sounds are generated when blood flow through the artery is altered by inflating the BP cuff that is wrapped around the extremity. Korotkoff sounds may be heard by listening over a pulse site that is distal to the BP cuff. As the air is released from the bladder of the cuff, the pressure on the artery changes from that which completely occludes blood flow to that which allows free flow. As the pressure against the artery wall decreases, five distinct sounds occur:

Phase I: The first audible sound heard as the cuff pressure is released. Sounds like clear tapping and correlates to systolic pressure (the force needed to pump the blood out of the heart).

Phase II: Sounds like swishing or a murmur. Created as the blood flows through blood vessels narrowed by the inflation of the BP cuff.

Phase III: Sounds like clear intense tapping. Created as blood flows through the artery but cuff pressure is still great enough to occlude flow during diastole.

Phase IV: Sounds are muffled and are heard when cuff pressure is low enough to allow some blood flow during diastole. The change from the tap of Phase III to the muffled sound of Phase IV is referred to as the first diastolic reading.

Phase V: No sounds are heard. Occurs when cuff pressure is released enough to allow normal blood flow. This is referred to as the second diastolic reading.

The pictogram in Figure 9-5 helps to visualize the relationship between the Korotkoff sounds and the phases they correspond to.

Measuring Blood Pressure

Systolic pressure represents the pressure exerted on the arterial wall during **systole,** when the ventricles are contracting. Diastolic pressure represents the pressure in the arteries when the ventricles are relaxed and filling. BP is recorded as a fraction with the top number representing the systole and the bottom number(s) representing the **diastole.** If first and second diastolic sounds are recorded, the first diastolic sound is written over the second. For example, 120/90/80 indicates that 120 mm Hg is the systolic pressure, 90 mm Hg is the first diastolic sound, and 80 mm Hg is the second diastolic sound. **Pulse pressure** is the difference between the diastolic and systolic blood pressures.

Measurement Sites

There are several potential sites for BP measurement. The preferred site is the brachial artery, which runs across the antecubital fossa. The posterior thigh, where the popliteal artery runs behind the knee joint, can also be used. A site should not be used if there is pain or injury around or near the site; for instance, a postmastectomy patient should have BP assessed on the unaffected side. Surgical incisions, intravenous, central venous, or arterial lines, or areas with poor perfusion should be avoided. Patients with arteriovenous (AV) fistulas or AV shunts should not have their BP measured in those extremities.

For the initial readings, it is recommended to take the BP in both arms (and legs if these are being used) with subsequent measures in the arm (or leg) with the highest reading.

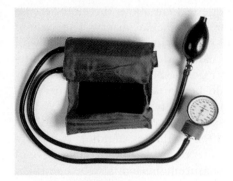

A. Aneroid Sphygmomanometer

B. Mercury Sphygmomanometer. *Courtesy of Omron Marshall Products, Inc.*

Figure 9-6 Sphygmomanometers.

Figure 9-7 Logo Endorsed by the Canadian Coalition and Control of Hypertension. *Reprinted from www.hypertension.ca with permission of the Canadian Hypertension Education Program.*

Equipment

BP is measured indirectly with a stethoscope or Doppler and a **sphygmomanometer,** which consists of the BP cuff, connecting tubes and air pump, and manometer. The size of the BP cuff bladder should be 80% of the circumference of the limb being assessed.[4] The cuff should completely encircle the limb.

A manometer is attached to the cuff via a second tube. There are two types of manometers: aneroid and mercury. The **aneroid manometer** is a calibrated dial with a needle that points to numbers representing the air pressure within the cuff. Aneroid devices should only be used if there is an established calibration check every 6–12 months.[5] The **mercury manometer** uses a calibrated column of mercury to provide the BP readings. An eye-level view of the meniscus of mercury is important in obtaining accurate readings. Figure 9-6 displays the two types of sphygmomanometers.

Electronic oscillometric devices are also available to measure BP. The CHEP recommends the use of devices that have met the standards of the Association for the Advancement of Medical Instrumentation (AAMI) and/or the British Hypertension Society (BHS), or the International Protocol (IP). For self blood pressure measurement devices, a logo (see Figure 9-7) on the packaging ensures that the device and model meet the international standards for accurate BP measurement.[6]

A Doppler ultrasonic stethoscope can also be used to obtain BP, especially when the BP sounds are difficult to hear, such as with infants or very obese patients.

E   1. Ensure that the patient has not had any caffeine in the preceding hour, nor nicotine products in the 15–30 minutes prior to testing. The patient should not be experiencing any acute anxiety, stress, or pain. Bladder and bowel should be comfortable.

2. Measurements should be taken with a sphygmomanometer known to be accurate. A recently calibrated aneroid or a validated and recently calibrated electronic device can be used. Aneroid devices or mercury columns need to be clearly visible at eye level.

3. Choose a cuff with an appropriate bladder width matched to the size of the arm (Figure 9-8). For measurements taken by auscultation, bladder width should be close to 40% of arm circumference and bladder length should cover 80%–100% of arm circumference. When using an automated device, select the cuff size as recommended by its manufacturer.

Cuff size

Arm circumference (cm)	Size of Cuff (cm)
From 18 to 26	9 x 18 (child)
From 26 to 33	12 x 23 (standard adult model)
From 33 to 41	15 x 33 (large, obese)
More than 41	18 x 36 (extra large, obese)

Figure 9-8 Cuff Size.
Source: *Reprinted from www.hypertension.ca with permission of the Canadian Hypertension Education Program.*

E	**Examination**	N	**Normal Findings**	A	**Abnormal Findings**	P	**Pathophysiology**

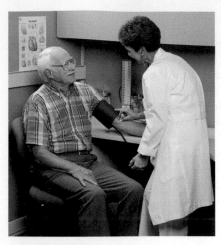

Figure 9-9 Position During Blood Pressure Measurement. © *Royalty-Free/Corbis*

4. Place the cuff so that the lower edge is 3 cm above the elbow crease and the bladder is centered over the brachial artery. The patient should be resting comfortably for 5 minutes in the seated position with back support. The arm should be bare and supported with the antecubital fossa at heart level, as a lower position will result in erroneously higher SBP and DBP. There should be no talking and patients' legs should not be crossed (Figure 9-9). At least two measurements should be taken in the same arm with the patient in the same position. Blood pressure also should be assessed after 2 minutes standing (with arm supported) and at times when patients report symptoms suggestive of postural hypotension. Supine BP measurements may also be helpful in the assessment of elderly and diabetic patients.

5. Increase the pressure rapidly to 30 mm Hg above the level at which the radial pulse is extinguished (to exclude the possibility of a systolic auscultatory gap).

6. Place the bell or diaphragm of the stethoscope gently and steadily over the brachial artery.

7. Open the control valve so that the rate of deflation of the cuff is approximately 2 mm Hg per heart beat. A cuff deflation rate of 2 mm Hg per beat is necessary for accurate systolic and diastolic estimation.

8. Read the systolic level—the first appearance of a clear tapping sound (phase I Korotkoff)—and the diastolic level (the point at which the sounds disappear (phase V Korotkoff). Continue to auscultate at least 10 mm Hg below phase V to exclude a diastolic auscultatory gap. Record the blood pressure to the closest 2 mm Hg on the manometer (or 1 mm Hg on electronic devices) as well as the arm used and whether the patient was supine, sitting or standing. Avoid digit preference by not rounding up or down. Record the heart rate. The seated blood pressure is used to determine and monitor treatment decisions. The standing blood pressure is used to examine for postural hypotension, which if present, may modify the treatment.

9. If Korotkoff sounds persist as the level approaches 0 mm Hg, then the point of muffling of the sound is used (phase IV) to indicate the diastolic pressure.

10. In the case of arrhythmia, additional readings may be required to estimate the average systolic and diastolic pressure. Isolated extra beats should be ignored. Note the rhythm and pulse rate.

11. Leaving the cuff partially inflated for too long will fill the venous system and make the sounds difficult to hear. To avoid venous congestion, it is recommended that at least 1 min should elapse between readings.

Nursing Alert

Palpating the Blood Pressure

The palpation method is used if the nurse is unable to hear a patient's BP and there is no electronic monitor or amplification device available. Obtain the BP as described in steps 1–6 using the brachial artery. When releasing air from the cuff, note when the brachial artery is palpable, which correlates with the systolic pressure. Document the BP as a number over palpated (e.g., 115/P).

Nursing Tip

Home Blood Pressure Monitoring Devices

Many patients monitor their BP at home to document their body's response to antihypertensive medications. Brachial artery–based monitors are the most accurate of home monitoring devices. The CHEP recommends that only devices that have met the standards of the AAMI, or the BHS, or the IP should be used. Patients should be instructed to bring their home device to their appointment so that a health care professional can observe the patient take his or her BP and assess the process for accuracy. Comparing the BP reading on the home device with that obtained in the office is useful to determine if there are any major discrepancies; generally, the measurements should correlate within 5 mm Hg of each other.

Nursing Alert

Automatic Blood Pressure Cuffs

Patients receiving drugs such as heparin, Aspirin, or thrombolytic therapy are more susceptible to bleeding complications (Figure 9-10). When an automatic BP cuff is used, the following precautions will prevent any bleeding complications that may occur in the arm that is being used for noninvasive BP monitoring:

1. Adjust the maximal inflation pressure on the automatic BP machine to the patient's last systolic BP. Otherwise, the BP cuff could inflate as high as to a systolic BP of 200 mm Hg.
2. Once the patient's BP is stable, increase the intervals between measurements. Otherwise, the BP cuff could inflate as often as every minute. Switching the mode to manual from automatic will avoid unnecessary inflations of the BP cuff.
3. Place the BP cuff on the arm opposite any intravenous infusions. If this is not possible, then try the thigh as a site for BP measurement.
4. Whenever permissible, rotate the cuff site and remove it at least every shift to assess the patient's skin.

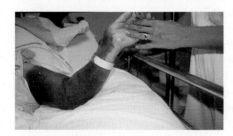

Figure 9-10 Proper placement and monitoring of an automatic blood pressure cuff will reduce the risk of injury or trauma to the patient. This patient had an automatic blood pressure cuff placed on the left arm while also receiving a heparin infusion in that arm.

Nursing Tip

Documenting Blood Pressure

The position of the patient during the BP measurement should be recorded. Use the following symbols to depict the patient's position:

○— supine   ○ sitting   ○ standing

Also, record where the BP was taken, using the following abbreviations:

RA = right arm   LA = left arm
RL = right leg   LL = left leg

Examples of BP readings are:

○— 160/122 LL (supine)

○ 98/52 RA sitting)

○ 118/85 LA (standing)

12. Blood pressure should be taken at least once in both arms and if an arm has a consistently higher pressure, that arm should be clearly noted and subsequently used for blood pressure measurement and interpretation.[7]

N Normal BP varies with age; it generally increases as a person ages (see Table 9-5). Normally, baroreceptors (located in the walls of most of the

TABLE 9-5	Blood Pressure: Normal Range According to Age and Gender*	
AGE (FEMALE)	**SYSTOLIC (mm Hg)**	**DIASTOLIC (mm Hg)**
1	97–103	52–56
5	103–109	66–70
10	112–118	73–76
15	120–127	78–81
≥18	<120	<80
AGE (MALE)	**SYSTOLIC (mm Hg)**	**DIASTOLIC (mm Hg)**
1	94–103	49–54
5	104–112	65–70
10	111–119	73–78
15	122–131	76–81
≥18	<120	<80

*The National Heart, Lung, and Blood Institute of the National Institutes of Health developed pediatric BP guidelines based on gender, age, and height percentiles. The measurements listed for pediatric patients are consolidated for ease in reporting. Normal BP is defined as the systolic (SBP) and diastolic (DBP) blood pressures that are below the 90th percentile for age and gender. High-normal BP is defined as the SBP or DBP being at the 90th percentile and above, but not including, the 95th percentile. Hypertension is defined as a SBP or DBP greater than or equal to the 95th percentile on three different occasions.

| E | Examination | N | Normal Findings | A | Abnormal Findings | P | Pathophysiology |

Nursing Alert

Risk Factors for Hypertension[8]

- Men >55 years of age
- Women >65 years of age
- Smoking
- Obesity
- Total cholesterol >6.5 mmol/L or LDL-C >4.0 mmol/L
- Family history of premature vascular disease
- Physical inactivity

Epidemiology

- Over one-fifth of Canadians have hypertension.[9]
- Hypertension is the one of the most common reasons for medical visits with over 4 million prescriptions for antihypertensive agents written every month in Canada.[10]
- 42% of people with hypertension either receive no treatment or are uncontrolled, despite treatment.[11]

Life 360°

Interpretation of Vital Signs

The early morning vital signs of a 23-year-old male patient who is scheduled for an inguinal hernia repair procedure are:

Temperature: 36.9°C (tympanic)
Pulse: 56
Respirations: 6
Blood Pressure: 69/55 LA,

What is your interpretation of these vital signs? Describe why some of the vital signs may be inaccurate and what errors may have led to such values.

TABLE 9-6	Errors in Blood Pressure Measurement
IF READING SHOWS	SUSPECT
Inaccurately high BP	BP cuff is too short or too narrow (e.g., using a regular BP cuff on an obese arm), or the brachial artery may be positioned below the heart. The patient may also be stressed, be in an emotional state, or have just completed physical activity.
High DBP	Unrecognized **auscultatory gap** (a silent interval between systolic and diastolic pressures that may occur in hypertensive patients or because the BP cuff deflated too rapidly); immediate reinflation of the cuff for multiple BP readings (resultant venous congestion makes the Korotkoff sounds less audible); if the patient supports his or her own arm, then sustained muscular contraction can raise the DBP by 10%.
Inaccurately low BP	BP cuff is too long or too wide; the brachial BP artery is above the heart.
Low SBP	Unrecognized auscultatory gap (a rapid deflation of the cuff pressure or immediate reinflation of the cuff for multiple readings can result in venous congestion, thus making the Korotkoff sounds less audible and the pressure appear lower).

great arteries that sense hypotension and initiate reflex vasoconstriction and tachycardia to bring the BP back to normal) help a patient to maintain normal BP when changing from a supine to a sitting or a standing position. Processes increasing cardiac output, such as exercise, will usually increase BP. Pulse pressure is normally 30 to 40 mm Hg. Table 9-6 lists errors in BP measurement.

A **Hypertension,** or high BP, is usually confirmed when an adult patient has sequential elevated BP readings. The CHEP recommends that the diagnosis of hypertension should be expedited with the goal of optimizing the diagnosis of hypertension. Compared to previous algorithms that took up to six office visits or six months to diagnose hypertension, it is now diagnosed in as few as 1–5 visits (see Table 9-7).

P The cause of hypertension in 90% of cases is unknown. It is thought that the mechanisms that maintain the therapeutic fluid volume in the body (e.g., the heart, kidneys, nervous system, renin-angiotensin-aldosterone system) may be abnormal. The other 10% of the population who have high BP have secondary hypertension. All of the following pathophysiologies of hypertension are secondary in nature.

P Arteriosclerosis reduces arterial compliance. Elastic and muscular tissues of arteries are replaced with fibrous tissue as part of the normal aging process, making the vessels less able to contract and relax in response to systolic and diastolic pressures. When the systolic pressure alone is elevated in the elderly, it is called isolated systolic hypertension.

| E | Examination | N | Normal Findings | A | Abnormal Findings | P | Pathophysiology |

TABLE 9-7 Canadian Recommendations for the Management of Hypertension

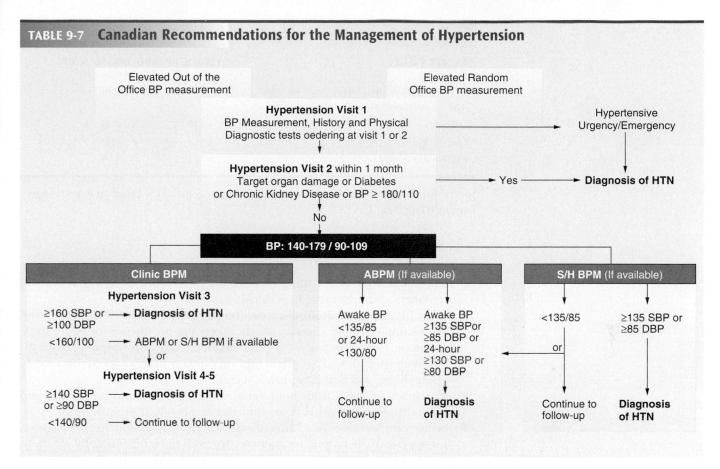

Source: Reprinted from www.hypertension.ca with permission of the Canadian Hypertension Education Program.

The CHEP offers health care practitioners three validated technologies to diagnose hypertension: office or clinic BP monitoring; self/home blood pressure measurement (S/H BMP) that involves BP measurement morning and evening for an initial seven-day period using approved monitoring devices (see Nursing Tip, Home Blood Pressure Monitoring Devices); ambulatory blood pressure monitoring (ABPM) by health professionals in the patients home (especially for those suspected of office-induced hypertension).

Hypertension is diagnosed in the following scenarios:

On **Visit 1** to a health care professional if a hypertensive urgency or emergency is present. Examples include: asymptomatic DBP ≥130 mm Hg, hypertensive encephalopathy, acute aortic dissection, acute left ventricular failure, acute myocardial ischemia

After Visit 2 to a health care professional if there is a sustained BP ≥180/110 mm Hg *or* sustained BP ≥140/90 mm Hg in the presence of diabetes, chronic kidney disease, or target organ damage.

After **3 Visits to a health care professional if there is s**ustained BP between 160–179 mm Hg or DBP between 100–109 mm Hg (and not already diagnosed using the above criteria).

After **5 Visits** to a health care professional if there is sustained SBP ≥140 mm Hg or DBP ≥90 mm Hg.

When S/H BPM yields **duplicate home readings** in the morning and evening for **one week** (excluding day 1) ≥135/85 mm Hg.

When **ambulatory blood pressure** monitoring (ABPM) yields **average daytime** BP ≥135/85 mm Hg or **24-hour average** BP ≥130/80 mm Hg.

See Table 9-8 for target values in treating hypertension.

P Processes decreasing the size of arterial lumen cause hypertension. Hypercholesterolemia results in deposits of plaque along the inner walls of the vessels, reducing the size of the lumen and increasing BP.

P Processes that increase the viscosity of the blood, such as sickle cell crisis, cause greater friction between molecules of the blood and, thus, higher BP.

TABLE 9-8	Target Values in the Treatment of Hypertension		
TARGET VALUES		**SYSTOLIC BP**	**AND DIASTOLIC BP**
Hypertension without target organ damage and no associated clinical condition		<140	<90
Diabetes		<130	<80
Chronic Kidney disease		<130	<80
Proteinuria >1 g/day		<125	<75

Source: Reprinted from www.hypertension.ca with permission of the Canadian Hypertension Education Program.

P Chronic steroid use, Cushing's syndrome, thyroid disease, and parathyroid dysfunction can all cause hypertension.

P High BP may result from diseases affecting other regulatory BP processes. For example, kidney disease, which affects the production of antidiuretic hormone (helps control body fluid balance), can cause hypertension. An adrenal gland tumour, or pheochromocytoma, can increase BP because of epinephrine and norepinephrine secretion.

P Overloads of fluids from poor renal function or indiscriminant IV fluid administration (particularly in children) can result in hypertension.

P Stress can increase BP. Stimulation of the sympathetic nervous system increases cardiac output and vasoconstriction, thus increasing BP.

P A patient's stress level can increase when in the presence of a health care provider. Patients who have elevated BP in a clinic or hospital environment only are said to have "white coat syndrome." When these patients have their BP taken in the community, it is frequently within an acceptable range.

A BP falling below normal range is considered to be **hypotension,** or low BP, which results in inadequate tissue perfusion and oxygenation. If the standing SBP is more than 30 mm Hg below the supine systolic pressure, it may indicate that the person has orthostatic hypotension (see Chapter 16). Slow response by baroreceptors when an individual transitions from a lying to a standing position can result in transitory orthostatic hypotension. When this occurs, the individual may feel dizzy and is at risk for falls.

P Processes drastically reducing circulatory blood volume, such as hypovolemic shock, cause hypotension.

P Medications such as nitroglycerin or antihypertensives lower BP.

P Anaphylactic shock, resulting from massive histamine release, and circulatory collapse cause severe hypotension.

A A difference of greater than 10–15 mm Hg between the BP in both arms is abnormal.

P This can be caused by coarctation of the aorta, aortic aneurysm, atherosclerotic obstruction, and subclavian steal syndrome. These conditions all result in an increased pressure proximal to the narrowing and a decreased pressure distal to the narrowing of the aorta or whatever is causing the obstruction.

E	Examination	N	Normal Findings	A	Abnormal Findings	P	Pathophysiology

TABLE 9-9 Lifestyle Recommendations for Hypertension

TOPIC	OBJECTIVE	RECOMMENDATION
Smoking	As a cardiovascular risk reduction strategy	Abstinence from smoking should be advised.
Weight excess	Attain/maintain a healthy BMI (18.5–24.9 kg/m^2) and waist circumference (<102 cm for men and <88 cm for women) in all normotensive and hypertensive individuals for prevention/ management of hypertension.	Encourage multidisciplinary approach to weight loss, including dietary education, increased physical activity and behavioural modification **BP may be reduced by 1.6/1.1 mmHg for every 1 kg of weight lost.**
Dietary	DASH diet and sodium reduction.	**DASH Diet:** Diet that emphasizes fresh fruits, vegetables and low-fat dairy products, and that is reduced in saturated fat and cholesterol. **Dietary sodium intake:** —Limited to 65-100 mmol/day in hypertensive patients —Target range for normotensive individuals at increased risk of developing hypertension and considered salt- sensitive[†]: less than 100 mmol/L per day. **In hypertensive patients, the DASH diet reduced BP by 11.4/5.5 mmHg.**
Physical activity	Should be prescribed to both hypertensive and normotensive individuals for prevention/ management of hypertension.	An accumulation of 30-60 minutes of dynamic exercise of moderate intensity (e.g.: walking, cycling, non-competitive swimming), on 4-7 days each week. Higher intensities of exercise are no more effective at reducing blood pressure.
Alcohol	Limited consumption.	Less than 2 drinks per day. Men: Less than 14 drinks per week. Women: Less than 9 drinks per week. **Limiting alcohol consumption can reduce blood pressure.**
Stress	Stress management.	Individualized cognitive behavior interventions are more likely to be effective when relaxation techniques are employed.

[†]Canadians of African descent, age over 45 years, and individuals with impaired renal function or diabetes.
Source: Reprinted from www.hypertension.ca with permission of the Canadian Hypertension Education Program.

A   A SBP that is greater in the arms than in the legs is abnormal.
P   This is caused by constriction or obstruction of the aorta, which can result from an increase in stroke volume ejection velocity, increased cardiac output, peripheral vasodilation, and decreased distensibility of the aorta or major arteries.
A   A decreased pulse pressure is abnormal.
P   A decreased pulse pressure can result from a decreased stroke volume (cardiac tamponade, shock, and tachycardia) or increased peripheral resistance

(aortic stenosis, coarctation of the aorta, mitral stenosis or mitral regurgitation, and cardiac tamponade).

A An increased pulse pressure is abnormal.

P An increased pulse pressure can result from increased stroke volume (aortic regurgitation) or increased peripheral vasodilatation (fever, anemia, heat, exercise, hyperthyroidism, and arteriovenous fistula).

PAIN

Pain is "an unpleasant sensory or emotional experience associated with actual or potential tissue damage, or described in terms of such damage."[12] It is a complex sensory experience that has received a lot of clinical attention in the past 35 years. Pain has become the focus of many clinical research projects as a single clinical phenomenon, not just a symptom of clinical pathology. Evidence about the prevalence and clinical significance of the pain experience has led to pain being classified as the 'fifth vital sign'.

Nociceptive Pain

Nociceptive pain arises from somatic or visceral stimulation. **Nociception,** or pain perception, is a multistep process that involves the nervous system as well as other body systems (Figure 9-11). A noxious stimulus (e.g., trauma, burn, chemical exposure, internal body inflammation, internal body growth of tissue) occurs that stimulates the **nociceptors** (receptive neurons of pain sensation that are located in the skin and various viscera). Transduction of the noxious stimulus travels to the spinal cord via the nociceptors, causing the conversion of one energy (travelling stimulus) from another (noxious stimulus). Cell damage from the noxious stimulus causes the release of certain chemicals or sensitizing nociceptors. Prostaglandins (PG), bradykinins (BK), serotonin (5 HT), substance P (SP), hydrogen (H^+), potassium (K^+), histamine (H), and leukotrienes are all sensitizing substances. SP is unique because it is only released when pain fibres are stimulated.

Activating the sensitizing substances leads to an action potential where the pain sensation is moved via afferent nerves to the spinal cord. Two types of nerve fibres participate in the action potential: A-delta fibres are myelinated neurons that transmit acute, sharp, shooting, and localized pain; C fibers are nonmyelinated neurons that transmit dull, throbbing, and poorly localized pain. These nerve fibers carry the pain impulse from the spinal cord via the spinothalamic tract to the brain stem and thalamus. The thalamus relays information to the cortex (which is capable of identifying past pain memories) and to the limbic system (where the emotional component of pain is formed). It is in these areas of the brain that pain is consciously perceived.

The last step of nociception is modulation, which inhibits nociceptor impulses. Neurons from the brain stem release neurotransmitters (e.g., norepinephrine [NE], gamma-aminobutyric acid [GABA], 5 HT, and endogenous opioids (e.g., enkephalins, dynorphins, b-endorphins) as the pain message descends from the brain stem to the spinal cord. Collectively, these substances block the transmission of pain and produce analgesia.

| **E** Examination | **N** Normal Findings | **A** Abnormal Findings | **P** Pathophysiology |

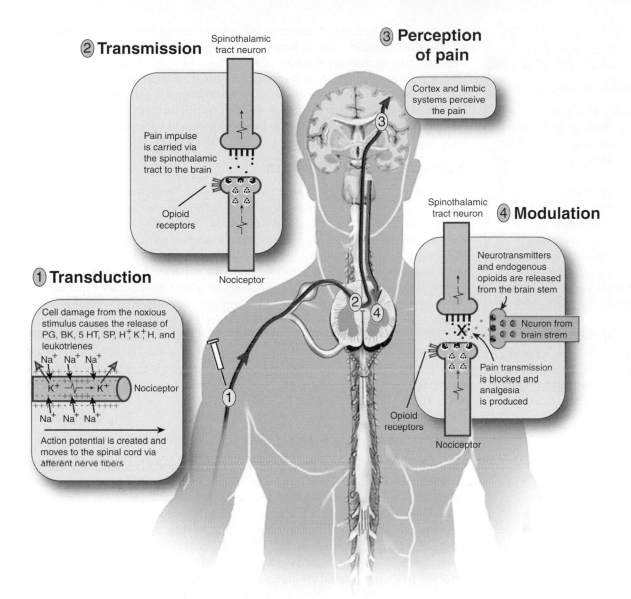

② **Transmission**

Spinothalamic tract neuron

Pain impulse is carried via the spinothalamic tract to the brain

Opioid receptors

Nociceptor

③ **Perception of pain**

Cortex and limbic systems perceive the pain

③

② ④

④ **Modulation**

Spinothalamic tract neuron

Neurotransmitters and endogenous opioids are released from the brain stem

Neuron from brain strem

Pain transmission is blocked and analgesia is produced

Opioid receptors

Nociceptor

① **Transduction**

Cell damage from the noxious stimulus causes the release of PG, BK, 5 HT, SP, H⁺, K⁺H, and leukotrlenes

Na^+ Na^+ Na^+

K^+ K^+

Nociceptor

Na^+ Na^+ Na^+

Action potential is created and moves to the spinal cord via afferent nerve fibers

Figure 9-11 The Nociception Process.

Neuropathic Pain

Neuropathic pain can result from lesions in the central nervous system (CNS) or peripheral nervous system (PNS). It is often characterized as a severe burning or tingling, such as that experienced with herpes zoster. Neuropathic pain may be difficult to treat clinically.

Types of Pain

Pain can be grouped by its origin as well as its duration. Cutaneous, somatic, visceral, and referred pain are the types grouped by origin. Cutaneous pain arises from the stimulation of cutaneous nerves and usually has a burning quality. Somatic pain originates from bone, tendons, ligaments, muscles, and nerves and is frequently caused by musculoskeletal injury. Visceral pain arises from the organs; diseased organs can change size, usually resulting in stretching of the organ, leading to pain. Acute appendicitis is an example of visceral pain. Referred pain is perceived in a location other than where the pathology is occurring. The location of the referred pain is in the dermatome of the spinal cord that is innervating the affected viscera and where the organ was located in its embryonic stage. An example of referred pain is the pain of pancreatitis felt on the left shoulder.

Acute, chronic malignant, and chronic nonmalignant pain are examples of pain grouped by their duration. Acute pain has a sudden onset, is of short duration, and is self-limiting. It ranges in intensity from mild to severe and usually has an identifiable cause, such as surgery or trauma. Chronic malignant pain is pain of more than six months' duration; for example, in a patient with cancer. This persistent pain can be due to a tumour, inflammation, blocked ducts, pressure on other body parts, and necrosis. Chronic nonmalignant pain also lasts more than six months and can occur with or without an identifiable cause. The pain can remain even after an initial injury is healed, such as in back pain and fibromyalgia.

Variables Affecting Pain

A patient's sex, age, previous experience with pain, and cultural expectations can affect an individual's response to pain. Studies have shown that females have a lower pain tolerance or threshold than males and report pain more frequently. Females tend to focus on the psychological aspects of pain, whereas males emphasize its physiological aspects.[15, 16] Typically, young children become sensitized to pain and may be greatly affected by the pain experience. As they reach adolescence, children may become more stoic about pain. Older adults, especially those who have chronic pain, may also not complain about their pain until it becomes debilitating. Failure to seek treatment for pain is frequently due to the perception that the pain means something is seriously wrong, or the patient may not have the resources to seek treatment. Older adults also have a lifetime of experiences with different types of pain, and that greatly influences how they choose to deal with new pain. Lastly, cultural norms can determine what the patient's pain experience will be. Refer to Chapter 5.

Effects of Pain on the Body

Pain affects everyone in different ways. Acute pain usually manifests itself differently from chronic pain, though there are some common elements. Physiological responses to pain include tachycardia, tachypnea, hypertension, diaphoresis, dilated pupils, and an altered immune response. Additional responses to pain include complaints of pain, crying, moaning, frowning, anger, fear, anxiety, depression, suicidal ideation, decreased appetite, sleep deprivation, altered concentration, pacing, and rubbing, protecting, or splinting the affected body part. Pain can affect every system in the human body, and unrelieved pain can take its toll on the health of the patient over time. Just as pain is a unique experience for the person in pain, so is the patient's response to pain.

Assessing Pain

Many patients present with a principle health issue or concern of pain. As with the experience of other symptoms, a thorough assessment includes asking questions about the following aspects of the pain experience:

- Location: Where is the pain located?
- Radiation: Does the pain move to another part of the body?
- Quality: How does the pain feel?
- Quantity: How severe is the pain?
- Associated manifestations: What other signs and symptoms are occurring with the pain?
- Aggravating factors: What makes the pain worse?
- Alleviating factors: What makes the pain better?
- Setting: Where were you (physically or emotionally or both) when the pain started?
- Timing: When did the pain start? How long does it last? How frequently does it occur?
- Meaning and impact: Does this pain have any special significance to you? How has it affected your life?

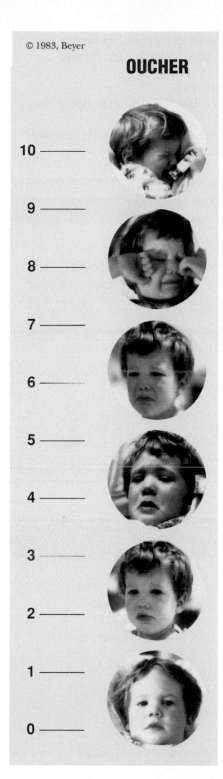

© 1983, Beyer

OUCHER

10 —

9 —

8 —

7 —

6 —

5 —

4 —

3 —

2 —

1 —

0 —

Figure 9-12 Oucher Pain Assessment Tool
Source: The Caucasian Version of the Oucher, developed and copyrighted by Judith E. Beyer, RN, PhD, 1983.

Nursing Tip

The PQRST Mnemonic Related to Pain Assessment

P – provoking (aggravating) factors and palliative measures (alleviating factors)
Q – quality of pain (how does the person describe the pain, e.g., burning, throbbing)
R – region (location) and radiation of pain
S – severity (quantity) and setting
T – timing

Pain intensity rating scales are available to assess the severity of a patient's pain experience. Examples of rating scales include the Oucher Pain Assessment Tool [17] (Figure 9-12), which is used with children 3–12 years old (Caucasian, Hispanic, and African American versions of this tool are available); the Wong-Baker FACES Pain Rating Scale[18] (Figure 9-13) which is recommended for children over the age of 3; and the Pain Intensity Scale[19] (Figure 9-14) which can be used with adults. Flow sheets can identify trends in the patient's pain e.g., is the pain being alleviated or is it worsening; are treatment methods being effective?

Other pain assessment tools include:

- FLACC[20] (Face, Legs, Activity, Cry, Consolability)—a behaviour pain assessment scale for use in nonverbal patients (young children) unable to provide reports of pain.
- Premature Infant Pain Profile (PIPP)[21]—measures behavioural, physiologic, and contextual indicators to assess acute pain in preterm and term neonates.

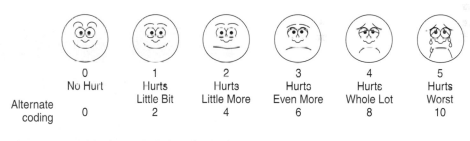

0	1	2	3	4	5
No Hurt	Hurts Little Bit	Hurts Little More	Hurts Even More	Hurts Whole Lot	Hurts Worst
Alternate coding 0	2	4	6	8	10

Figure 9-13 Wong-Baker FACES Pain Rating Scale.
Note. From Hockenberry, M., Wilson, D., & Winkelstein, M. (2005). *Wong's essentials of pediatric nursing* (7th ed.), St. Louis, MO: Mosby, Inc., p. 663. Reprinted with permission.

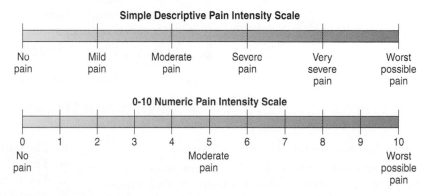

Simple Descriptive Pain Intensity Scale

No pain | Mild pain | Moderate pain | Severe pain | Very severe pain | Worst possible pain

0-10 Numeric Pain Intensity Scale

0 1 2 3 4 5 6 7 8 9 10
No pain | Moderate pain | Worst possible pain

Figure 9-14 Pain Intensity Scale.
Note. From Acute Pain Management Guideline Panel. (1992). Acute pain management: Operative or medical procedures and trauma. Clinical Practice Guideline (AHCPR Publication No. 92-0032), Rockville, MD: Agency for Health Care Policy and Research.

- Brief Pain Inventory (BPI)[22]—used for assessing pain and its impact on functioning in adults with cancer pain or pain from chronic disease. Translated versions of this tool are available at http://www.mdanderson.org/departments/PRG/
- Initial Pain Assessment Tool[23]—measures subjective pain experience, how pain is expressed, and the effects of pain.
- McGill Pain Questionnaire[24]—measures the subjective (sensory, affective, and evaluative) as well as quantitative pain experience.

Reflective Thinking

Using Clinical Judgment When Taking Vital Signs

Mr. Goldstein is a 75-year-old man hospitalized for pneumonia. He is wearing a 40% oxygen face mask. Mr. Goldstein has a history of confusion and combative behaviour, particularly at night. His IV had to be replaced last night because, in his confusion and agitation, he pulled it out. You are working the night shift and it is 2:00 a.m. Mr. Goldstein is sleeping comfortably. He has vital signs ordered every four hours. His signs were last taken at 10:00 p.m. and were as follows:

> Respirations: 14
> Pulse: 90
> Blood pressure: 132/88 (left arm)
> Temperature: 36.6°C (axilla)

- What are the major issues related to taking Mr Goldstein's vital signs right now?
- What are the possible actions you could take, and what are the potential consequences of each?

◄NURSING CHECKLIST►

General Survey, Vital Signs, and Pain

General Survey
- Physical presence
  - Stated age versus apparent age
  - General appearance
  - Body fat
  - Stature
  - Motor activity
  - Body and breath odours
- Psychological presence
  - Dress, grooming, and personal hygiene
  - Mood and manner
  - Speech
  - Facial expression
- Distress

Vital Signs
- Respiration
- Pulse
- Temperature
- Blood pressure

Pain

REVIEW QUESTIONS

Questions 1–4 refer to the following situation:

An unconscious 19-year-old male college student is brought to the Student Health Centre by his friends after drinking large quantities of alcohol. His vital signs are: T 36.4°C (tympanic); P 56; R 8; BP 98/62.

1. What conclusion do you make about this patient's respiratory status?

a. The patient is experiencing apnea.
b. The patient is experiencing bradypnea.
c. The patient is experiencing tachypnea.
d. The patient's respiratory status is normal.

The correct answer is (b).

2. What conclusion might you make about this patient's heart rate?
   a. Pain has altered the heart rate.
   b. He has most likely taken amphetamines in the past two hours.
   c. He is an active person who is in good physical condition.
   d. A male's heart rate is usually much higher than a female's heart rate.

   The correct answer is (c).

3. The patient's pulse volume is documented as 1+/3+. This means that the patient's pulse is:
   a. Absent
   b. Thready
   c. Normal
   d. Bounding

   The correct answer is (b).

4. What conclusion do you make about this patient's temperature?
   a. Tympanic temperatures should never be taken in an unconscious patient.
   b. An adult's temperature is greatly affected by the environment due to the large surface area of the head.
   c. Body temperature usually decreases with stimulation of the sympathetic nervous system.
   d. A patient's temperature can fluctuate with circadian rhythm patterns.

   The correct answer is (d).

5. Assessing a patient's psychological presence includes:
   a. Stated age versus apparent age, facial expressions
   b. Mood, manner, speech
   c. Dress, grooming, body and breath odours
   d. Stature, personal hygiene, speech

   The correct answer is (b).

6. The first audible sound heard as the blood pressure cuff is released is that of clear tapping. This best describes which phase of the Korotkoff sounds?
   a. Phase I
   b. Phase II
   c. Phase III
   d. Phase IV

   The correct answer is (a).

Questions 7 and 8 refer to the following situation:
Nat George is a 52-year-old man who presents for the evaluation of otalgia. His BP in his left arm while seated is 155/92. You note that the last time his BP was checked was two years ago and was 135/88. You recheck the BP in the right arm and obtain 168/98.

7. What might be the reason for the discrepancy in the BP readings?
   a. The patient's brachial artery was at the level of the heart.
   b. The patient rested for five minutes before the second BP reading.
   c. The cuff that was used for the first reading was too wide for the patient's arm.
   d. The patient refrained from having a cigarette before being seen.

   The correct answer is (c).

8. The nurse measures the BP of a patient on his third visit to a health clinic. The BP has been consistent at 150/90. According to CHEP:
   a. The patient should have been diagnosed with hypertension on his first visit.
   b. The patient is diagnosed with hypertension on this visit.
   c. The patient requires another follow-up visit for repeat measurement.
   d. The patient does not have hypertension.

   The correct answer is (c).

Questions 9 and 10 refer to the following situation:
Teri is a 30-year-old woman who got drunk in a bar last night. When she and her companions started to get rowdy, the bouncers grabbed Teri by her wrists and then put her in a headlock as they forcibly wrestled her to the ground. She presents today with numerous bruises and complaints of bodily pain.

9. Which type of pain is this patient most likely experiencing?
   a. Neuropathic pain
   b. Chronic pain
   c. Nociceptive pain
   d. Malignant pain

   The correct answer is (c).

10. This patient's pain experience occurred because the noxious stimulus caused a release of sensitizing substances. Which of the following is a sensitizing substance?
    a. Substance P
    b. Enkephalins
    c. GABA
    d. Norepinephrine

    The correct answer is (a).

Visit the Estes online companion resource at
www.healthassessment.nelson.com for additional content and study aids.

REFERENCES

[1]Schuh, S., Komar, L., Stephens, D, Chu, L., Read, S, & Allen, U. (2004). Comparison of the temporal artery and rectal thermometry in children in the emergency department. *Pediatric Emergency Care, 20*(11), 736–41.

[2] Canadian Paediatric Society (2005). *Temperature measurement in paediatrics*. Retrieved May 26, 2006, from http://www.cps.ca/english/statements/CP/cp00-01.htm

[3] Canadian Hypertension Education Program (CHEP) Recommendations (2006). Retrieved May 26, 2006, from http://www.hypertension.ca/CHEP2006/CHEP_2006_complete.pdf

[4] Canadian Hypertension Education Program (2005). *Canadian recommendations for the management of hypertension*. Retrieved May 26, 2006, from http://www.hypertension.ca/Documentation/Recommendation05_va.pdf

[5] Canadian Hypertension Education Program (CHEP) Recommendations (2006).

[6] Ibid.

[7] Reprinted from www.hypertension.ca with permission of the Canadian Hypertension Education Program.

[8] Canadian Hypertension Education Program (2005). *Canadian recommendations for the management of hypertension*.

[9] Joffres, M. R., Ghadirian, P., Fodor, J. G., Petrasovits, A., Chockalingam, A., & Hamet, P. (1997). Awareness, treatment, and control of hypertension in Canada. *American Journal of Hypertension, 10*, 1097–102.

[10] Campbell, N. R. C., McAlister, F. A., Brant, R., Levine, M., Drouin, D., & Feldman, R. (2003). Temporal trends in antihypertensive drug prescriptions in Canada before and after introduction of the Canadian Hypertension Education Program. *Journal of Hypertension, 21*, 1591–97.

[11] Joffres, M. R., Ghadirian, P., Fodor, J. G., Petrasovits, A., Chockalingam, A., & Hamet, P. (1997). Awareness, treatment, and control of hypertension in Canada.

[12] International Association for the Study of Pain (1979). *IASP pain terminology*. Retrieved May 26, 2006, from http://www.iasp-pain.org/terms-p.html

[13] Canadian Pain Coalition. *Charter of pain patients' rights*. Retrieved May 26, 2006, from http://www.painhurtscanada.ca/charter.htm

[14] Murray, M., Bullard, M., Grafstein, E., for the CTAS and CEDIS National Working Groups (2004). Revisions to the Canadian Emergency Department Triage and Acuity Scale implementation guidelines. *Canadian Journal of Emergency Medicine, 6*(6), 421–27.

[15] Fillingim, R. B., & Maixner, W. (1995). Gender differences in response to noxious stimuli. *Pain Forum, 4*, 209–11.

[16] Berkeley, K. J., & Holdcroft, A. (1999). Sex and gender differences in pain. In P. D. Wall & R. Melzack (Eds.), *Textbook of pain* (4th ed.). Edinburgh: Churchill Livingstone.

[17] Beyer, J. (1983). *The Caucasian version of the Oucher*. Developed and copyrighted by Judith E. Beyer, RN, PhD, 1983.

[18] Hockenberry, M., Wilson, D., Winkelstein, M., & Kline, N. (2003). *Wong's nursing care of infants and children* (7th ed.). St. Louis, MO: Mosby.

[19] Acute Pain Management Guideline Panel. (1992). *Acute pain management: Operative or medical procedures and trauma. Clinical practice guideline* (AHCPR Publication No. 92-0032). Rockville, MD: Agency for Health Care Policy and Research.

[20] Merkel, S. I., Voepel-Lewis, T., Shayevitz, J. R., & Malviya, S. (1997). The FLACC: A behavioral scale for scoring postoperative pain in young children. *Pediatric Nursing, 23*(3), 293–97.

[21] Ballantyne, M., Stevens, B., McAllister, M., Dionne, K. & Jack, A. (1999). Validation of the premature infant pain profile in the clinical setting. *Clinical Journal of Pain. 15*(4), 297–303.

[22] Cleeland, C.S., & Ryan, K.M. (1994). Pain assessment: Global use of the brief pain inventory. *Annals Academy of Medicine* (23), 129-138.

[23] McCaffery, M., & Pasero, F. (1999). *Pain: Clinical manual for nursing practice*. St. Louis, MO: Mosby.

[24] Melzack, R. (1987). The Short-Form McGill Pain Questionnaire. *Pain, 30*(2), 191–97.

BIBLIOGRAPHY

Abbott C., Schiffrin, E. L., Grover, S., Honos, G., Lebel, M., Mann, K., Wilson, T., Penner, B., Tremblay, G., Tobe, S. W., & Feldman, R. D. (2005). Canadian hypertension education program. The 2005 Canadian hypertension education program recommendations for the management of hypertension: Part 1—Blood pressure measurement, diagnosis and assessment of risk. *Canadian Journal of Cardiology. 21*(8), 645–56, Jun.

Bolli, P., Myers, M. & McKay, D. (2005). Applying the 2005 Canadian hypertension education program recommendations: 1. Diagnosis of hypertension. *Canadian Medical Association Journal, 173*(5), 480–83.

Campbell, N. R., Tu, K., Brant, R., Duong-Hua, M. & McAlister, F. A. (2006). Canadian hypertension education program outcomes research task force. The impact of the Canadian Hypertension Education Program on antihypertensive prescribing trends. *Hypertension, 47*(1), 22–28.

Canadian Hypertension Society (2005). Management of hypertension: A summary of the new and important aspects of the 2005 Canadian Hypertension Education Program recommendations for the management of hypertension. *The Canadian Nurse, 101*(5), 25.

Craig, J., Lancaster, G., Taylor, S., Williamson, P., & Smyth, R. (2002). Infrared ear thermometry compared with rectal thermometry in children: A systematic review. *The Lancet, 360* (9333), 603.

Guyton, A. C., & Hall, J. (2006). *Textbook of medical physiology* (11th ed.). Philadelphia: Saunders.

McMahon, S., & Koltzenburg, M. (2006). *Wall and Melzack's textbook of pain*. Philadelphia: Elsevier/Churchill Livingstone.

Registered Nurses' Association of Ontario (2002). *Assessment & management of pain*. Toronto: Registered Nurses' Association of Ontario.

WEB RESOURCES

The Canadian Hypertension Society
http://www.hypertension.ca/

Canadian Consortium on Pain Mechanisms Diagnosis & Management
http://www.curepain.ca/

Canadian Pain Society
http://www.canadianpainsociety.ca/

Pain Hurts Canada (Charter of Pain Patients' Rights and Responsibilities)
http://www.painhurtscanada.ca/

CHAPTER 10

Skin, Hair, and Nails

COMPETENCIES

1. Describe the anatomy and physiology of the integumentary system.

2. Explain the process of describing and classifying skin lesions.

3. Identify common skin lesions and discuss possible etiologies.

4. Identify pathophysiological changes to hair and nails and discuss possible etiologies.

5. State the warning signs of carcinoma in pigmented lesions.

6. Describe methods used to assess integumentary changes in both light- and dark-skinned patients.

*T*he skin, also known as the **integumentary system,** or cutaneous tissue, is the largest organ system of the body. It shelters most of the other organ systems, and if assessed carefully, it provides a noninvasive window to observe the body's level of functioning.

This chapter provides a review of the skin and its appendages, hair, and nails. Techniques for assessment of the integumentary system are addressed as well as an approach to evaluating skin lesions.

ANATOMY AND PHYSIOLOGY

The skin, hair, and nails, along with their functions, are discussed.

Skin

The surface area of the skin covers approximately 1.86 square metres (20 square feet) in the average adult, with a thickness varying from 0.2 mm to 1.5 mm, depending on the region of the body and the patient's age. Morphologically speaking, the skin is composed of three main layers: the epidermis, the dermis, and the subcutaneous tissue, or hypodermis (Figure 10-1).

Epidermis

The **epidermis** is a multilayered outer covering consisting of four layers throughout the body, except for the palms of the hands and soles of the feet, where there are five layers (Figure 10-2). The deepest layer of the epidermis is the **stratum germinativum,** or basal cell layer, which is composed of columnar-shaped cells that rest on a basement membrane. These columnar cells undergo continuous mitosis, producing new cells to replace the cells lost from the top layer of the epidermis. This layer provides the skin with tone and also creates pigment-producing melanocytes, which filter ultraviolet (UV) light. The **stratum**

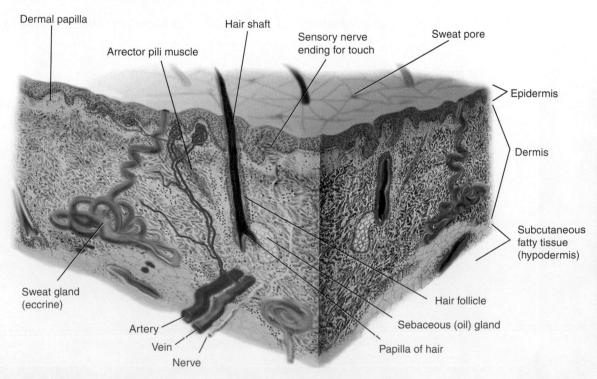

Figure 10-1 Structures of the skin

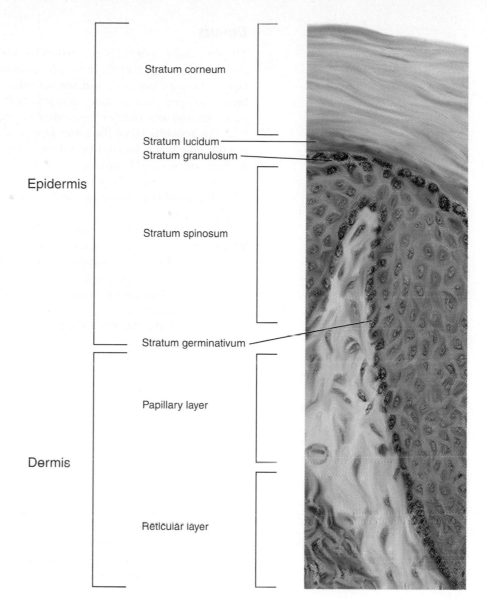

Epidermis

Stratum corneum

Stratum lucidum
Stratum granulosum

Stratum spinosum

Stratum germinativum

Dermis

Papillary layer

Reticular layer

Figure 10-2 Epidermal and dermal layers of the skin.

spinosum overlays the stratum germinativum and consists of layers of polyhedral-shaped cells. Intercellular bridges provide for the irregular shape. Skin cell death occurs in the **stratum granulosum,** which overlays the stratum spinosum. The stratum granulosum is composed of cells with shrivelled nuclei and strands of keratin.

The additional layer, which is found exclusively on the palmar and plantar surfaces, is the **stratum lucidum,** which contains a thin layer of translucent **eleidin** that aids in the formation of keratin. Finally, the **stratum corneum,** also known as the horny layer, completes the epidermis. The stratum corneum is composed of enucleated dead epithelial cells that contain keratin, which provides a waterproof barrier. This layer is in a continual state of **desquamation** (shedding) as new skin cells are pushed up from the lower layers; a complete turnover of cells occurs every 3 or 4 weeks.

The epidermis, with the exception of the palmar and plantar surfaces, is normally smooth. All epidermal surfaces are devoid of blood vessels, though blood pigments, such as oxyhemoglobin and reduced hemoglobin in the dermis, are responsible for the vascular colour transmitted to the skin's surface. Other factors that affect the skin's colour are various pigments such as melanin and carotene. Epidermal thickness and the ability of the skin to reflect light, known as the Tyndall effect, also influence integumentary colour.

Dermis

The **dermis,** or corium, is the second layer of the skin. It is approximately 20 times thicker than the epidermis in certain areas of the body and can be divided into two layers: the papillary layer and the reticular layer (see Figure 10-2). The **papillary layer,** or upper layer, is composed primarily of loose connective tissue, small elastic fibres, and an extensive network of capillaries that serve to nourish the epidermis. The **reticular layer,** the lower layer of the dermis, provides structural support for the skin and is formed by a dense bed of vascular connective tissue that also includes nerves and lymphatic tissue. In the deeper portions of the reticular layer, collagen and elastic fibres are surrounded by a gelatinous matrix. Intermeshed with the connective tissue are hair follicles, sweat glands, sebaceous glands, and adipose tissue.

The fibrous connective tissue in the dermis gives skin strength and elasticity. The tissue also provides structural support for the epidermis and forms dermal "ridges" to which the epidermis conforms and anchors, creating "epidermal ridges" known as fingerprints. These ridges develop during the first trimester of fetal development and though they enlarge with growth, their pattern remains the same throughout life and enhances with age.

In general, the dermis is thicker over the dorsal and lateral surfaces such as the palmar and plantar surfaces. It is much thinner over the ventral and medial surfaces, and is especially thin in the eyelids, scrotum, and penis.

Subcutaneous Tissue

Beneath the dermis is the **subcutaneous tissue,** or superficial fascia, composed of loose areolar connective tissue or adipose tissue, depending on its location in the body. The subcutaneous layers attach the skin to the underlying bones and act as a temperature insulator to help regulate body heat. These layers also encompass fat stores for energy use and contain an extensive venous plexus layer, which acts as a reservoir for the blood that warms the surface of the skin.

Distributed around the dermal blood vessels and the subcutaneous tissue are the skin's mast cells. **Mast cells** are the body's major source of tissue histamine and trigger the body's reaction to allergens; there are 7000–20,000 mast cells per cubic centimetre of skin.

Glands of the Skin

There are two main groups of glands in the skin: sebaceous glands and sweat glands.

Sebaceous Glands

The **sebaceous glands** are sebum-producing glands that are found almost everywhere in the dermis except for the palmar and plantar surfaces. They are part of the apparatus that contains the hair follicle and the **arrector pili muscle,** which contracts the skin and hair, resulting in "goose bumps." The ducts of the sebaceous glands open into the upper part of the hair follicle and produce **sebum,** an oily secretion that is thought to stop evaporation and water loss from the epidermal cells. Sebaceous glands are most prevalent in the scalp, forehead, nose, and chin.

Sweat Glands

The two main types of **sweat glands** are **apocrine glands,** which are associated with hair follicles, and **eccrine glands,** which are not associated with hair follicles. The secretory apparatus of both types of sweat glands is located in the subcutaneous tissue. Eccrine glands open directly onto the skin's surface and are widely distributed throughout the body. Apocrine glands are found primarily in the axillae, genital and rectal areas, nipples, and navel. These glands become functional during puberty, and secretion occurs during emotional stress or sexual stimulation. After puberty, apocrine glands are responsible for the characteristic body odour when sweat mixes with the natural bacterial flora normally present on the skin surface.

Hair

With few exceptions (the palmar and plantar surfaces, lips, nipples, and the glans penis), hair is distributed over the entire body surface. Its abundance and texture are dependent on an individual's age, sex, race, and heredity. **Vellus hair,** or fine, faint hair, covers most of the body. In general, **terminal hair** is the coarser, darker hair of the scalp, eyebrows, and eyelashes. In the axillary and pubic areas, terminal hair becomes increasingly evident in both males and females with the onset of puberty. Males also tend to develop coarser, thicker chest and facial hair.

Specialized epidermal cells are located in depressions at the base of each hair follicle and form each individual hair shaft. Blood vessels in the dermis nourish the cells so that they grow and divide, pushing the older cells toward the surface of the skin. Most hair shafts are composed of three layers: the cuticle, or outer layer; the cortex, or middle layer; and the medulla, or innermost layer. Hair colour is determined by the **melanocytes** produced in the cells at the base of each follicle; larger amounts of pigment produce darker hair colour and smaller amounts produce a lighter colour.

Nails

Nails are composed of keratinized, or horny, layers of cells that arise from undifferentiated epithelial tissue called the **matrix.** The **nail plate,** tissue that covers the distal portion of the digits and provides protection, is approximately 0.5–0.75 mm thick. The nails consists of the **nail root,** which lies posterior to the cuticle and is attached to the matrix; the **nailbed,** which is the vascular bed located beneath the nail plate; and the **periungual tissues,** which surround the nail plate and the free edge of the nail (Figure 10-3). At the proximal end of each nail is a white, crescent-shaped area known as the **lunula,** which is obscured by the cuticle in some individuals.

The normally translucent nail plate is given a pinkish cast by the underlying vascular bed in light-skinned individuals and a brownish cast in dark-skinned individuals. In many disease processes, the colour of the nailbed may vary. For instance, a decrease in oxygen content of the blood will cause the nailbeds to appear **cyanotic,** or blue.

The nail plate is continuously pushed forward by new growth from the germinative layer of the matrix. Normal growth for an adult is 0.1 mm to 1.0 mm per day, but this varies with age, season, nutrition, climate, health status, and activity.

Function of Skin

The skin has many functions, but perhaps the most important one is its ability to serve as a protective barrier against invasion from environmental hazards

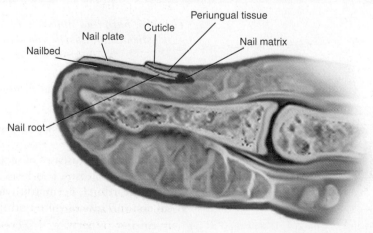

Figure 10-3 Structures of the nail.

and pathogens. It provides boundaries for materials that might enter the body, such as toxic chemicals, and for fluids and mobile tissues, such as blood, within the body. An intact integument also protects underlying organs that would otherwise be vulnerable to injury because of exposure.

Another function of skin is to regulate temperature through the production of perspiration. During states of increased body temperature, large quantities of sweat are produced by the eccrine glands. As perspiration reaches the skin's surface it rapidly evaporates, and the body's temperature begins to decrease. The skin's vascular system also plays a role in heat control. When vasodilation occurs, much of the heat can be lost through radiation and conduction. Conversely, vasoconstriction helps to maintain body heat.

The skin contains receptors for pain, touch, pressure, and temperature. These receptors originate in the dermis and terminate as either free nerve endings throughout the skin's surface or as special touch receptors that are encapsulated and found predominantly in the fingertips and lips. Each hair on the body contains a basal nerve fibre that acts as a tactile receptor. Sensory signals that help determine precise locations on the skin are transmitted along rapid sensory pathways, and less distinct signals such as pressure or poorly localized touch are sent via slower sensory pathways.

The skin excretes substances such as water, salts, and nitrogenous wastes, produces cells for wound repair, and is the site for the production of vitamin D. Nonverbal language and emotions, via blushing and facial expressions, are expressed through the skin. In addition, the skin may be used for the purpose of identification via fingerprints and birthmarks.

Function of Hair

Hair provides warmth, protection, and sensation to the underlying systems of the body. Terminal hair of the scalp and face provides warmth, shields against UV light, and filters dust and particulate matter. Vellus hair enhances tactile sensation and sensory perception. In many cultures, hair is a status symbol of beauty and wealth.

Function of Nails

Nails provide protection to the distal surface of the digits and can be used for self-protection. In many cultures, nail length in both men and women is a qualifier of social and economic status.

HEALTH HISTORY

The skin, hair, and nails health history provides insight into the link between a patient's life/lifestyle and skin, hair, and nails information and pathology.

PATIENT PROFILE   *Diseases that are age-, gender-, and race-specific for the skin, hair, and nails are listed.*

Age

Skin   Fungal infections, diseases of sebaceous glands, such as acne vulgaris (13–26)
Lupus erythematosus, psoriasis, hyperpigmented macular lesions, skin tags (acrochordon), dermatophyte infections (25–60)
Basal cell carcinoma (older adults)

Hair	Male pattern alopecia (adolescence to young adulthood) Thinning, graying, loss of hair in axillary and pubic areas, excessive facial hair (middle to old age)
Gender	
Skin	Male: Skin pathology is consistently more prevalent among males than females; dermatophyte infections; skin tumors; fungal infections and increased incidence of tumors related to occupational hazards and hygiene; Kaposi's sarcoma associated with immunodeficiency conditions
Hair	Female: Female pattern alopecia, increased facial hair with aging Male: Alopecia, increased coarse nose and ear hair with aging
Race	
Dark Skinned	**Keloid** formation, dermatosis papulosa nigra, hyper- and hypopigmentation, traumatic marginal alopecia, seborrheic dermatitis, pseudofolliculitis barbae, acne keloidalis, granuloma inguinale, Mongolian spots, albinism, hypopigmented sarcoidosis, granulomatosis skin lesions
Light Skinned	Squamous and basal cell carcinoma, actinic keratosis, psoriasis
HEALTH ISSUE/CONCERN	*Common health issues/concerns for the skin, hair, and nails are defined, and information on the characteristics of each sign and symptom is provided.*
Pruritus	Cutaneous itching that may have a multitude of etiologies
Location	Generalized or localized
Quality	Superficial or deep sensation of itching, intensity of itching, interference with sleep habits
Associated Manifestations	Rashes, lesions, edema, angioedema, anaphylaxis, excoriation or ulcers as the result of scratching, **lichenification** (thickening of the skin), systemic disease
Aggravating Factors	Exposure to chemicals, sunlight, plants, food, animals, stress, climate, parasites, xerosis, drug reaction, systemic disease processes, contact dermatitis, types of clothing (frequently wool)
Alleviating Factors	Dietary changes, medications, antihistamines, biofeedback, cool baths, types of clothing (frequently cotton), increased skin hydration, UV band light therapy
Setting	Work, home, school, or recreational environment
Timing	Pre- or postprandial, nocturnal, seasonal, during periods of stress, associated with menstrual cycle
Rash	A cutaneous eruption that may be localized or generalized
Lesion	A circumscribed pathological change in the tissues

continues

Location	Location of, where it started and spread, distribution over the body, percent of body involved, following dermatomes
Quantity	"Grouping or arrangement": **discrete**, grouped, **confluent, linear, annular, polycyclic,** generalized, **zosteriform**
Quality	"Morphology": **macule, patch, papule, plaque, nodule, cyst, wheal, vesicle, pustule, bullae, tumour,** lichenification, crust, **erosion, fissure, ulcer,** or **atrophy**
Associated Manifestations	Edema, angioedema, anaphylaxis, excoriation or ulcers as the result of scratching, lichenification, systemic disease, allergies, fever, induration
Aggravating Factors	Exposure to chemicals, sunlight, plants, food, animals, stress, climate, parasites, xerosis, drug reaction, systemic disease processes, contact dermatitis, radiation, types of clothing (frequently wool)
Alleviating Factors	Dietary changes, medications, antihistamines, biofeedback, cool baths, types of clothing (frequently cotton), increased skin hydration, UV band light therapy, surgery
Setting	Work, home, school, or recreational environment
Timing	When did it start, pre- or postprandial, nocturnal, seasonal, during periods of stress, associated with menstrual cycle
PAST HEALTH HISTORY	*The various components of the past health history are linked to skin, hair, and nail pathology and skin-, hair-, and nail-related information.*
Medical History	
Skin Specific	Allergies, eczema, atopic dermatitis, melanoma, albinism, vitiligo, psoriasis, skin cancer, athlete's foot, birthmarks, body piercing, tattoos, urticaria
Nonskin Specific	Renal disease, diabetes mellitus, lupus erythematosus, peripheral vascular disease, idiopathic thrombocytopenia purpura (ITP), Rocky Mountain spotted fever, liver disease, hepatitis, collagen diseases, cardiac dysfunction, sexually transmitted diseases, Lyme disease, arthritis, lymphoma, thyroid disease, pregnancy, Addison's disease, pernicious anemia, HIV, cytomegalovirus, Epstein-Barr virus, measles, mumps, rubella, coxsackievirus, adenovirus, typhoid, drug hypersensitivities, varicella, herpes zoster, herpes simplex, Kawasaki disease, toxic shock syndrome, carcinoma, asthma, tuberculosis, viral syndromes
Hair Specific	Allergies, alopecia, lice, bacterial or fungal infections of the scalp, brittle hair, rapid hair loss, trichotillomania, trauma, congenital anomalies
Nonhair Specific	Renal disease, diabetes mellitus, cardiac dysfunction, peripheral vascular disease, thyroid disease, pregnancy, Addison's disease, HIV, anemia, malnutrition, stress, chemotherapy, radiation therapy
Nail Specific	Allergies, psoriasis, bacterial or fungal infections, trauma, brittle nails, nail biting, congenital anomalies
Nonnail Specific	Iron deficiency anemia, chronic infection, malnutrition, Raynaud's disease, hypoxia, acute infections, syphilis

Surgical History	Keloid and scar formation, plastic surgery for birthmarks, skin grafts, reconstructive surgery, excision biopsy
Medications	Reaction manifested in skin changes after use of prescription or OTC drugs
Communicable Diseases	Varicella, roseola, measles, scabies, bacterial or fungal infections, HIV, and so on STIs: syphilis, gonorrhea, chancroid, genital warts (see Chapters 20 and 21 for further information)
Allergies	Medication, insect stings, foods, soaps, laundry detergent, chemicals, fibres (wool), metals (gold), animal dander, pollens, grasses, cosmetics, first manifestation of allergic reaction
Injuries/Accidents	Chemical inhalation, trauma, burns, toxin contamination
Special Needs	Poor eyesight can lead to poor hygiene, frequent skin trauma, prevents early detection and treatment of skin diseases, bedridden or wheelchair bound with possibility of pressure trauma and compromise of skin integrity
Blood Transfusions	Skin eruptions, pruritus
Childhood Illnesses	Refer to section on communicable diseases
FAMILY HEALTH HISTORY	*Skin, hair, and nail diseases that are familial in nature are listed.*
Skin Specific	Allergies, eczema, melanoma, albinism, vitiligo, psoriasis, nonmelonanomatous skin cancer
Hair Specific	Allergies, alopecia, brittle hair, hair loss
Nail Specific	Allergies, brittle nails
SOCIAL HISTORY	*The components of the social history are linked to skin, hair, and nail factors/pathology.*
Alcohol Use	Hepatotoxicity and subsequent skin manifestations that accompany liver failure, such as jaundice and pruritus; skin bruising and trauma from falls and ataxia; telangiectasia (spider veins) of the nose, neck, and upper chest
Drug Use	Skin manifestations from IV drug use, such as injection sites or tracks; these are especially prevalent in the forearms, behind the knees, toe and finger webs, and under the nails
Tobacco Use	Yellow discoloration of fingertips on smoking hand, leathery facial appearance
Sexual Practice	Various STIs may manifest in the genital region; these are discussed in Chapters 20 and 21
Travel History	Insect bites: insects indigenous to certain climates, such as the tsetse fly in Africa and the deer tick in wooded areas of southern Ontario and Lunenburg County, Nova Scotia, and parts of southern British Columbia as well as the northern and southeastern United States High-altitude areas: light-sensitive eruptions and winter eczema

continues

Work Environment	Chemical: contact dermatitis and burns Sunlight: skin eruptions, increased incidence of basal or squamous cell carcinoma, burns, wrinkles, senile freckles, lightened hair, excessive exposure to UV radiation Excessive exposure to water: drying and cracking of skin, pruritus, soft nails, damaged hair shafts Insect bites: rashes, urticaria, edema, angioedema, pruritus Operating heavy or sharp equipment: trauma, laceration Excessive exposure to wind and cold temperatures: aging, drying, and cracking of skin Pollution: contact dermatitis Tar and pitch: act as both photosensitizers and carcinogens
Home Environment	Chemicals used in cleaning can cause contact dermatitis; excessive exposure to water can cause dry, cracked skin, soft nails, and damaged hair shafts; excessive heat in the home can dry skin and cause pruritus; infected kittens and puppies may lead to tinea capitis
Hobbies/Leisure Activities	Gardening with exposure to chemicals, sunlight, contact dermatitis (e.g., poison ivy, poison oak) and insect bites; outdoor summer sports or activities increase sun and insect-bite exposure; outdoor winter activities increase frostbite and exposure; excessive exposure to chlorine and salt water damages hair; excessive use of tanning salons may lead to skin carcinoma
Stress	Skin eruptions such as eczema, urticaria, acne, and psoriasis may have a psychological component in some cases; body image disorder as a result of skin disease and hair loss
Economic Status	People who are homeless or lack finances to be able to access hygiene facilities or who must live in overcrowded living arrangements may develop skin eruptions associated with poor hygiene, contact spread, or malnutrition
HEALTH MAINTENANCE ACTIVITIES	*This information provides a bridge between the health maintenance activities and the skin, hair, and nail function.*
Sleep	Sleep disturbances caused by symptoms such as itching or burning
Diet	Allergies to food can cause skin eruptions such as urticaria; diets high in fat and cholesterol may be connected to the development of xanthelasmatous lesions; vitamin deficiencies result in skin, hair, and nail changes; see Chapter 7 for further information
Exercise	Increased risk for cutaneous trauma associated with contact sports and sun exposure with outdoor sports and activities
Use of Safety Devices	Sunblock with appropriate sun protection factor (SPF) to prevent UV exposure; lotions and creams to prevent drying and cracking of skin; apply products to hydrate skin; protective gloves when handling harsh irritating chemicals
Health Check-Ups	**Nevi** (moles) and birthmarks assessed for changes in size, shape, or colour; skin lesions from sun exposure assessed

◄NURSING CHECKLIST►

Specific Health History Questions Regarding the Skin, Hair, and Nails

Skin Care Habits

- Do you use lotions, perfumes, cologne, cosmetics, soaps, oils, shaving cream, after-shave lotion, or an electric or standard razor?
- What type of home remedies do you use for skin lesions and rashes?
- How often do you bathe or shower?
- Do you use a tanning bed or salon?
- What type of sun protection do you use?
- Have you ever had a reaction to jewelry that you wore?
- Do you wear hats, visors, gloves, long sleeves or pants, or sunscreen when in the sun?
- How much time do you spend in the sun?

Hair Care Habits

- Do you use shampoo, conditioner, hair spray, setting products?
- Do you colour, dye, bleach, frost, or use relaxants on your hair?
- What products do you use?
- Do you wear a wig or hairpiece?
- Do you have greying hair or hair loss?
- Do you use a hair dryer, heated curlers, or curling iron?
- Do you tightly braid your hair?

Nail Care Habits

- Do you get manicures or pedicures?
- What type of nail care do you practise (trimming, clipping, use of polish, nail tips, acrylics)?
- Do you bite your nails?
- Do you suffer from nail splitting or discoloration?

Nursing Alert

Skin Cancer

Epidemiology[1, 2]

- There are three main types of skin cancer: basal cell carcinoma, squamous cell carcinoma, and malignant melanoma.
- Most cases of skin cancer in Canada are either basal or squamous cell carcinoma. In 2006, there were an estimated 68,000 Canadians diagnosed with either squamous cell or basal cell carcinoma. These skin cancers tend to develop later in life on skin that has been exposed repeatedly to the sun, such as the face, neck, or hands. Both of these carcinomas progress slowly and rarely cause death because they usually do not spread to other parts of the body and are easily removed by surgery.
- Malignant melanomas account for only 1–2% of all skin cancers but are the most fatal. For every 25 Canadians who have malignant melanoma, 5 will die. Unlike other skin cancers, this type of cancer occurs earlier in life and progresses rapidly. Malignant melanomas can develop on almost any part of the body but are frequently located on the back and other areas that may be missed with self-inspection (see Figure 10-4).

continues

- The occurrence rate of melanoma is gradually increasing in men; it has remained relatively unchanged in women.

Risk Factors[3]

- Areas that are only exposed to the sun from *time to time*, such as the back, neck, and the backs of legs
- UV radiation exposure that is repeated and unprotected
- Family history of skin cancer (10% of melanomas are familial with mapping to Chromosome 1 and 9)
- Blonde or red hair
- Fair or freckled complexion
- Second-degree burns before age 18 and/or acute sunburns
- Melanocytic precursor lesion
- Smoking
- Male gender
- Chemical exposure
- Radiation exposure
- Long-term or severe skin inflammation or injury
- Psoralens and ultraviolet light treatment (PUVA) treatment for psoriasis
- Xeroderma pigmentosum
- Lots of nevi, particularly atypical ones (dysplastic nevi)
- Reduced immunity
- Human papillomavirus

The A, B, C, D, E's of Screening[4]

Patients should check nevi (moles) and other lesions in front of a mirror once a month. If a lesion is on a posterior surface, the patient should ask a partner to check it on a monthly basis. A photo can be taken for future comparisons. A skin lesion should be assessed further if any of the following are noted:

- *A*symmetry (Is the lesion asymmetrical?)
- *B*order irregularities (Are the borders of the lesion irregular?)
- *C*olour variegation (Is the colour of the lesion uneven, irregular, or multicoloured?)
- *D*iameter greater than 6 mm (Is the lesion greater than 6 mm?)
- *******E*nlargement or evolution of colour change, shape, or symptoms (Is the lesion getting bigger or changing in shape, size or sensation?)

**'E' was added to the ABCD mnemonic in 2004 when it was assessed that some lesions that were <6 mm were actually melanomatous; thus, the "enlargement or evolution" element was added to address important lesions that had not yet achieved the previously established diameter

Nursing Tip

Reducing Exposure to Integumentary Irritants

- In the workplace, always follow health and safety guidelines. Review any Material Safety Data Sheet (MSDS) sources for precautionary measures on working with dangerous products.
- Follow the directions on the labels of all products; pay special attention to warning labels.
- If using a personal care product for the first time, perform a patch test to evaluate for sensitivity.
- Use rubber gloves when handling toxins or caustic substances.
- Contact a poison control centre for treatment guidelines if exposed to toxic or caustic substances.
- Notify appropriate officials if a dangerous chemical or toxin exposure occurs.

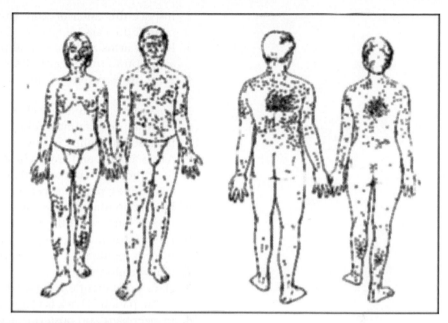

Figure 10-4 Body site distribution of Melanoma.
Source: http://www.utdol.com/utd/content/image.do?imageKey=prim_pix\body_dis.gif

EQUIPMENT

- Magnifying glass
- Good source of natural light
- Penlight
- Clean gloves
- Microscope slide
- Small centimeter ruler

For Special Techniques

- Wood's lamp
- #15 scalpel blade
- Microscope slide with cover slips
- Mineral oil
- Microscope

◄NURSING CHECKLIST►

General Approach to Skin, Hair, and Nail Assessment

1. Ensure that the room is well lit. Daylight is the best source of light, especially when determining skin colour. However, if access to daylight is not possible, overhead fluorescent lights should be added.
2. Use a handheld magnifying glass to aid in inspection when simple visual inspection is not adequate.
3. Explain to the patient each step of the assessment process prior to initiating the assessment.
4. Ensure patient privacy by providing drapes.
5. Ensure the comfort of the patient by keeping the room at an appropriate temperature.
6. Warm hands by washing them in warm water before the assessment.
7. Gather equipment on a table prior to initiating the assessment.
8. Ask the patient to undress completely and to put on a patient gown, leaving the back untied.
9. Perform assessment in a cephalocaudal fashion.
10. For episodic illness, the skin examination is incorporated into the regional physical exam.

ASSESSMENT OF THE SKIN, HAIR, AND NAILS

Inspection of the Skin

In each area, observe for: colour, bleeding, ecchymosis, vascularity, lesions, moisture, temperature, texture, turgor, and edema.
  E 1. Facing the patient, inspect the skin colour of the face, eyelids, ears, nose, lips, and mucous membranes.

| E Examination | N Normal Findings | A Abnormal Findings | P Pathophysiology |

2. Inspect the anterior and lateral aspects of the neck, then inspect behind the ears.
3. Inspect arms and dorsal and palmar surfaces of the hands. Pay special attention to the finger webs.
4. Have the patient move to a supine position, with arms placed over the head.
5. Lower gown to uncover chest and breasts.
6. Inspect intramammary folds and ridges. Pendulous breasts may need to be raised to complete this inspection.
7. Assess axillae, and cover chest and breasts with gown.
8. Raise gown to uncover abdomen and anterior aspect of the lower extremities; place a sheet over the genital area.
9. Inspect abdomen, anterior aspect of the lower extremities, dorsal and plantar surfaces of the feet, and toe webs.
10. Don gloves and uncover genital area.
11. Inspect inguinal folds and genitalia.
12. Remove gloves.
13. Have the patient turn to a side-lying position on the examination table so the patient's back is facing you.
14. Inspect back and posterior neck and scalp. Specifically look for nevi or other lesions.
15. Inspect posterior aspect of the lower extremities.
16. Don clean gloves and raise the gluteal cleft and inspect the gluteal folds and perianal area; then remove and discard the gloves.
17. Cover the patient and assist to a sitting position.
18. Wash hands.

Nursing Alert

Frostbite

Damage to tissues from freezing results because of the formation of ice crystals within cells, which leads to rupture of the cells and, ultimately, cell death.

Frostnip

Initially cold, burning pain; the affected area becomes blanched (usually hands, feet, face, or other exposed areas). With rewarming, the area becomes reddened. Frostnip generally does not lead to permanent damage because only the top layers of skin are involved. However, it can lead to long-term sensitivity to heat and cold.

Frostbite

If freezing continues, frostbite develops. Symptoms include cold burning pain that progresses to tingling, and later, numbness or a heavy sensation. The area becomes pale or white and rewarming causes pain.

If further freezing continues, deep frostbite occurs; all of the muscles, tendons, blood vessels, and nerves freeze. The extremity is hard, feels woody, and use is lost temporarily, and in severe cases, permanently. The involved area appears deep purple or red with blisters that are usually filled with blood. This type of severe frostbite may result in the loss of fingers and toes.

> ## Nursing Tip
>
> **Body Piercing and Tattoos**
>
> It is important to inspect the skin and note the presence and location of tattoos and body piercing. Some patients react to the ink in the tattoo and develop various skin disorders. Health Canada has deemed the use of the ingredient paraphenylenediamine (PPD) in "black henna" (temporary tattoo ink) as unsafe. Body piercing sites should be assessed for signs of infection (e.g., erythema, purulent discharge, increased skin temperature). Remember to assess all body areas and document the location of all tattoos and body piercing, such as the ears, umbilicus, eyebrows, lips, nares, tongue, labia, vagina, and scrotum. Health Canada warns that getting a tattoo or body piercing from an operator who does not use sterilized equipment or techniques places people at risk for blood-borne pathogens. Therefore, the nurse should screen patients with tattoos and body piercing for diseases such as hepatitis and HIV, among others.

Colour

E Assess for coloration.

N Normally, the skin is a uniform whitish pink or brown colour, depending on the patient's race. Exposure to sunlight results in increased pigmentation of sun-exposed areas. Dark-skinned persons may have a freckling of the gums, tongue borders, and lining of the cheeks; the gingiva may appear blue or variegated in colour.

A The appearance of **cyanosis** (blue discoloration) of fingers, nailbeds, lips, or mucous membranes is abnormal in both light-and dark-skinned individuals. In light-skinned individuals, the skin has a bluish tint. The earlobes, lower eyelids, lips, oral mucosa, nailbeds, and palmar and plantar surfaces may be especially cyanotic. Dark-skinned individuals have an ashen- grey to pale tint, and the lips and tongue are good indicators of cyanosis.

P Cyanosis occurs when there is greater than 50 g/L of deoxygenated hemoglobin in the blood and does not usually appear until arterial oxygen saturation falls to 75% (severe respiratory failure occurs when oxygen saturation falls to 85–90%). In order for cyanosis to be an accurate indicator of arterial oxygen (PaO$_2$), two conditions must be met. The patient must have normal hemoglobin and hematocrit as well as normal perfusion. For example, a patient with **polycythemia** (elevated number of red blood cells) can be cyanotic but have adequate oxygenation. The problem is that the patient has too many red blood cells rather than too little oxygen. Conversely, a patient with **anemia** (reduced number of red blood cells) can be hypoxemic but not cyanotic. In this case, the patient has too little hemoglobin. Central cyanosis is secondary to marked heart and lung disease; peripheral cyanosis can be secondary to systemic disease or vasoconstriction stimulated by cold temperatures or anxiety.

A The appearance of **jaundice** (yellow-green to orange cast) of skin, sclera, mucous membranes, fingernails, and palmar or plantar surfaces in the light-skinned individual is abnormal (Figure 10-5A). Jaundice in dark-skinned individuals may appear as yellow staining in the sclera, hard palate, and palmar or plantar surfaces.

P Jaundice is caused by an increased serum bilirubin level associated with liver disease or hemolytic disease and is only detected when the serum

| E | **Examination** | N | **Normal Findings** | A | **Abnormal Findings** | P | **Pathophysiology** |

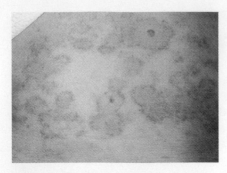

A. Jaundice drug eruption. *Courtesy of Robert A. Silverman, M.D., Clinical Associate Professor, Department of Pediatrics, Georgetown University.*

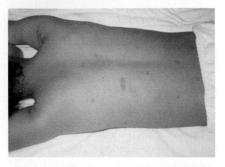

B. Café au lait spots.

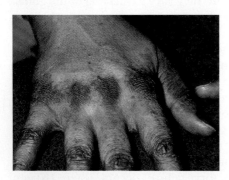

C. Acanthosis Nigricans.

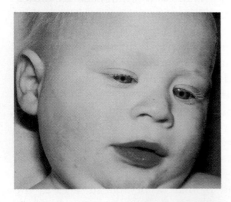

D. Note the lack of coloration in this child with albinism. *Courtesy of Robert A. Silverman, M.D., Clinical Associate Professor, Department of Pediatrics, Georgetown University.*

Figure 10-5 Skin coloration abnormalities.

bilirubin is greater than 34μmol/L (twice the normal upper limit). Severe burns and sepsis also can produce jaundice.

A A yellow discoloration of the palmar and digital creases is abnormal.

P Xanthoma striata palmaris is caused by hyperlipidemia.

A Orange-yellow coloration of palmar and plantar surfaces and forehead but no involvement of the mucous membranes is abnormal.

P **Carotenemia,** elevated levels of serum carotene, results from the excessive ingestion of carotene-rich foods such as carrots.

A A greyish cast to the skin is abnormal.

P A greyish cast is seen in renal patients and is associated with chronic anemia along with retained urochrome pigments. Slight jaundice may also be found in the renal patient.

A A combination of pallor and ecchymosis with a jaundiced appearance is abnormal.

P Uremia secondary to renal failure results in serum urochrome pigment retention.

A Sustained bright red or pink coloration in light-skinned individuals is abnormal. Dark-skinned individuals may have no underlying change in coloration. Palpation may be used to ascertain signs of warmth, swelling, or induration.

P Hyperemia occurs because of dilated superficial blood vessels, increased blood flow, febrile states, local inflammatory condition, or excessive alcohol intake.

A A bright red to ruddy sustained appearance that is evident on the integument, mucous membranes, and palmar or plantar surfaces is abnormal in both light- and dark-skinned individuals.

P Polycythemia, as noted earlier, is an increased number of red blood cells and results in this ruddy appearance.

A A dusky rubor of the extremities when in a dependent position, which can be associated with tissue necrosis, is abnormal.

P Venous stasis results from venule engorgement and diminished blood flow, which occurs in congestive heart failure and atherosclerosis.

A A pale cast to the skin that may be most evident in the face, mucous membranes, lips, and nailbeds is abnormal in light-skinned individuals. A yellow-brown to ashen-grey cast to the skin, along with pale or grey lips, mucous membranes, and nailbeds, is abnormal in dark-skinned individuals.

P **Pallor** (lack of colour) is due to decreased visibility of the normal oxyhemoglobin. This can occur when the patient has decreased blood flow in the superficial vessels, as in shock or syncope, or when there is a decreased amount of serum oxyhemoglobin, as in anemia. Localized pallor may be secondary to arterial insufficiency.

A A brown cast to the skin can be generalized or discrete.

P A brown coloration occurs when there is a deposition of melanin that can be caused by genetic predisposition, pregnancy, Addison's disease (deficiency in cortisol leads to enhanced melanin production), café au lait spots (Figure 10-5B), and sunlight.

P Acanthosis nigricans is a condition in which the skin becomes brownish and thicker, almost leathery in appearance (Figure 10-5C). This usually occurs in the axillae, on the flexoral surfaces of the groin and neck, and around the umbilicus. Acanthosis nigricans occurs in obesity, diabetes mellitus, and with medications such as steroids.

A A white cast to the skin as evidenced by generalized whiteness, including of the hair and eyebrows, is abnormal (Figure 10-5D).

P This lack of coloration is caused by **albinism,** a congenital inability to form melanin.

| E | Examination | N | Normal Findings | A | Abnormal Findings | P | Pathophysiology |

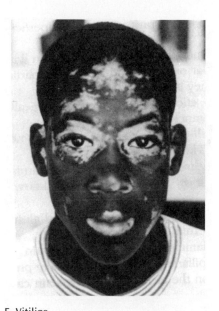

E. Vitiligo.

Figure 10-5 *continued.*

A **Vitiligo** is a condition marked by patchy symmetrical areas of white on the skin and is abnormal (Figure 10-5E).

P This condition can be caused by an acquired loss of melanin. Trauma can also lead to hypopigmentation, especially in dark-skinned individuals.

A An erythematous, confluent eruption in a butterfly-like distribution over the face is abnormal.

P Systemic lupus erythematosus, a connective tissue disorder, is the most likely etiology.

Bleeding, Ecchymosis, and Vascularity

E Inspect the skin for evidence of bleeding, ecchymosis, or increased vascularity.

N Normally, there are no areas of increased vascularity, ecchymosis, or bleeding.

A Bleeding from the mucous membranes, previous venipuncture sites, or lesions should be considered abnormal.

P Spontaneous bleeding can be indicative of clotting disorders, trauma, or use of antithrombolytic agents such as warfarin or heparin.

A **Petechiae** are violaceous (red-purple) discolorations of less than 0.5 cm in diameter (Figure 10-6A). Petechiae do not blanch. In dark-skinned individuals, evaluate for petechiae in the mucous membranes and axillae.

P Petechiae can indicate an increased bleeding tendency or embolism; causes include intravascular defects or infections.

A **Purpura** is a condition characterized by the presence of confluent petechiae or confluent ecchymosis over any part of the body (Figure 10-6B).

P Purpura or peliosis is characterized by hemorrhage into the skin and can be caused by decreased platelet formation. Lesions vary based on the type of purpura; pigmentation changes may become permanent.

A **Ecchymosis** is a violaceous discoloration of varying size, also called a black-and-blue mark (Figure 10-6C). In dark-skinned patients, these discolorations are deeper in colour.

P Ecchymosis is caused by extravasation of blood into the skin as a result of trauma and can also occur with heparin or warfarin use or liver dysfunction.

A An erythematous dilation of small blood vessels is abnormal (Figure 10-6D).

P This describes **telangiectasias.** They tend to appear on the face and thighs and occur more frequently in women.

A **Spider angiomas** are bright red and star-shaped (Figure 10-6E). There is often a central pulsation noted with pressure and this results in blanching

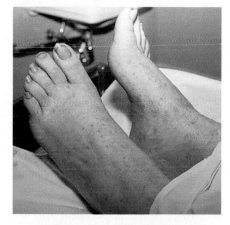

A. Petechiae. *Courtesy of Dr. Mark Dougherty, Lexington, KY*

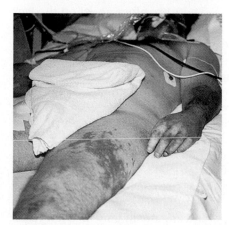

B. Purpura. *Courtesy of Dr. Mark Dougherty, Lexington, KY.*

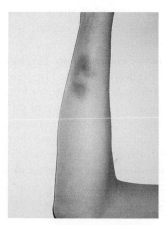

C. Ecchymosis.

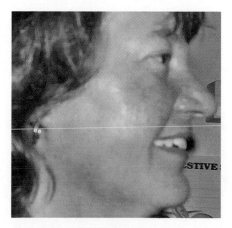

D. Telangiectasias usually occur more in women and on the face.

Figure 10-6 Bleeding, Ecchymosis, and Vascular abnormalities of the skin.

Nursing Alert

Signs of Abuse

Areas of ecchymosis at varying stages of healing (see Table 10-1) are often signs of trauma that could be the result of physical abuse. Ecchymotic areas at the base of the skull, or on the face, buttocks, breasts, or abdomen should warrant a high index of suspicion for abuse, especially if found in children or pregnant women, as should burns (e.g., cigarettes, iron) and ecchymoses that follow recognizable patterns (i.e., belt marks, fingerprints, bite marks). Any signs of abuse should be investigated further and referred as necessary.

TABLE 10-1

Estimating Age of Healing Bruises

COLOUR OF BRUISE	DAYS SINCE INJURY
Red	0–1
Bluish purple	1–4
Greenish yellow	5–7
Yellowish brown	8

Source: *Rudolph's Fundamentals of Pediatrics* (Rudolph and Kamei, 1998).

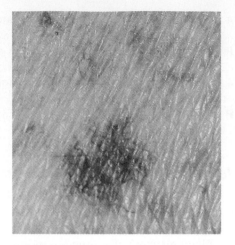

E. Spider angioma

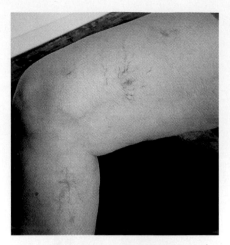

F. Venous star

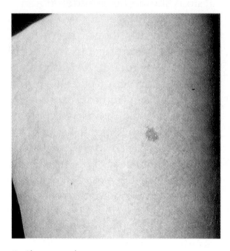

G. Cherry angioma

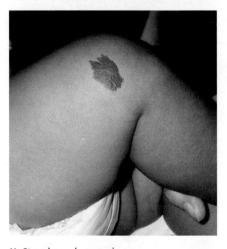

H. Strawberry hemangioma

Figure 10-6 *continued.*

in the extensions. Most often, these lesions are noted on the face, neck, and chest. They are a type of telangiectasia.

P Causes of spider angiomas include pregnancy, liver disease, and hormone therapy. They are normal in a small percentage of the population and are more prevalent in women.

A **Venous stars** are linear or irregularly shaped blue vascular patterns that do not blanch with pressure (Figure 10-6F). These are often noted on the legs near veins or on the anterior chest.

P Venous stars are caused by increased venous pressure in the superficial veins.

A **Cherry angiomas** are bright-red circumscribed areas that may darken with age (Figure 10-6G). They can be flat or raised and may show partial blanching with pressure. Most often, they are found on the trunk.

P These vascularities are of unknown etiology and are pathologically insignificant except for cosmetic appearance.

A A bright-red, raised area that has well-defined borders and does not blanch with pressure is abnormal (Figure 10-6H).

P **Strawberry hemangiomas,** or strawberry marks, are congenital malformations of closely packed immature capillaries. This condition is also known as nevus vascularis. They regress as the child grows and are usually gone in a few years.

E	Examination	N	Normal Findings	A	Abnormal Findings	P	Pathophysiology

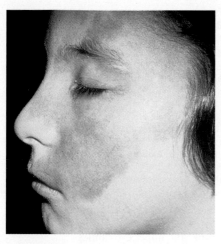

I. Nevus Flammeus. *Courtesy of Robert A. Silverman, M.D., Clinical Associate Professor, Department of Pediatrics, Georgetown University.*

Figure 10-6 *continued.*

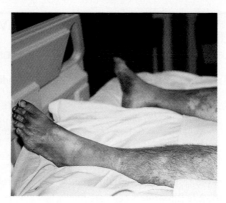

J. Necrosis. *Courtesy of Dr. Mark Dougherty, Lexington, KY.*

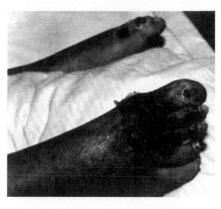

K. Gas gangrene

A   A burgundy, red, or violaceous macular vascular patch that is located along the course of a peripheral nerve is abnormal (Figure 10-6I).

P   This is a **nevus flammeus,** or port-wine stain. This type of nevus is composed of mature but thin-walled capillaries. The lesion is usually present at birth and is frequently located on the face. A port-wine stain can be indicative of underlying disorders, such as Sturge-Weber syndrome.

A   In light-skinned individuals, a purple to black discoloration is abnormal (Figure 10-6J). In dark-skinned individuals, very dark to black discoloration is abnormal.

P   These findings can indicate different stages of **necrosis,** or tissue death. Conditions that starve the affected body part of oxygen, whether in acute or chronic situations, such as in diabetes mellitus, disseminated intravascular coagulation, acute hypovolemia, and severe electric charge, can cause necrosis.

A   Dark-brown or blackened areas of skin that are edematous and painful are abnormal (Figure 10-6K). These areas may drain a thin liquid that has a sweet, foul odour. Crepitus may be palpated in the affected areas.

P   **Clostridial myonecrosis,** more commonly referred to as gas gangrene, is a gram-positive infection that affects skeletal muscles that have decreased oxygenation. The clostridia organisms are endogenous to the gastrointestinal tract and are also found in soil. Patients who experience circulatory compromise, such as in diabetes mellitus, arterial insufficiency, trauma, and constricting casts, are at risk for developing gas gangrene, as are patients who have contaminated wounds and decreased vascularity to the affected area.

Nursing Tip

Enhancement Techniques

Magnification: Use of a magnifying glass may be beneficial in the evaluation of lesions and discolorations for morphology.

Wood's Lamp: Also known as a UV light, it is valuable in the diagnosis of certain skin and hair diseases. Dermatophytosis and erythrasma are easily diagnosed by the fluorescent changes that occur under UV exposure. Dermatophytosis in the hair shaft will appear green to yellow, and erythrasma will appear coral red.

TABLE 10-2 Anatomic Locations of Various Skin Lesions

LESION	LOCATION
Basal cell carcinoma	Medial and lateral canthi and nasolabial fold
Rosacea	Face
Acne vulgaris	Face, back, shoulders, chest
Furuncle	Nose, neck, face, axillae, and buttocks
Lesions resulting from light exposure (squamous cell carcinoma, solar lentigo, solar keratosis)	Forehead, cheeks, tops of the ears, neck, dorsal surface of hands and forearms, and lateral arms
Seborrheic keratosis, spider angioma	Face, trunk, and upper extremities
Impetigo, verruca vulgaris (warts)	Arms, legs, buttocks, face, hands, fingers, and knees
Herpes zoster	Along the cutaneous spinal nerve tracks, almost always unilateral
Kaposi's sarcoma	Widespread: trunk, head, tip of nose, periorbital, penis, legs, palms, and soles
Erythema nodosum	Lower legs
Stasis dermatitis	Sock area
Cutaneous moniliasis	Moist folds behind the ears, under the breasts, in the axilla, umbilicus, along the inguinal and pudendal regions, and in the gluteal and perineal areas
Adult atopic eczema	Mainly flexor surfaces of the body
Psoriasis	Mainly scalp, elbows, and extensor surfaces of the body (rarely on the face and skin folds)
Contact dermatitis	Affects surfaces in contact with irritating agents
Pediculosis pubis	Pubic and axillary areas (may also include hairs of abdomen, thighs, eyebrows, eyelashes)

Lesions

E 1. Inspect the skin for lesions, noting the anatomic location. Lesions can be localized, regionalized, or generalized. They can involve exposed areas or skin folds (Table 10-2).
  2. Note the grouping or arrangement of the lesions: discrete, grouped, confluent, linear, annular, polycyclic, generalized, or zosteriform (Figure 10-7).
  3. Inspect the lesions for elevation (flat or raised).
  4. Using a ruler, measure the lesions.
  5. Describe the colour of the lesions.
  6. Note any exudate for colour or odour.
  7. Note the morphology of the skin lesions. Skin lesions can be primary (see Figure 10-8), originating from previously normal skin, or secondary (Figure 10-9), originating from primary lesions.

E	Examination	N	Normal Findings	A	Abnormal Findings	P	Pathophysiology

LESIONS   **EXAMPLES**   **LESIONS**   **EXAMPLES**

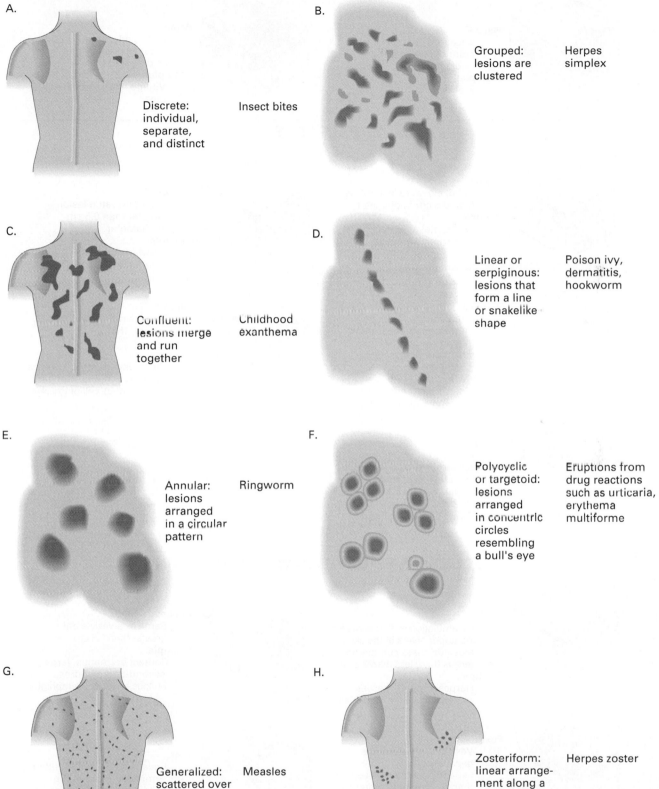

A.

Discrete: individual, separate, and distinct

Insect bites

B.

Grouped: lesions are clustered

Herpes simplex

C.

Confluent: lesions merge and run together

Childhood exanthema

D.

Linear or serpiginous: lesions that form a line or snakelike shape

Poison ivy, dermatitis, hookworm

E.

Annular: lesions arranged in a circular pattern

Ringworm

F.

Polycyclic or targetoid: lesions arranged in concentric circles resembling a bull's eye

Eruptions from drug reactions such as urticaria, erythema multiforme

G.

Generalized: scattered over the body

Measles

H.

Zosteriform: linear arrangement along a nerve root

Herpes zoster

Figure 10-7 Arrangement of lesions.

NONPALPABLE

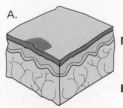

Macule:
Localized changes in skin color of less than 1 cm in diameter
Example:
Freckle

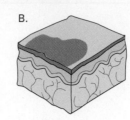

Patch:
Localized changes in skin color of greater than 1 cm in diameter
Example:
Vitiligo, stage 1 of pressure ulcer

PALPABLE

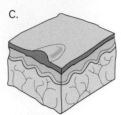

Papule:
Solid, elevated lesion less than 0.5 cm in diameter
Example:
Warts, elevated nevi, seborrheic keratosis

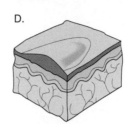

Plaque:
Solid, elevated lesion greater than 0.5 cm in diameter
Example:
Psoriasis, eczema, pityriasis rosea

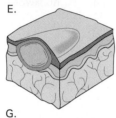

Nodules:
Solid and elevated; however, they extend deeper than papules into the dermis or subcutaneous tissues, 0.5-2.0 cm
Example:
Lipoma, erythema nodosum, cyst, melanoma, hemangioma

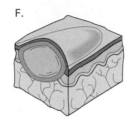

Tumor:
The same as a nodule only greater than 2 cm

Example:
Carcinoma (such as advanced breast carcinoma); **not** basal cell or squamous cell of the skin

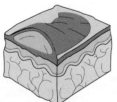

Wheal:
Localized edema in the epidermis causing irregular elevation that may be red or pale
Example:
Insect bite, hive, angioedema

FLUID-FILLED CAVITIES WITHIN THE SKIN

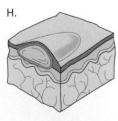

Vesicle:
Accumulation of fluid between the upper layers of the skin; elevated mass containing serous fluid; less than 0.5 cm
Example:
Herpes simplex, herpes zoster, chickenpox, scabies

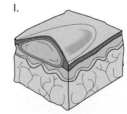

Bullae:
Same as a vesicle only greater than 0.5 cm
Example:
Contact dermatitis, large second-degree burns, bullous impetigo, pemphigus

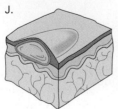

Pustule:
Vesicles or bullae that become filled with pus, usually described as less than 0.5 cm in diameter
Example:
Acne, impetigo, furuncles, carbuncles, folliculitis

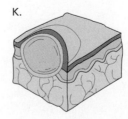

Cyst:
Encapsulated fluid-filled or semi-solid mass in the subcutaneous tissue or dermis
Example:
Sebaceous cyst, epidermoid cyst

Figure 10-8 Morphology of primary lesions.

ABOVE THE SKIN SURFACE

A.
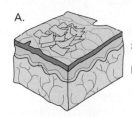
Scales:
    Flaking of the skin's surface
Example:
    Dandruff, psoriasis, xerosis

B.
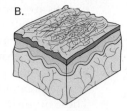
Lichenification:
    Layers of skin become
    thickened and rough as a
    result of rubbing over a
    prolonged period of time
Example:
    Chronic contact dermatitis

C.
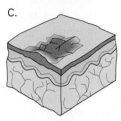
Crust:
    Dried serum, blood, or pus
    on the surface of the skin
Example:
    Impetigo, acute eczematous
    inflammation

D.
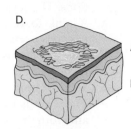
Atrophy:
    Thinning of the skin surface
    and loss of markings
Example:
    Striae, aged skin

BELOW THE SKIN SURFACE

E.
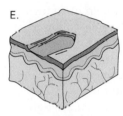
Erosion:
    Loss of epidermis
Example:
    Ruptured chickenpox vesicle

F.
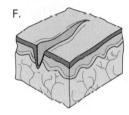
Fissure:
    Linear crack in the epidermis
    that can extend into the dermis
Example:
    Chapped hands or lips,
    athlete's foot

G.
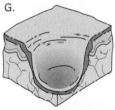
Ulcer:
    A depressed lesion of
    the epidermis and upper
    papillary layer of the dermis
Example:
    Stage 2 pressure ulcer

H.
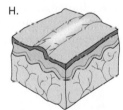
Scar:
    Fibrous tissue that replaces
    dermal tissue after injury
Example:
    Surgical incision

I.
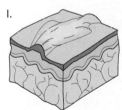
Keloid:
    Enlarging of a scar past
    wound edges due to excess
    collagen formation (more
    prevalent in dark-skinned
    persons)
Example:
    Burn scar

J.
Excoriation:
    Loss of epidermal layers
    exposing the dermis
Example:
    Abrasion

Figure 10-9 Morphology of secondary lesions.

N No skin lesions should be present except for freckles, birthmarks, or nevi (moles), which may be flat or elevated.

A A nonpalpable lesion that is less than 2 cm in size, light brown in colour, and appearing on the face, arms, and hands is abnormal (Figure 10-10A).

P This describes a **lentigo.** It is a hyperpigmented disorder that occurs in body areas that are exposed to the sun. They can increase in size as the person ages.

| E | Examination | N | Normal Findings | A | Abnormal Findings | P | Pathophysiology |

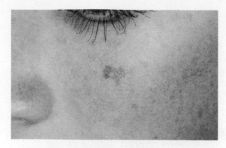

A. A lentigo occurs in sun-exposed areas of the body. *Courtesy of Robert A. Silverman, M.D., Clinical Associate Professor, Department of Pediatrics, Georgetown University.*

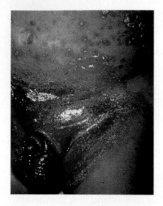

B. Moniliasis. *Courtesy of the Centers for Disease Control and Prevention.*

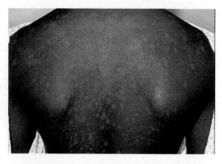

C. Tinea versicolor. *Courtesy of Robert A. Silverman, M.D., Clinical Associate Professor, Department of Pediatrics, Georgetown University.*

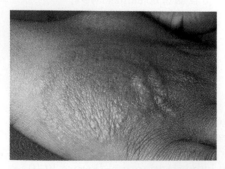

D. Tinea corporis. *Courtesy of Robert A. Silverman, M.D., Clinical Associate Professor, Department of Pediatrics, Georgetown University.*

A   **Intertriginous** (between folds or juxtaposed surfaces of the skin) exudative patches that are beefy red in colour, well demarcated, pruritic, and erythematous are abnormal.

P   Moniliasis, also known as candidiasis, is a yeast infection that may invade numerous areas of the body but normally occurs in the axillae, inframammary areas, groin, and gluteal regions (Figure 10-10B).

A   Scaly macular patches of white, reddish brown, or tan hyperpigmentation, or hypopigmentation of the skin is abnormal (Figure 10-10C).

P   These occur in tinea versicolor, which is caused by superficial fungal infections. The lesions usually occur on the trunk and proximal extremities.

A   A pink to red papulosquamous annular lesion with raised borders that expands peripherally and has a clearing centre is abnormal.

P   Tinea corporis (ringworm) is caused by a *Trichophyton,* a dermatophyte (fungal) infection (Figure 10-10D).

A   Toe web lesions that are macerated and have scaling borders are abnormal.

P   Tinea pedis (athlete's foot) is very common and often erupts in the third and fourth interdigital spaces; with time, the lesions will spread over the plantar surface. Tinea pedis is caused by *Trichophyton mentagrophytes* (Figure 10-10E).

A   A slightly erythematous, rose- or fawn-coloured, round or oval patch that may have slightly raised borders is abnormal (Figure 10-10F).

P   A herald patch is normally found on the trunk and is indicative of pityriasis rosea. This benign, self-limiting condition is often seen in young adults and may resemble ringworm. The herald patch is normally followed in 5 to 10 days by a generalized eruption of similar lesions. The etiology is thought to be viral.

A   Vesicles or bullae that measure 1 to 2 cm and become pustular and rupture easily, discharging straw-coloured fluid are abnormal. The purulent drainage becomes thick as it dries, producing crusts that are light brown or golden honey in colour (Figure 10-10G).

P   Impetigo is usually caused by group A streptococcus or *Staphylococcus aureus* and is highly contagious. It is typically found in preschoolers in the late summer and can be associated with poor hygiene, crowding, contact sports, and minor skin trauma that is untreated.

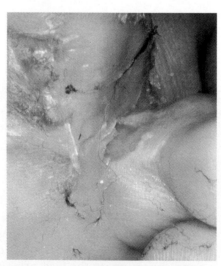

E. Tinea pedis. *Courtesy of Robert A. Silverman, M.D., Clinical Associate Professor, Department of Pediatrics, Georgetown University.*

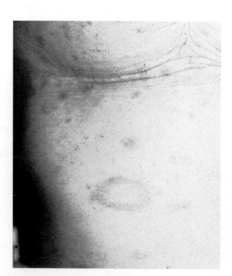

F. Pityriasis Rosea. *Courtesy of the Centers for Disease Control and Prevention.*

Figure 10-10 Common Skin Lesions.

| **E** | **Examination** | **N** | **Normal Findings** | **A** | **Abnormal Findings** | **P** | **Pathophysiology** |

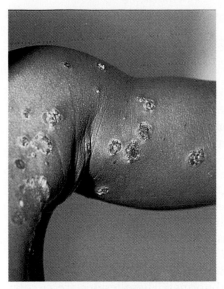

G. Impetigo. *Courtesy of Robert A. Silverman, M.D., Clinical Associate Professor, Department of Pediatrics, Georgetown University.*

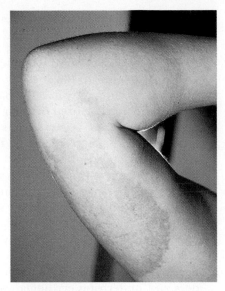

H. Erysipelas. *Courtesy of Robert A. Silverman, M.D., Clinical Associate Professor, Department of Pediatrics, Georgetown University.*

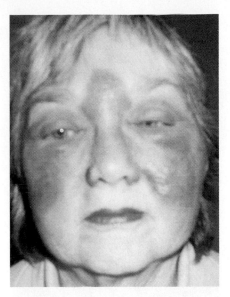

I. Cellulitis

J. Furuncle. *Courtesy of Robert A. Silverman, M.D., Clinical Associate Professor, Department of Pediatrics, Georgetown University.*

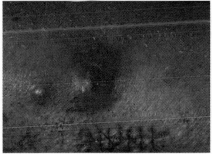

K. Acne papules and nodules are visible on this child's face. *Courtesy of Robert A. Silverman, M.D., Clinical Associate Professor, Department of Pediatrics, Georgetown University.*

Figure 10-10 *continued.*

A Red, shiny, indurated (with a peau d'orange appearance), and warm edematous lesions are abnormal. These lesions may be elevated, have defined margins, and may be painful. Vesicles and bullae may also be present (Figure 10-10H).

P Erysipelas is a type of superficial cellulitis that is usually found in older adults and in young children. Erysipelas can originate in cuts or incisions infected by group A streptococcus, either from the patient's respiratory tract or the respiratory tract of someone who was in close contact with the patient.

A A diffuse red area that is warm, edematous, painful, and indurated is abnormal (Figure 10-10I).

P These findings suggest cellulitis, an acute bacterial infection (usually staphylococcal or streptococcal) of the skin and subcutaneous tissues. Cellulitis can result from trauma to the skin, foreign bodies in the skin, and underlying infection.

A A lesion that starts as a tender, deep-red papule and develops into a well-defined, erythematous, and painful mass with purulent material (Figure 10-10J) is abnormal.

P This describes a furuncle, commonly called a boil. It can be a firm or fluctuant lesion. Furuncles are usually caused by staphylococci.

A A flat or raised lesion with a black interior is abnormal.

P A comedone, or blackhead, is usually seen on the face, chest, shoulders, or back. Comedones are due to increased keratinization in the hair follicle from an unknown etiology. They are associated with acne.

A Comedones accompanied by pustules (with yellow or white centres), red papules (Figure 10-10K), nodules, and cysts are abnormal.

P Acne vulgaris usually occurs in the middle to late teen years and is caused by an inflammation of the sebaceous follicles. Acne vulgaris is associated with hormonal changes. It can be located on the face, chest, shoulders, and back. Lesions that appear punched out may be present from scarring of previously active acne lesions (Figure 10-10L).

P Redness, with dilatation of the blood vessels on the cheeks and forehead, and acne are abnormal.

P Acne rosacea is a chronic inflammation seen primarily in middle-aged and older adults. The cause is unknown, though it is aggravated by alcohol,

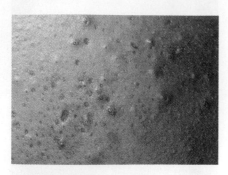

L. Acne scarring. *Courtesy of Robert A. Silverman, M.D., Clinical Associate Professor, Department of Pediatrics, Georgetown University.*

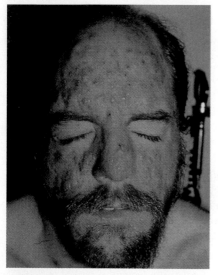

M. Acne rosacea. *Courtesy of Timothy Berger, M.D., San Francisco, CA.*

spicy food, hot liquids, sunlight, extremes in temperature, exercise, and stress (Figure 10-10M).

A   Rosacea that is red or purple on the lower nose and is accompanied by thickening of the affected skin and enlargement of the follicular orifices is abnormal (Figure 10-10N).

P   This is rosacea rhinophyma. The pathophysiology is the same as for rosacea.

A   Reddish salmon-coloured macular lesions are abnormal.

A   Elevated purple to brown lesions (in light-skinned patients) and bluish lesions (in dark-skinned patients) that are spongy, painful, and pruritic are abnormal (Figure 10-10O).

P   Both of these abnormal findings are typical lesions of Kaposi's sarcoma. The reddish lesions are early findings, and the purplish or bluish lesions are more advanced lesions. Kaposi's sarcoma is a neoplastic disorder that is thought to have a genetic, hormonal, and viral etiology. It is frequently found in patients infected with the AIDS virus, immunocompromised patients, and older adults.

A   Pruritic silvery scales of the epidermis that have clearly demarcated borders and underlying erythema are abnormal. These lesions are circular and are found primarily on the elbows, knees, and behind the ears (Figure 10-10P).

P   The etiology of psoriasis is unknown, but it has a genetic component and may be aggravated by cold weather, trauma, and infection.

A   A chronic superficial inflammation of the face, scalp, buttocks, or extremities that evolves into pruritic, red, weeping, crusted lesions is abnormal (Figure 10-10Q).

P   Eczema, also known as atopic dermatitis, is a multifaceted disease process that is often associated with asthma and allergic rhinitis. The etiology is unknown and a family history of related disorders is usually noted.

A   It is abnormal to have edema and erythema as well as red, pruritic vesicles that may discharge an exudate that leads to crusting (Figure 10-10R).

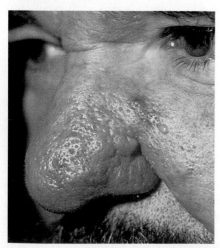

N. Rosacea rhinophyma. *Courtesy of Robert A. Silverman, M.D., Clinical Associate Professor, Department of Pediatrics, Georgetown University.*

O. Kaposi's sarcoma. *Courtesy of Robert A. Silverman, M.D., Clinical Associate Professor, Department of Pediatrics, Georgetown University.*

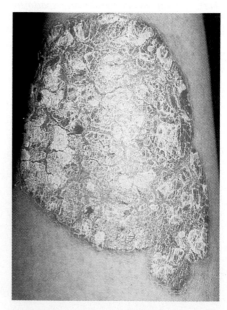

P. Psoriasis. *Courtesy of Robert A. Silverman, M.D., Clinical Associate Professor, Department of Pediatrics, Georgetown University.*

Figure 10-10 *continued.*

| E | Examination | N | Normal Findings | A | Abnormal Findings | P | Pathophysiology |

Q. Eczema. *Courtesy of the Centers for Disease Control and Prevention.*

R. Allergic contact Dermatitis. *Courtesy of the Centers for Disease Control and Prevention.*

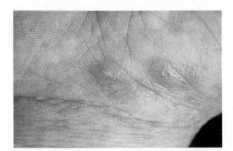

S. Scabies. *Courtesy of Robert A. Silverman, M.D., Clinical Associate Professor, Department of Pediatrics, Georgetown University.*

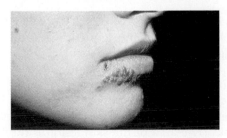

T. Herpes simplex Virus I. *Courtesy of Robert A. Silverman, M.D., Clinical Associate Professor, Department of Pediatrics, Georgetown University.*

P This describes allergic contact dermatitis. In Figure 10-10R, the allergen is poison oak. The patient must come in direct contact with the irritant to develop the dermatitis. Contact dermatitis is also caused by metals, such as nickel, and detergents, cosmetics, rubber, topical medications, food, shampoo, hair dye, and clothing.

A Red, pruritic papules or vesicles with S-shaped or straight-line burrows are abnormal (Figure 10-10S). These lesions can be intensely pruritic.

P Scabies is caused by the *Sarcoptes scabiei* mite, and may be visible as a small, dark area within the vesicle. It is highly contagious and can sometimes be spread through infected clothing or bedding.

A Red papules, vesicles, open sores, and crusting on the face, in the mouth, or on the genitalia are abnormal (Figure 10-10T).

P Herpes simplex virus (HSV) I is usually responsible for these lesions, which are more common on the face and in the mouth. After the initial exposure, the patient can often predict an outbreak because of the presence of burning, itching, or soreness at the eruption site.

A Red macular and papular lesions that are intensely pruritic are abnormal (see Figure 10-10U).

P Varicella, or chickenpox, usually starts on the trunk and proceeds to the extremities. Papules progress to thin-walled vesicles, pustules, and crusts. The patient may exhibit all of the different lesions simultaneously. Varicella is caused by the varicella-zoster virus, which is highly contagious, especially in children.

A Red, extremely painful vesicles with paresthesia that are closely grouped in a dermatomal pattern are abnormal (Figure 10-10V).

P Herpes zoster, or shingles, is caused by a reactivation of the varicella-zoster virus. The virus remains dormant after the initial varicella inoculation. It frequently occurs in elderly individuals. The lesions are similar to those of varicella, but they tend to develop more slowly.

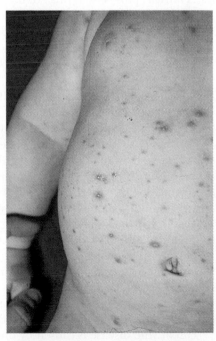

U. Varicella. *Courtesy of Robert A. Silverman, M.D., Clinical Associate Professor, Department of Pediatrics, Georgetown University.*

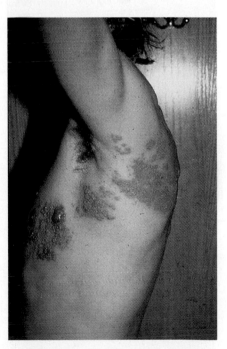

V. Herpes zoster. *Courtesy of Robert A. Silverman, M.D., Clinical Associate Professor, Department of Pediatrics, Georgetown University.*

Figure 10-10 *continued.*

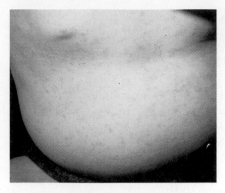

W. Roseola. *Courtesy of Robert A. Silverman, M.D., Clinical Associate Professor, Department of Pediatrics, Georgetown University.*

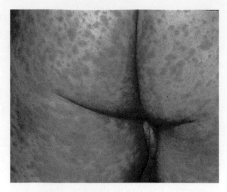

X. Rubeola. *Courtesy of the Centers for Disease Control and Prevention.*

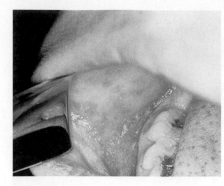

Y. Koplik's Spots in Rubeola. *Courtesy of the Centers for Disease Control and Prevention.*

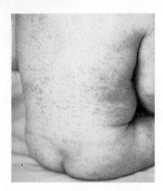

Z. Rubella. *Courtesy of the Centers for Disease Control and Prevention.*

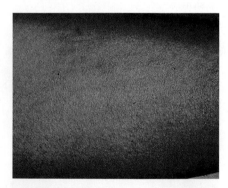

AA. Scarlet Fever. *Courtesy of the Centers for Disease Control and Prevention.*

Figure 10-10 *continued.*

A Discrete, pink macules or papular lesions with clear halos are abnormal. These lesions usually start on the trunk and progress to the face, neck, and extremities a few days after the patient has had a high fever (Figure 10-10W).

P Roseola, or exanthem subitum, is most likely viral in origin.

A A maculopapular rash that is brownish pink and starts around the ears, face, and neck then progresses over the trunk and limbs is abnormal (Figure 10-10X).

P Rubeola (measles) is a viral infection that is highly contagious and is characterized by high fever, cough, rash, and Koplik's spots (whitish-blue spots with a red halo) (Figure 10-10Y) on the buccal or labial mucosa.

P Rubella (German measles) displays a fine, pinkish, macular rash that becomes confluent and pinpoint after the second day (Figure 10-10Z). (The incidence of rubella is very low in Canada since immunization was introduced in 1969. However, it has been reported in pockets of the country where families have not chosen to immunize.[5])

P Rubella is caused by a virus; the rash spreads from the face and neck to the trunk.

A A diffuse, pinkish-red flush of the skin that is confluent over the entire body surface is abnormal (Figure 10-10AA).

P Scarlet fever (scarlatina) is caused by streptococcal bacteria (usually group A) and is associated with a strawberry tongue, circumoral pallor, fever, and chills. Linear petechiae (Pastia's sign) may be found in skin folds such as the antecubital fossa.

A A blotchy, maculopapular rash that may be reticular is abnormal (Figure 10-10BB).

P Erythema infectiosum (fifth disease) is caused by human parvovirus B19. The rash usually starts on the cheeks, giving a "slapped cheek" appearance, and spreads to the arms and trunk. This infection is usually a benign condition but it can cause severe complications in pregnant women.

A A maculopapular rash with erythemic borders that appears first on the wrists, ankles, palms, soles, and forearms and is associated with a high fever is abnormal (Figure 10-10CC).

P Rocky Mountain spotted fever is associated with a history of tick bites. This febrile disease is caused by *Rickettsia rickettsii* and is transmitted by several types of ticks. Severe headaches, myalgia, and vomiting can occur.

A A red papule that progresses to an erythematous circular lesion with central clearing (Figure 10-10DD) is abnormal.

P This lesion is erythema migrans, the characteristic skin lesion of Lyme disease. Lyme disease is caused by the spirochete *Borrelia burgdorferi*. It is transmitted by infected deer and avian ticks. The area of the skin lesion is the site of the tick bite.

| **E** Examination | **N** Normal Findings | **A** Abnormal Findings | **P** Pathophysiology |

BB. Erythema Infectiosums

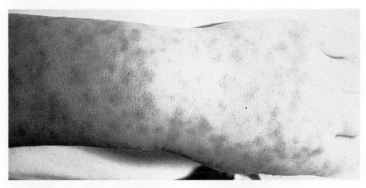

CC. Rocky Mountain Spotted Fever. *Courtesy of the Centers for Disease Control and Prevention*

DD. Erythema Migrans of Lyme Disease. *Courtesy of Robert A. Silverman, M.D., Clinical Associate Professor, Department of Pediatrics, Georgetown University.*

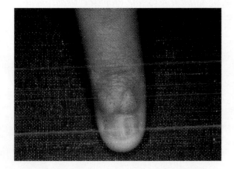

EE. Verruca Vulgaris (Wart). *Courtesy of Robert A. Silverman, M.D., Clinical Associate Professor, Department of Pediatrics, Georgetown University.*

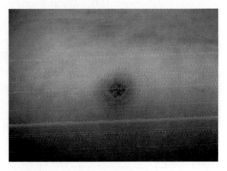

FF. Plantar Wart. *Courtesy of Robert A. Silverman, M.D., Clinical Associate Professor, Department of Pediatrics, Georgetown University*

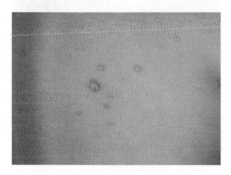

GG. Molluscum Contagiosum. *Courtesy of Robert A. Silverman, M.D., Clinical Associate Professor, Department of Pediatrics, Georgetown University.*

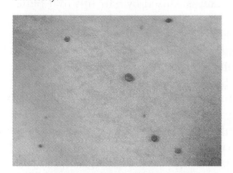

HH. Skin Tags. *Courtesy of Robert A. Silverman, M.D., Clinical Associate Professor, Department of Pediatrics, Georgetown University.*

Figure 10-10 *continued.*

A   Flesh-coloured, hyperkeratotic papules (Figure 10-10EE) that have black dots on them are abnormal.

P   Common warts, or verruca vulgaris, are viral in origin. The black dots represent thrombosed blood vessels. Warts that occur on the feet are called plantar warts (Figure 10-10FF).

A   Discrete, flesh-coloured, dome-shaped papules that are slightly umbilicated in the centre (see Figure 10-10GG) are abnormal.

P   This describes molluscum contagiosum, a self-limiting viral infection. The papules may appear anywhere on the body except the palmar and plantar surfaces. When found on the genitalia of children, sexual abuse must be considered.

A   A flesh-coloured or brown pedunculated nodule is abnormal.

P   Skin tags, or acrochordon, are benign nodules (Figure 10-10HH). They are frequently removed if they are in an area that receives repeated movement, such as a bra line, or if they are annoying to the patient.

A   Small, pinkish-brown papules that are slightly raised and retract beneath the skin when compressed are abnormal.

P   These are dermatofibromas, or benign papules. Occasionally they may also be scaly in appearance.

A   Pruritic, red **wheal**s (urticarial rash) that vary in size from very small to large and are sometimes accompanied by maculopapular eruptions, vesicles, and bullae are abnormal (Figure 10-10II).

P   Urticaria can be acute or chronic in nature. This itchy skin lesion is linked to histamine release within the body (Figure 10-10JJ). Exposure to food, drugs, infections, chemicals, physical stimuli (pressure, sun, cold weather or water, exercise) are among the causes of urticaria.

A   Lesions that are brownish tan, red, white, blue, pink, purple, or grey and that have irregular borders and notching are abnormal. The lesions can be flat or elevated.

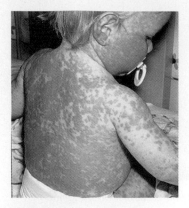

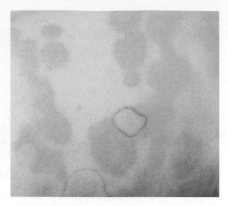

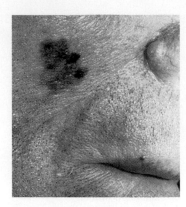

II. Exanthematous Drug Eruption. *Courtesy of Robert A. Silverman, M.D., Clinical Associate Professor, Department of Pediatrics, Georgetown University.*

JJ. Urticaria. *Courtesy of Robert A. Silverman, M.D., Clinical Associate Professor, Department of Pediatrics, Georgetown University.*

KK. Lentigo Malignant Melanoma. *Courtesy of Robert A. Silverman, M.D., Clinical Associate Professor, Department of Pediatrics, Georgetown University.*

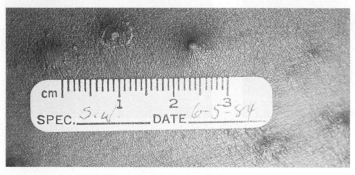

LL. Folliculitis. *Courtesy of Robert A. Silverman, M.D., Clinical Associate Professor, Department of Pediatrics, Georgetown University.*

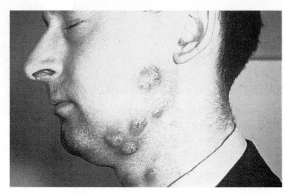

MM. Tinea Barbae. *Courtesy of the Centers for Disease Control and Prevention.*

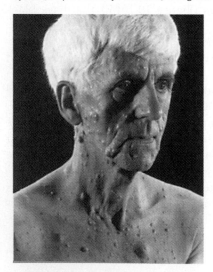

NN. Type I Neurofibromatosis (von Recklinghausen's Disease)

Figure 10-10 *continued.*

P Malignant melanoma is a cancerous lesion that is associated with repeated sun exposure. Malignant melanoma occurs earlier in life, spreads rapidly, and can occur on any part of the body. Individuals with light skin and blue eyes are particularly at risk for malignant melanoma. These neoplastic lesions can also be related to precancerous lesions such as nevi. Figure 10-10KK depicts lentigo malignant melanoma.

A Perifollicular papules are abnormal.

P Pseudofolliculitis barbae, or ingrown hair, is caused by hair tips that penetrate into the skin rather than exiting through the follicular orifice. It usually occurs in the beard area, particularly in Black men, because their hair may be curly and exit the skin at a sharp angle.

A Pustules at the opening of the hair follicle are abnormal (Figure 10-10LL).

P Folliculitis is an inflammation of the hair follicle. Figure 10-10LL depicts a staphylococcal folliculitis; however, the causative agent may be fungal and therefore called tinea barbae (Figure 10-10MM).

A Multiple pedunculated papules, nodules, or tumours, which are violaceous and soft (Figure 10-10NN), are abnormal.

P This describes neurofibromas, one of the hallmark findings of neurofibromatosis, type I (or von Recklinghausen's disease). Six or more café au lait spots are concurrently found on the patient's skin in neurofibromatosis, type I.

E	Examination	N	Normal Findings	A	Abnormal Findings	P	Pathophysiology

Nursing Tip

Wound Healing

Wound healing includes **re-epithelialization,** which is the migration of epithelial cells inward from the wound edges and from any surrounding hair follicles or eccrine glands. Scab (eschar) formation may prohibit re-epithelialization because of diminished moisture. Granulation tissue is a combination of inflammatory cells, new vessels, and white blood cells that form a matrix at the base of the wound, providing a foundation on which re-epithelialization occurs. New scars are thick, darkened, and vascular in appearance. Over time, the scar tissue flattens and becomes less vascular; however, old scars remain slightly darker or discoloured compared to the surrounding tissue.

Nursing Alert

Stages of Pressure Ulcers

Defined by the National Pressure Ulcer Advisory Panel[6]

Stage 1 An observable pressure-related alteration of intact skin whose indicators as compared to an adjacent or opposite area on the body may include changes in one or more of the following: skin temperature (warmth or coolness), tissue consistency (firm or boggy feel), and/or sensation (pain, itching). The ulcer appears as a defined area of persistent redness in lightly pigmented skin, whereas in darker skin tones, the ulcer may appear with persistent red, blue, or purple hues (Figure 10-11A).

Stage 2 Partial-thickness skin loss involving epidermis, dermis, or both. The ulcer is superficial and presents clinically as an abrasion, blister, or shallow crater (Figure 10-11B).

Stage 3 Full-thickness skin loss involving damage to, or necrosis of, subcutaneous tissue that may extend down to, but not through, underlying fascia. The ulcer presents clinically as a deep crater with or without undermining of adjacent tissue (Figure 10-11C).

Stage 4 Full-thickness skin loss with extensive destruction, tissue necrosis, or damage to muscle, bone, or supporting structures (e.g., tendon, joint, capsule). Undermining and sinus tracts also may be associated with Stage 4 pressure ulcers (Figure 10-11D).

Note: Wounds that are covered with debris and/or black discoloured tissue cannot be staged accurately because the full extent of the wound is not visualized.

Nursing Tip

Wound Evaluation

Remove the dressing from the wound and assess the wound for location, colour, drainage, odour, size, and depth. Measure the borders of the wound with a centimetre ruler and draw a picture in your notes, if necessary, to depict necrotic areas, drains, and so on. Describe the nature of any wound exudate if there is any. **Sanguinous** exudate is bloody; **serosanguineous** exudate contains both serum and blood; **serous** exudate is straw-coloured serum; and **mucopurulent** drainage contains mucus and pus (a protein-rich liquid inflammation product made up of leukocytes, serum, and cellular debris).

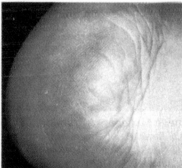

A. Stage 1

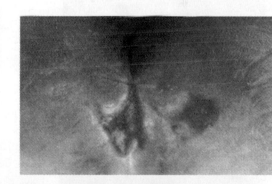

B. Stage 2

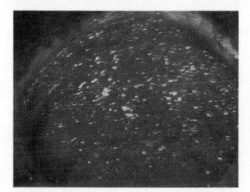

C. Stage 3

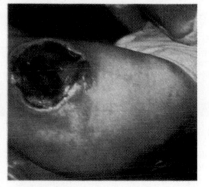

D. Stage 4.

Figure 10-11 Pressure Ulcers. *Courtesy of Emory University Hospital, Atlanta, Georgia.*

A. First-Degree Burn

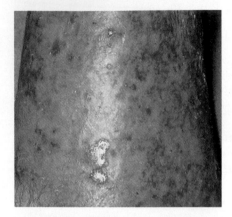

B. Second-Degree Burn

C. Third-Degree Burn

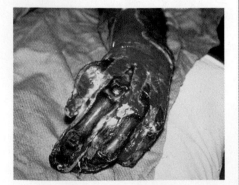

D. Fourth-Degree Burn

Figure 10-12 Types of Burns. *Courtesy of the Phoenix Society for Burn Survivors, Inc.*

Nursing Tip

The Braden Scale for Predicting Pressure Sore Risk (Table 10-3) enables nurses to identify patients at risk of pressure sores; accurate risk assessment helps to determine the nursing care plan to ensure the health of the patient.

Nursing Tip

Advise patients to follow the Canadian Cancer Society SunSense[7] Guidelines to reduce the risk of skin cancer.

- Reduce sun exposure between 11 a.m. and 4 p.m. or any time of the day when the UV Index™ is 3 or more.
- Seek shade or create your own shade by using an umbrella.
- *SLIP!* on clothing to cover your arms and legs—loose fitting, tightly woven, and lightweight.
- *SLAP!* on a wide-brimmed hat that covers the head, face, ears, and neck.
- *SLOP!* on a broad spectrum (anti UVA and UVB) sunscreen with SPF (sun protection factor) 15 or higher and SPF 30 if working outdoors or if outside for most of the day. Apply sunscreen generously, 20 minutes before outdoor activities. Reapply at least every 2 hours and after swimming or exercise that causes perspiration.
- Avoid artificial tanning equipment, beds, and lamps.
- Use sunglasses with even shading, medium to dark lenses (grey, brown or green tint), with UVA and UVB protection.

Nursing Tip

Identifying Burns

A burn patient frequently has varying degrees of injury on the body. Parts of the body may have first-degree burns, and other parts may have second-, third-, or fourth-degree burns. The following descriptions and photographs will assist you in identifying burn injuries:

First-Degree Burn (Figure 10-12A): the epidermis is injured or destroyed; there may be some damage to the dermis; hair follicles and sweat glands are intact; the skin is red and dry; painful.

Second-Degree Burn (Figure 10-12B): also called partial-thickness burn; the epidermis and upper layers of the dermis are destroyed; the deeper dermis is injured; hair follicles, sweat glands, and nerve endings are intact; the skin is red and blistery with exudate; painful.

Third-Degree Burn (Figure 10-12C): also called full-thickness burn; the epidermis and dermis are destroyed; subcutaneous tissue may be injured; hair follicles, sweat glands, and nerve endings are destroyed; the skin is white, red, black, tan, or brown with a leathery-looking appearance; painless because nerve endings are destroyed.

Fourth-Degree Burn (Figure 10-12D): the epidermis and dermis are destroyed; subcutaneous tissue, muscle, and bone may be injured; hair follicles, sweat glands, and nerve endings are destroyed; the skin is white, red, black, tan, or brown with exposed and damaged subcutaneous tissue, muscle, or bone; painless.

TABLE 10-3 BRADEN SCALE FOR PREDICTING PRESSURE SORE RISK

Patient's Name _____   Evaluator's Name _____   Date of Assessment _____

	1	2	3	4
SENSORY PERCEPTION ability to respond meaningfully to pressure-related discomfort	**1. Completely Limited** Unresponsive (does not moan, flinch, or grasp) to painful stimuli, due to diminished level of consciousness or sedation OR limited ability to feel pain over most of body.	**2. Very Limited** Responds only to painful stimuli. Cannot communicate discomfort except by moaning or restlessness OR has a sensory impairment which limits the ability to feel pain or discomfort over 1/2 of body.	**3. Slightly Limited** Responds to verbal commands, but cannot always communicate discomfort or the need to be turned OR has some sensory impairment which limits ability to feel pain or discomfort in 1 or 2 extremities.	**4. No Impairment** Responds to verbal commands. Has no sensory deficit which would limit ability to feel or voice pain or discomfort.
MOISTURE degree to which skin is exposed to moisture	**1. Constantly Moist** Skin is kept moist almost constantly by perspiration, urine, etc. Dampness is detected every time patient is moved or turned.	**2. Very Moist** Skin is often, but not always moist. Linen must be changed at least once a shift.	**3. Occasionally Moist** Skin is occasionally moist, requiring an extra linen change approximately once a day	**4. Rarely Moist** Skin is usually dry, linen only requires changing at routine intervals.
ACTIVITY degree of physical activity	**1. Bedfast** Confined to bed.	**2. Chairfast** Ability to walk severely limited or nonexistent. Cannot bear own weight and/or must be assisted into chair or wheelchair.	**3. Walks Occasionally** Walks occasionally during day, but for very short distances, with or without assistance. Spends majority of each shift in bed or chair.	**4. Walks Frequently** Walks outside room at least twice a day and inside room at least once every two hours during waking hours.
MOBILITY ability to change and control body position	**1. Completely Immobile** Does not make even slight changes in body or extremity position without assistance.	**2. Very Limited** Makes occasional slight changes in body or extremity position but unable to make frequent or significant changes independently.	**3. Slightly Limited** Makes frequent though slight changes in body or extremity position independently.	**4. No Limitation** Makes major and frequent changes in position without assistance.
NUTRITION usual food intake pattern	**1. Very Poor** Never eats a complete meal. Rarely eats more than 1/3 of any food offered. Eats 2 servings or less of protein (meat or dairy products) per day. Takes fluids poorly. Does not take a liquid dietary supplement OR is NPO and/or maintained on clear liquids or IVs for more than 5 days.	**2. Probably Inadequate** Rarely eats a complete meal and generally eats only about 1/2 of any food offered. Protein intake includes only 3 servings of meat or dairy products per day. Occasionally will take a dietary supplement OR receives less than optimum amount of liquid diet or tube feeding.	**3. Adequate** Eats over half of most meals. Eats a total of 4 servings of protein (meat, dairy products) per day. Occasionally will refuse a meal, but will usually take a supplement when offered OR is on a tube feeding or TPN regimen which probably meets most of nutritional needs.	**4. Excellent** Eats most of every meal. Never refuses a meal. Usually eats a total of 4 or more servings of meat and dairy products. Occasionally eats between meals. Does not require supplementation.

continues

TABLE 10-3 BRADEN SCALE FOR PREDICTING PRESSURE SORE RISK continued

FRICTION & SHEAR	1. Problem	2. Potential Problem	3. No Apparent Problem
	Requires moderate to maximum assistance in moving. Complete lifting without sliding against sheets is impossible. Frequently slides down in bed or chair, requiring frequent repositioning with maximum assistance. Spasticity, contractures or agitation leads to almost constant friction.	Moves feebly or requires minimum assistance. During a move skin probably slides to some extent against sheets, chair, restraints, or other devices. Maintains relatively good position in chair or bed most of the time but occasionally slides down.	Moves in bed and in chair independently and has sufficient muscle strength to lift up completely during move. Maintains good position in bed or chair.

Total Score

Source: http://www.bradenscale.com/bradenscale.htm

Palpation of the Skin

Moisture

E Palpate all nonmucous membrane skin surfaces for moisture using the dorsal surfaces of the hands and fingers.

N Normally, the skin is dry with a minimum of perspiration. Moisture on the skin will vary from one body area to another, with perspiration normally present on the hands, axilla, face, and in between the skin folds. Moisture also varies with changes in environment, muscular activity, body temperature, stress, and activity levels. Body temperature is regulated by the skin's production of perspiration, which evaporates to cool the body.

A Excessive dryness of the skin, **xerosis,** as evidenced by flaking of the stratum corneum and associated pruritus is abnormal.

P Hypothyroidism and exposure to extreme cold and dry climates can lead to xerosis.

A Very dry, large scales that are light coloured or brown are abnormal (Figure 10-13).

P Ichthyosis vulgaris is a skin abnormality originating from a keratin disorder. It can be associated with atopic dermatitis.

A **Diaphoresis** is the profuse production of perspiration. **Hyperhidrosis** is abnormally increased axillary, plantar, facial and/or truncal perspiration, in excess of that required for regulation of body temperature.

P Causes of diaphoresis include hyperthyroidism, increased metabolic rate, sepsis, anxiety, or pain. Primary hyperhidrosis is idiopathic; secondary hyperhidrosis can be related to endocrine disorders, obesity, or menopause.

Temperature

E Palpate all nonmucosal skin surfaces for temperature using the dorsal surfaces of the hands and fingers.

N Skin surface temperature should be warm and equal bilaterally. Hands and feet may be slightly cooler than the rest of the body.

A **Hypothermia** is a cooling of the skin and may be generalized or localized.

P Generalized hypothermia is indicative of shock or some other type of central circulatory dysfunction. Localized hypothermia is indicative of arterial insufficiency in the affected area.

A Generalized **hyperthermia** is the excessive warming of the skin and may be generalized or localized.

P Generalized hyperthermia may be indicative of a febrile state, hyperthyroidism, or increased metabolic function caused by exercise. Localized hyperthermia may be caused by infection, trauma, sunburn, or windburn.

Tenderness

E Palpate skin surfaces for tenderness using the dorsal surfaces of the hands and fingers.

N Skin surfaces should be nontender.

A Tenderness over the skin structures can be discrete and localized or generalized.

P Discrete tenderness may indicate a localized infection such as cellulitis; generalized tenderness can indicate systemic illness such as lymphoma or allergic reaction.

Figure 10-13 Ichthyosis Vulgaris. Courtesy of Robert A. Silverman, M.D., Clinical Associate Professor, Department Of Pediatrics, Georgetown University.

| E | Examination | N | Normal Findings | A | Abnormal Findings | P | Pathophysiology |

Texture

E **1.** Evaluate the texture of the skin using the finger pads.
   2. Evaluate surfaces such as the abdomen and medial surfaces of the arms first.
   3. Compare these areas to areas that are covered with hair.

N Skin should normally feel smooth, even, and firm except where there is significant hair growth. A certain amount of roughness can be normal.

A Roughness can occur on exposed areas such as the elbows, the soles of the feet, and the palms of the hands.

P Roughness can be due to wool clothing, cold weather, occupational exposures, or the use of soap. Generalized roughness can be associated with systemic diseases such as scleroderma, hypothyroidism, and amyloidosis. Localized thickening and roughness can be a result of chronic pruritus (lichenification) due to scratching, which causes a thickening of the epidermis.

A Areas of hyperkeratosis and increased roughness that are found in the lower extremities are abnormal.

P This type of texture change may be indicative of peripheral vascular disease, which causes abated circulation and diminished nourishment of cutaneous layers.

A The skin can feel very soft and silklike.

P Generalized softness can result from hyperthyroidism secondary to elevated metabolism.

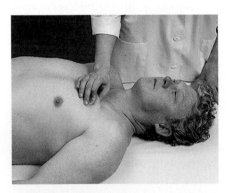

A. Skin Turgor

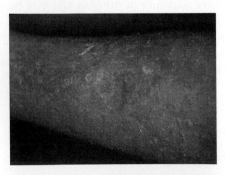

B. Pitting Edema. *Courtesy of Robert A. Silverman, M.D., Clinical Associate Professor, Department of Pediatrics, Georgetown University.*

Figure 10-14 Assessment of Skin Turgor and Edema.

Turgor

Palpate the skin **turgor,** or elasticity, which reflects the skin's state of hydration.

E **1.** Pinch a small section of the patient's skin between your thumb and forefinger. The anterior chest, under the clavicle, and the abdomen are optimal areas to assess.
   2. Slowly release the skin.
   3. Observe the speed with which the skin returns to its original contour when released (Figure 10-14A).

N When the skin is released, it should return to its original contour rapidly.

A Decreased skin turgor is present when the skin is released and it remains pinched, and slowly returns to its original contour.

P **Dehydration,** or lack of fluid in the tissues, is the main cause of decreased skin turgor. The aging process and scleroderma can also decrease the turgor of the skin.

A Increased turgor or tension causes the skin to return to its original contour too quickly.

P Increased turgor can be indicative of connective tissue disease caused by an increase of granulation tissue.

Edema

Palpate the skin for **edema,** or accumulation of fluid in the intercellular spaces.

E **1.** Firmly imprint your thumb against a dependent portion of the body (such as the arms, hands, legs, feet, ankle, or sacrum) for five seconds (see Figure 10-14B).
   2. Release pressure.
   3. Observe for an indentation on the skin.

| E | Examination | N | Normal Findings | A | Abnormal Findings | P | Pathophysiology |

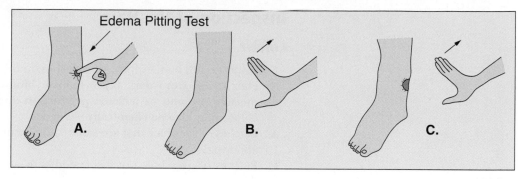

Edema Pitting Test

A. B. C.

C.

Figure 10-14 *continued.*
Source: http://www.moondragon.org/images/edemapitting.jpg

4. Rate the degree of edema. Pitting edema is rated on a 4-point scale:
   +0, no pitting
   +1, 1 cm pitting (mild)
   +2, 2 cm pitting (moderate)
   +3, 3 cm pitting (significant)
   +4, greater than 4 cm pitting (severe)
5. Check for symmetry and measure circumference of affected extremities.

N Edema is not normally present.

A Edema is present if the skin feels puffy and tight. It can be localized in one area (Figure 10-14C) or generalized throughout the body. There are many different types of edema (Table 10-4).

P Localized edema may be due to dependency; however, generalized or bilateral edema is caused by increased hydrostatic pressure, decreased capillary osmotic pressure, increased capillary permeability, or obstruction to lymph flow. This occurs in congestive heart failure or kidney failure.

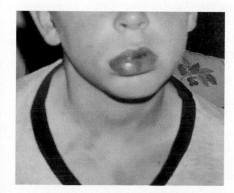

Figure 10-15 Angioedema of the Lips.

TABLE 10-4	Types of Edema
TYPE	**DESCRIPTION**
Pitting	Edema that is present when an indentation remains on the skin after applying pressure
Nonpitting	Edema that is firm with discoloration or thickening of the skin; results when serum proteins coagulate in tissue spaces
Angioedema	Recurring episodes of noninflammatory swelling of skin, brain, viscera, and mucous membranes (Figure 10-15); onset may be rapid, with resolution requiring hours to days
Dependent	Localized increase of extracellular fluid volume in a dependent limb or area
Inflammatory	Swelling due to an extracellular fluid effusion into the tissue surrounding an area of inflammation
Noninflammatory	Swelling or effusion due to mechanical or other causes not related to congestion or inflammation
Lymphedema	Edema due to the obstruction of a lymphatic vessel

Inspection of the Hair

Colour

E Inspect scalp hair, eyebrows, eyelashes, and body hair for colour.

N Hair varies from dark black to pale blond(e) based on the amount of melanin present. As melanin production diminishes, hair turns grey. Hair colour may also be chemically changed.

A Patches of grey hair that are isolated or occur in conjunction with a scar are abnormal.

P Patches of grey hair not associated with aging can be indicative of nerve damage.

Distribution

E Evaluate the distribution of hair on the body, eyebrows, face, and scalp.

N The body is covered in vellus hair. Terminal hair is found in the eyebrows, eyelashes, and scalp, and in the axilla and pubic areas after puberty. Males may experience a certain degree of normal balding and may also develop terminal facial and chest hair.

A The absence of pubic hair, unless purposefully removed, is abnormal in the adult.

P Diminished or absent pubic hair may be indicative of endocrine disorders, such as anterior pituitary adenomas, or chemotherapy.

A Male or female pattern baldness (**alopecia**) may be abnormal in some individuals if associated with pathology. Alopecia areata is a circumscribed bald area (Figure 10-16A).

P Androgenetic alopecia is a common, progressive hair loss that is caused by a combination of genetic predisposition and androgenetic effects on the hair follicle; however, alopecia may be secondary to chemotherapy and radiation, infection, stress, drug reactions, lupus, and traction. A pathological etiology of alopecia should be ruled out.

A Total scalp baldness, or alopecia totalis, is abnormal.

P Autoimmune diseases, emotional crisis, stress, or heredity can cause alopecia totalis.

A Hair loss in linear formations is abnormal (Figure 10-16B).

P Linear alopecia can be caused by frequent pressure on hair follicles, leading to their inability to produce new hair. In addition, traction alopecia can be caused by using curlers or wearing the hair in a tightly pulled ponytail where traction is continually applied, which is common among individuals who wear cornrows.

A Excess facial and body hair is abnormal (Figure 10-16C).

P **Hirsutism** is manifested by excessive body hair. It is indicative of endocrine disorders such as hypersecretion of adrenocortical androgens. In women, this disorder is manifested as excess facial and chest hair.

P Hirsutism can also result as a side effect of medications such as cyclosporin.

A Areas of broken-off hairs in irregular patterns with scaliness but no infection are abnormal (Figure 10-16D).

P Trichotillomania is the manipulation of the hair by twisting and pulling, leading to reduced hair mass. This can be an unconscious action or a sign of psychiatric illness.

A Broken-off hairs with scaliness and follicular inflammation is abnormal (Figure 10-16E). The area may be painful and purulent with boggy nodules.

P Tinea capitis (ringworm) is a fungal infection, frequently caused by dermatophytic trichomycosis.

| E | **Examination** | N | **Normal Findings** | A | **Abnormal Findings** | P | **Pathophysiology** |

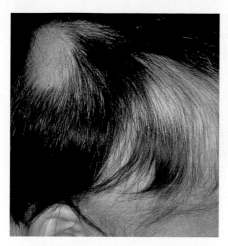

A. Alopecia Areata. *Courtesy of Robert A. Silverman, M.D., Clinical Associate Professor, Department of Pediatrics, Georgetown University.*

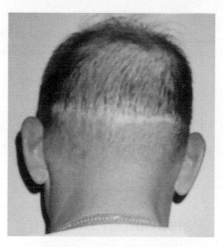

B. Linear alopecia developed in this man from daily wearing of his military uniform cap.

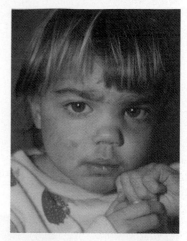

C. Hirsutism caused by the drug cyclosporin. *Courtesy of Robert A. Silverman, M.D., Clinical Associate Professor, Department of Pediatrics, Georgetown University.*

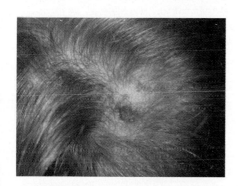

D. Trichotillomania. *Courtesy of Robert A. Silverman, M.D., Clinical Associate Professor, Department of Pediatrics, Georgetown University.*

E. Tinea Capitis. *Courtesy of Robert A. Silverman, M.D., Clinical Associate Professor, Department of Pediatrics, Georgetown University.*

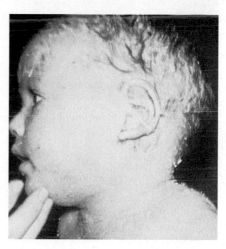

F. Seborrheic Dermatitis. *Courtesy of the Centers for Disease Control and Prevention.*

Figure 10-16 Abnormalities of the Head and Scalp.

Figure 10-17 Head Lice. *Courtesy of Hogil Pharmaceutical Corporation.*

A The scalp is covered with yellow-brown scales and crusts. The scalp may be oily. Edema may be present (Figure 10-16F).

P Seborrheic dermatitis is caused by increased production of sebum by the scalp.

Lesions

E 1. Don gloves and lift the scalp hair by segments.
   2. Evaluate the scalp for lesions or signs of infestation.

N The scalp should be pale white to pink in light-skinned individuals and light brown in dark-skinned individuals. There should be no signs of infestation or lesions. Seborrhea, commonly known as dandruff, may be present.

A Abnormal manifestations include head lice.

P Head lice (pediculosis capitis) may be distinguished from dandruff in that dandruff can be easily removed from the scalp or hair whereas nits (Figure 10-17), which are the lice larvae, are attached to the hair shaft and are difficult to remove. Both seborrhea and head lice may cause itching.

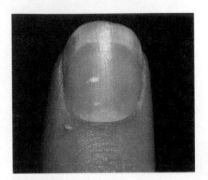

A. Leukonychia

B. Leukonychia Totalis. *Courtesy of Robert A. Silverman, M.D., Clinical Associate Professor, Department of Pediatrics, Georgetown University.*

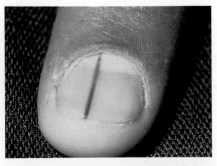

C. Longitudinal Melanonychia. *Courtesy of Robert A. Silverman, M.D., Clinical Associate Professor, Department of Pediatrics, Georgetown University.*

Figure 10-18 Abnormal Colour Changes of the Nailbed.

Palpation of the Hair

Texture

E 1. Palpate the hair between your fingertips.
   2. Note the condition of the hair from the scalp to the end of the hair.

N Hair may feel thin, straight, coarse, thick, or curly. It should be shiny and resilient when traction is applied and should not come out in clumps in your hands.

A Brittle hair that easily breaks off when pulled or hair that is listless and dull is abnormal.

P Brittle, dull hair, or hair that is broken off can be indicative of malnutrition, hyperthyroidism, use of chemicals such as permanents, or infections secondary to damage of the hair follicle.

Inspection of the Nails

Colour

E 1. Inspect the fingernails and toenails, noting the colour of the nails.
   2. Check capillary refill by depressing the nail until blanching occurs.
   3. Release the nail and evaluate the time required for the nail to return to its previous colour.
   4. Perform a capillary refill check on all four extremities.

N Normally, the nails have a pink cast in light-skinned individuals and are brown in dark-skinned individuals. Capillary refill is an indicator of peripheral circulation. Normal capillary refill may vary with age, but colour should return to normal within 2 or 3 seconds.

A White striations or dots in the nailbed are abnormal (Figure 10-18A).

P Leukonychia (Mees bands) may result from trauma, infections, vascular diseases, psoriasis, and arsenic poisoning.

A An entire nail plate that is white is abnormal (Figure 10-18B).

P Leukonychia totalis may result from hypercalcemia, hypochromic anemia, leprosy, hepatic cirrhosis, and arsenic poisoning.

A A brown colour in the nail plate is abnormal (Figure 10-18C).

P Melanonychia may result from Addison's disease and malaria.

A Bluish nails are abnormal.

P Bluish nails may result from cyanosis, venous stasis, and sulfuric acid poisoning.

A Red or brown linear streaks in the nailbed are abnormal (Figure 10-18D).

P Splinter hemorrhages can result from subacute bacterial endocarditis, mitral stenosis, trichinosis, cirrhosis, and nonspecific causes.

| E | **Examination** | N | **Normal Findings** | A | **Abnormal Findings** | P | **Pathophysiology** |

D. Splinter Hemorrhages

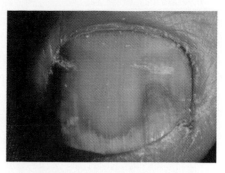

E. Onychomycosis. *Courtesy of Robert A. Silverman, M.D., Clinical Associate Professor, Department of Pediatrics, Georgetown University.*

Figure 10-18 *continued.*

Normal nail angle

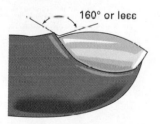

160°

Curved nail variant of normal

160° or less

Early clubbing

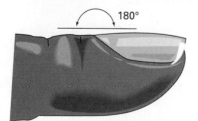

180°

Figure 10-19 Nail Angles.

A It is abnormal if the proximal end of the nailbed is white and the distal portion is pink.

P Lindsey's nails (half-and-half nails) can result from chronic renal failure and hypoalbuminemia.

A A yellow or white hue in a hyperkeratotic nailbed is abnormal (Figure 10-18E).

P Onychomycosis is a fungal infection of the nail.

Shape and Configuration

E 1. Assess the fingernails and toenails for shape, configuration, and consistency.
2. View the profile of the middle finger and evaluate the angle of the nail base.

N The nail surface should be smooth and slightly rounded or flat. Curved nails are a normal variant. Nail thickness should be uniform throughout, with no splintering or brittle edges. The angle of the nail base should be approximately 160° (Figure 10-19). Longitudinal ridging is a normal variant.

A Thin nail plates with cuplike depressions and concave, or spoon-shaped, nails are abnormal (Figure 10-20A).

P Koilonychia can result from iron deficiency anemia, chronic infections, malnutrition, or Raynaud's disease.

A An angle of the nail base greater than 160° (Figure 10-20B), along with sponginess of the nailbed is abnormal.

P Clubbing can result from long-standing hypoxia and lung cancer.

A A transverse furrow in the nail plate is abnormal (Figure 10-20C).

P Beau's line is caused by an arrest of nail growth at the matrix. It can be associated with an acute phase of an infectious disease, malnutrition, and anemia.

A Separation of the nail from the nailbed is abnormal (Figure 10-20D).

P Onycholysis can result from hypo- and hyperthyroidism, repeated trauma, Raynaud's disease, syphilis, eczema, and acrocyanosis.

A Painful, red swelling of the nail fold is abnormal (Figure 10-20E).

P Paronychia can be caused by *Candida albicans,* bacteria, and repeated exposure of the nails to moisture.

A Numerous horizontal depression ridges or a depression down the middle of the nail is abnormal.

P Habit tic deformity is caused by continuous picking of the cuticle and nail by a finger of the same hand. Trauma ensues to the nail base and nail matrix.

A Purpura or ecchymosis under the nail plate is abnormal (Figure 10-20F).

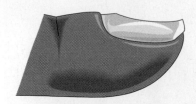

A. Koilonychia

B. Clubbing. *Courtesy of Robert A. Silverman, M.D., Clinical Associate Professor, Department of Pediatrics, Georgetown University.*

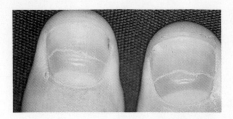

C. Beau's Lines. *Courtesy of Robert A. Silverman, M.D., Clinical Associate Professor, Department of Pediatrics, Georgetown University.*

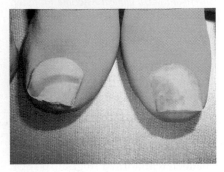

D. Onycholysis with Hyperkeratosis. *Courtesy of Judith A. Mysliborski, M.D., Albany, NY.*

E. Paronychia

F. Subungual Hematoma. *Courtesy of Robert A. Silverman, M.D., Clinical Associate Professor, Department of Pediatrics, Georgetown University.*

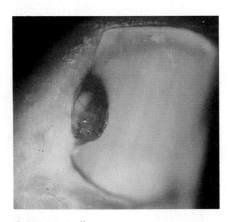

G. Ingrown Nail.

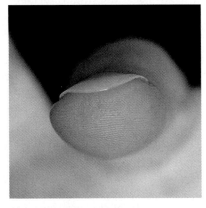

H. Eggshell Nails

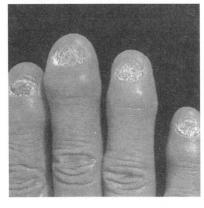

I. Onychatrophia

Figure 10-20 Abnormalities of the Shape and Configuration of the Nail.

P Subungual hematoma is caused by trauma to the digit and nail, leading to hemorrhage into the matrix and nailbed.

P The distal portion of the nail plate is embedded in periungual tissues (Figure 10-20G). The periungual tissues may become inflamed and have purulent discharge.

A Onychocryptosis (ingrown nail) is caused by growth of the distal nail plate into periungual tissues, secondary to increased lateral nail pressure, resulting in trauma to the tissues.

A Nails that become white, thin, and curved under the free edge are abnormal (Figure 10-20H).

P Eggshell nails may be caused by systemic diseases, medications, dietary deficiencies, nervous disorders, or sleeping with the hand fisted.

A Nails that atrophy, shrink, and fall off are abnormal (Figure 10-20I).

| **E** | **Examination** | **N** | **Normal Findings** | **A** | **Abnormal Findings** | **P** | **Pathophysiology** |

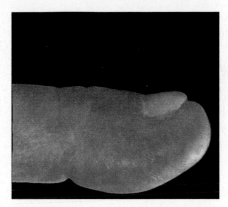

J. Onychauxis

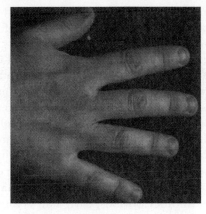

K. Onychophagy

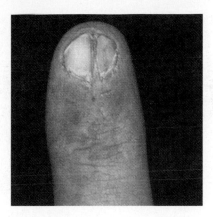

L. Onychorrhexis

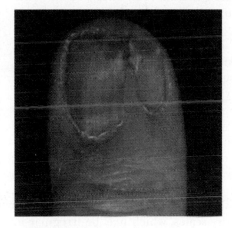

M. Pterygium

Figure 10-20 *continued.*

P Onychatrophia may result from injury to the nail matrix and from systemic diseases.
A Nails that hypertrophy (become abnormally thick and overgrown) are abnormal (Figure 10-20J).
P Onychauxis is caused by systemic infection, electrolyte imbalance, and hereditary predisposition.
A Nails deformed in shape are abnormal (Figure 10-20K).
P Onychophagy results from excessive biting of the nails.
A A nail that is split or brittle with lengthwise ridges is abnormal (Figure 10-20L).
P Onychorrhexis may result from trauma to the nail, toxic exposure to solvents, or harsh nail filing.
A It is abnormal for the cuticle to overgrow the nail and become attached to the nail (Figure 10-20M). The cuticle growth may persist to the free edge.
P Pterygium can occur in Raynaud's disease.

Palpation of the Nails

Texture

E 1. Palpate the nail base between your thumb and index finger.
   2. Note the consistency.
N The nail base should be firm on palpation.
A A spongy nail base is an early indication of clubbing.
P Clubbing is the result of impaired tissue oxygenation over a prolonged period of time, as in chronic bronchitis, emphysema, and heart disease. See Chapters 15 and 16 for further information.

GERONTOLOGICAL VARIATIONS

The most visible signs of aging are manifested in the skin and hair. These changes include wrinkles, sagging skin folds, greying hair, and hair loss. Also, skin disorders are more likely to occur as a person ages. Light-skinned individuals appear to manifest the changes of aging more rapidly than do dark-skinned individuals, and these changes are accelerated by sun exposure.

With aging, the epidermis thins, and elastic fibres that provide support to the dermis degenerate and lead to sagging skin folds. The number of sweat and sebaceous glands diminishes, as does the vascularity of the skin, which affects thermoregulation. There is increased incidence of hypothermia due to decreased vasodilation and vasoconstriction of the dermal arterioles, and loss of subcutaneous fat.

In elderly individuals, diminished inflammatory response and diminished perception of pain increase the risk of adverse effects from noxious stimuli. The elderly are at a greater risk for frostbite and burns because of diminished pain perception. Their injuries are more serious because of the thinning epidermis and prolonged wound healing. Re-epithelialization takes approximately twice as long in patients over the age of 75 compared to people in their twenties. Wrinkling is the change most associated with aging and is most prominent on the face and neck, areas that have the greatest sun exposure. Other factors leading to wrinkling are loss of subcutaneous fat and diminished elasticity of the skin.

Another obvious, early skin change associated with aging is hyperpigmentation. Senile **lentigo,** or liver spots (Figure 10-21A), are the result of the inability of the melanocytes to produce even pigmentation of the skin. Larger areas of hyperpigmentation are lentigines. These are generally seen on the backs of the hands and wrists of light-skinned individuals and are related to the degree of sun exposure.

Senile pruritus, the most common skin affliction in elderly individuals, is due to a decrease in water content of the skin and atrophy of the sweat glands. Dryness and itching are exacerbated during the winter months when humidity is low, indoor temperatures are high, and drying winds are present. The condition is aggravated by frequent bathing in hot water, which robs the skin of moisture. Generalized itching is also associated with systemic diseases such as diabetes mellitus, atherosclerosis, and liver disease. Thus, prolonged itching should receive medical attention. **Keratosis,** lesions on the epidermis and characterized by overgrowth of the horny layer, is also prevalent among the elderly population. Actinic keratosis, also known as solar keratosis, occurs in areas where sun exposure has been greatest (neck, ears, bald scalp, hands, forearms). The lesions are superficial, flattened papules covered by dry scales, which may be irregular in shape, and pink or tan in colour. Actinic keratosis is premalignant to squamous cell carcinoma; seborrheic keratosis is usually not premalignant (Figure 10-21B). The lesions of seborrheic keratosis are yellowish-brown and are found on the trunk, face, and scalp, and are covered with greasy, velvety textured scales.

Although cancer of the skin is common among elderly people, it is not usually life threatening. Basal cell carcinoma most often affects Caucasian males (Figure 10-21C) and is associated with prolonged exposure to sunlight, poor tanning ability, and previous therapy with X-rays for facial acne. Squamous cell carcinoma (see Figure 10-21D) is much less common than basal

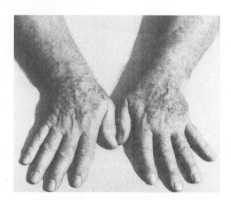

A. Senile Lentigo

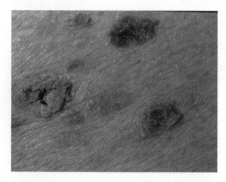

B. Seborrheic Keratosis. *Courtesy of Robert A. Silverman, M.D., Clinical Associate Professor, Department of Pediatrics, Georgetown University.*

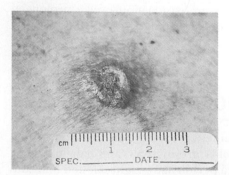

C. Basal Cell Carcinoma. *Courtesy of Robert A. Silverman, M.D., Clinical Associate Professor, Department of Pediatrics, Georgetown University.*

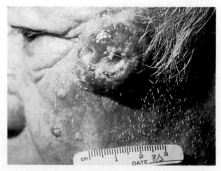

D. Squamous Cell Carcinoma. *Courtesy of Robert A. Silverman, M.D., Clinical Associate Professor, Department of Pediatrics, Georgetown University.*

Figure 10-21 Skin Changes in the Elderly.

Advanced Technique

Skin Scraping for Scabies

1. Place a drop of mineral oil on a sterile #15 scalpel blade.
2. Scrape the suspected papule or known scabies burrow vigorously in order to excavate the top of the papule or burrow. Flecks of blood will mix with the oil.
3. Place some of the oil and skin scrapings onto a microscope slide and cover with a cover slip.
4. Examine the slide for mites, ova, or feces.

cell carcinoma. It is almost twice as prevalent in males as in females; however, the incidence on the legs of females is higher. Risk factors include the ingestion of arsenic, prolonged exposure to sunlight, and exposure to gamma radiation and X-rays.

The number and thickness of terminal hairs generally diminish as a person ages, and there is a conversion of vellus hair to terminal hair in areas such as the rims of the ears and nose in men, and on the upper lip and chin in women. Decreased melanin production decreases the melanocytes at the hair follicle and thus leads to greying.

The nails in elderly persons may thicken and yellow. There may be an over-curvature of the toenails if tight shoes were worn for most of the individual's life.

Although most changes seen in aging are part of the normal aging process, many can also indicate underlying systemic or localized disease. Therefore, it is prudent not to generalize changes seen in elderly patients as routine.

Nursing Tip

Safety Tips to Help the Elderly Patient Avoid Integumentary Damage

1. Assist elderly patients in identifying hazards in the home that could cause trauma (e.g., loose rugs, sharp table edges, glass items in the bathroom, stoves, electric appliances, and the like).
2. Remind elderly patients that sensation to temperature diminishes with age, and therefore they should check their bath water with a thermometer (should not be warmer than 40.5°C).
3. Advise elderly patients to wear multiple layers of clothing in cooler temperatures, and gloves and socks to protect the distal extremities from hypothermia and frostbite.
4. Remind elderly patients to keep electric blankets and heating pads on a medium setting to prevent burns.
5. Advise elderly patients to apply emollient lotions to decrease xerosis and pruritus but to avoid lotions with a high alcohol content, which can cause further drying of the skin.
6. Warn elderly patients that their skin will tear more easily and be prone to shearing because their epidermal layers are thinner, and that because the integumentary system is slower to recover from trauma, healing will take longer.

CASE STUDY The Patient with Pityriasis Rosea

The case study illustrates the application and objective documentation of the skin, hair, and nail assessment.

Susan is a 45-year-old white female. Two weeks ago, she noticed a lesion on her abdomen. Ten days later she noticed similar small lesions over her abdomen and thorax.

HEALTH HISTORY

PATIENT PROFILE	45-yo woman; looks well
HEALTH ISSUE/CONCERN	"I have spots all over my stomach & breasts. I'm scared that I have skin cancer."
HISTORY OF ISSUE/CONCERN	Noticed a fawn-coloured, scaling lesion on the RLQ of her abd 2 wks ago; 10 days later she noticed similar small lesions over her abd & thorax; reports mild pruritus & temperature of 38.1°C; no discharge reported from lesion; she was bitten by a tick 4 wks ago on her Ⓛ forearm; pt applied OTC topical agents s̄ any change; recent URI; pt concerned she might have some form of Lyme dz
PAST HEALTH HISTORY	
Medical History	Iron-deficiency anemia, hypercholesteremia
Surgical History	Appendectomy at 10 yo, no complications
Medications	Multivitamin 1 daily, Evra (Norelgestromin/estrogen) patch q wk, calcium supplement 1200 mg daily
Communicable Diseases	Human papillomavirus at 21 yo
Allergies	Denies allergies to medication, food, animals, or environmental conditions
Injuries and Accidents	Fractured coccyx bone (fell from horse at age 26)
Special Needs	Denies
Blood Transfusions	Denies
Childhood Diseases	Mumps at 5 yo; varicella 6 yo
Immunizations	Influenza—2003, dT—2000; had childhood immunizations, no hepatitis vaccine

FAMILY HEALTH HISTORY

LEGEND

- 🔵 Living female
- 🔲 Living male
- ⊗ Deceased female
- ⊠ Deceased male
- ╱ Points to patient

CA = Cancer
HTN = Hypetension
MI = Myocardial infarction

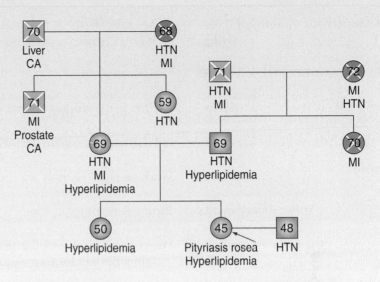

Denies family hx of skin dz or infestations, eczema, melanoma, or other skin cancers.

SOCIAL HISTORY

Alcohol Use	Occasional use (q Saturday); denies abuse or bingeing
Drug Use	Denies
Tobacco Use	Quit smoking 10 yrs ago; smoked 1 PPD × 10 yrs
Domestic and Intimate Partner Violence	Denies
Sexual Practice	Sexually active c̄ husband of 25 yrs
Travel History	Has not travelled out of Canada in the past 10 yrs
Home Environment	Lives c̄ husband on a farm in rural area
Hobbies and Leisure Activities	Riding horses
Stress	Concerned over present illness; finances tight at farm; she & husband have had recent arguments over finances; can never get away as full-time demands on farm & not many people to take over if they took a holiday
Education	2 yrs of college
Economic Status	Some worries as crops were less successful last year—didn't get as much for cattle as had hoped; "We make do but there are no frills."
Religion/Spirituality	"I have a lot of faith even if I don't go to church."

continues

Roles and Relationships	Wife, daughter, sister; states she & husband have had arguments about money but overall positive relations
Characteristic Patterns of Daily Living	Wakes at 05:00; she & husband work all day to maintain animals, crops. She & husband share cooking, house upkeep; supper at 18:00 then bed by 22:00

HEALTH MAINTENANCE ACTIVITIES

Sleep	6–7 hrs per night; occasional insomnia
Diet	No particular diet; she thinks she is about 3 kg overweight
Exercise	Work on farm—always "on the go"; no formal exercise program
Stress Management	Riding & reading
Use of Safety Devices	Wears seat belts; uses a hardhat when riding; has a smoke detector; uses lifting devices for farm work
Health Check-ups	Has had annual gyn exam; dental exams have not been done in 3 yrs

PHYSICAL ASSESSMENT

Inspection of Skin

Colour	Abd is pink $\bar{c}$ fawn-coloured, scaling lesions
Bleeding, Ecchymosis, and Vascularity	None
Lesions	Fawn-coloured scaling lesions, centre $\bar{c}$ a cigarette paper appearance; border has a ring of scale (also known as a collarette); lesions occur in a symmetric distribution & follow the cleavage lines of the trunk, which appears as a Christmas-tree pattern; there is a dominant patch in the RLQ that appears to be resolving slightly; it measures 3 cm × 6 cm & is oval in shape

Palpation of the Skin

Moisture	Skin surface is dry & slightly flaky
Temperature	Warm
Tenderness	Nontender
Texture	Lesions have a rough edge
Turgor	Skin returns to original contour immediately
Edema	No edema on affected surfaces

Inspection of the Hair

Colour	Vellus hair on abd light brown

Distribution	Body hair distribution appropriate for age & gender
Lesions	No lesions on scalp
Palpation of Hair	
Texture	Vellus hair of wrists & hands smooth & soft; no terminal hair growth noted in these areas
Inspection of Nails	
Colour	Pink c̄ capillary refill of 1 sec
Shape and Configuration	Smooth & flat; no splintering or brittle edges; nail edge <160°
Palpation of Nails	
Texture	Firm

◄NURSING CHECKLIST►

Skin, Hair, and Nail Assessment

Inspection of the Skin
- Colour
- Bleeding, ecchymosis, and vascularity
- Lesions

Palpation of the Skin
- Moisture
- Temperature
- Tenderness
- Texture
- Turgor
- Edema

Inspection of the Hair
- Colour
- Distribution
- Lesions

Palpation of the Hair
- Texture

Inspection of the Nails
- Colour
- Shape and configuration

Palpation of the Nails
- Texture

Advanced Technique
- Skin scraping for scabies

Reflective Thinking

Dealing with Pediculosis

As the school nurse in an elementary school, you are asked to conduct an assessment of each first-grade student's hair for lice and seven children are found to be infested with lice. You call the affected children's parents to pick up their children. One father screams at you on the phone, "My child is OK. You must be mistaken. Every few weeks you tell me that my daughter has lice. It's not my problem!"
- What is your response to this parent?
- What are your responsibilities for the well-being of the entire school?
- Plan an educational program to be disseminated to each class.

REVIEW QUESTIONS

1. You are caring for a 51-year-old morbidly obese, diabetic female who complains of weepy erythemic areas of the axillae, inframammary areas, groin, and gluteal region, which are extremely pruritic. This is very likely:
   a. Impetigo
   b. Moniliasis
   c. Xerosis
   d. Seborrhea
   The correct answer is (b).

2. Rubella is a viral infection that is highly contagious and characterized by a high fever, cough, and:
   a. Hyperkeratotic papules
   b. Pedunculated nodules
   c. Pastia's sign
   d. Koplik's spots
   The correct answer is (d).

3. Your patient has lesions on her arm that are arranged in a circular pattern. This arrangement of lesions is an example of which type of pattern?
   a. Discrete
   b. Confluent
   c. Annular
   d. Polycyclic
   The correct answer is (c).

4. You are evaluating a 5-year-old female who was given amoxicillin and now has developed an allergic reaction. Which of the following palpable lesions would you expect to find during your assessment?
   a. Patch
   b. Plaque
   c. Wheal
   d. Nodule
   The correct answer is (c).

5. Which type of sweat gland is primarily found in the axillae, genital and rectal areas, nipples, and navel?
   a. Sebaceous glands
   b. Eccrine glands
   c. Bartholin glands
   d. Apocrine glands
   The correct answer is (d).

6. A 42-year-old male, who has been clearing fence lines, comes into the office with the complaint of poison ivy. You would expect the lesions to be:

   a. Linear
   b. Concentric
   c. Zosteriform
   d. Generalized
   The correct answer is (a).

7. Which skin lesion presents as a bright red, star-shaped area with a central pulsation noted with pressure?
   a. Venous star
   b. Spider angioma
   c. Petechiae
   d. Cherry angioma
   The correct answer is (b).

8. A 78-year-old male who is bedridden is evaluated for a sacral pressure sore. You note a lesion measuring 4 cm $\times$ 7 cm that is oval in nature and has enhanced pigmentation. The epidermis is intact. This is an example of a:
   a. Stage 1 pressure sore
   b. Stage 2 pressure sore
   c. Stage 3 pressure sore
   d. Stage 4 pressure sore
   The correct answer is (a).

9. A 52-year-old female was burning leaves in her yard when her trousers caught fire. She sustained burns to her right calf. When you evaluate the injured area, you note that the epidermis and upper layers of the dermis are destroyed. The deeper dermis is injured. The skin is red and blistery with exudates and it is painful. This is an example of a:
   a. First-degree burn
   b. Second-degree burn
   c. Third-degree burn
   d. Fourth-degree burn
   The correct answer is (b).

10. A 72-year-old male presents to the office with shortness of breath and coarse cough. He is barrel chested with an A/P diameter greater than 1:2. You see he has COPD. You would expect his nail angle to be:
    a. Greater than 90°
    b. Less than 80°
    c. Less than 140°
    d. Greater than 160°
    The correct answer is (d).

The correct answer is (a).

9. A 52-year-old female was burning leaves in her yard when her trousers caught fire. She sustained burns to her right calf. When you evaluate the injured area, you note that the epidermis and upper layers of the dermis are destroyed. The deeper dermis is injured.

The skin is red and blistery with exudates and it is painful. This is an example of a:

a. First-degree burn
b. Second-degree burn
c. Third-degree burn
d. Fourth-degree burn

The correct answer is (b).

10. A 72-year-old male presents to the office with shortness of breath and coarse cough. He is barrel chested with an A/P diameter greater than 1:2. You see he has COPD. You would expect his nail angle to be:

a. Greater than 90°
b. Less than 80°
c. Less than 140°
d. Greater than 160°

The correct answer is (d).

REFERENCES

[1]Canadian Cancer Society/National Cancer Institute of Canada. (2006). *Canadian Cancer Statistics 2006.* Toronto, Canada.

[2]Health Canada. *Preventing skin cancer.* Retrieved May 26, 2006, from http://www.hc-sc.gc.ca/iyh-vsv/diseases-maladies/cancer_e.html

[3]Curiel-Lewandrowski, C. (2006). *Risk factors for the development of melanoma.* In UpToDate, Rose, B.D. (Ed.), UpToDate, Wellesley, MA.

[4]Abbasi, N. R., Shaw, H. M., Rigel, D. S., Friedman, R. J., McCarthy, W. H., Osman, I., Kopf, A.W., & Polsky, D. (2004). Early diagnosis of cutaneous melanoma: Revisiting the ABCD criteria. *Journal of the American Medical Association,* Dec 8; *292*(22), 2771–76.

[5]Health Canada. *Vaccine preventable diseases.* Retrieved October 16, 2006, from http://www.phac-aspc.gc.ca/im/vpd-mev/rubella_e.html

[6]National Pressure Ulcer Advisory Panel. NPUAP Staging Report. (2003). Retrieved October 16, 2006, from http://www.cancer.ca/ccs/internet/standard/0,2939,3172_273070_275853_langId-en,00.html

[7]Canadian Cancer Society. *SunSense guidelines.* Retrieved May 26, 2006, from http://www.cancer.ca/ccs/internet/standard/0,2939,3172_273070_275853_langId-en,00.html

BIBLIOGRAPHY

Bauer, A., Bong, J., Coenraads, P. J., Elsner, P., English, J., Williams, H. C. (2003). Interventions for preventing occupational irritant hand dermatitis. (Protocol) *The Cochrane Database of Systematic Reviews,* Issue 3.

Cartwright, M. (2000). Body piercing: What nurse practitioners need to know. *Journal of the American Academy of Nurse Practitioners, 12(5),* 171–74.

Dodd, C. S. Interventions for treating head lice. (2001). *The Cochrane Database of Systematic Reviews,* Issue 2. Art. No.: CD001165.

Droogan, J. (1999). Treatment and prevention of head lice and scabies. *Nursing Times, 95(29),* 44–45.

Elder, D., Elenitsas, R., Johnson, Jr., B., & Murphy, G. (Eds.). (2005). *Lever's histopathology of the skin* (9th ed.). Philadelphia: Lippincott-Raven.

First Nations and Inuit Health. *Clinical practice guidelines for nurses in primary care: Chapter 9: The skin.* Retrieved October 16, 2006, from http://www.hc-sc.gc.ca/fnih-spni/pubs/nursing-infirm/2000_clin-guide/chap_09_e.html

Gibbs, S., Harvey, I., Sterling, J. C., Stark, R. (2003). Local treatments for cutaneous warts. *The Cochrane Database of Systematic Reviews,* Issue 3. Art. No.: CD001781.

Hess, C. T. (2002). *Wound care* (4th ed.). Springhouse, PA: Springhouse.

James, W. (2005). *Andrews' diseases of the skin: Clinical dermatology* (10th ed.) Philadelphia: Elsevier Saunders.

Koning, S., Verhagen, A. P., van Suijlekom-Smit, L. W. A, Morris, A., Butler, C. C., van der Wouden, J. C. (2003). Interventions for impetigo. *The Cochrane Database of Systematic Reviews,* Issue 2. Art. No.: CD003261

Naldi, L., Buzzetti, R., Cecchi, C., Baldwin L., Battistutta, D., Benvenuto, C., Hanitta, M., Kanizsa, S., Parisi, A., Stoncham, M., Topalian, J. (2004). Educational programmes for skin cancer prevention. (Protocol) *The Cochrane Database of Systematic Reviews,* Issue 1. Art. No.: CD004686.

O'Brien, L., & Pandit, A. (2006). Silicon gel sheeting for preventing and treating hypertrophic and keloid scars. *The Cochrane Database of Systematic Reviews,* Issue 1. Art. No.: CD003826.

Paller, A. M., & Mancini, A. J. (2006). *Hurwitz clinical pediatric dermatology: A textbook of skin disorders of and adolescence* (3rd ed.). Philadelphia, PA: Elsevier Saunders.

NEL

CHAPTER 11

Head, Neck, and Regional Lymphatics

COMPETENCIES

1. Identify the anatomic structures of the head and neck.

2. Identify the lymph nodes of the head and neck.

3. Describe the system-specific health history for the head and neck.

4. Demonstrate the physical assessment of the head and neck.

5. Describe normal findings in the physical assessment of the head and neck.

6. List common abnormalities found in physical assessment of the head and neck.

7. Explain pathophysiology of common abnormalities found in physical assessment of the head and neck.

*A*ssessment of the head and neck is the gateway to a wide range of critical clues about the function of various body systems. As you assess the head and neck, you will learn about the skin, endocrine function, musculoskeletal integrity, and neurological function.

ANATOMY AND PHYSIOLOGY

The skull, face, neck, thyroid, lymphatics, and blood supply are discussed in the following sections.

Skull

The skull is a complex bony structure that rests on the superior end of the vertebral column (Figure 11-1). The skull protects the brain from direct injury and provides a surface for the attachment of the muscles that assist with mastication and produce facial expressions.

Cranial bones of the skull are connected by immovable joints called **sutures.** The most prominent sutures are the coronal suture, the sagittal suture, and the lambdoidal suture. The junction of the coronal and sagittal sutures is called the **bregma.**

Face

The face of every individual has its own unique characteristics, which are influenced by race, state of health, emotions, and environment. Facial structures are symmetrical so that eyes, eyebrows, nose, mouth, nasolabial folds, and palpebral fissures look the same on both sides.

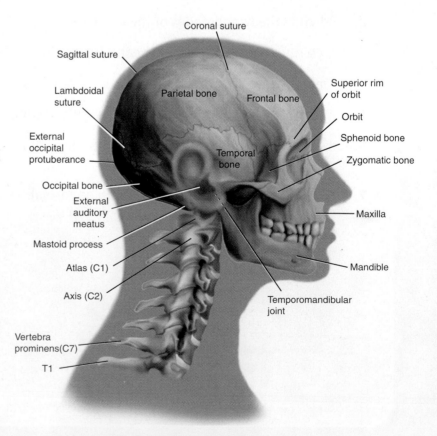

Figure 11-1 Bones of the Face and Skull (Lateral View).

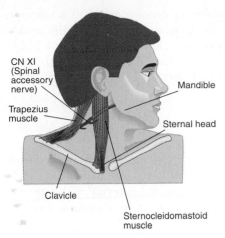

CN XI
(Spinal
accessory
nerve)

Trapezius
muscle

Mandible

Sternal head

Clavicle

Sternocleidomastoid
muscle

Figure 11-2 Major Cervical Muscles.

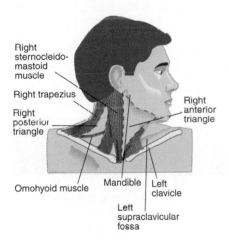

Right
sternocleido-
mastoid
muscle

Right trapezius

Right
posterior
triangle

Right
anterior
triangle

Omohyoid muscle   Mandible   Left
clavicle

Left
supraclavicular
fossa

Figure 11-3 Anterior and Posterior Cervical
Triangles.

Neck

The neck is made up of seven flexible cervical vertebrae that support the head while allowing it maximum mobility. The first vertebra, the **atlas,** articulates with the occipital condyles to support and balance the head. The second vertebra, the **axis,** has an odontoid process that extends into the ring of the atlas, allowing it to pivot as the head is turned from side to side. The seventh vertebra has a long spinous process called the **vertebra prominens,** which serves as a useful landmark during physical assessment of the neck, back, and thorax.

The major muscles of the neck are the sternocleidomastoids and the trapezii (Figure 11-2). The sternocleidomastoid muscles extend from the upper portion of the sternum and the clavicle to the mastoid process and allow the head to bend laterally, rotate, flex, and extend. They also divide each side of the neck into two triangles: the anterior cervical and the posterior cervical, which serve as assessment landmarks. The **anterior triangle** is formed by the mandible, the trachea, and the sternocleidomastoid muscle and contains the anterior cervical lymph nodes, the trachea, and the thyroid gland. The **posterior triangle,** the area between the sternocleidomastoid and the trapezius muscles with the clavicle at the base, contains the posterior cervical lymph nodes (Figure 11-3).

The trapezii extend from the occipital bone down the neck to insert at the outer third of the clavicles, at the acromion process of the scapula, and along the spinal column to the level of T12. They allow the shoulders and scapula to move up and down and rotate the scapula medially.

Thyroid

The thyroid gland, the largest endocrine gland in the body, secretes thyroxine (T_4) and triiodothyronine (T_3), which regulate the rate of cellular metabolism. The gland, a flattened, butterfly-shaped structure with two lateral lobes connected by the **isthmus,** weighs about 25 to 30 grams and is slightly larger in females (Figure 11-4). The isthmus rests on top of the trachea, inferior to the cricoid cartilage.

Lymphatics

An extensive system of lymphatic vessels is an important part of the immune system (Figure 11-5). Lymphatic tissue in the nodes filter and sequester pathogens and other harmful substances. Lymph nodes are usually less than

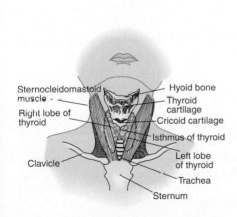

Sternocleidomastoid
muscle

Right lobe of
thyroid

Clavicle

Hyoid bone

Thyroid
cartilage

Cricoid cartilage

Isthmus of thyroid

Left lobe
of thyroid

Trachea

Sternum

Figure 11-4 Structures of the Thyroid Gland.

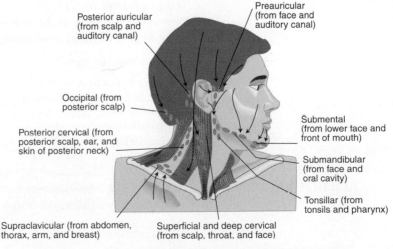

Posterior auricular
(from scalp and
auditory canal)

Preauricular
(from face and
auditory canal)

Occipital (from
posterior scalp)

Posterior cervical (from
posterior scalp, ear, and
skin of posterior neck)

Submental
(from lower face and
front of mouth)

Submandibular
(from face and
oral cavity)

Tonsillar (from
tonsils and pharynx)

Supraclavicular (from abdomen,
thorax, arm, and breast)

Superficial and deep cervical
(from scalp, throat, and face)

Figure 11-5 Lymph Nodes of the Head and Neck and Drainage Patterns.

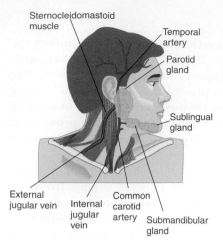

Figure 11-6 Major Veins and Arteries of the Neck.

1 cm, round or ovoid in shape, and smooth in consistency. If a tender or enlarged lymph node is found on the clinical examination, assess the entire lymph node area and note the direction in which each node drains (Figure 11-5). For example, if a patient's posterior cervical node is enlarged, examine the posterior scalp, the ear (both externally and internally), and the skin of the posterior neck for pathology.

Blood Supply

The blood supply to the head and neck is quite extensive, with arterial and venous patterns. Major arteries that carry blood to the head and neck include the common carotids (which bifurcate into the internal and external carotid arteries), the brachiocephalic artery (the right common carotid artery branches from this), the subclavian arteries, and the temporal arteries. Deoxygenated blood from the head and neck is returned to the heart via the internal and external jugular veins, the brachiocephalic vein, and the subclavian veins (Figure 11-6).

Nursing Tip

Cranial Nerve Assessment

The 12 cranial nerves that innervate the head and neck are integrated into this portion of the examination. See also Chapters 12 and 19.

HEALTH HISTORY

The head and neck health history provides insight into the link between a patient's life/lifestyle and head and neck information and pathology.

PATIENT PROFILE *Diseases that are age- and gender-specific for the head and neck are listed.*

Age Lymphadenopathies related to Hodgkin's disease (11–29)
Cervical spine trauma (young adults)
Hyperthyroidism (reproductive years in young women)
Temporal arteritis (elderly)
Decreased mobility of the cervical spine related to an inflammatory or degenerative process (elderly)

Gender

Female Hypo- or hyperthyroidism, thyroid cancer
Degenerative cervical bone disease

Male Lymphadenopathy related to Hodgkin's disease
Trauma-related cervical spine injury

HEALTH ISSUE/CONCERN *Common health issues/concerns for the head and neck are defined, and information on the characteristics of each sign or symptom is provided.*

Stiff Neck Painful movement of the neck that restricts range of motion

Quality	Limited range of motion, either passive or active
Associated Manifestations	Headache, neck tenderness, swelling, fever, numbness and tingling in arms or hands
Aggravating Factors	Position (sitting, standing, lying down), immobilization of position for a prolonged period, mobility, stress, weather
Alleviating Factors	Immobility or rest, certain position, analgesics, heat
Setting	Work, driving, stress
Timing	With all movements, with rotating movements only, with flexion and extension only, with weather changes; after falls, motor vehicle or other accidents
Hoarseness	Husky or harsh quality of the voice
Quality	Audible, inaudible
Associated Manifestations	Fever, sore throat, malaise
Aggravating Factors	Inhalation of chemicals or noxious fumes, smoking, overuse of voice, alcohol use, recent URIs, recent head and neck surgery, intubation, neck trauma
Alleviating Factors	Medications, adequate hydration, voice rest
Setting	Public speaking, singing, yelling, normal speech
Timing	Continuous, intermittent
Neck Mass	Discrete area of swelling found in the neck
Quality	Mobile, nonmobile, smooth, irregular, tender, nontender
Associated Manifestations	Shortness of breath, hoarseness, weight loss, fever and chills, dysphagia, ear pain
Aggravating Factors	Eating, talking, movement, tight clothing around the neck, swallowing
Alleviating Factors	Avoidance of tight clothing, analgesic medications, decreased dietary intake
Timing	Long-standing, recent
Headache	Pain felt within the head, behind the eyes, or at the nape of the neck (Table 11-1, Table 11-2)
Location	Temporal, frontal, occipital, orbital, hemicranial, neck, and upper shoulders
Quality	Neck pain: aching, sore, dull, sharp; head pain: throbbing, sharp, dull, aching
Associated Manifestations	Neck pain: fever, headache, swelling, tenderness; head pain: nausea and vomiting, aura, diplopia, blurred vision, irritability, sneezing, rhinorrhea, weakness, dizziness
Aggravating Factors	Neck pain: stress, trauma, aging, position, mobility, weather changes; head pain: stress, fatigue, foods, noxious odours, caffeine intake, coughing, alcohol intake, smoke, hunger, season, menstruation

continues

Alleviating Factors	Medications such as analgesics, anti-inflammatory agents, ergotamine, caffeinated drugs, antidepressants, or triptan medications; position change; rest; sleep; shaking head; food intake
Setting	Work, outdoors, relationship to biologic events, stressful environment
Timing	Neck pain: with movement, at rest, weather changes; head pain: constant, intermittent, in the morning, at the end of the day, premenstrual, seasonal
Head Injury	
Quality	Open, closed
Associated Manifestations	Lightheadedness, intolerance of bright light and noise, poor attention and concentration, sleep disturbances, depression, neck pain, nausea, vomiting, projectile vomiting, dizziness or vertigo, associated laceration, headache, seizure activity, loss of consciousness, amnesia, visual disturbances, gait disturbances, speech disturbances, confusion, drowsiness, abnormal behaviour, movement of extremities, change in respiratory pattern, discharge from nose or ear, head or neck lacerations/abrasions/ecchymoses
Alleviating Factors	Ice, analgesics, rest
Setting	Mechanism of injury, use of helmet or protective headgear, use of seat belt, violent activity, fall, sports injury, MVA, alcohol or drug use, concurrent history of seizure disorder, heart disease, or diabetes mellitus
PAST HEALTH HISTORY	*The various components of the past health history are linked to head and neck pathology and head- and neck-related information.*
Medical History	
Head and Neck Specific	Hypo- or hyperthyroidism, sinus infections, migraine headache, cancer, closed head injury or skull fracture
Nonhead and Neck Specific	Pheochromocytoma
Surgical History	Thyroidectomy, facial reconstruction, cosmetic surgery, neurosurgery, and other surgery related to the head or neck
Medications	Antibiotics, steroids, anticonvulsants, chemotherapy, thyroxine, propranolol, analgesics, oral contraceptives
Communicable Diseases	Meningitis, encephalitis
Injuries and Accidents	Obstruction caused by foreign bodies, trauma to the head or neck, chemical splashes to the face, noxious fumes, sports injuries, MVA
Special Needs	Tracheostomy, paralysis
FAMILY HEALTH HISTORY	*Head and neck diseases that are familial are listed.*
	Thyroid disease, headaches
SOCIAL HISTORY	*The components of the social history are linked to head and neck factors or pathology.*
Alcohol Use	Predisposes to accidents and head injury

Work Environment	Risk of head injury, exposure to toxins or chemicals
Home Environment	Risk of falls and head injury due to loose throw rugs or absence of handrails
Stress	Demands of employment, home, school
HEALTH MAINTENANCE ACTIVITIES	*This information provides a bridge between the health maintenance activities and head and neck function.*
Sleep	May be increased due to head injury
Diet	Recent weight gain or loss
Use of Safety Devices	Protective headgear for sports and work

Migraine

Although tension-type headaches are the most prevalent (approximately 70%) of all headaches, migraine headaches can be the most debilitating. Migraine is a primary neurobiologic disorder, resulting from dysfunction of the trigeminovascular system. The disorder manifests as recurring attacks, usually lasting 4–72 hours. The average number of migraine attacks is about three or four per month; some people only experience an attack once a year. Attacks involve unilateral throbbing headache pain of moderate to severe intensity and usually include nausea, sometimes vomiting, and sensitivity to light, sound, and other sensory stimuli. Some people experience "aura" symptoms such as unilateral visual disturbances, sensory disturbances, and muscular weakness prior to the headache.

TABLE 11-1 Classification of Headaches

VASCULAR ETIOLOGIES	Pheochromocytoma	Hypoglycemia
Migraine headaches	Premenstrual syndrome	
Cluster headaches		**DRUG ETIOLOGIES**
Subarachnoid hemorrhage	**FOOD-RELATED ETIOLOGIES**	Alcohol and alcohol withdrawal
Subdural hematoma	Nitrites (e.g., hot dogs, bacon)	Caffeine withdrawal
Infarction	Tyramine (e.g., red wine, cheese,	Nitrates
Cerebral aneurysm	chocolate)	Oral contraceptives
Temporal arteritis	Monosodium glutamate (e.g., Chinese	Estrogen
Vasculitis	food)	
	Food allergy	**ENVIRONMENTAL ETIOLOGIES**
MUSCLE CONTRACTION		Change in barometric pressure (from
Tension headache	**FACIAL OR CERVICAL ETIOLOGIES**	weather or altitude)
	Sinusitis	Carbon monoxide poisoning
INTRACRANIAL ETIOLOGIES	Temporomandibular joint (TMJ)	Tobacco smoke
Brain tumours	dysfunction	Glaring or flickering lights
Increased intracranial pressure from	Dental lesions	Odours
hydrocephalus, pseudotumor cerebri	Trigeminal neuralgia	
Intracranial infection, e.g., meningitis,	Cervical spine radiculopathies	**MISCELLANEOUS ETIOLOGIES**
encephalitis, abscess		Fever
Ischemic cerebrovascular disease	**OCULAR-RELATED ETIOLOGIES**	Influenza
	Narrow angle glaucoma	Head trauma
SYSTEMIC ETIOLOGIES	Uveitis	Otitis media
Infection	Extraocular muscle paralysis	Parotitis
Post-lumbar puncture	Eye strain	Pregnancy
Hypertension		Fatigue and decreased sleep
Exertion from coitus, cough, exercise	**METABOLIC ETIOLOGIES**	Psychogenic disorders
Postictal	Hypoxia	
	Hypercapnia	

TABLE 11-2 Migraine, Tension-type, Cluster, Chronic Daily Headache Characteristics

	Migraine	Tension-Type	Cluster	Chronic Daily Headache
Location of pain	One side or both sides of head	Both sides of head	One side of head	Both sides of head
Duration of pain	4 to 72 hours	2 hours to days	40 to 90 minutes; often once every 24 hours for weeks	Off/On—daily
Severity of pain	Mild, Moderate, or Severe	Mild or Moderate	Severe	Mild to Moderate
Nausea, sensitivity to light, sound, odors, movement	Yes (Maybe)	No	No	Maybe
Redness or tearing of eyes stuffy or runny nose	Maybe	No	Yes	No
Gender ratio (F:M)	3:1	1:1	1:4	1.8:1
Age of onset	Teens–20s	Any	27–31 years, typically	Adult, typically
Family history of headache	Usually	Not usually	Occasionally	Occasionally
Quality of pain	Throbbing	Pressure/ache	Stabbing/burning	Pressure/throbbing
Aura	10%–20% of patients	No	Rarely	Rarely

Adapted from: *Migraine and Other Headaches — A Patient Guide to Treatment,* 1998, American Medical Association - Migraine Support. Reprinted with permission from the American Medical Association, August 2006.

Source: http://www.w-h-a.org/wha2/index.asp; [PATH: go into section called 'understanding headache' then click on HIS classification system then click on 'quick glance at headache disorders']

Nursing Alert

Migraines

Epidemiology[1]

- An estimated 8% of Canadians aged 12 or older have received a clinical diagnosis of migraine.
- Migraine accounts for an estimated 7 million lost working days annually.
- In recent years, rates of migraine are increasing among women 25 to 54 years old.

Risk Factors for Migraine Headache

- Ages 5–50
- Female (three times more common in Canadian women than men)[2]
- Family history of migraines
- Allergies
- Raynaud's phenomenon
- History of motion sickness in childhood
- Increased stress
- Estrogen
- Caffeine intake
- Tyramine, MSG, sulfites, or nitrite consumption
- Sleep disorders

Nursing Alert

Tell patients that they need to seek help for a headache when:[3]

- They have a very sudden, severe, "thunderclap" headache that seems to come on instantly and is unlike any headache they have had before.
- It begins abruptly and they have no previous history of them, especially if the pain is sudden and severe.
- They experience any signs of a brain attack (stroke), such as sudden numbness, weakness, and inability to move one side of the entire body, or sudden problems speaking and understanding speech.
- A headache occurs with a stiff neck, fever, nausea, vomiting, lethargy, drowsiness, and confusion.
- A headache occurs with weakness, paralysis, numbness, visual disturbances, slurred speech, confusion, behaviour changes, or loss of consciousness.
- Headaches occur after a recent fall or blow to the head.
- Headaches develop gradually and occur with confusion, lethargy, problems with walking, or loss of bladder or bowel control.
- Headaches cause people to wake up at night.
- Headaches occur daily or become worse.
- Headaches occur after physical exercise, sexual activity, coughing, or sneezing.
- Life is being disrupted by the headaches (for example, missing work or school regularly).

Nursing Tip

Nonpharmaceutical Headache Remedies

Methods to alleviate headaches by nonchemical means include relaxation techniques, a quiet environment, a dark room, lying down, walking, music, muscle stretching, warm or cool compresses to the head, herbal tea, and a neck or temple massage. Encourage patients with headaches to experiment with these techniques to determine which method is effective for them.

Reflective Thinking

Preventing Head and Neck Injury

Ivan is a 20-year-old bicycle courier for a large business in the downtown area. He presents to the clinic with a swollen ankle that he sustained after running a red light and colliding with a car. You note that he has extensive bruises on his face. You inquire about his use of a helmet. He replies, "I'm careful. I don't need it." How would you respond to this comment? What teaching strategies might you use?

EQUIPMENT

- Stethoscope
- Cup of water

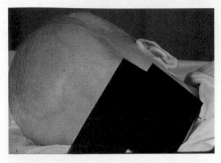

A. Hydrocephalus. *Courtesy of Armed Forces Institute of Pathology.*

B. Acromegaly (note wide nose, spaced teeth, and large lips). *Courtesy of Matthew C. Leinung, M.D., Acting Head, Division of Endocrinology, Albany Medical College, Albany, NY.*

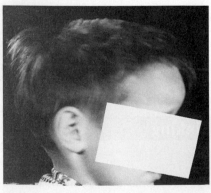

C. Craniosynostosis. *Courtesy of Armed Forces Institute of Pathology.*

Figure 11-7 Abnormal Head Shapes.

◄NURSING CHECKLIST►

General Approach to Head and Neck Assessment

1. Greet the patient and explain the assessment techniques that you will be using.
2. Ensure that the room temperature is at a comfortable level for the patient.
3. Use a quiet room free from interruptions.
4. Ensure that the light in the room provides sufficient brightness to allow adequate observation of the patient.
5. Place the patient in an upright sitting position on the examination table, or

   5a. Gain access to the head of the supine, bedridden patient by removing nonessential equipment or bedding (for patients who cannot tolerate the sitting position).
6. If the patient is wearing a wig or headpiece, ask the patient to remove it.
7. Visualize the underlying anatomic structures during the assessment process to permit an accurate description of the location of any pathology.
8. Always compare the right and left sides of the head, neck, and face to one another.
9. Use the same systematic approach every time an assessment is performed.

ASSESSMENT OF THE HEAD AND NECK

Inspection of the Shape of the Head

E 1. Have the patient sit in a comfortable position.
   2. Face the patient, with your head at the same level as the patient's head.
   3. Inspect the head for shape and symmetry.

N The head should be normocephalic and symmetrical.

A **Hydrocephalus** is an enlargement of the head without enlargement of the facial structures (Figure 11-7A).

P Hydrocephalus is caused by an abnormal accumulation of cerebrospinal fluid within the skull.

A **Acromegaly** is an abnormal enlargement of the skull and bony facial structures.

P Acromegaly is caused by excessive secretion of growth hormone from the pituitary gland (Figure 11-7B).

A **Craniosynostosis** is characterized by abnormal shape of the skull or bone growth at right angles to suture lines, exophthalmos, and drooping eyelids (Figure 11-7C).

P Craniosynostosis is caused by the premature closure of one or more sutures of the skull before brain growth is complete.

Palpation of the Head

E 1. Place the finger pads on the scalp and palpate all of its surface, beginning in the frontal area and continuing over the parietal, temporal, and occipital areas.
   2. Assess for contour, masses, depressions, and tenderness.

| E | Examination | N | Normal Findings | A | Abnormal Findings | P | Pathophysiology |

3. Palpate the superficial temporal artery, which is located anterior to the tragus of the ear.

N **The normal skull is smooth, nontender, and without masses or depressions. The temporal artery is usually a weaker peripheral pulse (1+/4+ or 1+/3+) than the other peripheral pulses of the body. The artery is nontender, smooth, and readily compressible.**

A Masses in the cranial bones that feel hard or soft are abnormal.

P These types of masses may be carcinomatous metastasis from other regions of the body or may result from lymphomas, multiple myeloma, or leukemia.

A Palpation elicits localized edema over the bony frontal portion of the skull.

P Osteomyelitis of the skull may develop following acute or chronic sinusitis if the infection extends out from the sinuses into the surrounding bone.

A Firm palpation reveals a softening of the outer bone layer.

P **Craniotabes** is a softening of the skull caused by hydrocephalus or demineralization of the bone due to rickets, hypervitaminosis A, or syphilis.

A A temporal artery that is hard in consistency and tender is abnormal.

P This can indicate temporal arteritis, and the temporal arteries may also be more tortuous.

Inspection and Palpation of the Scalp

E 1. Part the hair repeatedly all over the scalp and inspect for lesions or masses.
   2. Place the finger pads on the scalp and palpate for lesions or masses.

N The scalp should be shiny, intact, and without lesions or masses.

A A laceration, or a laceration with bleeding, is abnormal.

P Direct trauma can cause lacerations to the scalp.

A A gaping laceration with profuse bleeding is abnormal.

P If the laceration is gaping, it indicates a deep wound that may involve a compound skull fracture as a result of some type of trauma.

A Palpation reveals a localized, easily movable accumulation of blood in the subcutaneous tissue.

P Hematomas can result from direct trauma to the skull.

A Palpation may reveal either single or multiple masses that are easily movable. They are round, firm, nontender, and arise from either the skin or the subcutaneous tissue.

P These are sebaceous cysts that form as a result of a retention of secretions from sebaceous glands.

A Nonmobile, fatty masses with smooth, circular edges may be palpated deeper in the scalp.

P These masses are benign fatty tumours known as **lipomas.**

Inspection of the Face

Symmetry

E 1. Have the patient sit in a comfortable position facing you.
   2. Observe the patient's face for expression, shape, and symmetry of the eyebrows, eyes, nose, mouth, and ears.

N **The facial features should be symmetrical. Both palpebral fissures should be equal and the nasolabial fold should present bilaterally. It is important to remember that slight variations in symmetry are common. Slanted eyes with inner epicanthal folds are normal findings in patients of Asian descent.**

Figure 11-8 Bell's Palsy. © NIH/Phototake

Figure 11-9 Down Syndrome in Twin 12-Month-Old Girls. *Courtesy of Mary Ellen Estes.*

A   Structures are absent or deformed. There is a definite asymmetry of expression, the palpebral fissures, the nasolabial folds, and the corners of the mouth.

P   Asymmetry of the palpebral fissures, nasolabial folds, the mouth, and facial expression may indicate damage to the nerves innervating facial muscles (cranial nerve VII), as in stroke or **Bell's palsy** (Figure 11-8).

Shape and Features

E   1. Face the patient.
    2. Observe the shape of the patient's face.
    3. Note any swelling, abnormal features, or unusual movement.

N   The shape of the face can be oval, round, or slightly square. There should be no edema, disproportionate structures, or involuntary movements.

A   Inspection of the face may reveal slanted eyes with inner epicanthal folds; a short, flat nose; and a thick, protruding tongue.

P   These findings are likely to indicate the presence of **Down syndrome** (trisomy 21), a chromosomal aberration (Figure 11-9).

A   An abnormally wide distance between the eyes is **hypertelorism.**

P   Hypertelorism is a congenital anomaly.

A   Facial skin is shiny, contracted, and hard. The face appears to have furrows around the mouth (Figure 11-10).

P   Scleroderma is a collagen disease of unknown cause. Sclerosis of the skin, as well as visceral organs (esophagus, lungs, heart, muscles, and kidneys) occurs.

A   The face is thin with sharply defined features and prominent eyes (exophthalmos) in Graves' disease (Figure 11-11).

P   Graves' disease is an autoimmune disorder associated with increased circulating levels of T_3 and T_4.

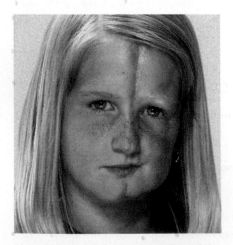

Figure 11-10 Scleroderma. *Courtesy of the Scleroderma Foundation (http://www.scleroderma.org).*

| E | Examination | N | Normal Findings | A | Abnormal Findings | P | Pathophysiology |

Figure 11-11 Exophthalmos of Graves' Disease. © *Chris Barry/Phototake*

Figure 11-12 Myxedema.

Figure 11-13 Cachectic face in a 40-year-old man with tuberculosis. Also note his cachectic torso *Courtesy of WHO/STD/Colors Magazine/ J. Mollison.*

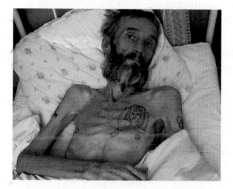

Figure 11-15 Allergic Facies.

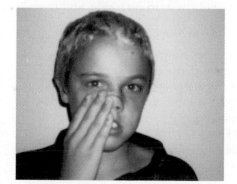

Figure 11-16 Young boy with characteristic nasal crease from the repeated action of the "nasal salute" caused by allergies.

A   The patient's face is round and swollen with characteristic periorbital edema and dry, dull skin (Figure 11-12).

P   This condition is known as myxedema and is associated with hypothyroidism.

A   The eyes are sunken and cheeks are hollow in cachexia (Figure 11-13).

P   Cachexia is a profound state of wasting of the vital tissues associated with cancer, malnutrition, and dehydration.

A   The patient's face is immobile and expressionless, with a staring gaze and raised eyebrows in Parkinson's disease (Figure 11-14).

P   Parkinson's disease is the degeneration of basal ganglia, resulting from a deficiency of the neurotransmitter dopamine.

A   The face of Caucasians shows a dusky blue discoloration beneath the eyes (allergic shiners), creases below the lower eyelids (Dennie's lines), and an open mouth due to mouth breathing (Figure 11-15).

P   The patient with chronic allergies develops this characteristic allergic facies or allergic gape. These findings are also typical of allergic rhinitis.

A   A transverse crease is noted across the nose.

P   This is a characteristic finding in patients with allergies and allergic rhinitis who frequently are observed to do the "nasal salute" or upward wiping of the nose (Figure 11-16).

A   The patient's face has a rounded "moonface," red cheeks, and excess hair on the jaw and upper lip (Figure 11-17).

P   This is the facies of Cushing's syndrome, which is caused by increased production of adrenocorticotropic hormone (ACTH) or prolonged steroid ingestion.

Figure 11-14 Parkinson's Disease. © *Ron Sachs/CNP/Corbis*

Figure 11-17 Cushing's Syndrome.

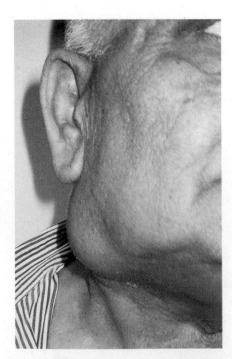

Figure 11-18 This right neck mass was identified as squamous cell carcinoma. *Courtesy of Dr. Daniel D. Rooney.*

Palpation and Auscultation of the Mandible

E 1. Use the fingertips of both index and middle fingers to locate the TMJ anterior to the tragus of the ear on both sides.
2. Hold the fingertips firmly in place over the joints and ask the patient to open and close the mouth.
3. As the patient opens and closes the mouth, observe the relative smoothness of the movement and whether or not the patient notices any discomfort.
4. Remove your hands.
5. Hold the bell of the stethoscope over the joint.
6. Listen for any sound while the patient opens and closes the mouth.

N The patient should experience no discomfort with movement. The TMJ should articulate smoothly, without clicking or crepitus.

A The patient complains of tenderness when the mouth is opened or closed. Palpation or auscultation reveals clicking or crepitus.

P Tenderness in the joint may be from the inflammation of migratory arthritis.

A Crepitus is present from the articulation of irregular bone surfaces found in osteoarthritis.

P Clicking may follow a "snapping" sound if there is displaced cartilage.

A The mouth remains in an open and fixed position.

P Following a wide yawn or trauma to the chin, the TMJ is dislocated and will not function. This condition requires reduction.

Inspection and Palpation of the Neck

Inspection of the Neck

E 1. Have the patient sit facing you, with the patient's head held in a central position.
2. Inspect for symmetry of the sternocleidomastoid muscles anteriorly, and the trapezii posteriorly.
3. Have the patient touch the chin to the chest, to each side, and to each shoulder.
4. Assess for limitation of motion.
5. Note the presence of a stoma or tracheostomy.

N The muscles of the neck are symmetrical with the head in a central position. The patient is able to move the head through a full range of motion without complaint of discomfort or noticeable limitation. The patient may be breathing through a stoma or tracheostomy.

A Asymmetry of the neck is abnormal (Figure 11-18).

P Asymmetrical masses can be benign or malignant, but they all must be evaluated further.

| E | Examination | N | Normal Findings | A | Abnormal Findings | P | Pathophysiology |

A The patient complains of pain with flexion or rotation of the head.

P Pain with flexion can be associated with the pain and muscle spasm caused by meningeal irritation of meningitis (see Chapter 19). Generalized discomfort may be related to trauma, spasm, inflammation of muscles, or diseases of the vertebrae.

A There is a slight or prominent lateral deviation of the patient's neck. The sternocleidomastoid muscles, and to a lesser extent the trapezius and scalene muscles, may also be prominent on the affected side. The muscles frequently hypertrophy as the result of powerful contractions.

P This condition is called **torticollis.** Causes can be:

    1. Congenital: resulting from a hematoma or partial rupture at birth of the sternocleidomastoid, causing a shortening of the muscle.

    2. Ocular: a head posture assumed to correct for ocular muscle palsy and resulting diplopia.

    3. Acute spasm: commonly associated with the inflammation of viral myositis or trauma such as sleeping with the head in an unusual position.

    4. Other: hysteria, phenothiazine therapy, and Parkinson's disease as the result of increased cholinergic activity in the brain.

A Range of motion of the neck is reduced.

P Degenerative changes of osteoarthritis may result in decreased ability for full range of motion. This condition is usually painless unless nerve root irritation has occurred. Crepitus, or a crunching sound on hyperextension of the neck, may also be observed.

Palpation of the Neck

E 1. Stand in front of the patient.

    2. Use your finger pads to palpate the sternocleidomastoids.

    3. Note the presence of masses or tenderness.

    4. Stand behind the patient.

    5. Palpate the trapezius with your finger pads.

    6. Note the presence of masses or tenderness.

N The muscles should be symmetrical without palpable masses or spasm.

A A mass is palpated in the musculature.

P A mass may be a tumour, either primary or metastatic.

A A spasm may be felt in the muscles.

P Muscle spasm may be the result of infections, trauma, chronic inflammatory processes, or neoplasms.

Inspection of the Thyroid Gland

E 1. Secure tangential lighting and shine it at an oblique angle on the patient's anterior neck.

    2. Face the patient.

    3. Ask the patient to look straight ahead with the head slightly extended.

    4. Have the patient take a sip of water and swallow twice.

    5. While the patient swallows, observe the front of the neck in the area of the thyroid and the isthmus for masses and symmetrical movement.

N Thyroid tissue moves up with swallowing but often the movement is so small it is not visible on inspection. In males, the thyroid cartilage, or Adam's apple, is more prominent than in females.

A A mass or enlargement of the thyroid that moves upward with swallowing is abnormal.

P Many **goiters** (enlarged thyroid glands) or thyroid nodules are visible and may indicate a variety of thyroid diseases.

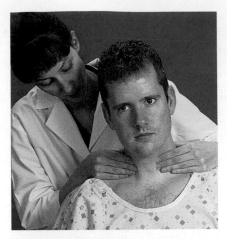

A. Posterior Approach.

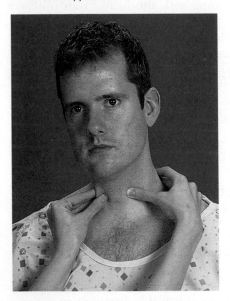

B. Anterior Approach.

Figure 11-19 Examination of the Thyroid Gland.

Nursing Tip

Assessment of the Neck's Vasculature

It is important to assess the superficial temporal artery, the carotid arteries, and the jugular veins at this point in the examination. Refer to Chapter 16 for a description of the technique.

Nursing Alert

Thyroid Cancer

Epidemiology[4]
- Thyroid cancer was the 12th leading cause of new cancers in 2006. However, it has a low death-to-case (DTC) ratio.
- Women accounted for 76.4% of new thyroid cancer diagnoses.
- The rate of thyroid cancer in Canadians has increased steadily since 1992, similar to trends in the United States and Europe, possibly because of improved detection practices that identify early stage cancers more frequently than was possible in the past.

Risk Factors
- Diets low in iodine (rare in Canada)
- History of head or neck radiation, especially in childhood
- Exposure to nuclear fallout
- Genetics
- Female gender

Palpation of the Thyroid Gland

Palpation of the thyroid gland may be done using both anterior and posterior approaches (Figure 11-19).

Posterior Approach

E 1. Have the patient sit comfortably. Stand behind the patient.
2. Have the patient lower the chin slightly in order to relax the neck muscles.
3. Place your thumbs on the back of the patient's neck and bring the other fingers around the neck anteriorly with their tips resting on the lower portion of the neck over the trachea.
4. Move the finger pads over the tracheal rings.
5. Instruct the patient to swallow. Palpate the isthmus for nodules or enlargement.
6. Have the patient incline the head slightly forward.
7. Press the fingers of the left hand against the left side of the thyroid cartilage to stabilize it while placing the fingers of the right hand gently against the right side.
8. Instruct the patient to swallow sips of water.
9. Note consistency, nodularity, or tenderness as the gland moves upward.
10. Repeat on the other side.

N/A/P Refer to Anterior Approach.

| E | Examination | N | Normal Findings | A | Abnormal Findings | P | Pathophysiology |

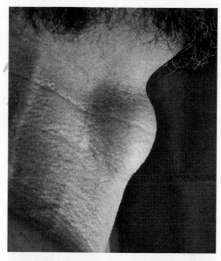

Figure 11-20 Solitary Thyroid Nodule. *Courtesy of Dr. Andrew B. Silva, Pediatric Otolaryngology.*

Anterior Approach

E 1. Stand in front of the patient.
   2. Ask the patient to flex the head slightly forward.
   3. Place the right thumb on the thyroid cartilage and displace the cartilage to the patient's right.
   4. Grasp the elevated and displaced right lobe of the thyroid gland with your thumb and index and middle fingers of the left hand.
   5. Palpate the surface of the gland for consistency, nodularity, and tenderness.
   6. Have the patient swallow, and palpate the surface again.
   7. Repeat the procedure on the opposite side.

N No enlargement, masses, or tenderness should be noted on palpation.

A Palpation reveals the gland to be smooth, soft, and slightly enlarged but less than twice the size of a normal thyroid gland.

P This is referred to as physiological hyperplasia and can be seen premenstrually, during pregnancy, or from puberty to young adulthood in females. Symmetrical enlargement may also be noted in patients who live in areas of iodine deficiency. These are referred to as nontoxic diffuse goiters or endemic goiters.

A Palpation reveals the gland to be two to three times larger than normal size.

P This is diffuse toxic hyperplasia of the thyroid, or Graves' disease, an autoimmune disorder that is the most common type of hyperthyroidism.

A Asymmetrical enlargement of the thyroid and the presence of two or more nodules are found.

P These are thyroid adenomas (benign epithelial tumours) that usually occur after the age of 30. A nontoxic diffuse goiter may become nodular as the patient ages.

A Palpation reveals a solitary nodule in the thyroid tissue.

P A solitary nodule is suggestive of carcinoma (Figure 11-20).

A Lateral deviation of the trachea is noted on palpation, but you are unable to identify a specific goiter.

P This may be a retrosternal goiter, which sometimes occurs in a patient with a short neck, or a goiter with many adenomatous nodules.

A Tenderness of the thyroid is found on palpation.

P Tenderness of an enlarged, firm thyroid suggests thyroiditis.

Auscultation of the Thyroid Gland

If the thyroid is enlarged, auscultation should be done.

E 1. Stand in front of the patient.
   2. Place the bell of the stethoscope over the right thyroid lobe.
   3. Auscultate for bruits.
   4. Repeat on the left thyroid lobe.

N Auscultation should not reveal bruits.

AP Auscultation reveals the presence of a bruit over an enlarged thyroid gland.

P Bruits occur with increased turbulence in a vessel and are due to the increased vascularization of a thyroid gland that is enlarged due to diffuse toxic goiter.

Inspection of the Lymph Nodes

E 1. Stand in front of the patient.
   2. Expose the area of the head and neck to be assessed.
   3. Inspect the nodal areas of the head and neck for any enlargement or inflammation.

N Lymph nodes should not be visible or inflamed.

A Enlargement and inflammation are present in specific nodes.

P Lymph nodes can be enlarged and inflamed when there is a localized or generalized infection in the body. This attempt to prevent the spread of infection occurs as a part of the body's immune response to infection.

Palpation of the Lymph Nodes

E **1.** Have the patient sit comfortably.

2. Face the patient and assess both sides of the neck simultaneously.

3. Move the pads and tips of your middle three fingers in small circles of palpation using gentle pressure.

4. Follow a systematic, routine sequence beginning with the preauricular, postauricular, occipital, submental, submandibular, and tonsillar nodes. Moving down to the neck, evaluate the anterior and the posterior cervical chains, and the supraclavicular nodes (Figure 11-21).

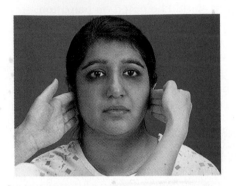

A. Preauricular

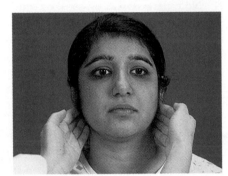

B. Postauricular

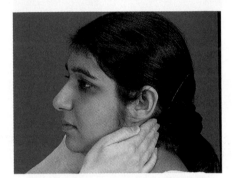

C. Occipital

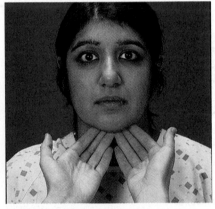

D. Submental

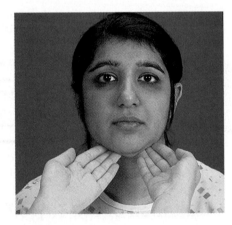

E. Submandibular

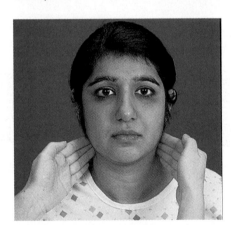

F. Tonsillar

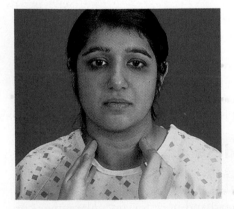

G. Anterior Cervical Chain

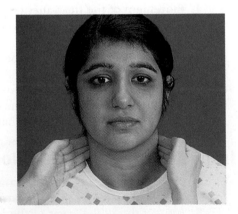

H. Posterior Cervical Chain

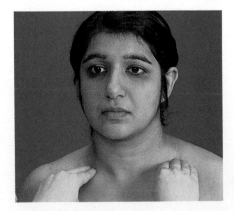

I. Supraclavicular

Figure 11-21 Palpation of Lymph Nodes.

E	Examination	N	Normal Findings	A	Abnormal Findings	P	Pathophysiology

     5. Note size, shape, delimitation (discrete or matted together), mobility, consistency, and tenderness.

N Lymph nodes should not be palpable in the healthy adult patient; however, small, discrete, movable nodes are sometimes present but are of no significance.

A Palpable lymph nodes are abnormal.

P Palpable lymph nodes are frequently seen in acute bacterial infections such as streptococcal pharyngitis. The anterior cervical nodes are usually affected and may be warm, firm, tender, and mobile.

A An enlarged postauricular node is sometimes found in patients with ear infections.

P Enlarged, hard, tender nodes are seen in lymphadenitis (inflammation of the lymph nodes). The affected node is the site of the inflammation.

A Enlarged nodes, particularly of the anterior and posterior cervical chains, may be found in infectious mononucleosis. These nodes are usually tender.

P An enlarged node in the left supraclavicular area (Virchow's node) may point to malignancy in the abdominal or thoracic regions.

A Nontender, firm, or hard nodes that are nonmobile may indicate a malignancy in the head and neck area, or metastasis from the region that the lymph node drains.

A Patients with malignant lymphomas may also present with nodes that are firm, hard, or rubbery; nontender; and fixed. In Hodgkin's disease, the cervical nodes are frequently the first to be palpable.

P Palpable lymph nodes can result from a variety of other pathological processes, including blood dyscrasias, AIDS, tuberculosis, surgical procedures that traumatize the nodes, blood transfusions, or chronic illness.

GERONTOLOGICAL VARIATIONS

Loss of subcutaneous fat and musculoskeletal changes due to the aging process affect the appearance and function of the head and neck. Facial symmetry may be altered because of the presence of dentures or loss of teeth. Neck veins may be more prominent due to loss of fat.

The head, neck, and lower jaw may be thrust forward, especially with a kyphotic posture. A "buffalo hump" may appear as an accumulation of fat over the posterior cervical vertebrae. Range of motion of the head may be limited, painful, or possible only with a jerking or "cogwheel" motion. Dizziness accompanying movement of the head may create safety problems. All of these changes may affect the elderly patient's ability to maintain normal activities of daily living.

CASE STUDY   The Patient with Cervical Strain

Mary is a 32-year-old mother of two young children. She says she awoke this morning with a stiff neck, especially on the left side. She has a busy life caring for her two children, ages 1 and 3, and taking care of their home.

HEALTH HISTORY

PATIENT PROFILE	32 yo woman, looks worried
HEALTH ISSUE/CONCERN	"I have had a stiff neck since yesterday."

continues

HISTORY OF ISSUES/CONCERN

Pt was in her usual state of good hl until yesterday when she developed pain & stiffness in her neck. The discomfort seemed to worsen during the night, & upon waking up this morning she found that she had significant pain & stiffness in her neck, particularly the Ⓛ side. She reports that she often carries her 1 yo son on her Ⓛ hip, shifting her wt to maintain balance. Yesterday, while walking & holding the child in this manner, she slipped on a wet floor & was barely able to maintain her balance s̄ falling. She noticed the stiffness beginning shortly p̄ this occurred; denies radiation. She denies any respiratory symptoms, fever, sweats, or chills, numbness & tingling in her hands, or △ in mental status. She feels fine otherwise. She took 200 mg ibuprofen about 2 hrs ago, which provided some relief. She reports feeling better when lying down but has little time to do this as must work & care for the children.

PAST HEALTH HISTORY

Medical History Denies serious medical problems. G2 P2

Surgical History C-sections c̄ both deliveries. Uncomplicated appendectomy at age 12

Medications Triphasil (OCP)

Communicable Diseases Varicella, age 6. Denies other childhood illnesses & STIs

Allergies Mild pollen allergy in spring s̄ tx

Injuries and Accidents fx Ⓛ ankle age 10 from bicycle fall—casted 6 wks; Ø sequelae

Special Needs Denies

Blood Transfusions Denies

Childhood Illnesses See communicable disease

Immunizations UTD; did not receive influenza vaccine this yr

FAMILY HEALTH HISTORY

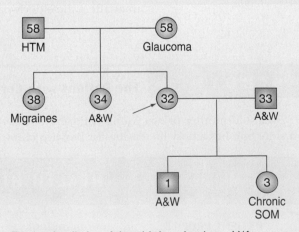

LEGEND
- ⬤ Living female
- ⬛ Living male
- ⊗ Deceased female
- ⊠ Deceased male
- ⟋ Points to patient

A&W = Alive and well
HTN = Hypertension
SOM = Serous otitis media

Denies family hx of thyroid dz, migraines, H/A.

SOCIAL HISTORY	
Alcohol Use	Glass or two of wine q Sat
Drug Use	Denies
Tobacco Use	Has never smoked cigarettes; no chewing tobacco or snuff
Domestic and Intimate Partner Violence	Denies
Sexual Practice	Monogamous c̄ partner of 5 yrs
Travel History	Summer vacations c̄ family at country cottage; occasional visits out of town for shopping or to visit family & friends
Work Environment	Works in a pharmacy as cashier
Home Environment	Lives c̄ 2 children & partner in their own home in suburban neighbourhood
Hobbies and Leisure Activities	Cooking, movies, playing c̄ children
Stress	Balancing work & home life; sometimes gets called to work at the last minute
Education	BA in English
Economic Status	Mortgage payments & living expenses take biggest chunk of earnings; has to watch what she spends, small debt on Visa
Religion/Spirituality	"I'm not the religious type."
Ethnicity	"I'm half Irish, half French."
Roles and Relationships	Close relationship c̄ partner & parents, sisters, friends. Says she has a "good life."
Characteristic Patterns of Daily Living	Wakens around 06:30; takes children to daycare for 08:00; works day or evening shift; if evenings then partner cares for children. Goes to Curves (gym) three times a week; works every other weekend so does house maintenance in week to "stay ahead"; plans weekends off carefully to spend time with family.
HEALTH MAINTENANCE ACTIVITIES	
Sleep	Usually gets 7–8 hours sleep. May nap in afternoon before going to evening shift.
Diet	Tries to have balanced diet c̄ plenty fruits & vegetables, lean meat, whole grain breads, dairy products
Exercise	Curves (exercise program for women) 2–3 times a wk; "chasing children"
Stress Management	Walking c̄ children, exercise, yoga, talking c̄ partner or friends, listening to music or watching movies
Use of Safety Devices	Always wears seat belt; home is child proofed

continues

Health Check-ups	Last exam $\cong$ 1 yr ago $\bar{p}$ birth of baby
PHYSICAL ASSESSMENT	
Inspection of the Shape of the Head	Normocephalic
Palpation of the Head	Skull smooth, $\bar{s}$ tenderness, masses, or depressions
Inspection and Palpation of the Scalp	Scalp smooth & intact $\bar{s}$ lesions or masses
Inspection of the Face	
Symmetry	Symmetrical $\bar{s}$ involuntary movements or swelling
Shape and Features	Round, $\bar{s}$ edema
Palpation and Auscultation of the Mandible	TMJ articulates smoothly $\bar{s}$ clicking or crepitus
Inspection of the Neck	Spasm noted in Ⓛ sternocleidomastoid & trapezius; $\downarrow$ rotation to the Ⓡ
Palpation of the Neck	Ⓛ sternocleidomastoid & trapezius are tender & tight to palpation
Inspection of the Thyroid Gland	No enlargement or asymmetry noted
Palpation of the Thyroid Gland	No enlargement, tenderness, masses, or nodules
Auscultation of the Thyroid Gland	Ø bruits
Inspection of the Lymph Nodes	Ø enlargement
Palpation of the Lymph Nodes	Ø adenopathy

◄NURSING CHECKLIST►

Head, Neck, and Regional Lymphatics Assessment

Inspection
- Shape of the head
- Scalp
- Face
  - Symmetry
  - Shape and features
- Neck
- Thyroid gland
- Lymph nodes

Palpation
- Head
- Scalp

- Mandible
- Neck
- Thyroid gland
  - Posterior approach
  - Anterior approach
- Lymph nodes

Auscultation
- Mandible
- Thyroid gland

REVIEW QUESTIONS

1. Risk factors for migraine headache include:
   a. Males, ages 20–50, allergies
   b. Males, history of motion sickness, tyramine
   c. Females, ages 5–50, caffeine intake
   d. Females, hypoxia, estrogen
   The correct answer is (c).

2. When inspecting the shape of the patient's head, you note an abnormal enlargement of the skull and bony facial structures. The term used to describe this finding is:
   a. Craniotabes
   b. Hydrocephalus
   c. Craniosynostosis
   d. Acromegaly
   The correct answer is (d).

3. Palpation of a normal temporal artery reveals:
   a. Softness of the surrounding bony structures
   b. Smooth, readily compressible, and nontender vessel
   c. Firm consistency and tenderness
   d. A stronger impulse than found with other peripheral pulses
   The correct answer is (b).

4. When inspecting your patient's face, you notice asymmetry of the palpebral fissures, nasolabial folds, and facial expression. These findings are characteristic of:
   a. Down syndrome
   b. Hypertelorism
   c. Parkinson's disease
   d. Bell's palsy
   The correct answer is (d).

5. Dusky blue discoloration beneath the eyes is known as:
   a. Allergic shiners
   b. Dennie's lines
   c. Myxedema
   d. Cachexia
   The correct answer is (a).

6. The face of a patient with Cushing's syndrome will have:
   a. Tenderness in the TMJ
   b. A transverse crease across the nose
   c. A rounded face with red cheeks and excess hair on the jaw and upper lip
   d. Thin, sharply defined features
   The correct answer is (c).

7. A solitary nodule found on palpation of the thyroid is suggestive of:
   a. Carcinoma
   b. Thyroid adenoma
   c. Retrosternal goiter
   d. Graves' disease
   The correct answer is (a).

8. When palpating your patient's thyroid using the posterior approach, you note that it is enlarged. Your next step is to:
   a. Order a CT scan of the thyroid
   b. Refer the patient to an endocrinologist
   c. Palpate the thyroid using the anterior approach
   d. Auscultate the thyroid for bruits
   The correct answer is (d).

9. Pain in the mandible during opening and closing of the mouth associated with a clicking sound suggests:
   a. TMJ dysfunction
   b. Vascular spasm
   c. Dental abscess
   d. Swollen lymph nodes
   The correct answer is (a).

10. When describing characteristics of an enlarged lymph node, you would note:
    a. Size, shape, colour, tenderness, mobility
    b. Size, shape, delimitation, mobility, consistency, tenderness
    c. Size, shape, tenderness, vertical mobility
    d. Size, shape, lateral movement, tenderness
    The correct answer is (b).

> **Visit the Estes online companion resource at**
> www.healthassessment.nelson.com **for additional content and study aids.**

[2]Ibid.

[3]British Columbia Ministry of Health. Headaches: When to call a doctor. Retrieved October 16, 2006, from http://www.bchealthguide.org/kbase/topic/major/hw116874/whn2call.htm

[4]Canadian Cancer Society/National Cancer Institute of Canada. (2006). *Canadian Cancer Statistics 2006*. Toronto, Canada.

REFERENCES

[1]Gilmour, H., & Wilkins, K. (2000). Statistics Canada: *Health Reports, 12*(2), 23–40.

BIBLIOGRAPHY

DeGroot, L. J., & Jameson, L. (2006). *Endocrinology* (5th ed). Philadelphia: Elsevier Saunders.

International Headache Society (1988). Classification and diagnostic criteria for headache disorders, cranial neuralgias and facial pain. Headache Classification Committee of the International Headache Society. *Cephalagia, 8* (suppl 7):1–96.

Lance, J. W., & Goadsby, P. (Eds.) (2006). *Mechanism and management of headache.* Philadelphia: Elsevier, Butterworth, Heinemann.

Nicholson, R., Penzien, D., McCrory, D. C., Gray, R. N., Nash, J., & Dickersin, K. (2004). Behavioral therapies for migraine. (Protocol) *The Cochrane Database of Systematic Reviews.* Issue 1. Art. No.: CD004601.

Molgat, C. V. & Patten, S. (2005). Comorbidity of major depression and migraine: A Canadian population-based study. *Canadian Journal of Psychiatry, 50,* 832–37.

Winner, P., & Lewis, D. W. (2005). *Young adult and pediatric headache management.* Hamilton, ON: Decker Inc.

WEB RESOURCES

MyThyroid.com (created by Dr. Drucker, a thyroid specialist in Toronto)
http://www.mythyroid.com/

OUCH Canada (Organization for Understanding Cluster Headaches)
http://www.clusterheadaches.ca/DesktopDefault.aspx

Thyroid Foundation of Canada
http://www.thyroid.ca/

T4Life Canada's Thyroid Magazine
http://www.t4life.com/

World Headache Alliance
http://www.w-h-a.org/wha2/index.asp

CHAPTER 12

Eyes

COMPETENCIES

1. Identify the structures and functions of the eyes.

2. Discuss the system-specific history for the eyes.

3. Describe normal findings in the physical assessment of the eyes.

4. Describe common abnormalities found in the physical assessment of the eyes.

5. Explain the pathophysiology of common abnormalities of the eyes.

6. Perform the physical assessment of the eyes.

*P*hysical assessment of the eyes provides information about the patient's nutritional, endocrine, cardiovascular, gastrointestinal, and neurological systems.

ANATOMY AND PHYSIOLOGY

External Structures

The external structures of the eyes comprise the eyelids or palpebra, the conjunctiva, the lacrimal glands, and the extraocular muscles. The eyelids consist of smooth muscle covered with a very thin layer of skin; they admit light to the eye while protecting and maintaining lubrication of the eye. The interior surface of the lid muscle is covered with a pink mucous membrane called the **palpebral conjunctiva.** Contiguous with the palpebral conjunctiva is the **bulbar conjunctiva,** which folds back over the anterior surface of the eyeball and merges with the cornea at the **limbus,** the junction of the sclera and the cornea (Figure 12-1). The conjunctiva contains blood vessels and pain receptors that respond quickly to outside insult. Eyelashes are evenly spaced along lid margins and curve outward to protect the eye by filtering particles of dirt and dust from the external environment. Eyebrows are symmetrical and evenly distributed above the eyelids.

The opening between the eyelids is called the **palpebral fissure.** Upper and lower eyelids meet at the inner **canthus** on the nasal side and at the outer canthus on the temporal side. Embedded just beneath the lid margins are the meibomian glands, which secrete a lubricating substance onto the surface of the eye. The **tarsal plates** are connective tissue that give shape to the upper lids.

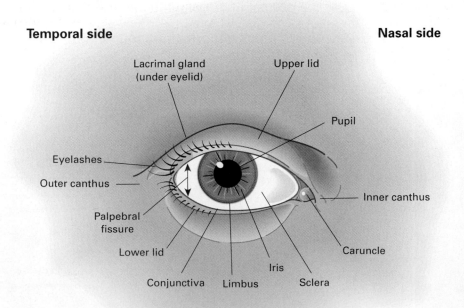

Temporal side   **Nasal side**

Lacrimal gland (under eyelid)   Upper lid

Pupil

Eyelashes

Outer canthus

Inner canthus

Palpebral fissure

Caruncle

Lower lid   Iris

Conjunctiva   Limbus   Sclera

RIGHT EYE

Figure 12-1 External View of the Eye.

Lacrimal Apparatus

The **lacrimal apparatus** is made up of the lacrimal gland and ducts. The lacrimal glands, located above and on the temporal side of each eye, are responsible for the production of tears, which lubricate the eye. Tears drain through the inferior and superior **puncta** at the inner canthus through the nasolacrimal duct and the lacrimal sac to the inferior turbinate in the nose. The **caruncle,** which contains sebaceous glands, is the round, red structure in the inner canthus.

Extraocular Muscles

Six extraocular muscles (superior, inferior, medial, and lateral recti, and the superior and inferior obliques) extend from the scleral surface of each eye and attach to the bony orbit. These voluntary muscles work in concert to move the eyes with great precision in several directions to provide a single image to the brain.

Internal Structures

The globes of the eyes are spherical structures that are encased in the protective bony orbits of the face along with the lacrimal gland and extrinsic muscles of the eye. Only a small portion of the anterior surface of the eye is exposed. The eye itself is approximately 2.5 cm in diameter and has three layers: a tough, outer, fibrous tunic (sclera); a middle, vascular tunic; and the innermost layer, which contains the retina (Figure 12-2).

Outer Layer

The outer tunic consists of the transparent cornea on the outer portion, which is continuous with the **sclera,** an opaque material that appears white and covers the structures inside the eye. The sclera protects the eye and is a surface for the attachment of the extraocular muscles. The posterior portion of the sclera contains an opening for the entrance of the optic nerve and various blood vessels. The **cornea** is a nonvascular, transparent surface that covers the iris and is continuous with the conjunctival epithelium.

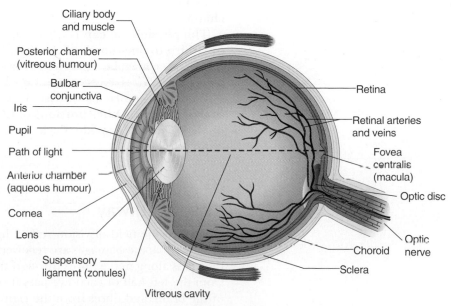

Figure 12-2 Lateral Cross Section of the Interior Eye.

Middle Layer

The pigmented, middle, vascular tunic, or uveal layer, is composed of the **choroid,** the ciliary body, and the iris. The choroid is a vascular tissue that lines the inner surface of the eye just beneath the retina. It provides nutrition to the retinal pigment epithelium and helps absorb excess light.

The **ciliary body** is an anterior extension of the uveal tract; it siphons serum from the systemic blood flow to produce the aqueous humour needed to nourish the corneal endothelium. Zonules are small strands of tissue extending from the ciliary body to the crystalline **lens.** Zonules hold the lens in place and allow it to change shape in order to refract light from various focusing distances. The **iris,** the most anterior portion of the uveal tract, provides a distinctive colour for the eye. It is comprised of smooth muscle that regulates the entrance of light. The **pupil,** an opening in the centre of the iris, regulates the amount of light entering the eye. The pupil reacts to light and closeness of objects by stimulation of the sympathetic nervous system, which dilates it, and parasympathetic nervous system, which constricts it.

The central cavity of the eye posterior to the lens is filled with a clear, gelatinous material called **vitreous humour,** which helps maintain the shape of the eye and the position of the internal structures.

Visual images pass through the structures and aqueous humour of the **anterior chamber** (the space anterior to the pupil and iris) and the vitreous humour of the **posterior chamber** (the space immediately posterior to the iris) to the fundus of the eye, where the retina is located.

Inner Layer

The innermost layer of the eyeball, or the **retina,** is an extension of the optic nerve, which lines the inside of the globe and receives light impulses that are transmitted to the occipital lobe of the brain. Paired retinal arteries and veins branch from the optic disc toward the periphery, growing smaller as they extend outward. Generally, retinal arteries are smaller and a lighter red than veins and often have a silver-looking "arterial light reflex." Normal arterial-to-venous width is a ratio of 2:3 or 4:5.

The **optic disc** is a round or oval area with distinct margins located on the nasal side of the retina. Retinal fibres join at the optic disc to form the optic nerve. Nerve fibres from the temporal visual fields cross at the optic chiasm.

The **physiologic cup** is a pale, central area in the optic disc occupying one-third to one-fourth of the disc. In the temporal area of the retina, the tiny, darker **macula,** with the **fovea centralis** at its centre, contains a high concentration of **cones** necessary for colour vision, reading ability, and other tasks requiring fine visual discrimination. The fovea is the area of sharpest vision. Other portions of the retina contain a high concentration of **rods,** which provide dark and light discrimination and peripheral vision.

Visual Pathway

Objects in the field of vision reflect light that is received by sensory neurons in the retina; these images are received upside down and reversed. From there they pass along nerve fibres through the optic disc and the optic nerve. Fibres from the left half of each eye pass through the optic chiasm to the right side of the brain, and fibres from the right side of each eye pass to the left side of the visual cortex of the occipital lobe of the brain (Figure 12-3).

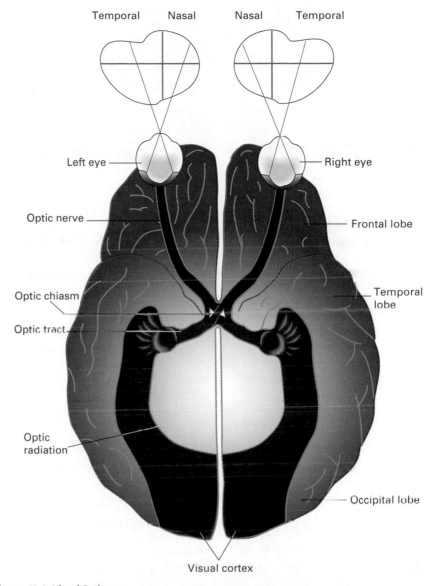

LEFT VISUAL FIELD

RIGHT VISUAL FIELD

Temporal Nasal Nasal Temporal

Left eye

Right eye

Optic nerve

Frontal lobe

Optic chiasm

Temporal lobe

Optic tract

Optic radiation

Occipital lobe

Visual cortex

Figure 12-3 Visual Pathway.

HEALTH HISTORY

The eye health history provides insight into the link between a patient's life/lifestyle and eye information and pathology.

PATIENT PROFILE   *Diseases that are age-, gender-, and race-specific for the eyes are listed.*

Age   Cataract (congenital, elderly)
Presbyopia (middle adulthood)
Hypertensive retinopathy (middle adulthood to elderly)
Glaucoma (middle adulthood to elderly)
Macular degeneration (elderly)
Entropion, ectropion (elderly)
Dry eyes (elderly)

continues

Gender	Female: Dry eyes, thyroid-related ophthalmopathy
Ethnicity	Glaucoma (Black descent, Inuit, Asian descent), melanoma of the eye (Caucasians)
	Trachoma (eye infection caused by Chlamydia Trachomatis—new immigrants from rural areas within Africa, Asia, Central & South America, & the Middle East)
HEALTH ISSUE/CONCERN	*Common health issues/concerns for the eyes are defined, and information on the characteristics of each sign or symptom is provided.*
Changes in Visual Acuity	Change in ability to see clearly
Location	One eye or both eyes
Quality	Dimming of vision, blurred vision, diplopia, visual field loss, legal blindness
Associated Manifestations	Headache, rhinorrhea, sneezing, vertigo, "floaters" (spots of different sizes that float across the visual field & are caused by changes in the vitreous humour), flashes of light, aura, nausea and vomiting, generalized muscle weakness, eye pain or pressure, infection (herpes simplex or cytomegalovirus)
Aggravating Factors	Allergens, stress, lack of sleep, decreased lighting, darkness (night), refractive changes, systemic diseases
Alleviating Factors	Improved lighting, medication, corrective glasses, rest or sleep, adequate hydration
Setting	Work environment, increased reading, computer work, night driving
Timing	With aging, at night, after trauma, with or after a headache, seasonal, sudden onset, gradual onset
Pain	Discomfort in the eye
Quality	Aching, sharp, throbbing, burning
Associated Manifestations	Drainage, conjunctival injection, decreased vision, herpes simplex or zoster lesions, increased tearing, headache
Aggravating Factors	Foreign body in the eye, sunlight or very bright light, contact lenses, trauma, allergens
Alleviating Factors	Closing of eye or eyes, removal of contacts, medications, sunglasses, avoiding allergens
Setting	Work environment (increased reading or computer work), recreational area, outdoors
Timing	Sudden onset, gradual onset, with reading
Drainage	Discharge of liquid from the eye
Quality	Type, colour
Associated Manifestations	Crusting on the lids, pain, itching, redness of the eye or the lids, headache
Aggravating Factors	Allergens, eye makeup, chlorine, poor hygiene, URI

Alleviating Factors	Medications, hypoallergenic or no eye makeup, avoiding allergens, good handwashing
Setting	Outdoors, swimming pool
Timing	In the morning, continuous, intermittent, seasonal
Itching	Irritation that causes the patient to scratch or rub
Quality	Mild, severe
Associated Manifestations	Rhinitis, sneezing, drainage, burning or gritty sensation in the eye, conjunctivitis, headache
Aggravating Factors	Allergens, contact lenses, eye makeup
Alleviating Factors	Medications, cold compresses to the eyes, removal of contacts, avoiding allergens and eye makeup
Setting	Indoors, outdoors
Timing	Seasonal, intermittent, continuous
Dryness	Reduced amount of lubricating secretions in the eye
Associated Manifestations	With systemic disease, redness of the eye, reduced tearing, itching
Aggravating Factors	Decreased humidity, wind, reading
Alleviating Factors	Artificial tears, humidified air
Setting	Outdoors, indoors with decreased humidity
Timing	With aging, during the winter (decreased humidity), post menopause
PAST HEALTH HISTORY	*The various components of the past health history are linked to eye pathology and eye-related information.*
Medical History	
Eye Specific	Myopia, hyperopia, strabismus, astigmatism, glaucoma, cataracts, conjunctivitis, hordeolum, pterygium, blepharitis, chalazion, trachoma, macular degeneration
Noneye Specific	Diabetes mellitus, renal disease, atherosclerotic disease, hypertension, inflammatory processes, infections (viral or bacterial), immunosuppressive disease, nutritional disturbances
Surgical History	Cataract extraction, lens implant, LASIK (laser-assisted in situ-keratomileusis) [laser vision correction], repair of detached retina, neurosurgery, enucleation of eye, optic nerve decompression
Medications	Antibiotics, antihistamines, decongestants, corticosteroids, artificial tears, mydriatics, myotics
Allergies	Pollen: watery or itchy eyes Insect stings: swelling around the eyes Animal dander: watery or itchy eyes
Injuries and Accidents	Foreign bodies; trauma to the eyes

continues

Special Needs	Legal blindness, low vision
Childhood Illnesses	Rubella and visual sequelae (blindness), congenital syphilis
FAMILY HEALTH HISTORY	*Eye diseases that are familial are listed.*
	Myopia, hyperopia, strabismus, colour blindness, cataracts, glaucoma, retinitis pigmentosa, retinoblastoma, neonatal blindness secondary to cataracts from mother contracting rubella in pregnancy
SOCIAL HISTORY	*The components of the social history are linked to eye factors and pathology.*
Work Environment	Exposure to toxins, chemicals, infections, allergens
Stress	Can be linked with decreased vision
HEALTH MAINTENANCE ACTIVITIES	*This information provides a bridge between the health maintenance activities and eye functions.*
Diet	Vitamin deficiencies may affect vision
Use of Safety Devices	Goggles or face shields for sports, job, or home projects
Health Check-Ups	Eye examination, intraocular pressure check

EQUIPMENT

- Ophthalmoscope
- Penlight
- Clean gloves
- Snellen chart, Snellen E chart, Rosenbaum near-vision pocket screening card
- Vision occluder
- Cotton-tipped applicator

Nursing Alert

Vision Issues in Canadians

- In 2001, Statistics Canada found that 610,950 Canadians identified themselves as having seriously impaired vision (defined as difficulty seeing ordinary newsprint or clearly seeing a face from 4 metres).[1]
- By the age of 65, 1 in 9 Canadians will experience severe vision loss.[2]
- By 2016, nearly 1 million Canadians will have severe vision loss.[3]
- According to a survey commissioned by the Canadian Ophthalmological Society, one-third of Canadians cannot name any causes of blindness and 5% incorrectly cited too much TV and computer use as causes.[4]

Nursing Alert

Glaucoma

Epidemiology

- Glaucoma is the second leading cause of blindness in people aged 50 and over, affecting 1 in 100 Canadians over 40.[5]
- At least 300,000 Canadians have glaucoma, with 50% of patients unaware of their disease. It affects men and women alike.[6]
- Half of Canadians do not know the symptoms of glaucoma and 74% are unaware of the risk factors.[7]
- Primary open-angle glaucoma (POAG) accounts for 90% of all cases. (In POAG, the aqueous cannot flow through the trabecular meshwork due to a

continues

blockage or malfunction of the eye's drainage system. This blockage causes intraocular pressure to increase.)[8]

Risk factors[9]

Glaucoma is asymptomatic until it is well advanced. Patients who wait for the appearance of symptoms before getting tested risk irreversible eye damage. The risk factors for glaucoma are:

- Advancing age (peaking after age 70), though glaucoma can develop at any age
- Family history of glaucoma
- High pressure in the eye
- African-Canadian descent
- Diabetes mellitus
- Myopia (nearsightedness)

Screening

Although there is no cure for glaucoma, it can be managed through treatment. Early detection is important. Individuals should have an eye examination every three to five years until the age of 40 and then every two to four years until the age of 65. As so many eye diseases tend to occur in the elderly, those over 65 should have an eye examination every two years—annually if they have any risk factors.[10]

Nursing Alert

Macular Degeneration

- Macular degeneration is the most common cause of severe vision loss in Canada, especially among the elderly. It usually occurs gradually over a few years.
- The most common form of the disease occurring in people over age 55 is age-related macular degeneration (ARMD).[11]

◄NURSING CHECKLIST►

General Approach to Eye Assessment

1. Greet the patient and explain the assessment techniques that you will be using.
2. Use a quiet room free from interruptions.
3. Ensure that the light in the room provides sufficient brightness to allow adequate observation of the patient.
4. Place the patient in an upright sitting position on the examination table.
5. Visualize the underlying structures during the assessment process to allow adequate description of findings.
6. Always compare right and left eyes.
7. Use a systematic approach that is followed consistently each time the assessment is performed.

ASSESSMENT OF THE EYE

Assessment of the eyes should be carried out in an orderly fashion, moving from the extraocular structures to the intraocular structures. The eye assessment usually includes testing of associated cranial nerves and can be performed in the following order:

1. Determination of visual acuity
2. Determination of visual fields
3. Assessment of the external eye and lacrimal apparatus
4. Evaluation of extraocular muscle function
5. Assessment of the anterior segment structures
6. Assessment of the posterior segment structures

Visual Acuity

The assessment of visual acuity (cranial nerve II, or CN II) is a simple, noninvasive procedure that uses a Snellen chart and also an occluder to cover the patient's eye. The **Snellen chart** contains letters of various sizes, with standardized visual acuity numbers at the end of each line of letters (Figure 12-4A). The

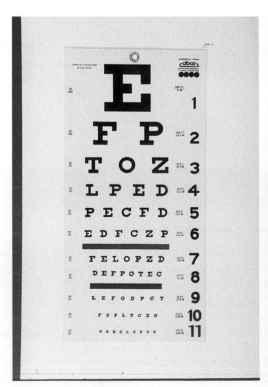

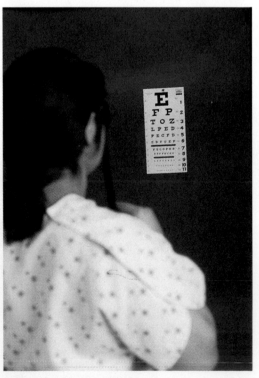

A. Snellen Vision Chart

B. Assessing Distance Vision

Figure 12-4 Visual Acuity Testing.

numbers indicate the degree of visual acuity when the patient is able to read that line of letters at a distance of 20 feet (approximately 6.1 metres).* For instance, a patient who has a visual acuity of 20/70 can read at 20 feet what a patient with 20/20 vision is able to read at 70 feet.

It can be difficult to find the adequate space required for the placement of the chart, but the distance can be simulated with the use of mirrors. For all vision screening, the chart should be illuminated with a diffuse light source to prevent spot lighting or glare.

Distance Vision

E   1. Ask the patient to stand or sit facing the Snellen chart at a distance of 20 feet (Figure 12-4B).
    2. If the patient normally wears glasses, ask that they be removed. Contact lenses may be left in the eyes.
    3. Instruct the patient to cover the left eye with the occluder and to read as many lines on the chart as possible.
    4. Note the number at the end of the last line the patient was able to read.
    5. If the patient is unable to read the letters at the top of the chart, move the patient closer to the chart. Note the distance at which the patient is able to read the top line.
    6. Repeat the test, occluding the right eye.
    7. If the patient normally wears glasses, the test should be repeated with the patient wearing the glasses, and it should be so noted (corrected or uncorrected).

N   The patient who has a visual acuity of 20/20 is considered to have normal visual acuity.

A   The patient is unable to read the chart with an uncorrected visual acuity of 20/30 in one eye, vision in both eyes is different by two lines or more, or acuity is absent.

P   The patient may have a refractive error related to a difference in the refractive power of the cornea. Figure 12-5A illustrates how light rays focus on the retina in a normal eye. In **myopia** (nearsightedness), the axial length of the globe is longer than normal, resulting in the image not being focused directly on the retina; this condition can be changed with corrective lenses (Figure 12-5B). If the patient is amblyopic, no corrective lenses will improve vision. **Amblyopia** is the permanent loss of visual acuity resulting from strabismus that has not been corrected in early childhood, or from certain medical conditions (alcoholism, uremia, and diabetes mellitus).

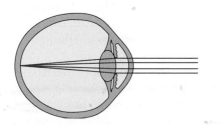

A. Normal eye
Light rays focus on the retina

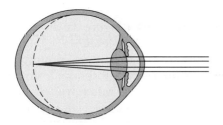

B. Myopia (nearsightedness)
Light rays focus in front
of the retina

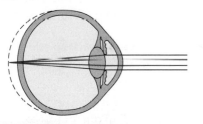

C. Hyperopia (farsightedness)
Light rays focus behind
the retina

Figure 12-5 Eye Refraction.

Nursing Tip

Use of the Snellen E Chart

When testing visual acuity of illiterate or preschool (ages 3 to 6) patients, use the Snellen E chart, which shows the letter "E" facing in different directions, rather than the standard Snellen alphabet chart. Ask the patient to identify the direction to which the "E" or "legs" of the E point (see Chapter 24).

| E | **Examination** | N | **Normal Findings** | A | **Abnormal Findings** | P | **Pathophysiology** |

---

*Although the metric system is used in Canada, the use of the 20-foot norm in relation to eye examinations remains popular and is what most people can identify with.

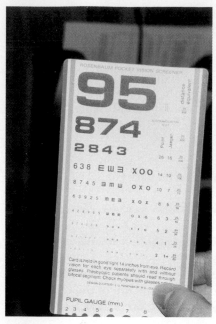

Figure 12-6 Rosenbaum Pocket Vision Screener.

P The patient may have corneal opacities that are congenital, from lesions that have scarred the cornea (e.g., herpes simplex), from trauma, or from degeneration and dystrophies.

P Visual acuity can be decreased because of opacities of the lens caused by senile or traumatic cataracts.

P Systemic autoimmune diseases such as inflammatory bowel disease, arthritis, or other collagen vascular diseases can be associated with inflammation of the iris (iritis), which will affect visual acuity. Iritis can also be idiopathic.

P Inflammation of the retina caused by toxoplasmosis or by the presence of blood in the vitreous humour following hemorrhage can be responsible for decreased visual acuity.

P Systemic diseases such as hypertension or diabetes mellitus and trauma may damage the choroid and retina, causing decreased visual acuity.

P Visual acuity can be impaired by pathology affecting the optic nerve, such as multiple sclerosis, tumours or abscesses of the nerve itself, optic atrophy, papilledema resulting from increased intracranial pressure, optic neuritis, or neovascularization of the optic nerve with resultant bleeding related to diabetes mellitus.

Near Vision

E 1. Use a pocket Snellen chart, Rosenbaum card (Figure 12-6), or any printed material written at an appropriate reading level.

2. If the pocket vision card is available, have the patient sit comfortably and hold the card 35 cm (14 inches) from the face without moving it.

3. Ask the patient to read the smallest line possible. If other printed material is used, you will be able to gain only a general understanding of the patient's near vision.

N Until a patient is in the late 30s to the late 40s, reading is generally possible at a distance of 35 cm.

A A patient in this age range who cannot read at 35 cm is considered presbyopic. Younger persons may have difficulty seeing up close because they have **hyperopia,** or farsightedness (Figure 12-5C).

P The normal aging process causes the lens to harden (nuclear sclerosis), decreasing its ability to change shape and therefore focus on near objects.

Colour Vision

E For routine testing of colour vision, test the patient's ability to identify primary colours found on the Snellen chart or in the examining room. For more specific testing, ask the patient to view Ishihara plates and identify the numerals on them.

N The patient who is able to identify all six screening Ishihara plates correctly has normal colour vision.

Nursing Tip

Low Vision versus Legal Blindness versus Blind

Be sure to describe visual loss correctly. For example, many more people are legally blind than totally blind; that is, they have no light perception. The following apply to all provinces and territories in Canada:

- Low vision is best corrected visual acuity of less than 20/60 and better than 20/200.
- Legal blindness or registered blindness is when corrected vision is 20/200 or worse, or peripheral vision is less than 20°.

A The colour vision defect is designated as red/green, blue/yellow, or complete when the patient sees only shades of grey.

P Defects in colour vision can result from diseases of the optic nerve, macular degeneration, pathology of the fovea centralis, nutritional deficiency, or heredity.

Visual Fields

The confrontation technique is used to test visual fields of each eye (CN II). The visual field of each eye is divided into quadrants, and a stimulus is presented in each quadrant.

E 1. Sit or stand approximately 60–90 cm (2–3 feet) opposite the patient, with your eyes at the same level as the patient's (Figure 12-7).
   2. Have the patient cover the right eye with the right hand or an occluder.
   3. Cover your left eye in the same manner.
   4. Have the patient look at your uncovered eye with his or her uncovered eye.
   5. Hold your free hand at arm's length equidistant from you and the patient, and move your hand, or a held object such as a pen, into your and the patient's field of vision from nasal, temporal, superior, inferior, and oblique angles.
   6. Ask the patient to say "now" when your hand is seen moving into the field of vision. Use your own visual fields as the control for comparison to the patient's.
   7. Repeat the procedure for the other eye.

N The patient is able to see the stimulus at about 90° temporally, 60° nasally, 50° superiorly, and 70° inferiorly.

A If the patient is unable to identify movement that you perceive, a defect in the visual field is presumed. The portion of the visual field loss should be noted (Figure 12-8).

P Defects in the patient's visual field can be associated with tumours or strokes, or neurological diseases such as glaucoma or retinal detachment.

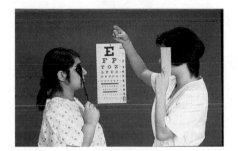

Figure 12-7 Testing Visual Fields by Confrontation.

External Eye and Lacrimal Apparatus

The assessment of the external eye includes the eyelids and the lacrimal apparatus. Pathology of the eyelids is among the most common eye complaint of patients.

Eyelids

E 1. Ask the patient to sit facing you.
   2. Observe the patient's eyelids for drooping, infection, tumours, or other abnormalities.
   3. Note the distribution of the eyelashes and eyebrows.

E	Examination	N	Normal Findings	A	Abnormal Findings	P	Pathophysiology

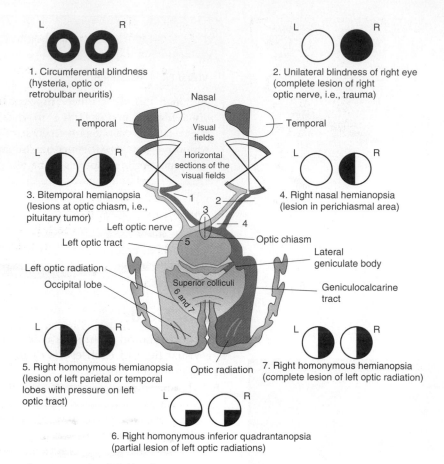

Figure 12-8 Visual Field Defects.

4. Instruct the patient to focus on an object or a finger held about 25–30 cm (10–12 inches) away and slightly above eye level.
5. Move the object or finger slowly downward and observe for a white space of sclera between the upper lid and the limbus.
6. Observe the blinking of the eyes.
7. Ask the patient to elevate the eyelids.

N The eyelids should appear symmetrical with no drooping, infections, or tumours of the lids. Eyelids of people of Asian descent normally slant upward. When the eyes are focused in a normal frontal gaze, the lids should cover the upper portion of the iris. The patient can raise both eyelids symmetrically (CN III). Slight ptosis, or drooping of the lid, can be normal. When the eye is closed, no portion of the cornea should be exposed. Normal lid margins are smooth with the lashes evenly distributed and sweeping upward from the upper lids and downward from the lower lids. Eyebrows are present bilaterally and are symmetrical and without lesions or scaling.

A The patient has either unilateral or bilateral, constant or intermittent ptosis of the lid (Figure 12-9). If part of the pupil is occluded, there may be wrinkling of the forehead above the affected eye in an attempt to compensate by using the frontalis muscle to lift the lid.

P Ptosis can be either congenital or acquired. In congenital ptosis there is failure of the levator muscle to develop, which may be associated with pathology of the superior rectus muscle as well. If the ptosis is acquired, it is related to one of three factors:

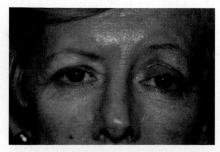

Figure 12-9 Mild Ptosis. *Courtesy of Salim I. Butrus, M.D., Senior Attending, Department of Ophthalmology, Washington Hospital Center, Washington, DC & Associate Clinical Professor, Georgetown University Medical Center, Washington, DC.*

| E | Examination | N | Normal Findings | A | Abnormal Findings | P | Pathophysiology |

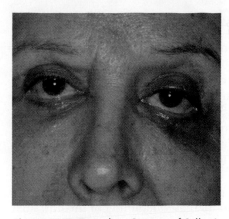

Figure 12-10 Ectropion. *Courtesy of Salim I. Butrus, M.D., Senior Attending, Department of Ophthalmology, Washington Hospital Center, Washington, DC & Associate Clinical Professor, Georgetown University Medical Center, Washington, DC.*

1. Mechanical: heavy lids from lesions, adipose tissue, swelling, or edema.
2. Myogenic: muscular diseases such as myasthenia gravis or multiple sclerosis.
3. Neurogenic: paralysis from damage or interruption of the neural pathways.

A An area of white sclera appears between the upper lid and the limbus, widening as the object is moved downward.

P This condition is called lid lag and may indicate the presence of thyrotoxicosis or increased circulating levels of free thyroxine or triiodothyronine.

A The patient is unable to bring about complete lid closure. This is generally a unilateral condition.

P This condition is referred to as **lagophthalmos** and can be associated with Bell's palsy, stroke, trauma, or **ectropion** (everted eyelid) (Figure 12-10).

A During inspection of the lids, a disparity of the palpebral fissure is noted with apparent lid retraction, indicating a protrusion of the globe. This condition may be unilateral or bilateral.

P This abnormality is **exophthalmos** (or proptosis) and can be present unilaterally in orbital tumours, thyroid disease, trauma, or inflammation. Bilateral exophthalmos is related to thyroid disease.

A There is apparent disparity in the size of the globe, manifested by a narrowing of the palpebral fissure.

P Enophthalmos is a backward displacement of the globe in the orbit, generally caused by an orbital blowout fracture due to trauma. When this occurs, the orbital contents herniate through the fracture site.

A The turning inward, or inversion, of the lower lid is referred to as **entropion** and can cause severe discomfort to the patient because the eyelashes abrade the cornea (trichiasis) (Figure 12-11). If left untreated, it can cause inflammation, corneal scarring, and eventual ulceration.

P Entropion is caused by spasms or advancing age (senile). In senile entropion, there is a loss of muscle tone, which causes the lid to fold inward.

A The turning outward, or eversion, of the lower lid is referred to as ectropion and may be unilateral or bilateral (see Figure 12-10). With ectropion, the lower lids appear to be sagging outward.

P The normal aging process can cause the muscles to lose their tone and relax, or they may be affected by Bell's palsy.

A The patient exhibits excessive blinking that may or may not be accompanied by increased tearing and pain.

P The causes of excessive blinking are:
1. Voluntary: irritation to the cornea or the conjunctiva, or stress and anxiety (usually disappears when stimulus is removed).
2. Involuntary: tonic spasms of the orbicularis oculi muscle, called blepharospasm; often seen in elderly individuals and in patients with CN VII lesions, irritation of the eye, fatigue, and stress.

A The lids are black and blue, bluish, yellow, or red, depending on race and skin colour.

P Colour changes in the lids can result from the following:
1. Redness: generalized redness is nonspecific; however, redness in the nasal half of the lid may indicate frontal sinusitis. Redness adjacent to the lower lid can indicate disease of the lacrimal sac or nasolacrimal duct, such as dacryocystitis; and redness in the temporal portion of the lid can result from dacryoadenitis, an inflammation of the lacrimal gland.
2. Bluish: cyanosis can result from orbital vein thrombosis, orbital tumours, or aneurysms in the orbit.
3. Black and blue: ecchymosis is caused by bleeding into the surrounding tissues following trauma (black eye).

A Swelling or edema is noted in the eyelid.

P Swelling or edema may be noted in nonocular conditions such as inflammation associated with allergies, systemic diseases, medications that contribute

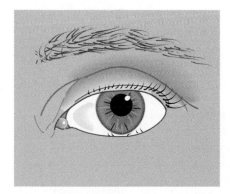

Figure 12-11 Entropion.

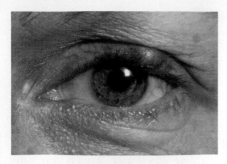

Figure 12-12 Hordeolum.

to swelling from fluid overload, trichinosis, early myxedema, thyrotoxicosis, or contact dermatitis.

A There is an acute localized inflammation, tenderness, and redness, with pain in the infected area (Figure 12-12). This is called a **hordeolum.**

P *Staphylococcus* is generally the infecting organism that causes a hordeolum. There are two types of hordeolum:

1. Internal: affects the meibomian glands, is usually large, and can point either to the skin or to the conjunctival side of the lid.

2. External: often called a sty, is an infection of a sebaceous gland that usually points to the skin side of the lid and extends to the lid margin. Infections of the glands of the eyelid can be caused by improper removal of makeup, dry eyes, or seborrhea. There may be some connection between a hordeolum and increased handling of the lids, such as inserting and removing contact lenses.

A There is a chronic inflammation of the meibomian gland in either the upper or the lower lid (Figure 12-12). It generally forms over several weeks and, in many cases, points toward the conjunctival side of the lid, usually not on the lid margin. There is no redness or tenderness.

P This inflammation is referred to as a **chalazion** and its cause is unknown.

A The lids are inflamed bilaterally and are red rimmed, with scales clinging to both the upper and the lower lids. The patient complains of itching and burning along the lid margins. There may also be some loss of the eyelashes.

P This is chronic marginal **blepharitis,** which may be either staphylococcal or seborrheic. Often a patient has both types simultaneously. If the patient has seborrheic infections elsewhere (scalp or eyebrows), it is more likely that the blepharitis is of the seborrheic type.

A Raised, yellow, nonpainful plaques are present on upper and lower lids near the inner canthus.

P These lesions are **xanthelasma,** a form of xanthoma frequently associated with hypercholesterolemia.

Nursing Tip

Extraocular Muscles

One method of remembering names of extraocular muscles and associated cranial nerves is: LR (lateral rectus) VI; SO (superior oblique) IV; all others (superior, inferior, and medial rectus and inferior oblique) are III.

Reflective Thinking

The Patient with Suspected Physical Abuse

How would you react to a patient who has swollen and discoloured eyelids that you believe to be the result of physical abuse? What would be an appropriate verbal response? What resources are available in your community or institution to support and assist victims of physical abuse?

| E | Examination | N | Normal Findings | A | Abnormal Findings | P | Pathophysiology |

Lacrimal Apparatus

Inspection

E **1.** Have the patient sit facing you.

2. Identify the area of the lacrimal gland. Note any swelling or enlargement of the gland or elevation of the eyelid. Note any enlargement, swelling, redness, increased tearing, or exudate in the area of the lacrimal sac at the inner canthus.

3. Compare this eye to the other eye in order to determine whether there is unilateral or bilateral involvement.

N **There should be no enlargement, swelling, or redness, no large amount of exudate, and minimal tearing.**

A There is inflammation and swelling in the upper lateral aspect of one or both eyes, and pain in the affected area.

P Acute inflammation of the lacrimal gland is called **dacryoadenitis;** it does not occur commonly and may result from trauma or may be found in association with measles, mumps, and mononucleosis.

A There is inflammation and painful swelling beside the nose and near the inner canthus and possibly extending to the eyelid.

P **Dacryocystitis** is caused by inflammatory or neoplastic obstruction of the lacrimal duct.

Palpation

E **1.** To assess the lacrimal sac for obstruction, don gloves.

2. Gently press the index finger near the inner canthus, just inside the rim of the bony orbit of the eye.

3. Note any discharge from the punctum.

N There should not be excessive tearing or discharge from the punctum.

A Mucopurulent discharge is noted.

P Obstruction anywhere along the system from the lacrimal sac to the point at which the ducts empty below the inferior nasal turbinate can cause mucopurulent discharge.

A There is an overflowing of tears from the eye.

P This condition is epiphora, which is caused by obstruction of the lacrimal duct.

Extraocular Muscle Function

Six extraocular muscles control the movement of each eye in relation to three axes: vertical, horizontal, and oblique (Figure 12-13). Assessing extraocular function is carried out by observing corneal light reflex or alignment, using the cover/uncover test, and by testing the six cardinal fields of gaze (CN III, IV, and VI).

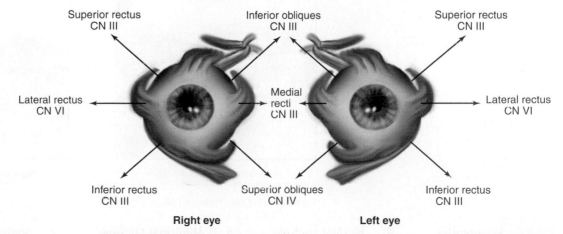

Superior rectus
CN III

Inferior obliques
CN III

Superior rectus
CN III

Lateral rectus
CN VI

Medial recti
CN III

Lateral rectus
CN VI

Inferior rectus
CN III

Superior obliques
CN IV

Inferior rectus
CN III

Right eye

Left eye

Figure 12-13 Direction of Movement of Extraocular Muscles.

CORNEAL LIGHT REFLEX

A. Right Esotropia

B. Right Exotropia

Figure 12-14 Strabismus.

Corneal Light Reflex (Hirschberg Test)

E 1. Instruct the patient to look straight ahead.
2. Focus a penlight on the corneas from a distance of 30–38 cm away at the midline.
3. Observe the location of reflected light on the cornea.

N The reflected light (light reflex) should be seen symmetrically in the centre of each cornea.

A There is a discrepancy in the placement of one of the light reflections.

P Asymmetrical corneal light reflexes indicate an extraocular muscle imbalance that may be related to a variety of causes, depending on the patient's age and medical condition: neurological, such as myasthenia gravis, multiple sclerosis, stroke, neuropathies of diabetes mellitus; uncorrected childhood strabismus (misalignment); trauma; or hypertension. The condition of one eye constantly being deviated is called **strabismus,** or tropia: **esotropia** is an inward turning of the eye; **exotropia** is an outward turning of the eye (Figure 12-14).

Cover/Uncover Test

E 1. Ask the patient to look straight ahead and to focus on an object in the distance.
2. Place an occluder over the patient's left eye for several seconds and observe for movement in the uncovered right eye.
3. As the occluder is removed, observe the covered eye for movement.
4. Repeat the procedure with the same eye, having the patient focus on an object held close to the eye.
5. Repeat on the other side.

N If the eyes are in alignment, there will be no movement of either eye.

A If the uncovered eye shifts position as the other eye is covered, or if the covered eye shifts position as it is uncovered, a **phoria,** or latent misalignment of an eye, exists.

P This condition is a mild weakness elicited by the cover/uncover test and has two forms: **esophoria,** nasal or inward drift, and **exophoria,** a temporal or outward drift (Figure 12-15).

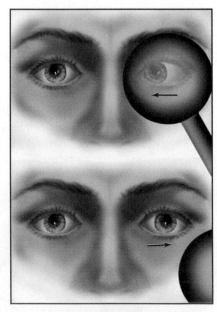

Left covered eye is weaker.
(Left Exophoria)

Right uncovered eye is weaker.
(Right Esophoria)

Figure 12-15 Cover/Uncover Test.

| **E** Examination | **N** Normal Findings | **A** Abnormal Findings | **P** Pathophysiology |

Cardinal Fields of Gaze (Extraocular Muscle Movements)

E 1. Place the patient in a sitting position facing you.
2. Place your nondominant hand just under the patient's chin or on top of the patient's head as a reminder to hold the head still.
3. Ask the patient to follow an object (finger, pencil, or penlight) with the eyes.
4. Move the object through the six fields of gaze (Figure 12-16) in a smooth and steady manner, pausing at each extreme position to detect any **nystagmus,** or involuntary movement, and returning to the centre after each field is tested.
5. Note the patient's ability to move the eyes in each direction.
6. Move the object forward to about 12 cm (5 inches) in front of the patient's nose at the midline.
7. Observe for convergence of gaze.

N Both eyes should move smoothly and symmetrically in each of the six fields of gaze and converge on the held object as it moves toward the nose. A few beats of nystagmus with extreme lateral gaze can be normal.

A There is a lack of symmetrical eye movement in a particular direction.

P Inability to move the eye in a given direction indicates a weakness in the muscle that moves the eye in that direction.

A Abnormal eye movements consist of failure of an eye to move outward (CN VI), inability of the eye to move downward when deviated inward (CN IV), or other defects in movement (CN III).

P Traumatic ophthalmoplegia may be caused by fracture of the orbit near the foramen magnum, causing damage to the extraocular muscles or CN II, III, IV, and VI. Basilar skull fractures that involve the cavernous sinus may also cause extraocular muscle palsy

P Vitamin deficiency, especially thiamine (which may occur in chronic alcoholism), may cause extraocular muscle palsy and nystagmus. Usually CN VI is affected.

A Herpes zoster, syphilis, scarlet fever, whooping cough, or botulism are infections that may affect CN III, IV, and VI, causing extraocular muscle palsy.

A Ophthalmoplegia is paralysis of one or more of the optic muscles.

P Increased intracranial pressure may cause strangulation of CN VI. CN VI palsy occurs late after the onset of increased intracranial pressure.

P Parasellar meningiomas or tumours in the sphenoid sinus may impinge on the wall of the cavernous sinus and involve one or more cranial nerves (CN III, IV, and VI).

A Vertical gaze is a paralysis of upward gaze and is abnormal.

P Destruction at the area of the midbrain–diencephalic junction or the medial longitudinal fasciculus, or tumours of the pineal gland that press on the brain stem at the superior colliculus can cause a vertical gaze deviation.

A Paralysis of horizontal gaze is abnormal.

P Damage to the motor areas of the cerebral cortex causes the inability of both eyes to look to the contralateral side, so the eyes tend to deviate toward the side of the lesion.

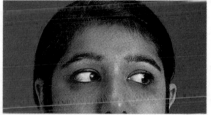

A. Eyes Midline

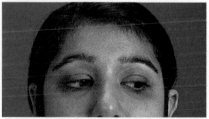

B. Left Lateral Gaze

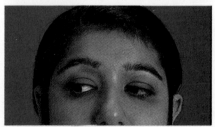

C. Left Lateral Inferior Gaze

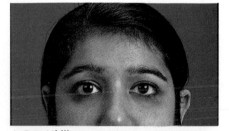

D. Right Lateral Inferior Gaze

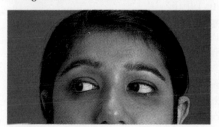

E. Right Lateral Gaze

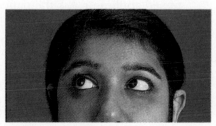

F. Right Lateral Superior Gaze

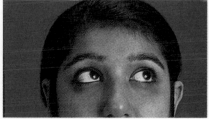

G. Left Lateral Superior Gaze

Figure 12-16 Cardinal Fields of Gaze.

A With internuclear ophthalmoplegia, the eyes are unable to look medially, but convergence may be maintained because the pathway for convergence is different from that for conjugate gaze.

P The medial rectus muscle is involved, so the eyes are unable to look medially. Internuclear ophthalmoplegia may be caused by demyelinization due to multiple sclerosis.

A If one eye deviates down and the other eye deviates up, it is called skew deviation.

P Cerebellar disease or a lesion in the pons on the same side as the eye that is deviated down may cause skew deviation.

A There is a rhythmic, beating, involuntary oscillation of the eyes as the object is held at points away from the midline. Movement is usually lateral, vertical, or rotary. Nystagmus can be jerky, with fast and slow components, or rhythmic, similar to the pendulum of a clock.

P Nystagmus may be caused by a lesion in the brain stem, cerebellum, vestibular system, or along the visual pathways in the cerebral hemispheres.

Anterior Segment Structures

Conjunctiva

To assess the bulbar conjunctiva:

E 1. Separate the patient's lid margins with your fingers.
2. Have the patient look up, down, and to the right and left.
3. Inspect the surface of the bulbar conjunctiva for colour, redness, swelling, exudate, or foreign bodies. Note whether **injection** or redness is around the cornea, foreign bodies, or toward the periphery.
4. With your thumb, gently pull the lower lid toward the cheek and inspect the surface of the bulbar conjunctiva for colour, inflammation, edema, lesions, or foreign bodies.

N The bulbar conjunctiva is transparent with small blood vessels visible in it. It should appear white except for a few small blood vessels, which are normal. No swelling, injection, exudate, foreign bodies, or lesions are noted.

A/P Refer to palpebral conjunctiva.

The palpebral conjunctiva is examined only when there is a concern about its condition. To examine the palpebral conjunctiva of the upper lid:

E 1. Explain the procedure to the patient to alleviate the fear of pain or damage to the eye.
2. Don gloves, and have the patient look down to relax the levator muscle (Figure 12-17A).
3. Gently pull the eyelashes downward and place a sterile, cotton-tipped applicator about 1 cm above the lid margin.
4. Gently exert downward pressure on the applicator while pulling the eyelashes upward to evert the lid (Figure 12-17B).
5. Inspect the palpebral conjunctiva for injection, swelling or **chemosis,** exudate, and foreign bodies.
6. Return the lid to its normal position by instructing the patient to look up and then pulling the eyelid outward and removing the cotton-tipped applicator. Ask the patient to blink.

N The palpebral conjunctiva should appear pink and moist. It is without swelling, lesions, injection, exudate, or foreign bodies.

A Bilateral injected conjunctiva with purulent, sticky discharge and lid edema are noted.

P These findings usually indicate the presence of bacterial conjunctivitis.

A Unilateral injection with moderate pain and without purulent discharge is noted but the patient complains of increased lacrimation.

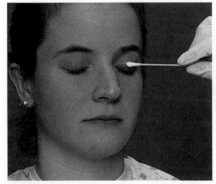

A. Patient Position

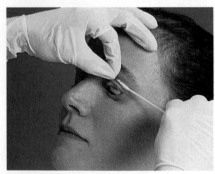

B. Everting the Eyelid

Figure 12-17 Assessing Palpebral Conjunctiva.

| E | **Examination** | N | **Normal Findings** | A | **Abnormal Findings** | P | **Pathophysiology** |

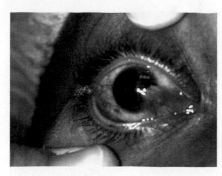

Figure 12-18 Pterygium. *Courtesy of Salim I. Butrus, M.D., Senior Attending, Department of Ophthalmology, Washington Hospital Center, Washington, DC & Associate Clinical Professor, Georgetown University Medical Center, Washington, DC.*

P   These symptoms indicate that the conjunctivitis is viral. Viral conjunctivitis is most commonly due to adenovirus, which may become epidemic. Herpes simplex may also be a viral cause of conjunctivitis. A preauricular node is often felt on palpation.

A   Mild inflammation and injection and follicles of palpebral conjunctiva are present with scant discharge. The patient reports an itching and burning sensation as well as increased lacrimation.

P   This is allergic conjunctivitis and is often associated with hay fever.

A   A yellow nodule is noted on the nasal side of the bulbar conjunctiva adjacent to the cornea. It may be on the temporal side as well. This lesion is painless unless it becomes inflamed.

P   This lesion is called a **pinguecula.** It is a nodular degeneration of the conjunctiva and is thought to be a result of increased exposure to UV light.

A   A unilateral or bilateral triangle-shaped encroachment onto the conjunctiva is abnormal (Figure 12-18). This lesion always occurs nasally and remains painless unless it becomes ulcerated. If the lesion covers the cornea, loss of vision may occur.

P   This lesion is called a **pterygium** and is also caused by excessive UV light exposure.

A   The patient exhibits a sudden onset of a painless, bright-red appearance on the bulbar conjunctiva.

P   This is a subconjunctival hemorrhage and may result from the pressure exerted during coughing, sneezing, or a Valsalva maneuver. It can also be attributed to anticoagulant medications or uncontrolled hypertension.

Sclera

E   While assessing the conjunctiva, inspect the sclera for colour, exudate, lesions, and foreign bodies.

N   In light-skinned individuals, the sclera should be white with some small, superficial vessels and without exudate, lesions, or foreign bodies. In dark-skinned individuals, the sclera may have tiny brown patches of melanin or a greyish blue or "muddy" colour.

A   The colour of the sclera is uniformly yellow.

P   This condition is known as jaundice or scleral icterus and is due to colouring of the sclera with bilirubin, which infiltrates all tissues of the body. This is an early manifestation of systemic conditions such as hepatitis, sickle cell disease, gallstones, and physiological jaundice of the newborn.

A   The sclera is blue.

P   This finding is a distinctive feature of osteogenesis imperfecta and is due to the thinning of the sclera, which allows the choroid to show through.

Cornea

E   1. Stand in front of the patient.
    2. Shine a penlight directly on the cornea.

Nursing Alert

Screening for Retinopathy in People with Diabetes Mellitus

- Initiate screening five years after diagnosis of type 1 diabetes mellitus (DM) in all individuals 15 years of age and older. In the absence of retinopathy, rescreen annually.
- Screen all individuals at diagnosis of type 2 DM. In the absence of retinopathy, rescreen every one to two years.
- For all people with DM, review the ABC's (A1C, blood pressure, and cholesterol).[12]

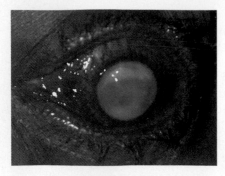

Figure 12-19 Corneal Ulceration. Note the injection and hypopyon (purulent material in the anterior chamber), which frequently occurs with corneal ulceration. *Courtesy of Salim I. Butrus, M.D., Senior Attending, Department of Ophthalmology, Washington Hospital Center, Washington, DC & Associate Clinical Professor, Georgetown University Medical Center, Washington, DC.*

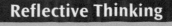

Reflective Thinking

Corneal Abrasion

You are examining a 25-year-old male with severe eye pain, photophobia, and tearing. This is his fourth visit in the past three months. His previous three visits were for confirmed corneal abrasions caused by sleeping in his hard contact lenses. While you are examining the patient, he tells you that he got drunk again and fell asleep with his contact lenses in his eyes. What type of physical examination would you perform? What additional information would you elicit from his history?

3. Move the light laterally and view the cornea from that angle, noting colour, discharge, and lesions.

N The corneal surface should be moist and shiny, with no discharge, cloudiness, opacities, or irregularities.

A A greyish, well-circumscribed ulcerated area on the cornea is abnormal (Figure 12-19).

P The most common cause of this is a corneal ulceration resulting from a bacterial invasion.

A A treelike configuration on the corneal surface is identified. The patient complains of mild discomfort, photophobia, and in some cases blurred vision (depending on the location of the lesions).

P This type of ulceration is caused by the herpes simplex virus. The patient usually has a history of having had a cold sore somewhere on the face.

A There is a hazy grey ring about 2 mm in width just inside the limbus (Figure 12-20).

P This common finding is **arcus senilis,** a bilateral, benign degeneration of the peripheral cornea. It can be found at any age but is most common in older individuals. If found in a young person, it may be associated with hypercholesterolemia.

A A steamy or cloudy cornea is abnormal. The patient also has ocular pain.

P Glaucoma is caused by increased intraocular pressure. Refer to Anterior Chamber assessment.

A Any irregularities in the appearance of the cornea are abnormal.

P Keratoconus (Figure 12-21) is the conical protrusion of the centre of the cornea. It is a noninflammatory condition in which the cornea thins, sometimes leading to the need for corneal transplant surgery.

P A corneal scar (Figure 12-22) forms at the site of past injury or inflammation.

P Corneal laceration (Figure 12-23) can occur secondary to trauma.

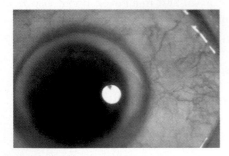

Figure 12-20 Arcus Senilis. *Courtesy of Salim I. Butrus, M.D., Senior Attending, Department of Ophthalmology, Washington Hospital Center, Washington, DC & Associate Clinical Professor, Georgetown University Medical Center, Washington, DC.*

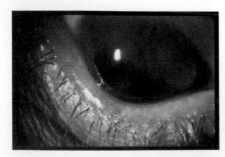

Figure 12-21 Keratoconus. *Courtesy of Salim I. Butrus, M.D., Senior Attending, Department of Ophthalmology, Washington Hospital Center, Washington, DC & Associate Clinical Professor, Georgetown University Medical Center, Washington, DC.*

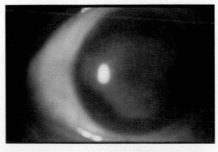

Figure 12-22 Corneal Scar. *Courtesy of Salim I. Butrus, M.D., Senior Attending, Department of Ophthalmology, Washington Hospital Center, Washington, DC & Associate Clinical Professor, Georgetown University Medical Center, Washington, DC.*

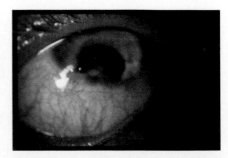

Figure 12-23 Corneal Laceration. *Courtesy of Salim I. Butrus, M.D., Senior Attending, Department of Ophthalmology, Washington Hospital Center, Washington, DC & Associate Clinical Professor, Georgetown University Medical Center, Washington, DC.*

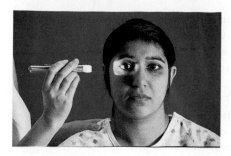

Figure 12-24 Examining the Anterior Chamber.

Anterior Chamber

The anterior chamber is found between the cornea and the iris. The space between the flat plane of the iris and the periphery of the cornea must be adequate to allow drainage of aqueous fluid out of the eye. If this angle is too narrow, drainage is inadequate, the pressure of the aqueous fluid in the anterior chamber increases, and **glaucoma** develops. If intraocular fluid pressure remains high, optic nerve damage and visual field loss occur.

To differentiate a normal from a narrowed angle:

E **1.** Face the patient and shine a light obliquely through the anterior chamber from the lateral side toward the nasal side (Figure 12-24).

 2. Observe the distribution of light in the anterior chamber (Figure 12-25).

 3. Repeat the procedure with the other eye.

N In a normal eye, the entire iris will be illuminated.

A The eye has a narrow angle, with the decreased space between the iris and the cornea appearing as a crescent-shaped shadow on the far portion of the iris.

P The narrow angle is an anatomic variant that can predispose an individual to the development of angle closure glaucoma. As aging progresses, the lens thickens, which may cause even further narrowing of the angle.

Iris

E With the penlight, inspect the iris for colour, nodules, and vascularity.

N Normally, the colour is evenly distributed over the iris, although there can be a mosaic variant. It is normally smooth and without apparent vascularity.

A There is a heavily pigmented, slightly elevated area visible in the iris.

P This lesion can be a benign iris nevus or a malignant melanoma. An iris nevus is much more common than melanoma.

A The inferior portion of the iris is obscured by blood.

P This is a **hyphema** and is caused by bleeding from vessels in the iris as a result of direct trauma to the globe. It can also occur as a result of eye surgery.

A An absent wedge portion of the iris is abnormal.

P The shape of the iris changes after surgical removal of a cataract; the pupil may also have an irregular shape.

Pupil

E **1.** Stand in front of the patient in a darkened room.

 2. Note the shape and size of the pupils in millimetres.

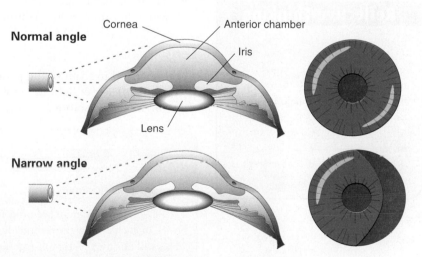

Figure 12-25 Evaluating the Angle of the Anterior Chamber.

E **Examination** N **Normal Findings** A **Abnormal Findings** P **Pathophysiology**

A. Starting Position with Penlight to Side of Pupil

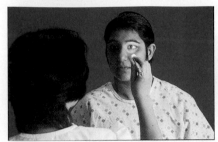

B. Move Penlight Directly in Front of Pupil

Figure 12-26 Pupil Assessment.

3. Move a penlight from the side to the front of one eye without allowing the light to shine on the other eye (Figure 12-26).
4. Observe the pupillary reaction in that eye. This is the direct light reflex. Note the size of the pupil receiving light stimulus and the speed of pupillary response to light.
5. Repeat in the other eye.
6. Move the penlight in front of one eye and observe the other eye for pupillary constriction. This is the consensual light reflex.
7. Repeat the procedure on the other eye.
8. Instruct the patient to shift the gaze to a distant object for 30 seconds.
9. Instruct the patient to then look at your finger or an object held in your hand about 10 cm from the patient.
10. Note the reaction and size of the pupils. **Accommodation** occurs when pupils constrict and converge to focus on objects at close range.

N The pupils should be deep black, round, and of equal diameter, ranging from 2–6 mm. Pupils should constrict briskly to direct and consensual light and to accommodation (CN III). Small differences in pupil size (anisocoria) may be normal in some people.

A The pupil that constricts to less than 2 mm in diameter is termed miotic. The pupil that dilates to more than 6 mm in diameter is termed mydriatic.

P Abnormal pupillary size can be caused by medications such as sympathomimetics or parasympathomimetics, iritis, or disorders such as CN III paralysis, which can occur as a result of a carotid artery aneurysm. These abnormalities may also be due to nerve damage or trauma (see Table 12-1 for further pathologies).

A The pupil has an irregular shape.

P This is a common finding associated with the surgical removal of cataracts and iridectomy.

A When the direct light reflex is defective, the pupil dilates in response to light, but consensual reaction is appropriate. This is called a Marcus Gunn pupil.

P Optic nerve damage in the optic chiasm, such as in trauma, results in destruction of the afferent pathways of the pupillary light reflex (deaffernated pupil).

A The hippus phenomenon occurs after the pupil has been stimulated by direct light. Light causes the pupil to constrict, but then the pupil appears to rhythmically vacillate in size from a larger to a smaller diameter.

P Hippus may be caused by a lesion in the midbrain.

A The presence of midposition, round, regular, and fixed (5 to 6 mm) pupils that may show hippus is abnormal.

P These signs usually indicate midbrain damage that interrupts the light reflex but may leave accommodation intact.

Lens

E 1. Stand in front of the patient.
2. Shine a penlight directly on the pupil. The lens is behind the pupil.
3. Note the colour.

Reflective Thinking

Pupil Assessment

You are examining a teenager and note that his pupils are unequal but reactive to light. What additional assessment techniques would you perform? What health history questions would you ask? What additional assessments should be undertaken?

Nursing Tip

Assessment of the Pupils

The beginning examiner should focus the beam of light a total of four times, twice in each eye, to assess direct light reflex and to assess consensual light reflex. This will ensure accuracy of examination.

| E | Examination | N | Normal Findings | A | Abnormal Findings | P | Pathophysiology |

TABLE 12-1	**Pupil Abnormalities**

A.

A: The size of pupils is unequal but both pupils react to light and accommodation.
P: Inequality of pupillary size is called **anisocoria** and may be congenital or due to inflammation of ocular tissue or disturbances of neurophthalmic pathways.

B.

A: A fixed and dilated pupil is observed on one side. The abnormal pupil does not react to direct or consensual light stimulation and does not accommodate. Ptosis and lateral downward deviation may also be noted.
P: This abnormality is caused by **oculomotor nerve damage** due to head trauma and increased intracranial pressure. Atropine-like agents applied topically may cause an even more widely fixed and dilated pupil.

C.

A: A unilateral, small, regularly shaped pupil is observed. Both pupils react directly and consensually and accommodate. Ptosis and diminished or absent sweating on the affected side may also be noted.
P: This finding is **Horner's syndrome,** which is caused by a lesion of the sympathetic nerve pathway.

D.

A: Pupils are bilaterally small and irregularly shaped. They react to accommodation but sluggishly or not at all to light.
P: These abnormalities are **Argyll Robertson** pupils and are usually caused by central lesions of neurosyphilis. Other causes include encephalitis, drugs, diabetes, brain tumors, and alcoholism.

E.

A: A unilateral, large, regularly shaped pupil is noted. The affected pupil's reaction to light and accommodation is sluggish or absent. The patient may report blurred vision because of the slow accommodation. You may observe diminished ankle and knee deep-tendon reflexes.
P: This abnormality, a tonic or **Adie's** pupil, is due to impaired sympathetic nerve supply.

F.

A: Both pupils are **small, fixed,** regularly shaped, and do not react to light or accommodation.
P: This abnormality may be caused by opiate ingestion, topical application of miotic drops, or lesions in the brain.

A: Pupils are small, equal, and reactive.
P: Diencephalic injury or metabolic coma may cause these findings.

G.

A: Both pupils are **dilated** and **fixed,** and do not react to light or accommodation.
P: Severe head trauma, brain stem infarction, cardiopulmonary arrest (after 4 to 6 min).

H.   Blind eye

Light

A: Light shone into a blind eye (amaurotic pupil) will cause no reaction (direct or consensual) in either pupil. If light is shone in the other eye, and CN III is intact, both pupils should constrict.
P: Due to a lesion in the retina or the optic nerve, the light stimulus shown in the amaurotic pupil is unable to pass along the sensory pathway; therefore, the oculomotor response in both eyes is absent.

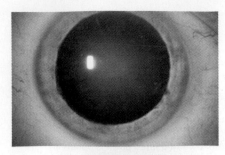

Figure 12-27 Cataract. *Courtesy of Salim I. Butrus, M.D., Senior Attending, Department of Ophthalmology, Washington Hospital Center, Washington, DC & Associate Clinical Professor, Georgetown University Medical Center, Washington, DC.*

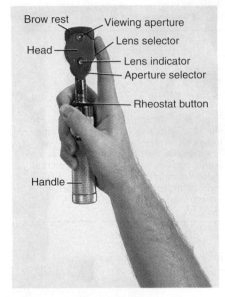

Figure 12-28 Ophthalmoscope.

N The lens is transparent in colour.

A One or more of the pupils are not deep black.

P In an adult, a pearly grey appearance of one or both pupils may indicate an opacity (cloudiness) in the lens (**cataract**) (Figure 12-27).

P A senile cataract is the most common type. Progressively blurred distance vision is the main symptom, though near vision may be improved because of greater convexity of the lens.

P A unilateral cataract may occur soon after an eye injury caused by a foreign body. Along with the lens opacity, there may be intraocular hemorrhage or aqueous or vitreous humour leaking from the globe. The patient reports an immediate blurring of vision.

P Bilateral cataracts found in infants or young children are congenital cataracts. These cataracts are probably genetically determined, though maternal rubella in the first trimester can also be responsible.

Posterior Segment Structures

The funduscopic assessment (CN II) requires the use of a direct ophthalmoscope to assess the structures in the posterior segment of the eye (Figure 12-28). The ophthalmoscope consists of two parts: the head and the handle. To activate the light source in the head, depress the rheostat button and move it as far as possible. Move the aperture selector to produce the largest beam of light that can be visualized by focusing the beam of light on the palm of your hand. The larger beam is preferred when assessing an average-sized pupil, and the smaller beam makes assessment of a smaller pupil easier. Table 12-2 lists the various apertures of the ophthalmoscope and their uses. The lens selector allows you to choose lenses of varying power for different parts of the assessment. These lenses are marked with red and black numbers, signifying different focal lengths. The 0 lens sits between the red- and black-numbered lenses and has no correction. In some ophthalmoscopes, there is no colour designation (red or black) and the lens power is signified by + or − signs in front of the numbers. A + sign is equivalent to black and focuses closer to the ophthalmoscope; a − sign is equivalent to red and focuses further from the instrument. These lenses compensate for the refractive error of both the patient and the nurse.

Retinal Structures

In a darkened room, ask the patient to remove eyeglasses; contact lenses may be left in place.

TABLE 12-2	**Apertures of the Ophthalmoscope**	
○	Small round light	Used to examine eyes with small, undilated pupils
◯	Large round light	Used for routine eye examinations and examination of dilated eyes
⊞	Grid	Used to assess size and location of funduscopic lesions
▯	Slit light	Assesses anterior eye and determines elevation of funduscopic lenses
●	Green light (red-free filter)	Used to assess retinal hemorrhages (which appear black) and small vessel changes

| E | **Examination** | N | **Normal Findings** | A | **Abnormal Findings** | P | **Pathophysiology** |

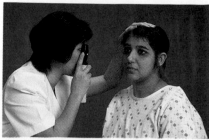

A. Eliciting the Red Reflex

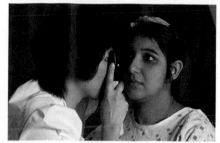

B. Funduscopic Examination

Figure 12-29 Examining Retinal Structures.

E 1. Instruct the patient to look at a distant object across the room. This will help to dilate the eyes.

2. Set the ophthalmoscope on the 0 lens and hold it in front of your right eye with your index finger on the lens selector.

3. From a distance of 20–30 cm (8–12 inches) from the patient and about 15° to the lateral side, shine the light into the patient's right pupil, eliciting a light reflection from the retina; this is called the red reflex (Figure 12-29A).

4. While maintaining the red reflex in view, move closer to the patient and move the lens selector from 0 to the + or black numbers in order to focus on the anterior ocular structures.

5. For optimum visualization, keep the ophthalmoscope within an inch of the patient's eye (Figure 12-29B).

6. At this point, move the lens selector from the + or black numbers, through 0, and into the × or red numbers in order to focus on structures progressively more posterior.

7. Focus on the optic disc at the nasal side of the retina by following any retinal vessels centrally (Figure 12-30).

8. You may need to reverse direction along the vessel if the disc does not appear.

9. Observe the retina for colour and lesions; the retinal vessels for configuration and characteristics of their crossing; and the optic disc for colour, shape, size, margins, and comparison of cup-to-disc ratio.

10. Describe the size, position, and location of any abnormality. Use the diameter of the disc (DD) as a guide to describe the distance of the abnormality from the optic disc. Use the optic disc as a clock face as a reference point to describe the location of the abnormality. Describe the size of the abnormality in relation to the size of the optic disc.

11. Repeat on the left eye.

N Refer to Table 12-3. The red reflex is present. The optic disc is pinkish orange in colour, with a yellow-white excavated centre known as the physiologic cup (Figure 12-30). The ratio of the cup diameter to that of the entire disc is 1:3. The border of the disc may range from a sharp, round demarcation from the surrounding retina to a more blended border, but should be on the same plane as the retina. In general, there are four main vascular branches emanating from the disc, each branch consisting of an arteriole and a venule. The venules are approximately four times the size of the accompanying arterioles and are darker in colour. Light often

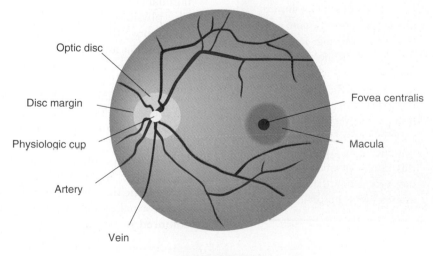

LEFT EYE

Figure 12-30 Optic Disc.

TABLE 12-3 Retinal Colour Variations

Findings	Characteristics
Fair-skinned individual	• Retina appears a lighter red-orange colour
	• Tessellated appearance of the fundi (pigment does not obscure the choroid vessels)
Dark-skinned individual	• Fundi appear darker in colour; greyish purple to brownish (from increased pigment in the choroid and retina)
	• No tessellated appearance
	• Choroidal vessels usually obscured
Aging individual	• Vessels are straighter and narrower
	• Choroidal vessels are easily visualized
	• Retinal pigment epithelium atrophies and causes the retinal colour to become paler

Life 360°

Cataract Surgery

Many elderly people remember their parents having to spend days in bed following cataract surgery. More recent interventions have led to same-day surgery and a range of approaches. Here are the results of two systematic reviews that will help you help your clients see the value in the newer techniques.

• Different surgical techniques can be used to remove a lens that has become cloudy due to cataract. The removed lens can be replaced either by an intraocular lens, aphakic glasses, or contact lens. There is evidence for the safety and effectiveness of all the major techniques for cataract extraction and that use of an intraocular lens improved vision, even better than wearing glasses.[13]

• Phacoemulsification is a newer method of cataract surgery that reduces the length of the procedure and leads to quicker recovery, making day surgery a possibility. There is evidence that day surgery for this type of cataract extraction may be cheaper than and just as effective as hospitalization.[14]

produces a glistening "light reflex" from the arteriolar vessel. Normal arterial-to-venous width is a ratio of 2:3 or 4:5.

A The red reflex is absent.

P The presence of cataracts can prevent the red reflex from being observed due to the opacity of the lens.

A The red reflex is absent and the pupil appears white.

P Leukocoria, or white reflex, is found in retinoblastoma, congenital cataracts, and retinal detachment. This is often referred to as the cat's eye reflex.

A The optic disc is pale.

P Pallor is due to optic atrophy caused by increased intracranial pressure or from congenital syphilis; an intracranial space-occupying lesion, for example, meningioma; or end-stage glaucoma.

A Optic atrophy is abnormal.

P Optic atrophy occurs in retinitis pigmentosa (Figure 12-31A). Arteriole narrowing and "bone spicule" are also noted on the fundus. There is a loss of central or peripheral vision, night blindness, and glare sensitivity in this familial condition.

A The physiologic cup exceeds the normal 1:3 ratio. The disc appears elevated above the plane of the surrounding retina.

P Disc edema and loss of vision are caused by the papillitis resulting from optic neuritis. The disc is hyperemic, the margins are blurred, and the disc surface is elevated.

P Disc edema and an elevated disc without loss of vision are found in papilledema (Figure 12-31B), which is caused by increased intracranial pressure obstructing return blood flow from the eye. This is also called a "choked disc."

P Glaucomatous cupping (Figure 12-31C) occurs due to increased intraocular pressure. The physiologic cup is enlarged and may extend to the edge of the optic disc. Blood vessels are displaced nasally.

A The normal white stripe of retinal arteries appears instead as a copper-coloured stripe.

E	Examination	N	Normal Findings	A	Abnormal Findings	P	Pathophysiology

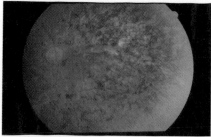

A. Retinitis Pigmentosa. *Courtesy of Salim I. Butrus, M.D., Senior Attending, Department of Ophthalmology, Washington Hospital Center, Washington, DC & Associate Clinical Professor, Georgetown University Medical Center, Washington, DC.*

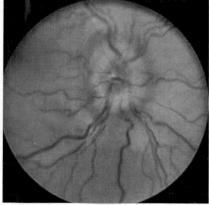

B. Papilledema. *Courtesy of Salim I. Butrus, M.D., Senior Attending, Department of Ophthalmology, Washington Hospital Center, Washington, DC & Associate Clinical Professor, Georgetown University Medical Center, Washington, DC.*

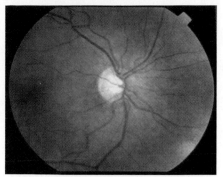

C. Glaucomatous Cupping. *Courtesy of Salim I. Butrus, M.D., Senior Attending, Department of Ophthalmology, Washington Hospital Center, Washington, DC & Associate Clinical Professor, Georgetown University Medical Center, Washington, DC.*

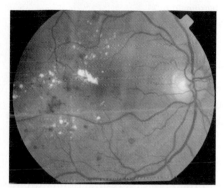

D. Microaneurysms with Exudate and Dot Hemorrhages. *Courtesy of Salim I. Butrus, M.D., Senior Attending, Department of Ophthalmology, Washington Hospital Center, Washington, DC & Associate Clinical Professor, Georgetown University Medical Center, Washington, DC.*

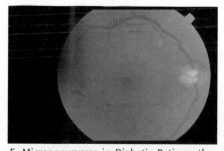

E. Microaneurysms in Diabetic Retinopathy. *Courtesy of Salim I. Butrus, M.D., Senior Attending, Department of Ophthalmology, Washington Hospital Center, Washington, DC & Associate Clinical Professor, Georgetown University Medical Center, Washington, DC.*

Figure 12-31 Retinal Abnormalities.

P   This is the copper wire appearance of retinal arteries characteristic of hypertensive changes.

A   At the crossing of retinal arteries over veins, the vein is not seen on either side of the overlying artery.

P   This finding is arteriovenous (A-V) nicking, a sign of retinal arteriolar sclerosis that occurs as the walls become thickened and obscure portions of the veins that lie underneath. This can also occur in hypertension.

A   Superficial retinal hemorrhages are flame-shaped hemorrhages found in the fundi, or they may appear as red hemorrhages with white centres called Roth's spots. These hemorrhages form a pattern related to the nerve fibres that radiate from the optic disc.

P   These hemorrhages may be due to severe hypertension, occlusion of the central retinal vein, and papilledema. Roth's spots are sometimes associated with infective endocarditis.

A   Deep retinal hemorrhages, or dot hemorrhages, appear as small red dots or irregular spots in the deep layer of the retina (Figure 12-31D).

P   Deep retinal hemorrhages can be associated with diabetes mellitus.

A   Diffuse preretinal hemorrhages occur in the small space between the vitreous and the retina.

P   Preretinal hemorrhages may occur in conjunction with a sudden increase in intracranial pressure.

A   Microaneurysms are tiny, round, red dots that can be seen in peripheral and macular areas of the retina (Figure 12-31E).

P   These dots are small retinal vessels that dilate in diabetic retinopathy.

A   Neovascularization is the formation of new vessels that are very narrow and disorderly in appearance and may extend into the vitreous (Figure 12-31F). These vessels may bleed, resulting in a loss of vision.

P   Neovascularization occurs in proliferative diabetic retinopathy.

A   Fluffy white or grey slightly irregular areas that appear on the retina and are ovoid in shape are abnormal (Figure 12-31G).

P   Cotton wool spots represent microscopic infarcts of the nerve fibre layer and are due to diabetic or hypertensive retinopathy.

P   Drusen are small white dots in the fundus that are arranged in an irregular pattern. They may also occur on the optic disc, and may become shiny with calcification.

P   Drusen are findings of the normal aging process. They may cause loss of vision if they occur in the macular region.

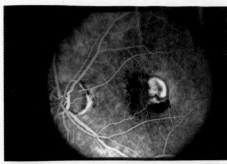

F. Subretinal Neovascularization in Age-Related Exudative Macular Degeneration. *Courtesy of Salim I. Butrus, M.D., Senior Attending, Department of Ophthalmology, Washington Hospital Center, Washington, DC & Associate Clinical Professor, Georgetown University Medical Center, Washington, DC.*

Figure 12-31 *continued.*

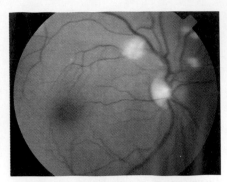

G. Cotton Wool Spots. *Courtesy of Salim I. Butrus, M.D., Senior Attending, Department of Ophthalmology, Washington Hospital Center, Washington, DC & Associate Clinical Professor, Georgetown University Medical Center, Washington, DC.*

A Hard exudates are yellow with distinct borders and are small unless they coalesce. They are arranged in round, linear, or star-shaped patterns.

P Hard exudates are associated with diabetes mellitus or hypertension.

A A cleft defect of the choroid and retina is abnormal. The size ranges from medium to large.

P **Coloboma** is a congenital abnormality.

A The red-orange retinal reflex is absent in the area of a retinal detachment. The area appears pearly grey and is elevated and wrinkled.

P A detached retina may be associated with severe myopia, cataract surgery, or diabetic retinopathy, or it may be caused by trauma.

A Fibrous white bands that obscure the retinal vessels are abnormal. Neovascularization may also be present.

P These findings occur in proliferative diabetic retinopathy.

Macula

When the retinal structures and the optic disc have been assessed:

E 1. Move the ophthalmoscope approximately two disc diameters temporally to view the macula, or ask the patient to look at the light. The red-free filter lens of the ophthalmoscope may be helpful in assessing the macula, which is not clearly demarcated and is very light sensitive. The patient tends to turn away when the light strikes the fovea, making it difficult to assess details of the macular area.

2. Note the fovea centralis and observe for colour, shape, and lesions.

3. Repeat with the other eye.

N The macula is a darker, avascular area with a pinpoint reflective centre known as the fovea centralis.

A The retina is pale with the macular region appearing as a cherry-red spot.

P This finding is central retinal artery occlusion, an indication of Tay-Sachs disease.

A An enlarged macula is abnormal (Figure 12-32).

P Macular edema is caused by the leakage of fluid from retinal blood vessels. This can occur in diabetes mellitus, hypertension, ARMD, and retinal blood vessel obstruction.

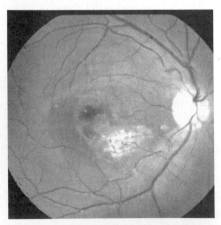

Figure 12-32 Macular Edema with Bleeding. *Courtesy of Salim I. Butrus, M.D., Senior Attending, Department of Ophthalmology, Washington Hospital Center, Washington, DC & Associate Clinical Professor, Georgetown University Medical Center, Washington, DC.*

| E | **Examination** | N | **Normal Findings** | A | **Abnormal Findings** | P | **Pathophysiology** |

A   Sharply defined, small red spots are found in and around the macula.

P   These microaneurysms are pathognomonic of diabetes mellitus.

A   Macular borders are blurred, with a few spots of pigment near the macula; a hole may appear to be present in the centre of the region, or a hemorrhage may have occurred.

P   This finding is characteristic of ARMD. Hemorrhages, patches of retina atrophy, and pigmented areas may also be associated with this condition.

GERONTOLOGICAL VARIATIONS

The four main causes of age-related vision loss in Canada are: ARMD, glaucoma, diabetic retinopathy, and cataract. Visual impairment of some form affects 13% of elderly people with almost 8% of them having severe impairment (blindness in both eyes or inability to read newsprint even with glasses).[15] Prevention of sensory impairment as well as early detection of problems in this area are challenges for patients and health care providers.

During the aging process, the eye undergoes significant changes. By the mid-forties, the lens cortex becomes denser, compromising its ability to change shape and focus. This condition, **presbyopia,** is responsible for farsightedness and the need for bifocals. Next, there is a tendency for the lens to yellow and become cloudy, which impairs a person's ability to discern various colours, especially blues and greens. In addition, pupils become smaller, so that the amount of light reaching the retina is reduced. As a consequence, elderly people need more light to see and their eyes take longer to accommodate to darkness and glare. Finally, a decrease in tear production predisposes the individual to corneal irritation and conjunctivitis.

Cataracts involve opacity and yellowing of the lens, which results in dimmed and blurred vision. Cataracts can be surgically removed.

Individuals experiencing loss of central vision, or ARMD, require the use of magnification to compensate for visual loss. Systemic diseases that aggravate macular degeneration include diabetes mellitus and hypertension.

Increased intraocular pressure and inability of aqueous humour to flow out into collecting channels places pressure on the optic nerve. Early detection of glaucoma is critical.

Inspection of the eyelids of the older individual often reveals slightly drooping upper and lower lids. The globe appears to be deeper in the socket, and the lacrimal gland may be visible because of lost subcutaneous fat around the eye.

Diabetic retinopathy is due to microvascular damage in the retina as a result of chronic hyperglycemia. Partial occlusion of the small vessels of the retina can give rise to microaneurysms and subsequent leakage of capillary fluid, retinal edema, and possibly hemorrhages. After 15 years with type 2 diabetes mellitus, almost 80% will have some form of diabetic retinopathy.

Nursing Tip

Night Driving

Many older persons find that driving at night is not safe because of their decreased nighttime vision. Being unable to drive at night results in major changes in the ability to participate in activities such as shopping and social events.

CASE STUDY — The Patient with Entropion

Martin is a resident of an assisted living facility.

HEALTH HISTORY

PATIENT PROFILE	79 yo widowed man of Black descent, looks tired
HEALTH ISSUE/CONCERN	"My ® eye has been red & irritated for 2 wks."
HISTORY OF ISSUE/CONCERN	Pt was in his usual state of hl until 2 wks ago when he started noticing that his OD was red at times & felt irritated as if something was in it. He's also noticed that he seems to have excessive amounts of tearing in that eye. He rubs it occasionally to try to relieve the discomfort but that doesn't help. He denies vision changes, photophobia, crusting of the lashes, trauma or foreign bodies; denies using any eye medications or products.

PAST HEALTH HISTORY

Medical History	HTN controlled by medication. Had MI at age 72.
Surgical History	Cataract sgy, age 70, Ø sequelae; appendectomy, age 32, Ø sequelae.
Medications	Captopril 25 mg tid, ASA 81 mg daily, MVI daily
Communicable Diseases	Denies hepatitis, AIDS, STIs
Allergies	Penicillin: Bronchospasm, hives
Injuries and Accidents	Closed head injury in MVA, age 53
Special Needs	Occasionally uses a cane for assistance in walking
Blood Transfusions	Denies
Childhood Illnesses	Pertussis, age 3
Immunizations	Tetanus booster 2002; pneumovax, 1999; annual flu shots

FAMILY HEALTH HISTORY

LEGEND

- ◯ Living female
- ▢ Living male
- ⊗ Deceased female
- ⊠ Deceased male
- ╱ Points to patient

A&W = Alive & well
CRF = Chronic renal failure
CVA = Cerebrovascular accident
DM = Diabetes mellitus
HTN = Hypertension
MI = Myocardial infarction
MVA = Motor vehicle accident
RA = Rheumatoid arthritis

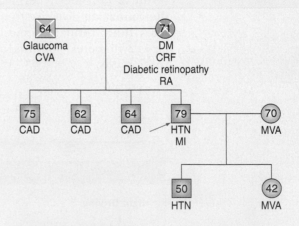

Denies family hx of hyperopia, strabismus, colour blindness, cataracts, glaucoma, retinitis pigmentosa.

SOCIAL HISTORY	
Alcohol Use	Denies
Drug Use	Denies
Tobacco Use	$\dotplus$ PPD × 35 yrs; quit 1972
Domestic and Intimate Partner Violence	Denies
Sexual Practice	Sporadic (every couple of months) relations with a woman who lives in the residence
Travel History	None recent $\bar{x}$ for occasional visits to son's home in nearby neighborhood
Work Environment	Retired factory worker; lives in assisted living facility
Home Environment	Lives in small apt; has meals in group dining room; cleaning and laundry service provided
Hobbies and Leisure Activities	Watches TV; crossword and Sudoku; visits with friends in group activity room
Stress and Coping	Feels lonesome at times, "I miss my wife and daughter." Son is "my greatest support."
Education	Graduated from high school
Economic Status	Saved adequately for retirement; can afford modest living arrangement & has money to treat others
Religion/Spirituality	United Church; "I rely on my religion a lot."
Ethnic Background	"I'm a Canadian, my grandparents came from Jamaica."
Roles and Relationships	Has close friends who live in same facility & in town; close to son who lives nearby; describes very positive relationship with son
Characteristic Patterns of Daily Living	Wakes around 07:30, goes to dining room for breakfast & activity room to watch TV $\bar{c}$ friends; attends morning activity sessions before lunch; rests in his room during early afternoon & then watches TV there; may have visitors in afternoon or early evening; occasionally goes to son's home on weekends or holidays; usually watches TV in his room in the evening & goes to bed around 22:00.
HEALTH MAINTENANCE ACTIVITIES	
Sleep	8–9 hrs most nights. Up to the bathroom 1–2 q night.
Diet	Takes most meals in dining room but has some snacks in his apt & occasionally eats out c son or friends who live in town
Exercise	Walks daily in the hall or outside the facility; participates in light exercise program in activity room 3 × wk
Stress Management	Says he is generally not stressed
Use of Safety Devices	Wears seat belt regularly; uses cane to assist balance at times

continues

Health Check-ups	Has regular check-ups c̄ family physician; nurse comes to residence weekly for BP check
PHYSICAL ASSESSMENT	
Eyes	
Visual Acuity	(c̄ glasses): 20/30 OS, 20/40 OD Near vision: Reads newspaper s̄ errors Colour vision: deferred
Visual Fields	Intact
External Eye and Lacrimal Apparatus	Lower Ⓡ eyelid is turned in toward the eye, causing lower lashes to brush against the eye; no ptosis, no lid lag; lacrimal apparatus s̄ enlargement, swelling, or redness; excess clear tears from OD; no purulent drainage
Extraocular Muscle Function	Corneal light reflex: Symmetric s̄ strabismus Cover/uncover test: Deferred Cardinal fields of gaze: Intact s̄ nystagmus
Anterior Segment Structures	Conjunctiva: Peripheral injection of lower bulbar conjunctiva of OD, OS = clear Sclera: mud colour s̄ lesions Cornea: s̄ opacities Anterior chamber: clear Iris: brown Pupils: PERRLA 5 mm Lens: clear
Posterior Segment Structures	Retinal structures: ⊕ red reflex bilaterally; discs flat c̄ sharp margins; vessels have copper wire appearance & are in 2:3 ratio c̄ some A/V nicking; background brownish colour; s̄ hemorrhages or exudates Macula: colour = even

◀NURSING CHECKLIST▶

Eye Assessment

Visual Acuity

- Distance vision
- Near vision
- Colour vision

Visual Fields

External Eye and Lacrimal Apparatus

- Eyelids
- Lacrimal apparatus
  Inspection
  – Palpation

continues

Extraocular Muscle Function

- Corneal light reflex
- Cover/uncover test
- Cardinal fields of gaze

Anterior Segment Structures

- Conjunctiva
- Sclera
- Cornea
- Anterior chamber
- Iris
- Pupil
- Lens

Posterior Segment Structures

- Retinal structures
- Macula

REVIEW QUESTIONS

1. An asymmetrical corneal light reflex with one eye constantly turned inward is called:
   a. Esotropia
   b. Exotropia
   c. Esophoria
   d. Exophoria
   The correct answer is (a).

2. When checking the visual acuity of a patient, you notice vision changes due to the length of the globe of the eye being longer than normal so that the image is not focused directly on the retina. This condition is called:
   a. Amblyopia
   b. Presbyopia
   c. Myopia
   d. Hyperopia
   The correct answer is (c).

3. During inspection of your patient's eyelids, you notice raised, yellow, nontender plaques on the upper and lower lids near the inner canthus. This condition is called:
   a. Blepharitis
   b. Lagophthalmos
   c. Pterygium
   d. Xanthelasma
   The correct answer is (d).

4. Involuntary movement of an eye following its uncovering during the cover/uncover test indicates that:
   a. A muscle weakness or muscle imbalance exists
   b. Nystagmus is present

   c. Pupillary accommodation is impaired
   d. Decreased sensitivity of the corneal blink reflex is present
   The correct answer is (a).

5. An acute, localized area of pain and swelling in the skin of the eyelid is called:
   a. Chalazion
   b. Hordeolum
   c. Ectropion
   d. Pinguecula
   The correct answer is (b).

6. The colour of normal sclera in light-skinned individuals is:
   a. White
   b. Brown
   c. Blue
   d. Yellow
   The correct answer is (a).

7. Observation of a treelike configuration on the surface of the cornea is indicative of:
   a. Corneal laceration
   b. Corneal abrasion
   c. Arcus senilis
   d. Herpes simplex infection
   The correct answer is (d).

8. While performing an eye assessment, you notice that the patient has unilateral eversion of the lower lid. This condition is called:
   a. Ectropion
   b. Entropion

c. Lagophthalmos
d. Enophthalmos
The correct answer is (a).

9. Which is characteristic of retinal changes in an aging individual?
a. Fundi are darker in colour
b. Pigment does not obscure the vessels
c. Vessels are usually obscured
d. Vessels are straighter and narrower
The correct answer is (d).

10. During funduscopic examination, you notice that your patient has disc edema. Which of these conditions is associated with this finding?
a. Retinitis pigmentosa
b. Hypertension
c. Diabetes mellitus
d. Increased intracranial pressure
The correct answer is (d).

Visit the Estes online companion resource at
www.healthassessment.nelson.com **for additional content and study aids.**

REFERENCES

[1]Statistics Canada. (2001). *A profile of disability in Canada.* Ottawa, ON.

[2]CNIB (Canadian National Institute for the Blind). National Consultation of the Crisis of Vision Loss. Toronto: Oct 2–5, 1998. Retrieved October 16, 2006, from http://www.cnib.ca/eng/publications/pamphlets/nccvl/chapter2.htm

[3]Statistics Canada. (2001). *Age (122) and sex (3) for population, for Canada, province, territories, census metropolitan area and census agglomerations, 2001 census – 100% data.* Ottawa, ON.

[4]Canadian Ophthalmological Association. Glaucoma Awareness Survey. Retrieved October 16, 2006 from http://www.eyesite.ca/english/press/glaucoma_backgrounder.html

[5]CNIB, .National Consultation of the Crisis of Vision Loss.

[6]Elolia, R., & Stokes, J. (2000). Monograph series on aging-related diseases: Glaucoma. Chronic Disease in Canada, 19 (4). Published by authority of the Minister of Health © Minister of Public Works and Government Services Canada 1999.

[7]Ibid.

[8]Ibid.

[9]Ibid.

[10]Patterson C. (1994). Screening for visual impairment in the elderly. In: Canadian Task Force on the Periodic Health Examination. *The Canadian Guide to Clinical Preventive Health Care.* Ottawa, ON; Health Canada.

[11]CNIB. *Eye conditions: Macular degeneration.* Retrieved May 27, 2006, from http://www.cnib.ca/eng/eye_con/mclrdegn.htm

[12]Canadian Diabetes Association. Clinical Practice Guidelines Expert Committee. (2003). *Clinical practice guidelines: Retinopathy.* Retrieved October 16, 2006, from http://www.diabetes.ca/cpg2003/downloads/retinopathy.pdf

[13]Snellingen, T., Evans, J. R., Ravilla, T., & Foster, A. (2002). Surgical interventions for age-related cataract. *The Cochrane Database of Systematic Reviews,* Issue 2. Art. No.: CD001323.

[14]Fedorowicz, Z., Lawrence, D., & Gutierrez, P. (2005). Day care versus in-patient surgery for age-related cataract. *The Cochrane Database of Systematic Reviews,* Issue 1 Art. No.: CD004242.

[15]CNIB, National Consultation of the Crisis of Vision Loss.

BIBLIOGRAPHY

Palay, D. A., & Krachmer, J. H. (2005). *Primary care ophthalmology* (2nd ed.). St. Louis, MO: Mosby.

Spalton, D. (Ed.) (2005). *Atlas of clinical ophthalmology.* Philadelphia: Elsevier Mosby.

Yanoff, M., & Fine, B. (2002). *Ocular pathology* (5th ed.). St. Louis, MO: Mosby.

WEB RESOURCES

Alliance for the Quality of Blind Canadians
http://www.blindcanadians.ca/

Canadian Council of the Blind
http://www.ccbnational.net/

The Canadian National Institute for the Blind
http://www.cnib.ca/

Canadian Ophthalmological Society – Information Service
http://www.eyesite.ca/

Fondation des Aveugles du Québec
http://www.aveugles.org/

National Organization for Albinism and Hypopigmentation
http://www.albinism.org/

CHAPTER 13

Ears, Nose, Mouth, and Throat

COMPETENCIES

1. Identify the structures and functions of the ears, nose, mouth, and throat.

2. Discuss the system-specific history for the ears, nose, mouth, and throat.

3. Describe normal findings in the physical assessment of the ears, nose, mouth, and throat.

4. Describe common abnormalities found in the physical assessment of the ears, nose, mouth, and throat.

5. Explain the pathophysiology of common abnormalities of the ears, nose, mouth, and throat.

6. Perform the physical assessment of the ears, nose, mouth, and throat.

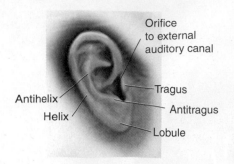

Figure 13-1 External Ear.

𝒫hysical assessment of the ears, nose, sinuses, mouth, and throat provides a wealth of information about the integrity of many body systems and serves as the foundation for assessment of the neurological, respiratory, endocrine, gastrointestinal, musculoskeletal, and cardiovascular systems.

ANATOMY AND PHYSIOLOGY

Ear

The ear has three sections: the external, the middle, and the inner ear.

External Ear

The external ear, also called the **auricle** or pinna, extends through the auditory canal to the tympanic membrane (TM) (Figure 13-1). The auricle is composed of cartilage and receives sound waves and funnels them through the auditory canal to produce vibrations on the TM.

The external auditory canal (EAC) is an S-shaped tube approximately 2.5 cm in length, with the outer third made up of cartilage and the remainder of bone covered by a thin layer of skin (Figure 13-2). The canal is lined with tiny hairs and modified sweat glands that secrete a thick, waxlike substance called **cerumen,** which can vary in consistency from dry and flaky to wet and waxy. Cerumen ranges from a pale, honey colour in light-skinned individuals to dark-brown or black in dark-skinned people.

Middle Ear

The middle ear is composed of the TM, the ossicles, and the tympanic cavity. The cavity is an air-filled compartment that separates the external ear from the

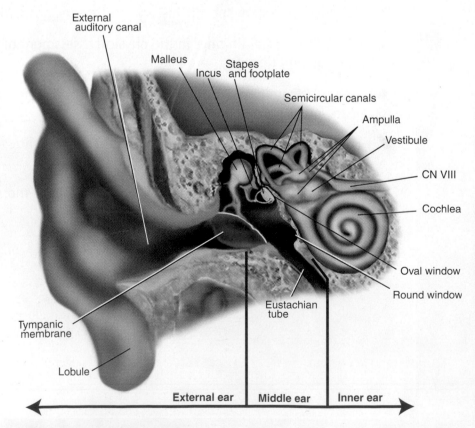

Figure 13-2 Cross Section of the Ear.

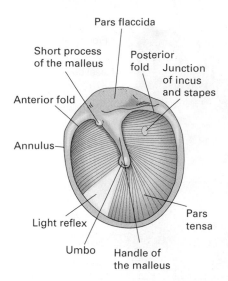

Figure 13-3 Landmarks of the Left Tympanic Membrane.

internal ear. The TM, which is circular or oval and is about 2.5 cm in diameter, sits in an oblique position in the external canal so that it leans slightly forward. The rim of the TM is called the annulus, the superior portion is the pars flaccida, and the tighter, largest area of the drum is the pars tensa (Figure 13-3).

The **ossicles** are three tiny bones—the malleus (hammer), the incus (anvil), and the stapes (stirrup)—that play a crucial role in the transmission of sound. The long handle, or manubrium, of the malleus extends downward from the short process and meets the TM at the umbo. The stapes is held against the wall of the TM at the oval window by tiny ligaments. The head of the malleus articulates with the incus, which in turn articulates with the stapes; they work as a unit when the TM begins to vibrate. Vibrations set up in the TM by sound waves reaching it through the EAC are transmitted to the inner ear by rapid movement of the ossicles.

The tensor tympani and the stapedius are two tiny muscles involved in movement of the ossicles. The tensor tympani maintains the tension of the TM and pulls the malleus inward when it contracts. The stapedius works in opposition by pulling the stapes outward. This coordinated movement is an important mechanism in reducing the intensity of loud sounds that might otherwise result in serious damage to hearing receptors in the inner ear.

The middle ear is connected to the nasopharynx by the auditory or **eustachian tube** (ET), which serves as a channel through which air pressure within the cavity can be equalized with air pressure outside to maintain normal hearing. Equalization of pressure is aided by yawning or swallowing, which opens up the valvelike flaps that cover the eustachian tubes.

Inner Ear

The inner ear is a complex, closed, fluid-filled system of interconnecting tubes called the **labyrinth,** which is essential for hearing and equilibrium. The labyrinth has bony and membranous portions. The bony labyrinth is composed of the cochlea, the semicircular canals, and the vestibule. The **vestibule,** which is important in both hearing and balance, is located between the cochlea and the **semicircular canals.** The three semicircular canals are located at right angles to each other and provide equilibrium for the body. The **cochlea** is a snail-shaped structure made up of three compartments. The first two compartments contain perilymph, and the third contains endolymph. As sound waves travel through the ear, they cause the perilymph and the endolymph to vibrate, stimulating the thousands of hearing-receptor cells of the organ of Corti. Nearby nerve fibres transmit impulses along the cochlear branch of the vestibulocochlear nerve to the brain, allowing us to hear. The human ear is capable of hearing within a frequency range of 20 to 20,000 Hz, and a decibel (dB) range of 0 to 140.[1] There is no known risk of hearing loss associated with sound levels below 70 dB. Figure 13-4 illustrates the decibel levels of commonly heard sounds.

Nose

The nose consists of the external or outer nose, and the nasal fossae or internal nose (Figure 13-5). The outer nose is made up of bone and cartilage and is divided internally into two nasal fossae by the nasal septum, and externally by the columella. Anterior openings into the nasal fossae are nostrils, or nares. Each fossa has a lateral extended "wing" portion called the ala nasi on the outside and a vestibule just inside the nostril. Superior, middle, and inferior meatuses or grooves are located on the lateral walls of the nostrils just below the corresponding conchae, or **turbinates.** The nasal turbinates are covered by mucous membranes and greatly increase the surface area of mucous membrane in the nose because of their shape. Kiesselbach's plexus is a vascular area on the nasal septum and is the most common site of nosebleeds.

Air enters the anterior nares, passes through the vestibule, which contains nasal hairs and sebaceous glands, and enters the fossa. The fossae have both

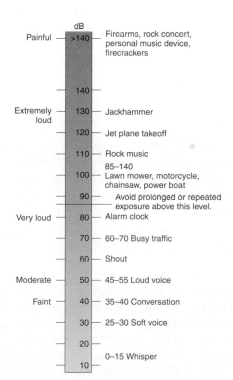

Figure 13-4 Decibel Scale of Frequently Heard Sounds

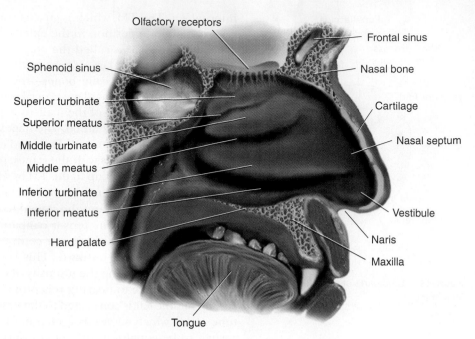

Figure 13-5 Lateral Cross Section of the Nose.

olfactory and respiratory functions. To protect the lungs from noxious agents, these structures of the nose clean, filter, humidify, and control the temperature of inspired air. The mucous covering in the nose and sinuses traps fine dust particles, and lysosomes kill most of the bacteria. The tiny hairs of the nose (cilia) transport the mucus and the particles to the pharynx to be swallowed.

The nasal mucosa is capable of adding large amounts of water to inspired air through evaporation from its surface. The rich vascular supply to the turbinates radiates heat to the incoming air as it passes through the nasal cavity.

Olfactory receptor cells are located in the upper parts of the nasal cavity, the superior nasal conchae, and on parts of the nasal septum and are covered by cilia that project into the cavity. The chemical component of odours binds with the receptors, causing nerve impulses to be transmitted to the olfactory cortex, located in the base of the frontal lobe.

Sinuses

Air-filled cavities lined with mucous membranes are present in some of the cranial bones and are referred to as **paranasal sinuses** (Figure 13-6), which lighten the weight of the skull and add resonance to the quality of the voice. The frontal, maxillary, ethmoid, and sphenoid paranasal sinuses open into the nose. Only the frontal and maxillary sinuses can be assessed in the physical examination.

Mouth and Throat

The lips are sensory structures at the opening of the mouth (Figure 13-7). The labial tubercle is the small projected area in the midline of the upper lip. The area where the upper and lower lips meet is the labial commissure. The vermilion zone is the reddish or reddish-brown area of the lips; the area where the lips meet the facial skin is called the vermilion border. The median groove superior to the upper lip is called the philtrum. The cheeks form the lateral walls of the mouth and are lined with buccal mucosa. The posterior pharyngeal wall is at the back of the mouth.

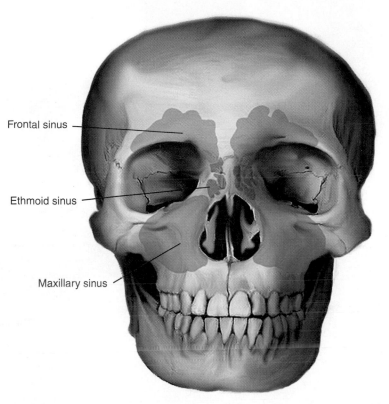

Figure 13-6 Location of the Sinuses (Sphenoid sinuses are directly behind ethmoid sinuses.)

The roof of the mouth consists of the hard palate anteriorly and the soft palate posteriorly (Figure 13-8). The **linear raphe** is a linear ridge in the middle of the hard palate that is formed by two palatine bones and part of the superior maxillary bone. The mucous membrane on either side of the linear raphe is thick, pale, and corrugated, whereas the posterior mucous membrane is thin, a deeper pink, and smooth.

Situated in the floor of the mouth, the tongue is a muscular organ connected to the hyoid bone posteriorly and to the floor of the mouth anteriorly by the **frenulum.** The tongue assists with mastication, swallowing, speech, and mechanical cleansing of the teeth.

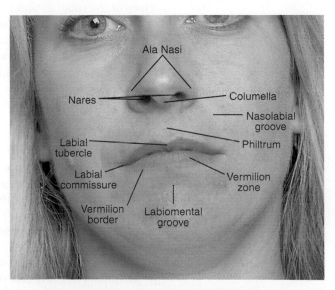

Figure 13-7 Landmarks of the Area around the Mouth.

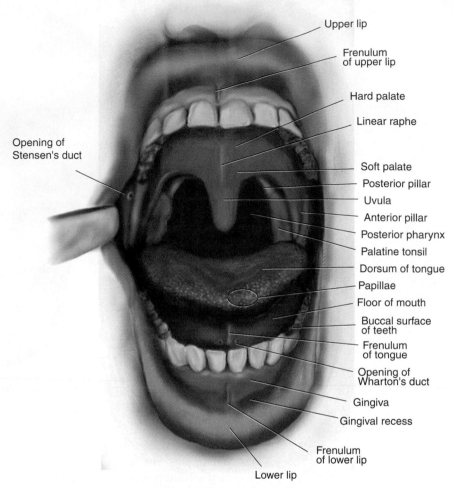

Figure 13-8 Structures of the Mouth.

The mucous membrane covering the upper surface of the tongue has numerous projections called **papillae** that assist in handling food and contain taste buds. Four qualities of taste are found in taste buds distributed over the surface of the tongue: bitter is located at the base, sour along the sides, and salty and sweet near the tip. The **sulcus terminalis** is the midline depression that separates the anterior two-thirds of the tongue from the posterior one-third.

Two of the three pairs of salivary glands open into the mouth on the ventral surface of the tongue. Submaxillary glands secrete fluid through **Wharton's ducts,** located on both sides of the frenulum. Sublingual glands open into the floor of the mouth posteriorly to Wharton's ducts. The larger parotid glands are located in the cheeks and secrete amylase-rich fluid through **Stensen's ducts,** located just opposite the upper second molars.

Salivary glands produce 1000 to 1500 mL of saliva per day to assist with digestion of food and maintenance of oral hygiene. Saliva prevents dental caries and bacterial damage of healthy oral tissue by washing away bacteria and destroying it with antibodies and proteolytic enzymes. Gums, or gingivae, hold the teeth in place and appear pink or coral in light-skinned individuals, and brown with a darker melanotic line along the edges in dark-skinned individuals.

Adults have 32 permanent teeth: four incisors, two canines, four premolars, and six molars in each half of the mouth (Figure 13-9). The three parts of the tooth are the top, or the crown, the root, which is embedded in the gum, and

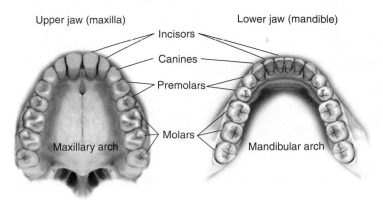

Figure 13-9 Permanent Teeth.

the neck, which connects the root and the crown. Incisors provide strong cutting action, and molars provide strong grinding action.

The soft palate is suspended from the posterior border of the hard palate and extends downward as folds, called palatine arches or pillars, forming an incomplete septum between the mouth and the nasopharynx. The **uvula** is a fingerlike projection of tissue that hangs down from the centre of the soft palate. Two palatine tonsils containing primarily lymphoid tissue are connected to the palatine arches; they vary greatly in size from one individual to another. Lymphoid tissue in the tonsils plays a role in the control of infection.

HEALTH HISTORY

The ears, nose, mouth, and throat health history provides insight into the link between a patient's life and lifestyle, and ears, nose, mouth, and throat information and pathology.

PATIENT PROFILE *Diseases that are age- and gender-specific for the ears, nose, mouth, and throat are listed.*

Age

Ears Hearing loss related to presbycusis (hearing loss commonly found in the elderly), sensorineural degeneration or otosclerosis (elderly)
Excessive or impacted cerumen (elderly)

Nose Decrease in ability to smell (elderly)

Mouth and Throat Orthodonture (middle age)
Tooth loss and gum disease (elderly)
Thrush related to immunosuppression (elderly)
Decrease in ability to taste (elderly)

Gender

Ears Female: Calcifications of the ossicles

Nose Male: Rhinophyma, deviated septum related to trauma, polyps

Mouth and Throat Male: Singer's nodule on the larynx (over 30), cancer of the larynx, leukoplakia of the tongue, gums, and buccal mucosa

HEALTH ISSUE/CONCERN *Common health issues/concerns for the ears, nose, mouth, and throat are defined, and information on the characteristics of each sign or symptom is provided.*

continues

	Ear
Change in or Loss of Hearing	Reduction in the perception of sound
Location	Unilateral, bilateral
Quality	Loud sounds heard, soft sounds heard
Quantity	Partial or complete
Associated Manifestations	Tinnitus, vertigo, drainage, swelling, fever, ear pain
Aggravating Factors	Loud noises, excessive or impacted cerumen, swimming
Alleviating Factors	Hearing aid, removal of excessive cerumen, turning up volume when possible, cupping the ear, facing the speaker
Setting	Work (jobs with loud background noise)
Timing	Constant, intermittent, after drug therapy, onset sudden, gradual, or slow
Otorrhea	Drainage of liquid from the ear
Location	Unilateral or bilateral
Quality	Painful or nontender, watery, bloody or purulent, foul odour
Associated Manifestations	Hearing loss, headache, fever, vertigo, URI
Aggravating Factors	Upright or supine position
Alleviating Factors	Upright or supine position
Timing	Following trauma, continuous, intermittent
Otalgia	Discomfort in the ear
Location	Unilateral or bilateral, in jaw region, in pinna region
Quality	Aching, dull, sharp
Associated Manifestations	Drainage, tinnitus, dysphagia, sore throat, vertigo, diminished hearing
Aggravating Factors	Tooth infection, URI, perforated TM, insect bites in the ear, upright or supine position, objects in ear, change in air pressure
Alleviating Factors	Analgesics, upright or supine position, avoiding swimming and pressure changes, removal of objects, change in air pressure
Setting	Outdoors, high altitudes, noisy environments
Timing	Continuous, intermittent, after swimming, following trauma to the head or ear, following loud noises, after pressure changes, flying
Tinnitus	"Ringing" in the ears
Location	Unilateral or bilateral
Quality	Pulsatile, buzzing, high-pitched ringing
Associated Manifestations	Vertigo, drainage, pain, nausea, fullness or pressure in the ears, hearing loss, URI, allergies, middle ear infection, inner ear lesions, ET inflammation

Aggravating Factors	Medications, fluid in the middle ear, perforation of the TM, position, pressure on the neck, excessive cerumen
Alleviating Factors	Discontinuing medications, position change, avoiding allergens
Setting	Work (high noise levels), outdoors
Timing	Long-standing, recent, constant, intermittent, following drug therapy, after exposure to loud noises
Nose	
Pain	Discomfort in the nose
Quality	Aching, throbbing, sharp
Associated Manifestations	Fever, chills, visual changes, swelling, sneezing, nasal discharge
Aggravating Factors	Exposure to allergens, decreased humidity indoors, cocaine use
Alleviating Factors	Use of medications (decongestant or antihistamine), removal of allergens, humidification of the environment, discontinuation of cocaine
Setting	Outdoors, dry heat, low humidity
Timing	Seasonal, in the morning
Drainage	Excessive discharge of nasal secretions
Quality	Unilateral or bilateral, amount, viscosity, colour, odour
Associated Manifestations	Fever, sneezing, pain, mouth breathing, swelling, skin irritation around drainage site, itchy eyes
Aggravating Factors	Allergens, infections
Alleviating Factors	Medication, hydration, avoiding allergens
Setting	Outdoors, indoors
Timing	In the morning, seasonal, after trauma
Blockage or Congestion	Reduced ability to move air through the nose secondary to obstruction
Quality	Complete, partial
Associated Manifestations	Mouth breathing, snoring, pain, disfigurement, sneezing, itchy eyes, sinus infection
Aggravating Factors	Infection, allergens, medications, objects in nose
Alleviating Factors	Mouth breathing, medications, avoidance of allergens, removal of objects
Setting	Outdoors, indoors
Timing	Following drug therapy, trauma after oral intake, after nasal surgery
Mouth and Throat	
Halitosis	Unpleasant odour of the breath (bad breath)

continues

Quality	Ammonia, acetone, "fruity," newly mown grass or old wine odour, foul (i.e., fetor hepaticus of liver disease due to mercaptan/sulphur)
Associated Manifestations	Gum disease, caries, systemic disease (DM, liver disease), sinusitis, pharyngitis, gastroesophageal reflux disease (GERD)
Aggravating Factors	Poor oral hygiene, poor nutrition, poor diabetic control, alcohol intake, decreased hydration, inadequate renal function
Alleviating Factors	Good oral hygiene, control of systemic diseases, breath mints, good nutrition, adequate dental care, treatment of infection
Timing	Associated with systemic disease or acute infectious process
Lesions	Disruptions in the mucosa of the mouth or tongue
Quality	Tender, nontender
Associated Manifestations	Malnutrition, odour, pain, swelling, fever, stress
Aggravating Factors	Eating, drinking, spices, smoking, hot or cold stimuli, alcohol, dehydration
Alleviating Factors	Medications, avoiding eating, hydration, proper nutrition, avoiding smoking & alcohol
Timing	Associated with systemic disease, intermittent, continuous
Swelling	Edema of the pharynx
Quality	Mild, moderate, severe
Associated Manifestations	Dysphagia, urticaria, wheezing, pruritus, rhinorrhea, difficulty breathing, lesions, chills, sweats, fever, sneezing, itchy eyes
Aggravating Factors	Exposure to allergens, heat
Alleviating Factors	Medications, avoiding allergens, ice, saltwater gargles
Timing	Following drug therapy, after eating, after an insect bite, after trauma, during or after an infectious process
PAST HEALTH HISTORY	*The various components of the past health history are linked to ears, nose, mouth, and throat pathology and ears-, nose-, mouth-, and throat-related information.*
Medical History	
Ear Specific	**Acute otitis media** (AOM), acute otitis externa (AOE), serous otitis media, hearing difficulties
Nose Specific	Polyps, septal deviation, sinus infection, allergic rhinitis, anosmia
Mouth and Throat Specific	Tonsillitis, caries, herpes simplex virus, *Candida* infections, strep throat, frequent URIs, tonsillar abscess
Non-Ear, Nose, Mouth, and Throat Specific	DM, renal disease, atherosclerotic disease, hypertension, inflammatory processes, infections (viral or bacterial), immunosuppressive disease, dental pathology, blood dyscrasias, STIs, anaphylaxis, nutritional disturbances

Surgical History	Neurosurgery, tonsillectomy, adenoidectomy, tumour removal, cosmetic surgery of head or neck, repair of septal deviation, oral surgery, tympanostomy tube placement
Medications	Antibiotics, antihistamines, decongestants, steroids, chemotherapy, immunotherapy immunosuppressive drugs
Allergies	Pollen: sneezing, nasal congestion, watery or itchy eyes, cough Insect stings: swelling of the throat, around the eyes Animal dander: sneezing, nasal congestion, watery or itchy eyes, cough
Injuries and Accidents	Foreign bodies; trauma to the ears, nose, mouth, throat; noxious fumes; sports injuries, MVAs
Special Needs	Deafness, speech disorders
Childhood Illnesses	Frequent tonsillitis, frequent ear infections
FAMILY HEALTH HISTORY	*Ears, nose, mouth, and throat diseases that are familial are listed.*
	Hearing loss, otosclerosis, neonatal blindness secondary to cataracts from mother contracting rubella in pregnancy
SOCIAL HISTORY	*The components of the social history are linked to ears, nose, mouth, and throat factors and pathology.*
Alcohol Use	Predisposes the patient to cancer of the oral cavity as well as decreased nutrition leading to cheilosis
Drug Use	Snorting cocaine may cause perforation of the nasal septum
Tobacco Use	Snuff or chewing tobacco predisposes the patient to mouth, lip, or throat cancer
Sexual Practice	Herpes simplex viruses I and II and gonorrhea can be contracted from oral sex
Work Environment	Exposure to toxins, chemicals, infections, excess noise, allergens
Home Environment	Exposure to loud music may cause hearing loss
Hobbies and Leisure Activities	Prolonged exposure (loud music, rock concerts, chain sawing) or sudden exposure (gun firing) without proper ear protection may cause hearing loss
Stress	Relationship to frequent URIs, decreased hearing
HEALTH MAINTENANCE ACTIVITIES	*This information provides a bridge between the health maintenance activities and ears, nose, mouth, and throat functions.*
Sleep	Deprivation may be associated with frequent URIs
Diet	Deficiencies may affect integrity of nasal and oral mucosa
Use of Safety Devices	Use of mouth guard for sports participants; face shields for sports, job, or home projects; ear protection when around loud noise to prevent damage to hearing
Health Check-ups	Hearing assessment, dental examination

EQUIPMENT

- Otoscope with earpieces of different sizes and pneumatic attachment
- Nasal speculum
- Penlight
- Tuning fork, 512 Hz
- Tongue blade
- Watch
- Gauze square
- Clean gloves
- Transilluminator
- Cotton-tipped applicator

◄NURSING CHECKLIST►

General Approach to Ears, Nose, Mouth, and Throat Assessment

1. Greet the patient and explain the assessment techniques that you will be using.
2. Use a quiet room free from interruptions.
3. Ensure that the light in the room provides sufficient brightness to allow adequate observation of the patient.
4. Place the patient in an upright sitting position on the examination table, or
4a. For patients who cannot tolerate the sitting position, gain access to the patient's head so that it can be rotated from side to side for assessment.
5. Visualize the underlying structures during the assessment process to allow adequate description of findings.
6. Always compare right and left ears, as well as right and left sides of the nose, sinuses, mouth, and throat.
7. Use a systematic approach that is followed consistently at each assessment.

Nursing Tip

The Patient with Decreased Hearing

Observe the patient for signs of hearing difficulty and deafness during the health history and physical exam. Turning the head to facilitate hearing, lip reading, speaking in a loud voice, or asking you to write words are signs of hearing difficulty. If the patient is wearing a hearing device, ask if it is turned on, when the batteries were last changed, and if the device causes any irritation of the ear canal.

Reflective Thinking

A woman who has unilateral deafness from complications following acoustic neuroma surgery arrives in your clinic for a complete health and physical assessment. How would you approach the assessment differently than if she had no difficulties hearing? How would you react if she kept asking you to repeat yourself or did not respond to your questions?

ASSESSMENT OF THE EAR

Physical assessment of the ear consists of three parts:

1. Auditory screening (CN VIII)
2. Inspection and palpation of the external ear
3. Otoscopic assessment

Auditory Screening

Voice-Whisper Test

E   1. Instruct the patient to occlude one ear with a finger.
   2. Stand 0.6 metres behind the patient's other ear and whisper a two-syllable word or phrase that is evenly accented.
   3. Ask the patient to repeat the word or phrase.
   4. Repeat the test with the other ear.

N   The patient should be able to repeat words whispered from a distance of 0.6 metres.

| E | Examination | N | Normal Findings | A | Abnormal Findings | P | Pathophysiology |

A The patient is unable to repeat the words correctly or states that he or she was unable to hear anything.

P This indicates a hearing loss in the high-frequency range that may be caused by excessive exposure to loud noises.

Tuning Fork Tests

Weber and **Rinne tests** help to determine whether the type of hearing loss the patient is experiencing is conductive or sensorineural. In order to understand how these tests are evaluated, it is important to know the difference between air and bone conduction. Air conduction refers to the transmission of sound through the ear canal, TM, and ossicular chain to the cochlea and auditory nerve. Bone conduction refers to the transmission of sound through the bones of the skull to the cochlea and auditory nerve.

Weber Test

E 1. Hold the handle of a 512 Hz tuning fork and strike the tines on the ulnar border of the palm to activate it.
   2. Place the stem of the fork firmly against the middle of the patient's forehead, on the top of the head at the midline, or on the front teeth (Figure 13-10).
   3. Ask the patient if the sound is heard centrally or toward one side.

N **The patient should perceive the sound equally in both ears or "in the middle." No lateralization of sound is known as a negative Weber test.**

A The sound lateralizes to the affected ear.

P This occurs with unilateral conductive hearing loss because the sound is being conducted directly through the bone to the ear. Conductive hearing loss occurs when there are external or middle ear disorders such as impacted cerumen, perforation of the TM, serum or pus in the middle ear, or a fusion of the ossicles.

A The sound lateralizes to the unaffected ear.

P This occurs with sensorineural loss related to nerve damage in the impaired ear. Sensorineural hearing loss occurs when there is a disorder in the inner ear, the auditory nerve, or the brain; disorders include congenital defects, effects of ototoxic drugs, and repeated or prolonged exposure to loud noise.

Rinne Test

E 1. Stand behind or to the side of the patient and strike the tuning fork.
   2. Place the stem of the tuning fork against the patient's right mastoid process to test bone conduction (Figure 13-11A).
   3. Instruct the patient to indicate if the sound is heard.
   4. Ask the patient to tell you when the sound stops.
   5. When the patient says that the sound has stopped, move the tuning fork, with the tines facing forward, in front of the right auditory meatus, and ask the patient if the sound is still heard. Note the length of time the patient hears the sound (testing air conduction) (Figure 13-11B).
   6. Repeat the test on the left ear.

N **Air conduction is heard twice as long as bone conduction when the patient hears the sound through the external auditory canal (air) after it is no longer heard at the mastoid process (bone). This is denoted as AC>BC.**

A The patient reports hearing the sound longer through bone conduction; that is, bone conduction is equal to or greater than air conduction.

P This occurs when there is a conductive hearing loss resulting from disease, obstruction, or damage to the outer or middle ear.

A Bone conduction is prolonged in the context of a normal TM, patent ET, and middle ear disease.

P These findings are typical of otosclerosis.

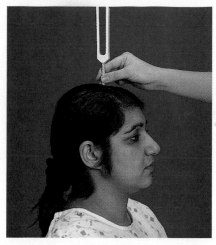

Figure 13-10 Weber Test.

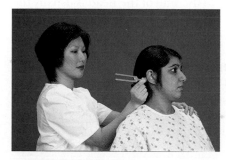

A. Assessing Bone Conduction

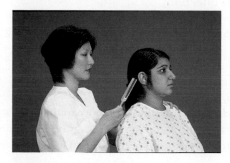

B. Assessing Air Conduction

Figure 13-11 Rinne Test.

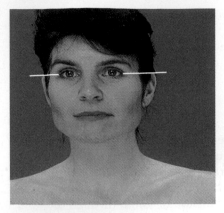

Figure 13-12 Normal Ear Alignment.

Nursing Alert

Cerebrospinal Fluid Drainage from the Ear

If the patient has cerebrospinal fluid (clear liquid that tests positive for glucose on Dextrostix) leaking from the ear, use a good handwashing technique and avoid placing any objects into the ear canal, in order to prevent the development of meningitis. A patient with this finding needs immediate referral to a qualified specialist.

External Ear

Inspection

E   1. Inspect the ears and note their position, colour, size, and shape.
     2. Note any deformities, nodules, inflammation, or lesions.
     3. Note colour, consistency, and amount of cerumen.

N   The ear should match the flesh colour of the patient's skin and should be positioned centrally and in proportion to the head. The top of the ear should cross an imaginary line drawn from the outer canthus of the eye to the occiput (Figure 13-12). Cerumen should be moist and not obscure the TM. There should be no foreign bodies, redness, drainage, deformities, nodules, or lesions.

A   The ears are pale, red, or cyanotic.

P   Vasomotor disorders, fevers, hypoxemia, and cold weather can account for various colour changes.

A   The ears are abnormally large or small.

P   These abnormalities can be congenitally determined or the result of trauma. Figure 13-13 depicts microtia, or an unusually small external ear. Frequently, this is accompanied by an absent external ear canal and middle ear, but an intact inner ear.

A   An ear that is grossly misshapen, damaged, or mutilated is abnormal.

P   Blunt trauma, such as in contact sports, to the side of the head is usually the cause.

A   An external ear that is erythematous, edematous, warm to the touch, and painful is abnormal.

P   Perichondritis is an inflammation of the fibrous connective tissue that overlies the cartilage of the ear (Figure 13-14).

A   A tumour on the external ear is abnormal.

P   Basal cell and squamous cell carcinoma are the most common external ear tumours. Prolonged sunlight exposure is a predisposing factor for these tumours.

A   Purulent drainage is abnormal.

P   Purulent drainage usually indicates an infection.

A   Clear or bloody drainage is present.

P   Clear or bloody drainage may be due to cerebrospinal fluid leaking as a result of head trauma or surgery.

A   A hematoma behind an ear over the mastoid bone is abnormal.

P   This is called Battle's sign and indicates head trauma to the temporal bone of the skull.

A   A hard, painless, irregular-shaped nodule on the pinna is abnormal.

P   Tophi are uric acid nodules and may indicate the presence of gout. These are usually located near the helix. Many other nodules are benign fibromas.

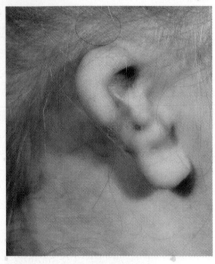

Figure 13-13 Microtia. *Courtesy of Dr. Andrew B. Silva, Pediatric Otolaryngology.*

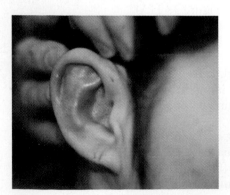

Figure 13-14 Perichondritis. *Courtesy of Dr. Andrew B. Silva, Pediatric Otolaryngology.*

| E | Examination | N | Normal Findings | A | Abnormal Findings | P | Pathophysiology |

A Sebaceous cysts are abnormal.

P Sebaceous cysts or retention cysts form as a result of the blockage of the ducts to the sebaceous gland.

A Lymph nodes anterior to the tragus or overlying the mastoid are abnormal.

P Lymph nodes may be enlarged due to a malignancy or an infection such as external otitis.

Palpation

E **1.** Palpate the auricle between your thumb and the index finger, noting any tenderness or lesions. If the patient has ear pain, assess the unaffected ear first, then cautiously assess the affected ear.

     2. Using the tips of the index and middle fingers, palpate the mastoid tip, noting any tenderness.

     3. Using the tips of the index and middle fingers, press inward on the tragus, noting any tenderness.

     4. Hold the auricle between the thumb and the index finger and gently pull up and down, noting any tenderness.

N The patient should not complain of pain or tenderness during palpation.

A Auricular pain or tenderness is noted.

P Auricular pain is a common finding in external ear infection and is called acute otitis externa (AOE).

A There is tenderness over the mastoid process.

P Mastoid tenderness is associated with middle-ear inflammation or mastoiditis.

A The tragus is edematous or sensitive.

P This finding may indicate inflammation of the external or middle ear.

Otoscopic Assessment

E **1.** Ask the patient to tip his or her head away from the ear being assessed.

     2. Select the largest speculum that will comfortably fit the patient.

     3. Hold the otoscope securely in your dominant hand, with the patient's head held downward, and the handle held like a pencil between your thumb and forefinger.

     4. Rest the back of your dominant hand on the right side of the patient's head (Figure 13-15).

     5. Use the ulnar aspect of your free hand to pull the right ear in a manner that will straighten the canal. In adults, and in children over 3 years old, pull the ear up and back. See Chapter 24 for the assessment of children.

     6. If hair obstructs visualization, moisten the speculum with water or a water-soluble lubricant.

     7. If wax obstructs visualization, it should be removed only by a skilled practitioner, either by curettement (if the cerumen is soft or the TM is ruptured) or by irrigation (if the cerumen is dry and hard and the TM is intact).

     8. Slowly insert the speculum into the canal, looking at the canal as the speculum passes.

     9. Assess the canal for inflammation, exudates, lesions, and foreign bodies.

    10. Continue to insert the speculum into the canal, following the path of the canal until the TM is seen.

    11. If the TM is not visible, gently pull the pinna slightly farther in order to straighten the canal to allow an adequate view.

    12. Identify the colour, light reflex, umbo, the short process, and the long handle of the malleus. Note the presence of perforations, lesions, bulging or retraction of the TM, dilatation of blood vessels, bubbles, or fluid.

Figure 13-15 Position for Otoscopic Examination.

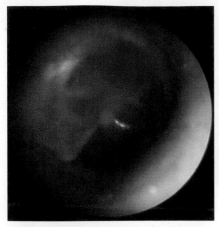

Figure 13-16 Normal Tympanic Membrane. *Courtesy of Dr. Andrew B. Silva, Pediatric Otolaryngology.*

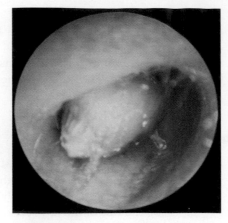

Figure 13-17 EAC Foreign Body (a bean). *Courtesy of Dr. Andrew B. Silva, Pediatric Otolaryngology.*

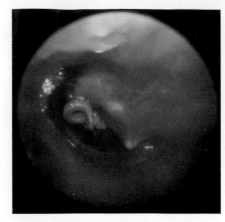

Figure 13-18 PE Tube. *Courtesy of Dr. Andrew B. Silva, Pediatric Otolaryngology.*

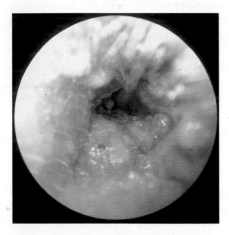

Figure 13-19 Furunculosis. *Courtesy of Bruce Black, M.D., Brisbane, Australia.*

13. Ask the patient to close the mouth, pinch the nose closed, and blow gently while you observe for movement of the TM. A pneumatic attachment may be used to create this movement if one is available.

14. Gently withdraw the speculum and repeat the process with the left ear.

N The ear canal should have no redness, swelling, tenderness, lesions, drainage, foreign bodies, or scaly surface areas. Cerumen varies in amount, consistency, and colour. The TM should be pearly grey with clearly defined landmarks and a distinct cone-shaped light reflex extending from the umbo toward the anteroinferior aspect of the membrane. This light reflex is seen at 5 o'clock in the right ear and at 7 o'clock in the left ear. Blood vessels should be visible only on the periphery, and the membrane should not bulge, be retracted, or have any evidence of fluid behind it (Figure 13-16). The TM should move when the patient blows against resistance.

A A foreign body in the EAC is abnormal (Figure 13-17).

P Both adults and children can have foreign bodies in the EAC. Some objects are more difficult to remove than others; for instance, vegetables in the EAC can swell with time and make removal challenging.

P Tympanostomy tubes, or pressure equalization (PE) tubes (Figure 13-18), are surgically placed for prolonged otitis media with effusion (OME). The tubes allow drainage of the effusion, normal vibration of the ossicles, and equalization of pressures across the TM. When a myringotomy has been performed with tympanostomy tube placement, the presence of the tubes (or lack of) needs to be documented.

A A painful, boil-like pustule in the EAC is abnormal (Figure 13-19).

P Furunculosis is an infection of a hair follicle. EAC edema and otorrhea may also be present.

A Black or brown spores (Figure 13-20A), yellow or orange spores (Figure 13-20B), or white fluffy hyphae in the EAC are abnormal.

P Prolonged use of aural antibiotics can cause otomycosis, or a fungal infection, in the ear. Different strains of fungi cause the variations in appearance.

A Bony, hard lesions in the deep EAC (Figure 13-21) are abnormal.

P These are exostoses. Patients who frequently participate in cold-water activities are at risk for developing exostoses. If an exostosis becomes large enough, it can block the EAC and trap debris between it and the TM, which can lead to infection.

| E | Examination | N | Normal Findings | A | Abnormal Findings | P | Pathophysiology |

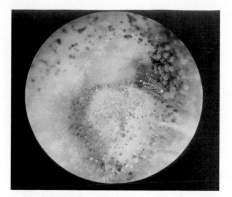

A. Aspergillus Nigra

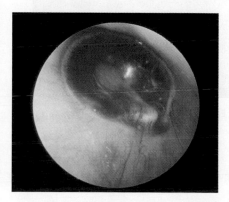

B. Aspergillus Flavum

Figure 13-20 Otomycosis. *Courtesy of Bruce Black, M.D., Brisbane, Australia.*

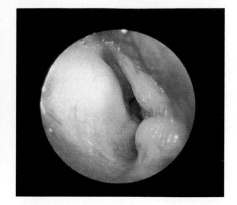

Figure 13-21 Exostoses. *Courtesy of Bruce Black, M.D., Brisbane, Australia.*

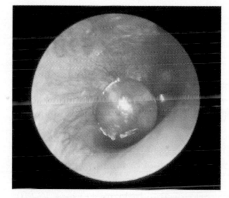

Figure 13-22 Bullous Myringitis. *Courtesy of Bruce Black, M.D., Brisbane, Australia.*

A Exquisite pain accompanied by erythema deep into the EAC and on the TM, along with serous-filled blebs (Figure 13-22), is abnormal.

P This describes viral bullous myringitis. This can easily be mistaken for AOM.

A The appearance of chalk patches on the TM (Figure 13-23) is abnormal.

P These are calcifications found in myringosclerosis, which can occur after TM surgery, infection, or inflammation. Myringosclerosis can be associated with a gradual hearing loss. Involvement of the entire TM is called tympanosclerosis.

A Air bubbles on the TM (Figure 13-24) are abnormal.

P Conditions such as coryza and influenza and changes in extratympanic pressure (such as in scuba diving, airplane travel) can lead to ET failure.

A The presence of blood in the middle ear is abnormal (Figure 13-25).

P Hemotympanum occurs as a result of trauma to the head. The TM can have a bluish hue or be red in appearance.

A A severely retracted TM has exaggerated landmarks (Figure 13-26). Mobility of the TM is decreased.

P Retraction of the TM can occur when the intratympanic membrane pressures are reduced, as in ET blockage caused by OME or allergies. Repeated negative pressure in the middle ear sucks in the TM and leads to retractions. Over time, keratinized epithelial debris accumulate in these retraction pockets and leads to ossicle fixation and to cholesteatoma (Figure 13-27). Foul-smelling ear discharge, as well as deafness, may accompany cholesteatoma.

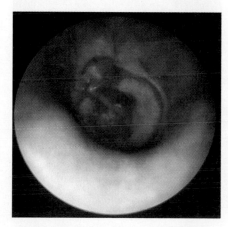

Figure 13-23 Myringosclerosis and OME. *Courtesy of Dr. Andrew B. Silva, Pediatric Otolaryngology.*

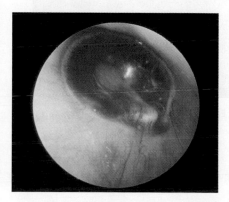

Figure 13-24 Barotrauma Caused by Scuba Diving. *Courtesy of Bruce Black, M.D., Brisbane, Australia.*

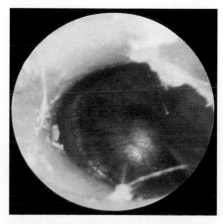

Figure 13-25 Hemotympanum. *Courtesy of Dr. Andrew B. Silva, Pediatric Otolaryngology.*

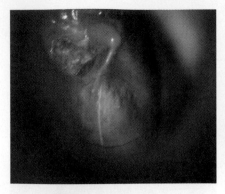

Figure 13-26A Tympanic Membrane Retraction. *Courtesy of Dr. Andrew B. Silva, Pediatric Otolaryngology.*

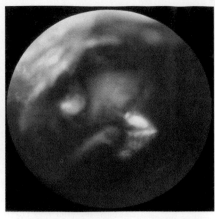

Figure 13-26B Severe Tympanic Membrane Retraction. *Courtesy of Dr. Andrew B. Silva, Pediatric Otolaryngology.*

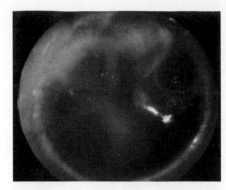

Figure 13-27 Cholesteatoma. *Courtesy of Dr. Andrew B. Silva, Pediatric Otolaryngology.*

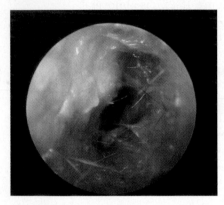

Figure 13-28 Acute Otitis Externa. *Courtesy of Bruce Black, M.D., Brisbane, Australia.*

A There is redness, swelling, narrowing, and pain of the external ear (Figure 13-28). Drainage may be present.

P AOE is caused by infectious organisms or allergic reactions. Predisposing factors include excessive moisture in the ear related to swimming, trauma from cleansing the ears with a sharp instrument, or allergies to substances such as hairspray.

A Hard, dry, and very dark yellow-brown cerumen is abnormal.

P Old cerumen is harder and drier, and may become impacted if not removed.

A The TM is red, with decreased mobility and possible bulging (Figure 13-29).

P This is acute **otitis media** (AOM), or an inflammation of the middle ear. Pain, fever, otalgia, decreased hearing, irritability, disturbed sleep, and otorrhea may accompany the middle ear infection. Twenty-five percent of AOMs are viral; bacterial infections are generally caused by *Haemophilus influenza, Moraxella catarrhalis, Staphylococcus aureus, Streptococcus pneumonia,* and *Streptococcus pyogenes.*[2]

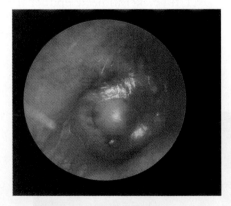

A. Early AOM. Note the bulging TM.

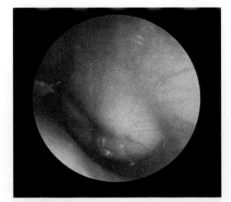

B. More Advanced AOM with Bleb Formation. Note the bulging TM and purulent effusion behind it. The pressure behind the membrane caused a vesicle to form on the pars tensa.

Figure 13-29 Acute Otitis Media. *Courtesy of Bruce Black, M.D., Brisbane, Australia.*

| E | Examination | N | Normal Findings | A | Abnormal Findings | P | Pathophysiology |

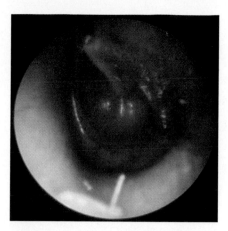

Figure 13-30 Otitis Media with Effusion. *Courtesy of Dr. Andrew B. Silva, Pediatric Otolaryngology.*

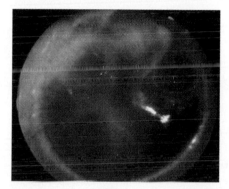

Figure 13-31 Serous Otitis Media. *Courtesy of Dr. Andrew B. Silva, Pediatric Otolaryngology.*

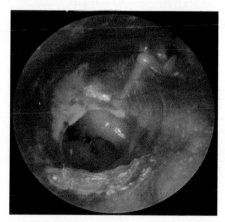

Figure 13-32 Tympanic Membrane Perforation. *Courtesy of Dr. Andrew B. Silva, Pediatric Otolaryngology.*

A Along with a bulging eardrum and decreased mobility, the landmarks are diffuse, displaced, or absent.

P The late stage of AOM causes landmarks to become progressively obscured.

A Amber-yellow fluid on the TM is abnormal and may be accompanied by a fluid line or bubbles behind the membrane. Bulging may be present and mobility of the eardrum may be decreased (Figures 13-30 and 13-31). The patient may complain of ear popping, pain, and decreased hearing.

P OME or serous otitis media can be caused by allergies, infections, and a blocked ET. Table 13-1 compares AOM, OME, and otitis externa.

A The TM appears to have a darkened area or a hole.

P A perforated eardrum is caused by an untreated ear infection secondary to increasing pressure or by trauma to the ear canal (Figure 13-32).

A The TM is pearly grey and has dark patches.

P These patches are usually old perforations in the TM.

A The TM is pearly grey and has dense white plaques.

P These plaques represent calcific deposits of scarring of the TM from frequent past episodes of otitis media.

Nursing Tip

Integrating Research Findings about Otitis Media

- Antibiotics provide a small benefit for AOM in children, however, because most cases of AOM resolve spontaneously, the benefit of antibiotics must be weighed against their possible adverse reactions.[3]
- There is not enough evidence to support the use of decongestants or antihistamines for AOM in children.[4]
- Systematic reviews on the use of topical analgesia for treating the pain associated with AOM,[5] and the use of influenza vaccine to prevent AOM in infants and children[6] will provide helpful guidance for parents and clinicians.
- Quinolone antibiotic drops (e.g., ciprofloxacin) are better than oral or injected antibiotics at drying the ear in children with chronic suppurative otitis media (an infection of the middle ear with pus and a persistent perforation in the eardrum).[7]

Nursing Alert

Risk Factors for Otitis Media

- Less than 2 years of age
- Frequent upper respiratory tract infections
- Males
- Family history (parents, siblings)
- Pacifier use after 6 months of age
- Passive smoking
- Day care attendance
- Bottle fed
- Down syndrome
- Craniofacial disorders

Nursing Alert

Hearing Loss Risk Factors

- Noise exposure (see Nursing Tip, Hearing Safety)
- Smoking
- Ototoxic drugs (i.e., aminoglycosides)
- Congenital or heredity
- Cardiovascular disease
- Aging
- Tumours (i.e., acoustic neuroma)
- Trauma
- Chronic infection
- Systemic disease
- Tympanic membrane perforation
- Ménière's disease
- Barotrauma

Nursing Tip

Hearing Safety[8]

- Health Canada's Hazardous Products Act states that no children's toy, as ordinarily used, should produce sound levels exceeding 100 dB.
- When using personal stereo systems, keep the sound at enjoyable but safe levels. If someone a metre away must shout to be understood, the sound level of the music is probably higher than 85 dB, and may be hazardous.
- For sound levels higher than 70 dB, the duration of daily exposure becomes an important risk factor.
- Exposure to 85 dB for eight hours daily, has been adopted by several Canadian provinces as the limit for occupational noise.

TABLE 13-1	Comparison of AOM, OME, and AOE		
	AOM	**OME**	**AOE**
TM colour	Diffuse red, dilated peripheral vessels	Yellowish	WNL
TM appearance	Bulging	Bubbles, fluid line	WNL
TM landmarks	Decreased	Retracted with prominent malleus	WNL
Movement of tragus	Painless	Painless	Painful
Hearing	WNL/decreased	WNL/decreased	WNL
EAC	WNL	WNL	Erythematous, edematous

ASSESSMENT OF THE NOSE

External Inspection

E Inspect the nose, noting any trauma, bleeding, lesions, masses, swelling, and asymmetry.

N The shape of the external nose can vary greatly among individuals. Normally, it is located symmetrically in the midline of the face and is without swelling, bleeding, lesions, or masses.

A The nose is misshapen, broken, or swollen.

P The shape of the nose is determined by genetics; however, changes can occur because of trauma or cosmetic surgery.

Patency

E 1. Have the patient occlude one nostril with a finger.
   2. Ask the patient to breathe in and out through the nose as you observe and listen for air movement in and out of the nostril.
   3. Repeat on the other side.

N Each nostril is patent.

A You observe or the patient states that air cannot be moved through the nostril(s).

P Occlusion of the nostrils can occur with a deviated septum, foreign body, URI, allergies, or nasal polyps.

A Nasal drainage is observed from only one side of the nose.

P Unilateral nasal drainage may be a sign of nasal obstruction.

Internal Inspection

E 1. Position the patient's head in an extended position.
   2. Place your nondominant hand firmly on top of the patient's head.
   3. Using the thumb of the same hand, lift the tip of the patient's nose.
   4. Gently insert a nasal speculum or an otoscope with a short, wide nasal speculum (Figure 13-33). If using a nasal speculum, use a penlight to view the nostrils.
   5. Assess each nostril separately.
   6. Inspect the mucous membranes for colour and discharge.

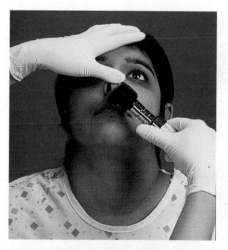

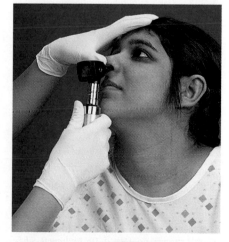

A. Use of Otoscope with Nasal Speculum   B. Lateral View of Internal Nose Assessment

Figure 13-33 Internal Inspection of the Nose.

| E | **Examination** | N | **Normal Findings** | A | **Abnormal Findings** | P | **Pathophysiology** |

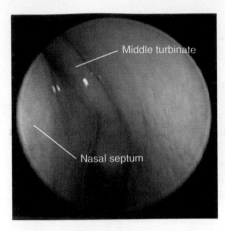

Figure 13-34 Deviated Septum. *Courtesy of Dr. Andrew B. Silva, Pediatric Otolaryngology.*

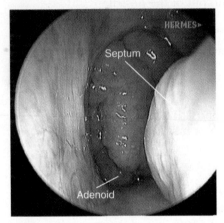

Figure 13-35 Nasal Cavity Blocked by Adenoid. *Courtesy of Dr. Andrew B. Silva, Pediatric Otolaryngology.*

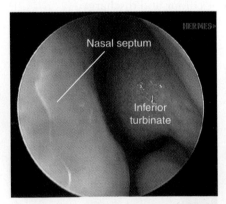

Figure 13-36 Edematous inferior turbinate causing almost total occlusion of the nasal cavity. Note the slight difference in colour between the septum and the turbinate. These findings can occur in patients with allergic rhinitis. *Courtesy of Dr. Andrew B. Silva, Pediatric Otolaryngology.*

7. Inspect the middle and inferior turbinates and the middle meatus for colour, swelling, drainage, lesions, and polyps.

8. Observe the nasal septum for deviation, perforation, lesions, and bleeding.

N The nasal mucosa should be pink or dull red without swelling or polyps. The septum is at the midline and without perforation, lesions, or bleeding. A small amount of clear, watery discharge is normal.

A A nasal septum that is "pushed" to one side can be an abnormal finding (Figure 13-34).

P A deviated septum can be a naturally occurring finding, or it can be caused by trauma to the face and nasal area.

A A nasal cavity that is occluded is abnormal.

P There are many causes of an occluded nasal cavity. Foreign bodies may be present, especially in children. Trauma may induce nasal edema, sinus infection may produce copious discharge, an adenoid may be so large that it occludes the nasal cavity (Figure 13-35), and allergies can lead to edematous turbinates (Figure 13-36).

A The nasal mucosa is red and swollen with copious, clear, watery discharge. This is called rhinitis, an inflammation of the nasal mucosa.

P These findings indicate the occurrence of the common cold (coryza) when there is an acute onset of symptoms. Discharge may become purulent if a secondary bacterial infection develops.

A Nasal mucosa is pale and edematous with clear, watery discharge.

P These findings usually indicate the presence of allergies or hay fever.

A Following trauma to the head, there is a clear, watery nasal discharge with normal-appearing mucosa. This discharge tests positive for glucose.

P These findings indicate the presence of cerebrospinal fluid. This may occur following head injury or complications of nose or sinus surgery or dental work. Immediate referral is warranted.

A Nasal mucosa is red and swollen with purulent nasal discharge (Figure 13-37). These findings are usually worse on one side but may be found bilaterally.

P These are common findings in bacterial sinusitis.

A Smooth, round masses that are pale and shiny are noted protruding from the middle meatus.

P These masses are nasal polyps (Figure 13-38), which may obstruct air passages. They are usually found bilaterally and are often seen in patients with chronic allergic rhinitis, asthma, and cystic fibrosis. A unilateral polyp is suspect for a malignancy until proven otherwise.

A Bleeding is noted from an area of the lower portion of the nasal septum.

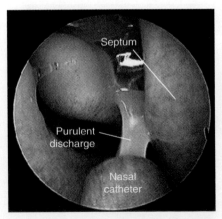

Figure 13-37 Purulent Discharge in the Nasal Cavity at the Middle Turbinate. *Courtesy of Dr. Andrew B. Silva, Pediatric Otolaryngology.*

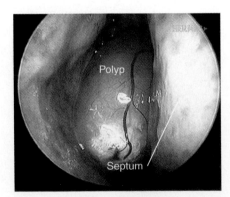

Figure 13-38 Nasal Polyp. *Courtesy of Dr. Andrew B. Silva, Pediatric Otolaryngology.*

| E | Examination | N | Normal Findings | A | Abnormal Findings | P | Pathophysiology |

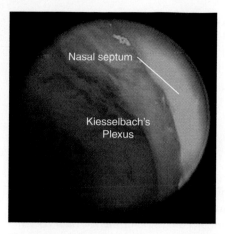

Figure 13-39 Kiesselbach's Plexus. *Courtesy of Dr. Andrew B. Silva, Pediatric Otolaryngology.*

P Kiesselbach's plexus is the site of most nosebleeds (Figure 13-39). Repeated nosebleeds warrant attention for blood dyscrasias, environmental causes, and malignancies.

A There is unilateral purulent discharge; however, the patient does not experience other symptoms of an URI. Nasal mucosa on the unaffected side appears normal.

P Unilateral purulent discharge without other findings of an URI indicates the development of a local infection. A common cause of localized infection is the presence of a foreign body.

A Nasal mucosa is inflamed and friable with possible septal perforation. There is no infection present.

P These findings may indicate nasal inhalation of cocaine or amphetamines or the overuse of nasal spray.

ASSESSMENT OF THE SINUSES

Inspection

E Observe the patient's face for any swelling around the nose and eyes.

N There is no evidence of swelling around the nose and eyes.

A Swelling is noted above or below the eyes.

P Acute sinusitis may result in swelling of the face around the eyes due to inflammation and accumulation of purulent material in the paranasal sinuses.

Palpation and Percussion

To palpate and percuss the frontal sinuses:

E 1. Stand facing the patient.
2. Gently press your thumbs under the bony ridge of the upper orbits (Figure 13-40A). Avoid applying pressure on the globes themselves.
3. Observe for the presence of pain.
4. Percuss the areas using the middle or index finger of your dominant hand (immediate percussion).
5. Note the sound.

N/A/P Refer to maxillary sinuses.

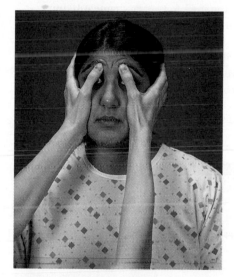

A. Palpation of Frontal Sinuses

To palpate and percuss the maxillary sinuses:

E 1. Stand in front of the patient.
2. Apply gentle pressure in the area under the infraorbital ridge using your thumb or middle finger (Figure 13-40B).
3. Observe for the presence of pain.
4. Percuss the area using your dominant middle or index finger.
5. Note the sound.

N The patient should experience no discomfort during palpation or percussion. The sinuses should be air filled and therefore resonant to percussion.

A The patient complains of pain or tenderness at the site of palpation or percussion.

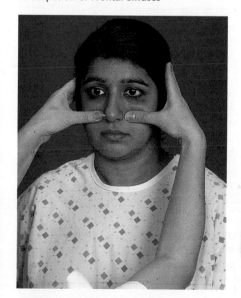

B. Palpation of Maxillary Sinuses

Figure 13-40 Palpation of Sinuses.

Reflective Thinking

Septal Perforation

You note that your patient has a small septal perforation. She adamantly denies snorting cocaine, even though her friends do. She admits to using other illegal substances in the past, and you are aware that she was recently released from a drug rehab program. What questions would you ask this patient? What other physical assessments would be appropriate?

P Sinusitis can be due to viral, bacterial, or allergic processes that cause inflammation of the mucous membranes and obstruction of the drainage pathways.

A Percussion of the sinuses elicits a dull sound.

P Dullness can be caused by fluid or cells present in the sinus cavity from an infectious or allergic process, or congenital absence of a sinus.

Nursing Alert

Epistaxis—Nosebleeds

- Epistaxis can occur in the anterior-inferior nasal septum or at the point where the inferior turbinates meet the nasopharynx. Usually unilateral, they may seem bilateral as blood runs from the bleeding side to the alternate nare. Epistaxis may be mild to severe and possibly life threatening.[9]
- Nosebleeds in children usually stop by themselves or after pinching the nose. Some children get repeated nosebleeds with no specific cause (recurrent idiopathic epistaxis). Treatments are cautery (sealing with heat) and/or antiseptic cream.[10]
- Have the patient sit with his or her head tilted forward, breathing through the mouth. Pinch the entire soft part of the nose for approximately 10 minutes (or until bleeding stops), and coach the patient to stay quiet and avoid coughing, spitting, or sniffing.
- If the patient has severe epistaxis, take vital signs and monitor for signs of hypovolemic shock. If hypovolemic, have the patient lie down and turn his or her head to the side to prevent blood from draining down the back of the throat. Monitor airway patency and seek medical help (the patient may need nasal packing to stop the bleeding).[11]

Advanced Technique

Transillumination of the Sinuses

If palpation and percussion of the sinuses suggest sinusitis, transillumination of the frontal and maxillary sinuses should be performed.

To evaluate the frontal sinuses:

E 1. Place the patient in a sitting position facing you in a dark room.
  2. Place a strong light source, such as a transilluminator, penlight, or the tip of an otoscope with the speculum, under the bony ridge of the upper orbits (Figure 13-41A).
  3. Observe the red glow over the sinuses and compare the symmetry of the two sides.

To evaluate the maxillary sinuses:

E 1. Place the patient in a sitting position facing you in a dark room.
  2. Place the light source firmly under each eye and just above the infraorbital ridge (Figure 13-41B).
  3. Ask the patient to open his or her mouth; observe the red glow on the hard palate, and compare the two sides.

N The glow on each side is equal, indicating air-filled frontal and maxillary sinuses.

A Absence of glow is abnormal.

P Absence of glow suggests sinus congestion or the congenital absence of a sinus.

A An extremely bright glow is abnormal.

P This phenomenon may be present in an elderly patient with decreased subcutaneous fat.

| E | **Examination** | N | **Normal Findings** | A | **Abnormal Findings** | P | **Pathophysiology** |

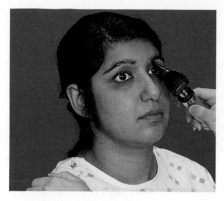

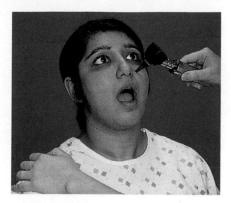

A. Frontal Sinus

B. Maxillary Sinus

Figure 13-41 Transillumination of Sinuses.

> ## ◄NURSING CHECKLIST►
>
> **Preparing for the Assessment of the Mouth and Throat**
>
> 1. Physical assessment of the oral cavity should include the following: breath, lips, tongue, buccal mucosa, gums and teeth, hard and soft palates, throat (oropharynx), and temporomandibular joint (see Chapters 11 and 18).
> 2. If the patient is wearing dentures or removable orthodontia, ask that they be removed before the examination begins.
> 3. Use gloves and a light source for optimum visualization of the oral cavity and pharynx.

ASSESSMENT OF THE MOUTH AND THROAT

Assessment of the Mouth

Breath

E **1.** Stand facing the patient and about 30 cm away.

    2. Smell the patient's breath.

N The breath should smell fresh.

A The breath smells foul.

P The foul smell of halitosis can be a symptom of tooth decay, poor oral hygiene, or diseases of the gums, tonsils, or sinuses.

A The breath smells of acetone.

P Acetone or "fruity" breath is common in patients who are malnourished or who have diabetic ketoacidosis. The patient may also be on a low-carbohydrate diet.

A The breath smells musty.

P Fetor hepaticas is the musty smell of the breath of a patient in liver failure and is caused by the breakdown of nitrogen compounds.

A The breath smells of ammonia.

P The smell of ammonia can be detected in a patient in end-stage renal failure (uremia) because of the inability to eliminate urea.

Lips

Inspection

E **1.** Observe the lips for colour, moisture, swelling, lesions, or other signs of inflammation.

    2. Instruct the patient to open his or her mouth.

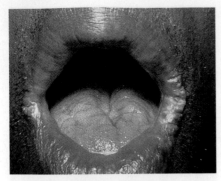

A. Angular Cheilosis. *Courtesy of Dr. Joseph Konzelman, School of Dentistry, Medical College of Georgia.*

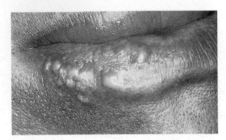

B. Fever Blister (Herpes Simplex Virus). *Courtesy of Dr. Joseph Konzelman, School of Dentistry, Medical College of Georgia.*

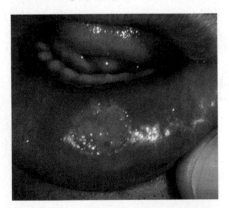

C. Chancre from Primary Syphilis

D. Squamous Cell Carcinoma. *Courtesy of Dr. Joseph Konzelman, School of Dentistry, Medical College of Georgia.*

Figure 13-42 Lip Abnormalities.

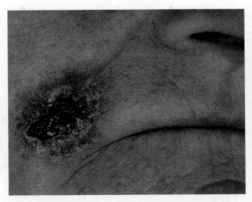

E. Basal Cell Carcinoma. © Lester V. Bergman/ CORBIS.

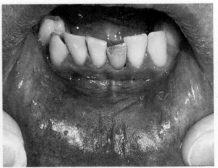

F. Leukoplakia. *Courtesy of Dr. Joseph Konzelman, School of Dentistry, Medical College of Georgia.*

3. Use a tongue blade to inspect the membranes that connect the upper and lower lips to the gums for colour, inflammation, lesions, and hydration.

N   The lips and membranes should be pink and moist with no evidence of lesions or inflammation.

A   The lips are pale or cyanotic.

P   Refer to Chapter 16.

A   The lips are dry and cracked.

P   Chapping or superficial cracking of the lips may be due to exposure to wind, sun, or a dry environment, dehydration, or persistent licking of the lips.

A   Swelling of the lips is noted.

P   Allergic reactions to medications, foods, or other allergens can result in swelling of the lips.

A   The skin at the outer corners of the mouth is atrophic, irritated, and cracked (Figure 13-42A).

P   Angular cheilosis may be due to increased accumulation of saliva in the corners of the mouth or constant drooling from the mouth. This occurs in nutritional deficiencies (such as riboflavin), poorly fitting dentures, and deficiencies of the immune system. *Candida* infections may also be present.

A   Vesicles on erythematous bases with serous fluid are found on the lips, gums, or hard palate, either singly or in clusters. They later rupture, crust over, and become painful (Figure 13-42B).

P   These are herpes simplex lesions, which are also called cold sores or fever blisters. This common viral infection may be precipitated by febrile illness, sunlight, stress, or allergies.

A   A round, painless lesion with central ulceration (Figure 13-42C) is noted and may become crusted.

P   This is a chancre, the primary lesion of syphilis.

A   A plaque, wart, nodule, or ulcer is noted, usually on the lower lip.

P   This may be squamous cell carcinoma, the most common form of oral cancer, which is more frequent in males (Figure 13-42D).

P   Basal cell carcinoma lesions can have pearly borders, crusting, and central ulcerations (Figure 13-42E).

A   Persistent, painless, white, painted-looking patches are noted on the lips (Figure 13-42F). They are associated with heavy smoking and the use of chewing tobacco.

| E | Examination | N | Normal Findings | A | Abnormal Findings | P | Pathophysiology |

P   These patches are called leukoplakia and are considered premalignant lesions. They often occur at sites of chronic irritation from dentures, tobacco, or excessive alcohol intake.

Palpation

E   1. Don clean gloves.
2. Gently pull down the patient's lower lip with the thumb and index finger of one hand and pull up the patient's upper lip with the thumb and index finger of the other hand.
3. Note the tone of the lips as they are manipulated.
4. If lesions are present, palpate them for consistency and tenderness.

N   Lips should not be flaccid and lesions should not be present.

N/A/P   See inspection of the lips for pathologies.

Tongue

E   1. Ask the patient to stick out his or her tongue (CN XII assesses tongue movement).
2. Observe the dorsal surface for colour, hydration, texture, symmetry, fasciculations, atrophy, position in the mouth, and the presence of lesions.
3. Ask the patient to move the tongue from side to side and up and down.
4. With the patient's tongue back in the mouth, ask the patient to press it against the cheek. Provide resistance with your finger pads held on the outside of the cheek. Note the strength of the tongue and compare bilaterally.
5. Ask the patient to touch the tip of the tongue to the roof of the mouth. You may also grasp the tip of the tongue with a gauze square held between the thumb and the index finger of the gloved hand (Figure 13-43).
6. Inspect the ventral surface of the tongue, the frenulum, and Wharton's ducts for colour, hydration, lesions, inflammation, and vasculature.
7. With the gauze square, pull the tongue to the left and inspect and palpate the tongue using your finger pads.
8. Repeat with the tongue held to the right side.

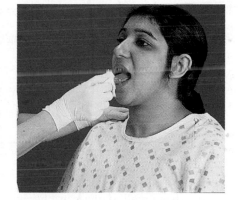

Figure 13-43 Tongue Assessment.

N   The tongue is in the midline of the mouth. The dorsum of the tongue should be pink, moist, rough (from the taste buds), and without lesions. The tongue is symmetrical and moves freely. The strength of the tongue is symmetrical and strong. The ventral surface of the tongue has prominent blood vessels and should be moist and without lesions. Wharton's ducts are patent and without inflammation or lesions. The lateral aspects of the tongue should be pink, smooth, and lesion free.

A   The tongue is enlarged.

P   An enlarged tongue may be associated with myxedema, acromegaly, Down syndrome, or amyloidosis. Transient enlargement may be associated with glossitis, stomatitis, cellulitis of the neck, angioneurotic edema, hematoma, or abscess.

A   The tongue is red and smooth with absent papillae.

P   This indicates glossitis caused by a vitamin B_{12}, iron, or niacin deficiency. It may also be a side effect of chemotherapy.

A   There is a thick, white, curdlike coating on the tongue that leaves a raw, red surface when it is scraped off (Figure 13-44A).

P   This is candidiasis, or thrush, which may also be red in the absence of the coating. Thrush can result from changes in the normal oral flora due to chemotherapy, radiation therapy, disorders of the immune system such as AIDS, antibiotic therapy, or excessive use of alcohol, tobacco, or cocaine.

A   Thin, pearly white lesions that coalesce and become thick and palpable are noted on the sides of the tongue. The white lesions are firmly attached to the underlying tissue and will not scrape off.

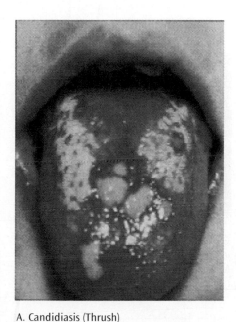

A. Candidiasis (Thrush)

Figure 13-44 Tongue Conditions.

B. Leukoplakia of the Tongue. *Courtesy of Dr. Daniel D. Rooney.*

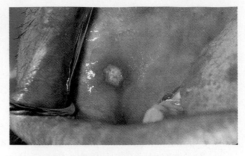

C. Aphthous Ulcer (Canker Sore). *Courtesy of Dr. Joseph Konzelman, School of Dentistry, Medical College of Georgia.*

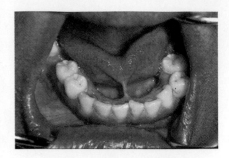

D. Ankyloglossia. *Courtesy of Dr. Joseph Konzelman, School of Dentistry, Medical College of Georgia.*

Figure 13-44 *continued.*

P This is leukoplakia. It is considered a premalignant lesion. Some leukoplakia progresses from dysplasia to a malignancy (Figure 13-44B).

A A painful, small, round, white, ulcerated lesion with erythematous borders is abnormal (Figure 13-44C).

P This is an aphthous ulcer (canker sore), which can be associated with stress, extreme fatigue, food allergies, and oral trauma.

A A short lingual frenulum is observed (Figure 13-44D).

P Ankyloglossia is a congenital abnormality.

A The tongue has a hairy appearance and is yellow, black, or brown (Figure 13-44E).

P This is known as oral hairy leukoplakia, or hairy tongue, a benign condition that can result from antibiotic therapy. The hairy appearance is caused by elongated papillae.

A Lesions are noted on the ventral surface of the tongue.

P The ventral surface of the tongue is an area where malignancies are likely to develop, especially in patients who drink alcohol and smoke or use smokeless tobacco.

A Indurations, or ulcerations, are present on the lateral surfaces of the tongue.

P Most lingual cancers are located in this area and are associated with use of alcohol and tobacco.

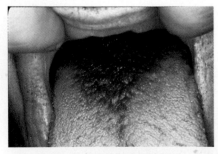

E. Oral Hairy Leukoplakia. *Courtesy of Dr. Joseph Konzelman, School of Dentistry, Medical College of Georgia.*

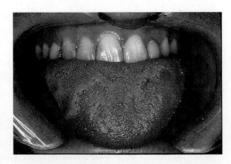

F. Geographic Tongue. *Courtesy of Dr. Joseph Konzelman, School of Dentistry, Medical College of Georgia.*

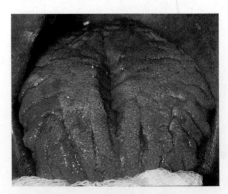

G. Fissured Tongue (Scrotal Tongue). *Courtesy of Dr. Joseph Konzelman, School of Dentistry, Medical College of Georgia.*

Figure 13-44 *continued.*

| E | Examination | N | Normal Findings | A | Abnormal Findings | P | Pathophysiology |

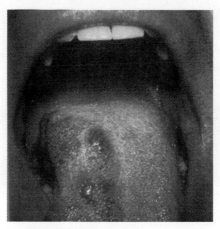

H. Hemangioma. *Courtesy of Dr. Joseph Konzelman, School of Dentistry, Medical College of Georgia.*

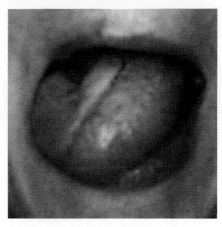

I. Cranial Nerve XII (Hypoglossal) Palsy

Figure 13-44 *continued.*

A   Patches of red denuded areas on the lingual surface of the tongue, frequently at the papillae, surrounded by ridges of pale-yellow epithelium are abnormal (Figure 13-44F).

P   This harmless condition, known as geographic tongue, has no known cause. Its name is derived from the patterns of regular and irregular surfaces on the tongue that resemble a map.

A   Numerous furrows or grooves are observed, often radiating horizontally from the midline of the dorsal surface of the tongue (Figure 13-44G).

P   This is a harmless and often inherited condition known as fissured or scrotal tongue. It is different from syphilitic glossitis, which is characterized by longitudinal furrows.

A   Engorged blood vessels of the tongue are abnormal (Figure 13-44H).

P   A hemangioma of the tongue is a benign overgrowth of vascular tissue.

A   Deviation of the tongue toward one side (Figure 13-44I), atrophy, and asymmetrical shape of the tongue are abnormal.

P   Unilateral paralysis of the tongue muscles will cause the tongue to deviate toward the affected side because the muscles on the paralyzed side are unable to oppose the strong muscles of the unaffected side. The patient is unable to push the tongue toward the nonparalyzed side. Lesions of the hypoglossal nucleus or nerve fibre cause these unilateral symptoms.

A   Atrophy of the tongue and the inability to protrude the tongue are abnormal.

P   Bilateral paralysis of the tongue muscles will prevent the patient from protruding the tongue. Syringobulbia or trauma to CN XII may cause hypoglossal nerve paralysis.

Buccal Mucosa

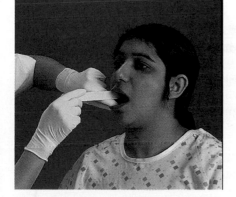

Figure 13-45 Assessment of the Buccal Mucosa.

E   1. Ask the patient to open his or her mouth as wide as possible.
    2. Use a tongue depressor and a penlight to assess the inner cheeks and the openings of Stensen's ducts (Figure 13-45).
    3. Observe for colour, inflammation, hydration, and lesions.

N   The colour of the oral mucosa on the inside of the cheek may vary according to race. Blacks have a bluish hue; Caucasians have pink mucosa. Freckle-like macules may appear on the inside of the buccal mucosa. The buccal mucosa should be moist, smooth, and free of inflammation and lesions. Some patients may have torus mandibularis (Figure 13-46A), which are bony nodules in the mandibular region.

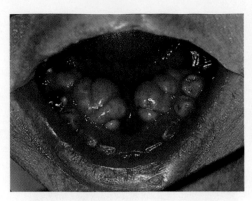

A. Torus Mandibularis. *Courtesy of Dr. Joseph Konzelman, School of Dentistry, Medical College of Georgia.*

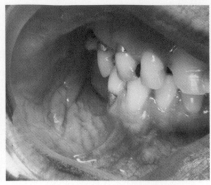

B. Leukoplakia Caused by Snuff. *Courtesy of Dr. Joseph Konzelman, School of Dentistry, Medical College of Georgia.*

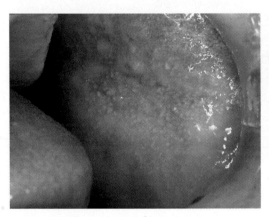

C. Fordyce's Spots. *Courtesy of Dr. Joseph Konzelman, School of Dentistry, Medical College of Georgia.*

D. Left Parotitis

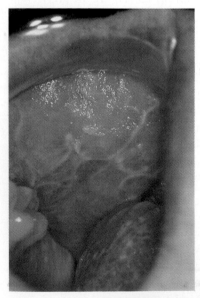

E. Lichen Planus. *Courtesy of Dr. Joseph Konzelman, School of Dentistry, Medical College of Georgia.*

Figure 13-46 Buccal Mucosa Conditions.

A   Leathery, painless, white, painted-looking patches are noted.

P   Leukoplakia may be found in the buccal mucosa. Figure 13-46B shows leukoplakia caused by snuff.

A   Yellow patches on the buccal mucosa are present.

P   Fordyce's spots are small sebaceous glands (Figure 13-46C).

A   The orifice of Stensen's duct is erythematous and edematous. It may be tender to palpation.

P   This is seen in parotitis, an inflammation of the parotid gland. The area between the ear lobule and angle of the mandible may not be visible due to the swelling of the parotid gland (Figure 13-46D). Acute unilateral swelling may be seen in mumps.

A   The mucosa is pale.

P   This can be caused by anemia or vasoconstriction that may occur when the sympathetic nervous system is stimulated, such as in shock.

A   The mucosa is cyanotic.

P   Cyanosis can indicate systemic hypoxemia. See Chapters 10 and 16.

A   The mucosa is erythematous.

P   Erythema can be associated with stomatitis.

A   There is excessive dryness of the mucosa.

E	Examination	N	Normal Findings	A	Abnormal Findings	P	Pathophysiology

Nursing Alert

Oral Cancer

Epidemiology[12]
- Oral cancer is the 9th leading cause of new cancers and the 11th leading cause of cancer-related deaths in Canadian men; It is the 15th leading cause of new cancers and death in Canadian women.

Risk Factors[13]
- Male gender
- Age >50 years
- Tobacco use (snuff, chewing tobacco, pipes, cigars, cigarettes)
- Chewing betel nut
- Excessive alcohol use
- Excessive sun exposure to the lips
- History of leukoplakia or erythroplakia

Screening
- Oral cancer has a low survival rate, largely because the disease is often not diagnosed until it is advanced. Screening the general population for oral cancer might make it possible to detect cases of the disease earlier. The most common method is visual inspection, but other techniques include the use of toluidine blue and fluoroscene imaging. A systematic review concluded that there is not enough evidence to decide whether screening by visual inspection reduces the death rate for oral cancer.[14]

P   This is xerostomia, which occurs when salivary gland activity is decreased or obstructed, or when the patient is hypovolemic, breathes through the mouth, or has Sjögren's syndrome.

A   Excessive moisture is noted in the mouth.

P   This condition may be noted in the early stages of inflammation or when the patient is hypervolemic.

A   Flat-topped papules with thin, bluish white spider-web lines (Figure 13-46E) resembling leukoplakia are noted on the mucosa or tongue.

P   Wickham's striae are the lesions of lichen planus, which is an inflammatory and pruritic disease of the skin and mucous membranes. It is usually a benign disease and the cause is unknown.

Gums

E   1. Instruct the patient to open his or her mouth.
   2. Observe dentures or orthodontics for fit.
   3. Remove any dentures or removable orthodontia.
   4. Shine the penlight in the patient's mouth.
   5. Use the tongue depressor to move the tongue to visualize the gums.
   6. Observe for redness, swelling, bleeding, retraction from the teeth, or discoloration.

N   In light-skinned individuals, the gums have a pale-red stippled surface. Patchy brown pigmentation may be present in dark-skinned patients. The gum margins should be well defined with no pockets existing between the gums and the teeth and no swelling or bleeding.

A   The gingiva are red, tender, and swollen and bleed easily (Figure 13-47).

P   This describes gingivitis, which may be caused by poor dental hygiene, improperly fitted dentures, and scurvy. Gingivitis can also occur with

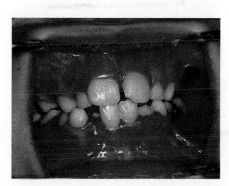

Figure 13-47 Gingivitis with Herpes Simplex Virus. *Courtesy of Dr. Joseph Konzelman, School of Dentistry, Medical College of Georgia.*

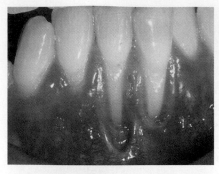

Figure 13-48 Gingival Recession. *Courtesy of Gary Shellerud, DDS.*

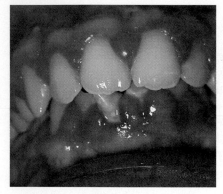

Figure 13-49 Gingival Hyperplasia. *Courtesy of Dr. Joseph Konzelman, School of Dentistry, Medical College of Georgia.*

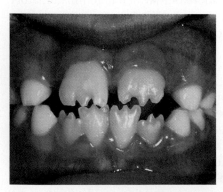

Figure 13-50 Hutchinson's Incisors. *Courtesy of Dale Ruemping, DDS, MSD.*

stomatitis that occurs in mouth infections and upper respiratory tract infections.

A Gingival borders are red and there is infection of the pockets formed between receding gums and teeth. Purulent drainage may be present.

P This is periodontitis, which is an inflammation of the periodontium due to chronic gingivitis. This condition is caused by poor oral hygiene.

A Blue lines are noted approximately 1 mm from the gingival margin.

P These are lead bismuth lines caused by chronic exposure to lead or bismuth.

A The gums are brownish.

P This occurs in association with Addison's disease.

A A greyish membrane is noted over an inflamed and ulcerated area of the mucosa.

P This condition is Vincent's stomatitis, or trench mouth, a bacterial infection of the gums that may extend into pharyngeal structures and bones.

A A nontender, immobile tumour lighter than the gums is noted on the gum.

P This lesion is epulis, a fibrous tumour of the gums.

A The gums are retracted from the teeth (Figure 13-48), sometimes exposing the roots of the teeth.

P This recession of the gums often occurs in older individuals due to poor oral hygiene.

A Hypertrophy of gum tissue is abnormal (Figure 13-49).

P This is called gingival hyperplasia and is usually painless; it occurs in pregnancy, in wearers of orthodontic braces, by dental plaque, or with the use of medications such as phenytoin.

A Small ulcers or folds of excess tissue are noted on the gums under an ill-fitting denture. Inflamed and swollen nodules may be seen in the area of the palate.

P Continued irritation of the gums by ill-fitting dentures results in hyperplasia.

Teeth

E 1. Instruct the patient to open his or her mouth.
   2. Count the upper and lower teeth.
   3. Observe the teeth for discoloration, loose or missing teeth, caries, malocclusion, and malformation.

N The adult normally has 32 teeth, which should be white with smooth edges, in proper alignment, and without caries.

A Teeth are absent.

P This problem may be due to loss or failure of development. The patient's nutritional status may be seriously impaired when the teeth are insufficient.

A There are white or black patches on the surface of a tooth. These patches may become eroded as damage progresses.

P These are dental caries, or cavities, resulting from poor oral hygiene.

A The teeth are worn at an angle.

P Biting surfaces of the teeth may become worn down by repetitive biting on hard substances or objects or grinding of teeth, called bruxism, especially at night.

A A tooth is dark in colour and the patient reports insensitivity to cold.

P This is usually a dead tooth, which results in a darkening of the enamel.

A Teeth that have serrated edges (Figure 13-50) are abnormal.

P These are called Hutchinson's incisors. Pregnant women with syphilis can have abnormal fetal dentition because of the effects of the disease on tooth development.

| E | Examination | N | Normal Findings | A | Abnormal Findings | P | Pathophysiology |

Reflective Thinking

The Patient with Poor Oral Hygiene

You are assigned to care for a woman who has lacerations on her left hand. You note that she has foul-smelling breath. On further assessment of her mouth, you note that she has very poor oral hygiene with many broken, carious, rotting teeth. How would you react? How would you begin to discuss the importance of oral hygiene and dental consultation with her?

Palate

E 1. Ask the patient to tilt his or her head back and open the mouth as wide as possible.
2. Shine the penlight in the patient's mouth.
3. Observe both the hard and the soft palates.
4. Note their shape and colour, and the presence of any lesions or malformations.

N **The hard and soft palates are concave and pink. The hard palate has many ridges; the soft palate is smooth. No lesions or malformations are noted.**

A The palates are red, swollen, tender, or with lesions.

P These findings are symptoms of infection.

A There is a bony ridge in the midline of the hard palate (Figure 13-51).

P This is a benign condition called torus palatinus, which develops in adulthood.

A A fibrous, encapsulated tissue growth on the palate is abnormal (Figure 13-52).

P A fibroma may be idiopathic or neoplastic in origin. Chronic trauma can also lead to fibroma formation.

A A lesion that has become eroded is noted on the palate.

P This may be a cancerous lesion in the epithelium of the hard palate.

A The palate is highly arched.

P This finding is associated with Turner's syndrome and Marfan's syndrome.

A There is a hole in the hard palate.

P Palatine perforation is related to syphilis or radiation therapy.

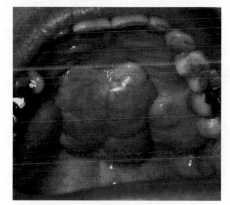

Figure 13-51 Torus Palatinus. *Courtesy of Dr. Joseph Konzelman, School of Dentistry, Medical College of Georgia.*

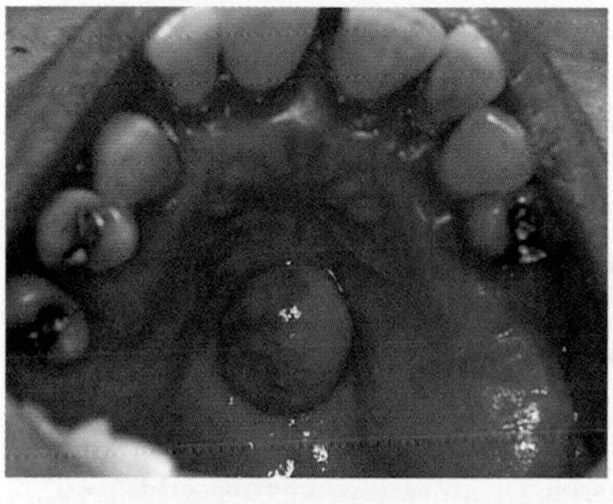

Figure 13-52 Fibroma. *Courtesy of Dr. Joseph Konzelman, School of Dentistry, Medical College of Georgia.*

Inspection of the Throat

P 1. Ask the patient to tilt his or her head back and to open the mouth widely. The patient can either stick out the tongue or leave it resting on the floor of the mouth.
2. Use your right hand to place the tongue blade on the middle third of the tongue.
3. With your left hand, shine a light at the back of the patient's throat.
4. Ask the patient to say "ah."
5. Observe the position, size, colour, and general appearance of the tonsils and uvula.
6. Touch the posterior third of the tongue with the tongue blade.
7. Note movement of the palate and the presence of the gag reflex.
8. Assess the colour of the oropharynx. Note any swelling, exudate, or lesions.

N **When the patient says "ah," the soft palate and the uvula should rise symmetrically (CN IX and X). The uvula is midline. The throat is normally pink and vascular and without swelling, exudate, or lesions. Normal tonsillar size is evaluated as 1+ to 2+. (See Figure 13-53 for grading scale.) This indicates that both tonsils are behind the pillars. The patient's gag reflex should be present but is congenitally absent in some patients (CN IX and X).**

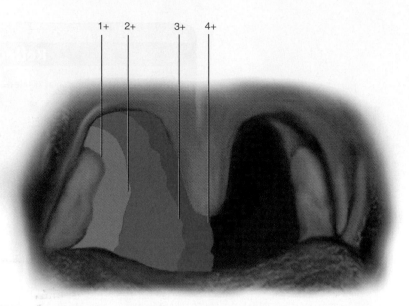

Figure 13-53 Grading of Tonsils: 1+ tonsils are visible, 2+ tonsils are between the pillars and uvula, 3+ tonsils are touching uvula, 4+ one or both tonsils extend to the midline of the oropharynx.

Nursing Tip

Eliciting the Gag Reflex

Before eliciting the gag reflex, be sure to warn the patient about what to expect during your assessment. It may not be necessary to elicit the gag reflex if the palate and uvula rise symmetrically with phonation.

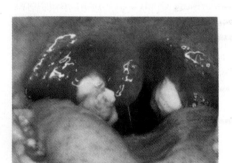

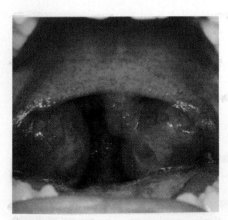

Figure 13-54 Streptococcal Pharyngitis.

Figure 13-55 Left tonsil is 4+ and right tonsil is 3+.

A The posterior pharynx is red with white patches. The tonsils are large and red with white patches, and the uvula is red and swollen.

P Viral pharyngitis and tonsillitis are common illnesses with these findings.

A Tonsils, pillars, and uvula are very red and swollen, with patches of white or yellow exudate on the tonsils (Figure 13-54). The posterior pharynx is bright red. The patient reports soreness of the throat with swallowing.

P These findings are typical of streptococcal pharyngitis and tonsillitis and are usually associated with significant lymphadenopathy. However, diagnosis requires throat culture or rapid strep test.

A There is a greyish membrane covering the tonsils, uvula, and soft palate.

P These findings are typical of diphtheria, acute tonsillitis, or infectious mononucleosis.

A The patient speaks with a hoarse voice and the oropharynx is red.

P Causes of hoarseness are varied and may include overuse of the voice, inflammation due to viral or bacterial infection, lesions of the larynx, foreign bodies, pressure on the larynx from masses, or an enlarged thyroid gland.

A The patient has difficulty opening the mouth and is noted to have unilateral tonsillar swelling. Unusual phonation is also observed.

P These findings are associated with peritonsillar abscess, which is most commonly seen in older children and young adults with a history of frequent tonsillitis.

A Chronic 3+ or 4+ tonsils (Figure 13-55) are abnormal.

P Large tonsils frequently lead to loud snoring and obstructive sleep apnea.

| **E** Examination | **N** Normal Findings | **A** Abnormal Findings | **P** Pathophysiology |

GERONTOLOGICAL VARIATIONS

Hearing loss, **presbycusis,** is a common problem among elderly individuals. Conductive hearing loss occurs in the outer or middle ear and usually makes things sound softer. However, the more common age-related hearing loss is sensorineural, which involves the inner ear. Otoscopic assessment may reveal more pronounced landmarks if atrophic or sclerotic changes have occurred. It is estimated that up to 60% of seniors over the age of 65 have hearing loss requiring assistive devices to help them maintain communication and improve their quality of life. Seniors with undiagnosed hearing loss are in greater danger of becoming isolated, less active and risk depression and personal safety.[15]

Taste may not diminish with age but may become less reliable. As one ages, the ability to taste sweetness remains, and the ability to taste bitterness declines. Sense of smell also diminishes slightly with age.

Common alterations in the mouths of elderly individuals are precancerous and cancerous lesions, untreated caries, periodontal disease, tooth loss resulting from oral disease, oral alterations related to systemic disease, side effects from medications, and orofacial pain. The increased incidence of chronic systemic disease, depression, and physical limitations in elderly individuals contribute to development of these problems.

A loss of teeth may affect closure of the mouth. The amount of saliva is reduced, and the mucosa is shinier, thinner, and less vascular. Gums are likely to be paler, and the teeth appear larger as the gums recede with the resorption of supporting bone.

Changes in a person's ability to hear, taste, or swallow often prevent him or her from participating in day-to-day social occasions due to embarrassment over these declining functions. For example, eating in a restaurant or with a group of other people may be difficult for a person with dysphagia who requires special food preparation and extended time for eating.

Life 360°

Diminished Sense of Taste

If a patient is experiencing some loss of taste, you can suggest adding seasonings to the diet, such as garlic, pepper, and curry. Heavy use of salt should be avoided. You can also suggest preparing aromatic foods that first stimulate the olfactory sense to enhance appetite.

CASE STUDY

The Patient with Otitis Externa

Jacques is a 15-year-old high school student, competitive swimmer who is complaining of pain in his Ⓡ ear.

HEALTH HISTORY

PATIENT PROFILE	15 yo male, looks tired
CHIEF COMPLAINT	"My Ⓡ ear has been painful for 3 days."
HISTORY OF ISSUE/CONCERN	Pt was in his usual state of good hl until 3 days ago when he developed gradual onset of Ⓡ otalgia. Has been swimming 3–4 daily × 5 d as he prepares for competition. States pain is worse when lying on his Ⓡ side. He has tried to clean the ear out c̄ a cotton swab but that has made the pain worse. Denies fever, chills, sweats, itching, hearing loss, other respiratory symptoms, bleeding, or other drainage from the ear. Has taken acetaminophen with relief, but isn't sure how much he has taken.

continues

PAST HEALTH HISTORY

Medical History	No major illnesses
Surgical History	Nil
Medications	Takes occasional acetaminophen for H/A or backaches
Communicable Diseases	No childhood illnesses other than mild URI
Allergies	NKA
Injuries and Accidents	Nondisplaced Ⓛ wrist fx at age 10 casted × 4 wks s̄ sequelae
Special Needs	Denies
Blood Transfusions	Denies
Childhood Illnesses	Varicella age 2 s̄ sequelae
Immunizations	UTD; has had hepatitis B series

FAMILY HEALTH HISTORY

LEGEND

- ⬤ Living female
- ◼ Living male
- ⊗ Deceased female
- ⊠ Deceased male
- ╱ Points to patient

dz = Disease
CAD = Coronary artery disease
HOH = Hard of hearing
HTN = Hypertension
NIDDM = Non-insulin dependent diabetes mellitus (Type II)

39 — 66
Depression "Heart
Suicide trouble"

44 — 85
Farming HOH
accident Parkinson's dz

45 — 42
CAD HTN
NIDDM

15 17
Myopia

Denies family hx of otosclerosis.

SOCIAL HISTORY

Alcohol Use	Denies
Drug Use	Denies
Tobacco Use	Denies
Domestic and Intimate Partner Violence	Denies
Sexual Practice	Not sexually active & never has been
Travel History	Travel to US & across Canada for swim competitions

Work Environment	Attends high school in urban area; part-time work doing chores at home & for neighbours
Home Environment	Lives c̄ parents & 1 brother in single-family home
Hobbies and Leisure Activities	Swims 2–3 hours daily (more with competitions); visits c̄ friends in their homes
Stress and Coping	Trying to meet school demands; thrives on the stress of competition
Education	Grade 11—doing well in school
Economic Status	No worries; parents have saved for university.
Religion/Spirituality	"I don't go to church—I was christened Catholic but I don't know if I will stay with it."
Ethnicity	"I'm French Canadian."
Roles and Relationships	Very close to family members; has several close friends from school & his neighbourhood
Characteristic Patterns of Daily Living	Wakes at 06:00, eats breakfast; goes to pool for 2-hour practice; school all day until 15:30; swims another 1–2 hours before going home; eats supper, does homework, may watch TV; bed by 22:30
HEALTH MAINTENANCE ACTIVITIES	
Sleep	7–8 hrs on school nights; 9–10 hrs on weekends
Diet	"I eat very healthy to stay in shape;" regular snacks to provide energy for swimming
Exercise	See above re swimming
Stress Management	Talking to mom, swimming, friends
Use of Safety Devices	Uses seat belts regularly; only swims in known pools/lakes
Health Check-ups	At 12 yrs of age
PHYSICAL ASSESSMENT	
Ears	

Auditory Screening	Voice whisper test—intact
	Tuning fork tests
	    Weber—midline s̄ lateralization
	    Rinne—air conduction > bone conduction (AC > BC) & = bilaterally

External Ear	Pain elicited by movement of Ⓡ tragus; Ⓡ EAC c̄ erythema & moderate edema; some debris is noted in canal, Ⓛ EAC clear s inflammation; small amount light brown cerumen present. No mastoid tenderness on Ⓡ or Ⓛ sides
Otoscopic Assessment	Both TMs are shiny grey & mobile c̄ visible light reflexes; s̄ bulging or perforation

continues

Nose	
External Inspection	Midline s̄ swelling, bleeding, lesions, or masses
Patency	Nares patent
Internal Inspection	Mucosa pink & moist s̄ swelling or purulent discharge; septum pink s̄ lesions or perforation
Sinuses	
Inspection	No swelling of frontal or maxillary sinuses
Palpation and Percussion	Nontender
Mouth and Throat	
Mouth	
Breath	No odour
Lips	Pink & moist s̄ lesions
Tongue	Midline, pink, well papillated & s̄ fasciculations, lesions, swelling, or bleeding
Buccal Mucosa	Pink, moist s̄ lesions
Gums	Pink & moist s̄ swelling or bleeding
Teeth	32 present in good repair & in good alignment
Palate	Intact, rises c̄ phonation
Throat	Pink & moist c̄ 1+ tonsils & no exudates; uvula midline; gag reflex ⊕

◄NURSING CHECKLIST►

Ears, Nose, Mouth, and Throat Assessment

Ears
- Auditory screening
  - Voice-whisper test
  - Tuning fork tests
    Weber test
    Rinne test
- External ear
  - Inspection
  - Palpation
- Otoscopic Assessment

Nose
- External inspection
- Patency
- Internal inspection

Sinuses
- Inspection
- Palpation and percussion

Mouth and Throat
- Mouth
  - Breath
  - Lips
    Inspection
    Palpation
  - Tongue
  - Buccal mucosa
  - Gums
  - Teeth
  - Palate
- Throat

Advanced Technique
- Transillumination of the sinuses

REVIEW QUESTIONS

1. Which of the following describes a typical exam finding of AOM?
   a. Landmarks are retracted with prominent malleus
   b. Movement of the tragus is painful
   c. TM is diffuse red in colour with dilated peripheral vessels
   d. Bubbles and a fluid line are noted
   The correct answer is (c).

2. A common finding when assessing the ears of elderly individuals is:
   a. Costochondritis
   b. Presbycusis
   c. Coryza
   d. Coloboma
   The correct answer is (b).

3. Risk factors for oral cancer are:
   a. Female gender, excessive alcohol use
   b. Male gender, tobacco use
   c. Male gender, age <50 years
   d. Male gender, nonsmoker
   The correct answer is (b).

4. Vincent's stomatitis or trench mouth is best described as:
   a. A greyish membrane that extends over an inflamed and ulcerated area of the gingival mucosa
   b. The gums are retracted from the teeth, thereby exposing the roots of the teeth
   c. A pale, nontender, immobile tumour seen on the gum
   d. Gingival borders are red and signs of infection are found in the pockets between receding gums and teeth
   The correct answer is (a).

5. The most frequent site of bleeding from the nose is:
   a. Dorsum nasi
   b. Inferior turbinate
   c. Kiesselbach's plexus
   d. Middle concha
   The correct answer is (c).

6. After examining the tonsils of a 10-year-old child, you record your findings as "tonsils are 3+," which means that:
   a. Tonsils are touching the uvula
   b. Tonsils extend to the midline of the oropharynx
   c. Tonsils are visible
   d. Tonsils are between the pillars and the uvula
   The correct answer is (a).

7. During examination of your patient's nares, you note smooth round masses protruding from the middle meatus of both nostrils. This finding is commonly associated with:
   a. Acute sinusitis
   b. Nasal inhalation of cocaine
   c. Nasal polyps
   d. Traumatic perforation
   The correct answer is (c).

8. Which structure can be found in the buccal mucosa just opposite the upper second molars?
   a. Sulcus terminalis
   b. Linear raphae
   c. Wharton's ducts
   d. Stensen's ducts
   The correct answer is (d).

9. Which statement describes a normal Weber test?
   a. The sound lateralizes to the affected ear.
   b. The sound lateralizes to the unaffected ear.
   c. When a tuning fork is placed in the middle of the forehead, the sound is heard equally in both ears.
   d. AC > BC
   The correct answer is (c).

10. As you prepare to examine a young adult's TM using an otoscope, you straighten the ear canal by pulling the ear:
    a. Down and back
    b. Down and forward
    c. Up and back
    d. Up and forward
    The correct answer is (c).

Visit the Estes online companion resource at www.healthassessment.nelson.com for additional content and study aids.

REFERENCES

[1]O'Donoghue, G. M., Narula, A. A., & Bates, G. J. (2000). *Clinical ENT: An illustrated textbook.* San Diego, CA: Singular.

[2]Springhouse (2007). *The professional guide to signs and symptoms* (5th ed). Philadelphia: Lippincott Williams & Wilkins.

[3]Glasziou, P. P., Del Mar, C. B., Sanders, S. L., & Hayem, M. (2004). Antibiotics for acute otitis media in children. *The Cochrane Database of Systematic Reviews*, Issue 1. Art. No.: CD000219.

[4]Flynn, C. A., Griffin, G. H., & Schultz, J. K. (2004). Decongestants and antihistamines for acute otitis media in children. *The Cochrane Database of Systematic Reviews*, Issue 3. Art. No.: CD001727.

[5]Foxlee, R., Johansson, A., Wejfalk, J., Ullrich, K., Dawkins, J., Dooley, L., & Del Mar, C. (2006). Topical analgesia for acute otitis media. (Protocol) *The Cochrane Database of Systematic Reviews*, Issue 1. Art. No.: CD005657.

[6]Kay, E., Ng, K., Salmon, A., & Del Mar, C. (2005). Influenza vaccine for preventing acute otitis media in infants and children. (Protocol) *The Cochrane Database of Systematic Reviews*, Issue 3. Art. No.: CD005438.

[7]Macfadyen, C. A., Acuin, J. M., & Gamble, C. (2006). Systemic antibiotics versus topical treatments for chronically discharging ears with underlying eardrum perforations. *The Cochrane Database of Systematic Reviews*, Issue 1. Art. No.: CD005608.

[8]Health Canada. (2005). *Hearing loss and leisure noise*. Retrieved October 17, 2006, from *http://www.hc-sc.gc.ca/iyh-vsv/environ/leisure-loisirs_e.html*

[9]Springhouse, *The professional guide to signs and symptoms*.

[10]Burton, M. J., & Doree, C. J. (2004). Interventions for recurrent idiopathic epistaxis (nosebleeds) in children. *The Cochrane Database of Systematic Reviews*, Issue 1. Art. No.: CD004461.

[11]Health Canada. (2000). Clinical practice guidelines for nurses in primary care: Ears, nose, and throat (ENT). Retrieved October 15, 2006, from http://www.hc-sc.gc.ca/fnih-spni/pubs/nursing-infirm/2000_clin-guide/chap_02a_e.html#2-5

[12]Canadian Cancer Society/National Cancer Institute of Canada. (2005). *Canadian Cancer Statistics 2005*. Toronto, Canada.

[13]Canadian Cancer Society: *Oral cancer*. Retrieved October 17, 2006, from http://www.cancer.ca/ccs/internet/standard/0,3182,3543_10175_272695_langId-en,00.html

[14] Kujan, O., Glenny, A. M., Duxbury, A. J., Thakker, N., & Sloan, P. (2003). Screening programmes for the early detection and prevention of oral cancer. *The Cochrane Database of Systematic Reviews*, Issue 4. Art. No.: CD004150.

[15]Springhouse, *The professional guide to signs and symptoms*.

BIBLIOGRAPHY

Davies, A., & Finlay, I. (Eds.). (2005). *Oral care in advanced disease*. Oxford, NY: Oxford University Press.

Goodheart, H. (2002). Disorders of the mouth, lips, and tongue, part 4: Intraoral lesions. *Women's Health in Primary Care, 6*(2), 58–62.

Sataloff, R.T. & Sataloff, J. (2005). *Hearing loss*. New York: Taylor & Francis.

WEB RESOURCES

Canadian Association of the Deaf
http://www.cad.ca/

Canadian Cultural Society of the Deaf
http://www.ccsdeaf.com/

Canadian Dental Association
http://www.cda-adc.ca/

The Hearing Foundation of Canada
http://www.hearingfoundation.ca/

CHAPTER 14

Breasts and Regional Nodes

COMPETENCIES

1. Describe the anatomy and physiology of the breasts and regional lymphatics, including age-related variations.

2. Demonstrate assessment techniques for the evaluation of the breasts and regional lymphatics.

3. Distinguish common variations and abnormal changes of the breasts.

4. Discuss methods of teaching breast self-examination to patients.

5. Identify risk factors for breast cancer.

*T*he breasts hold significant symbolism in our society. In women, they are an external symbol of sexuality, femininity, and nurturance. In men, they symbolize strength, fitness, and masculinity. Breast cancer is the most common cancer among Canadian women, and its devastating effects have come to the forefront of public attention in recent years. Although incidence rates have increased significantly over the past 50 years, survival rates remain constant despite increased research dollars and public attention.

This chapter focuses primarily on the female breast because its structure is more complicated than the male gland and because of the higher incidence of breast disease in women.

ANATOMY AND PHYSIOLOGY

The breasts and regional nodes are discussed, as is the development of the breasts during adolescence.

Breasts

The female **breasts** are a pair of mammary glands located on the anterior chest wall, extending vertically from the second to the sixth rib and laterally from the sternal border to the axilla. Anatomically, the breast can be divided into four quadrants: the upper inner quadrant, the lower inner quadrant, the upper outer quadrant, and the lower outer quadrant (Figure 14-1). The upper outer quadrant, which extends into the axilla, is known as the **tail of Spence.** The breasts are supported by a bed of muscles: the pectoralis major and minor, latissimus dorsi, serratus anterior, rectus abdominus, and external oblique muscles, which extend vertically from the deep fascia (Figure 14-2). **Cooper's ligaments** extend vertically from the deep fascia through the breast to the inner layer of the skin, providing support for the breast tissue (Figure 14-3).

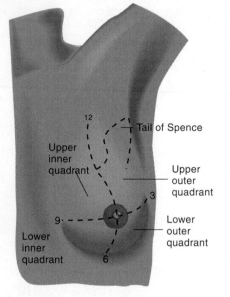

Figure 14-1 Quadrants of the Left Breast.

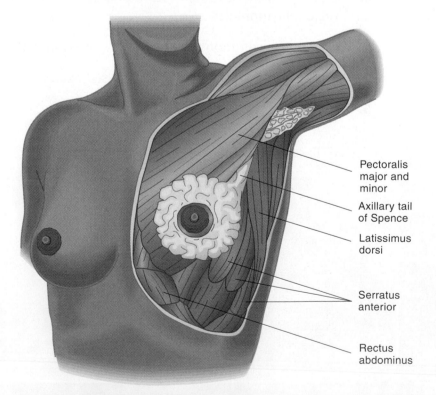

Figure 14-2 Muscles Supporting the Breast.

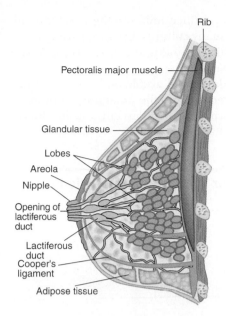

Figure 14-3 Cross Section of the Left Breast.

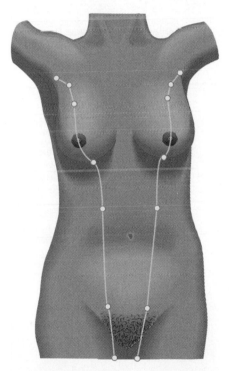

A. These bands develop in utero and later atrophy

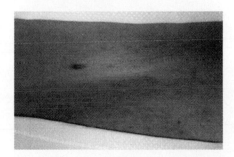

B. Supernumerary Nipple

Figure 14-4 Ectodermal Galactic Bands.

In the centre of each breast is the **nipple,** a round, hairless, pigmented protrusion of erectile tissue approximately 0.5 to 1.5 cm in diameter. The nipple becomes more erect during sexual excitement, pregnancy, lactation, cold temperatures, and certain phases of the menstrual cycle. The 12 to 20 minute openings on the surface of the nipple consist of **lactiferous ducts** through which milk and colostrum are excreted.

The **milk line,** or **ectodermal galactic band** (Figure 14-4A), develops from the axilla to the groin during the fifth week of fetal development. Most of the band atrophies except in the thoracic area, where it forms a mammary ridge. Incomplete atrophy of the galactic band results in the development of extra nipples or breast tissue known as **supernumerary nipples** (Figure 14-4B), which develop along the milk lines and are a normal variant in a small percentage of adult women.

Surrounding the nipple is the **areola,** a pigmented area approximately 2.5 to 10 cm in diameter, with hair follicles punctuating the border. The size and pigmentation of the areola vary from woman to woman. Several sebaceous glands (**Montgomery's tubercles**) that are present on the surface of the areola lubricate the nipple, helping to keep it supple during lactation.

The breast is composed of glandular, connective (Cooper's ligaments), and adipose tissue. Glandular tissue is arranged radially in the form of 12 to 20 **lobes,** a disbursement similar to a bicycle wheel—each lobe represents a spoke of the wheel and extends from a central point (the nipple) to the outermost border (Figure 14-5). Each lobe is composed of 20 to 40 **lobules** that contain milk-producing glands called **alveoli** or **acini.** The lobules are arranged in grapelike bunches that cluster around several ducts to gradually form one main lactiferous (excretory) duct per lobe. Each lactiferous duct widens to form a sinus that acts as a reservoir for milk during lactation. The duct opens onto the surface of the nipple. The lobes are lodged in tissue composed of subcutaneous and **retromammary adipose tissue,** and it is this tissue that composes the bulk of the breast.

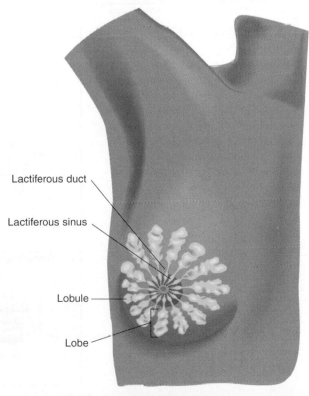

Figure 14-5 Glandular Tissue of the Right Breast.

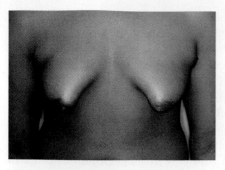

Figure 14-6 Gynecomastia. *Courtesy of Steven M. Lynch, M.D.*

The function of the female breast is to produce milk for the nourishment and protection of neonates and infants. In many cultures, breasts provide pleasure during sexual foreplay and breastfeeding, in addition to providing some protection to the anterior thoracic chest wall.

The male breast is composed of a well-developed areola and a small nipple that has immature tissue underneath. **Gynecomastia,** the enlargement of male breast tissue (Figure 14-6), may occur normally in adolescent and in elderly males. The condition is normally unilateral and temporary.

TABLE 14-1 **Sexual Maturity Rating for Female Breast Development**

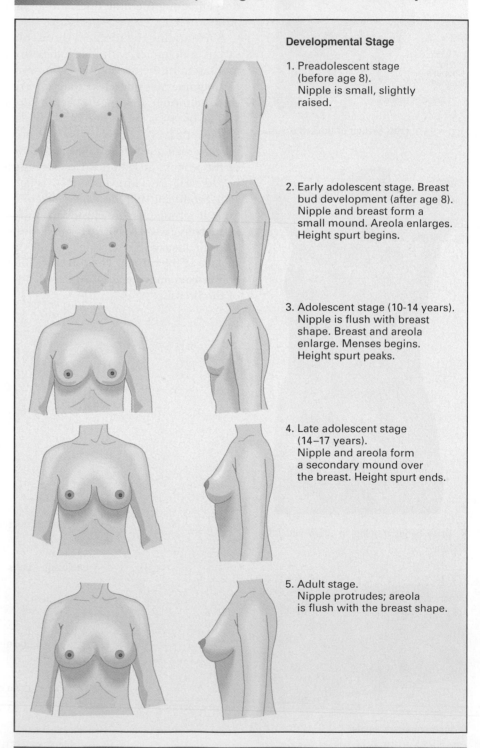

Developmental Stage

1. Preadolescent stage (before age 8). Nipple is small, slightly raised.

2. Early adolescent stage. Breast bud development (after age 8). Nipple and breast form a small mound. Areola enlarges. Height spurt begins.

3. Adolescent stage (10-14 years). Nipple is flush with breast shape. Breast and areola enlarge. Menses begins. Height spurt peaks.

4. Late adolescent stage (14–17 years). Nipple and areola form a secondary mound over the breast. Height spurt ends.

5. Adult stage. Nipple protrudes; areola is flush with the breast shape.

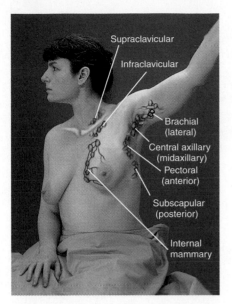

Figure 14-7 Regional Lymphatics and Drainage Patterns of the Left Breast.

Regional Nodes

The **lymphatic drainage** (the yellow alkaline drainage composed primarily of lymphocytes) of the breast is via a complex network of lymph vessels and nodes (Figure 14-7). It is estimated that a majority of the lymph from the breast flows to the axillary nodes. The **axillary nodes** are composed of four groups: central axillary nodes (midaxillary), pectoral nodes (anterior), subscapular nodes (posterior), and brachial nodes (lateral). The central axillary nodes receive lymph from the three other nodal groups. The lymph is then channelled from the central axillary nodes to the infraclavicular and supraclavicular nodes. The remainder of the lymph flows into the internal mammary chain or directly to the infraclavicular chain via the Rotter's nodes, deep into the chest or abdominal cavity, or to the other breast.

Because of their superficial location, axillary nodes can be easily palpated. The internal mammary nodes, however, are very deep in the chest wall and are inaccessible by palpation.

Breast Development

Female breast development usually begins at 8 to 10 years of age and is stimulated by estrogen release during puberty. Enhanced fat deposition increases the size of the breasts, while the ductal system, lobes, and lobules increase in number and in size. Asymmetry in breast development is not abnormal. Tanner's sexual maturity ratings describe the pattern of adolescent breast development (Table 14-1).

HEALTH HISTORY	
	The breasts and regional nodes health history provides insight into the link between a patient's life and lifestyle and breast information and pathology.
PATIENT PROFILE	*Diseases that are age-, gender-, and race-specific for the breasts and regional nodes are listed.*
Age	Early menarche increases the risk of breast cancer (puberty) Gynecomastia (adolescent and elderly males) Fibroadenoma (15–20) Benign breast disease (cystic hyperplasia) (30–55) Mastitis and plugged milk ducts (childbearing years) Increasing risk of breast cancer (first pregnancy after 30, or nulliparous) Paget's disease (postmenopausal) Incidence of breast cancer increases (50 or older) Breast cancer incidence rates increased only in those aged 50 and older from 1986 to 2006
Gender	
Female	An estimated 22,300 new cases of breast cancer were diagnosed in Canadian women during 2006[1] 99% of all breast disease is in women One in every nine women in Canada will develop breast cancer during her life time[2]
Male	In 2006 there were an estimated 160 new cases of male breast cancer[3] Gynecomastia (adolescent and elderly men)

continues

Ethnicity	Breast cancer survival is lower in Northern First Nations women[4] Breast cancer incidence is highest in North American and European women; relatively uncommon in Asian and Latin American women[5] An estimated 1 in 100 women of Ashkenazi Jewish origin are at greater risk of breast cancer due to a mutation of the *BRCA 1* gene
HEALTH ISSUE/CONCERN	*Common issues/concerns for the breasts and regional nodes are defined and information on the characteristics of each sign or symptom is provided.*
Breast Mass	Presence of a lump in the breast
Location	Anywhere in the breast or axilla; usually in the upper outer quadrant, unilateral or bilateral
Quality	Size, size in relationship to menstrual cycle, shape, consistency, mobility, delineation of borders
Quantity	Number of masses
Associated Manifestations	Tenderness, presence of dimpling, nipple retraction, nipple discharge, tender palpable lymph nodes
Aggravating Factors	Methylxanthines, recent injury to breast
Alleviating Factors	Aspiration, biopsy, surgery, radiation, chemotherapy
Timing	Incidence rises with age, in relation to menses and ovulation
Breast Tenderness	Sensation of discomfort in the breast
Location	Pinpoint, discrete, generalized, unilateral or bilateral
Quality	Sharp, dull, pulling
Associated Manifestations	Mass, dimpling, nipple retraction, breast swelling, premenstrual syndrome symptoms, induration, discharge, palpable nodes, fever, breastfeeding
Aggravating Factors	Recent injury to breast, palpation, vigorous exercise, oral contraceptives, chlorpromazine, or alpha-methyldopa
Alleviating Factors	Warm compresses, analgesics, massage, support bras, aspiration, biopsy, surgery, breastfeeding, cessation of aggravating medications
Timing	In relation to menses or ovulation, pregnancy, lactation, activity
Breast Discharge	Abnormal substance expressed from the breast
Location	From the nipple or sebaceous gland, unilateral or bilateral
Quality	Colour, odour, consistency
Associated Manifestations	Redness, swelling, induration, mass, dimpling, nipple retraction, breast swelling, palpable nodes, lactation, headaches, history of pituitary disorders, fever
Aggravating Factors	Trauma to breast, breastfeeding, pituitary tumour, hyperthyroidism, chlorpromazine, alpha-methyldopa, digitalis, diuretics, oral contraceptives, papillomas, carcinomas of the ducts
Alleviating Factors	Breastfeeding, biopsy, surgery, cessation of medications

Timing	In relation to pregnancy, menses, lactation, ovulation
PAST HEALTH HISTORY	*The various components of the past health history are linked to breasts and regional nodes pathology and related information.*
Medical History	
Breast Specific	Benign breast disease, cysts, fibroadenomas, intraductal papillomas, mammary duct ectasia, mastitis, areas of greater density, breast cancer, masses, breast abscess, Paget's disease
Nonbreast Specific	Thyroid disorders, pituitary tumour, chest radiation, cancer of ovary or endometrium, obesity
Surgical History	Breast biopsy, lumpectomy, quadrantectomy, partial mastectomy, radical mastectomy, breast reduction or augmentation
Medications	Oral contraceptives, chlorpromazine, alpha-methyldopa, diuretics, digitalis, steroids, and tricyclics may precipitate nipple discharge; use of hormone replacement therapy has been linked with increased incidences of breast cancer
Allergies	Localized rashes of breast, contact dermatitis
Injuries and Accidents	May cause hematoma or edema; lumps may result from previous trauma to soft tissue
Childhood Illnesses	Varicella scarring of cutaneous tissue
FAMILY HEALTH HISTORY	*Breasts and regional nodes diseases that are familial are listed.*
	8% to 20% of breast cancers are thought to have a familial link via a primary relative, for example, mother, sister, grandmother. The link is stronger if the family history includes bilateral breast cancer. *BRCA 1* or *BRCA 2* gene mutation (*BRCA 1* and *2* are defective genes associated with the development of familial breast cancer)
	Benign breast disease
SOCIAL HISTORY	*The components of the social history are linked to breasts and regional nodes factors and pathology.*
Alcohol Use	Loose association between alcohol intake of more than three glasses per day and increased incidence of breast cancer
Tobacco Use	No association between smoking and breast cancer
Work Environment	Radiation exposure
Home Environment	Increased incidence of breast cancer noted in urban dwellers
Economic Status	Increased incidence of breast cancer in women of upper socioeconomic status
HEALTH MAINTENANCE ACTIVITIES	*This information provides a bridge between the health maintenance activities and breasts and regional nodes function.*
Diet	No longer a correlation between high-fat diet and incidence of breast cancer; increased incidence of benign breast disease with caffeine use
Exercise	Strong correlation between obesity and incidence of breast cancer

continues

Use of Safety Devices	Use of restraining devices in motor vehicles prevents chest trauma
Health Check-ups	*Screening clinical examination and mammography* every 1–2 years for women aged 50–69 years[6]
	Current evidence does not support the recommendation that screening mammography be included in or excluded from the periodic health examination of women aged 40–49 at average risk of breast cancer[7]
	Breast self-examination
	The Canadian Task Force on Preventive Health Care Guidelines recommends against the teaching of breast self-examination (BSE) as part of the periodic health examination, however, many women will ask to be taught BSE[8, 9] (See Nursing Tip: The Debate about BSE)
	Many breast tumours are discovered by women themselves, and though the evidence does not support routinely teaching BSE, women should be instructed to promptly report any breast changes or concerns[10]

Nursing Tip

The Debate about BSE

Many Canadian women likely feel confused as to whether or not they should perform BSE. For years women have been taught this technique and many public health awareness campaigns have encouraged women to do so. It is only recently, after years of research on this practice, that there is sufficient evidence to draw conclusions about the effectiveness of BSE in influencing the morbidity and mortality rates of breast cancer. Although the Canadian Task Force on Preventive Health Care Guidelines discourages the teaching of BSE, the Canadian Cancer Society continues to recommend it.

Drawbacks to BSE:[11]

- Increased number of unnecessary biopsies and inherent risks (scarring, breast deformity, anxiety).
- Relatively low sensitivity of BSE in detecting lesions (no difference in breast cancer mortality, or stage at diagnosis, between women taught BSE and control subjects).
- It is costly to teach BSE, which could potentially divert from resources for other preventive strategies.
- Screening women 50–69 with BSE is not effective in reducing breast cancer mortality if they do not receive mammography or routine clinical breast examinations.

Benefits of BSE:

- Familiarity with one's breast tissue and usual changes.
- If current methods of detecting breast cancer are flawed (mammograms fail to detect 10–15% of tumours and also expose women to ionizing radiation) and there is no evidence-based alternative on the horizon, the lifesaving potential of BSE may be less important than its ability to give women some control on deciding what is best for their health and well-being.[12]
- BSE may help detect changes in breast tissue that are of importance, particularly in women who do not access clinical breast examination and screening mammography resources.
- Many women might willingly undergo investigation to reassure themselves that they do not have breast cancer.[13]
- Women may feel that their BSE is more thorough than the clinical examination they receive by health care professionals who are rushed or who have not learned proper clinical breast examination.

Nursing Tip

Hope for Women—Preventing Breast Cancer

A five-year prospective clinical trial research study, ExCel, is testing whether the drug exemestane (Aromasin™) can help prevent breast cancer in women who are at increased risk for the disease. This study (Canada, United States, Spain) commenced in 2005 and is coordinated by the National Cancer Institute of Canada Clinical Trials Group (NCIC CTG). Exemestane is an aromatase inhibitor that suppress estrogen production, a key component in the development of some types of breast cancer. Information on this study is found at http://www.excelstudy.com/

Nursing Tip

Male Breast Cancer[14]

- About one man gets breast cancer for every 100–150 women.
- Compared to female breast cancer, male breast cancers are more often diagnosed at higher stages of disease (metastatic) due to men ignoring lumps in their breast tissue; there is a higher percentage of men than women who are estrogen receptor positive.

EQUIPMENT

- Towel
- Drape
- Centimetre ruler
- Teaching aid for BSE

◀NURSING CHECKLIST▶

General Approach to Clinical Breast Examination

Prior to the assessment:

1. When possible, instruct the patient to neither use creams, lotions, or powders, nor shave her underarms 24 to 48 hours before the scheduled examination. These products may mask or alter the nature of the surface integument of the breasts, and shaving the underarms may cause folliculitis, which may result in pain upon palpation.
2. Encourage the patient to express any anxieties and concerns about the physical examination. Acknowledge anxieties and validate concerns. Many women avoid having their breasts assessed because they fear abnormal findings.
3. Inform the patient that the examination should not be painful but may be uncomfortable at times. This is especially true if the patient is currently experiencing menses, ovulation, or pregnancy.
4. Adopt a nonjudgmental and supportive attitude and remain sensitive to the patient's views of having her breasts touched by another person.
5. Be aware of the impact of the patient's culture on the breast examination. Women of certain cultures may not accept a male performing this assessment; even within the dominant Canadian culture, some women may feel uncomfortable with the clinical breast examination because of beliefs about the potential sexual nature of the procedure.
6. Instruct the patient to remove any jewelry that might interfere with the assessment.
7. Ensure that the room is warm enough to prevent chilling, and provide additional draping material as necessary.

continues

8. Warm your hands with warm water or by rubbing them together prior to the assessment.

9. Ensure that privacy is maintained during the examination by providing screens, closing doors, and posting a door sign stating that an examination is in progress.

During the assessment:

1. Inform the patient of what you are going to do before you do it.

2. Use this time to educate the patient about her body.

3. Offer the patient the opportunity to ask questions about her body and sexuality.

4. Keep body areas not being assessed appropriately draped.

5. Always compare right and left breasts.

6. Wear gloves if the patient has any discharge from the breast.

After the assessment:

1. Assess whether the patient needs assistance in dressing.

2. After the patient is dressed, discuss the experience with her, invite questions and comments, listen carefully, and provide her with information regarding the examination.

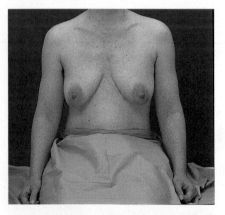

Figure 14-8 Position of Patient for Breast Inspection: Arms at Side.

ASSESSMENT OF THE FEMALE BREASTS AND REGIONAL NODES

Physical assessment produces feelings of fear, anxiety, embarrassment, and loss of control in many women. These feelings may be reduced by the sensitivity of the nurse before, during, and after assessment of the breasts. Assessment of the female breasts and regional nodes includes inspection and palpation.

Inspection of the Breasts

E 1. Position the patient uncovered to the waist, seated at the edge of the examination table, and facing you.

2. Instruct the patient to let her arms relax by her sides (Figure 14-8).

3. Inspect the breasts, axillae, areolar areas, and nipples for colour, vascularity, thickening, edema, size, symmetry, contour, lesions or masses, and exudates.

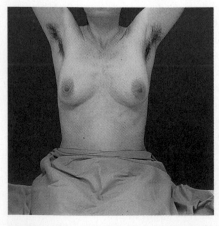

Figure 14-9 Position of Patient for Breast Inspection: Arms Overhead.

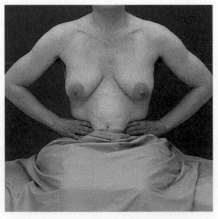

Figure 14-10 Position of Patient for Breast Inspection: Hands Pressed against Hips.

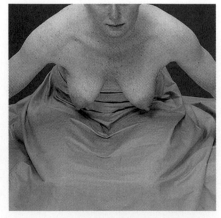

Figure 14-11 Position of Patient for Breast Inspection: Leaning Forward.

| E | **Examination** | N | **Normal Findings** | A | **Abnormal Findings** | P | **Pathophysiology** |

Figure 14-12 Striae Secondary to Inflammatory Breast Cancer. Also note peau d'orange. *Courtesy of Dr. S. Eva Singletary, University of Texas, M.D. Anderson Cancer Center.*

4. Repeat the above inspection sequence with the patient's arms raised over her head (Figure 14-9). This will accentuate any retraction (tissue drawn back) if present.
5. Repeat inspection sequence with patient pressing hands into hips, which will contract the pectoral muscles (Figure 14-10). Once again, if retraction is present, it will be more pronounced with this maneuver.
6. Have the patient lean forward to allow the breasts to hang freely away from the chest wall (Figure 14-11), and repeat the inspection sequence. Provide support to the patient as necessary.

Colour

E   Inspect the breasts, areolar areas, nipples, and axillae for coloration.
N   **The breasts and axillae are flesh-coloured and the areolar areas and nipples are darker in pigmentation. This pigmentation is normally enhanced during pregnancy. Moles and nevi are normal variants, and terminal hair may be present on the areolar areas.**
A   Reddened areas of the breasts, nipples, or axillae need further assessment.
P   Redness may be an indication of inflammation, an infection such as mastitis, or inflammatory carcinoma.
A   Striae (Figure 14-12) are streaks over the breasts or axillae and are abnormal. In light-skinned individuals, new striae are red and become silver to white in coloration with age. In dark-skinned individuals, new striae are a ruddy, dark-brown colour, and older striae become lighter than the skin colour.
P   Striae are caused by rapid stretching of the skin, which damages the elastic fibres found in the dermis. Although normal in pregnancy, striae are often observed with obesity.

Vascularity

E   Observe the entire surface of each breast for superficial vascular patterns.
N   **Normal superficial vascular patterns are diffuse and symmetrical.**
A   Abnormal patterns of vascularity are focal or unilateral.
P   Focal or unilateral superficial vascular patterns (Figure 14-13) occur as the result of an increased blood supply and may indicate tumour formation, which requires increased vascularization and blood supply.

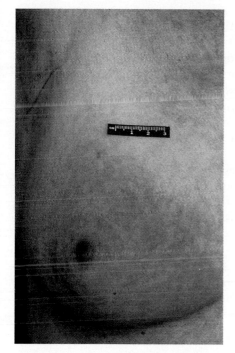

Figure 14-13 Erythema with Abnormal Vascular Pattern Secondary to Inflammatory Breast Cancer. *Courtesy of Dr. S. Eva Singletary, University of Texas, M.D. Anderson Cancer Center.*

Thickening or Edema

E   Observe the breasts, axillae, and nipples for thickening or edema.
N   **Normally, thickening or edema is not found in the breasts, axillae, or nipples.**
A   Thickening or edema of the breast tissue or nipple may present as enlarged skin pores that give the appearance of an orange rind (**peau d'orange**). It may be more prevalent in the dependent or inferior portions of the breast (Figure 14-14).
P   This peau d'orange appearance may be indicative of obstructed lymphatic drainage due to a tumour.

Size and Symmetry

E   Observe the breasts, axillae, areolar areas, and nipples for size and symmetry.
N   **It is not unusual for there to be some difference in the size of the breasts and areolar areas, with the breast on the side of the dominant arm being larger. Bilateral hypertrophy of the breasts may be normal for some patients (Figure 14-15). Nipple inversion, which is present from puberty, is a normal variant and is of no clinical consequence except for difficulty in breast-feeding. Nipples should point upward and laterally, or they may point outward and downward (Figure 14-16A). Supernumerary nipples are a variant of normal and have no pathological significance in either males or females.**

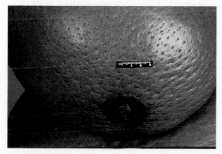

Figure 14-14 Peau d'orange. *Courtesy of Dr. S. Eva Singletary, University of Texas, M.D. Anderson Cancer Center.*

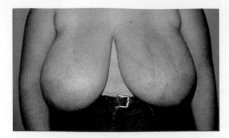

Figure 14-15 Massive Hypertrophy of Breasts. *Courtesy of Steven M. Lynch, M.D.*

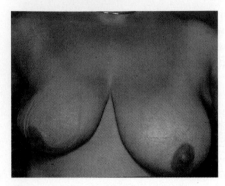

Figure 14-17 Asymmetry of Breasts Due to Cancer. *Courtesy of Dr. S. Eva Singletary, University of Texas, M.D. Anderson Cancer Center.*

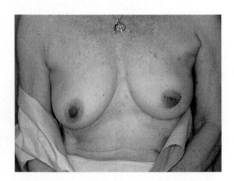

Figure 14-18 Nipple Retraction of Left Breast. *Courtesy of Steven M. Lynch, M.D.*

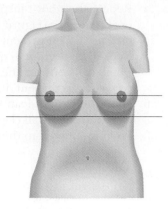
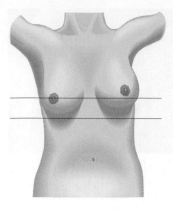

A. Symmetrical without Deviation   B. Asymmetrical with Deviation

Figure 14-16 Deviation of Nipples.

A Asymmetry in the directions in which the nipples are pointed is an abnormal finding (Figure 14-16B).

P Asymmetrical nipple direction is suggestive of an underlying invasive process that is contorting nipple tissue. Often the direction of nipple deviation is toward the underlying process.

A Significant differences in the size or symmetry of the breasts, axillae, areolar areas, or nipples are abnormal (Figure 14-17).

P Significant enlargement of one breast, axilla, or areola may be indicative of tumour formation.

A Recent inversion, flattening, or depression of a nipple is abnormal.

P A sudden onset of nipple inversion, flattening, or depression is indicative of nipple retraction, which is suggestive of an underlying cancer (Figure 14-18).

A Nipples that have been inverted since puberty and become broader or thicker are abnormal.

P Additional broadening or thickening of a previously inverted nipple may be indicative of tumour formation.

A Lack of breast tissue unilaterally is abnormal.

P Unilateral reduction of breast tissue or structures may result from trauma, mastectomy, or breast reduction.

Contour

E 1. Assess the breasts for contour.
2. Compare the breasts to each other.

N The breast is normally convex, without flattening, retractions, or dimpling.

A Dimpling, retractions, flattening (Figure 14-19), or other changes in breast contour are abnormal.

P Changes in contour are highly suggestive of cancer. The invasive process that causes the contour changes is the result of fibrotic shortening and disablement of the Cooper's ligament. Fat necrosis and mammary duct ectasia may also cause retraction, dimpling, and puckering.

Lesions or Masses

E Inspect the breasts, axillae, areolar areas, and nipples for lesions or masses.

N The breasts, axillae, areolar areas, and nipples are free of masses, tumours, and primary or secondary lesions.

A Breast masses, tumours, nodules, or cysts of any kind are abnormal.

| E | Examination | N | Normal Findings | A | Abnormal Findings | P | Pathophysiology |

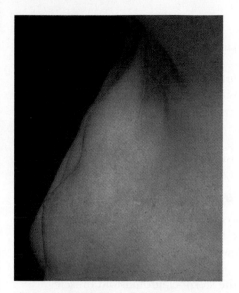

Figure 14-19 Dimpling of Left Breast Tissue. *Courtesy of Dr. S. Eva Singletary, University of Texas, M.D. Anderson Cancer Center.*

TABLE 14-2 Characteristics of Common Breast Masses

	Gross Cyst	Fibroadenoma	Carcinoma
Age	30–50; diminishes after menopause	puberty to menopause; peaks between ages 20–30	most common after 50 years
Shape	round	round, lobular, or ovoid	irregular, stellate, or crab-like
Consistency	soft to firm	usually firm	firm to hard
Discreteness	well defined	well defined	not clearly defined
Number	single or grouped	most often single	usually single
Mobility	mobile	very mobile	may be mobile or fixed to skin, underlying tissue, or chest wall
Tenderness	tender	nontender	usually nontender
Erythema	no erythema	no erythema	may be present
Retraction/ dimpling	not present	not present	often present

P See Table 14-2 for common pathologies of breast masses.

A A scaly, eczema-like erosion of the nipple, or persistent dermatitis of the areola and nipple, is abnormal.

P Persistent eczematous dermatitis of the areola and nipple region is suggestive of **Paget's disease,** a malignant neoplasm, which is usually unilateral in its involvement.

Discharge

E Observe for spontaneous discharge from the nipples or other areas of the breast.

N In the nonpregnant, nonlactating female, there should be no discharge. During pregnancy and up through the first week after birth, there may be a yellow discharge known as colostrum. During lactation, there is a white discharge of breast milk.

A The presence of a nipple discharge in the nonpregnant, nonlactating woman is abnormal.

P Nipple discharge may be caused by the use of medications such as tranquilizers and oral contraceptives, manual stimulation, pituitary tumour, or infection. It may also be indicative of malignant or benign breast disease.

Palpation

Palpation is performed in a sequential manner:

1. Supraclavicular and infraclavicular lymph node areas
2. Breasts, with the patient in sitting position
   a. Arms at side
   b. Arms raised over head
3. Axillary lymph node regions
4. Breasts, with the patient in supine position

Supraclavicular and Infraclavicular Lymph Nodes

E 1. Have patient seated and uncovered to the waist.
   2. Encourage the patient to relax the muscles of her head and neck because this pulls the clavicles down and allows a thorough exploration of the supraclavicular area.
   3. Flex the patient's head to relax the sternocleidomastoid muscle.
   4. Standing in front of the patient, in a bilateral and simultaneous motion, place your finger pads over the patient's clavicles, lateral to the tendinous portion of the sternocleidomastoid muscles.
   5. Using a rotary motion of the palmar surfaces of the fingers, probe deeply into the scalene triangles in order to palpate the supraclavicular lymph nodes (Figure 14-20).

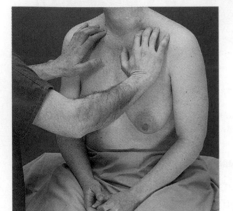

Figure 14-20 Palpation of Supraclavicular Nodes.

Nursing Tip

Ductal Lavage

Sometimes referred to by women as a "pap smear of the breast," this new procedure uses a microcatheter to lavage mammary ducts to obtain epithelial cells for cytological evaluation. The procedure takes approximately 30 minutes and can be performed in a clinic environment. The nipple is anesthetized and a small tube is inserted into the milk ducts on the nipple. The duct is rinsed and cells are sent for evaluation to see if they are atypical. The procedure is used in the United States for women who are assessed to be at high risk of breast cancer; the procedure is not commonly used in Canada.

Nursing Tip

The GAIL model, named after Dr. Mitchell H. Gail, consists of a set of calculations that evaluate the relative risk of breast cancer based on age at menarche, number of breast biopsies, age at first live birth, number of first-degree relatives with breast cancer, and a woman's age.

Nursing Alert

Examining Nipple Discharge

If a patient is found to have abnormal nipple discharge:

1. Don gloves before proceeding with the assessment.
2. Note the colour, odour, consistency, and amount of discharge, and whether the discharge is unilateral or bilateral, and spontaneous or provoked.
3. With a sterile, cotton-tipped swab, obtain a sample of the discharge so that a culture, sensitivity, and gram stain can be obtained.
4. Consider checking the sample for occult blood.
5. Follow your institution's guidelines for sample preparation.

| E | Examination | N | Normal Findings | A | Abnormal Findings | P | Pathophysiology |

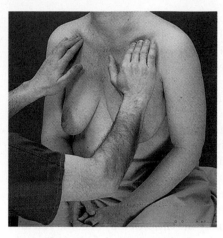

Figure 14-21 Palpation of Infraclavicular Nodes.

6. Palpate the infraclavicular nodes using the same rotary motion of the palmar surfaces of the fingers (Figure 14-21).

N Palpable lymph nodes less than 1 cm in diameter are usually considered normal and clinically insignificant provided that there are no additional enlarged lymph nodes found in other regions such as the axilla. Palpation should not elicit pain.

A Fixed, firm, immobile, irregular lymph nodes more than 1 cm in diameter are considered abnormal.

P These nodes are considered suspicious for metastasis from a variety of sources or primary lymphoma.

A Enlarged, painful, or tender nodes that are matted together are abnormal.

P Tender, enlarged nodes may indicate systemic infection or carcinoma.

Breasts: Patient in Sitting Position

E **1.** Place the patient in a sitting position with arms at her sides.
2. Stand to the patient's right side, facing the patient.
3. Using the palmar surfaces of the fingers of your dominant hand, begin the palpation at the outer quadrant of the patient's right breast.
4. Use the other hand to support the inferior aspect of the breast.

Nursing Alert

Risk factors for breast cancer in women

- One in 8.9 women develop breast cancer in her lifetime; 1 out of 27 is expected to die from it.
- Breast cancer is the leading cause of new cases of cancer in women and the second leading cause of death (following lung cancer).[15]

There is no single cause of breast cancer but some factors appear to increase the risk of developing it.[16, 17]

Factors which have been consistently found to increase risk

- Being overweight or obese (only after menopause), based on BMI
- Taking hormone replacement therapy (estrogen plus progestin for more than 5 years)
- Exposure of the breasts to high levels of ionization radiation (e.g., X-rays) or lower levels before age 2
- Having a first baby after age 30 or never having a baby
- Never breastfeeding
- Having a close relative(s) with breast cancer (especially in a mother, sister, or daughter diagnosed before menopause or if the *BRCA 1* or *BRCA 2* genes are present)
- Age (breast cancer can occur in women of any age but increases with age, especially after 50)
- Early menstruation (before the age of 12); late menopause (after age 55)
- Significant mammographic breast density (this indicates greater amount of glandular tissue)

Factors which have been *less* consistently found to increase breast cancer risk

- Drinking alcohol
- Being physically inactive
- Smoking tobacco
- Taking birth control pills appears to slightly increase a woman's risk of breast cancer, though the risk of ovarian cancer is decreased.

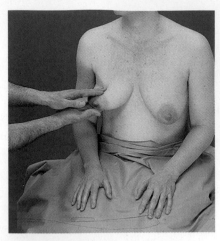

Figure 14-22 Bimanual Palpation of the Breasts while Patient Is Sitting.

5. In small-breasted patients, the dominant hand can palpate the tissue against the chest wall, but if the breasts are pendulous, use a bimanual technique of palpation (Figure 14-22).

6. Palpate in a downward fashion, sweeping from the outer quadrants to the sternal border of each breast.

7. Repeat this sequence on the other breast.

8. Repeat the entire assessment with the patient's arms raised over her head to enhance any potential retraction.

N   The consistency of the breasts is widely variable, depending on age, time in menstrual cycle, and proportion of adipose tissue. The breasts may have a nodular or granular consistency that may be enhanced prior to the onset of menses. The inferior aspect of the breast will be somewhat firmer due to a transverse inframammary ridge. Palpation should not elicit significant tenderness, though the breasts and especially the nipples may become full and slightly tender premenstrually. Breasts that feel fluid-filled or firm throughout with accompanying inferior suture-line scars are indicative of breast augmentation.

A   The presence of any lump, mass, thickening, or unilateral granulation that is noticeably different from the rest of the breast tissue should be considered suspicious and abnormal.

P   For a description of breast masses and their pathologies, see Table 14-2.

A   Significant breast tenderness is abnormal and may indicate mammary duct ectasia.

P   This is a benign condition in which lactiferous ducts become inflamed.

A   Erythema and swelling of the breast with possible pitting edema is abnormal and usually indicates mastitis.

P   This condition is usually seen postpartum and is an inflammation of the breast usually caused by *Staphylococcus aureus*.

Axillary Lymph Node Region

E   **1.** Stand at the patient's right side, facing the patient.

2. Tell the patient to take a deep breath and to relax her shoulders and arms (this relaxes the areas to be palpated).

3. Using your left hand, adduct the patient's right arm so that it is close to her chest wall. This maneuver relaxes the muscles.

4. Support the patient's right arm with your left hand.

5. Using the palmar surfaces of the finger pads of your right hand, place your fingers into the apex of the axilla so that they are positioned behind the pectoral muscles.

6. Gently roll the tissue against the chest wall and axillary muscles as you work downward.

7. Locate and palpate the four axillary lymph node groups:

a. Brachial (lateral) at the inner aspect of the upper part of the humerus, close to the axillary vein.

b. Central axillary (midaxillary) at the thoracic wall of the axilla.

c. Pectoral (anterior) behind the lateral edge of the pectoralis major muscle.

d. Subscapular (posterior) at the anterior edge of the latissimus dorsi muscle.

8. Repeat this method of palpation with the patient's arm abducted—instruct the patient to remain in the same position and lift the upper arm and elbow away from her body. Support the patient's abducted arm on your left shoulder (Figure 14-23).

9. Palpate the patient's left axilla using the same technique.

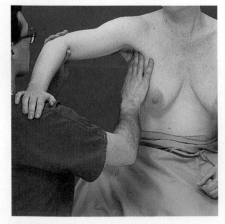

Figure 14-23 Palpation of Axillary Nodes.

| E | **Examination** | N | **Normal Findings** | A | **Abnormal Findings** | P | **Pathophysiology** |

N Palpable lymph nodes less than 1 cm in diameter are usually considered normal and clinically insignificant provided that there are no additional enlarged lymph nodes found in other regions. Palpation should not elicit pain.

A Fixed, firm, immobile, irregular lymph nodes more than 1 cm in diameter, are clinically significant.

P These nodes are considered suggestive of metastasis from a variety of sources or primary lymphoma.

A Enlarged, painful, or tender nodes that are matted together are abnormal.

P Tender, enlarged nodes may be indicative of a systemic infection or carcinoma.

Breasts: Patient in Supine Position

E 1. Keep the patient uncovered to the waist.
   2. Instruct the patient to assume a supine position, which spreads the breast tissue thinly and evenly over the chest wall. Palpation is more accurate when there is the least amount of breast tissue between the skin and the chest wall.
   3. If the breasts are large, place a small towel or folded sheet under the patient's right shoulder. This helps to flatten the breast more.
   4. Stand at the patient's right side. Palpation can be performed with the patient's arms at her sides or with her right arm above her head.
   5. Using the palmar surfaces of your fingers, palpate the right breast by compressing the mammary tissues gently against the chest wall. Do not press too hard; you may mistake a rib for a hard breast mass. Palpation may be performed from the periphery to the nipple, in either concentric circles, in wedge sections, or parallel lines (Figure 14-24).
   6. Palpation must include the tail of Spence, periphery (Figure 14-25A), and areola (Figure 14-25B).
   7. Finally, don gloves and compress the nipple to express any discharge (Figure 14-25C). If discharge is noted, palpate the breast along the wedge radii to determine from which lobe the discharge is originating.
   8. Repeat procedure on opposite breast.

N See previous section on normal breast tissue findings upon palpation. The nipple should be elastic and return readily to its previous shape. No discharge should be expressed in the nonpregnant, nonlactating patient.

Refer to Table 14-2 for a description of breast masses. Table 14-3 offers a list of breast mass characteristics that are used to evaluate abnormal findings.

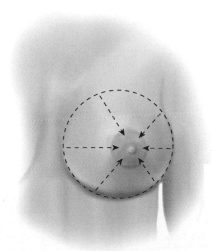

A. Wedge

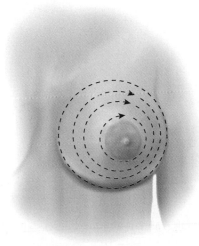

B. Concentric Circles

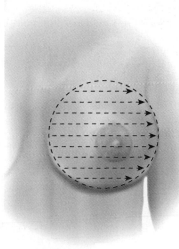

C. Parallel Lines

Figure 14-24 Breast Palpation Methods.

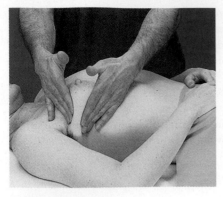

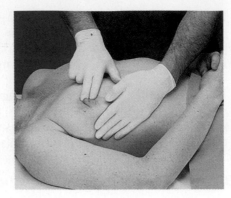

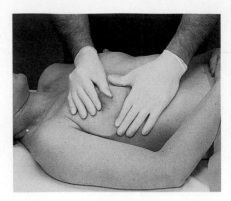

A. Palpation of the Glandular Tissue   B. Palpation of the Areola   C. Compression of the Nipple

Figure 14-25 Palpation of the Breasts while Patient Is Supine.

TABLE 14-3 Evaluation of Breast Mass Characteristics

If a mass is noted during palpation, the following information should be obtained regarding the mass. Always note if one or both breasts are involved.

Location
Identify the quadrant involved or visualize the breast with the face of a clock superimposed upon it. The nipple represents the centre of the clock. Note where the mass lies in relation to the nipple, for example, "3 cm from the nipple in the 3 o'clock position."

Size
Determine size in centimetres in all three planes (height, width, and depth).

Shape
Masses may be round, ovoid, matted, or irregular.

Number
Note if mass is singular or multiple. Note if one or both breasts are involved.

Consistency
Masses may be firm, hard, soft, fluid, or cystic.

Definition
Note if the mass borders are discrete or irregular.

Mobility
Determine if the mass is fixed or freely movable in relation to the chest wall.

Tenderness
Note if palpation elicits pain.

Erythema
Note any redness over involved area.

Dimpling or Retraction
Observe for dimpling or retraction as the patient raises arms overhead and presses her hands into her hips.

Lymphadenopathy
Note if the mass involves any of the regional lymph nodes, and indicate whether there is associated lymphadenopathy.

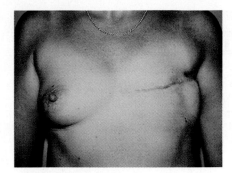

A. Modified Radical

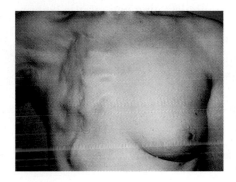

B. Radical

Figure 14-26 Mastectomy Patients. *Courtesy of Steven M. Lynch, M.D.*

Nursing Tip

The Patient With a Mastectomy

There are four types of **mastectomy** (excision of the breast) procedures. In a simple mastectomy, just the breast is removed. In a modified radical procedure, the breast and lymph nodes from the axilla are removed (Figure 14-26A). In a radical mastectomy, the breast, lymph nodes from the axilla, and pectoral muscles are removed (Figure 14-26B); this procedure is rarely performed. In a subcutaneous mastectomy, the skin and nipple are left intact, but the underlying breast tissue and lymph nodes are removed. The patient who has undergone a simple, modified radical, or radical mastectomy literally has had the breast amputated from the chest wall.

Reconstruction techniques include synthetic implants, tissue expansion techniques (in which a temporary device is placed in a subpectoralis-subserratus position between the anterior chest wall and skin and is then inflated with saline over a period of weeks), and latissimus dorsi myocutaneous flap breast reconstruction. A myocutaneous flap reconstruction involves transferring skin from the back or the abdomen to the anterior chest wall.

Assessment of the mastectomy patient is guided by the type of mastectomy and the presence or absence of reconstructive surgery. Follow the standard assessment procedures and modify your technique to suit the amount of breast tissue and the presence, if any, of a nipple. Always begin the assessment on the unaffected breast. Mastectomy patients should continue to perform a monthly BSE to determine if masses have returned to the excised area. Annual clinical evaluations and mammography are also recommended.

Nursing Tip

Breast Augmentation and Reduction

Breast augmentation, or **augmentation mammoplasty,** involves the use of implants. It is the second most popular form of cosmetic surgery in Canada (following liposuction). Saline-filled implants have been in use for many years while silicone gel-filled implants are now only back on the Canadian market as of 2006 after a moratorium on their use since 1999 because of concerns about systemic illnesses that might be associated with them.

A patient who has recently had this type of surgery will likely have incision sites in the axillae, circumareolar areas, and inframammary creases. Potential complications from augmentation include hematoma, infection, scarring, loss of nipple or skin sensation, pain from engorgement, asymmetry, and malpositioning. Breakage of the implant can lead to **granulomatous reaction** in the breasts in which small, nodular, inflammatory lesions develop, and a capsular membrane forms over the breasts. The augmented breast will feel firmer upon palpation and remain more erect when the patient is supine.

Breast reduction is usually performed on patients who complain of back, neck, or shoulder pain caused by breast hypertrophy. The type of procedure used to reduce the breasts (either free nipple graft or dermal pedicles) can be ascertained from observing the postoperative scarring. A free nipple graft leaves scars around the nipple and at the inferior mammary fold. A dermal pedicles procedure leaves "keyhole" scars over the breasts. Recently, breast liposuction has become popular. Potential complications from breast reduction procedures are hematoma, infection, nipple or skin necrosis, fat necrosis, and asymmetry. Palpation results will depend on the type of procedure that was carried out and the amount of scar tissue formed.

Life 360°

Attitude of Older Women and Breast Cancer

The nurse is conducting a seminar on female health to residents of an assisted living residence. The nurse reviews the guidelines for clinical breast examination and mammography in detecting cancer. The nurse hears comments such as:

"My breasts are so sagging, no need to worry."

"I had one breast removed for cancer and the other breast is OK."

"If I haven't gotten breast cancer by now, I doubt I will ever get it."

How might the nurse respond to these comments?

Reflective Thinking

The Patient with a New Breast Mass

What nursing care would you offer a patient who has a newly diagnosed breast mass? How would you answer her questions about cancer, death, or cure rates? How could you provide helpful support and education within your nursing practtice?

A Loss of nipple elasticity or nipple thickening is abnormal.

P Loss of elasticity in the nipple may indicate tumour formation.

A Milky-white discharge in a nonpregnant, nonlactating patient may be non-puerperal galactorrhea.

P Nonpuerperal galactorrhea is either hormonally induced from lesions of the anterior pituitary gland or drug induced.

A Nonmilky discharge from the nipple, which may be green, brown, straw coloured, or grey, is abnormal.

P Nonmilky discharge may be indicative of benign or malignant breast disease such as duct ectasia.

A Bleeding from the nipple is abnormal.

P Bleeding from the nipple is often seen in the benign condition of intraductal papilloma.

Inspection and Palpation of the Male Breasts

Assessment of the male breasts is completed in essentially the same manner as that of the female breasts. Modify the technique for a smaller breast with less tissue bulk. Having the patient lean forward is usually not necessary unless gynecomastia is present. Males should perform a BSE every month and have clinical examinations of the breast every 1 to 3 years.

DIAGNOSTIC TECHNIQUES

Etiologic determination of breast or lymphatic masses can be accurately assessed only via a combination of the diagnostic techniques listed below.

1. Mammography: roentgenographic examination of the breasts by means of X-rays, ultrasound, or nuclear magnetic resonance. There is contradictory evidence as to whether mammography saves lives.
2. Ultrasonography: the location, measurement, and delineation of deep structures by measuring the reflection of ultrasonic waves.
3. Needle aspiration: the withdrawal of fluid or tissue from a cavity via a hollow needle with an aspirator tube attached to one end.
4. Biopsy: the process of removing tissue from a suspicious area for examination. Methods include needle biopsy, punch biopsy, excisional biopsy, core biopsy, and stereotactic biopsy.
5. Thermography: measuring the regional temperature of a body part or organ. Malignant lesions are often warmer than nonmalignant areas and are called "hot spots."
6. Ductal lavage: a method of rinsing the milk duct to obtain cells for analysis of atypia.

E Examination	**N** Normal Findings	**A** Abnormal Findings	**P** Pathophysiology

GERONTOLOGICAL VARIATIONS

The adipose tissue of the breast atrophies with age and is replaced by connective tissue. The glandular tissue gradually decreases and the breasts feel granular instead of lobular. The breasts become smaller, pendulous, and wrinkled. The nipples become smaller and flatter. Ductal tissue becomes more palpable, especially around the nipple, and may become firm and stringy. In addition, the musculature around the breast tends to atrophy, which contributes to the overall droopiness of the breasts.

There is increased incidence of breast cancer after the age of 50. In women, it is the second major cause of cancer death, exceeded only by lung cancer.

Nursing Tip

Breast Self-Examination—The BSE steps are provided for the women who want to learn BSE.

Teaching BSE can be quick and simple.

1. BSE should be performed once a month, 8 days following menses or on any given fixed date. Advise the patient to avoid the time when her breasts might be tender due to menstruation or ovulation. Encourage her to put the BSE on her calendar and include her significant other in the process.
2. **B** (bed): Show the patient how to palpate her breast while supine in bed using the palmar surfaces of her fingers. She should start by placing her right arm over her head and palpating the right breast with the left hand, moving in concentric circles from the periphery inward, including the periphery, tail of Spence, and areola (Figure 14-27A). Finally, instruct her to squeeze the nipple to examine for discharge. Using the reverse procedure, she should examine the other breast.
3. **S** (standing): Instruct the patient to repeat the above palpation method while standing (Figures 14-27B and 14-27C).
4. **E** (examination before a mirror): The patient should stand in front of a mirror with her arms at her sides (Figure 14-27D), then with her arms raised over her head (Figure 14-27E), and finally with her hands pressed into her hips (Figure 14-27F). She should examine her breasts for symmetry, retractions, dimpling, inverted nipples, and nipple deviation.

Nursing Alert

Breast Mass

Any new breast mass or change in a previously benign breast mass must be referred for evaluation.

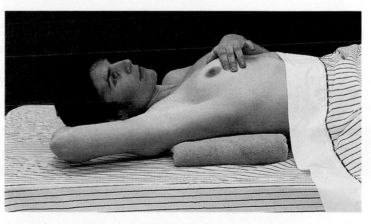

A. In Bed

Figure 14-27 Breast Self-Examination.

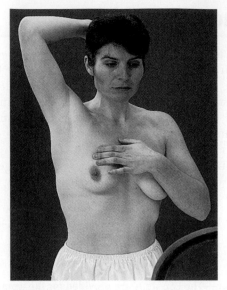

B. Standing

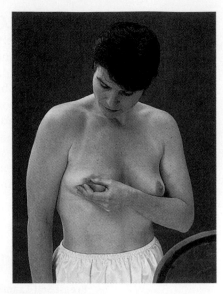

C. Compression of the Nipple

D. Before a Mirror: Arms at Side

E. Before a Mirror: Arms Overhead

F. Before a Mirror: Hands Pressed into Hips

Figure 14-27 *continued*

CASE STUDY

The Patient with Spontaneous Nipple Discharge of the Left Breast

The case study illustrates the application and objective documentation of the breasts and regional nodes assessment.

Ms. Sloan arrives at the health clinic with a complaint of nipple discharge.

HEALTH HISTORY

PATIENT PROFILE	54-yo divorced woman who looks worried
HEALTH ISSUE/CONCERN	"I have a green discharge coming out of my left nipple."

HISTORY OF ISSUE/ CONCERN	States she has a dark green nipple discharge, which spontaneously expresses from the Ⓛ nipple. This first occurred 1 month ago c̄ her noticing a few drops in her bra each day. Now she notices the discharge also stains her gown at night. She states she has had dull Ⓛ breast pain for approximately 4 mos. She denies any masses, dimpling, or retractions. Has been menopausal for 4 yrs & has never taken HRT. "I am scared that I have breast cancer. If I get sick, there is no one to care for me."
PAST HEALTH HISTORY	
Medical History	Denies a history of benign breast disease, cysts, fibroadenomas, mastitis, breast cancer, endometrial or ovarian cancer. She had an abnormal mammogram 1 year ago c̄ ↑ densities seen in the Ⓛ breast. She never went for the follow-up mammogram that was scheduled 6 mos later. HTN & hyperlipidemia controlled c̄ medication; denies thyroid disease, pituitary disorders, or exposure to chest radiation; onset of menarche age 12
Surgical History	C-section age 32; laparoscopic cholecystectomy age 52
Medications	Amlodipine (Norvasc) 10 mg, atorvastatin (Lipitor) 20 mg, & calcium 1500 mg daily, occasional ibuprofen for pain for H/A & occasional back pain
Communicable Disease	Denies
Allergies	No known food or drug allergies
Injuries and Accidents	Broken Ⓡ foot age 15, casted; Ø sequelae
Special Needs	Denies
Blood Transfusions	Denies
Childhood Illnesses	Mumps age 6
Immunizations	dT 2002, annual flu vaccine
FAMILY HEALTH HISTORY	

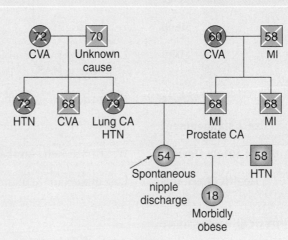

LEGEND

- ⬤ Living female
- ⬛ Living male
- ⊗ Deceased female
- ⊠ Deceased male
- ╱ Points to patient
- – – – – = Separated
- A&W = Alive & well
- CA = Cancer
- CVA = Cerebrovascular accident
- HTN = Hypertension
- MI = Myocardial infarction

Denies family hx of breast dz.

continues

SOCIAL HISTORY

Alcohol Use	3–4 glasses wine on wkds
Drug Use	Denies
Tobacco Use	Never smoked
Domestic and Intimate Partner Violence	Denies
Sexual Practice	Has a male partner; uses condoms
Travel History	Goes to Mexico every winter
Work Environment	Works in the local poultry factory
Home Environment	Large home in a rural setting
Hobbies and Leisure Activities	Gardens, hobby farming
Stress and Coping	Worries about her daughter who has finished HS and now "has no direction;" talks things over with a few friends who are "very good listeners."
Education	High school
Economic Status	"I have no worries unless I will have to keep supporting my daughter."
Religion/Spirituality	"I believe in God but not in going to church."
Ethnicity	"My parents were from Scotland."
Roles and Relationships	Mother, employee, daughter
Characteristic Patterns of Daily Living	Wakes 05:00, at work by 07:00; home by 16:00, cares for animals, eats $\bar{c}$ daughter, in bed by 21:30.

HEALTH MAINTENANCE ACTIVITIES

Sleep	7–8 hr/night
Diet	Lots of fresh vegetables, fruits; meat from her own cattle & poultry, NAS
Exercise	No formal program but active with animal care
Stress Management	Talks with friends; may have a glass of wine to unwind sometimes
Use of Safety Devices	Wears seat belt, smoke detector in home
Health Check-ups	Last gyn exam & mammogram >1 yr ago, does not perform BSE

PHYSICAL ASSESSMENT

Inspection

Colour	Breasts & axillae flesh-coloured c̄ striae bilaterally over breasts & axillae; areolar areas & nipples dark in pigmentation
Vascularity	Symmetrical, no enhanced vascular patterns
Thickening or Edema	No thickening or edema
Size and Symmetry	Breasts large & pendulous, symmetrical, no nipple inversion; both nipples facing downward & outward bilaterally
Contour	Breasts convex in shape & symmetrical s̄ dimpling, retraction, or flattening
Lesions or Masses	No fissures or erosion; no supernumerary nipples; no obvious lesions or masses
Discharge	Ø
Palpation	
Supraclavicular and Infraclavicular Lymph Nodes	Nonpalpable
Breasts: Patient in Sitting Position	No tenderness; no nodes or masses palpable; breast tissue granular & uniform throughout bilaterally; green black discharge expressed from Ⓛ nipple; ⊕ for blood
Axillary Lymph Node Region	Discrete, < 1 cm s̄ tenderness
Breasts: Patient in Supine Position	No nodes or masses palpable; breast tissue granular & uniform throughout bilaterally; green black discharge expressed from Ⓛ nipple; ⊕ for blood
DIAGNOSTIC DATA	
Mammography	Densities noted in Ⓛ breast

◄NURSING CHECKLIST►

Breasts and Regional Nodes Assessment

Inspection
- Colour
- Vascularity
- Thickening or edema
- Size and symmetry
- Contour
- Lesions or masses
- Discharge

Palpation
- Supraclavicular and infraclavicular lymph nodes
- Breasts: Patient in sitting position
- Axillary lymph node region
- Breasts: Patient in supine position

REVIEW QUESTIONS

1. When inspecting the breast, the patient should be placed in this position:
   a. Arms at side, arms overhead, leaning forward, hands on knees
   b. Arms at side, arms overhead, hands pressed on shoulders, leaning forward
   c. Arms at sides, arms overhead, hands pressed on hips, leaning forward
   d. Arms at side, arms overhead, hands pressed on hips, leaning backward
   The correct answer is (c).

2. Most breast masses tend to occur in which quadrant?
   a. Lower outer quadrant
   b. Lower inner quadrant
   c. Upper outer quadrant
   d. Upper inner quadrant
   The correct answer is (c).

3. A 58-year-old patient presents to the office with a breast mass. Which diagnostic technique might be used to evaluate her breast mass?
   a. CT scan, mammography, ultrasonography, needle biopsy
   b. Mammography, needle biopsy, ultrasonography, thermography
   c. Thermography, needle biopsy, CT scan, mammography
   d. CT scan, MRI, needle biopsy, mammography
   The correct answer is (b).

4. In palpating the breast tissue, the nurse starts at the outermost rim of the breast and gradually works in a circular pattern to the nipple. This palpation uses which technique?
   a. Wedge
   b. Concentric circles
   c. Parallel lines
   d. Perpendicular lines
   The correct answer is (b).

5. Which is a risk for breast cancer?
   a. Multiparous
   b. Breastfeeding
   c. Late menopause
   d. Late menarche
   The correct answer is (c).

6. A 35-year-old woman presents at the clinic to discuss her risk of breast cancer since her mother and aunt were just diagnosed with the disease. Which best describes familial risks and breast cancer?
   a. Eight percent to 20% of breast cancers are thought to have a familial link.
   b. A primary or secondary relative with the disease places a woman at risk.
   c. The link is stronger if the family history includes unilateral breast disease.
   d. Benign breast disease in a primary relative increases the risk.
   The correct answer is (a).

7. A mother is concerned that her 13-year-old daughter is not developing appropriately. In evaluating sexual maturity rating for female breast development, which would you expect?
   a. Nipple is small and slightly raised.
   b. Nipple and breast form a mound.
   c. Nipple is flush with breast shape; breast and areola are enlarged.
   d. Nipple protrudes; areola is flush with breast shape.
   The correct answer is (c).

8. The breast is composed of glandular, connective, and adipose tissue. The milk-producing glands are called acini. These glands compose the:
   a. Montgomery tubercles
   b. Lobules
   c. Alveoli
   d. Adipose tissue
   The correct answer is (b).

9. A 32-year-old woman arrives at the clinic for a clinical breast examination. During the exam, you find a mass in the left breast. The mass is round, firm, well defined, singular, mobile, tender without erythema, without retraction or dimpling. It is most likely a:
   a. Carcinoma
   b. Fibroadenoma
   c. Gross cyst
   d. Calcification
   The correct answer is (c).

10. Gynecomastia is the enlargement of male breast tissue. This may be a normal finding in:
    a. Prepubescent boys
    b. Elderly men
    c. Men using testosterone
    d. Men who are on beta blockers
    The correct answer is (b).

Visit the Estes online companion resource at
www.healthassessment.nelson.com for additional content
and study aids.

REFERENCES

[1]Canadian Cancer Society/National Cancer Institute of Canada. (2006). *Canadian Cancer Statistics 2006.* Toronto, Canada.

[2]Ibid.

[3]Ibid.

[4]Cancer Care Ontario. (2004). *First Nations cancer research and surveillance priorities for Canada: Report of a workshop September 23–24, 2003.* Ottawa, Canada.

[5]National Cancer Institute of Canada. *Cancer statistics: International variation in cancer incidence, 1993–1997.* Retrieved October 17, 2006, from http://www.ncic.cancer.ca/ncic/internet/standard/0,3621,84658243_85787780_91036643_langId-en,00.html

[6]Morrison, B. J. (1994). Screening for breast cancer. In: Canadian Task Force on the Periodic Health Examination. *Canadian Guide to Clinical Preventive Health Care.* Ottawa. Health Canada.

[7]Ringash, J. & the Canadian Task Force on Preventive Health Care (2001). Preventive health care, 2001 update: Screening mammography among women aged 40–49 years at average risk of breast cancer. *Canadian Medical Association Journal, 164*(4), 469–76.

[8]Baxter N., with the Canadian Task Force on Preventive Health Care. (2001). Preventive health care, 2001 update: Should women be routinely taught breast self-examination to screen for breast cancer? *Canadian Medical Association Journal, 161*(13), 1837–46.

[9]Kösters, J. P., & Gøtzsche, P. C. (2003). Regular self-examination or clinical examination for early detection of breast cancer. *The Cochrane Database of Systematic Reviews*, Issue 2. Art. No.: CD003373.

[10]Baxter & CTFPHC. *Preventive health care, 2001 update: Should women be routinely taught breast self-examination to screen for breast cancer?*

[11]Ibid.

[12]DeKoning, K. (2002). Early detection: An unresolved controversy. *Network News, 7*(1), 3–5. Ottawa, ON: Canadian Breast Cancer Network.

[13]Ibid.

[14]BC Cancer Agency. *Male breast cancer.* Retrieved October 17, 2006, from http://www.bccancer.bc.ca/PPI/TypesofCancer/Breast/Male.htm

[15]Canadian Cancer Society, *Canadian Cancer Statistics 2006.*

[16]Canadian Cancer Society. (2006). *What causes breast cancer.* Retrieved May 27, 2006, from http://www.cancer.ca/ccs/internet/standard/0,3182,3172_10175_272579_langId-en,00.html

[17]Health Canada. *Risks of developing breast cancer.* Retrieved May 27, 2006, from http://www.hc-sc.gc.ca/iyh-vsv/diseases-maladies/breast-sein_e.html

BIBLIOGRAPHY

Cruickshank, S., Kennedy, C., Lockhart, K., Dosser, I., & Dallas, L. (2006). Specialist breast care nurses for supportive care of women with breast cancer. *The Cochrane Database of Systematic Reviews,* Issue 1. Art. No.: CD005634.

Finkel, M. L. (2005). *Understanding the mammography controversy: Science, politics, and breast cancer screening.* Westport, CT: Praeger.

Grunfeld, E., Dhesy-Thind, S., Levine, M., for the Steering Committee on Clinical Practice Guidelines for the Care and Treatment of Breast Cancer (2005). Clinical practice guidelines for the care and treatment of breast cancer: Follow-up after treatment for breast cancer (2005 update). *Canadian Medical Association Journal. 172*(10), 1319–20.

Harris, J. R. (2004). *Diseases of the breast.* Philadelphia; London: Lippincott Williams & Wilkins.

Heft, B. (2002). My journey with breast cancer: Past, present, and future. *Network News. Canadian Breast Cancer Network, 7*(1), 1–5.

Lerner, B. (2002). When statistics provide unsatisfying answers: Revisiting the breast self-examination controversy. *Canadian Medical Association Journal, 166*(2), 199–201.

Manning, A. P., Abelovich, D., Ghadirian, P., Provencher, D. M., Mes-Masson, A. M., Foulkes, W. F., Narod, S. A., Morgan, K., & Tonin, P. N. (2001). Haplotype analysis of BRCA2 8765delAG mutation carriers in French Canadian and Yemenite Jewish hereditary breast cancer families. *Human Heredity, 52,* 116–20.

Oktay, J. S. (2005). *Breast cancer: Daughters tell their stories.* New York: Haworth Press

Steering Committee on Clinical Practice Guidelines for the Care and Treatment of Breast Cancer (1998). The palpable breast lump: Information and recommendations to assist decision making when a breast lump is detected. *Canadian Medical Association Journal, 158* (3 Suppl).

Working Group on the Integration of Screening and Diagnosis for the Canadian Breast Cancer Screening Initiative. *Waiting for a diagnosis after an abnormal breast screen in Canada.* Ottawa, ON: Canadian Breast Cancer Screening Initiative Working Group on the Integration of Screening and Diagnosis 2000.

WEB RESOURCES

Breast Cancer Society of Canada
http://www.bcsc.ca/

Breast Cancer Support
http://www.breastcancersupport.org/CoverStories/centerStories/news.html

Breast Self-Examination: A Handbook for Women with Disabilities
http://dawn.thot.net/BSE_Handbook.html

Canadian Breast Cancer Network
http://www.cbcn.ca/english/

Canadian Breast Cancer Research Alliance
http://www.breast.cancer.ca/language/default.asp?thisUrl=%2FDefault%2Easp

First Nations Breast Cancer Society
http://www.fnbreastcancer.bc.ca/

For a complete list of provincial and territorial breast cancer support and educational agencies, visit http://www.phac-aspc.gc.ca/ccdpc-cpcmc/bc-cds/links_e.html

NEL

CHAPTER 15

Thorax and Lungs

COMPETENCIES

1. Identify the anatomic landmarks of the thorax.

2. Describe the characteristics of the most common respiratory health issues or concerns.

3. Perform inspection, palpation, percussion, and auscultation on a healthy adult and on a patient with pulmonary pathology.

4. Explain the pathophysiology for abnormal findings.

5. Document respiratory assessment findings.

6. Describe the changes that occur in the lungs with the aging process.

The respiratory system extends from the nose to the alveoli (Figure 15-1). The normal air pathway is nose, pharynx, larynx, trachea, mainstem bronchus, right and left main bronchi, lobar/secondary bronchi, tertiary/segmental bronchi, terminal bronchioles, respiratory bronchioles, alveolar ducts, alveolar sacs, and alveoli.

The respiratory system is divided into the upper and lower tracts. The upper respiratory tract comprises the nose, pharynx, larynx, and the upper trachea. The nose and pharynx are discussed in Chapter 13. The lower respiratory tract is composed of the lower trachea to the lungs. This chapter deals only with those components of the respiratory system that are located in the thorax.

ANATOMY

Thorax

The thorax is a cone-shaped structure (narrow at the top and wide at the bottom) that consists of bones, cartilage, and muscles. Of these, the bones are the supportive structure of the thorax. On the anterior thorax, these bones are the 12 pairs of ribs and the sternum. Posteriorly, there are the 12 thoracic vertebrae and the spinal column.

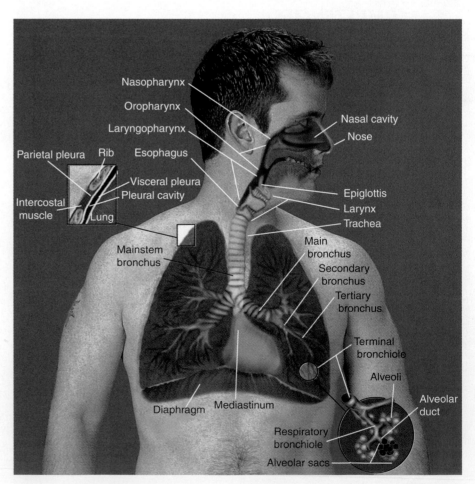

Figure 15-1 The Respiratory Tract.

Sternum

The sternum, or breastbone, is a flat, narrow bone approximately 15 cm long. It is located at the median line of the anterior chest wall and is divided into three sections: the **manubrium** (the upper bone of the sternum that articulates with the clavicles and the first pair of ribs), the body, and the **xiphoid process** (a cartilaginous process at the base of the sternum that does not articulate with the ribs).

Ribs

The first seven pairs of ribs are articulated to the sternum via the costal cartilages and are called the **vertebrosternal** or **true ribs.** The **false ribs,** or rib pairs 8–10, articulate with the costal cartilages just above them. The remaining two pairs of ribs (11 and 12) are termed **floating ribs** and do not articulate at their anterior ends. The 10th rib is the lowest rib that can be palpated anteriorly. The 11th rib is palpated on the lateral thorax, and the 12th rib is palpated on the posterior thorax. All ribs articulate posteriorly to the vertebral column. When a rib is palpated, the costal cartilage cannot be distinguished from the rib itself (Figure 15-2).

Intercostal Spaces

Each area between the ribs is called an **intercostal space** (ICS). There are 11 ICSs.

Lungs

The lungs are cone-shaped organs that fill the lateral chamber of the thoracic cavity. The lower outer surface of each lung is concave where it meets the convex diaphragm. Likewise, the medial aspect is concave to allow room for the heart, with the left lung having a more pronounced concavity (cardiac notch). The lungs lie against the ribs anteriorly and posteriorly.

Nursing Tip

Counting Anterior Intercostal Spaces

Use the angle of Louis as a landmark for identifying the rib number. Count the ribs in the midclavicular line. Each ICS is named for the number of the rib directly above it. For example, the space between the third and fourth ribs would be called the third ICS.

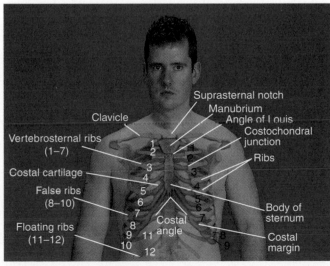

A. Anterior View

B. Posterior View

Figure 15-2 Thorax: Rib number is shown on the patient's right; intercostal space number is shown on the patient's left.

Nursing Tip

Identifying Thoracic Landmarks

Anterior
- Sternum
- Clavicles
- Nipples
- **Suprasternal notch:** With the finger pad of your index finger, feel in the midsternal line above the manubrium; the depression is the suprasternal notch.
- **Angle of Louis** (or **manubriosternal junction** or **sternal angle**): With your finger pads, feel for the suprasternal notch and move your finger pads down the sternum until they reach a horizontal ridge (the junction of the manubrium and the body of the sternum); this is the angle of Louis; the second rib articulates with this landmark and serves as a convenient reference point for counting the ribs and ICSs (the first rib is difficult to palpate).
- **Costal angle:** Place your right finger pads on the bottom of the patient's anterior left rib cage (10th rib); place your left finger pads on the bottom of the anterior right rib cage (10th rib); move both hands horizontally towards the sternum until they meet in the midsternal line; the angle formed by the intersection of the ribs creates the costal angle.

Posterior
- **Vertebra prominens:** Flex the neck forward; palpate the posterior spinous processes; if two processes are palpable, the superior process is C7 (vertebra prominens) and the inferior is T1; this landmark is useful in counting ribs to the level of T4; beyond T4 the spinous processes project obliquely and no longer correspond to the rib of the same number as the vertebral process.
- **Inferior angle of scapula:** Locate the inferior border of the scapula; this level corresponds to the seventh rib or seventh ICS.
- Spine.
- **Twelfth rib:** Palpate the lower thorax in the scapular line. Move your hand laterally to palpate the free tip of the 12th rib.

The right lung is broader than the left lung because of the position of the heart. Inferiorly, the right lung is about 2.5 cm shorter than the left lung because of the upward displacement of the diaphragm by the liver. The right lung consists of three lobes (upper, middle, and lower), and the left lung has two lobes (upper and lower). The **apex** denotes the top of the lung, and the **base** refers to the bottom of the lung. Anteriorly, the apices of the lung extend 2.5–4 cm superior to the inner third of the clavicles, and posteriorly, the apices lie near the T1 process. On deep inspiration posteriorly, the lower lung border extends to the level of T12, and to T10 on deep expiration. The anterior inferior border of the lungs is at the sixth rib at the **midclavicular line** (MCL: vertical line drawn from the midpoint of the clavicle) and at the eighth rib at the **midaxillary line** (MAL: vertical line drawn from the apex of the axillae and lying midway between the anterior and the posterior axillary lines) (Figure 15-3).

The lobes of the right and left lungs are divided by grooves called fissures. It is important to know the locations of the fissures to describe clinical findings. Figure 15-4 illustrates the right oblique (or diagonal) fissure, the right horizontal fissure, and the left oblique (or diagonal) fissure.

When assessing the thorax, it is helpful to envision it as a rectangular box, with the four sides being the anterior, posterior, right lateral, and left lateral thoraxes. Figure 15-5 illustrates the imaginary thoracic lines on each of the four sides. These landmarks are helpful in discussing clinical findings.

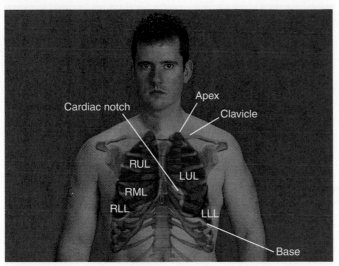

A. Anterior View

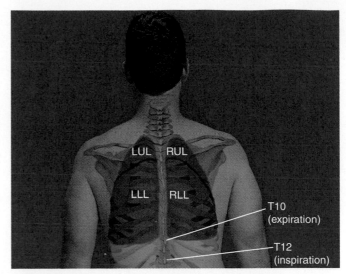

B. Posterior View

Figure 15-3 Lungs: RUL = Right Upper Lobe, RML = Right Middle Lobe, RLL = Right Lower Lobe, LUL = Left Upper Lobe, LLL = Left Lower Lobe.

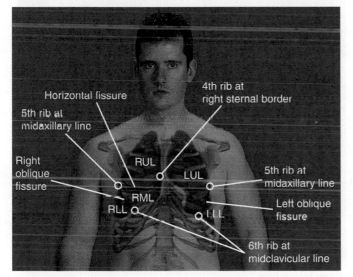

A. Anterior View

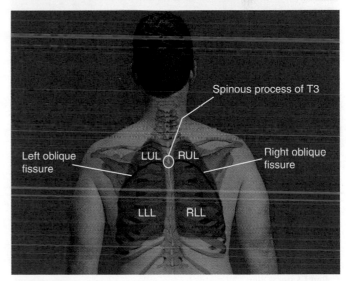

B. Posterior View

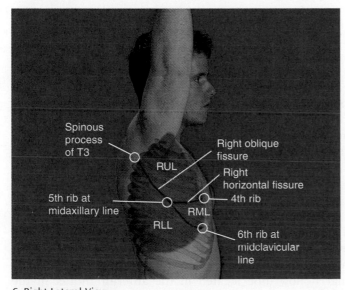

C. Right Lateral View

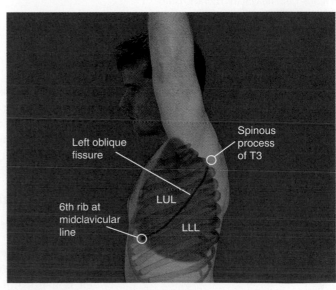

D. Left Lateral View

Figure 15-4 Lung Fissures.

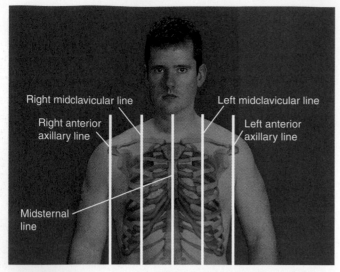

Right midclavicular line

Left midclavicular line

Right anterior axillary line

Left anterior axillary line

Midsternal line

A. Anterior View

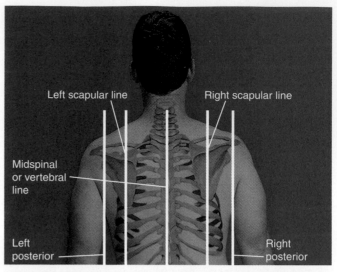

Left scapular line

Right scapular line

Midspinal or vertebral line

Left posterior

Right posterior

B. Posterior View

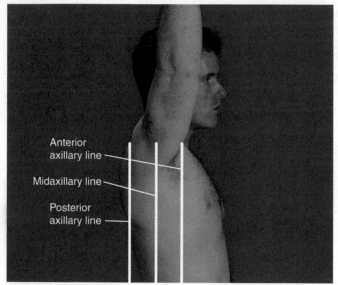

Anterior axillary line

Midaxillary line

Posterior axillary line

C. Right Lateral View

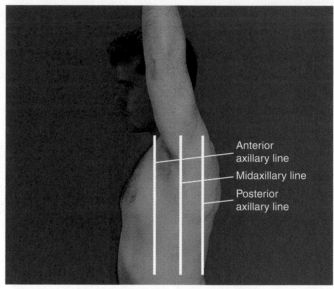

Anterior axillary line

Midaxillary line

Posterior axillary line

D. Left Lateral View

Figure 15-5 Imaginary Thoracic Lines.

Pleura

Each lung is encased in a serous sac, or **pleura.** The **parietal pleura** lines the chest wall and the superior surface of the diaphragm. The **visceral pleura** lines the external surface of the lungs. Usually, a small amount of fluid is found in the space between the pleurae; this fluid prevents the pleurae from rubbing against each other and is a cushioning agent for the lungs.

Mediastinum

The **mediastinum,** or **interpleural space,** is the area between the right and left lungs. It extends from the sternum to the spinal column and contains the heart, great vessels, trachea, esophagus, and lymph vessels. The only respiratory structures in the mediastinum are the trachea and the pulmonary vasculature. The trachea is a fibromuscular hollow tube located in the anterior thorax in the median plane. It is 11–13 cm in length and 2–3 cm in width. The trachea lies anterior to the esophagus.

Nursing Tip

Thoracic Anatomic Topography

Additional landmarks that are useful when describing assessment findings are:

- **Anterior axillary line:** vertical line drawn from the origin of the anterior axillary fold and along the anterolateral aspect of the thorax.
- **Midspinal (vertebral) line:** vertical line drawn from the midpoint of the spinous process.
- **Midsternal line:** vertical line drawn from the midpoint of the sternum.
- **Posterior axillary line:** vertical line drawn from the posterior axillary fold.
- **Scapular line:** vertical line drawn from the inferior angle of the scapula.

Bronchi

The trachea bifurcates into the left and right mainstem bronchi at the level of the fourth or fifth vertebral process posteriorly and the sternal angle anteriorly. The right mainstem bronchus is wider, shorter, and more vertical than the left. This anatomic difference is critical because it makes the right mainstem bronchus more susceptible to aspiration and endotracheal intubation. The mainstem bronchi further divide into lobar or secondary bronchi. Each lobar bronchus supplies a lobe of the lung. The bronchi transport gases as well as trap foreign particles in their mucus. Cilia aid in sweeping the foreign particles upward in the respiratory tract for possible elimination. Culmination of the tracheobronchial tree is in the alveoli.

Nursing Alert

Tuberculosis

- The number of reported cases of tuberculosis (TB) in Canada has shown a continual decrease over the past decade; however, the incidence in Canadian residents born outside the country has remained relatively constant. In 2002, TB among foreign-born individuals accounted for 67% of all reported cases in Canada. Canadian-born Aboriginal cases represented 15% of the total cases; Canadian-born non-Aboriginal individuals accounted for 16%. (Birthplace was unknown for 3% of cases.)
- In 2002, 1634 cases (5.2 per 100,000) of new active and relapsed TB were reported to the Canadian Tuberculosis Reporting System (CTBRS). The highest rate of 93.4 per 100,000 was reported from Nunavut. TB incidence was lowest in Nova Scotia where the reported rate was less than 1.0 per 100,000. The three most populous provinces (British Columbia, Ontario, and Quebec) accounted for 77% of the total reported cases.[1]

Risk Factors for Tuberculosis[2]

- travel to countries where TB is common
- aboriginal background
- homelessness
- alcoholism
- working or living in a prison
- age over 65 years
- being HIV positive
- working with high-risk groups (i.e., health care workers)

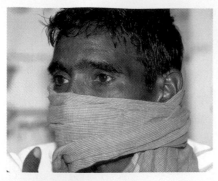

Figure 15-6 Since TB is spread via droplet nuclei, the infected person needs to wear a mask or other barrier device. *Courtesy of WHO/P. Virot.*

Nursing Alert

Personal Respiratory Protection (Masks) for Respiratory Infections Transmitted by Large Droplets or Contact[3]

- Suspected or possible respiratory tract infections include colds, pharyngitis, croup bronchiolitis, pneumonia and confirmed infections with adenovirus, influenza, parainfluenza virus, respiratory syncytial virus, metapneumovirus, rhinovirus, or coronavirus.
- Masks should be worn when within 1 metre of a coughing patient or when performing activities that are likely to generate splashes or sprays of blood, body fluids, or secretions.
- The patient should wear a surgical mask when not in a confined room.
- Carefully remove masks using the straps to avoid self-contamination; discard any mask that is crushed, wet, or contaminated by secretions, and wash hands after removing a mask.
- Masks should be changed if they become moist, hard to breath in, physically damaged, or visibly soiled.
- High-risk patients should wear masks when in contact with people who have contagious diseases, and they should be tested regularly for TB (Figure 15-6).
- Disposable N95 respirators that have been fitted properly are used for airborne isolation precautions in patients with active TB or severe acute respiratory syndrome (SARS).

Nursing Alert

SARS[4]

SARS, caused by a coronavirus, is a relatively new respiratory illness that is spread through close contact with an infected person. People who live in the same household, provide care to someone with SARS, or have direct contact with respiratory secretions and body fluids of an infected person are most at risk for contracting SARS. The first Canadian cases were identified in 2003 in people who had travelled to Hong Kong and returned to Canada. The majority of cases were in Ontario, but cases were also reported in British Columbia, Alberta, New Brunswick, Prince Edward Island, and Saskatchewan. Flu vaccination does not protect against SARS; however, it may help reduce the number of "false alarms."

If a patient presents with *fever (>38 Celsius) and cough or difficulty breathing:*

- The health care professional (HCP) doing the initial screening should stand 1 metre from the patient.
- The HCP, patient, and anyone accompanying the patient, should don a surgical mask; all should perform hand hygiene, and the patient (and family member) should be placed in a separate area.
- The HCP should don eye protection if there is a potential for splattering or spraying of blood, body fluids, secretions or excretions.
- The HCP asks the following screening questions—a positive answer to any of these indicates risk of SARS: Do you have new or worsening cough or shortness of breath? Have you had a fever or chills? Have you been to (insert country where cases have recently been reported by public health authorities) in the last 14 days? Have you had contact with a sick person who has travelled to (same country) in the last 14 days?

Alveoli

The **alveoli** are the smallest functional units of the respiratory system. It is here that gas exchange occurs. Approximately 300 million alveoli are present in each lung. This aerating surface is about equal to 100 times the body surface area of an adult. Each alveolus has its own blood supply and lymphatic drainage. Branches of the pulmonary artery carry blood to the capillaries surrounding the alveoli to be oxygenated. Branches of the pulmonary vein transport oxygenated blood from the alveoli to the heart.

Diaphragm

The diaphragm, which is innervated by the phrenic nerve, is a dome-shaped muscle that forms the inferior border of the thorax. Anteriorly, its right edge is located at the fifth rib—fifth ICS at the MCL. The left dome of the diaphragm is at the sixth rib—sixth ICS at the MCL. The presence of the liver below the right dome of the diaphragm accounts for the elevated border on that side. On expiration posteriorly, the diaphragm is located at the level of the 10th vertebral process, and at T12 on inspiration. Laterally, the diaphragm is found at the eighth rib at the midaxillary line. The diaphragm is the principal muscle of respiration. Contraction of the diaphragm leads to an increase in volume in the thoracic cavity.

External Intercostal Muscles

The external intercostal muscles are located in the ICS. During inspiration, the external intercostal muscles elevate the ribs, thus increasing the size of the thoracic cavity. The internal intercostal muscles draw adjacent ribs together, thereby decreasing the size of the thoracic cavity during expiration.

Accessory Muscles

Accessory respiratory muscles are used to accommodate increased oxygen demand. Exercise and some diseases lead to the use of accessory muscles. The accessory muscles are the scalene, sternocleidomastoid, trapezius, and abdominal rectus.

PHYSIOLOGY

Ventilation

The primary function of the respiratory system is to deliver oxygen to the lungs and to remove carbon dioxide from the lungs. The breathing process includes inspiratory and expiratory phases. During inspiration, the pressure inside the lungs becomes subatmospheric when the diaphragm and external intercostal muscles contract. The diaphragm lowers, and the ribs elevate, thus increasing the intrapulmonic volume. As a result of the negative intra-alveolar pressure, atmospheric air is pulled into the respiratory tract until intra-alveolar pressure equals atmospheric pressure. The lungs increase in size with the air.

Expiration is a passive process and occurs more rapidly than inspiration. During expiration, the diaphragm and external intercostal muscles relax, decreasing the volume of the thoracic cavity. The diaphragm rises. The intrapulmonic volume decreases and the intrapulmonic pressure increases above the atmospheric pressure. The lungs possess elastic recoil capabilities that allow air to be expelled until intrapulmonic pressure equals atmospheric pressure.

External Respiration

External respiration is the process by which gases are exchanged between the lungs and the pulmonary vasculature. Oxygen diffuses from the alveoli into the blood, and carbon dioxide diffuses from the blood to the alveoli. Diffusion is a passive process in which gases move across a membrane from an area of higher concentration to an area of lower concentration. In the lungs, the membrane is the alveolar–capillary network.

Internal Respiration

Internal respiration is the process by which gases are exchanged between the pulmonary vasculature and the body's tissues. Oxygen from the lungs diffuses from the blood into body tissue; carbon dioxide diffuses from the tissue into the blood. The blood is then carried back to the right side of the heart for reoxygenation.

Control of Breathing

Control of breathing is influenced by neural and chemical factors. The pons and medulla are the central nervous system structures primarily responsible for involuntary respiration. The stimulus for breathing is an increased carbon dioxide level, a decreased oxygen level, or an increased blood pH level.

Life 360°

Tobacco Use

- How do you feel about people who smoke?
- How do you feel about patients who have pathology related to tobacco use?
- Do you treat patients who smoke any differently from nonsmoking patients?
- How do you feel about health care professionals who smoke?

HEALTH HISTORY

The thorax and lungs health history provides insight into the link between a patient's life and lifestyle and thorax and lungs information and pathology.

PATIENT PROFILE	*Diseases that are age-, gender-, and race-specific for the thorax and lungs are listed.*
Age	Bronchiectasis (birth–20) Cystic fibrosis (CF) (birth–30) Pneumothorax (20–40) Sarcoidosis (30–40) Chronic bronchitis (>35) Pneumonia (>60) Emphysema (50–60) Idiopathic pulmonary fibrosis (60–70)
Gender	
Female	Sarcoidosis
Male	Mesothelioma, idiopathic pulmonary fibrosis, pneumothorax
HEALTH ISSUE/CONCERN	*Common health issues/concerns for the thorax and lungs are defined and information on the characteristics of each sign or symptom is provided.*
Dyspnea	Subjective feeling of shortness of breath (SOB)
Quantity	The number of steps that can be climbed before SOB occurs; distance that can be walked; number of pillows needed to sleep comfortably
Associated Manifestations	Palpitations, leg pain, faintness, anxiety, fatigue, cough, sputum, wheezing, diaphoresis, cyanosis, pain, fever

Aggravating Factors	Smoking, exercise, poorly ventilated rooms
Alleviating Factors	Pillow orthopnea, side-lying position, tripod position, fresh air, medications (e.g., bronchodilators), supplemental oxygen, resting
Timing	Nighttime (paroxysmal nocturnal dyspnea)
Cough	Stimulation of afferent vagal endings, which helps clean the airway of extraneous material by producing a sudden, forceful, and noisy expulsion of air from the lungs
Quality	Dry, wet, hacking, barking, congested, harsh, brassy, high pitched, whooping, bubbling
Associated Manifestations	SOB, wheezing, sputum, pleuritic pain, chest pain, fever, hemoptysis, coryza, anxiety, diaphoresis
Aggravating Factors	Position of patient, exposure to noxious stimuli, exercise
Alleviating Factors	Medications (e.g., nebulizer, inhaler, antitussive), humidity, cool air, cool liquids
Setting	Temperature and humidity of environment, exertion
Timing	Winter, early morning, bedtime, middle of the night, after eating, prior to fainting, continuous
Sputum	Substance produced by the respiratory tract that can be expectorated or swallowed; it is composed of mucus, blood, purulent material, microorganisms, cellular debris, and, occasionally, foreign objects
Quality	Colour: white or clear, purulent, blood tinged, yellow or green, mucoid, rust, black, pink Consistency: thick, thin, moderate; frothy—separates into layers Odour: malodorous
Quantity	Normal daily sputum production is 60–90 mL (normally this is not expectorated); small, moderate, copious
Associated Manifestations	Cough, fever, dyspnea
Aggravating Factors	Exposure to allergens, smoking
Alleviating Factors	Medications (e.g., guaifenesin), liquids
Setting	Sleep, exposure to allergen
Timing	Early morning
Chest Pain	Pain can have a pulmonary, cardiac, gastrointestinal, or musculoskeletal etiology. Chapter 16 differentiates the types of chest pain.
PAST HEALTH HISTORY	*The various components of the past health history are linked to thorax and lung pathology and thorax- and lung-related information.*
Medical History	
Respiratory Specific	Asthma, bronchitis, croup, frequent coryza, CF, emphysema, epiglottitis, pleurisy, pneumonia, pneumothorax, pulmonary edema, pulmonary embolus, lung cancer, TB

continues

Nonrespiratory Specific	Lupus, drug-induced respiratory pathology, rheumatoid arthritis, congenital musculoskeletal chest defects, severe scoliosis, multiple sclerosis, amyotrophic lateral sclerosis
Surgical History	Lobectomy, pneumonectomy, tracheostomy, wedge resection, bronchoscopy
Medications	Antibiotics, bronchodilators, cough expectorant, cough suppressant, oxygen
Communicable Diseases	Coryza: sneezing, coughing TB: pulmonary fibrosis and calcification Influenza: pneumonia AIDS: *Pneumocystis carinii* pneumonia Hantavirus: bilateral pulmonary infiltrates, respiratory failure SARS: pneumonia, respiratory failure
Allergies	Asthma is the predominant manifestation of allergies in the respiratory patient. Hypersensitivity to drugs, food, pets, dust, cigarette smoke, perfume, or pollen should be closely scrutinized. In addition, any common signs of allergies, such as cough, sneeze, and sinusitis, should be closely evaluated.
Injuries and Accidents	Chest trauma, near drowning
Special Needs	Oxygen dependent, phrenic pacer dependent, ventilator dependent
Childhood Illnesses	Pertussis and measles: bronchiectasis
FAMILY HEALTH HISTORY	*Thorax and lung diseases that are familial are listed.* Allergies, alpha$_1$-antitrypsin deficiency, asthma, bronchiectasis, cancer, CF, emphysema, sarcoidosis, TB
SOCIAL HISTORY	*The components of the social history are linked to thorax and lung factors and pathology.*
Alcohol Use	Decreases efficiency of lung defense mechanisms, predisposes to aspiration pneumonia; patients with carbon dioxide retention are more sensitive to alcohol's depressant effect
Drug Use	Heroin: pulmonary edema Barbiturates or narcotic overdose: respiratory depression Cocaine: tachypnea
Tobacco Use	Cigarette smoking is the primary risk factor for chronic bronchitis, emphysema, and lung cancer, as well as other disorders.
Travel History	Prolonged exposure to confined space with recirculated air (e.g., airplane) TB (Haiti, Southeast Asia) Pneumonic plague (India)
Work Environment	Repeated exposure to materials in the workplace can create respiratory complications that range from minor problems to life-threatening events. Numerous categories of respiratory diseases have been identified from repeated exposure to toxic substances. These diseases are listed along with the industries and agents related to them.

Silicosis: glass making, tuning, stonecutting, mineral mining, insulation work, quarrying, cement work, ceramics, foundry work, semiconductor manufacturing

Asbestosis: mining, shipbuilding, construction

Coal worker's pneumoconiosis: coal mining

Pneumoconioses: tin and aluminum production, welding, insecticide manufacturing, rubber industry, fertilizer industry, ceramics, cosmetic industry

Occupational asthma: electroplating, grain working, woodworking, photography, printing, baking, painting

Chronic bronchitis: coal mining, welding, firefighting

Byssinosis: cotton mill dust, flax

Extrinsic allergic alveolitis (hypersensitivity pneumonia): animal hair, contamination of air conditioning or heating systems, mouldy hay, mouldy grains, mouldy dust, sugarcane

Toxic gases and fumes: welding, cigarette smoke, auto exhaust, chemical industries, firefighting, hair spray

Pulmonary neoplasms: radon gas, mustard gas, printing ink, asbestos

Pneumonitis: furniture polish, gasoline, or kerosene ingestion; mineral oil, olive oil, and milk aspiration

Home Environment	Air pollution, cigarette smoke, wood-burning stoves, gas stoves and heaters, kerosene heaters, radon gas, pet hair and dander
Hobbies and Leisure Activities	Birds (bird breeder's lung), mushroom growers (mushroom grower's lung), scuba diving (lung rupture, oxygen toxicity, decompression sickness), high-altitude activities (skiing, climbing: pulmonary edema and pulmonary embolus)
Stress	Asthma can be exacerbated by stress
Economic Status	Poor sanitation and densely populated areas are ideal conditions for the spread of communicable respiratory illnesses
HEALTH MAINTENANCE ACTIVITIES	*This information provides a bridge between the health maintenance activities and thorax and lung function*
Sleep	Sleep apnea syndrome: absence of inspiratory muscle activation; upper airway occlusion Chronic obstructive pulmonary disease (COPD) or neuromuscular disease: nocturnal oxygen desaturation caused by hypoventilation without apnea
Diet	Obesity: chronic hypoventilation, obstructive apnea (Pickwickian syndrome)
Exercise	Regular exercise improves pulmonary function
Use of Safety Devices	Mask worn when exposed to toxic substances; other occupational precautions as mandated by Canadian and provincial health and safety legislation; knowledge of Heimlich maneuver
Health Check-ups	Respiratory rate, lung auscultation, chest X-ray, sputum culture and sensitivity, pulmonary function test, 2-step purified protein derivative (tuberculin) (PPD), influenza and pneumococcal vaccines, immunotherapy (allergy desensitization injections) Current evidence does not support systematic screening for lung cancer with chest radiography or sputum cytology. Frequent chest X-ray screening might be harmful.[5]

Nursing Alert

Avian Influenza H5N1 Virus (Bird Flu)

Avian influenza viruses, such as the H5 virus present in Asia, may, on rare occasions, cause disease in humans. Human transmission has occurred to people having prolonged contact with heavily contaminated environments. Human-to-human transmission of avian influenza is extremely limited.[6]

Due to the potential for human infection, it is recommended that people working with or in contact with poultry suspected of being infected with avian influenza wear protective clothing, including face masks, goggles, gloves and boots.[7]

◄NURSING CHECKLIST►

Maintaining Respiratory Health—The Movement for Clean Air Now[*]

- Avoid smoking; encourage those living with you to stop.
- Never smoke around infants and children.
- If you must live with a smoker, ask that smoking be confined to one well-ventilated room, or preferably outside.
- If dust and mould are allergy triggers or aggravating factors for other respiratory ailments, clean house frequently, avoid wall-to-wall carpeting, use easily washed curtains, and don't have a cluttered room.
- Change filters on furnace, heaters, air conditioners, exhaust systems, and range hoods as frequently as the manufacturer specifies.
- Have chimneys cleaned at the beginning of each season and more frequently if used heavily.
- Have home inspected for radon and take remedial steps as needed.
- Check carbon monoxide and smoke detectors on a monthly basis.
- Walking, taking public transport, and avoiding car idling are all measures to reduce emissions.
- Make scent-free choices.

_____

[*]The Canadian Lung Association's environmental health program proposes simple actions to make a positive difference to the air Canadians breathe. For more information visit http://www.lung.ca/cando/sitemap.html.

◄NURSING CHECKLIST►

General Approach to Thorax and Lung Assessment

1. Greet the patient and explain the assessment techniques that you will be using.
2. Ensure that the examination room is at a warm, comfortable room temperature to prevent patient chilling and shivering.
3. Use a quiet room free from interruptions.
4. Ensure that the light in the room provides sufficient brightness to adequately observe the patient.
5. Instruct the patient to remove all street clothes from the waist up and to don an examination gown.
6. Place the patient in an upright sitting position on the examination table, or
6a. For patients who cannot tolerate the sitting position, rotate the supine, bedridden patient from side to side to gain access to the thorax.
7. Expose the entire area being assessed. Provide a drape that women can use to cover their breasts (if desired) when the posterior thorax is assessed.
8. When palpating, percussing, or auscultating the anterior thorax of female or obese patients, ask them to displace the breast tissue. Assessing directly over breast tissue is not an accurate indicator of underlying structures.
9. Visualize the underlying respiratory structures during the assessment process in order to accurately describe the location of any pathology.
10. Always compare the right and left sides of the anterior thorax and the posterior thorax to one another, as well as the right and left lateral thorax.
11. Use a systematic approach every time the assessment is performed. Proceed from the lung apices to the bases, right to left to lateral.

Nursing Tip

Influenza Vaccine

The Canadian Task Force on Preventive Health Care recommends annual influenza vaccination in *all* healthy adults and children (grade A recommendation). Adults over age 65 should also receive the pneumococcal vaccine.[8]

Nursing Alert

Lung Cancer

- Lung cancer is often described as the most preventable of all cancers. While it is the primary cause of cancer deaths among men, their mortality rate from lung cancer is gradually declining because of a decrease in male tobacco consumption. On the other had, mortality rates among women are steadily increasing, with lung cancer now surpassing breast cancer as the number one cause of cancer deaths among women.[9, 10]

Risk Factors for Lung Cancer

- Smoking tobacco and secondhand tobacco exposure
- Hereditary predisposition for some smokers
- Occupational or environmental exposure to known carcinogens (e.g., asbestos, radon, heavy metals)

Smoking Trends and Smoke Cessation Programs available across Canada are found in Chapter 3.

EQUIPMENT

- Stethoscope
- Centimetre ruler or tape measure
- Washable marker
- Watch with second hand

ASSESSMENT OF THE THORAX AND LUNGS

Inspection

Shape of Thorax

E 1. Stand in front of the patient.
   2. Estimate visually the transverse diameter of the thorax.
   3. Move to either side of the patient.
   4. Estimate visually the width of the anteroposterior (AP) diameter of the thorax.
   5. Compare the estimates of these two visualizations.

N In the normal adult, the ratio of the AP diameter to the transverse diameter is approximately 1:2 to 5:7. In other words, the normal adult is wider from side to side than from front to back. The normal thorax is slightly elliptical in shape. A barrel chest is normal in infants and sometimes in older adults. See Chapter 24 for a discussion of the pediatric patient. Figure 15-7 illustrates the normal and abnormal configurations of the thorax.

A In **barrel chest,** the ratio of the AP diameter to the transverse diameter is approximately 1:1. The patient's chest is circular or barrel-shaped in appearance.

P The patient with COPD has a barrel chest due to air trapping in the alveoli and subsequent lung hyperinflation. Lung volume thus increases and the diaphragm flattens over time. The ribs are forced upward and outward. Collectively these changes result in the barrel chest appearance.

A **Pectus carinatum,** or pigeon chest, is a marked protrusion of the sternum. This increases the AP diameter of the thorax.

P Pectus carinatum can result from a congenital anomaly. A patient with severe pectus carinatum will exhibit respiratory difficulty.

P Rickets results from a vitamin D deficiency in which the bones become demineralized and weak. The loss of bone strength allows the intercostal muscles to pull the ribs and sternum forward, resulting in pectus carinatum.

| E | Examination | N | Normal Findings | A | Abnormal Findings | P | Pathophysiology |

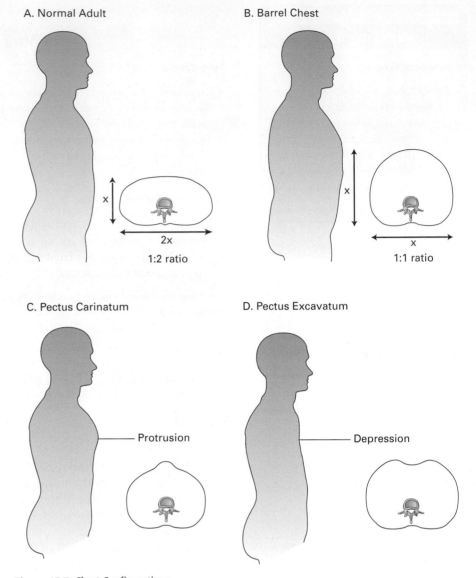

A. Normal Adult

B. Barrel Chest

x

2x
1:2 ratio

x

x
1:1 ratio

C. Pectus Carinatum

D. Pectus Excavatum

Protrusion

Depression

Figure 15-7 Chest Configurations.

A **Pectus excavatum,** or fun chest, is a depression in the body of the sternum that can compress the heart and cause myocardial disturbances. The AP diameter of the chest decreases.

P Pectus excavatum results from a congenital anomaly. Respiratory insufficiency can ensue from the compression of the lungs in marked pectus excavatum.

A **Kyphosis,** or humpback, is an excessive convexity of the thoracic vertebrae. Gibbus kyphosis is an extreme deformity of the spine.

P The majority of kyphosis cases are idiopathic. Respiratory compromise is manifested only in severe cases.

A **Scoliosis** is a lateral curvature of the thorax or lumbar vertebrae. See Chapter 18 for further discussion.

P The majority of the cases of scoliosis are idiopathic, though scoliosis can also result from neuromuscular diseases, connective tissue diseases, and osteoporosis. Marked scoliosis can interfere with normal respiratory function. The total lung capacity and vital capacity decline in proportion to the severity of the scoliosis.

| **E** **Examination** | **N** **Normal Findings** | **A** **Abnormal Findings** | **P** **Pathophysiology** |

Symmetry of Chest Wall

E   **1.** Stand in front of the patient.

     2. Inspect the right and the left anterior thoraxes.

     3. Note the shoulder height. Observe any differences between the two sides of the chest wall, such as the presence of masses.

     4. Move behind the patient.

     5. Inspect the right and the left posterior thoraxes, comparing right and left sides.

     6. Note the position of the scapula.

N   The shoulders should be at the same height. Likewise, the scapula should be the same height bilaterally. There should be no masses.

A   Having one shoulder or scapula higher than the other is abnormal.

P   The presence of scoliosis can lead to a shoulder or a scapula that is higher than its corresponding part. Marked scoliosis impairs lung function.

A   The presence of a visible mass is abnormal.

P   A visible chest mass is always abnormal. Likely etiologies are mediastinal tumours or cysts. If large enough, they can compress lung tissue and impair lung function.

Presence of Superficial Veins

E   **1.** Stand in front of the patient.

     2. Inspect the anterior thorax for the presence of dilated superficial veins.

N   In the normal adult, dilated superficial veins are not seen.

A   The presence of dilated superficial veins on the anterior chest wall is an abnormal finding.

P   Dilated veins on the anterior thorax may be indicative of superior vena cava obstruction. Due to the obstruction, the superficial veins and collateral vessels become engorged with blood and dilate. Venous return to the heart is diminished, compromising oxygenation. A patient may present with dyspnea.

Costal Angle

E   **1.** Stand in front of the patient.

     2. In a patient whose thoracic skeleton is easily viewed, visually locate the **costal margins** (medial borders created by the articulation of the false ribs).

     3. Estimate the angle formed by the costal margins during exhalation and at rest. This is the costal angle.

     4. In a heavy or obese patient, place your fingertips on the lower anterior borders of the thoracic skeleton.

     5. Gently move your fingertips medially to the xiphoid process.

     6. As your hands approach the midline, feel the ribs as they meet at the apex of the costal margins. Visualize the line that is created by your fingers as they move up the floating ribs toward the sternum. This is the costal angle (Figure 15-8A). Approximate this angle.

N   The costal angle is less than 90° during exhalation and at rest. The costal angle widens slightly during inhalation due to the expansion of the thorax.

A   A costal angle greater than 90° is abnormal.

P   Processes where hyperinflation of the lungs (emphysema) or dilation of the bronchi (bronchiectasis) occurs also result in a costal margin angle greater than 90°. The diaphragm flattens out and the ribs are forced upward and outward, leading to the change in the costal margin angle.

Angle of the Ribs

E   **1.** Stand in front of the patient.

     2. In a patient whose thoracic skeleton is easily viewed, visually locate the midsternal area.

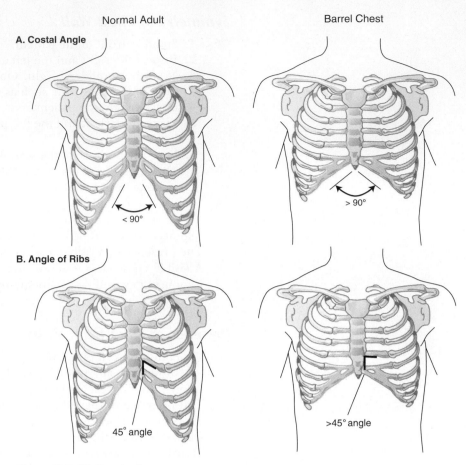

Figure 15-8 Rib Cage Angles.

3. Estimate the angle at which the ribs articulate with the sternum.
4. In a heavy or obese patient, place your fingertips on the midsternal area.
5. Move your fingertips along a rib laterally to the anterior axillary line. Visualize the line that is created by your hand as it traces the rib. Approximate this angle. See Figure 15-8B.

N   The ribs articulate at a 45° angle with the sternum.

A   An angle greater than 45° is considered abnormal. Patients with particular respiratory pathology may have ribs that are nearly horizontal and perpendicular to the sternum.

P   Conditions characterized by an increased AP diameter, such as emphysema, bronchiectasis, and CF, result in an angle greater than 45° because the lungs are forced out due to hyperinflation or dilation of the bronchi.

Intercostal Spaces

E   1. Stand in front of the patient.
    2. Inspect the ICS throughout the respiratory cycle.
    3. Note any bulging of the ICS and any retractions.

N   There should be an absence of retractions and of bulging of the ICS.

A   The presence of retractions is abnormal. Retractions occur during inspiration.

P   Conditions that obstruct the free inflow of air may lead to retractions. These include emphysema, asthma, tracheal or laryngeal obstruction, and the presence of a foreign body or tumour that compresses the respiratory tract.

A   The presence of bulging of the ICS is abnormal. Bulging of the ICS tends to occur during expiration.

| E | **Examination** | N | **Normal Findings** | A | **Abnormal Findings** | P | **Pathophysiology** |

P Abnormal bulging of the ICS occurs when there is an obstruction to the free exhalation of air, such as in emphysema, asthma, an enlarged heart, aortic aneurysm, massive pleural effusion, tension pneumothorax, and tumours.

Muscles of Respiration

E 1. Stand in front of the patient.
   2. Observe the patient's breathing for a few respiratory cycles, paying close attention to the anterior thorax and the neck.
   3. Note all of the muscles that are being used by the patient.

N No accessory muscles are used in normal breathing.

A The use of the accessory muscles is a pathological finding.

P Any condition that creates a state of hypoxemia or hypermetabolism may lead to the use of accessory muscles. Accessory muscles attempt to create an extra respiratory effort to inhale needed oxygen. Patients experiencing hypermetabolic states such as exercise, fever, and infection, or hypoxic events such as COPD, pneumonia, pneumothorax, pulmonary edema, and pulmonary embolus usually present with accessory muscle use.

Respirations

The inspection of the respiration process includes seven components: rate, pattern, depth, symmetry, audibility, patient position, and mode.

Rate

E 1. Stand in front of the patient or to the right side.
   2. Observe the patient's breathing without stating what you are doing—the patient may change the respiratory rate (increase or decrease it) if aware that you are watching the chest rising and falling. This assessment can be conducted simultaneously with the pulse rate assessment.
   3. Count the number of respiratory cycles that the patient has for one full minute. A respiratory cycle consists of one inhaled and one exhaled breath.

N In the resting adult, the normal respiratory rate is 12–20 breaths per minute. This type of breathing is termed eupnea, or normal breathing.

A A respiratory rate greater than 20 breaths per minute is termed **tachypnea.**

P Tachypnea is frequently present in hypermetabolic and hypoxic states. By increasing the respiratory rate, the body is trying to supply additional oxygen to meet the body's demands. Tachypnea occurs in many disease states, such as pneumonia, bronchitis, asthma, and pneumothorax.

P Tachypnea is often a sign of stress. In stressful situations, the body releases catecholamines that elevate the respiratory rate to supply sufficient oxygen.

A A respiratory rate lower than 12 breaths per minute is termed **bradypnea.**

P Injury to the brain may cause bradypnea because of excessive intracranial pressure applied to the respiratory centre in the medulla oblongata.

P In drug overdoses (barbiturates, alcohol, and opiates), bradypnea is a sign of the drug's depressant effect on the respiratory centre.

P Bradypnea occurs in sleep because of the lowered metabolic state of the body. The respiratory rate also slows in non-REM sleep due to changes in the response of the respiratory centre to chemical signals.

A **Apnea** is the lack of spontaneous respirations for 10 or more seconds.

P Traumatic brain injury may lead to apnea because of herniation of the brain stem.

P Sleep apnea can be central or obstructive in nature. In central sleep apnea, the respiratory drive is altered, leading to periods of respiratory cessation. In obstructive sleep apnea, enlarged upper airway anatomy leads to a physical blockage in the oropharynx.

Nursing Alert

Respiratory Rate Emergencies

Extreme tachypnea (greater than 30 breaths per minute in an adult), bradypnea, and apnea are emergency conditions. Immediate intervention is necessary to prevent complications.

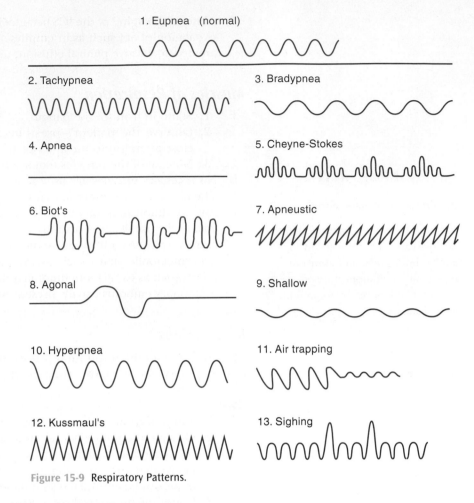

Figure 15-9 Respiratory Patterns.

Pattern (Figure 15-9)

E **1.** Stand in front of the patient.

2. While counting the respiratory rate, note the rhythm or pattern of the breathing for regularity or irregularity.

N Normal respirations are regular and even in rhythm.

A **Cheyne-Stokes respirations** occur in crescendo and decrescendo patterns interspersed between periods of apnea that can last 15–30 seconds. This can be a normal finding in elderly patients and in young children. Cheyne-Stokes respiration is an example of a regularly irregular respiratory pattern; that is, the respirations predictably or regularly become irregular.

P Central cerebral or high brain-stem lesions that occur in brain injury produce Cheyne-Stokes respirations.

P Cheyne-Stokes respirations can also appear in sleep due to alterations in the respiratory centre's ability to accurately perceive chemical and mechanical stimuli.

A **Biot respirations,** or **ataxic respirations,** is an example of an irregularly irregular respiratory pattern. In an irregularly irregular rhythm, there is no identifiable pattern to the respiratory cycle. There is an absence of a crescendo and decrescendo pattern. Deep and shallow breaths occur at random intervals interspersed with short and long pauses. Periods of apnea can be long and frequent.

P Biot's breathing indicates damage to the medulla.

| E | **Examination** | N | **Normal Findings** | A | **Abnormal Findings** | P | **Pathophysiology** |

A   **Apneustic respirations** are characterized by a prolonged gasping during inspiration followed by a very short, inefficient expiration. These pauses can last 30–60 seconds.

P   Injury to the upper portion of the pons can lead to apneustic breathing.

A   **Agonal respirations** are irregularly irregular respirations. They are of varying depths and patterns.

P   Impending death, where there is little or no oxygen supplying the brain, or compression of the respiratory centre, may lead to agonal breaths.

Depth

E   **1.** Stand in front of the patient.

     2. Observe the relative depth with which the patient draws a breath during inspiration.

N   The normal depth of inspiration is nonexaggerated and effortless.

A   In hypoventilation, or shallow respirations, the chest wall is moved minimally during inspiration and expiration. A small tidal volume is being inspired.

P   Obese patients frequently have small tidal volumes due to the sheer weight of the chest wall and the effort it takes to move it with each breath.

P   The patient in pain or with a recent abdominal or thoracic incision has shallow respirations due to the discomfort of moving the rib cage, the integument, and the respiratory muscles with each breath.

P   Shallow respirations are also seen in conditions where lung pathology exists and breathing is painful: pulmonary embolus, pneumonia, pneumothorax.

A   **Hyperpnea** is a breath that is greater in volume than the resting tidal volume. The respiratory rate is normal and the pattern is even.

P   In the warm-up and cool-down periods of exercise, hyperpnea is present. The deep breath is drawn to meet the increased metabolic needs of the body.

P   Patients in highly emotional states exhibit hyperpnea as the body attempts to meet the increased oxygen demand.

P   Patients who are thrust into high-altitude regions will become hyperpneic due to the decreased partial pressure of oxygen. Deep breaths and slight tachypnea represent an attempt to supply the oxygen needs of the body.

A   **Air trapping** is an abnormal respiratory pattern with rapid, shallow respirations and forced expirations.

A   Patients with COPD have difficulty with exhaling. When these patients exercise or experience increased heart rate, they have insufficient time to fully exhale. As a result, air is trapped in the lungs, and, over time, the chest overexpands. Likewise, an asthmatic patient experiencing an acute attack has difficulty exhaling due to increased mucus and bronchial constriction. Air trapping ensues.

A   **Kussmaul's respirations** are characterized by extreme increased depth and rate of respirations. These respirations are regular and the inspiratory and expiratory processes are both active.

P   Diabetic ketoacidosis and metabolic acidosis may result in Kussmaul's respirations. The body is lowering its $PaCO_2$ level, thereby raising the pH and attempting to correct the acidosis.

A   **Sighing** is characterized by normal respirations interrupted by a deep inspiration and followed by a deep expiration. It may be accompanied by an audible sigh. Sighing is pathological if it occurs frequently.

P   Excessive sighing can occur in central nervous system lesions.

Symmetry

E   **1.** Stand in front of the patient.

     2. Observe the symmetry with which the chest rises and falls during the respiratory cycle.

N   The healthy adult's thorax rises and falls in unison in the respiratory cycle. There is no paradoxical movement.

A   Unilateral expansion of either side of the thorax is abnormal.

P Conditions where the lung is absent or collapsed (pneumonectomy, pneumothorax) are characterized by unilateral thoracic expansion secondary to the lack of active alveolar expansion on inspiration.

A Absence of expansion is evident on the affected lung side in a patient with pulmonary fibrosis due to the thickening of the lung and decreased elasticity.

P Acute pleurisy and massive atelectasis are pathologies where pain and collapsed alveoli, respectively, interfere with the respiratory process and prevent adequate bilateral and equal chest symmetry.

A Paradoxical, or seemingly contradictory, chest wall movement is always abnormal. In paradoxical chest wall movement, the unaffected part of the thorax will rise during inspiration while the affected area will fall. Conversely, during expiration the unaffected part of the thorax will fall while the affected area will rise.

P Broken ribs from trauma to the chest wall or flail chest interferes with the normal rib cage dynamics during the respiratory process and may lead to paradoxical chest wall movement.

A Hoover's sign is the paradoxical inward movement of the lower ICS during inspiration. This occurs when the diaphragm is flat instead of its normal dome shape. Muscle fibres are horizontal, and diaphragmatic contraction pulls the rib cage inward rather than down.

P Broken ribs from trauma to the chest wall or flail chest interferes with the normal rib cage dynamics during the respiratory process and may lead to the presence of Hoover's sign.

Audibility

E 1. Stand in front of the patient.
   2. Listen for the audibility of the respirations.

N A patient's respirations are normally heard by the unaided ear a few centimetres from the patient's nose or mouth.

A It is abnormal to hear audible breathing when standing a few feet from the patient. Upper airway sounds may also be heard but should not be confused with pulmonary sounds.

P Any condition where air hunger exists has the potential to create audible and noisy breathing. The body is attempting to meet its oxygen demands. Examples of these states are exercise, COPD, pneumonia, and pneumothorax.

Patient Position

E 1. Ask the patient to sit upright for the respiratory assessment.
   2. View the patient either before or after the assessment and note the assumed position for breathing. Ask if the assumed position is required for respiratory comfort.
   3. Note if the patient can breathe normally when in a supine position.
   4. Note if pillows are used to prop the patient upright to facilitate breathing.

N The healthy adult breathes comfortably in a supine, prone, or upright position.

A Orthopnea is difficulty breathing in positions other than upright.

P COPD, congestive heart failure, and pulmonary edema exemplify conditions where orthopnea may be present. The upright position maximizes the use of the respiratory muscles in patients who might otherwise be unable to breathe in a supine position, secondary to fluid in the lungs. Patients with COPD may assume the tripod position to breathe easier and make breathing look natural (Figure 15-10). The tripod position allows for easier use of accessory muscles.

Figure 15-10 Tripod Position.

| E | Examination | N | Normal Findings | A | Abnormal Findings | P | Pathophysiology |

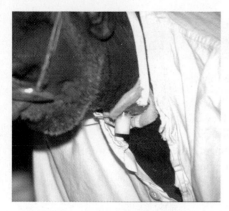

Figure 15-11 Tracheostomy. *Courtesy of WHO/P. Virot.*

Nursing Tip

Assisting the Patient in Expectoration

- Increase fluid intake.
- Humidify environment.
- Splint painful areas with a pillow during coughing.
- Teach patient effective coughing technique.
- Use postural drainage and chest physiotherapy prior to cough, when indicated.

TABLE 15-1

Pathologies Associated with Different Colours of Sputum

SPUTUM COLOUR	PATHOLOGY
Mucoid	Tracheobronchitis, asthma, coryza
Yellow or green	Bacterial infection
Rust or blood tinged	Pneumococcal pneumonia, pulmonary infarction, TB, lung cancer
Black	Black lung disease
Pink	Pulmonary edema

Mode of Breathing

E **1.** Stand in front of the patient.
2. Note whether the patient is using the nose, the mouth, or both, to breathe.
3. Note for which part of the respiratory cycle each is used.

N Normal findings vary among individuals but generally, most patients inhale and exhale through the nose.

A Continuous mouth breathing is usually abnormal.

P Any type of nasal or sinus blockage obstructs the normal breathing passageway and leads to mouth breathing.

A Pursed-lip breathing is performed by patients who need to prolong the expiration phase of the respiratory cycle. It appears that the patient is trying to blow out a candle or is preparing for a kiss.

P Pursed-lip breathing is performed by patients with COPD. It is the patient's innate mechanism to apply positive-pressure breathing to prevent total alveolar collapse with every breath. Less energy is expended with each breath because the alveoli do not completely collapse after expiration.

A Patients may breathe through a stoma or tracheostomy (Figure 15-11).

P Patients with laryngeal cancer who have had a surgical removal of the larynx breathe initially through a tracheostomy and then through a stoma. This is their normal mode of breathing.

Sputum

E **1.** Ask the patient to expectorate a sputum sample.
2. If the patient is unable to expectorate, ask the patient for a recent sputum sample from a handkerchief or tissue.
3. Note the colour, odour, amount, and consistency of the sputum.

N A small amount of sputum is normal in every individual. The colour is light yellow or clear. Normal sputum is odourless. Depending on the hydration status of the patient, the sputum can be thick or thin.

A Colours of sputum that are abnormal are mucoid, yellow or green, rust or blood tinged, black, and pink (and frothy).

P Table 15-1 lists the pathologies that are associated with different colours of sputum.

A Foul-smelling sputum is always abnormal.

P Anaerobic infections produce foul-smelling sputum.

A A large amount of sputum can be pathological.

P Chronic bronchitis produces a large amount of sputum as a result of the irritation to the respiratory tract.

A Patients with pneumonia expectorate large quantities of sputum. The sputum is produced in reaction to the infectious process.

P An excessive amount of sputum is found in pulmonary edema, from the fluid that has leaked from pulmonary capillary membranes into large airways.

A Very thick sputum can be abnormal.

P Water is a normal component of the sputum. Therefore, when a patient is dehydrated, the sputum will be thicker because the mucus, blood, purulent material, and cellular debris form the bulk of the sputum.

A Sputum that has a thin consistency can be abnormal.

P In overhydration, the extra fluid tends to dilute the remaining components of the sputum. In pulmonary edema, the sputum is thin, pink, and frothy.

Palpation

General Palpation

General palpation assesses the thorax for pulsations, masses, thoracic tenderness, and crepitus.

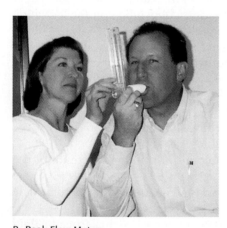

A. Pulse Oximeter

B. Peak Flow Meter

Figure 15-12 Respiratory Assistive Devices.

◄NURSING CHECKLIST►

Assessing Patients with Respiratory Assistive Devices

- Oxygen
  - Mode of delivery (e.g., nasal cannula, face mask)
  - Percentage of oxygen that is being delivered (e.g., 24%, 40%)
  - Flow rate of the oxygen (e.g., 2 litres per minute, 4 litres per minute)
  - Humidification provided and oxygen warmed
- Incentive Spirometer
  - Frequency of use
  - Volume achieved (e.g., 1,000 mL, 1,500 mL)
  - Number of times patient reaches goal with each use
- Endotracheal Tube
  - Size of endotracheal tube
  - Nasal or oral insertion
  - Tube secured to the patient
  - Length of the endotracheal tube as it exits the nose or the mouth (e.g., 24 cm at the lips or 27 cm at the tip of the left nare)
  - Cuff inflated or deflated
- Tracheostomy Tube
  - Size of tracheostomy tube
  - Cuff present; if yes, cuff inflated or deflated
  - Tracheostomy ties secure the tube
- Mechanical Ventilation
  - Type of ventilator
  - FiO_2 setting
  - Mode used (e.g., assist, intermittent mandatory ventilation)
  - Amount of positive end-expiratory pressure
  - Rate and tidal volume
  - Peak inspiratory pressure
  - Temperature of the humidification
  - Alarms set
- Pulse Oximeter (Figure 15-12A)
  - Determine the monitor's settings.
  - The monitor's alarms are on. The appropriate limits are set.
  - If using the probe on a nail, the patient's nail polish has been removed.
  - If using the probe on the ear, the skin is intact and earrings are not interfering.
- Peak Flow Meter (Figure 15-12B)
  - Patient is seated while performing the manoeuvre.
  - Indicator line is lowered to the baseline level.
  - Patient exhales as quickly and deeply as possible while maintaining a firm seal with the lips around the mouthpiece.
  - Patient does not obstruct the exhalation outlet.

To perform anterior palpation:

E 1. Stand in front of the patient.
   2. Place the finger pads of your dominant hand on the apex of the right lung (above the clavicle).
   3. Using light palpation, assess the integument of the thorax in that area.
   4. Move the finger pads down to the clavicle and palpate.

| E | Examination | N | Normal Findings | A | Abnormal Findings | P | Pathophysiology |

5. Proceed with the palpation, moving down to each rib and ICS of the right anterior thorax. Palpate any area(s) of tenderness last.
6. Repeat the procedure on the left anterior thorax.

To perform posterior palpation:

E 1. Stand behind the patient.
   2. Place the finger pads of the dominant hand on the apex of the right lung (approximately at the level of T1).
   3. Using light palpation, assess the integument of the thorax in that area.
   4. Move the finger pads down to the first thoracic vertebra and palpate.
   5. Proceed with the palpation, moving down to each thoracic vertebra and ICS of the right posterior thorax.
   6. Repeat the procedure on the left posterior thorax.

To perform lateral palpation:

E 1. Stand to the patient's right side.
   2. Have the patient lift his or her arms overhead.
   3. Place the finger pads of your dominant hand beneath the right axillary fold.
   4. Using light palpation, assess the integument of the thorax in that area.
   5. Move the finger pads down to the first rib beneath the axillary fold.
   6. Proceed with the palpation, moving down to each rib and ICS of the right lateral thorax.
   7. Move to the patient's left side.
   8. Repeat steps 2–6 for the left lateral thorax.

> ### Nursing Tip
>
> **Assessing the Thoracic Skin**
>
> When palpating the thorax, remember to assess temperature, turgor, moisture, texture, and edema. See Chapter 10.

Pulsations

N No pulsations should be present.
A The presence of pulsations on the thorax is abnormal.
P A thoracic aortic aneurysm that is large may be seen pulsating on the anterior chest wall.

Masses

N No masses should be present.
A The presence of a thoracic mass is abnormal.
P The presence of a thoracic tumour or cyst should be closely evaluated and malignancy ruled out.

Thoracic Tenderness

N No thoracic tenderness should be present.
A Fractured ribs may cause thoracic tenderness.
P Blunt chest trauma can affect any component of the respiratory tract, as well as the heart and great vessels. The region involved, the type of injury, and the impact of the injury dictate the amount of internal damage.

Crepitus

N Crepitus should be absent.
A The presence of **crepitus,** also referred to as subcutaneous emphysema, is always an abnormal finding. Fine beads of air escape the lung and are trapped in the subcutaneous tissue. As this area is palpated, a crackling sound may be heard. This air is slowly absorbed by the body. Crepitus is usually felt earliest in the clavicular region, but it can easily be found in the neck, face, and torso. It can also be described as feeling similar to bubble packing material that can be palpated and popped.
P Any condition that interrupts the integrity of the pleura and the lungs has the potential to lead to crepitus. Pathologies where crepitus is frequently found are pneumothorax, chest trauma, thoracic surgery, mediastinal emphysema, alveolar rupture, and tearing of pleural adhesions.

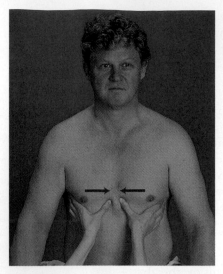

A. Anterior

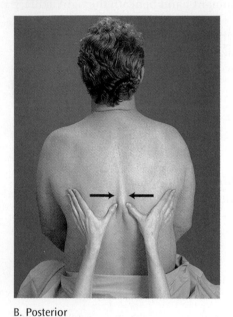

B. Posterior

Figure 15-13 Thoracic Expansion.

Thoracic Expansion

Thoracic expansion assesses the extent of chest expansion and the symmetry of chest wall expansion. Anterior and posterior thoracic expansions can be assessed (Figure 15-13).

To perform anterior thoracic expansion:

E 1. Stand directly in front of the patient. Place the thumbs of both hands on the costal margins and pointing toward the xiphoid process. Gather a small fold of skin between your thumbs to help you see the results of this technique.
2. Lay your outstretched palms on the anterolateral thorax.
3. Instruct the patient to take a deep breath.
4. Observe the movement of your thumbs, both in direction and in distance.
5. Ask the patient to exhale.
6. Observe the movement of your thumbs as they return to the midline.

To perform posterior thoracic expansion:

E 1. Stand directly behind the patient. Place the thumbs of both hands at the level of the 10th spinal vertebra, equidistant from the spinal column and approximately 2.5–7.5 cm. apart. Gather a small amount of skin between your thumbs as directed for the anterior expansion.
2. Place your outstretched palms on the posterolateral thorax.
3. Instruct the patient to take a deep breath.
4. Observe the movement of your thumbs, both in direction and in distance.
5. Ask the patient to exhale.
6. Observe the movement of your thumbs as they return to the midline.

N The thumbs separate an equal amount from the spinal column or xiphoid process (distance) and remain in the same plane of the 10th spinous vertebra or costal margin (direction). The normal distance for the thumbs to separate during thoracic expansion is 3–5 cm.

A Unilateral decreased thoracic expansion is abnormal.

P Unilateral decreased thoracic expansion on the affected or pathological side occurs in pneumothorax, pneumonia, atelectasis, lower lobe lobectomy, pleural effusion, and bronchiectasis. In these conditions, the alveoli are either not present or not fully expanding on the affected side due to pathology inside or external to the lung.

A Bilateral decreased thoracic expansion is an abnormal finding.

P Bilateral disease external or internal to the lungs must be present in order for bilateral decreased thoracic expansion to be present. Hypoventilation, emphysema, pulmonary fibrosis, and pleurisy exemplify diseases where the alveoli do not fully expand.

A Displacement of thumbs from the 10th spinal vertebra region (thumbs will not meet in the midline when the patient exhales) is abnormal.

P In scoliosis, the spine is laterally deviated to a particular side. Thus, when the patient takes a deep breath, there may be a slight or marked expansion of the lungs in an unequal fashion due to the compression of the lungs by the spine.

Tactile Fremitus

Tactile or **vocal fremitus** is the palpable vibration of the chest wall that is produced by the spoken word and is useful in assessing the underlying lung tissue and pleura. The anterior, posterior, and lateral chest walls are assessed. Three different aspects of the hand can be used to perform this technique: the palmar bases of the fingers, the ulnar aspect of the hand, and the ulnar aspect of a closed fist (Figure 15-14). The beginning nurse may wish to experiment with

E Examination	**N** Normal Findings	**A** Abnormal Findings	**P** Pathophysiology

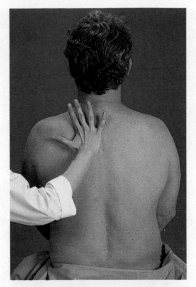

A. Using Palmar Base of Fingers

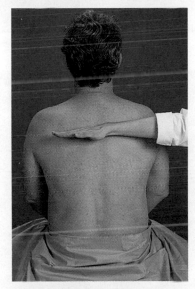

B. Using Ulnar Aspect of Hand

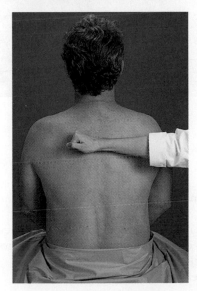

C. Using Ulnar Aspect of Closed Fist

Figure 15-14 Tactile Fremitus.

each technique and decide which is the most comfortable. The ulnar aspect of the hand should be used initially because this exposes the least amount of surface area, and therefore more discrete areas can be assessed.

To perform tactile fremitus:

E 1. Firmly place the ulnar aspect of your open hand (or palmar base of the fingers or ulnar aspect of a closed fist) on the patient's right anterior apex (remember that this is above the clavicle).

2. Instruct the patient to say the words "99" or "1, 2, 3" with the same intensity every time you place your hand on the thorax.

3. Feel any vibration on the ulnar aspect of the hand as the patient phonates. If no fremitus is palpated, ask the patient to speak more loudly.

4. Move your hand to the same location on the left anterior thorax.

5. Repeat steps 2 and 3.

6. Compare the vibrations palpated on the right and left apices.

7. Move your hand down 5–7.5 cm and repeat the process on the right and then on the left. Ensure that your hand is in the ICS in order to avoid the bony structures. Minimal or no fremitus will be felt over the ribs because they lie on top of the lungs.

8. Continue this process down the anterior thorax to the base of the lungs.

9. Repeat this procedure for the lateral chest wall and compare symmetry. Either do the entire right then the entire left thorax, or alternate right and left at each ICS

10. Repeat this procedure for the posterior chest wall. Figure 15-15 illustrates the progression of the assessment.

N Normal fremitus is felt as a buzzing on the ulnar aspect of the hand. The fremitus will be more pronounced near the major bronchi (second ICS anteriorly, and T1 and T2 posteriorly) and the trachea, and will be less palpable in the periphery of the lung. The diaphragm is approximately at the level of T10–T12 posteriorly, and it is slightly higher on the right because of the presence of the liver.

A Increased tactile fremitus is abnormal.

P Diseases that involve consolidation, such as pneumonia, atelectasis, and bronchitis, also involve increased tactile fremitus in the affected area. A compressed lung exhibits increased tactile fremitus because solids conduct sound better than does air.

A Decreased or absent tactile fremitus is a pathological finding.

P Because porous materials conduct vibrations less effectively than do fluids and solids, decreased tactile fremitus will be present in pneumothorax, emphysema, and asthma.

P In a pleural effusion, the exudate is external to the alveoli and therefore acts as a blockade to the transmission of sound waves. This results in decreased tactile fremitus.

P A patient with a large chest wall or an obese patient will have decreased tactile fremitus because the sound waves are dampened as they pass through a greater distance.

A A high diaphragm level is abnormal.

P The diaphragm level is abnormally high in a patient with a lower lobe lobectomy. Tactile fremitus will be present above the surgical site.

A Three additional findings can be revealed during tactile fremitus: pleural friction fremitus, tussive fremitus, and rhonchal fremitus.

P **Pleural friction fremitus** is a palpable grating sensation that feels more pronounced on inspiration when there is an inflammatory process between the visceral and the parietal pleurae.

P **Tussive fremitus** is the palpable vibration produced by coughing.

P **Rhonchal fremitus** is the coarse palpable vibration produced by the passage of air through thick exudate in large bronchi or the trachea. This can clear with coughing.

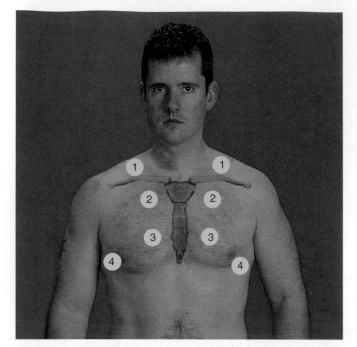

A. Anterior Thorax

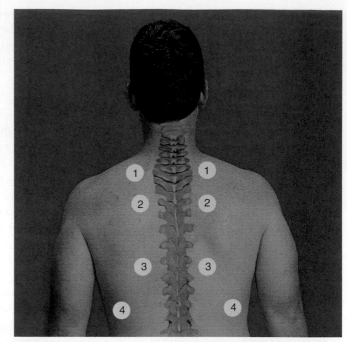

B. Posterior Thorax

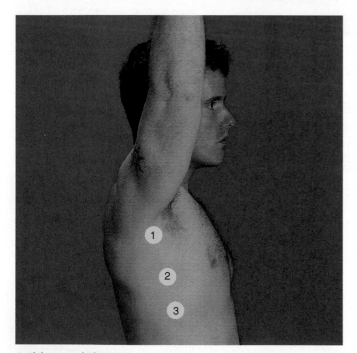

C. Right Lateral Thorax

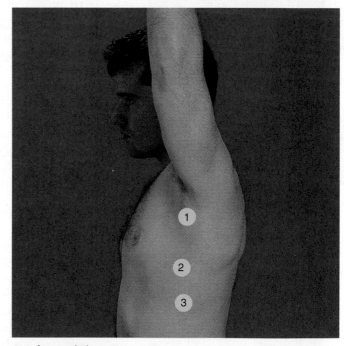

D. Left Lateral Thorax

Figure 15-15 Pattern for Tactile Fremitus.

Tracheal Position

To assess the position of the trachea:

E 1. Place the finger pad of your index finger on the patient's trachea in the suprasternal notch (Figure 15-16).

2. Move the finger pad laterally to the right and gently move the trachea in the space created by the border of the inner aspect of the sterno-cleidomastoid muscle and the clavicle.

3. Move the finger pad laterally to the left and repeat the procedure.

E	**Examination**	N	**Normal Findings**	A	**Abnormal Findings**	P	**Pathophysiology**

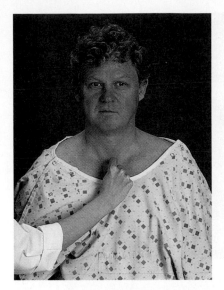

Figure 15-16 Assessing Tracheal Position.

The trachea can also be palpated by:

E   1. Gently placing the finger pad of your index finger in the midline of the suprasternal notch.
    2. Palpate for the position of the trachea.
N   The trachea is midline in the suprasternal notch.
A   Tracheal deviation to the affected side is abnormal.
P   The normal midline position of the trachea is maintained by the counterbalancing forces of the air in the alveoli in the right and left lungs. In atelectasis and pneumonia, alveoli are closed to some degree or filled with exudate. Fewer aerating alveoli are present and therefore the trachea is slightly pushed by the healthy lung to the affected side, which contains less air.
P   The mechanical pulling force of ventilator tubing that is attached to an endotracheal tube or tracheostomy for a prolonged period of time can cause tracheal deviation toward the side of the pulling.
A   Tracheal deviation to the unaffected side is abnormal.
P   A tension pneumothorax, pleural effusion, or a tumour may each generate sufficient pressure to force the trachea toward the unaffected side.
P   An enlarged thyroid may also deviate the trachea via its space-occupying capacity.

Percussion

Indirect or mediate percussion is used to further assess the underlying structures of the thorax. Remember that percussion reverberates a sound that is generated from structures approximately 5 cm below the chest wall. Deep pathological conditions will not be revealed during the percussion process.

General Percussion

Figure 15-17 demonstrates the percussion pattern for the anterior, posterior, right lateral, and left lateral thoraxes.

To perform anterior thoracic percussion:

E   1. Place the patient in an upright sitting position with the shoulders back.
    2. Percuss two or three strikes along the right lung apex.
    3. Repeat this process at the left lung apex.
    4. Note the sound produced from each percussion strike and compare the sounds from each. If different sounds are produced or if the sound is not resonant, then pathology is suggested.
    5. Move down approximately 5 cm, or every other ICS, and percuss in that area.
    6. Percuss in the same position on the contralateral side.
    7. Continue to move down until the entire lung has been percussed.

To perform posterior thoracic percussion:

E   1. Place the patient in an upright sitting position with a slight forward tilt. Have the patient bend the head down and fold the arms in front at the waist. These actions move the scapula laterally and maximize the lung area that can be percussed (Figure 15-18).
    2. Percuss the right lung apex located along the top of the shoulder. Approximately three percussion strikes should be struck along this area.
    3. Repeat the process on the left lung apex.
    4. Note the sound produced from each percussion strike and compare the sounds from each. If different sounds are produced or if the sound is not resonant, then pathology is suggested.
    5. Move down approximately 5 cm, or every other ICS, and percuss in that area.

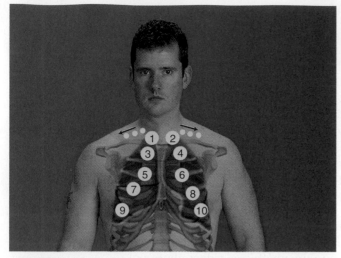

A. Anterior Thorax

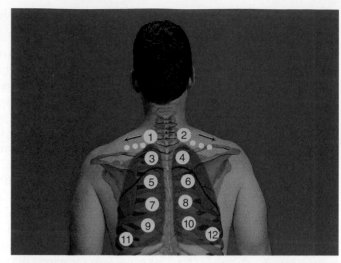

B. Posterior Thorax

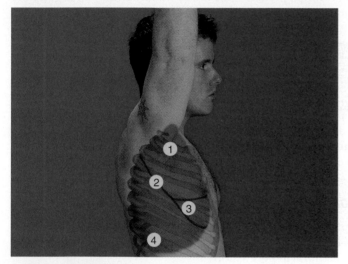

C. Right Lateral Thorax

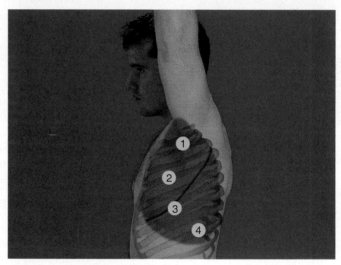

D. Left Lateral Thorax

Figure 15-17 Percussion Patterns.

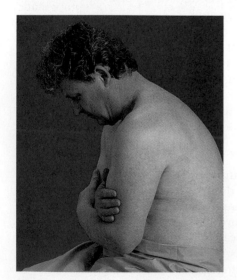

Figure 15-18 Patient Position for Posterior Percussion.

6. Percuss in the same position on the contralateral side.

7. Continue to move down the thorax until the entire posterior lung field has been percussed.

To perform lateral thoracic percussion:

E **1.** Place the patient in an upright sitting position, with arms raised directly overhead. This position allows for the greatest exposure of the thorax.

2. Either percuss the entire right lateral thorax and then the entire left lateral thorax, or alternate right and left sides. Start to percuss in the ICS directly below the axilla.

3. Note the sound produced from that strike.

4. Percuss approximately 5 cm below the original location, or about every other ICS.

5. Percuss down to the base of the lung.

N Normal lung tissue produces a resonant sound. The diaphragm and the cardiac silhouette emit dull sounds. Rib sounds are flat. Hyperresonance is normal in thin adults and in patients with decreased musculature.

A The presence of hyperresonance in the majority of adults is abnormal.

| E | Examination | N | Normal Findings | A | Abnormal Findings | P | Pathophysiology |

P Hyperresonance is percussed in air-filled spaces. It can be elicited in pneumothorax, emphysema, asthma, and an emphysematous bulla.

A The healthy human lung never produces a dull sound.

P Dullness is found in solid or fluid-filled structures. Pneumonia, atelectasis, pulmonary edema, pleural effusion, pulmonary fibrosis, hemothorax, empyema, and tumours are dull to percussion.

Diaphragmatic Excursion

Diaphragmatic excursion provides information on the patient's depth of ventilation by measuring the distance the diaphragm moves during inspiration and expiration (Figure 15-19).

To perform diaphragmatic excursion:

E 1. Position the patient for posterior thoracic percussion.
   2. With the patient breathing normally, percuss the right lung from the apex (resonance in healthy adults) to below the diaphragm (dull). Note the level at which the percussion note changes quality to orient your assessment to the patient's percussion sounds. If full posterior thoracic percussion has already been performed, then this step can be eliminated.
   3. Instruct the patient to inhale as deeply as possible and hold that breath.
   4. With the patient holding the breath, percuss the right lung in the scapular line from below the scapula to the location where resonance changes to dullness.
   5. Mark this location and tell the patient to exhale and breathe normally.
   6. When the patient has recovered, instruct the patient to inhale as deeply as possible, exhale fully, and hold the exhaled breath.
   7. Repercuss the right lung below the scapula in the scapular line in a caudal direction. Mark the spot where resonance changes to dullness.
   8. Measure the distance between the two marks.
   9. Repeat steps 1–8 for the left posterior thorax.

N The measured distance for diaphragmatic excursion is normally 3–5 cm. The level of the diaphragm on inspiration is T12, and T10 on expiration. The right side of the diaphragm is usually slightly higher than the left.

A A diaphragmatic excursion that is less than 3 cm is abnormal.

P Conditions involving hypoventilation, where the patient is unable to inhale deeply or hold that breath, can lead to a reduction in the diaphragmatic excursion. Pain, obesity, lung congestion, emphysema, asthma, and pleurisy are examples.

A A high diaphragm level suggests lung pathology.

P Surgical intervention can elevate the diaphragm. If a lower lobe lobectomy is performed, the diaphragm will move upward to partially fill the empty space. Likewise, after a pneumonectomy the paralyzed diaphragm will move upward, leading to a high diaphragm level.

P Space-occupying states such as ascites and pregnancy will lead to an elevated diaphragm due to the upward displacement of the lungs and diaphragm.

P If atelectasis or a pleural effusion is present in a lower lobe, then the diaphragm will seem abnormally high, because these conditions are dull to percussion as is the diaphragm. The border between the diaphragm and the dull lung will thus be indistinguishable.

Auscultation

The aim of respiratory auscultation is to identify the presence of normal breath sounds, abnormal lung sounds, adventitious (or added) lung sounds, and adventitious pleural sounds. The anterior, posterior, and lateral aspects of the chest are auscultated. A stethoscope is required for this assessment. If an acoustic stethoscope is used, the diaphragm, which transmits high-pitched sounds, is the headpiece of choice.

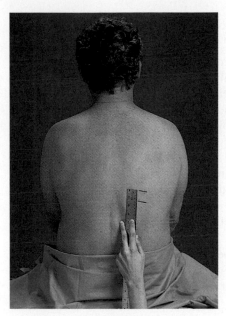

Figure 15-19 Diaphragmatic Excursion.

General Auscultation

To perform anterior thoracic auscultation:

E   1. Place the patient in an upright sitting position with the shoulders back.
    2. Instruct the patient to breathe only through the mouth. Mouth breathing, when compared to nasal breathing, decreases air turbulence and can interfere with the interpretation of breath sounds. Have the patient inhale and exhale deeply and slowly every time the stethoscope is felt or when instructed to do so.
    3. Place the stethoscope on the apex of the right lung and listen for one complete respiratory cycle (one inhalation and one exhalation).
    4. Note the sound that is auscultated.
    5. Repeat on the left apex.
    6. Note the breath sound auscultated in each area and compare one side to the other.
    7. Continue to move the stethoscope down approximately 5 cm, or every other ICS, comparing contralateral sides. Remember to visualize the anatomic topography of the chest during auscultation.

To perform posterior thoracic auscultation:

E   1. Place the patient in an upright sitting position with a slight forward tilt, head bent down, and arms folded in front at the waist (Figure 15-18). These actions move the scapula laterally and maximize the lung area that can be auscultated.
    2. Place the stethoscope firmly on the patient's right lung apex. Ask the patient to inhale and exhale deeply and slowly every time the stethoscope is felt on the back.
    3. Repeat this process on the left lung apex.
    4. Move the stethoscope down approximately 5 cm, or every other ICS, and auscultate in that area.
    5. Auscultate in the same position on the contralateral side.
    6. Continue to move inferiorly with the auscultation until the entire posterior lung has been assessed. See Figure 15-17 from the percussion section for the recommended stethoscope location for each auscultation.

To perform lateral thoracic auscultation:

E   1. Place the patient in an upright sitting position with the hands and arms directly overhead.
    2. Auscultate the entire right thorax first, then the entire left thorax, or auscultate the right and left lateral thoraxes by comparing side to side. The stethoscope should initially be placed in the ICS directly below the axilla.
    3. Instruct the patient to breathe only through the mouth. Have the patient inhale and exhale deeply and slowly every time the stethoscope is felt on the lateral thorax.
    4. Note the sound that is auscultated and continue to move the stethoscope inferiorly approximately every 5 cm, or every other ICS, until the entire thorax has been auscultated.

Breath Sounds

N   Air rushing through the respiratory tract during inspiration and expiration generates different breath sounds in the normal patient. There are three distinct types of normal breath sounds (Figure 15-20):
    1. Bronchial (or tubular)
    2. Bronchovesicular
    3. Vesicular

E	**Examination**	N	**Normal Findings**	A	**Abnormal Findings**	P	**Pathophysiology**

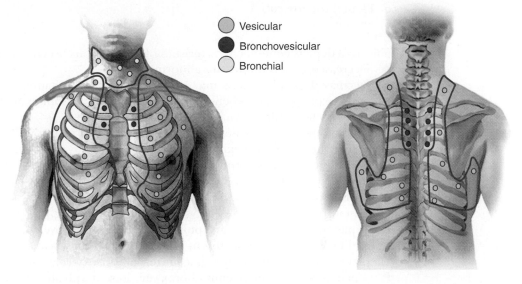

Vesicular
Bronchovesicular
Bronchial

A. Anterior Thorax

B. Posterior Thorax

Figure 15-20 Location of Breath Sounds.

Normal breath sounds are unique in their pitch, intensity, quality, relative duration in the inspiratory and expiratory phases of respiration, and location (Table 15-2). It is abnormal to auscultate these breath sounds in locations other than where they are usually found. For example, a patient with emphysema may have bronchial breath sounds in the peripheral lung parenchyma, where vesicular sounds are expected to be found. Also keep in mind that heart sounds may obscure some of the breath sounds during the anterior chest auscultation.

Breath sounds that are not normal can be classified as either abnormal or adventitious breath sounds. Abnormal breath sounds are characterized by decreased or absent breath sounds. **Adventitious breath sounds** are superimposed sounds on the normal bronchial, bronchovesicular, and vesicular breath sounds. There are six adventitious breath sounds:

1. Fine crackle
2. Coarse crackle
3. Sonorous wheeze
4. Sibilant wheeze

Nursing Tip

Upper Airway Sounds

If the patient has secretions in the oropharynx (upper airway), whether from allergies, infection, coryza, and so on, the patient's respirations may be loud and gurgling. It may sound as if the patient is having difficulty breathing. Ask the patient to clear the throat, then reassess the breath sounds.

TABLE 15-2	Characteristics of Normal Breath Sounds				
BREATH SOUND	PITCH	INTENSITY	QUALITY	RELATIVE DURATION OF INSPIRATORY AND EXPIRATORY PHASES	LOCATION
Bronchial	High	Loud	Blowing or hollow	I < E ⋀	Trachea
Bronchovesicular	Moderate	Moderate	Combination of bronchial and vesicular	I = E ⋀	Between scapulae, first and second ICS lateral to the sternum
Vesicular	Low	Soft	Gentle rustling or breezy	I > E ⋀	Peripheral lung

5. Pleural friction rub
6. Stridor

Table 15-3 depicts general characteristics of adventitious breath sounds.

A Decreased breath sounds are abnormal.

P Decreased breath sounds may be noted when auscultating a large chest because of the distance between the lungs, where the sounds are generated, and the chest wall.

P An emphysematous patient may have decreased breath sounds due to the inability to inhale and exhale deeply.

P Conditions such as bronchial obstruction and atelectasis may lead to decreased breath sounds because a foreign object or sputum occludes some portion of the respiratory tract, thus blocking the passage of air.

A Absent breath sounds are always a pathological finding.

P A pleural effusion, tumour, pulmonary fibrosis, empyema, hemothorax, and hydrothorax lead to absent breath sounds. These states occupy or displace normal aerating lung space internally or externally to the lungs.

P A patient with a large pneumothorax can present with absent breath sounds due to the collapse of the lung.

P Absent breath sounds occur when the lung has been removed (pneumonectomy).

P Blocked passageways in the respiratory tract explain the etiology for absent breath sounds in pulmonary edema, massive atelectasis, and complete airway obstruction.

Voice Sounds

The assessment of **voice sounds** will reveal whether the lungs are filled with air or fluid, or are solid. This auscultation need be performed only if an abnormality is detected during the general auscultation, percussion, or palpation. There are three techniques by which voice sounds can be assessed:

1. Bronchophony
2. Egophony
3. Whispered pectoriloquy

Only one of these techniques needs to be performed because they all provide the same information. The voice sound findings will parallel those obtained during tactile fremitus. Thus, voice sounds will be heard loudest over the trachea and softest in the lung's periphery.

To perform **bronchophony:**

E 1. Position the patient for posterior, lateral, or anterior chest auscultation. The area to be auscultated will be that in which an abnormality was found during percussion or palpation or in which adventitious breath sounds were heard.
2. Place the stethoscope in the appropriate location on the patient's chest.
3. Instruct the patient to say the words "99" or "1, 2, 3" every time the stethoscope is placed on the chest or when told to do so.
4. Auscultate the transmission of the patient's spoken word.

To perform **egophony:**

E 1. Repeat steps 1 and 2 from the bronchophony procedure.
2. Instruct the patient to say the sound "ee" every time the stethoscope is placed on the chest or when told to do so.
3. Auscultate the transmission of the patient's spoken word.

Advanced Technique

Forced Expiratory Time

Forced expiratory time is a gross measurement of the forced expiratory volume (FEV).

To perform this assessment:

E 1. Place your stethoscope over the patient's trachea.
2. Instruct the patient to inhale as deeply as possible and then exhale forcefully through the mouth (as if blowing out a candle).
3. Time the exhalation phase.

N Normal exhalation occurs in less than four seconds.

A The forced expiratory time is abnormal if it is greater than four seconds.

P Patients with COPD have a prolonged forced expiratory time and FEV because of the air trapping in the lungs. A complete exhalation is difficult to achieve.

E	Examination	N	Normal Findings	A	Abnormal Findings	P	Pathophysiology

TABLE 15-3 Characteristics of Adventitious Breath Sounds

BREATH SOUND	RESPIRATORY PHASE	TIMING	DESCRIPTION	CLEAR WITH COUGH	ETIOLOGY	CONDITIONS
Fine crackle (rale)	Predominantly inspiration	Discontinuous	Dry, high-pitched crackling, popping, short duration; roll hair near ears between your fingers to simulate this sound	No	Air passing through moisture in small airways that suddenly reinflate	COPD, congestive heart failure (CHF), pneumonia, pulmonary fibrosis, atelectasis
Coarse crackle (coarse rale)	Predominantly inspiration	Discontinuous	Moist, low-pitched crackling, gurgling; long duration	Possibly	Air passing through moisture in large airways that suddenly reinflate	Pneumonia, pulmonary edema, bronchitis, atelectasis
Sonorous wheeze (rhonchi)	Predominantly expiration	Continuous	Low pitched; snoring	Possibly	Narrowing of large airways or obstruction of bronchus	Asthma, bronchitis, airway edema, tumor, bronchiolar spasm, foreign body obstruction
Sibilant wheeze (wheeze)	Predominantly expiration	Continuous	High pitched; musical	Possibly	Narrowing of large airways or obstruction of bronchus	Asthma, chronic bronchitis, emphysema, tumor, foreign body obstruction
Pleural friction rub	Inspiration and expiration	Continuous	Creaking, grating	No	Inflamed parietal and visceral pleura; can occasionally be felt on thoracic wall as two pieces of dry leather rubbing against each other	Pleurisy, tuberculosis, pulmonary infarction, pneumonia, lung abscess
Stridor	Predominantly inspiration	Continuous	Crowing	No	Partial obstruction of the larynx, trachea	Croup, foreign body obstruction, large airway tumor

To perform **whispered pectoriloquy:**

E 1. Repeat steps 1 and 2 from the bronchophony procedure.
2. Instruct the patient to whisper the words "99" or "1, 2, 3" every time the stethoscope is placed on the chest or when told to do so.
3. Auscultate the transmission of the patient's spoken word.

N **The normal finding when performing tests for bronchophony, egophony, and whispered pectoriloquy is an unclear transmission or muffled sounds.**

A Positive (or present) voice sounds are:
Bronchophony: clear transmission of "99" or "1, 2, 3" with increased intensity.
Egophony: transformation of "ee" to "ay" with increased intensity; the voice has a nasal or bleating quality.
Whispered pectoriloquy: clear transmission of "99" or "1, 2, 3" with increased intensity.

P Any type of consolidation process, such as pneumonia, will produce positive voice sounds. Remember that sound is transmitted reasonably well by a fluid medium.

A Voice sounds are absent or even more decreased than in the normal lung in conditions where the lung is more air filled than usual.

P Air conducts sound poorly. Therefore, air-filled lungs (emphysema, asthma, pneumothorax) will produce absent voice sounds (Figure 15-21).

Table 15-4 compares physical assessment findings for 12 respiratory conditions.

GERONTOLOGICAL VARIATIONS

The aging patient undergoes changes that involve the external and internal anatomy of the thorax and lungs and that affect the respiratory process. As a result, the physiology of the respiratory system also becomes altered. The resulting state of the patient depends on the extent of the changes and the condition of the body prior to these changes. The gerontological variations of the respiratory system include four broad areas:

1. Anatomic changes
2. Alveolar gas exchange
3. Regulation of ventilation
4. Lung defense mechanisms

Older adults experience degeneration of the intervertebral discs, stiffening of ligaments and joints, and calcification of the costochondral cartilage, all of which limit chest wall expansion during the respiratory cycle. Muscles atrophy and the diaphragm flattens out. Collectively, these changes make respiratory effort more difficult for the older patient. Strenuous exercise is taxing secondary to decreased oxygen uptake and decreased elastic recoil of the lung parenchyma. Most older adults will have barrel chest and some kyphosis. Forced vital capacity decreases, residual volume and functional residual capacity increase, and total lung capacity remains unchanged.

The second major change in the gerontological population is the alveolar gas exchange. The lung's decreased elastic recoil causes the closure of the airways for a portion of the respiratory cycle, particularly in the lower lobes of the lungs. As a result, the apices and the bases of the lower lobes have a ventilation–perfusion mismatch. Loss of lung tissue and alveolar capillaries, and pulmonary wall thickening also contribute to loss of alveolar gas exchange. In essence, this creates a situation in which there is less surface area for diffusion, and this surface area

---

Nursing Tip

Preventing Respiratory Complications

To minimize respiratory complications, instruct the older adult to:

- Avoid large crowds, especially in enclosed areas, if ill.
- Obtain annual influenza immunization.
- Obtain pneumococcal immunization (for most people, a single vaccination is adequate for lifetime protection).
- Chew food completely and do not talk while eating.
- Avoid eating in a supine position (if possible).
- Avoid strenuous exercise if not part of normal activity.

E **Examination** N **Normal Findings** A **Abnormal Findings** P **Pathophysiology**

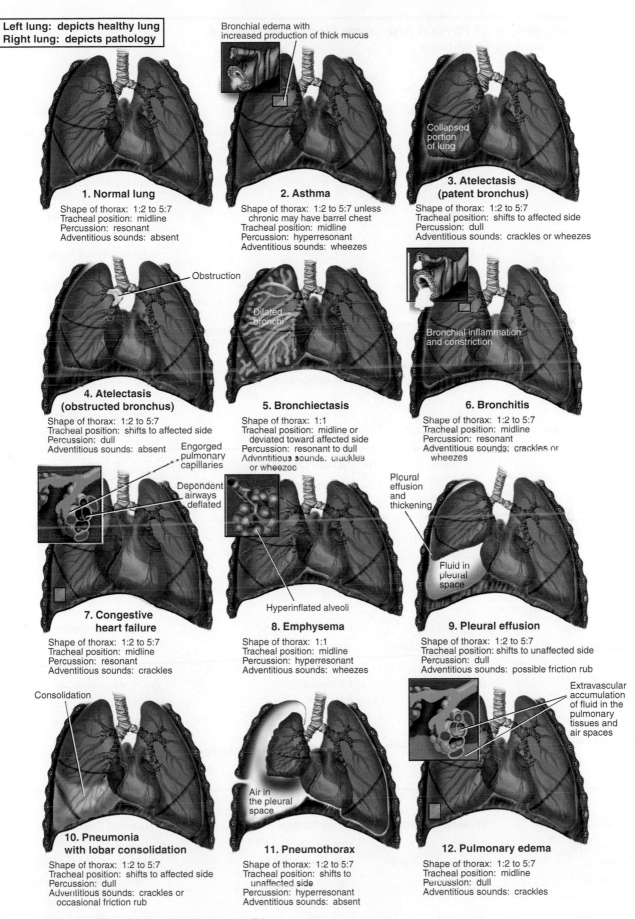

Left lung: depicts healthy lung
Right lung: depicts pathology

Bronchial edema with increased production of thick mucus

Collapsed portion of lung

1. Normal lung

Shape of thorax: 1:2 to 5:7
Tracheal position: midline
Percussion: resonant
Adventitious sounds: absent

2. Asthma

Shape of thorax: 1:2 to 5:7 unless chronic may have barrel chest
Tracheal position: midline
Percussion: hyperresonant
Adventitious sounds: wheezes

3. Atelectasis (patent bronchus)

Shape of thorax: 1:2 to 5:7
Tracheal position: shifts to affected side
Percussion: dull
Adventitious sounds: crackles or wheezes

Obstruction

Dilated bronchi

Bronchial inflammation and constriction

4. Atelectasis (obstructed bronchus)

Shape of thorax: 1:2 to 5:7
Tracheal position: shifts to affected side
Percussion: dull
Adventitious sounds: absent

5. Bronchiectasis

Shape of thorax: 1:1
Tracheal position: midline or deviated toward affected side
Percussion: resonant to dull
Adventitious sounds: crackles or wheezes

6. Bronchitis

Shape of thorax: 1:2 to 5:7
Tracheal position: midline
Percussion: resonant
Adventitious sounds: crackles or wheezes

Engorged pulmonary capillaries

Dependent airways deflated

Hyperinflated alveoli

Pleural effusion and thickening

Fluid in pleural space

7. Congestive heart failure

Shape of thorax: 1:2 to 5:7
Tracheal position: midline
Percussion: resonant
Adventitious sounds: crackles

8. Emphysema

Shape of thorax: 1:1
Tracheal position: midline
Percussion: hyperresonant
Adventitious sounds: wheezes

9. Pleural effusion

Shape of thorax: 1:2 to 5:7
Tracheal position: shifts to unaffected side
Percussion: dull
Adventitious sounds: possible friction rub

Consolidation

Air in the pleural space

Extravascular accumulation of fluid in the pulmonary tissues and air spaces

10. Pneumonia with lobar consolidation

Shape of thorax: 1:2 to 5:7
Tracheal position: shifts to affected side
Percussion: dull
Adventitious sounds: crackles or occasional friction rub

11. Pneumothorax

Shape of thorax: 1:2 to 5:7
Tracheal position: shifts to unaffected side
Percussion: hyperresonant
Adventitious sounds: absent

12. Pulmonary edema

Shape of thorax: 1:2 to 5:7
Tracheal position: midline
Percussion: dull
Adventitious sounds: crackles

Figure 15-21 Comparison of Selected Respiratory Conditions.

TABLE 15-4 Comparison of Physical Assessment Findings in Selected Respiratory Conditions

INSPECTION

Condition	Skin Color: Shape of Thorax	Lips and Nails	Clubbing, Angle of Ribs
A. Normal lung	1:2 to 5:7	Pink in light-skinned individuals; darker than normal in dark-skinned individuals	No clubbing, rib angle 45°
B. Asthma	If chronic, may have barrel chest	Pale or cyanotic in acute attack	No clubbing, rib angle 45°
C. Atelectasis (patent bronchus)	1:2 to 5:7	Pale or cyanotic	No clubbing, rib angle 45°
D. Atelectasis (obstructed bronchus)	1:2 to 5:7	Pale or cyanotic	No clubbing, rib angle 45°
E. Bronchiectasis	1:1 (barrel chest)	Pale or cyanotic if severe	Clubbing possible, rib angle >45°
F. Bronchitis	1:2 to 5:7	Possibly pale	No clubbing, rib angle 45°
G. Congestive heart failure	1:2 to 5:7	Pale or cyanotic	Clubbing possible, rib angle 45°
H. Emphysema	1:1 (barrel chest)	Pale	Clubbing, rib angle >45°
I. Pleural effusion	1:2 to 5:7	Pale or cyanotic	No clubbing, rib angle 45°
J. Pneumonia with lobar consolidation	1:2 to 5:7	Pale or cyanotic	No clubbing, rib angle 45°
K. Pneumothorax	1:2 to 5:7	Pale or cyanotic	No clubbing, rib angle 45°
L. Pulmonary edema	1:2 to 5:7	Pale or cyanotic	No clubbing, rib angle 45°

INSPECTION continued

Condition	Capillary Refill	Retractions or Bulging of ICS	Respiratory Rate
A. Normal lung	Brisk	Absent	12–20/min eupnea
B. Asthma	Sluggish in acute attack	Retractions	>20/min tachypnea
C. Atelectasis (patent bronchus)	Sluggish to moderate	Absent	>20/min tachypnea
D. Atelectasis (obstructed bronchus)	Sluggish	Absent	>20/min tachypnea
E. Bronchiectasis	Sluggish if severe	Retractions if severe	>20/min tachypnea
F. Bronchitis	Sluggish to moderate	Absent	>20/min tachypnea
G. Congestive heart failure	Sluggish	Retractions	>20/min tachypnea
H. Emphysema	Sluggish	Both present	>20/min tachypnea
I. Pleural effusion	Sluggish	Bulging	>20/min tachypnea
J. Pneumonia with lobar consolidation	Sluggish	Absent	>20/min tachypnea
K. Pneumothorax	Sluggish	Bulging	>20/min tachypnea
L. Pulmonary edema	Sluggish	Absent	>20/min tachypnea

PALPATION

Condition	Thoracic Expansion	Tactile Fremitus	Tracheal Position
A. Normal lung	3–5 cm	Moderate (normal)	Midline
B. Asthma	Decreased in attack	Decreased	Midline
C. Atelectasis (patent bronchus)	Decreased	Increased	Shifts to affected side
D. Atelectasis (obstructed bronchus)	Decreased	Increased	Shifts to affected side

TABLE 15-4   Comparison of Physical Assessment Findings in Selected Respiratory Conditions   *continued*

PALPATION *continued*

Condition	Thoracic Expansion	Tactile Fremitus	Tracheal Position
E. Bronchiectasis	Decreased on affected side	Increased	Midline or deviated toward affected side
F. Bronchitis	Possibly decreased	Moderate or increased	Midline
G. Congestive heart failure	May be decreased	Moderate	Midline
H. Emphysema	Decreased	Decreased	Midline
I. Pleural effusion	Decreased	Decreased	Shifts to unaffected side
J. Pneumonia with lobar consolidation	Decreased	Increased	Shifts to affected side
K. Pneumothorax	Decreased	Absent or decreased	Shifts to unaffected side
L. Pulmonary edema	Decreased	Increased	Midline

PERCUSSION

Condition	General Percussion	Diaphragmatic Excursion
A. Normal lung	Resonant	3–5 cm
B. Asthma	Hyperresonant	Decreased
C. Atelectasis (patent bronchus)	Dull	Decreased
D. Atelectasis (obstructed bronchus)	Dull	Decreased
E. Bronchiectasis	Resonant to dull	Decreased
F. Bronchitis	Resonant	Decreased if severe
G. Congestive heart failure	Resonant	Decreased
H. Emphysema	Hyperresonant	Decreased
I. Pleural effusion	Dull	Decreased
J. Pneumonia with lobar consolidation	Dull	Decreased
K. Pneumothorax	Hyperresonant	Decreased
L. Pulmonary edema	Dull	Decreased

AUSCULTATION

Condition	Breath Sounds	Adventitious Sounds	Voice Sounds
A. Normal lung	Vesicular in periphery	Absent	Muffled
B. Asthma	Decreased or absent in severe obstruction	Wheezes	Decreased
C. Atelectasis (patent bronchus)	Bronchial	Crackles or wheezes	Increased or muffled
D. Atelectasis (obstructed bronchus)	Absent or decreased	Absent	Absent or muffled
E. Bronchiectasis	Vesicular or bronchial if severe	Crackles or wheezes	Muffled or decreased
F. Bronchitis	Vesicular or bronchial	Crackles or wheezes	Increased or muffled
G. Congestive heart failure	Vesicular	Crackles	Muffled
H. Emphysema	Bronchial and decreased	Wheezes	Decreased
I. Pleural effusion	Absent or decreased	Possible friction rub	Decreased or absent
J. Pneumonia with lobar consolidation	Bronchial	Crackles or occasional friction rub	Increased
K. Pneumothorax	Absent or decreased	Absent	Decreased or absent
L. Pulmonary edema	Absent or decreased	Crackles	Increased

is thicker. In addition, hemoglobin's affinity for oxygen decreases, which leads to a decrease in the partial pressure of oxygen.

Third, the aging patient experiences changes in the regulation of ventilation. The medulla is less sensitive to changes in carbon dioxide and oxygen levels that normally trigger the respiratory apparatus. Neural output to respiratory muscles is decreased. Both peripheral and central chemoreceptors are affected.

The last area of gerontological variation is in lung defense mechanisms. There is less ciliary activity, which increases susceptibility to infection. The cough reflex decreases. The risk of aspiration increases with this weakened defense mechanism.

CASE STUDY The Patient with Pneumonia

The case study illustrates the application and objective documentation of the thorax and lungs assessment.

Bill Victor comes to the clinic after not breathing well for a few days this winter.

HEALTH HISTORY

PATIENT PROFILE	54 yo man who looks tired, in no acute distress
HEALTH ISSUE/CONCERN	"It's getting worse. I keep coughing and can't catch my breath."
HISTORY OF ISSUE/CONCERN	Pt was in usual state of hl until 1 wk ago; was cleaning out basement that had suffered water damage from recent flooding; started to feel "winded" going up steps; 2 d later could only make it half way up steps when he needed to stop to catch his breath; sleeping on 2 pillows at night; congested cough started 4 d ago; reports sm amt of blood-tinged green sputum; diaphoretic at rest & c̄ coughing; musical sound coming from lungs when he gets very SOB; feels he has a fever but has never taken temp; has been taking some cough medicine (type?) s̄ relief; pt is concerned b/c his mother died from pneumonia when she was 57 yo.
PAST HEALTH HISTORY	
Medical History	HTN × 10 yrs; takes BP wkly on home machine (no recent calibration); denies h/o asthma, bronchitis frequent colds
Surgical History	T & A age 4
Medications	Hydrochlorothiazide (HCTZ) 25 mg po daily
Communicable Diseases	Denies TB exposure; ≠ recall having PPD skin test
Allergies	NKDA
Injuries and Accidents	"Nothing major"
Special Needs	Denies
Blood Transfusions	Denies
Childhood Illnesses	Does not remember any
Immunizations	Believes he had childhood vaccines; no influenza or pneumococcal vaccines

FAMILY HEALTH HISTORY

LEGEND

 Living female

 Living male

 Deceased female

 Deceased male

⟋ Points to patient

CA = Cancer

AR = Allergic rhinitis

A&W = Alive & well

HI = Health

HTN = Hypertension

IBS = Irritable bowel syndrome

MI = Myocardial infarction

MVA = Motor vehicle accident

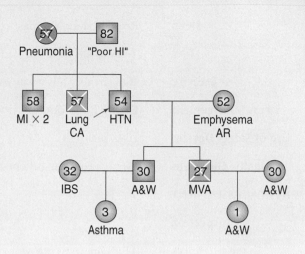

Denies family hx of cystic fibrosis, TB, allergies, bronchiectasis, sarcoidosis.

SOCIAL HISTORY	
Alcohol Use	2–3 beers q Fri/Sat
Drug Use	Denies
Tobacco Use	Smoked 1 PPD for 10 yrs; quit 24 yrs ago
Domestic and Intimate Partner Violence	Denies
Sexual Practice	Deferred
Travel History	Goes to Maritimes to visit family twice a year
Work Environment	Electrician
Home Environment	Lives in 2-floor suburban house
Hobbies and Leisure Activities	Plays guitar, volunteers at local nursing home
Stress and Coping	Worries about his grandchildren as his 2 sons are struggling financially; talks about problems with wife & friends.
Education	Technical college
Economic Status	"I'm OK but I might run into problems if I keep having to bail my kids out!"
Religion/Spirituality	Roman Catholic
Ethnicity	"I'm a displaced Maritimer!"
Roles and Relationships	"Happily" married 32 yrs; children & grandchildren live nearby—visit wkly
Characteristic Patterns of Daily Living	Deferred

continues

HEATH MAINTENANCE ACTIVITIES	
Sleep	Restless sleep the past couple of nights
Diet	Tries to eat well. No added salt, balanced meat/vegetables/fruit/grains.
Exercise	"On my feet all day at work."
Stress Management	Eating junk food, playing cards
Use of Safety Devices	Uses seat belt
Health Check-ups	Twice a year for BP check and medication renewal.
PHYSICAL ASSESSMENT	
Inspection	
Shape of Thorax	AP diameter/transverse diameter = 5:7, $\ominus$ barrel chest/pectus carinatum/pectus excavatum/kyphoscoliosis
Symmetry of Chest Wall	Shoulder & scapula ht =; Ø masses
Presence of Superficial Veins	Ø
Costal Angle	<90°
Angle of the Ribs	45° c̄ sternum
Intercostal Spaces	Ø bulging/retractions
Muscles of Respiration	Minimal use of SCM muscles
Respirations	Rate: 28/min, Pattern: reg Depth: shallow Symmetry: no paradoxical mvt Audibility: heard upon entering room Patient position: sitting upright Mode of breathing: predominantly mouth
Sputum	Blood-tinged dark yellow
Palpation	
General Palpation	Pulsations: Ø Masses: Ø Thoracic tenderness: Ø Crepitus: Ø
Thoracic Expansion	Ant expansion 3.5 cm c̄ ↓ mvt on Ⓛ; post expansion 2.5 cm c̄ Ø mvt on Ⓛ
Tactile Fremitus	↑ Post thorax from Ⓛ base to mid-back
Tracheal Position	Sl deviated to Ⓛ
Percussion	
General Percussion	Dullness post thorax from Ⓛ base to mid-back; dullness ant thorax Ⓛ base
Diaphragmatic Excursion	Unable to hold breath

Auscultation	
General Auscultation	Bronchial over trachea, bronchovesicular b/t scapula, ↓ vesicular Ⓛbase ant & post thorax; coarse crackles that clear c̄ coughing in post LLL; exp wheezing post LUL/LLL
Voice Sounds	⊕ Bronchophony post LLL
Assistive Devices	Pulse Oximeter: 92–94% (nl = 97–99%) Peak flow meter: 260 mL, 310 mL, 230 mL (predicted value = 556 cc based on sex, ht, & age)
DIAGNOSTIC DATA	
Chest X-ray	General impression: no previous film with which to compare. Consolidation of LLL with mild linear scarring in the posterior aspect of the LLL. The heart size is WNL. There are no pleural effusions.

◄NURSING CHECKLIST►

Thorax and Lung Assessment

Inspection
- Shape of thorax
- Symmetry of chest wall
- Presence of superficial veins
- Costal angle
- Angle of the ribs
- Intercostal spaces
- Muscles of respiration
- Respirations
  – Rate
  – Pattern
  – Depth
  – Symmetry
  – Audibility
  – Patient position
  – Mode of breathing
- Sputum

Palpation
- General palpation
  – Pulsations
  – Masses
  – Thoracic tenderness
  – Crepitus
- Thoracic expansion
- Tactile fremitus
- Tracheal position

Percussion
- General percussion
- Diaphragmatic excursion

Auscultation
- General auscultation
- Breath sounds
- Voice sounds

Advanced Techniques
- Forced expiratory time

Assistive Devices
- Oxygen
- Incentive spirometer
- Endotracheal tube
- Tracheostomy tube
- Mechanical ventilation
- Pulse oximeter
- Peak flow meter

REVIEW QUESTIONS

Questions 1 and 2 refer to the following situation:

A patient is admitted to the emergency department with SOB after blunt trauma to the thorax that resulted from an assault. Physical examination revealed a possible fracture to the left 10th rib.

1. The 10th rib is also referred to as a:
   a. True rib
   b. Vertebrosternal rib
   c. False rib
   d. Floating rib
   The correct answer is (c).

2. On further examination you palpate beads of air over the anterior thorax. This assessment finding is called:
   a. Crepitus
   b. Thoracic tenderness
   c. Dermal emphysema
   d. Pulmonary nodule
   The correct answer is (a).

3. While conducting an assessment of the thorax and lungs you ask the patient to flex the neck forward as you palpate the spinous process in this area. The superior process that you palpate is called the:
   a. Suprasternal notch
   b. Angle of Louis
   c. Costal angle
   d. Vertebra prominens
   The correct answer is (d).

4. During inspection you note that the patient's costal angle is 85°. This patient has:
   a. A normal finding
   b. Bronchiectasis
   c. Pneumonia
   d. Pneumothorax
   The correct answer is (a).

5. You might expect an unconscious drunk patient to have which respiratory rate?
   a. Eupnea
   b. Tachypnea
   c. Bradypnea
   d. Apnea
   The correct answer is (c).

6. Which palpation finding would you expect to find in atelectasis of the left lung?
   a. Tracheal deviation to the left
   b. Low diaphragm level
   c. Absent tactile fremitus
   d. Increased thoracic expansion
   The correct answer is (a).

7. While performing diaphragmatic excursion, you measure a distance of 4 cm. This finding suggests:
   a. A normal distance
   b. High diaphragm level
   c. Hypoventilation
   d. Pneumonectomy
   The correct answer is (a).

8. A breath sound that is low in pitch, soft in intensity, and has an inspiratory component that is longer than its expiratory component is called:
   a. Bronchial
   b. Tubular
   c. Bronchovesicular
   d. Vesicular
   The correct answer is (d).

9. In which condition might you expect to find dull lung percussion and possibly a friction rub?
   a. Asthma
   b. Pulmonary edema
   c. Pleural effusion
   d. Pneumothorax
   The correct answer is (c).

10. During bronchophony you hear a clear transmission of "99." In which condition might this occur?
    a. Asthma
    b. Pneumothorax
    c. Pneumonia
    d. Emphysema
    The correct answer is (c).

Visit the Estes online companion resource at www.healthassessment.nelson.com for additional content and study aids.

REFERENCES

[1] Public Health Agency of Canada. (2004). *Tuberculosis in Canada 2002.* Health Canada: Ottawa: Canada.

[2] Ibid.

[3] Health Canada—Public Health Agency. *Infection control precautions for respiratory infections transmitted by large droplet and contact: Infection control guidelines in a non-outbreak setting.* Retrieved October 19, 2006, from http://www.phac-aspc.gc.ca/sars-sras/pdf/sars-icg-nonoutbreak_e.pdf

[4] Ibid.

[5] Manser, R. L., Irving, L. B., Stone, C., Byrnes, G., Abramson, M., & Campbell, D. (2003). Screening for lung cancer. *The Cochrane Database of Systematic Reviews,* Issue 1. Art. No.: CD001991.

[6] Canadian Food Inspection Agency. *Avian influenza.* Retrieved from http://www.inspection.gc.ca/english/anima/heasan/disemala/avflu/avflufse.shtml

[7] Ibid.

[8] Langley, J. M., Faughnan, M. E., & the Canadian Task Force on Preventive Health Care. Prevention of influenza in the general population: Recommendation statement from the Canadian Task Force on Preventive Health Care. *Canadian Medical Association Journal, 171,* 1169–70.

[9] Canadian Cancer Society/National Cancer Institute of Canada. (2006). *Canadian cancer statistics 2006.* Toronto, Canada.

[10] Public Health Agency of Canada. (2004). *Progress report on cancer control in Canada.* Ottawa: Health Canada.

BIBLIOGRAPHY

Boulet, L.-P., Bai, T. R., Becker, A., et al. (2001). What is new since the last (1999) Canadian asthma consensus guidelines? *Canadian Respiratory Journal, 8* (Suppl A): 5A–27A.

Fraser, R. S., Muller, N. L., Colman, N., Muller, N. L., & Pare, P. D. (2005). *Synopsis of diseases of the chest* (3rd ed.). Philadelphia: Saunders.

Hendrick, D., Beckett, W., Burge, S. P., & Churg, A. (2002). *Occupational disorders of the lung.* Philadelphia: Saunders.

Kacmarek, R. M., Dimas, S., & Mack, C. W. (2005). *The essentials of respiratory care.* St. Louis, MO: Elsevier Mosby.

Kleinman, A., & Watson, J. L. (Eds.) (2006). *SARS in China: Prelude to pandemic?* Stanford, CA: Stanford University Press.

Registered Nurses' Association of Ontario. (2005). *Nursing care of dyspnea: The 6th vital sign in individuals with chronic obstructive pulmonary disease (COPD).* Toronto: Registered Nurses' Association of Ontario

WEB RESOURCES

Asthma in Canada
http://www.asthmaincanada.com/

Canadian COPD Alliance
http://www.lung.ca/CCA/

Canadian Council for Tobacco Control
http://www.cctc.ca/index_html?set_language=en&cl=en

Canadian Lung Association
http://www.lung.ca/

SARS—Public Health Agency of Canada
http://www.phac-aspc.gc.ca/sars-sras/index.html

Public Health Agency of Canada—Respiratory Infections (Information for Health Professionals)
http://www.phac-aspc.gc.ca/sars-sras/prof_e.html

R.A.L.E. Repository (website offering lung sounds)
http://www.rale.ca/

NEL

CHAPTER 16

Heart and Peripheral Vasculature

COMPETENCIES

1. Identify the anatomic landmarks of the chest and periphery.

2. Describe the characteristics of the most common cardiovascular issues or concerns.

3. Elicit a health history from a patient with cardiovascular pathology.

4. Perform a cardiovascular assessment on a healthy adult.

5. Perform a cardiovascular assessment on a patient with cardiovascular pathology.

6. Provide scientific rationale for abnormal cardiovascular assessment findings.

7. Describe the changes that occur in the cardiovascular system in the elderly.

*T*he heart's primary function is to pump blood to all parts of the body. The circulating blood not only brings oxygen and nutrients to the body's tissues but also helps to take away the body's waste products. The body's activities determine the amount of blood that is pumped. The heart will beat faster or slower and the blood vessels will expand or relax in order to properly distribute the blood that the body demands.

ANATOMY AND PHYSIOLOGY

Heart

In a resting, healthy adult, the heart contracts 60 to 100 times while pumping four to five litres of blood per minute. The human heart is only about the size of a clenched fist and is remarkably efficient considering its size in relation to the rest of the body.

The heart is located in the thoracic cavity between the lungs and above the diaphragm in an area known as the mediastinum (Figure 16-1). The **base** of the heart is the uppermost portion, which includes the left and right atria as well as the aorta, pulmonary arteries, and the superior and inferior venae cavae. These structures lie behind the upper portion of the sternum. The **apex,** or lower portion of the heart, extends into the left thoracic cavity, causing the heart to appear as if it is lying on its right ventricle.

Pericardium

The heart and roots of the great vessels lie within a sac called the pericardium, which is composed of fibrous and serous layers. The fibrous layer is the outermost

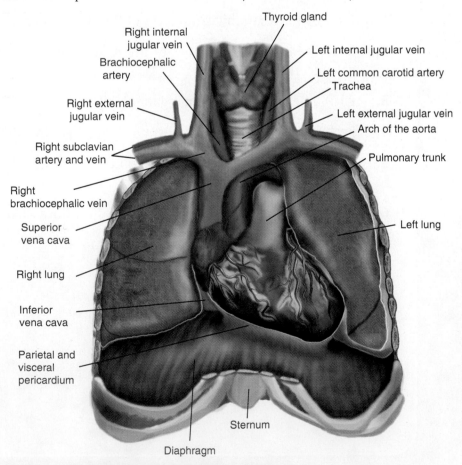

Figure 16-1 Position of the Heart in the Thoracic Cavity.

layer and is connected to the diaphragm and sternum by ligaments and tendons. Its major role is to limit the stretching of the myocardial muscle, especially during strenuous activity or hypervolemia.

There are two serous layers of the pericardium: the **parietal** layer, which lies close to the fibrous tissues, and the **visceral** layer, which lies against the actual heart muscle. This visceral layer is often referred to as the epicardium. Between the two serous layers is a small space that contains approximately 20 to 50 mL of pericardial fluid. This pericardial fluid serves to facilitate the movement of the heart muscle and protect it via its lubricant effect.

Chambers of the Heart

The heart is divided into four chambers, which are separated laterally by walls known as the vertical **septa.** These vertical septa divide the heart into the right and the left atria (interatrial septum) and the right and the left ventricles (interventricular septum). The right atrium is the collection point for the blood returning from the systemic circulation for reoxygenation in the lungs. The left atrium receives its freshly oxygenated blood via the four pulmonary veins, which are the only veins in the body that carry oxygenated blood. The walls of the left ventricle are three times thicker than those of the right ventricle because of its greater workload as it pumps blood through the high-pressure systemic arterial system. Left ventricular pressures are five times greater than those in the right ventricle. Figure 16-2 shows the configuration of the heart's chambers, the pressures, and normal oxygen content of the blood contained therein.

Heart Valves

As blood empties into the two atria, the **atrioventricular (A-V) valves** prevent it from prematurely entering the ventricles. The A-V valve between the right atrium and the right ventricle is known as the tricuspid valve, named for its three flaps or cusps. The A-V valve between the left atrium and the left ventricle is the bicuspid valve, named for its two flaps or cusps; it is commonly known as the mitral valve. When the tricuspid and mitral valves are closed, blood cannot flow from the atria into the ventricles. In a normal heart, they open only as atrial pressures increase with progressive filling.

The semilunar valves are also known as outflow valves because blood exits the heart through them. Blood flows from the right ventricle to the pulmonary vasculature for oxygenation by way of the pulmonic valve. Blood is pumped from the left ventricle into the systemic and coronary circulation through the aortic valve.

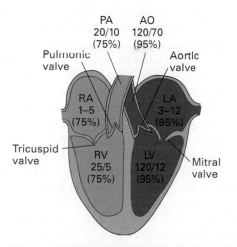

Figure 16-2 The Configuration, Normal Pressures, and Oxygen Content of the Heart Chambers.

Legend:
AO = Aorta
PA = Pulmonary artery
RA = Right atrium
LA = Left atrium
RV = Right ventricle
LV = Left ventricle
% = O_2 content
Numbers = Normal cardiac pressures in mm Hg

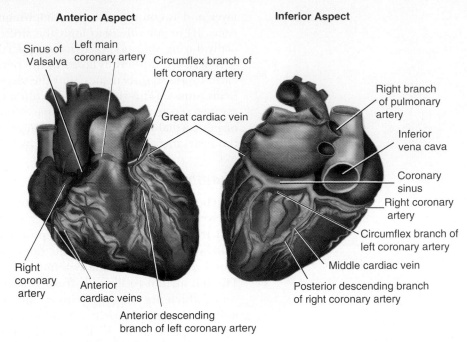

Figure 16-3 The Coronary Arteries and Major Veins of the Heart (Anterior and Inferior Views).

Coronary Circulation

The exterior surface of the heart muscle contains a critical and intricate blood supply. Two major coronary arteries arise from the small openings in the aorta known as the sinuses of Valsalva, located just behind the aortic valve. Figure 16-3 demonstrates the position of the coronary arteries as they exit from the aorta to cover the myocardium with an arterial network. The left and right coronary arteries run superficially across the heart muscle, but the smaller branches of these two main arteries actually penetrate deeply into the myocardium, carrying with them a nutritious blood supply. Blood flow to the coronary arteries is greatest during diastole because the force of the ventricular contraction during systole actually impedes flow through the sinuses of Valsalva.

The myocardium is extremely dependent on a constant supply of oxygen that is delivered through the coronary arterial system. The heart's oxygen requirements increase when it is stimulated by conditions such as exercise. If the coronary blood supply is not sufficient to meet the needs of the heart, the result may be **ischemia** (local and temporary lack of blood supply to the heart), injury (beyond ischemia but still reversible), or an **infarction** (necrosis) of the heart muscle itself. Myocardial ischemia is often manifested as chest, neck, or arm pain known as **angina pectoris.**

The left main coronary artery branches into the left circumflex coronary artery and the left anterior descending (LAD) coronary artery. Any obstruction to blood flow prior to the branch point of the left main coronary artery can be lethal.

The LAD supplies blood to the anterior wall and apex of the left ventricle as well as to the anterior portion of the interventricular septum. The smaller arterial branches that supply the septum also nourish the ventricular conduction system, including the bundle of his and the right and left bundle branches. The left circumflex (LCX) branch supplies arterial blood to the left atrium and to the lateral and posterior portions of the left ventricle. In some individuals, the sinoatrial (S-A) node and the A-V node are also supplied by this branch.

The right coronary artery (RCA) supplies nutrients and oxygen to the right atrium, the right ventricle, and the inferior wall of the left ventricle. In most individuals, the RCA supplies the S-A and the A-V nodes as well as the posterior portion of the interventricular septum. In inferior wall infarction, the RCA is most likely the vessel that has been occluded. In anterior wall infarction, the LAD branch is the most likely source of occlusion with resulting complications in the ventricular conduction system, such as bundle branch blocks or ventricular dysrhythmias.

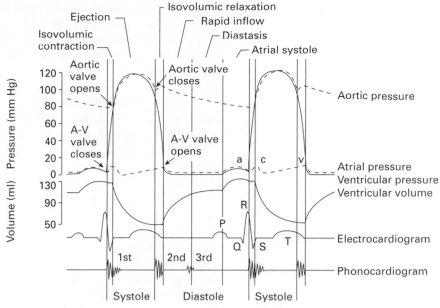

Figure 16-4 Events of the Cardiac Cycle.

Reproduced with permission from *Textbook of Medical Physiology* (11th ed.), by A. C. Guyton and J. E. Hall, 2006, Philadelphia: W. B. Saunders Company.

Venous drainage from the myocardium is carried by the coronary sinus, anterior cardiac veins, and thebesian veins. About 75% of the venous blood empties into the right atrium via the coronary sinus. The thebesian veins carry only a small portion of the unoxygenated blood that is emptied directly into all four chambers of the heart.

Cardiac Cycle

Figure 16-4 illustrates the electrical and mechanical events in the heart. Physical assessment findings can be correlated with these electrophysiological mechanisms.

The cardiac cycle consists of two phases: systole and diastole. In **systole,** the myocardial fibres contract and tighten to eject blood from the ventricles (for the purpose of this chapter, any mention of systole will mean ventricular systole unless specifically called atrial systole). **Diastole** is a period of relaxation and reflects the pressure remaining in the blood vessels after the heart has pumped.

Systole is divided into three phases, beginning with the isovolumic (or isometric) contraction phase, which marks the onset of a ventricular contraction. During this phase, the pressure is increasing but no blood is entering or leaving the ventricle. As the pressure rises in the left ventricle, the mitral valve closes (similar events occur in the right ventricle with the tricuspid valve). Closure of these A-V valves produces the first heart sound, known as S_1 (depicted as "1st" on the phonocardiogram [a recording of the heart sounds] curve in Figure 16-4).

Once the pressure in the left ventricle exceeds that in the aorta, and the pressure in the right ventricle exceeds that in the pulmonary artery, the semilunar (aortic and pulmonic) valves open, and blood is rapidly ejected. This rapid ejection phase is also referred to as early systole. It is followed by a third phase of reduced ejection, which is known as late systole.

Ventricular diastole begins with the isovolumic, or isometric, relaxation phase. During this phase, ventricular ejection ceases and the pressure in the left ventricle is reduced to less than that in the aorta. This permits a backflow of blood from the aorta to the left ventricle, causing the aortic valve to close (similar events occur in the pulmonary artery to cause the pulmonic valve to close). The closure of the semilunar valves produces the second heart sound, known as S_2 (depicted as "2nd" on the phonocardiogram curve in Figure 16-4). When the A-V and semilunar valves are closed, the pressure in the left ventricle falls rapidly.

Atrial pressures then rise as a result of the large amount of blood accumulating in the atria because of the closed A-V valves. When systole is over and the ventricular pressures fall, the high pressure in the atria forces the A-V valves to open to allow for rapid ventricular filling (rapid inflow) during early diastole. Filling then slows during a phase called diastasis or mid-diastole. Seventy percent of ventricular filling occurs in a passive manner during these early and mid-diastolic filling periods.

The final phase of diastole is known as atrial systole. The atria contract to complete the remaining 20% to 30% of ventricular filling, which is often referred to as **atrial kick.** After atrial systole, the cardiac cycle starts all over again.

The **electrocardiogram (ECG)** in Figure 16-4 shows the P, Q, R, S, and T waves. These waves are electrical voltages produced by the heart and recorded by ECG leads placed on the body. When the atria depolarize, the P wave is produced on the ECG. During this period, the pressure in the atria exceeds that in the ventricles, thus forcing the blood from the atria into the ventricles. Approximately 0.16 seconds after the appearance of the P wave, the QRS complex on the ECG occurs as the ventricles are electrically depolarized. As the ventricles begin to repolarize, the T wave appears on the ECG. The downslope of the T wave indicates the end of ventricular repolarization and the beginning of a relaxation period. Note that the ECG contains an **isoelectric line,** or flat line, after the T wave, indicating a period of electrical rest.

Excitation of the Heart

The **sinoatrial (S-A) node** is the normal pacemaker of the heart and is located about 1 mm below the right atrial epicardium at its junction with the superior vena cava. It initiates a rhythmic impulse approximately 70 times per minute. The infranodal atrial pathways conduct the impulse initiated in the S-A node to the **atrioventricular (A-V) node** via the myocardium of the right atrium. The three infranodal pathways are the anterior, middle, and posterior tracts. Meanwhile, the Bachmann's bundle conducts the impulse from the S-A node to the left atrium. In the absence of a signal from the S-A node, the A-V node has its own intrinsic rate of 40 to 60 impulses per minute. The A-V node, also known as the A-V junction, delays the impulse received from the atria before transmitting it to the ventricles in order to give them time to fill prior to the next systole. The impulse then travels very rapidly from the A-V node to the bundle branch system via the bundle of His. The bundle branch system comprises the right bundle branch (RBB) and the left bundle branch (LBB). The RBB carries the impulse down the right side of the interventricular septum into the right ventricle. The LBB separates into three fascicles that relay the impulse to the left ventricle. Finally, the Purkinje fibres arising from the distal portions of the bundle branches transmit the impulse into the subendocardial layers of both ventricles. Barring interference with the connections described above, the final transmission of the impulse allows depolarization of the ventricles to occur followed by a normal systole. Figure 16-5 depicts the normal conduction pathways of the heart. If A-V node disease causes transmission of the electrical signal to be blocked, the intrinsic rate of the ventricles kicks in at a rate of fewer than 40 beats per minute.

The cardiac impulse is transmitted from the S-A node to the A-V node via the internodal pathways and Bachmann's bundle, and then on to the bundle of His and down the left and right bundle branches to the Purkinje fibres, which distribute the impulse to the rest of the ventricles.

Peripheral Vasculature

The circulatory system consists of arterial pathways, which are the distribution routes, and venous pathways, or the collection system that returns the blood to a central pumping station, the heart. Figure 16-6 demonstrates the journey of the blood through the systemic and pulmonary circuits.

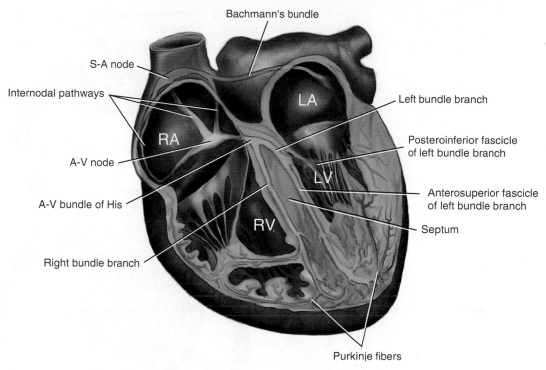

Figure 16-5 Excitation of the Heart.

Labels: Bachmann's bundle, S-A node, Internodal pathways, A-V node, A-V bundle of His, Right bundle branch, RA, LA, LV, RV, Left bundle branch, Posteroinferior fascicle of left bundle branch, Anterosuperior fascicle of left bundle branch, Septum, Purkinje fibers.

Nursing Tip

Exercise and Cardiovascular Health

Teach your patients the following about exercise:

- Always consult with your health care provider before starting an exercise program to determine how much exercise is right for you. This may be determined through stress, bicycle, or treadmill tests.
- Avoid activities that have caused previous cardiac problems.
- Avoid strenuous activity in extremes of temperature or after a heavy meal because this may predispose to angina.
- Stop any exercise and notify the physician if dizziness, faintness, lightheadedness, or angina occurs.

Nursing Tip

Calculating Target Heart Rate

1. Subtract the patient's age in years from 220.
2. The target heart rate (THR) is 80% of the value obtained in step 1. For example, a 50-year-old patient's THR is calculated as: $(220 - 50) \times 0.80 = 136$ (THR).

Arterial walls are composed of three coats or linings. The innermost lining is known as the tunica intima and is composed of the endothelium and some connective tissue. The tunica media is the middle layer and is composed of both smooth muscle and an elastic type of connective tissue. The outer layer, the tunica externa or adventitia, has a more fibrous connective tissue that is arranged longitudinally.

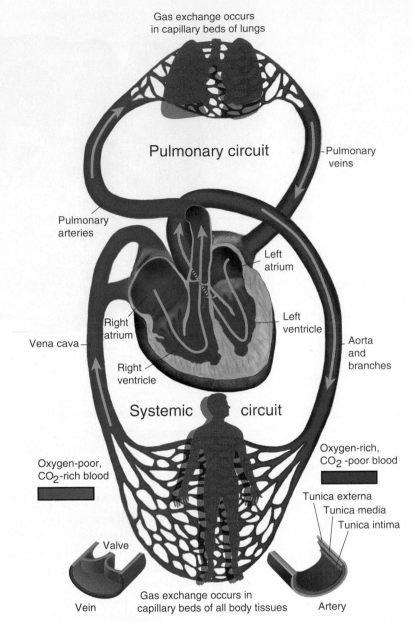

Gas exchange occurs
in capillary beds of lungs

Pulmonary circuit

Pulmonary
veins

Pulmonary
arteries

Left
atrium

Right
atrium

Left
ventricle

Vena cava

Aorta
and
branches

Right
ventricle

Systemic   circuit

Oxygen-poor,
CO_2-rich blood

Oxygen-rich,
CO_2-poor blood

Tunica externa
Tunica media
Tunica intima

Valve

Vein

Gas exchange occurs in
capillary beds of all body tissues

Artery

Figure 16-6 The Systemic and Pulmonary Circuits. The systemic pump consists of the left side of the heart, and the pulmonary circuit pump represents the right side of the heart.

As the arterial system branches and subdivides on its way to the periphery, the diameters of the vessels decrease. Arterioles are the smallest group of arteries, with a diameter of less than 0.5 mm. It is here that the rapid velocity of blood flow found in the larger arteries begins to decrease. Blood flow becomes even slower in the capillaries arising from each arteriole. The walls of the capillaries are only one cell thick, which, coupled with the slow rate of blood flow, provides optimal conditions for the exchange of nutrients and wastes and the transfer of fluid volume between the plasma and the interstitium.

After leaving the capillaries, the blood flows into the low-pressure venous system beginning with vessels known as venules. Veins are similar in construction to arteries, but they have much less elasticity, thinner walls, and greater diameters. One-way valves are found in most veins where blood is carried against the force of gravity, such as in the lower extremities. Arteries do not have valves.

As blood passes from the arterial system through the capillaries, there is a change from the pulsatile character of arterial flow to a steady flow in the venous system. Arterial pulsations are caused by the intermittent contractions of the left ventricle. Figures 16-7 and 16-8 illustrate the arterial and venous networks of blood flow.

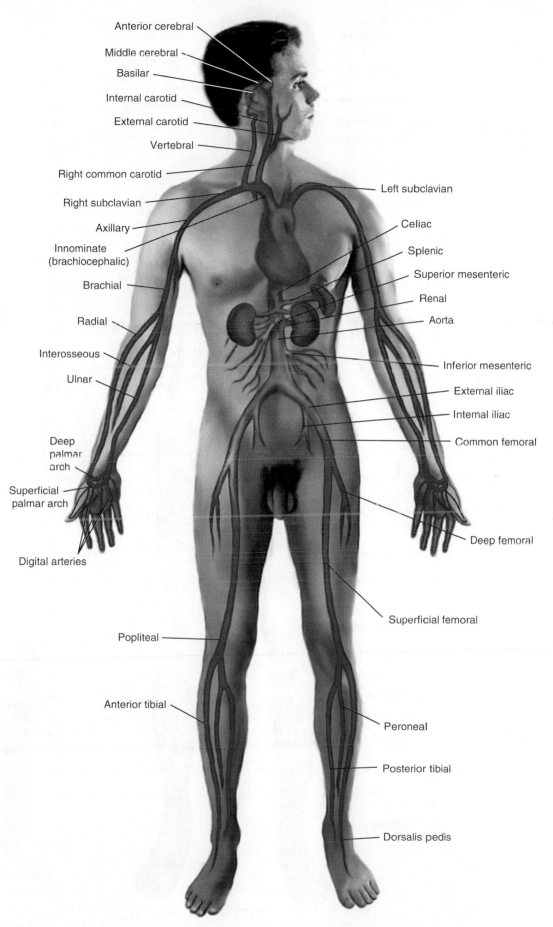

Figure 16-7 Arterial System Anatomy.

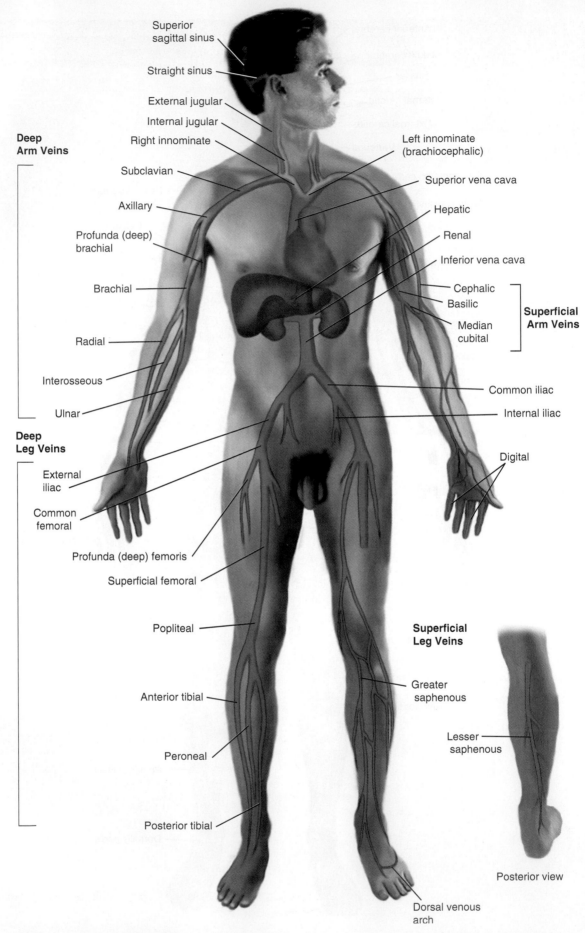

Deep Arm Veins

Superior sagittal sinus

Straight sinus

External jugular

Internal jugular

Right innominate

Left innominate (brachiocephalic)

Subclavian

Superior vena cava

Axillary

Hepatic

Profunda (deep) brachial

Renal

Inferior vena cava

Brachial

Cephalic

Basilic

Superficial Arm Veins

Median cubital

Radial

Interosseous

Ulnar

Common iliac

Internal iliac

Deep Leg Veins

Digital

External iliac

Common femoral

Profunda (deep) femoris

Superficial femoral

Popliteal

Superficial Leg Veins

Anterior tibial

Greater saphenous

Peroneal

Lesser saphenous

Posterior tibial

Dorsal venous arch

Posterior view

Figure 16-8 Venous System Anatomy.

HEALTH HISTORY

The heart and peripheral vasculature health history provides insight into the link between a patient's life and lifestyle and heart and peripheral vasculature information and pathology.

PATIENT PROFILE

Diseases that are age-, gender-, and race-specific for the heart and peripheral vasculature are listed. Table 16-1 differentiates the common cardiovascular disorders. Table 16-2 differentiates congenital cardiovascular defects.

Age

Raynaud's disease (18–50)
Rheumatic fever (5–15)
Mitral valve prolapse (20–50)
Hypertension (HTN) (20–70)
Valve **stenosis** (narrowing or constriction of a diseased heart valve) or **regurgitation** (backward flow of blood through a heart valve) (30–50)
Coronary artery disease (CAD) (40–60)
Dilated or congestive cardiomyopathy (40–60)
Myocardial infarction (MI) (40–60)
Arteriosclerosis (50–70)
Cerebrovascular accident (CVA) (50–70)
Abdominal aortic aneurysm (AAA) (60–70)

Gender

Female

Higher mortality rate after a severe MI; marked rise in CAD after menopause; atrial septal defect (ASD); Raynaud's disease

Male

Marked predisposition to CAD; ventricular septal defect (VSD)

Ethnicity

Canadians of European, South Asian descent: ↑ CVD; Canadians of Chinese origin have low rates of CVD.[1] Black Canadians and Aboriginal people have > CVD. Note: disparities in ethnic groups across Canada are narrowing, likely due to immersion in Canadian lifestyle trends.

HEALTH ISSUE/CONCERN

Common health issues/concerns for the heart and peripheral vasculature are defined, and information on the characteristics of each sign or symptom is provided.

Chest Pain

Subjective sense of discomfort in the thorax; also referred to as angina pectoris if it is caused by myocardial ischemia; not all chest pain is angina; Table 16-3 differentiates different origins of chest pain

Radiation

Arm, shoulder, neck, jaw, teeth

Quality

Crushing, heavy, tight, stabbing, burning, squeezing, aching, smothering, or perceived as indigestion

Associated Manifestations

Nausea and vomiting, shortness of breath (SOB), restlessness, anxiety, weakness, feeling of impending doom, diaphoresis, faintness, dizziness

Aggravating Factors

Exercise, stress

Alleviating Factors

Medication (e.g., nitroglycerin), rest, position change

Setting

While dreaming, eating, excited, stressed, exercising, or resting; hot or cold environment

continues

Timing	Early morning is more common but can be any time of the day
Syncope	Fainting caused by a transient decrease in cerebral blood flow
Associated Manifestations	Nausea, perspiration, palpitations, yawning, seizures, flushed face, cessation of breathing during episode, aura prior to episode
Aggravating Factors	Exercise, medications, fever, lack of food
Alleviating Factors	Rest
Setting	Heavy activity, hot environment, buttoning the collar of a shirt
Timing	Early morning, after medication, after exercise, arising from a supine or sitting position
Palpitations	Irregular heart beats; the sensation of a rapidly throbbing or fluttering heart
Quality	Skipped heart beats, throbbing, pounding, fluttering
Associated Manifestations	Anxiety, weakness, nausea, SOB, chest pain, perspiration, fainting
Aggravating Factors	Smoking, caffeine, exercise
Alleviating Factors	Rest
Setting	Resting, smoking, exercising, drinking or eating food containing caffeine
Timing	After exercise or at rest
Peripheral Edema	Swelling of the extremities, usually the feet and hands
Quality	Imprints on swollen areas after applying pressure
Associated Manifestations	Recent weight gain, pain in upper right half of abdomen, swollen abdomen, shoes tighter, rings difficult to remove from fingers
Aggravating Factors	Continuous standing, high salt intake
Alleviating Factors	Lying down or elevating the feet
Extremity Pain	Sense of discomfort usually occurring in the legs or feet; claudication
Quality	Temperature change in feet or leg
Associated Manifestations	Swelling in the affected extremity, discoloration of the skin, tenderness, change in skin temperature
Aggravating Factors	Continual standing, walking, exercise, cold weather, smoking, stress
Alleviating Factors	Rest, elevation, dangling the extremity to a dependent position if the pain is caused by arterial insufficiency (but pain actually worsens with venous insufficiency)
Setting	Walking, exercise
Timing	Late night, early morning
PAST HEALTH HISTORY	*The various components of the past health history are linked to heart and peripheral vasculature pathology and heart- and peripheral-vasculature-related information.*

Medical History	
Cardiac Specific	Abdominal aortic aneurysm (AAA), thoracic aortic aneurysm (TAA), angina, cardiogenic shock, cardiomyopathy, chest trauma, congenital anomalies, congestive heart failure (CHF), CAD, endocarditis, hyperlipoproteinemia, HTN, MI, myocarditis, pericarditis, peripheral vascular disease (PVD), rheumatic fever, valvular disease
Non-cardiac Specific	Bleeding or blood disorder, diabetes mellitus, gout, Marfan's syndrome, pheochromocytoma, primary aldosteronism, renal artery disease, CVA, thyroid disease
Surgical History	Ablation of accessory pathways, aneurysm repair, cardiac catheterization, chest surgery for trauma, congenital heart repair, coronary artery bypass graft (CABG), coronary stents, directional coronary atherectomy (DCA), electrophysiology studies (EPS), heart transplant, implantable or internal cardioverter/defibrillator (ICD) placement, myotomy or myectomy, percutaneous laser myoplasty, pacemaker insertion, percutaneous transluminal coronary angioplasty (PTCA), pericardial window, pericardiectomy, pericardiotomy, peripheral vascular grafting and bypass, valve replacement
Medications	Antianginals, antidysrhythmics, anticoagulants, antihypertensives, antilipemics, diuretics, inotropics, thrombolytic enzymes, vasodilators
Communicable Diseases	Rheumatic fever (valvular dysfunction), untreated syphilis (aortic regurgitation, aortitis, and aortic aneurysm), viral myocarditis (cardiomyopathy)
Childhood Illnesses	Rheumatic fever (valvular dysfunction)
Allergies	Aspirin (most patients who are recovering from an MI receive aspirin), intravenous pyelogram (IVP) dye, seafood (both contain iodine compounds used in the dye that is injected during a cardiac catheterization), latex (found in gloves used for procedures), betadine (which is used as a skin surface prep for cardiac and vascular procedures)
Injuries and Accidents	Chest trauma (falls, motor vehicle accidents, blunt force)
FAMILY HEALTH HISTORY	*Heart and peripheral vasculature diseases that are familial are listed.*
	Aneurysm, CVA, CAD, HTN, hypertrophic cardiomyopathy, Marfan's syndrome, mitral valve prolapse (MVP), MI, Raynaud's disease, rheumatic fever, sudden cardiac death
SOCIAL HISTORY	*The components of the social history are linked to heart and peripheral vasculature factors and pathology.*
Alcohol Use	Prolonged use of alcohol can interfere with the normal pumping function and electrical activity of the heart, leading to **cardiomegaly** (enlargement of the heart), poor left ventricular contractility, ventricular dilatation, palpitations, peripheral edema, fatigue, and SOB. Thiamine deficiencies that usually occur concurrently with alcohol abuse may contribute to dysrhythmias and heart failure. Excessive alcohol intake may play a role in the pathogenesis of dilated cardiomyopathy, angina, CAD, hypertension, dysrhythmias, stroke, and beriberi heart disease. On the other hand, the use of alcohol in moderation, up to 60 mL a day, is inversely related to the development of CAD due to the protective effect of the increased HDL cholesterol.

continues

Drug Use	Intravenous drug use: Increased risk for contracting infective endocarditis because of the use of non-sterile needles and the embolization of localized infections from the injection site. Amphetamines, cocaine, and heroin: Tachycardia, severe hypertension, hypotension, coronary vasospasm, MI, dysrhythmias, aortic rupture or dissection, coronary artery dissection, stroke, and dilated cardiomyopathy.
Tobacco Use	Nicotine increases catecholamine release, leading to elevated cardiac output, heart rate, and blood pressure. Nicotine also inhibits the development of collateral circulation, causes peripheral vasoconstriction, thickens cardiac arterioles, causes platelet aggregation, leads to dysrhythmias, and neutralizes heparin thus increasing the risk of thrombus formation. The tobacco habit contributes to the pathogenesis of CAD, angina, and atherosclerosis.
Sexual Practice	Effect of intercourse on the heart (such as exertional chest pain) or eliciting a vagal response (which may occur with anal intercourse), thus making the patient prone to syncope and other sequelae Patients who use nitrate drugs should never take phosphodiesterase type 5 inhibitors
Travel History	Arsenic poisoning: Systemic arterial disease, including gangrene and PVD; traced to the elevated arsenic content in drinking water and soil in Taiwan and Chile Chagas' disease: Severe dysrhythmias, mitral regurgitation or insufficiency, and cardiomegaly; caused by a protozoan parasite endemic to Central America, South America, and the Southwestern United States
Work Environment	Table 16-4 lists toxic substances that can cause profound cardiac pathology.
Home Environment	A dirty fireplace may cause a smoky environment that leads to the worsening of chest pain.
Hobbies and Leisure Activities	Any activity that involves exertion may contribute to a decline in status in a patient with cardiovascular pathology.
Stress	Atherosclerosis, tachycardia, HTN, dysrhythmias, sudden death
HEALTH MAINTENANCE ACTIVITIES	*This information provides a bridge between the health maintenance activities and heart and peripheral vasculature function.*
Sleep	Dyspnea, orthopnea, or paroxysmal nocturnal dyspnea (PND)
Diet	Foods high in vitamin K may reduce the effectiveness of anticoagulants. Tap water and home water softeners may contain sodium. Caffeine (in coffee, tea, soft drinks, chocolate, and over-the-counter medications) is a sympathomimetic amine that increases blood pressure and heart rate, elevates the serum catecholamine level, and can lead to dysrhythmias (especially premature atrial contractions).
Exercise	Physical exercise may have either deleterious or beneficial effects on the heart, depending on the type of activity performed, the amount, and the condition of the exerciser. The aim of an individual's cardiovascular fitness program should be the attainment of the THR (also known as perceived rate of exertion) to increase cardiovascular tone. In general, it is believed that aerobic exercise or sustained physical activity for at least 15 to 30 minutes per day, three or four times per week, positively affects one's cardiovascular conditioning.

Stress Management	Exercise, time management, pet therapy, reading, listening to music, eating, biofeedback, yoga, imagery, massages, transcendental meditation, and participation in a variety of support groups
Use of Safety Devices	Patients with older pacemakers should avoid areas with microwaves; cellular phones (especially digital cellular phones) may cause interference with pacemakers.
Health Check-ups	ECG, chest X-ray, blood pressure, pulse, serum triglyceride, serum cholesterol
PATIENT CLASSIFICATION	The Canadian Cardiovascular Society has outlined four classifications for patients with cardiac pathologies leading to angina.

Grade I: Ordinary physical activity does not cause angina (walking or climbing stairs does not cause angina but strenuous or rapid or prolonged exertion does)

Grade II: Slight limitation of ordinary activity (angina occurs walking or stair climbing after meals, in cold, in wind, under emotional stress or only during the few hours after awakening, walking more than two blocks on a level surface or climbing more than one flight of ordinary stairs)

Grade III: Marked limitation of ordinary activity (angina occurs walking 1–2 blocks on a level surface or climbing one flight of stairs)

Grade IV: Inability to carry on any physical activity without discomfort (angina syndrome may be present at rest)

Nursing Alert

Cardiovascular Disease (CVD)

Health Canada defines cardiovascular diseases as all diseases of the circulatory system including acute myocardial infarction, ischemic heart disease, valvular heart disease, peripheral vascular disease, arrhythmias, high blood pressure, and stroke. (See Chapter 19 for a discussion of stroke.)

- CVD is the leading cause of death in Canada, accounting for 36% of all deaths.[2]
- 54% of all cardiovascular deaths are due to coronary artery disease (CAD).[3]
- Fortunately, mortality rates for ischemic heart disease and acute myocardial infarction are decreasing.
- There is a lack of data on congenital heart disease in Canada.[4]

Warning Signs of Potential Cardiovascular Problems

- Change in colour of lips, face, or nails
- Chest pain
- Diaphoresis (extreme)
- Dizziness
- Dyspnea
- Edema
- Extremity pain
- Fatigue
- Feeling of doom
- Numbness in the extremities
- Pain that limits self-care
- Palpitations
- Syncope
- Tingling in the extremities

Risk Factors for Cardiovascular Disease

Unmodifiable

- Age, gender, race, family history

continues

Nursing Alert

Emergency Interventions: Cardiopulmonary Respiration

To review the *2005 Guidelines for Cardiopulmonary Resuscitation (CPR) and Emergency Cardiovascular Care (ECC)* visit http://ww2.heartand-stroke.ca

Nursing Alert

See Chapter 9 for extensive discussion of hypertension control.

Modifiable

The Canadian Heart and Stroke Foundation asks that we help our patients **Know the Nine.** According to a Canadian-led global study,[5] the following nine factors collectively account for a full 90% of first heart attacks:

- cigarette smoking
- abnormal blood lipid ratios
- high blood pressure
- diabetes control
- abdominal obesity (waist circumference greater than 102 cm for men and 88 cm for women)
- stress
- lack of daily consumption of vegetables
- lack of daily consumption of fruit
- lack of daily exercise

Nursing Alert

Hormone Replacement Therapy for Postmenopausal Women

The *Canadian Consensus on Menopause and Osteoporosis*[6] makes the following recommendations about HRT and CVD:

- HRT should not be initiated or continued for the sole purpose of preventing future cardiovascular events.
- All women should be counselled about the beneficial effects of lifestyle modifications (smoke cessation, heart-healthy diet, maintenance of ideal body weight) on reducing the risk of cardiovascular events.

Nursing Tip

Terminology

Arteriosclerosis: A group of diseases characterized by thickening and loss of elasticity of arterial walls. Popularly called "hardening of the arteries." Three forms of arteriosclerosis: atherosclerosis (most common), medial calcific sclerosis (affecting tunica media), and arteriolar sclerosis (affecting small arteries—arterioles)

Atherosclerosis: A type of arteriosclerosis in which deposits of yellowish plaques (atheromas) containing cholesterol, lipid material, and lipophages are formed in the inner layer (tunica interna) of the large and medium-sized arteries. An atheroma can increase in size and harden over time, reducing blood flow, and can potentially result in a thrombosis or bleeding into and subsequently clotting of an artery, resulting in a myocardial infarction.

Ischemic Heart Disease: Any condition in which heart muscle is damaged or works inefficiently because of any sense or relative deficiency of its blood supply; most often caused by atherosclerosis, it includes angina pectoris, acute myocardial infarction, chronic ischemic heart disease, and sudden death. Also called coronary heart disease (CHD).

TABLE 16-1 Cardiovascular Disorders

DISORDER	DEFINITION	COMMON FINDINGS
Acute myocardial infarction; Acute Coronary Syndrome (ACS)	Sometimes called heart attack; a manifestation of ischemic heart disease, describing a severe sudden onset of myocardial necrosis due to the formation of a thrombus in the coronary arterial system obstructing arterial blood flow to that section of cardiac muscle	Chest pain that is similar to angina except that it is more intense and more persistent (>30 minutes); not fully relieved by rest or nitroglycerin; and accompanied by systemic symptoms (e.g., nausea, sweating, or apprehension)
Aneurysm (Abdominal Aortic Aneurysm: AAA; Thoracic Aortic Aneurysm: TAA)	Localized abnormal dilation of a blood vessel; it may be filled with fluid or clotted blood, often forming a pulsating tumour	AAA: dulled abdominal or lower back pain; nausea and vomiting; ruptured AAA—severe, sudden, and continuous pain that radiates to back TAA: sudden, tearing pain in chest radiating to shoulders, neck, and back; dysphagia; dyspnea
Aortic regurgitation or insufficiency	Backflow of blood from the aorta to the left ventricle during diastole because of an incompetent valve	Dyspnea; PND; orthopnea; palpitations; insufficiency angina; fatigue; syncope; diastolic murmur
Aortic stenosis	A narrowing or constriction of the aortic valve causing an obstruction to the ejection of blood from the left ventricle during systole	Syncope; fatigue; weakness; palpitations; angina; systolic murmur
Atherosclerosis (coronary artery disease)	A type of arteriosclerosis; process in which deposits of yellowish plaques (atheromas) containing cholesterol, lipid material, and lipophages are formed within large and medium-sized arteries	Angina; MI; CHF; sudden cardiac death; dysrhythmias
Cardiac tamponade	Compression of the heart resulting from the accumulation of excess fluid in the pericardium	Beck's triad (hypotension, distended neck veins, and distant heart sounds); pulsus paradoxus
Cardiogenic shock	A shock of cardiac origin caused by pump failure	Pulmonary congestion; peripheral edema; hypotension; tachycardia; decreased pulse pressure; cool, pale, and clammy skin
Cardiomyopathy • congestive or dilated • hypertrophic • restrictive	Heart muscle disease	CHF-type symptoms; cardiomegaly with dilated or congestive form; familial history with hypertrophic form
Cerebrovascular accident (stroke, brain attack)	A condition that results in a reduction of blood flow to a region of the brain resulting in the death of brain tissue; may be embolic, thrombotic, or hemorrhagic cause	Decreased neurological function; headaches; hemiparesis; hemiplegia; aphasia; coma; abnormal cranial nerve findings
Congestive heart failure	An inability of the heart to deliver blood at a rate commensurate with the requirements of the metabolizing tissues at rest or during light exercise; left, right, or both ventricles may fail	Left-sided: anxiety, diaphoresis, crackles, S_3, cough, PND, fatigue; right-sided: dependent pitting edema, hepatomegaly, weight gain, hepatojugular reflux
Deep vein thrombosis (DVT)	The formation of a blood clot in a deep vein (most commonly in the leg or pelvis); inflammation of a vein due to a blood clot	Unilateral edema; calf pain or tenderness; and thrombophlebitis temperature and colour changes in the affected leg; cyanosis in the foot
Endocarditis (bacterial)	Infection of the endocardial surface or the heart valves	Fever; chills; fatigue; anorexia; nausea and vomiting; arthralgia; back pain; dyspnea; splinter hemorrhages of the nails; petechiae
Hypertension (See Chapter 9 for detailed discussion)	Elevated blood pressure	Systolic blood pressure (SBP) ≥ 140 mm Hg; diastolic blood pressure (DBP) ≥ 90 mm Hg for most people; SBP ≥ 130; DBP > 80 mm

continues

TABLE 16-1 Cardiovascular Disorders *continued*

DISORDER	DEFINITION	COMMON FINDINGS
		Hg for people with diabetes or renal failure; most often asymptomatic; headaches or epistaxis; see Chapter 9, Table 9-7 and 9-8 for *Canadian Recommendations for the Management of Hypertension* and *Target Values in the Treatment of Hypertension*
Marfan's syndrome	A syndrome of congenital collagen deficiency affecting the connective tissues	Patient may be tall and thin with hyperextensive joints and long arms, legs, and fingers; aortic dissection; aortic regurgitation; mitral regurgitation; dysrhythmias
Mitral regurgitation	The backflow of blood from the left ventricle to the left atrium during systole and resulting from an incompetent valve	CHF-type symptoms; history of rheumatic insufficiency fever, infection, trauma, or mitral valve prolapse; systolic murmur
Mitral stenosis	A narrowing or constriction of the mitral valve causing an obstruction of blood flow from the left atrium to the left ventricle during diastole	CHF-type symptoms; history of rheumatic heart disease or congenital heart defect; diastolic murmur; thrill at apex
Myocardial infarction	An area of coagulation necrosis in a tissue due to local ischemia resulting from obstruction of circulation to the area, most commonly by a thrombus or embolus	Nausea and vomiting; diaphoresis; shortness of breath; abnormal heart and lung sounds; angina; dysrhythmias; CHF; cardiogenic shock
Myocarditis	Inflammation of the heart's muscular tissue	History of rheumatic fever; viral or parasitic infection; irregular pulse; tenderness over the pericardium; may lead to dilated cardiomyopathy
Pericarditis	An inflammation of the pericardium; origin may be viral, malignant, or autoimmune	Precordial pain that increases with inspiration or in the supine position; pain may be relieved by leaning forward; fever; fatigue; pulsus paradoxus; pericardial friction rub
Peripheral vascular	Vascular disorders of the arteries and veins that supply the extremities (usually refers to arterial disease)	Intermittent claudication; pain in the toes; ulcers that don't heal; impotence; loss of pulses; severe extremity pain; paresthesia
Pulmonary regurgitation or insufficiency	The backflow of blood from the pulmonary artery to the right ventricle because of an incompetent valve	Shortness of breath on exertion (SOBOE); fatigue; diastolic murmur
Pulmonary stenosis	A narrowing or constriction of the pulmonary artery causing an obstruction to the ejection of blood from the right ventricle	SOBOE; fatigue; right-sided heart failure symptoms; systolic murmur
Raynaud's disease	A condition caused by abnormal blood vessel spasms in the extremities, especially in response to cold temperatures	Finger or toe becomes pale, cold, and numb, then becomes red, hot, and tingling
Tricuspid regurgitation or insufficiency	The backflow of blood from the right ventricle to the right atrium because of an incompetent valve	Dyspnea; fatigue; systolic murmur
Tricuspid stenosis	A narrowing or constriction of the tricuspid valve causing an obstruction of blood flow from the right atrium to the right ventricle	Dyspnea; fatigue; diastolic murmur; right-sided CHF
Ventricular aneurysm	The dilatation of a portion of necrosed ventricular wall after an MI	Tachydysrhythmias; CHF-type symptoms; cardiac tamponade; systolic murmur

TABLE 16-2 Congenital Cardiovascular Defects

A congenital cardiovascular defect (CCD)—previously known as congenital heart disease—occurs when the heart or blood vessels near the heart do not develop normally before birth. CCDs occur in about 1% of live births. Although there are few cures for CCD, more patients are now surviving to adulthood. Often the cause of the defect is unknown but it may be related to teratogenic, genetic, or random factors. The majority of patients with congenital cardiovascular defects require long-term follow-up for the management of persistent problems such as electrophysiologic sequelae, myocardial changes, ventricular failure, prosthetic materials, orendocarditis.

Most CCDs either obstruct blood flow in the heart or vessels near the heart, or cause blood to flow through the heart in an abnormal pattern. Another rare defect occurs when the right or left side of the heart is not completely formed.

CLASSIFICATION	DISORDER	DEFINITION	COMMON FINDINGS	TREATMENT OPTIONS	SPECIAL CONSIDERATIONS
Obstruction Defects	Pulmonary stenosis (PS)	Occurs when a defective pulmonary valve does not open properly. Thus, the right ventricle must pump harder than normal to overcome the obstruction.	If stenosis is severe, especially in babies, then cyanosis may occur. Older children may not have symptoms. A pulmonic systolic ejection click, murmur, and/or a diminished S_2, possibly with a wide split, may be auscultated. Patient may also have a thrill.	Required when the pressure in the right ventricle is higher than normal. Obstruction can be relieved by balloon valvuloplasty or open-heart surgery.	Patients need subacute bacterial endocarditis (SBE) prophylaxis. Before and after, treatment for their CCD, patients need to take antibiotics before certain dental and surgical procedures to prevent endocarditis.
	Aortic stenosis (AS)	Occurs when the aortic valve is narrowed. This makes it hard for the heart to pump blood to the body.	Chest pain, DOE, unusual tiring, dizziness, or fainting may occur. A systolic ejection murmur may be auscultated. Patient may also have a thrill.	The need for surgery depends on how bad the stenosis is. The stenosis may be relieved by enlarging the valve opening. Eventually, the valve may need to be replaced with an artificial valve.	• Patients need SBE prophylaxis. • Lifelong follow-up is required.
	Coarctation of the aorta (COA)	When the aorta is constricted, blood flow to the lower part of the body is obstructed. Also, the blood pressure above the obstruction is increased.	Symptoms of CHF and hypertension may develop in the week after birth. Blood pressure that is higher in the upper extremities than the lower extremities is suggestive of COA. A systolic murmur will often be present. Absent or weak femoral pulses is another hallmark sign. A heave over the left ventricle may be observed. In adulthood, the upper body may be more developed thar the lower body.	Balloon angioplasty or surgery, or both.	• Patients need SBE prophylaxis. • Defect may reoccur. • Hypertension may ensue even after repair. • Lifelong follow-up is required.

continues

TABLE 16-2 Congenital Cardiovascular Defects continued

CLASSIFICATION	DISORDER	DEFINITION	COMMON FINDINGS	TREATMENT OPTIONS	SPECIAL CONSIDERATIONS
	Bicuspid aortic valve	Occurs when the bicuspid valve has only two cusps, rather than the normal three.	There may be no symptoms in childhood but by adulthood, the valve can become stenotic or regurgitant. Thus, a diastolic or systolic murmur may be auscultated depending on the condition of the valve.	Treatment depends on how well the valve works.	Patients need SBE prophylaxis.
	Subaortic stenosis	Refers to a narrowing of the left ventricle just below the aortic valve. Thus, blood flow out of the left ventricle is limited. This condition may be congenital or it may be the result of a type of cardiomyopathy known as idiopathic hypertrophic subaortic stenosis (IHSS).	Patient may have an ejection murmur and thrill.	Treatment depends on the cause and severity of the narrowing and may include drugs or surgery.	Patients need SBE prophylaxis.
	Ebstein's anomaly	Occurs when the tricuspid valve is displaced downward into the right ventricle. It is usually associated with an atrial septal defect (ASD).	In mild cases, there are no symptoms. Later, patients may complain of tiredness, palpitations, or an abnormal heart beat. In severe cases, children may turn cyanotic and have CHF.	Medications for mild cases and surgery for severe cases.	Patients need SBE prophylaxis.
Septal Defects	Atrial septal defects (ASD)	Occurs when there is an opening between the heart's upper chambers. Thus, blood from the left atrium flows into the right atrium instead of flowing through the left ventricle, out of the aorta, and through the rest of the body.	Many children have few, if any, symptoms. A systolic ejection murmur, a diastolic murmur, a fixed widely split S_2, or a heave may be auscultated. Signs of CHF may occur in older patients.	Open-heart surgery in some cases.	
	Ventricular septal defect (VSD)	Occurs when there is an opening between the heart's lower chambers. Thus, blood that has returned from the lungs and has been pumped into the left	Patient may have high pulmonary pressures. A lift is often observed, a thrill may be palpated, and a harsh holosystolic murmur may be	Open-heart surgery for a large defect.	• Patient need SBE prophylaxis. • After a VSD has been successfully fixed with surgery, prophylactic antibiotics are usually not required.

TABLE 16-2   Congenital Cardiovascular Defects   *continued*

CLASSIFICATION	DISORDER	DEFINITION	COMMON FINDINGS	TREATMENT OPTIONS	SPECIAL CONSIDERATIONS
		ventricle flows into the right ventricle instead of being pumped directly though the aorta. The heart may enlarge because it has to pump extra blood and thus may become overworked.	auscultated Children with VSDs may have poor weight gain, slow growth, feeding difficulties, DOE and failure to thrive (FTT).		• Lifelong follow-up is required.
	Eisenmenger's complex or syndrome	Consists of both a VSD and pulmonary hypertension. Therefore, blood shunts from the right side of the heart to the left, causing the right ventricle to enlarge. It may also include an overriding aorta whereby a malpositioned aorta receives ejected blood from both ventricles.	Severe CHF and cyanosis with a right to left shunt. Patients may have healthy childhoods but become progressively cyanotic in adulthood, with poor exercise tolerance. Syncope may occur. Problems might not arise until pregnancy or some other type of cardiovascular stress occurs.	Surgery followed by a possible heart or heart–lung transplant.	• Patients need SBE prophylaxis. • Lifelong follow-up is required.
	Atrioventricular canal defect (also known as endocardial cushion defect or atrioventricular septal defect)	Consists of both a large hole in the center of the heart plus a single, large valve (which is a combination of the tricuspid and mitral valves) that crosses the defect. Eventually, the heart may enlarge because it has to pump extra blood and thus may become overworked. The defect may be complete, intermediate, or partial (the most common form).	Babies may become under-nourished because they don't grow normally. Pulmonary hypertension occurs because there is increased blood flowing to the lungs. Patients may present with CHF. S_2 may be widely split. Diastolic and systolic murmurs may be auscultated.	Surgery	• Patients need SBE prophylaxis. • A reconstructed valve may not work normally. • About 40% to 50% of patients with the defect have Down syndrome.
Cyanotic Defects	Tetralogy of Fallot	Has four components: 1. VSD 2. Stenosis at or beneath the pulmonic vavle 3. Right ventricular hypertrophy 4. Dextroposition of the aorta (the aorta now lies directly over the VSD)	Cyanosis may occur soon after birth or with rapid breathing. Older children may faint during exercise because not enough blood flows to the lungs to supply the body with oxygen. Subsequently, clubbing of the fingers and toes may occur. Patients may have a heave as well as a systolic ejection murmur, a loud S_2, and a thrill.	Surgery	Patients need SBE prophylaxis.

continues

TABLE 16-2 Congenital Cardiovascular Defects *continued*

CLASSIFICATION	DISORDER	DEFINITION	COMMON FINDINGS	TREATMENT OPTIONS	SPECIAL CONSIDERATIONS
	Transposition of the great arteries	Occurs when the positions of the pulmonary artery and the aorta are reversed. The aorta is connected to the right ventricle so most of the blood returning to the heart from the body has not gone through the lungs to be oxygenated. The pulmonary artery is connected to the left ventricle so most of the blood returning from the lungs goes back to the lungs again.	Cyanosis, tachypnea without respiratory distress, loud S_2, poor feeding in infants.	Surgery	• Patients need SBE prophylaxis. • Lifelong follow-up is required. • This defect is rare (<1% of all congenital heart defects).
	Tricuspid atresia	With this defect, there is no tricuspid valve; therefore, blood cannot flow from the right atrium to the right ventricle. Thus, the right ventricle is small and under-developed. The child's survival depends on whether there is both an ASD and a VSD.	Cyanosis	If left untreated, patients will die. Thus, surgery is required.	• Patients need SBE prophylaxis. • Lifelong follow-up is required.
	Pulmonary atresia	With this defect, there is no pulmonary valve; therefore, blood cannot flow from the right ventricle into the pulmonary artery and on into the lungs. The right ventricle may be small and underdeveloped. The tricuspid valve may also be abnormal. An ASD allows blood to exit the right side of the heart. A coexisting PDA is the only source of lung blood flow.	Cyanosis, clubbing, dyspnea, or tachypnea.	Medications and surgery	• Patients need SBE prophylaxis. • Lifelong follow-up is required.
	Truncus arteriosus	Consists of only one artery that arises from the heart and forms the aorta and the pulmonary artery. May also have a VSD.	Cyanosis, CHF, tachypnea, or poor feeding. A systolic ejection click is often heard, as well as a harsh pansystolic murmur.	Medications and surgery	• Patients need SBE prophylaxis. • Lifelong follow-up is required.

TABLE 16-2 Congenital Cardiovascular Defects *continued*

CLASSIFICATION	DISORDER	DEFINITION	COMMON FINDINGS	TREATMENT OPTIONS	SPECIAL CONSIDERATIONS
		There are four types of this defect depending on how the pulmonary arteries originate from the single arterial vessel.			
	Total anomalous pulmonary venous connection	Occurs when the pulmonary veins do not connect to the left atrium. Instead, they drain through abnormal connections to the right atrium.	Cyanosis	Surgery	Lifelong follow-up is required.
Miscellaneous	Hypoplastic left heart syndrome	Results in an underdeveloped left side of the heart. May also have an ASD, PDA, or both.	Babies become ashen within days of birth, sometimes cyanotic. They will also have rapid breathing and difficulty in feeding. CHF, shock, and multisystem organ failure may be present.	Compassionate care, medications, surgery, and/or possibly a heart transplant.	• This heart defects is usually fatal without treatment. • Patients need SBE prophylaxis. • Lifelong follow-up is required.
	Patent ductus arteriosus (PDA)	This defect occurs when the ductus, which is patent in-utero, fails to close after birth. This allows blood to mix between the pulmonary artery and aorta. Consequently, the right ventricle has to work harder and pulmonary hypertension may ensue.	If ductus is large, children may tire quickly, grow slowly, breathe rapidly, and catch pneumonia easily. A continuous, harsh, loud and machine-like murmur is often heard throughout systole and diastole.	Surgery	

TABLE 16-3 Differentiating Chest Pain

All of these conditions (excluding musculoskeletal) are life threatening and require immediate attention.

CARDIAC ISCHEMIA (also known as acute coronary syndrome)

Pain: burning, squeezing or aching, heaviness, smothering

- Not reproducible by palpation of the chest wall, may be relieved with rest or oxygen, and may or may not be accompanied by EKG changes.
- Myocardial ischemia may lead to myocardial infarction; when in doubt, assume a cardiac cause and follow your institution's chest pain protocol.

AORTIC (THORACIC) DISSECTION

Pain: sudden, sharp, and tearing, and radiates to shoulders, neck, back, and abdomen

- Neurological complications: hemiplegia, sensory deficits secondary to carotid artery occlusion.
- May present with a new murmur, bruits, or unequal blood pressure in upper extremities.

PERICARDITIS

Pain: positional ache, dyspnea

- May also present with a pericardial friction rub or distended neck veins.

PULMONARY EMBOLUS

Pain: sudden onset, sharp or stabbing, varies with respiration

- May also present with dyspnea, tachypnea, fever, tachycardia, diaphoresis, or DVT.

PNEUMOTHORAX

Pain: sudden onset, tearing or pleuritic, worsened by breathing

- May also have dyspnea, tachycardia, decreased breath sounds, and a deviated trachea. Refer to Chapter 15 for further information.

PNEUMONIA

Pain: stabbing that is exacerbated by coughing and deep breathing

- Presents with fever, chills, productive cough, tachypnea. Refer to Chapter 15 for further information.

ESOPHAGEAL RUPTURE

Pain: sudden onset upon swallowing or constant retrosternal, epigastric pain

- May mimic signs and symptoms of a pneumothorax.
- Consider esophageal rupture when a patient has experienced penetrating trauma, a severe epigastric blow, or a first or second rib fracture.

MISCELLANEOUS: MUSCULOSKELETAL

Pain: reproducible by chest wall palpation

- May be relieved by position changes.

MISCELLANEOUS: RECREATIONAL DRUG USE (cocaine, amphetamines, or stimulants)

Pain: Cardiac ischemia pain (as listed above)

- May produce a direct, toxic effect on the myocardium.

TABLE 16-4	Work-Related Exposures to Cardiotoxic Substances

PHYSICAL

- Extremes of oxygen pressure, barometric pressure, gravity, acceleration, noise, temperature, and humidity

BIOLOGICAL

- Laboratory-acquired infections
- Work in endemic areas

CHEMICAL

- Arsenic
- Carbon disulfide
- Carbon monoxide
- Cobalt
- Fibrogenic dust found in asbestos
- Fluorocarbons found in solvents and propellants
- Halogenated hydrocarbons
- Heavy metals such as lead

EQUIPMENT

- Stethoscope
- Sphygmomanometer
- Watch with second hand
- Tape measure

◄NURSING CHECKLIST►

General Approach to Heart Assessment

1. Explain to the patient what you are going to do.
2. Ensure that the room is warm, quiet, and well lit.
3. Expose the patient's chest only as much as is needed for the assessment.
4. Position the patient in a supine or sitting position.
5. Stand to the patient's right side. The light should come from the opposite side of where you are standing so that shadows can be accentuated.

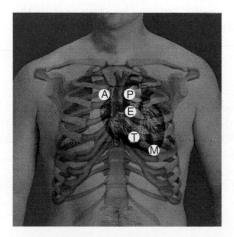

Figure 16-9 The Cardiac Landmarks.
A = Aortic Area; P = Pulmonic Area; E = Erb's Point; T = Tricuspid Area; M = Mitral Area

ASSESSMENT OF THE PRECORDIUM

The cardiovascular physical assessment has two major components:

1. Assessment of the **precordium** (the area on the anterior surface of the body overlying the heart, great vessels, pericardium, and some pulmonary tissue) and
2. Assessment of the periphery.

Inspection, palpation, and auscultation should be performed in a systematic manner, using certain cardiac landmarks. Percussion has limited usefulness in the cardiovascular assessment because X-rays and other diagnostic tests provide the same information in a much more accurate manner. The cardiac landmarks (Figure 16-9) are defined as follows:

1. The aortic area is the second intercostal space (ICS) to the right of the sternum.
2. The pulmonic area is the second ICS to the left of the sternum.

E	Examination	N	Normal Findings	A	Abnormal Findings	P	Pathophysiology

3. The midprecordial area, Erb's point, is located in the third ICS to the left of the sternum.

4. The tricuspid area is the fifth ICS to the left of the sternum. Other terms for this area are the right ventricular area or the septal area.

5. The mitral area is the fifth ICS at the left midclavicular line. Other terms for this area are the left ventricular area or the apical area.

These cardiac landmarks are the locations where the heart sounds are heard best, not where the valves are actually located. The mitral area correlates anatomically with the apex of the heart; the aortic and pulmonic areas correlate anatomically with the base of the heart. Assessment of the heart should proceed in an orderly fashion from the base of the heart to the apex, or from the apex of the heart to the base.

Inspection

Aortic Area

E 1. Lightly place your index finger on the angle of Louis.
2. Move your finger laterally to the right of the sternum to the rib. This is the second rib.
3. Move your finger down beneath the second rib to the ICS. The aortic area is located in the second ICS to the right of the sternum.

N No pulsations should be visible.

A A pulsation in the aortic area is abnormal.

P A pulsation in the aortic area may indicate the presence of an aortic root aneurysm. The aneurysm's dilation may become bigger when the patient experiences hypertension. A rupture can occur at any time but the risk is greater when the aneurysm becomes 5 cm or more in diameter.

Pulmonic Area

E 1. Lightly place your index finger on the left second ICS.
2. The pulmonic area is located at the second ICS to the left of the sternum.

N No pulsations should be visible.

A A pulsation or bulge in the pulmonic area is an abnormal finding.

P Pulmonary stenosis, which is usually congenital, impedes blood flow from the right ventricle into the lungs, causing a bulge. The right side of the heart then dilates and the right ventricle becomes hypertrophied in order to accommodate the load.

Midprecordial Area

E 1. Lightly place your index finger on the left second ICS.
2. Continue to move your finger down the left rib cage, counting the third rib and the third ICS.
3. The midprecordial area, or Erb's point, is located at the third ICS, left sternal border. Both aortic and pulmonic murmurs may be heard here.

N No pulsations should be visible.

A The presence of a pulsation or a systolic bulge in the midprecordial area is not normal.

P A left ventricular aneurysm can produce a midprecordial pulsation. Ventricular aneurysms can develop several weeks following an acute MI.

E	**Examination**	N	**Normal Findings**	A	**Abnormal Findings**	P	**Pathophysiology**

With an MI, the hydraulic stress on the infarcted area may cause the damaged ventricular wall to bulge and become extremely thin during systole.

A A retraction in the midprecordial area is abnormal.

P Pericardial disease can produce retractions in this area (retractions occur when there is a pulling in some of the tissues of the precordium, depending on the activities of the heart).

Tricuspid Area

E 1. Lightly place your index finger on the left third ICS.
   2. Continue to move your finger down the left rib cage, counting the fourth rib, the fourth ICS, and the fifth rib followed by the fifth ICS.
   3. The tricuspid area is located at the fifth ICS, left of the sternal border.

N No pulsations should be visible.

A A visible systolic pulsation in the tricuspid area is abnormal.

P A visible systolic pulsation can result from right ventricular enlargement secondary to an increased stroke volume. Anxiety, hyperthyroidism, fever, and pregnancy are clinical situations that produce an increased stroke volume.

Mitral Area

E 1. Lightly place your index finger on the left fifth ICS.
   2. Move your finger laterally to the midclavicular line. This is the mitral landmark. In a large-breasted patient, have the patient displace the left breast upward and to the left so you can locate the mitral landmark.

N Normally, there is no movement in the precordium except at the mitral area, where the left ventricle lies close enough to the skin's surface that it visibly pulsates during systole. The apical impulse at the mitral landmark is generally visible in about half of the adult population. This pulsation is also known as the point of maximal impulse (PMI) and occurs simultaneously with the carotid pulse.

A **Hypokinetic** (decreased movement) pulsations at the mitral area are considered abnormal.

P Conditions that place more fluid between the left ventricle and the chest wall, such as a pericardial effusion or cardiac tamponade, produce a hypokinetic or absent pulsation. In obese individuals, excess subcutaneous tissue dampens the apical impulse. Low output states such as shock produce a less palpable apical impulse from the reduced blood volume and decreased myocardial contractility. Keep in mind that absent pulsations are normal in half of the adult population.

A **Hyperkinetic** (increased movement) pulsations are always abnormal when located at the mitral area.

Nursing Tip

PMI versus Apical Impulse

The term *PMI* has fallen out of favour because it can be a misnomer if cardiac pathology causes a stronger impulse in a different region. Any movement other than the apical impulse is abnormal and should be described in terms of type, location, and timing in relation to the cardiac cycle.

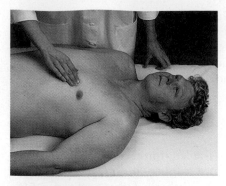

Figure 16-10 Palpating for Pulsations.

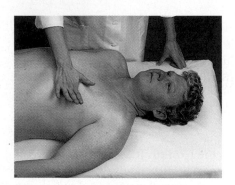

Figure 16-11 Palpating for Thrills.

P   High-output states such as mitral regurgitation, thyrotoxicosis, severe anemia, and left-to-right heart shunts are potential causes of hyperkinetic pulsations.

Palpation

Inspection and palpation of the heart go hand in hand. Again, you must be systematic in this part of the assessment and palpate the cardiac landmarks starting at either the base or the apex of the heart. During palpation, assess for the apical impulse, pulsations, **thrills** (vibrations that feel similar to what one feels when a hand is placed on a purring cat), and **heaves** (lifting of the cardiac area secondary to an increased workload and force of left ventricular contraction; also referred to as lift). The patient should be in a supine position for this portion of the assessment.

E   Palpate the cardiac landmarks for:

1. Pulsations: Using the finger pads, locate the cardiac landmark and palpate the area for pulsations (Figure 16-10).
2. Thrills: Using the palmar surface of the hand, at the base of the fingers (also known as the ball of the hand), locate the cardiac landmark and palpate the area for thrills (Figure 16-11).
3. Heaves: Follow step 2 and palpate the area for heaves.

Aortic Area

E   Palpate the aortic area for pulsations, thrills, and heaves.
N   No pulsations, thrills, or heaves should be palpated.
A   Palpation of a thrill in the aortic area is abnormal.
P   Aortic stenosis and aortic regurgitation create turbulent blood flow in the left ventricle, which may be palpated as a thrill.

Pulmonic Area

E   Palpate the pulmonic area for pulsations, thrills, and heaves.
N   No pulsations, thrills, or heaves should be palpated.
A   Palpation of a thrill in the pulmonic area is abnormal.
P   Pulmonic stenosis and pulmonic regurgitation create turbulent blood flow in the right ventricle, which may be palpated as a thrill.

Midprecordial Area

E   Palpate the midprecordial area for pulsations, thrills, and heaves.
N   No pulsations, thrills, or heaves should be palpated.
A   Palpation of pulsations in the midprecordial area is abnormal.
P   Both a left ventricular aneurysm and an enlarged right ventricle can produce a pulsation in the midprecordial area.

Tricuspid Area

E   Palpate the tricuspid area for pulsations, thrills, and heaves.
N   No pulsations, thrills, or heaves should be felt.
A   Palpation of a thrill in the tricuspid area is abnormal.
P   Tricuspid stenosis and tricuspid regurgitation create turbulent blood flow in the right atrium, which may be palpated as a thrill.
A   Palpation of a heave in the tricuspid area is abnormal.

E   **Examination**   N   **Normal Findings**   A   **Abnormal Findings**   P   **Pathophysiology**

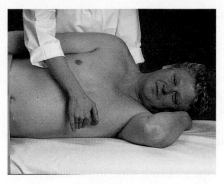

Figure 16-12 Palpating the Apical Impulse with the Patient on the Left Side.

P Right ventricular enlargement may produce a heave in the tricuspid area secondary to an increased workload.

Mitral Area

E Palpate the mitral area for pulsations, thrills, and heaves. If a pulsation (apical impulse) is not palpable, turn the patient to the left side and palpate in this position (Figure 16-12). This position facilitates palpation because the heart shifts closer to the chest wall.

N The apical impulse is palpable in approximately half of adults. It is felt as a light, localized tap that is 1 to 2 cm in diameter. The amplitude is small and it can be felt immediately after the first heart sound, lasting for about one-half of systole. This impulse may be exaggerated in young patients. A thrill is not found in the normal adult population. A heave is absent in the healthy adult.

A A thrill palpated at the fifth ICS at the left midclavicular line is considered abnormal.

P Mitral stenosis and mitral regurgitation may produce a thrill from the turbulent blood flow found in the left atrium.

A A visible heave, or sustained apex beat, displaced laterally to the left sixth ICS at the anterior axillary line is abnormal. It is usually more than 3 cm in diameter and has a large amplitude.

P Left ventricular hypertrophy produces a laterally displaced apical impulse because of the increased size of the left ventricle in the thorax and the subsequent shifting of the heart. In addition, the hypertrophied muscle works harder during a contraction to produce a heave or sustained apex. This frequently occurs in conditions such as aortic stenosis, systemic hypertension, and idiopathic hypertrophic subaortic stenosis (it is a form of hypertrophic cardiomyopathy).

◄NURSING CHECKLIST►

General Approach to Heart Auscultation

1. Explain to the patient what you are going to do.
2. Expose the patient's chest only as much as is needed for the assessment. Never auscultate through any type of clothing.
3. Position the patient in a supine or sitting position. The left lateral position may be used for auscultation of the mitral and tricuspid areas. Also, the upright, leaning forward position may be used for thorough auscultation of the aortic area.
4. Stand to the patient's right side.
5. Use the correct headpiece of the stethoscope. The diaphragm transmits high-frequency sounds whereas the bell is used for low-pitched sounds. Keep in mind when using the bell that it should rest lightly on the skin. If too much pressure is applied, the bell will act like a diaphragm.
6. Warm the headpiece in your hands prior to touching it to the patient.
7. Listen to all four of the valvular cardiac landmarks at least twice. During the first auscultation, identify S_1 and S_2, and then listen for a possible S_3 and S_4. During the second auscultation, listen for murmurs and friction rubs. As you gain expertise, you may be able to listen for S_1, S_2, S_3, S_4, murmurs, and friction rubs all at the same time.
8. Listen for at least a few cardiac cycles (10 to 15 seconds) in each area.

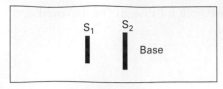

A. Normal S₂

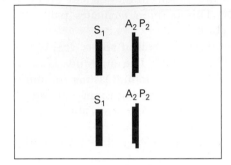

B. Intensified A2, Diminished A₂

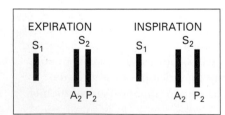

C. Aortic Ejection Click

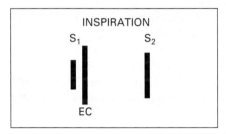

D. Normal Physiological Split of S₂

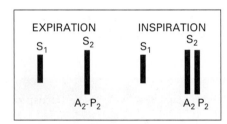

E. Wide Splitting of S₂

Figure 16-13 Summation of Heart Sounds.

A Hypokinetic pulsations, usually less than 1 to 2 cm in diameter and of small amplitude, are abnormal.

P Conditions that place more fluid between the left ventricle and the chest wall, such as a pericardial effusion or cardiac tamponade, produce a hypokinetic or absent pulsation. In obesity, the excess subcutaneous tissue dampens the apical impulse. Low-output states such as shock produce a less palpable apical impulse from the reduced blood volume and decreased myocardial contractility.

A Hyperkinetic pulsations, usually greater than 1 to 2 cm in diameter and of increased amplitude, are abnormal.

P High-output states such as mitral regurgitation, thyrotoxicosis, severe anemia, and left-to-right heart shunts are potential causes of hyperkinetic pulsations.

Auscultation

Aortic Area

E Place the diaphragm of the stethoscope on the aortic landmark and listen for S_2.

N S_2 is caused by the closure of the semilunar valves. S_2 corresponds to the "dub" sound in the phonetic "lub-dub" representation of heart sounds. S_2 heralds the onset of diastole. S_2 is louder than S_1 at this landmark (Figure 16-13A).

A The components of S_2 are A_2 (aortic) and P_2 (pulmonic). A greatly intensified or diminished A_2 is considered abnormal (Figure 16-13B).

P Arterial hypertension, which increases the pressure in the aorta, may be suspected in the case of a greatly intensified A_2. Aortic stenosis, where the aortic valve is calcified or thickened, may be the cause of a diminished A_2.

A An ejection **click** is an abnormal systolic sound that is high pitched and can radiate in the chest wall. It is created by the opening of the damaged valve and it does not vary with the respiratory cycle. An ejection click follows S_1 (Figure 16-13C).

P An ejection click can be auscultated in aortic stenosis, where the calcified valve produces this sound on opening.

Pulmonic Area

E Place the diaphragm of the stethoscope on the chest wall at the pulmonic landmark and listen for S_2.

N S_2 is also heard in the pulmonic area. S_2 is louder than S_1 at this landmark as depicted in Figure 16-13A. It is softer than the S_2 auscultated in the aortic area because the pressure on the left side of the heart is greater than that on the right. There is a normal physiological splitting of S_2 that is heard best at the pulmonic area. The components of a split S_2 are A_2 (aortic) and P_2 (pulmonic) (Figure 16-13D). The aortic component occurs slightly before the pulmonic component during inspiration. The physiology of a split S_2 is that during inspiration, because of the more negative intrathoracic pressure, the venous return to the right side of the heart increases. Thus, pulmonic closure is delayed because of the extra time needed for the increased blood volume to pass through the valve. Normally, the A_2 component of the split S_2 is louder than the P_2 component because of the greater pressures in the left side of the heart.

E Examination	**N** Normal Findings	**A** Abnormal Findings	**P** Pathophysiology

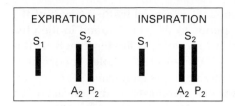

F. Fixed Splitting of S₂

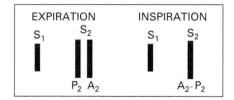

G. Paradoxical Splitting of S₂

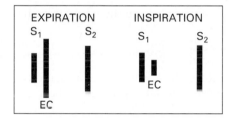

H. Pulmonic Ejection Click

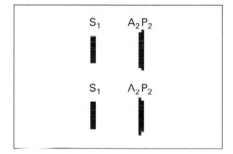

I. Intensified P₂, Diminished P₂

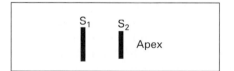

J. Normal S₁

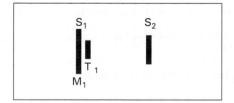

K. Normal Physiological Split of S₁

Figure 16-13 *continued.*

A When a split S_2 occurs that is abnormally wide, the aortic valve closes early and the pulmonic valve closes late. There is a split on both inspiration and expiration, but a wider split on inspiration, as shown in Figure 16-13E.

P Delayed closure of the pulmonic valve may be due to a delay in the electrical stimulation of the right ventricle, as seen with right bundle branch block.

A Fixed splitting, a wide splitting that does not change with inspiration or expiration, is abnormal (Figure 16-13F). The pulmonic valve consistently closes later than the aortic valve. The right side of the heart is already ejecting a large volume, so filling cannot be increased during inspiration.

P Right ventricular failure that results in a prolonged right ventricular systole or a large atrial septal defect can lead to fixed splitting.

A In paradoxical splitting, the aortic valve closes after the pulmonic valve because of the delay in left ventricular systole. This occurs during expiration and disappears with inspiration. It is considered abnormal (Figure 16-13G).

P Left bundle branch block, aortic stenosis, patent ductus arteriosus, severe hypertension, and left ventricular failure are conditions in which paradoxical splitting may be auscultated.

A A pulmonic ejection click always indicates an abnormality (Figure 16-13H).

P A pulmonic ejection click is caused by the opening of a diseased pulmonic valve. It is heard loudest on expiration and is quieter on inspiration. It occurs early in systole and it does not radiate.

A A P_2 that is louder than or equal in volume to A_2 is abnormal, as is a greatly diminished P_2 (Figure 16-13I).

P A loud P_2 is expected in pulmonary hypertension, where the pressures in the pulmonary artery are abnormally high; pulmonic stenosis, where the pulmonic valve is calcified or thickened, may be the cause of a diminished P_2.

Midprecordial Area

Both aortic and pulmonic murmurs may be auscultated at Erb's point. Refer to the discussion on murmurs later in this chapter for additional information.

Tricuspid Area

E Place the diaphragm of the stethoscope on the chest wall at the tricuspid landmark to listen for S_1.

N S_1 in the tricuspid area is softer than the S_1 auscultated in the mitral area because the pressure in the left side of the heart is greater than that in the right. S_1 is louder than S_2 at this landmark (Figure 16-13J). There is a normal physiological splitting of S_1 that is best heard in the tricuspid area (Figure 16-13K). This split occurs because the mitral valve closes slightly before the tricuspid valve due to greater pressures in the left side of the heart. The components of a split S_1 are M_1 (mitral) and T_1 (tricuspid). Physiological splitting disappears when the patient holds his or her breath.

A A split S_1 with an abnormally wide split is pathological (Figure 16-13L). The split is wider than usual during inspiration and is still heard on expiration.

P A split S_1 is usually due to electrical malfunctions such as right bundle branch block or mechanical problems such as mitral stenosis. In mitral stenosis, the tricuspid valve can close before the mitral valve closes because of calcification of the diseased mitral valve.

Mitral Area

E 1. Place the diaphragm of the stethoscope over the mitral area to identify S_1.
   2. If you are unable to distinguish S_1 from S_2, palpate the carotid artery with the hand closest to the head while auscultating the mitral landmark. You will hear S_1 with each carotid pulse beat.

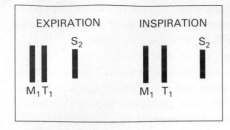

L. Wide Split of S$_1$

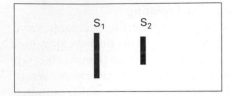

M. Loud S$_1$

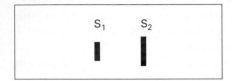

N. Soft S$_1$

O. Variable S$_1$

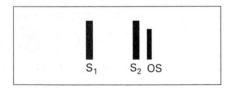

P. Opening Snap

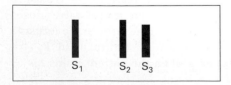

Q. S$_3$

Figure 16-13 *continued.*

N S$_1$ is heard the loudest in the mitral area. S$_1$ is caused by the closure of the mitral and tricuspid valves. S$_1$ corresponds to the "lub" sound in the phonetic "lub-dub" representation of heart sounds. S$_1$ is louder than S$_2$ at this landmark (Figure 16-13J). S$_1$ also heralds the onset of systole. At normal or slow heart rates, systole (the time occurring between S$_1$ and S$_2$) is usually shorter than diastole. Diastole constitutes two-thirds of the cardiac cycle and systole constitutes the other third. The intensity of S$_1$ depends on:

1. The adequacy of the A-V cusps in halting the ventricular blood flow
2. The mobility of the cusps
3. The position of the cusps and the rate of ventricular contraction

A An abnormally loud S$_1$ occurs when the mitral valve is wide open when systolic contraction begins, then slams shut (Figure 16-13M).

P A loud S$_1$ occurs in mitral stenosis, short PR interval syndrome (0.11 to 0.13 second), or in high-output states such as tachycardia, hyperthyroidism, and exercise.

A A soft S$_1$ is abnormal (Figure 16-13N).

P A soft S$_1$ can occur as a result of rheumatic fever, where the mitral valve has only limited motion.

A A variable abnormal S$_1$ occurs when diastolic filling time varies. Both a soft and a loud S$_1$ can be auscultated (Figure 16-13O).

P A variable S$_1$ can occur with complete heart block, where the atria and the ventricles are beating independently, and in atrial fibrillation, where the ventricles are beating irregularly.

A An opening snap is an early diastolic sound that is high-pitched. It is abnormal (Figure 16-13P).

P An opening **snap** is caused by the opening of a diseased valve and can be auscultated in mitral stenosis. The sound does not vary with respirations and can radiate throughout the chest. It follows S$_2$ and can be differentiated from an S$_3$ because it occurs earlier than an S$_3$.

A In tachycardia, the heart rate increases, diastole shortens, and systole and diastole become increasingly difficult to distinguish. Tachycardia is abnormal.

P Tachycardia can occur in exercise, fever, anxiety, pregnancy, and conditions that lead to hypertrophy, such as heart failure.

Mitral and Tricuspid Area (S$_3$)

Auscultation of the mitral and tricuspid areas is repeated for low-pitched sounds, specifically an S$_3$ (otherwise known as a ventricular diastolic **gallop,** or extra heart sound). An S$_3$ is an early diastolic filling sound that originates in the ventricles and is therefore heard best at the apex of the heart. A right-sided S$_3$ (tricuspid area) is heard louder during inspiration because the venous return to the right side of the heart increases with a more negative intrathoracic pressure. An S$_3$ sound occurs just after an S$_2$ (Figure 16-13Q).

E 1. Place the bell of the stethoscope lightly over the mitral landmark. When the S$_3$ originates in the left ventricle, it is heard best with the patient in a left lateral decubitus position and exhaling.

2. When originating in the right ventricle, an S$_3$ can best be heard by placing the bell of the stethoscope lightly over the third or fourth ICS at the left sternal border.

3. Auscultate for 10 to 15 seconds for a left- or right-sided S$_3$.

N An S$_3$ heart sound can be a normal physiological sound in children and in young adults. After the age of 30, a physiological S$_3$ is very infrequent. An S$_3$ can also be normal in high-output states such as the third trimester of pregnancy.

| E | **Examination** | N | **Normal Findings** | A | **Abnormal Findings** | P | **Pathophysiology** |

R. S_4

S. Summation Gallop

Figure 16-13 *continued.*

A In an adult, an S_3 heart sound may be one of the earliest clinical findings of cardiac dysfunction. A loud, persistent S_3 can be an ominous sign. The average life expectancy after a persistent S_3 sound is detected is approximately four to five years.

P An S_3 is caused by rapid ventricular filling. An S_3 sound may occur with ventricular dysfunction, excessively rapid early diastolic ventricular filling, and restrictive myocardial or pericardial disease. It often indicates congestive heart failure and fluid overload.

Mitral and Tricuspid Area (S_4)

An S_4 heart sound, or atrial diastolic gallop, is a late diastolic filling sound associated with atrial contraction. An S_4 can be either left- or right-sided and is therefore heard best in the mitral or tricuspid area. An S_4 is a late diastolic filling sound that occurs just before S_1 (Figure 16-13R).

Sometimes, the S_3 and the S_4 heart sounds can occur simultaneously in mid-diastole, thus creating one loud diastolic filling sound. This is known as a summation gallop (Figure 16-13S).

E 1. Place the bell of the stethoscope lightly over the mitral area.
   2. Place the bell of the stethoscope lightly over the tricuspid area.
   3. Auscultate for 10 to 15 seconds for a left- or right-sided S_4.

N An S_4 heart sound may occur with or without any evidence of cardiac decompensation. A left-sided S_4 is usually louder on expiration. A right-sided S_4 is usually louder on inspiration.

A The presence of an S_4 can be indicative of cardiac decompensation.

P An S_4 heart sound can be auscultated in conditions that increase the resistance to filling because of a poorly compliant ventricle (e.g., MI, CAD, CHF, and cardiomyopathy) or in conditions that result in systolic overload (e.g., HTN, aortic stenosis, and hyperthyroidism).

Murmurs

Murmurs are distinguished from heart sounds by their longer duration. Murmurs may be classified as innocent (which are always systolic and are not associated with any other abnormalities), functional (which are associated with high-output states), or pathological (which are related to structural abnormalities). Murmurs are produced by turbulent blood flow in the following situations:

1. Flow across a partial obstruction
2. Increased flow through normal structures
3. Flow into a dilated chamber
4. Backward or regurgitant flow across incompetent valves
5. Shunting of blood out of a high-pressure chamber or artery through an abnormal passageway

When assessing for a murmur, analyze the murmur according to the following seven characteristics:

1. Location: area where the murmur is heard the loudest (e.g., mitral, pulmonic, etc.).
2. Radiation: transmission of sounds from the specific valves to other adjacent anatomic areas. For example, mitral murmurs can often radiate to the axilla.
3. Timing: phase of the cardiac cycle in which the murmur is heard. Murmurs can be either systolic or diastolic. If the murmur occurs simultaneously with the pulse, it is a systolic murmur. If it does not, it is a diastolic murmur. Murmurs can further be characterized as **pansystolic** or **holosystolic,** meaning that the murmur is heard throughout all of systole. Murmurs can also be characterized as early, mid-, or late systolic or diastolic murmurs.

Nursing Tip

S_3 Heart Sound

Phonetically, an S_3 heart sound is thought to resemble the pronunciation of the word *Kentucky*:

S_1	S_2	S_3
KEN	TÚC	KY

Nursing Tip

S_4 Heart Sound

Phonetically, an S_4 heart sound is thought to resemble the pronunciation of the word *Tennessee*:

S_4	S_1	S_2
TEN	NES	SÉE

TABLE 16-5

Grading Heart Murmurs

GRADE	CHARACTERISTICS
I	Very faint; heard only after a period of concentration
II	Faint; heard immediately
III	Moderate intensity
IV	Loud; may be associated with a thrill
V	Loud; stethoscope must remain in contact with the chest wall in order to hear; thrill palpable
VI	Very loud; heard with stethoscope off of chest wall; thrill palpable

A. Crescendo

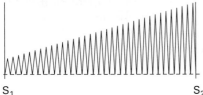

S_1 S_2

B. Decrescendo

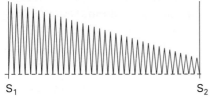

S_1 S_2

C. Crescendo-decrescendo

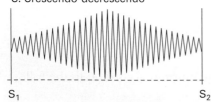

S_1 S_2

D. Plateau

S_1 S_2

Figure 16-14 Characteristic Patterns of Murmurs.

4. Intensity: See Table 16-5 for the six grades of loudness or intensity. The murmur is recorded with the grade over the roman numeral "VI" to show the scale being used (e.g., III/VI).
5. Quality: harsh, rumbling, blowing, or musical.
6. Pitch: high, medium, or low. Low-pitched murmurs should be auscultated with the bell of the stethoscope whereas high-pitched murmurs should be auscultated with the diaphragm of the stethoscope.
7. Configuration: pattern that the murmur makes over time (Figure 16-14). The configuration of a murmur can be described as **crescendo** (soft to loud), **decrescendo** (loud to soft), crescendo-decrescendo (soft to loud to soft), and plateau (sound is sustained).

E 1. The patient should be in the same position for murmur auscultation as that which was used for the first auscultation (i.e., supine or sitting).
    2. Auscultate each of the following cardiac landmarks for 10 to 15 seconds:
       a. Aortic and pulmonic areas, with the diaphragm of the stethoscope
       b. Mitral and tricuspid areas, with the diaphragm of the stethoscope
       c. Mitral and tricuspid areas, with the bell of the stethoscope
    3. Label the murmur using the characteristics of location, radiation, timing, configuration, intensity, pitch, and quality. See Table 16-5 for information on grading heart murmurs.
    4. You may also have the patient sit up, lean forward, completely exhale, and hold his or her breath while you listen at the right and left second and third ICSs for aortic murmurs (especially aortic regurgitation).

N No murmur should be heard; however, a physiological or functional murmur in children and adolescents may be innocent. These murmurs are usually systolic, short, grade I or II, vibratory, heard at the left sternal border, and do not radiate. No cardiac symptoms accompany the murmur.

A Abnormal murmurs of stenosis can be found in each of the four valvular cardiac landmarks.

P Stenosis occurs when a valve that should be open remains partially closed. It produces an increased **afterload,** or pressure overload. Stenosis may develop from rheumatic fever, congenital defects of the valves, or calcification associated with the aging process.

A Abnormal murmurs of regurgitation or insufficiency can be auscultated in each of the four valvular cardiac landmarks.

P Regurgitation or insufficiency occurs when a valve that should be closed remains partially open. An insufficient valve causes volume overload, or increased **preload.** Regurgitation frequently results from the effects of rheumatic fever and congenital defects of the valves.

Nursing Tip

Pericardial Friction Rub versus Pleural Friction Rub

- A pericardial friction rub produces a *high*-pitched, multiphasic, and scratchy (may be leathery or grating) sound that *does not* change with respiration. It is a sign of pericardial inflammation.
- A pleural friction rub produces a *low*-pitched, coarse, and grating sound that *does* change with respiration. When the patient holds his or her breath, the sound disappears. The patient may also complain of pain upon breathing. It is a sign of visceral and parietal pleurae inflammation.

E	Examination	N	Normal Findings	A	Abnormal Findings	P	Pathophysiology

Pericardial Friction Rub

E **1.** Position the patient so that he or she is reclining in the sitting position, in the knee-chest position, or leaning forward.

2. Auscultate from the sternum (third to fifth ICS) to the apex (mitral area) with the diaphragm of the stethoscope for 10 to 15 seconds.

3. Characterize any sound according to its location, radiation, timing, quality, and pitch.

N No pericardial friction rub should be auscultated.

A A pericardial friction rub is always an abnormal finding. It is heard best during held inspiration or expiration. It does not change with the respiratory cycle. See Table 16-6 for additional information on pericardial friction rubs.

P Pericardial friction rubs are caused by the rubbing together of the inflamed visceral and parietal layers of the pericardium. They may be present in conditions such as **pericarditis** (inflammation of the pericardium) and renal failure.

Prosthetic Heart Valves

N Prosthetic heart valves can be located in any of the four heart valves, although mitral and aortic valve replacements are the most common. Refer to the aortic and mitral valve auscultation discussions.

A Prosthetic heart valves produce abnormal heart sounds. Furthermore, mechanical prosthetic valve sounds can sometimes be heard without the use of a stethoscope.

TABLE 16-6   Murmurs and Pericardial Friction Rub

HEART SOUND	LOCATION/RADIATION	QUALITY/PITCH	CONFIGURATION
Systolic Murmurs			
Aortic stenosis	Second right ICS; may radiate to neck or left sternal border	Harsh/medium	Crescendo/decrescendo
Pulmonic stenosis	Second or third left ICS; radiates toward shoulder and neck	Harsh/medium	Crescendo/decrescendo
Mitral regurgitation	Apex; fifth ICS, left midclavicular line; may radiate to left axilla and back	Blowing/high	Holosystolic/plateau
Tricuspid regurgitation	Lower left sternal border; may radiate to right sternum	Blowing/high	Holosystolic/plateau
Diastolic Murmurs			
Aortic regurgitation	Second right ICS and Erb's point; may radiate to left or right sternal border	Blowing/high	Decrescendo
Pulmonic regurgitation	Second left ICS; may radiate to left lower sternal border	Blowing/high	Decrescendo
Mitral stenosis	Apex; fifth ICS, left midclavicular line; may get louder with patient on left side; does not radiate	Rumbling/low	Crescendo/decresoendo
Tricuspid stenosis	Fourth ICS, at sternal border	Rumbling/low	Crescendo/decrescenda
Pericardial Friction Rub	Third to fifth ICS, left of sternum; does not radiate	Leathery, scratchy, grating/high	Three components: 1. Ventricular systole 2. Ventricular diastole 3. Atrial systole

Note: Timing is described as systolic or diastolic; intensity is described in Table 16-5.

◄NURSING CHECKLIST►

General Approach to Peripheral Vasculature Assessment

1. Explain to the patient what you are going to do.
2. Use a drape and uncover only those areas that are necessary as the assessment is done.
3. Position the patient in a supine or sitting position.

P Mechanical prosthetic valves (caged-ball, tilting disk, and bileaflet valves) produce "clicky" opening and closing sounds. Homograft (human tissue) and heterograft (animal tissue) valves produce sounds that are similar to those of the human valves; however, they usually produce a murmur.

ASSESSMENT OF THE PERIPHERAL VASCULATURE

Assessment of the periphery is the second major component of a comprehensive cardiovascular assessment. The components of the assessment of the periphery include:

1. Inspection of the jugular venous pressure (JVP)
2. Inspection of the hepatojugular reflux
3. Palpation and auscultation of the arterial pulses
4. Inspection and palpation of peripheral perfusion
5. Palpation of the epitrochlear node

Inspection of the Jugular Venous Pressure

Identify the internal and external jugular veins (Figure 16-15) with the patient in a supine position with the head elevated to 30° or 45° so that the jugular veins are visible. Tangential lighting (lighting across the veins rather than on

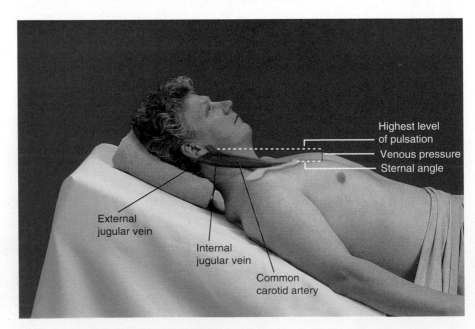

Figure 16-15 Inspection of Jugular Venous Pressure.

| E | **Examination** | N | **Normal Findings** | A | **Abnormal Findings** | P | **Pathophysiology** |

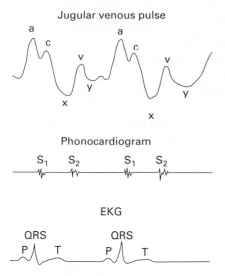

Figure 16-16 Jugular Venous Pulse Waves in Relation to the Phonocardiogram and Electrocardiogram.

top of the veins) will facilitate the assessment. Both sides of the neck should be assessed. The external jugular veins are more superficial than the internal jugular (IJ) veins and traverse the neck diagonally from the centre of the clavicle to the angle of the jaw. The IJ veins are larger and are located deep below the sternocleidomastoid muscle adjacent to the carotid arteries. The pulsations of the IJ veins can be difficult to identify visually because the veins are deep and the pulsations can be confused with the adjacent carotid arteries.

Jugular vein pulsations consist of two or three waves (Figure 16-16). These waves are called the *a, c,* and *v* waves. The *a* wave is produced by the contraction of the right atrium and it reflects the backflow of blood into the venae cavae as the right atrium ejects blood into the right ventricle. The *a* wave occurs just before S_1.

The *c* wave occurs at the end of S_1 and is produced when the right ventricle begins to contract. The *c* wave is caused by both the slight backflow of blood into the right atrium when the ventricular contraction occurs and by the bulging of the tricuspid valve backward toward the right atrium because of increased right ventricular pressure.

The *v* wave results from the slow buildup of blood in the right atrium during the ventricular contraction (when the tricuspid valve is closed) and occurs during late systole. The *v* wave disappears when the tricuspid valve opens and blood flows rapidly into the right ventricle.

Two negative slopes, the *x* and *y* descents, also occur in the jugular venous pulse. The *x* descent occurs after the *v* wave and reflects the fall of the right atrial pressure when the tricuspid valve closes and the right atrium relaxes. The *y* descent follows the *v* wave and occurs when the tricuspid valve opens and blood flows rapidly from the right atrium into the right ventricle.

E   1. To *indirectly* estimate a patient's CVP, estimate the JVP (Figure 16-15):
     a. Place the patient at a 30° to 45° angle (the highest position where the neck veins remain visible).
     b. Measure the vertical distance in centimetres from the patient's sternal angle to the top of the distended neck vein. This will give you the JVP.
     c. Knowing that the sternal angle is roughly 5 cm above the right atrium, take the JVP measurement obtained in the previous step and add 5 cm to get an estimate of the CVP. For example, a JVP of 2 cm at a 45° angle estimated on a patient's right side is equivalent to a CVP of 5 + 2, or 7, cm.

   2. Direct CVP measurements in the patient with a central venous cannula should be obtained with the patient in the supine position or reclining at no more than a 45° angle.
     a. Do not forget to level the transducer at the patient's right atrium (phlebostatic axis—fourth ICS, midaxillary line) prior to obtaining any CVP reading.
     b. When recording CVP measurements, chart the angle of the patient when the measurement was taken.

N   A JVP reading less than 4 cm is considered normal. Normally, the jugular veins are:

   1. Most distended when the patient is flat because gravity is eliminated and the jugular veins fill
   2. 1 to 2 cm above the sternal angle when the head of the bed is elevated to a 45° angle
   3. Absent when the head of the bed is at a 90° angle
   Normal direct CVP readings are 3–8 cm H2O or 0–8 mm Hg.

A   A JVP greater than 4 cm is considered abnormal.

P   An elevated JVP can be due to an increased right ventricular pressure, increased blood volume, or an obstruction to right ventricular flow.

A   Bilateral jugular venous distension (JVD) is abnormal.

P JVD indicates an increased JVP.

A Unilateral JVD is abnormal.

P Unilateral JVD indicates a local vein blockage.

A JVD with the head of the bed elevated to a 90° angle is abnormal.

P JVD at a 90° angle indicates more serious pathology such as severe right ventricular failure, constrictive pericarditis, or cardiac tamponade.

A An increased *a* wave is abnormal.

P An increased *a* wave can occur with stenosis of the tricuspid valve (because the right atrium has difficulty emptying blood into the right ventricle) or when the right ventricle is enlarged and the right atrium needs to more forcefully contract to fill it. An increased *a* wave can also occur in complete heart block because the right atrium contracts at its own pace against a closed tricuspid valve.

A An enlarged *v* wave is abnormal.

P An enlarged *v* wave can occur with tricuspid regurgitation or insufficiency. It is exaggerated when the tricuspid valve allows blood to flow back from the right ventricle to the right atrium during systole, thus causing the *x* slope to be replaced by a large *c–v* wave. It can also occur with right-sided heart failure, where the right ventricle becomes so enlarged that it forces the tricuspid valve to stretch and allow blood back into the right atrium.

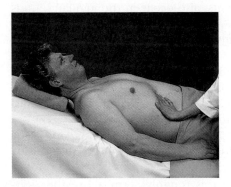

Figure 16-17 Hepatojugular Reflux.

Inspection of the Hepatojugular Reflux

Hepatojugular reflux is a test that is very sensitive in detecting right ventricular failure. This procedure is performed if the CVP is normal but right ventricular failure is suspected.

E 1. Place the patient flat in bed, or elevated to a 30° angle if the jugular veins are visible. Remind the patient to breathe normally.

2. Using single or bimanual deep palpation, press firmly on the right upper quadrant for 30 to 60 seconds. Press on another part of the abdomen if this area is tender.

3. Observe the neck for an elevation in JVP (Figure 16-17).

N Normally, this pressure should not elicit any change in the jugular veins.

A A rise of more than 1 cm in JVP is abnormal.

P A rise in JVP that occurs with this technique is suggestive of right-sided congestive heart failure or fluid overload. The heart simply cannot accept the increase in venous return.

Palpation and Auscultation of Arterial Pulses

Information concerning the function of the right ventricle is gained via the assessment of the venous pulses; however, assessment of the arterial pulses provides information about the left ventricle. The pulses to be evaluated are the temporal, carotid, brachial, radial, femoral, popliteal, posterior tibial, and the dorsalis pedis. The arteries that are most frequently examined are the radial arteries due to their easy accessibility. In a cardiac arrest situation, the carotid pulse is the artery of choice for palpation.

E 1. The arterial pulse assessment is best facilitated with the patient in a supine position with the head of the bed elevated at 30° to 45°. If the patient cannot tolerate such a position, then the supine position alone is acceptable.

2. Using your dominant hand, palpate the pulses with the pads of the index and middle fingers. The number of fingers used will be determined by the amount of space where the pulse is located.

| E | Examination | N | Normal Findings | A | Abnormal Findings | P | Pathophysiology |

Nursing Alert

Palpation of Carotid Pulses

The carotid pulses should not be palpated together because excessive stimulation can elicit a vagal response and slow down the heart. Palpating both carotid pulses at the same time could also cut off circulation to the patient's head and brain.

3. Evaluate the pulse in terms of:
   a. Rate
   b. Rhythm: If there is an irregularity in the pulse rate, then auscultate the heart.
   c. Amplitude: Refer to Table 9-2 for grading scales.
   d. Symmetry: Palpate the pulses on both sides of the patient's body simultaneously (with the exception of the carotid pulses).
4. Using the bell of the stethoscope, auscultate the temporal, carotid, and femoral pulses for **bruits,** which are blowing sounds heard when blood flow becomes turbulent as it rushes past an obstruction. Ask the patient to hold his or her breath during auscultation of the carotid pulse because respiratory sounds can interfere with auscultation.

N Refer to Chapter 9, for normal pulse rate, rhythm, and amplitude. When assessing symmetry, the pulses should be equal bilaterally. No bruits should be auscultated in the carotid or femoral pulses.

A/P Figure 16-18 illustrates abnormal pulses with possible etiologies.

A Asymmetrical pulses are abnormal.

P Variations in the symmetry of pulses can occur because of anatomic differences in the depths and locations of the arteries.

A Auscultation of bruits at the temporal, carotid, and femoral areas is abnormal.

P Bruits in these areas can be caused by an obstruction related to atherosclerotic plaque formation, a jugular vein–carotid artery fistula, or high-output states such as anemia or thyrotoxicosis.

Advanced Technique

Assessing for Pulsus Paradoxus

During inspiration, the blood flow into the right side of the heart is increased, the right ventricular output is enhanced, and pulmonary venous capacitance is increased, resulting in less blood reaching the left ventricle. These mechanisms account for a decrease in both the left ventricular stroke volume and arterial pressure. An exaggerated form of this mechanism is referred to as **pulsus paradoxus.**

E 1. Place the patient in a supine position. Instruct the patient to breathe normally.
   2. Apply the blood pressure cuff.
   3. Inflate the cuff to 20 mm Hg above the patient's last systolic blood pressure reading.
   4. Slowly deflate the cuff until the first systolic sound is heard.
   5. Observe the patient's respirations because the systolic sound may disappear during normal inspiration.
   6. Slowly deflate the cuff again and note the point at which all of the systolic sounds are heard regardless of respirations.

N The difference between the first systolic sound and the point at which all the systolic sounds are heard is the paradox. The paradox should be less than or equal to 10 mm Hg.

A A paradox greater than 10 mm Hg is considered abnormal.

P Pulsus paradoxus can occur in conditions such as cardiac tamponade, pericardial effusion, constrictive pericarditis, restrictive cardiomyopathy, severe chronic obstructive lung disease, and superior vena cava obstruction because all of these conditions can result in a decreased blood return to the left ventricle.

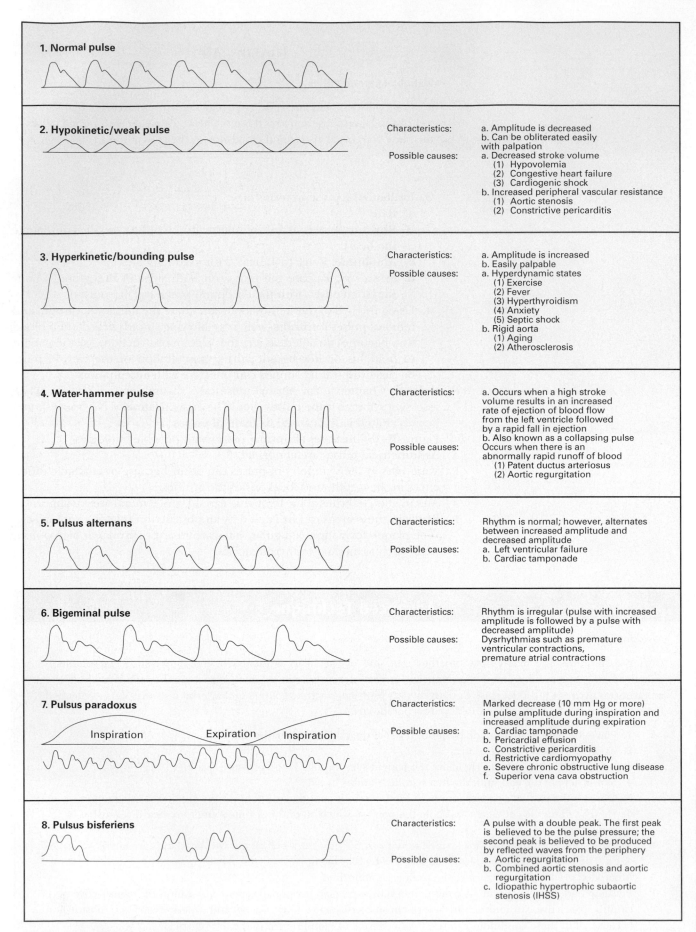

1. Normal pulse

2. Hypokinetic/weak pulse

Characteristics:
a. Amplitude is decreased
b. Can be obliterated easily with palpation

Possible causes:
a. Decreased stroke volume
  (1) Hypovolemia
  (2) Congestive heart failure
  (3) Cardiogenic shock
b. Increased peripheral vascular resistance
  (1) Aortic stenosis
  (2) Constrictive pericarditis

3. Hyperkinetic/bounding pulse

Characteristics:
a. Amplitude is increased
b. Easily palpable

Possible causes:
a. Hyperdynamic states
  (1) Exercise
  (2) Fever
  (3) Hyperthyroidism
  (4) Anxiety
  (5) Septic shock
b. Rigid aorta
  (1) Aging
  (2) Atherosclerosis

4. Water-hammer pulse

Characteristics:
a. Occurs when a high stroke volume results in an increased rate of ejection of blood flow from the left ventricle followed by a rapid fall in ejection
b. Also known as a collapsing pulse

Possible causes:
Occurs when there is an abnormally rapid runoff of blood
  (1) Patent ductus arteriosus
  (2) Aortic regurgitation

5. Pulsus alternans

Characteristics:
Rhythm is normal; however, alternates between increased amplitude and decreased amplitude

Possible causes:
a. Left ventricular failure
b. Cardiac tamponade

6. Bigeminal pulse

Characteristics:
Rhythm is irregular (pulse with increased amplitude is followed by a pulse with decreased amplitude)

Possible causes:
Dysrhythmias such as premature ventricular contractions, premature atrial contractions

7. Pulsus paradoxus

Inspiration   Expiration   Inspiration

Characteristics:
Marked decrease (10 mm Hg or more) in pulse amplitude during inspiration and increased amplitude during expiration

Possible causes:
a. Cardiac tamponade
b. Pericardial effusion
c. Constrictive pericarditis
d. Restrictive cardiomyopathy
e. Severe chronic obstructive lung disease
f. Superior vena cava obstruction

8. Pulsus bisferiens

Characteristics:
A pulse with a double peak. The first peak is believed to be the pulse pressure; the second peak is believed to be produced by reflected waves from the periphery

Possible causes:
a. Aortic regurgitation
b. Combined aortic stenosis and aortic regurgitation
c. Idiopathic hypertrophic subaortic stenosis (IHSS)

Figure 16-18 Alterations in Arterial Pulses.

Advanced Technique

Orthostatic Hypotension Assessment

When an individual stands, blood pools in the lower part of the body and the blood pressure falls transiently. However, in the healthy individual, **baroreceptors** (receptors located in the walls of most of the great arteries) located in the carotid sinus area sense the decrease in blood pressure and initiate reflex vasoconstriction and increase the heart rate. These mechanisms bring the blood pressure back to normal. When this mechanism fails, **orthostatic hypotension** may ensue and an evaluation must be made. When assessing for orthostatic hypotension, take the patient's blood pressure and heart rate with the patient in supine, sitting, and standing positions. This set of orthostatic vital signs is commonly referred to as **tilts.**

E 1. First check the blood pressure in a supine position. In this position, the patient should be flat for at least five minutes. (This time ensures that no reflex mechanisms from the upright position are influencing the blood pressure.) Record the blood pressure and the heart rate as the first set of tilts.

2. Next, assist the patient to a sitting position with the feet dangling. Wait one to three minutes. (There is no consensus in the literature regarding how long to wait after a position change before obtaining the next set of vital signs.) Retake the blood pressure and heart rate. This waiting period allows time for the reflex mechanisms to activate and ensure a normal blood pressure. Record the blood pressure and the heart rate as the second set of tilts. Also, ask the patient about any symptoms of weakness or dizziness related to the position change. If the patient becomes weak or dizzy, assist the patient back to a supine position.

3. Finally, assist the patient to a standing position. Measure the blood pressure and heart rate again after one to three minutes. Again, ask the patient about any symptoms of weakness or dizziness related to the position change. If the patient becomes weak or dizzy, assist the patient back to a supine position.

N Wide discrepancies in the literature exist regarding the magnitude of the orthostatic response. The latest studies reveal that there is no relationship between orthostatic vital signs and volume status, yet tilts are still frequently used as indicators of intravascular volume status. Many normal patients may have what has been considered in the past to be positive tilts consistent with hypovolemia even though they are not hypovolemic.

A Orthostatic vital signs that have been considered positive in the past include a systolic or a diastolic blood pressure decrease of more than 10 mm Hg or a heart rate increase of more than 20 beats per minute. However, tilts have fallen out of favour with many for the reason previously stated.

P Orthostatic hypotension can occur in patients who are hypovolemic, have a neurogenic problem, or are experiencing side effects from a prescribed medication.

Nursing Tip

Peripheral Perfusion

Refer to Chapter 10 for **E, N, A,** and **P** on colour, clubbing, capillary refill, skin temperature, edema, skin texture, and hair distribution.

Nursing Tip

Central Cyanosis

When assessing a patient's periphery, remember to look for cyanosis in the mucous membranes, the earlobes, and the cheeks.

Nursing Tip

Capillary Refill

A delayed return of colour in the nailbeds suggests that there is an impairment of blood flow in the microcirculation. A delayed capillary refill may occur with CHF, shock, or PVD. Refer to Chapter 10 for further information on capillary refill.

| E | Examination | N | Normal Findings | A | Abnormal Findings | P | Pathophysiology |

Inspection and Palpation of Peripheral Perfusion

Peripheral perfusion can be impaired with any pathological state that affects the flow of blood through the peripheral arteries and veins. Components of peripheral perfusion assessment include peripheral pulse, colour, clubbing, capillary refill, skin temperature, edema, ulcerations, skin texture, hair distribution, and special techniques for the assessment of arterial and venous blood flow.

E **1.** Inspect the fingers, toes, or points of trauma on the feet and legs for ulceration. Inspect the sides of the ankles for ulceration.

  2. Advanced techniques for assessing the venous system (discussed in more detail later):
    a. Homan's sign
    b. Manual compression

  3. Advanced techniques for examining the arterial system (discussed in more detail later):
    a. Pallor
    b. Colour return (CR) and venous filling time (VFT)
    c. Allen Test

N Ulcerations: No ulcerations should be noted.

A Arterial ulcerations are abnormal.

  1. Location: occurs at toes or points of trauma on the feet or the legs.
  2. Characteristics: well-defined edges; black or necrotic tissue; a deep, pale base and lack of bleeding; hairlessness or disruption of the hair along with shiny, thick, waxy skin.
  3. Pain: exceedingly painful; claudication related to chronic arterial insufficiency is relieved by rest; pain at rest is relieved by dependency.

P The location and characteristics of ulceration are due to inadequate arterial flow, such as in peripheral vascular disease and diabetes mellitus. Most distal arterial beds are prone to ulceration. The pain is caused by ischemia.

P Arterial ulcers on the tips of the fingers, toes, or nose can be caused by Raynaud's disease (Figure 16-19A). Arteriolar spasms lead to pallor and pain in the affected area, followed by cyanosis, with numbness, tingling, and burning; rubor also develops. Over time, the affected area may develop an ulcer. Attacks occur bilaterally and last minutes to hours.

A Venous ulcerations are abnormal (Figure 16-19B).

  1. Location: occurs at the sides of the ankles.
  2. Characteristics: uneven edges and ruddy granulation of tissue; thin, shiny skin that lacks the support of subcutaneous tissue; disruption of hair pattern, or hairlessness.
  3. Pain: deep muscular pain (associated with inadequate venous flow) with acute DVT; aching and cramping are relieved with elevation.

P Ulcers are due to inadequate venous flow that results when communication between the superficial and deep veins is compromised. Both the characteristics and the pain are related to inadequate venous blood flow.

A. Raynaud's Disease. *Courtesy of Marvin Ackerman, M.D., Scarsdale, NY.*

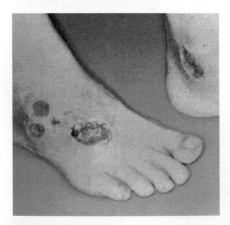

B. Venous Ulceration

Figure 16-19 Ulcerations.

Advanced Technique

Assessing the Venous System

Homan's Sign

It is important to note that because a Homan's sign has a **low sensitivity** (an indication of the frequency of a positive test result in a population with

continues

| E | **Examination** | N | **Normal Findings** | A | **Abnormal Findings** | P | **Pathophysiology** |

the disease) for thrombophlebitis, the use of this test has fallen out of favour with some health care providers. *A positive Homan's sign is present in less than 20% of all DVT cases.*

E **1.** With the patient's knee slightly bent, sharply dorsiflex the patient's foot and ask the patient if this manoeuvre elicits pain in the calf.

2. Repeat this technique with the other foot.

N There should be no complaints of calf pain when this is evaluated.

A A positive Homan's sign may be abnormal.

P A positive Homan's sign may indicate thrombophlebitis or DVT. Early detection of thrombophlebitis is essential because it can lead to life-threatening complications such as pulmonary emboli, which occurs when a thrombus breaks loose from the vein and travels to the lung. Three factors can disrupt the balance between blood-clotting activators and inhibitors. Known as Virchow's triad, they are stasis of blood flow, an injured venous wall, and hypercoagulability. All three of these factors can predispose a patient to thrombosis. Thrombosis can occur in either deep or superficial veins.

Manual Compression

Manual compression tests the competency of the saphenous vein's valves.

P **1.** Palpate the dilated vein with one hand.

2. Use the other hand to compress the same vein 20 cm higher in the leg.

3. Note if an impulse is felt.

N If the valves are competent, you will not feel the impulse because competent valves block transmission of the impulse.

A An impulse felt with manual compression is abnormal.

P Varicose veins are dilated, tortuous veins that are caused by incompetent valves (Figure 16-20). They are most prevalent in the saphenous veins of the lower extremities.

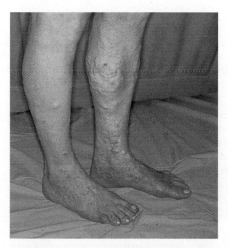

Figure 16-20 Varicose Veins. *Courtesy of the Armed Forces Institute of Pathology.*

Nursing Alert

Risk Factors for Varicose Veins

Varicose veins affect approximately 10% of the adult population and occur four times more often in women than in men. The pathogenesis of varicose veins remains unknown; however, it is not uncommon to find varicose veins in patients:

- Who have a family history of varicose veins
- Whose occupation requires long periods of standing
- Who are obese
- Who are pregnant

Measures to prevent unnecessary pressure on the leg veins include:

- Avoid heavy lifting.
- Avoid excessive weight gain.
- Do not cross legs.
- Wear support pantyhose.
- Stop smoking.
- Elevate feet while sitting.
- Exercise.

Advanced Technique

Assessing the Arterial System

Pallor

E 1. Instruct the patient to raise the extremities.

2. Note the time it takes for pallor, or lack of colour, to develop.

N Normally no pallor develops within 60 seconds.

A Pallor that develops quickly in the extremities when the extremities are lifted is abnormal.

P Pallor that develops quickly is indicative of arterial insufficiency. The quicker the pallor develops, the more severe the disease.

Colour Return and Venous Filling Time

E 1. To drain the patient's feet of venous blood, elevate the supine patient's legs approximately 30 cm and ask the patient to move the feet up and down at the ankles for approximately one minute.

2. Next, place the patient in a sitting position on the edge of the bed, with the legs dangling over the side.

3. Note the time it takes for the colour to return to the legs and for the superficial veins to refill.

N Normal colour return (CR) is 10 seconds and venous filling time (VFT) is 15 seconds.

A A delayed CR of 15 to 25 seconds or a VFT of 20 to 30 seconds is abnormal.

P These scores indicate moderate ischemia.

A A delayed CR of 40 seconds or more or a VFT of 40 seconds or more is abnormal.

P These scores indicate severe ischemia.

Allen Test

The Allen test is used to assess the patency of the radial and ulnar arteries (Figure 16-21). This test is usually performed prior to radial artery cannulation because radial artery cannulation is commonly associated with radial artery thrombosis. If the radial artery becomes occluded with a thrombus, continued viability of the hand depends on collateral blood flow from the ulnar artery.

E 1. Ask the patient to make a tight fist. If the patient is unresponsive, raise the arm above the heart for several seconds to force blood to leave the hand.

continues

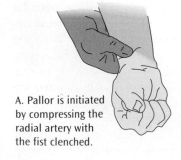

A. Pallor is initiated by compressing the radial artery with the fist clenched.

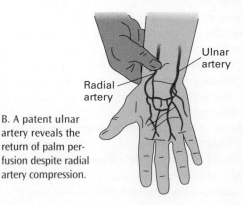

B. A patent ulnar artery reveals the return of palm perfusion despite radial artery compression.

Ulnar artery

Radial artery

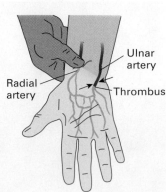

C. An occluded ulnar artery results in continued pallor of the hand while the radial artery is still compressed.

Ulnar artery

Radial artery

Thrombus

Figure 16-21 The Allen Test.

| **E** Examination | **N** Normal Findings | **A** Abnormal Findings | **P** Pathophysiology |

2. Apply direct pressure on the radial and ulnar arteries to obstruct blood flow to the hand as the patient opens and closes the fist.

3. Instruct the patient to open the hand, with the radial artery remaining compressed. If the patient is unresponsive, keep the arm above the heart level.

4. Examine the palmar surface of the hand for a blush or pallor within 15 seconds.

N If the radial artery is compressed, the blood flow through the ulnar artery should be sufficient to maintain the normal palm colour after the patient unclenches the fist. Also, if the ulnar artery is compressed, the blood flow through the radial artery should be sufficient to maintain the normal palm colour. This is a positive Allen test.

A If the colour does not return to normal within six seconds after the patient unclenches the fist, then obstruction of either the radial or the ulnar arteries may be present. This is a negative Allen test. Thus, the radial artery should not be punctured for an arterial blood gas or invasive arterial line.

P Atherosclerosis or a thrombus can cause either artery to be not patent.

GERONTOLOGICAL VARIATIONS

As adults age, their cardiovascular systems undergo physiological changes that in many instances are complicated by disease processes. In the normal individual, the size of the cardiac muscle begins to decrease with age. As fibrotic and sclerotic changes take place in the atria and the ventricles, cardiac output can fall by as much as 35% at rest after the age of 70. Skeletal changes that sometimes occur in the elderly, such as kyphosis or collapsed vertebrae from osteoporosis, can alter the position of the heart within the thoracic cavity, giving rise to changes in the electrocardiographic data. Obesity that results in an increased abdominal girth with subsequent diaphragmatic elevation can also displace the heart within the chest.

With the aging process, intracardiac valves may develop calcifications or fibrosis that results in systolic or diastolic murmurs. If the left ventricle has thickened or enlarged, thus losing its compliance, an S_4 heart sound can be heard on auscultation. Changes in the conduction system resulting from electrolyte imbalances, debilitating states or pharmacotherapy, or thickened myocardial fibres can cause cardiac irritability leading to a variety of dysrhythmias.

Vascular integrity is also susceptible to the aging process. The arterial system becomes increasingly rigid as the vessels become fibrotic. If a pathological process such as atherosclerosis is added, the insult to the vascular tree becomes even greater. Elasticity is lost, the vessel lumen is narrowed, and peripheral vascular resistance is increased, thus impeding blood flow. Other conditions that cause vascular spasm, such as smoking, contribute to a decrease in vascular flow. In the venous system, there is intimal thickening with dilation and loss of valvular competency. Venous return to the heart is affected, and edema or varicosities may develop. The baroreceptors located in the aortic arch and the carotid sinuses are also affected by vascular integrity. In the presence of impaired compliance, these structures are altered in their abilities to respond to changes in blood pressure.

In addition to cardiovascular changes associated with the aging process, diseases affecting other body systems may also affect the heart and vessels. For example, right-sided heart failure may be precipitated by chronic obstructive lung disease, and diabetes mellitus can have deleterious effects on the peripheral vasculature.

Alterations in cerebral perfusion related to atherosclerosis or arteriosclerotic heart disease can cause patients to become confused or forgetful, thus making history taking difficult. The patient may tire easily because of decreased cardiac output, and thus may require periods of rest during the interview and assessment.

It is interesting to note that more elderly people die of cardiovascular problems than of any other single disease. Keep in mind that a majority of these patients do not have chest pain with MI. Instead, they may present with dyspnea, palpitations, or complaints of weakness. Among elderly persons with hypertension in addition to CAD, the mortality rate is even higher. Age-related changes may delay the peak effect of cardiovascular drugs, thus creating the possibility for additional cardiovascular problems in the elderly patient.

CASE STUDY   The Patient with Chest Pain

John Goodal is a 66-year-old man with a history of cardiovascular disease. He is experiencing chest pain that is increasing in intensity.

HEALTH HISTORY

PATIENT PROFILE	66 yo man, obese (BMI 35), arrives with his sister
HEALTH ISSUE/CONCERN	"I'm having chest pain"
HISTORY OF ISSUE/CONCERN	Presents to the emergency department at 09:00 c̄ complaints of CP that began around MN. Pt describes the CP as a dull, achy pain c̄ radiation to the neck. He now rates it as a 4/10. Pt went to bed with 3/10 CP & awoke c̄ 5/10 CP. Pt denies diaphoresis, dizziness, SOBOE, SOB, or any other associated sx. Pt states that he was out of his sublingual NTG tablets; therefore, he did not take any NTG for his CP. Pt denies any association of CP c̄ activity or food. Pt reports that his CP is different in nature from his prior experiences with anginal CP. In the ED, pt received a GI cocktail, Ranitidine (Zantac) (IV), & NTG (sublingual, q 5 minutes × 3). Pt reports that CP was unrelieved. BP 177/77 Ⓛ arm
PAST HEALTH HISTORY	
Medical History	HTN, CAD; hyperlipidemia; hiatal hernia; GERD c̄ Barrett's esophagus; AAA (3 cm confirmed by angiogram); DVT in RLE 20 yrs ago
Surgical History	CABG (3-vessel) 5 yrs ago. Cardiac catheterization 1 yr ago revealed that both grafted vessels were patent. Ⓛ carotid endarterectomy 5 yrs ago.
Medications	Atenolol 100 mg po daily Captopril 50 mg po tid ASA 81 mg po daily Simvastatin (Zocor) 20 mg po qhs Omeprazole (Losec) 10 mg po bid NTG sl prn chest pain
Communicable Diseases	Denies
Allergies	NKDA
Injuries and Accidents	Denies
Special Needs	Denies
Blood Transfusions	Denies
Childhood Illnesses	Pt thinks he has had "all the usual;" no rheumatic heart disease
Immunizations	Received tetanus booster 2 yrs ago; receives annual influenza vaccine

FAMILY HEALTH HISTORY

LEGEND

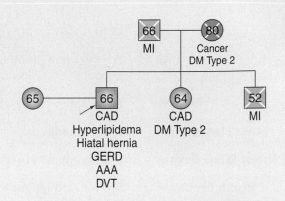

 Living female

 Living male

 Deceased female

 Deceased male

╱ Points to patient

AAA = Abdominal aortic aneurysm

CAD = Coronary artery disease

DM = Diabetes mellitus

DVT = Deep vein thrombosis

GERD = Gastroesophageal reflux disease

MI = Myocardial infarction

66 MI — 80 Cancer DM Type 2

65 — 66 CAD Hyperlipidema Hiatal hernia GERD AAA DVT

64 CAD DM Type 2

52 MI

Denies family hx of CVA, MVP, rheumatic fever, hypertrophic cardiomyopathy, sudden cardiac death.

SOCIAL HISTORY

Alcohol Use	Pt states he is a "social" drinker
Drug Use	Denies
Tobacco Use	3 PPD × 5 yrs; quit 15 yrs ago
Domestic and Intimate Partner Violence	Denies
Sexual Practice	Pt reports a monogamous relationship c̄ his wife of 40 yrs; does not use sildenafil citrate (Viagra)
Travel History	Never travelled outside Canada
Work Environment	Retired transportation official
Home Environment	Lives in a 2-bedroom apartment with 5 stairs to reach his apartment's landing
Hobbies and Leisure Activities	Likes to "play cards;" walks daily
Stress and coping	"I am really worried that I have had a heart attack. I've managed before so I guess I will manage whatever happens now."
Education	College graduate
Economic Status	No financial worries
Religion/Spirituality	Jehovah's Witness
Ethnicity	"I'm Jamaican but have lived in Canada for 30 years."
Roles and Relationships	Pt reports that he is married to "my best friend;" Ø children living at home
Characteristic Patterns of Daily Living	Arises at 09:00 & eats breakfast. Likes to walk every morning to the local market for his daily newspaper (stays around to visit). Returns home by noon for lunch. May take a nap in his lounge chair. Eats dinner around 18:00, watches TV, goes to bed around 22:00.

continues

HEALTH MAINTENANCE ACTIVITIES	
Sleep	11 hr/night
Diet	Tries to limit salt intake; is correct in his knowledge about what foods contain salt; prefers fresh fruits & vegetables to processed foods
Exercise	Walks approximately 30 minutes q morning
Stress Management	Talking things out $\bar{c}$ his wife
Use of Safety Devices	Does not have a pacemaker
Health Check-ups	Saw his cardiologist 6 mos ago
RISK FACTORS	
Unmodifiable	Age, gender, family history
Modifiable	Diet, weight, lipid levels, activity
PHYSICAL ASSESSMENT	
Assessment of the Precordium	
Inspection	Aortic area: Neg Pulmonic area: Neg Midprecordial area: Neg Tricuspid area: Neg Mitral area: Neg
Palpation	Aortic area: Neg Pulmonic area: Neg Midprecordial area: Neg Tricuspid area: Neg Mitral area: Neg
Auscultation	Aortic area: $\oplus$ S_2 Pulmonic area: $\oplus$ S_2 Midprecordial area: Neg Tricuspid area: $\oplus$ S_1, $\ominus$ S_3 Mitral area: $\oplus$ S_1, $\ominus$ S_3 Murmurs: $\oplus$ II/VI holosystolic murmur heard best at LSB, 5th ICS Pericardial friction rub: Neg
Assessment of the Peripheral Vasculature	
Inspection of JVP (Indirect)	Unable to visualize
Inspection of Hepatojugular Reflux	Neg
Palpation and Auscultation of Arterial Pulses	Arterial Pulses Rate: 42 Rhythm: Regular Amplitude: Symmetry: All symmetrical Bruits: Neg carotid/femoral

Inspection and Palpation of Peripheral Perfusion	Colour: Normal for race, mucous membranes pink Clubbing: Neg Capillary refill: Less than 2 seconds Skin temperature: Warm Edema: None Ulcerations: None Skin texture: Smooth, even Hair distribution: Even distribution, s̄ alopecia
Palpation of the Epitrochlear Node	Non-palpable
Advanced Technique	⊕ Homan's Sign in Ⓡ leg
DIAGNOSTIC DATA	
Chest X-ray	No infiltrates
ECG	Sinus bradycardia, Q waves in III, AVF (findings new when compared with previous ECG from 1 yr ago); no acute changes
Echocardiogram	Ejection fraction of 60% (Normal: 55–65%)
CT Spiral	⊖ for PE; ⊕ DVT Ⓡ leg, 3 cm
LABORATORY DATA	

	Patient's Values	Normal Range
Total Cholesterol	6.22	<5.19 mmol/L
Triglycerides	4.14	<1.7 mmol/L
HDL-C	0.9	>1.3–1.54 (acceptable); > 1.55 mmol/L (desirable)
LDL-C	3.1	<2.5 mmol/L (optimal); 2.5–3.5 (near optimal)
Total Cholesterol: HDL-C ratio	6.9	at least <4
Chemistries		
Sodium	142	135–145 mmol/L
Potassium	4.1	3.5–5.0 mmol/L
Chloride	107	97–107 mmol/L
Bicarbonate	24	24–28 mmol/L
BUN	11.06	2.9–7.5 mmol/L
Creatinine	106	male: 53–106 μmol/L
Glucose	5.8	fasting: 3.6–5.5 mmol/L
Calcium	2.2	male: 2.05–2.55 mmol/L
Magnesium	0.95	0.66–1.07 mmol/L
Cardiac Enzymes	550	male: 38–174 U/L
Troponin T	0.72	<0.2 μg/L (elevation is consistent with MI)

continues

Hematology

WBC	8.2	$4.5-11 \times 10^9$/L
HGB	120	male: 126–174 mmol/L
HCT	0.36	male: 0.43–0.49
PLT	238	$150-450 \times 10^9$/L

Clotting Studies

PT	15.5	10–13 seconds
PTT	32	25–39 seconds
INR	1.5	<2.0

Arterial Blood Gas

Oxygen Saturation	95%	> 95%
pH	7.38	7.35–7.45
$paCO_2$	36	35–45 mm Hg
pO_2	92	80–95 mm Hg
HCO_3^-	18	18–23 mmol/L

◄NURSING CHECKLIST►

Heart and Peripheral Vasculature Assessment

Assessment of the Precordium

- Inspection
  - Aortic area
  - Pulmonic area
  - Midprecordial area
  - Tricuspid area
  - Mitral area
- Palpation
  - Aortic area
  - Pulmonic area
  - Midprecordial area
  - Tricuspid area
  - Mitral area
- Auscultation
  - Aortic area
  - Pulmonic area
  - Midprecordial area
  - Tricuspid area
  - Mitral area
  - Mitral and tricuspid area (S_3)
  - Mitral and tricuspid area (S_4)
  - Murmurs
  - Pericardial friction rub
  - Prosthetic heart valves

Assessment of the Peripheral Vasculature

- Inspection of the jugular venous pressure
- Inspection of the hepatojugular reflux
- Palpation and auscultation of arterial pulses
- Inspection and palpation of peripheral perfusion
  - Peripheral pulse
  - Colour
  - Clubbing
  - Capillary refill
  - Skin temperature
  - Edema
  - Ulcerations
  - Skin texture
  - Hair distribution
- Palpation of the epitrochlear node

Advanced Techniques

- Orthostatic hypotension assessment
- Assessing for pulsus paradoxus
- Assessing the venous system
  - Homan's sign
  - Manual compression
- Assessing the arterial system
  - Pallor
  - Colour return and venous filling time
  - Allen test

REVIEW QUESTIONS

1. In assessing a patient's ECG strip, it is understood that the QRS complex represents contraction of the ventricles. Which phase of the cardiac cycle does this represent?
   a. Systole
   b. Diastole
   c. Isovolumetric contraction
   d. Diastasis
   The correct answer is (a).

2. When assessing an elderly patient, which finding should be reported immediately to the patient's provider?
   a. Pulse of 62 beats/minute, regular
   b. Blood pressure of 120/82
   c. Capillary refill of less than three seconds
   d. Detection of an S_3
   The correct answer is (d).

3. The fourth heart sound (S_4):
   a. Occurs during atrial contraction
   b. Is a normal finding in children
   c. Occurs after ventricular contraction
   d. Is best heard with a diaphragm of the stethoscope
   The correct answer is (a).

4. Your patient is a 55-year-old man diagnosed with hypertension (BP 178/102). What factor in the patient's history is a known modifiable risk factor for cardiovascular disease?
   a. Obesity
   b. Gender
   c. Sex
   d. Family history
   The correct answer is (a).

5. When assessing a patient who is thought to have pericarditis, which finding would strongly support this diagnosis?
   a. Dysphagia
   b. Pain in the left shoulder
   c. Bilateral lung crackles
   d. Pericardial friction rub
   The correct answer is (d).

6. When assessing a patient with congestive heart failure, which clinical manifestations are most suggestive of left ventricular heart failure?
   a. Distended neck veins and hepatomegaly
   b. Hemoptysis, orthopnea, and ascites
   c. Fatigue and lung crackles
   d. Angina, weight gain, and pitting edema
   The correct answer is (c).

7. Your patient has been admitted for evaluation of aortic regurgitation. Assessment of the patient will reveal a:
   a. Diastolic murmur that is loudest over the aortic area
   b. Systolic murmur that is loudest over the aortic area
   c. Diastolic pressure that is increased and a narrowed pulse pressure
   d. Systolic murmur that is loudest over the pulmonic area
   The correct answer is (a).

8. Patients with heart valve regurgitation will experience problems with the flow of blood _____, whereas patients with stenosis of heart valves will experience complications with the flow of blood _____.
   a. Forward, backward
   b. Forward, forward
   c. Backward, forward
   d. Backward, backward
   The correct answer is (c).

9. Which sign and symptom is consistent with chronic arterial insufficiency?
   a. Edema and blistering
   b. Shiny, waxy skin and sparse hair growth
   c. Thick, tough skin and dermatitis
   d. Reddish skin discoloration
   The correct answer is (b).

10. Virchow's triad, which explains the phenomenon that predisposes patients to pulmonary emboli, includes all of the following *except*:
    a. Stasis of blood flow
    b. Inadequate amounts of ATP
    c. Injured vessel wall
    d. Hypercoagulability
    The correct answer is (b).

Visit the Estes online companion resource at www.healthassessment.nelson.com for additional content and study aids.

REFERENCES

[1]Sheth, T., Nair, C., Nargundkar, M., Anand, S., & Yusul, S. (1999). Cardiovascular and cancer mortality among Canadians of European, South Asian and Chinese origin from 1979 to 1993: An analysis of 1.2 million deaths. *Canadian Medical Association Journal*, 161 (2): 132–38.

[2]Statistics Canada—Laboratory Centre for Disease Control (2002). *Mortality data: Leading causes of death both sexes combined, all*

ages, 1999, Canada. Retrieved October 29, 2006, from http://dsol-smed.phac-aspc.gc.ca/dsol-smed/cvd/c_quik_e.html

[3]Ibid.

[4]Ibid.

[5]Yusuf, S; Hawken, S., Ôunpuu, S., & Dans, T. (2004). Effect of potentially modifiable risk factors associated with myocardial infarction in 52 countries. *Lancet*, 364 (9438): 937–52.

[6]Society of Obstetricians and Gynaecologists of Canada. (2002). *The Canadian Consensus Conference on Menopause and Osteoporosis—2002 Update* (SOGC guideline no. 108). Ottawa.

BIBLIOGRAPHY

Alspach, J. (Ed.) (2006). *Core curriculum for critical care nursing* (6th ed.). St. Louis: Saunders Elsevier.

Chambers, L., Kaczorowski, J., Dolovich, L., Karwalajtys, T., et al. (2005). A community-based program for cardiovascular health awareness. *Canadian Journal of Public Health, 96* (4): 294–99.

Fahey, V. A. (2003). *Vascular nursing* (4th ed.). Philadelphia: W. B. Saunders.

Guyton, A. C., & Hall, J. E. (2006). *Textbook of medical physiology* (11th ed.). Philadelphia: W. B. Saunders.

Oneill, B. J., Brophy, J. M., Simpson, C. S., Sholdice, M. M., et. al. (2005). General commentary on access to cardiovascular care in Canada: Universal access but when? Treating the right patient at the right time. *Canadian Journal of Cardiology, 21*(14): 1272–76.

Pipes, D. P. (2005). Epidemiology and mechanisms of sudden cardiac death. *Canadian Journal of Cardiology, 21,* Suppl A (May 15): 27A–40A.

Stein, R. (2006). *Outliving heart disease. The 10 new rules for prevention and treatment.* New York: New Market W.W. Norton.

Wheatley, E. E. (2006). *Bodies at risk: An ethnography of heart disease.* Burlington, VT: Ashgate Pub. Co.

Woods, S. L., Sivarajan Froelicher, E. S., & Motzer, S. A. (2005). *Cardiac nursing* (5th ed.). Philadelphia: Lippincott Williams & Wilkins.

WEB RESOURCES

The Auscultation Assistant (audio clips for heart sounds)
http://www.wilkes.med.ucla.edu

Canadian Adult Congenital Heart Network
http://www.cachnet.org

Canadian Cardiovascular Society
http://www.ccs.ca/home/index_e.aspx

Canadian Institutes of Health Research: Institute of Circulatory and Respiratory Health
http://www.cihr-irsc.gc.ca/e/8663.html

Canadian Pediatric Cardiology Association
http://www.cardioped-canada.org/gen/links.asp

Centre for Chronic Disease Prevention and Control: Cardiovascular Disease
http://www.phac-aspc.gc.ca/ccdpc-cpcmc/cvd-mcv/index_e.html

Healthy Heart Kit
http://www.phac-aspc.gc.ca/ccdpc-cpcmc/hhk-tcs/english/guide/pdf_e/book_intro.pdf

Heart and Stoke Foundation of Canada
http://ww2.heartandstroke.ca

CHAPTER 17

Abdomen

COMPETENCIES

1. Identify the physiological function of the gastrointestinal organs.

2. Assess the health status of a patient with a gastrointestinal complaint.

3. Demonstrate the techniques of gastrointestinal assessment.

4. Relate abnormal physical gastrointestinal findings to pathological processes.

5. Outline the gastrointestinal variations associated with the aging process.

*A*ssessing the abdomen requires a complete understanding of anatomic and abdominal assessment norms. Examination of the abdomen provides significant information about the various functions of the gastrointestinal, cardiovascular, and genitourinary systems.

ANATOMY AND PHYSIOLOGY

Abdominal Cavity

The abdomen is the largest cavity of the body. It is located between the diaphragm and the symphysis pubis. It is oval shaped and contains several vital organs. The posterior wall of the cavity includes the lumbar vertebrae, the sacrum, and the coccyx. The iliac bones and the lateral portion of the ribs shape the sides of the abdominal cavity (Figures 17-1 and 17-2). These bony structures are held together by muscular tissue that surrounds the entire abdominal cavity. The muscles of the abdomen include the rectus abdominis, transversus abdominis, external oblique, and internal oblique. The **linea alba**, a tendinous tissue that extends from the sternum to the symphysis pubis in the midline of the abdomen, is situated between the rectus abdominis muscles (Figure 17-3).

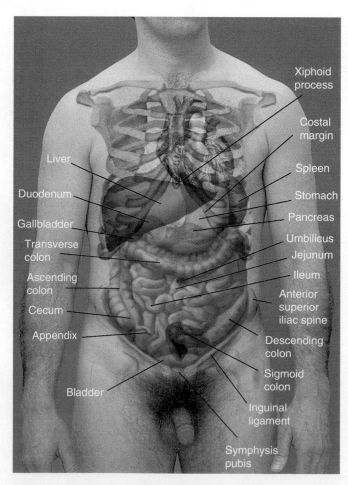

Figure 17-1 Structures of the Abdomen: Anterior View.

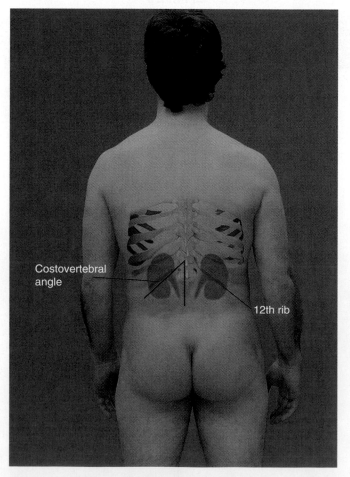

Figure 17-2 Structures of the Abdomen: Posterior View.

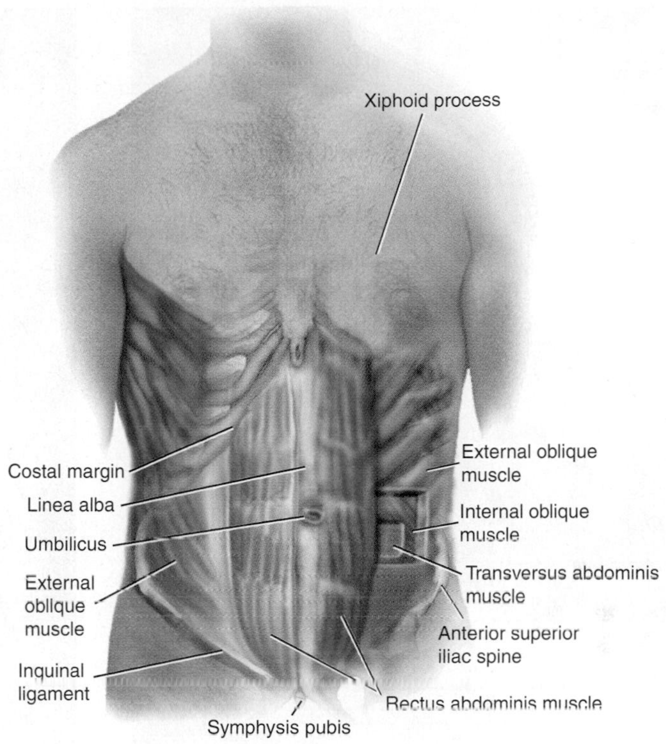

Figure 17-3 Abdominal Musculature.

Peritoneum

The endothelial lining of the abdominal cavity consists of membranes called peritoneal serous membranes. The serous layer that lines the walls of the cavity itself is called the parietal peritoneum and that which covers the organs is called the visceral peritoneum. The potential space between the two layers is referred to as the peritoneal cavity. In the male, this cavity is completely closed, whereas in the female, openings exist for the fallopian tubes.

The organs covered with peritoneum and held in place by mesentery are referred to as intraperitoneal organs. The intraperitoneal organs are the spleen, gallbladder, stomach, liver, bile duct, small intestine, and large intestine. In contrast, the organs situated behind the peritoneum and without mesenteric attachment are known as retroperitoneal organs. The retroperitoneal organs are the pancreas, kidneys, ureters, and bladder.

Abdominal Vasculature

The aorta is the largest artery in the body. Below the level of the diaphragm, the descending aorta becomes the abdominal aorta, giving rise to arterial vessels that supply the abdominal wall and gastrointestinal organs with blood (Figure 17-4). At about the fourth lumbar vertebra, the aorta bifurcates to become the right and left common iliac arteries.

Anatomic Mapping

Anatomic maps serve as a frame of reference during assessment of the abdomen. The abdominal cavity can be subdivided using two methods: quadrants or nine regions.

The most commonly used assessment approach in clinical practice is the four-quadrant technique (Figure 17-5). For accuracy in documentation, the abdominal surface is divided into four sections by imaginary vertical and

Life 360°

Abdominal Pathologies and Alcoholism

Many abdominal pathologies such as pancreatitis, cirrhosis, and portal hypertension can be caused by excessive alcohol intake. Reflect on the last time you provided care to a patient who had an alcohol-induced illness. Did you find it difficult to provide care for that patient? Did you treat that patient in a manner that was different from patients without histories of alcohol abuse?

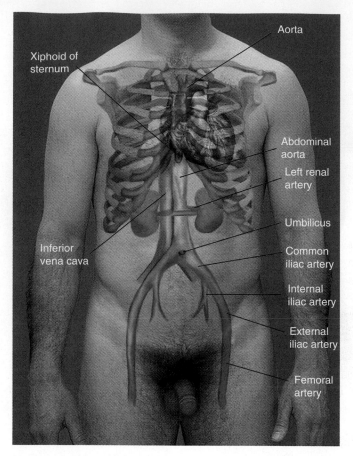

Figure 17-4 Abdominal Vasculature.

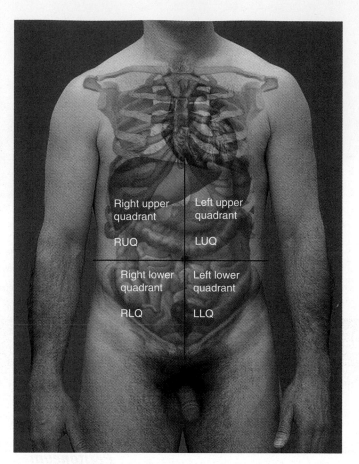

Figure 17-5 Abdominal Quadrants.

TABLE 17-1 Four-Quadrant Anatomic Map

RIGHT UPPER QUADRANT (RUQ)

- Liver
- Gallbladder
- Pylorus
- Duodenum
- Pancreas (head)
- Portion of right kidney and adrenal gland
- Hepatic flexure of colon
- Section of ascending and transverse colons

RIGHT LOWER QUADRANT (RLQ)

- Appendix
- Cecum
- Lower pole of right kidney
- Right ureter
- Right ovary (female)
- Right spermatic cord (male)

LEFT UPPER QUADRANT (LUQ)

- Left lobe of liver
- Stomach
- Spleen
- Pancreas (body)
- Portion of left kidney and adrenal gland
- Splenic flexure of colon
- Sections of transverse and descending colons

LEFT LOWER QUADRANT (LLQ)

- Sigmoid colon
- Section of descending colon
- Lower pole of left kidney
- Left ureter
- Left ovary (female)
- Left spermatic cord (male)

horizontal lines intersecting at the umbilicus. Commit to memory the location of abdominal organs according to quadrants (Table 17-1). Table 17-2 lists pathologies by the quadrant or region where the pain is perceived.

Another strategy for pinpointing the location of abdominal assessment findings is via nine abdominal anatomic regions (Figure 17-6). You can also use the anatomic landmarks in Figure 17-7.

TABLE 17-2 Etiologies of Abdominal Pain: Anatomical Regions where They Are Perceived

RIGHT UPPER QUADRANT	EPIGASTRIUM	LEFT UPPER QUADRANT
Biliary stone	Abdominal aortic aneurysm	Gastric ulcer
Cholecystitis	Appendicitis (early)	Gastritis
Cholelithiasis	Biliary stone	Myocardial infarction
Duodenal ulcer	Cholecystitis	Pneumonia
Gastric ulcer	Diverticulitis	Splenic enlargement
Hepatic abscess	Gastroesophageal reflux disease	Splenic rupture
Hepatitis	Hiatal hernia	
Hepatomegaly		
Pancreatitis		
Pneumonia		
	PERIUMBILICAL	
	Abdominal aortic aneurysm	
	Appendicitis (early)	
	Diverticulitis	
	Intestinal obstruction	
	Irritable bowel syndrome	
	Pancreatitis	
	Peptic ulcer	
	Recurrent abdominal pain (in children)	
	Volvulus	
RIGHT LOWER QUADRANT		**LEFT LOWER QUADRANT**
Appendicitis		Diverticulitis
Crohn's disease		Ectopic pregnancy (ruptured)
		Endometriosis
Diverticulitis		Hernia (strangulated)
Ectopic pregnancy (ruptured)		Irritable bowel syndrome
Endometriosis		Mittelschmerz
Hernia (strangulated)		Ovarian cyst
Irritable bowel syndrome		Pelvic inflammatory disease
Mittelschmerz		Renal calculi
		Salpingitis
Ovarian cyst		Ulcerative colitis
Pelvic inflammatory disease		
Renal calculi		
Salpingitis		
	DIFFUSE	
	Gastroenteritis	
	Peritonitis	

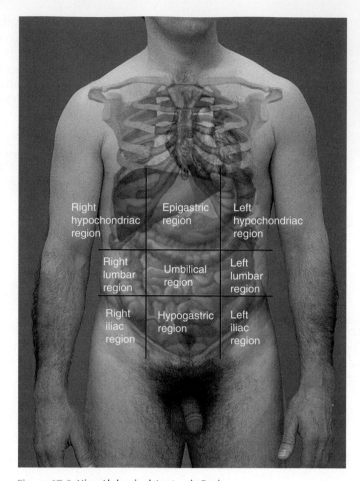

Figure 17-6 Nine Abdominal Anatomic Regions.

Right hypochondriac region

Epigastric region

Left hypochondriac region

Right lumbar region

Umbilical region

Left lumbar region

Right iliac region

Hypogastric region

Left iliac region

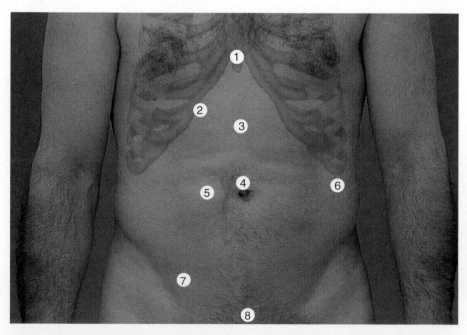

Figure 17-7 Abdominal Assessment Landmarks. When describing pathology of the abdomen, it is useful to use these anatomic landmarks: 1. Xiphoid Process; 2. Costal Margin; 3. Abdominal Midline; 4. Umbilicus; 5. Rectus Abdominis Muscle; 6. Anterior Superior Iliac Spine; 7. Inguinal Ligament (Poupart's Ligament); 8. Symphysis Pubis.

Abdominal Viscera (Organs)

Stomach

The stomach is a J-shaped pouchlike organ located in the left upper quadrant of the abdomen beneath the diaphragm; it lies to the right of the spleen and is partially covered by the liver.

The stomach functions as a reservoir where the complex mechanical and chemical processes of digestion occur. Hydrochloric acid and digestive enzymes are secreted by the stomach to aid digestion. Little absorption of foodstuffs occurs in the stomach. Foodstuffs are liquefied via gastric secretions into a semisolid substance called chyme. The usual capacity of the stomach is 1 to 1.5 litres. In a regulated manner, chyme is released into the small intestine's duodenum for further digestion and absorption.

Small Intestine

The small intestine is a tubular-shaped organ extending from the pyloric sphincter to the ileocecal valve at the opening of the large intestine. The majority of foodstuffs are digested and absorbed in the small intestine. The convoluted loops of intestine are relatively mobile and can measure from 3 to 9 m, depending on the degree of muscular relaxation of the intestinal wall and the size of the individual. Portions of the small intestine can be found in all four abdominal quadrants. The three segments of the small intestine are the duodenum, the jejunum, and the ileum. The duodenum is the first and shortest section. It plays a significant role in digestion because hormonal secretions are released, and both the common bile and main pancreatic ducts open into the duodenum. The jejunum, the second component, is composed of circular mucosal folds that provide surface area for nutrient absorption. The ileum absorbs bile salts and vitamin B_{12}. The ileum terminates at the ileocecal valve.

Large Intestine

The large intestine is a tubular-shaped organ extending from the ileocecal valve to the anus. It has a greater diameter than the small intestine and can vary considerably in length, depending on the size of the individual, but generally is 1.5 metres in length.

The four segments of the large intestine are the ascending, transverse, descending, and sigmoid colons. The cecum is the blind pouch that is continuous with the ascending colon, the large intestine located in the lower right quadrant of the abdomen.

The work of the large intestine is to form stool from cellulose, indigestible fibres, fat, bacteria, cellular debris, and inorganic materials, and then carry these intestinal contents to the end of the gastrointestinal tract. An additional function of the large intestine is the absorption of water and electrolytes. Water

---

Nursing Alert

Clostridium difficile (C. difficile)

This bacterium causes diarrhea and conditions such as colitis. It is the most common cause of infectious diarrhea in hospitalized patients in the industrialized world. Symptoms include watery diarrhea (at least three bowel movements/day for two or more days), fever, loss of appetite, nausea, abdominal pain/tenderness.[1] *C. difficile* produces spores that are resistant to destruction by many environmental influences, including a number of chemicals. Spread of *C. difficile* occurs due to inadequate hand hygiene and environmental cleaning, therefore, proper control is achieved though consistent hand hygiene and thorough cleaning of the patient environment.

Nursing Alert

Risk for Fluid Imbalance

If the patient is vomiting, there is a risk of dehydration and electrolyte imbalance. Remember to assess skin turgor, mucous membranes, and orthostatic blood pressure. See Chapters 10, 13, and 16.

Nursing Alert

Bloody Vomitus

Hematemesis, or the vomiting of blood, may be attributed to gastrointestinal ulcers or esophageal varices. Active bleeding is a medical emergency, and the patient should be treated promptly.

absorption occurs primarily in the ascending colon under the influence of the osmotic pressure gradient produced by sodium ions. The large intestine has limited digestive function.

Liver

The liver is the largest solid organ in the body. It lies directly below the diaphragm. The liver is located in the right upper quadrant, but extends across the midline into the left upper quadrant. In the right upper quadrant, the superior aspect of the liver is at the fifth rib, or at the nipples. The lower border does not extend more than 1 to 2 cm below the right costal margin.

The functions of the liver are complex and varied, and can be divided into:

- Storage (carbohydrates, amino acids, vitamins, minerals, and blood)
- Detoxification and filtration (drugs, hormones, and bacteria)
- Metabolism (carbohydrates, proteins, fat, ammonia to urea)
- Synthesis and secretion (bile production—600 to 1,000 mL/day, formation of lymph, bile salts, plasma proteins, fibrinogen, blood-clotting substances, and antibodies)

Nursing Tip

Cause of Flatulence

Most gases are nitrogen and oxygen derived from swallowing. Bacterial gas formation occurs in the large intestine and is expelled as flatus.

Gallbladder

The gallbladder is a pear-shaped sac located in the right upper quadrant of the abdomen. It is attached to the inferior surface of the liver.

The primary role of the gallbladder is to store and concentrate the bile produced by the liver. Bile contributes to fat digestion and absorption. The gallbladder stores approximately 30 to 50 mL of bile and releases bile in the presence of cholecystokinin, pancreozymin, and parasympathetic stimulation. As the gallbladder contracts, bile is released through the cystic duct into the common bile duct, which drains into the duodenum.

Pancreas

The pancreas is an elongated accessory organ of digestion. It lies in a transverse position along the posterior abdominal wall. It is located in the upper right and upper left quadrants of the abdomen. The pancreas is both an exocrine gland that secretes bicarbonate and pancreatic enzymes (which aid in digestion), and an endocrine gland that secretes the hormones insulin, glucagon, and gastrin.

Spleen

The spleen is the largest lymph organ in the body. It is oval in shape and is composed of white pulpy lymphoid tissue and red pulp containing capillaries and venous sinuses. It is located behind the fundus of the stomach, below the diaphragm and above the left kidney and splenic flexure. The spleen is found in the upper left quadrant of the abdomen.

The spleen is part of the reticuloendothelial system and serves the body as a filter and a reservoir for red blood cell mass. During events that can cause vasoconstriction, such as hemorrhage or exercise, the spleen contributes needed blood to the general circulation. As a filter, the spleen rids the body of old or deformed red blood cells and platelets.

Vermiform Appendix

The vermiform appendix extends off the lower cecum in the right lower quadrant. This fingerlike appendage fills with digestive materials from the cecum. The vermiform appendix may not empty completely, causing obstruction and subsequent infection.

Kidneys, Ureters, and Bladder

The kidneys are bean-shaped organs that lie tucked against the posterior abdominal wall. The left kidney is slightly larger in some individuals. Because of the superior placement of the liver over the right kidney, that kidney tends to hang about 1.25 cm lower than the left, between T12 and L3.

The primary function of the kidneys is to rid the body of waste products and to maintain homeostasis through regulation of the acid–base balance, fluid and electrolyte balance, and arterial blood pressure.

Urine leaves the kidneys via the ureters. Peristaltic waves move the waste products to the bladder. The bladder stores the urine. Normally the bladder holds 200 to 400 mL of urine; however, its capacity is greater.

Lymph Nodes

The inguinal area contains deep and superficial lymph nodes. Only the superficial nodes are palpable. These lymph nodes are grouped into superior and inferior chains. The superior chain of lymph nodes is located horizontally near the inguinal ligament. The inferior chain of lymph nodes lies vertically below the junction of the saphenous and femoral veins (Figure 17-8).

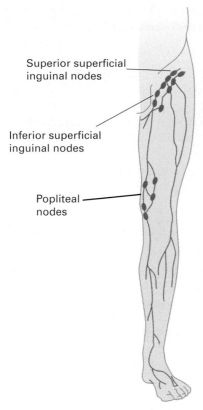

Superior superficial inguinal nodes

Inferior superficial inguinal nodes

Popliteal nodes

Figure 17-8 Inguinal Lymph Nodes.

HEALTH HISTORY

The abdominal health history provides insight into the link between a patient's life and lifestyle and abdominal information and pathology.

PATIENT PROFILE	*Diseases that are age- and gender-specific for the abdomen are listed.*
Age	Recurrent abdominal pain (2–15) Appendicitis (young child–30) Peptic ulcer disease (> 30, with an increased incidence in the elderly) Cholecystitis (40–50) Diabetes mellitus (type 2 > 45) Colonic diverticulosis (> 50) Bladder cancer (50–70) Pancreatic cancer (60–70s) Mesenteric arterial insufficiency or infarct (more prevalent in the elderly, especially those with arteriosclerotic or atherosclerotic disease)
Gender	
Female	Gallbladder disease, mittelschmerz (ovulatory pain)
Male	Pancreatic cancer, gastric cancer, cancer of the kidney and bladder, cirrhosis, duodenal ulcer, diverticulosis
Ethnicity	**Stomach cancer:** highest rates in Latin America, most of Asia and Eastern Europe

continues

Primary liver cancer: high incidence in east and Southeast Asia, particularly among men

Esophageal cancer: common in China, India, Japan and England; "esophageal cancer belt" crosses central Asia

Hepatitis A: high prevalence in the areas of Africa, Asia, and Central and South America with very poor sanitary/hygienic conditions[2]

Hepatitis B: high in immigrant populations, the Inuit; intermediate among First Nations[3]

HEALTH ISSUE/CONCERN	*Common health issues/concerns for the abdomen are defined and information on the characteristics of each sign or symptom is provided.*
Nausea	An uncomfortable sensation in the stomach and abdominal region
Quality	Retching (dry heaves)
Associated Manifestations	Vomiting, medication use, fever, chills, foods eaten, fluids consumed, diarrhea, pregnancy
Aggravating Factors	Noxious odours
Alleviating Factors	Flat soda, dry crackers, sleep, antiemetics
Timing	Early morning, bedtime, middle of the night, after eating, after missed menstrual period
Vomiting	Expulsion of contents from the upper gastrointestinal tract via contraction of abdominal wall muscles and relaxation of the esophageal sphincter
Quality	Colour (bright red: fresh blood; coffee grounds appearance: "old" blood that has had time to mix with digestive juices; dark brown or black: bile; other colours may occur secondary to food intake), projectile
Associated Manifestations	Nausea, medications, fever, chills, abdominal pain, headache, foods eaten, fluids consumed, diarrhea, pregnancy
Aggravating Factors	Noxious odours
Alleviating Factors	Flat soda, dry crackers, sleep, antiemetic medications, NPO for brief period if >2 vomits
Timing	Early morning, bedtime, middle of the night, after eating, after missed menstrual period
Diarrhea	Frequent watery stools resulting in the loss of essential electrolytes
Quality	Colour; presence of blood, mucous, or fat; odour
Associated Manifestations	Abdominal cramping, pain, physical weakness, weight loss, fever, stress
Aggravating Factors	Food, medications, stress
Alleviating Factors	Diet (bananas, rice, apples, toast), medications, fluids with electrolyte supplement, physical rest
Timing	Recent travel, especially areas with unpotable water; recent antibiotic use

continues

Constipation	Infrequent stools resulting in the passage of dry, hard fecal waste
Quality	Colour, odour, appearance of blood
Associated Manifestations	Physical discomfort, rectal fullness, nausea, bloating, pain with defecation
Aggravating Factors	Dietary fibre < 25–30 g/day, medications (e.g., iron, opioids, anticholinergics, hypnotics, sedatives), stress, fluid intake < 1.5–2 L/day
Alleviating Factors	High-fibre diet, medications (e.g., laxatives, stool softeners, enemas), physical activity, increased fluid intake
Setting	Lack of privacy, inability to assume squat position
Timing	Inability to respond to defecation urge
Abdominal Distension	Protuberance of the abdomen
Quantity	Degree of distension and frequency (may need to measure abdomen)
Associated Manifestations	Constipation, abdominal discomfort, ascites, enlarged liver, enlarged spleen
Aggravating Factors	Food, medications, stress
Alleviating Factors	Diet, medications, physical activity
Abdominal Pain	Discomfort in the abdomen; may be visceral, parietal, or referred pain (Table 17-3)
Quality	Dull, burning, sharp, gnawing, stabbing, cramping (severe cramping is referred to as colic pain), aching, gradual, sudden
Associated Manifestations	Bleeding, flank pain, weight loss, nausea and vomiting, eructation, fever or chills, changes in bowel habits, flatus, prolonged immobility, menstrual cycle
Aggravating Factors	Position, stress, eating, smoking, medications (e.g., aspirin, steroids, NSAID), alcohol or drug use
Alleviating Factors	Antacids, proton pump inhibitors (PPI), histamine-2 antagonists, rest, diet, stress management, position change
Setting	Home environment, work environment, mealtimes, social occasions involving alcohol or drug use
Timing	Pre- or postprandial, nighttime, seasonal, stressful situations, menstruation
Increased Eructation	Belching, or the oral expression of air (gas) from the stomach
Quantity	Marked increase over patient's normal status
Aggravating Factors	Ingestion of milk products, certain foods, carbonated beverages, beer
Increased Flatulence	Passage of excess gas via the rectum
Quantity	Marked increase over patient's normal status
Associated Manifestations	Ingestion of certain foods (onions, cabbage, beans, cauliflower, corn, wheat, barley, rye)
Aggravating Factors	Food or medications
Alleviating Factors	Avoidance of particular foods that are fermentable

continues

Timing	Following meals
Dysuria	Painful urination
Location	Suprapubic, near urinary meatus
Quality	Burning, stabbing
Associated Manifestations	Abdominal/flank/testicular pain, fever, chills, current bacterial infection, hematuria, dribbling, urethral discharge, decreased urinary flow, urgency, hesitancy, nocturia, recent sexual intercourse
Aggravating Factors	Presence of prostatic stones or renal calculi, decreased oral intake
Alleviating Factors	Medications (antibiotics, pyridium, analgesics), passage or surgical removal of stone, transurethral resection of the prostate, increased oral intake
Setting	New sexual partner in the last six months, a sexual partner known to have other sexual partners, unprotected intercourse, wiping genitalia back to front (female)
Timing	At start of urination, midstream, throughout stream, sense of urgency, pregnancy
Nocturia	Night arousal to void
Associated Manifestations	Hesitancy, decrease in force of urinary stream, postvoid dribbling, urge incontinence
Aggravating Factors	Enlarged prostate, diabetes mellitus, diuretics, urinary tract infection, alcohol ingestion, anticholinergic medications, decongestants, and cough medicines
Alleviating Factors	Adrenergic antagonists, 5–alpha-reductase inhibitors, transurethral resection of prostate, elimination of causative medications
Urinary Incontinence	
Quality	Constant, intermittent, dribbling, large volumes, hesitancy
Quantity	Frequency, urgency, number of pads used
Associated Manifestations	Recent surgery, coughing, sneezing, crying, laughing, heavy lifting, activity, medications, urinary tract infection, constipation, spinal cord lesions, neurological disease
Aggravating Factors	Medications, caffeine intake, alcohol intake, inadequate fluid intake (concentrated urine stimulates urination)
Alleviating Factors	Pelvic floor muscle rehabilitation, bladder training, biofeedback, anti-incontinence devices, medications
Setting	Accessibility of toilet, distance to toilet, adequate lighting to toilet, grab bars by toilet, height of toilet seat
Timing	Nocturia
PAST HEALTH HISTORY	*The various components of the past health history are linked to abdominal pathology and abdomen-related information.*

continues

Abdomen Specific	Malignancies, peritonitis, cholecystitis, appendicitis, pancreatitis, small bowel obstruction, ulcerative colitis, hepatitis, hiatal hernia, diverticulitis, diverticulosis, peptic ulcer disease, Crohn's disease, acute renal failure, chronic renal failure, gallstones, kidney stone, irritable bowel syndrome, gastroesophageal reflux disease, urinary tract infection, parasitic infections, food poisoning, cirrhosis, infectious mononucleosis, hyper- or hypoadrenalism, malabsorption syndromes
Non-Abdomen Specific	Pulmonary tuberculosis, malaria, heart disease, thyroid or parathyroid disease, pneumonia, upper respiratory infections, allergies, postnasal discharge, sinusitis, stress, sexually transmitted infection (STI), puberty, menopause, diabetes, ketoacidosis, ectopic pregnancy, cystic fibrosis, endometriosis, lupus, sickle cell anemia
Surgical History	Cholecystectomy, gastrectomy, Billroth I or II, ileostomy, colostomy, appendectomy, colectomy, nephrectomy, pancreatectomy, ileal conduit, portal caval shunt, splenectomy, hiatal hernia repair, umbilical hernia repair, femoral or inguinal hernia repair, removal of renal calculi, liver transplant, renal transplant, bariatric surgery
Medications	Histamine-2 antagonists, PPI, antibiotics, lactulose, antacids, vitamins, antiparasitics, anticholinergics, tranquilizers, steroids, antidiarrheals, electrolytes, laxatives, stool softeners, insulin, antiemetics, antiflatulents
Communicable Diseases	STI, HIV infection, hepatitis, tuberculosis, infectious mononucleosis, and intestinal parasites
	HIV opportunistic infections: enteric pathogens—*Cryptosporidium* causes weight loss from malabsorption syndrome and persistent debilitating diarrhea. Kaposi's sarcoma lesions can cause bowel occlusion, leading to constipation.
Allergies	Ingestion of certain food types or medications may cause gastric irritation, nausea, and vomiting, lactose intolerance.
Injuries and Accidents	Abdominal trauma such as ruptured or bruised organs, gunshot wounds, or knife stabbings; swallowing of foreign bodies
FAMILY HEALTH HISTORY	*Abdominal diseases and disorders that are familial are listed.*
	Malignancies of the stomach, liver, pancreas, or colon, peptic ulcer disease, diabetes mellitus, familial polyposis, inflammatory bowel disease, irritable bowel syndrome, polycystic kidney disease, colitis, malabsorption syndromes (celiac disease, cystic fibrosis)
SOCIAL HISTORY	*The components of the social history are linked to abdomen factors and pathology.*
Alcohol Use	Altered nutrition, impaired gastric absorption, at risk for upper and lower gastrointestinal bleeding, cirrhosis of liver
Drug Use	Opioids reduce peristalsis and are associated with the development of constipation.
Travel History	Infectious diarrhea may be produced by bacteria such as *Escherichia coli* and parasites that may not be indigenous to the patient's usual environment. Hepatitis A in areas with poor sanitation

continues

Work Environment	Improper food preparation and handling, water contamination, and poor sanitation can lead to hepatitis and *Escherichia coli* infections.
Home Environment	Public water versus well water; lead-based paint in homes built before 1976
Hobbies and Leisure Activities	Sports often associated with traumatic injuries, such as hockey, football, and boxing
Economic Status	Bacterial and parasitic diseases from poor sanitation
Stress	Abdominal cramping or discomfort, stress ulcers associated with stress response
HEALTH MAINTENANCE ACTIVITIES	*This information provides a bridge between the health maintenance activities and abdominal function.*
Sleep	Nocturnal pain with peptic ulcer disease; hiatal hernia discomfort in recumbent position
Diet	Healthy diet as a means of avoiding problems (fruits, vegetables, fibre, alcohol in moderation, decreased intake of fat and prepared foods); gallbladder attacks after fatty meals; caffeinated beverages, coffee, tea, and alcohol exacerbate GERD.
Exercise	Regular exercise facilitates gastrointestinal functioning.
Stress Management	High stress levels are associated with stress ulcers.
Use of Safety Devices	Shoulder and lap restraints in automobiles to prevent abdominal injuries; appropriate sports safety equipment to protect abdominal region
Health Check-Ups	Blood chemistry: Elevated glucose might indicate onset of diabetes mellitus.
	Blood count: Anemia could reflect silent gastrointestinal bleeds.
	Urinalysis: Dark colour may signify bilirubin in urine.
	See Chapter 22 for screening guidelines for colorectal cancer.

TABLE 17-3 Differentiating Abdominal Pain

	VISCERAL PAIN	PARIETAL PAIN	REFERRED PAIN
Origin	Originates in the abdominal organs	Originates in the parietal peritoneum	Originates from abdominal organs to nonabdominal locations (e.g., chest, spine, or pelvis); refer path to abdominal region
Cause	Hollow structures become painful when they contract forcefully or when distended (e.g., intestines); solid organs become painful when stretched	Inflammation	Nerve innervation
Characteristics	Deep, dull, poorly localized; usually begins as dull pain, but when it becomes intense, is associated with nausea, vomiting, pallor, and diaphoresis	Sharp, precisely localized; usually serve from the onset and intensifies with movement	Well localized; pain is from a disorder in another site; for example: Duodenal pain: back and right shoulder; Pancreatic pain: back and left shoulder

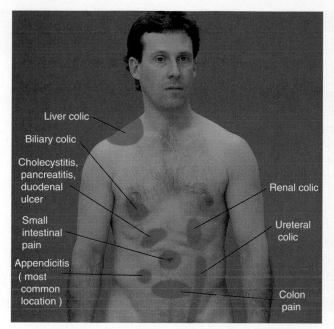

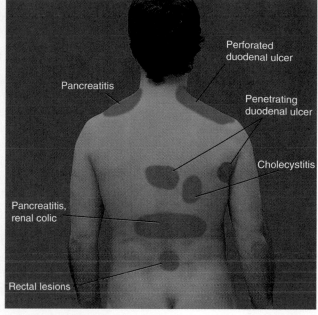

A. Anterior View

B. Posterior View

Figure 17-9 Areas of Referred Pain.

Nursing Alert

Acute Abdominal Pain and Analgesia

Acute abdominal pain can be difficult to assess as there are many possible causes such as appendicitis, cholecystitis, bowel obstruction, urinary colic, gastritis, peptic ulcer disease, gastroenteritis, pancreatitis, diverticulitis, gynecologic disorders in women, and other reasons. Pain originating from the liver, spleen, pancreas, stomach, and duodenum may be referred (Figure 17-9). There is a controversy about management of acute abdominal pain. Some clinicians argue that analgesia should be withheld until a diagnosis is made for fear of "masking" the symptoms; others argue that analgesia does not interfere with the diagnosis and may even facilitate it, as a more extensive physical examination can be performed. As well, the analgesia is unlikely to remove all pain so there still remains a "symptom" for assessment. Fortunately, the Cochrane Collaboration has launched a systematic review on the topic of analgesia for patients with acute abdominal pain.[4]

EQUIPMENT

- Drapes
- Small pillow for under knee
- Tape measure or small ruler with centimetre markings
- Marking pencil
- Gooseneck lamp for tangential lighting
- Stethoscope
- Sterile safety pin or sterile needle

ASSESSMENT OF THE ABDOMEN

The order of abdominal assessment is inspection, auscultation, percussion, and palpation. Auscultation is performed second because percussion and palpation can alter bowel sounds.

Nursing Tip

Abdominal Inspection

1. Position tangential light lengthwise across the patient's abdomen at a right angle.
2. Position yourself on a horizontal plane looking at the patient's abdomen, or slightly higher.

Nursing Tip

7 Fs of Abdominal Distension

Seven possible causes of abdominal distension are:

- Fat
- Fluid (ascites)
- Flatus
- Feces
- Fetus
- Fatal growth (malignancy)
- Fibroid tumour

◄ NURSING CHECKLIST ►

General Approach to Abdominal Assessment

1. Greet the patient and explain the assessment technique.
2. Ensure that the room is at a warm, comfortable temperature to prevent patient chilling and shivering.
3. Use a quiet room that will be free from interruptions.
4. Utilize an adequate light source. This includes both a bright overhead light and a freestanding lamp for tangential lighting.
5. Ask the patient to urinate before the exam.
6. Drape the patient from the xiphoid process to the symphysis pubis, and then expose the patient's abdomen.
7. Position the patient comfortably in a supine position with knees flexed over a pillow or position the patient so that the arms are either folded across the chest or at the sides to ensure abdominal relaxation.
8. Stand to the right side of the patient for the examination.
9. Visualize the underlying abdominal structures during the assessment process in order to accurately describe the location of any pathology.
10. Have the patient point to tender areas; assess these last. Mark these and other significant findings (scars, dullness, and so on) on the body diagram in the patient's chart.
11. Watch the patient's face closely for signs of discomfort or pain.
12. Help the patient relax by using an unhurried approach, diverting attention with questions, and so on.
13. Ensure that your hands and the stethoscope are warm to promote patient comfort.

Inspection

Contour

E View the contour of the patient's abdomen from the costal margin to the symphysis pubis.

N **In the normal adult, the abdominal contour is flat (straight horizontal line from costal margin to symphysis pubis) or rounded (convexity of abdomen from costal margin to symphysis pubis). See Figure 17-10.**

A Assessment reveals a large convex symmetrical profile from the costal margin to the symphysis pubis.

P A large convex abdomen can result from one of the 7 Fs. Refer to 7 Fs of Abdominal Distension Nursing Tip.

A A convex abdomen that has a marked increase at the height of the umbilicus is abnormal.

P A protuberant abdomen may result from a wide range of disorders. Taut stretching of the skin across the abdominal wall may be present. Refer to the 7 Fs of Abdominal Distension Nursing Tip.

A A concave symmetrical profile from the costal margin to the symphysis pubis is abnormal.

P A scaphoid abdomen reflects a decrease in fat deposits, a malnourished state, or flaccid muscle tone.

Symmetry

E 1. View the symmetry of the patient's abdomen from the costal margin to the symphysis pubis.
   2. Move to the foot of the examination table and recheck the symmetry of the patient's abdomen.

Flat

Rounded

Scaphoid

Protuberant

Figure 17-10 Abdominal Configurations.

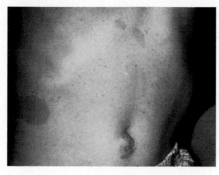

Figure 17-11 von Recklinghausen's Disease. *Courtesy of the Armed Forces Institute of Pathology.*

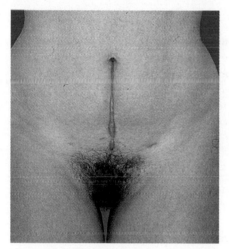

Figure 17-12 Abdominal Scar from a Hysterectomy.

N The abdomen should be symmetrical bilaterally.

A Assessment reveals an asymmetrical abdomen.

P Asymmetry may be caused by a tumour, cysts, bowel obstruction, enlargement of abdominal organs, or scoliosis. Bulging at the umbilicus can indicate an umbilical hernia.

P If the abdomen is asymmetrical at the site of a surgical incision or scar, suspect an incisional hernia.

Rectus Abdominis Muscles

E 1. Instruct the patient to raise the head and shoulders off the examination table.

   2. Observe the rectus abdominis muscles for separation.

N The symmetry of the abdomen remains uniform; no ridge is observed parallel to the umbilicus or between the rectus abdominis muscles.

A A ridge between the rectus abdominis muscles is observed.

P This abnormality is known as diastasis recti abdominis and is attributed to marked obesity or past pregnancy. The observed separation of rectus abdominis muscles is caused by increased intra-abdominal pressure and is not considered to be harmful or ominous.

Pigmentation and Colour

E View the colour of the patient's abdomen from the costal margin to the symphysis pubis.

N The abdomen should be uniform in colour and pigmentation.

A Uneven skin colour or pigmentation is abnormal.

P The presence of jaundice suggests liver dysfunction. The yellow discoloration of the skin in light-skinned patients is due to the accumulation of bilirubin in the blood. The average level for visible jaundice is 35 μmol/L.

P In light-skinned individuals, the observation of a blue tint at the umbilicus suggests free blood in the peritoneal cavity, known as **Cullen's sign**. Such bleeding can occur either following rupture of a fallopian tube secondary to an ectopic pregnancy or with acute hemorrhagic pancreatitis.

P Irregular patches of tan skin pigmentation (café au lait spots) may be attributed to von Recklinghausen's disease (Figure 17-11), a familial condition associated with the formation of neurofibromas.

P Engorged abdominal veins are abnormal.

P The appearance of engorged or dilated veins around the umbilicus is called **caput medusae**. It is associated with circulatory obstruction of the superior or the inferior vena cava. In some instances, this condition is related to obstruction of the portal vein or to emaciation.

Scars

E Inspect the abdomen for scars from the costal margin to the symphysis pubis.

N There should be no abdominal scars present.

A Scars are present (Figure 17-12).

P The site of the scars discloses useful information about the patient's surgical history. Dense, irregular, collagenous scars are keloids, which are more common in dark-skinned individuals and may be associated with traumatic injuries or burns. The presence of surgical scars may indicate internal adhesions.

A A network of dilated veins on the abdomen is abnormal.

P This occurs in portal hypertension, cirrhosis, and vena cava obstruction secondary to increased venous pressures.

E	Examination	N	Normal Findings	A	Abnormal Findings	P	Pathophysiology

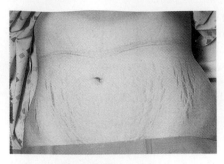

Figure 17-13 Abdominal Striae.

Striae

E   Observe the abdominal skin for **striae** (stretch marks), or abdominal atrophic lines or scars.

N   No evidence of striae is present.

A   Striae are present (Figure 17-13).

P   Striae, atrophic lines or streaks, occur when there has been rapid or prolonged stretching of the skin. Abdominal striae may be caused by Cushing's syndrome, abdominal tumours, obesity, ascites, or pregnancy. Following pregnancy, striae are a normal finding.

Reflective Thinking

Hepatitis B Risks

A 29-year-old man who recently immigrated to Canada from an area of the world with a high incidence of hepatitis B is seeking follow-up care for abdominal pain and jaundice. Laboratory data indicate that he has hepatitis B. He tells you that he is worried about telling his wife about his diagnosis because he thinks she may accuse him of having an extramarital affair. How would you respond?

Nursing Alert

Hepatitis A

Accounts for 20 to 40% of acute hepatitis in adults. The most common mode of transmission is via the fecal–oral route, either directly through interpersonal contact or indirectly through ingestion of contaminated food or water.[5] Hepatitis A is reportable in Canada, and vaccination is recommended by the National Advisory Committee for Immunization (NACI) for individuals at increased risk. Incubation period is from 10 to 50 days, depending on dose; average is 28 to 30 days.[6]

Risk Factors

- Overcrowded living quarters
- Poor personal hygiene (poor handwashing, especially after defecation)
- Poor sanitation (sewage disposal)
- Food and water contamination
- Ingestion of shellfish caught in contaminated water
- Travel to endemic area (many developing countries)
- Those in close personal contact with infected individual
- Day care centres, especially those with children wearing diapers

Hepatitis B

Hepatitis B is an important vaccine-preventable infectious disease in Canada. Hepatitis B is transmitted through blood or body fluids contaminated with the virus. Incubation period is usually 24 to 180 days; average 60 to 90 days.[7]

Risk Factors

- Injection drug use with shared needles
- Receipt of multiple transfusions of blood and blood products (oncology and hemodialysis patients, hemophiliacs)
- Frequent contact with blood (health care workers such as nurses, doctors)
- Heterosexual activities such as having multiple heterosexual partners
- Sex with hepatitis B-infected individuals
- Male homosexual activity
- Perinatal transmission
- Travel to endemic areas (e.g., China)
- Sharing blood-contaminated toothbrushes, razors

Hepatitis C

A key feature of hepatitis C infection is the high frequency (75% to 85%) with which acute infection progresses to chronic infection, with serious sequelae

continues

appearing decades following infection.[8] Many Canadians will remember the 1980s controversial Krever Inquiry established to investigate tainted blood transfusions that led to many people becoming infected with hepatitis C (and HIV). Transmission of the virus from therapeutic blood or blood products has plummeted since 1990, when donor screening was introduced in Canada.[9] Hepatitis C is transmitted through blood or body fluids contaminated with the virus. Incubation period is usually seven to ten weeks.

Risk Factors

- Injection drug use with shared needles
- Sex with HCV-infected individuals
- Vertical transmission (from mother to baby) can occur but is inefficient
- Unapparent parenteral exposure, such as tattooing, body piercing, and sharing of personal hygiene items, is presumed to be a risk factor only if the instruments or items for such activities are contaminated with blood or body fluids

Hepatitis D

Incubation period between 2 to 12 weeks; shorter in hepatitis B virus carrier individuals. While there is no vaccine for hepatitis D, vaccination against hepatitis B will protect against the hepatitis D virus.[10]

Risk Factors

- See hepatitis B risk factors
- Coinfection with hepatitis B or superinfection with chronic hepatitis B virus infection
- Perinatal transmission (rare)

Hepatitis E

Rarely seen in Canada—currently not a notifiable disease according to Canadian National Surveillance; transmitted by fecal–oral route; high prevalence in subtropical areas (including South Asia, North Africa, and Central America).[11]

Hepatitis G

Thought to be a different strain of hepatitis C, there is little proof that hepatitis G causes serious liver disease at any age, though it is being monitored for possible health impact.[12]

Respiratory Movement

E   Observe the abdomen for smooth, even respiratory movement.

N   There is no evidence of respiratory retractions. Normally, the abdomen rises with inspiration and falls with expiration.

A   Abnormal respiratory movements and retractions are observed.

P   The origin of abnormal respirations due to an abdominal disorder may include appendicitis with local peritonitis, pancreatitis, biliary colic, or a perforated ulcer.

Masses or Nodules

E   Observe the abdominal skin for nodules or masses.

N   No masses or nodules are present.

A   Abdominal masses or nodules are present.

P   The presence of abdominal masses or nodules may indicate tumours, metastases of an internal malignancy, or pregnancy.

| E | Examination | N | Normal Findings | A | Abnormal Findings | P | Pathophysiology |

Visible Peristalsis

E   Observe the abdominal wall for surface motion.

N   **Ripples of peristalsis may be observed in thin patients. Peristalsis movement slowly traverses the abdomen in a slanting downward direction.**

A   Strong peristaltic contractions are observed.

P   Peristaltic waves may indicate intestinal obstruction.

Pulsation

E   Inspect the epigastric area for pulsations.

N   **In the patient with a normal build, a non-exaggerated pulsation of the abdominal aorta may be visible in the epigastric area. In heavier patients, pulsation may not be visible.**

A   Marked, strong abdominal pulsations are observed.

P   Widened pulse pressure and strong epigastric pulsations may indicate an aortic aneurysm. An exaggerated pulsation can also occur in aortic regurgitation and in right ventricular hypertrophy.

Umbilicus

E   1. Observe the umbilicus in relation to the abdominal surface.

    2. Ask the patient to flex the neck. Perform the valsalva manoeuvre.

    3. Observe for protrusion of the intestine through the umbilicus.

N   **The umbilicus is depressed and beneath the abdominal surface.**

A   The umbilicus protrudes above the abdominal surface.

P   Umbilical hernia in the adult is the protrusion of part of the intestine through an incomplete umbilical ring. Umbilical hernia is confirmed by inserting the index finger into the navel and feeling an opening in the fascia. It can often be seen when the patient's intra-abdominal pressure increases during coughing, sneezing, laughing, and straining.

P   The umbilicus that appears as a nodule may be the manifestation of abdominal carcinoma with metastasis to the umbilicus. This physical finding is known as Sister Mary Joseph's nodule.

P   Intra-abdominal pressure from ascites, masses, or pregnancy can cause the umbilicus to protrude.

Nursing Tip

Nasogastric Tube Suction

Prior to assessing the abdomen, if the patient has a nasogastric tube that is connected to suction, discontinue the suction in order to avoid interfering with auscultation findings. Remember to turn the suction on after your assessment.

◀NURSING CHECKLIST▶

Assessing Patients with Abdominal Tubes and Drains

For all tubes, drains, and intestinal and urinary diversions, note colour, odour, amount, consistency, and the presence of blood in any drainage. Check for an obstruction if there is no drainage. The skin around the device should be intact without excoriation.

Tubes

1. Enteral Tubes
   - Nasogastric, nasoduodenal, or nasojejunal.
   - Check the residual amount on a frequent basis. If greater than 100 mL, stop the feeding; restart the feeding based on further inspection of residual amounts.
2. Nasogastric (NG) Suction Tubes
   - Ensure that the suction setting (intermittent or continuous) is set at the appropriate suction level.

continues

3. Intestinal Tubes
   - Ensure that tube is advancing with peristalsis as expected.
   - Ensure that the suction setting is at the appropriate suction level.

4. Gastrostomy
   - With intermittent feedings, clamp is applied when not in use.
   - Tube should be secured to abdomen; check that dressing is applied.

Drains

1. Abdominal Cavity Drain (e.g., Hemovac, Jackson-Pratt)
   - To self-suction or wall suction; if wall suction, ensure that it is set at appropriate level.

2. Biliary Drain (T-Tube)
   - Tube is below insertion site.

Intestinal Diversions

1. Ileostomy, Colostomy
   - Stoma is pink; skin barrier should be used around stoma if appliance is worn.
   - Ileostomy drainage varies from liquid to pasty; colostomy drainage is generally formed stool.

Urinary Diversions

1. Ileal Conduit
   - Stoma is pink; skin barrier is used with appliance.

2. Ureteral Stents
   - Stent is secured to avoid pulling; no bleeding from insertion site.

3. Indwelling Catheter
   - Balloon inflated; catheter secured to patient to prevent dislodgement.
   - Urinary collecting bag is closed and below level of bladder and without kinks.

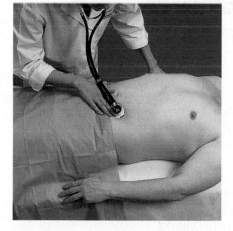

Figure 17-14 Technique of Abdominal Auscultation.

Nursing Alert

Palpation Contraindication

Never palpate over areas where bruits are auscultated. Palpation may cause rupture. Refer the patient immediately.

Auscultation

Bowel Sounds

E **1.** Place the diaphragm lightly on the abdominal wall beginning at the RLQ.
   2. Listen to the frequency and character of the bowel sounds. It is necessary to listen for at least five minutes in an abdominal quadrant before concluding that bowel sounds are absent.
   3. Move diaphragm to RUQ, LUQ, LLQ (Figure 17-14).

N Bowel sounds are heard as intermittent gurgling sounds throughout the abdominal quadrants. Usually, they are high-pitched sounds and occur 5 to 30 times per minute. Bowel sounds result from the movement of air and fluid through the gastrointestinal tract. Normally, bowel sounds are always present at the ileocecal valve area (RLQ).

N Normal hyperactive bowel sounds are called borborygmi. They are loud, audible, gurgling sounds. Borborygmi may be due to hyperperistalsis ("stomach growling") or the sound of flatus in the intestines.

A Absent bowel sounds are abnormal.

P Absent bowel sounds are indicative of late intestinal obstruction, both mechanical and non-mechanical in nature. Mechanical obstruction of the bowel may result from extraluminal lesions such as adhesions, hernias, and

---

E	**Examination**	**N**	**Normal Findings**	**A**	**Abnormal Findings**	**P**	**Pathophysiology**

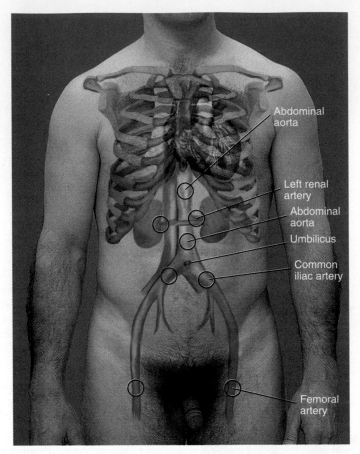

Figure 17-15 Stethoscope Placement for Auscultating Abdominal Vasculature.

masses. In non-mechanical obstruction, the gastrointestinal lumen remains unobstructed, but the muscles of the intestinal wall cannot move its contents. This type of obstruction can be caused by physiological, neurogenic, or chemical imbalances that result in paralytic ileus.

A   Hypoactive bowel sounds are abnormal.

P   Hypoactive or diminished bowel sounds indicate decreased motility of the bowel and can occur with peritonitis and non-mechanical obstruction. Other causes include inflammation, gangrene, electrolyte imbalances, and intraoperative manipulation of the bowel.

A   Hyperactive bowel sounds are abnormal.

P   Hyperactive or increased bowel sounds signify increased motility of the bowel and can result from gastroenteritis, diarrhea, laxative use, and subsiding ileus.

P   Auscultation of high-pitched tinkling hyperactive bowel sounds is indicative of partial obstruction. These sounds are caused by the powerful peristaltic action of the bowel segment attempting to eject its contents through a narrow, constricted area. Frequently, patients complain of abdominal cramping.

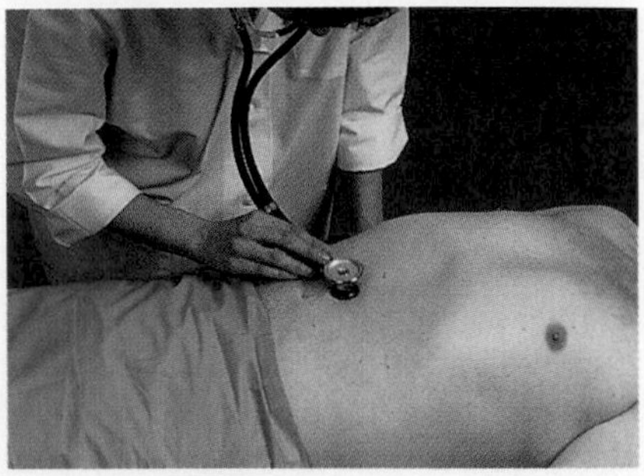

Vascular Sounds

E   1. Place the bell of the stethoscope over the abdominal aorta, renal arteries, iliac arteries, and femoral arteries (Figure 17-15).

    2. Listen for bruits over each area (Figure 17-16).

N   No audible bruits are auscultated.

A   Audible bruits are auscultated.

Figure 17-16 Auscultation of Aortic Bruits with Bell of Stethoscope.

P A bruit over an abdominal vessel indicates turbulence of blood flow and suggests a partial obstruction. Bruits can occur with abdominal aortic aneurysm, renal stenosis, and femoral stenosis.

Venous Hum

E Using the bell of the stethoscope, listen for a **venous hum**, or a continuous, medium-pitched sound, in all four quadrants.

N Venous hums are normally not present in adults.

A A continuous pulsing or fibrillary sound is auscultated.

P A venous hum in the periumbilical area is usually due to obstructed portal circulation. Portal hypertension caused by cirrhosis of the liver impedes portal circulation.

Friction Rubs

E 1. Using the diaphragm of the stethoscope, listen for friction rubs over the right and left costal margins, the liver, and the spleen.

 2. Listen for friction rubs in all four quadrants.

N No friction rubs should be present.

A Friction rubs are high-pitched sounds that resemble the sound produced by two pieces of sandpaper being rubbed together. The sound increases with inspiration.

P Friction rubs occur when tumours, inflammation, or infarct cause the visceral layers of the peritoneum to rub together over the liver and the spleen.

Percussion

General Percussion

E 1. Percuss all four quadrants in a systematic manner. Begin percussion in the RLQ, moving upward to the RUQ, crossing over to the LUQ, and moving down to the LLQ (Figure 17-17).

 2. Visualize each organ in the corresponding quadrant; note when tympany changes to dullness.

N Tympany is the predominant sound heard because air is present in the stomach and in the intestines. It is a high-pitched sound of long duration. In obese patients it may be difficult to elicit tympany due to the quantity of adipose tissue. Dullness is normally heard over organs such as the liver or a distended bladder. Dull sounds are high pitched and of moderate duration.

A Dullness over areas where tympany normally occurs, such as over the stomach and intestines, is considered abnormal.

P Dullness may be caused by a mass or tumour, pregnancy, ascites, or a full intestine.

Liver Span

E 1. Stand to the right side of the patient.

 2. Begin at the right midclavicular line below the umbilicus and percuss upward to determine the lower border of the liver (Figure 17-18A).

 3. With a marking pen, mark where the sound changes from tympany to dullness.

 4. Then, at the right midclavicular line, percuss downward from an area of lung resonance to one of dullness.

 5. With a tape measure or ruler, measure the two marks in centimetres (Figure 17-18B).

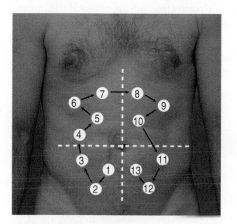

Figure 17-17 Direction of Pattern of Abdominal Percussion.

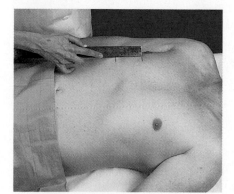

A. Determining Lower Liver Border

B. Measuring Liver Span

Figure 17-18 Percussing Liver Span.

| E | **Examination** | N | **Normal Findings** | A | **Abnormal Findings** | P | **Pathophysiology** |

N Normally, the distance between the two marks is 6 to 12 cm in the midclavicular line. There is a direct correlation between body size and the size of the liver. The mean span for a man is 10.5 cm and for a woman it is 7.0 cm.

A A liver span greater than 12 cm or less than 6 cm is considered abnormal.

P The liver span is increased when the liver becomes enlarged. Hepatomegaly can occur with various liver diseases such as hepatitis, cirrhosis, cardiac or renal congestion, cysts, or metastatic tumours.

P The liver span can be falsely increased when the upper border is obscured by the dullness of lung consolidation with pneumonia or pleural effusion.

P The liver span can be decreased in the later stages of cirrhosis when the disease causes liver atrophy.

P The liver span can be falsely decreased when gas in the colon, tumours, or pregnancy push the lower border of the liver upward.

Nursing Alert

Stomach Cancer

In 2006, stomach cancer was the 14th leading cause of new cancers in Canadians with men accounting for 65% of new cases. The incidence is declining, which may reflect improved diets and the role of infectious agents and their treatment (e.g., *Helicobacter pylori* therapy).[13]

Risk Factors

- Diet high in smoked foods, lacking in significant quantities of fruits and vegetables
- Pernicious anemia
- Possible hereditary factors
- Chronic stomach inflammation such as with *H. pylori* infection

---

Nursing Alert

Helicobacter pylori

H. pylori has been linked to gastroduodenal disease (over 60% of duodenal ulcers and 40% of gastric ulcers are associated with this bacteria) and is considered a cocarcinogen for gastric cancer. Patients who are diagnosed with *H. pylori* can expect to receive quadruple therapy (Proton Pump Inhibitor, bismuth, tetracycline, and metronidazole).[14]

Liver Descent

E 1. Percuss the liver descent by asking the patient to take a deep breath and to hold it (because on inspiration, the diaphragm moves downward).

2. Again, percuss the lower border of the liver at the right midclavicular line by percussing from tympany to dullness. Have the patient exhale.

3. Repercuss the liver–lung border.

4. Mark where the change in sound takes place.

5. Measure the difference in centimetres between the two lower borders of the liver.

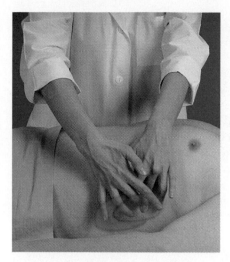

Figure 17-19 Percussion of the Spleen.

N Normally, the area of lower border dullness descends 2 to 3 cm.
A The liver descent is considered abnormal if it is greater or less than 2 to 3 cm.
P The liver descent is greater than 2 to 3 cm due to hepatomegaly, as in cirrhosis.
P The liver descent is less than 2 cm due to abdominal tumours, pregnancy, or ascites.

Spleen

E 1. Percuss the lower level of the left lung slightly posterior to the midaxillary line and continue downward (Figure 17-19).
   2. Percuss downward until dullness is ascertained. In some individuals, the spleen is positioned too deeply to be discernable by percussion.
N Normally, the upper border of dullness is found 6 to 8 cm above the left costal margin. Splenic dullness may be heard from the sixth to the tenth rib.
A Dullness beyond the 8 cm line is indicative of splenic enlargement. However, a full stomach or a feces-filled intestine may mimic the dullness of splenic enlargement. Moreover, gastric or colonic air may obscure the dullness of the spleen.
P Splenic enlargement can be due to portal hypertension resulting from liver disease; other potential causes are mononucleosis, thrombosis, stenosis, atresia, angiomatous deformities of the portal or splenic vein, cysts, or aneurysm of the splenic artery.

Stomach

E Percuss for a gastric air bubble in the LUQ at the left lower anterior rib cage and left epigastric region.
N The tympany of the gastric air bubble is lower in pitch than the tympany of the intestine.
A An increase in size of the gastric air bubble is abnormal.
P This increase in size accompanied by gastric distension can suggest gastric dilation.

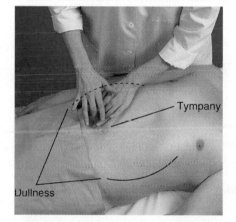

A. Patient Supine

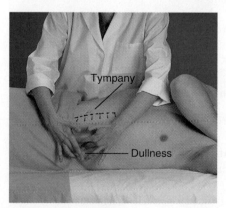

B. Patient on Left Side

Figure 17-20 Percussion for Ascites: Shifting Dullness.

Advanced Technique

Assessing for Ascites: Shifting Dullness and Puddle Sign

Assess the patient for **ascites,** or excess accumulation of fluid in the abdominal cavity. There are two methods for this assessment: **shifting dullness** and **puddle sign.**

Shifting Dullness

E 1. Standing to the right, with the patient supine, percuss over the top of the abdomen, beginning at the midline.
   2. Percuss outward toward the right side of the patient, following a downward direction (Figure 17-20A).
   3. Mark on the abdomen where percussion changes from tympany to dullness because this change is indicative of settled fluid in the flanks of the abdominal cavity.
   4. Turn the patient onto the right side.
   5. Repercuss the upper side of the abdomen, moving downward.

continues

| E | **Examination** | N | **Normal Findings** | A | **Abnormal Findings** | P | **Pathophysiology** |

Figure 17-21 Percussion for Ascites: Puddle Sign.

6. If the percussion sound changes from tympany to dullness above the prior-marked fluid line, this shifting dullness is positive for ascites.

7. Repeat the same assessment technique on the left side of the patient. Change the patient's position from the right to the left side (Figure 17-20B).

8. Mark where the percussion changes from tympany to dullness.

N There should be no change from tympany to dullness.

A There is a marked change from tympany to dullness as you percuss outward and downward. Ascites is present in the abdominal cavity.

P Ascitic fluid sinks with gravity, which accounts for the dullness in dependent areas. Ascites is found in cirrhosis and in other liver diseases.

Puddle Sign

E 1. Ask the patient to kneel and assume the knee–chest position for several minutes.

2. Percuss the umbilical area (Figure 17-21).

N The umbilical area should remain tympanic.

A The umbilical area percusses dull.

P The ascitic fluid pools in the dependent area of the umbilicus because of gravity.

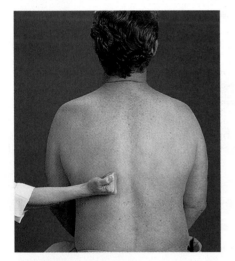

Figure 17-22A Direct Fist Percussion of the Left Kidney

Nursing Alert

Risk Factors for Ascites

- Increased vascular resistance to hepatic outflow
- Increased hepatic lymph flow and extravasation of fluid into the peritoneal cavity
- Portal hypertension and increased capillary filtration pressure
- Hypoalbuminemia and decreased colloid osmotic pressure of the serum
- Disordered kidney function
- Hyperaldosteronism
- Excessive secretion of antidiuretic hormone

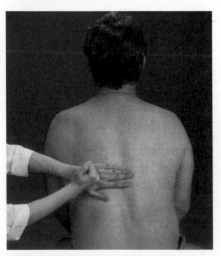

Figure 17-22B Indirect Fist Percussion of the Left Kidney

Fist Percussion

Fist percussion is done over the kidneys and liver to check for tenderness.

Kidney

E 1. Place the patient in a sitting position.

2. Strike the costovertebral angle with a closed fist (direct fist percussion, Figure 17-22A) or

2A. Place the palmar surface of one hand over the costovertebral angle (CVA). Strike that hand with the ulnar surface of the fist of the other hand (indirect fist percussion, Figure 17-22B).

3. Ask the patient what was felt. Observe the patient's reaction.

4. Repeat on the other side.

N No tenderness should be elicited.

A Tenderness or pain over the costovertebral angle is abnormal.

P Costovertebral angle tenderness can occur in pyelonephritis.

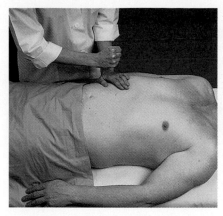

Figure 17-23 Indirect Fist Percussion of the Liver.

Liver

E 1. Place the patient in a supine position.
   2. Place the palmar surface of one hand over the lower right rib cage (where the liver was percussed).
   3. Strike that hand with the ulnar surface of the fist of the other hand (Figure 17-23).
   4. Ask the patient what was felt. Observe the patient's reaction.

N **No tenderness should be elicited.**

A Tenderness or pain that can be elicited over the liver is abnormal.

P Liver tenderness can occur in conjunction with cholecystitis or hepatitis.

Bladder

E 1. Percuss upward from the symphysis pubis to the umbilicus.
   2. Note where the sound changes from dullness to tympany.

N **A urine-filled bladder is dull to percussion. A recently emptied bladder should not be percussable above the symphysis pubis.**

A It is abnormal to percuss a bladder that has recently been emptied. The urine that remains in the bladder after urination is called residual urine. A bladder may also be dull to percussion when the patient has difficulty voiding.

P The inability to completely empty the bladder occurs in the elderly, in post-operative, bedridden, and acutely ill patients, and in patients with neurogenic bladder dysfunction.

P Difficult voiding can occur in conjunction with benign prostatic hypertrophy (see Chapter 22 for additional information), urethral pathology, and some medications (antipsychotics: phenothiazine; anticholinergics: atropine; antihypertensives: hydralazine).

Palpation

Light Palpation

E 1. With your hands and forearm on a horizontal plane, use the pads of the approximated fingers to depress the abdominal wall 1 cm (Figure 17-24).
   2. Avoid short, quick jabs.
   3. Lightly palpate all four quadrants in a systematic manner.

N **The abdomen should feel smooth with consistent softness.**

A Light palpation reveals changes in skin temperature, tenderness, or large masses.

P Tenderness and elevated skin temperature can be due to inflammation. Large masses can be due to tumours, feces, or enlarged organs.

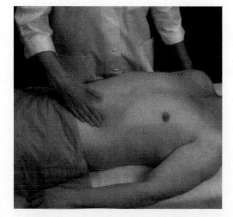

Figure 17-24 Light Palpation of the Abdomen.

Abdominal Muscle Guarding

To determine whether muscle guarding is involuntary:

E 1. Perform light palpation of the rectus muscles during expiration.
   2. Note muscle tensing.

N **Muscle guarding, or tensing of the abdominal musculature, is absent during expiration. The abdomen is soft. Normally, during expiration the patient cannot exercise voluntary muscle tensing.**

A Muscle guarding of the rectus muscles occurs during expiration.

P Involuntary muscle guarding suggests irritation of the peritoneum, as in peritonitis.

| E | Examination | N | Normal Findings | A | Abnormal Findings | P | Pathophysiology |

Deep Palpation

In performing deep palpation of all four quadrants, you can use either a one-handed or a two-handed method.

E 1. With the one-handed method, use the palmar surface of the extended fingers to depress the skin approximately 5 to 8 cm in the RLQ (Figure 17-25A).

2. A two-handed approach is used when palpation is difficult because of obesity or muscular resistance. With the bimanual technique, the non-dominant hand is placed on top of the dominant hand. The bottom hand is used for sensation, and the top hand is used to apply pressure (Figure 17-25B).

3. Identify any masses and note location, size, shape, consistency, tenderness, pulsation, and degree of mobility.

4. Continue palpation of RUQ, LUQ, and LLQ.

N No organ enlargement should be palpable, nor should there be any abnormal masses, bulges, or swelling. Normally, only the aorta and the edge of the liver are palpable. When the large colon or the bladder is full, palpation is possible.

A The gallbladder, liver, spleen, fecal-filled colon, or flatus-filled cecum should not be palpable. Masses, bulges, and swellings are also considered abnormal.

P Organomegaly can be caused by many pathological states such as cholecystitis, hepatitis, or cirrhosis; masses, bulges, or swelling can be due to tumours, fluids, feces, flatus, or fat.

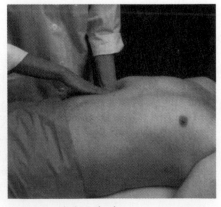

A. One-Handed Method

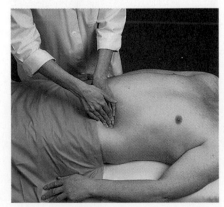

B. Bimanual Method

Figure 17-25 Deep Palpation.

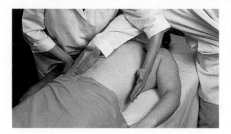

Figure 17-26 Palpation for Ascites: Fluid Wave.

Advanced Technique

Assessing for Ascites: Fluid Wave

E 1. With the patient in a supine position, stand at the patient's right side.

2. Have the patient or a second nurse firmly place the ulnar side of the right hand midline on the abdomen to prevent displacement of fat.

3. Place your right hand on the patient's right hip or flank area. Reach across the patient with your left hand and deliver a blow to the patient's left hip or flank area (Figure 17-26).

4. Assess if a fluid wave is felt on the right hand of the patient or the other nurse.

N No fluid wave should be felt.

A A fluid wave is easily felt if a large amount of ascites is present. This sign is often negative until the ascites is obvious. In addition, the fluid wave is sometimes positive in people without ascites.

P The factors that contribute to the development of ascites are outlined in the nursing alert on page 584.

Nursing Alert

Liver Encephalopathy

Early recognition of signs and symptoms of liver encephalopathy may minimize complications.

- Slowed mentation or mental confusion
- Asterixis (liver flap)
- Uncoordinated muscle movements
- Elevated values for serum BUN, ammonia, liver enzymes, and osmolarity. Increased values reflect systemic effects of liver dysfunction.

Nursing Alert

Liver Cancer

Incidence rates of hepatocellular carcinoma have increased substantially, consistent with the reported increase in the prevalence of hepatitis C Virus (HCV) and hepatitis B Virus (HBV) infections in recent decades.[15]

Risk Factors for Liver Cancer

- Cirrhosis
- Hepatitis B, C
- Cigarette smoking
- Alcohol use
- Exposure to toxic substances such as arsenic or vinyl chloride
- Primary malignancy

Liver

Liver palpation can be performed by one of two methods: the bimanual method or the hook method.

Bimanual Method

E 1. Stand at the patient's right side, facing the patient's head.

2. Place the left hand under the patient's right flank at about the 11th or 12th rib.

3. Press upward with the left hand to elevate the liver toward the abdominal wall.

4. Place the right hand parallel to the midline at the right midclavicular line below the right costal margin or below the level of liver dullness.

5. Instruct the patient to take a deep breath.

E	Examination	N	Normal Findings	A	Abnormal Findings	P	Pathophysiology

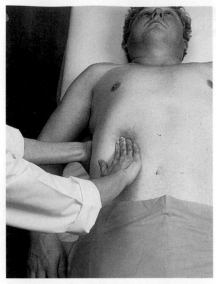

A. Bimanual Method

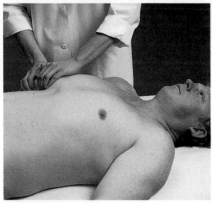

B. Hook Method

Figure 17-27 Palpation of the Liver.

6. Push down deeply and under the costal margin with your right fingers. On inspiration, the liver will descend and contact the hand (Figure 17-27A).
7. Note the level of the liver.
8. Note the size, shape, consistency, and any masses.

Hook Method

E 1. Stand at the patient's right side, facing the patient's feet.
2. Place both hands side by side on the right costal margin below the border of liver dullness.
3. Hook the fingers in and up toward the costal margin and ask the patient to take a deep breath and hold it.
4. Palpate the liver's edge as it descends (Figure 17-27B).
5. Note the level of the liver.
6. Note the size, shape, consistency, and any masses.

N A normal liver edge presents as a firm, sharp, regular ridge with a smooth surface. Normally, the liver is not palpable, although it may be felt in extremely thin adults.

A If the liver is palpable below the costal margin both medially and laterally, it is abnormal.

P An enlarged liver can be due to congestive heart failure, hepatitis, encephalopathy, cirrhosis, cysts, or cancer.

A A liver that is enlarged and has an irregular border and nodules and is hard is abnormal.

P These findings suggest liver malignancy. Tenderness may or may not be present.

Advanced Technique

Assessing for Cholecystitis: Murphy's Sign

E 1. With the patient supine, stand at the patient's right side.
2. Palpate below the liver margin at the lateral border of the rectus muscle.
3. Have the patient take a deep breath.

N No pain is elicited.

A Pain is present with palpation. The patient may stop inhaling to guard against the pain. This is known as Murphy's sign.

P Murphy's sign is positive in inflammatory processes of the gallbladder, such as cholecystitis.

Spleen

Use the bimanual technique to palpate the spleen.

E 1. Stand at the patient's right side.
2. Reach across and place the left hand beneath the patient and over the left costovertebral angle. Press upward to lift the spleen anteriorly toward the abdominal wall.
3. With the right hand, press inward along the left costal margin while asking the patient to take a deep breath (Figure 17-28).
3A. The procedure can be repeated with the patient lying on the right side, with the hips and knees flexed. This position will facilitate the spleen coming forward and to the right because the spleen is located retroperitoneally.
4. Note the size, shape, consistency, and any masses.

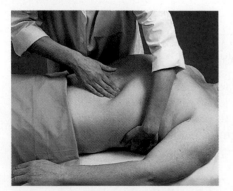

Figure 17-28 Palpation of the Spleen.

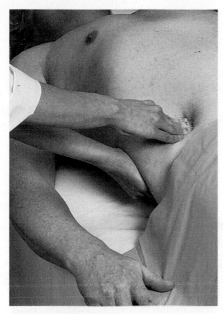

Figure 17-29 Palpation of the Right Kidney.

N The spleen should not be palpable.

A Because of its retroperitoneal position in the body, the spleen becomes palpable only when it has become enlarged to three times its normal size. An enlarged spleen is usually very tender.

P Splenomegaly can be due to inflammation, congestive heart failure, cancer, cirrhosis, or mononucleosis.

Kidneys

E 1. Stand at the patient's right side.
   2. Place one hand on the right costovertebral angle on the patient's back.
   3. Place the other hand below and parallel to the costal margin.
   4. As the patient takes a deep breath, press hands firmly together and try to feel the lower pole of the kidney (Figure 17-29).
   5. At the peak of inspiration, press the fingers together with greater pressure from above than from below.
   6. Ask the patient to exhale and to hold the breath briefly.
   7. Release the pressure of your fingers.
   8. If the kidney has been "captured," it can be felt as it slips back into place.
   9. Note the size, shape, and consistency. Note any masses.
   10. For the left kidney, reach across the patient and place the left hand under the patient's left flank.
   11. Apply downward pressure with the right hand below the left costal margin and repeat steps 4 to 9.

N The kidneys should not be palpable in the normal adult. However, the lower pole of the right kidney may be felt in very thin individuals. Kidneys are more readily palpable in the elderly due to loss of muscle tone and muscle bulk.

A Enlarged kidneys are abnormal. The right kidney may be difficult to distinguish from an enlarged liver. Left kidney enlargement may be difficult to distinguish from an enlarged spleen.

P Enlarged, palpable kidneys can be caused by hydronephrosis, neoplasms, or polycystic kidney disease.

Nursing Alert

Risk for Spleen Rupture

Palpate the spleen gently because an enlarged spleen will be very tender and may rupture.

Nursing Alert

Risk for Aortic Rupture

Do not palpate an aorta that you suspect has an aneurysm. Notify the patient's physician immediately if you suspect an abdominal aortic aneurysm because it may dissect and cause renal failure, loss of limbs, and eventually death if left untreated.

Nursing Tip

Differentiating Kidney Palpation

The distinguishing features between an enlarged liver and an enlarged kidney include:
1. The edge of the liver tends to be sharper and to extend medially and laterally, whereas the pole of the kidney is more rounded.
2. In addition, the edge of the liver cannot be "captured," whereas an enlarged kidney can be.

Distinguishing features between an enlarged left kidney and an enlarged spleen include:
1. A palpable notch on the medial edge of the organ favours the spleen.
2. Percussion of the spleen produces dullness because the bowel is displaced downward; however, resonance is heard over the left kidney because of the intervening bowel.

| E | Examination | N | Normal Findings | A | Abnormal Findings | P | Pathophysiology |

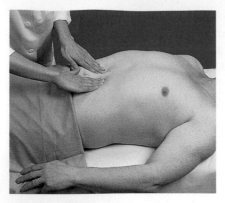

Figure 17-30 Palpation of the Aorta.

Aorta

E 1. Press the upper abdomen with one hand on each side of the abdominal aorta, slightly to the left of the midline.
    2. Assess the width of the aorta (Figure 17-30).

N The aorta width is 2.5 to 4.0 cm, and the aorta pulsates in an anterior direction.

A Aorta width greater than 4.0 cm is abnormal. Lateral pulsation of the aorta is also abnormal.

P A widened aorta and lateral pulsations suggest an abdominal aortic aneurysm.

Advanced Technique

Assessing for Abdominal Inflammation: Rebound Tenderness (Blumberg's Sign)

Rebound tenderness is assessed if pain has been elicited during palpation, or the patient has reported pain. Rebound tenderness is an abnormal finding frequently associated with peritoneal inflammation or appendicitis. Be prepared to recognize that rebound tenderness assessment could elicit a strong pain response from the patient. It is imperative to test for rebound tenderness away from the site where pain is initially determined and to conclude abdominal assessment with this test. If other tests are positive, omit this assessment.

E 1. Apply several seconds of firm pressure to the abdomen, with the hand at a 90° angle (perpendicular to the abdomen) and the fingers extended (Figure 17-31A).
    2. Quickly release the pressure (Figure 17-31B).

N Pain is not elicited.

A As the abdominal wall returns to its normal position, the patient complains of pain at the pressure site (direct rebound tenderness) or at another site (referred rebound tenderness).

P Rebound tenderness may indicate peritoneal irritation. The rebound effect of the internal structures indented by this technique causes sharp pain in the area of inflammation.

P Pain in the RLQ can indicate appendicitis. This location is known as McBurney's point.

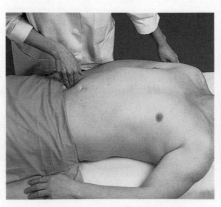

A. Apply firm pressure to the abdomen

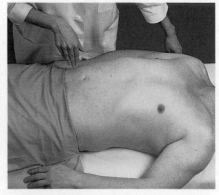

B. Quickly release the pressure

Figure 17-31 Rebound Tenderness.

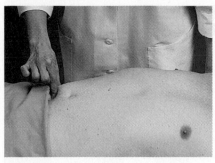

A. Lift a fold of skin away from the underlying muscle

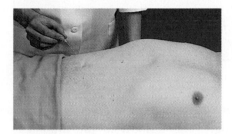

B. Stimulate the skin with a sterile needle

Figure 17-32 Assessment of Cutaneous Hypersensitivity.

Advanced Technique

Assessing for Appendicitis: Rovsing's Sign

Rovsing's sign is a differential technique to elicit referred pain, reflective of peritoneal inflammation secondary to appendicitis.

- **E** 1. Press deeply and evenly in the LLQ for five seconds.
  2. Note the patient's response.
- **N** No pain should be elicited.
- **A** Abdominal pain felt in the RLQ is abnormal and is a positive Rovsing's sign.
- **P** This sign is based on the concept that changes in intraluminal pressure will be transmitted through the intestine when the ileocecal valve is competent. Pressing the LLQ traps air within the large intestine and increases the pressure in the cecum. When the appendix is inflamed, this increase in pressure causes pain.

Advanced Technique

Assessing for Abdominal Inflammation: Cutaneous Hypersensitivity

On stimulation with a sterile pin or by lifting a fold of skin away from the musculature, cutaneous hypersensitivity zones of sensory nerves initiate a painful response. The irritative stimulus detects specific zones of peritoneal irritation.

- **E** 1. Lift a fold of skin away from the underlying muscle (Figure 17-32A) or stimulate the skin by gently jabbing the abdominal surface with a sterile pin (Figure 17-32B).
  2. Observe for pain response.
- **N** No adverse reaction should be noted.
- **A** The patient experiences an exaggerated sense of pain.
- **P** Cutaneous hypersensitivity indicates a zone of peritoneal irritation. Localized pain in all or part of the RLQ may accompany appendicitis. Midepigastrium pain could signal a peptic ulcer.

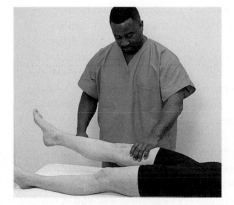

Figure 17-33 Iliopsoas Muscle Test.

Advanced Technique

Assessing for Appendicitis: Iliopsoas Muscle Test

When a patient presents with acute abdominal pain, an inflamed or perforated appendix may be distinguished via irritation of the lateral iliopsoas muscle.

- **E** 1. Place your hand over the right thigh and push downward as the patient raises the leg, flexing at the hip (Figure 17-33).
  2. Observe for pain response in the RLQ as described by the patient.
- **N** The patient should experience no pain.
- **A** The patient experiences pain in the RLQ.
- **P** This pain indicates an inflammation of the iliopsoas muscle in the groin and is caused by an inflamed appendix.

| E Examination | N Normal Findings | A Abnormal Findings | P Pathophysiology |

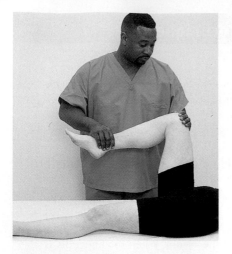

Figure 17-34 Obturator Muscle Test.

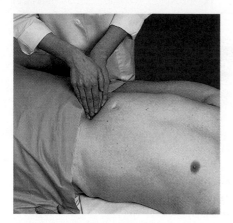

Figure 17-35 Palpation of the Bladder.

Advanced Technique

Assessing for Appendicitis or Pelvic Abscess: Obturator Muscle Test

Another differential technique used to help determine if the patient is experiencing appendicitis is eliciting the **obturator sign.** This test can be used when pelvic abscess is suspected. Both conditions may cause irritation of the obturator internus muscle.

E 1. Flex the right leg at the hip and knee at a right angle.
2. Rotate the leg both internally and externally (Figure 17-34).
3. Observe for pain response.

N No pain is elicited with this manoeuvre.

A Pain is elicited in the hypogastric area.

P This pain indicates irritation of the obturator muscle and can be caused by a ruptured appendix or pelvic abscess.

Bladder

E 1. Using deep palpation, palpate the abdomen at the midline, starting at the symphysis pubis and progressing upward to the umbilicus (Figure 17-35).
2. If the bladder is located, palpate the shape, size, and consistency.

N An empty bladder is not usually palpable. A moderately full bladder is smooth and round, and it is palpable above the symphysis pubis. A full bladder is palpated above the symphysis pubis, and it may be close to the umbilicus.

A A bladder that is nodular or asymmetrical to palpation is abnormal.

P A nodular bladder may indicate a malignancy. An asymmetrical bladder may result from a tumour in the bladder or an abdominal tumour that is compressing the bladder.

A It is abnormal to palpate a bladder that has been recently emptied.

Life 360°

Urinary Incontinence

Can you remember the last time that you sneezed or coughed and experienced some loss of bladder control? How did that make you feel? Did you soil your clothes? Now imagine what it must be like for a patient who has urinary incontinence on a regular basis. Interview a patient with urinary incontinence and ask him or her how it affects his or her life. Does the patient perform "bathroom mapping" when out in public? Familiarize yourself with the Registered Nurses of Ontario Best Practice Guideline on *Promoting Continence Using Prompted Voiding.*[16]

TABLE 17-4	Types of Urinary Incontinence	
TYPE	**DEFINITION**	**ETIOLOGY**
Stress	Involuntary loss of urine with activities that increase abdominal pressure (e.g., sneezing, coughing, laughing, heavy lifting, physical activity)	Childbirth, previous abdominal surgery, prostate surgery, radiation therapy
Urge	Involuntary loss of urine due to detrusor hyperactivity; usually associated with a strong desire to void with a larger volume of urine	Stroke, dementia, multiple sclerosis, Parkinson's disease, brain tumour, urinary tract tumours
Overflow	Involuntary loss of urine due to an overextended bladder; incontinence occurs when bladder pressure exceeds urethral pressure; usually small amount of urine occurs during dribbling; may be some hesitancy and frequency	Fecal impaction, diabetic neuropathy, obstruction of the bladder or urethra (due to prostate cancer, benign prostatic hypertrophy)
Functional	Involuntary loss of urine due to the inability to reach the toilet because of physical, cognitive, or environmental impairments	Immobility, dementia, inaccessible toilet, inappropriate lighting, physical restraints

E Examination	**N** Normal Findings	**A** Abnormal Findings	**P** Pathophysiology

P   Men with benign prostatic hypertrophy may be unable to completely empty their bladder because of the pressure that the enlarged prostate places on the bladder.

P   Various types of urinary incontinence, due to altered mental status, muscle function, medications, and other causes, can lead to incomplete bladder emptying. See Table 17-4 for additional information on urinary incontinence.

Inguinal Lymph Nodes

E   1. Place the patient in a supine position, with the knees slightly flexed.
    2. Drape the genital area.
    3. Using the finger pads of the second, third, and fourth fingers, apply firm pressure and palpate with a rotary motion in the right inguinal area.
    4. Palpate for lymph nodes in the left inguinal area.

N   It is normal to palpate small, movable nodes less than 1 cm in diameter. Palpable nodes are non-tender.

A   Presence of inguinal lymph nodes greater than 1 cm in diameter or elicitation of non-movable, tender lymph nodes is abnormal.

P   Large, palpable nodes can be attributed to localized or systemic infections. More serious pathology includes processes associated with cancer or lymphomas.

GERONTOLOGICAL VARIATIONS

In the process of aging, the abdominal musculature diminishes in mass and loses much of its tone. At the same time, the fat content of the body increases, leading to increased fat deposition in the abdominal area. The mucosal lining of the gastrointestinal tract becomes less elastic, and changes in gastric motility result in alterations in digestion and absorption. Gastric acid secretion decreases and pepsin secretion is thought to diminish.

Gastrointestinal complaints such as gas or epigastric discomfort constitute many of the reasons for the elderly to seek care. Although many of these complaints may be functional in nature, other cues should be investigated. Prolonged gastric irritation from gastric acid or excessive use of medications such as aspirin may cause occult bleeding that goes undetected until profound anemia occurs.

With an increase in age comes an increase in the incidence of malignant disease.

Constipation is a frequent digestive complaint of the elderly. Changes in bowel habits may be benign manifestations of diet, medications, a loss of sphincter tone, or lack of exercise. However, in the elderly, these symptoms could signify the presence of gastric or colonic malignancies. As the intestinal wall weakens, diverticuli (outpouching) can develop and sometimes progress to inflammation and obstruction. Chronic ulcerative colitis and Crohn's disease, usually thought of as occurring in a younger population, occur with equal incidence after the age of 50.

There is little evidence that the liver function changes significantly with age. However, weight, blood flow, and regenerative capacity decrease progressively with age. The decrease in liver mass and blood flow alters the pharmacokinetic effects of various drugs.

Persistent jaundice in the elderly is generally thought to be due to malignant obstruction of the biliary system. Multiple-drug therapy may cause hepatitis-like reactions that mimic viral hepatitis. Cholelithiasis, which occurs in one-third of the population between the ages of 70 and 80, is also a frequent cause of jaundice.

The small and large intestines are subject to acute and chronic ischemia when atherosclerosis is extensive. Vascular occlusions that are embolic in origin, from the heart for example, can cause life-threatening infarctions of the gut. Non-occlusive intestinal infarctions may also result in the presence of congestive heart failure.

CASE STUDY

The Patient with Appendicitis

The case study illustrates the application and objective documentation of abdominal assessment.

Uri Mogilevsy presents at the Emergency Department with abdominal pain.

HEALTH HISTORY

PATIENT PROFILE	34 yo arrives with wife
HEALTH ISSUE/CONCERN	"My stomach is killing me. I have such bad diarrhea."
HISTORY OF ISSUE/CONCERN	woke at MN c̄ intense (10/10) abd pain in all quads s̄ radiation; Ø N/V; 2 bouts diarrhea of loose brown stool s̄ gross blood; usually BM q AM; fetal position makes pain sl better, walking/activity makes pain worse; hurts to walk & stand up straight; denies recent travel; nobody at home sick; ate salmon at lunch yesterday at restaurant; colleague ate salmon & was fine until 21:00 last evening; pt = stressed b/c of big report due in 24 hrs for client
PAST HEALTH HISTORY	
Medical History	No illnesses
Surgical History	Wisdom teeth excised age 21 s̄ complications
Medications	MVI daily
Communicable Diseases	None
Allergies	None
Injuries and Accidents	fx Ⓛ radius/ulna age 7; Ø sequelae
Special Needs	Denies
Blood Transfusions	Denies
Childhood Illnesses	Varicella age 7, frequent strep throat
Immunizations	UTD; receives annual influenza vaccine

FAMILY HEALTH HISTORY

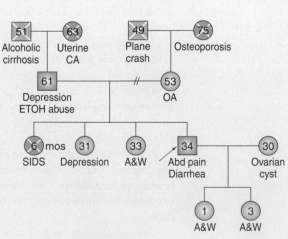

LEGEND

- ◯ Living female
- ▢ Living male
- ⊗ Deceased female
- ⊠ Deceased male
- ╱ Points to patient
- —#— = Divorced
- A&W = Alive & well
- CA = Cancer
- ETOH = Ethyl alcohol
- OA = Osteoarthritis
- SIDS = Sudden infant death syndrome

Denies family hx of malignancies of stomach, liver, or pancreas, DM, familial polyposis, inflammatory bowel dz, polycystic kidney dz, colitis, PUD, IBS, malabsorption syndromes.

SOCIAL HISTORY

Alcohol Use	2–3 Bourbons q Sat
Drug Use	Marijuana in college
Tobacco Use	None
Domestic and Intimate Partner Violence	Deferred
Sexual Practice	Deferred
Travel History	Italy 4 wks ago
Work Environment	Accountant at major accounting firm × 7 yrs; enjoys work & colleagues
Home Environment	Lives in suburban community, small bungalow
Hobbies and Leisure Activities	Golf 2–3 × q wk; likes to read spy novels
Stress	Work, especially at tax time
Education	Has Bachelor of Commerce degree
Economic Status	"Comfortable lifestyle"
Religion/Spirituality	Deferred
Ethnicity	"I'm Ukrainian"
Roles and Relationships	Husband/father/son; "great relationship with my kids"
Characteristic Patterns of Daily Living	Wakes at 05:00, goes to gym & works out; at office by 08:00 & home by 19:00 plays $\bar{c}$ children & has family dinner; reads/watches TV until 22:00; weekends active with sports and family get together.

HEALTH MAINTENANCE ACTIVITIES

Sleep	7–8 hrs q night & feels rested in AM
Diet	"I eat everything—try to stay healthy"; infrequent fast foods; caffeine 3–4/d
Exercise	Treadmill for 30 min wkdays followed by weights; works $\bar{c}$ trainer at gym
Stress Management	Running, yoga
Use of Safety Devices	Wears seat belts
Health Check-ups	4 yrs ago had complete physical $\bar{c}$ labs—WNL

PHYSICAL ASSESSMENT

Inspection

Contour	Flat
Symmetry	Symmetrical
Rectus Abdominis Muscle	Intact, Ø separation
Pigmentation and Colour	Uniform dark brown pigmentation
Scars	Ø
Striae	Ø

continues

Respiratory Movement	Ø retractions
Masses or Nodules	Ø
Visible Peristalsis	Ø
Pulsation	Sl visible in epigastrium
Umbilicus	Ø hernia
Auscultation	
Bowel Sounds	Absent
Vascular Sounds	Ø
Venous Hum	Ø
Friction Rub	Ø
Percussion	
General	Dull
Liver Span	8 cm in ® MCL
Liver Descent	2 cm
Spleen	Unable to percuss
Stomach	Dull
Fist Percussion (Indirect)	⊕ CVA tenderness
Bladder	Dull superior to symphysis pubis
Palpation	
Light Palpation	Smooth, warm
Abdominal Muscle Guarding	⊕ guarding
Deep Palpation	Exquisitely tender epigastrium Liver: Ø hepatomegaly Spleen: Ø splenomegaly Kidneys: Non-palpable Aorta: 3 cm c̄ ant pulsation Bladder: Non-palpable Inguinal Lymph Nodes: Ø lymphadenopathy
Advanced Techniques	Rebound Tenderness: ⊕ pain McBurney's point Rovsing's Sign: ⊕ Iliopsoas & Obturator Muscles Tests: ⊕ Cutaneous Hypersensitivity: Deferred
LABORATORY DATA	SMAC, amylase, lipase: WNL

	Patient's Values	Normal Range
RBC:	4.8×10^{12}/L	$4\text{--}5.2 \times 10^{12}$/L
Hct:	0.45	male: 0.43–0.49
Hgb:	150 g/L	male: 126–174 g/L
MCV:	90 fL	85–95 fL
MCH:	29 pg	28–32 pg
MCHC:	330 g/dl	330–350g/L
PLT:	380×10^9/L	$150\text{--}450 \times 10^9$/L
WBC:	13.7×10^9/L	$4.5\text{--}11 \times 10^9$/L

Differential		
Neutrophils:	9.8×10^9	$1.8–7.7 \times 10^9$
Bands	10%	3%
Segments	49%	56%
Lymphocytes:	3.3×10^9	$1.4–4.8 \times 10^9$
Monocytes:	0.4×10^9	$0.0–0.8 \times 10^9$
Eosinophils:	0.1×10^9	$0.0–0.45 \times 10^9$
Basophils:	0.08×10^9	$0.0–0.2 \times 10^9$
ESR:	33 mm/hr	0.0–10 mm/hr (Westergren method)

Abdominal CT with Contrast   Negative

Pelvic CT with Contrast   No free fluid. Slightly thickened loop of bowel with only perinephric stranding. This demonstrates a so-called bull's-eye appearance of an inflamed appendix. Suspicious for a focal early acute appendicitis.

◄NURSING CHECKLIST►

Abdominal Assessment

Inspection
- Contour
- Symmetry
- Rectus abdominis muscles
- Pigmentation and colour
- Scars
- Striae
- Respiratory movement
- Masses or nodules
- Visible peristalsis
- Pulsation
- Umbilicus

Auscultation
- Bowel sounds
- Vascular sounds
- Venous hum
- Friction rubs

Percussion
- General percussion
- Liver span
- Liver descent
- Spleen
- Stomach
- Fist percussion
  - Kidney
  - Liver
- Bladder

Palpation
- Light palpation
- Abdominal muscle guarding
- Deep palpation
- Liver
  - Bimanual method
  - Hook method
- Spleen
- Kidneys
- Aorta
- Bladder
- Inguinal lymph nodes

Advanced Techniques
- Assessing for ascites
  - Shifting dullness
  - Puddle sign
- Fluid wave
- Murphy's sign
- Rebound tenderness (Blumberg's sign)
- Rovsing's sign
- Cutaneous hypersensitivity
- Iliopsoas muscle test
- Obturator muscle test

Abdominal tubes and drains
- Tubes
  - Enteral tube
  - Nasogastric suction tube
  - Intestinal tube
  - Gastrostomy
- Drains
  - Abdominal cavity drain
  - Biliary drain
- Intestinal diversions
  - Colostomy
  - Ileostomy
- Urinary diversions
  - Ileal conduit
  - Ureteral Stent
  - Indwelling catheter

REVIEW QUESTIONS

1. While palpating a patient's abdominal LUQ, you visualize the underlying organs that include:
   a. Stomach, body of pancreas, splenic flexure of colon
   b. Body of pancreas, gallbladder, and spleen
   c. Splenic flexure of colon, duodenum, cecum
   d. Appendix, pylorus, hepatic flexure of colon
   The correct answer is (a).

2. After assessing a patient's abdomen, you suspect that she may be experiencing pan creatitis. In which abdominal area is the patient most likely experiencing pain?
   a. Epigastrium
   b. Right upper quadrant
   c. Periumbilical
   d. Left lower quadrant
   The correct answer is (b).

3. You see a nurse in a rural setting where the village has frequent sewage difficulties. This situation poses a risk to contract what type of hepatitis?
   a. Hepatitis A
   b. Hepatitis B
   c. Hepatitis C
   d. Hepatitis D
   The correct answer is (a).

4. A woman who is eight months pregnant would have which abdominal contour?
   a. Flat
   b. Rounded
   c. Scaphoid
   d. Protuberant
   The correct answer is (d).

5. Auscultation of the patient's abdomen reveals loud bowel sounds every two seconds. What might be the etiology of this finding?
   a. Normal gastrointestinal finding
   b. Gastroenteritis
   c. Paralytic ileus
   d. Gangrene
   The correct answer is (b).

6. You are assessing a patient with ascites by having the patient assume the knee–chest position. After a few minutes, you percuss the umbilical area. This technique for assessing ascites is called:
   a. Shifting dullness
   b. Fluid wave
   c. Puddle sign
   d. Cullen's sign
   The correct answer is (c).

7. Indirect fist percussion is performed bilaterally. The patient experiences left CVA tenderness. What condition might this patient have?
   a. Hepatitis
   b. Cholecystitis
   c. Pyelonephritis
   d. Appendicitis
   The correct answer is (c).

Questions 8–10 refer to the following situation:

An 82-year-old man with advanced Alzheimer's disease and prostate enlargement experiences frequent urinary incontinence.

8. You percuss and palpate the abdomen from the symphysis pubis to the umbilicus. The percussion notes are tympanic and the bladder is non-palpable. This finding indicates:
   a. An empty bladder
   b. A nodular bladder
   c. A full bladder
   d. An asymmetrical bladder
   The correct answer is (a).

9. The patient experiences an involuntary loss of urine due to the inability to reach the toilet. This type of urinary incontinence is called:
   a. Stress incontinence
   b. Urge incontinence
   c. Overflow incontinence
   d. Functional incontinence
   The correct answer is (d).

10. Which is a gerontological variation that occurs to the gastrointestinal system?
    a. Abdominal musculature increases in mass
    b. Gastric acid secretion decreases.
    c. Intestinal walls and sphincter tone strengthen
    d. Fat deposition in the abdominal area decreases
    The correct answer is (b).

Visit the Estes online companion resource at
www.healthassessment.nelson.com for additional
content and study aids.

REFERENCES

[1]Public Health Agency of Canada. *Clostridium difficile.* Retrieved October 29, 2006, from http://www.phac-aspc.gc.ca/c-difficile

[2]National Cancer Institute of Canada. Cancer Statistics: International variation in cancer incidence, 1993–1997. Retrieved October 29, 2006, from http://www.ncic. cancer.ca/ncic/internet/standard/0,3621,84658243_85787780_langId-en,00.html

[3]Zhang, J., Zou, S., & Giulivi, A. (2001). Hepatitis B in Canada. *Canada Communicable Disease Report,* Vol. 27S3, (September). Ottawa: Public Health Agency of Canada.

[4]Manterola, C., Astudillo, P., Losada, H., Pineda, V., Sanhueza, A., & Vial, M. Analgesia for patients with acute abdominal pain. (Protocol) *The Cochrane Database of Systematic Reviews* 2006. Iss. 1, Art. No. CD005660.

[5]Wu, J., Zou, S., & Giulivi, A. (2001) Hepatitis A and its control. *Canada Communicable Disease Report,* Vol. 27S3 (September). Ottawa: Public Health Agency of Canada.

[6]Minister of Public Works and Government Services Canada (2002). *Canadian immunization guide,* 6th ed. Ottawa: Health Canada

[7]Zhang, J., Zou, S., & Giulivi, A. *Hepatitis B in Canada.*

[8]Zou, S., Tepper M., & Giulivi A. (2000). Current status of hepatitis C in Canada. *Canadian Journal of Public Health* 91, Supp. 1: S10-5, S10-6 (July–August).

[9]Patrick, D.M., Buxton, J.A., Bigham, M., et al. (2000). Public health and hepatitis C. *Canadian Journal of Public Health,* 91, Supp. 1, S18–S21 (July–August).

[10]Blood Safety Surveillance and Health Care Acquired Infections Division—Public Health Agency of Canada. *Hepatitis D Fact Sheet.* Retrieved October 29, 2006, from http://www.phac-aspc.gc.ca//hcai-iamss/bbp-pts/hepatitis/hep_d_e.html

[11]———. *Hepatitis E Fact Sheet.* Retrieved October 29, 2006, from http://www.phac-aspc.gc.ca/hcai-iamss/bbp-pts/hepatitis/hep_e_e.html

[12]———. *Hepatitis G Fact Sheet.* Retrieved October 29, 2006, from http://www.phac-aspc.gc.ca/hcai-iamss/bbp-pts/hepatitis/hep_g_e.html

[13]Canadian Cancer Society/National Cancer Institute of Canada. (2006). *Canadian Cancer Statistics 2006.* Toronto.

[14]Hunt, R., Fallone, C., vanZanten, S. V., Sherman, P., Smaill, F., Flook, N., Thomson, A., and all participants of CHSG 2004 (2004). Canadian Helicobacter Study Group Consensus Conference: Update on the management of *Helicobacter pylori*—An evidence-based evaluation of six topics relevant to clinical outcomes in patients evaluated for H pylori infection. *Canadian Journal of Gastroenterology,* 18 (9): 547–54.

[15]elSaadany S., Tepper, M., Mao, Y., Semenciw, R., & Giulivi A. (2002). An epidemiologic study of hepatocellular carcinoma in Canada. *Canadian Journal of Public Health. Revue Canadienne de Sante Publique,* 93 (6) (November–December): 443–46.

[16]Registered Nurses' Association of Ontario. (2005). *Promoting continence using prompted voiding.* Toronto: Registered Nurses' Association of Ontario.

BIBLIOGRAPHY

Aspinall, R. J., & Taylor-Robinson, S. D. (2002). *Mosby's Color Atlas and Text of Gastroenterology and Liver Disease.* St. Louis, MO: Mosby.

Canadian Liver Foundation (2000). Hepatitis C: Medical information update. *Canadian Journal of Public Health* vol 91, supp. 1 (July–August): S4–S9.

Chen, T.M. (Ed.) (2006). *New Developments in Liver Cirrhosis Research.* New York: Nova Biomedical Books.

Health Canada: Bloodborne Pathogens Section—Health Care Acquired Infections Division (2001). *Acute and Chronic Hepatitis C in Canada, 2001: Enhanced Hepatitis Strain Surveillance System.* Ottawa: Health Canada.

Riben, P., Bailey, G., Hudson, S., McCulloch, K., Dignan, T., & Martin, D. (2000). Hepatitis C in Canada's First Nations and Inuit populations: An unknown burden. *Canadian Journal of Public Health,* 91 (July–August) Suppl 1: S16–18.

Talley, N. J. (2006). *Conquering Irritable Bowel Syndrome : A Guide to Liberating Those Suffering with Chronic Stomach or Bowel Problems.* Hamilton, ON: BC Decker.

WEB RESOURCES

Canadian Association for Study of the Liver
http://www.hepatology.ca/cm/

Canadian Association for Enterostomal Therapy
http://www.caet.ca

Canadian Association of Gastroenterology
http://www.cag-acg.org/home.htm

Canadian Association of Hepatology Nurses
http://www.livernurses.org

Canadian Hepatitis C Information Centre
http://www.hepc.cpha.ca

Canadian Liver Foundation
http://www.liver.ca/Home.aspx

Crohn's and Colitis Foundation of Canada
http://www.ccfc.ca

Hepatitis C Society of Canada
http://www.hepatitiscsociety.com

HepNet—the Hepatitis Information Network
http://www.hepnet.com/index.html

NEL

CHAPTER 18

Musculoskeletal System

COMPETENCIES

1. Elicit a health history from a patient with health issues or concerns regarding the musculoskeletal system.

2. Perform inspection and palpation of the musculoskeletal system.

3. Describe the range of motion movements of the major joints.

4. Use a range of assessment techniques related to the musculoskeletal system.

5. Document the findings of the musculoskeletal assessment.

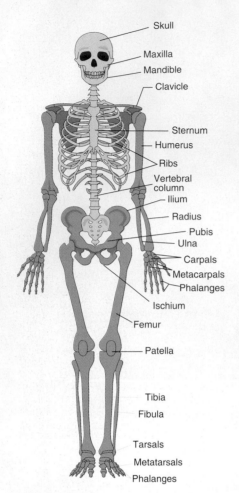

Appendicular skeleton (blue)
Axial skeleton (grey)

Figure 18-1 Adult Skeleton: Anterior View.

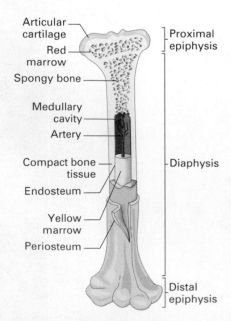

Figure 18-2 Structure of a Long Bone.

*T*he musculoskeletal system provides the ability to maintain and change body position in response to both internal and external stimuli. Muscle tone and bone strength allow an individual to maintain an upright and erect posture position. Muscle contraction and joint movement allow an individual to move toward positive stimuli and away from noxious stimuli. Changes in the musculoskeletal system will affect the individual's ability to complete activities of daily living, occupation, and recreation. The musculoskeletal system functions closely with the neurological system, such that a disturbance in the neurological system can grossly impact the musculoskeletal system.

ANATOMY AND PHYSIOLOGY

The musculoskeletal system consists of an intricate framework of bones, joints, skeletal muscles, and supportive connective tissue (cartilage, tendons, and ligaments). Although the primary purpose of the musculoskeletal system is to support body position and promote mobility, it also protects underlying soft organs and allows for mineral storage. In addition, it produces select blood components (platelets, red blood cells, and white blood cells). Only those aspects of the musculoskeletal system that are responsible for body position and mobility are discussed in this chapter.

Bones

The adult human skeleton comprises 206 bones (Figure 18-1). Bone is ossified connective tissue. The skeleton is divided into the central **axial skeleton** (facial bones, skull, auditory ossicles, hyoid bone, ribs, sternum, and vertebrae) and the peripheral **appendicular skeleton** (limbs, pelvis, scapula, and clavicle). A bone's size and shape are directly related to the mobility and weight-bearing function of that bone. In some cases, bone size and shape are also related to the protection of underlying internal organs and tissues (e.g., the ribs in relation to the lungs, heart, and thoracic aorta).

Shape and Structure

Bones have long, short, flat, rounded, and irregular shapes. The long bone is a shaft (**diaphysis**) with two large ends (**epiphyses**). The two epiphyses each articulate with another bone to form a joint. A 1 to 4 cm layer of cartilage covers each epiphysis in order to minimize stress and friction on the bone ends during movement and weight bearing. The thickness of the cartilage layer varies, depending on the amount of stress placed on that joint. The interior of the diaphysis is the **medullary cavity**, which contains the bone marrow (Figure 18-2).

Short bones are found in the hands (carpals) and feet (tarsals). Flat bones, such as the skull and parts of the pelvic girdle, are associated with the protection of nearby soft body parts. Rounded, or sesamoid, bones are often encased in the fascia or in a tendon near a joint, such as is the patella. Irregular bones include the mandible, vertebrae, and the auditory ossicles of the inner ear.

Muscles

There are over 600 muscles in the human body, and they can be characterized as one of three types. Cardiac and smooth muscles are involuntary, meaning that the individual has no conscious control over the initiation and termination

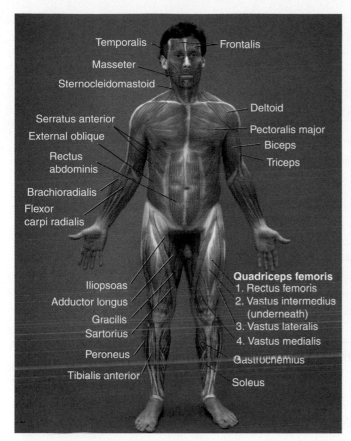

A. Anterior View

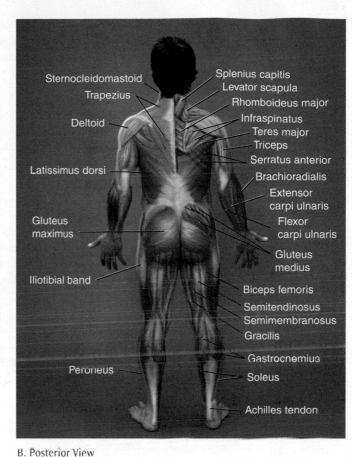

B. Posterior View

Figure 18-3 Muscles of the Body.

of the muscle contraction. The largest type of muscle, and the only type of voluntary muscle, is called skeletal muscle. Skeletal muscle provides for mobility by exerting a pull on the bones near a joint. In addition, skeletal muscle provides for body contour and contributes to overall body weight. Figure 18-3 illustrates the major muscles. It is estimated that 40% to 50% of adult body weight is due to the weight of the skeletal muscles. Muscles vary in size and strength in every person and are affected by age, sex, exercise, and nutrition.

Tendons

A strong connective tissue sheath (**epimysium**) acts as the outer covering of the muscle belly. The ends of the epimysium extend beyond the **muscle belly** (the wide central aspect of the muscle) to form the **tendons** of the muscle. The tendon attaches the muscle to a bone (Figure 18-4).

Cartilage

Cartilage is an avascular, dense connective tissue that covers the ends of opposing bones. Its resilience allows it to withstand increased pressure and tension.

Ligaments

Ligaments comprise strong fibrous connective tissue. They connect bones to each other at the joint level and encase the joint capsule. Ligaments may be

Figure 18-4 Connective Tissue Structures of the Leg.

seen as oblique to or parallel to a joint (e.g., knee) or encircling the joint (e.g., hip). Ligaments support purposeful joint movement and prevent joint movement that is detrimental to that type of joint.

Bursae

Bursae are sacs filled with fluid. Bursae act as cushions between two nearby surfaces (e.g., between tendon and bone or between tendon and ligament) to reduce friction. They can also develop in response to prolonged friction or pressure.

Joints

A **joint** is a union between two bones. Joints secure the bones firmly together but allow for some degree of movement between the two bones. Contraction of overlying skeletal muscle will act to alter the angle of the two bones by pulling the distal bone toward or away from the proximal bone. Terms used for joint range of motion are described in Table 18-1.

TABLE 18-1 Descriptive Terms for Joint Range of Motion

TERM	DESCRIPTION	CHANGE IN JOINT ANGLE
Flexion	Bending of a joint so that the articulating bones on either side of the joints are moved closer together	Decreased
Extension	Bending the joint so that the articulating bones on either side of the joint are moved farther apart	Increased
Hyperextension	Extension beyond the neutral position	Increased beyond the angle of extension
Adduction	Moving the extremity medially and toward the midline of the body	Decreased
Abduction	Moving the extremity laterally and away from the midline of the body	Increased
Internal rotation	Rotating the extremity medially along its own axis	No change
External rotation	Rotating the extremity laterally along its own axis	No change
Circumduction	Moving the extremity in a conical fashion so that the distal aspect of the extremity moves in a circle	No change
Supination	Rotating the forearm laterally at the elbow so that the palm of the hand turns laterally to face upward	No change
Pronation	Rotating the forearm medially at the elbow so that the palm of the hand turns medially to face downward	No change
Opposition	Moving the thumb outward to touch the little finger of the same hand	No change
Eversion	Tilting the foot inward, with the medial side of the foot lowered	No change
Inversion	Tilting the foot outward, with the lateral side of the foot lowered	No change
Dorsiflexion	Flexing the foot at the ankle so that the toes move toward the chest	Decreased
Plantar flexion	Moving the foot at the ankle so that the toes move away from the chest	Increased
Elevation	Raising a body part in an upward direction	No change
Depression	Lowering a body part	No change
Protraction	Moving a body part anteriorly along its own axis (parallel to the ground)	No change
Retraction	Moving a body part posteriorly along its own axis (parallel to the ground)	No change
Gliding	One joint surface moves over another joint surface in a circular or angular nature	No change

TABLE 18-2	Categories of Skeletal Joints	
CATEGORY	**DEGREE OF MOVEMENT**	**EXAMPLES**
Diarthroses (synovial)	Freely movable	Shoulder, elbow, wrist, thumb, hip, knee, ankle, and proximal cervical vertebrae
Amphiarthroses	Slightly movable	Vertebrae, manubriosternal joint, radioulnar joint, and symphysis pubis
Synarthroses	Immovable	Epiphyseal growth plate (adult), skull sutures (child), between the distal ends of the radius and ulna, between the distal ends of the tibia and fibula, and the attachment of the root of a tooth to the alveolar process of the maxilla or mandible

Of the three classifications of skeletal joints found in the adult human skeleton (synarthroses, amphiarthroses, and diarthroses), only the synovial joint (diarthroses) is considered freely movable. Examples of each joint are provided in Table 18-2. Table 18-3 shows categories of the major synovial joints. The synovial joint allows body movement.

A synovial membrane lines the interior of the joint space (Figure 18-5). The primary purpose of the synovial membrane is to secrete fluid for joint lubrication, nourishment, and waste removal. Normally, the joint space contains only 1 to 3 mL of synovial fluid. Excessive synovial joint fluid is called a **synovial effusion**.

TABLE 18-3	Categories of Synovial Joints	
CATEGORY	**DESCRIPTION**	**EXAMPLES**
Uniaxial Joints		
Hinge joint	Angular movement in one axis and in one plane	Elbow, fingers, knee
Pivot joint (trochoid)	Rotary movement in one axis; a ring rotates around a pivot, or a pivotlike process rotates within a ring	Radioulnar joint, atlantoodontal joint of the first and second cervical vertebrae
Biaxial Joints		
Saddle joint (sellar)	Articulating surface of one bone is convex and articulating surface of second bone is concave	Metacarpal bone of thumb, trapezium bone of carpus
Condyloid joint	Angular motion in two planes without axial rotation	Wrist between the distal radius and the carpals
Multiaxial Joints		
Ball and socket (spheroidal) joint	Round end of bone fits into cuplike cavity of another bone; provides movement around three or more axes, or in three or more planes	Shoulder, hip
Gliding joint	Gliding movement	Vertebrae, tarsal bones of ankle

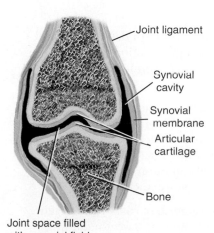

Joint ligament

Synovial cavity

Synovial membrane

Articular cartilage

Bone

Joint space filled with synovial fluid

Figure 18-5 Synovial Joint.

HEALTH HISTORY

The musculoskeletal health history provides insight into the link between a patient's life and lifestyle and musculoskeletal information and pathology.

PATIENT PROFILE

Diseases that are age-, gender-, and race-specific for the musculoskeletal system are listed.

Age

Osteosarcoma (10–20 and 50–60)
Ankylosing spondylitis (20–40)
Bursitis (20–40)
Rheumatoid arthritis (onset 20–40 unless juvenile form of the disease)
Systemic lupus erythematosus (SLE) (25–35)
Low back pain (30–50)
Gout (onset over 30, postmenopausal female)
Type I osteoporosis (menopausal female)
Carpal tunnel syndrome (pregnant or menopausal female)
Degenerative joint disease or osteoarthritis (onset after 55 in the female and before 45 in the male)
Type II osteoporosis (onset 50–70)
Multiple myeloma (50–70)
Paget's disease (50–70)

Gender

Female

Type I osteoporosis, rheumatoid arthritis, scoliosis, carpal tunnel syndrome, SLE, postmenopausal gout, polymyalgia rheumatica, scleroderma, myasthenia gravis, multiple sclerosis (MS), senile kyphosis

Male

Type II osteoporosis, ankylosing spondylitis, gout, Paget's disease, Reiter's syndrome, Dupuytren's contracture, psoriatic arthritis, muscular dystrophy (MD), amyotrophic lateral sclerosis (ALS), low back pain

Ethnicity

Caucasian

Rheumatoid arthritis, primary osteoarthritis, polymyalgia rheumatica, type I osteoporosis, Paget's disease, Dupuytren's contracture, ALS, ankylosing spondylitis

African descent

SLE, rheumatoid arthritis

HEALTH ISSUE/CONCERN

Common health issues/concerns for the musculoskeletal system are defined and information on the characteristics of each sign or symptom is provided.

Pain

The subjective sense of discomfort in the axial or appendicular skeleton

Location

Muscle, bone, tendon, ligament, or joint

Quantity

Degree of interruption in the patient's usual activities of daily living (ADL) (changes in walking, bathing, dressing, food preparation, working, sitting, transfer to a sitting or standing position, climbing stairs, lifting, pushing, and pulling)

Associated Manifestations

Inflammation, skin abrasion, laceration, bruising, hematoma, stiffness, deformity, muscle spasm, paresthesia, decreased joint mobility, restriction of weight bearing and movement, excessive weakness or fatigue, mental depression, insomnia, guarding of the painful area, crying, moaning, facial grimacing, anxiety, social withdrawal, agitation, restlessness, diaphoresis, tachycardia, elevated blood pressure, tachypnea

Aggravating Factors

Muscle contraction, muscle spasm, joint movement, partial or full weight bearing, obesity, dependent position, cold and damp weather, non-compliance to physical or occupational therapy guidelines

continues

Alleviating Factors	Restriction of movement, position change, nonweight-bearing, limb elevation and rest, ice, heat, analgesics, anti-inflammatory agents, steroids, muscle relaxants, local anesthetic agents, whirlpool therapy, transcutaneous electrical nerve stimulation (TENS), acupuncture, acupressure, assistive devices for use during weight bearing and mobility, splints
Setting	Recent untreated streptococcal infection
Timing	Sudden, insidious, intermittent, continuous
Weakness	The subjective sense of an overall decrease in strength and endurance
Location	Local or diffuse, central or peripheral
Quantity	Effect on ADL
Associated Manifestations	Fatigue, muscle atrophy, decreased sensation, decreased joint mobility, decreased muscle strength, discomfort, decreased ability to do ADL
Aggravating Factors	Overexertion, fatigue, immobility, non-compliance to physical or occupational therapy guidelines, physical or emotional stress
Alleviating Factors	Rest, adequate nutrition and hydration, electrolyte replacement therapy, physical and occupational therapy geared toward muscle-strengthening exercises and adaptive techniques
Limited Movement	Decrease in mobility caused by a problem with impulse transmission to the muscle, stimulation of a muscle, the ability of that muscle to contract sufficiently to move the joint, or bone stability
Location	Diffuse, or localized to a specific joint
Quantity	Range of joint motion compared to maximum potential or previous measurement
Associated Manifestations	Pain, inflammation, stiffness, muscle atrophy, weakness, deformity, crepitus, joint effusion
Aggravating Factors	Overexertion, immobility, excessive weight gain, non-compliance to medication regime (e.g., anti-inflammatory agents), non-compliance to physical and occupational therapy guidelines
Alleviating Factors	Physical and occupational therapy, anti-inflammatory agents, analgesics, ice, heat, rest, reduction of fractures, correction of dislocation or subluxation
Stiffness	The subjective sense of inflexibility
Location	Diffuse, or localized to a specific joint
Quantity	Effect on ADL
Associated Manifestations	Joint inflammation, muscle atrophy, deformity, contracture, immobility, pain, palpable joint crepitus, limited range of joint motion
Aggravating Factors	Immobility, aging, overexertion (especially without adequate warming-up and cooling-down sessions during exercise), non-compliance to medication regime (e.g., anti-inflammatory agents), non-compliance to physical and occupational therapy guidelines
Alleviating Factors	Physical and occupational therapy, exercise, anti-inflammatory agents, analgesics, heat, rest, massage, muscle relaxants
Setting	Cold and damp environment
Timing	Sudden or insidious, time of day (e.g., morning stiffness for more than 30 minutes is associated with rheumatoid arthritis), in relation to vigorous or excessive physical exercise

continues

Deformity	The congenital or acquired alteration in the configuration of the axial or appendicular skeleton
Location	General (e.g., decreased overall body size) or localized (e.g., disruption in limb length and alignment due to a fracture)
Quality	Degree of cosmetic alteration, degree of musculoskeletal dysfunction (adverse changes in mobility, weight bearing, and the ability to maintain body posture and position)
Associated Manifestations	Enlarged skull, jaw protrusion, forehead protrusion, abnormal joint angle, limb malalignment, missing or extra digits, missing limb, discrepancy in limb length or width, abnormal posture, muscle atrophy, joint contractures
Aggravating Factors	Certain body positions or movements
Alleviating Factors	Surgery, skeletal or skin traction, manual reduction of a fracture or dislocation, limb elevation, ice, physical therapy, splint, cast, brace
Timing	Sudden or insidious, temporary or permanent
PAST HEALTH HISTORY	*The various components of the past health history are linked to musculoskeletal pathology and musculoskeletal-related information.*
Medical History	
Musculoskeletal Specific	Rheumatoid arthritis, osteoarthritis, osteoporosis, Paget's disease, gout, ankylosing spondylitis, osteogenesis imperfecta, loosening or malfunction of joint prosthesis, aseptic necrosis, chronic low back pain, herniated nucleus pulposus, chronic muscle spasms or cramps, scoliosis, poliomyelitis, polymyalgia rheumatica, osteomalacia, rickets, Marfan's syndrome, scleroderma, spina bifida, congenital deformity, MD, MS, myasthenia gravis, ALS, Guillain-Barré syndrome, Reiter's syndrome, carpal tunnel syndrome, paralysis
Non-musculoskeletal Specific	Immunosuppression, necrotizing faciitis, gas gangrene, tetanus, sickle cell anemia, SLE, Lyme disease, blood dyscrasias (including hemophilia), diabetes mellitus with or without peripheral neuropathy, hypo- or hypercalcemia, hypo- or hyperpituitarism, hyper- or hypoparathyroidism, hyper- or hypothyroidism, peripheral vascular disease with or without claudication, malnutrition, obesity, menopause
Surgical History	Joint aspiration, therapeutic joint arthroscopy, joint arthroplasty, joint replacement, synovectomy, meniscectomy, arthrodesis, open reduction and internal fixation (ORIF), discectomy, laminectomy, spinal fusion, Harrington rod placement or other spinal instrumentation, repair of torn rotator cuff, debridement, limb or digit amputation, reattachment of a limb or digit
Medications	Narcotic analgesics, non-narcotic analgesics, anti-inflammatory agents, antigout agents, muscle relaxants, steroids, calcitonin, calcium, and vitamin D supplements, intra-articular injections, bisphosphonates, selective estrogen receptor modulator, human parathyroid hormone
Communicable Diseases	Poliomyelitis
Injuries and Accidents	Fracture, dislocation, subluxation, tendon tear, tendonitis, muscle contusion, joint strain or sprain, spinal cord injury, torn rotator cuff, traumatic amputation of a digit or limb, crush injury, back injury (including herniated vertebral disc), sports-related injury (e.g., golf elbow, pitcher's shoulder), cartilage damage. See Table 18-4 for age-related trauma.
Special Needs	Amputation, hemiplegia, paraplegia, quadriplegia, need for brace or splint, limb in a cast, need for supportive devices, muscle atrophy

continues

Childhood Illnesses	Poliomyelitis, juvenile arthritis
FAMILY HEALTH HISTORY	*Musculoskeletal diseases that are familial are listed.*
	Rheumatoid arthritis, osteoporosis, ankylosing spondylitis, gout, Paget's disease, Dupuytren's contracture, SLE, Marfan's syndrome, osteomalacia, congenital defect
SOCIAL HISTORY	*The components of the social history are linked to musculoskeletal factors and pathology.*
Alcohol Use	Increased use associated with increased risk of osteoporosis
Tobacco Use	Increased use associated with increased risk of osteoporosis
Work Environment	Manual movement of heavy objects (lifting, pushing, pulling), duties requiring repetitive motions (e.g., keyboard use), duties requiring prolonged standing or walking, use of hazardous equipment, availability and use of safety equipment (e.g., lifting equipment, availability of back support vest or brace)
Home Environment	Design of home (e.g., number of floors, width of doorways, stairs, location of bedroom and bathroom), elevated toilet seat, bar in bathtub or shower
Roles and Relationships	Decreased self-esteem, decreased independence, or isolation secondary to immobility or pain
Hobbies and Leisure Activities	Basketball, wrestling, gymnastics, hockey, ballet, aerobics, use of free weights and exercise machines, baseball, football, lacrosse, rugby, cycling, running, horseback riding, skiing, hiking, tennis, racquetball, swimming, camping, gardening, painting, needlepoint, carpentry, rollerblading, skateboarding
HEALTH MAINTENANCE ACTIVITIES	*This information provides a bridge between the health maintenance activities and musculoskeletal function.*
Sleep	Sleeping positions, need for pillow support, need for firm mattress
Diet	Intake of dairy products and protein, use of dietary supplements or vitamins (especially calcium and vitamin D)
Exercise	Prevents disuse atrophy, promotes bone growth (especially weight-bearing exercise), can aggravate existing musculoskeletal conditions and cause musculoskeletal trauma
Use of Safety Devices	Use of back support vest or lifting equipment for movement of heavy objects (e.g., Hoyer lift, forklift), safety shields when using hazardous equipment, protective padding (wrist or knee guards), helmet
Health Check-ups	Immunizations up to date, especially polio and tetanus, DEXA scan

Nursing Tip

Weakness Rating Scale

A 0–10/10 scale can be used to obtain the patient's subjective rating of the intensity of the weakness. When a 0–10/10 scale is being utilized, 0 represents complete absence of weakness and 10 represents weakness necessitating complete bed rest.

TABLE 18-4 Common Age-Related Trauma

AGE RANGE	COMMON TRAUMA
10 to 20	Sports-related injuries, motorcycle accidents, high-energy falls (e.g., downhill skiing or cycling)
20 to 50	Sports-related injuries, stress or overuse injuries (e.g., stress fractures, tendonitis), pedestrian accidents
50 to 65+	Recreation-related injuries, falls, pathological fractures, pedestrian accidents

Nursing Tip

Stiffness Rating Scale

When assessing a patient's ability to complete ADL, question the patient's family as well as the patient. The changes in activities of daily living over time may be too subtle to have been noticed by the patient, or the patient may have developed compensatory measures so that these activities can still be accomplished (although they may take longer to complete). A 0–10/10 scale can be used to obtain the patient's subjective rating of the intensity of the stiffness. When utilizing a 0–10/10 scale, 0 represents the complete absence of stiffness and 10 represents total inflexibility.

Life 360°

Assessing Home Safety

Examine the safety of your personal living quarters and the immediate outside environment. Next, re-examine your living quarters for safety as if you had an 85-year-old person living with you. Are there internal or external changes that would need to be made for the safety of the older person?

Nursing Tip

Ensuring Home Safety

To ensure a safe home environment, encourage patients (especially those who have an increased risk for injury in the home) to avoid:
- Loose or unsecured rugs (e.g., scatter rugs, rugs on stairways)
- Stairways without banisters or stairways with loose banisters
- Stairs with a slippery surface
- Dim lighting, especially near stairways or steps
- Ill-fitting shoes, loose non-laced shoes, shoes with high heels, or shoes with slippery soles
- Household clutter beneath waist level
- Electrical or phone cords that are too long and fall on the floor
- Only one phone or a phone that is not easily accessible during most of the day
- Wet or waxed floors
- Unrestrained small pets
- Bathtubs or shower stalls without a non-skid surface
- Lack of grab bars in the bathroom near the toilet and tub or shower stall
- Objects that are not within easy reach
- Wet or icy outdoor steps and sidewalks

◄NURSING CHECKLIST►

General Approach to Musculoskeletal Assessment

1. Assist the patient to a comfortable position.
2. Offer pillows or folded blankets to support a painful body part.
3. If necessary because of a painful body part or limited mobility, provide the patient assistance in disrobing. Allow the patient extra time to remove clothing.
4. To maximize patient comfort during the physical assessment, maintain a warm temperature in the exam room.
5. Be clear in your instructions to the patient if you are asking the patient to perform a certain body movement or to assume a certain position. Demonstrate the desired movement if necessary.
6. Notify the patient before touching or manipulating a painful body part.
7. Inspection, palpation, range of motion, and muscle testing are performed on the major skeletal muscles and joints of the body in a cephalocaudal, proximal-to-distal manner. Always compare paired muscles and joints.

continues

8. Examine non-affected body parts before examining affected body parts.

9. Avoid unnecessary or excessive manipulation of a painful body part. If the patient complains of pain, stop the aggravating motion.

10. If necessary because of a painful body part or limited mobility, provide the patient assistance in dressing after the physical assessment. Allow the patient extra time to get dressed.

11. Some musculoskeletal disorders may affect the patient more during certain times of the day. Arrange for the follow-up appointment to be during the patient's time of optimal function.

Equipment

- Measuring tape: cloth tape measure that will not stretch
- **Goniometer:** protractor-type instrument with two movable arms to measure the angle of a skeletal joint during range of motion
- Sphygmomanometer and blood pressure cuff
- Felt-tip marker

ASSESSMENT OF THE MUSCULOSKELETAL SYSTEM

General Assessment

Overall Appearance

E 1. Obtain height and weight. Refer to Chapter 7.

2. Observe the patient's ability to tolerate weight bearing on the lower limbs during standing and walking. Assess the amount of weight bearing placed on each of the lower limbs. See Table 18-5 for a description of weight-bearing terms.

3. Identify obvious structural abnormalities (e.g., atrophy, scoliosis, kyphosis, amputated limbs, contractures).

4. Note indications of discomfort (e.g., restricted weight bearing or movement, frequent shifting of position, facial grimacing, excessive fatigue).

TABLE 18-5 Weight-Bearing Status

DEGREE OF WEIGHT BEARING	DESCRIPTION
Nonweight bearing	Patient does not bear weight on the affected extremity. The affected extremity does not touch the floor.
Touchdown weight bearing	Patient's foot of the affected extremity may rest on the floor, but no weight is distributed through that extremity.
Partial weight bearing	Patient bears 30% to 50% of his or her weight on the affected extremity.
Weight bearing as tolerated	Patient bears as much weight as can be tolerated on the affected extremity without undue strain or pain.
Full weight bearing	Patient bears weight fully on the affected extremity.

Source: Reprinted with permission from *Orthopedic Nursing* (3rd ed.), A. Maher, S. Salmond, & T. Pellino, Copyright 2002, Philadelphia: Elsevier.

E	**Examination**	N	**Normal Findings**	A	**Abnormal Findings**	P	**Pathophysiology**

Figure 18-6 Dwarfism.

N The Body Mass Index is in the normal range (see Chapter 7). The patient should be able to enter the assessment area via independent walking. Structural defects should be absent. There should be no outward indications of discomfort during rest, weight bearing, or joint movement. There should be a distinct and symmetrical relationship among the limbs, torso, and pelvis.

A An excessively tall or short, or overweight or underweight patient is abnormal.

P Marfan's syndrome affects multiple systems. The musculoskeletal changes are increased height for age due to an increased length of the distal limbs, extra digits, joint instability, pectus excavatum, and kyphosis.

P Dwarfism, a congenital disorder, is manifested by a decreased body size. This decreased size is regarded as proportionate if both limb and trunk size are smaller than average. The decreased size may affect only the limbs, which then appear out of proportion to the torso size (Figure 18-6).

P Severe osteoporosis and ankylosing spondylitis can result in height loss due to vertebral compression fractures and thoracic kyphosis.

P Obesity is considered to be a factor in both degenerative joint disease and low back pain.

A Any weight-bearing status other than full weight bearing is abnormal.

P Low back pain may cause a patient to lean forward or toward the affected side.

A Structural defects are abnormal.

P **Acromegaly,** due to hyperpituitary function, may result in an enlarged skull with jaw protrusion, and an increase in the size of the hands, feet, and long bones. The increased length of the long bones can contribute to increased height.

P A missing limb can be due to a congenital defect, surgery, or trauma.

P Pectus excavatum and pectus carinatum are abnormal findings. See Chapter 15.

P Scoliosis and kyphosis are abnormal findings (further discussed on page 650-651).

Figure 18-7 Deviation of Normal Posture.

Preventing Falls in Long-Term Care Facilities (LTC)

Programs that target the broad range of both environmental and resident-specific risk factors to prevent falls and hip fractures for all individuals admitted to long-term care facilities are recommended.[2] Because the factors that lead to admission to LTCs parallel those that predispose older adults to falls, fall prevention must be a priority. Programs should involve in-depth assessment of medical history, cognition, strength and balance, nutrition, medications, and environmental hazards. A multi-disciplinary approach is advised.

| E | Examination | N | Normal Findings | A | Abnormal Findings | P | Pathophysiology |

Morse Fall Scale

Fall risk is based upon fall risk factors and it is more than a total score. Determine fall risk factors and target interventions to reduce risks. Complete on admission, at change of condition, transfer to new unit, and after a fall.

Variables			Score	
History of Falling	no	0		
	yes	25	————	
Secondary Diagnosis	no	0		
	yes	15	————	
Ambulatory Aid	None/bed rest/nurse assist	0		
	Crutches/cane/walker	15	————	
	Furniture	30		
IV or IV access	no	0		
	yes	20	————	
Gait	Normal/bed rest/wheelchair	0		
	Weak	10	————	
	Impaired	20		
Mental status	Knows own limits	0		
	Overestimates or forgets limits	15	————	
		Total	————	

Definition of Variables for the Morse Scale

History of falling
- Yes (scored 25) if a previous fall is recorded during the present admission or if there is immediate history of physiological falls (i.e., from seizures, impaired gait) prior to admission.

Secondary diagnosis
- Yes (15) if more than one medical diagnosis is listed on the patient chart.

Ambulatory aids
- Scored 0 if patient walks without a walking aid even if assisted by a nurse or is on bedrest.
- Scored 15 if ambulatory with crutches, cane, or walker.
- Scored 20 if clutches for support.

Intravenous therapy
- Scored 20 if has an IV apparatus or heparin lock.

Gait
- Normal gait scored 0 if patient is able to walk with head erect, arms swinging freely at the side, & strides unhesitantly.
- Weak gait scored 10 if patient is stooped but able to lift head while walking. Furniture support may be sought but is of feather-weight touch, almost for reassurance. Steps are short, and the patient may shuffle.
- Impaired gait scored 20 if patient is stooped, may have difficulty rising from the chair, attempts to rise by pushing on the arms of the chair and/or by "bouncing". The patient's head is down, and because balance is poor the patient grasps the furniture, a person, or walking aid for support and cannot walk without assistance. Steps are short and patient shuffles. If patient is wheelchair-bound, the patient is scored according to the gait used when transferring from the wheelchair to the bed.

Mental Status
- The patient is asked if s/he is able to go to the bathroom alone or if she/he is permitted up. If the patient's response is consistent with the ambulatory orders on the Kardex, the score is 0.
- If the response is not consistent with the orders or if the patient's assessment is unrealistic, score is 15.
- Each institution can determine its own cut-off for high risk or address each targeted (greater than 0) risk factor.

Figure 18-8 Morse Fall Scale.

Posture

E   **1.** Stand in front of the patient.
     2. Instruct the patient to stand with the feet together.
     3. Observe the structural and spatial relationship of the head, torso, pelvis, and limbs. Assess for symmetry of the shoulders, scapulae, and iliac crests.
     4. Ask the patient to sit; observe posture.

N   In the standing position, the torso and head are upright. The head is midline and perpendicular to the horizontal line of the shoulders and pelvis. The shoulders and hips are level, with symmetry of the scapulae and iliac crests. The arms hang freely from the shoulders. The feet are aligned and the toes point forward. The extremities are proportional to the overall body size and shape, and the limbs are also symmetrical with each other. The knees face forward, with symmetry of the level of the knees. There is usually less than a 5 cm interval between the knees when the patient stands with the feet together, facing forward. When full growth is reached, the arm span is equal to the height. In the sitting position, both feet should be placed firmly on the floor surface, with toes pointing forward.

A   Forward slouching of the shoulders produces a false thoracic kyphosis.

P   These findings can be caused by poor posture habits.

Gait and Mobility

E   **1.** Instruct the patient to walk normally across the room.
     2. Ask the patient to walk on toes and then on the heels of the feet.
     3. Ask the patient to walk by placing one foot in front of the other, in a "heel-to-toe" fashion (tandem walking).
     4. Instruct the patient to walk forward, then backward.
     5. Ask the patient to side step to the left, then to the right.
     6. Instruct the patient to ambulate forward a few steps with the eyes closed.
     7. Observe the patient during transfer between the standing and sitting position.

N   Walking is started in one smooth, rhythmic fashion. The foot is lifted 2.5 to 5 cm off the floor and then propelled 30 to 45 cm forward in a straight path. As the heel strikes the floor, body weight is then shifted onto the ball of that foot. The heel of the foot is then lifted off the floor before the next step forward. The patient remains erect and balanced during all stages of gait. Step height and length are symmetrical for each foot. The arms swing freely at the side of the torso but in opposite direction to the movement of the legs. The lower limbs are able to bear full body weight during standing and walking. Prior to turning, the head and neck turn toward the intended direction, followed by the rest of the body. The patient should be able to transfer easily to various positions.

A   Indications of gait disturbance include hesitancy or multiple attempts to initiate walking, unsteadiness, staggering, grasping for external support, high stepping, foot scraping due to inability to raise the foot completely off the floor, persistent toe or heel walking, excessive pointing of the toes inward or outward, asymmetry of step height or length, limping, stooping during walking, wavering gait, shuffling gait, waddling gait, excessive swinging of the shoulders or pelvis, and slow or rapid step speed. Table 18-6 provides examples of abnormal gait patterns.

| E | **Examination** | N | **Normal Findings** | A | **Abnormal Findings** | P | **Pathophysiology** |

TABLE 18-6	Examples of Abnormal Gait Patterns	
TYPE OF ABNORMAL GAIT	**ETIOLOGY**	**DESCRIPTION**
Antalgic	Degenerative joint disease of the hip or knee	Limited weight bearing is placed on an affected leg in an attempt to limit discomfort.
Short leg	Discrepancy in leg length, flexion contracture of the hip or knee, congenital hip dislocation	A limp is present during ambulation unless shoes have been adapted to compensate for length discrepancy.
Spastic hemiplegia	Cerebral palsy, unilateral upper motor neuron lesion (e.g., stroke)	Extension of one lower extremity with plantar flexion and foot inversion; arm is flexed at the elbow, wrist, and fingers. The patient walks by swinging the affected leg in a semicircle. The foot is not lifted off the floor. The affected arm does not swing with the gait.
Scissors	Multiple sclerosis, bilateral upper motor neuron disease	Adduction at the knee level produces short, slow steps. Gait is uncoordinated, stiff, and jerky. The foot is dragged across the floor in a semicircle.
Cerebellar ataxia	Cerebellar disease	Gait is broad based and uncoordinated, and the patient appears to stagger and sway during ambulation.
Sensory ataxia	Disorders of peripheral nerves, dorsal roots, and posterior column that interfere with proprioceptive input	Stance is broad based. Patient lifts feet up too high and abruptly slaps them on the floor, heel first. The patient watches the floor carefully to help ensure correct foot placement because the patient is unaware of position in space.
Festinating	Parkinson's disease	Decreased step height and length, but increased step speed, resulting in "shuffling" (feet barely clearing the floor). Patient's posture is stooped and patient appears to hesitate both in initiation and in termination of ambulation. Rigid body position, with flexion of the knees during standing and ambulation.
Steppage or footdrop	Peroneal nerve injury, paralysis of the dorsiflexor muscles, damage to spinal nerve roots L5 and S1 from poliomyelitis	Hip and knee flexion are needed for step height in order to lift the foot off the floor. Instead of placing the heel of the foot on the floor first, the whole sole of the foot is slapped on the floor at once. May be unilateral or bilateral.
Apraxic	Alzheimer's disease, frontal lobe tumors	Patient has difficulty with walking despite intact motor and sensory systems. The patient is unable to initiate walking, as if stuck to the floor. After walking is initiated, the gait is slow and shuffling.
Trendelenburg	Developmental dysplasia of hip, muscular dystrophy	During ambulation, pelvis of the unaffected side drops when weight bearing is performed on the affected side. When both hips are affected, a "waddling" gait may be evident.

Source: Reprinted with permission from *Orthopedic Nursing* (3rd ed.), A. Maher, S. Salmond, & T. Pellino, Copyright 2002, Philadelphia: Elsevier.

P Causes of abnormal gait include muscle weakness, joint deterioration, malalignment of the lower limbs, paralysis, lack of coordination or balance, fatigue, and pain.

P Limited mobility due to stiffness is associated with degenerative joint disease, rheumatoid arthritis, Paget's disease, and Parkinson's disease.

P Severe thoracic kyphosis will alter the body's centre of gravity and affect balance during both standing and walking.

P Pathological fracture of the femoral shaft during the stress of weight bearing may occur during standing or walking. Pathological fracture can occur

TABLE 18-7 **Transfer Techniques**

TECHNIQUE	DESCRIPTION
Independent	The patient is safe with transfers and requires no assistance.
Standby assist of 1	The patient is basically independent but may need verbal cues or observation.
Contact guard of 1	The patient transfers well with hands-on contact by a nurse. This method is used if the patient's judgment is questionable or for patients with slightly decreased balance.
Minimal assistance of 1	The patient requires minimal physical assistance from a nurse to stand or sit (e.g., for lower extremity placement on footrest of wheelchair).
Maximal assistance of 1	The patient requires maximal physical assistance and many verbal cues from a nurse to transfer (e.g., for extremity placement, trunk placement).
Maximal assistance of 2	Same as for the previous example but requires two nurses. This necessitates good body mechanics and often calls for assistive devices (e.g., Hoyer lift, total lift).

Source: Reprinted with permission from *Orthopedic Nursing* (3rd ed.), A. Maher, S. Salmond, & T. Pellino, Copyright 2002, Philadelphia: Elsevier.

if the bone has been significantly weakened by malignancy, osteoporosis, Paget's disease, or osteomalacia.

A When rising from or sitting in a chair, the patient may have to lean on the armrest for external support. The patient may also tend to rock forward and push off from the armrest for propulsion upward into the standing position. Discomfort felt while bearing the body's weight in the standing position may be reduced in the sitting position. In Table 18-7, transfer techniques that will assist you in documenting the type of patient transfer are described.

P Because of stiffness and discomfort, the patient with degenerative joint disease of the hip joint often has difficulty rising from a sitting position without assistance.

Inspection

Muscle Size and Shape

E 1. Survey the overall appearance of the muscle mass.
2. Ask the patient to contract the muscle without inducing movement (isometric muscle contraction), relax the muscle, and then repeat the muscle contraction.
3. Look for any obvious muscle contraction.

N Muscle contour will be affected by the exercise and activity patterns of the individual. Muscle shape may be accentuated in certain body areas (e.g., the limbs and upper torso) but should be symmetrical. There may be hypertrophy in the dominant hand. During muscle contraction, you should be able to visualize sudden tautness of the muscle area. Muscle relaxation will be associated with termination of muscle tautness. There is no involuntary movement.

E	**Examination**	N	**Normal Findings**	A	**Abnormal Findings**	P	**Pathophysiology**

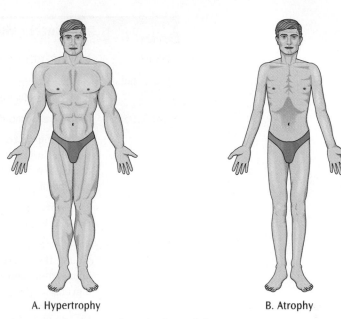

A. Hypertrophy   B. Atrophy

Figure 18-9 Variances of Muscle Size and Shape.

N   Hypertrophy refers to an increase in muscle size and shape due to an increase in the muscle fibres. Hypertrophy is detected as a unilateral or bilateral increase in the contour of the muscle. During contraction, the borders of the muscle will become accentuated. An increase in muscle strength will accompany the increase in muscle size (Figure 18-9A). Bilateral hypertrophy is common among athletes involved in weight lifting or other activities that require repetitive motion against opposing resistance. Hypertrophy of the proximal arms is often seen in patients who are dependent on a wheelchair for mobility yet are able to propel the wheelchair manually.

A   **Atrophy** describes a reduction in muscle size and shape. Atrophy is evidenced by the appearance of thin, flabby muscles. The contour of the skeletal muscle is less distinct than usual. The muscle will appear relaxed, even during voluntary isometric contraction. Atrophy may be local or diffuse (Figure 18-9B).

P   Generalized atrophy is directly related to prolonged immobility of the body as a whole (disuse atrophy), unless isometric exercises were routinely performed during the period of immobility. It is accentuated by poor nutrition.

P   Generalized atrophy may also be noted in grossly obese patients who lead sedentary lifestyles.

P   Local atrophy is often detected in the limb or limbs affected by hemiparesis, paraplegia, or quadriplegia. It is also seen following the removal of a limb cast or splint.

A   There is involuntary muscle movement.

P   See Table 18-8.

Advanced Technique

Measuring Limb Circumference

Limb circumference is measured when a limb looks larger or smaller than its counterpart during inspection.

E   1. During muscle relaxation or nonweight-bearing, measure the limbs at exactly the same distance from a nearby joint (e.g., the knee or elbow) at the site of maximal limb diameter (Figure 18-10).

continues

TABLE 18-8	Involuntary Muscle Movements
TYPE	**DESCRIPTION**
Fasciculation	Visible twitching of a group of muscle fibers that may be stimulated by the tapping of a muscle.
Fibrillation	Ineffective, uncoordinated muscle contraction that resembles quivering.
Spasm	Sudden muscle contraction. A cramp is a muscle spasm that is strong and painful. Clonic muscle spasms are contractions that alternate with a period of muscle relaxation. A tonic muscle spasm is a sustained contraction with a period of relaxation.
Tetany	Paroxysmal tonic muscle spasms, usually of the extremities. The face and jaw may also be affected by spasm. Tetany may be associated with discomfort.
Chorea	Rapid, irregular, and jerky muscle contractions of random muscle groups. It is unpredictable and without purpose. It can involve the face, upper trunk, and limbs. Sometimes, the patient tries to incorporate the movement into voluntary movement, which may appear grotesque and exaggerated. The patient may have difficulty with chewing, speaking, and swallowing.
Tremors	A period of continuous shaking due to muscle contractions. Although the quality of the tremors will be influenced by the cause, the amplitude and the frequency should remain the same. Tremors may be fine or coarse, rapid or slow, continuous or intermittent. They may be exacerbated during rest and attempts at purposeful movements, or by certain body positions.
Tic	Sudden, rapid muscle spasms of the upper trunk, face, or shoulders. The action is often repetitive and may decrease during purposeful movement. It can be persistent or limited in nature.
Ballism	Jerky, twisting movements due to strong muscle contraction.
Athetosis	Slow, writhing, twisting type of movement. The patient is unable to sustain any part of the body in one position. The movements are most often in the fingers, hands, face, throat, and tongue, although any part of the body can be affected. The movements are generally slower than in chorea.
Dystonia	Similar to athetosis but differing in the duration of the postural abnormality, and involving large muscles such as the trunk. The patient may present with an overflexed or overextended posture of the hand, pulling of the head to one side, torsion of the spine, inversion of the foot, or closure of the eyes along with a fixed grimace.
Myoclonus	A rapid, irregular contraction of a muscle or group of muscles, such as the type of jerking movement that occurs when drifting off to sleep.
Tremors at rest	Asymmetrical and coarse movements that disappear or diminish with action. They tend to diminish or cease with purposeful movement.
Action tremors	Symmetrical or asymmetrical movements that increase in states of fatigue, weakness, drug withdrawal, hypocalcemia, uremia, or hepatic disease. This type of tremor may be induced in a normal individual when he or she is required to maintain a posture that demands extremes of power or precision. Action tremors are also called postural tremors.
Intention tremors	These tremors may appear only on voluntary movement of a limb and may intensify on termination of movement.
Asterixis	This is a variant of a tremor. The rate of limb flexion and extension is irregular, slow, and of wide amplitude. The outstretched limb temporarily loses muscle tone.

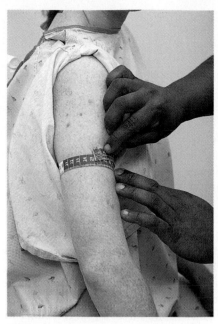

Figure 18-10 Measuring Limb Circumference.

N Bilateral measurements should be within 1 to 3 cm of each other. A slight increase in the girth of the dominant arm is normal.

A A discrepancy in limb girth of 3 cm or more is abnormal.

P Atrophy results from disuse of a limb, as may occur in stroke.

P Swelling following trauma to soft tissue or bone (e.g., crush injury or fracture) results in an increased limb circumference.

P Unilateral hypertrophy can result from selected activities that use one side of the body more than the other (e.g., tennis arm).

P Unilateral hypertrophy may also be the result of compensating for a deficit in the corresponding limb. For example, a patient with hemiparesis of a limb will present with some degree of hypertrophy of the non-affected arm muscles.

P A unilateral increase in calf girth may indicate a deep vein thrombosis.

Joint Contour and Periarticular Tissue

E 1. Observe the shape of the joint while the joint is in its neutral anatomic position.

2. Visually inspect the 5 to 7.5 cm of skin and subcutaneous tissue surrounding that joint. Assess the periarticular area for erythema, swelling, bruising, nodules, deformities, masses, skin atrophy, or skin breakdown.

N Joint contour should be somewhat flat in extension, and smooth and rounded in flexion. You should be unable to detect any difference between periarticular tissue, the skin, and subcutaneous tissue. Bilateral joints should be symmetrical in position and appearance. There should be no observable erythema, swelling, bruising, nodules, deformities, masses, skin atrophy, or skin breakdown.

A Enlargement of the joint is an abnormal finding.

P Joint inflammation can result from inflammatory disorders such as rheumatoid arthritis and gout.

P Trauma to the joint and its extra-articular structures will also result in joint inflammation.

A Deformity of the joint capsule is an abnormal finding.

P Immobility results in joint contractures, which cause the joint to be permanently fixated in one position. The acquired joint position may be one within its normal range of joint motion or an abnormal joint position.

P Joint destruction from rheumatoid arthritis may result in a joint becoming fixated in one position.

P Joint dislocation or subluxation will alter the normal contour of a joint. **Dislocation** refers to a complete dislodgment of one bone out of the joint cavity. **Subluxation** is a partial dislodgment of a bone from its place in the joint cavity.

A Alteration in periarticular skin and subcutaneous tissue is an abnormal finding.

P Trauma to the joint results in inflammation and bruising of the periarticular tissue. Joint trauma may include strain, sprain, contusion, dislocation, subluxation, or fracture within or near the joint capsule.

P The patient with rheumatoid arthritis often presents with periarticular skin atrophy and subcutaneous nodules near a joint (e.g., elbow).

P Synovial effusion within the joint capsule may cause a bulging appearance that extends into the periarticular area.

| E | Examination | N | Normal Findings | A | Abnormal Findings | P | Pathophysiology |

Palpation

Muscle Tone

E 1. Palpate the muscle by applying light pressure with the finger pads of the dominant hand.
   2. Note the change in muscle shape as the muscle belly tapers off to become a tendon.
   3. Ask the patient to alternately perform muscle relaxation and isometric muscle contraction. Note the change in palpable muscle tone between relaxation and isometric contraction.
   4. Palpate the muscle belly during contraction induced by voluntary movement of a nearby joint.
   5. Perform passive range of motion to all extremities and note whether these movements are smooth and sustained.

N Muscle tone refers to the partial muscle contraction state that is maintained in order for the muscle to respond quickly to the next stimulus. On palpation, the muscle should feel smooth and firm, even during the phase of muscle relaxation. Normal muscle tone provides light resistance to passive stretch. During muscle contraction, especially against moderate external resistance to nearby joint movement, you will be able to palpate a significant overall increase in the firmness of the muscle belly. Muscle tone increases during anxiety or excitable states. Tone decreases during rest and sleep. You will be able to palpate the muscle belly and detect a change in its shape as it tapers down to become a tendon. The hypertrophied muscle will have a distinctive contour. You will detect muscle tautness even during the phase of relaxation.

A **Hypotonicity** (flaccidity) is a decrease in muscle tone. When the muscle is palpated, it feels flabby and soft to the touch. When a flaccid limb is held away from the body and then released, it falls quickly with gravity.

P Etiology of flaccidity may include diseases involving the muscles, anterior horn cells, or peripheral nerves.

P **Spasticity** refers to an increase in muscle tension on passive stretching (especially rapid or forced stretching of the muscle). It is often noted with extreme flexion or extension.

P Upper motor neuron dysfunction is associated with spasticity.

A The atrophied muscle will feel small and flabby, even during the phase of muscle contraction.

P See page 617.

A A muscle spasm represents persistent muscle contraction without relaxation. The muscle belly will feel taut and the patient may complain of discomfort over the muscle area. The spasm may also result in involuntary joint movement or a change in body position.

P Spasm follows fracture and may alter the distance between the bone fragments. Spasm is also common in the affected limbs of patients with paralysis, electrolyte imbalance, peripheral vascular disease, and cerebral palsy.

A Crepitus refers to a grating or crackling sensation caused by two rough musculoskeletal surfaces rubbing together. Crepitus is more commonly detected with joint movement than it is with muscle contraction.

P Crepitus detected during palpation of muscle contraction, especially in a non-articulating area, may indicate shaft fracture due to trauma or loss of bone density. Muscle spasm following fracture may bring bone fragments in contact with each other, resulting in crepitus.

A Muscle masses detected on palpation are to be considered an abnormal finding.

E	Examination	N	Normal Findings	A	Abnormal Findings	P	Pathophysiology

P Muscle rupture (e.g., of the long head of the biceps muscle) will present as an inappropriate muscle mass above the joint. The muscle mass may be accentuated by muscle contraction.

P Tendon rupture may also result in an inappropriate muscle mass. An example is a complete rupture of the Achilles tendon, resulting in a mass noted in the calf area.

P Displaced fracture (e.g., of the femoral shaft near the hip joint) will often result in palpation of the displaced bone near a muscle.

P Complete dislocation (e.g., of the hip joint) will also result in palpation of the displaced bone near a muscle.

Joints

E 1. With the joint in its neutral anatomic position, begin palpating the joint by applying light pressure with the finger pads of the dominant hand 5 to 7 cm away from the centre of the joint.
2. Palpate from the periphery inward to the centre of the joint.
3. Note any swelling, pain, tenderness, warmth, or nodules.

N When the major skeletal joints are palpated in their neutral anatomic positions, the external joint contour will feel smooth, strong, and firm. The shape of the joint corresponds to that specific joint type. The area surrounding the joint (periarticular tissue) is free from swelling, pain, tenderness, warmth, or nodules. As the joint is moved through its normal range of motion, it should be able to articulate in proper alignment without any visible or palpable deformity. Palpation of joint movement produces a smooth sensation, without tactile detection of grating or popping. A synovial membrane is not palpable under normal circumstances.

A Bony enlargement or bony deformities of the joint are considered abnormal findings. See Table 18-9, which provides a tool for grading joint swelling, tenderness, and limitations.

P Urate deposits associated with gout will result in a reactive synovitis, producing joint enlargement. Urate crystals accumulate in the joint as a result

TABLE 18-9	Grading of Joint Swelling, Tenderness, and Limitation		
GRADE	**SWELLING (S)**	**TENDERNESS (T)**	**LIMITATION (L)**
0	None	None	None
1	Mild	Mild but tolerable tenderness upon palpation	25% decrease in joint range of motion
2	Moderate	Moderate tenderness upon palpation (which the patient can tolerate but prefers not to)	50% decrease in joint range of motion
3	Marked	Light pressure or palpation induces an intolerable tenderness	75% decrease in joint range of motion
4	Maximum	Slight skin motion or sensation induces an intolerable tenderness	Complete loss of joint range of motion

0 = *normal* 2 = *moderate abnormality* 4 = *maximum abnormality*
1 = *mild abnormality* 3 = *marked abnormality*

Example: S3/T3/L4 = marked joint swelling with intolerable joint tenderness upon light pressure and with complete loss of joint range of motion.

of a prolonged elevation of serum uric acid. The affected joint will be extremely warm and tender to the touch. Although the great toe is most commonly affected, gout can also affect other joints.

A Subcutaneous nodules detected in the periarticular area are abnormal.

P Rheumatoid arthritis is associated with subcutaneous nodules over the bony prominences and extensor joint surfaces (e.g., olecranon process of the elbow). These nodules are painless, firm but movable, and of normal skin colour. They are more of a cosmetic concern than a threat to nearby joint function, although the overlying skin is at risk for breakdown due to irritation or pressure.

P Tophi nodules may be detected in the patient with chronic gout, and they represent soft tissue reaction to uric acid crystal deposition. They are often found on the great toes.

A Palpable, audible, severe crepitus that presents as more of a coarse than a fine sensation is abnormal.

P Crepitus is often palpated in joints affected by acute rheumatoid arthritis and degenerative joint disease due to the contact of bone surfaces.

P Bony overgrowth, muscle contracture, dislocation, and subluxation are associated with joint crepitus.

A Any tenderness felt on light touch or joint palpation is considered abnormal. You must differentiate between tenderness on palpation of the joint at rest versus palpation during joint movement.

P Joint pain due to septic arthritis can occur 10 to 14 days after an untreated streptococcal pharyngitis or tonsillitis.

P Increased joint capsule pressure with a significant joint effusion may induce discomfort with light touch or pressure to the joint in the neutral position.

P Localized joint tenderness may be detected in the presence of joint contusion, infection, or synovitis.

A Periarticular warmth, with temperature exceeding overall body temperature, indicates an underlying problem.

P Joint inflammation (e.g., due to acute rheumatoid arthritis or recent trauma) and gout produce significant joint warmth because of the increased localized perfusion associated with the inflammatory process.

Range of Motion (ROM)

E 1. Ask the patient to move the joint through each of its various ROM movements.
   2. Note angle of each joint movement.
   3. Note any pain, tenderness, or crepitus.
   4. If the patient is unable to perform active ROM, then passively move each joint through its ROM.
   5. Always stop if the patient complains of pain, and never push a joint beyond its anatomic angle.
   6. Use a Goniometer to determine exact ROM in joints with limited ROM. Refer to the Advanced Technique on page 623.

Muscle Strength

Each muscle group is assessed for strength via the same movements as are performed in range of motion.

E 1. Note whether muscle groups are strong and equal.
   2. Always compare right and left sides of paired muscle groups.
   3. Note involuntary movements.

| E | Examination | N | Normal Findings | A | Abnormal Findings | P | Pathophysiology |

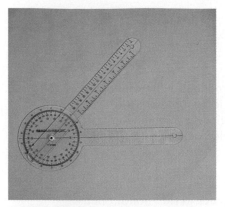

A. Goniometer

B. Use of Goniometer

Figure 18-11 Goniometer and Its Use.

N Normal muscle strength allows for complete voluntary range of joint motion against both gravity and moderate to full resistance. Muscle strength is equal bilaterally. There is no observed involuntary muscle movement.

A A decrease in skeletal muscle strength is significant if complete range of joint motion is either impossible or possible only without resistance or gravity.

P Local decrease in muscle strength will accompany muscle atrophy of the limbs secondary to disuse.

P Diffuse reduction in muscle strength is associated with general atrophy, severe fatigue, malnutrition, muscle relaxant medications, long-term steroid use, and deteriorating neuromuscular disorders. These deteriorating neuromuscular diseases include but are not limited to ALS, MD, MS, myasthenia gravis, and Guillain-Barré syndrome.

A One-sided muscle weakness or paralysis is considered abnormal.

P Unilateral weakness or paralysis is indicative of **hemiparesis** (**hemiplegia**) from a cerebrovascular accident, brain tumour, or head trauma.

Advanced Technique

Assessing Joint ROM: Using a Goniometer

E 1. With the joint in its neutral position, place the centre of the Goniometer over the joint so that the two distal arms of the Goniometer are in alignment with the proximal and distal bones adjacent to that joint.

2. Move the joint through its ROM and note the degree of the joint angle visible on the centre of the Goniometer (Figure 18-11).

N Refer to the specific sections on joints for the ROM for each joint movement.

A Abnormalities of joint function are indicated by the inability of the patient to voluntarily and comfortably move a joint in the directions and to the degrees that are considered the norms for that joint.

P Degenerative joint disease, rheumatoid arthritis, and joint trauma are some of the many musculoskeletal disorders that prevent the affected joint from moving through its normal ROM.

Nursing Alert

Assessing Muscle Strength

Muscle strength can be assessed indirectly by reviewing the patient's ability to perform daily activities that involve lifting, pushing, pulling, grasping, walking, climbing stairs, and transferring to a sitting position. Muscle strength can be assessed directly using the Muscle Strength Grading Scale (Table 18-10).

TABLE 18-10 Muscle Strength Grading Scale

FUNCTIONAL ABILITY DESCRIPTION	SCALE (%)	0–5/5 SCALE
Complete range of joint motion against both gravity and full manual resistance from the nurse.	100%	5/5 Normal (N)
Complete range of joint motion against both gravity and moderate manual resistance from the nurse.	75%	4/5 Good (G)
Complete range of joint motion possible only without manual resistance from the nurse.	50%	3/5 Fair (F)
Complete range of joint motion possible only with the joint supported by the nurse to eliminate the force of gravity and without any manual resistance from the nurse.	25%	2/5 Poor (P)
Muscle contraction detectable but insufficient to move the joint even when the forces of both gravity and manual resistance have been eliminated.	10%	1/5 Trace (Tr)
Complete absence of visible and palpable muscle contraction.	0%	0/5 None (0)

Examination of Joints

Temporomandibular Joint

E **1.** Stand in front of the patient.

    2. Inspect the right and left temporomandibular joints (Figure 18-12).

    3. Palpate the temporomandibular joints (Figure 18-13).

      a. Place your index and middle fingers over the joint.

      b. Ask the patient to open and close the mouth.

      c. Feel the depression into which your fingers move with an open mouth.

      d. Note the smoothness with which the mandible moves.

      e. Note any audible or palpable click as the mouth opens.

    4. Assess ROM (Figure 18-14). Ask the patient to:

      a. Open the mouth as wide as possible.

      b. Push out the lower jaw.

      c. Move the jaw from side to side.

    5. Palpate the strength of the masseter and temporalis muscles as the patient clenches the teeth. This assesses cranial nerve V.

N It is normal to hear or palpate a click when the mouth opens. The mouth can normally open 3 to 6 cm with ease. The lower jaw protrudes without deviating to the side and moves 1 to 2 cm with lateral movement.

A Pain, limited ROM, and crepitus can occur in temporomandibular joint dysfunction.

P Temporomandibular joint dysfunction can occur secondary to malocclusion, arthritis, dislocation, poorly fitting dentures, myofacial dysfunction, and trauma.

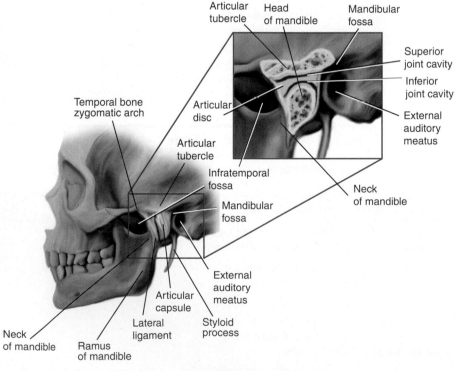

Figure 18-12 Anatomy of the Temporomandibular Joint (Sagittal Section).

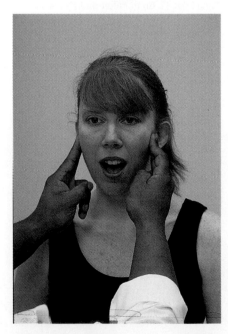

Figure 18-13 Palpation of the Temporomandibular Joint.

| E | Examination | N | Normal Findings | A | Abnormal Findings | P | Pathophysiology |

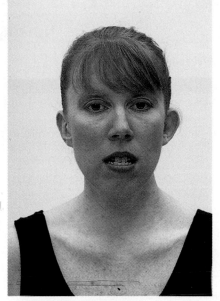

A. Pushing out the Lower Jaw   B. Moving the Jaw from Side to Side

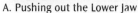
Figure 18-14 Range of Motion of the Temporomandibular Joint.

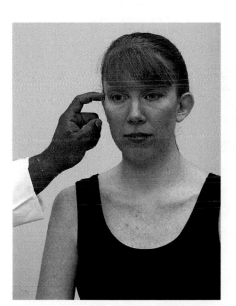

Figure 18-15 Assessing for Chvostek's Sign.

Advanced Technique

Assessing for Neuroexcitability: Chvostek's Sign

E   1. The patient can be assessed in the standing, sitting, or supine position.
     2. While the patient is facing forward, tap the side of the face just below the temple area, using the middle or index finger (Figure 18-15).
     3. Observe for ipsilateral changes in facial expression immediately after tapping the face.
     4. Repeat the procedure on the other side of the face.

N   There will be no change in the patient's facial expression when the temple area is stimulated.

A   A positive Chvostek's sign, indicated by ipsilateral muscle spasm of the mouth and cheek, is abnormal. The muscle spasm will occur in an upward direction, toward the temple.

P   A positive Chvostek's sign is suggestive of neuroexcitability associated with hypocalcemia and tetanus infection.

Advanced Technique

Assessing for Neuroexcitability: Trousseau's Sign

E   1. Place the patient in a sitting or a supine position.
     2. Apply a blood pressure cuff to the patient's upper arm.
     3. Inflate the blood pressure cuff to 10 mm Hg above the patient's systolic blood pressure for one to three minutes.
     4. Observe for twitching of the hand and fingers on the side being tested.

N   There will be no visible twitching of the hand and fingers during cuff inflation.

A   A positive Trousseau's sign, indicated by visible ipsilateral twitching of the hand and fingers during cuff inflation, is abnormal.

P   A positive Trousseau's sign is suggestive of neuroexcitability associated with hypocalcemia and tetanus infection.

Nursing Alert

Preventing Neck Injury

Never move the head or neck of a patient with a suspected neck injury. Movement can result in permanent spinal cord injury. Refer the patient to an orthopedist or a neurosurgeon immediately.

Use caution when applying mild to moderate resistance during neck assessment, especially when the patient has a known musculoskeletal disorder.

Cervical Spine

E 1. Stand behind the patient.
   2. Inspect the position of the cervical spine.
   3. Palpate the spinous processes (Figure 18-16) of the cervical spine and the muscles of the neck.

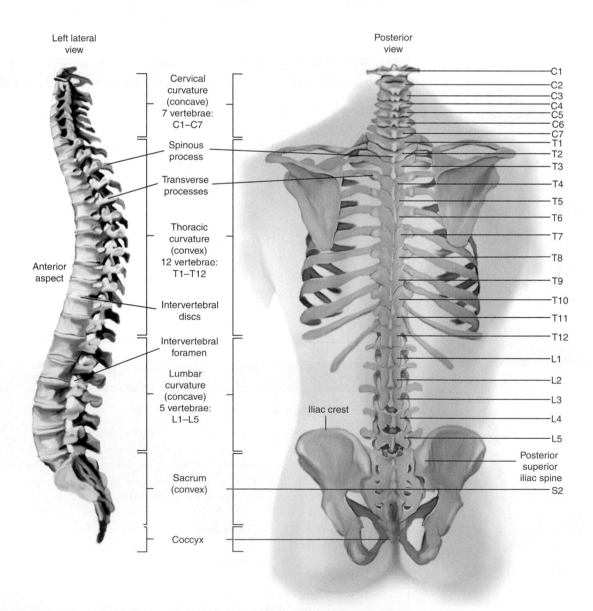

Figure 18-16 Anatomy of the Spine.

4. Stand in front of the patient.
5. Assess the ROM of the cervical spine (Figure 18-17). Ask the patient to:
   a. Touch the chin to the chest (flexion).
   b. Look up at the ceiling (hyperextension).
   c. Move each ear to the shoulder on its respective side without elevating the shoulder (lateral bending).
   d. Turn the head to each side to look at the shoulder (rotation).
6. Assess strength of the cervical spine by repeating the movements in step 5d while applying opposing force. This also assesses the function of cranial nerve XI.

N The cervical spine's alignment is straight and the head is held erect. The normal ROM for the cervical spine is flexion—45°, hyperextension—55°, lateral bending—40° to each side, rotation—70° to each side. Hypertrophy of the neck muscles due to weight-lifting exercises will produce the appearance of a thick neck.

A A neck that is not erect and straight is abnormal.

P Degenerative joint disease of the cervical vertebrae may result in lateral tilting of the head and neck.

P Torticollis is discussed on page 347.

A A change in the size of the neck is abnormal.

P Klippel-Feil syndrome is the congenital absence of one or more cervical vertebrae along with fusion of the upper cervical vertebrae and bilateral elevation of the scapulae, resulting in a shortened neck appearance. It may be accompanied by a low hairline, webbing of the neck, and decreased neck mobility.

A Inability of the patient to perform ROM, and pain and tenderness on palpation are abnormal.

P Osteoarthritis, neck injury, disc degeneration (among aging patients or from occupational stress), and spondylosis can cause these cervical spine signs or symptoms.

Shoulders

E 1. Stand in front of the patient.
   2. Inspect the size, shape, and symmetry of the shoulders (Figure 18-18).

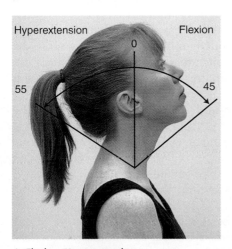

A. Flexion, Hyperextension

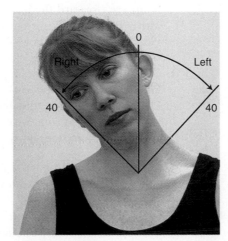

B. Lateral Bending

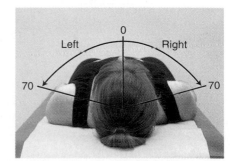

C. Rotation

Figure 18-17 Range of Motion of the Cervical Spine.

| E | Examination | N | Normal Findings | A | Abnormal Findings | P | Pathophysiology |

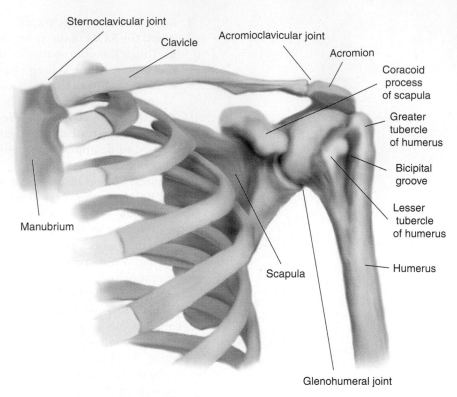

Figure 18-18 Anatomy of the Shoulder Joint.

3. Move behind the patient and inspect the scapula for size, shape, and symmetry.
4. Palpate the shoulders and surrounding muscles.
    a. Move from the sternoclavicular joint along the clavicle to the acromioclavicular joint.
    b. Palpate the acromion process, subacromial area, greater tubercle of the humerus, the anterior aspect of the glenohumeral joint, and the biceps groove.
5. Assess ROM of the shoulders (Figure 18-19). Ask the patient to:
    a. Place arms at the side, elbows extended, and move the arms forward in an arc (forward flexion).
    b. Move the arms backward in an arc as far as possible (hyperextension).
    c. Place arms at side, elbows extended, and move both arms out to the sides in an arc until the palms touch together overhead (abduction).
    d. Move one arm at a time in an arc toward the midline and cross it as far as possible (adduction).
    e. Place hands behind the back and reach up, trying to touch the scapula (internal rotation).
    f. Place both hands behind the head with elbows flexed (external rotation).
    g. Shrug the shoulders. This assesses cranial nerve XI function.
6. Assess strength of the shoulders by applying opposing force to the ROM movement in step 5g.

N The shoulders are equal in height. There is no fluid palpable in the shoulder area. Crepitus is absent. The normal ROM for the shoulder is forward flexion—180°, hyperextension—50°, abduction—180°, adduction—50°, internal rotation—90°, external rotation—90°.

| **E** | **Examination** | **N** | **Normal Findings** | **A** | **Abnormal Findings** | **P** | **Pathophysiology** |

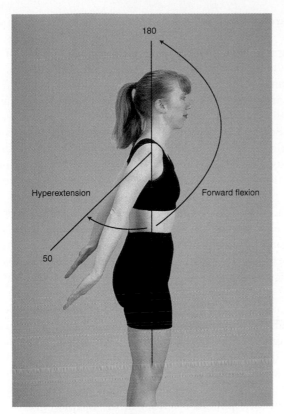

A. Forward Flexion, Hyperextension

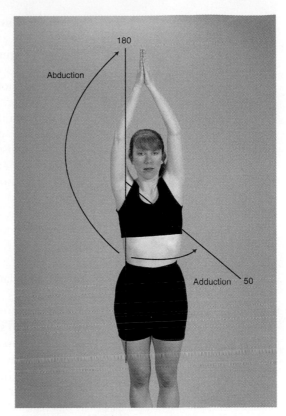

B. Abduction, Adduction

C. Internal Rotation

D. External Rotation

Figure 18-19 Range of Motion of the Shoulder Joint.

A Increased outward prominence of the scapula (winging) is an abnormal finding.

P Scapular winging is indicative of serratus anterior muscle injury or weakness.

A Decreased movement, pain with movement, swelling from fluid, and asymmetry are abnormal.

P These findings are associated with immobility, osteoarthritis, and injury. Swelling from fluid is usually best seen anteriorly.

P A significant decrease in shoulder ROM is seen in frozen shoulder (adhesive capsulitis). In frozen shoulder, the glenohumeral joint gradually loses function, especially abduction and external rotation. Stroke with loss of shoulder movement and rotator cuff pathology are common etiologies.

P Bursitis of the shoulder can result from overuse of the shoulder in repetitive activity (either a new activity such as leaf raking and car polishing or a familiar activity such as swimming).

P An acromioclavicular joint separation (separated shoulder) causes pain in the acromioclavicular joint. Swelling frequently occurs at the distal end of the clavicle.

P Shoulder subluxation and dislocation are common athletic injuries. Patients with recurrent subluxations may feel the glenohumeral joint pop out of the socket and pop back in without medical intervention. The shoulder may lose its usual rounded contour. With an anterior dislocation, fluid is usually seen anteriorly, whereas with a posterior dislocation, fluid is usually best seen posteriorly.

P In biceps tendinitis, the patient is tender in the bicipital groove. Excessive straining, as with lifting heavy objects, can rupture an inflamed biceps tendon. This can lead to a bulge in the antecubital fossa.

Nursing Alert

Differentiating the Cause of Shoulder Pain

Shoulder pain that is not induced by palpation and ROM often occurs in patients experiencing cardiac dysfunction, such as a myocardial infarction (MI). See Chapter 16. Be alert to other signs and symptoms of an MI, such as chest pain, nausea, vomiting, indigestion, shortness of breath, and diaphoresis. If the patient complains of any of these symptoms, immediately refer the patient to an appropriate health care facility.

Advanced Technique

Assessing for Rotator Cuff Damage: Drop Arm Test

The rotator cuff comprises four muscles (supraspinatus, infraspinatus, teres minor, and subscapularis) and their tendons. The tendons insert into the humeral tuberosities. The rotator cuff stabilizes the glenohumeral joint.

The drop arm test assesses for rotator cuff damage.

E 1. Manually abduct the patient's affected arm.

2. Ask the patient to slowly lower the raised arm to the side while maintaining extension of the arm.

3. Observe the speed at which the patient lowers the arm.

N The patient will be able to slowly lower the arm to the side while maintaining the arm in extension.

A An abnormal drop arm test is manifested by the inability of the patient to slowly lower the arm to the side (e.g., the arm quickly falls to the side of the torso), or by severe pain occurring in the shoulder while the arm is slowly lowered to the side.

P An abnormal drop arm test is indicative of a rotator cuff tear. It is caused by trauma to the shoulder.

Elbows

E 1. Stand to the side of the elbow being examined.

2. Support the patient's forearm on the side that is being examined (approximately 70°).

| E | **Examination** | N | **Normal Findings** | A | **Abnormal Findings** | P | **Pathophysiology** |

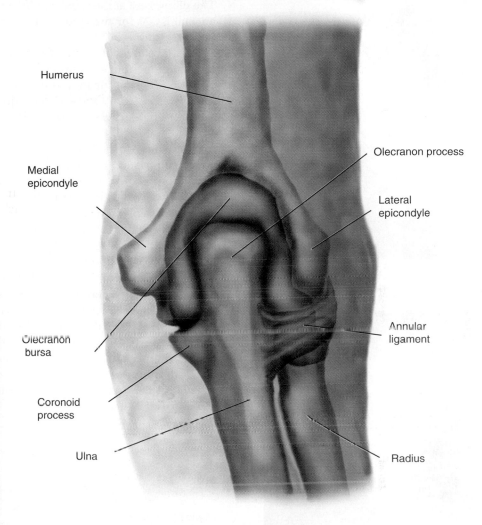

Right elbow—posterior view

Figure 18-20 Anatomy of the Elbow Joint (Posterior View, Right Elbow).

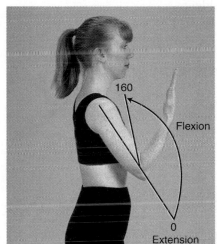

A Flexion, Extension

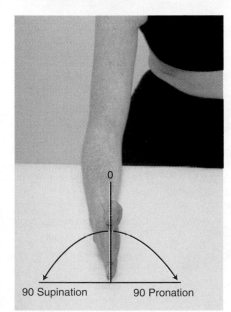

B. Supination, Pronation

Figure 18-21 Range of Motion of the Elbow Joint.

3. Inspect the elbow in flexed and extended positions. Note the olecranon process and the grooves on each side of the olecranon process (Figure 18-20).
4. Using your thumb and middle fingers, palpate the elbow. Note the olecranon process, the olecranon bursa, the groove on each side of the olecranon process, and the medial and lateral epicondyles of the humerus.
5. Assess ROM of the elbows (Figure 18-21). Ask the patient to:
   a. Bend the elbow (flexion).
   b. Straighten the elbow (extension).
   c. Hold the arm straight out, bent at the elbow, and turn the palm upward toward the ceiling (supination).
   d. Turn the palm downward toward the floor (pronation).
6. Assess strength of the elbow:
   a. Stabilize the patient's arm at the elbow with your non-dominant hand. With your dominant hand, grasp the patient's wrist.
   b. Ask the patient to flex the elbow (pulling it toward the chest) while you apply opposing resistance (Figure 18-22).
   c. Ask the patient to extend the elbow (pushing it away from the chest) while you apply opposing resistance.

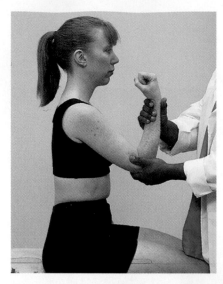

Figure 18-22 Muscle Strength of the Elbow.

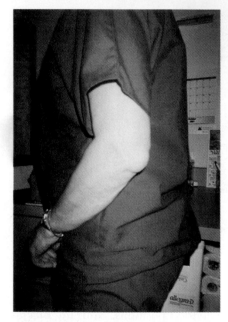

Figure 18-23 Olecranon Bursitis.

Nursing Tip

Suspected Radial Head Fractures

Any patient, particularly an elderly person, who complains of elbow pain after suffering a fall must be carefully assessed for a radial head fracture.

N The elbows are at the same height and are symmetrical in appearance. The normal ROM for the elbow is flexion—160°, extension—0°, supination—90°, pronation—90°.

A Elbows that are not symmetrical are abnormal. The forearm is not in its usual alignment. Pain is present.

P These findings occur in a dislocation or a subluxation of the elbow. They usually occur from sports-related injuries, falls, or motor vehicle accidents.

A Localized tenderness and pain with elbow flexion, extension, or both are abnormal.

P Epicondylitis occurs from repetitive motions such as swinging a tennis racquet, hammering, using a screwdriver, tight gripping, and other activities involving repetitive movements of the forearm. Lateral epicondylitis (tennis elbow) is caused by injury to the extensor tendon at the lateral epicondyle, and medial epicondylitis (golfer's elbow) is caused by injury to the flexor tendon at the medial epicondyle.

P Radial head fractures usually result from falls. Frequently, the elbow is flexed in a 90° position.

P A flexion contracture of the elbow may be seen in a patient with hemiparesis following a cerebrovascular accident.

A Red, warm, swollen, and tender areas in the grooves beside the olecranon process are abnormal. Synovial fluid may be palpable and is soft or boggy.

P Inflammatory processes such as gouty arthritis, rheumatoid arthritis, and SLE can cause these clinical manifestations.

P Olecranon bursitis (Figure 18-23) is classified as an overuse syndrome. It usually results from repetitive motions rather than from an acute injury. ROM is usually not affected.

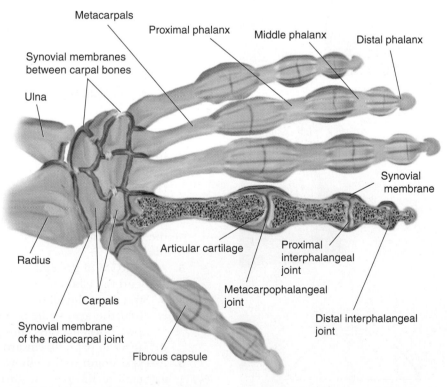

Figure 18-24 Anatomy of the Wrist and Hand.

| E | Examination | N | Normal Findings | A | Abnormal Findings | P | Pathophysiology |

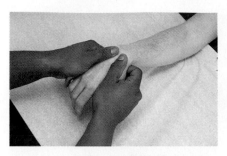

Figure 18-25 Palpating the Wrist Joint.

A. Metacarpophalangeal Joint

B. Interphalangeal Joint

Figure 18-26 Palpating the Hand Joints.

Wrists and Hands

E 1. Stand in front of the patient.
2. Inspect the wrists and the palmar and dorsal aspects of the hands. Note the shape, position, contour, and number of fingers (Figure 18-25).
3. Inspect the **thenar eminence** (the rounded prominence at the base of the thumb).
4. Support the patient's hand in your two hands, with your fingers underneath the patient's hands and your thumbs on the dorsum of the patient's hand.
5. Palpate the joints of the wrists by moving your thumbs from side to side. Feel the natural indentations (Figure 18-25).
6. Palpate the joints of the hand:
   a. Use your thumbs to palpate the metacarpophalangeal joints, which are immediately distal to and on each side of the knuckle (Figure 18-26A).
   b. Between your thumb and index finger, gently pinch the sides of the proximal and distal interphalangeal joints (Figure 18-26B).
7. Assess the ROM of the wrists and hands (Figure 18-27). Ask the patient to:
   a. Straighten the hand (extension) and bend it up at the wrist toward the ceiling (hyperextension).
   b. Bend the hand down at the wrist toward the floor (flexion).
   c. Bend the fingers up at the metacarpophalangeal joint toward the ceiling (hyperextension).
   d. Bend the fingers down at the metacarpophalangeal joint toward the floor (flexion).
   e. Place the hands on a flat surface and move them side to side (radial deviation is movement toward the thumb, and ulnar deviation is movement toward the little finger) without moving the elbow.
   f. Ask the patient to make a fist with the thumb on the outside of the clenched fingers.
   g. Spread the fingers apart.
   h. Touch the thumb to each fingertip. Touch the thumb to the base of the little finger.
8. Assess the strength of the wrists. Ask the patient to:
   a. Place the arm on a table with the forearm supinated. Stabilize the forearm by placing your non-dominant hand on it.

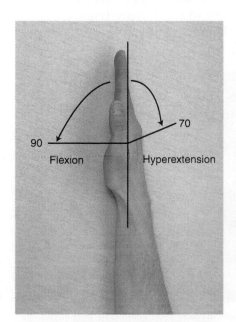

A. Hyperextension and Flexion of the Wrist

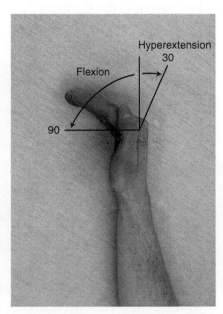

B. Flexion and Hyperextension of the Fingers

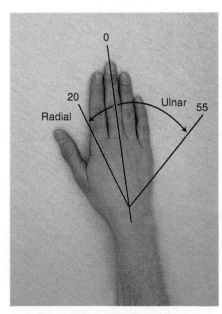

C. Radial and Ulnar Deviation of the Wrist

Figure 18-27 Range of Motion of the Wrist and Hand Joints.

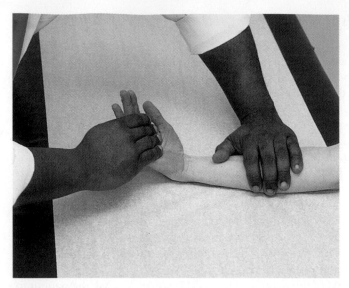

Figure 18-28 Muscle Strength of the Wrist.

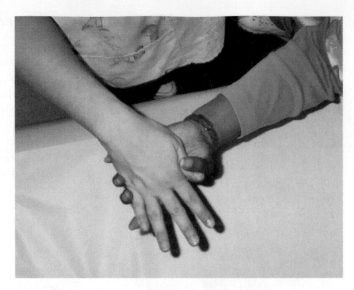

Figure 18-29 Muscle Strength of the Fingers.

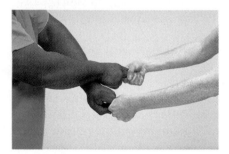

Figure 18-30 Muscle Strength of the Hand Grasp.

b. Flex the wrist while you apply resistance with your dominant hand (Figure 18-28).

c. Extend the wrist while you apply resistance.

9. Assess the strength of the fingers. Ask the patient to:

a. Spread the fingers apart while you apply resistance (Figure 18-29).

b. Push the fingers together while you apply resistance.

10. Assess the strength of the hand grasp. Ask the patient to:

a. Grasp your dominant index and middle fingers in the patient's dominant hand and your non-dominant index and middle fingers in the patient's non-dominant hand (Figure 18-30).

b. Squeeze your fingers as hard as possible.

c. Release the grasp.

N   There are five fingers on each hand. The normal range of motion for the wrists is extension—0°, hyperextension—70°, flexion—90°, radial deviation—20°, ulnar deviation—55°. The normal range of motion for the metacarpophalangeal joints is hyperextension—30° and flexion—90°.

A   Extra fingers, loss of fingers, or webbing between fingers is abnormal.

P   **Polydactyly** is the congenital presence of extra digits (Figure 18-31A). **Syndactyly** is the congenital webbing or fusion of fingers or toes (Figure 18-31B).

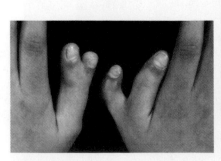

A. Polydactyly in Fingers. *Biophoto Associates/ Photo Researchers, Inc.*

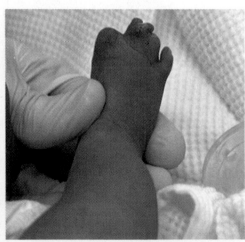

B. Syndactyly in Toes. *Courtesy of Mary Ellen Estes*

Figure 18-31 Digit Anomalies.

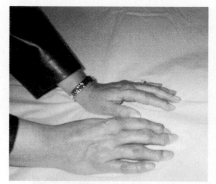

Figure 18-32 Bouchard's Nodes, Heberden's Nodes, and Swan-Neck Deformity.

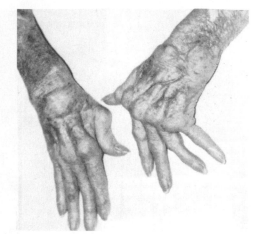

Figure 18-33 Ulnar Deviation.

Nursing Tip

Significance of Hand Grasp Strength

Although some nurses measure hand grasp strength as part of assessment, the true significance of this measurement may be in representing the patient's ability to respond to a command. A strong hand grasp around an object (e.g., the nurse's fingers or hand) as demonstrated by patients with brain disorders may actually represent a reflex action. When assessing muscle strength, arm muscle strength should thus always be considered more representative of muscle strength than is hand grasp strength.

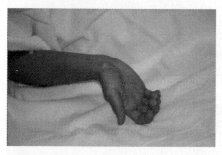

Figure 18-34 Ganglion Cyst. *Courtesy of Mary A. Hitcho.*

A   Bony enlargement or bony deformities of the joints of the hand are abnormal.

P   Osteoarthritis is associated with bony enlargement of the proximal interphalangeal joint (**Bouchard's node**) and the distal interphalangeal joint (**Heberden's node**) of the finger. These enlargements are hard and nontender. Bony enlargement may be masked by subcutaneous swelling. Bony enlargement is usually symmetrical (Figure 18-32).

P   Rheumatoid arthritis results in ulnar deviation (Figure 18-33), swan-neck deformity (Figure 18-32), and boutonniere deformities of the fingers. In ulnar deviation, the fingers deviate to the ulnar side of the body. In swan neck deformity, there is flexion of the metacarpophalangeal joint, hyperextension of the proximal interphalangeal joint, and flexion of the distal interphalangeal joint. In other words, the finger appears to go up, down, and up again. In boutonniere deformity, there is flexion of the proximal interphalangeal joint with hyperextension of the distal interphalangeal joint. The patient frequently complains of pain, especially early in the morning. The joints may feel boggy on palpation. ROM may be restricted.

A   A round, cystic growth near the tendons of the wrist or joint capsule is abnormal.

P   A **ganglion** is a benign growth that is usually non-tender and more prominent on the dorsum of the hand and wrist (Figure 18-34). Its etiology is unknown.

A   Flexion of the fingers is abnormal.

P   Dupuytren's contracture is a flexion contracture that affects the little finger, ring finger, and middle finger. Pain does not normally accompany this disorder. It is caused by the progressive contracture of the palmar fascia from an unknown etiology (Figure 18-35).

A   Muscular atrophy of the thenar eminence is abnormal.

P   This disorder occurs in median nerve compression such as in carpal tunnel syndrome.

A   Severe flexion ankylosis of the wrist is abnormal.

P   Flexion ankylosis can be caused by rheumatoid arthritis or severe disuse (Figure 18-36).

A   Tenderness over the distal radius is abnormal.

P   This can occur in Colles fracture or fracture of the distal radius. This is the most common type of wrist fracture.

A   Wrist drop, demonstrated by the inability of the patient to flex the fisted hand downward at the wrist, is abnormal.

P   Radial nerve injury may cause wrist drop.

A   Inability of the patient to prevent moving of spread fingers together is abnormal.

| E | Examination | N | Normal Findings | A | Abnormal Findings | P | Pathophysiology |

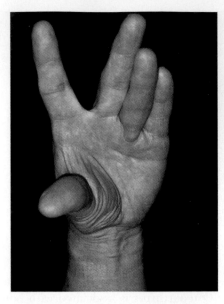

Figure 18-35 Dupuytren's Contracture.

Figure 18-36 Flexion Ankylosis.

P Ulnar nerve injury causes weakness of the fingers.

A Weakness of opposition of the thumb and ipsilateral finger against resistance is abnormal.

P Median nerve disorders, such as carpal tunnel syndrome, affect thumb opposition. Weak thumb opposition usually occurs from injuries where the hand is outstretched during a fall or from a twisting motion.

Figure 18-37 Assessing Grip Strength Using a Blood Pressure Cuff.

Advanced Technique

Assessing Grip Strength Using a Blood Pressure Cuff

E **1.** Roll up a blood pressure cuff into a ball and inflate the cuff to 20 mm Hg.
   2. Ask the patient to squeeze the inflated cuff (to determine the strength of the hand grasp action).
   3. Note the increase in mm Hg during the grasp (Figure 18-37).
   4. Assess the strength of the other hand.

N A healthy individual can usually achieve 150 mm Hg during a strong hand grasp action.

A A hand grasp that measures below 150 mm Hg is abnormal.

P Neurological pathology, such as in stroke and myasthenia gravis, as well as musculoskeletal disease such as MS, and rheumatoid arthritis can lead to decreased grip strength.

Advanced Technique

Assessing for Carpal Tunnel Syndrome: Tinel's Sign

The median nerve lies within the carpal tunnel of the wrist (Figure 18-38). Compression of the tunnel leads to median nerve neuropathy. The patient may complain of paresthesias and burning, especially in the first three fingers,

continues

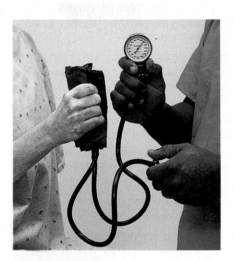

Transverse carpal ligament (flexor retinaculum)

Median nerve

Carpal canal

Figure 18-38 Anatomy of the Carpal Tunnel.

E	**Examination**	N	**Normal Findings**	A	**Abnormal Findings**	P	**Pathophysiology**

Figure 18-39 Assessing for Tinel's Sign.

pain in the wrist and forearm, and a decreased ability to grasp objects due to a weak grip.

E 1. Place the patient in a sitting position with the arm flexed at the elbow and the palm facing up.
2. Using the index or middle finger of the dominant hand, briskly tap the centre of the patient's wrist (median nerve) (Figure 18-39).
3. Ask the patient to describe the sensations that occur in the forearm, hands, thumb, or fingers.
4. Repeat the technique on the other wrist.

N There will be no tingling or burning noted in the hand, thumb, or fingers.

A A positive Tinel's sign, indicated by a tingling or pricking sensation that occurs in the hand, thumb, and index and middle fingers when the median nerve is tapped, is abnormal.

P A positive Tinel's sign is indicative of median nerve compression (carpal tunnel syndrome).

Advanced Technique

Assessing for Carpal Tunnel Syndrome: Phalen's Sign

E 1. Place the patient in a sitting position with the arms flexed at the elbow and the backs of the hands pressed together (Figure 18-40).
2. Ask the patient to maintain the wrist flexion of 90° for at least one minute.
3. Ask the patient to describe the sensations that occur in the hands and fingers.

N There will be no change in the sensation of the hands and fingers.

A A positive Phalen's test, indicated by sensations of numbness and paresthesia in the palmar aspect of the hand and in the fingers (especially the first three fingers), is abnormal. These sensations disappear when the wrist joint is returned to its neutral anatomic position.

P A positive Phalen's test is indicative of carpal tunnel syndrome.

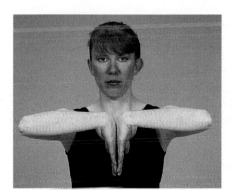

Figure 18-40 Assessing for Phalen's Sign.

Advanced Technique

Assessing for Hip Dislocation: Trendelenburg Test

E 1. Ask the patient to stand on one foot, with the knee of the non-weight-bearing leg flexed to raise the foot off the floor.
2. Assess the symmetry of the iliac crests while the patient is standing on one leg.
3. Repeat this technique on the other leg.

N The iliac crest on the side opposite the weight-bearing leg elevates slightly.

A It is abnormal for the iliac crest on the nonweight-bearing leg to drop.

P This finding is a positive Trendelenburg test and it is indicative of hip dislocation. The weakness of the gluteus medius muscle causes the hip on the unaffected side to drop.

Hips

E 1. While the patient is standing, inspect the iliac crests (refer to the Advanced Technique for the Trendelenburg test), size and symmetry of the buttocks, and number of gluteal folds (Figure 18-41).

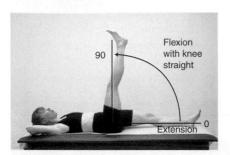

90

Flexion
with knee
straight

0
Extension

A. Flexion with Knee Straight

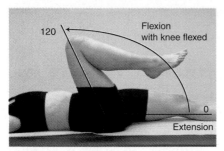

120

Flexion
with knee flexed

0
Extension

B. Flexion with Knee Flexed

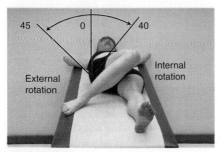

45   0   40

External
rotation

Internal
rotation

C. Internal and External Rotation

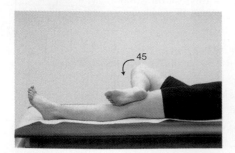

45

D. Position of the Leg for Full External Rotation

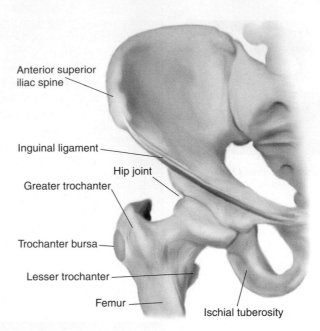

Anterior superior
iliac spine

Inguinal ligament

Hip joint

Greater trochanter

Trochanter bursa

Lesser trochanter

Femur

Ischial tuberosity

Figure 18-41 Anatomy of the Hip Joint.

2. Observe the patient's gait, if not previously assessed (see General Assessment).
3. Assist the patient to a supine position on the examination table with the legs straight and the feet pointing toward the ceiling.
4. Palpate the hip joints.
5. Assess ROM of the hips (Figure 18-42). Ask the patient to:
   a. Raise the leg straight off the examination table with the knee extended (hip flexion with knee straight). The other leg should remain on the table.
   b. With the knee flexed, raise the leg off the examination table toward the chest as far as possible (hip flexion with knee flexed). The other leg should remain on the table. This is called the Thomas test.
   c. Flex the hip and knee. Move the flexed leg medially as the foot moves outward (internal rotation).
   d. Flex the hip and knee. Move the flexed leg laterally as the foot moves medially (external rotation).
   e. With the knee straight, swing the leg away from the midline (abduction).
   f. With the knee straight, swing the leg toward the midline (adduction).
   g. Roll over onto the abdomen and assume a prone position.
   h. From the hip, move the leg back as far as possible while maintaining the pelvis on the table (hyperextension). This can also be performed while the patient is standing.
6. Assist the patient to a supine position.

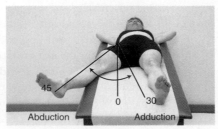

45   0   30

Abduction   Adduction

E. Abduction and Adduction

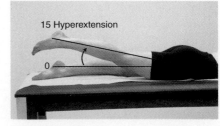

15 Hyperextension

0

F. Hyperextension

Figure 18-42 Range of Motion of the Hip Joint.

| E | Examination | N | Normal Findings | A | Abnormal Findings | P | Pathophysiology |

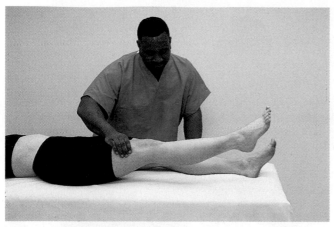

A. Flexion with Opposing Force

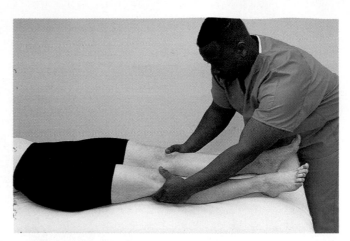

B. Abduction with Opposing Force

Figure 18-43 Muscle Strength of the Hip.

7. Assess strength of the hips.
   a. Place the palm of your hand on the anterior thigh, above the knee. Instruct the patient to raise the leg against your resistance (Figure 18-43A). Repeat on the other leg.
   b. Place the palm of your hand posteriorly above and behind the knee. Instruct the patient to lower the leg against your resistance. Repeat on the other leg.
   c. Place your hands on the lateral aspects of the patient's legs at the level of the knee. Instruct the patient to move the legs apart against your resistance (Figure 18-43B).
   d. Place your hands on the medial aspects of the patient's legs just above the knee. Instruct the patient to move the legs together against your resistance.

N The normal ROM for the hips is flexion with knee straight—90°, flexion with knee flexed—120°, internal rotation—40°, external rotation—45°, abduction—45°, adduction—30°, hyperextension—15°.

A A leg that is externally rotated and painful on movement is abnormal.

P These findings occur in hip fractures, which usually result from falls (especially in elderly persons). The affected leg may also be shorter. See the Advanced Technique for guidelines on measuring limb length.

A A positive Thomas test, when the patient is unable to flex one knee and hip while simultaneously maintaining the other leg in full extension, is abnormal. There may be slight to moderate hip and knee flexion of the extended leg.

P Flexion contractures of the hip joint, such as in long-term degenerative joint diseases, will result in a positive Thomas test. This test will identify hip flexion contractures that are masked by lumbar lordosis.

Advanced Technique

Measuring Limb Length

E 1. Place the patient in a supine position on the examination table with the legs extended.
   2. Measure the leg from the anterior superior iliac spine to the medial malleolus (Figure 18-44).
   3. Repeat on the other limb.
   4. Compare measurements.

N Limb length measurements should be within 1 to 3 cm of each other.

A A more than 3 cm difference in the length of limbs is abnormal.

continues

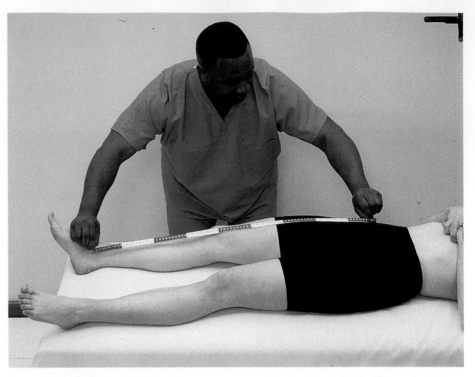

Figure 18-44 Measuring Limb Length.

P	Unilateral discrepancy in lower limb length may be a congenital defect.
P	Sudden unilateral decrease in limb length occurs with fracture and dislocation of the hip and leg.
P	A displaced proximal femoral shaft fracture (hip fracture) can result in limb shortening and internal or external rotation. Internal rotation is common if the patient fell forward during the fall, and external rotation is common if the patient fell onto the buttocks. The patient is unable to straighten the leg into its neutral anatomic position.

Knees

1. With the patient standing, note the position of the knees in relation to each other and in relation to the hips, thighs, ankles, and feet.
2. Ask the patient to sit on the examination table with the knees flexed and resting at the edge of the table.
3. Inspect the contour of the knees. Note the normal depressions around the patella (Figure 18-45).
4. Inspect the suprapatellar pouch and the prepatellar bursa.
5. Note the quadriceps muscle, located on the anterior thigh.
6. Palpate the knees. The patient may assume a supine position if this is more comfortable.
   a. Grasp the anterior thigh approximately 10 cm above the patella, with your thumb on one side of the knee and the other four fingers on the other side of the knee (Figure 18-46).
   b. As you palpate, gradually move your hand down the suprapatellar pouch.
7. Palpate the tibiofemoral joints. It is best to have the knee flexed to 90° when performing this assessment.
   a. Place both thumbs on the knee, with the fingers wrapped around the knee posteriorly.

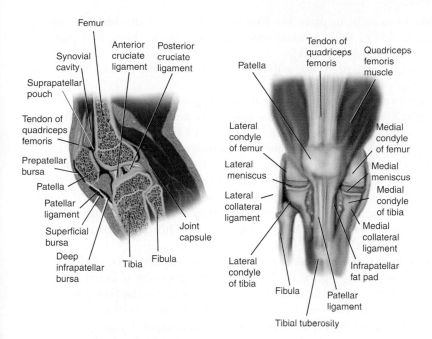

Figure 18-45 Anatomy of the Right Knee Joint.

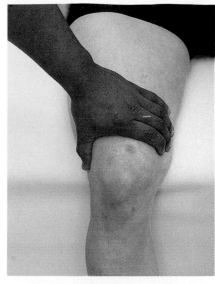

Figure 18-46 Palpating the Knee.

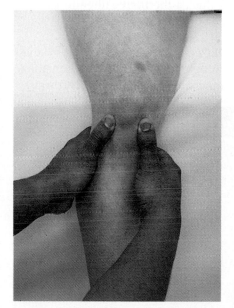

Figure 18-47 Palpating the Tibiofemoral Joint.

b. Press in with the thumbs as you palpate the tibial margins (Figure 18-47).
c. Palpate the lateral collateral ligament.
8. If knee fluid is suspected, test for the bulge sign and ballottement. See the Advanced Techniques on pages 642.
9. Assess ROM of the knees (Figure 18-48). Ask the patient to stand and:
   a. Bend the knee (flexion).
   b. Straighten the knee (extension). The patient may also be able to hyperextend the knee during this movement.
10. Assess strength of the knees with the patient seated and the legs hanging off the table.
    a. Ask the patient to bend the knee. Place your non-dominant hand under the knee and place your other hand over the ankle.
    b. Instruct the patient to straighten the leg against your resistance (Figure 18-49).

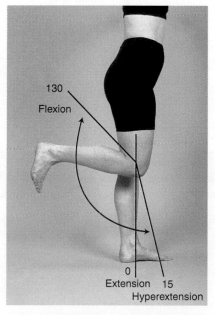

Figure 18-48 Range of Motion of the Knee Joint: Flexion, Extension, and Hyperextension.

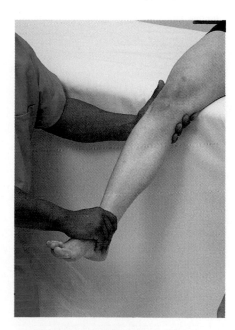

Figure 18-49 Strength of Knee Joint.

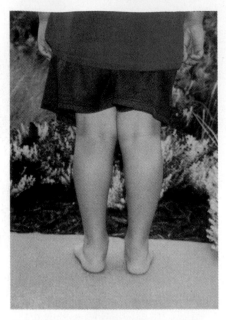

Figure 18-50 Genu Valgum.

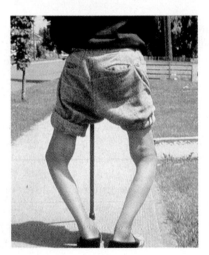

Figure 18-51 Genu Varum.

c. Ask the patient to place the foot on the bed and the knee at approximately 45° of flexion. Place one hand under the knee and place the other hand over the ankle.

d. Instruct the patient to maintain the foot on the table despite your attempts to straighten the leg.

N The knees are in alignment with each other and do not protrude medially or laterally. The normal ROM for the knees is flexion—130°, extension—0°; in some cases, hyperextension is possible up to 15°.

A Alteration in lower limb alignment is considered an abnormal finding.

P **Genu valgum** (knock knees) is inward deviation toward the midline at the level of the knees (Figure 18-50). Both legs are usually affected by the disorder. It is detected as an increased distance between the medial malleoli when the femoral condyles are close together and the patella are facing forward. The knees appear closer together than is normal. Genu valgum can be congenital or acquired (rickets).

P **Genu varum** (bow legs) is outward deviation away from the midline at the level of the knees (Figure 18-51). Both legs are usually affected by the disorder. It is detected as an increased distance between the femoral condyles when the medial malleoli are close together and the patella are facing forward. The knees appear farther apart than is normal. Genu varum can be congenital or acquired. This syndrome is common in horse jockeys due to the stretching of the nearby ligaments. It may also be seen in rickets, rheumatoid arthritis, and osteomalacia due to the body's attempt to bend bone shape in order to tolerate the weight of the upper body.

A A knee effusion is present.

P A knee effusion can be associated with a Baker cyst. A Baker cyst is a cystic mass in the medial popliteal fossa. If large enough, it can decrease the anatomic ROM of the knee. It is often detected in patients with rheumatoid arthritis.

Advanced Technique

Assessing for Small Effusions: Bulge Sign

The bulge sign tests for small effusions (4 to 8 mL) in the knee.

E 1. Place the patient in a supine position with the legs extended.
2. Firmly milk upward the medial aspect of the patella several times. This displaces any fluid (Figure 18-52A).
3. Press or tap the lateral aspect of the knee.
4. Observe the hollow on the medial aspect of the knee for a bulge of fluid (Figure 18-52B).

N Normally there is no fluid return to the knee. This is a negative bulge sign.

A The return of fluid to the medial aspect of the patella is abnormal.

P A positive bulge sign is present in joint effusion.

Advanced Technique

Assessing for Large Effusions: Patellar Ballottement

Ballottement is performed to detect large effusions in the knee.

E 1. Place the patient either in a supine position with the legs extended or sitting up with the knees flexed at 90° and hanging over the edge of the examination table.

continues

E	**Examination**	**N**	**Normal Findings**	**A**	**Abnormal Findings**	**P**	**Pathophysiology**

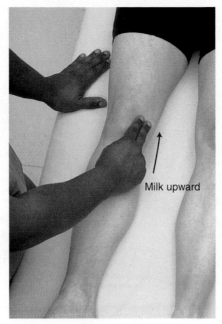

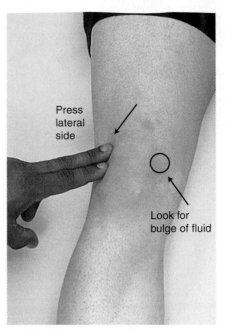

A. Milking the Patella

B. Observing for Fluid

Figure 18-52 Assessing for Bulge Sign.

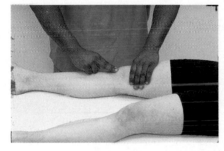

Figure 18-53 Patellar Ballottement.

2. Firmly grasp the thigh (with your thumb on one side and the four fingers on the other side) just above the patella. This compresses fluid out of the suprapatellar pouch.

3. With your other hand, push the patella back toward the femur (Figure 18-53).

4. Feel for a click.

N There is no palpable click. Normally, the patella is close to the femur because there is no excess fluid.

A A palpable click is abnormal.

P When fluid is present between the femur and the patella, the patella "floats" on top of the femur. As the patella is pushed back, fluid is displaced and a palpable click is felt when the patella hits the femur.

Advanced Technique

Assessing for Meniscal Tears: McMurray's Sign

This test is performed to assess the integrity of the meniscus of the knee.

E 1. Place the patient in a supine position on the examination table and stand on the affected side.

2. Manually flex the hip and knee. Hold the patient's heel with one hand and stabilize the knee with the other hand (Figure 18-54).

3. Using the hand that is holding the heel, internally rotate the leg while applying resistance to the medial aspect of the knee joint. This assesses the medial meniscus.

4. Move the knee to a position of full extension. Note if full extension of the knee joint can be achieved or tolerated by the patient.

5. Flex the hip and knee and externally rotate the leg. While stabilizing the knee joint, apply resistance to the lateral aspect of the knee joint. This assesses the lateral meniscus.

6. Assess for an audible or palpable click of the knee joint.

continues

Figure 18-54 Assessing for McMurray's Sign.

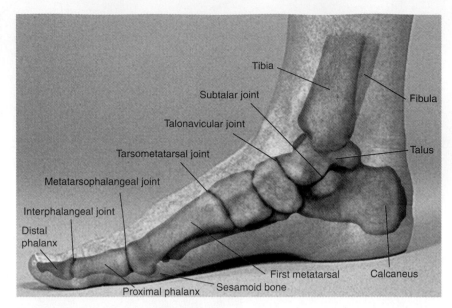

Figure 18-55 Anatomy of the Ankle and Foot.

N	The patient will be able to extend the leg at the knee joint and there will be no audible or palpable click detected.
A	A positive McMurray's sign is indicated when the patient is unable to extend the leg at the knee joint or when an audible or palpable click is detected.
P	A positive McMurray's sign is suggestive of torn meniscus cartilage of the knee. The patient may also state that full extension of the knee joint is impossible, that the knee joint "locks into place," or that "it feels like something is in the knee joint." If the torn meniscus cartilage is obstructing the articulating function of the joint, knee joint extension will be limited.

Ankles and Feet

E 1. Inspect the ankles and feet (Figure 18-55) as the patient stands, walks, and sits (bearing no weight).

2. Inspect the alignment of the feet and toes with the lower leg.

3. Inspect the shape and position of the toes.

4. Assist the patient to a supine position on the examination table.

5. Stand by the patient's feet.

6. Palpate the ankle and foot (Figure 18-56).

   a. Grasp the heel with the fingers of both hands. Palpate the posterior aspect of the heel at the calcaneus.

   b. Use your thumbs to palpate the medial malleolus (bony prominence on the distal medial aspect of the tibia) and the lateral malleolus (bony prominence on the distal lateral aspect of the fibula).

   c. Move your hands forward and palpate the anterior aspects of the ankle and foot, particularly at the joints.

   d. Palpate the inferior aspect of the foot over the plantar fascia.

   e. Use your finger pads to palpate the Achilles tendon.

   f. Palpate with your thumb and index finger each metatarsophalangeal joint.

   g. Between your thumb and index finger, palpate the medial and lateral surfaces of each interphalangeal joint.

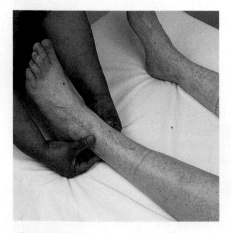

Figure 18-56 Palpation of the Ankle.

| E | **Examination** | N | **Normal Findings** | A | **Abnormal Findings** | P | **Pathophysiology** |

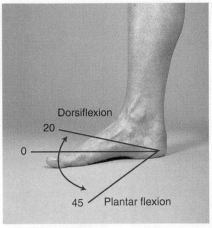
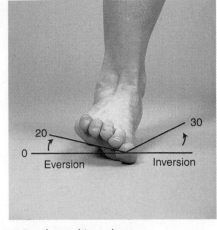
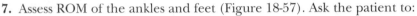

A. Plantar Flexion and Dorsiflexion   B. Eversion and Inversion

Figure 18-57 Range of Motion of The Ankle And Foot.

Figure 18-58 Strength of The Ankle And Foot.

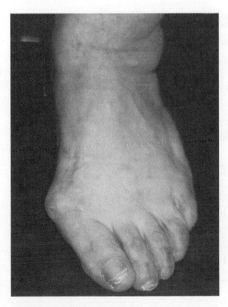

Figure 18-59 Hallux Valgus. *Courtesy of Mary A. Hitcho.*

7. Assess ROM of the ankles and feet (Figure 18-57). Ask the patient to:
   a. Point the toes toward the chest by moving the ankle (dorsiflexion).
   b. Point the toes toward the floor by moving the ankle (plantar flexion).
   c. Turn the soles of the feet outward (eversion).
   d. Turn the soles of the feet inward (inversion).
   e. Curl the toes toward the floor (flexion).
   f. Spread the toes apart (abduction).
   g. Move the toes together (adduction).
8. Assess strength of the ankles and feet.
   a. Assist the patient to a supine position on the examination table with the legs extended and the feet slightly apart.
   b. Stand at the foot of the examination table.
   c. Place your left hand on top of the patient's right foot and place your right hand on top of the patient's left foot.
   d. Ask the patient to point the toes toward the chest (dorsiflexion) despite your resistance.
   e. Place your left hand on the sole of the patient's right foot and place your right hand on the sole of the patient's left foot.
   f. Ask the patient to point the toes down (plantar flexion) despite your resistance. This technique can also be performed one foot at a time as demonstrated in Figure 18-58.

N The foot is in alignment with the lower leg. The foot has a longitudinal arch. There is no pain over the plantar fascia. The normal ROM for the ankles and feet is dorsiflexion—20°, plantar flexion—45°, eversion—20°, inversion—30°, abduction—30°, and adduction—10°.

A An alteration in the shape and the position of the foot is considered abnormal.

P **Pes varus** describes a foot that is turned inward toward the midline.

P **Pes valgus** occurs when the foot is turned laterally away from the midline.

P **Pes planus** (flat foot) refers to a foot with a low longitudinal arch.

P **Pes cavus** refers to a foot with an exaggerated arch height.

P In **hallux valgus** (bunion), the big toe is deviated laterally while the first metatarsal is deviated medially (Figure 18-59). The metatarsophalangeal joint enlarges and becomes inflamed from the pressure. A bursa may form at this point. Hallux valgus can be congenital or caused by narrow shoes and arthritis.

P Tight shoes can also cause **hammertoe**. In hammertoe, there is a flexion of the proximal interphalangeal joint and hyperextension of the distal metatarsophalangeal joint. A corn or callus can develop from undue pressure at the point of flexion (Figure 18-60).

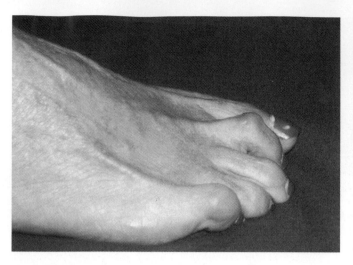

Figure 18-60 Hammertoe with Corn.

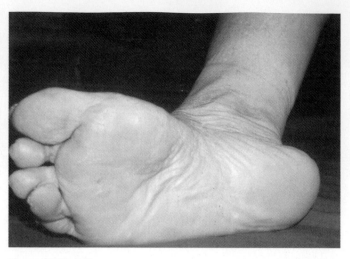

Figure 18-61 Callus.

P A **corn** is a conical area of thickened skin. It extends into the dermis and can be painful. Corns are caused by pressure on the affected area, particularly over bony prominences. Tight shoes and hammertoe can cause corns.

P A **callus** is a thickening of the skin due to prolonged pressure (Figure 18-61). It usually occurs on the sole of the foot and is not painful.

A Pain over the plantar fascia is abnormal.

P Plantar fasciitis (heel-spur syndrome) is an inflammation of the plantar fascia where it attaches to the calcaneus. The pain tends to be worse first thing in the morning, and with prolonged standing, sitting, or walking.

A A swollen, red, warm, and painful metatarsophalangeal joint is abnormal.

P The first metatarsophalangeal joint is usually affected in acute gouty arthritis.

A Decreased ROM of the ankle is abnormal.

P The patient with an ankle sprain or fracture secondary to injury or trauma complains of pain on palpation and ROM. Crepitus may be present in an ankle fracture. Ankle sprain cannot always be differentiated from ankle fracture without the use of X-rays. Refer these patients to an orthopedist.

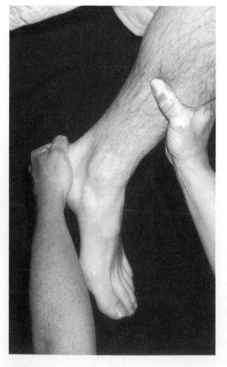

Figure 18-62 Anterior Drawer Test of the Ankle.

Advanced Technique

Assessing for Ankle Sprain: Anterior Drawer Test

E 1. Have the patient sit with the feet hanging freely.
   2. Grasp the heel of the foot with the injured ankle with the left hand.
   3. Place the right hand over the anterior aspect of the tibia on the affected side and firmly grasp the leg about 6 cm above the joint line (Figure 18-62).
   4. Firmly hold the tibia as you apply an anterior forward motion with your left hand.
   5. Note any movement of the ankle.

N There should be no forward movement of the ankle.

A It is abnormal to have anterior movement of the ankle.

P Anterior movement of the ankle indicates a possible tear in the anterior talofibular ligament (Figure 18-63).

| E | Examination | N | Normal Findings | A | Abnormal Findings | P | Pathophysiology |

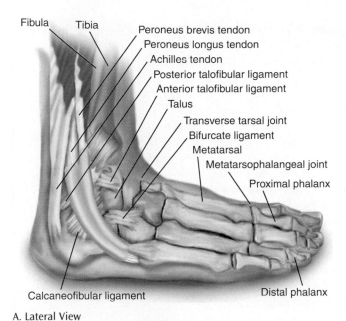

A. Lateral View

Fibula · Tibia · Peroneus brevis tendon · Peroneus longus tendon · Achilles tendon · Posterior talofibular ligament · Anterior talofibular ligament · Talus · Transverse tarsal joint · Bifurcate ligament · Metatarsal · Metatarsophalangeal joint · Proximal phalanx · Distal phalanx · Calcaneofibular ligament

B. Medial View

Tibia · Anterior tibialis tendon · Medial malleolus · Tibiotalar joint · Achilles tendon · **Deltoid ligament:** Tibiocalcaneal ligament · Anterior tibiotalar ligament · Tibionavicular ligament · Flexor hallucis longus tendon · Posterior tibialis tendon · Longitudinal arch · Calcaneus

Figure 18-63 Ligaments of the Ankle.

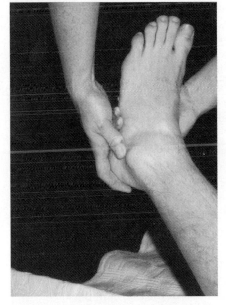

Figure 18-64 Talar Tilt Test.

Advanced Technique

Assessing for Ankle Sprain: Talar Tilt Test

F 1. Have the patient sit with the feet hanging freely.
2. Place your hands around the ankle of the affected leg so that the thumbs are inferior to the malleoli.
3. Passively invert and evert the ankle through range of motion (Figure 18-64).
4. Note the movement of the ankle.
5. Compare with the unaffected ankle.

N Normally, there should be an equal talar tilt, or range of motion, through inversion and eversion of both ankles.

A It is abnormal if the injured ankle has a talar tilt that is more than 5 to 10° greater than the unaffected ankle.

P A talar tilt more than 5 to 10° greater may indicate a tear in the calcaneofibular ligament.

Advanced Technique

Assessing Neurovascular Status of Distal Limbs and Digits

When you suspect distal limb or digit hypoperfusion due to trauma, injury, or pathology, conduct the following assessment:

E 1. Uncover the distal aspects of both limbs being assessed. A bilateral assessment allows for comparison of the affected and unaffected limbs. When assessing an injured limb, assess the limb areas proximal and distal to the site of injury.
2. Assess for swelling.
3. Assess the vascular status of the distal limb and its digits (peripheral pulses, skin colour, skin temperature, and capillary refill).

continues

4. Ask the patient to perform specific movements of the distal limb on command.
   a. To assess the ulnar nerve, ask the patient to perform abduction of the fingers.
   b. To assess the radial nerve, ask the patient to perform hyperextension of the thumb or wrist.
   c. To assess the median nerve, ask the patient to perform opposition of the thumb to the little finger of the same hand.
   d. To assess the peroneal nerve, ask the patient to perform dorsiflexion of the toes and ankle.
   e. To assess the tibial nerve, ask the patient to perform plantar flexion of the toes and ankle.
5. When assessing sensation, instruct the patient to close the eyes to prevent biased results. Use the thumb and index finger of the dominant hand to pinch certain areas of the distal limb.
   a. To assess the ulnar nerve, pinch the finger pad of the little finger.
   b. To assess the radial nerve, pinch the web space between the thumb and the index finger.
   c. To assess the median nerve, pinch the distal aspect of the index finger.
   d. To assess the peroneal nerve, pinch the lateral aspect of the great toe and the medial surface of the second toe.
   e. To assess the tibial nerve, pinch the medial and lateral surfaces of the sole of the foot.

N **The individual with normal perfusion to the limbs and digits will appear comfortable during rest and muscle contraction. Pain will not occur with movement of the distal limb or digits. Limb perfusion will be manifested by strong peripheral pulses, warm skin temperature, and a brisk capillary refill. There will be complete motor and sensory function of the distal limb and digits. The patient will not experience any numbness or tingling.**

A Neurovascular deterioration, manifested by the "5 Ps" (pain, pallor, decreased perfusion, paresthesia, and paralysis) is abnormal.

P Neurovascular deterioration can occur in compartment syndrome. It is a severe complication of musculoskeletal trauma in which swelling is limited due to a confined space. Pain is the most significant and the earliest clinical manifestation of acute compartment syndrome. It occurs distal to the site of injury and is induced by the contraction of the muscle compartment being compressed. Pain results from stretching of a muscle that is experiencing vascular compromise.

P Inadequate arterial flow is a complication of digit or limb replantation following traumatic amputation.

P Arterial occlusion may also be detected as a complication of fracture or dislocation.

P Inadequate venous flow from the distal limb or digits, manifested by cyanosis, mottling, skin temperature that is warmer than usual, immediate capillary refill, and a distended or tense tissue turgor, is abnormal.

P Inadequate venous flow is a complication of digit or limb replantation following traumatic amputation.

Nursing Tip

Differentiating Back Pain

Keep in mind that tenderness of the costovertebral angle can indicate a musculoskeletal problem or a kidney problem. Integrate the information obtained during the health history with clinical findings to guide your nursing interventions.

Spine

E 1. Ask the patient to stand and to leave the back of the gown open.
2. Stand behind the patient so that you can visualize the posterior anatomy.

E Examination	**N** Normal Findings	**A** Abnormal Findings	**P** Pathophysiology

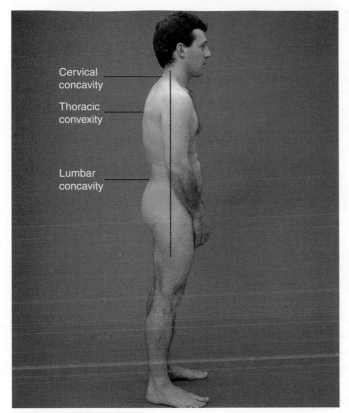

A. Lateral View

B. Posterior View

Figure 18-65 Alignment of Spinal Landmarks

3. Inspect the position and alignment of the spine from a posterior and a lateral position.
4. Draw an imaginary line:
   a. From the head down through the spinous processes (Figure 18-65A).
   b. Across the top of the scapula (Figure 18-65B).
   c. Across the top of the iliac crests.
   d. Across the bottom of the gluteal folds.
5. Palpate the spinous processes with your thumb.
6. Palpate the paravertebral muscles.

A. Flexion and Hyperextension

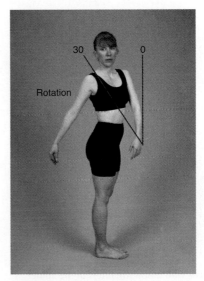

B. Lateral Bending

C. Rotation

Figure 18-66 Range of Motion of the Spine.

7. Assess ROM of the spine (Figure 18-66). Ask the patient to bend forward from the waist and touch the toes (flexion).
8. If necessary, stabilize the patient's pelvis with your hands during the ROM assessment. Ask the patient to:
   a. Bend to each side (lateral bending).
   b. Bend backward (hyperextension).
   c. Twist the shoulders to each side (rotation).

N The normal spine has a cervical concavity, a thoracic convexity, and a lumbar concavity. An imaginary line can be drawn from the head straight down the spinous processes to the gluteal cleft. The imaginary lines drawn from the scapula, iliac crests, and gluteal folds are symmetrical with each other. The normal ROM of the spine is flexion—90°, hyperextension—30°, lateral bending—35°, and rotation—30°. As the patient flexes forward, the concavity of the lumbar spine disappears and the entire back assumes a convex C shape.

A From a posterior view, **scoliosis** (lateral curvature of the thoracic or lumbar vertebrae) may be detectable (Figure 18-67A, B) and is an abnormal finding. The curvature is visible despite voluntary attempts at proper posture. This is structural scoliosis. The curvature becomes accentuated on forward flexion from the waist. Scoliosis may also be accompanied by asymmetry of the clavicles, uneven shoulder and iliac crest levels, and a visible prominence of a scapula. If the lateral curvature is allowed to progress beyond 55°, cardiopulmonary problems can occur. Surgery may be indicated if the curve exceeds 40°.

P Structural scoliosis occurs most frequently in adolescence, especially in females.

A Functional scoliosis, which manifests itself only in a standing position, is abnormal.

P Functional scoliosis is due to unequal leg length or poor posture. Limb length should be measured.

A **Kyphosis**, an excessive convexity of the thoracic spine (Figure 18-67C), is abnormal. The patient with kyphosis presents with the chin tilted downward onto the chest and with abdominal protrusion. There is also a decrease in the interval between the lower rib cage and the iliac crests. This appearance is due to forward and downward hunching of the head, neck, shoulders, and upper back.

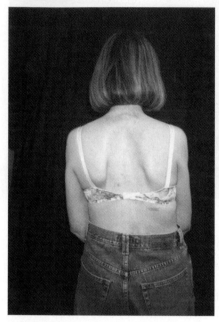

A. Scoliosis

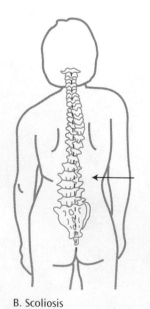

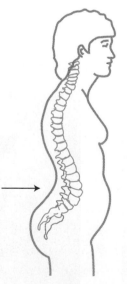

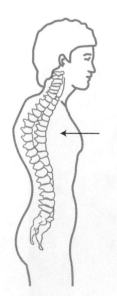

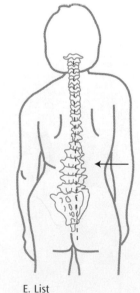

B. Scoliosis   C. Kyphosis   D. Lordosis   E. List

Figure 18-67 Abnormalities of the Spine.

| E | **Examination** | N | **Normal Findings** | A | **Abnormal Findings** | P | **Pathophysiology** |

P Kyphosis is seen in elderly patients and in patients with osteoporosis, ankylosing spondylitis, and Paget's disease.

A **Lordosis**, an excessive concavity of the lumbar spine (Figure 18-67D), is abnormal.

P Lordosis is accentuated in obesity and pregnancy due to the change in the centre of gravity.

A A **list**, a leaning of the spine (Figure 18-67E), is abnormal. If an imaginary line is drawn straight down from T1, the gluteal cleft is lateral to it. In scoliosis, the imaginary line rests in the gluteal cleft, and the spine deviates from this straight line.

P A list can result from a herniated vertebral disc and painful paravertebral muscle spasms.

A It is abnormal to have iliac crests that are unequal in height.

P Scoliosis and congenital or acquired limb length discrepancies lead to iliac crests that are not equal in height.

A Decreased ROM is abnormal. This is usually accompanied by pain.

P These clinical findings are found in back injury, osteoarthritis, and ankylosing spondylitis.

A. Scoliometer

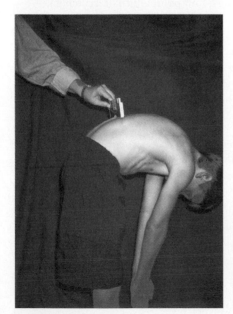

B. Use of Scoliometer

Figure 18-68 Scoliometer and Its Use.

Advanced Technique

Assessing for Scoliosis: Adams Forward Bend Test and Use of the Scoliometer

E 1. Instruct the patient to undress to underwear.
   2. Have the patient stand upright with the feet together.
   3. Stand behind the patient.
   4. Ask the patient to bend forward from the waist with the hands held downward toward the feet with palms together (similar to a diving position). The head should be down with the patient looking at the floor.
   5. Inspect and palpate the progression of the spinous processes, starting at the cervical spine and progressing in an inferior direction to the sacral area.
   6. Draw an imaginary line through the spinous processes (or use a felt-tipped marker to connect the spinous processes).
   7. Place the scoliometer (Figure 18-68A) on the thoracic vertebrae in the midspinal line. Measure the angle of trunk rotation on the scoliometer.
   8. Place the scoliometer on the lumbar vertebrae (Figure 18-68B) in the midspinal line and measure the angle of trunk rotation.

N The imaginary (or real) line drawn through the spinous processes should be straight or have minimal deviation. The angle of trunk rotation reading on the scoliometer should be less than 7°.

A It is abnormal to have moderate to severe lateral deviation of the spine. An angle of trunk rotation reading greater than 7° indicates scoliosis.

P Structural scoliosis usually develops in adolescence.

Advanced Technique

Assessing for Herniated Disc: Straight Leg-Raising Test (Lasègue's Test)

E 1. Assist the patient to a supine position on the examination table.
   2. Place one hand on the heel of the right foot and place the other hand behind the upper calf area of the same leg.

continues

Figure 18-69 Straight Leg-Raising Test.

3. Maintain the foot in its neutral anatomic position.
4. Raise the leg to the angle at which low back pain occurs.
5. With the extended leg still raised to its maximum height, manually dorsiflex the foot (Figure 18-69).
6. Repeat the technique on the left leg.

N The patient will be able to flex the hip joint and raise the straight leg to a hip flexion angle of 90°. There will be no low back pain with lifting of the extended leg or with dorsiflexion of the foot while the leg is raised.

A The patient who is unable to raise the extended leg to a 90° angle of hip joint flexion is considered to have a positive straight-leg raising test; this result is abnormal. Low back pain will occur with any lifting of the straight leg, and this discomfort will increase when the foot is dorsiflexed while the leg is in the raised position.

P Irritation of the nerve roots of the lumbosacral area causes pain in the sciatic nerve. Pain at less than 40° generally means an irritated nerve root caused by a herniated vertebral disc in the lumbosacral area. Pain may also occur in the other leg.

◄ NURSING CHECKLIST ►

Assessing Patients with Musculoskeletal Assistive Devices

Assistive devices may be necessary to support musculoskeletal structure and function. The need for such devices automatically indicates an underlying musculoskeletal disorder. For each assistive device, determine the reason for its use.

Crutches

Determine the following:
1. Amount of weight bearing allowed on affected lower limb
2. Appropriate crutch height
3. Type of crutch gait and appropriateness for the amount of weight bearing on affected leg: two-point crutch gait (partial weight bearing); three-point crutch gait (partial or nonweight-bearing); four-point alternate crutch gait (partial or full weight bearing); swing gait (nonweight-bearing)
4. Condition of crutches (padded handles, rubber tips)
5. Ease of transfer into and out of a chair
6. Ease of stair climbing with the crutches
7. Patient wearing flat, properly fitted shoes with non-skid surfaces
8. Signs or symptoms of skin breakdown or distal limb hypoperfusion

Cane

Determine the following:
1. Shape of handle (C or T)
2. Number of points on contact surface
3. Appropriateness for patient's height
4. Cane used on unaffected side
5. Refer to numbers 4 to 8 in the section on crutches

Walker

Determine the following:
1. Amount of weight bearing allowed on the lower limb
2. Type of walker (e.g., rolling or pickup walker)
3. Appropriateness for patient's height

continues

TABLE 18-11

Risk Factors for Osteoporotic Fractures in Postmenopausal Women

Major

- Age ≥ 65 yr
- Vertebral compression fracture
- Fragility fracture after age 40 yr
- Family history of osteoporotic fracture (especially hip fracture in mother)
- Systemic glucocorticoid therapy ≥ 3 mo
- Malabsorption syndrome
- Primary hyperparathyroidism
- Propensity to fall
- Appearance of osteopenia on radiograph
- Hypogonadism and early menopause (< 45 yr)

Minor

- Rheumatoid arthritis
- History of clinical hyperthyroidism
- Long-term anticonvulsant therapy
- Weight loss > 10% of body weight at age 25 yr
- Weight <57 kg
- Smoking
- Excess alcohol intake
- Excess caffeine intake
- Low dietary calcium intake
- Long-term heparin therapy

These risk factors were taken from the Osteoporosis Society of Canada 2002 clinical practice guidelines. Additional risk factors for osteoporotic fractures include: being Caucasian or Asian, not on HRT, having low BMI, low physical activity, impaired vision, dementia, recent falls, poor health, and being frail.

Sources: "Prevention of Osteoporosis and Osteoporosis Fractures in Postmenopausal Women: Recommendation Statement from the Canadian Task Force on Preventive Health Care." (May 25, 2004). Reprinted from *Canadian Medical Association Journal, 170*(11), 1665–1667. By permission of the publisher. © 2004 Canadian Medical Association.

4. Patient's ability to grip and propel the walker forward with rolling walker; patient's ability to grip, lift, and propel the walker forward with pickup walker
5. Refer to numbers 4 to 8 in the section on crutches

Brace, Splint, Immobilizer

Determine the following:
1. Location of device (e.g., limb, neck, torso, lower back, or pelvis)
2. Joint position maintained by device (e.g., extension, flexion, or abduction)
3. Joint motion allowed by device
4. If a movable device is used, is the hinge joint of the device aligned with the skeletal joint
5. Padding under pressure points of device
6. Amount of weight bearing allowed on the affected leg (lower leg device)
7. Refer to numbers 7 and 8 in the section on crutches

Cast

Determine the following:
1. Plaster or non-plaster (e.g., synthetic, fibreglass)
2. Location of cast
3. Joint position maintained (e.g., extension, flexion, or abduction)
4. Joint motion allowed
5. Edges of the cast covered ("petaled") with tape to prevent skin irritation
6. Amount of weight bearing allowed (lower leg cast)
7. Damage to cast (e.g., cracked, flaking or crumbling, dented, wet, softening)
8. Visible discoloration on the cast (e.g., from underlying wound drainage or bleeding)
9. Significant odour around the cast (e.g., a musty or foul smell)
10. Refer to number 8 in the section on crutches

Nursing Alert

Osteoporosis

Osteoporosis Canada refers to osteoporosis as the "Silent Thief."

Epidemiology

- One in four women over the age of 50 has osteoporosis; one in eight men over 50 also has the disease.[3]
- Estimates suggest that a 50-year-old Caucasian woman has a remaining lifetime fragility fracture risk of 40% (for hip, vertebra, or wrist).[4]
- The one-in-six lifetime risk of getting a hip fracture is greater than the one-in-nine risk of developing breast cancer, and the death rate is higher from hip fractures.[5]
- 50% of women who suffer a hip fracture need to depend on others, with about 20% requiring long-term care.[6]

Risk Factors[7] (See Table 18-11)

Screening for Bone Marrow Density Indicators of Osteoporosis and Interventions[8]

- Screening postmenopausal women to prevent fragility fractures is recommended. Although there is no direct evidence that screening reduces fractures, there is good evidence that screening is effective in identifying

continues

postmenopausal women with low bone mineral density and that treating osteoporosis can reduce the risk of fractures in this population.

- For women without documented osteoporosis, there is fair evidence that calcium and vitamin D supplementation alone prevents osteoporotic fractures.
- There is fair evidence that combined estrogen–progestin therapy decreases the incidence of total, hip, and non-vertebral fractures; however, for most women the risks may outweigh the benefits.
- Women who screen positive for osteoporosis may be prescribed therapy with alendronate, risedronate, or raloxifene to prevent osteoporotic fractures.
- Healthy daily calcium and vitamin D intake recommendations are[9]:
  - Prepubertal children (ages 4 to 8): 800 mg calcium
  - Adolescents (ages 9 to 18): 1300 mg calcium
  - Women and men (ages 19 to 50): 1000 mg calcium; 400 IU vitamin D
  - Women and men (ages > 50): 1500 mg calcium; 800 IU vitamin D
  - Pregnant or lactating women: 1000 mg calcium; 400 IU vitamin D
- Men and women should be encouraged to participate in exercise, particularly in weight-bearing exercises including walking, running, or dancing, or sports such as tennis, bowling, or soccer.

Nursing Alert

Osteoarthritis Risk Factors

- Obesity
- Family history
- Age > 40
- Joint abnormality
- Overuse of joint
- History of joint trauma

GERONTOLOGICAL VARIATIONS

With age, bone density decreases due to an increased rate of bone reabsorption that exceeds the rate of bone cell replenishment. Bone density loss is accentuated in the elderly female due to the estrogen deficiency that accompanies menopause. Although components of bone tissue become calcified with age, the loss of bone density results in a weaker bone that is more susceptible to fracture. For example, the elderly patient with osteoporosis is at risk for hip or wrist fracture from a minor fall. Other changes seen as a result of bone density loss include thoracic kyphosis and a reduction in height. Thoracic kyphosis will cause a change in the patient's centre of gravity, making the patient more prone to loss of balance and to falls.

With age, muscle fibres deteriorate and are replaced by fibrous connective tissue. Muscle atrophy is accompanied by a reduction in muscle mass, a loss of muscle strength against resistance, and a reduction in overall body mass. The fat content of the body increases, with particular distribution around the waistline.

The elderly patient may be less able to perform heavy physical activity or activities of daily living, especially if these activities are prolonged in duration. The severity of muscle atrophy will be influenced by the patient's activity level and by peak muscle mass. Because muscle atrophy with aging is a gradual process, some elderly patients are able to compensate for the loss in muscle strength, and changes in activities of daily living may be minimal. The ability to maintain an active lifestyle, including physical exercise, will act to prevent disuse muscle atrophy and will maximize muscle strength.

There is a decrease in water content of cartilage, which leads to a narrowing of joint spaces, possibly pain, crepitus, and decreased movement of the affected area. There is also a reduction in the ability of cartilage to repair itself following trauma or surgery. Articulating cartilage will deteriorate slightly due to a lifetime of wear and tear.

A decrease in the water content of the intervertebral discs occurs with age, resulting in a reduction of vertebral flexibility. Thinning of the discs, which results in a decrease in height, makes the elderly patient prone to back pain and injury.

The degree of thoracic kyphosis, muscle atrophy, articulating cartilage deterioration, and vertebral inflexibility seen with aging will directly affect the mobility of the elderly patient. During walking, a reduction in step height and length is common, and results from joint inflexibility and reduced muscle strength. Steps may become slower or more rapid in speed (e.g., shuffling). Transfers in and out of a sitting position will be more difficult because of vertebral inflexibility and reduced muscle strength. Stair climbing will also be affected by the reduction in muscle strength. The elderly patient may require some degree of external support to rise from a chair, to walk, or to climb stairs.

Nursing Alert

Scoliosis Screening

According to the Canadian Task Force on the Periodic Health Examination[10], there is insufficient evidence to indicate that screening for idiopathic scoliosis in adolescents is either effective or ineffective in improving the outcome. It is reasonable for clinicians to include periodic visual inspection of the back in their examination of adolescents seen for other reasons.

Nursing Alert

Elder Abuse and Neglect

Unfortunately, there is physical abuse and neglect among the elderly. Etiological factors may include stress related to financial difficulties, multiple family members residing in limited space, the lack of nearby family members, and the stress of dealing with an elderly relative with dementia or incontinence. Possible indications of physical abuse include unexplained bruises, swelling, hematomas, burns, fractures, poor hygiene, and poor nutritional status. Health care providers are obligated to investigate these symptoms further when they are unexplained or when the explanation is inappropriate for the location and severity of the trauma. Be familiar with your institution's policy on elder abuse.

Life 360°

Recognizing Possible Elder Abuse and Neglect

A 78-year-old woman with Alzheimer's disease is admitted through the emergency department with a diagnosis of probable aspiration pneumonia. Chest X-ray not only reveals pulmonary infiltrates consistent with the diagnosis of pneumonia but also multiple old rib fractures. Further assessment of the patient indicates cachexia, poor general hygiene, urinary and fecal incontinence, fecal impaction, decubiti of the sacral area, bruising of both arms in a "grip" fashion, and multiple bruises and abrasions of the buttocks and lower legs. The patient moans in pain frequently during the physical assessment. Follow-up limb X-rays reveal an old healed fracture of the left humerus. The patient is a widow and has been living with her divorced daughter for the last year. The daughter is the patient's only child as well as the patient's primary caregiver. During the day, the daughter works full time and the patient is cared for by hired help. The hired caregiver claims that the patient "falls frequently during the day."

- What is your initial reaction to these clinical findings?
- Do the findings of the physical assessment indicate possible physical abuse or neglect? Explain.
- What would you say to the patient's daughter?
- What questions would you ask the patient?

CASE STUDY   The Patient with Musculoskeletal Pain

The case study illustrates the application and objective documentation of the musculoskeletal assessment.

Crystal Conway is a physical education teacher at an elementary school who presents to your clinic today in pain.

HEALTH HISTORY

PATIENT PROFILE	28 yo divorced woman, no children
HEALTH ISSUE/CONCERN	"My back & neck are so painful. My hands are numb."
HISTORY OF HEALTH ISSUE/CONCERN	Pt was in Mexico 2 mos ago on spring break when she was involved in a MVA. Car was stopped when a 2nd vehicle ran into her at 50 kph. Pt wearing seat belt. Experienced cervical neck pain & exacerbation of LBP. Transported to local hospital where spinal X-rays were taken. X-rays neg. Pt discharged on codeine 60 mg c̄ acetaminophen 650 mg q 6 & cyclobenzaprine (skeletal muscle relaxant) 10 mg po tid. Both meds taken for 10 days. Pt had been feeling better until yesterday at 8 AM when she slipped on ice on her way to work. Denies ↓ LOC, lacerations/abrasions, bleeding. Felt ok so continued on to work. Since that time her back & neck pain have returned. Cervical neck pain is throbbing (6/10 intensity), s̄ radiation, aggravated by mvt; took codeine/acetaminophen × 2 doses s̄ relief; denies numbness/tingling in arms/hands, denies △ in mobility/coordination. Exacerbation of longstanding midspinal LBP. Achy sensation c̄ shooting pains down both legs (9/10 intensity). Mild tingling in Ⓡ lateral calf & foot. Denies loss of bowel/bladder control or incoordination of legs. Sitting & lying down make pain worse. Standing, leaning onto a chair is the only tolerable position. Pt also c/o burning pain (4/10 intensity s̄ radiation) in Ⓡ index & middle fingers, unable to maintain good grip on tennis racket; pt is Ⓡ handed. Pt is a new PE teacher (in her probationary period) at local school & needs to get back to work. Concerned that this injury may jeopardize her job as she cannot conduct or demonstrate athletics in accord c̄ her job description.
PAST HEALTH HISTORY	
Medical History	Asthma dx age 9; minor exacerbation with URTI. LBP started 3 yrs ago p̄ football game when she was tackled; intermittent tx c̄ NSAIDs & heating pad Genital herpes since age 21; Ø recent outbreaks Wisdom teeth excision age 19 s̄ sequelae
Surgical History	
Medications	Ibuprofen 400 mg po 2–3 × qwk Alesse (Levonorgestrel & estrogen) oral contraception
Communicable Diseases	Genital herpes age 21; usually 2–3 outbreaks q̄ yr, especially when stressed
Allergies	Perennial allergies to grasses, ragweed, pollen
Injuries and Accidents	MVA as per HPI Back injury sustained in tackle football game age 25
Special Needs	Denies
Blood Transfusions	Denies
Childhood Illnesses	Not sure if she had varicella
Immunizations	Hepatitis A for travel to Mexico; usually gets influenza vaccine at work q yr

FAMILY HEALTH HISTORY

LEGEND

 Living female

Living male

Deceased female

Deceased male

Points to patient

————//———— = Divorced

A&W = Alive & well

COPD = Chronic obstructive
    pulmonary disease

GSW = Gunshot wound

HTN = Hypertension

PE = Pulmonary embolus

RA = Rheumatoid arthritis

77 Osteoporosis — **81** HTN Alzheimer's disease

59 RA Osteoporosis — **62** COPD HTN

38 PE   **17** GSW   **33** Asthma   **28** Asthma Allergies Genital herpes —//— **31** A&W

Denies family hx of ankylosing spondylitis, lupus, gout, Paget's dz, Dupuytren's contracture.

SOCIAL HISTORY

Alcohol Use 2–3 beers q wkend night

Drug Use At university tried amphetamines, cocaine; denies use in past 5 yrs

Tobacco Use 1/2 PPD over wkend × 10 yrs

Domestic and Intimate Partner Violence Denies

Sexual Practice Sexually active, Ø use condoms c̄ multiple partners (8 per yr); married age 23, divorced 3 yrs later; now defines self as lesbian; monogamous re/ship with current partner (1 year)

Travel History Mexico 2 mo ago

Work Environment Suburban elementary school; new faculty member, learning the system— feels like she has to "produce" to keep job.

Home Environment Lives in condo by herself; "comfortable home"

Hobbies and Leisure Activities Likes to play tennis; rec softball league in spring; runs (usually daily but not since pain started)

Stress New job, current pain & its effect on her ability to do her job; = also girls' tennis team coach & season = about to start

Education BA in education

Economic Status "Nothing luxurious"

Religion/Spirituality Protestant; "I go to church when I can. I try different churches all the time."

Ethnicity "I am of Scottish descent"

Roles and Relationships Good relationship with parents & siblings; Ø contact c̄ ex-husband; talks on phone c̄ significant other daily, spends wkends c̄ her

continues

Characteristic Patterns of Daily Living	Wakes at 05:00 & runs 5 km; showers, leaves for work by 08:00 arrives at 08:30; conducts classes until 15:00; prepares lesson plans for next day; arrives home 16:30; eats dinner, goes for neighborhood walk; reads, watches TV, in bed by 21:30

HEALTH MAINTENANCE ACTIVITIES

Sleep	7 1/2 hrs q night; sometimes has difficulty falling & staying asleep
Diet	Low in fat; avoids fast foods
Exercise	Runs 5 km q wkday; more on wkends
Stress Management	Runs; c̄ current pain unable to run & is feeling very "uptight"
Use of Safety Devices	Wears seat belt; no helmet when rollerblades
Health Check-ups	Ø PAP in past 4 yrs; had physical ā started this new job—was told she = healthy

PHYSICAL ASSESSMENT

General Assessment

Overall Appearance	Slender; pt standing, leaning on exam table breathing deeply & clenching teeth
Posture	Stooped over exam table c̄ Ⓛ foot in front of Ⓡ; extremities proportional to body size/shape; head = looking down
Gait and Mobility	Slow gait in non-erect position; leads only c̄ Ⓛ foot c̄ gait; has difficulty c̄ position Δ 2° pain

Inspection

Muscle Size and Shape	Well developed/contoured leg muscles; Ø involuntary mvt
Joint Contour and Periarticular Tissue	Intact s̄ rashes, deformities, erythema, ecchymosis, swelling, enlgment, masses, nodules

Palpation

Muscle Tone	WNL s̄ masses, tenderness, spasm
Joints	Joints smooth, strong, firm; periarticular tissue s̄ swelling, tenderness, pain, warmth, nodules
Range of Motion	Cervical spine: flexion 25°, hyperextension 30°, lateral bending 15°, rotation 20° Hands/fingers: WNL Spine: flexion 20°, hyperextension 5°, lateral bending 10°, rotation, 10° All other joints: WNL
Muscle Strength	Cervical spine: 4/5 Hands/fingers: Ⓡ hand grip 3–4/5 Spine: deferred 2° to pain All other joints: WNL
Advanced Techniques	Phalen's Sign: Pain in Ⓡ index & middle fingers p̄ 30 sec Tinel's Sign: Tingling in Ⓡ index finger Straight Leg Raising Test: Pain c̄ dorsiflexion of Ⓡ foot at 30° Assessing Status of Distal Limbs and Digits: 3/3 peripheral pulses, warm skin, brisk cap refill in UE & LE

◄NURSING CHECKLIST►

Musculoskeletal Assessment

General Assessment
- Overall appearance
- Posture
- Gait and mobility

Inspection
- Muscle size and shape
- Joint contour and periarticular tissue

Palpation
- Muscle tone
- Joints

Range of Motion

Muscle Strength

Examination of Joints
- Temporomandibular joint
- Cervical spine
- Shoulders
- Elbows
- Wrists and hands
- Hips
- Knees
- Ankles and feet
- Spine

Advanced Techniques
- Measuring limb circumference
- Using a Goniometer
- Chvostek's sign (assessing for neuroexcitability)
- Trousseau's sign (assessing for neuroexcitability)
- Drop arm test (assessing for rotator cuff damage)
- Assessing grip strength using a blood pressure cuff
- Tinel's sign (assessing for carpal tunnel syndrome)
- Phalen's sign (assessing for carpal tunnel syndrome)
- Trendelenburg test (assessing for hip dislocation)
- Measuring limb length
- Bulge sign (assessing for small effusions)
- Patellar ballottement (assessing for large effusions)
- McMurray's sign (assessing for meniscal tears)
- Anterior drawer test (assessing for ankle sprain)
- Talar tilt test (assessing for ankle sprain)
- Assessing neurovascular status of distal limbs and digits
- Adams forward bend test (assessing for scoliosis) and use of the scoliometer
- Straight leg-raising test (Lasègue's test) (assessing for herniated disc)

Assistive Devices

- Crutches
- Cane
- Walker
- Brace, splint, immobilizer
- Cast

REVIEW QUESTIONS

1. A patient moves his shoulder medially and toward the midline of the body. What terms describe this joint and its movement?
   a. Adduction, diarthroses, ball- and -socket joint
   b. Abduction, synovial, hinge joint
   c. Flexion, amphiarthroses, gliding joint
   d. Extension, synarthroses, saddle joint
   The correct answer is (a).

2. Which illustrates the proper method to conduct a musculoskeletal assessment?
   a. Always conduct the assessment first thing in the morning
   b. Assess the painful body part first
   c. Assess the musculoskeletal system in a proximal-to-distal manner
   d. Manipulate each joint through its full anatomic ROM even if pain occurs
   The correct answer is (c).

3. When the patient walks into the public health department, you note a gait that is uncoordinated, stiff, and jerky. The patient is dragging a foot across the floor in a semicircle. What type of gait does this patient demonstrate?
   a. Antalgic gait of degenerative joint disease of the hip
   b. Spastic hemiplegia gait of cerebral palsy
   c. Scissors gait of multiple sclerosis
   d. Festinating gait of Parkinson's disease
   The correct answer is (c).

   Questions 4 and 5 refer to the following situation:

   Mrs. Nguyen is a 71-year-old woman with cervical neck pain that started yesterday while she was watching TV. You ask her to perform ROM of the cervical spine. Your findings are flexion 20°, hyperextension 30°, lateral bending 20°, rotation 35°.

4. Which conclusion do you make concerning Mrs. Nguyen's cervical neck pain?
   a. Her ROM is within normal limits, so it is probably an acute strain.
   b. She most likely has osteoarthritis.
   c. Her anatomic ROM is increased due to her age.
   d. The pain is congenital in nature.
   The correct answer is (b).

5. Mrs. Nguyen is most likely experiencing which musculoskeletal change that occurs with aging?
   a. Muscle fibres replace fibrous connective tissue.
   b. The water content of cartilage increases, leading to a widening of joint spaces.
   c. Step length increases due to joint laxity.
   d. There is an increased rate of bone reabsorption.
   The correct answer is (d).

6. When you manually squeeze the calf muscle of a prone patient's leg, there is an absence of plantar flexion. What is the significance of this finding?
   a. It suggests a ruptured Achilles tendon.
   b. It suggests a fracture of the tibia.
   c. It suggests plantar fasciitis.
   d. It is normal.
   The correct answer is (a).

7. Which assessment technique is used to determine if the meniscus of the knee is intact?
   a. McMurray's sign
   b. Trousseau's sign
   c. Talar tilt test
   d. Straight leg-raise test
   The correct answer is (a).

8. While performing passive ROM, your patient has a strong, painful muscle contraction. What is this involuntary movement called?
   a. Fasciculation
   b. Spasm
   c. Tremor
   d. Asterixis
   The correct answer is (b).

9. You ask the patient to sit with the arms flexed at the elbow and the back of the hands pressed together for one minute. The patient experiences numbness in the index and middle fingers. This test indicates that there is pressure placed on which nerve?
   a. Radial nerve
   b. Ulnar nerve
   c. Median nerve
   d. Peroneal nerve
   The correct answer is (c).

10. Which would you perform to assess the neurovascular status of the ulnar nerve?
    a. Phalen's sign
    b. Ask the patient to perform opposition of the thumb to the little finger of the same hand.
    c. Trousseau's sign
    d. Pinch the finger pad of the little finger.
    The correct answer is (d).

> Visit the Estes online companion resource at
> www.healthassessment.nelson.com for additional
> content and study aids.

REFERENCES

1. Registered Nurses' Association of Ontario. (2005). *Prevention of falls and fall injuries in the older adult.* Toronto: Registered Nurses' Association of Ontario.
2. Norris, M.A., Walton, R. E., Patterson, C., Feightner, J. W. and the Canadian Task Force on Preventive Health Care (2003). *Prevention of falls in long-term care facilities: Systematic review and recommendations.* CTFPHC Technical Report June 2003. London, ON: Canadian Task Force.
3. Osteoporosis Canada. *What is osteoporosis. Fact sheet.* retrieved November 2, 2006, from http://www.osteoporosis.ca/english/about%20osteoporosis/default.asp?s=1
4. Tenenhouse, A., Joseph L., Kreiger, N., Poliquin, S., Murray, T.M., Blondeau, L., et al. (2000). *Estimation of the prevalence of low bone density in Canadian women and men using a population-specific DXA reference standard: The Canadian Multicentre Osteoporosis Study (CaMOS). Osteoporosis International,* 11, 897–904.
5. Ibid.
6. Ibid.
7. Cheung, A., Feig, D. S., Kapral, M., Diaz-Granados, N, & Dodin, S., and The Canadian Task Force on Preventive Health Care (2004). Prevention of osteoporosis and osteoporotic fractures in postmenopausal women: Recommendation statement from the Canadian Task Force on Preventive Health Care. *Canadian Medical Association Journal, 170* (11), 1665–1667.
8. Brown, J. P., Jossse, R. G., et al. (2002). Clinical practice guidelines for the diagnosis and management of osteoporosis in Canada. *Canadian Medical Association Journal, 167* (10 Suppl): S1–S34.
9. Tenenhouse, A., Joseph L., Kreiger, N., Poliquin, S., Murray, T. M., Blondeau, L., et al. (2000). *Estimation of the prevalence of low bone density in Canadian women and men using a population-specific DXA reference standard: The Canadian multicentre osteoporosis study* (CaMOS).
10. Goldbloom R. B. Screening for idiopathic adolescent scoliosis. (1994). In Canadian Task Force on the Periodic Health Examination. *Canadian Guide to Clinical Preventive Health Care.* Ottawa: Health Canada, 346–354.

BIBLIOGRAPHY

Brown, D. E., & Neumann, R. D. (2003). *Orthopedic secrets* (3rd ed.). Philadelphia: Hanley & Belfus.

Maher, A., Salmond, S., & Pellino, T. (2002). *Orthopedic nursing* (3rd ed.). Philadelphia: Elsevier.

Society of Obstetricians and Gynaecologists of Canada. (2002). *The Canadian Consensus Conference on Menopause and Osteoporosis—2002 update* [SOGC guideline no. 108]. Ottawa: The Society; 2002.

Wilens, N. (2005). Osteoporosis in men: Early detection promotes quality of life. *Advance for Nurse Practitioners, 13*(4), 31–34.

WEB RESOURCES

Arthritis Society of Canada
http://www.arthritis.ca

Institute of Musculoskeletal Health and Arthritis (IMHA)
http://www.fp.ucalgary.ca/imhadb

Osteoporosis Canada
http://www.osteoporosis.ca

NEL

CHAPTER 19

Mental Status and Neurological Techniques

COMPETENCIES

1. Discuss the divisions of the nervous system and their functions.

2. Relate blood flow to the brain to the functional area supplied.

3. Describe the characteristics of the most common neurological health issues and concerns.

4. Perform a mental status assessment and document the results.

5. Assess the neurological system in a systematic manner and document the results.

6. Explain the pathophysiology of any abnormal results obtained.

7. Document a complete health history as it relates to the neurological system.

*T*he nervous system controls all body functions and thought processes. The complex interrelationships among the various divisions of the nervous system permit the body to maintain homeostasis; receive, interpret, and react to stimuli; and control voluntary and involuntary processes, including cognition.

ANATOMY AND PHYSIOLOGY

The structure and function of the central nervous system and the peripheral nervous system are discussed.

Macrostructure

The scalp and skull are two protective layers covering the brain. The scalp performs a unique function in that it moves freely, helping to protect and cushion the head from traumatic injury. The skull is a rigid, bony cavity that has a fixed volume of approximately 1500 mL.

Meninges

There are three layers of meninges (protective membranes), known as the dura mater, arachnoid mater, and pia mater, located between the brain and the skull (Figure 19-1). The dura mater is the thick, tough outermost layer. Below the dura mater is a small, serous space known as the subdural space.

The arachnoid mater lies between the dura mater and the pia mater. Below the arachnoid mater is the subarachnoid space, where cerebrospinal fluid (CSF) is circulated. Portions of the arachnoid mater, called arachnoid villi, project into the subarachnoid space (also shown in Figure 19-1). These serve to absorb CSF.

The pia mater is thin and vascular. It is the innermost layer of the meninges. The pia mater helps form the choroid plexuses, which are vascular structures located in the ventricles of the brain that form CSF.

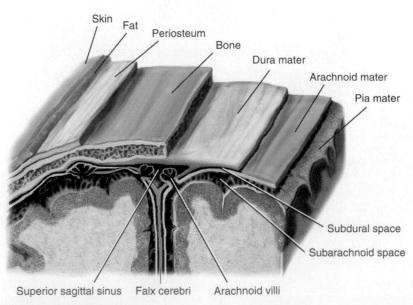

Figure 19-1 The Meninges.

Central Nervous System

The brain and the spinal cord make up the central nervous system (CNS). The brain is divided into four main components: the cerebrum, the diencephalon, the cerebellum, and the brain stem. Each of these areas is subdivided into various anatomic areas.

Cerebrum

The cerebrum is the largest portion of the brain. It is incompletely divided into right and left hemispheres by the longitudinal fissure. The two hemispheres are connected by the corpus callosum, which serves as a communication link between the left and right hemispheres.

The cerebral cortex, or the outermost layer of the cerebrum, contains grey matter. Higher cognitive functioning is dependent on the cerebral cortex and its interaction with other parts of the nervous system. The cerebral cortex is involved in memory storage and recall, conscious understanding of sensation, vision, hearing, and motor function. The basal ganglia are located deep within the cerebral hemispheres and function intricately with the cerebral cortex and the cerebellum in regulating motor activity.

Each cerebral hemisphere is divided into four lobes: the frontal, parietal, temporal, and occipital lobes. The locations and functions of each of the cerebral lobes are illustrated in Figure 19-2. A fifth lobe called the limbic lobe is anatomically part of the temporal lobe and is involved in emotional behaviour and self-preservation.

Diencephalon

The diencephalon, a relay centre for the brain, is composed of the thalamic structures: the thalamus, the epithalamus, and the hypothalamus. The hypothalamus

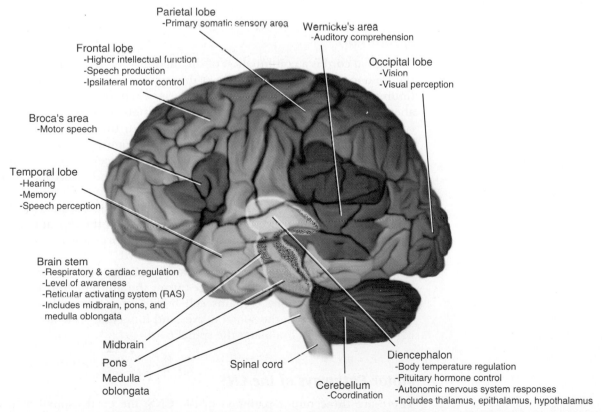

Figure 19-2 The Locations and Functions of the Cerebral Lobes, Diencephalon, Cerebellum, and Brain Stem.

is important in body temperature regulation, pituitary hormone control, and autonomic nervous system responses. It also plays a role in behaviour via its connections with the limbic system.

Cerebellum

The cerebellum lies inferior to the occipital lobe and behind the brain stem. It is divided into two lateral lobes and a medial part called the vermis. The vermis is the part of the cerebellum concerned primarily with maintenance of posture and equilibrium. Each cerebellar hemisphere is responsible for coordination of movement of the ipsilateral (same) side of the body.

Brain Stem

The brain stem is located immediately below the diencephalon and is divided into the midbrain, the pons, and the medulla oblongata. The reticular formation, a complex network of sensory fibres in the brain stem, contains centres that control respiratory, cardiovascular, and vegetative functions. The ascending reticular activating system (RAS) is located in the brain stem and extends to the cerebral cortex. The RAS is mostly excitatory and is essential for arousal from sleep, maintaining attention, and perception of sensory input.

The midbrain contains the nuclei of cranial nerves III (oculomotor) and IV (trochlear), which are associated with control of eye movements. The pons is located between the midbrain and the medulla oblongata. Sensory and motor nuclei of cranial nerves V (trigeminal), VI (abducens), VII (facial), and VIII (acoustic) are located in the pons. The medulla oblongata is located between the pons and the spinal cord. It contains the nuclei of cranial nerves IX (glossopharyngeal), X (vagus), XI (spinal accessory), and XII (hypoglossal). Also located in the medulla oblongata are the centres for reflexes such as sneezing, swallowing, coughing, and vomiting, as well as the centres regulating the respiratory and cardiovascular systems.

Spinal Cord

The spinal cord is a continuation of the medulla oblongata. It exits the skull at the foramen magnum and begins at the upper border of the atlas (C1), continuing downward to the conus medullaris, a tapered ending of the cord at about the level of the first or second lumbar vertebrae (Figure 19-3A). From the conus medullaris is a connective tissue filament, the filum terminale, which continues down to its attachment at the coccyx (Figure 19-3B).

A cross-section of the spinal cord shows that the central part of the cord is grey matter. The grey matter is in the shape of an H and is surrounded by white matter.

The grey matter comprises nerve cell bodies and short segments of unmyelinated fibres. The posterior portion of the H is called the dorsal horn, and the anterior portion is the ventral horn. Small lateral horns are also present in thoracic and upper lumbar sections of the spinal cord.

The dorsal horn contains cell bodies of sensory (afferent) neurons, which receive and transmit sensory messages from the afferent fibres in the spinal nerve. The ventral horn contains cell bodies of motor (efferent) neurons, which send axons into the spinal nerves and innervate skeletal muscles, carrying signals from the brain and the spinal cord.

Motor Pathways of the CNS

There are three motor pathways in the CNS: the corticospinal or pyramidal tract, the extrapyramidal tract, and the cerebellum.

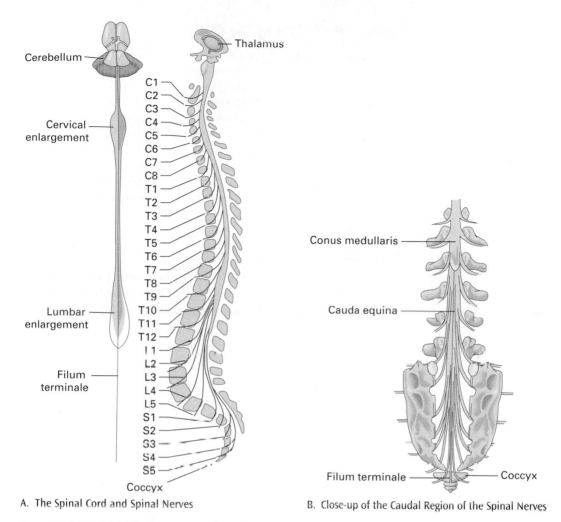

A. The Spinal Cord and Spinal Nerves

B. Close-up of the Caudal Region of the Spinal Nerves

Figure 19-3 The Spinal Cord.

Pyramidal Tract

The corticospinal pathway descends from the motor area of the cerebral cortex, through the midbrain, the pons, and the medulla. At the level of the medulla, 90% of the fibres of the corticospinal tract decussate (cross) to travel down the opposite side of the spinal cord, becoming the lateral corticospinal tract. The remaining fibres travel down the spinal cord in a tract known as the anterior corticospinal tract. Fibres of the lateral corticospinal tract synapse in the anterior horn (grey matter) at all levels of the cord just before they leave the cord (Figure 19-4). The motor neurons above this synapse in the anterior horn are known as upper motor neurons. Upper motor neurons connect the cerebral cortex with the anterior horn and are entirely contained within the CNS. Lower motor neurons are motor neurons below the level of the upper motor neurons. Lower motor neuron cell bodies are located in the anterior horn, where they connect with the corticospinal tract. Lower motor neurons innervate skeletal muscle at the myoneural junction. They are responsible for purposeful, voluntary movement.

Extrapyramidal Tract

This pathway includes all motor neurons in the motor cortex, basal ganglia, brain stem, and spinal cord that are outside the corticospinal, or pyramidal, tract (henceforth referred to as extrapyramidal). The extrapyramidal tract is responsible for controlling body movement, particularly gross automatic movements (e.g., walking), and controlling muscle tone.

Figure 19-4 Motor Pathways of the CNS.

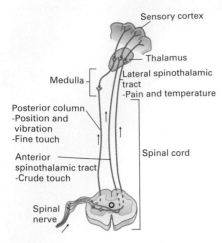

Figure 19-5 Sensory Pathways of the CNS.

Sensory Pathways of the CNS

The sensory portion of the peripheral nervous system consists of afferent neurons divided into somatic afferent and visceral afferent neurons. Somatic afferent fibres originate in skeletal muscles, joints, tendons, and skin. Visceral fibers originate in the viscera. Both types of afferent fibres carry impulses from both the external and the internal environments to the CNS.

Afferent fibres containing impulses, or messages, enter the spinal cord through the dorsal roots. From the spinal cord the message travels via the spinothalamic tracts or the posterior column to the thalamus and sensory cortex. The thalamus receives the message and interprets a general sensation. The impulse synapses with another sensory neuron to the sensory cortex, where the message is fully interpreted (Figure 19-5).

Spinothalamic Tracts

In the spinal cord, the spinothalamic tracts synapse with a second sensory neuron and then decussate to the opposite side. The message is then carried up the tract. The lateral spinothalamic tract carries pain and temperature sensations, and the anterior spinothalamic tract carries the sensation of crude or light touch.

Posterior Column

The posterior column carries position, vibration, and fine-touch sensations. The nerve impulse enters the spinal cord and travels upward to the medulla, where a synapse with a second sensory neuron occurs. The neuron decussates to the opposite side of the medulla and continues on to the thalamus and sensory cortex.

Blood Supply

Blood is supplied to the brain by two pairs of arteries, the internal carotid arteries (anterior circulation) and the vertebral arteries (posterior circulation). At the base of the brain lies the circle of Willis, an arterial anastomosis that links the anterior and posterior blood supplies (Figure 19-6). The functional areas supplied by each of the main cerebral arteries are listed in Table 19-1.

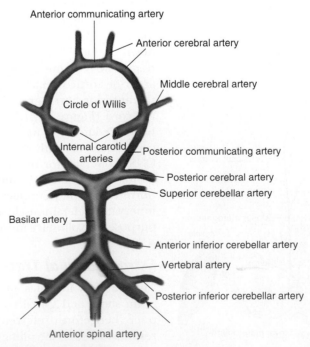

Figure 19-6 Major Arteries of the Brain.

TABLE 19-1   Cerebral Blood Supply

ARTERY	FUNCTIONAL AREA
Anterior cerebral artery	Medial and inferior surfaces of each hemisphere: • Frontal lobe • Parietal lobe
Middle cerebral artery	Lateral surface of each hemisphere: • Frontal lobe • Temporal lobe • Parietal lobe • Occipital lobe
Posterior cerebral artery	Medial and inferior surfaces of each hemisphere: • Temporal lobe • Medial occipital lobe • Midbrain
Basilar artery	• Midbrain • Upper brain stem • Medulla oblongata
Cerebellar arteries	• Pons • Midbrain • Cerebellum

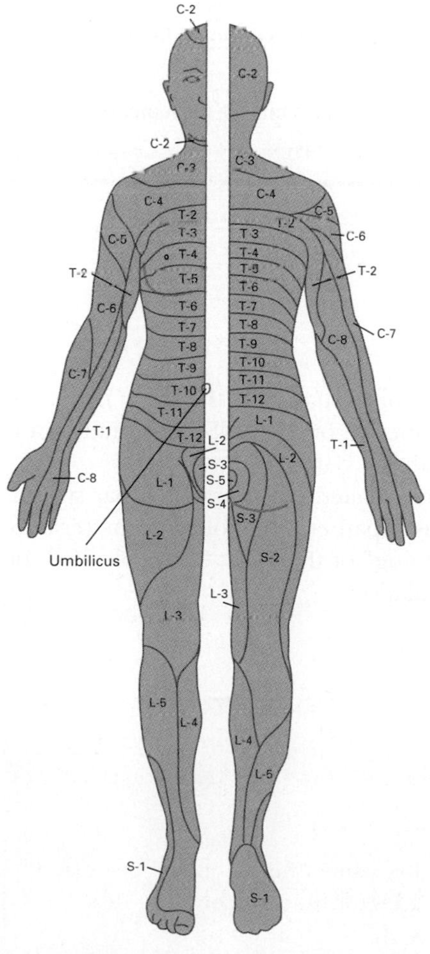

Figure 19-7 Anterior and Posterior Dermatomal Distributions.

Peripheral Nervous System

The peripheral nervous system consists of nervous tissue found outside the CNS, including the spinal nerves, cranial nerves, and the autonomic nervous system.

Spinal Nerves

The 31 pairs of spinal nerves include 8 cervical, 12 thoracic, 5 lumbar, 5 sacral, and 1 coccygeal. Each spinal nerve is made up of a dorsal (afferent) root and a ventral (efferent) root. Each afferent spinal nerve root innervates a specific area of the skin, called a **dermatome**, for superficial cutaneous sensations. Figure 19-7 illustrates both the anterior and the posterior dermatomal distributions. Spinal nerves leaving the right side of the cord supply the right side of the body, and those leaving the left side supply muscles on the left side.

Each of the eight cervical nerves exits above its corresponding vertebra. Each of the spinal nerves below the cervical portion exits below its corresponding vertebra. The spinal cord is not as long as the vertebral column, so the lumbar and sacral nerves are comparatively long. These longer roots are called the cauda equina, meaning "horse's tail" (Figure 19-3B).

Cranial Nerves

There are 12 pairs of cranial nerves. They are designated in order of their position with Roman numerals I through XII. Some cranial nerves have purely motor functions and some have only sensory functions. Others have mixed sensory and motor functions. Table 19-2 summarizes the functions of the cranial nerves.

Autonomic Nervous System

The autonomic nervous system (ANS) is divided into two functionally different subdivisions: the sympathetic and parasympathetic nervous systems.

TABLE 19-2 The 12 Cranial Nerves and Their Functions

NAME AND NUMBER	FUNCTION
Olfactory (I)	Smell
Optic (II)	Visual acuity, visual fields, funduscopic examination
Oculomotor (III)	Cardinal fields of gaze (EOM movement), eyelid elevation, pupil reaction, doll's eyes phenomenon
Trochlear (IV)	EOM movement
Trigeminal (V)	Motor: strength of temporalis and masseter muscles Sensory: light touch, superficial pain and temperature to face, corneal reflex
Abducens (VI)	EOM movement
Facial (VII)	Motor: facial movements Sensory: taste anterior two-thirds of tongue *Parasympathetic: tears and saliva secretion
Acoustic (VIII)	Cochlear: gross hearing, Weber and Rinne tests Vestibular: vertigo, equilibrium, nystagmus
Glossopharyngeal (IX)	Motor: soft palate and uvula movement, gag reflex, swallowing, guttural and palatal sounds Sensory: taste posterior one-third of tongue *Parasympathetic: carotid reflex, chemoreceptors
Vagus (X)	Motor and Sensory: same as CN IX *Parasympathetic: carotid reflex, stomach and intestinal secretions, peristalsis, involuntary control of bronchi, heart innervation
Spinal Accessory (XI)	Sternocleidomastoid and trapezius muscle movements
Hypoglossal (XII)	Tongue movement, lingual sounds

Cannot be directly assessed.
EOM = extraocular muscle; CN = cranial nerve.

The ANS functions without voluntary control to maintain the body in a state of homeostasis. Most organs under the influence of the ANS have dual innervation of both sympathetic and parasympathetic systems.

The sympathetic nervous system, sometimes called the thoracolumbar system, controls "fight or flight" actions. The parasympathetic nervous system (craniosacral) is responsible for "general housekeeping" of the body. See Table 19-3 for specific system responses to autonomic stimulation.

Nursing Tip

Cranial Nerve Mnemonics

Mnemonics can assist you in remembering the name of each cranial nerve and whether each nerve has a sensory function, a motor function, or both. Read the columns vertically to see the mnemonics.

continues

First Letter of Cranial Nerve	Number of Cranial Nerve	Function of Cranial Nerve
On (**O**lfactory)	I	Some
Old (**O**ptic)	II	Say
Olympus's (**O**culomotor)	III	Marry
Towering (**T**rochlear)	IV	Money
Tops (**T**rigeminal)	V	But
A (**A**bducens)	VI	My
Finn (**F**acial)	VII	Brother
And (**A**coustic)	VIII	Says
German (**G**lossopharyngeal)	IX	Bad
Viewed (**V**agus)	X	Business
Some (**S**pinal Accessory)	XI	Marry
Hops (**H**ypoglossal)	XII	Money

For cranial nerve function: S = sensory nerve, M = motor nerve, B = both sensory and motor nerve

Reflexes

A reflex action, a specific response to an adequate stimulus, occurs without conscious control. The stimulus can occur in a joint, muscle, or the skin, and is transmitted to the CNS by one or more afferent, or sensory, neurons. The impulse enters the spinal cord through the dorsal root of a spinal nerve, where it synapses. Following synapse in the cord, the anterior motor neurons send an impulse via efferent neurons to the endplates of the skeletal muscle, causing the effector muscle to react (Figure 19-8).

A monosynaptic reflex, such as the patellar reflex, involves two neurons: one afferent and one efferent. Polysynaptic reflexes involve many neurons in addition to the afferent and efferent limbs of the reflex arc. Reflexes are classified into three main categories: muscle stretch, or deep tendon reflexes (DTR); superficial reflexes; and pathological reflexes.

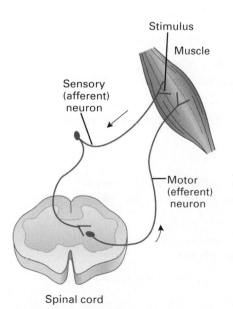

Figure 19-8 Monosynaptic Reflex Arc.

TABLE 19-3 Symphathetic versus Parasympathetic Response

SYSTEM	SYMPATHETIC RESPONSE	PARASYMPATHETIC RESPONSE
Neurological	Pupils dilated Heightened awareness	Pupils normal size
Cardiovascular	Increased heart rate Increased myocardial contractility Increased blood pressure	Decreased heart rate Decreased myocardial contractility
Respiratory	Increased respiratory rate Increased respiratory depth Bronchial dilation	Bronchial constriction
Gastrointestinal	Decreased gastric motility Decreased gastric secretions Increased glycogenolysis Decreased insulin production Sphincter contraction	Increased gastric motility Increased gastric secretions Sphincter dilatation
Genitourinary	Decreased urine output Decreased renal blood flow	Normal urine output

HEALTH HISTORY

The neurological health history provides insight into the link between a patient's life and lifestyle and neurological information and pathology.

PATIENT PROFILE — *Diseases that are age-, gender-, and race-specific for the neurological system are listed.*

Age
Multiple sclerosis (MS) (20–40)
Myasthenia gravis (20–30)
Fibromyalgia (25–50)
Syringomyelia (30)
Huntington's chorea (30–40)
Parkinson's disease (>50)
Alzheimer's disease (middle–old age)

Gender

Female
Myasthenia gravis, MS, meningiomas, pseudotumour cerebri, migraine headaches, fibromyalgia

Male
Cervical spine injuries, cluster headache, dyslexia (boys)

Ethnicity
Aboriginal Canadians, and people of African, Hispanic, South Asian, and Black descent have higher rates of high blood pressure and diabetes—conditions that can lead to stroke.
Caucasian, Northern European: Multiple sclerosis
Jewish descent: Tay-Sachs disease

HEALTH ISSUE/CONCERN — *Common health issues/concerns for the neurological system are defined and information on the characteristics of each sign or symptom is provided.*

Headache
See Chapter 11

Seizure
A transient disturbance of cerebral function caused by an excessive discharge of neurons

Location
Body parts involved

Quality
General or localized

Quantity
Number of minutes or seconds, weekly, monthly, every few months

Associated Manifestations
Incontinence, injury (tongue, cheeks, limbs), memory loss, cyanosis, respiratory arrest; postictal headache, somnolence, or confusion

Aggravating Factors
Television viewing, bright lights, sleep deprivation, stress, flashing lights, hyperventilation, fever in children or infants, alcohol (use or withdrawal), hyperglycemia, hypoglycemia

Alleviating Factors
Medications

Setting
Sequence of events: warning (aura) such as headache, abdominal discomfort, euphoria or depression, visual hallucination; phases: tonic, clonic, postictal, fugue states

Timing
First occurrence, age at onset of seizures, associated trauma or presumed cause, sleeping hours, first awakening, menses

Syncope
Abrupt loss of consciousness of brief duration due to decreased oxygen or glucose supply to the brain

continues

Quality	Total versus partial loss of consciousness
Quantity	Duration of seconds, minutes, or hours; daily, monthly
Associated Manifestations	Nausea, diaphoresis, dimmed vision, increased salivation, gastrointestinal bleeding, dyspnea, chest pain, palpitations, hemiparesis, transient focal deficits, seizures, migraine headache, associated illness (myocardial infarction, insulin-dependent diabetes mellitus)
Aggravating Factors	Injury, intense emotion, carotid occlusion, cardiovascular disorders, exertion, anemia, hypoglycemia, insulin peak, crowded space, decreased atmospheric oxygen
Alleviating Factors	Cool air, change in position, oxygen, glucose, medication, volume infusions
Setting	Hot, stuffy room; standing still for long periods of time
Pain	A sensation of discomfort, distress, or suffering
Location	Anatomic location (e.g., lower back, head)
Quality	Aching, stabbing, throbbing, cramping
Associated Manifestations	Crying, hysteria, muscular tenseness, depression, shortness of breath, diaphoresis, splinting or protective behaviours, focal deficits, limited range of motion
Aggravating Factors	Stress, excessive exercise, lifting, coughing or sneezing, posture changes, trauma, illness, extreme temperatures, humidity
Alleviating Factors	Medications, heat, cold, distraction, physical therapy
Timing	Minutes to constant; early morning, late day; daily, monthly
Paresthesia	Abnormal sensations such as numbness, pricking, tingling
Location	Anatomic location (e.g., arms, hands, legs, feet)
Quality	Aching, stabbing, pins and needles, numbness
Associated Manifestations	Pain, stiffness, changes in gait, pulseless extremities, pallor, injury, ulcers, muscle wasting, traumatic injury
Aggravating Factors	Activity, extreme cold, diabetes mellitus
Alleviating Factors	Medication, warmth, position changes
Disturbances in Gait	Abnormal way of moving on foot, walking, or running
Quality	Ataxic, spastic hemiplegia, hemiplegic, scissors, festinating, steppage, antalgic, apraxic, Trendelenburg
Associated Manifestations	Vertigo, visual impairments, blackouts, stroke, focal weakness, muscle wasting, abnormal movements or posture, spasticity, falling
Aggravating Factors	Fatigue, alcohol ingestion, vitamin D deficiency
Alleviating Factors	Rest, assistive devices
Setting	Level ground versus uneven terrain, stroke, neuromuscular pathology

continues

Visual Changes	Changes in visual acuity, visual fields, colour perception, depth perception
Quality	Blindness in particular field of vision; scotoma; perception of flashing, bright lights; blurriness
Associated Manifestations	Vertigo, dizziness, nausea, weakness, headache
Aggravating Factors	Darkness, fatigue, bright light, reading, alcohol ingestion, medication
Alleviating Factors	Rest, medications, glasses
Timing	Abrupt, gradual, constant, intermittent, morning, evening
Vertigo	The sensation of moving in space or objects moving around the person; also may be referred to as dizziness, lightheadedness
Quality	Spinning sensations, dizziness, or lightheadedness
Associated Manifestations	Nausea, vomiting, headache, tinnitus, deafness, discharge from ear, cranial nerve palsies, hemiparesis, seizure, loss of consciousness, chest pain, palpitations, falling
Aggravating Factors	Motion, movement of head, changes in atmospheric pressure (weather), heights, amusement rides, anxiety, alcohol ingestion, pain, medications
Alleviating Factors	Medications, lying down, maintaining a still posture
Setting	Amusement rides, glassed-in elevators, rising from a seated or supine position
Timing	Sudden, gradual; seconds, minutes, days, months; constant, intermittent
Memory Disorders	Change in ability to remember events or facts
Quality	Recent or remote memory loss
Associated Manifestations	Irritability, anxiety, agitation, confabulation, associated trauma, depression
Aggravating Factors	Distraction, anxiety, medications, alcohol ingestion, drug abuse, unfamiliar environment, sleep deprivation, anesthesia, hypoxia, electrolyte imbalance, high altitude
Alleviating Factors	Visual or auditory cues, familiarity with environment, oxygen, electrolyte replacement, narcotic reversal, detoxification
Setting	Unfamiliar environment
Timing	Nighttime, upon awakening
Difficulty with Swallowing or Speech	Inability to swallow food or drink, choking, or aspiration; changes in enunciation of words, volume of speech, content of speech, or comprehension of written or verbal language
Associated Manifestations	Excessive drooling and saliva, paresis, dysarthria, weight loss, dehydration, irritability, depression, disease or damage to the CNS, such as stroke or cerebral palsy
Aggravating Factors	Fatigue, position, prolonged tracheal intubation, alcohol intake
Alleviating Factors	Rest, quiet environment, thickened liquids, soft foods, varied communication tools
Setting	Loud, chaotic environment; after prolonged intubation

continues

PAST HEALTH HISTORY	*The various components of the past health history are linked to neurological pathology and neurology-related information.*
Medical History	
Neurologic Specific	Amyotrophic lateral sclerosis (ALS), multiple sclerosis (MS), tumours, Guillain-Barré syndrome, cerebral aneurysm, arteriovenous malformations (AVM), stroke (brain attack), migraines, Alzheimer's disease, myasthenia gravis, congenital defects, metabolic disorders, childhood seizures, head trauma, neuropathies, peripheral vascular disease, Parkinson's disease
Non-neurologic Specific	Hypertension, heart disease, cardiac surgery, invasive procedures, diabetes mellitus, leukemia, hypoglycemia
Surgical History	Craniotomy, laminectomy, carotid endarterectomy, transsphenoidal hypophysectomy, cordotomy, aneurysmectomy or repair
Medications	Antidepressants, antiseizure medications, narcotics, antianxiety medications, antipsychotic medications
Communicable Diseases	Encephalitis, meningitis or poliomyelitis, AIDS dementia, botulism, syphilis, cat scratch disease, rickettsial infections, toxoplasmosis
Injuries and Accidents	Closed head injury, chronic subdural hematoma, spinal cord injury, peripheral nerve damage
FAMILY HEALTH HISTORY	*Neurological diseases that are familial are listed.*
	Congenital defects such as neural tube defects, hydrocephalus, arteriovenous malformation (AVM), headaches, epilepsy, Alzheimer's disease, Huntington's chorea, muscular dystrophies, lipid storage diseases, Gaucher's disease, Niemann-Pick's disease
SOCIAL HISTORY	*The components of the social history are linked to neurological factors and pathology.*
Alcohol Use	Patients suffering from chronic alcoholism may exhibit the following abnormal findings: Korsakoff's psychosis, polyneuropathy, Wernicke's encephalopathy, tremor
Drug Use	Neurological signs of drug use are listed in Table 19-4.
Tobacco Use	Increased risk of stroke
Sexual Practice	Neurosyphilis; impotence secondary to neuropathies, MS, or lower motor neuron lesions
Travel History	Arthropod-borne encephalitis (Venezuelan equine, Japanese B, Murray-Valley, Russian spring-summer, Central European, Colorado tick), malaria
Work Environment	Exposure to continuous loud noise, performing repetitive-motion tasks, toxic chemical exposure (carbon dioxide, insecticides)
Home Environment	Exposure to toxic chemicals (carbon dioxide, insecticides), lead paint
Hobbies and Leisure Activities	Use of protective equipment; participation in contact sports or high-risk activities such as football, soccer, hockey, boxing, race car driving, motorcycling; hobbies involving repetitive motion (needlework)
Stress	Headaches

continues

HEALTH MAINTENANCE ACTIVITIES	*This information provides a bridge between the health maintenance activities and neurological function.*
Sleep	Narcolepsy, insomnia
Diet	Beriberi (vitamin B_1), pellagra (niacin)
Exercise	Increased muscle strength, increased coordination
Use of Safety Devices	Helmet, seat belt
Health Check-ups	Developmental milestones

TABLE 19-4 **Neurological Signs of Drug Ingestion**

ASSESSMENT PARAMETER	DRUG				
	Hallucinogens	*Cannabis (Marijuana)*	*Narcotics*	*Sedative-Hypnotics*	*CNS Stimulants*
Pupils	Dilated React to light	Normal	Pinpoint Fixed	Normal	Dilated React to light
Deep tendon reflexes	Hyperactive	Normal	Normal	Hypoactive	Hyperactive
Speech	Normal	Often normal	Normal or dulled	Slurred	N/A
Coordination	Normal	Normal	Normal or unsteady	Ataxia	N/A
Sensorium	Often clear	Usually clear	Dulled	Confusion	May be confused
Sensory perception	Distorted	Distorted	Dulled	Dulled	Heightened
Memory	Unchanged	Transient loss	Unchanged	Impaired	Unchanged
Hallucinations	Any type	Rare	Rare	N/A	N/A
Delusions	Variable	Paranoid	N/A	N/A	Paranoid

N/A = not applicable.

Nursing Alert

Brain Attack (Stroke, Cerebrovascular Accident)

There has been a gradual shift in terminology from stroke or cerebrovascular accident (CVA) to "*brain attack*" as health care practitioners try to educate Canadians that a stroke, just like a heart attack, is a life-threatening emergency. Many Canadians still believe that nothing can be done if you have a stroke; however, since the advent of thrombolytic therapy in the mid-90s, more and more people are surviving and experiencing improved outcomes following this experience. So, to make sure people act quickly (people experiencing a stroke must get to hospital within three hours after onset of symptoms!), we hope they start to think of a stroke as equally risky yet treatable as a heart attack. [As some people say, "**time is brain.**"]

continues

Brain attack is a condition that results in a reduction of blood flow to a region of the brain resulting in the "death" of brain tissue, specifically, infarction from hemorrhage, thrombolitic/embolitic, or rupturing aneurysm. Thrombolytic strokes are due to cerebral thrombosis often superimposed on a plaque of atherosclerosis with symptom onset ranging from minutes to days. Embolic strokes are due to cerebral embolism and usually have a sudden onset of symptoms reflecting abrupt loss of blood flow to the brain region of the occluded artery.

Epidemiology

- Stroke is the fourth leading cause of death in Canada. Each year, about 16,000 Canadians die from stroke; more women than men die from stroke.[1]
- Of people who have a stroke, 15% die; 10% recover completely; 25% recover with a minor impairment/disability; 40% have a moderate to severe impairment; 10% are so severely disabled they require long-term care.[2]

Risk Factors[3]

Unmodifiable

Age
- Over 2/3 of all strokes occur in people over 65 years; a woman's risk of having a stroke increases significantly after menopause.

Gender
- Men have a higher risk than women; however, as women tend to live longer than men and the risk of dying from stroke increases with age, each year more women than men die from stroke.

Ethnicity
- Aboriginal Canadians and people of African, Hispanic, South Asian, and Black descent have higher rates of high blood pressure and diabetes—conditions that can lead to stroke.
- New immigrants have lower rates initially, but as they adopt Canadian lifestyles, they develop increased rates of cardiovascular diseases.

Family History
- Risk of having a stroke is higher if a parent or sibling had a stroke before the age of 65.

Modifiable

Hypertension
- High blood pressure is the single most important modifiable risk factor for stroke. Evidence shows that 65% of all strokes are associated with HBP.

Diabetes Mellitus
- Diabetics have a two to four times greater risk of stroke than people without diabetes.

Smoking
- Men who smoke have a 40% greater chance of having a stroke than those who do not smoke. Women who smoke have a 60% greater chance of having a stroke compared to non-smoking women. Women who smoke and take the birth control pill have an even higher risk for stroke.

continues

Heart disease/Atrial fibrillation
- Coronary heart disease (e.g., angina or heart attack), valve disorders, heart rhythm disorders, and other heart diseases increase risk of stroke.
- About 6% of the population age 65 and older has atrial fibrillation; AF increases the risk that blood clots will form, possibly leading to stroke.

High blood cholesterol
- Elevated blood cholesterol contributes to the development of atherosclerotic plaque along the walls of the blood vessels.

Inactivity
- People who are physically inactive are at twice the risk for stroke.

Excessive alcohol consumption
- Heavy drinking, especially binge drinking, is associated with stroke.

Signs and symptoms [**] **(any one of the following can be significant)**
- Weakness, numbness, or paralysis
- Difficulty speaking or understanding
- Blurred vision or loss of vision
- Dizziness or loss of consciousness
- Sudden, severe headache

[**]**If a patient experiences any of these signs or symptoms he or she must seek prompt assessment.** The Canadian Alteplase for Stroke Effectiveness Study (CASES) has found that administration of tissue Plasminogen Activator (t-PA) is safe and effective in treating acute ischemic stroke. It must be administered within *three hours* of symptoms to be effective.[4]

EQUIPMENT

- Cotton wisp
- Cotton-tipped applicators
- Penlight
- Tongue blade
- Tuning fork: 128 Hz or 256 Hz
- Reflex hammer
- Sterile needle, either a 22-gauge needle or a sterile safety pin
- Familiar small objects (coins, key, paperclip)
- Vials containing odorous materials (coffee, orange extract, vinegar)
- Vials containing hot and cold water
- Vials with solutions for tasting: quinine (bitter), glucose solution (sweet), lemon or vinegar (sour), saline (salty)
- Snellen chart or Rosenbaum pocket screener
- Pupil gauge in millimetres

◄NURSING CHECKLIST►

General Approach to Neurological Assessment

1. Greet the patient and explain the assessment techniques that you will be using.
2. Maintain a quiet, unhurried, self-confident demeanour to help relieve any feelings of anxiety or discomfort, and to help the patient relax during the assessment.
3. Provide a warm, quiet, and well-lit environment.
4. After the mental status examination, instruct the patient to remove all street clothes, and provide an examination gown for the patient to put on.
5. Begin the assessment with the patient in a comfortable upright sitting position, or for the patient on bed rest, position the patient comfortably, preferably with the head of the bed elevated, or flat, whichever is tolerated best or is within activity orders for the patient.

ASSESSMENT OF THE NEUROLOGICAL SYSTEM

A complete neurological assessment includes an assessment of mental status, sensation, cranial nerves, motor function, cerebellar function, and reflexes. For patients with minor or intermittent symptoms, a rapid screening assessment may be used as outlined in Table 19-5.

Nursing Tip

Patient History and Mental Status Assessment

1. Begin your assessment as the patient approaches you. Observe gait, posture, mode of dress, involuntary movements, voice, and other features that will help guide and refine your assessment priorities.
2. The history should be holistic because neurological disorders can affect all body systems.
3. The history should be age-sensitive:
   - Use other family members when appropriate.
   - Acknowledge adolescents' ability to speak for themselves.
   - Do not make assumptions regarding elderly patients' ability to relate their own health histories.
4. Allow the patient to remain clothed during the history and mental status assessment.
5. Consider language and cultural norms when obtaining the history and performing the mental status assessment.

TABLE 19-5 Neurological Screening Assessment

ASSESSMENT PARAMETER	ASSESSMENT SKILL	COMMENTS
Mental status	Note general appearance, affect, speech content, memory, logic, judgment, and speech patterns during the history.	If any abnormalities or inconsistencies are evident, perform full mental status assessment.
	Perform Glasgow Coma Scale (GCS) with motor assessment component and pupil assessment.	If GCS <15, perform full assessment of mental status and consciousness. If motor assessment is abnormal or asymmetrical, perform complete motor and sensory assessment.
Sensation	Assess pain and vibration in the hands and feet, light touch on the limbs.	If deficits are identified, perform a complete sensory assessment.
Cranial nerves	Assess CN II, III, IV, VI: visual acuity, gross visual fields, funduscopic examination, pupillary reactions, and extra-ocular movements. Assess CN VII, VIII, IX, X, XII: facial expression, gross hearing, voice, and tongue.	If any abnormalities exist, perform complete assessment of all 12 cranial nerves.

continues

TABLE 19-5	Neurological Screening Assessment (*Continued*)	
Motor system	• Muscle tone and strength • Abnormal movements • Grasps	If deficits are noted, perform a complete motor system assessment.

Cerebellar function	Observe the patient's:
	1. Gait on arrival
	2. Ability to:
	  • Walk heel-to-toe
	  • Walk on toes
	  • Walk on heels
	  • Hop in place
	  • Perform shallow knee bends
	3. Check Romberg's test
	4. Finger-to-nose test
	5. Fine repetitive movements with hands
		If any abnormalities exist, perform complete cerebellar assessment.

Reflexes	Assess the deep tendon reflexes and the plantar reflex.	If an abnormal response is elicited, perform a complete reflex assessment.

Nursing Tip

Focusing the Mental Status Assessment

In most cases, the information obtained during the health history is sufficient to assess mental status. A more specific mental assessment should be performed if the following are noted:
• Known brain lesion (stroke, tumours, trauma)
• Suspected brain lesion (new seizures, headaches, behavioural changes)
• Memory deficits
• Confusion
• Vague behavioural complaints (by significant others if patient is unaware of or denies behavioural changes)
• Aphasia
• Irritability
• Emotional lability

Nursing Tip

Influences on Dress and Grooming

Dress and grooming are influenced by the patient's economic status, age, home situation, and ethnic background. Information obtained during the health history will assist you in determining appropriate dress and grooming for each patient. It is helpful to directly ask the patient about grooming routines and clothing choices when there is a question as to appropriateness.

Mental Status

Much of the mental status assessment should be done during the interview, with the patient comfortably positioned facing you. Mental status may also be assessed throughout the neurological assessment. Assess physical appearance and behaviour, communication, level of consciousness, cognitive abilities, and mentation while talking with the patient.

Physical Appearance and Behaviour

Posture and Movements

E 1. Observe the patient's ability to wait patiently.
   2. Note if patient's posture is relaxed, slumped, or stiff.
   3. Observe the patient's movements for control and symmetry.
   4. Observe the patient's gait (see Chapter 18).

N The patient should appear relaxed with the appropriate amount of concern for the assessment. The patient should exhibit erect posture, a smooth gait, and symmetrical body movements.

A Restlessness, tenseness, and pacing can be abnormal.

P These may be signs of anxiety or metabolic disorders, which should alert you to further investigate these problems.

A Slumped posture, slow gait, poor eye contact, and slow responses can be abnormal findings.

P These may be signs of depression.

A Stooped, flexed, or rigid posture, drooping neck, deformities of the spine, and tics are abnormal findings.

P Patients with kyphosis, scoliosis, Parkinson's disease, cerebral palsy, osteoporosis, schizophrenia, muscular atrophy, myasthenia gravis, or stroke may exhibit these signs.

Dress, Grooming, and Personal Hygiene

E 1. Note the appearance of the patient's clothing, specifically:
      a. Cleanliness
      b. Condition
      c. Age appropriateness
      d. Weather appropriateness
      e. Appropriateness for the patient's socioeconomic group
   2. Observe the patient's personal grooming (hair, skin, nails, teeth) for:
      a. Adequacy
      b. Symmetry
      c. Odour

N The patient should be clean and well groomed, and should wear appropriate clothing for age, weather, and socioeconomic status.

A Poor personal hygiene such as uncombed hair, body odour, or unkempt clothing is abnormal.

P These signs may be indications of depression, schizophrenia, or dementia.

A Excessive, meticulous care and attention to clothing and grooming are abnormal behaviours.

P These signs may indicate obsessive-compulsive behaviour.

A Obvious one-sided differences in grooming and dressing or the use of only one side of the body is abnormal.

P Stroke in the parietal lobe may cause the patient to be aware of only one side of the body, which is termed one-sided neglect.

| E | **Examination** | N | **Normal Findings** | A | **Abnormal Findings** | P | **Pathophysiology** |

Facial Expression

E Observe for appropriateness of, variations in, and symmetry of facial expressions.

N Facial expressions should be appropriate to the content of the conversation and should be symmetrical.

A Extreme, inappropriate, or unchanging facial expressions, or asymmetrical facial movements are abnormal.

P Abnormal facial expressions demonstrate anxiety, depression, or the unchanging facial expression of a patient with Parkinson's disease. They may also indicate a lesion in the facial nerve (CN VII).

Affect

E 1. Observe the patient's interaction with you, paying particular attention to both verbal and non-verbal behaviours.
     2. Note if the patient's affect appears labile, blunted, or flat.
     3. Note the variations in the patient's affect with a variety of topics.
     4. Note any extreme emotional responses during the interview.

N The appropriateness and degree of affect should vary with the topics and the patient's cultural norms, and be reasonable, or eurhythmic (normal).

A Blunted affect, manifested by the patient shuffling into the examination room, slumping into a chair, moving slowly and not making eye contact, is abnormal.

P A blunted affect may indicate depression.

A Unresponsive, inappropriate affect is abnormal.

P A flat, unresponsive affect may indicate depression or schizophrenia.

A Anger, hostility, and paranoia are abnormal responses in most clinical situations.

P These may be the responses of a paranoid schizophrenic individual.

A Euphoric, dramatic, disruptive, irrational, or elated behaviours are abnormal in most clinical situations.

P A manic-depressive patient might display these responses during the manic phase.

Communication

Communication skills should be assessed throughout the entire interview and physical assessment.

E 1. Note voice quality, which includes voice volume and pitch.
     2. Assess articulation, fluency, and rate of speech by engaging the patient in normal conversation. Ask the patient to repeat words and sentences after you or to name objects you point out.
     3. Note the patient's ability to carry out requests during the assessment, such as pointing to objects within the room as requested. Ask questions that require "yes" and "no" responses.
     4. Write simple commands for the patient to read and perform, for example "point to your nose" or "tap your right foot." Reading ability may be influenced by the patient's educational level or visual impairment.
     5. Ask the patient to write the name, birthday, a sentence the patient composes, or a sentence that you dictate. Note the patient's spelling, grammatical accuracy, and logical thought process.

N The patient should be able to produce spontaneous, coherent speech. The speech should have an effortless flow with normal inflections, volume, pitch, articulation, rate, and rhythm. Content of the message should make sense. Comprehension of language should be intact. The patient's ability to read and write should match the patient's educational level. Non-native speakers may exhibit some hesitancy or inaccuracy in written and spoken language.

A **Aphasia**, an impairment of language functioning, is abnormal.

P Aphasias are classified by involved anatomy, behavioural speech manifestations, fluency of speech (fluent: rhythm, grammar, and articulation are normal; non-fluent: speech production is limited and speech is poorly articulated), and comprehension (receptive) versus expression (expressive) deficits. Other categories include amnesic, inability to recall specific types of words, and central, a deficit in the coordination among the speech areas. See Table 19-6 for a summary of the characteristics and pathophysiology of

---

Nursing Tip

Handedness

Note handedness prior to language testing. Handedness and cerebral dominance for language are closely allied. Patients with dominant hemisphere lesions will frequently show communication abnormalities, for example, aphasia in the right-handed individual almost always indicates left-hemisphere pathology.

TABLE 19-6 Classification of Aphasias

APHASIA	PATHOPHYSIOLOGY	EXPRESSION	CHARACTERISTICS
Broca's aphasia	Motor cortex lesion, Broca's area	Expressive Nonfluent	Speech slow and hesitant, the patient has difficulty in selecting and organizing words. Naming, word and phrase repetition, and writing impaired. Subtle defects in comprehension.
Wernicke's aphasia	Left hemisphere lesion in Wernicke's area	Receptive Fluent	Auditory comprehension impaired, as is content of speech. Patient unaware of deficits. Naming severely impaired.
Anomic aphasia	Left hemisphere lesion in Wernicke's area	Amnesic Fluent	Patient unable to name objects or places. Comprehension and repetition of words and phrases intact.
Conduction aphasia	Lesion in the arcuate fasciculus, which connects and transports messages between Broca's and Wernicke's areas	Central Fluent	Patient has difficulty repeating words, substitutes incorrect sounds for another (e.g., *dork* for *fork*).
Global aphasia	Lesions in the frontal-temporal area	Mixed Fluent	Both oral and written comprehension severely impaired; naming, repetition of words and phrases, ability to write impaired.
Transcortical sensory aphasia	Lesion in the periphery of Broca's and Wernicke's areas (watershed zone)	Fluent	Impairment in comprehension, naming, and writing. Word and phrase repetition intact.
Transcortical motor aphasia	Lesion anterior, superior, or lateral to Broca's area	Nonfluent	Comprehension intact. Naming and ability to write impaired. Word and phrase repetition intact.

E	**Examination**	N	**Normal Findings**	A	**Abnormal Findings**	P	**Pathophysiology**

Nursing Alert

The Patient with Dysphonia

Patients with signs of dysphonia (impaired laryngeal speech) are at high risk for dysphagia (difficulty with swallowing) and therefore aspiration. A thorough assessment of swallowing is warranted before the patient may eat unassisted.

Nursing Alert

The Confused Patient

The confused patient should be thoroughly assessed for aphasia. A missed diagnosis because of "confusion" can be fatal if aphasia is present and due to a subdural hematoma. Check for other signs associated with a subdural hematoma, including headache, slow cerebration, decreasing level of consciousness, and ipsilateral pupil dilatation with a sluggish response to light.

Nursing Tip

Application of Painful Stimuli

1. Application of painful stimuli is extremely upsetting to family members and therefore should not be performed in their presence or without a comprehensive explanation.
2. Apply only the amount of pressure needed to elicit a response.
3. Alternate sites when possible.
4. Pain applied centrally (e.g., trapezius muscle squeeze) that results in a response always indicates involvement of the cerebrum. Pain applied to an extremity (e.g., pen pressure on a nailbed) may elicit a reflex response or cerebral response, or both. Great care is needed when interpreting the significance of response to pain with patients in profound coma.

specific aphasias. Most patients with an aphasia will have some components of several aphasia classifications (e.g., transcortical motor aphasia will usually have some degree of transcortical sensory aphasia).

A   **Dysarthria**, a disturbance in muscular control of speech, is abnormal.

P   Dysarthria is due to ischemia affecting motor nuclei of CN X and CN XII; defects in the premotor or motor cortex that provide motor input for the face, throat, and mouth; or cerebellar disease.

A   **Dysphonia**, difficulty making laryngeal sounds, is abnormal and can progress to **aphonia** (total loss of voice).

P   Dysphonia is usually caused by lesions of CN X or swelling and inflammation of the larynx.

A   **Apraxia**, the inability to convert the intended speech into the motor act of speech, is abnormal.

P   Apraxia is due to dysfunction in the precentral gyrus of the frontal lobe.

A   **Agraphia**, the loss of the ability to write, is abnormal.

P Agraphia is caused by lesions of Broca's and Wernicke's areas in the dominant side of the brain.

A **Alexia**, the inability to grasp the meaning of written words and sentences (word blindness), is abnormal.

P Alexia is usually due to a lesion of the angular gyrus and the occipital lobe.

Level of Consciousness (LOC)

Consciousness is the level of awareness of the self and the environment. Conscious behaviour requires arousal, or wakefulness, and awareness, or cognition and affect. Arousal is controlled by the reticular activating system (RAS). The RAS activates the cortex after receiving stimuli from the somatic and special sensory pathways. Awareness is a higher-level function of the cerebral cortex, which interprets incoming sensory stimuli. Aspects of awareness at a higher level include judgment and thinking, which are generally assessed as part of the cognitive assessment. Orientation is awareness of self and environment.

E **1.** Observe the patient's eyes when entering the room (environmental stimuli). Note whether the patient's eyes are open or whether they open when you enter the room (prior to any verbalization). Note the patient's response to any general environmental stimuli, such as noises or lights.

2. If the patient's eyes are closed, call out the patient's name (verbal stimuli). Observe whether the patient's eyes open, whether he responds verbally and appropriately, and whether he follows verbal commands.

3. If the patient does not respond to verbal stimuli, lightly touch the patient's hand or gently shake the patient awake.

4. If the patient is not responding to environmental or verbal stimuli, proceed to the application of a painful stimulus.
  a. Apply pressure with a pen to the nailbed of each extremity, or
  b. Firmly pinch the trapezius muscle, or
  c. Apply pressure to the supraorbital ridge or the manubrium.

5. Observe the patient's reaction to the painful stimulus. Note whether the patient's eyes open.

6. Observe whether the patient can localize the painful stimulus by reaching for the area being stimulated. Strength of the patient's extremities can be assessed by the strength and distance of movement during his attempt to reach the painful stimulus. Note any abnormal motor responses.

7. Compare the motor responses and strength of the responses of right versus left sides of the patient.

8. Note whether the patient responds verbally to the painful stimulus.

9. Assess orientation by asking questions related to person, place, and time:
  a. Person: name of the patient, name of spouse or significant other
  b. Place: where the patient is now (what town, what province), where the patient lives
  c. Time: the time of day, month, year, season

10. Determine the **Glasgow Coma Scale** (GCS) (Figure 19-9) score, an international method for grading neurological responses of the injured or severely ill patient. It is monitored in patients who have the potential for rapid deterioration in level of consciousness. The GCS assesses three parameters of consciousness: eye opening, verbal response, and motor response.

E	Examination	N	Normal Findings	A	Abnormal Findings	P	Pathophysiology

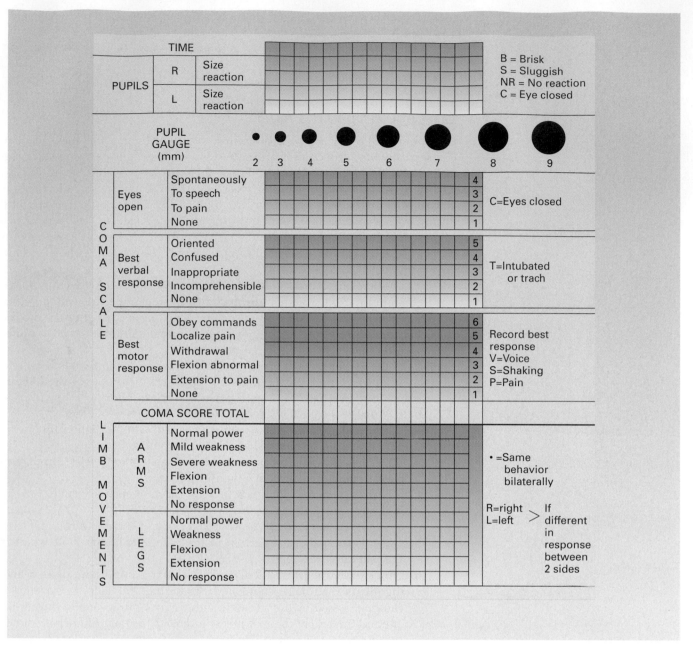

Figure 19-9 Neurological Flow Sheet, including Glasgow Coma Scale.

Nursing Alert

Airway Protection

Patients with altered LOC may be unable to protect their airways. A complete airway assessment is required to determine the need for intubation.

N The patient's best response to each of these categories is recorded. The sum of the three categories is the total GCS score. The highest score of responsiveness is 15 and the lowest is 3. A score of 15 would indicate a fully alert, oriented individual.

A/P See Table 19-7.

Cognitive Abilities and Mentation

Assessment of cognitive function includes testing for attention, memory, judgment, insight, spatial perception, calculation, abstraction, thought processes, and thought content.

| E | Examination | N | Normal Findings | A | Abnormal Findings | P | Pathophysiology |

TABLE 19-7 Levels of Consciousness: Abnormalities and Pathophysiology

LOC	GCS	RESPONSE TO STIMULI	PUPIL RESPONSE	PATHOPHYSIOLOGY	PROGNOSIS
Confusion	14	Spontaneous but may be inappropriate Memory faulty Reflexes intact	Normal	Metabolic derangements Diffuse brain dysfunction	Good chance of recovery Must treat primary cause
Lethargy	13–14	Requires stimulus to respond (verbal, touch) Reflexes intact	Normal to unequal	Metabolic derangements Medications Increased ICP	Good chance of recovery Must treat primary cause
Stupor	12–13	Requires vigorous, continuous stimuli to respond Reflexes intact	Normal, unequal, or sluggish	Metabolic derangements Medications Increased ICP	Good chance of recovery Must treat primary cause
Permanent vegetative state	8–10	Responds to pain No cognitive response Reflexes abnormal	Normal	Anoxic ischemic insults	Irreversible
Locked-in syndrome	6	Awake and aware	Normal	Lesion in ventral pons All four extremities and lower cranial nerves paralyzed Myasthenia gravis Acute polyneuritis	Poor prognosis
Coma	3–6	Abnormal Varied response to pain Reflexes abnormal or absent	Abnormal Dilated or pinpoint	Anoxia Traumatic injury Space-occupying lesion Cerebral edema	Prognosis dependent on length of time in coma
Brain death	3	No response Reflexes abnormal or absent	Abnormal Dilated or pinpoint	Anoxia Structural damage	Irreversible

LOC = level of consciousness; GCS = Glasgow Coma Scale; ICP = intracranial pressure.

◄NURSING CHECKLIST►

Assessment of Cognitive Function

You should have on hand:
- Preprinted lists of objects, phrases, and numbers for patient recall and explanation
- Answers to long-term memory questions to accurately assess recall
- Alternate tests prepared for patients with language barriers, aphasia, deafness, blindness, etc.
- Paper and pencils for patient to use to respond

Nursing Tip

Cognitive Mental Status Screening

The Mini Mental State Exam (MMSE) is a tool for assessing cognitive mental status, detecting impairment, following the course of an illness, and monitoring response to treatment. The MMSE is most useful in screening for the cognitive deficits seen in syndromes of dementia and delirium.

The MMSE contains 11 cognitive tasks and takes five to ten minutes to administer. Orientation to time and place, immediate and short-term memory recall, serial 7s, reading, writing, drawing, and verbal/motor comprehension compose the bulk of the examination. The maximum score on the MMSE is 30, and scores greater than 24 are considered within the normal range. Patients with scores less than 24 require a more detailed neuropsychological evaluation.

Sample items from the MMSE include:

Time Orientation: "What is the date?"

Registration: "Listen carefully. I am going to say three words. You say them back after I stop. Ready? Here they are . . . APPLE (pause), PENNY (pause),

(continues)

TABLE (pause). Now repeat those words back to me." [Repeat up to 5 times, but score only the first trial.]

Naming: "What is this?" [Point to a pencil or pen.]

Reading: "Please read this and do what it says." [Show examinee the words on the stimulus form.] CLOSE YOUR EYES

Attention

E 1. Pronounce a list of numbers slowly (approximately one second apart), starting with a list of two numbers and progressing to a series of five or six numbers. For example: 2, 5; 3, 7, 8; 1, 9, 4, 3; 1, 5, 4, 9, 0.

2. Ask the patient to repeat the numbers in correct order, both forward and backward.

3. Give the patient a different series of the same number of digits if the patient is unable to repeat the first series correctly. Stop after two misses of any length series.

4. Serial 7s is another way of assessing attention and concentration. Instruct the patient to begin with the number 100 and to count backward by subtracting 7 each time: 100, 93, 86, 79, 72, 65, etc.

5. The patient may also try serial 3s (counting backward from 100 by threes) if unable to perform serial 7s.

N The patient should be able to correctly repeat the series of numbers up to a series of five numbers. The patient should be able to recite serial 7s or serial 3s accurately to at least the 40s or 50s from 100 within one minute.

A If the patient has a short attention span, the patient will not be able to repeat the numbers in sequence or perform serial 7s or 3s.

P Dementia, neurological injury or disease, and mental retardation may impair attention.

Memory

E 1. Assess immediate recall in conjunction with attention span as discussed previously.

2. Give a list of three items that the patient is to remember and repeat in five minutes. Have the patient repeat the items to check initial understanding. During the five minutes, carry on conversation as usual. Ask the patient to repeat the items again after the five-minute time frame.

3. If the patient is unable to remember one or more of the objects, show a list containing the objects along with others, and check recognition.

4. Record the number of objects remembered over the number of objects given.

5. Long-term memory is memory that is retained for at least 24 hours. Commonly asked questions for testing long-term memory include name of spouse, spouse's birthday, mother's maiden name, name of the prime minister, or the patient's birthday.

N The patient should be able to correctly respond to questions and identify all the objects as requested.

A Memory loss is abnormal.

P Memory loss may be caused by pathologies such as nervous system infection, trauma, stroke, tumours, Alzheimer's disease, seizure disorders, alcohol, and drug toxicity. Memory is located in the temporal lobe and the hippocampus. Damage to these areas, in the form of hemorrhage, ischemia, compression, or herniation, will cause memory impairment.

Judgment

E 1. During the interview, assess whether the patient is responding appropriately to social, family, and work situations that are discussed.

2. Note whether the patient's decisions are based on sound reasoning and decision making.

3. Present hypothetical situations and ask the patient to make decisions as to what his or her responses would be. For example: "What would you do if followed by a police car with flashing lights?" or "What would you do if you saw a house burning?"

4. Interview the patient's family or directly observe the patient to assess judgment more carefully.

N The patient should be able to evaluate and act appropriately in situations requiring judgment.

A Impaired judgment, the inability to act appropriately in situations, is abnormal.

P Frontal lobe damage, dementia, psychotic states, and mental retardation may cause the patient to exhibit lack of appropriate judgment.

Insight

Insight is the ability to realistically understand oneself.

E 1. Ask the patient to describe personal health status, reason for seeking health care, symptoms, current life situation, and general coping behaviours.

2. If the patient describes symptoms, ask what life was like prior to the appearance of the symptoms, what life changes the illness has introduced, and whether the patient feels a need for help.

3. Ask the patient to draw a self-portrait; note the emphasis put on specific body parts, the patient's ability to reproduce figures on paper, and the representation of any part of the self-portrait. Note the facial features and the feelings portrayed by the picture.

N The patient should demonstrate a realistic awareness and understanding of self.

A Unrealistic perceptions of self are abnormal.

P Lack of insight may occur in the euphoric stages of bipolar affective disorders, endogenous anxiety states, or depressed states.

Spatial Perception

Spatial perception is the ability to recognize the relationships of objects in space.

E 1. Ask the patient to copy figures that you have previously drawn, such as a circle, triangle, square, cross, and a three-dimensional cube.

2. Ask the patient to draw the face of a clock, including the numbers around the dial.

3. Ask the patient to identify a familiar sound while keeping the eyes closed, for example, a closing door, running water, or a finger snap.

4. Have the patient identify right from left body parts.

N The patient should be able to draw the objects without difficulty and as closely as possible to the original drawing, and to identify familiar sounds and left and right body parts.

A **Agnosia**, the inability to recognize the form and nature of objects or persons, is abnormal. It may be visual, auditory, or somatosensory. For example, the patient may be unable to name or recognize objects, faces, or familiar objects by touch, or to identify the meaning of non-verbal sounds.

| E | **Examination** | N | **Normal Findings** | A | **Abnormal Findings** | P | **Pathophysiology** |

Diamond   Patient's drawing

Figure 19-10 Constructional Apraxia.

P Lesions in the non-dominant parietal lobe impair the patient's ability to appreciate self in relation to the environment and to conceive three-dimensional objects. Lesions in the occipital lobe will cause visual agnosia, and temporal lesions will cause auditory agnosia.

A Apraxia, the inability to perform purposeful movements despite the preservation of motor ability and sensation, is abnormal. **Constructional apraxia** is the inability to reproduce figures on paper (Figure 19-10).

P Apraxia is usually associated with lesions of the precentral gyrus of the frontal lobe.

Calculation

The patient's ability to perform serial 7s was discussed in the section on attention and is also an assessment of calculation.

E 1. Ask the patient to add 3 to 100, then 3 to that number, until numbers greater than 150 are reached.
   2. Note the amount of time and difficulty associated with the calculations.

N The patient should be able to calculate the correct numbers upon subtraction or addition within educational abilities and with fewer than four errors in less than 1 1/2 minutes.

A **Dyscalculia**, the inability to perform calculations, is abnormal.

P Dyscalculia may be caused by depression or anxiety, dementia, or mental retardation. The most common cause of dyscalculia is focal lesions in the dominant parietal lobe; however, calculation deficits have also been ascribed to focal lesions in the frontal, temporal, and occipital lobes.

Nursing Tip

Proverbs from Different Origins

Afghan	Hach guli ba char mast.	No rose is without thorns.
Chinese	老子	Give a man a fish and you feed him for a day. Teach him how to fish and you feed him for a lifetime.
French	C'est la goutte d'eau qui fait déborder le vase.	It's the drop of water that makes the vase overflow.
Italian	Non giudicare un libro dalla relativa copertura.	Don't judge a book by its cover.
Japanese	七転び八起き (Nana-korobi ya-oki.)	Literal: Fall down seven times, get up eight. English proverb equivalent: If at first you don't succeed, try, try again.
Romanian	Pãcatul mãrturisit este pe jumãtate iertat.	A fault confessed is half redressed.
Swahili	Atakae hachoki.	A person in need never gets tired.

Visit http://en.wikipedia.org/wiki/List_of_English_proverbs for proverbs from many other origins.

Abstract Reasoning

E **1.** Ask the patient to describe the meaning of a familiar fable, proverb, or metaphor. Use examples that are meaningful within the context of the patient's culture and language. Some examples from dominant Canadian culture are below; see Nursing Tip: Proverbs from Different Cultural Backgrounds for more ideas.
- The squeaky wheel gets the grease.
- A stitch in time saves nine.
- It's easier said than done.
- Don't count your chickens before they hatch.

    2. Note the degree of concreteness versus abstraction in the answers.

N **Patients should be able to give the abstract meanings of proverbs, fables, or metaphors within their cultural understanding.**

A Conceptual concreteness—the inability to describe in abstractions, to generalize from specifics, and to apply general principles—is abnormal.

P Alterations of cognitive processes causing concreteness in thought may occur in patients with dementia, frontal tumours, or schizophrenia. Concreteness in thought processes may also indicate low intelligence.

Thought Process and Content

E **1.** Observe the patient's pattern of thought for relevance, consistency, coherence, logic, and organization.

    2. Listen throughout the interview for flaws in content of conversation.

N **Thought processes should be logical, coherent, and goal oriented. Thought content should be based on reality.**

A Unrealistic, illogical thought processes and interruptions of the thinking processes, such as blocking, are abnormal. Blocking is demonstrated when an extended pause occurs during a sentence due to repressed subject matter. Sometimes, the thoughts following are unrelated to what the patient was discussing.

P Abnormal thought processes are often due to schizophrenia.

A Flight of ideas, demonstrated when the patient changes from subject to subject within a sentence, is abnormal. This is frequently due to distractions or word associations with a resultant lack of sense of purpose of the conversation.

P Patients suffering from manic episodes of bipolar affective disorder often demonstrate flight of ideas.

A **Confabulation**, the making up of answers unrelated to facts, is abnormal.

P Confabulation is often related to aging, memory loss, disorientation, Korsakoff's psychosis, and psychopathic disorders.

A **Echolalia**, the involuntary repetition of a word or sentence that was uttered by another person, is abnormal.

P Schizophrenics and patients suffering from dementia often demonstrate echolalia.

A **Neologism**, a word coined by the patient that is meaningful only to the patient, is an abnormal finding.

P Patients who are delirious or schizophrenic may exhibit neologism.

A Delusions of persecution, grandiose delusions, hallucinations, illusions, obsessive-compulsiveness, and paranoia are examples of abnormal thoughts.

P Abnormal thought content is demonstrated in patients suffering from schizophrenia or dementia and may be the result of drug toxicities or adverse effects of certain medications.

| E | Examination | N | Normal Findings | A | Abnormal Findings | P | Pathophysiology |

Nursing Alert

Suicide—Epidemiology

- The suicide rate among Canadian men and women is 19.5 and 5.1/100,000 respectively, among the highest in the industrialized world.[5]
- While suicide rates have dropped or remained stable in most regions of Canada, the rate is increasing in Quebec and in Aboriginal peoples.[6]
- The Aboriginal suicide rate is two to three times higher than the non-Aboriginal rate for Canada,[7] and within the youth age group, the suicide rate of Aboriginal youth is five to six times higher, and in the Inuit youth, 11 times higher than the national average.[8]
- Unfortunately, suicide is the second leading cause of death in youth aged 10 to 24 (following motor vehicle accidents).
- Immigrants, especially those who move into tight-knit immigrant communities in large urban centres like Montreal, Vancouver, and Toronto, are much less likely to suicide than native-born Canadians, with approximately half the suicide rate.[9]
- Suicide rates among male Canadian farm operators are generally lower than in other Canadian men. It is hypothesized that social support traditionally available in Canadian farm communities may serve a protective function.[10]

Risk Factors for Suicide

- Male (more successful suicides)
- Female (more suicide attempts)
- Aboriginal teens and gay and lesbian teens may be at particularly high risk, depending on the community they live in and their self-esteem
- Prior suicide attempts
- Family member with attempt history
- Drug abuse
- Mental illness (especially those with command hallucinations or delusions of grandeur)
- Unwillingness to seek help because of stigma
- Barriers to accessing mental health treatment
- Stressful life events or loss
- Feeling isolated and hopeless
- Easy access to lethal methods such as guns
- Suicidal ideation with or without a plan

Nursing Alert

The Older Adult—Delirium, Dementia, and Depression

According to the RNAO Best Practices Guidelines[11]
- Nurses should maintain a high index of suspicion for delirium, dementia, and depression in the older adult.
- Delirium, dementia, and depression present with overlapping clinical features and may co-exist in the older adult.
- Cognitive changes should be assessed objectively using one or more standardized tools in order to substantiate clinical observations.
- If you determine the patient is exhibiting features of delirium, dementia, and/or depression, make a referral for a medical diagnosis to specialized geriatric services, specialized geriatric psychiatry services, neurologists, and/or members of the multidisciplinary team, as indicated by screening findings.
- Table 19-8 compares and contrasts the various clinical parameters that distinguish dementia, depression, delirium, and acute confusion.

TABLE 19-8 Distinguishing Dementia, Depression, Delirium, and Acute Confusion

PARAMETER	DEMENTIA	DEPRESSION	DELIRIUM	ACUTE CONFUSION
Definition	Deterioration of all cognitive function with little or no disturbance of consciousness or perception Onset: gradual	An abnormal emotional state characterized by feelings of sadness, despair, and discouragement Onset: variable	A disorder of perception with heightened awareness, hallucinations, vivid dreams, and intense emotional disturbances Onset: sudden	An inability to think with customary speed, clarity, and coherence Onset: variable
Pathophysiology	Alzheimer's disease Metabolic disorders Stroke Head injury	Inherited: neurochemical abnormalities Situational: acute loss of significant person CVA Parkinson's disease Alzheimer's disease Medications (e.g., steroids)	Withdrawal from alcohol and other drugs Drug intoxications Encephalitis Traumatic injury Febrile states Hypoxia Fluid and electrolyte imbalance	Metabolic disorders Drug intoxication Traumatic injury Febrile states
Attention	Impaired	Intact	Impaired: heightened or dulled	Impaired: dulled
Memory	Short term: impaired first Long term: intact for awhile	Intact	Short term: impaired Long term: intact	Short term: impaired Long term: may be intact
Judgment	Impaired	Intact	Grossly impaired Impulsive Volatile	Impaired
Insight	Impaired	Impaired if in manic phase	Impaired	Impaired
Spatial perception	Impaired	Intact	Intact	May be impaired
Calculation	Impaired	May be intact	May be intact	Impaired
Abstract reasoning	Impaired	Intact	Impaired	Impaired
Thought process and content	Impaired	Intact but may demonstrate flight of ideas	Impaired, hallucinations present	Impaired, incoherent

CVA = *cerebrovascular accident.*

Nursing Alert

Alzheimer's Disease

Alzheimer's disease is a progressive, degenerative disease. Many Canadians inaccurately associate this disease with "normal aging" and may even joke at memory lapses saying "I have Alzheimer's—or 'old timers' disease." People may even delay seeking assessment as they view changes as normal. On the other hand, many Canadians will worry that any lapse in memory or change in memory might be Alzheimer's. The Alzheimer Society of Canada has developed a list of ten warning signs so Canadians can make better health care decisions:

Alzheimer's Disease: Ten Warning Signs

1. **Memory loss that affects day-to-day function**

   It's normal to occasionally forget appointments, colleagues' names, or a friend's phone number and remember them later. A person with Alzheimer's disease may forget things more often and not remember them later, especially things that have happened more recently.

2. **Difficulty performing familiar tasks**

   Busy people can be so distracted from time to time that they may leave the carrots on the stove and only remember to serve them at the end of a meal. A person with Alzheimer's disease may have trouble with tasks that have been familiar to them all their lives, such as preparing a meal.

3. **Problems with language**

   Everyone has trouble finding the right word sometimes, but a person with Alzheimer's disease may forget simple words or substitute words, making her sentences difficult to understand.

4. **Disorientation of time and place**

   It's normal to forget the day of the week or your destination—for a moment. But a person with Alzheimer's disease can become lost on their own street, not knowing how they got there or how to get home.

5. **Poor or decreased judgment**

   People may sometimes put off going to a doctor if they have an infection, but eventually seek medical attention. A person with Alzheimer's disease may have decreased judgment, for example, not recognizing a medical problem that needs attention or wearing heavy clothing on a hot day.

6. **Problems with abstract thinking**

   From time to time, people may have difficulty with tasks that require abstract thinking, such as balancing a cheque book. Someone with Alzheimer's disease may have significant difficulties with such tasks, for example, not recognizing what the numbers in the cheque book mean.

7. **Misplacing things**

   Anyone can temporarily misplace a wallet or keys. A person with Alzheimer's disease may put things in inappropriate places: an iron in the freezer or a wristwatch in the sugar bowl.

continues

8. **Changes in mood and behaviour**

Everyone becomes sad or moody from time to time. Someone with Alzheimer's disease can exhibit varied mood swings—from calm to tears to anger—for no apparent reason.

9. **Changes in personality**

People's personalities can change somewhat with age. But a person with Alzheimer's disease can become confused, suspicious or withdrawn. Changes may also include apathy, fearfulness, or acting out of character.

10. **Loss of initiative**

It's normal to tire of housework, business activities, or social obligations, but most people regain their initiative. A person with Alzheimer's disease may become very passive, and require cues and prompting to become involved.

Source: http://www.alzheimer.ca/english/disease/warningsigns.htm. Used with permission of the Alzheimer Society of Canada.

Nursing Tip

Depression Acronym

An easy way to remember the symptoms of clinical depression is to use the acronym "IN SAD CAGES."

IN Interest (loss of pleasure)
S   Sleep disturbance
A   Appetite change (increases or decreases)
D   Depressed mood
C   Concentration difficulties
A   Activity level (retardation or agitation)
G   Guilt feelings (low self-esteem)
E   Energy loss (fatigue)
S   Suicidal ideation

Suicidal Ideation

E If the patient has expressed feelings of sadness, hopelessness, despair, worthlessness, or grief, explore his or her feelings further with more specific questions such as:

1. Have you ever felt so bad that you wanted to hurt yourself?
2. Do you feel like hurting yourself now?

N **The patient should provide a negative response and be able to verbalize his or her self-worth.**

A An affirmative response is abnormal and requires probing such as:
- Do you have a plan to hurt yourself?
- What would happen if you were dead?

Continued affirmative responses and expressions of worthlessness and hopelessness should be interpreted as suicidal ideation, a psychiatric emergency that requires immediate referral to a specialist.

P Suicidal ideation is associated with mental disorders, particularly depression, substance abuse, and schizophrenia.

E	**Examination**	N	**Normal Findings**	A	**Abnormal Findings**	P	**Pathophysiology**

Mental Illness

Mental illness touches the lives of all Canadians. Approximately 20% of Canadians will experience a mental illness in their lifetime with the remainder likely to be touched by mental illness in family members or friends.[12] Findings during the cognitive functioning examination may indicate the need for further screening. Table 19-9 summarizes findings common to mental illness that may lead the practitioner to refer the patient for further diagnostic study.

TABLE 19-9 Mental Illnesses

DISORDER (excludes addictions)	DEFINING CHARACTERISTICS	POPULATION CHARACTERISTICS
Anxiety Disorders • Panic • Phobias • Generalized anxiety disorder • Obsessive-compulsive disorder • Acute and posttraumatic stress disorders	A group of conditions that share extreme or pathological anxiety as the principal disturbance of mood or emotional tone.	• Common across cultures • Affects 12% of Canadians • Early age onset • Relapsing or recurrent episodes • Periods of disability • Significant overlap with mood and substance abuse disorders
Panic Disorder • Panic attack • Panic disorder	Repeated and unexpected attacks of intense fear and anxiety accompanied by physiological manifestations such as palpitations, chest pain, smothering or choking, dizziness, sweating, nausea or abdominal distress, trembling or hot flushes or chills.	• 1.3% of Canadians • Twice as common in women as men • Onset most common between adolescence and mid-adult life • Significant overlap with mood, substance abuse, and panic disorders
Phobias • Agoraphobia • Social phobia • Specific phobias	Marked fear of specific objects or situations.	• Experienced by approximately 8% of the population • Typically begin in childhood • There is a second peak in the middle 20s of adulthood
Generalized Anxiety Disorder	Protracted period of anxiety and worry accompanied by multiple associated physical and cognitive symptoms.	• Approximately 6% of Canadians • Twice as common in women as men • Half of cases begin in childhood or adolescence • Symptoms increase with life stress or difficulties
Obsessive-Compulsive Disorder	Obsessions are recurrent, intrusive thoughts, impulses, or images that are perceived as inappropriate, grotesque, or forbidden. Compulsions are repetitive behaviours or mental acts that reduce the anxiety that accompanies an obsession.	• 0.8% Canadians • Equally common among the sexes • Begins in adolescence to young adult life in males • Female onset typically is young adult life • Familial pattern • Strongly associated with Tourette's disorder • Significant overlap with other anxiety disorders and major depressive disorder

continues

TABLE 19-9 Mental Illnesses *Continued*

Acute and Posttraumatic Stress Disorders	Acute: The anxiety and behavioral disturbances that develop within the first month after exposure to an extreme trauma. If the symptoms persist for more than one month and are associated with functional impairment the diagnosis is changed to posttraumatic stress disorder. Symptoms in relation to the event include: At least one of: intrusive thoughts or images, dreams or nightmares, flashbacks or illusions, distress when reminded of the event, physical arousal when reminded of the event; At least three of: avoidance of thoughts or talk about the event, avoidance of activities or people that are reminders, inability to recall important aspects of event, emotional detachment from others, restricted emotions, sense of foreshortened future (fear of the future or death in the future); and At least two of: insomnia, irritability or anger, difficulty concentrating, hypervigilance (always on guard), exaggerated startle response.	• Twice as prevalent in females as males • Develop in approximately 9% of those exposed to extreme trauma such as rape, physical assault, near-death experience, witnessing murder and combat • Current estimates indicate that up to 40% of Canada's returning peacekeepers will experience some form of PTSD[13]
Mood Disorders • Major depressive disorder • Dysthymia • Bipolar disorder • Cyclothymia	A cluster of mental disorders best recognized by depression or mania.	• Rank among the top ten causes of worldwide disability • More prevalent in women • Leading cause of absenteeism and diminished productivity at work • Common comorbidities include anxiety disorder, personality disorders, and chronic medical conditions • May be caused by: – Dominant hemispheric strokes – Hyperthyroidism – Cushing's disease – Pancreatic cancer – Antihypertensives – Oral contraceptives – Alcohol withdrawal
Major Depressive Disorder	Five or more of the following symptoms have been present for the same two-week period and represent a change from previous functioning; at least one symptom is either depressed mood or loss of interest or pleasure: • Depressed mood • Loss of interest or pleasure • Significant weight loss when not dieting • Insomnia or hypersomnia • Psychomotor agitation or retardation • Fatigue or loss of energy • Feeling of worthlessness	• Approximately 8% of Canadian adults will experience major depression at some time in their lives • More common among women • Most severe depressions more common among the elderly • At least 50% will recur

continues

TABLE 19-9 Mental Illnesses *Continued*

	• Diminished ability to think or concentrate; indecisiveness • Recurrent thoughts of death or suicidal ideation	
Dysthymia	A chronic form of depression, symptoms are constant for a 2-year period (1 year for children).	• Twice as many women as men are diagnosed • Affects about 2% of adults each year • If onset is childhood, associated strongly with subsequent substance abuse • Susceptible to major depression episode superimposed on dysthymia
Bipolar Disorder • Type I (prior mania) • Type II (prior hypomanic episodes only)	Recurrent mood disorder featuring one or more episodes of mania or mixed episodes of mania and depression.	• Equally common in men and women • Affects about 1–2% of adult Canadian population
Cyclothymia	Manic and depressive states of insufficient intensity or duration to merit a diagnosis of bipolar disorder or major depressive disorder.	• 33% higher risk than general population to develop bipolar disorder
Schizophrenia	Profound disruption in cognition and emotion. Two or more of the following symptoms persist for a significant portion of a time during a 1-month period: – Delusions – Hallucinations – Disorganized speech – Grossly disorganized or catatonic behaviour – Negative symptoms: affective flattening, alogia (inability to express oneself through speech), or avolition (lack of motivation for work or other goal-directed activity)	• Affects 1% of Canadians • Onset during young adulthood • Women experience later onset than men • Associated with significantly higher mortality rate than the general population • Suicide • Comorbid medical illness: visual and dental problems, hypertension, diabetes, and sexually transmitted infections

Source: Information condensed from Health Canada (2002), A report on mental illnesses in Canada, Ottawa;[14] Statistics Canada (2003), Canadian community health survey mental health and well-being;[15] U.S. Department of Health and Human Services, Substance Abuse and Mental Health Services Administration, Center for Mental Health Services, National Institutes of Health, National Institute of Mental Health, 1999, A report of the Surgeon General, Rockville, MD.

◄NURSING CHECKLIST►

Assessing Sensation

1. Explain the procedure to the patient before starting the assessment.
2. The sensory assessment is carried out with the patient's eyes closed.
3. For a thorough sensory examination, the patient should be in a supine position.
4. The patient should be cooperative and reliable, although the pain assessment may be performed on comatose patients.
5. Note the patient's ability to perceive the sensation.

continues

6. Much of the sensory component of the neurological assessment is subjective; observe the reactions of the patient by watching the face for grimacing, or withdrawal of the stimulated extremity.
7. Compare the patient's sensation on the corresponding areas bilaterally.
8. Note whether any sensory deficits follow a dermatome distribution.
9. The borders of any area exhibiting changes in sensation should be mapped by dermatomes (Figure 19-7).

Sensory Assessment

Sensation should be tested early in the neurological assessment because of the detail involved and because the cooperation of the patient is required. The conclusions of the assessment may be unreliable if the patient becomes fatigued.

The sensory assessment is divided into three sections. First, the exteroceptive sensations (superficial sensations that originate in the sensory receptors in the skin and mucous membranes) are tested. These are the sensations of light touch, superficial pain, and temperature.

Next, the proprioceptive sensations (deep sensations, with sensory receptors in the muscles, joints, tendons, and ligaments) are assessed. **Proprioception** is tested with the modalities of motion and position, and vibration sense.

Finally, the cortical sensations (those that require cerebral integrative and discriminative abilities) are assessed. Stereognosis, graphesthesia, two-point discrimination, and extinction are tested.

Exteroceptive Sensation

For the entire exteroceptive sensation assessment, expose the patient's legs, arms, and abdomen.

Light Touch

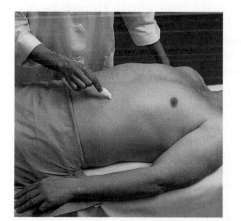

Figure 19-11 Assessment of Light Touch.

E
1. Use a wisp of cotton and apply the stimulus with very light strokes (Figure 19-11). If the skin is calloused, or for thicker skin on the hands and soles, the stimulus may need to be intensified, although care must be taken not to stimulate subcutaneous tissues.
2. Begin with distal areas of the patient's limbs and move proximally.
3. Test the hand, lower arm, abdomen, foot, and leg. Assessment of sensation of the face is discussed in the cranial nerve section.
4. To prevent the patient from being able to predict the next touch, alter the rate and rhythm of stimulation. Also, vary the sites of stimulation, keeping in mind that the right and left sides must be compared.
5. Instruct the patient to respond by saying "now" or "yes" when the stimulus is felt, and to identify the area that was stimulated either verbally or by pointing to it.

N/A/P   Refer to Temperature on following page.

Superficial Pain

E
1. Use a sharp object: sterile needle or sterile safety pin.
2. Establish that the patient can identify sharp and dull sensations by touching the patient with each stimulus and asking the patient to describe what is felt. This will help alleviate some of the fears the patient may have about being touched with a sharp object.

| E | Examination | N | Normal Findings | A | Abnormal Findings | P | Pathophysiology |

3. Hold the object loosely between the thumb and first finger to allow the sharp point to slide if too much pressure is applied.
4. Begin peripherally, moving in a distal to proximal direction and following the dermatomal distribution. If impaired sensation is identified, move from impaired sensation to normal sensation for comparison. Attempt to define the area of impaired sensation (mapping) by proceeding from the analgesic area to the normal area.
5. Alternate the sharp point with the dull end to test the patient's accuracy of shear sensation.
6. Instruct the patient to reply "sharp," "dull," or "I don't know" as quickly as the stimulus is felt and to indicate areas of the skin that perceive differences in pain sensation.
7. Again, compare the two sides, taking care not to proceed too quickly or to cue the patient with regularity in the stimulus presentation.

N/A/P   Refer to Temperature, following.

Temperature

Assess temperature sensation only if abnormalities in superficial pain sensation are noted.

E   1. Use glass vials containing warm water (40° to 45°C) and cold water (5° to 10°C). Hotter or colder temperatures will stimulate pain receptors.
2. Touch the warm or cold test tubes on the skin, distal to proximal and following dermatome distribution.
3. Instruct the patient to respond "hot," "cold," or "I can't tell" and to indicate where the sensation is felt.

N   The patient should be able to perceive light touch, superficial pain, and temperature accurately, and be able to correctly perceive the location of the stimulus.

A   **Anesthesia** refers to an absence of touch sensation. **Hypesthesia** is a diminished sense of touch; this may also be called hypoesthesia. **Hyperesthesia** is marked acuteness to the sensitivity of touch. **Paresthesia** is numbness, tingling, or pricking sensation. **Dysesthesia** is an abnormal interpretation of a stimulus such as burning or tingling from a stimulus such as touch or superficial pain. All of these findings are abnormal.

P   Peripheral nerve lesions may cause anesthesia, hypesthesia, or hyperesthesia, which may be mapped out in the specific sensory distribution of the affected nerve. Lesions of the nerve roots produce areas of anesthesia and hypesthesia limited to the segmental distribution of the roots involved. Lesions in the brain stem or spinal cord can cause anesthesia, paresthesia, or dysesthesia.

A   **Analgesia** refers to insensitivity to pain. **Hypalgesia** refers to diminished sensitivity to pain. **Hyperalgesia** is increased sensitivity to pain. These findings are abnormal.

P   Lesions of the thalamus and the peripheral nerves and nerve roots can cause analgesia, hypalgesia, and hyperalgesia.

A   Total unilateral loss of all forms of sensation is an abnormal finding.

P   This is due to an extensive lesion of the thalamus and results in gross disability.

A   A "saddle" pattern of sensation loss is abnormal.

P   A lesion of the cauda equina produces the "saddle" pattern of sensation loss, the loss of leg reflexes, and the loss of sphincter control. If touch is preserved, the lesion is in or near the conus medullaris.

A   The loss of touch sensation in the hands and lower legs (glove and stocking anesthesia) is abnormal.

P   Glove and stocking anesthesia is common in polyneuritis of any cause.

A   Unilateral loss of all exteroceptive sensation is abnormal.

P   This is caused by a partial lesion of the thalamus or a lesion laterally situated in the upper brain stem. It may also be caused by hysteria.

Proprioceptive Sensation

Motion and Position

E 1. Grasp the patient's index finger with your thumb and index finger. Hold the finger at the sides (parallel to the plane of movement) in order not to exert upward or downward pressure with your fingers and thus give the patient any clues as to which direction the finger is moving. The patient's fingers should be relaxed.

2. Have the patient shut the eyes and show the patient what "up" and "down" feel like by moving the finger in those directions.

3. Use gentle, slow, and deliberate movements. Begin with larger movements that become smaller and less perceptible.

4. Instruct the patient to respond "up," "down," or "I can't tell" after each time you raise or lower the finger.

5. Repeat this several times. Vary the motion in order not to establish a predictable pattern.

6. Repeat steps 2 through 5 with the finger of the patient's opposite hand, and then with the great toes.

7. If there appears to be a deficit in motion sense, proceed to the proximal joints such as wrists or ankles, and repeat the test.

N **The patient should be able to correctly identify the changes of position of the body.**

A Inability to perceive direction of movement is abnormal.

P Peripheral neuropathies will interfere with position sense. A lesion of the posterior column will cause an ipsilateral loss of position sense. Lesions of the sensory cortex, the thalamus, or the connections between them (thalamocortical connections) may also disrupt position sense.

Vibration Sense

E 1. Strike the prongs of a low-pitch tuning fork (128 or 256 Hz) against the ulnar surface of your hand or your knuckles, and place the base of the fork firmly on the patient's skin over bony prominences (Figure 19-12). Be sure that your fingers touch only the stem of the fork, not the tines.

2. Begin with distal prominences such as a toe or finger, testing each extremity by touching the base of the fork against it.

3. Instruct the patient to say "now" when the vibrating tuning fork is felt, and to report immediately when the vibrations are no longer felt.

4. Ensure that the patient is reporting the vibration sense rather than hearing a humming sound or just feeling pressure from the tuning fork.

5. After the patient can no longer feel the vibrations, determine whether the vibrations can, in fact, still be felt by holding the prongs while the tuning fork is left on the patient.

6. If you detect a deficit in vibratory sense in the peripheral bony prominences, progress toward the trunk by testing ankles, knees, wrists, elbows, anterior superior iliac crests, ribs, sternum, and spinous processes of the vertebrae.

N **Normally, the patient should be able to perceive vibration over all bony prominences.**

A The inability to perceive vibration sense is abnormal.

P Vibratory sense may be lost as a result of polyneuropathies (e.g., diabetic) or spinal cord lesions involving the posterior columns. Vibratory sensation is normally lower in patients over age 65.

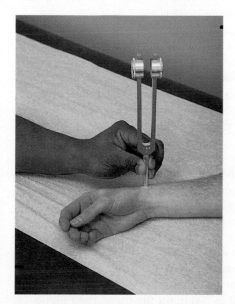

Figure 19-12 Assessment of Vibration.

| E | Examination | N | Normal Findings | A | Abnormal Findings | P | Pathophysiology |

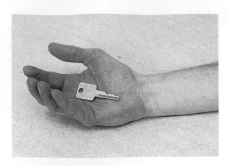

Figure 19-13 Assessment of Stereognosis.

Cortical Sensation

Stereognosis

Stereognosis is the ability to identify objects by manipulating and touching them.

E 1. Place a familiar object (coin, button, closed safety pin, key) into the patient's hand (Figure 19-13).
   2. Ask the patient to manipulate the object, appreciating size and form.
   3. Ask the patient to name the object.
   4. Repeat in the opposite hand with a different object.

N **The patient should be able to identify the objects by holding them.**

A The inability to recognize the nature of objects by touch manipulation, termed **astereognosis**, is abnormal.

P Astereognosis is related to dysfunction of the parietal lobe, where the sensory cortex is located.

Figure 19-14 Assessment of Graphesthesia.

Graphesthesia

The ability to identify numbers, letters, or shapes drawn on the skin is termed **graphesthesia**.

E 1. Draw a number or letter with a blunt object (such as a closed pen or the stick of a cotton-tipped applicator) on the patient's outstretched palm. Ensure the number or letter is facing the patient's direction (Figure 19-14).
   2. Ask the patient to identify what has been written.
   3. Repeat on the opposite side.

N **The patient should be able to identify the number or letter written on the palm or other skin surface.**

A Graphanesthesia is the inability to recognize a number or letter drawn on the skin and is abnormal.

P Graphanesthesia, in the presence of intact peripheral sensation, indicates parietal lobe dysfunction.

Two-Point Discrimination

Two-point discrimination is tested by simultaneously and closely touching various parts of the body with two identical, sharp objects.

E 1. With two sterile pins, tips of opened paperclips, or broken cotton-tipped applicators, simultaneously touch the tip of the patient's finger, starting with the objects far apart.
   2. Ask the patient whether one or two points are felt.
   3. Continue to move the two points closer together until the patient is unable to distinguish two points. Note the minimum distance between the two points at which the patient reports feeling the objects separately.
   4. Irregularly alternate, using one or two pins throughout the test to verify that the patient is feeling two points.
   5. Repeats steps 1 to 4 with the fingers of the opposite hand.
   6. Other areas of the body that may be tested include the dorsum of the hand, the tongue, the lips, the feet, or the trunk.

N **The patient should be able to identify two points at 5 mm apart on the fingertips. Other parts of the body vary widely in normal distance of discrimination, such as the dorsum of the hand or feet, where a separation of as much as 20 mm may be necessary for discrimination. The patient may be able to detect two points as close as 2 to 3 mm on the tip of the tongue.**

A Distances greater than those described previously that are required to identify two points are abnormal.

P Lesions in the parietal lobe impair two-point discrimination (with intact tactile sensation).

Nursing Alert

Neuropathy and the Patient with Diabetes Mellitus

Detection of peripheral neuropathy in diabetes should be conducted by assessing loss of sensitivity to the 10 g Semmes-Weinstein monofilament at the great toe or loss of sensitivity to vibration (128 Hz tuning fork) at the great toe.[16]

Nursing Tip

Olfactory Assessment

- Determine whether the nasal passages are patent by asking the patient to breathe through first one nostril and then through the other while occluding the opposing nostril by pressing against it with a finger. Assessment of the olfactory nerve may be delayed if the patient has a severe cold, allergic rhinitis, or nasal packing; had recent oral surgery; or has used nasal steroids for a prolonged period.
- Keep aromatic substances such as cloves, coffee, orange, or chocolate in closed glass vials until they are presented to the patient.
- Avoid using noxious odours such as alcohol, camphor, ammonia, acetic acid, or formaldehyde, which may stimulate the trigeminal nerve endings in the nasal mucosa.

Extinction

Extinction (sensory inattention) is tested by simultaneously touching opposite sides of the body at the identical site. Use cotton-tipped applicators or your fingers.

E 1. Ask the patient if one or two points are felt and where they are felt.
   2. Remove the stimulus from one side while maintaining the stimulus on the opposite side.
   3. Ask the patient if one or two points are felt and where the sensations are felt.

N The patient should be able to feel both stimuli.

A The inability to feel the two points simultaneously and to discriminate that one point has been removed is abnormal.

P A lesion in one parietal lobe may prevent the patient from feeling the stimulus on the opposite side of the body even if sensation is intact on that side during routine assessment.

Cranial Nerves

A complete assessment of the 12 cranial nerves is necessary when a baseline assessment is desired, if a tumour of a specific cranial nerve is suspected, or if periodic assessment is needed after surgery or radiation treatments. An abbreviated cranial nerve assessment is an integral part of a neurological screening examination. The screening examination would include cranial nerves II, III, IV, and VI: visual acuity

| E | **Examination** | N | **Normal Findings** | A | **Abnormal Findings** | P | **Pathophysiology** |

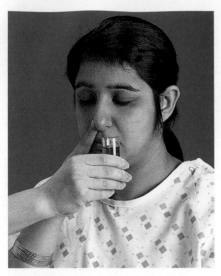

Figure 19-15 Assessment of CN I.

and gross visual fields, funduscopic examination, pupillary reactions, and extra-ocular movements; cranial nerves VII, VIII, IX, X, and XII: facial musculature and expression, gross hearing, voice, and inspection of the tongue.

Olfactory Nerve (CN I)

E **1.** Ask the patient to close the eyes.

2. Test each side separately by asking the patient to occlude one nostril by pressing against it with a finger.

3. Ask the patient to inhale deeply in order to cause the odour to surround the mucous membranes and adequately stimulate the olfactory nerve (Figure 19-15).

4. Ask the patient to identify the contents of each vial.

5. Present one odour at a time and alternate them from nostril to nostril.

6. Allow enough time to pass between presentation of vials to prevent confusion of the olfactory system.

7. Record the number of substances tested and the number of times the patient was able to correctly identify the contents.

8. Note whether a difference between the right and the left sides was apparent.

N The patient should be able to distinguish and identify the odours with each nostril.

A **Anosmia**, the loss of the sense of smell, is abnormal.

P Total loss of the sense of smell may be caused by trauma to the cribriform plate, sinusitis, colds, or heavy smoking. Unilateral anosmia may be the result of an intracranial neoplasm, such as a meningioma of the sphenoid ridge compressing the olfactory tract or bulb.

Optic Nerve (CN II)

Visual Acuity (ENAP: See Chapter 12.)
Visual Fields (ENAP: See Chapter 12.)
Funduscopic Examination (ENAP: See Chapter 12.)

Oculomotor Nerve (CN III)

Cardinal Fields of Gaze (ENAP: See Chapter 12.)
Eyelid Elevation (ENAP: See Chapter 12.)
Pupil Reactions (Direct, Consensual, Accommodation) (ENAP: See Chapter 12.)

Normal (reflex present)

Head rotated to the right   Eyes move to the left

Abnormal (reflex absent)

Head rotated to the right   Eyes follow

Figure 19-16 Assessing the Oculocephalic Reflex.

Advanced Technique

Doll's Eyes Phenomenon

Assess doll's eyes phenomenon (oculocephalic reflex) (CN III) in the unconscious patient. This tests the intactness of the vestibular and oculomotor pathways. Doll's eyes phenomenon should not be tested in the patient with suspected neck injury.

E **1.** Hold the patient's eyelids open and rotate the head of the patient from the centre to one side and then to the opposite side, holding briefly at the end points.

2. Watch for eye movement.

3. Further evaluate the oculocephalic reflex by alternately flexing and extending the head with the eyelids held as before.

N Normally, the eyes should deviate in the direction opposite the head (e.g., head up, eyes look down; head turned to the right, eyes look left) (Figure 19-16).

continues

> **A** The patient whose eyes remain fixed with neither lateral nor vertical deviation in response to head movement is said to exhibit *doll's eyes phenomenon* (Figure 19-16) because the eyes appear to be painted onto the head as a doll's eyes are.
>
> **P** Patients with low brain stem lesions will exhibit abnormal doll's eyes phenomenon.

Trochlear Nerve (CN IV)

Cardinal Fields of Gaze (ENAP: See Chapter 12.)

Trigeminal Nerve (CN V)

Motor Component

E **1.** Instruct the patient to clench the jaw.

2. Palpate the contraction of the temporalis (Figure 19-17A) and masseter (Figure 19-17B) muscles on each side of the face by feeling for contraction of the muscles with the finger pads of the first three fingers.

3. Ask the patient to move the jaw from side to side against resistance from your hand. Feel for weakness on one side or the other as the patient pushes against resistance.

4. Test the muscles of mastication by having the patient bite down with the molars on each side of a tongue blade and comparing the depth of the impressions made by the teeth. If you can pull the tongue blade out while the patient is biting on it, there is weakness of the muscles of mastication.

5. Observe for fasciculation and note the bulk, contour, and tone of the muscles of mastication.

Sensory Component

E **1.** Instruct the patient to close the eyes.

2. Test light touch by using a cotton wisp to lightly stroke the patient's face in each area of the sensory distribution of the trigeminal nerve (Figure 19-18).

3. Instruct the patient to respond by saying "now" each time the touch of the cotton wisp is felt.

4. Test and compare both sides of the face.

5. To assess superficial pain sensation, use a sterile needle or open paperclip. Before testing, show the patient how the sharpness of the needle or paperclip feels compared to the dullness of the opposite, blunt end. Testing with the blunt end will give some reliability to the assessment.

    a. Instruct the patient to respond by saying "sharp" or "dull" when each sensation is felt.

    b. Irregularly alternate the sharp and dull ends, and again test each distribution area of the trigeminal nerve on both sides of the face.

6. Test temperature sensation if other abnormalities have been detected. Use vials of hot and cold water.

    a. Touch the vials to each dermatomal distribution area, irregularly alternating hot and cold.

    b. The patient should respond by saying "hot" or "cold."

7. Because sensation to the cornea is supplied by the trigeminal nerve, test the corneal reflex (the motor component is CN VII). The corneal reflex should not be routinely assessed in conscious patients, unless there is a clinical suspicion of trauma to CN V or CN VII.

    a. Ask the patient to open the eyes and look away from you.

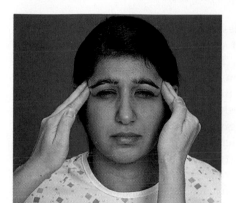

A. Temporalis muscles

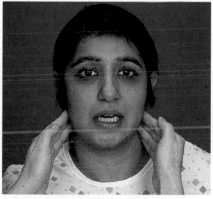

B. Masseter Muscles

Figure 19-17 Assessment of the Motor Component of CN V.

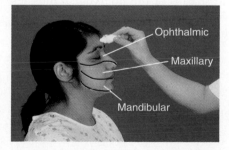

Ophthalmic

Maxillary

Mandibular

Figure 19-18 Assessment of the Sensory Component of CN V: Light Touch.

E	**Examination**	**N**	**Normal Findings**	**A**	**Abnormal Findings**	**P**	**Pathophysiology**

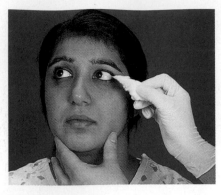

Figure 19-19 Assessment of the Sensory Component of CN V and Motor Component of CN VII: Corneal Reflex.

b. Approach the patient out of the line of vision to eliminate the blink reflex. You can stabilize the patient's chin with your hand if it is moving.

c. Lightly stroke the cornea with a slightly moistened cotton wisp (to avoid irritating the cornea, see Figure 19-19). Avoid stroking just the sclera or the lashes of the eye. An alternative technique is to instill normal saline eye drops instead of a light stroke of a cotton wisp.

d. Observe for bilateral blinking of the eyes.

e. Repeat on the opposite eye.

N The temporalis and masseter muscles should be equally strong on palpation. The jaw should not deviate and should be equally strong during side-to-side movement against resistance. The volume and bulk of the muscles should be bilaterally equal. Sensation to light touch, superficial pain, and temperature should be present on the sensory distribution areas of the trigeminal nerve. The corneal reflex should cause bilateral blinking of eyes.

A Lesions of the trigeminal nerve may give rise to either reduced sensory perception or to facial pain, both of which are abnormal.

P Aneurysms of the internal carotid artery next to the cavernous sinus may give rise to severe pain in the ophthalmic or mandibular distribution of the trigeminal nerve due to the pressure of the aneurysm on the nerve. Neoplasms that compress the gasserian ganglion or root, such as meningiomas, pituitary adenomas, and malignant tumours of the nasopharynx, may cause facial pain and impairment of sensation. Head injuries, especially basilar skull fractures, may give rise to facial anesthesia and paralysis of the muscles of mastication.

A Trigeminal neuralgia (tic douloureux), characterized by brief, paroxysmal unilateral facial pain along the distribution of the trigeminal nerve, is abnormal. The pain can be provoked by touch or movement of the face, such as in tooth brushing, yawning, chewing, or talking. There is no associated motor weakness.

P Trigeminal neuralgia may occur in patients with multiple sclerosis due to demyelinization of the root of CN V. The patient with a posterior fossa tumour may have trigeminal neuralgia. In most cases, there is no etiology found.

A Postherpetic neuralgia is found most often in the elderly. The pain is continuous and is described as a constant, burning ache with occasional stabbing pains. The stabbing pain may begin spontaneously or may be provoked by touch. The pain is unilateral and tends to follow the distribution of the ophthalmic distribution of the trigeminal nerve. It is abnormal.

P Herpes zoster involvement of the trigeminal nerve causes postherpetic neuralgia. Inflammatory lesions are found throughout the trigeminal pathways.

A Tetanus is characterized by tonic spasms interfering with the muscles that open the jaw (trismus). Dysphagia and spasms of the pharyngeal muscles are also observed in tetanus. Tetanus is abnormal.

P Motor root involvement of the trigeminal nerve causes the spasm of the masseter muscles.

Abducens Nerve (CN VI)

Cardinal Fields of Gaze (ENAP: See Chapter 12.)

Facial Nerve (CN VII)

Motor Component

E 1. Observe the patient's facial expressions for symmetry and mobility throughout the assessment.

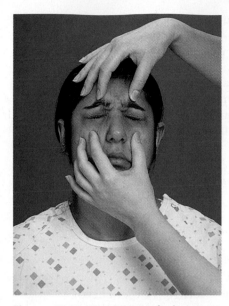

Figure 19-20 Assessment of the Motor Component of CN VII: Opening the Patient's Eyes against Resistance.

2. Note any asymmetry of the face, such as wrinkles or lack of wrinkles on one side of the face or one-sided blinking.
3. Test muscle contraction by asking the patient to:
   a. Frown
   b. Raise the eyebrows
   c. Wrinkle the forehead while looking up
   d. Close the eyes lightly and then keep them closed against your resistance (Figure 19-20)
   e. Smile, show teeth, purse lips, and whistle
   f. Puff out the cheeks against the resistance of your hands
4. Observe for symmetry of facial muscles and for weakness during the above manoeuvres.
5. Note any abnormal movements such as tremors, tics, grimaces, or immobility.

N Normal findings of the motor portion of the facial nerve include symmetry between the right and the left sides of the face as well as the upper and lower portions of the face at rest and while executing facial movements. There should be an absence of abnormal muscle movement.

A **Bell's palsy** (idiopathic facial palsy), characterized by complete flaccid paralysis of the facial muscles on the involved side, is abnormal. The affected side of the face is smooth, the eye cannot close, the eyebrow droops, the labiofacial fold is gone, and the mouth may droop. Loss of the sensation of taste in the anterior two-thirds of the tongue may occur.

P Bell's palsy is caused by damage to the facial nerve. It is a lower motor neuron paralysis because the damage occurs along the facial nerve from its origin to its periphery.

A Supranuclear facial palsy is characterized by paralysis in the lower one-third to two-thirds of the face; the upper portion of the face is spared. The nasolabial fold is flat, and the eye on the affected side can close, although more weakly. The patient may be unable to keep the eye closed against resistance applied by the nurse. The muscles of the upper portion of the face remain intact. Supranuclear facial palsy is abnormal.

P Supranuclear facial palsy is due to an upper motor neuron lesion of the facial nerve.

Sensory Component

E 1. Sensory assessment of the facial nerve is limited to testing taste. The portions of the tongue that are tested are:
   a. The tip of the tongue for sweet and salty tastes
   b. Along the borders and at the tip for sour taste
   c. The back of the tongue and the soft palate for bitter taste
2. Test both sides of the tongue with each solution.
3. The patient's tongue should protrude during the entire assessment of taste, and talking is not allowed. In order for the patient to identify the substance, the words sweet, salty, bitter, and sour should be written on a card so the patient can point to what is tasted. Be sure the patient does not see which solution is being tested.
4. Cotton swabs may be used as applicators, using a different one for each solution.
5. Dip the cotton swab into the solution being tested and place it on the appropriate part of the tongue.
6. Instruct the patient to point to the word that best describes taste perception.
7. Instruct the patient to rinse the mouth with water before the next solution is tested.

| E | Examination | N | Normal Findings | A | Abnormal Findings | P | Pathophysiology |

8. Repeat steps 5 to 7 until each solution has been tested on both sides of the tongue.

N   Normal sensation would be accurate perceptions of sweet, sour, salty, and bitter tastes.

A   **Ageusia** (loss of taste) and **hypogeusia** (diminution of taste) are abnormal.

P   Age, excessive smoking, extreme dryness of the oral mucosa, colds, medications, lesions of the medulla oblongata, or lesions of the parietal lobe may cause alterations in the sense of taste.

Acoustic Nerve (CN VIII)

Cochlear Division
Hearing. (ENAP: See Chapter 13.)
Weber and Rinne Tests. (ENAP: See Chapter 13.)

Vestibular Division
The vestibular division of CN VIII assesses for vertigo.

E   **1.** During the history, ask the patient if vertigo is experienced.

2. Note any evidence of equilibrium disturbances. Refer to the section on cerebellar assessment.

3. Note the presence of nystagmus.

N   Vertigo is not normally present.

P   Vertigo describes an uncomfortable sensation of movement of the environment or the movement of self within a stationary environment; it is often accompanied by nausea, vomiting, and nystagmus.

P   Vertigo is caused by a disorder of the labyrinth or the vestibular nerve. Causative factors may include migraine headache, which causes a disruption in the supply of the internal auditory artery. Tumours of the cerebellopontine angle may cause vertigo by compressing the vestibular nerve. Head injuries that involve the labyrinth may cause vertigo. Blockage of the eustachian tube during ascent in an airplane may lead to vertigo.

A   Ménière's disease, characterized by vertigo that lasts for minutes or hours, low-pitched roaring tinnitus, progressive hearing loss, nausea, and vomiting, is abnormal. The patient also experiences pressure in the ear.

P   The main pathological finding is distension of the endolymphatic system, with degenerative changes in the organ of Corti.

Glossopharyngeal and Vagus Nerves (CN IX and CN X)

The glossopharyngeal and vagus nerves are tested together because of their overlap in function.

E   **1.** Examine soft palate and uvula movement and gag reflex as described in Chapter 13.

2. Assess the patient's quality of speech for a nasal quality or hoarseness. Ask the patient to produce guttural and palatal sounds, such as *k*, *q*, *ch*, *b*, and *d*.

3. Assess the patient's ability to swallow a small amount of water. Observe for regurgitation of fluids through the nose. If the patient is unable to swallow, observe how oral secretions are handled.

4. The sensory assessment of the glossopharyngeal and vagus nerves is limited to taste on the posterior one-third of the tongue. This assessment was previously discussed in the section on CN VII.

N   Refer to Chapter 13 for normal soft palate and uvula movement and gag reflex findings. The speech is clear, without hoarseness or a nasal quality. The patient is able to swallow water or oral secretions easily. Taste (sweet, salty, sour, and bitter) is intact in the posterior one-third of the tongue.

A   Unilateral lowering and flattening of the palatine arch, weakness of the soft palate, deviation of the uvula to the normal side, mild dysphagia, regurgitation of fluids, nasal quality of the voice, loss of taste in the posterior one-third of the tongue, and hemianesthesia of the palate and pharynx are abnormal.

P Unilateral glossopharyngeal and vagal paralysis, such as with trauma or skull fractures at the base of the skull, will cause these symptoms.

A Marked nasal quality of the voice, difficulty with guttural and palatal sounds, severe dysphagia with liquids, and inability of the palate to elevate on phonation are abnormal.

P Bilateral vagus nerve paralysis will cause these more marked symptoms, and often occurs simultaneously with signs and symptoms of other lower brain stem cranial nerve dysfunction such as in progressive bulbar palsy in amyotrophic lateral sclerosis (ALS).

Spinal Accessory Nerve (CN XI)

E 1. Place the patient in a seated or a supine position. Inspect the sternocleidomastoid muscles for contour, volume, and fasciculation.
   2. Place your right hand on the left side of the patient's face. Instruct the patient to turn the head sideways against the resistance of your hand (Figure 19-21A).
   3. Use the other hand to palpate the sternocleidomastoid muscle for strength of contraction. Inspect the muscle for contraction.
   4. Repeat steps 2 and 3 in the opposite direction. Compare the strength of the two sides.
   5. To assess the function of the trapezius muscle, stand behind the patient and inspect the shoulders and scapula for symmetry of contour. Note any atrophy or fasciculation.
   6. Place your hands on top of the patient's shoulders and instruct the patient to raise the shoulders against the downward resistance of your hands (Figure 19-21B). This can be performed in front of or behind the patient.
   7. Observe the movements and palpate the contraction of the trapezius muscles. Compare the strength of the two sides.

N **The patient should be able to turn the head against resistance with a smooth, strong, and symmetrical motion. The patient should also demonstrate the ability to shrug the shoulders against resistance with strong, symmetrical movement of the trapezius muscles.**

A Inability to turn the head toward the paralyzed side, and a flat, non-contracting muscle on that side are abnormal findings. The contralateral sternocleidomastoid muscle may be contracted.

P These findings are the result of unilateral paralysis of the sternocleidomastoid muscle due to trauma, tumours, or infection affecting the spinal accessory nerve.

A The inability of the patient to elevate one shoulder, asymmetrical drooping of the shoulder and scapula, and a depressed outline of the neck are abnormal findings. The involved shoulder may also show atrophy and fasciculation of the muscles.

P Unilateral paralysis of the trapezius muscle may be suspected, usually due to trauma, tumours, or infection.

A/P For information on torticollis, see Chapter 11.

Hypoglossal Nerve (CN XII)

E 1. See Chapter 13 for assessment of tongue movement.
   2. Assess lingual sounds by asking the patient to say "la la la."

N See Chapter 13 for normal tongue movements. Lingual speech is clear.

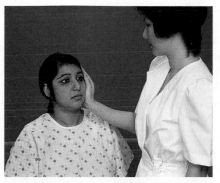

A. Strength of Sternocleidomastoid Muscle

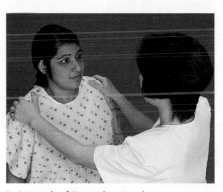

B. Strength of Trapezius Muscle

Figure 19-21 Assessment of CN XI.

| E | Examination | N | Normal Findings | A | Abnormal Findings | P | Pathophysiology |

A Inability or difficulty in producing lingual sounds is abnormal. The speech sounds lispy and clumsy.

P Lesions of the hypoglossal nerve will cause difficulty in pronunciation of lingual sounds.

Motor System

For ENAP on muscle size, tone, and strength, and involuntary movements, see Chapter 18. See following for additional A & P.

A Extrapyramidal rigidity is evident when resistance is present during passive movement of the muscles in all directions and lasts throughout the entire range of motion. It may involve both flexor and extensor muscles and is abnormal.

P Extrapyramidal rigidity is due to lesions located in the basal ganglia.

A **Decerebrate rigidity** (decerebration) is characterized by rigidity and sustained contraction of the extensor muscles and is abnormal. The arms are adducted, extended, and hyperpronated. The legs are stiffly extended and the feet are plantar flexed (Figure 19-22A). The back and neck may be arched and the teeth clenched (opisthotonos).

P Decerebration may be found in unconscious patients with deep, bilateral diencephalic injury that progresses to midbrain dysfunction. Decerebrate rigidity may also occur due to midbrain and pontine damage, which occurs with compression of these structures due to expanding cerebellar or posterior fossa lesions. Severe metabolic disorders that depress diencephalic and forebrain function may also cause decerebration.

A **Decorticate rigidity** (decortication) is characterized by hyperflexion of the arms (flexion of the arm, wrist, and fingers, adduction of the arms), hyperextension and internal rotation of the legs, and plantar flexion (Figure 19-22B). It is abnormal.

P Decorticate rigidity is found in unconscious patients with cerebral hemisphere lesions that interfere with the corticospinal tract.

Nursing Tip

Patients Who Require Corrective Lenses for Coordination

Ensure that patients who wear corrective lenses (eyeglasses or contacts) are wearing them prior to assessing their coordination.

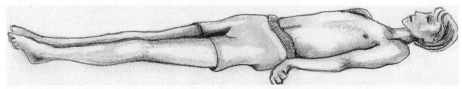

A. Decerebrate Rigidity (Abnormal Extension)

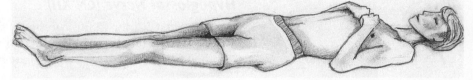

B. Decorticate Rigidity (Abnormal Flexion)

Figure 19-22 Motor System Dysfunction.

Pronator Drift

E 1. Have the patient extend the arms out in front with palms up for 20 seconds.

2. Observe for downward drifting of an arm.

N There should be no downward drifting of an arm.

A Downward drifting of an arm is abnormal.

P Downward drifting of an arm may indicate hemiparesis, such as in stroke.

Cerebellar Function (Coordination, Station, and Gait)

Motor coordination refers to smooth, precise, and harmonious muscular activity. Movement requires the coordination of many muscle groups. Coordination is an integrated process, involving complicated neural integration of the motor and premotor cortex, basal ganglia, cerebellum, vestibular system, posterior columns, and peripheral nerves.

Equilibratory coordination refers to maintenance of an upright stance and depends on the vestibular, cerebellar, and proprioceptive systems. Non-equilibratory coordination refers to smaller movements of the extremities and involves the cerebellar and proprioceptive mechanisms.

Incoordination is categorized into three different types of syndromes: cerebellar, vestibular and posterior column syndromes. Incoordination is not considered to be secondary to involuntary movements, paresis, or alterations of muscle tone.

Station refers to the patient's posture, and gait refers to the patient's manner of walking.

Figure 19-23 Assessment of Coordination: Fingertip-to-Nose Touch.

Coordination

E 1. Instruct the patient to sit comfortably facing you, with eyes open and arms outstretched.

2. Ask the patient to first touch the index finger to the nose, then to alternate rapidly with the index finger of the opposite hand.

3. With the patient's eyes closed, have the patient continue to rapidly touch the nose with alternate index fingers (Figure 19-23).

4. With the patient's eyes open, ask the patient to again touch finger to nose. Next, ask the patient to touch your index finger, which is held about 45 cm away from the patient.

5. Change the position of your finger as the patient rapidly repeats the manoeuvre with one finger.

6. Repeat steps 4 and 5 with the other hand.

7. Observe for intention tremor or overshoot or undershoot of the patient's finger.

8. To assess rapid alternating movements, ask the patient to rapidly alternate patting the knees, first with the palms and then alternating palms with the backs of the hands (rapid supinating [Figure 19-24A] and pronating [Figure 19-24B] of the hands).

9. Ask the patient to repeatedly touch the thumb to each of the fingers of the hand in rapid succession from index to the fifth finger, and back.

10. Repeat step 9 with the other hand.

11. Observe coordination and the ability of the patient to perform these in rapid sequence.

12. With the patient in a seated or supine position, ask the patient to place the heel just below the knee on the shin of the opposite leg and to slide it down to the foot (Figure 19-25).

| E | Examination | N | Normal Findings | A | Abnormal Findings | P | Pathophysiology |

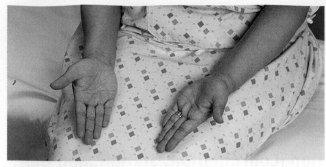

A. Supination

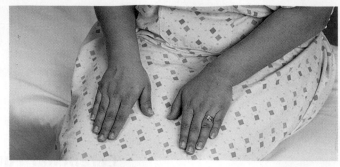

B. Pronation

Figure 19-24 Assessment of Coordination: Rapid Alternating Hand Movements.

Figure 19-25 Assessment of Coordination: Heel Slide.

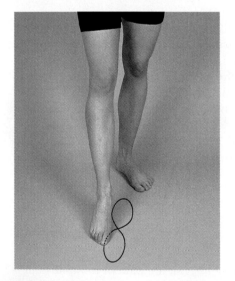

Figure 19-26 Assessment of Coordination: Figure 8.

13. Repeat with the opposite foot.
14. Observe coordination of the two legs.
15. Ask the patient to draw a circle or a figure 8 with the foot either on the ground or in the air (Figure 19-26).
16. Repeat with the other foot.
17. Observe for coordination and regularity of the figure.
18. Test the lower extremities for rapid alternating movement by asking the patient to rapidly extend the ankle ("tap your foot") or to rapidly flex and extend the toes of one foot.
19. Repeat with the opposite foot.
20. Note rate, rhythm, smoothness, and accuracy of the movements.

N   The patient is able to rapidly alternate touching finger to nose and moving finger from nose to your finger in a coordinated fashion. The patient is able to perform alternating movements in a purposeful, rapid, coordinated manner. The patient demonstrates the ability to purposefully and smoothly run heel down shin with equal coordination in both feet and to draw a figure 8 or circles with the foot.

A   **Dyssynergy**, the lack of coordinated action of the muscle groups, is abnormal. The patient is unable to carry out smooth, coordinated movements. The patient's movements appear jerky, irregular, and uncoordinated.

A   **Dysmetria**, impaired judgment of distance, range, speed, and force of movement, is abnormal. The patient misjudges distance and overshoots.

A   **Dysdiadochokinesia**, the inability to perform rapid alternating movements, is abnormal. The patient is unable to abruptly stop one movement and begin another opposite movement.

P   Cerebellar disease causes all of these abnormal findings.

Gait

E   1. See Chapter 18 for gait assessment technique.
2. Ask the patient to walk on tiptoes, then on heels.
3. Ask the patient to walk in a straight line, touching heel to toe (tandem walking). The arms should be held at the side and the eyes should be open.
4. Note the patient's ability to maintain balance.
5. Ask the patient to hop in place first on one foot and then on the other.

N   See Chapter 18 for normal gait findings. The patient should be able to walk unaided on tiptoes and heels, and walk heel to toe in a straight line without losing balance. The patient should also be able to maintain balance while hopping on one foot, with bilateral equal strength.

A/P   See Chapter 18.

Advanced Technique

Romberg Test

E **1.** Ask the patient to stand erect, feet together and arms at side, first with eyes open, then closed.

2. Note the patient's ability to maintain balance with eyes first open then closed.

N The patient should be able to maintain balance with eyes open or closed for 20 seconds and with minimum swaying.

A Romberg test is positive if the patient becomes unsteady and tends to fall when the eyes are closed.

P In cerebellar disease, the patient remains unsteady with the eyes open and closed. In posterior column disease with proprioceptive loss, the patient becomes appreciably more unsteady with eye closure.

Nursing Alert

Romberg Test

Stand close to the patient during this test in order to catch the patient if he or she begins to fall.

◄NURSING CHECKLIST►

Assessing Reflexes

1. When testing reflexes, the patient should be relaxed and comfortable.
2. Position the patient so the extremities are symmetrical.
3. To elicit true reflexes, distract the patient by talking about another topic.
4. Hold the reflex hammer loosely between the thumb and index finger and strike the tendon with a brisk motion from the wrist. The reflex hammer should make contact with the correct point on the tendon in a quick, direct manner.
5. Observe the degree and speed of response of the muscles after the reflex hammer makes contact. Grading of DTR is as follows:
   0: absent
   + (1+): present but diminished
   ++ (2+): normal
   +++ (3+): mildly increased but not pathological
   ++++ (4+): markedly hyperactive, clonus may be present
6. Compare reflex responses of the right and the left sides. The normal response to taps in the correct area should elicit a brisk (++ or +++) contraction of the muscles involved.
7. When documenting the DTRs, you may use a stick figure. See page 722.

Nursing Tip

Deep Tendon Reflex Reinforcement

Even when the deep tendon reflex (DTR) is stimulated correctly, the patient may not exhibit a DTR because of conscious thought. If this occurs, reinforcement may be necessary. Reinforcement is a technique used to distract conscious thought of the DTR by concentrating on another action. Examples include the patient clenching the teeth, grasping the thigh with the hand not being assessed, and grasping and pulling the wrists with the contralateral hand.

| **E** | **Examination** | **N** | **Normal Findings** | **A** | **Abnormal Findings** | **P** | **Pathophysiology** |

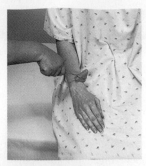

A. Brachioradialis

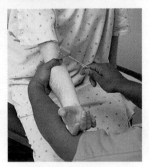

B. Biceps

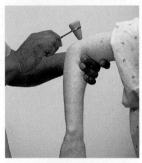

C. Triceps

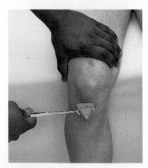

D. Patellar

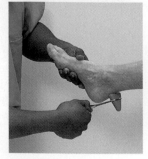

E. Achilles

Figure 19-27 Assessment of Deep Tendon Reflexes.

Reflexes

Deep Tendon Reflexes

Brachioradialis

E 1. Flex the patient's arm to 45°.
   2. Support the patient's relaxed arm either on the lap or semipronated on your forearm.
   3. With the blunt end of the reflex hammer, strike the tendon of the brachioradialis above the styloid process of the radius (a few centimetres above the wrist on the thumb side) (Figure 19-27A).

N Observe for flexion and supination of the forearm. An exaggerated reflex may also show flexion of the wrist and fingers and adduction of the forearm. Innervation of this reflex is through the radial nerve, with segmental innervation of C5, C6.

A/P See Achilles, below.

Biceps

E 1. Flex the patient's arm to between 45° and 90°.
   2. Support the patient's forearm on your forearm.
   3. Place your thumb firmly on the biceps tendon just above the crease of the antecubital fossa (Figure 19-27B).
   4. Wrap your fingers around the patient's arm and rest them on the biceps muscle to feel it contract.
   5. Tap the thumb briskly with the pointed end of the reflex hammer.

N Observe for contraction of the biceps muscle and flexion of the elbow. Innervation of the biceps reflex is through the musculocutaneous nerve with segmental innervation of C5, C6.

A/P See Achilles, below.

Triceps

E 1. Flex the patient's arm to between 45° and 90°.
   2. Support the patient's arm either on the lap or on your hand as shown in Figure 19-27C.
   3. With the pointed end of the reflex hammer, tap the triceps tendon just above its insertion above the olecranon process (elbow).

N Observe for contraction of the triceps muscle and extension of the arm. Innervation of the triceps reflex is through the radial nerve, with segmental innervation of C7, C8.

A/P See Achilles, below.

Patellar

E 1. Ask the patient to sit in a chair or at the edge of the examination table.
   2. Place your hand over the quadriceps femoris muscle to feel contraction.
   3. With the other hand, tap the patellar tendon just below the patella with the blunt end of the reflex hammer (Figure 19-27D).
   4. If the patient cannot tolerate a sitting position, support the flexed knee with your hand under it so the foot is hanging freely.

N There should be contraction of the quadriceps muscle and extension of the leg. Innervation of the patellar reflex is through the femoral nerve, with segmental innervation of L2, L3, L4.

A/P See Achilles, below.

Achilles

E 1. Ask the patient to sit with the feet dangling.
   2. Slightly dorsiflex the patient's foot.
   3. With the blunt end of the reflex hammer, tap the Achilles tendon just above its insertion in the heel.

4. If the patient is lying down, flex the leg at the knee and externally rotate the thigh. Place your non-dominant hand under the foot to produce dorsiflexion (Figure 19-27E). Apply the stimulus as described in step 3.

N The normal response is contraction of the muscles of the calf (gastrocnemius, soleus, and plantaris) and plantar flexion of the foot. Innervation of the Achilles reflex is through the tibial nerve, with segmental innervation of L5, S1, S2.

A Absent or decreased deep tendon reflexes are abnormal.

P Diminished deep tendon reflexes usually result from interference in the reflex arc, and an absence may indicate a break in the reflex arc. Deep tendon reflexes are lost in deep coma, narcosis, or deep sedation. Hypothyroidism, sedative or hypnotic drugs, and infectious diseases may also diminish reflexes. Patients with increased intracranial pressure frequently show decreased or absent deep tendon reflexes. Spinal shock also causes loss of these reflexes.

A Hyperactive deep tendon reflexes are abnormal. Hyperactive deep tendon reflexes are characterized by an increase in speed of response and enhancement of the vigour of movement. The muscle contraction is sustained, with a minimal stimulus needed to elicit the response. Sometimes the adjacent muscles may also contract. Clonus may be present.

P Hyperactivity is associated with a loss of inhibition of the higher centres in the cortex and reticular formation, and in lesions of the pyramidal system. Muscle stretch reflexes are also exaggerated in light coma, tetany, and tetanus.

Superficial Reflexes

Abdominal

E **1.** Drape and place the patient in a recumbent position, arms at sides and knees slightly flexed. Stand to the right of the patient.
2. Use a moderately sharp object to stroke the skin, such as the wooden tip of a cotton-tipped applicator or a split tongue blade.
3. To elicit the upper abdominal reflex, stimulate the skin of the upper abdominal quadrants. From the tip of the sternum, stroke in a diagonal (downward and inward) fashion (Figure 19-28).
4. Repeat step 3 on the opposite side.
5. To elicit the lower abdominal reflex, stimulate the skin of the lower abdominal quadrants. From the area below the umbilicus, stroke in a diagonal (downward and inward) fashion to the symphysis pubis.
6. Repeat step 5 on the opposite side.

N Observe for contraction of the upper abdominal muscles upward and outward with a deviation of the umbilicus toward the stimulus. The upper abdominal reflex is innervated by the intercostal nerves through T7, T8, T9. Observe for contraction of the lower abdominal muscles and contraction of the umbilicus toward the stimulus. The lower abdominal reflex is innervated by the lower intercostal, iliohypogastric, and ilioinguinal nerves through segments T10, T11, T12.

A/P See Bulbocavernosus on following page.

Plantar

E **1.** With the handle of the reflex hammer, stroke the outer aspect of the sole of the foot from the heel across the ball of the foot to just below the great toe (Figure 19-29).
2. Repeat on the opposite foot.

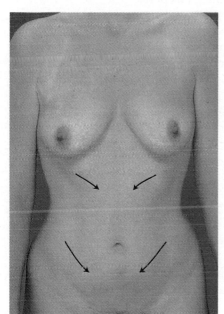
Figure 19-28 Assessment of Superficial Reflexes: Direction of Stimulus for Abdominal Reflexes.

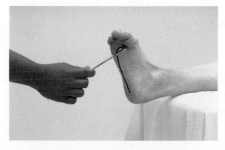
Figure 19-29 Assessment of Superficial Reflex: Plantar.

| E | Examination | N | Normal Findings | A | Abnormal Findings | P | Pathophysiology |

N Observe for plantar flexion of the toes. The plantar reflex is innervated by the tibial nerve with segmental innervation of L5, S1, S2.

A/P See Bulbocavernosus below.

Cremasteric

E 1. The male patient should be lying down with the thighs exposed and the testicles visible.
   2. Stroke the skin of the inner aspect of the thigh near the groin in a downward movement (Figure 19-30).
   3. Repeat step 2 on the opposite side.

N Observe contraction of the cremasteric muscle with corresponding elevation of the ipsilateral testicle. Innervation of the cremasteric reflex is through the ilioinguinal and genitofemoral nerves with segmental innervation of T12, L1, L2.

A/P See Bulbocavernosus, next.

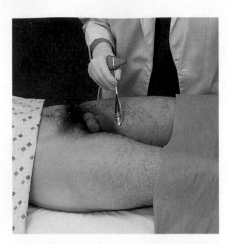

Figure 19-30 Assessment of Superficial Reflex: Cremasteric.

Bulbocavernosus

E 1. Pinch the skin of the foreskin or the glans penis.
   2. Observe for a contraction of the bulbocavernosus muscle in the perineum at the base of the penis.

N Contraction of the bulbocavernosus muscle occurs. The presence of this reflex in a paraplegic patient after acute spinal cord injury indicates that the initial stage of spinal shock is past. The bulbocavernosus reflex is innervated by segments S3 and S4.

A Decreased or absent superficial reflexes are abnormal.

P Superficial reflexes are diminished or absent with dysfunction of the reflex arc as in the muscle stretch reflexes. Superficial reflexes are complex because they involve the parietal areas and the motor centres of the premotor area and the pyramidal system. Lesions in the pyramidal tracts will cause decrease or absence of superficial reflexes. These reflexes may also be lost in deep sleep and coma.

Pathological Reflexes

All the reflexes described following are abnormal findings in adults and are not usually assessed unless the patient's clinical presentation warrants it.

Glabellar

E 1. With your finger, tap the patient on the forehead between the eyebrows.
   2. Observe for a hyperactive blinking response.

A The presence of this reflex is abnormal.

P Patients with lesions of the corticobulbar pathways from the cortex to the pons, patients with Parkinson's disease, and patients with glioblastoma of the corpus callosum will have this reflex.

Clonus

E 1. Have the patient assume a recumbent position. Stand to the side.
   2. Support the patient's knee in a slightly flexed position.
   3. Quickly dorsiflex the foot and maintain it in that position.
   4. Assess for **clonus** (a rhythmic oscillation of involuntary muscle contraction).

A Sustained clonus is an abnormal finding.

P Sustained clonus, in combination with muscle spasticity and hyperreflexia, indicates upper motor neuron disease. Table 19-10 summarizes the findings associated with upper and lower motor neuron dysfunction.

P Women with preeclampsia and eclampsia can also demonstrate clonus.

TABLE 19-10	Comparison of Upper Motor Neuron and Lower Motor Neuron Lesions	
PARAMETER	UPPER MOTOR NEURON	LOWER MOTOR NEURON
Muscle tone	Spasticity	Flaccidity
Muscle bulk	Late atrophy from disease; no fasciculations	Atrophy; fasciculations
Pronator drift	Positive	Absent
Deep tendon reflexes	Hyperreflexia	Hyporeflexia or absent
Babinski's reflex	Positive	Absent
Clonus	Present	Absent

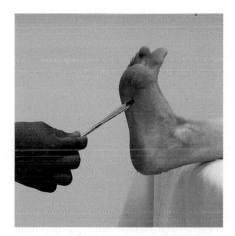

Figure 19-31 Assessment of Pathological Reflexes: Babinski.

Babinski

E With the handle of the reflex hammer, stroke the patient's sole as you did for the plantar reflex. Use a slow and deliberate motion.

N A Babinski reflex is normal in infants and toddlers until 15 to 18 months of age.

A A positive Babinski's reflex is noted when the patient's toes abduct (fan) and the great toe dorsiflexes (Figure 19-31).

P Patients with lesions in the pyramidal system, such as in stroke or trauma, display a positive Babinski's reflex.

Advanced Technique

Meningeal Irritation

To assess the patient for signs of meningeal irritation, look for nuchal rigidity, Kernig's sign, and Brudzinski's sign, all abnormal findings. Other signs and symptoms include violent headache, photophobia, fever, nausea and vomiting, decreasing level of consciousness, and seizures. Definitive diagnosis is obtained through cultures of cerebrospinal fluid.

Nuchal Rigidity

Nuchal rigidity is the tendency by the patient to maintain the head in an immobile, extended position. The patient resists movement of the neck. Severe pain and spasms occur with movement.

E 1. Place the patient in a supine position.
2. Flex the patient's neck.

A The patient resists the movement.

P Nuchal rigidity can be caused by meningeal irritation such as in meningitis. Meningitis is an infectious process of the meninges caused by bacteria, viruses, mycobacteria, fungi, or spirochetes. The organisms enter the subarachnoid space, causing an acute inflammatory response.

P Irritation of the subarachnoid space due to subarachnoid hemorrhage may cause meningeal irritation.

continues

E	**Examination**	N	**Normal Findings**	A	**Abnormal Findings**	P	**Pathophysiology**

Kernig's Sign

E 1. Place the patient in a recumbent position.
2. Lift the patient's leg and flex the knee at a right angle.
3. Attempt to extend the patient's knee by pushing down on it.

A A positive Kernig's sign is a resistance to extension and pain (due to spasm of the hamstring), preventing extension of the leg.

P Kernig's sign is caused by stretching of irritated nerve roots and meninges.

Brudzinski's Sign

E 1. Place one hand under the patient's neck and the other hand on top of the patient's chest to prevent elevation of the body.
2. Flex the patient's neck with a deliberate motion.

A Brudzinski's sign is positive if the patient responds with flexion of one or both legs up to the pelvis. The arms may also flex.

P Refer to nuchal rigidity.

GERONTOLOGICAL VARIATIONS

The nervous system in the aging adult is particularly vulnerable to illness and to dysfunction of other body systems. The brain is dependent on blood flow for oxygen and nutrients. Changes in the cardiovascular system that lead to a decreased oxygen supply to the brain, such as arteriosclerosis of the cerebral arteries, affect cerebral functions such as mental acuity, sensory interpretation, and motor ability.

Neuronal changes occur with aging. The myelin sheath surrounding the nerve begins to degenerate, decreasing nerve conduction rate. The axons become smaller. Biochemically, the amount of neurotransmitter produced in the neuron is diminished, and the activity of the enzymes that degrade the neurotransmitter increases. Changes in neurotransmitters are known to affect sleep, temperature control, and mood. Depression, for example, is associated with decreased levels of the neurotransmitter norepinephrine, a common finding among the elderly. A score of 5 or greater on the Geriatric Depression Scale is evidence of depression (Table 19-11). Also, see Nursing Alert "The Older Adult—Delirium, Dementia, and Depression" on page 692.

Total brain weight, the number of synapses, and the number of neurons diminish with aging, beginning at age 50. Most of the loss occurs in the cerebral cortex and the cerebellum; and less so in the brain stem. The brain atrophies, causing a widening of the sulci and gyri, especially in the frontal lobes. The tendency of the brain to atrophy increases the size of the subdural space, leaving the cortical bridging veins vulnerable to trauma, bleeding, and the formation of a chronic subdural hematoma. The ventricles increase in size and the amount of cerebrospinal fluid increases to fill the space.

Sensory changes in the elderly are related to vision, hearing, vestibular alterations, and proprioception. The elderly have decreased visual acuity, visual fields, colour sensitivity, and pupillary size, and diminished pupillary responses to light. The elderly person's hearing also diminishes due to ossification of the ossicles and degenerative changes in the auditory nerve. Elderly persons also demonstrate difficulties with balance as well as changes in coordination and equilibrium.

Cognitive changes characteristic of aging include decreased memory, primarily short-term memory, increased learning time, and changes in affect, mood, and orientation. Dementia may be a chronic or reversible problem. Delirium or acute mental confusion may be seen in elderly patients suffering from infection, dehydration, or CNS damage. As previously mentioned, depression, another problem among the elderly, may have a neurological base.

TABLE 19-11 Geriatric Depression Scale

Directions: Have the patient reflect over the last week and choose the best answer for how they have felt. Score 1 point for each shaded answer.

1.	Are you basically satisfied with your life?	YES	**NO**
2.	Have you dropped many of your activities and interests?	**YES**	NO
3.	Do you feel that your life is empty?	**YES**	NO
4.	Do you often get bored?	**YES**	NO
5.	Are you in good spirits most of the time?	YES	**NO**
6.	Are you afraid that something bad is going to happen to you?	**YES**	NO
7.	Do you feel happy most of the time?	YES	**NO**
8.	Do you often feel helpless?	**YES**	NO
9.	Do you prefer to stay at home rather than going out and doing new things?	**YES**	NO
10.	Do you feel you have more problems with memory than most?	**YES**	NO
11.	Do you think it is wonderful to be alive now?	YES	**NO**
12.	Do you feel pretty worthless the way you are now?	**YES**	NO
13.	Do you feel full of energy?	YES	**NO**
14.	Do you feel that your situation is hopeless?	**YES**	NO
15.	Do you think that most people are better off than you are?	**YES**	NO

5 points indicates that the patient is depressed and further evaluation is indicated.

Source: Adapted from "Development of a Comprehensive Assessment Toolbox for Stroke," P. W. Duncan, 1999, *Clinics in Geriatric Medicine, 15*(4), pp. 885–894.

CASE STUDY · The Patient with a Metastatic Brain Tumour

The case study illustrates the application and objective documentation of the neurological assessment.

Ms Essex is a 61-year-old journalist, divorced for several years, and is employed by a national news magazine in a large west coast city.

HEALTH HISTORY

PATIENT PROFILE	61 yo, Ⓡ handed
HEALTH ISSUE/CONCERN	Difficulty walking & Ⓛ -sided weakness
HISTORY OF ISSUE/CONCERN	Reports a 2 wk gradual decline in ambulation & new onset of Ⓛ -sided weakness. She went to work this morning & felt OK, but on her way home noticed she was having trouble walking from her car to her apartment. She reached her lobby & fell to her Ⓛ, landing on a large chair. Her son was c̄ her & he called 911.
PAST HEALTH HISTORY	
Medical History	Breast cancer 6 yrs ago Hypothyroidism × 30 yrs

continues

HTN × 21 yrs
Hypercholesterolemia × 18 yrs
Postmenopause × 10 yrs

Surgical History	Total Ⓡ mastectomy c̄ reconstruction 6 yrs ago
Medications	Takes all meds once daily: levothyroxine 0.1 mg, atenolol 25 mg, simvastatin 20 mg, glucosamine 500 mg, calcium carbonate 500 mg, vitamin E 400 IU
Communicable Diseases	Ø
Allergies	Latex (urticaria)
Injuries and Accidents	Sprained Ⓛ ankle 3 wks ago, no medical tx sought
Special Needs	Ø
Blood Transfusion	Ø
Childhood Illnesses	Varicella age 5, mumps age 7
Immunizations	Tetanus 2 yrs PTA, annual flu vaccination; Hep A for travel

FAMILY HEALTH HISTORY

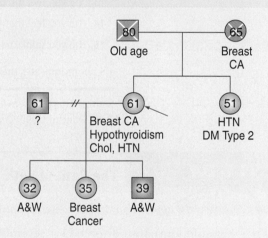

LEGEND

 Living female
 Living male
⊗ Deceased female
⊠ Deceased male
╱ Points to patient
———//——— = Divorced
A&W = Alive & well
CA = Cancer
DM = Diabetes mellitus
HTN = Hypertension

No known family hx of CVA, H/A, sz disorder, Alzeimer's dz, or other neurological disorders.

SOCIAL HISTORY

Alcohol Use	1–2 glasses of wine c̄ dinner q PM
Drug Use	Ø
Tobacco Use	Ø
Domestic and Intimate Partner Violence	Denies
Sexual Practice	Divorced, monogamously active
Travel History	Frequent travel to Europe & South America for work (q 1–2 mos)
Work Environment	Office & field work as a journalist
Hobbies and Leisure Activities	Photography, crossword puzzles, hiking, swimming

Stress	Work 60–80 hrs/wk, frequent travel
Education	BA
Economic Status	Financially comfortable
Religion/Spirituality	"I'm Jewish"
Ethnicity	"I'm Canadian but my parents were from England"
Roles and Relationships	Mother, journalist
Characteristic Patterns of Daily Living	Awakens at 05:00, breakfast at home, swims × 30 mins, usually works from 06:30 to 19:30. Has lunch at her desk, or "on the run." Returns home after work; usually invites friends over for dinner. Retires between 22:00 and 23:00.
HEALTH MAINTENANCE ACTIVITIES	
Sleep	6–7 hrs/night
Diet	Vegetarian
Exercise	30 min swimming q AM
Stress Management	See Hobbies and Leisure Activities and exercise
Use of Safety Devices	Seat belt
Health Check-ups	2 mos ago $\bar{c}$ internist
PHYSICAL ASSESSMENT	

Mental Status	1. Physical appearance and behaviour:
	  a. Posture & movements: Sitting on side of bed $\bar{c}$ mild Ⓛ hemiparesis & leaning to the Ⓛ.
	  b. Dress, grooming, & personal hygiene: hospital gown, clean & well-groomed hair, skin, & nails
	  c. Facial expression: slight Ⓛ facial droop
	  d. Affect: appropriate
	2. Communication: Normal voice quality, rapid speech, fluent & appropriate
	3. Level of consciousness: Alert and oriented; GCS = 15
	4. Cognitive abilities/mentation:
	  a. Attention: short, easily distracted
	  b. Memory: long-term intact, recent memory impaired
	  c. Judgment: impaired
	  d. Insight: appropriate
	  e. Spatial perception: intact
	  f. Calculations: intact
	  g. Abstract reasoning: intact
	  h. Thought processes and content: inconsistent
	  i. Suicidal ideation: denies

Sensory	1. Exteroceptive sensation:
	  a. Light touch: intact on Ⓡ, diminished on Ⓛ face/arm/leg
	  b. Superficial pain: intact
	  c. Temperature: intact
	2. Proprioceptive sensation:
	  a. Motion & position: intact on Ⓡ, diminished on Ⓛ
	  b. Vibration sense: intact

continues

	3. Cortical sensation:
	a. Stereognosis, graphesthesia, 2-point discrimination, extinction: intact
Cranial Nerves	I: Intact
	II: Ⓡ superior homonymous quadrantanopsia. Visual acuity 20/50 OS, 20/40 OD; funduscopic: mild papilledema OD, normal OS;
	III, IV, & VI: EOM intact; Ø nystagmus; pupils equal, round, briskly reactive to light (PERRL) at 5 mm to 3 mm, ⊕ accommodation, Ø ptosis
	V: Nl strength of masseter & temporalis muscles, sensation of superficial pain & light touch intact
	VII: Mild Ⓛ flattening of nasolabial folds
	VIII: Hearing grossly intact, Rinne: AC > BC, Weber: Ø lateralization
	IX & X: Symmetrical excursions of the soft palate; uvula midline; ⊕ gag
	XI: Intact
	XII: Tongue midline

Motor	1. Size: = bilaterally
	2. Tone: firm & supple on Ⓡ, Ø on Ⓛ
	3. Strength: LUE 3/5, RUE 5/5, LLE 4/5, RLE 5/5
	4. Involuntary movements: none
	5. Pronator drift: Ⓛ drift

Cerebellar Function	1. Coordination
	a. Finger to nose: intact bilaterally c̄ eyes closed & open
	b. Rapid alternating movements: rapid supination & pronation of the hands: intact bilaterally; heel slide: intact bilaterally
	2. Gait
	a. Tip toes and heel walking: intact
	b. Heel to toe in a straight line: intact
	c. Hopping on one leg: intact bilaterally

Reflexes Deep tendon reflexes

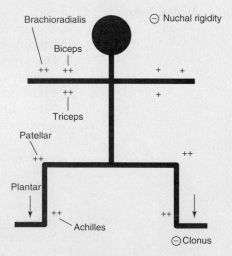

Superficial	Deferred
Pathological	Babinski: ⊕ L
	Glabellar: ⊖
Advanced Technique	Romberg test: steady c̄ eyes open & closed
LABORATORY DATA	CBC & metabolic profile WNL
DIAGNOSTIC DATA	CT scan s̄ contrast: Low density structure most likely metastatic disease c̄ edema in the Ⓛ parietal region c̄ a mild shift to the Ⓛ side
	MRI c̄ and s̄ contrast: 3.3 cm Ⓡ parietal enhancing mass consistent c̄ metastatic tumour

◄NURSING CHECKLIST►

Mental Status Assessment and Neurological Techniques

Mental Status Assessment
- Physical appearance and behaviour
  - Posture and movements
  - Dress, grooming, and personal hygiene
  - Facial expression
  - Affect
- Communication
- Level of consciousness
- Cognitive abilities and mentation
  - Attention
  - Memory
  - Judgment
  - Insight
  - Spatial perception
  - Calculation
  - Abstract reasoning
  - Thought process and content
    Suicidal Ideation

Sensory Assessment
- Exteroceptive sensation
  - Light touch
  - Superficial pain
  - Temperature
- Proprioceptive sensation
  - Motion and position
  - Vibration sense
- Cortical sensation
  - Stereognosis
  - Graphesthesia
  - Two-point discrimination
  - Extinction

Cranial Nerves Assessment
- Olfactory nerve (CN I)
- Optic nerve (CN II)
  - Visual acuity
  - Visual fields
  - Funduscopic examination
- Oculomotor nerve (CN III)
  - Cardinal fields of gaze
  - Eyelid elevation
  - Pupil reactions
- Trochlear nerve (CN IV)
  - Cardinal fields of gaze
- Trigeminal nerve (CN V)
  - Motor component
  - Sensory component
- Abducens nerve (CN VI)
  - Cardinal fields of gaze

- Facial nerve (CN VII)
  - Motor component
  - Sensory component
- Acoustic nerve (CN VIII)
  - Cochlear division
    Hearing
    Weber test
    Rinne test
  - Vestibular division
- Glossopharyngeal nerve (CN IX)
- Vagus nerves (CN X)
- Spinal accessory nerve (CN XI)
- Hypoglossal nerve (CN XII)

Motor System Assessment
- Muscle size
- Muscle tone
- Muscle strength
- Involuntary movements
- Pronator drift

Cerebellar Function
- Coordination
- Gait

Reflexes
- Deep tendon reflexes
    Brachioradialis
  - Biceps
  - Triceps
  - Patellar
  - Achilles
- Superficial reflexes
  - Abdominal
  - Plantar
  - Cremasteric
  - Bulbocavernosus
- Pathological reflexes
  - Glabellar
  - Clonus
  - Babinski

Advanced Techniques
- Doll's eyes phenomenon
- Romberg's test
- Meningeal irritation
  - Nuchal rigidity
  - Kernig's sign
  - Brudzinski's sign

REVIEW QUESTIONS

1. You are assessing a patient's language function and you note slurred speech. This abnormality is called:
   a. Dysarthria
   b. Dysphonia
   c. Dyslexia
   d. Dyspraxia
   The correct answer is (a).

2. You are asked to assess your patient's olfactory nerve (CN I) function. Which would be an appropriate collection of aromatic substances?
   a. Coffee, strawberries
   b. Alcohol, chocolate
   c. Coffee, cloves
   d. Cloves, formaldehyde
   The correct answer is (c).

3. During the neurological examination, you have your patient close the eyes. You place a closed safety pin in the patient's hand and ask him or her to identify the object. What are you testing?
   a. Two-point discrimination
   b. Graphesthesia
   c. Extinction
   d. Stereognosis
   The correct answer is (d).

4. The physical examination of a 22-year-old male who fell off a second-story balcony and landed on his head reveals the following: his eyes open when painful stimuli are applied, he has incomprehensible speech, and he withdraws to pain. Using the Glasgow Coma Scale to document these findings the nurse assigns the patient a score of:
   a. 4
   b. 6
   c. 8
   d. 9
   The correct answer is (c).

5. You are caring for a 77-year-old male patient who underwent a total knee replacement two days ago. He has been progressing appropriately with his physical therapy. Your patient's daughter approaches you to discuss her concerns about her father's mental status. She describes a gradual decline in his ability to care for himself at home. This description is most consistent with which disorder?
   a. Delirium
   b. Dementia

   c. Depression
   d. Acute confusion
   The correct answer is (b).

6. You perform a test for the Babinski reflex by stroking the sole of your patient's foot with the handle of your reflex hammer. A positive reflex is described as:
   a. Toes remain still and the great toe dorsiflexes
   b. Toes abduct and the great toe dorsiflexes
   c. Toes remain still and the great toe flutters
   d. Toes adduct and the great toe hyperextends
   The correct answer is (b).

7. The corneal reflex requires adequate function of which two cranial nerves?
   a. Sensory V and motor VII
   b. Sensory III and motor X
   c. Sensory VII and motor VI
   d. Sensory I and motor II
   The correct answer is (a).

8. You ask your patient to explain the meaning of the statement "The squeaky wheel gets the grease." What are you assessing?
   a. Aphasia
   b. Concentration
   c. Abstract reasoning
   d. Articulation
   The correct answer is (c).

9. You observe your patient eating his meal. You notice great difficulty with placing his hand on the cup of water. After the meal, you perform an assessment and discover that he cannot consistently perform a fingertip-to-nose touch test. This is an example of:
   a. Hyperreflexia
   b. Paresis
   c. Ataxia
   d. Dysmetria
   The correct answer is (d).

10. Your patient is able to speak in full sentences and make her needs known but is unable to follow commands or name basic objects. This form of aphasia can be classified as:
    a. Expressive (Broca's) aphasia
    b. Non-fluent aphasia
    c. Receptive (Wernicke's) aphasia
    d. Dysarthria
    The correct answer is (c).

Visit the Estes online companion resource at
www.healthassessment.nelson.com for additional content
and study aids.

REFERENCES

[1]Canadian Heart and Stroke Foundation. *Stroke statistics.* Retrieved November 3, 2006, from http://ww2.heartandstroke.ca/Page.asp?PageID=33&ArticleID=1078&Src=news&From=SubCategory

[2]Canadian Heart and Stroke Surveillance System (CHSSS). *The changing face of heart and stroke disease in Canada (2000).* Public Health Agency of Canada. Retrieved November 3, 2006, from http://www.phac-aspc.gc.ca/ccdpc-cpcmc/cvd-mcv/publications/hdsc_2000_e.html

[3]Canadian Heart and Stroke Foundation. *Stroke risk factors.* Retrieved Retrieved November 3, 2006, from http://ww2.heartand-stroke.ca/Page.asp?PageID=33&ArticleID=438&Src=stroke&From=SubCategory

[4]Hill, M. D. & Buchan, A. M. for the Canadian Alteplase for Stroke Effectiveness Study (CASES). (2005). Thrombolysis for acute ischemic stroke: Results of the Canadian Alteplase for Stroke Effectiveness Study. *Canadian Medical Association Journal, 172,* 1307–12.

[5]World Health Organization. (2003). *Mental health: Suicide rates.* Retrieved November 3, 2006, from http://www.who.int/mental_health/prevention/suicide/suiciderates/en/

[6]Health Canada. (October 2002). *A report on mental illness in Canada.* Ottawa. Retrieved November 3, 2006, from http://www.phac-aspc.gc.ca/publicat/miic-mmac/pdf/mcn_ill_e.pdf

[7]Advisory Group on Suicide Prevention–Health Canada. (2003). *Acting on what we know: Preventing youth suicide in First Nations.* Retrieved Retrieved November 3, 2006, from http://www.hc-sc.gc.ca/tnih-spni/pubs/suicide/prev_youth-jeunes/index_e.html

[8]Health Canada. *Aboriginal health.* Retrieved November 3, 2006, from http://www.hc-sc.gc.ca/hcs-sss/delivery-prestation/fptcollab/2004-fmm-rpm/fs-if_02_e.html

[9]Malenfant, E. (2004, March). Suicide in Canada's immigrant population. *Statistics Canada: Health Reports,* 15(2), 9–17.

[10]Pickett, W., King, W. D., Faelker, T., Lees, R. E. M., Morrison, H. I., & Bienefeld, M. (2000). Suicides among Canadian farm operators. *Chronic Diseases in Canada, 20*(3). Retrieved November 19, 2006, from http://www.phac-aspc.gc.ca/publicat/cdic-mcc/20-3/a_e.html

[11]Registered Nurses' Association of Ontario (2003). *Screening for delirium, depression, and dementia in older people.* Toronto: Registered Nurses' Association of Ontario.

[12]Health Canada. (2002, October). *A report on mental illness in Canada.* Ottawa. Retrieved November 2, 2006, from http://www.phac-aspc.gc.ca/publicat/miic-mmac/pdf/men_ill_e.pdf

[13]Weir, E. (2000). Veterans and post-traumatic stress disorder. *Canadian Medical Association Journal,* 163(9), 1187.

[14]Health Canada. (2002, October). *A report on mental illness in Canada.*

[15]Statistics Canada (2003). *Canadian community health survey— Mental health and well-being.* Retrieved November 2, 2006, from http://www.statcan.ca/english/freepub/82-617-XIE/index.htm

[16]Canadian Diabetes Association—Clinical Practice Guidelines Expert Committee (2003). *Clinical practice guidelines: Neuropathy.* Retrieved November 3, 2006, from http://www.diabetes.ca/cpg2003/downloads/neuropathy.pdf

BIBLIOGRAPHY

Bader, M. K., & Littlejohns, L. R. (Eds.). (2004). *AANN Core Curriculum for Neuroscience Nursing* (4th ed.). St. Louis, MO: Saunders.

Heart and Stroke Foundation of Canada. (2003). *The Growing Burden of Heart Disease and Stroke in Canada 2003.* Ottawa.

Folstein, M. F., Folstein, S. E., & McHugh, P. R. (1975). "Mini-Mental State:" A practical method for grading the cognitive state of patients for the clinician. *Journal of Psychiatric Research, 12,* 189–98.

Hagen, B., & Reimer, M. (2000). Getting an earful: A primer in acoustic neuroma. *The Canadian Nurse, 96*(2), 23–30.

Henry, G. L., Little, N., Jagoda, A., & Pellegrino, T. R. (2003). *Neurologic Emergencies: A Symptom-Oriented Approach.* New York: McGraw-Hill Professional.

Hickey, J. V. (Ed.). (2003). *The Clinical Practice of Neurological and Neurosurgical Nursing* (5th ed.). Philadelphia: Lippincott, Williams, & Wilkins.

Lindsay, M. P., Kapral, M. K., Holloway, R., Gladstone, D. J., Tu, J. V, Laupacis, A., et al. (2005). Canadian Stroke Quality of Care Study: Identification of performance indicators for acute stroke care. *Canadian Medical Association Journal, 772*(3), 1–8.

Stuart, G., & Laraia, M. (Eds.) (2005). *Principles and Practice of Psychiatric Nursing* (8th ed.). St. Louis, MO: Elsevier Mosby.

Weir, E., & Wallington, T. (2001). Suicide: The hidden epidemic. *Canadian Medical Association Journal, 165*(5), 9–17.

Wijdicks, E. F. M. (2004). *Catastrophic Neurological Disorders in the Emergency Department* (2nd ed.). New York: Oxford University Press.

WEB RESOURCES

ALS Society Canada
http://www.als.ca

Anxiety Disorders Association of Canada
http://www.anxietycanada.ca

Brain Attack Coalition
http://www.stroke-site.org

Canadian Alliance on Mental Illness and Mental Health
http://www.camimh.ca/key.htm

Canadian Association of Neuroscience Nurses
http://www.cann.ca

Canadian Congress of Neurological Sciences
http://www.ccns.org

Canadian Heart and Stroke Foundation
http://ww2.heartandstroke.ca

Canadian Mental Health Association
http://www.cmha.ca/bins/index.asp

Canadian Stroke Network
http://www.canadianstrokenetwork.ca/media/releases.php

Canadian Syringomyelia Network
http://www.csn.ca

Epilepsy Canada
http://www.epilepsy.ca

Mood Disorders Society of Canada
http://www.mooddisorderscanada.ca

Public Health Agency of Canada: Mental Health
http://www.phac-aspc.gc.ca/mh-sm/mentalhealth

Schizophrenia Society of Canada
http://www.schizophrenia.ca

ThinkFirst Foundation—National Brain and Spinal Cord
Injury Prevention
http://www.thinkfirst.ca/default.asp

CHAPTER 20

Female Genitalia

COMPETENCIES

1. Describe the anatomy and physiology of the female genitalia, including age-relevant transformations.

2. Demonstrate the techniques necessary for assessment of the female genitalia, including patient positioning, external and internal inspection, speculum procedures, and palpation methods.

3. Identify anatomic landmarks during bimanual vaginal, uterine, and rectovaginal examinations.

4. Identify normal findings as well as atypical findings of the vulva, vagina, cervix, uterus, and adnexa.

5. Describe procedures for genital and anal smears and cultures.

*A*ssessment of the genitalia is often the last phase of a woman's physical assessment. Deaths attributed to uterine and cervical cancers have declined by more than 50% since the 1960s. This decline in morbidity and mortality rates can be attributed to early detection by physical assessment and Papanicolaou Test (Pap smears) and, to a lesser extent, increased patient knowledge of routine screening techniques. However, previous experiences of painful or embarrassing examinations may contribute to the patient's apprehension of the assessment process. By using a few common-sense techniques to diminish patient discomfort and by empowering the patient through education and participation in the assessment process, you can encourage the patient in the management of her own health care. The female reproductive system is an area in which you have a major impact on patient health through routine screening, education, and integrating the patient in the process of self-care.

ANATOMY AND PHYSIOLOGY

External Female Genitalia

The components of the external female genitalia are collectively referred to as the vulva. They consist of the mons pubis, labia majora, labia minora, clitoris, vulval vestibule and its glands, urethral meatus, and vaginal introitus (Figure 20-1).

The **mons pubis** is a pad of subcutaneous fatty tissue lying over the anterior symphysis pubis. At puberty, a characteristic triangular pattern of coarse, curly hair known as **escutcheon** develops over the mons pubis. The function of the mons pubis is to protect the pelvic bones, especially during coitus.

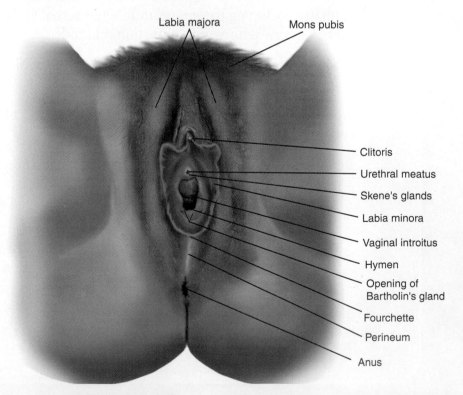

Figure 20-1 External Female Genitalia.

The **labia majora** are two longitudinal folds of adipose and connective tissue. They extend from the clitoris anteriorly and gradually narrow to merge and form the posterior commissure of the perineum. The outer surface of the labia majora becomes pigmented, wrinkled, and hairy at puberty. The inner surface is smoother and softer, and contains sebaceous glands. The function of the labia majora is to protect the vulva components that it surrounds.

Tucked within the labia majora are the **labia minora**, which enclose the vestibule. They are two thin folds of skin that extend to form the prepuce, or hood, of the clitoris anteriorly and a transverse fold of skin forming the **fourchette**, or frenulum, posteriorly.

The labia minora contain sebaceous glands, erectile tissue, blood vessels, and involuntary muscle tissue but no adipose tissue or hair follicles. The secretions of the sebaceous glands are bactericidal and aid in lubricating the vulval skin and protecting the skin from urine. Both the labia majora and the labia minora contain genital corpuscles that transmit erotic sensation.

The **clitoris** is a cylinder-shaped erectile body approximately 2.5 cm in length and 0.5 cm in diameter, but normally less than 2.0 cm of the body is visible on inspection. It is located at the superior aspect of the vulva between the labia minora. The clitoris contains erectile tissue and has a significant supply of nerve endings.

The **vestibule** is the area between the two skin folds of the labia minora. The vestibule is a boat-shaped area that contains the urethral meatus, openings of the Skene's glands, hymen, openings of the Bartholin's glands, and vaginal introitus.

The external urethral meatus is located in the superior aspect of the vestibule, approximately 2.5 cm inferior to the clitoris. It is characterized as an elongated dimple or slit. Surrounding the urethral meatus are **Skene's glands**, also known as paraurethral glands, which provide lubrication to protect the skin. These tiny glands open in a posterolateral position to the urethral meatus, but they are not readily visible.

The **vaginal introitus** or orifice is situated at the inferior aspect of the vulval vestibule and is the entrance to the vagina. The size and shape of the vaginal introitus may vary. Surrounding the vaginal introitus is the **hymen**, an avascular, thin fold of connective tissue. It may be annular or crescentic in shape. The hymen may be broken by first-time sexual intercourse, strenuous physical activity, tampons, masturbation, or menstruation, or it may be congenitally absent. Once the hymenal ring is perforated, small, irregular tags of tissue may be visible at the vaginal opening.

In the cleft between the labia minora and the hymenal ring lie the **Bartholin's glands**, also known as the greater vestibular glands. Bartholin's glands are small, pea-shaped glands located deep in the perineal structures. The ductal openings are not usually visible. The glands secrete a clear, viscid, odourless, alkaline mucous that improves the viability and motility of sperm along the female reproductive tract.

The **perineum** is located between the fourchette and the anus. Its composition of muscle, elastic fibres, fascia, and connective tissue gives it an exceptional capacity for stretching during childbirth. The **anal orifice** is located at the seam of the gluteal folds, and it serves as the exit to the gastrointestinal tract.

Internal Female Genitalia

The components of the internal female genitalia are the vagina, uterus, fallopian tubes, and ovaries (Figure 20-2).

The **vagina** is a pink, hollow, muscular tube extending from the cervix to the vulva. It is located posterior to the bladder and anterior to the rectum, and it slopes backward at an angle of approximately 45° with the vertical plane of the

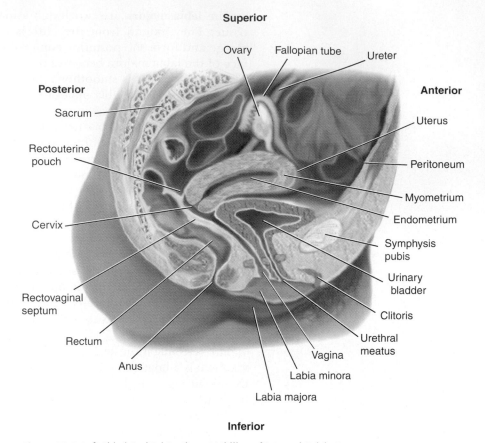

Figure 20-2 Left-Sided Sagittal Section at Midline of Internal Pelvic Organs.

body. The cervix projects into the vagina. This projection creates pouchlike recesses around the cervix. These recesses are divided into anterior, posterior, and lateral **fornices**. Abdominal organs such as the uterus, ovaries, appendix, cecum, colon, ureters, and distended bladder can be palpated through the thin walls of these fornices.

The vaginal walls consist of an outer layer of longitudinal and circular muscle fibres and a stratified squamous epithelium arranged in folds called rugae. Lactic acid is formed by the normal vaginal flora in conjunction with glycogen, which is contained in the superficial cells of the vagina. This maintains the vaginal pH and assists in the prevention of vaginal infections.

The **uterus** is an inverted pear-shaped, hollow, muscular organ in which an impregnated ovum develops into a fetus. The inferior aspect is the **cervix**; the superior aspect is the **fundus**. The most common position of the uterus is anteverted, but it may also be anteflexed, retroverted, retroflexed, or in midplane position (Figure 20-3). The mature non-pregnant uterus weighs about 60 gm and is approximately 5.5 to 8.0 cm long, 3.5 to 4.0 cm wide, and 2.0 to 2.5 cm thick. The uterus of a parous patient, or one who has given birth, may be enlarged by 2 to 3 cm in any of the above dimensions.

Anatomically, the uterus can be divided into three parts: the body, the isthmus, and the cervix (Figure 20-4). The body consists of the fundus, a raised, dome-shaped area on the superior portion of the uterus, and the cornu, the points of insertion of the fallopian tubes. The uterine body has three layers: an outer layer of peritoneum; a middle layer of muscle, called the myometrium; and an inner layer of columnar epithelium, mucous glands, and stroma, called the endometrium. It is this innermost layer that is shed and regenerated under normal hormonal influence during the menstrual cycle. The outer layer of the peritoneum forms a deep recess called the **rectouterine pouch**, or pouch of Douglas. It is the lowest point in the pelvic cavity and encompasses the lower posterior wall of the uterus, the upper portion of the vagina, and the intestinal surface of the rectum.

The **isthmus** is a constricted area between the body of the uterus and the cervix. The cervix is an open-ended canal approximately 2 to 3 cm in length and diameter. Its internal os (opening) is at the isthmus and its external os extends into the vagina. The os of the **nulliparous** woman, one who has not given birth, will be closed and tight. The os of a **parous** woman, one who has given birth to one or more neonates, may be open by 1 cm and the orifice may be elongated and irregular. The endocervical canal is lined with mucous-secreting columnar epithelium. The ectocervix, which protrudes into the vagina, is covered with the same squamous epithelial cells that line the vagina. The point at which the two types of cells merge is the **squamocolumnar junction**. Its exact location varies with age but is clinically important because it is the point at which most cervical cancer originates.

The **adnexa** of the uterus consists of the fallopian tubes, the ovaries, and their supporting ligaments. The **fallopian tubes** extend from the cornu of the uterus to the ovaries and are supported by the broad ligaments. The tubes are approximately 8 to 14 cm long. The distal, funnel-shaped end of the fallopian tube is called the infundibulum. It has moving, fingerlike projections called fimbriae, which help direct ova from the ovary into the tube, where fertilization takes place. The fallopian tubes are lined with ciliated squamous epithelium. The movement of the cilia and the peristaltic waves of the muscular layer of the tube propel the ovum toward the uterus, where implantation occurs.

The **ovaries** are a pair of almond-shaped glands, approximately 3 to 4 cm in length, in the upper pelvic cavity. **Oogenesis**, the development and formation of an ovum, and hormonal production are the ovaries' principal functions.

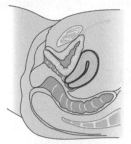

Anteverted
(most common)

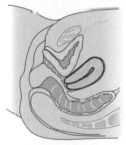

Anteflexed

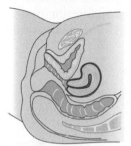

Midposition
(midplane)

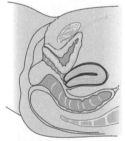

Retroverted
(palpable only during
rectovaginal exam)

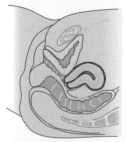

Retroflexed
(palpable only during
rectovaginal exam)

Figure 20-3 Positions of the Uterus.

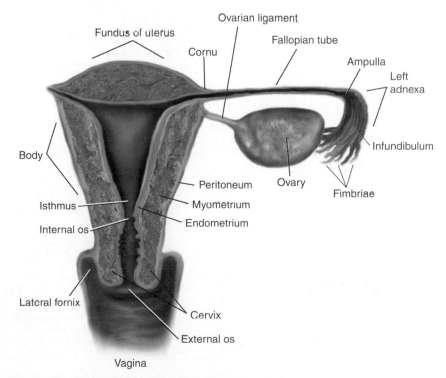

Figure 20-4 Coronal Section of Uterus and Adnexal Structures.

The rectovaginal septum separates the rectum from the posterior aspect of the vagina.

THE FEMALE REPRODUCTIVE CYCLE

The female reproductive cycle consists of two interrelated cycles called the ovarian and the menstrual cycles. These cycles occur synchronously under neurohormonal control from the hypothalamus and the anterior pituitary gland.

The ovarian cycle consists of two phases: the follicular phase and the luteal phase. During the follicular phase, the actions of the follicle-stimulating hormone (FSH) and the luteinizing hormone (LH) from the anterior pituitary gland stimulate the ripening of one ovarian follicle called the graafian follicle. The

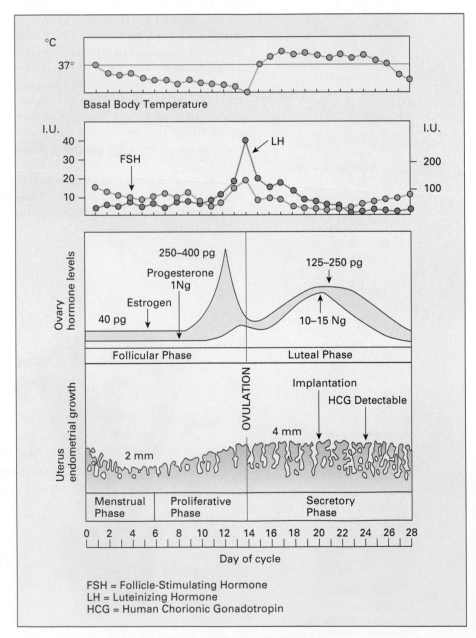

Figure 20-5 Cyclic Changes Associated with the Menstrual Cycle.

TABLE 20-1

Sexual Maturity Rating (SMR) for Female Genitalia

DEVELOPMENTAL STAGE	DESCRIPTION
Stage 1 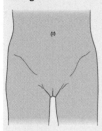	**Preadolescent Stage** (before age 8) No pubic hair, only body hair (vellus hair)
Stage 2 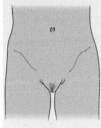	**Early Adolescent Stage** (ages 8 to 12) Sparse growth of long, slightly dark, fine pubic hair, slightly curly and located along the labia
Stage 3 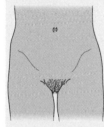	**Adolescent Stage** (ages 12 to 13) Pubic hair becomes darker, curlier, and spreads over the symphysis
Stage 4 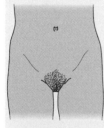	**Late Adolescent Stage** (ages 13 to 15) Texture and curl of pubic hair is similar to that of an adult but not spread to thighs
Stage 5 	**Adult Stage** Adult appearance in quality and quantity of pubic hair; growth is spread to inner aspect of thighs and abdomen

remaining follicles are suppressed by LH. Ovulation occurs when high levels of LH cause the release of the ovum from the graafian follicle. During the luteal phase, LH stimulates the development of the corpus luteum. This yellow pigment that fills the graafian follicle produces high levels of progesterone and low levels of estrogen. The basal body temperature rises, indicating that ovulation has occurred.

The menstrual cycle begins if implantation does not occur. The corpus luteum degenerates and the levels of progesterone and estrogen decrease, causing the endometrium to degenerate and shed. The menstrual flow lasts from two to seven days and the cycles continue every 25 to 34 days, with the average being 28 days. The first day of the cycle is the first day of menstruation. The menstrual flow consists of blood and mucous and normally does not exceed 150 mL. Menstrual blood lacks fibrin; therefore, it does not clot. If clots do occur, they usually form in the vagina and are a combination of red blood cells, glycoproteins, and mucous. Cyclic changes associated with the menstrual cycle are shown in Figure 20-5.

The proliferative phase of the menstrual cycle occurs when the endometrial lining begins to regenerate under the influence of estrogen. Changes in the cervical mucosa also occur during this phase. The cervical mucous becomes clearer, thinner, and threadlike.

If conception and implantation of the fertilized ovum occur, the corpus luteum is maintained by the presence of human chorionic gonadotropin (HCG), which is secreted by the implanting blastocyst. HCG is the hormone tested in at-home pregnancy kits.

The female reproductive cycle begins at **menarche**, the onset of menstruation, which occurs between 9 and 16 years of age, and ends at menopause, which occurs between 45 and 55 years of age. The onset of puberty, which occurs between the ages of eight and nine, is marked by significant increases in estrogen production and the development of secondary sex characteristics such as breast enlargement, hair distribution on the mons pubis, and contour changes of the hips and abdomen. Tanner's stages of pubic hair development provide objective criteria for the evaluation of developmental changes in the appearance of female genitalia (Table 20-1).

Nursing Tip

Patient Education on the Reproductive Cycle

Educating the patient about the reproductive cycle and its effects on the body will help the patient to better understand her own body's functioning and assist her in planning for gynecological examinations and birth control measures. The cervical mucous becomes clearer, thinner, and threadlike, indicating the onset of ovulation. The patient can perform her own **spinnbarkeit** test, the point at which the mucous can be drawn to a maximal length, by stretching vaginal mucous between her thumb and index finger. Tell the patient it is normal to feel low abdominal or flank pain when the ovum is released during ovulation. Rise in basal body temperature indicates that ovulation has occurred. Spotting may also be present after ovulation.

HEALTH HISTORY

The female genitalia health history provides insight into the link between a patient's life and lifestyle and female genitalia information and pathology.

PATIENT PROFILE	*Diseases that are age- and race-specific for the female genitalia are listed.*
Age	Sexually transmitted infections (STIs) (increased incidence 15–25) Uterine myomas (30–50) Cervical cancer (40–60) Vulval cancer (postmenopause) Uterine prolapse (postmenopause) Cystocele (postmenopause) Rectocele (postmenopause) Atrophic vaginitis (postmenopause) Endometrial cancer (diagnosis is usually made between 55 and 69) Vaginal cancer (over 60) Ovarian cancer (risk increases with age; highest rates are between 65 and 84)
Ethnicity	Fibroids are more common in African Americans (women of African descent who live in other countries do not appear to have as high an incidence of fibroids)
HEALTH ISSUE/CONCERN	*Common health concerns/issues for the female genitalia are defined and information on the characteristics of each sign or symptom is provided.*
Uterine Bleeding	The presence of bleeding from the endometrium
Quality	Odour, consistency, colour
Quantity	Amount (number and size of tampons or pads used in 24 hours), duration and frequency of flow
Associated Manifestations	Abdominal pain or cramping, passage of clots or tissue
Aggravating Factors	Stress, anxiety, medications (aspirin, NSAIDs), rapid weight loss or gain, obesity, sexual intercourse
Alleviating Factors	Medication, dilatation and curettage, surgery
Setting	Traumatic abortion or dilatation and curettage
Timing	Relationship to menses (intermenstrual, oligomenorrhea, polymenorrhea, menometrorrhagia, metrorrhagia), to use of intrauterine device (IUD)
Vaginal Discharge	The presence of a leaky discharge of fluid from the vagina
Quality	Colour, consistency, odour
Quantity	Number and size of tampons or pads used in 24 hours
Associated Manifestations	Itching, presence of discharge in sexual partner, **dyspareunia** (painful sexual intercourse), dysuria, abdominal pain, or cramping
Aggravating Factors	Tight pants, wet bathing suits, antibiotics, birth control pills, diet, pregnancy, deodorant tampons, bubble bath, chemical douches, lubricated condoms, contraceptive creams, pre-existing disease such as diabetes mellitus, increased number of sexual partners, semen, vaginal films, latex products
Alleviating Factors	Position, loose-fitting pants, cotton underpants and pantyhose with cotton crotch, medication

continues

Timing	Post coitus, while taking antibiotics
Urinary Symptoms	Changes in the normal voiding pattern and in characteristics of the urine
Quality	Colour: straw, amber; microscopic or macroscopic hematuria; consistency: clear, cloudy; presence of particles; odour
Quantity	Polyuria, oliguria, or anuria
Associated Manifestations	Flank pain, abdominal pain or cramping, dysuria, abdominal distention, vaginal discharge, urgency and frequency in voiding, stress incontinence, pneumaturia, fever
Aggravating Factors	Douches, intravaginal devices, traumatic coitus, alcohol, caffeine, spices, delaying urination
Alleviating Factors	Medication, warm baths, hydration
Setting	Post coitus
Timing	At beginning, throughout, or end of stream
Pelvic Pain	The subjective sense of discomfort in the pelvis
Quality	Stabbing, burning, cramping, aching, throbbing, drawing, pulling
Associated Manifestations	Abdominal distension, pelvic fullness, vaginal discharge or bleeding, gastrointestinal symptoms, menstruation, fever, ectopic pregnancy, pelvic inflammatory disease (PID)
Aggravating Factors	Exercise, sexual activity
Alleviating Factors	Rest, medication, surgery, heating pad, NSAIDs
Setting	During coitus, ovulation
Timing	Sudden or gradual onset, association with activity, duration, recurrence, relation to menstrual cycle
PAST HEALTH HISTORY	*The various components of the past health history are linked to female genitalia pathology and female genitalia-related information.*
Medical History	
Female Genitalia Specific	See Table 20-2
Non-Female Genitalia Specific	Diabetes mellitus, thyroid disease, incontinence, constipation, urinary tract infections
Surgical History	Hysterectomy, myomectomy, salpingectomy, oophorectomy, dilatation and curettage, laparoscopy, vulvectomy, tubal ligation, colpotomy, cesarean section, colposcopy, cryotherapy, uterine cryoablation
Medications	Antibiotics may increase incidence of *Candida* vaginosis and lessen the effectiveness of oral contraceptives.
Communicable Diseases	STI: gonorrhea, syphilis, herpes, HIV/AIDS, hepatitis, *chlamydia*, human papillomavirus (HPV), hepatitis B and C, trichomoniasis, chancroid, molluscum contagiosum
Allergies	Numerous feminine hygiene products may cause allergic reactions or increase the incidence of *Candida* vaginosis. Be aware of any latex allergies; condoms and diaphragms are usually made of latex. The spermicide nonoxynol 9 may also cause allergic reactions.

continues

Injuries and Accidents	Abdominal trauma, rape, sexual abuse, vaginal trauma or injuries, pelvic fractures, lumbar spine, sacrococcygeal injuries
Special Needs	Paraplegic and quadriplegic patients are at increased obstetric risk depending on level of injury, tone of uterus, and competency of cervix.
Childhood Illnesses	Fetal diethylstilbestrol (DES) exposure
FAMILY HEALTH HISTORY	*Female genitalia diseases that are familial are listed.*
	Cancers of the reproductive organs, mother received DES while pregnant with patient, transfer of STIs during delivery, placental transfer of hepatitis B and hepatitis C, HIV/AIDS, multiple pregnancies, congenital anomalies
SOCIAL HISTORY	*The components of the social history are linked to female genitalia factors and pathology.*
Alcohol/Drug Use	There is a significant positive correlation between alcohol use and acquaintance rape in the postsecondary-aged population. Alcohol, pot, cocaine, ecstasy, and crystal meth use can reduce inhibitions and caution, leading to unsafe sex practices.[1]
Tobacco Use	There is an increased incidence of strokes and thrombotic events in women who concurrently smoke and use hormonal therapy. Smoking is a risk factor for cervical cancer.
Sexual Practice	Sexually active women < 25, women with multiple partners or who are monogamous but whose partners have had a series of partners; women who have unprotected sex, share sex toys, have sex with blood exchange, are sex workers or have "survival sex" (sex for food, shelter, drugs), or are victims of sexual assault/abuse, are at increased risk for STIs, HIV/AIDS, hepatitis, and cervical carcinoma (an increase in the number of partners increases the risk of human papillomavirus, which can lead to dysplasia and possible cervical cancer).[2]
Home Environment	Poor sanitation may lead to numerous forms of vaginitis and infections; overcrowding is an ideal condition for mite infestation.
Hobbies and Leisure Activities	Wearing wet bathing suits for extended periods of time may increase the likelihood of *Candida* vaginosis. Strenuous equestrian sports and off-road cycling increase the likelihood of external genitalia trauma from saddle injuries. Female athletes may suffer from **amenorrhea** (absent menses).
Stress	Stress can have significant effects on menstruation, causing amenorrhea and exacerbating genital herpes simplex.
HEALTH MAINTENANCE ACTIVITIES	*This information provides a bridge between the health maintenance activities and female genitalia function.*
Sleep	Lack of sleep or extreme fatigue can lead to amenorrhea.
Diet	Increased levels of refined sugars, salt, and caffeine enhance PMS symptomology. Extreme dieting can affect menstruation and lead to amenorrhea. Elevated sugar and lactose can lead to vaginal candidiasis.
Exercise	Exercise may diminish **dysmenorrhea** (pain or cramping during menses) and **menorrhagia** (heavy menses).
Use of Safety Devices	Condom use
Health Check-ups	Date of last Pap smear and results, last STI screen

Nursing Tip

Late Onset of Menarche

Late onset of menarche can result from a multiplicity of pathologies. Women who have not experienced the onset of menstruation by 16 years of age or 14 years of age when secondary sex characteristics are present experience primary amenorrhea. Evaluate the patient for the following:

1. Pregnancy
2. Inadequate nutrition or eating disorders
3. Chronic diseases such as Crohn's disease, thyroid disease
4. Environmental stressors
5. Intensive athletic training
6. Use of opiates or steroids
7. Polycystic ovarian syndrome
8. Autoimmune diseases
9. Anatomic obstruction to menstrual flow
10. Genetic or chromosomal syndromes
11. Hypothalamic–pituitary ovarian axis disorders

TABLE 20-2 Female Reproductive Health History

MENSTRUAL HISTORY

Age of menarche, last menstrual period (LMP), length of cycle, regularity of cycle, duration of menses, amenorrhea, menorrhagia, presence of clots or vaginal pooling, number and type of tampons or pads used during menses, dysmenorrhea, spotting between menses, missed menses.

PREMENSTRUAL SYNDROME (PMS)

Symptoms occur from 3 to 7 days before the onset of menses with cessation of symptoms after second day of cycle. Symptoms include: breast tenderness, bloating, moodiness, cravings for salt, sugar, or chocolate, fatigue, weight gain, headaches, joint pain, nausea and vomiting.

OBSTETRIC HISTORY

See Chapter 23.

MENOPAUSE HISTORY

Menopause (cessation of menstruation), spotting, associated symptoms of menopause (such as hot flashes, palpitations, numbness, tingling, drenching sweats, mood swings, vaginal dryness, itching), treatment for symptoms (including estrogen replacement therapy), feelings about menopause.

VAGINAL DISCHARGE

See Health Issue/Concern Section.

HISTORY OF UTERINE BLEEDING

See Health Issue/Concern Section.

SEXUAL FUNCTIONING

Sexual preference, number of partners, interest, satisfaction, dyspareunia, inorgasmia.

REPRODUCTIVE MEDICAL HISTORY

Vaginal infections, yeast infections, salpingitis, endometritis, endometriosis, cervicitis, fibroids, ovarian cysts, cancer of the reproductive organs, infertility, Pap smear records.

METHOD OF BIRTH CONTROL

Type, frequency of use, methods to prevent STI's, any associated problems with birth control or STI prevention methods, such as a reaction to the spermicides used with the vaginal sponges, diaphragms, and condoms.

Life 360°

Thought-Provoking Scenarios

Think how you would respond to a female patient who told you the following during the health history:

- I really want a baby but my boyfriend doesn't, so I stopped taking my pills.
- I have had three abortions. It's an easier method of birth control than trying to remember to take a pill every day.
- My uncle is sexually abusing me and I can't take it anymore.
- Some guy put something in my drink at a party and I woke up in a strange bed. I don't know if I contracted an STI or HIV.

Nursing Tip

Maintaining Gynecological Health

Encourage patients to adopt healthy gynecological practices:

1. Avoid douches and feminine hygiene sprays or films, or use sparingly because these products disrupt the natural vaginal flora and increase the vaginal pH.
2. Do not leave tampons in the vagina for longer than eight hours at a time because of the increased risk of toxic shock syndrome.
3. Always wash and wipe the vaginal area from front to back to prevent contamination of the vagina and urethra with fecal material.
4. Thoroughly wash diaphragms, pessaries (device used to maintain the position of the uterus/bladder), and sexual aid devices before and after each use.
5. Void immediately after coitus.

EQUIPMENT

Assemble items before placing the patient on the examination table; materials should be arranged in order of use and within easy reach.

- Examination table with stirrups
- Stool, preferably mounted on wheels
- Large hand mirror
- Gooseneck lamp
- Clean gloves
- Linens for draping
- Vaginal specula (Figure 20-6):
  - Graves' bivalve specula, sizes medium and large, useful for most adult sexually active women
  - Pederson bivalve specula, sizes small and medium, useful for non-sexually active women, children, menopausal women
- Cytological materials (Figure 20-7):
  - Wood spatulas i.e., Ayre
  - Cervical broom
  - Cytobrushes
  - Cotton-tipped applicators
  - Liquid-based preparation vials
  - Microscope slides, cover slips, culture plates labelled with the patient's name, identification number, and date specimen was collected
  - Cytology fixative spray
  - Reagents: normal saline solution, potassium hydroxide (KOH), acetic acid (white vinegar)
- Warm water

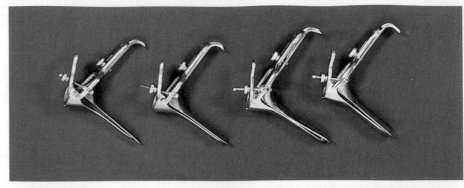

A. Lateral View

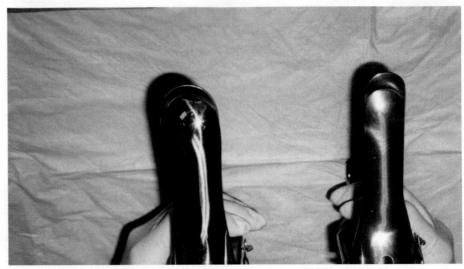

B. Superior View: Graves' Speculum (left), Pederson Speculum (right)

Figure 20-6 Vaginal Specula.

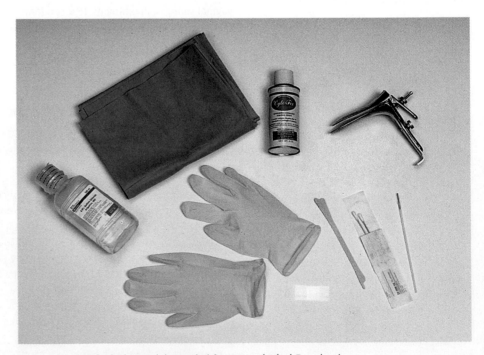

Figure 20-7 Cytological Materials Needed for Gynecological Examination.

ASSESSMENT OF THE FEMALE GENITALIA

Assessment of the female reproductive system consists of inspection and palpation only, and includes assessment of the abdomen (see Chapter 17), inspection of the external genitalia, palpation of the external genitalia, speculum assessment of the internal genitalia, collection of specimens for laboratory analysis, inspection of the vaginal walls, bimanual examination, and rectovaginal assessment (see Chapter 22 for the complete rectal examination). The assessment process requires somewhat uncomfortable positioning for the patient; therefore, it should be completed as quickly and as efficiently as possible.

Nursing Tip

Preparing for a Gynecological Examination

If you are a beginning nurse or if you have not performed a gynecological examination:
- Ask another nurse to assist you with the first few examinations.
- Familiarize yourself with the equipment. Practise opening and closing the speculum. Plastic specula make significant audible clicking sounds when opening and closing, so you should prepare the patient for this event.
- Review the anatomy and physiology of the female genitalia; visualize the underlying structures of the anatomic landmarks.
- Review and practise any procedures to be done. Some nurses find it difficult to prepare slides and cultures without assistance if they are novices to these procedures.
- Know your institution's policies regarding the option of having a female nurse present if a male nurse is performing the gynecological exam.

Nursing Tip

Liquid-Based Cervical Cytology

Liquid-based cervical cytology (Thin-Layer cytology) is becoming popular in Canada for the detection of squamous epithelial abnormalities (Figure 20-8). While the conventional PAP screening procedure involves smearing cells (including mucous, inflammatory cells, and some red blood cells) on a glass slide, the liquid-based procedure cleans the specimens for Pap smears by removing blood and mucous prior to mounting the cells on the slide. The cell sample is placed in a preservative vial, and the specimen is centrifuged, filtered, or both at the laboratory. It is likely that within a few years most, if not all, cervical cytology in Canada will be liquid-based.[3]

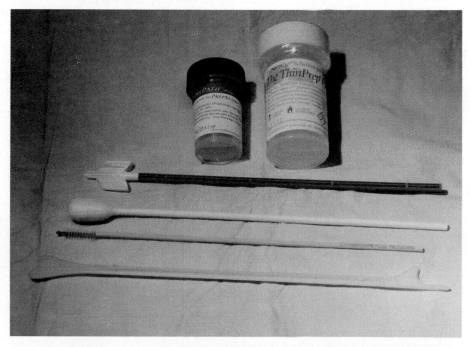

Figure 20-8 Liquid-Based Cervical Cytology Preparations.

◄NURSING CHECKLIST►

General Approach to Female Genitalia Assessment

Prior to the assessment:

1. Ensure that the patient will not be menstruating at the time of the examination for optimal cytological specimen collection.
2. Instruct the patient not to use vaginal sprays, to douche, or to have coitus 24 to 48 hours before the scheduled physical assessment. The products of coitus and commercial sprays and douches may affect the Pap smear and other vaginal cultures.
3. Encourage the patient to express any anxieties and concerns about the physical assessment. Reassure the patient by acknowledging anxieties and validating concerns. Virgins need reassurance that the pelvic assessment should not affect the hymen.
4. Show the speculum and other equipment to the patient and allow her to touch and explore any items that do not have to remain sterile.
5. Inform the patient that the assessment should not be painful but may be uncomfortable at times, and tell her to inform you if she is experiencing any pain.
6. Instruct the patient to empty her bladder and then to undress from the waist to the ankles.
7. Ensure that the room is warm enough to prevent chilling, and provide additional draping material as necessary.
8. Place drapes or sheep skin over the stirrups to increase patient comfort.
9. Warm your hands with warm water prior to gloving.
10. Ensure that privacy will be maintained during the assessment. Provide screens and a closed door.
11. Warm the speculum with warm water or a warming device before insertion.

During the assessment:

1. Inform the patient of what you are going to do before you do it. Tell her she may feel pressure when the speculum is opened and a pinching sensation when the Pap smear is done.
2. Adopt a non-judgmental and supportive attitude.
3. Maintain eye contact with the patient as much as possible to reinforce a caring relationship.
4. Use a mirror to show the patient what you are doing and to educate her about her body. Help her with positioning the mirror during the examination so she will feel comfortable using this technique at home to assess her genitalia.
5. Offer the patient the opportunity to ask questions about her body and sexuality.
6. Encourage the patient to use relaxation techniques such as deep breathing or guided imagery to prevent muscle tension during the assessment.

After the assessment:

1. Assess whether the patient needs assistance in dressing.
2. Offer tissues with which to wipe excess lubrication.
3. After the patient is dressed, discuss the experience with her, invite questions and comments, listen carefully, and provide her with information regarding the assessment and any laboratory information that is available.
4. Tell the patient she may experience a small amount of spotting following the Pap smear.

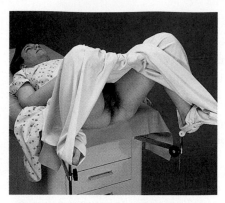

Figure 20-9 Patient Positioning and Draping for Gynecological Examination.

Inspection of the External Genitalia

1. With the patient seated, place a drape over the patient's torso and thighs until positioning is completed.
2. Instruct the patient to first sit on the examination table between the stirrups, facing the foot of the table.
3. Assist the patient in assuming a dorsal recumbent or lithotomy position on the examination table. Assist the patient in placing her heels in the stirrups, thus abducting her legs and flexing her hips.
4. Don clean gloves.
5. Assist the patient as she moves her buttocks down to the lower end of the examination table so that the buttocks are flush with the edge of the table. If the patient desires, raise the head of the examination table slightly to elevate her head and shoulders. This position allows you to maintain eye contact with the patient and prevents abdominal muscle tension (Figure 20-9).
6. Readjust the drape to cover the abdomen, thighs, and knees; adjust the stirrups as necessary for patient comfort. Push the drape down between the patient's knees so you can see the patient's face.
7. Sit on a stool at the foot of the examination table facing the patient's external genitalia.
8. Adjust your lighting source and provide the patient with a mirror. Instruct her on how to hold the mirror in order to view the examination prior to touching the patient's genitalia.
9. Finally, remember to inform the patient of each step of the assessment process before it is performed, and be gentle.

Pubic Hair

E 1. Observe the pattern of pubic hair distribution.
   2. Note the presence of nits or lice.

N The distribution of the female pubic hair should be shaped like an inverse triangle. There may be some growth on the abdomen and upper inner thighs. A diamond-shaped pattern from the umbilicus may be due to cultural or familial differences. There are no nits or lice.

A Extensive hair extending beyond the pubic hair triangle to the abdomen and upper inner thighs is abnormal.

P This distribution pattern may occur with hirsutism, which is indicative of an endocrine disorder.

A Hair distribution is sparse or hair is absent at the genitalia area. This is called **alopecia** and it is abnormal.

P Alopecia in the genital area may result from genetic factors, aging, or local or systemic disease. These include developmental defects and hereditary disorders, infection, neoplasms, physical or chemical agents, endocrine diseases, deficiency states (nutritional or metabolic), destruction, damage to the follicles, and obesity.

A The presence of nits or lice is abnormal.

P Pubic lice (pediculosis pubis) is the infestation of the hairy regions of the body, usually the pubic area, but it sometimes involves the hairy aspects of the abdomen, chest, and axillae.

| E | Examination | N | Normal Findings | A | Abnormal Findings | P | Pathophysiology |

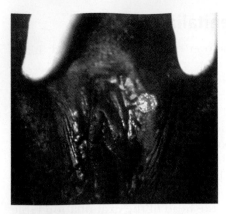

Figure 20-10 Syphilitic Chancre. *Courtesy of Centers for Disease Control and Prevention (CDC).*

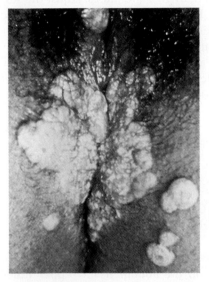

Figure 20-11 Secondary Syphilis (Condyloma Latum). *Courtesy of Centers for Disease Control and Prevention (CDC).*

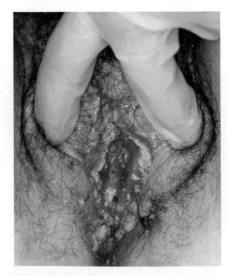

Figure 20-12 Genital Warts (Condyloma Acuminatum). *Courtesy of Centers for Disease Control and Prevention (CDC).*

Skin Colour and Condition

Mons Pubis and Vulva

E 1. Observe the skin coloration and condition of the mons pubis and vulva.
  2. Inform the patient that you will touch the inside of her thigh before you touch her genitals.
  3. With gloved hands, separate the labia majora using the thumb and index finger of the dominant hand.
  4. Observe both the labia majora and the labia minora for coloration, lesions, or trauma.

N The skin over the mons pubis should be clear except for nevi and normal hair distribution. The labia majora and minora should appear symmetrical with a smooth to somewhat wrinkled, unbroken, slightly pigmented skin surface. There should be no ecchymosis, excoriation, nodules, swelling, rash, or lesions. An occasional sebaceous cyst is within normal limits. These cysts are non-tender, yellow nodules that are less than 1 cm in diameter.

A Ecchymosis over the mons pubis or labia is abnormal.

P This may be due to blunt trauma that may have resulted from an accident or intentional abuse.

A Edema or swelling of the labia is an abnormal finding.

P This may be due to hematoma formation, Bartholin's cyst, or obstruction of the lymphatic system.

A Broken areas on the skin surface are abnormal.

P These may be due to ulcerations or abrasions secondary to infection or trauma.

A Rash over the mons pubis and labia is abnormal.

P Rashes have multiple etiologies including contact dermatitis and infestations.

A A non-tender, reddish, round ulcer with a depressed centre, and raised, indurated edges (**chancre**) is an abnormal finding (Figure 20-10).

P A chancre appears during the primary stages of syphilis at the site where the *Treponema* enters the body. The chancre lasts for four weeks and then disappears.

A Flat or raised, round, wartlike papules that have moist surfaces covered by grey exudate (condyloma latum) are abnormal (Figure 20-11).

P These lesions occur during the secondary stage of syphilis.

A White, dry, cauliflower-like growths that have narrow bases are suggestive of condyloma acuminatum (Figure 20-12) and are abnormal.

P These warts are caused by the human papillomavirus and may be dysplastic.

A Small, swollen, red vesicles that fuse together to form a large, burning ulcer that may be painful and itch (Figure 20-13) are abnormal.

P These ulcers are indicative of herpes simplex virus (HSV). Primary HSV (or genital herpes) outbreaks can last up to 21 days. Recurrent HSV outbreaks are usually shorter in duration and last about two weeks. Serologic testing must be performed to determine if an outbreak is HSV-1 or HSV-2.

A Firm, painless, papular, granular lesions that are beefy red are abnormal (Figure 20-14).

P Granuloma inguinale is caused by the bacteria *Calymmatobacterium granulomatis*. It is also referred to as donovanosis and granuloma venereum. This STI tends to occur on the external genitalia, inguinal region, and anus.

A A painless mass that may be accompanied by pruritus or a mass that develops into a cauliflower-like growth is an abnormal finding.

P This type of mass is highly suggestive of malignancy.

A Venous prominences of the labia may be abnormal.

P Varicose veins may develop due to a congenital predisposition, prolonged standing, pregnancy, or aging.

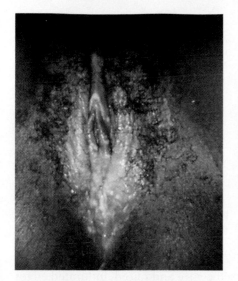

Figure 20-13A Genital Herpes Simplex Virus. *Courtesy of Centers for Disease Control and Prevention (CDC).*

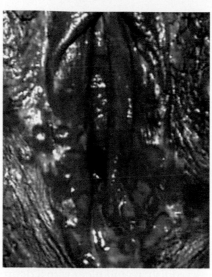

Figure 20-13B Primary Herpes Simplex Virus, First Episode. Serology tests are negative for HSV. *Copyright GlaxoSmithKline. Used with permission.*

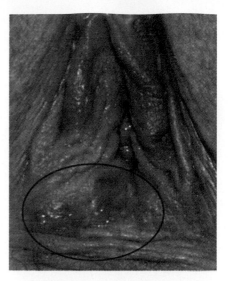

Figure 20-13C Non-Primary Herpes Simplex Virus, First Episode. Serology tests are positive for HSV (type 1 or type 2), meaning the patient has had previous exposure to the virus at another body site. *Copyright GlaxoSmithKline. Used with permission.*

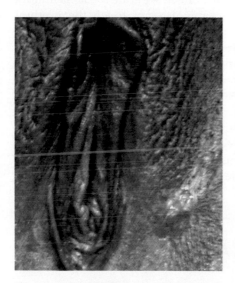

Figure 20-13D Recurrent HSV. After the initial primary outbreak, frequent recurrences (four to eight episodes per year) can occur at the primary outbreak site. *Copyright GlaxoSmithKline. Used with permission.*

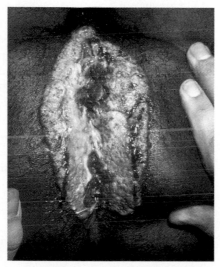

Figure 20-14 Granuloma Inguinale. *Courtesy of Centers for Disease Control and Prevention (CDC).*

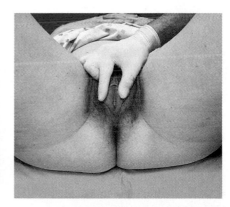

Figure 20-15 Inspection of the External Genitalia.

Clitoris

E   **1.** Using the dominant thumb and index finger, separate the labia minora laterally to expose the prepuce of the clitoris (Figure 20-15).
   2. Observe the clitoris for size and condition.

N   The clitoris is approximately 2.0 cm in length and 0.5 cm in diameter and without lesions.

A   Hypertrophy of the clitoris is an abnormal finding.

P   This may indicate female pseudohermaphroditism due to androgen excess.

E	**Examination**	**N** **Normal Findings**	**A** **Abnormal Findings**	**P** **Pathophysiology**

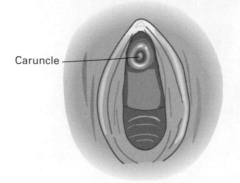

Caruncle

Figure 20-16 Urethral Caruncle.

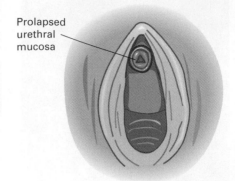

Prolapsed urethral mucosa

Figure 20-17 Prolapse of the Urethral Meatus.

A A reddish, round ulcer with a depressed centre and raised, indurated edges (chancre) is an abnormal finding.

P Refer to the chancre discussion on page 742.

Urethral Meatus

E 1. Using the dominant thumb and index finger, separate the labia minora laterally to expose the urethral meatus. Do not touch the urethral meatus; this may cause pain and urethral spasm.

2. Observe the shape, colour, and size of the urethral meatus.

N The urethral opening is slit-like in appearance and midline; it is free of discharge, swelling, or redness and is about the size of a pea.

A Discharge of any colour from the meatus is an abnormal finding.

P Discharge indicates possible urinary tract infection.

A Swelling or redness around the urethral meatus is an abnormal finding.

P Swelling indicates possible infection of the Skene's glands, urethral caruncle (small, red growth that protrudes from the meatus, shown in Figure 20-16), urethral carcinoma, or prolapse of the urethral mucosa (Figure 20-17).

Nursing Alert

Risk Factors for Vaginal Infections

The following may increase vaginal discharges and infections:

- Anatomy of the genital area
- Underlying skin diseases
- Increasing age
- Antibiotic use
- Immunodeficiency
- Oral contraceptive use
- Estrogen deficiency
- High sugar or milk intake
- Diabetes mellitus
- Steroid use
- Menses
- Douches
- Alkalinization from semen or chemical products
- Pregnancy
- Increased number of sexual partners
- Sexual abuse
- Hygiene

Nursing Alert

Female Genital Mutilation (FGM)

Female genital mutilation (FGM) is the collective term given to several different procedures that involve the cutting of female genitalia and permanently mutilating the sexual organs of young females for non-medical reasons. While the practice has its roots in countries in Africa, the Arabian Peninsula, Asia, and South America, global migration patterns have brought the practice to Canada. FGM includes any or all of the following: the removal of the hood of the clitoris; the complete removal of the clitoris along with labia minora excisions; the complete removal of the clitoris and surrounding tissues, and suturing of the vaginal opening (infibulation). There is a growing recognition of FGM as a violation of human rights and is considered child assault in Canada and thus prohibited. Immigrant and refugee movements, governments, and advocacy organizations in Canada have acknowledged the need to deal with FGM as an internationally recognized health and human rights concern.[4] The nurse performing an examination of the female genitalia must be sensitive in that women who have undergone FGM may not be open to such an examination for fear of being judged or embarrassed. As well, the woman or girl may present for possible complications from this procedure such as infection.

Vaginal Introitus

E   **1.** Keep the labia minora retracted laterally to inspect the vaginal introitus.
      2. Ask the patient to bear down.
      3. Observe for patency and bulging.

N   **The introitus mucosa should be pink and moist. Normal vaginal discharge is clear to white and free of foul odour; some white clumps may be seen that are mass numbers of epithelial cells. The introitus should be patent and without bulging.**

A   Pale colour and dryness of the introitus are abnormal.

P   Possible etiologies include atrophy from topical steroids, the aging process, and estrogen deficiency.

A   Foul-smelling discharge that is any colour other than clear to slightly pale white is abnormal. Malodorous white, yellow, green, or grey discharge that may be purulent are some possible findings.

P   Gonorrhea, *chlamydia*, *Candida* vaginosis, *Trichomonas* vaginitis, bacterial vaginosis, atrophic vaginitis, or cervicitis are possible infectious processes or vectors (Table 20-3).

A   An external tear or impatency of the vaginal introitus is abnormal.

P   Possible causes include trauma and fissure of the introitus. An external tear may indicate trauma from sexual activity or abuse, and a fissure may indicate a congenital malformation or childbirth trauma.

A   Bulging of the anterior vaginal wall indicates a **cystocele** (Figure 20-18) and is abnormal.

P   The upper two-thirds of anterior vaginal wall along with the bladder push forward into the introitus due to weakened supporting tissues and ligaments.

A   Bulging of the anterior vaginal wall, bladder, and urethra into the vaginal introitus indicates a **cystourethrocele** (Figure 20-19) and is abnormal.

P   The etiology is usually a weakening of the entire anterior vaginal wall. A fissure may define the urethrocele and cystocele.

A   Bulging of the posterior vaginal wall with a portion of the rectum indicates a **rectocele** (Figure 20-20) and is abnormal.

P   This is caused by a weakening of the entire posterior vaginal wall.

Perineum and Anus

E   **1.** Observe for colour and shape of the anus.
      2. Observe texture and colour of the perineum.

N   **The perineum should be smooth and slightly darkened. A well-healed episiotomy scar is normal after vaginal delivery. The anus should be dark pink to brown and puckered. Skin tags are not uncommon around the anal area.**

A   A fissure or tear of the perineum is an abnormal finding.

P   Possible causes include trauma, abscess, or unhealed episiotomy.

A   Venous prominences of the anal area indicate external hemorrhoids and are abnormal.

P   An external hemorrhoid is the varicose dilatation of a vein of the inferior hemorrhoidal plexus and is covered with modified anal skin.

Palpation of the External Genitalia

Labia

E   **1.** Palpate each labium between the thumb and the index finger of your dominant hand.
      2. Observe for swelling, induration, pain, or discharge from a Bartholin's gland duct.

E   **Examination**   **N**   **Normal Findings**   **A**   **Abnormal Findings**   **P**   **Pathophysiology**

TABLE 20-3 Vaginal Discharge—Diagnostic Features and Laboratory Diagnosis

	BACTERIAL VAGINOSIS	CANDIDIASIS	TRICHOMONIASIS
Sexual transmission	• Not usually considered sexually transmitted	• Not usually considered sexually transmitted	• Sexually transmitted
Predisposing factors	• Often absent • More common if sexually active • New sexual partner • IUD use	• Often absent • More common if sexually active • Current or recent antibiotic use • Pregnancy • Corticosteroids • Poorly controlled diabetes • Immunocompromised	• Multiple partners
Symptoms	• Vaginal discharge • Fishy odour • 50% asymptomatic	• Vaginal discharge • Itch • External dysuria • Superficial dyspareunia • Up to 20% asymptomatic	• Vaginal discharge • Itch • Dysuria • 10–50% asymptomatic
Signs	• White or grey, thin, copious discharge	• White, clumpy, curdy discharge • Erythema and edema of vagina and vulva	• Off-white or yellow, frothy discharge • Erythema of vulva and cervix ("strawberry cervix")
Vaginal pH Wet mount	• >4.5 • PMNs • Clue cells*	• <4.5 • Budding yeast • Pseudohyphae	• >4.5 • Motile flagellated protozoa (38–82% sensitivity)
Gram stain	• Clue cells • Decreased normal flora • Predominant Gram-negative curved bacilli and coccobacilli	• PMNs • Budding yeast • Pseudohyphae	• PMNs • Trichomonads
Whiff test Preferred treatment	• Positive • Metronidazole • Clindamycin	• Negative • Antifungals	• Negative • Metronidazole • Treat partner

IUD = intrauterine device

PMN = polymorphonuclear leukocytes

*Clue cells are vaginal epithelial cells covered with numerous coccobacilli.

†Culture is more sensitive than microscopy for *T vaginalis*.

Source: Compiled from information on the Health Canada website.

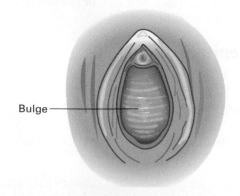

Figure 20-18 Cystocele.

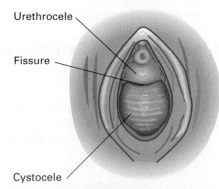

Figure 20-19 Cystourethrocele.

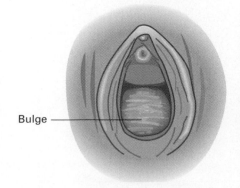

Figure 20-20 Rectocele.

Nursing Alert

The Sexually Abused Patient

No patient, regardless of age, should be excluded from evaluation for sexual abuse. Physical signs of sexual abuse include bruising of the mons pubis, labia, or perineum, and vaginal or rectal tears. The presence of STIs in the very young or the very old patient suggests abuse. Emotional signs such as lack of eye contact during the examination, extreme anxiety or guarding during the assessment, or refusing to assume certain positions may all indicate a history of abuse. Document all signs of suspected sexual abuse.

Know your institution's policy regarding the reporting of sexual abuse. All provinces and territories have mandatory reporting policies for sexual abuse in children and teenagers.

Assure the patient that she is safe with you and refer her to the appropriate social services or sexual assault services. *See Chapter 3, p. 70-71 on further assessment of abuse.*

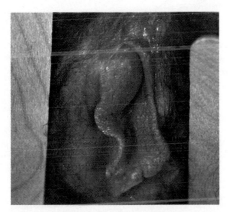

Figure 20-21 Bartholinitis. *Courtesy of Centers for Disease Control and Prevention (CDC).*

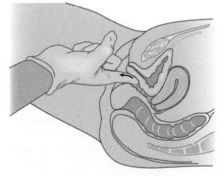

Figure 20-22 Milking the Urethra.

N   The labium should feel soft and uniform in structure with no swelling, pain, induration, or purulent discharge.

A   Swelling, redness, induration, or purulent discharge from the labial folds with hot, tender areas are abnormal findings (Figure 20-21).

P   These findings indicate a probable Bartholin's gland infection. Causative organisms include gonococci, *chlamydia trachomatis*, and syphilis.

A   A firm mass that is possibly painful in the labia majora is abnormal.

A   This might indicate an inguinal hernia. If this is suspected, repalpate the mass with the patient in a standing position. See Chapter 21 for a more thorough explanation of hernias.

Urethral Meatus and Skene's Glands

E   1. Insert your dominant index finger into the vagina.
    2. Apply pressure to the anterior aspect of the vaginal wall and milk the urethra (Figure 20-22).
    3. Observe for discharge and patient discomfort.

N   Milking the urethra should not cause pain or result in any urethral discharge.

A   Pain on contact and discharge from the urethra are abnormal findings.

P   These findings indicate a Skene's gland infection or urinary tract infection.

Vaginal Introitus

E   1. While your finger remains in the vagina, ask the patient to squeeze the vaginal muscles around your finger.
    2. Evaluate muscle strength and tone.

N   Vaginal muscle tone in a nulliparous woman should be tight and strong; in a parous woman, it will be diminished.

A   Significantly diminished or absent vaginal muscle tone and bulging of vaginal or pelvic contents are abnormal findings.

P   Weakened muscle tone may result from injury, age, childbirth, or medication. Bulging results from cystocele, rectocele, or uterine prolapse (Figure 20-23).

E	**Examination**	N	**Normal Findings**	A	**Abnormal Findings**	P	**Pathophysiology**

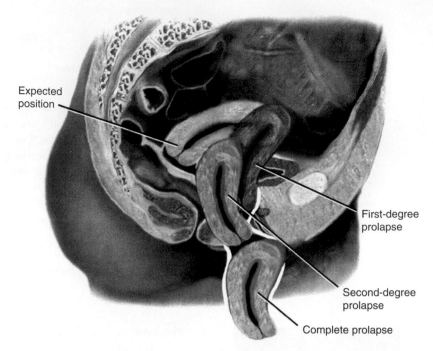

Expected
position

First-degree
prolapse

Second-degree
prolapse

Complete prolapse

Figure 20-23 In first-degree prolapse, the cervix is contained within the vagina with straining. In second-degree prolapse, the cervix is at the introitus with straining, and in third-degree prolapse, complete prolapse, the cervix, uterus, and vagina are outside the introitus, even without straining.

Nursing Tip

Examining Urethral Discharge

If discharge is noted from the urethra, swab the discharge with a cotton-tipped applicator and spread the sample on a microscope slide for further evaluation. Consider sending a sample for culture and sensitivity.

Nursing Tip

Genital Self-Examination

Teach the patient to inspect and palpate the external genitalia and glands for lesions, irritations, and ulcerations, which may indicate disease. The use of a mirror facilitates genital self-examination.

Nursing Alert

Hormone Replacement Therapy (HRT)

The use of HRT/ERT (hormone replacement therapy/estrogen replacement therapy) can be a concern of many menopausal women as the benefits and risks have been subject to much discussion. The Society of Obstetricians and Gynaecologists of Canada (SOGC) Menopause Consensus Report (2006) [5, 6] notes the following:
- Hormone therapy is the most effective option for the medical management of moderate or severe menopausal symptoms i.e., hot flashes, night sweats. HRT is given in the lowest dose possible.
- Local estrogen therapy should be used for urogenital sexual health such as vaginal dryness.
- Breast cancer risk after five years of combined systemic hormone therapy is in similar magnitude to lifestyle variables such as obesity, alcohol and cigarette use, and physical inactivity. As such, the benefits and risks of HRT/ERT in relation to other lifestyle variables must be considered.
- The risks and benefits must be weighed if ERT is used solely for the purpose of fracture prevention.

Nursing Alert

Primary Dysmenorrhea (PD)

- The majority of Canadian women will suffer from dysmenorrhea at some time during their reproductive years. Young age, smoking, and non-use of oral contraceptives are independent risk factors for PD.[7]
- Therapeutic options may include NSAIDS as a first-line treatment for the relief of pain, high-frequency TENS, oral contraceptives; there is limited support yet ongoing study of the use of complementary and alternative medicines such as vitamin B_1, vitamin E, fish oil, magnesium, vitamin B_6, and Neptune krill oil.[8]

Perineum

E 1. Withdraw your finger from the introitus until you can place only your dominant index finger posterior to the perineum and place the dominant thumb anterior to the perineum.
   2. Assess the perineum between the dominant thumb and index finger for muscular tone and texture.

N The perineum should be smooth, firm, and homogenous in the nulliparous woman, and thinner in the parous woman. A well-healed episiotomy scar is also within normal limits for a parous woman.

A A thin, tissue-like perineum, fissures, or tears are abnormal.

P A thin perineum is indicative of atrophy, and fissures and tears may indicate trauma or an unhealed episiotomy.

Speculum Examination of the Internal Genitalia

Cervix

E 1. Select the appropriate-sized speculum. This selection should be based on the patient's history, size of vaginal introitus, and vaginal muscle tone. See page 738 for description of specula.
   2. Lubricate and warm the speculum by rinsing it under warm water. Do not use other lubricants because they may interfere with the accuracy of cytological samples and cultures.
   3. Hold the speculum in your dominant hand with the closed blades between the index and middle fingers. The index finger should rest at the proximal end of the superior blade. Wrap the other fingers around the handle, with the thumbscrew over the thumb (Figure 20-24).
   4. Insert your non-dominant index and middle fingers, ventral sides down, just inside the vagina and apply pressure to the posterior vaginal wall. Encourage the patient to bear down. This will help to relax the perineal muscles.
   5. Encourage the patient to relax by taking deep breaths. Be careful not to pull on pubic hair or pinch the labia.
   6. When you feel the muscles relax, insert the speculum at an oblique angle on a plane parallel to the examination table until the speculum reaches the end of the fingers that are in the vagina (Figure 20-25A).

Figure 20-24 Holding the Speculum.

| E Examination | N Normal Findings | A Abnormal Findings | P Pathophysiology |

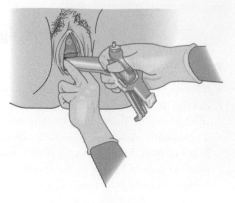

A. Opening of the Vaginal Introitus

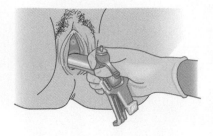

B. Oblique Insertion of the Speculum

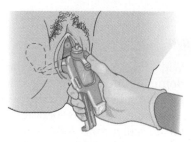

C. Final Advancement of the Speculum

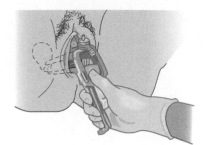

D. Opening the Speculum Blades

Figure 20-25 Speculum Examination.

7. Withdraw the fingers of your non-dominant hand.
8. Gently rotate the speculum blades to a horizontal angle and advance the speculum at a 45° downward angle against the posterior vaginal wall until it reaches the end of the vagina (Figures 20-25B and C).
9. Using your dominant thumb, depress the lever to open the blades and visualize the cervix (Figure 20-25D).
10. If the cervix is not visualized, close the blades and withdraw the speculum 2 to 3 cm and reinsert it at a slightly different angle to ensure that the speculum is inserted far enough into the vagina.
11. Once the cervix is fully visualized, lock the speculum blades into place. This procedure varies based on the type of speculum being used.
12. Adjust your light source so that it shines through the speculum.
13. If any discharge obstructs the visualization of the cervix, clean it away with a cotton-tipped applicator.
14. Inspect the cervix and the os for colour, position, size, surface characteristics such as polyps or lesions, discharge, and shape.

Colour

N The normal cervix is a glistening pink; it may be pale after menopause or blue (Chadwick's sign) during pregnancy.
A Cyanosis not associated with pregnancy is abnormal.
P Possible causes include venous congestion of the area or systemic hypoxia as in congestive heart failure.
A Redness or a friable appearance is an abnormal finding.
P Possible causes include infection and inflammation, such as *chlamydia* or gonorrhea.

Figure 20-26 Nabothian Cysts.

Figure 20-27 Cervical Polyp.

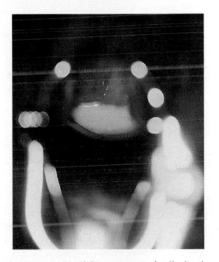

Figure 20-28 *Trichomonas vaginalis* is the cause of the purulent cervical discharge. *Courtesy of Centers for Disease Control and Prevention (CDC).*

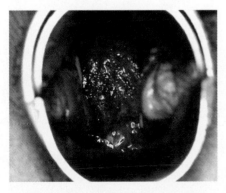

Figure 20-29 This woman's cervix is erythematous with erosions due to *chlamydia*. *Courtesy of Centers for Disease Control and Prevention (CDC).*

Position

N The cervix is located midline in the vagina with an anterior or posterior position relative to the vaginal vault and projecting approximately 2.5 cm into the vagina.

A Lateral positioning of the cervix may present as an abnormal finding.

P Possible causes include tumour or adhesions that would displace the cervix.

A Projection of the cervix into the vaginal vault greater than normal limits is suspect.

P Uterine prolapse is caused by weakened vaginal wall muscles and pelvic ligaments, and may push the cervix into the vaginal vault.

Size

N Normal size is 2.5 cm.

A Cervical size greater than 4 cm is indicative of hypertrophy and is abnormal.

P Inflammation or tumour could result in the morbid enlargement of the cervix.

Surface Characteristics

N The cervix is covered by the glistening pink squamous epithelium, which is similar to the vaginal epithelium, and the deep pink to red columnar epithelium, which is a continuation of the endocervical lining.

A A reddish circle around the os may be abnormal.

P This is known as **ectropion** or **eversion**. It occurs when the squamocolumnar junction appears on the ectocervix. It results from lacerations during childbirth or possibly from congenital variation.

A Small, cystic, yellow lesions on the cervical surface indicate **nabothian cysts** (Figure 20-26), which are abnormal.

P These benign cysts result from the obstruction of cervical glands.

A A bright-red, soft protrusion through the cervical os indicates a cervical polyp (Figure 20-27) and is abnormal.

P Polyps originate from the endocervical canal; they are usually benign but tend to bleed if abraded.

A Hemorrhages dispersed over the surface and known as strawberry spots are abnormal. There may also be a foul-smelling, frothy, green or yellow discharge (Figure 20-28).

P These may be seen in conjunction with trichomonal infections.

A Mucopurulent discharge, erythema, and friability of the cervix are abnormal (Figure 20-29).

P Many women with *chlamydia trachomatis* are asymptomatic; others can have pelvic pain, fever, and dysuria. *Chlamydia* is the most common STI in Canada.[9] Patients infected with this STI frequently have gonorrhea.

A Irregularities of the cervical surface that may look cauliflower-like are abnormal.

P Carcinoma of the cervix may manifest as a cauliflower-like overgrowth (Figure 20-30).

A Columnar epithelium covering most of the cervix and extending to the vaginal wall (vaginal ad enosis), and a collar-type ridge between the cervix and the vagina are abnormal (Figure 20-31).

P This denotes fetal exposure to DES.

| E | **Examination** | N | **Normal Findings** | A | **Abnormal Findings** | P | **Pathophysiology** |

Figure 20-30 Carcinoma of the Cervix.

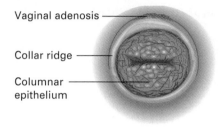

Vaginal adenosis

Collar ridge

Columnar epithelium

Figure 20-31 Fetal Exposure to DES.

Nursing Alert

Cancer of the Female Genitalia

Epidemiology[10]
- Cancer of the body of the uterus is the 4th most common cause of new cancer cases in Canadian women, after breast, lung, and colorectal cancer.
- Ovarian cancer is the 7th most common cause of new cancer cases in Canadian women; the majority of women who present with ovarian cancer are in the late stages of the illness. The National Ovarian Cancer Association of Canada refers to this form of cancer as "the disease that whispers."
- Cervical cancer is the 11th most common cause of cancer diagnosis in Canadian women; it is the third most common cancer among women aged 20 to 49.

Risk Factors for Female Genitalia Cancer
Evaluate each patient for risk factors, and counsel the patient regarding diminishing risk factors that are behaviour dependent. Suspected carcinoma of the female genitalia requires an immediate referral.

Cervical Cancer
Risk Factors
- Early age at first intercourse (before 17 or 18 years of age)
- Multiple sex partners or male partners who have had multiple partners
- Prior history of human papillomavirus, herpes simplex virus
- Current or prior human papillomavirus or condylomata, or both
- Family history
- Tobacco use
- Drug use
- HIV
- Immunosuppressed
- History of STIs, cervical dysplasia or cervical cancer, endometrial, vaginal, or vulvar cancer
- Women of lower socioeconomic state

Endometrial Cancer
- Early or late menarche (before age 11 or after age 16)
- History of infertility
- Failure to ovulate
- Unopposed estrogen therapy
- Use of tamoxifen
- Obesity
- Family history

*Ovarian Cancer**
- Advancing age
- Nulliparity
- History of breast cancer
- Family history of ovarian cancer
- Infertility treatment

Vaginal Cancer
- Daughters of women who ingested DES during pregnancy
- Prior human papillomavirus

Ovarian Cancer Signs and Symptoms[11]
Changes in bowel function (constipation, diarrhea); abdominal bloating, distention or discomfort; nausea, indigestion, flatulence; urinary frequency/nocturia; menstrual irregularities; back pain; pelvic discomfort, heaviness; weight gain or loss; fatigue/sleep changes.

Nursing Alert

DES (diethylstilbestrol) Exposure

Most patients with DES exposure were born prior to 1971. These patients are at greater risk for carcinoma of the upper vagina.

Nursing Alert

Screening for Ovarian Cancer

Unfortunately, the use of biomarkers, e.g. CA 125 or investigations such as pelvic examination and transvaginal ultrasound, for early detection of ovarian cancer have not been associated with a reduction in mortality rates from this illness. Like lung cancer, there are currently no national screening recommendations for ovarian cancer in healthy and asymptomatic women.[12]

Nursing Alert

Screening for Cervical Cancer

The Programmatic Guidelines for Screening for Cancer of the Cervix in Canada[13] recommend:
- Annual screening using Papanicolaou (Pap) smears upon initiation of sexual intercourse or at 18 years.
- After two normal tests, screening every three years until age 69.
- More frequent testing may be considered for women at high risk (first intercourse at < 18 yrs., multiple sexual partners, consort with multiple sexual partners, smoking, low socioeconomic status, immunocompromised, HIV positive). *The Society of Obstetricians and Gynaecologists of Canada recommends that women of **all** sexual orientations require regular assessment for cervical cancer.*

The most recent data on screening for cervical cancer indicates that there are disparities in which Canadian women are being adequately screened. Women in New Brunswick and the Yukon report the highest levels of screening (85% and 88% respectively) while women in Quebec and Nunavut report the lowest (76% and 70% respectively).[14]

Nursing Alert

Human Papillomavirus (HPV) Infections[15]

- HPV causes skin or mucosal infections, particularly in moist areas like the genitalia. Some types of HPV pose low risk for cervical cancer while others, such as HPV 16 and 18, are associated with a high risk of cervical cancer.
- Fortunately, regular cervical screening is effective in reducing rates of cervical cancer.
- Gardasil™ vaccine, the first and only vaccine against HPV, is approved in Canada for females aged 9 to 26 years (further research is being conducted on the use of this vaccine in older women). This vaccine is effective for HPV types 6, 11, and 18.

Normal

Nulliparous

Parous

Lacerations

Unilateral transverse

Bilateral transverse

Stellate

Figure 20-32 Shapes of the Cervical Os.

Discharge

E Note characteristics of any discharge.
E/A/P 1. See Table 20-3.

Shape of the Cervical Os

N In the nulliparous woman, the os is small and either round or oval. In the parous woman who has had a vaginal delivery, the os is a horizontal slit.
A A unilateral transverse, bilateral transverse, stellate, or irregular cervical os is abnormal (Figure 20-32).
P Possible causes include cervical tears that have occurred during rapid second-stage childbirth delivery, forceps delivery, and trauma.

| E | **Examination** | N | **Normal Findings** | A | **Abnormal Findings** | P | **Pathophysiology** |

Collecting Specimens for Cytological Smears and Cultures

After inspection of the cervix and the cervical os, obtain any laboratory specimens that are indicated.

Collect the Pap smear first, followed by the gonococcal and any other vaginal smears. There are many accepted variations among laboratories regarding the collection and fixing of vaginal specimens. It is wise to identify the procedure recommended by the laboratory testing the specimens.

Papanicolaou (Pap) Smear

The Pap smear is actually a collection of three specimens that are obtained from three sites: the endocervix (covered by columnar epithelium), cervix (or transformative zone—covered by metaplastic epithelium), and the vaginal pool (also called the exocervix or posterior fornix—covered by squamous epithelium). The purpose of the Pap smear is to evaluate cervicovaginal cells for pathology that may indicate carcinoma. The Programmatic Guidelines for Screening for Cancer of the Cervix in Canada recommend that all females at the age of 18 or any female who is sexually active (whichever comes first) undergo this screening examination on a yearly basis. If the patient has three or more consecutive normal Pap smears, screening may be done every three years unless the patient is high risk (see Nursing Alert: Screening for Cervical Cancer). If the patient had a hysterectomy for benign disease, discontinue routine Pap screening. In women with hysterectomy for non-benign disease the Pap smear screens for cervical cancer. If the patient has CIN II or CIN III, screen three times and then discontinue screening if normal. Though Pap smears can be spaced every three years, a woman should have an annual pelvic examination at least until age 80–85.

A separate slide may be used for each specimen collected from the three areas, or one slide that is divided and labelled in three sections may be used. Two methods can be used to screen for cervical cancer: a glass slide fixed with Cytospray (conventional) or liquid-based cytology (LBC). Access to LBC is limited to a small number of jurisdictions in Canada but use of this method is growing.[16]

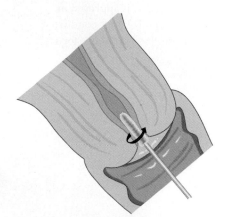

Figure 20-33 Endocervical Smear.

Endocervical Smear

E
1. Using your dominant hand, insert the Cytobrush or cervical broom through the speculum into the cervical os approximately 1 cm. Many patients find that this procedure causes a cramping sensation, so forewarn your patient that she may feel discomfort during this element of the assessment.
2. Rotate the Cytobrush between your index finger and thumb 90° clockwise, then counterclockwise. Keep the Cytobrush in contact with the cervical tissue (Figure 20-33). Note: If you have to use a cotton-tipped applicator instead of a Cytobrush, leave the applicator in the cervical os for 30 seconds to ensure saturation. If you use the cervical broom, rotate the broom six times clockwise and place the broom in the liquid-based preparation container.
3. Remove the Cytobrush and, using a rolling motion, spread the cells on the section of the slide marked *E*, if a sectional slide is being used. Do not press down hard or wipe the Cytobrush back and forth because doing so will destroy the cells.
4. Discard the brush.

N/A/P   Refer to Vaginal Pool Smear, following.

Cervical (Transformative Zone) Smear

E
1. Insert the bifurcated end of the wooden spatula through the speculum base. Place the longer projection of the bifurcation into the cervical os. The shorter projection should be snug against the ectocervix.

2. Rotate the spatula 360° one time only (Figure 20-34). Make sure the transformation zone is well sampled.

3. Remove the spatula and gently spread the specimen on the section of the slide labelled *C*, if a sectional slide is being used.

N/A/P   Refer to Vaginal Pool (Exocervical) Smear, following.

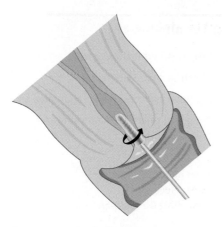

Figure 20-34 Cervical Smear.

Vaginal Pool (Exocervical) Smear

E   **1.** Reverse the spatula and insert the rounded end into the posterior vaginal fornix and gently scrape the area. *Note:* a cotton-tipped applicator can also be used to obtain the smear. The cotton-tipped applicator may be the preferred vehicle for obtaining the specimen if vaginal secretions are viscous or dry. By moistening the cotton-tipped applicator with normal saline solution, viscous secretions can be removed with less trauma to the surrounding membranes (Figure 20-35).

2. Remove the spatula and gently spread the specimen on the section of the slide marked *V*, if a sectional slide is being used.

3. Dispose of the spatula or cotton-tipped applicator.

4. Spray the entire slide or the slides with cytological fixative.

5. Submit the specimens to the appropriate laboratory following your institution's guidelines for cytology specimens.

N   Normal classifications for cervicovaginal cytology (meaning no pathogenesis) include "within normal limits (WNL)" (using Bethesda System); or "no abnormal cells" or "metaplasia noted" (using the CIN/Modified Walton System) (Table 20-4).[17]

A   A report finding of benign cellular changes is abnormal.

P   Benign cellular changes have a multiplicity of causes including fungal, bacterial, protozoan, or viral infections.

A   A report finding of "atypical squamous cells of undetermined significance" is abnormal.

P   Causes of this finding include inflammatory or infectious processes, a preliminary lesion, or an unknown phenomenon.

A   A report finding of epithelial cell abnormalities is aberrant.

P   This finding is indicative of squamous intraepithelial lesion, which may or may not be transient; squamous cell carcinoma; or glandular cell abnormalities that are seen in postmenopausal women who are not on hormone replacement therapy.

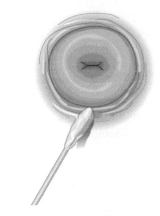

Figure 20-35 Vaginal Pool Smear.

Chlamydia Culture Specimen

P   **1.** Insert a sterile cotton swab applicator 1 cm into the cervical os.

2. Hold the applicator in place for 20 seconds.

3. Remove the swab.

4. Place the swab in a viral, *chlamydia*, or mycoplasma culture transport tube.

5. Dispose of the cotton swab applicator.

6. Submit the specimens to the appropriate laboratory following your institution's guidelines for culture specimens.

N   Cervicovaginal tissues are normally free of *Candida albicans*. There should be no odour.

A   It is abnormal to find *trachomatis*, serotypes D through K, or obligate, intracellular bacteria in cervicovaginal secretions.

P   *Trachomatis* may invade the cervix or fallopian tubes, but it is often asymptomatic in women.

Note: Non-culture laboratory test methods include direct fluorescent antibody (DFA), enzyme immunoassay (EIA), DNA probes, or polymerase chain reaction (PCR).

E	**Examination**	N	**Normal Findings**	A	**Abnormal Findings**	P	**Pathophysiology**

TABLE 20-4 Cervico-Vaginal Reporting Terminologies

The Bethesda System	CIN/Modified Walton System
Unsatisfactory: state reason	Unsatisfactory: state reason
Within normal limits	No abnormal cells; metaplasia noted
Benign cellular changes	Abnormal cells consistent with reactive atypia (non-dysplastic)
Trichomonas vaginalis Fungal organisms morphologically consistent with *Candida spp.* Cellular changes associated with Herpes Simplex virus	Trichomonas effect Yeast effect Viral effect (Herpes type)
Benign cellular changes	Abnormal cells consistent with reactive atypia (non-dysplastic)

Reactive cellular changes associated with:
  Inflammation
  Radiation
  Other
	
	Inflammatory effect
	Irradiation effect
	Other

ASCUS	Abnormal cells consistent with atypia (possibly dysplastic) Atypical metaplasia Atypical parakeratosis Other (add comment)
LSIL	Abnormal cells consistent with condyloma (HPV § effect)
LSIL	Mild dysplasia/CIN§§ I
HSIL	Moderate dysplasia/CIN II
HSIL	Severe dysplasia/CIS/CIN III
Carcinoma Squamous cell carcinoma Adenocarcinoma Unspecified	Abnormal cells consistent with malignancy Consistent with invasive squamous carcinoma Consistent with adenocarcinoma Type unspecified
AGUS	
Other	Abnormal cells not specifically classified Add comment

ASCUS = atypical squamous cells of undetermined significance
LSIL = low grade squamous intraepithelial lesion
HSIL = high grade intraepithelial lesion
AGUS = atypical glandular cells of undetermined significance
HPV = human papillomavirus
CIN = cervical intraepithelial neoplasia
Source: Cervico-Vaginal Reporting Terminologies from page 22, http://www.phac-aspc.gc.ca/ccdpc-cpcmc/cc-ccu/pdf/screening.pdf. Reproduced with the permission of the Minister of Public Works and Government Services Canada, 2006.

Gonococcal Culture Specimen

E 1. Insert a sterile cotton swab applicator 1 cm into the cervical os.
   2. Hold the applicator in place for 20 to 30 seconds.
   3. Remove the swab.

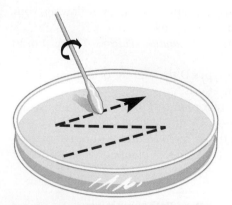

Figure 20-36 Inoculation of a Culture Plate.

4. Roll the swab in a large Z pattern over the culture plate. Simultaneously rotate the swab as you roll it to ensure that all of the specimen is used (Figure 20-36).

5. Dispose of the swab.

6. Submit the specimens to the appropriate laboratory following your institution's guidelines for culture specimens.

N Cervicovaginal tissues are normally free of *Neisseria gonorrhoeae.*

A It is abnormal to find a large number of Gram-negative diplococci present in cervicovaginal secretions.

P *N. gonorrhoeae* are Gram-negative diplococci organisms that prefer to invade columnar and stratified epithelium.

Saline Mount or Wet Mount

This test is performed for the rapid evaluation of white blood cells and protozoa.

E 1. Spread a sample of the cervical or vaginal pool specimen onto a microscope slide, add one drop of normal saline (0.9%) solution, and apply a cover slip.

2. Examine under a microscope.

N The sample should have fewer than ten white blood cells (WBCs) per field.

A A sample with more than ten WBCs per field, protozoa (Figure 20-37), bacteria-filled epithelial cells (clue cells) (Figure 20-38), or other organisms is abnormal.

P A large number of WBCs can be indicative of an inflammatory response, *chlamydia trachomatis,* or a bacterial infection. Protozoa are indicative of *trichomoniasis.*

Whiff Test or KOH Prep

This test is performed for the rapid evaluation of *Candida.*

P 1. Spread a sample of the cervical or vaginal pool specimen onto a microscope slide, add one drop of 10% KOH (potassium hydroxide), and apply a cover slip.

2. Note any odour.

3. Examine under a microscope.

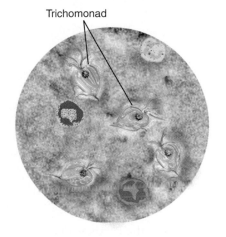

Trichomonad

Figure 20-37 Microscopic View of Trichomonas.

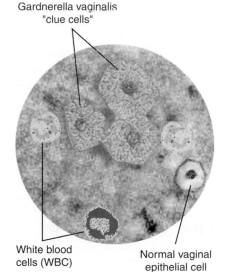

Gardnerella vaginalis "clue cells"

White blood cells (WBC)

Normal vaginal epithelial cell

Figure 20-38 Microscopic View of Clue Cells.

Nursing Alert

Lesbian Health Issues

Women whose primary emotional and sexual relationships are with women may not get the care they need because they do not believe they have certain needs or because health care providers are not aware of lesbian health issues. Canadian lesbians use the health care system with approximately the same frequency as other women; however, they are less likely to undergo screening tests, specifically Pap smears, mammograms, and breast examination, even when needed.[18] Women may believe that because they are not having sex with men that they do not require Pap testing when they do. Health care providers may assume lesbians are not having sex with men or may feel uncomfortable conducting a sexual history. As you conduct a health history with any client, think about how that person's sexual orientation influences the scope and depth of your exploration and the way you relate to this person.

E Examination	N Normal Findings	A Abnormal Findings	P Pathophysiology

Reflective Thinking

Examining the Patient with an STI

Your patient has told you that she has noticed an odourless greenish discharge from her vagina during the past two weeks. She has been married for 37 years and has not had any sexual partners other than her husband during that time. You observe that her vulva is erythematous, and there is pus in her cervical os. How would you further assess this patient? What additional questions would you ask? What anticipatory guidance would you provide?

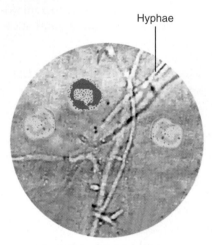

Hyphae

Figure 20-39 Microscopic View of Hyphae.

N Cervicovaginal tissues are normally free of *Candida albicans* except in a small percentage of women. There should be no odour.

A The presence of yeast and pseudohyphae forms (chains of budding yeast) (Figure 20-39) is abnormal.

P The presence of budding yeast is indicative of an overgrowth of *Candida*.

A An odour is abnormal.

P An amine (fishy odour) indicates bacterial vaginosis.

Five Percent Acetic Acid Wash*

E After completing all other vaginal specimens, swab the cervix with a cotton-tipped applicator that has been soaked in 5% acetic acid.

P The normal response is no change in the appearance of the cervix.

A A rapid acetowhitening or blanching with jagged borders is an abnormal finding.

P The cause may be the human papillomavirus, which is the causative agent of genital warts.

* Aceto-acid testing has a high false-positive rate in both female and male patients; however, it can provide useful information, in conjunction with other sources of data, for single-visit approaches to cervical prevention in low-resource settings.[19]

Anal Culture

E 1. Insert a sterile cotton swab applicator 1 cm into the anal canal.
2. Hold the applicator in place for 20 to 30 seconds.
3. Remove the swab. If fecal material is collected, discard the applicator and start again.
4. Roll and rotate the swab in a large Z pattern over a culture plate.
5. Dispose of the swab.

N Anal tissues are normally free of *Neisseria gonorrhoeae*.

A The presence of a large number of Gram-negative diplococci is abnormal.

P This is indicative of *N. gonorrhoeae*.

Inspection of the Vaginal Wall

E 1. Disengage the locking device of the speculum.
2. Slowly withdraw the speculum but do not close the blades.
3. Rotate the speculum into an oblique position as you retract it to allow full inspection of the vaginal walls. Observe vaginal wall colour and texture.

N The vaginal walls should be pink, moist, deeply rugated, and without lesions or redness.

A   Spots that appear as white paint on the walls are abnormal.

P   A possible cause is leukoplakia from *Candida albicans*. Repeated occurrences even after treatment may indicate HIV infection.

A   Pallor of the vaginal walls is abnormal.

P   Possible causes include anemia and menopause.

A   Redness of the vaginal walls is abnormal.

P   Possible causes include inflammation, hyperemia, and trauma from tampon insertion or removal.

A   Vaginal lesions or masses are abnormal findings.

P   Possible causes include carcinoma, tumours, and DES exposure.

Bimanual Examination

E   1. Observe the patient's face for signs of discomfort during the assessment process.

2. Inform the patient of the steps of the bimanual assessment, and warn her that the lubricant gel may be cold.

3. Squeeze water-soluble lubricant onto the fingertips of your dominant hand.

4. Stand between the legs of the patient as she remains in the lithotomy position, and place your non-dominant hand on her abdomen and below the umbilicus.

5. Insert your dominant index and middle fingers 1 cm into the vagina. The fingers should be extended with the palmar side up. Exert gentle posterior pressure.

6. Inform the patient that pressure from palpation may be uncomfortable. Instruct the patient to relax the abdominal muscles by taking deep breaths.

7. When you feel the patient's muscles relax, insert your fingers to their full length into the vagina. Insert your fingers slowly so that you can simultaneously palpate the vaginal walls.

8. Remember to keep your thumb widely abducted and away from the urethral meatus and clitoris throughout the palpation in order to prevent pain or spasm.

Vagina

E   Complete steps 1–8 from bimanual examination. Rotate the wrist so that the fingers are able to palpate all surface aspects of the vagina.

N   **The vaginal wall is non-tender and has a smooth or rugated surface with no lesions, masses, or cysts.**

A   The presence of lesions, masses, scarring, or cysts is abnormal.

P   These findings may be indicative of benign lesions such as inclusion cysts, myomas, or fibromas. The most common site for malignant lesions of the vagina is the upper one-third of the posterior vaginal wall.

Cervix

E   1. Position the dominant hand so that the palmar surface faces upward.

2. Place the non-dominant hand on the abdomen approximately one-third of the way down between the umbilicus and the symphysis pubis.

3. Use the palmar surfaces of the dominant hand's finger pads, which are in the vagina, to assess the cervix for consistency, position, shape, and tenderness.

| E | **Examination** | N | **Normal Findings** | A | **Abnormal Findings** | P | **Pathophysiology** |

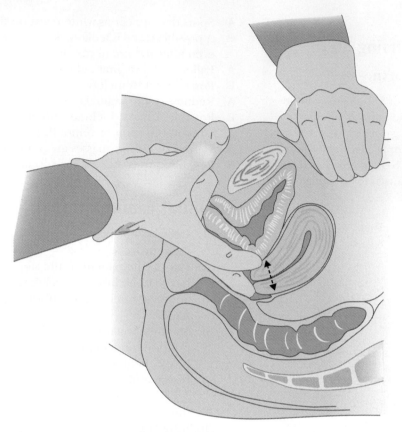

Figure 20-40 Assessment of Cervical Mobility.

    4. Grasp the cervix between the fingertips and move the cervix from side to side to assess mobility (Figure 20-40).

N The normal cervix is mobile without pain, smooth and firm, symmetrically rounded, and midline.

A The presence of pain on palpation or the assessment of mobility is a positive **Chandelier's sign** and is abnormal.

P This is indicative of possible pelvic inflammatory disease or ectopic pregnancy.

A Softening of the cervix (Goodell's sign) is a significant finding.

P This sign is seen at the fifth to sixth week of pregnancy.

A Irregular surface, immobility, or nodular surface structure of the cervix indicates abnormality.

P Possible causes include malignancy, fibroids, nabothian cysts, and polyps.

Fornices

E **1.** With the fingertips and palmar surfaces of the fingers, palpate around the fornices.
     2. Note nodules or irregularities.

N The walls should be smooth and without nodules.

A The presence of nodules or irregularities is abnormal.

P Possible causes include malignancy, polyps, and herniations if the walls of the fornices are impatent.

Uterus

E **1.** With the dominant hand, which is in the vagina, push the pelvic organs out of the pelvic cavity and provide stabilization while the non-dominant hand, which is on the abdomen, performs the palpation (Figure 20-41).

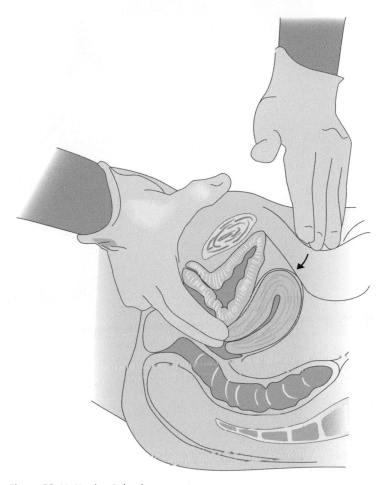

Figure 20-41 Uterine Palpation.

2. Press the hand that is on the abdomen inward and downward toward the vagina, and try to grasp the uterus between your hands.
3. Evaluate the uterus for size, shape, consistency, mobility, tenderness, masses, and position.
4. Place the fingers of the intravaginal hand into the anterior fornix and palpate the uterine surface.

N   The size of the uterus varies based on parity; it should be pear-shaped in the non-gravid patient and more rounded in the parous patient. The uterus should be smooth, firm, mobile, non-tender, and without masses. For uterine positions, see Figure 20-3. A uterus may be non-palpable if it is retroverted or retroflexed. The uterus in these positions can be assessed only via rectovaginal examination. A non-palpable uterus in the older woman may be a normal finding secondary to uterine atrophy.

A   Significant exterior enlargement and changes in the shape of the uterus are abnormal.

P   Uterine enlargement indicates possible intrauterine pregnancy or tumour.

A   Presence of nodules or irregularities indicates leiomyomas.

P   Leiomyomas are tumours containing muscle tissue.

A   Inability to assess the uterus may be abnormal.

P   A hysterectomy may account for a non-palpable uterus.

| E | **Examination** | N | **Normal Findings** | A | **Abnormal Findings** | P | **Pathophysiology** |

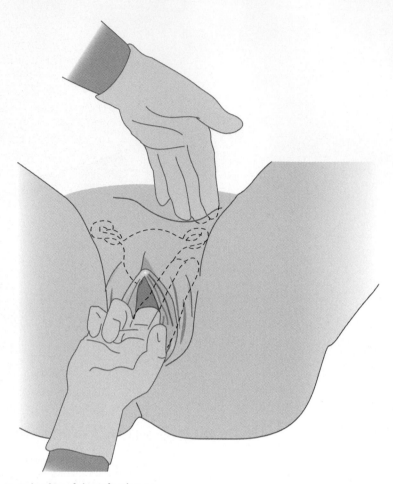

Figure 20-42 Palpation of the Left Adnexa.

Adnexa

Fallopian tubes are rarely palpable, and palpation of the ovaries depends on patient age and size. Many times, the ovaries are not palpable, and this procedure can be painful to the patient during the luteal phase of the menstrual cycle (postovulation) or due to normal visceral tenderness.

E 1. Move the intravaginal hand to the right lateral fornix, and the hand on the abdomen to the right lower quadrant just inside the anterior iliac spine. Press deeply inward and upward toward the abdominal hand.
   2. Push inward and downward with the abdominal hand and try to catch the ovary between your fingertips.
   3. Palpate for size, shape, consistency, and mobility of the adnexa.
   4. Repeat the above manoeuvres on the left side (Figure 20-42).

N **The ovaries are normally almond shaped, firm, smooth, and mobile without tenderness.**

A Presence of enlarged ovaries that are irregular, nodular, painful, with decreased mobility, or pulsatile indicate pathology.

P Abnormal adnexal presentation may indicate ectopic pregnancy, ovarian cyst, pelvic inflammatory disease, or malignancy.

Rectovaginal Examination

E 1. Withdraw your dominant hand from the vagina and change gloves. Apply additional lubricant to the fingertips of your dominant hand.
   2. Tell the patient you will be inserting one finger into her vagina and one finger into her rectum. Remind her that the lubricant jelly will feel cold and that the rectal examination will be uncomfortable.

3. Insert the dominant index finger back into the vagina.
4. Ask the patient to strain down as if she is having a bowel movement in order to relax the anal sphincter. Assess anal sphincter tone.
5. Insert the middle finger of the dominant hand into the patient's rectum as she strains down (Figure 20-43). If the rectum is full of stool, carefully remove the stool digitally from the rectum.
6. Advance the rectal finger forward while using the non-dominant hand to depress the abdomen. Assess the rectovaginal septum for patency, the cervix and uterus for anomalies such as posterior lesions, and the rectouterine pouch for contour lesions.
7. On completion of the assessment, withdraw the fingers from the vagina and rectum, and if any stool is present on the glove, test for occult blood.
8. Clean the patient's genitalia and anal area with a tissue and assist her back to a sitting position.

N   The rectal walls are normally smooth and free of lesions. The rectal pouch is rugated and free of masses. Anal sphincter tone is strong. The cervix and uterus, if palpable, are smooth. The rectovaginal septum is smooth and intact. Refer to Chapter 22 for further information on the complete rectal examination.

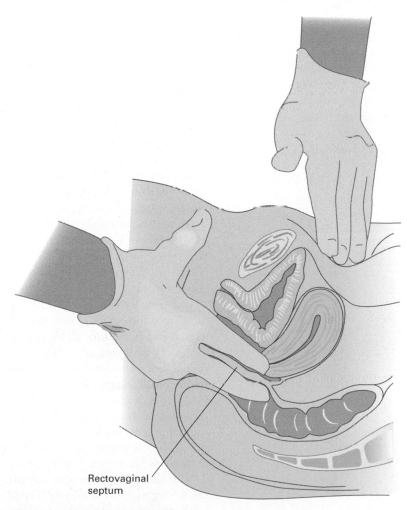

Rectovaginal septum

Figure 20-43 Rectovaginal Examination.

E	**Examination**	N	**Normal Findings**	A	**Abnormal Findings**	P	**Pathophysiology**

Nursing Tip

Examining the Patient with a Hysterectomy

If the patient has had a hysterectomy, follow the same assessment sequence but omit the following items: cervical palpation, uterine inspection and palpation, endocervical smear, and cervical smear. The vaginal walls and adnexa are evaluated if they were not surgically removed during the hysterectomy.

Life 360°

Gynecological Assessments for Women after Hysterectomies

Some women feel that it is unnecessary to have gynecological examinations after hysterectomies. However, many of these women had surgery because of malignancy and therefore are at risk for recurrence. All women who have had this type of surgery must be encouraged to continue seeking annual gynecological examinations. Yearly monitoring helps to determine if malignancy has returned or if other pathologies have developed; for instance, women whose ovaries were not removed in the hysterectomy are still at risk for ovarian cancer.

How can you publicize this topic? How can you increase women's awareness of the need for annual gynecological check-ups even if they have had hysterectomies?

Life 360°

Sexuality in Older Women

Think back to the last time you conducted a sexual history on an older woman. Did you ask her the same questions as you would pose to a 25-year-old female? Did you introduce any gender bias? Economic bias? Education bias? What are your personal views on sexuality in a 50-year-old female? 60-year-old? 70-year-old? 80-year-old? 90-year-old?

A The presence of masses or lesions indicates pathology.
P Possible causes include malignancy and internal hemorrhoids.
A Lax sphincter tone is an abnormal finding.
P Possible causes include perineal trauma from childbirth or anal intercourse and neurological disorders.

GERONTOLOGICAL VARIATIONS

The aging woman undergoes definite physical changes in her internal and external genitalia and her reproductive system. These changes begin with menopause, which usually occurs between the ages of 45 and 55. Menopause is characterized by low estrogen levels, which cause the cessation of the menstrual cycle. As aging progresses, a generalized atrophy of the external and internal female reproductive organs evolves.

Atrophy of the external reproductive organs results in a smaller clitoris and smaller labia. The labia also become flatter and lose their pigmentation. The skin of the labia becomes thin, shiny, avascular, and dry. There is a loss of subcutaneous fat in the pubic area, and the pubic hair becomes sparse and turns grey or white.

Atrophy of the internal reproductive organs causes the ovaries and fallopian tubes to diminish in size so that they are rarely palpable. The uterus atrophies so that it may be difficult to palpate. The cervix becomes smaller, paler, and less mobile. The cervical os becomes smaller but should remain palpable. The vagina becomes shorter, narrower, and thinner. The introitus may be constricted due to atrophy. There is a loss of rugae in the vaginal walls, and therefore a loss of elasticity in the walls. These changes in the vagina may cause the patient to complain of dyspareunia. Also, a delayed and reduced production of vaginal secretions may cause alterations in sexual response. An increase in the pH of the vaginal secretions and a decrease in the normal vaginal flora leads to an increase in vaginal infections in elderly women.

The pelvic muscles also atrophy, causing a decrease in the support of the pelvic organs. These muscles are often already weakened by trauma from childbirth; therefore, prolapse of the uterus and vaginal walls are common in elderly women.

CASE STUDY

The Patient with Herpes Simplex Virus

Linda is a 20-Year-Old Single Mother with a History of Sexually Transmitted Infections

HEALTH HISTORY

PATIENT PROFILE	20 yo woman, looks worried
HEALTH ISSUE/CONCERN	"I have a sore on my bottom that really hurts."
HISTORY OF ISSUE/CONCERN	States that she felt a tingling on her Ⓛ labia 2 d ago & now she has a blisterlike lesion in the same area that is quite tender to touch & causes extreme pain when she voids. Warm baths help the pain. Feels flu like & achy c̄ a sore throat; unable to state whether she has a fever since she does not have a thermometer. She took ASA s̄ relief then borrowed Empracet from a friend "that helped a bit." Pain prevents her from wearing her jeans, & walking is more difficult.
PAST HEALTH HISTORY	
Medical History	
Female Reproductive Health History	Menstrual hx: menarche age 11, 28–31 d cycle c̄ mod flow lasting 5–7 d; LMP lasted 6 d & flow was nl, but was 6 wks ago
	Premenstrual syndrome: States she occasionally has bloating & irritability 1 wk prior to her menses
	Obstetrical hx: G: 2 P: 2 T:2 P: OA:O E:O LC: 2, SVD × 2, uncomplicated pregnancies
	Menopause hx: N/A
	Vaginal discharge: clear
	Hx of uterine bleeding: denies
	Sexual functioning: sexually active for 6 yrs, had at least 16 different male partners; present partner × 2 weeks; denies engaging in anal intercourse; denies dyspareunia, inorgasmia
	Reproductive medical hx: has had 3 abnormal Pap smears; pt. cannot remember what they were and did not follow up.
	Method of birth control: occasionally condoms but inconsistent use
Surgical History	Umbilical hernia repair, age 2
Medications	Denies
Communicable Diseases	hx ⊕ for *chlamydia* × 2, gonorrhea × 1 (not sure if treated), genital warts, Trichomonas; denies testing for HIV or hepatitis
Allergies	Denies food or drug allergies
Injuries and Accidents	Stabbed in Ⓛ arm, age 15, 10 sutures required
Special Needs	Denies
Blood Transfusions	Denies
Childhood Illnesses	Denies
Immunizations	States she does not know; had some to get into elementary school

continues

FAMILY HEALTH HISTORY   *States she does not know her father's family*

LEGEND

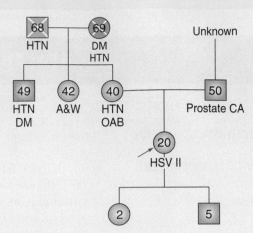

- ⬤ Living female
- ⬛ Living male
- ⊗ Deceased female
- ⊠ Deceased male
- ╱ Points to patient

A&W = Alive & well
CA = Cancer
DM = Diabetes mellitus
HTN = Hypertension
HSVII = Herpes simplex
        virus, type II
OAB = Overactive bladder

Denies family hx of cancer of female reproductive organs, DES exposure, congenital anomalies.

SOCIAL HISTORY

Alcohol Use	Drinks 2 beers daily on wkend
Drug Use	Occasional marijuana use
Tobacco Use	1 PPD for 5 yrs
Domestic and Intimate Partner Violence	Former boyfriend beat her up a few times; never reported events or went to the hospital
Sexual Practice	Refer to med hx
Travel History	Denies
Work Environment	Unemployed
Home Environment	Lives in low-cost housing project c̄ 2 children & her mother
Hobbies and Leisure Activities	Denies
Stress & coping	"I worry about not having any skills to get a job . . . my children take so much of my energy. I try to find pleasure in the simple things in life and am going to meet a counsellor to help me find some training program so I might get a job. My mother is really supportive and helps me a lot with the children."
Education	Quit high school in grade 10 to care for children
Economic Status	Unemployed, receives government assistance, food vouchers from local church
Religion/Spirituality	"I don't go to church"
Ethnicity	"I'm half French and half English"
Roles and Relationships	Occasionally argues c̄ mother but overall positive; children irritate her at times but "I love them so much."

continues

Characteristic Patterns of Daily Living	Awakens when children wake her; has breakfast; cares for and plays with children; goes to park or community centre with children in afternoon; feeds children at noon and about 17:00; bathes children; sometimes she goes out c̄ friends in the evening when mother can babysit
HEALTH MAINTENANCE ACTIVITIES	
Sleep	5–6 hours per night
Diet	Followed Canada's Food Guide but generally can't afford fresh vegetables or "good meat."
Exercise	Regular walks with children; no formal exercise program.
Stress Management	Playing with children, talking with mother, some socializing with friends.
Use of Safety Devices	Uses public transportation; has a smoke detector but does not think it has a battery
Health Check-Ups	Annual gyn exam, has not had dental exam in 5 years
PHYSICAL ASSESSMENT	
Inspection of the External Genitalia	
Pubic Hair	Inverse triangle formation, no nits or lice
Skin Colour and Condition	Clitoris, mons pubis, & vulva: mons pubis s̄ discoloration; Ⓛ labia majora c̄ 2 cm ulcerative, vesicular lesion c̄ raised edges near lower border, labia minora s̄ lesion, s̄ hypertrophy or ulceration Urethral meatus: midline, no swelling or discharge Vaginal introitus: pink s̄ lesion, no discharge noted Perineum and anus: pink-brown perineum, old episiotomy scar well healed; anus dark brown, old hemorrhoid tag at inferior edge
Palpation of the External Genitalia	
Labia	Tender to palpation
Urethral Meatus and Skene's Glands	No pain or discharge
Vaginal Introitus	Tone strong c̄ no bulging of pelvic contents
Perineum	Palpable episiotomy scar non-tender
Speculum Examination of the Internal Genitalia	
Cervix	Colour: pink Position: midline Size: 3.0 cm Surface characteristics: nabothian cyst at 3:00 position; laceration at 3:00 position Discharge: none Shape of the cervical os: parous

continues

Inspection of Vaginal Walls	Pink c̄ rugae
Bimanual Examination	
Vagina	No masses, non-tender
Cervix	Mobile, non-tender firm, palpable nabothian cyst
Fornices	Smooth, no herniation or polyps
Uterus	Parous, smooth, mobile, anteverted, non-tender, firm consistency
Adnexa	Mobile, round s̄ masses or tenderness, no pulsations
Rectovaginal Examination	Septum intact, no masses or fissures; uterus and cx WNL, strong anal sphincter tone, no occult blood
LABORATORY DATA	HSV culture: positive HSV II IgG: positive Pregnancy test: negative VDRL: negative HIV antibody: negative Gonorrhea and *chlamydia* culture: negative Pap smear: negative for intraepithelial lesion or malignancy

◄NURSING CHECKLIST►

Female Genitalia Assessment

Inspection of the External Genitalia

- Pubic hair
- Skin colour and condition
  - Mons pubis and vulva
  - Clitoris
  - Urethral meatus
  - Vaginal introitus
  - Perineum and anus

Palpation of the External Genitalia

- Labia
- Urethral meatus and Skene's glands
- Vaginal introitus
- Perineum

Speculum Examination of the Internal Genitalia

- Cervix
  - Colour
  - Position
  - Size
  - Surface characteristics
  - Discharge
  - Shape of the cervical os

Collecting Specimens for Cytological Smears and Cultures

- Pap smear
  - Endocervical smear
  - Cervical smear
  - Vaginal pool smear
- *Chlamydia* culture specimen
- Gonococcal culture specimen
- Saline mount or Wet mount
- KOH prep
- Five percent acetic acid wash
- Anal culture

Inspection of the Vaginal Wall

Bimanual Examination

- Vagina
- Cervix
- Fornices
- Uterus
- Adnexa
- Rectovaginal Examination

REVIEW QUESTIONS

1. The Pap smear collects specimens from these three sites:
   a. Skene's gland, endocervix, vaginal pool
   b. Endocervix, cervix, vaginal pool
   c. Uterus, vaginal pool, urethra
   d. Labia, urethra, Skene's gland
   The correct answer is (b).

2. While checking the cervix during the bimanual exam, the patient states that she has pain on palpation and evaluation of mobility. This finding is known as:
   a. Chandelier's sign
   b. Chadwick's sign
   c. Ectropion
   d. Goodell's sign
   The correct answer is (a).

3. You suspect your patient has a sexually transmitted infection. When you evaluate the cervix, you note reddened spots over the surface, known as "strawberry spots." This is a sign of which STI?
   a. Human papillomavirus
   b. Trichomoniasis
   c. *Candida*
   d. Gonorrhea
   The correct answer is (b).

4. Which of the following STIs requires reporting to both public health officials and sexual partners?
   a. *Chlamydia*, gonorrhea, pelvic inflammatory disease
   b. *Chlamydia*, gonorrhea, mucopururlent cervicitis
   c. Gonorrhea, mucopururlent cervicitis, primary syphilis
   d. *Chlamydia*, gonorrhea, primary syphilis
   The correct answer is (d).

5. Your patient complains of severe vulvar pain for the past three days. On evaluation you note that she has unilateral swelling of the right labia minora cleft. You palpate a lobular 2-cm mass that is exquisitely tender. This is most likely a:
   a. Rectocele
   b. Urethral caruncle
   c. Secondary syphilis
   d. Bartholin's gland infection
   The correct answer is (d).

6. Your 48-year-old patient had a total abdominal hysterectomy two years ago. She has both ovaries intact and is on estrogen replacement therapy. How often should she have a pelvic examination?
   a. Every three years
   b. Every year
   c. Every five years
   d. She no longer requires pelvic examinations
   The correct answer is (b).

7. Which two hormones stimulate the ripening of the graafian follicle?
   a. TSH and FSH
   b. FSH and SBGH
   c. LH and FSH
   d. HCG and LH
   The correct answer is (c).

8. Your patient is 17 years old and has never had a menstrual cycle. Which condition may cause primary amenorrhea?
   a. Hypothalamic–pituitary ovarian axis disorder
   b. Use of nonsteroidal anti-inflammatory medications
   c. Early age of first coital activity
   d. Parathyroid disease
   The correct answer is (a).

9. Your patient has a low-grade intraepithelial lesion of the cervix, CIN I. In evaluating her risk factors, which would increase her risk of cervical cancer?
   a. Unopposed estrogen therapy
   b. Fetal exposure to DES
   c. Smoking
   d. Failure to ovulate
   The correct answer is (c).

10. The leading cause of hysterectomies in Canada is:
    a. Uterine cancer
    b. Postpartum hemorrhage
    c. Leiomyomas
    d. Ovarian cancer
    The correct answer is (c).

> Visit the Estes online companion resource at
> www.healthassessment.nelson.com **for additional content and study aids.**

REFERENCES

[1]Fisher, W., Sevigny, C., & Stebenn, M. (2006). Primary care and sexually transmitted infections. *Canadian Guidelines on Sexually Transmitted Infections 2006 Edition Public Health Agency of Canada.* Retrieved November 16, 2006, from http://www.phac-aspc.gc.ca/std-mts/sti_2006/sti_intro2006_e.html

[2]Ibid.

[3] Chapman, W. (2002). HPV testing and cervical cancer screening. *Canadian Journal of Diagnosis, December 2002,* 64–70.

[4]Ontario Human Rights Commission. *Policy on Female Genital Mutilation (FGM).* Retrieved November 6, 2006, from http://www.ohrc.on.ca/english/publications/fgm-policy.shtml.

[5]Society of Obstetricians and Gynaecologists of Canada. (2006). Canadian consensus conference on menopause, 2006 update. *Journal of Obstetrics and Gynaecology of Canada, No. 171,* S7–S10.

[6]Ibid., S95–S96.

[7]Burnett, M.A., Antao, V., Black, A., Feldman, K., Grenville, A., Lea, R., Lefebvre, G., Pinsonneault, O., & Robert, M. (2005). Prevalence of primary dysmenorrhea in Canada. *Journal of Obstetrics and Gynaecology of Canada, 27*(8), 765–770.

[8]Society of Obstetricians and Gynaecologists of Canada. (2005). Primary dysmenorrhea consensus guidelines. *Journal of Obstetrics and Gynaecology of Canada, 169,* (December), 1119–1120.

[9]Fisher, W., Sevigny, C., & Stebenn, M. (2006). Primary care and sexually transmitted infections.

[10]Canadian Cancer Society/National Cancer Institute of Canada. (2006). *Canadian Cancer Statistics 2006.* Toronto.

[11]National Ovarian Cancer Association. The disease that whispers: Think ovarian! Retrieved November 16, 2006, from http://www.ovariancancercanada.ca/EN/awareness/symptoms.asp

[12]Canadian Cancer Society/National Cancer Institute of Canada. (2006). *Canadian Cancer Statistics 2006.*

[13]Health Canada and the Society of Gynecologic Oncologists of Canada. (1998). *Programmatic Guidelines for Screening for Cancer of the Cervix.* Ottawa, Retrieved November 6, 2006, from http://www.phac-aspc.gc.ca/ccdpc-cpcmc/cc-ccu/pdf/screening.pdf

[14]Canadian Cancer Society/National Cancer Institute of Canada (2006). *Canadian Cancer Statistics 2006.*

[15]Fisher, W., Sevigny, C., & Stebenn, M. (2006). Primary care and sexually transmitted infections.

[16]Steben, M. (2006). Genital human papillomavirus (HPV) infections. Canadian Guidelines on Sexually Transmitted Infections 2006 Edition. Retrieved November 6, 2006, from http://www.phac-aspc.gc.ca/std-mts/sti_2006/pdf/papillomavirus_e.pdf

[17]National Ovarian Cancer Association. The disease that whispers: Think ovarian!

[18]Davis, V. and the Social and Sexual Issues Committee (2000). Lesbian health guidelines. *Journal of Obstetrics and Gynaecology of Canada, 22* (3), 202–205.

[19]Society of Obstetricians and Gynaecologists of Canada (2004). Cervical cancer prevention in low-resource settings. *Journal of Obstetrics and Gynaecology of Canada, 26*(3), 205–208.

BIBLIOGRAPHY

Al Kadri, H., AL Fozan, H., Hajeer, A., & Hassan, S. (2006). Hormone therapy for endometriosis and surgical menopause. (Protocol) *The Cochrane Database of Systematic Reviews* 2006, Issue 2. Art. No.: CD005997.

Carlson, C., Eisinstat, S., Frigoletto, F., & Schiff, I. (2002). *Primary Care of Women* (2nd ed.). St. Louis, MO: Mosby.

Federal Interdepartmental Working Group on Female Genital Mutilation. (1999). *Female genital mutilation and health care—an exploration of the needs and roles of affected communities and health care providers in Canada.* Ottawa: Health Canada.

Fitch, M. & Turner, F. (2006). Ovarian cancer. *The Canadian Nurse, 102*(1), 16.

Greer, I., Cameron, I., Kitchener, H., & Prentice, A. (2001). *Mosby's Color Atlas and Text of Obstetrics and Gynecology.* St. Louis, MO: Mosby.

Gruszecki, L., Forchuk, C., & Fisher, W.A. (2005). Factors associated with common sexual concerns in women: Findings from the Canadian Contraception Study. *Canadian Journal of Human Sexuality, 14* (1/2), 1–13.

Health Canada (1999). *Women's health surveillance: A plan of action for Health Canada.* Ottawa: Minister of Public Works and Government Services Canada.

Tweedy, A. (2000). Polycystic ovary disease. *Journal of the American Academy of Nurse Practitioners, 12*(3), 101–105.

Worcester, N., & Whatley, M.H. (2006). *Canada–USA women's health forum preventive/health promotion strategies—Women's health promotion and disease prevention: Shifting the emphasis to earliest and lifelong health promotion for a diversity of women.* Retrieved November 6, 2006, from http://www.hc-sc.gc.ca/hl-vs/pubs/women-femmes/can-usa/am-back-promo_7_e.html.

Youngkin, E. Q., & Davis, M. S. (2003). *Women's Health: A Primary Care Clinical Guide* (3rd ed.). Stamford, CT: Appleton & Lange.

WEB RESOURCES

Canadian Women's Health Network
http://www.cwhn.ca/indexeng.html

Female Genital Mutilation
http://www.cirp.org/pages/female

Ovarian Cancer Canada
http://www.ovariancancercanada.ca

Rural, Remote, and Northern Women's Health: Policy and Research Directions Summary Report.
http://www.pwhce.ca/ruralAndRemote.htm

The Society of Obstetricians and Gynaecologists of Canada (SOGC)
http://sogc.medical.org/index_e.asp

CHAPTER 21

Male Genitalia

COMPETENCIES

1. Identify the anatomic landmarks of the male genitalia.

2. Describe the characteristics of the most common male reproductive health issues and concerns.

3. Perform inspection, palpation, and auscultation on an adult male.

4. Explain the pathophysiological rationale for abnormal findings.

5. Document male reproductive assessment findings.

6. Describe the pathological changes that occur in the male reproductive system with the aging process.

*T*he male reproductive system includes essential and accessory organs, ducts, and supporting structures (Figure 21-1). The essential organs are the testes, or male gonads. The accessory organs include the seminal vesicles and bulbourethral glands. There are also several ducts, including the epididymis, ductus (vas) deferens, ejaculatory ducts, and urethra. The supporting structures include the scrotum, penis, and spermatic cords. The prostate is discussed in Chapter 22.

ANATOMY

Organs, ducts, supporting structures, and sexual development are discussed.

Essential Organs

The **testes**, or testicles, are two oval glands located in the scrotum. Each measures about 5 cm in length and 2.5 cm in width. The testes are partially covered by a serous membrane called the tunica vaginalis (Figure 21-2). This membrane separates the testes from the scrotal wall. Interior to the tunica vaginalis is a dense, whitish membrane covering each testicle called the tunica albuginea. This membrane enters the testes and divides each testis into sections called lobules, which contain tightly coiled tubules called the seminiferous tubules. These coiled structures are the main component of testicular mass, and they produce sperm by spermatogenesis.

Accessory Organs

The **seminal vesicles** are two pouches located posteriorly to and at the base of the bladder. They contribute about 60% of the volume of semen. The fluid secreted by the seminal vesicles is rich in fructose and helps provide a source of energy for sperm metabolism. Prostaglandins, which contribute to sperm motility and viability, are also produced by the seminal vesicles.

The **bulbourethral glands**, or Cowper's glands, are pea-sized glands located just below the prostate. Secretions are emptied from the bulbourethral glands at the time of ejaculation. The bulbourethral glands secrete an alkaline substance that protects sperm by neutralizing the acidic environment of the vagina. These glands also provide lubrication at the end of the penis during sexual intercourse.

Ducts

The **epididymis** is a comma-shaped, tightly coiled tube that is located on the top and behind the testis and inside the scrotum. Each epididymis comprises three parts: the head, which is connected to the testis; the body; and the tail, which is continuous with the vas deferens. Sperm mature and develop the power of motility as they pass through the epididymis.

The **ductus (vas) deferens** is an extension of the tail of the epididymis. Each duct ascends from the scrotum and permits sperm to exit from the scrotal sac upward into the abdominal cavity. The ductus deferens loops over the side and down the posterior surface of the bladder. This is where the duct enlarges into the ampulla of the vas deferens and joins the duct from the seminal vesicles to form the ejaculatory ducts.

The **ejaculatory ducts** are two short tubes posterior to the bladder. They descend through the prostate gland and terminate in the urethra. The ducts eject spermatozoa into the prostatic urethra just prior to ejaculation.

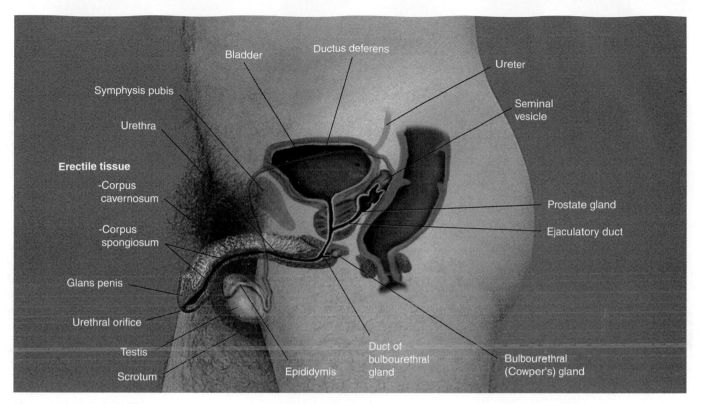

Figure 21-1 Male Genitalia.

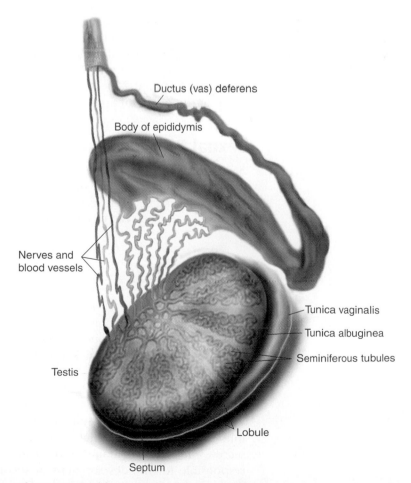

Figure 21-2 Testicle.

The **urethra** is the terminal duct of the seminal fluid passageway. It measures about 20 cm in length, passes through the prostate gland and penis, and terminates at the external urethral orifice.

Supporting Structures

The **scrotum** is a pouchlike supporting structure for the testes and consists of rugated, deeply pigmented, loose skin. Inside, the scrotum is divided by a single septum into two sacs, each containing a single testis. The production and survival of sperm requires a temperature that is 1°C cooler than normal body temperature (37°C). This is achieved by the scrotum's exposed location.

The **penis**, or male organ of copulation and urination, is hairless, slightly pigmented, and cylindrical in shape. It consists of three compartments of erectile tissue. The corpus spongiosum surrounds the urethra and is located ventromedially. The two corpora cavernosa are located on the dorsolateral sides of the corpus spongiosum. Distally, the corpus spongiosum expands to form the **glans penis**, or the bulbous end of the penis. In the uncircumcised male, a fold of loose skin, the **prepuce** (foreskin), covers the glans penis. The corona forms the border between the glans penis and the penile shaft. The penis contains the urethra, a slitlike opening on the tip of the glans. The urethra terminates at the urethral meatus and is the passageway for urine.

The **spermatic cord** is made up of testicular arteries, autonomic nerves, veins that drain the testicles, lymphatic vessels, and the cremaster muscle. The testicles are suspended by the spermatic cord. The left side of the spermatic cord is longer than the right side, causing the left testicle to be lower in the scrotal sac. The cremaster muscle elevates the testes during sexual stimulation and exposure to cold. It also surrounds the testicles. The spermatic cord and ilioinguinal nerves pass through the inguinal canal into the abdomen. The inguinal canal is an oblique passageway in the anterior abdominal wall. The canal is about 4 to 5 cm long. It originates at the deep inguinal ring. The distal opening of the inguinal canal is called the external inguinal ring and is accessible to palpation. Superior to the inguinal canal lies the inguinal ligament, or Poupart's ligament. The inguinal ligament extends from the anterior iliac spine to the pubic tubercle.

Sexual Development

Sexual development can be assessed according to the five stages described by Tanner (Table 21-1). Most of the changes in the male genitalia occur during puberty, starting between ages $9\frac{1}{2}$ and $13\frac{1}{2}$. The development of male genitalia to adult size and shape can take two to five years, with three years being the average.

PHYSIOLOGY

The primary function of the male reproductive system is to produce sperm to fertilize eggs. In order for this to be achieved, there are several essential features of male reproduction that must take place. These are the manufacture of sperm and the deposition of sperm into the female genital tract.

Spermatogenesis

The testes produce sperm by a process called **spermatogenesis**. Specialized cells found between the seminiferous tubules, called the interstitial cells of Leydig, secrete the male hormone testosterone. Testosterone is an androgen and is responsible for the development of secondary sexual characteristics and the attainment of reproductive capacity. Testosterone is responsible for male sexual

---

Life 360°

References to Male Genitalia

Just as people are different, so are the words that refer to the male genitalia. Jot down as many slang terms for male genitalia and erections that come to mind. Pair up with a classmate and compare words. Did you learn any new slang terms? Do you think you can use these terms with patients without becoming embarrassed?

TABLE 21-1 Sexual Maturity Rating (SMR) for Male Genitalia

DEVELOPMENTAL STAGE	PUBIC HAIR	PENIS	SCROTUM
1.	No pubic hair, only fine body hair (vellus hair)	Preadolescent; childhood size and proportion	Preadolescent; childhood size and proportion
2.	Sparse growth of long, slightly dark, straight hair	Slight or no growth	Growth in testes and scrotum; scrotum reddens and changes texture
3.	Becomes darker and coarser; slightly curled and spreads over symphysis	Growth, especially in length	Further growth
4.	Texture and curl of pubic hair is similar to that of an adult but not spread to thighs	Further growth in length; diameter increases; development of glans	Further growth; scrotum darkens
5.	Adult appearance in quality and quantity of pubic hair; growth is spread to medial surface of thighs	Adult size and shape	Adult size and shape

feelings and performance as well as muscle development. The testes prepare for sperm production at approximately 13 years of age.

Male Sexual Function

The male sexual act consists of four stages: erection, lubrication, emission, and ejaculation. Erection of the penis is the first stage and is achieved through either physical or psychogenic stimulation of sensory nerves in the genital area. Parasympathetic impulses from the sacral portion of the spinal cord cause a vascular effect. The arterioles dilate and blood fills the corpora cavernosa, causing the penis to expand and become rigid. The corpora cavernosa can hold from 20 to 50 mL of blood. The veins from the tissue are compressed to occlude venous outflow.

Parasympathetic impulses at the same time cause the bulbourethral glands to secrete mucus, which provides lubrication during intercourse. When the sexual stimulus reaches a critical intensity, the reflex centres of the spinal cord send sympathetic impulses to the genital organs, and an orgasm occurs. Emission begins with contraction of the epididymis and the vas deferens, causing expulsion of sperm into the internal urethra. Ejaculation follows with contractions of the penile urethra.

HEALTH HISTORY

The male genitalia health history provides insight into the link between a patient's life and lifestyle and male genitalia information and pathology.

PATIENT PROFILE	*Diseases that are age-specific for the male genitalia are listed.*
Age	*Chlamydia trachomatis* (14–35) Testicular torsion (12–25) Varicocele (15–35) Testicular cancer (16–35) Gonococcal urethritis (< 35) Epididymitis, sexually associated (< 35) Epididymitis, urinary pathogens (> 35) Hydrocele (> 30) Spermatocele (> 30) Bladder cancer (> 50) Testicular lymphoma (> 50) Erectile dysfunction (> 50) Bacteriuria (> 65)
HEALTH ISSUE/CONCERN	*Common health issues/concerns related to the male genitalia are defined and information on the characteristics of each sign or symptom is provided.*
Urethral Discharge	Excretion of substance from the urethra
Quality	Colour: clear, white, purulent, blood-tinged, green, yellow, pink; consistency: thin, moderate, thick, mucoid; foul odour
Quantity	Absent, scant, mild, moderate, copious
Associated Manifestations	Dysuria, painful ejaculation, fever, urethral meatal discharge, change in frequency of urination, pruritus, conjunctivitis, arthritis, dermatological rash, STI

continues

Aggravating Factors	Urethral trauma
Alleviating Factors	Medications (antibiotics, analgesics)
Setting	A new sexual partner in the last 6 months, multiple partners, a partner known to have other partners, unprotected intercourse
Timing	More prominent in the morning before urinating
Palpable Mass	A lump in the male genitalia
Quality	Firm, smooth, stellate, soft, mobile, non-mobile, well circumscribed, poorly circumscribed, "bag of worms," hard, heavy, transilluminating, non-transilluminating, fluctuant, separate from testes
Associated Manifestations	Pain, scrotal enlargement, absence of pain, vague back or abdominal pain, gynecomastia (if mass produces estrogen or human chorionic gonadotropin), nausea, vomiting, generalized edema
Aggravating Factors	Positioning, palpation or pressure, obesity, lifting, edema
Alleviating Factors	Medications, surgical removal or repair, positioning
Setting	Post trauma, recurrent testicular pain
Timing	Mumps orchitis present 7–10 days following parotitis
Scrotal Pain	Discomfort in the scrotal sac
Quality	Dull, sharp, heavy
Associated Manifestations	Scrotal swelling, groin pain, lower abdominal pain, flank pain, dysuria, urinary frequency, fever, nausea, vomiting, pyuria, urethral discharge, scrotal edema, erythema, infertility
Aggravating Factors	Sexual encounter, urinary tract infection, scrotal trauma
Alleviating Factors	Medications (antibiotics, analgesics), bed rest, scrotal elevation, surgery
Setting	New sexual partner in the past six months, unprotected intercourse, recent urinary instrumentation
Timing	Epididymitis may present months following a new or unprotected sexual encounter; it may also present shortly after a urinary tract infection
Erectile Dysfunction	The inability or decrease in ability to achieve and maintain a penile erection or to ejaculate seminal fluid
Quality	Inability to achieve erection (failed nocturnal tumescence test), ability to achieve with failure to maintain erection, inability to achieve complete erection, inability to ejaculate
Associated Manifestations	Anxiety, systemic disease (diabetes mellitus, hypertension, coronary artery disease), decreased libido, phimosis, decreased or absent cremasteric reflex, decreased femoral pulses, trauma, recent transurethral resection of the prostate or prostatectomy surgery, testicular atrophy
Aggravating Factors	Medications (beta blockers, diuretics, reserpine, monoamine oxidase inhibitors, selective serotonin reuptake inhibitors, diazepam, alprazolam, chemotherapeutic agents, codeine, oxycodone propoxyphene), anxiety, unsupportive partner, alcohol, smoking, elevated blood sugar, hyperthyroidism, hypothyroidism

continues

Alleviating Factors	Medications (hormone therapy, yohimbine, anxiolytics, sildenafil, alprostadil), injections, implants, vascular surgery, sex counselling, avoiding alcohol, smoking cessation, change in diet (avoiding foods high in saturated fat or cholesterol), maintaining ideal body weight, reducing tension and stress, vacuum erectile device
Setting	Uncomfortable physical environment, stress
Timing	Nocturnal tumescence
Penile Lesion	A growth on the penis
Quality	Colour: erythematous, hyperpigmented, hypopigmented, pink, brown, black; presentation: flat, raised, indurated, papular, macular, multiple, isolated, ulcerated, warty, exudative (clear, purulent, bloody drainage)
Associated Manifestations	Fever, malaise, inguinal lymphadenopathy, pain, prodromal numbness and tingling at lesion site, myalgias, headache, pruritus, immunosuppression, systemic illness, recurrent herpes simplex virus (HSV), human papillomavirus (HPV)
Aggravating Factors	Stress, systemic illness, immunosuppression
Alleviating Factors	Medications (antivirals, antibiotics), surgical removal, lifestyle changes
Setting	Unprotected intercourse, multiple sexual partners
Timing	Lymphogranuloma venereum: papule appears 1–3 weeks after inoculation; primary HSV: lesions appear 2–7 days after inoculation, vesicles ulcerate in 3–4 days; recurrent HSV: lesions appear a few hours to days after prodromal symptoms, lesions last approximately 10 days
PAST HEALTH HISTORY	*The various components of the past health history are linked to male genitalia pathology and male genitalia-related information.*
Medical History	
Male Genitalia Specific	Prior history of STI, prostatitis, urinary tract infection, nephrolithiasis, cryptorchidism, trauma, cancer, benign prostatic hypertrophy (BPH), congenital or acquired deformity (epispadias, hypospadias), premature ejaculation, impotence, infertility
Non-male Genitalia Specific	Mumps, rashes, joint pain, conjunctivitis, viral illness, renal disease, congestive heart failure, spinal cord injury, pelvic fracture, diabetes mellitus, hypertension, tuberculosis, multiple sclerosis, depression, anxiety
Surgical History	Prostatectomy, transurethral prostatectomy (TURP), circumcision, orchiectomy, correction of malposition of testes, vasectomy, lesion or nodule removal, epispadias repair, hypospadias repair, hernia repair
Medications	Antibiotics, hormone replacements, 5-alpha-reductase inhibitors, antihypertensives, psychotropic agents
Communicable Diseases	HSV, HPV, molluscum contagiosum, condyloma acuminata, syphilis, penile lesion, *chlamydia*, gonorrhea, ureaplasma

continues

Allergies	Contact dermatitis from topical preparations, condoms, nonoxynol 9 or other spermicides
Injuries and Accidents	Trauma, testicular torsion
Special Needs	Urinary incontinence, indwelling or intermittent urinary catheter, penile prosthesis, suprapubic urinary catheter
Childhood Illnesses	Mumps: orchitis, infertility
FAMILY HEALTH HISTORY	*Male genitalia diseases that are familial are listed.*
	Varicocele, testicular cancer, hypospadias, infertility, mother's use of hormones (diethylstilbestrol [DES]) during pregnancy
SOCIAL HISTORY	*The components of the social history are linked to male genitalia factors and pathology.*
Alcohol Use	Impairs gonadotropin release and accelerates testosterone metabolism, causing impotence and loss of libido; large doses can acutely depress the sexual reflexes; chronic alcoholism causes high levels of circulating estrogens, which decrease libido; alcohol intoxication may impair judgment, decreasing incidence of safe sex practices and increasing risk of exposure to STIs
Drug Use	May impair judgment, increasing the risk for unsafe sex practices and STI exposure Cocaine: priapism with chronic abuse, impotence, increased sexual excitability Barbiturates: impotence Amphetamines: increased libido and delayed orgasm in moderate users, impotence in chronic users
Tobacco Use	Cigarette smoking increases risk of atherosclerotic disease, which may decrease penile blood flow; it is also associated with an increased risk of bladder cancer
Sexual Practice	Multiple partners, partner with multiple partners, new sexual partner, condom use (frequency and accuracy of use), sexual orientation, anal or oral intercourse
Work Environment	Radiation exposure has been linked to cancer of the male genitalia; bladder cancer associated with certain dyes
HEALTH MAINTENANCE ACTIVITIES	*This information provides a bridge between the health maintenance activities and male genitalia function.*
Sleep	Nocturia secondary to urethritis
Diet	Erectile dysfunction: food high in saturated fat or cholesterol
Exercise	Trauma to the testicle may cause a hydrocele
Use of Safety Devices	Condoms used for vaginal and anal intercourse; supportive device worn while participating in sports
Health Check-ups	Testicular exam

EQUIPMENT

- Non-sterile gloves
- Penlight
- Stethoscope
- Culturette tube
- Sterile cotton swabs
- Absorbent underpad
- Culture plate
- 10 × power magnifying lens

ASSESSMENT OF THE MALE GENITALIA

◄NURSING CHECKLIST►

General Approach to Male Genitalia Assessment

1. Greet the patient and explain the assessment techniques that you will be using.
2. Ensure that the examination room is at a warm, comfortable room temperature to prevent patient chilling and shivering.
3. Use a quiet room that will be free from interruptions.
4. Ensure that the light in the room provides sufficient brightness to adequately observe the patient.
5. Assess the patient's apprehension level about the assessment and address this with him, reassuring him that this is normal.
6. Instruct the patient to remove his pants and underpants.
7. Place the patient on the examination table in the supine position with the legs spread slightly, and cover with a drape sheet. Stand to the patient's right side or
7a. Have the patient stand in front of you while you are sitting.
8. Don clean gloves.
9. Expose the entire genital and groin area.

Inspection

Sexual Maturity Rating

E   1. Using the Tanner stages in Table 21-1, assess the developmental stage of the pubic hair, penis, and scrotum.
   2. Determine the SMR.

N   Males usually begin puberty between the ages of $9\frac{1}{2}$ and $13\frac{1}{2}$. The average male proceeds through puberty in about three years, with a possible range of two to five years.

A   An SMR that is less than expected for a male's age is abnormal.

P   Delayed puberty may be familial or caused by chronic illnesses.

A   A normally formed but diminutive penis is abnormal. There is a discrepancy between the penile size and the age of the individual.

P   A **microphallus** can result from a disorder in the hypothalamus or pituitary gland. It may be secondary to primary testicular failure due to partial androgen insensitivity. Maternal DES exposure has teratogenic effects caused by defects in nonandrogen-dependent regulatory agents. Microphallus can also be idiopathic in nature.

A   It is abnormal when the penis appears larger than what is generally expected for the stated age. This condition is usually evident only before the age of normal puberty.

P   Hormonal influence of tumours of the pineal gland or hypothalamus, tumours of the Leydig cells of the testes, tumours of the adrenal gland, or precocious genital maturity may cause penile hyperplasia.

A   A testicle that is smaller and softer than normal (less than 5 cm × 2.5 cm) is abnormal.

P   An atrophic testicle may be the result of Klinefelter's syndrome (hypogonadism), hypopituitarism, estrogen therapy, or orchitis.

Life ↻360°

Sensitivity during the Male Genitalia Examination

Remember that, regardless of culture, assessing genitalia requires sensitivity on the part of the nurse to both the patient and the nurse's own level of comfort. Consider the role of your patient's cultural background in determining if a female nurse can examine a male patient or if a male nurse can examine a male patient. Reflect on general societal beliefs about people of the same sex or opposite sex touching the genitalia.

Hair Distribution

E **1.** Note hair distribution pattern.
2. Note the presence of nits or lice.
N Pubic hair is distributed in a triangular form. It is sparsely distributed on the scrotum and inner thigh and absent on the penis. Genital hair is more coarse than scalp hair. There are no nits or lice.
A Hair distribution is sparse or hair is absent at the genitalia area. This is called **alopecia** and it is abnormal.
P Alopecia in the genital area may result from genetic factors, aging, or local or systemic disease. These include developmental defects and hereditary disorders, infection, neoplasms, physical or chemical agents, endocrine diseases, deficiency states (nutritional or metabolic), destruction, or damage to the follicles.
A The presence of nits or lice is abnormal.
N/A/P See Chapter 10.

Penis

E **1.** Inspect the glans, foreskin, and shaft for lesions, swelling, and inflammation. If the patient is uncircumcised, ask him to retract the foreskin so that the underlying area can be inspected. Ensure the foreskin is replaced after the assessment.
2. Inspect the anterior surface of the penis first. Then lift the penis to check the posterior surface.
3. Note the shape of the penis.
N Skin is free of lesions and inflammation. The shaft skin appears loose and wrinkled in the male without an erection. The glans is smooth and without lesions, swelling, and inflammation. The foreskin retracts easily and there is no discharge. There may be a small amount of smegma, a white, cottage cheese-like substance, present. The dorsal vein is sometimes visible. The penis is cylindrical in shape. The glans penis varies in size and shape and may appear rounded or broad.
P Inflammation of the glans penis is abnormal.
A This inflammation is called balanitis. The prepuce may also be affected. This is a bacterial infection that is associated with phimosis and is seen in diabetic men.

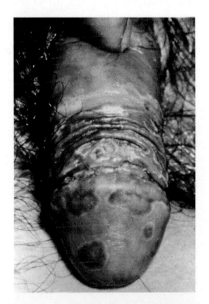

Figure 21-3 Balanitis of the Glans Penis. *Courtesy of Centers for Disease Control and Prevention (CDC).*

| E Examination | N Normal Findings | A Abnormal Findings | P Pathophysiology |

Reflective Thinking

Embarrassing Situations Encountered during the Male Genitalia Assessment

The genitalia examination may cause the patient to feel uncomfortable or embarrassed. How would you handle the following situations if they were to occur during the genitalia assessment?

- The patient has an erection during the examination.
- The patient asks you if you would like to go out with him for dinner.

P Balanitis can occur with sexually transmitted infections. The patient in Figure 21-3 had balanitis of the glans penis from a chlamydial infection (non-gonococcal urethritis) caused by *Chlamydia trachomatis*.

A A small papular lesion that enlarges and undergoes superficial necrosis to produce a sharply marginated ulcer on a clean base is abnormal (Figure 21-4).

P The **chancre** is the lesion of primary syphilis. It contains a multitude of *Treponema pallidum* spirochetes and is highly infectious. The tissue reacts to the organism with infiltration of lymphocytes, fibroblasts, and plasma cells that cause swelling and proliferation of the endothelial tissue, manifesting as a chancre.

A A tender, painful, ulcerated, exudative, papular lesion with an erythematous halo, surrounding edema, and a friable base is abnormal (Figure 21-5).

P **Chancroid** is caused by inoculation of *Haemophilus ducreyi* through small breaks in epidermal tissue. Acute inflammatory response causes bubo formation. This is usually accompanied by inguinal adenopathy.

A Penile lesions that range from a relatively subtle induration to a small papule, pustule, warty growth, or exophytic lesion are abnormal. The distribution of lesions is most commonly on the glans and prepuce.

P Penile carcinoma usually begins with a small lesion that gradually extends to involve the entire glans, shaft, and corpora. Circumcision has been well established as a prophylactic measure that will eliminate the occurrence of penile carcinoma.

A Pinhead papules to cauliflower-like groupings of filiform, skin-coloured, pink, or red lesions are abnormal (Figure 21-6).

P **Condyloma acuminatum** (genital warts) are caused by HPV infection of the epithelial cells. HPV may remain dormant for months to years after infection. There is a high incidence of recurrence of condyloma following appropriate treatment because of the persistence of latent HPV in normal-appearing skin.

A Multifocal maculopapular lesions that are tan, brown, pink, violet, or white are abnormal.

P This describes intraepithelial neoplasia. HPV oncogenic types 16, 18, 31, and 33 infection cause epidermal proliferation and koilocytotic, dyskeratotic cells. Female partners may have a history of cervical intraepithelial neoplasm (CIN). The majority of lesions are distributed on the glans penis and prepuce. Changes of squamous cell carcinoma in situ are seen on histological examination.

A Erythematous, painful ulcers developing into vesicular lesions that may become pustular are abnormal (Figure 21-7).

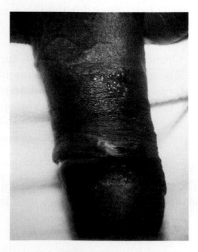

Figure 21-4 Syphilitic Chancre. *Courtesy of Centers for Disease Control and Prevention (CDC).*

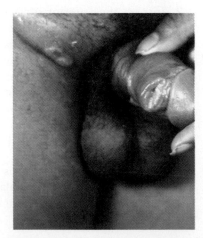

Figure 21-5 Chancroid of the Penis with Right Inguinal Lymphadenopathy. *Courtesy of Centers for Disease Control and Prevention (CDC).*

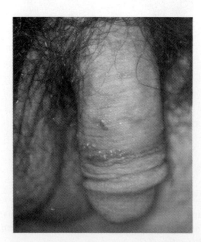

Figure 21-6 Genital Warts. *Courtesy of Centers for Disease Control and Prevention (CDC).*

Figure 21-7A Herpes Simplex Virus of the Penis. *Courtesy of Centers for Disease Control and Prevention (CDC).*

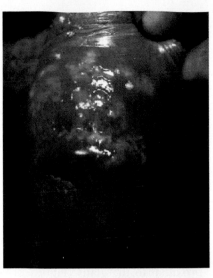

Figure 21-7B Primary Herpes Simplex Virus, First Episode. Serology tests are negative for HSV. *Copyright GlaxoSmithKline. Used with permission.*

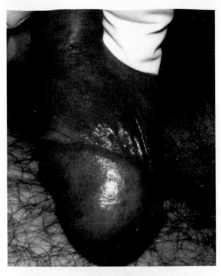

Figure 21-7C Primary Herpes Simplex Virus, First Episode. Serology tests are positive for HSV (type 1 or type 2), meaning the patient has had a previous exposure to the virus at another body site. This patient had a cold sore (herpes labialis) two years ago. *Copyright Glaxosmithkline. Used with permission.*

P   This describes genital herpes simplex virus infection. Skin-to-skin contact infection of HSV 1 and 2 causes epidermal degeneration, acanthosis, and intraepidermal vesicles. Lesions become ulcerated and eroded and are moist or crusted. Epithelial changes resolve in two to four weeks and hyper- or hypopigmentation of these areas is common. Postinflammatory scarring is rare. Recurrent herpes lesions are smaller. Diagnosis may be confirmed by Tzanck test for microscopic acanthocytes, viral culture, or serology for HSV antibodies.

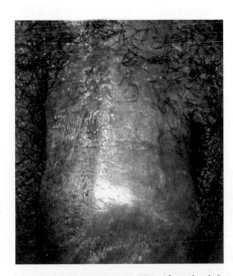

Figure 21-7D Recurrent HSV. After the initial primary outbreak, frequent recurrences (four to eight episodes per year) can occur at the primary outbreak site. This outbreak was the second episode in 4 months for this patient. *Copyright GlaxoSmithKline. Used with permission.*

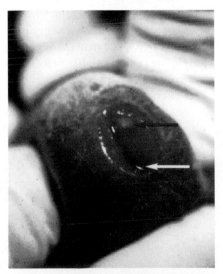

Figure 21-7E Atypical Recurrent HSV Presentation. The black arrow points to the herpetic urethritis, and the yellow arrow points to the urethral discharge. *Copyright GlaxoSmithKline. Used with permission.*

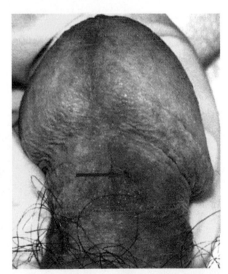

Figure 21-7F Atypical Recurrent HSV Presentation. The arrow points to a healed crusted lesion surrounded by erythema. *Copyright GlaxoSmithKline. Used with permission.*

| E | Examination | N | Normal Findings | A | Abnormal Findings | P | Pathophysiology |

Figure 21-8 Phimosis. *Courtesy Of Dr. James Mandell, Children's Hospital, Boston, MA.*

Figure 21-9 Paraphimosis. *Courtesy of Dr. James Mandell, Children's Hospital, Boston, MA.*

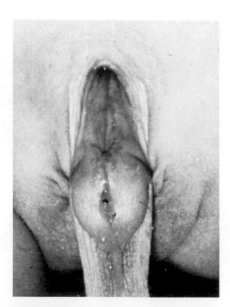

Figure 21-10 Epispadias. *Courtesy of Dr. James Mandell, Children's Hospital, Boston, MA.*

A Multiple, discrete, flat pustules with slight scaling and surrounding edema are abnormal.

P *Candida* is a superficial mycotic infection of moist cutaneous sites. Predisposing factors include moisture, diabetes mellitus, antibiotic therapy, and deficiencies in systemic immunity.

A Erythematous plaques with scaling, papular lesions with sharp margins, and occasionally clear centres, and pustules, are abnormal.

P Tinea cruris is a fungal infection of the groin, usually caused by *Epidermophyton floccosum* or *Trichophyton rubrum*. Predisposing factors are a warm, humid environment, tight clothing, and obesity.

A An unusually long foreskin or one that cannot be retracted over the glans penis is abnormal.

P **Phimosis** occurs in uncircumcised males (Figure 21-8). Inability to retract the foreskin is normal in infancy. In later years, an acquired constricting circumferential scar may follow healing of a split foreskin.

A It is abnormal when the retracted foreskin develops a fixed constriction proximal to the glans (Figure 21-9). The penis distal to the foreskin may become swollen and gangrenous.

P This is called **paraphimosis**. If the foreskin is retracted and not returned to its original position, such as following cleansing, paraphimosis can ensue. The foreskin acts as a circulatory constrictor, causing decreased blood flow, edema, and potential tissue necrosis.

A A continuous and pathological erection of the penis is abnormal.

P The cause of **priapism** is unclear in most patients; however, it does not occur as the result of sexual desire. Some of the cases are associated with leukemia, metastatic carcinoma, sickle cell anemia, intracavernous injection, alcohol abuse, genital trauma, and neurologic disorders. Some drugs, such as antihypertensives, antipsychotics, and antidepressants, have also been associated with prolonged erections. The patient may also present after having used a medication for erectile dysfunction. Priapism is created by the positive imbalance between the arterial blood supply and its return, created by venous drainage.

A Penile curvature, or chordee, is either a ventral or a dorsal curvature of the penis and is abnormal.

P Curvature is usually congenitally caused by a fibrous band along the usual course of the corpus spongiosum. Ventral chordee is seen mostly with **epispadias** (Figure 21-10), when the urethral meatus opens dorsally on the glans. In cases of congenital penile curvature without epispadias or **hypospadias** (when the urethral meatus opens ventrally on the glans), there is no additional tissue on or in any portion of the corpora cavernosa (Figure 21-11). This is caused by congenital maldevelopment of the tunica albuginea of the corpora.

Nursing Alert

STIs Affecting Male Genitalia

- *Chlamydia* is the most commonly diagnosed and reported bacterial STI in Canada. It is most common in men aged 20–29; its rates are steadily increasing.[1]
- Men account for two-thirds of cases of gonorrhea in Canada, especially men aged 20–29 and men who have sex with men (MSM).[2]
- Syphilis rates have increased dramatically since 1997, especially in MSM aged 30–39; outbreaks have occurred in Vancouver, Yukon, Calgary, Edmonton, Toronto, Ottawa, Montreal, and Halifax. A large number of MSM who have syphilis are also HIV positive.[3, 4]

continues

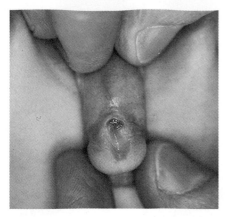

Figure 21-11 Hypospadias. *Courtesy of Dr. James Mandell, Children's Hospital, Boston, MA.*

- Lymphogranuloma venereum has previously been rare in Canada but recent outbreaks in MSM have been noted.[5]
- Genital herpes (HSV-1 and 2) is relatively common in MSM.

Signs and symptoms
- Urethral discharge, bloody or purulent
- Scrotal or testicular pain
- Burning or pain during urination
- Penile lesion, rashes

Health maintenance activities
- Avoiding or minimizing unprotected anal, vaginal, anal-oral intercourse; minimizing other sexual activities that involve exchange of bodily fluids such as sharing of sex toys.[6]
- Avoiding the use of products with nonoxynol-9 (N-9) during intercourse (N9 found on spermicidally lubricated condoms may provide added protection against pregnancy but does not effectively protect against infection with HIV or other STIs and may irritate the genital mucosal lining, facilitating transmission).[7]
- Ensure consistent and correct use of condoms for vaginal intercourse and both insertive and receptive anal intercourse.
- Avoid or minimize sexual encounters with multiple or anonymous partners, as well as the use of recreational drugs in conjunction with sex.

Reporting of STIs
- Reporting of STIs to public health officials and partners is an important means of ensuring the health of all Canadians. See Appendix B for a list of reportable STIs, traceback periods, and the contacts that must be notified.

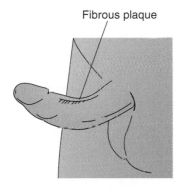

Fibrous plaque

External view

Figure 21-12 Dorsal Curvature of the Penis in Peyronie's Disease.

P Peyronie's disease is a condition of penile curvature that occurs with erection (Figure 21-12). The dorsal surface of the corpora cavernosa becomes hardened with palpable, non-tender plaques. Its cause is unknown.

Scrotum

E 1. Displace the penis to one side in order to inspect the scrotal skin.
   2. Lift up the scrotum to inspect the posterior side.
   3. Observe for lesions, inflammation, swelling, and nodules.
   4. Note size and shape.
   5. The patient should then stand with legs slightly spread apart.
   6. Have the patient perform the Valsalva manoeuvre.
   7. Observe for a mass of dilated testicular veins in the spermatic cord above and behind the testes.

P Scrotal skin appears rugated and thin and appears more deeply pigmented than body colour. The skin should hug the testicles firmly in the young male and become elongated and flaccid in the elderly male. All skin areas should be free of any lesions, nodules, swelling, or inflammation. Scrotal size and shape vary greatly from one individual to another. The left scrotal sac is lower than the right. There should be no dilated testicular veins.

P Condyloma acuminatum, tinea cruris, and *Candida* are abnormal findings. See page 782–784.

A Enlargement of or masses within the scrotum are abnormal.

P Scrotal masses can arise from benign or malignant conditions. Scrotal swelling is seen with inguinal hernia, hydrocele, varicocele, spermatocele, tumour, and edema.

| E | **Examination** | N | **Normal Findings** | A | **Abnormal Findings** | P | **Pathophysiology** |

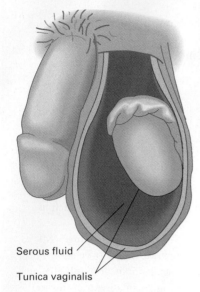

Serous fluid

Tunica vaginalis

Figure 21-13 Hydrocele.

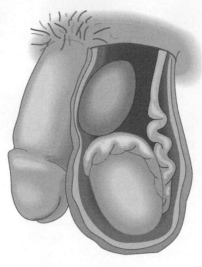

Figure 21-14 Spermatocele.

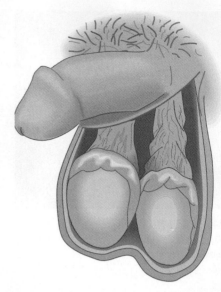

Figure 21-15 Variocele.

A   A large, pear-sized mass in the scrotum is abnormal (Figure 21-13). The scrotal skin is stretched, shiny, and erythematous, which may give the penis a shortened appearance.

P   A **hydrocele** is created by the accumulation of fluid between the two layers of the tunica vaginalis. Hydroceles may be idiopathic or due to trauma, inguinal surgery, epididymitis, or testicular tumour.

A   A well-defined cystic mass on the superior testis or in the epididymis is abnormal. It is usually < 2 cm in diameter (Figure 21-14). Multiple masses may be present.

P   This is called **spermatocele**. Blockage of the efferent ductules of the rete testis causes formation of sperm-filled cysts at the top of the testis or in the epididymis.

A   In light-skinned individuals, a scrotal mass with a bluish discoloration is abnormal (Figure 21-15).

P   Dilated veins in the pampiniform plexus of the spermatic cord cause **varicocele** formation and are usually accompanied by a decreased sperm count. Most appear in the left hemiscrotum; the remainder are bilateral. A right-sided varicocele may indicate an obstruction at the vena cava. Acute onset of a right-sided varicocele may be pathognomonic for a renal tumour extending into the renal vein or compression of the renal vein. It may increase in size with the Valsalva manoeuvre, and decrease or disappear with supine positioning.

A   Round, firm, cystic nodules confined within the scrotal skin are abnormal.

P   A sebaceous cyst contains sebum, an oily, fatty matter secreted by the sebaceous glands. The cyst may result from a decrease in localized circulation and closure of sebaceous glands or ducts.

Urethral Meatus

E   1. Note the location of the urethral meatus.
    2. Observe for discharge.
    3. Obtain a culture of any discharge (see Advanced Technique on page 788).
    4. If the patient complains of penile discharge but none is present, ask the patient to milk the penis from the shaft to the glans. This manoeuvre may express a discharge that can then be cultured.

N   The urethral meatus is located centrally. It is pink and without discharge.

A   Erythema and swelling at the urethral meatus are abnormal.

P Urethritis is a localized tissue inflammation resulting from bacterial, viral, or fungal infection as well as from urethral trauma.

A It is abnormal for the urethral meatus to be displaced dorsally (see Figure 21-10).

P Epispadias is a congenital abnormality caused by a complete or partial dorsal fusion defect of the urethra.

A It is abnormal for the urethral meatus to open on the ventral aspect of the glans penis (see Figure 21-11). The urethral meatus may also open at the perineum.

P Hypospadias is a congenital abnormality, usually associated with chordee. Complications of this defect include urethral meatal stenosis, inability to direct the urine stream, and sexual dysfunction.

Inguinal Area

E 1. If the patient is supine, ask the patient to stand.
   2. Stand facing the patient.
   3. Observe for swelling or bulges.
   4. Ask the patient to bear down.
   5. Observe for swelling or bulges.

N The inguinal area is free of any swelling or bulges.

A A bulge in the inguinal area is abnormal.

P Hernia pathology is discussed further in the section on palpation.

Palpation

Penis

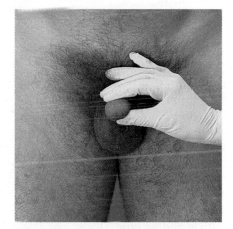

Figure 21-16 Palpation of the Penis.

E 1. Stand in front of the patient's genital area.
   2. Don clean gloves.
   3. Between the thumb and the first two fingers, palpate the entire length of the penis (Figure 21-16).
   4. Note any pulsations, tenderness, masses, or plaques.

N Pulsations are present on the dorsal sides of the penis. The penis is nontender. No masses or firm plaques are palpated.

A It is abnormal to palpate fibrotic plaques or ridges along the dorsal shaft.

P Plaques develop from perivascular inflammation between the tunica albuginea and the underlying spongy erectile tissue.

A Vascular insufficiency is evidenced by diminished or absent palpable pulse or pulsations and is abnormal.

P Systemic disease, localized trauma, and localized disease may adversely affect normal blood flow in the penis.

A It is abnormal for the penis to be enlarged in a non-erect state. Generalized penile swelling may be present.

P Fluid accumulation in the loose tissue of the penile integument results from anasarcic states. Obstruction of the penile veins or inflammation of the penis results in local edema. Trauma to the penis may cause swelling secondary to penile contusion and extravasation of blood. Gentle finger pressure may cause pitting.

Urethral Meatus

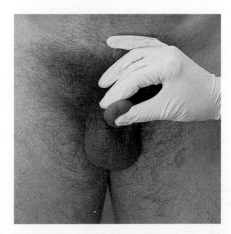

Figure 21-17 Palpation of the Urethral Meatus.

E 1. Stand in front of the patient's genital area.
   2. Between the thumb and forefinger, grasp the glans and gently squeeze to expose the meatus (Figure 21-17).
   3. If discharge is seen, or if the patient complains of a urethral discharge, a culture should be taken.

| E | Examination | N | Normal Findings | A | Abnormal Findings | P | Pathophysiology |

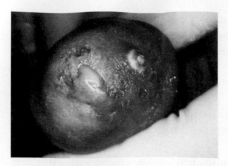

Figure 21-18 Purulent Penile Discharge from Gonorrhea. *Courtesy of Centers for Disease Control and Prevention (CDC).*

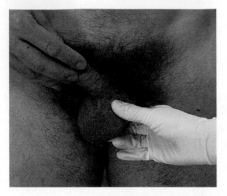

Figure 21-19 Palpation of the Testicle.

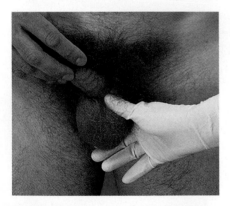

Figure 21-20 Palpation of the Epididymis.

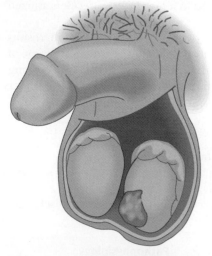

Figure 21-21 Testicular Tumour.

N The urethral meatus is free of discharge and drainage.

A A urethral discharge of pus and mucus shreds is abnormal (Figure 21-18). The discharge may vary in colour, consistency, and amount.

P Bacterial infection of the genitourinary tract causes inflammation and formation of a liquid composed of albuminous substances, leukocytes, shedding tissue cells, and bacteria.

Advanced Technique

Urethral Culture: Identifying Penile Pathogens

Equipment: sterile cotton swabs, Culturette tube, culture plate.

1. Explain to the patient what you are going to do and that some discomfort may be involved.
2. Place the patient in the supine position.
3. Note the colour, consistency, and odour of the discharge.
4. With the non-dominant hand, hold the penis. With the dominant hand, roll a sterile cotton swab in the discharge.
5. Place the swab in a Culturette tube.
6. With a second sterile cotton swab, obtain another specimen for a gonorrheal culture.
7. Roll the swab over a culture plate in a Z pattern.
8. Label both cultures and send them to the laboratory for analysis.

Scrotum

E 1. Between the thumb and the first two fingers, gently palpate the left testicle (Figure 21-19).
2. Note the size, shape, consistency, and presence of masses.
3. Palpate the epididymis (Figure 21-20).
4. Note the consistency and presence of tenderness or masses.
5. Between the thumb and the first two fingers, palpate the spermatic cord from the epididymis to the external ring.
6. Note the consistency and presence of tenderness or masses.
7. Repeat on the left side.

N The scrotum contains on each side a testicle and an epididymis. The testicles should be firm (but not hard), ovoid, smooth, and equal in size bilaterally. They should be sensitive to pressure but not tender. The epididymis is comma-shaped and should be distinguishable from the testicle. The epididymis should be insensitive to pressure. The spermatic cord should feel smooth and round.

A A unilateral mass palpated within or about the testicle is abnormal (Figure 21-21).

P Intratesticular masses should be considered malignant until proven otherwise. They are nodular and associated with painless swelling. The majority of intratesticular masses arise from germinal elements. Extratesticular tumours are uncommon and usually are benign. They can arise from any of the surrounding structures, including the epididymis, the testicular tunica vaginalis, or the spermatic cord. Testicular cancer should be suspected if a hard, fixed nodule is palpated.

P Inguinal hernia is discussed on pages 792 to 794.

P Refer to the section on scrotal inspection for a description of spermatocele.

A A large, pear-shaped mass with a smooth wall is abnormal.

P Refer to the section on scrotal inspection for a description of hydrocele. The entire testicle must be palpated because underlying malignancies cause a small percentage of all hydroceles. Sonography must be performed if the entire testicle is not palpable.

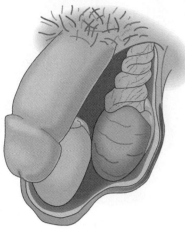

Figure 21-22 Testicular Torsion.

A A soft testis is abnormal.

P This might indicate hypogonadism.

A Palpation of a scrotal mass superior to the testis that reveals a "bag of worms" is abnormal.

P Refer to the section on scrotal inspection for a description of varicocele.

A It is abnormal for the testicle to be enlarged, retracted, in a lateral position, and/or extremely sensitive (Figure 21-22). Sometimes it is difficult to distinguish between testicular torsion and epididymitis. Refer to the Advanced Technique on Prehn's Sign.

Advanced Technique

Prehn's Sign: Assessing for Testicular Torsion

E 1. Elevate the scrotum with towels until it is fully supported.
2. Observe the patient's pain response.

N The patient with epididymitis will have decreased scrotal pain with scrotal elevation.

A/P The patient with testicular torsion will not have any change in his scrotal pain with this manoeuvre.

P Testicular torsion is a surgical emergency. Twisting or torsion of the testis causes venous obstruction, secondary edema, and eventual arterial obstruction. Doppler ultrasonography reveals absence of perfusion to the testicle.

A Palpation reveals an indurated, swollen, tender epididymis (Figure 21-23).

P Epididymitis results from the retrograde spreading of pathogenic organisms from the urethra to the epididymis. The majority of infections are caused by bacterial pathogens such as *chlamydia trachomatis* and *Neisseria gonorrhoeae*. An associated hydrocele may be present. The testis may also be enlarged and tender.

A It is abnormal for one or both testes to be undescended (Figure 21-24).

P The causes of **cryptorchidism** are not established but may be multiple and related to testicular failure, deficient gonadotrophic stimulation, mechanical obstruction, or gubernacular defects. The undescended testis is usually smaller than its normally descended mate. Unilateral cryptorchidism is more common than is bilateral. The undescended testicle is usually located in the inguinal canal or less commonly intra-abdominally. Spontaneous descent is unusual after one year of age.

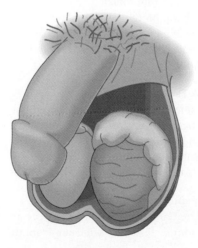

Figure 21-23 Epididymitis.

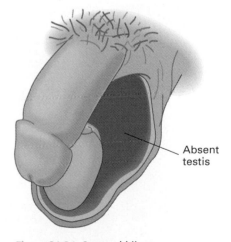

Absent testis

Figure 21-24 Cryptorchidism.

E	**Examination**	**N**	**Normal Findings**	**A**	**Abnormal Findings**	**P**	**Pathophysiology**

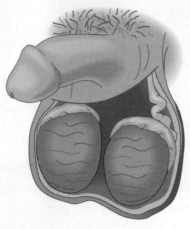

Figure 21-25 Orchitis.

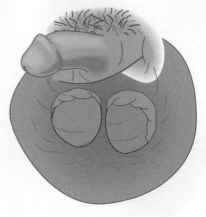

Figure 21-26 Scrotal Edema.

A An acute, painful onset of swelling of the testicle along with warm scrotal skin is abnormal (Figure 21-25). The patient may complain of heaviness in the scrotum.

P **Orchitis** can be caused by mumps, coxsackievirus B, infectious mononucleosis, and varicella. Involvement of the testes is via the hematogenous route. Orchitis is unilateral in the majority of cases, but onset in the second testicle may occur up to one week after that in the first.

A In light-skinned individuals, it is abnormal for the scrotum to be enlarged, taut with pitting edema, and reddened (Figure 21-26).

Nursing Alert

Testicular Cancer[8, 9]

- Testicular cancer is the most common cancer in men aged 15 to 34 years.
- While there is a relatively low incidence of testicular cancer in Canada—1.1% of cancers in men—the rates have been increasing, particularly in Ontario and the more westerly regions of Canada. Quebec and the Atlantic provinces report rates about 40% lower than Ontario and the West.
- Testicular cancer generally has a very good prognosis. For example, of the 840 men diagnosed with testicular cancer in 2006, 95% will be alive in five years.

Signs and symptoms[10]
- A lump on the testicle (almost always painless)
- Feeling of heaviness in the lower abdomen or scrotum
- Dull ache in lower abdomen and groin
- Infertility

Risk Factors
- Caucasian race, especially Scandinavian background
- Higher socioeconomic status
- Unmarried
- Rural resident
- History of cryptorchidism (even if previously repaired)

Screening
- The Canadian Cancer Society recommends that all men should perform monthly testicular self-exam from the time they are 15 years old.[11]

| E | **Examination** | N | **Normal Findings** | A | **Abnormal Findings** | P | **Pathophysiology** |

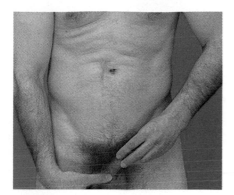

A. Palpating the Testis

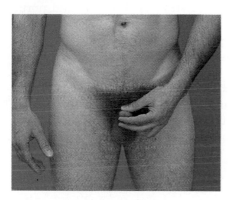

B. Assessing for Penile Discharge

Figure 21-27 Testicular Self-Examination.

Nursing Alert

Bladder Cancer

Epidemiology[12]
- Bladder cancer is the fourth leading cause of new cancers and the eighth leading cause of death in Canadian men (these facts may be influenced by under-reporting of bladder cancer, especially bladder cancer in situ across provinces).
- Bladder cancer is much more common in men (73% of new cases are male).

Signs and symptoms[13]
Early
- Hematuria (most common presenting sign)
- Frequent urination (daytime and nocturnal)
- Difficulty starting to urinate
- Urgency
- Bladder spasms
- Dysuria
- Reduced bladder capacity

Advanced bladder cancer may cause:
- Weight loss
- Loss of appetite
- Fever
- Bone pain
- Pain in the rectal, anal, and pelvic areas

Risk Factors
- Age (particularly over 50)
- Male
- Smoking plays major role
- Exposure occupational exposure to certain substances (possibly mineral, cutting, or lubricating oil, asbestos, dyes, and benzidine[14])
- Caffeine

Nursing Tip

Teaching Testicular Self-Examination

Testicular self-examination (TSE) should be taught to the patient during the scrotal examination.
- Ask the patient if monthly testicular self-examination is performed.
- Explain the rationale for the examination. Monthly testicular examination will allow for earlier detection of testicular cancer.
- Tell the patient to pick a date to perform the exam every month. The best time to perform the examination is after a warm shower when both hands and the scrotum are warm.
- Instruct the patient to gently feel each testicle using the thumb and first two fingers (Figure 21-27A).
- Remind the patient that the testicles are ovoid and movable, and that they feel firm and rubbery. The epididymis is located on top and behind the testis, is softer, and feels ropelike.
- Instruct the patient to report any changes from these findings, including any lumps and nodules, especially if they are non-mobile.
- Instruct the patient to squeeze the tip of the penis and check for any discharge (Figure 21-27B).

Life 360°

Teaching Testicular Self-Examination

You are teaching a group of male grade 11 students the importance of performing a testicular self-examination. You proceed to demonstrate the technique on a mannequin. After the class is over, one student shyly approaches you and says that he is not sure if he can perform testicular self-examination because "it is masturbation." How could you respond to the student?

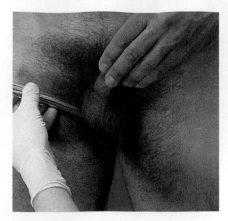

Figure 21-28 Transillumination of the Scrotum.

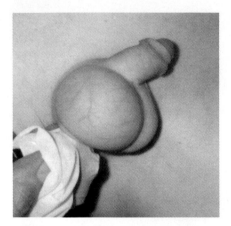

Figure 21-29 Transillumination of a Hydrocele.

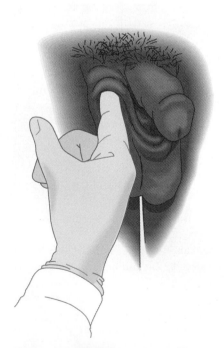

Figure 21-30 Palpation for an Inguinal Hernia.

Advanced Technique

Transillumination of the Scrotum: Assessing for a Scrotal Mass

If a scrotal mass or enlargement is detected, the scrotum should be transilluminated.

> **E** 1. Tell the patient what you are going to do and that it should not be painful.
> 2. Darken the room.
> 3. Using a penlight, apply the light source to the unaffected side behind the scrotum and direct it forward.
> 4. Apply the light source to the side of the scrotal enlargement or mass.
> 5. Note whether there is transmission of a red glow (Figure 21-28).
>
> **N** A normal testicle does not transilluminate (i.e., there is no red glow).
>
> **A** The transmission of a red glow indicates a serous fluid within the scrotal sac (Figure 21-29). This can occur in hydrocele and spermatocele and is abnormal. Vascular structures such as a hernia and a tumour do not transilluminate.

P Scrotal edema accompanies edema associated with the lower half of the body, such as in congestive heart failure (CHF), renal failure, and portal vein obstruction. Scrotal edema may also be the result of local inflammation. Scrotal contents are usually non-palpable.

A Acute, painful, scrotal swelling may occur with a history of trauma. This is abnormal.

P Trauma is a major cause of acute scrotal swelling. Scrotal or testicular hematoma formation as well as testicular rupture may be present. A small percentage of all diagnosed testicular tumours are diagnosed through medical attention for trauma; therefore, any intratesticular hematoma must be followed to rule out neoplasm.

Inguinal Area

E 1. With the index and middle fingers of the right hand, palpate the skin overlying the inguinal and femoral areas for lymph nodes.
2. Note size, consistency, tenderness, and mobility.
3. Ask the patient to bear down while you palpate the inguinal area.
4. Place the right index finger in the patient's right scrotal sac above the right testicle and invaginate the scrotal skin. Follow the spermatic cord until you reach a triangular, slitlike opening (the external inguinal ring).
5. The finger is placed with the nail facing inward and the finger pad outward (Figure 21-30).
6. If the inguinal ring is large enough, continue to advance the finger along the inguinal canal and ask the patient to turn his head and cough.
7. Note any masses felt against the finger.
8. Repeat on the left side using the left hand to perform the palpation.
9. Palpate the femoral canal. Ask the patient to bear down.

N It is normal for there to be small (1 cm), freely mobile lymph nodes present in the inguinal area. There should not be any bulges present in the inguinal area. There should not be any palpable masses in the inguinal canal. No portions of the bowel should enter the scrotum. There should be no palpable mass at the femoral canal.

A Unilateral enlargement of the lymph nodes along with erythematous overlying skin that may contain adhesions is abnormal.

P Three of the 15 strains of *chlamydia trachomatis*, specifically L1, L2, and L3, cause lymphogranuloma venereum (LV). These serovars are more invasive

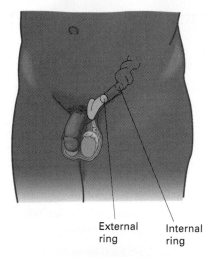

External
ring

Internal
ring

Figure 21-31 Indirect Inguinal Hernia.

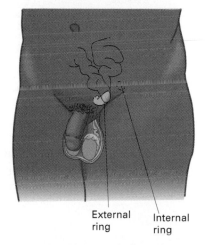

External
ring

Internal
ring

Figure 21-32 Direct Inguinal Hernia.

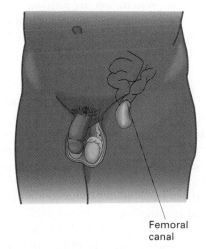

Femoral
canal

Figure 21-33 Femoral Hernia.

and virulent and selectively infect lymphoid tissue rather than columnar epithelial cells. Firm inguinal masses result when buboes involve.

A Unilateral or bilateral enlargement of the inguinal lymph nodes is abnormal. The nodes may be tender or painless.

P Lymphadenopathy occurs when the immune system responds to bacterial infections, trauma, or carcinoma. Bacterial infections commonly associated with inguinal lymphadenopathy include syphilis, chancroid, and gonorrhea.

P An **indirect inguinal hernia** palpated at the inguinal ring is abnormal (Figure 21-31). An impulse may be felt on the fingertip when the patient is asked to cough. A larger indirect inguinal hernia may feel like a mass at the inguinal canal.

P Portions of the bowel or omentum enter the inguinal canal through the internal ring and exit at the external inguinal ring. All indirect hernias are congenitally related to a patent processus vaginalis. The severity of a combination of the congenital abnormality and a condition that increases abdominal pressure (e.g., obesity, chronic obstructive pulmonary disease [COPD], hard physical labour, coughing, ascites) determines the onset and degree of the hernia.

A Oval swelling found at the pubis on inspection represents a **direct inguinal hernia** and is abnormal (Figure 21-32). Coughing causes enlargement on palpation of the mass.

P In direct hernias, portions of the bowel or omentum protrude directly through the external inguinal ring. Direct hernias are acquired masses that are influenced by increases in intra-abdominal pressure and weakening of the inguinal structures as part of the normal aging process. Other related factors include heavy lifting, obesity, and COPD.

A Palpation of a mass medial to the femoral vessels and inferior to the inguinal ligament is indicative of a **femoral hernia** and is abnormal (Figure 21-33).

P A femoral hernia is caused by protrusion of the omentum or bowel through the femoral wall. Onset and size of the hernia may be affected by a congenitally large femoral ring, degradation of collagen and tissue attenuation associated with aging, increased intra-abdominal pressure, and presence of preperitoneal fat.

Table 21-2 compares the different types of hernias.

Nursing Tip

Reducing a Direct Inguinal Hernia

An attempt should be made by a qualified practitioner to reduce hernia (to return the bowel to the abdominal cavity) if nausea, vomiting, and tenderness are absent. Have the patient lie down and gently push the hernia back into the abdominal cavity. An incarcerated hernia cannot be pushed back into the abdominal cavity. If nausea, vomiting, and tenderness are present, they may indicate a strangulated hernia (no blood supply to the affected bowel), which should be referred immediately to a physician.

Auscultation

Auscultation is performed if a scrotal mass is found on inspection or palpation.

Scrotum

E 1. Place the patient in a supine position.
  2. Stand at the patient's right side at the genitalia area.

| E | Examination | N | Normal Findings | A | Abnormal Findings | P | Pathophysiology |

TABLE 21-2 Comparison of Inguinal and Femoral Hernias

FEATURE	INDIRECT INGUINAL HERNIA	DIRECT INGUINAL HERNIA	FEMORAL HERNIA
Occurrence	More common in infants <1 year and males 16 to 25 years of age.	Middle-aged and elderly men.	More frequent in women.
Origin of Swelling	Above inguinal ligament. Hernia sac enters canal at internal ring and exits at external ring. Can be found in the scrotum.	Above inguinal ligament. Directly behind and through external ring.	Below inguinal ligament.
Cause	Congenital or acquired.	Acquired weakness brought on by heavy lifting, obesity, COPD.	Acquired, due to increased abdominal pressure and muscle weakness.
Signs and Symptoms	Lump or fullness in the groin that may be associated with a cough or crying.	Lump or fullness in the groin area. It may cause an aching or dragging sensation	Firm a rubbery lump in the groin. Plain may be severe.

Reflective Thinking

Dealing with Changes in Sexual Function

You are a gerontological nurse practitioner who works in an assisted living facility. You are performing a physical examination of Mr. Darcy, a new resident. He tells you that his wife will be joining him after her discharge from the hospital. He tells you that he and his wife are sexually active but he voices concerns about difficulty in sustaining an erection in the past few weeks. What additional questions would you ask him? What anticipatory guidance would you provide?

3. Place your stethoscope over the scrotal mass.
4. Listen for the presence of bowel sounds.
P   No bowel sounds are present in the scrotum.
A   An indirect inguinal hernia is present if bowel sounds are present in the enlarged scrotum.
P   Loops of bowel extending into the scrotum via an indirect hernia continue to produce bowel sounds unless the hernia is strangulated (lack of blood flow to bowel tissue) and bowel tissue becomes ischemic or necrotic.

GERONTOLOGICAL VARIATIONS

Physiological changes in the male reproductive system occur with aging. Assessment of the external genitalia reveals thinner pubic hair. The penis has an atrophic appearance and the testicles may appear or feel small or atrophied. The scrotal sac loses its elasticity. In most individuals, there is a reduction in testosterone levels by the age of 50.

Testicular degeneration seems to occur in patchy distribution, which allows normal spermatogenesis to be present in the majority of men until 70 years of age. Sperm output may be slightly decreased.

Aging is associated with the development of a variety of disease processes that may have direct effects on gonadal function. Systemic disease (COPD, sarcoidosis, cirrhosis, renal failure, depression, or hypo- or hyperthyroidism), for example, can alter hormonal release and metabolism at various levels. Systemic disease can also have direct toxic effects on the testes, cause pituitary damage and hypothalamic disease, and alter hormonal metabolism.

The ability to obtain or maintain an erection is affected by aging. Testosterone levels decline slightly with age but are related to impotence in only a small minority of men who have low hormone levels. The normal changes of aging are often misunderstood by patients, which can lead to misconceptions and anxiety. Aging brings a significant delay in erectile attainment, and erection is also often not as complete. An absence or marked reduction of pre-ejaculatory fluid emission is often associated with advancing age. The refractory period before re-arousal, after a cycle of erection and ejaculation, lengthens with age. This physiologic change in what used to be an almost automatic erection is often perceived by men as the onset of impotence.

Nursing Tip

Erectile Function

Treatment for impotence varies greatly depending on the cause and may include any of the following:

- Patience and a relaxed atmosphere
- Oral medication: Halotestin, yohimbine HCl, phosphodiesterase type 5 inhibitors
- Penile prosthesis
- Intracavernosal injections
- Vacuum erection device
- Transurethral suppositories

The man becomes increasingly anxious, which triggers further erectile difficulties. Information from the health care provider about these natural changes of aging can be extremely reassuring.

A marked increase in the prevalence of impotence is associated with increased aging. The most common cause of impotence in the older male is vascular disease, which accounts for half of the cases. Other causes may include diabetes mellitus, hypogonadal states, and psychological stimuli. The older population has a tendency to take more of those medications that can contribute to impotence.

Nursing Tip

Sildenafil (Viagra), Vardenafil (Levitra), and Tadalafil (Cialis)

There are three phosphodiesterase type 5 inhibitors (PDE 5) now available for erectile dysfunction. All three are available only by prescription. PDE 5 inhibitors improve vasodilation and smooth muscle relaxation. Libido is not affected by PDE 5 inhibitors. All three have a contraindication in men using organic nitrates.

Sildenafil citrate, the first of the PDE 5s to be available, has been widely used in Canada since 1999. The recommended starting dose is a 50 mg tablet taken 30 to 60 minutes before initiating sexual activity, and it has a half-life of four to five hours. A 100 mg dose is recommended for patients who do not respond to the 50 mg dose. Sildenafil citrate should be taken on an empty stomach or after a low-fat meal. Ingesting a high-fat meal within one to two hours can reduce the onset of action by up to 70%. A blue discoloration of vision may be experienced.

Vardenafil is supplied in 5 mg, 10 mg, and 20 mg tablets. Initial starting dose is 10 mg taken one hour before sexual activity; it has a half-life of four to five hours. All alpha blockers are contraindicated in patients taking vardenafil due to potential orthostatic hypotension. Vardenafil can be taken without regard to food.

Tadalafil is marketed in 10 mg and 20 mg tablets. Patients should start with a 10 mg dose and increase to 20 mg if needed. It is taken 30 to 60 minutes before sexual activity. Tadalafil has a half-life of 17.5 hours. All alpha blockers except tamsulosin (Flomax) are contraindicated in patients taking tadalafil. Tadalafil can be taken without regard to food.

Side effects of all three drugs may include headache, nasal congestion, and flushing. Only rarely do these side effects cause men to stop using the drug. Immediate medical attention must be sought if sudden vision loss or vision-related problems occur while taking these drugs.[15]

CASE STUDY | The Patient with Erectile Dysfunction Due to Hypogonadism

Sam is a 58-year-old unemployed truck driver who comes alone to the health clinic.

HEALTH HISTORY

PATIENT PROFILE	58 yo married man; looks well
HEALTH ISSUE/CONCERN	"I'm having a loss of libido & difficulty c̄ my erections."

continues

HISTORY OF ISSUE/CONCERN

Pt. c/o a gradual onset of difficulty in achieving & maintaining an erection during the past 2 yrs; morning erections have ↓ in frequency; reduced sex frequency with wife to abstinence for 3 mo. Two casual sexual encounters in past month to see if libido/erection would "improve" but was "unable to function;" 2 children; denies any urinary symptoms; denies any new medication, no recent sgy or traumatic injury to the genital area. During the past 6 mos noticed frontal throbbing H/A & some trouble c̄ vision, which he associates c̄ stress at work. Hot flashes started 6 wks ago.

PAST HEALTH HISTORY

Medical History

Wt gain of 5 kg & problems c̄ constipation during the last yr

Surgical History

Kidney stone removal ages 45 & 54

Medications

None

Communicable Diseases

Hx of *chlamydia* (22 yo), denies history of other STIs

Allergies

Penicillin (urticaria & SOB)

Injuries and Accidents

MVA 8 yrs ago, fractured Ⓡ femur (casted s̄ sequelae)

Special Needs

Denies

Blood Transfusions

Denies

Childhood Illnesses

Mumps (6), scarlet fever (8), Ø complications

Immunization

"Up to date," last tetanus 5 yrs ago

FAMILY HEALTH HISTORY

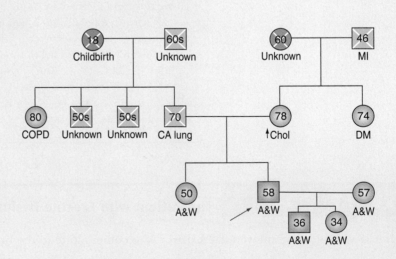

LEGEND

⬤ Living female

■ Living male

⊗ Deceased female

⊠ Deceased male

╱ Points to patient

—‖— Divorced

A&W = Alive & well
CA = Cancer
Chol = Cholesterol
COPD = Chronic obstructive
           pulmonary disease
DM = Diabetes mellitus
MI = Myocardial infarction

Denies family hx of varicocele, testicular CA, hypospadias.

SOCIAL HISTORY

Alcohol Use

Drinks 3–4 beers/night since unemployed

Drug Use

Denies

continues

Tobacco Use	Smokes 1 ppd × 20 yrs
Domestic and Intimate Partner Violence	Denies
Sexual Practice	No sex with wife for 3 months; 2 sexual encounters in last month without protection; no sex with men
Travel History	Drives his truck across country to deliver products
Work Environment	Unemployed at this time
Home Environment	Small rented apartment in the city
Hobbies and Leisure Activities	Watching TV, listening to music, going to local clubs
Stress and coping	Being unemployed—trying to be positive about finding work but "it is so discouraging;" "I feel so guilty about cheating on my wife . . . I thought it might be her but it is me. I wouldn't be surprised if she leaves me."
Education	High school graduate
Economic status	"My kids have to help me pay the rent."
Religion/Spirituality	"I am not a religious man but I hope God forgives me for what I have done"
Ethnicity	"I'm Canadian"
Roles and Relationships	Lives with wife; married 25 yrs; 2 children, 4 grandchildren, who he sees/talks to q 2–3 wks; states good relationship with his children. Generally a positive relationship with his wife but he has not mentioned his "problem" to her.
Characteristic Patterns of Daily Living	Wakes up anywhere from 09:00 to 10:00. Has no set daily schedule since loss of job 3 mos ago. Has breakfast/lunch/supper alone at home. Goes a local club & watches television & has 3–4 beers/night. Leaves the club around 23:00. At home, usually falls asleep in front of the television watching sports. Wakes 2 × during the night to void.
HEALTH MAINTENANCE ACTIVITIES	
Sleep	9 hrs/night
Diet	Breakfast/lunch usually combined because of getting up late; mostly fast food
Exercise	None
Stress Management	Beer, hanging out at the club c̄ friends; tries not to talk about problems.
Use of Safety Devices	Wears seat belt while driving
Health Check-ups	Last physical was 2 yrs ago
PHYSICAL ASSESSMENT	
Inspection	
Sexual Maturity Rating	Tanner stage 5

continues

Hair Distribution	Triangular distribution of pubic hair
Penis	Circumcised, no erythema at meatus, skin free of lesions & inflammation, rounded glans penis, size equates $\bar{c}$ developmental stage, no penile curvature
Scrotum	Scrotal skin rugated, no testicular swelling, no masses or nodules, no erythema
Urethral Meatus	Centrally located, no erythema
Inguinal Area	No swelling or bulges
Palpation	
Penis	Pulsations present on dorsal aspect, no masses or firm plaques
Urethral Meatus	No discharge expressed from the urethral meatus
Scrotum	Testicles palpated bilaterally very soft, no masses or tenderness
Inguinal Area	No inguinal nodes, no hernial masses
Auscultation	
Scrotum	No bowel sounds
Advanced Technique	Transillumination of the scrotum: no red glow

LABORATORY DATA

Hematology (CBC)

	Pt's Values	Normal Range
RBC	4.5×10^{12}/L	$4.71–5.14 \times 10^{12}$/L (men)
WBC	9.5×10^{9}/L	$4.0–11 \times 10^{9}$/L
PLT	310×10^{9}/L	$150–450\ 10^{9}$/L
HgB	142 g/L	male: 126–174 g/L
Hct	0.46	male: 0.43–0.49

Luteinizing Hormone	2 IU/L	5–15 IU/L
Follicle-Stimulating Hormone	7 IU/L	5–15 IU/L
Testosterone	3.29 nmol/L	10.4–34.7 nmol/L
TSH	3 mU/L	0.5–5 mU/L
T$_4$	51.6 nmol/L	64.5–154.8 nmol/L
T$_3$ Uptake	0.22	0.25–0.35
PSA	1.3 µg/ml	0–4 µg/ml

◀ **NURSING CHECKLIST** ▶

Male Genitalia Assessment

Inspection
- Sexual maturity rating
- Hair distribution
- Penis
- Scrotum
- Urethral meatus
- Inguinal area

Palpation
- Penis
- Urethral meatus

- Scrotum
- Inguinal area

Auscultation
- Scrotum

Advanced Techniques
- Urethral culture: Identifying penile pathogens
- Prehn's sign: Assessing for testicular torsion
- Transillumination of the scrotum: Assessing for a scrotal mass

REVIEW QUESTIONS

1. Which would be best evaluated with the patient in the standing position and performing the Valsalva manoeuvre?
   a. Hydrocele
   b. Spermatocele
   c. Varicocele
   d. Sebaceous cyst
   The correct answer is (c).

2. During the testicular exam you palpate a unilateral mass in the scrotum. You are unable to palpate the entire testicle. What is the first thing you should do?
   a. Obtain a testicular sonogram.
   b. Obtain a urethral culture and treat for infection.
   c. Refer the patient to a surgeon.
   d. Attempt to transilluminate the mass.
   The correct answer is (d).

3. What is the greatest risk factor for developing penile cancer?
   a. 20–30 years of age
   b. Cigarette smoking
   c. Intact foreskin
   d. Good hygiene
   The correct answer is (c).

4. Which could be a cause of a patient's priapism?
   a. Hypothyroidism
   b. Genital trauma
   c. Cigarette smoking
   d. Hypertension
   The correct answer is (b).

5. Which physiological change in the male reproductive system would you expect to find in an elderly man?
   a. Thick pubic hair
   b. Testicles ovoid and firm
   c. Scrotal sac loss of elasticity
   d. Indirect inguinal hernia
   The correct answer is (c).

6. A male patient is diagnosed with *chlamydia*. Which of the following is true with respect to reporting of this STI?
   a. No reporting is required.
   b. The infection must be reported to public health officials but not to any previous partners.
   c. The infection must be reported to public health officials and to sexual partners within the last 30 days.
   d. The infection must be reported to public health officials and to sexual partners within the last 60 days or the last sexual partner if no partners in last 60 days.
   The correct answer is (d).

7. Which medication is associated with erectile dysfunction?
   a. Amoxicillin
   b. Fluticasone
   c. Sildenafil
   d. Metoprolol
   The correct answer is (d).

8. Which is a surgical emergency?
   a. Testicular torsion
   b. Epididymitis
   c. Cryptorchidism
   d. Orchitis

   The correct answer is (a).

9. Mrs. Davis brings her ten-month-old son, Josh, into the office with a lump in the right groin. She notices that it appears larger when he cries. What would you expect to find on Josh?

   a. Femoral hernia
   b. Cryptorchidism
   c. Indirect inguinal hernia
   d. Direct inguinal hernia

   The correct answer is (c).

10. Which pathology presents with scrotal swelling?
    a. Indirect inguinal hernia
    b. Cryptorchidism
    c. Hydrocele
    d. Condyloma acuminatum

    The correct answer is (d).

> **Visit the Estes online companion resource at**
> **www.healthassessment.nelson.com for additional**
> **content and study aids.**

REFERENCES

[1]Fisher, W., Sevigny, C., & Stebenn, M. (2006). Primary care and sexually transmitted infections. *Canadian guidelines on sexually transmitted infections 2006 edition.* Public Health Agency of Canada. Retrieved November 9, 2006, from http://www.phac-aspc.gc.ca/std-mts/sti_2006/sti_intro2006_e.html

[2]Ibid.

[3]Public Health Agency of Canada. (n.d.). *Reported infectious syphilis cases and rates in Canada by province/territory and sex, 1993–2002.* Retrieved November 9, 2006, from http://www.phac-aspc.gc.ca/std-mts/stddata_pre06_04/tab3-2_e.html

[4]Sarwal, S., Shahin, R., Ackery, J. A., Wong, T. Infectious syphilis in MSM, 2002: Outbreak investigation. Paper presented at Annual Meeting of the International Society for STD Research, July 2003. Ottawa: Abstract 0685.

[5]Fisher, W., Sevigny, C., & Stebenn, M. (2006). Primary care and sexually transmitted infections.

[6]Kropp, R. (2006). Men who have sex with men (MSM)/Women who have sex with women. *Canadian guidelines on sexually transmitted infections 2006 edition.* Public Health Agency of Canada. Retrieved November 9, 2006, from http://www.phac-aspc.gc.ca/std-mts/sti_2006/pdf/wm-hf_e.pdf

[7]Public Health Agency of Canada (2004, May). Nonoxynol-9 and the risk of HIV transmission. HIV/AIDS Epi Update. Retrieved November 9, 2006, from http://www.phac-aspc.gc.ca/publicat/epiu-aepi/epi_update_may_04/16_e.html

[8]Canadian Cancer Society/National Cancer Institute of Canada. (2006). *Canadian cancer statistics 2006.* Toronto: NCIC.

[9]Cancer Care Ontario. *Cancer statistics—testis.* Retrieved November 9, 2006, from http://www.cancercare.on.ca/index_statisticsTestis.htm

[10]Ibid.

[11]Canadian Cancer Society. (n.d.) Testicular self exam. Retrieved November 9, 2006, from http://www.cancer.ca/ccs/internet/standard/0,3182,3172_10175_275318_langId-en,00.html

[12]Canadian Cancer Society/National Cancer Institute of Canada. (2006). *Canadian cancer statistics 2006.*

[13]Donat, S. M., Dalbagni, G. & Herr, H. (2006). Clinical presentation, diagnosis, and staging of bladder cancer. In *UpToDate,* B.D. Rose (Ed.). Waltham, MA .

[14]Ugnat, A. M., Luo, W., Semenciw, R., Mao, Y. & The Canadian Cancer Registries Epidemiology Research Group (2004). Occupational exposure to chemical and petrochemical industries and bladder cancer risk in four western Canadian provinces. *Chronic diseases in Canada,* 25 (2):7–15.

[15]Health Canada. (2005). Advisory 2005–83: Health Canada advises about vision problems possibly associated with Viagra, Cialis and Levitra. Retrieved November 9, 2006, from http://www.hc-sc.gc.ca/ahc-asc/media/advisories-avis/2005/2005_83_e.html

BIBLIOGRAPHY

Campbell, M. F., Walsh, P. C. & Retik, A. B. (2002). *Campbell's urology* (Vols. 1–4). Philadephia: W. B. Saunders.

Cole, F. L., & Vogler, R. (2004). The acute, nontraumatic scrotum: Assessment, diagnosis, and management. *Journal of the American Academy of Nurse Practitioners, 16*(2), 50–56.

Epperly, T. D., & Moore, K. E. (2000). Health issues in men: Part I. Common genitourinary disorders. *American Family Physician, 61*(12), 3657–3664. Retrieved December 23, 2004, from http://www.aafp.org/afp/20000615/3657.html

Esposito, K., Giugliano, F., DiPalo, C., Giuliano, G., Marfella, R., D'Andrea, F., et al. (2004). Effect of lifestyle changes on erectile dysfunction in obese men: A randomized controlled trial. *JAMA, 291*(24), 2978–2984.

Fillingham, S. (2004). *Urological nursing* (3rd ed.). Philadelphia: W. B. Saunders.

Gray, M. (2005). Andropause and the aging man: Separating evidence from speculation. *Advance for Nurse Practitioners, 13*(4), 22–27.

Mahmud, S. M., Fong, B., Fahmy, N., Tanguay, S. & Aprikian, A.G. (2006). Effect of preoperative delay on survival in patients with bladder cancer undergoing cystectomy in Quebec: A Population Based Study. *Journal of Urology*, 175 (Iss. 1), 78–83.

Mrdjenovich, A., Bischof, G., & Menichello, J.L. (2005). A biopsychosocial systems approach to premature ejaculation. *The Canadian Journal of Human Sexuality*, 13(1), 45–56.

Mullen, B. A. (2004). Testicular complaints and the young man. *Journal of the American Academy of Nurse Practitioners*, *16*(11), 490–495.

Westheimer, R. & Lopater, S. (2005). *Human sexuality: A psychosocial perspective*. Baltimore, MD: Lippincott Williams & Wilkins.

WEB RESOURCES

Canadian Health Network: Men
http://www.canadian-health-network.ca/servlet/
ContentServer?cid= 1041887104229&pagename=CHN-RCS%
2FPage%2FGTPageTemplate&c=Page&lang=En

Health Canada: Diseases and Conditions—Sexually Transmitted Infections (STI)
http://www.hc-sc.gc.ca/dc-ma/sti-its/index_e.html

Male Health Center
http://www.malehealthcenter.com

NEL

CHAPTER 22

Anus, Rectum, and Prostate

COMPETENCIES

1. Identify anatomic landmarks of the rectum and the prostate gland.

2. Describe the characteristics of the most common rectal and prostatic chief health issues and concerns.

3. Perform inspection and palpation of the anus, rectum, and prostate on an adult.

4. Explain the pathophysiological rationale for abnormal findings.

5. Document assessment findings.

6. Describe the changes that occur in the rectum and the prostate with the aging process.

*T*he anorectal examination is an important part of the physical examination. In the male patient, this examination includes assessment of the anus, rectum, and prostate gland. In the female patient, assessment of the anus and rectum is performed. These assessments are usually performed last and should be performed on a regular basis because they provide vital screening for anorectal and prostate cancers. As with assessing the male or female genitalia, this part of the physical examination requires sensitivity on the part of the nurse.

ANATOMY AND PHYSIOLOGY

Rectum

The large intestine is composed of the cecum, colon, rectum, and anal canal. The cecum and colon are discussed in Chapter 17. The sigmoid colon begins at the pelvic brim. Beyond the sigmoid colon, the large intestine passes downward in front of the sacrum. This portion is called the **rectum** (Figure 22-1). The rectum contains three transverse folds, or valves of Houston. These valves work to retain fecal material so it is not passed along with flatus.

Anus

The terminal 3 to 4 cm of the large intestine is called the **anal canal**. The anal canal fuses with the rectum at the anorectal junction, or the dentate line, and together these structures form the **anorectum**. The anal orifice is located at the seam of the gluteal folds; it serves as the exit to the gastrointestinal tract and it is marked by corrugated skin. The anal orifice lies 2 cm below the dentate line. The lower 2 cm of the anal canal is lined by **anoderm**, a thin, pale, stratified squamous epithelium that contains no hair follicles, sweat glands, or sebaceous glands.

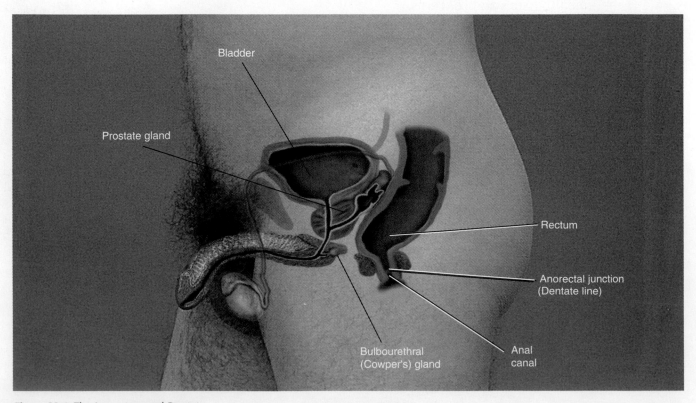

Figure 22-1 The Anorectum and Prostate.

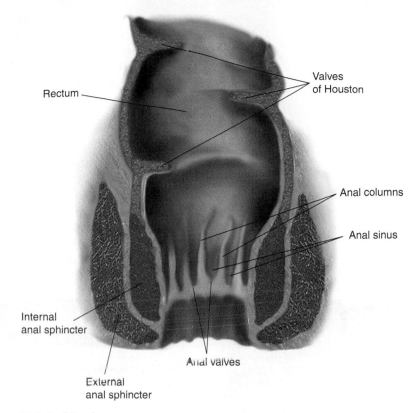

Rectum

Valves of Houston

Anal columns

Anal sinus

Internal anal sphincter

Anal valves

External anal sphincter

Figure 22-2 Anal Canal.

In the superior half of the anal canal are **anal columns**, which are longitudinal folds of mucosa (also called columns of Morgagni). The **anal valves** are formed by inferior joining anal columns. There are pockets located superior to the valves and are called the **anal sinuses**. These sinuses secrete mucus when they are compressed by feces, providing lubrication that eases fecal passage during **defecation** (Figure 22-2).

The anal canal opens to the exterior through the anus. Internal and external anal sphincter muscles surround the anus. Smooth muscle, which is under involuntary control, forms the internal sphincter. Skeletal muscle forms the external sphincter and is under voluntary control, allowing a person to control bowel movements.

The motility of the large intestine is controlled mainly by its nerves. There are two types of nerves: those that lie within the large intestine (the intrinsic nerves) and those that lie outside it (the extrinsic nerves). The rectum has more segmental contractions than does the sigmoid colon. These contractions keep the rectum empty by retrograde movement of contents into the sigmoid colon. As fecal material is forced into the rectum by mass peristaltic movements, the stretching of the rectal wall initiates the defecation reflex. A parasympathetic reflex signals the walls of the sigmoid colon and rectum to contract and the internal anal sphincter to relax. During defecation, the musculature of the rectum contracts to expel the feces.

Prostate

Contiguous with part of the anterior rectal wall in the male is the **prostate** gland. The prostate is an accessory male sex organ the size and shape of a chestnut, approximately 3.5 cm long by 3 cm wide. It consists of glandular tissue and muscle, and its small ducts drain into the urethra. The prostate lies just below the bladder and encircles the urethra like a doughnut.

The prostate has five lobes: anterior, posterior, median, and two lateral. The median sulcus is the groove between the lateral lobes. The right and left lateral lobes are accessible to examination.

Prostatic secretions are thin, milky, and alkaline. The secretions are made up of many different components. Citrate, a major component of prostatic fluid, provides a good transport medium for spermatozoa by maintaining the osmotic equilibrium of the seminal fluid. Prostatic fluid composes 15% to 30% of the ejaculate. Prostatic secretions have high levels of prostatic acid phosphatase (PAP) and prostate-specific antigen (PSA).

The prostate is primarily involved in reproduction, but it also provides a certain measure of protection against urinary tract infections. Semen contains high levels of zinc, which is derived from the prostate. Zinc is what provides the antibacterial properties to the prostate.

Within the prostatic cells, testosterone is converted to an androgen called dihydrotestosterone (DHT). DHT is the major androgen responsible for the benign enlargement of the prostate gland.

HEALTH HISTORY

The anus, rectum, and prostate health history provides insight into the link between a patient's life and lifestyle and anal, rectal, and prostatic information and pathology.

PATIENT PROFILE	*Diseases that are age-, gender-, and race-specific for the anus, rectum, and prostate are listed.*
Age	Pilonidal cyst or sinus (20–35)
	Crohn's disease of the anorectum (20–40)
	Anal fissure (20–45)
	Rectal condylomata acuminata (20–50)
	Ulcerative colitis (20–50)
	Gonococcal proctitis (20–50)
	Herpes proctitis (20–50)
	Prostatitis (20–60)
	Anal stenosis (> 25)
	Pruritus ani (> 25)
	Anal skin tags (< 30)
	Acute bacterial prostatitis (> 30)
	Anorectal abscess (30–40)
	Anorectal fistula (30–40)
	Hemorrhoids (40–65)
	Prostatic abscess (> 40)
	Fecal incontinence (> 40)
	Benign prostatic hypertrophy (> 40)
	Rectal cancer (> 55)
	Prostate cancer (> 50)
	Fecal impaction (> 60)
	Rectal prolapse (60–80)
Gender	
Female	Rectal prolapse, fecal incontinence
Male	Anorectal abscess, anorectal fistula, pruritus ani, rectal cancer, pilonidal cyst or sinus, hemorrhoids, gonococcal proctitis, herpes proctitis, benign prostatic hypertrophy, prostatitis, prostate abscess, prostate cancer

continues

Ethnicity	**Prostate cancer** incidence higher among U.S. whites, Australians and Canadians; U.S. black men have the highest incidence in the world, at a rate 70% higher than that of U.S. whites[1] **Colorectal** cancer highest in Western Europe, the United States, Canada, Australia, and parts of Asia (Singapore, China, and Japan)[2]
HEALTH ISSUE/CONCERN	Common health issues/concerns for the anus, rectum, and prostate are defined and information on the characteristics of each sign or symptom is provided.
Rectal Bleeding	Discharge of blood from the rectum
Quality	Occult, melena, hematochezia, massive hemorrhage
Quantity	Scant, spotty, dripping, massive
Associated Manifestations	Pain, absence of pain, malaise, fever, mass at anus
Aggravating Factors	Defecation, constipation, diarrhea, minor trauma, pelvic irradiation
Alleviating Factors	Increased fibre diet, bulk agents, exercise, increased fluid intake, hemorrhoidectomy
Timing	Constant, intermittent
Rectal Pain	The subjective phenomenon of a sensation indicating real or potential tissue damage in the rectum
Quality	Acute, sharp, tearing, burning, throbbing
Associated Manifestations	Swelling, fever, blood, abdominal pain
Aggravating Factors	Defecation, sitting, movement, foreign bodies, pregnancy
Alleviating Factors	High-fiber diet, bulk agents, exercise, increased fluid intake, warm sitz bath, topical emollients, surgery, removal of foreign body, lying down
Timing	More prominent with defecation; constant or episodic
Anal Incontinence	The involuntary passage of stool
Associated Manifestations	Diarrhea, urgency, rectal prolapse, prolapsed hemorrhoids, gaping anus
Aggravating Factors	Diarrhea, impaction, cognitive impairment, anxiety, physical handicaps, neurological disorders, trauma
Alleviating Factors	Bulk fibre, constipating agents, laxatives, enemas, biofeedback, anal continence plugs
Constipation	The infrequent, difficult passage of stool
Quantity	Fewer than three bowel movements per week
Associated Manifestations	Pain, blood, mucus, hard stool, straining with defecation, flatulence, decreased appetite
Aggravating Factors	Low-fibre diet, lack of exercise, drugs (e.g., opiates, calcium channel blockers) chronic use of laxatives, ignoring urge to defecate, weak abdominal muscles, inadequate fluid intake, rectocele, rectal prolapse, anal stenosis

continues

Alleviating Factors	High-fibre diet, bulking agents, increased fluid intake, defecation schedule, exercise, laxatives, digital removal, suppositories
Diarrhea	Increased volume, fluidity, or frequency of bowel movements relative to the person's usual pattern
Associated Manifestations	Abdominal pain, blood, steatorrhea, weight changes, appetite changes
Aggravating Factors	Viral infection, bacterial infection, antibiotics, laxatives, fecal impaction, Crohn's disease, ulcerative colitis, lactose intolerance, specific foods (very individualized), irritable bowel syndrome, caffeine, alcohol
Alleviating Factors	Constipating agents, anticholinergics, fluid replacement, certain foods (bananas, rice, apples, toast), antibiotics
Setting	Stressful situations, recent ingestion of improperly stored or prepared food, recent travel abroad
Pruritus	Itching of the anal and perianal skin
Associated Manifestations	Erythema, edema, psoriasis, candidiasis, contact dermatitis, hemorrhoids, anal fissures, rectal carcinoma
Aggravating Factors	Psoriasis, eczema, contact dermatitis, infections, parasites, oral antibiotics, diabetes mellitus, liver disease, obesity, poor hygiene, tight underclothes, wet clothing
Alleviating Factors	Discontinuing current antibiotics and topical agents; eliminating coffee, tea, cola, milk, beer, and wine; discontinuing laxatives; good rectal hygiene; loose clothing; non-medicated talcum powder; topical fungicides
Palpable Mass	A mass at the anus, in the anal canal, or on the prostate
Quality	Firm, smooth, soft, mobile, non-mobile, nodular, fibrotic
Associated Manifestations	Pain, absence of pain, blood, pus, mucus, fever, hemorrhoids, rectal prolapse
Alleviating Factors	Warm sitz baths, high-fibre diet, bulk agents, surgery
PAST HEALTH HISTORY	*The various components of the past health history are linked to anal, rectal, and prostatic pathology and anal-, rectal-, and prostatic-related information.*
Medical History	
Anorectal Specific	Trauma, inflammatory bowel disease, prior history of STIs, polyps, rectal cancer, hemorrhoids, pruritus ani, constipation, diarrhea, incontinence
Non-anorectal Specific	Radiation, lymphogranuloma venereum, childbirth, arthritis, endocarditis, high serum testosterone, endometrial cancer, ovarian cancer, breast cancer, cervical cancer, HIV infection, penile or vaginal STIs
Prostate Specific	Prostate cancer, prostatitis, benign prostatic hypertrophy
Surgical History	
Anorectal	Sigmoidoscopy, colonoscopy, rubber band ligation, injection sclerotherapy, hemorrhoidectomy, drainage of fistula or abscess
Prostate	Prostatectomy, transurethral resection of the prostate (TURP)

continues

Medications	Laxatives, constipating agents, alpha blockers, 5-alpha-reductase inhibitors, antifungals, astringent ointments, suppositories
Communicable Diseases	HIV, *Neisseria gonorrhoeae*, *Treponema pallidum* (syphilis), *chlamydia trachomatis*, human papillomavirus (HPV), herpes simplex virus (HSV)
Allergies	Contact dermatitis of perianal area
Injuries and Accidents	Rectal trauma, foreign body in rectum
Childhood Illnesses	Anal stenosis, Hirschsprung's disease (with rectal pullthrough)
FAMILY HEALTH HISTORY	*Anal, rectal, and prostatic diseases that are familial are listed.*
	Rectal polyps, rectal cancer, pilonidal cyst, prostate cancer
SOCIAL HISTORY	*The components of the social history are linked to anal, rectal, and prostatic factors and pathology.*
Alcohol Use	Excess intake of alcohol associated with pruritus ani; increased amount of alcohol associated with rectal and prostate cancers
Drug Use	Illicit drug use may distort the user's perception, increasing the risk for unsafe sexual practices and STI exposure.
Tobacco Use	Cigarette smoking increases the risk for anal carcinoma and exacerbates Crohn's disease.
Sexual Practice	Rectal penetration increases the risk for anal carcinoma and anorectal STIs. Use of foreign objects in the rectum can lead to anal valve incompetence.
Work Environment	Excessive sitting causes direct pressure and increases venous pooling, which can lead to hemorrhoids.
Hobbies and Leisure Activities	Weight lifting (hemorrhoids, rectal prolapse)
Stress	Pruritus ani can be exacerbated by stress; diarrhea can be caused by stress; constipation can be caused by depression.
HEALTH MAINTENANCE ACTIVITIES	*This information provides a bridge between the health maintenance activities and anal, rectal, and prostatic function.*
Sleep	Nocturia secondary to an enlarged prostate
Diet	Increased amounts of dietary fats, cured and smoked meats, and charcoal-broiled foods, and decreased amounts of fibre, fruits, and vegetables are associated with prostate and rectal cancers; excessive intake of milk, coffee, tea, cola, and spices is associated with pruritus ani. Vitamins A, C, E, and folate may protect against developing rectal cancer.
Exercise	Exercise promotes regular bowel evacuation.
Use of Safety Devices	Condoms used with vaginal and anal intercourse
Health Check-ups	Hemoccult cards, digital rectal exam, flexible sigmoidoscopy, colonoscopy

EQUIPMENT

- Non-sterile gloves
- Water-soluble lubricant
- Hemoccult cards
- Gooseneck lamp

ASSESSMENT OF THE ANUS, RECTUM, AND PROSTATE

◄NURSING CHECKLIST►

General Approach to Anus, Rectum, and Prostate Assessment

1. Greet the patient and explain the assessment techniques that you will be using.
2. Ensure that the examination room is at a warm, comfortable temperature to prevent patient chilling and shivering.
3. Use a quiet room that will be free from interruptions.
4. Ensure that the light in the room provides sufficient brightness to adequately observe the patient. It may be helpful to have a gooseneck lamp available for additional lighting when lesions are observed.
5. Instruct the patient to void prior to the assessment.
6. Instruct the patient to remove pants and underpants and to cover up with a drape sheet.
7. Assess the patient's apprehension level about the assessment and reassure the patient that apprehension is normal.
8. For inspection, place the patient in the left lateral decubitus position and visualize the perianal skin (Figure 22-3A). This position can also be used for palpation.
9. For palpation, have the patient stand at the side or end of the examination table, bending over the table resting the elbows on the table and spreading the legs slightly apart (Figure 22-3B).
   - 9a. For the patient who cannot stand, have the patient assume the knee-chest position (Figure 22-3C).
   - 9b. For the female who is undergoing a rectovaginal examination, have her assume the lithotomy position. See Chapter 20.
10. Don non-sterile gloves.
11. Use a systematic approach every time the assessment is performed. Proceed from the anus to the rectum in the female patient. Proceed from the anus to the prostate in the male patient.

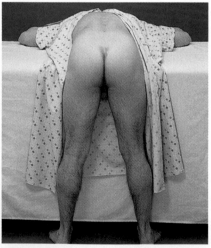

A. Left Lateral Decubitus

B. Standing

Nursing Tip

Rectal Examination of the Female Patient

If a woman is to undergo a rectal examination without a vaginal exam, then the left lateral decubitus, standing, or knee-chest position can be used for the assessment.

C. Knee-Chest

Figure 22-3 Patient Positions for the Anus, Rectum, and Prostate Examination.

Nursing Tip

Skin Assessment during Rectal Examination

As you examine the perineum and the sacrococcygeal area, perform a skin assessment. See Chapter 10 to review this examination.

Inspection

Perineum and Sacrococcygeal Area

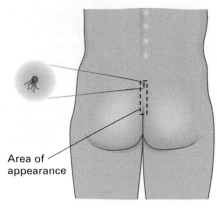

Figure 22-4 Pilonidal Cyst.

Area of
appearance

E   Inspect the buttocks and sacral region for lesions, swelling, inflammation, and tenderness.

N   This area should be smooth and free of lesions, swelling, inflammation, and tenderness. There should be no evidence of feces or mucus on the perianal skin.

A   It is abnormal for one or several tiny openings to be seen in the midline over the sacral region, often with hair protruding from them (Figure 22-4).

P   Pilonidal disease is an acquired condition of the midline coccygeal skin region induced by local stretching forces. There can be a cyst, an acute abscess or chronic draining sinuses in the sacrococcygeal area. Small skin pits representing enlarged hair follicles precede development of the draining sinus or abscess. Lesions are often secondarily invaded by hair.

A   Areas of hyperpigmentation, coupled with excoriation and thickened skin in the perianal area, are abnormal. The area may be intensely pruritic.

P   Pruritus ani is caused by pinworms in children and by fungal infections in adults. The lesions are dull, greyish pink.

A   Well-demarcated, erythematous, sometimes itchy, exudative patches of varying size and shape and rimmed with small, red-based pustules are abnormal.

P   *Candida albicans* occurs in sites where heat and maceration provide a fertile environment. Systemic antibacterial, corticosteroid, or antimetabolic therapy; pregnancy; obesity; diabetes mellitus; blood dyscrasias; and immunologic defects increase susceptibility to candidiasis.

Anal Mucosa

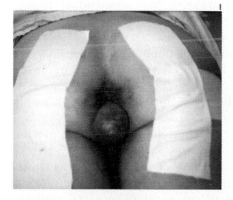

Figure 22-5 Thrombosed Hemorrhoid.
Courtesy of Dr. Haider Goussous, Albany, NY.

E   1. Spread the patient's buttocks apart with both hands, exposing the anus.
    2. Instruct the patient to bear down as though moving the bowels.
    3. Examine the anus for colour, appearance, lesions, inflammation, rash, and masses.

N   The anal mucosa is deeply pigmented, coarse, moist, and hairless. It should be free of lesions, inflammation, rash, masses, or additional openings. The anal opening should be closed. There should not be any leakage of feces or mucus from the anus with straining and there should not be any tissue protrusion.

A   A spherical, bluish lump that appears suddenly at the anus, and that ranges in size from a few millimetres to several centimetres in diameter (Figure 22-5) is abnormal. The overlying anal skin may be tense and edematous. Pain and pruritus may be present in the perianal region.

P   **Hemorrhoids** result from dilatation of the superior and inferior hemorrhoidal veins. These hemorrhoidal veins form a hemorrhoidal plexus, or cushion, in the submucosal layer of the anorectum. An external hemorrhoid is located below the dentate line. Thrombosed external hemorrhoids (blood clots within subcutaneous hemorrhoidal veins) occur as a result of heavy lifting, childbirth, straining to defecate (which may be due to a low-fibre diet), or other vigorous activity. Bleeding may occur with defecation.

A   Excess anal or perianal tissue of varying sizes that is soft, pliable, and covered by normal skin is abnormal.

P   Anal skin tags are the result of residual resolved thrombosed external hemorrhoids, pregnancy, or anal operations. In some cases, there is no known cause.

E	**Examination**	N	**Normal Findings**	A	**Abnormal Findings**	P	**Pathophysiology**

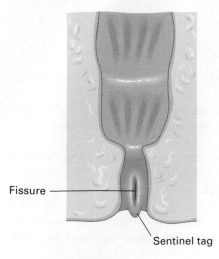

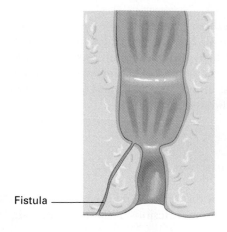

Figure 22-6 Anal Fissure.

Skin
surface
opening

Figure 22-7 Anorectal Fistula.

Figure 22-8 Rectal Prolapse.

A Linear tears in the epidermis of the anal canal beginning below the dentate line and extending distally to the anal orifice are abnormal (Figure 22-6). Extreme pain, pruritus, and bleeding may accompany these findings.

P **Anal fissures** are the result of trauma, such as the forced passage of a large, hard stool, and anal intercourse, especially forced intercourse. Fissures occur most often in the area of the posterior coccygeal midline and less frequently in the anterior midline. This is because of weakness in the superficial external sphincter in these sectors. Predisposition to fissure is increased by perianal inflammation that causes the anoderm to lose its normal elasticity. A senti skin tag may be visible inferior to the anal fissure and at the anal margin. Sphincter spasms may occur during the examination. The use of a local anesthetic may be necessary to thoroughly examine the area.

A Undrained collections of perianal pus of the tissue spaces in and adjacent to the anorectum are abnormal.

P The most common cause of **anorectal abscesses** is infection of the anal glands, usually located posteriorly and situated between the internal and the external sphincters. These glands normally drain via the internal sphincter through small ducts into anal crypts. When these ducts are occluded by impacted fecal material or trauma, ductal stasis and abscess formation results. An indurated mass with overlying erythema displaces the anus in cases of superficial abscess.

A An inflamed, red, raised area with purulent or serosanguinous discharge on the perianal skin is abnormal (Figure 22-7).

P An **anorectal fistula** is a hollow, fibrous tract lined by granulation tissue and having an opening inside the anal canal or rectum and one or more orifices in the perianal skin. Fistulas are usually the result of incomplete healing of drained anorectal abscesses. However, they may occur in the absence of an abscess history. If this is the case, other causes for the fistula must be explored. Additional predisposing factors are inflammatory bowel disease, infectious disease, malignancy, Crohn's disease, radiation therapy, chemotherapy, chlamydial infections, and trauma.

A Soiling of the skin with stool and gaping of the anus are abnormal.

P **Anal incontinence** may be caused by neurological diseases, traumatic injuries, or surgical damage to the puborectalis or sphincter muscles. Perineal or intestinal disorders, diarrhea, fecal impaction, and constipating agents may also cause anal incontinence.

A The protrusion of the rectal mucosa (pinkish red doughnut with radiating folds) through the anal orifice is abnormal (see Figure 22-8).

P **Rectal prolapse** is associated with poor tone of the pelvic musculature, chronic straining at stool, fecal incontinence, and, sometimes, neurological disease or traumatic damage to the pelvis. A complete rectal prolapse involves the entire bowel wall. It is larger, red, and moist looking, and has circular folds.

A Erythematous plaques that develop into vesicular lesions that may become pustules and ulcerate are abnormal (Figure 22-9).

P These lesions are suggestive of HSV. Most anorectal herpes is due to HSV-2, and infections are related to anal intercourse.

A Warts or lesions that are beefy red, flesh coloured, irregular, and pedunculated are abnormal findings (Figure 22-10). The lesions may involve the anoderm but may also extend deep into the anal canal and involve the rectal mucosa. There may be a few scattered lesions or extensive involvement of the entire anus.

P Condylomata acuminatum are caused by HPV. Coital trauma allows entry into the anal epidermis in those in whom wart virus is latent in the anorectum. Anal warts may also develop in women via extension of genital warts along the perineum. Of the 50 strains of HPV, types 16, 18, and 31 have been associated with malignant lesions.

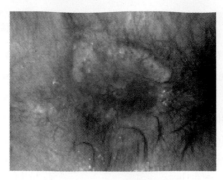

Figure 22-9 Perianal Herpes Simplex Virus. *Courtesy of Centers for Disease Control and Prevention (CDC).*

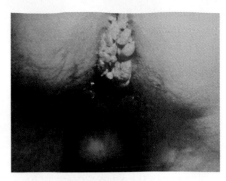

Figure 22-10 Human Papilloma Virus in the Anal Region. *Courtesy of Centers for Disease Control and Prevention (CDC).*

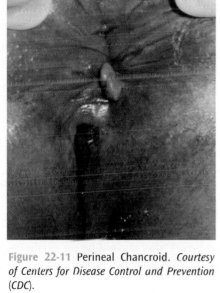

Figure 22-11 Perineal Chancroid. *Courtesy of Centers for Disease Control and Prevention (CDC).*

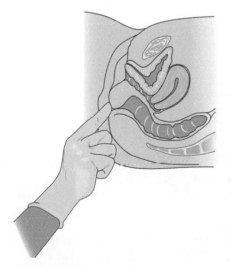

Figure 22-12 Position of the Index Finger for Anorectal Palpation.

P Perineal chancroids (Figure 22-11) are caused by *Haemophilus ducreyi.* Chancroids can be seen on the genitalia as well as the perineal and perianal regions.

A Mucoid or creamy exudate, possibly blood, from the rectum is abnormal.

P Gonococcal proctitis is most often seen in homosexual men as a result of direct inoculation, but it also occurs in women through contamination by vaginal discharge.

A Perianal fissures and edematous skin tags of varying degrees are abnormal.

P Anorectal involvement occurs in the majority of patients with Crohn's disease. Perianal disease may precede the onset of intestinal Crohn's disease by several years. Perianal disease may proceed to anal stricture and incontinence. The development of perianal Crohn's disease has no relation to other extraintestinal manifestations of the disease.

Palpation

Anus and Rectum

To perform anal and rectal wall palpation:

E 1. Have the patient assume one of the positions described on page 810.
2. Reassure the patient that sensations of urination and defecation are common during the rectal assessment.
3. Lubricate a gloved index finger.
4. Place your finger by the anal orifice and instruct the patient to bear down (Valsalva manoeuvre) as you gently insert the flexed tip of your gloved finger into the anal sphincter, with the tip of the finger toward the anterior rectal wall (pointed toward the umbilicus) (Figure 22-12). The anus should never be approached at a right angle (with the index finger extended).

Nursing Tip

Documenting Abnormalities of the Anus

When documenting any abnormalities found in the anus, describe them with regard to anatomic location: e.g., posterior toward the patient's back; anterior toward the patient's abdomen; right and left, respectively. Be sure to note patient position and orientation.

E **Examination** N **Normal Findings** A **Abnormal Findings** P **Pathophysiology**

TABLE 22-1 Common Stool Findings and Etiologies

STOOL FINDING	ETIOLOGY
Black, tarry (**melena**)	Upper gastrointestinal bleeding
Bright red	Rectal bleeding
Black	Iron or bismuth ingestion
Gray, tan	Obstructive jaundice
Pale yellow, greasy, fatty (**steatorrhea**)	Malabsorption syndromes (e.g., celiac disease), cystic fibrosis
Mucus with blood and pus	Ulcerative colitis, acute diverticulitis
Maroon or bright red	Diverticulosis

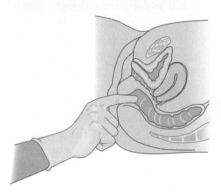

Figure 22-13 Position of the Index Finger in the Anorectum.

TABLE 22-2

Common Causes of Rectal Bleeding

- Cancer of the colon
- Benign polyps of the colon
- Hemorrhoids
- Anal fissure
- Inflammatory bowel disease
- Forced or vigorous anal intercourse
- Traumatic sexual practices

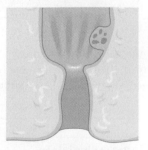

Figure 22-14 Internal Hemorrhoids.

4a. If the patient tightens the sphincter, remove your finger, reassure the patient, and try again, using a relaxation technique such as deep breathing.

5. Feel the sphincter relax. Insert finger as far as it will go (Figure 22-13). Note anal sphincter tone.

6. Palpate the lateral, posterior, and anterior walls of the rectum in a sequenced manner. The lateral walls are felt by rotating the finger along the sides of the rectum. Palpate for nodules, irregularity, masses, and tenderness.

6a. Ask the patient to bear down again (which may help to palpate masses).

7. Slowly withdraw the finger; inspect any fecal matter on your glove and test it for occult blood. Table 22-1 lists common stool findings and etiologies. Table 22-2 lists the common causes of rectal bleeding.

8. Offer the patient tissues to wipe off any remaining lubricant.

N The rectum should accommodate the index finger. There should be good sphincter tone at rest and with bearing down. There should be no excessive pain, tenderness, induration, irregularities, or nodules in the rectum or rectal wall.

A It is abnormal for the anal canal to be tight (making insertion of the index finger very difficult and painful or impossible).

P Anal stenosis can occur congenitally, but this condition usually is acquired. Anorectal operations, diarrheal disease, inflammatory conditions, and the habitual use of laxatives may cause anal stenosis. Chlamydial infections and malignancy must be excluded.

A Internal masses of vascular tissue in the anal canal are abnormal (Figure 22-14).

Nursing Tip

Successful Rectal Examination

The digital rectal exam is usually reserved for the last portion of the assessment after the nurse–patient relationship has been established. A step-by-step explanation, description of expected sensations, reassurance, and a gentle technique will minimize patient embarrassment and discomfort. It is also important for the health professional to feel at ease about performing this examination. Task trainers are available that provide opportunities to learn this technique.

Life 360°

Situations Encountered during the Rectal Assessment

The rectal examination may cause the patient to feel uncomfortable or embarrassed. How would you handle the following situations?
- The patient develops an erection during the examination.
- The patient loses bowel control.
- The patient passes flatus during the examination.
- The patient states "you must hate doing this procedure."

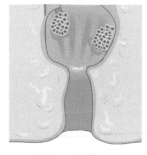

Figure 22-15 Rectal Polyps.

Reflective Thinking

Rectal Assessment

A wide range of situations may be encountered during the rectal assessment. Consider how you would react in each of the following situations:

- Mr. DiCicco presents because he wants to know if he has prostate cancer. He tells you that his father died of prostate cancer and that one of his brothers is now awaiting prostatectomy for treatment of cancer.
- Mrs. Kelly visits the office today for a pap smear and pelvic examination. She states, "I am embarrassed to talk about this, but my husband would like me to participate in anal intercourse and I feel the need to discuss this with someone."
- Mr. Singh has a painful anal fissure. He asks when he can start having sex again with his male partner.

P Internal hemorrhoids arise from the superior (internal) hemorrhoidal vascular plexuses above the dentate line; they are covered by mucosa. Internal hemorrhoids are usually painless unless they are thrombosed or prolapsed through the anal orifice.

A A soft nodule or nodules in the rectum are abnormal (Figure 22-15).

P Rectal polyps occur frequently in the general population. Occasionally, they can be palpated, but more often they are diagnosed by proctoscopy. They vary in size and may be accompanied by rectal bleeding. Rectal polyps are of two types: pedunculated (attached to a stalk) or sessile (adhering to the rectal mucosal wall). A biopsy of the tissue is required to determine if the polyp is benign or malignant.

A A tender, indurated mass in the anorectum is abnormal.

P This may be an anorectal abscess. Refer to page 812.

A An indurated cord palpated in the anorectum is abnormal.

P Anorectal fistula tracts may be palpated from the secondary orifice toward the anus. Digital rectal examination helps to determine the course of the tract. A drop of purulent drainage can be expressed from the opening if the opening is patent.

A A small, symmetrical projection 2 to 4 cm long is abnormal.

P Rectal prolapse is best assessed with the patient in a squatting position. The anal sphincter is lax and palpation between the finger and thumb reveals only two layers of mucosa. Refer to page 812 for additional information.

A Foreign bodies palpated in the rectum are abnormal.

P Thermometers, enema catheters, vibrators, bottles, and phallic objects may be introduced into the anus by accident, for erotic purposes, for concealment, for self-treatment, or by assault. Complications may include perforation of the rectum, obstruction, and pararectal infections.

A A hard mass in the anal canal is abnormal.

P This finding usually indicates anal carcinoma. There is a strong association between anal carcinoma (squamous cell) and HPV types 16 and 18.

A A firm, sometimes rocklike but often rubbery, puttylike mass is abnormal.

P In fecal impaction, the feces accumulates in the rectum because the colon does not respond to the usual stimuli promoting evacuation, or because accessory stimuli normally provided by eating and physical activity are lacking. Drugs, such as opiates, may compound the problem. Rectal sensitivity may be dulled by habitual disregard of the urge to defecate. The prolonged use of laxatives or enemas may also decrease rectal sensitivity.

| **E** Examination | **N** Normal Findings | **A** Abnormal Findings | **P** Pathophysiology |

Nursing Alert

Colorectal Cancer (CRC)[3]

- CRC is the third most common cancer in Canada, after breast and lung cancer in women and prostate and lung cancer in men.
- It is the second most common cancer-related cause of death for men and the third most common for women.
- CRC is believed to develop from a benign tumour or polyp in the bowel and therefore difficult to detect; it develops over a period of time (at least 10 years).
- Approximately 2/3 of colorectal cancers are found in the large intestine and 1/3 in the rectum.
- Symptoms of CRC depend on the lesion's location, type, extent and complications, and may include fatigue and weakness; a change in bowel habit (alternating constipation and increased stool frequency); stool streaked or mixed with blood; and discomfort or pain in the lower abdomen.
- Rates in Canada show an east-to-west gradient, higher in Atlantic provinces and lower in the West with Ontario's rates in the middle range.

Risk Factors for Colorectal Cancer[4]

- Over 50 years of age (most of those diagnosed are 70 years or older)
- Family history of colorectal cancer
- Personal history of adenomatous polyps and/or chronic inflammatory bowel disease (ulcerative colitis, Crohn's disease)
- Personal history of endometrial, ovarian, or breast cancer
- Diet high in red meat and low in fruits and vegetables; high-fat diet
- Obesity
- Lack of physical activity
- Alcohol consumption, especially beer
- Smoking

Screening for Colorectal Cancer[5, 6, 7]

Biennial Fecal Occult Blood Testing in asymptomatic individuals over 50 years of age with a negative family history using Hemoccult 11 or equivalent; begin at age 40 if one first-degree relative with cancer or adenomatous polyp affected at age >60 or two or more second-degree relatives with polyps or cancer.

Patients with risk of hereditary non-polyposis colorectal cancer (HNPCC) or familial adenomatous polyposis (FAP) or who have one first-degree relative with cancer or adenomatous polyp at age < 60 or two or more first-degree relatives with polyp or colon cancer at any age require special screening with colonoscopy or sigmoidoscopy.

Fecal Occult Blood Test (FOBT)

The FOBT is a relatively easy and painless chemical test used to detect hidden (occult) blood in the stools. This test is not diagnostic; rather, it provides important information to determine if further assessment is needed. Generally, the patient is given a kit (see Figure 22-16) and stool samples are collected over a three-day period. Because a variety of foods and medications can give a false-positive result, the following instructions are generally given: for 7 days before and during the stool collection period, avoid nonsteroidal anti-inflammatory drugs or aspirin (no more than one adult aspirin a day). For 3 days before and during the stool collection period avoid vitamin C in excess of 250 mg a day from supplements; citrus fruits or juices; and red meats (including beef, lamb, and liver).

| E | Examination | N | Normal Findings | A | Abnormal Findings | P | Pathophysiology |

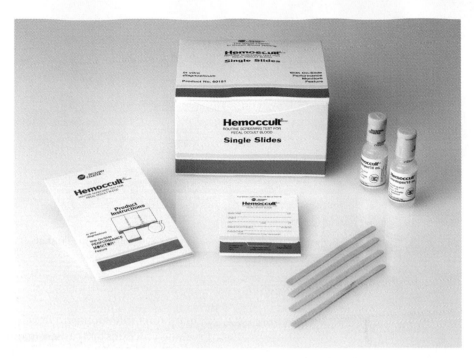

Figure 22-16 Fecal Occult Blood Testing (FOBT) *Used by permission of Beckman Coulter, Inc.*

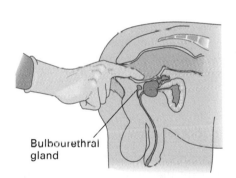

Figure 22-17 Bidigital Palpation of the Bulbourethral Gland.

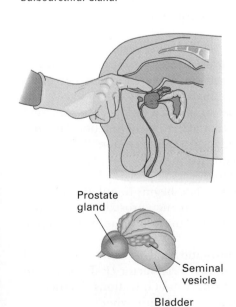

Figure 22-18 Prostatic Palpation.

Prostate

E To perform prostatic palpation:

1. Position the patient as tolerated (the standing position is preferred).
2. Reassure the patient that sensations of urination and defecation are common during the prostatic assessment.
3. Use a well-lubricated, gloved index finger.
4. Insert the gloved index finger and proceed as described in steps 4 and 5 on pages 813 and 814.
5. Perform bidigital examination of the bulbourethral gland by pressing your gloved thumb into the perianal tissue while pressing your gloved index finger toward it (Figure 22-17). Assess for tenderness, masses, or swelling.
6. Release pressure of the thumb and index finger. Remove thumb from the perianal tissue and advance your index finger.
7. Palpate the posterior surface of the prostate gland (Figure 22-18). Note the size, shape, consistency, sensitivity, and mobility of the prostate. Note whether the median sulcus is palpable.
8. Attempt to palpate the seminal vesicles by extending your index finger above the prostate gland. Assess for tenderness and masses.
9. Slowly withdraw the finger; inspect any fecal matter on your glove and test it for occult blood (if not previously performed).

N The prostate gland should be small, smooth, mobile, and non-tender. The median sulcus should be palpable.

A A soft, tender, enlarged prostate gland is abnormal (Figure 22-19).

P The development of benign prostatic hypertrophy (BPH) is related to aging and the presence of testosterone, which converts to dihydrotestosterone and leads to prostatic cell growth. The size of the prostate gland on rectal assessment is not always indicative of the degree of symptoms because the lobes may not be palpable or they may be causing obstruction. In BPH, the median sulcus may not be palpable.

A A firm, tender, or fluctuant mass on the prostate is abnormal.

P A high percentage of patients with prostatic abscess have diabetes mellitus. An abscess is suspected in the patient with acute bacterial prostatitis or

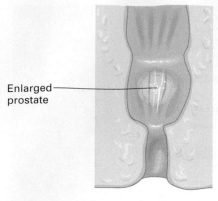

Enlarged prostate

Figure 22-19 Benign Prostatic Hypertrophy.

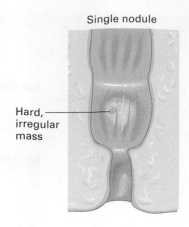

Single nodule

Hard, irregular mass

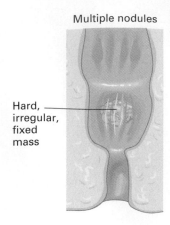

Multiple nodules

Hard, irregular, fixed mass

Figure 22-20 Cancer of the Prostate.

urinary tract infection who develops a spiked fever along with rectal pain. Prostatic abscesses are caused mainly by *Escherichia coli*.

A   Firm, hard, or indurated nodules on the prostate are abnormal (Figure 22-20).

P   The nodules of prostate cancer may be single or multiple. Early in the disease the nodules may be small, but late in the disease the entire prostate may seem irregular, hard, immobile, and quite large.

A   An exquisitely tender and warm prostate is abnormal.

P   Bacterial prostatitis is usually caused by *Escherichia coli*. When patients present with a sudden onset of high fever, chills, malaise, myalgias, and arthralgias, acute bacterial prostatitis is suspected.

GERONTOLOGICAL VARIATIONS

There are age-related changes associated with the rectum and prostate. Anorectal function changes due to the loss of muscle elasticity in the rectum. Older adults also have reduced maximum tolerated volumes in the rectum, with higher rectal pressures in response to distension. Rectal prolapse is most commonly seen in elderly women.

Fecal incontinence in elderly individuals is usually the result of impairment of more than one of the factors that ordinarily maintain continence and may be a sign of an underlying acute medical problem. Table 22-3 lists some of the causes of fecal incontinence in elderly individuals.

Constipation is also common and may be caused by a variety of factors, such as lack of exercise, poor diet, medications that affect bowel function, intrinsic slowing of large bowel transit, and decreased fecal water excretion. Patients usually respond to advice on how to prevent constipation.

The prostate undergoes changes related to the aging process. The most obvious change that occurs is that of size. The prostate begins to enlarge after the age of 40, which often leads to the development of benign prostatic hypertrophy. The prostate capsule may contract and prostatic urethral tone may increase, resulting in urinary obstruction.

There are lower levels of zinc in the prostatic fluid of older men, which appear to reduce the amount of prostatic antibacterial factor (PAF), therefore making the older man more susceptible to urinary tract infections. An increase in the prevalence of prostate cancer is also associated with aging.

TABLE 22-3

Causes of Fecal Incontinence in Elderly Patients

- Diarrhea
- Fecal impaction
- Irritable bowel syndrome
- Anorectal carcinoma
- Rectal trauma
- Stroke
- Diabetes mellitus
- Dementia
- Multiple sclerosis
- Rectal prolapse

Nursing Alert

Prostate Cancer[8]

- Prostate cancer is the most frequently diagnosed cancer and the third most common cause of cancer-related deaths among Canadian men.
- One in 7 Canadian men will develop prostate cancer during his lifetime (mostly after the age of 70); one in 26 men will die of it.
- There were an estimated 20,700 newly diagnosed cases and 4,200 deaths as a result of prostate cancer in Canada in 2006.
- The majority (98% of cases) of prostate cancer is found in men over 50 years of age.
- Fortunately, overall death rates from prostate cancer are declining.

Risk Factors for Prostate Cancer[9]
- Family history of prostate cancer
- Age (particularly after 65; uncommon in men under 50)
- Ethnicity—African ancestry

Research is ongoing into other potential risk factors including dietary factors; sexual factors including sexually transmitted infections; occupational exposures; and hormonal factors.

Screening[10]
- The Canadian Task Force on Preventive Health Care Guidelines *excludes* routine screening for Prostate-Specific Antigen (see Nursing Tip below) from the periodic health examination of asymptomatic men on the basis of low positive predictive value.
- Routine screening using Digital Rectal Examination (DRE) results in increased detection of early cancers but the manoeuvre can detect only small cancers in the posterior and lateral aspects of the prostate. The Canadian Task Force on Preventive Health Care notes that there is insufficient evidence that DRE be included or excluded from periodic health examination for men over 50 years; however, professionals who currently include DRE in their examinations are not advised to change that behaviour.

Nursing Tip

Prostatic-Specific Antigen

The normal value for a serum PSA (prostatic-specific antigen) is 0–4 µg/ml. Serum elevations occur as a result of disruption of the normal prostatic architecture that allows PSA to diffuse into the prostatic tissue and gain access to the circulation. Because PSA is produced by the epithelial cells of the prostate rather than cancer-specific cells, its elevation can be caused by such benign conditions as prostatitis or benign hypertrophy of prostate tissue instead of or as well as prostate cancer. Prostate manipulation with prostate massage and prostate biopsy may also cause increases in the PSA level. There is no significant change, however, in PSA with a digital rectal exam.

Compared to digital rectal exam, the principal advantage of PSA is its ability to detect prostate cancer at an earlier stage. However, like all early detection tests, its test characteristics and ability to contribute to the net benefit of patients requires careful evaluation. Unfortunately, the PSA test identifies not only those cancers that should be treated but also small and slowly growing prostate cancers that

continues

would never have caused symptoms in the person's lifetime. Not only are the detection and treatment of these cancers unnecessary, but also there is risk of substantial complications including postoperative mortality, incontinence, and impotence.

Pickles[11] (2004) cites "widespread enthusiasm for PSA screening has been replaced with a more cautious, individualized approach. If a man wants to minimize risk of prostate cancer and maximize his chance of living as long as possible, PSA screening might be appropriate. If a man wants to maximize his quality of life, minimize his risk of complications (such as impotence and incontinence), and undergo only medical tests that we know to be beneficial, PSA screening is unlikely to be of value to him."

CASE STUDY

The Patient with Acute Bacterial Prostatitis

The case study illustrates the application and objective documentation of the anal, rectal, and prostatic assessment.

Mr. Huong is a 45-year-old male with urinary frequency.

HEALTH HISTORY

PATIENT PROFILE	45 yo man, looks tired and worried.
HEALTH ISSUE/CONCERN	"I feel like I have the flu, and I have to pee all the time."
HISTORY OF ISSUE/CONCERN	Mr. H. woke this morning c̄ 38.9°C temperature, chills, low "achy" back pain 3/10, & "sore all over." Felt well yesterday, never experienced these s/s before. Feels better when lying down. "I want to get better so I can go to work—I am so busy." Constant desire to urinate & is voiding small amounts of cloudy dark urine. States that he was up during the night to urinate 3 times, which is unusual for him. Denies any previous UTIs, difficulty voiding, STIs, hematuria, or hx of renal stones.
PAST HEALTH HISTORY	
Medical History	HTN dx. 1 yr ago by family MD, controlled by diet and smoke cessation; Hypothyroidism dx. 3 yr ago.
Surgical History	Ⓡ knee injury 5 yrs ago while skiing, Ⓡ arthroscopy to repair torn cartilage, no complications
Medications	levothyroxine 0.25 mg daily
Communicable Diseases	Denies rheumatic fever, STIs, TB; Voluntary HIV testing—Neg
Allergies	Penicillin causes a rash over his trunk area
Injuries and Accidents	Refer to surgical section
Special Needs	Denies
Blood Transfusions	Denies
Childhood Illnesses	Varicella age 6
Immunizations	Tetanus 8 yrs ago

continues

FAMILY HEALTH HISTORY

LEGEND

 Living female

 Living male

 Deceased female

 Deceased male

/ Points to patient

A&W = Alive & well

CA = Cancer

CVA = Cerebrovascular accident

HTN = Hypertension

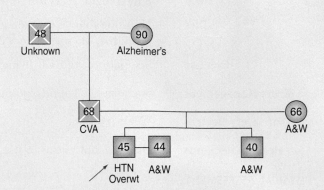

Denies family hx of pilonidal cyst, colorectal CA, rectal polyps, prostate CA.

SOCIAL HISTORY

Alcohol Use	1 beer 3–4 night/wk × 10 yrs
Drug Use	Denies
Tobacco Use	Quit 1 year ago
Domestic and Intimate Partner Violence	Denies
Sexual Practice	Monogamous homosexual relationship for 8 yrs; Ø condom use; engages in oral & anal sex
Travel History	Annual vacation Caribbean
Work Environment	Hairdresser for 20 yrs, has owned his business for 10 yrs
Home Environment	Lives c̄ significant other, no children, 2 dogs; condominium residence
Hobbies and Leisure Activities	Gardening, travelling, reading, going to the gym
Stress and coping	Strained relations with parents since moving in with partner; "I try to see their side and be patient with them." Stress c̄ managing his own business; copes by keeping physically active.
Education	Technical college
Economic Status	Denies financial concerns
Religion/Spirituality	Roman Catholic; feels conflicted with teachings of church and sexual orientation
Ethnicity	"I'm Vietnamese-Canadian"
Roles and Relationships	Describes good relationship c̄ partner, employees, & many friends; attends community events. Strained relations with parents but "things are getting better."
Characteristic Patterns of Daily Living	Wakes at 07:00; goes to the gym 5 days a wk & works out for 1½ hrs; returns home, gets ready for work; works from 12:00–19:00; usually goes out to dinner c̄ friends from work; goes to bed around 23:00

continues)

HEALTH MAINTENANCE ACTIVITIES	
Sleep	8 hr q night, feels rested in AM
Diet	States he follows Canada Food Guide; eats out at restaurants approx. 5 nights/wk and is "very careful;" avoids salt and fatty foods
Exercise	See patterns of daily living
Stress Management	Socializing $\bar{c}$ friends, going to the gym
Use of Safety Devices	Wears seat belt
Health Check-ups	Has had 2 physicals in the last 5 years; weekly self-monitoring of BP
PHYSICAL ASSESSMENT	
Inspection	
Perineum and Sacrococcygeal Area	Skin smooth & even, no lesions, inflammation or swelling
Anal Mucosa	Deeply pigmented, coarse, moist, & hairless; no lesions, inflammation, rashes, or masses
Palpation	
Anus and Rectum	Pain & tenderness $\bar{c}$ rectal exam, ⊕ sphincter tone, Ø irregularities, Ø nodules in the rectum or rectal wall
Prostate	Exquisitely tender, swollen prostate, firm throughout & warm to touch

LABORATORY DATA

Hematology (CBC)

	Pt's Values	Normal
RBC	$4.2 \times 10^{12}/L$	$4.71\text{–}5.14 \times 10^{12}/L$ (men)
WBC	$12 \times 10^{9}/L$	$4.5\text{–}11 \times 10^{9}/L$
PLT	$250 \times 10^{9}/L$	$150\text{–}450 \times 10^{9}/L$
Hgb	150 g/L	male: 126–174 g/L
Hct	0.46	male: 0.43–0.49

Chemistry Panel   PSA   25 µg/ml   0–4 µg/ml

◄NURSING CHECKLIST►

Anus, Rectum, and Prostate Assessment

Inspection
- Perineum and sacrococcygeal area
- Anal mucosa

Palpation
- Anus and rectum
- Prostate B

REVIEW QUESTIONS

1. Which lobes of the prostate are accessible to examination?
   a. Right and left lateral lobes
   b. Anterior and posterior lobes
   c. Median and anterior lobes
   d. Median and posterior lobes
   The correct answer is (a).

2. Which person would be at the highest risk for developing colorectal cancer?
   a. 28-year-old female with a paternal grandmother with colon cancer
   b. 56-year-old male who had an adenomatous polyp removed 1 year ago
   c. 35-year-old male with a high-fat, low-fibre diet
   d. 78-year-old obese female with limited physical activity
   The correct answer is (b).

3. You are examining a 40-year-old-female. During inspection, which physical assessment finding would cause you to suspect rectal abuse from repeated anal intercourse?
   a. Rectal prolapse
   b. Anal skin tags
   c. External hemorrhoids
   d. Anal fissures
   The correct answer is (d).

4. Which etiology would you suspect if your patient had the complaint of blood, pus, and mucus in the stool?
   a. Rectal bleeding
   b. Ulcerative colitis
   c. Upper gastrointestinal bleeding
   d. Iron ingestion
   The correct answer is (b).

5. During Mr. Jones' rectal exam, you are unable to palpate the median sulcus. Which physical finding does this indicate?
   a. Prostate cancer
   b. Benign prostatic hypertrophy
   c. Bacterial prostatitis
   d. Prostatic abscess
   The correct answer is (b).

   Questions 6 and 7 refer to the following situation:

Mr. Miller, a 34-year-old homosexual male, presents to you with hematochezia, anorectal pain, and pruritus. On assessing him, you observe anorectal vesicular lesions.

6. What do you suspect is the cause of Mr. Miller's lesions?
   a. Rectal cancer
   b. Anorectal fistula
   c. Anal fissure
   d. Anorectal herpes simplex virus
   The correct answer is (d).

7. The most likely cause of this patient's hematochezia is:
   a. Internal hemorrhoids
   b. Upper gastrointestinal bleeding
   c. Obstructive jaundice
   d. Malabsorption syndrome
   The correct answer is (a).

8. A 75-year-old man has been experiencing constipation. Which is most likely the cause of his constipation?
   a. Enlarged prostate
   b. Intrinsic slowing of large bowel transit
   c. Hemorrhoids
   d. Rectal prolapse
   The correct answer is (b).

9. During inspection of the anal mucosa, which would you find during a normal examination?
   a. Excess anal tissue
   b. A spherical bluish lump
   c. Coarse, deeply pigmented mucosa
   d. Linear tear in the epidermis
   The correct answer is (c).

10. Which statement is correct in regard to performing a successful rectal examination?
   a. Perform at the beginning of the physical examination to decrease patient anxiety.
   b. The less information given about the exam the better.
   c. Perform at the end of exam after a trusting relationship has been established.
   d. Ask the patient if he or she would like to skip this part of the exam.
   The correct answer is (c).

Visit the Estes online companion resource at
www.healthassessment.nelson.com for additional
content and study aids.

REFERENCES

[1]National Cancer Institute of Canada. (n.d.). *Cancer statistics: International variation in cancer incidence, 1993–1997.* Retrieved November 9, 2006, from http://www.ncic.cancer.ca/ncic/internet/standard/0,3621,84658243_85787780__langId-en,00.html

[2]Ibid.

[3]Public Health Agency of Canada. (2004). *Progress report on cancer control in Canada.* Ottawa: Health Canada.

[4]Health Canada, 2005. Screening for colorectal cancer. Retrieved November 9, 2006, from http://www.hc-sc.gc.ca/iyh-vsv/diseases-maladies/colorectal_e.html

[5] Public Health Agency of Canada. (2002, May). *Technical report for the National Committee on Colorectal Cancer Screening.* Ottawa: Health Canada.

[6]Leddin, D., Hunt R., Champion, M., Cockeram, A., Flook, N., Gould, M., Kim, Y.I., Love, J., Morgan, D., Natsheh, S. & Sadowski, D. and Canadian Association of Gastroenterology. Canadian Digestive Health Foundation. Canadian Association of Gastroenterology and the Canadian Digestive Health Foundation (2004). Guidelines on colon cancer screening. *Canadian Journal of Gastroenterology.* 18(2): 93–9.

[7]Towler, B.P., Irwig, L., Glaszio,u P., Weller, D., Kewenter, J. Screening for colorectal cancer using the faecal occult blood test, Hemoccult. *The Cochrane Database of Systematic Reviews* 1998, Issue 2. Art. No.: CD001216.

[8]National Cancer Institute of Canada. (2006). Canadian cancer statistics 2006. Toronto.

[9]Centre for Chronic Disease Prevention and Control (2005). Prostate Cancer. Retrieved November 17, 2006, from http://www.phac-aspc.gc.ca/ccdpc-cpcmc/topics/cancer_prost_e.html#desc

[10]Pickles, T. (2004). Current status of PSA screening. *Canadian Family Physician,* 50: 57–63.

[11]Ibid.

BIBLIOGRAPHY

Fazio, V., Church, J., & Delaney, C. (2005). *Current therapy in colon and rectal surgery* (2nd ed.). St. Louis, MO, Mosby.

Ezer, H. (2003) Predictors of adaptation in wives during the initial psychosocial phase of prostate cancer. Doctoral Dissertation, Université de Montreal.

Held-Warmkessel, J. (Ed.) (2006). *Contemporary issues in prostate cancer: A nursing perspective.* Sudbury, MA: Jones and Bartlett Publishers.

Kemp C., & Potyk D. (2005, August). Cancer screening: principles & controversies. *Nurse Practitioner: American Journal of Primary Health Care* 30(8): 46–50.

Lin, O., Roy, P., Schembre, D.B., Kozarek, R.A. (2005). Screening sigmoidoscopy and colonoscopy for reducing colorectal cancer mortality in asymptomatic persons. (Protocol) *The Cochrane Database of Systematic Reviews* Issue 2. Art. No.: CD005201.

Kopec, J. A., Goel, V., Bunting, P. S., Neuman, J., Sayre, E. C., Warde, P., Levers, P., & Fleshner, N. (2005). Screening with prostate specific antigen and metastatic prostate cancer risk: A population based case-control study. *The Journal of Urology,* 174, 495–499.

Meyrier, A. & Fekete, T. (2006). Acute and chronic bacterial prostatitis. In *Up-To-Date,* B.D. Rose (Ed.). Waltham, MA.

Pachler, J., & Wille-Jørgensen, P. (2005). Quality of life after rectal resection for cancer, with or without permanent colostomy. *The Cochrane Database of Systematic Reviews* Issue 2. Art. No.: CD004323.

Porche, D. J. (2005, September). Prostate cancer: screening and early detection. *Journal for Nurse Practitioners* 1(2): 70–71.

WEB RESOURCES

Canadian Prostate Cancer Research Initiative
http://www.prostateresearch.ca

Canadian Prostate Cancer Network
http://www.cpcn.org

Canadian Prostate Health Council
http://www.canadian-prostate.com

Canadian Urological Association
http://www.cua.org

Colorectal Cancer Association of Canada
http://www.ccac-accc.ca

UNIT 4

Special Populations

For it may safely be said, not that the habit of ready and correct observation will by itself make us useful nurses, but that without it we shall be useless with all our devotion.

—Florence Nightingale

CHAPTER 23

Pregnant Patient

COMPETENCIES

1. Describe the characteristics of the most common pregnancy-related health issues or concerns.

2. Assess the psychosocial status of a pregnant woman.

3. Differentiate the normal changes of pregnancy from pathological changes.

4. Perform a physical assessment on a pregnant woman.

5. Assess the learning needs of a pregnant woman.

*P*regnancy brings about many physiological, hormonal, and psychological changes in a woman during the 280 days, or approximately 40 (normal range 37 to 40) weeks, of gestation. The pregnancy is subdivided into trimesters of a little more than 13 weeks each, and various symptoms and problems can be specific to each trimester. You are encouraged to review Chapters 14 and 20 before beginning this chapter.

Much of prenatal care centres on assessing the health of mother and fetus as well as educating the pregnant patient and her family about the many changes that result from pregnancy. With the availability of accurate home pregnancy tests, a woman may know she is pregnant within two weeks of conception. Nurses are often the primary contact during the pregnancy and can play a critical role in helping to ensure a healthy pregnancy. With active listening and a supportive attitude, nurses assess for health and potential complications throughout the pregnancy as well as provide anticipatory guidance for the issues or challenges that arise during and after the pregnancy.

The trend is for women to wait longer and longer to have their first child. Almost half of Canadian women are 28 and older when they give birth to their first child, with women in Ontario and British Columbia being the oldest first-time mothers. In contrast, in Nunavut the average age of first-time mothers is 21.7 years. The number of births continues to decline over the years with 1.5 children per family becoming the norm.[1]

Overall, Canada's standard of perinatal care ranks among the highest in the world. Maternal mortality rates have dropped from 6.1 per 100,000 live births in 1979–81 to 2.5 per 100,000 live births in 1997–99 and are among the lowest in the world. Causes of mortality include hypertensive disorders, pulmonary embolism, hemorrhage, puerperal infection and ectopic pregnancy. While the infant mortality rate in Canada is among the lowest in the world (5.2/1,000 live births in 2001), other industrialized countries like Sweden, Norway, and Singapore have even lower rates of 3 to 4/1,000. Infant mortality due to congenital anomalies has especially decreased likely because of increased prenatal diagnosis and termination of affected pregnancies together with improvements in care of infants with congenital anomalies. However, preterm birth rates are gradually increasing, possibly linked to the increase in multiple birth rates from 1.8/100 total births in 1974 to 2.7 in 2000. As well, use of technologies such as ultrasound has likely led to the earlier delivery of compromised fetuses. The increase in multiple births is linked to a higher proportion of older women giving birth and the increase in use of infertility treatments. Some regional discrepancies exist in Canada with stillbirth and perinatal mortality rates in registered Indians estimated to be about double the Canadian average; rates among the Inuit in the Northwest Territories are about 2.5 times the rates for Canada as a whole.[2, 3, 4, 5]

ANATOMY AND PHYSIOLOGY

Physiological changes during pregnancy affect every system in the body. These changes occur to maintain maternal health and accommodate the growth of a healthy fetus. This chapter provides an overview of these changes; it is not all-inclusive.

Skin and Hair

The skin is subjected to the influence of hormones during pregnancy. There is an increased subdermal fat deposit, along with thickening of the skin. Acne may develop or improve during pregnancy. Other changes include an increase in sweat and sebaceous gland production, which, along with the increase in superficial capillaries and peripheral vasodilation, serves to dissipate heat. Existing pigmentation increases in the nipples, areolae, external genitalia, and the anal

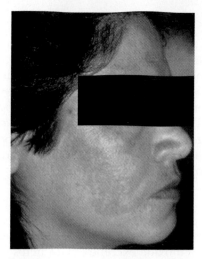

Figure 23-1 Melasma or Chloasma. *Courtesy of Timothy Berger, MD, Chief, Department of Dermatology at San Francisco General Hospital, San Francisco, CA.*

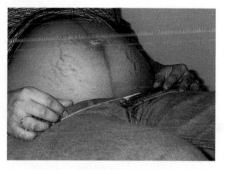

Figure 23-2 Linea Nigra with Striae Gravidarum.

region. The face may develop **melasma**, or **chloasma** (Figure 23-1), known as the mask of pregnancy, which manifests as blotchy, irregular pigmentation. Linea nigra, or darkening of the linea alba, may present on the abdomen as a darkened vertical midline between the fundus and the symphysis pubis (Figure 23-2). **Linea nigra** regresses, or fades, after delivery, but does not totally disappear. Nevi—circumscribed, pigmented areas of skin—may be stimulated to grow; and skin tags, molluscum fibrosum gravidarum, may develop from epithelial hyperplasia, especially on the upper body. With connective tissue changes of pregnancy, **striae gravidarum** (stretch marks) often develop on the abdomen, breasts, and upper thighs; after delivery, they regress or fade but do not totally disappear.

> ### Nursing Tip
>
> **Breast Care during Pregnancy**
>
> Teach your patients to properly care for their breasts during pregnancy by:
> - Wearing a supportive bra that accommodates the breasts' changing size
> - Avoiding nipple stimulation, which may cause either leakage of colostrum, pain in already tender breasts, or premature contractions
> - Washing the breasts with warm water only, because soap may irritate the skin and sore nipples
> - Patting instead of rubbing the breasts dry after bathing
> - Wearing nursing pads in the bra and air drying the breasts if colostrum leakage is significant

Vascular changes reflected in the skin can include the development or enlargement of spider angiomas, hemangiomas, varicosities, and palmar erythema, which may become more pronounced as pregnancy progresses.

Facial hair may increase, but the scalp hair may shed and thin, especially in the postpartum period. The scalp hair may become oily.

Head and Neck

The thyroid gland may increase in size after approximately 12 weeks of gestation (although studies are conflicting as to whether or not there is an increase), related to the increase in vascularity. This may result in a shift in thyroid tests.

Eyes, Ears, Nose, Mouth, and Throat

Corneal thickening and edema (especially in the third trimester) may occur and the pregnant woman may experience visual changes. These changes may be discussed with the patient's ophthalmologist or optometrist, but pregnancy changes in vision are typically not treated because they may resolve shortly after delivery. Contact lens wearers may also experience blurry vision secondary to increased lysozyme in tears, which may lead to an oily sensation.

Increased vascularity and increased mucous production often lead to nasal stuffiness, snoring, congestion and epistaxis, impaired hearing or fullness in the ears, and a decreased sense of smell. The pregnant woman should be reassured that these are normal experiences that usually resolve after delivery.

Increased vascularity and hormonal changes often lead to soft, edematous, and bleeding gums, commonly noticed when brushing teeth. Epulis, or erythematous gingival nodules that bleed easily, can be present. **Ptyalism**, excessive secretion of saliva, may be an annoying symptom and, if marked, may require evaluation for other causes such as goiter. Vocal changes or cough may be noted due to hormonally induced changes in the larynx.

Breasts

Early breast changes may include enlargement, tingling, and tenderness secondary to hormonal changes. As the pregnancy progresses, the breasts continue to enlarge and the mammary glands prepare for lactation after delivery (alveoli increase in both number and size, Montgomery's tubercles enlarge, and lactiferous ducts proliferate). This may cause the breasts to feel more nodular on palpation than in the non-pregnant state. The areolae may darken. The nipples may become darker and more erect. **Colostrum**, a thick, yellow discharge known as early breast milk, may be secreted as early as the second trimester. Veins in the breasts may become more apparent and blue as they become engorged from increased vascularization.

Thorax and Lungs

The demands of the physiological changes of pregnancy and of the fetus lead to increased oxygen consumption and carbon dioxide excretion. This helps to increase oxygen use by the fetus and facilitate the transfer of carbon dioxide from the fetus to the maternal circulation for elimination. With advancing pregnancy, the diaphragm elevates approximately 4 cm and the movement of the diaphragm increases, so that most respiratory effort is diaphragmatic. Stimulated by progesterone, the thoracic cage relaxes and expands by 5 to 7 cm in circumference to accommodate these increased respiratory demands, and may cause discomfort or pain as the intercostal muscles stretch. The tidal volume increases by 30% to 40% during pregnancy, probably due to the stimulatory effects of increased levels of progesterone. These physiological changes often lead to an increased respiratory rate, hyperventilation, or shortness of breath, especially on exertion such as climbing stairs.

Heart and Peripheral Vasculature

Largely as an increase in plasma, blood volume increases by 30% to 50% (more with multiple births), thus increasing the cardiac output. This process begins at 12 weeks of gestation and peaks at 28 to 34 weeks. This increase protects the mother from hemorrhage at delivery, increases oxygen transport, increases renal filtration, and dissipates fetal heat production. With cardiac dilatation (maximal by ten weeks), the mother's heart lies more horizontally and shifts upward and to the left along with the apical impulse. Heart rate increases by 10 to 15 beats per minute, a split first heart and S_3 sound may be heard, physiological systolic murmurs of grade 2/6 may be heard, and blood pressure varies according to position and trimester. In addition, the increased breast vascularization may lead to a continuous murmur, especially near the end of the pregnancy, known as the "mammary souffle." Supine hypotension, resulting from the weight of the uterus on the inferior vena cava, is common; it is recommended that pregnant women avoid a supine position starting at 20 weeks, unless there is a left uterine tilt.

Systolic pressure is not significantly different throughout pregnancy, whereas the diastolic pressure may lower by 5 mm Hg in the second trimester and then rise to first trimester levels after midpregnancy. The lower blood pressure in the second trimester occurs as the body adjusts to the changes in the intravascular volume and to the hormonal effects on the vascular walls. Monitoring of blood pressure during pregnancy is an important factor in determining complications such as pre-eclampsia. Many pregnant women also experience dependent edema partially due to peripheral vasodilation and decreased vascular resistance. This swelling is most commonly seen in the feet but can also occur in the hands and face.

Abdomen

The growing uterus gradually displaces the abdominal contents, leading to decreased tone and motility, decreased bowel sounds, and an increased emptying time for the stomach and intestines. These changes often bring about

---

Nursing Tip

Nausea and Vomiting during Pregnancy

As many as 90% of women experience nausea and vomiting during pregnancy. The following recommendations may be helpful:[6]

- Dietary and lifestyle changes such as eating several small, frequent meals of foods that are appealing; avoiding spicy and fatty foods or cold, sweet beverages; and avoiding noxious sensory stimuli such as strong odours.
- Alternative therapies such as ginger supplementation, acupuncture, and acupressure.
- Rest to avoid exacerbation of nausea and vomiting associated with fatigue.
- Medical prescription of doxylamine/pyridoxine (e.g., Diclectin), or H1 receptor antagonist (e.g., dimenhydrinate— Gravol; hydroxyzine—Atarax)

Nursing Tip

Maintaining Urinary Health during Pregnancy

Pregnant women are reminded to:

- Drink eight to ten glasses of water a day and avoid fluids with caffeine.
- Void frequently, especially after intercourse.
- Gently wash the external genitalia before and after intercourse.
- Always wipe front to back after urination and defecation.

Nursing Alert

Centre of Balance during Pregnancy

Warn the pregnant woman that she is more vulnerable to falls and accidents because of the change in her centre of balance. Pregnant women should exercise caution when changing position, moving over uneven surfaces, ascending and descending stairs, and participating in activities such as riding a bicycle.

increased flatulence and constipation and can contribute to the development of hemorrhoids.

Indigestion (heartburn) is often experienced by the pregnant woman due to the relaxation of the esophageal sphincter, subsequent reflux, and slowed gastric emptying. Nausea and vomiting are common early in pregnancy and may even lead to a weight loss in the first trimester.

Increased emptying time and chemical changes in bile composition can put the pregnant woman at increased risk for cholelithiasis, the presence or formation of bilestones or calculi in the gallbladder or duct, and estrogen may augment any tendency to develop cholestasis (arrest of bile excretion).

Some women will also experience a separation of the rectus muscle of the abdominal wall, known as **diastasis recti**, which may be asymptomatic and noticed only as a vertical protrusion midline. Diastasis requires no medical intervention.

Urinary System

Secondary to the increased intravascular volume, the glomerular filtration rate (GFR) increases by approximately 50% and the reabsorption rate of various chemicals, especially sodium and water, changes. Urinary frequency usually increases in the first trimester. **Glycosuria**, glucose in the urine, is common in pregnancy. There is also an increased loss of amino acids that may show as **proteinuria** on a urine dipstick. Dilation of the ureters and renal pelvises, a decrease in bladder tone, and the short female urethra place the pregnant woman at risk for urinary tract infections. In both early and late pregnancy the bladder is encroached upon by the enlarging uterus and fetal presenting parts. **Nocturia**, or excessive night-time urination, may disrupt the pregnant woman's sleep pattern.

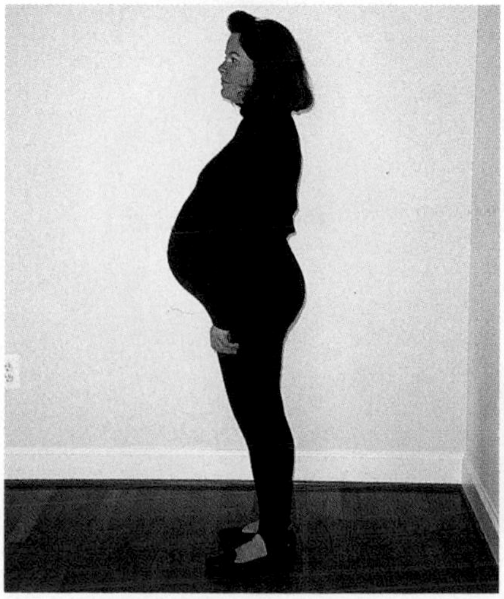

Figure 23-3 Lordosis of Pregnancy.

Musculoskeletal System

The hormones relaxin and progesterone affect all joints in the pregnant woman's body. This leads to a widening (and, occasionally, a separation) of the symphysis pubis at approximately 28 to 32 weeks, increased pelvic mobility to accommodate vaginal delivery, and an unsteady gait known as the "waddle of pregnancy." These hormones also allow the thoracic cage to change shape, which can lead to complaints of upper back or rib pain.

Developing lordosis (Figure 23-3) of the lumbar spine keeps the centre of gravity over the legs and is often associated with lower back pain. Sciatic nerve pain may present as lower back pain, a shooting pain down the leg, or leg weakness. For unknown reasons, muscle cramps, particularly in the calves, thighs, and buttocks, may develop, especially at night.

Shoe size may increase by as much as one full size as pregnancy progresses, due to edema and relaxation of foot joints. Fat deposits increase throughout the body and are most noticeable on the hips and buttocks.

Neurological System

The most commonly experienced neurological changes of pregnancy include headaches, numbness, and tingling. The more bothersome neuropathies include carpal tunnel syndrome, foot drop, facial palsy, fatigue, and difficulty remaining asleep at night. After ruling out any underlying disorder, reassure the patient that these are temporary symptoms. Headaches may be relieved by small frequent meals, adequate rest, and posture and work environment adjustments. Seizure activity with no prior history may indicate the development of **eclampsia**, or seizures associated with pregnancy-induced hypertension (PIH). Dizziness and lightheadedness may be due to the fetus's pressure on the vena cava. Lapses of memory are common and the etiology is poorly understood.

Female Genitalia

The pelvic organs experience vascular, hormonal, and structural changes. Uterine vessels dilate and at term can hold one-sixth of the maternal circulation with a blood flow of 500 mL/min. With the increased blood flow, the pregnant woman may note a feeling of pelvic congestion as well as vulvar edema. Amenorrhea, secondary to the hormonal changes of pregnancy, is generally the first noticeable sign.

The pregnant woman's enlarging uterus begins as a pelvic organ, becoming, with bimanual examination, palpably enlarged at six to seven weeks (Figures 23-4 and 23-5), and progresses to an abdominal organ at approximately 12 weeks of gestation. At 16 weeks the fundus of the uterus is midway between the symphysis pubis and the umbilicus, and at 20 weeks the fundus is typically at the umbilicus.

Between weeks 18 and 32 of gestation, the height of the uterine fundus above the symphysis pubis is measured in centimetres and is used to confirm the gestational age in weeks. After 32 weeks, although still used, this measurement is less accurate.

The round and broad ligaments elongate to accommodate the growing fetus, and may cause the patient lower quadrant pain. **Lightening**, also called dropping, is a decrease in fundal height due to the descent of the presenting fetal part into the pelvis. This typically occurs approximately three weeks prior to the onset of labour in a nulliparous woman, and is often indicated by increased pressure in the pelvis and increased frequency of urination. In a multiparous woman, lightening may not occur until after active labour begins. **Braxton Hicks contractions**, which are irregular and usually painless, begin as early as the first trimester.

> ### Nursing Tip
>
> **Avoiding Vaginal Yeast Infections during Pregnancy**
>
> Perineal care during pregnancy includes:
> 1. Avoiding clothing that fits tightly in the crotch
> 2. Choosing underwear with a cotton rather than a nylon crotch
> 3. Removing a wet bathing suit promptly
> 4. Reporting recurrent yeast infections (suggestive of glucose intolerance)

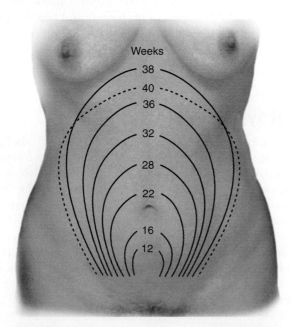

Figure 23-4 Uterine and Abdominal Enlargement of Pregnancy.

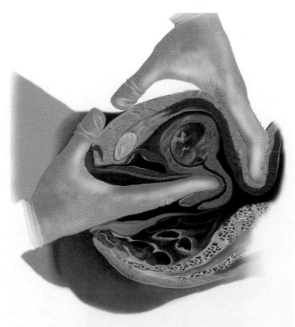

Figure 23-5 Bimanual Examination and Hegar's Sign.

TABLE 23-1	Changes in Pelvic Organs in Pregnancy	
NAME	**GESTATIONAL AGE**	**DESCRIPTION**
Ladin's sign	5–6 weeks	Softening of cervical–uterine junction
Goodell's sign	6 weeks	Cervical softening
McDonald's sign	7–8 weeks	Easy flexion of fundus on cervix
Chadwick's sign	8 weeks	Cervical bluish hue
Hegar's sign	8 weeks	Softening of uterine isthmus

The cervix experiences increased vascularity and increased **friability**, or susceptibility to bleeding, especially following a Pap smear or intercourse. Table 23-1 lists additional changes in the cervix and uterus in pregnancy. The endocervical glands increase in number and size, which causes a softening of the cervix. Mucous production occurs to form an endocervical protective plug (referred to as the mucous plug), and the vaginal mucosa thickens secondary to hormonal changes. Throughout pregnancy, the vaginal discharge increases and is typically of a white, milky consistency. From 36 weeks on, vaginal discharge may become noticeably thicker and clumps may be present when the mucous plug is expelled. The hormonally induced changes in the vaginal environment lead to an increased risk of yeast infection.

Nursing Alert

Physiological Anemia and Pregnancy Induced Hypertension (PIH)

Failure of the normal physiological anemia of pregnancy to occur in the third trimester may be associated with PIH. PIH is commonly known as toxemia of pregnancy. Complications can include **HELLP syndrome** (hemolysis, elevated liver enzymes, and low platelets), which may lead to significant blood loss. Immediately refer patients with these symptoms for further evaluation.

Life 360°

Providing Care to the Abused Patient

Women who are abused may be reluctant to seek help, sometimes out of fear (of retaliation from her partner), sometimes out of the hope that the partner will change and the abuse will end, and sometimes because of low self-esteem. Will you feel comfortable asking directly whether your client is being hurt or abused in any way? Do you know what resources are available to the patient if there is an affirmative answer? What would you do if the woman denies any abuse yet you believe she is at risk? What are the laws in your province or territory that would influence how you act in such cases?

Nursing Alert

Identifying Abuse in Pregnant Women

The Canadian Perinatal Surveillance System (CPSS)[7] has identified that women reporting physical abuse during pregnancy is an important health care issue. While data on physical abuse during pregnancy are limited and no standard of physical abuse is used in the Canadian literature, the CPSS reports that the prevalence of physical abuse during pregnancy likely ranges from 5% to 7%. The majority of these women will have previously been abused, but approximately 40% will experience their first episode of abuse during pregnancy. Women who were previously abused may experience an increase in abuse during pregnancy, and it is worrisome that pregnant women may be up to four times more likely than nonpregnant women to experience serious violence such as being beaten, sexually assaulted, choked, or sustaining injury to the head, neck, and abdomen.

The Society of Obstetricians and Gynaecologists of Canada recommends that screening for abuse during pregnancy should be part of routine prenatal care. Physical abuse should be suspected when women make multiple visits to care providers' offices with health issues or concerns such as:[8]
- headaches, insomnia
- choking sensations, hyperventilation
- gastrointestinal symptoms, chronic pain
- shyness, fear, embarrassment
- evasiveness, passivity
- frequent crying
- a male partner who often accompanies her but who is reluctant to leave
- drug and alcohol abuse or overdose
- attempts at self-harm or suicide
- depression
- sexual problems
- injuries not consistent with stated cause

Anus and Rectum

Decreased gastrointestinal tract tone and motility produce a sense of fullness, indigestion, constipation, bloating, and flatulence. Development of hemorrhoids is common and can become very problematic. As pregnancy progresses and the uterus enlarges, mechanical pressure may aggravate constipation and hemorrhoids. Vitamin and iron supplementation may increase the above symptoms and commonly darken the stool.

Hematological System

Common hematological changes include increased white blood cell count (WBC), increased total red blood cell (RBC) volume, increased plasma volume, decreased number and increased size of platelets, and increased fibrinogen and clotting factors VII through X. The relatively larger increase in plasma volume compared to RBC volume leads to physiological anemia of pregnancy. The coagulation changes protect against hemorrhage at birth but may also put the pregnant woman at increased risk for thromboembolic disease, for example, deep vein thrombosis (DVT).

Endocrine System

The basal metabolic rate (BMR) increases by 15% to 25% due to the increased oxygen consumption and to fetal metabolic demands. This can often lead to feelings of warmth and heat intolerance.

As pregnancy progresses, an increasing resistance to insulin develops, causing pregnancy to be called a "diabetogenic state." Causes for this phenomenon are incompletely understood but are partially related to placental manufacture of the enzyme insulinase. This process occurs to ensure adequate amounts of glucose for fetal demands. Glycosuria may be noted because the distant renal tubules cannot respond to the increased amounts and duration of glucose in the circulatory system. Pregnancy-induced glucose intolerance can be a risk factor for future development of insulin-dependent diabetes mellitus. The maternal immunological system is less resistant to infection due to a decreased cellular immune response.

HEALTH HISTORY

The pregnant patient health history provides insight into the link between a patient's life and lifestyle and pregnancy-related information and pathology.

The health history for the pregnant woman is generally taken on a form designed specifically for pregnancy. Data about the trajectory of the pregnancy from the preconception visit (if there is one) through delivery are collected. A standard health history is taken as well as specific assessment of any prior obstetric history, genetic predispositions, current signs and symptoms including those of pregnancy, any change in normal routine, physical assessment, and laboratory data. This comprehensive approach is essential for directing risk factor assessment and developing a plan of management. Table 23-2 illustrates a typical obstetric history.

PATIENT PROFILE   *Diseases that are age- and ethnicity-specific for pregnancy are listed.*

continues

Age	Being under 17 or over 35 puts women at risk for various pregnancy complications such as PIH, gestational diabetes, and genetic disorders. The prevalence of Down syndrome in women 25–27 is 7.2/100,000 births compared to 28.3/100,000 in 35–39-year-old women.[9] Almost 13% of births are to women 35–39. The birth rate among teenagers is declining except in Nunavut. Ectopic pregnancy rates increase with age.[10]
Ethnicity	People of Asian, Asian Indian, or Mediterranean origin (Greece, Italy, Cyprus, Middle Eastern): thalassemia Ashkenazi Jews: Tay-Sachs and Gaucher's diseases French Canadians: Tay-Sachs disease
HEALTH ISSUE/CONCERN	The pregnant woman may have a myriad of concerns as discussed throughout the chapter.
PAST HEALTH HISTORY	*The various components of the past health history are linked to pregnancy pathology and pregnancy-related information.*
Medical History	Asthma, diabetes mellitus, cardiac disease, renal disease, seizure disorder, autoimmune disorders
Surgical History	Uterine surgery, cone or excisional biopsy of the cervix, abdominal surgery leading to internal or external scarring or adhesions
Medications	Certain medications for chronic conditions may be continued during pregnancy, such as methyldopa and hydralazine for hypertension. Other medications may be changed due to the teratogenic effect on the fetus; for example, Coumadin would be changed to heparin, and an oral diabetic agent would be changed to insulin. Medications for seizure disorders or psychiatric conditions should be discussed with the health care provider in terms of risk–benefit ratio for mother and the fetus, as well as any possible alternate medications for use prior to conception and during pregnancy. Some OTC medications such as acetaminophen are considered safe during pregnancy, but any pregnant (or possibly pregnant) woman should consult her health care provider before taking any medications or therapies.
Communicable Diseases	TORCH diseases (toxoplasmosis, rubella, cytomegalovirus, herpes), measles, varicella, mumps, human parvovirus B19, HIV, hepatitis B. A rubella titer, VDRL, and hepatitis B surface antigen are routinely drawn on pregnant patients. HIV testing is recommended, if the patient agrees to it. Rubella (German measles), especially in the first trimester, and syphilis during pregnancy can cause anomalies and complications. Other infectious diseases may affect the pregnancy depending on their severity and the gestational age at which the disease is contracted; e.g., varicella may present a problem to the fetus if active at the time of delivery. Other infectious diseases to review include tuberculosis and sexually transmitted illnesses (STIs).
Allergies	Symptoms may change with pregnancy; it is best to review all current allergy medications to ensure compatibility with pregnancy.
Injuries and Accidents	Any injury during pregnancy is of concern, especially those involving the abdomen, pelvis, or back.
Special Needs	Disabilities and handicaps do not generally interfere with pregnancy. Some neuromuscular disorders such as myasthenia gravis may affect muscle response as pregnancy progresses and during labour. Paralysis does not

continues

interfere with pregnancy other than with regard to the patient's decreased ability to note significant changes in her physical status, e.g., uterine contractions.

Childhood Illnesses

Rheumatic heart disease, if mitral valve prolapse (MVP) developed, may put the patient at risk for endocarditis with an extremely long or complicated labour or delivery and could require prophylactic antibiotics with delivery. Knowledge of childhood diseases leading to immunity may decrease anxiety if exposure to those illnesses occurs during pregnancy.

Immunizations

Typically, immunizations should be avoided during pregnancy, though the hepatitis B series is not contraindicated. Any unavoidable travel to an area with known infectious disease risk requires a discussion of the risk–benefit ratio of immunization. Immune status testing should be encouraged at any preconception visit. If immune status is unknown or immune status testing reveals a lack of adequate titers, rubella and varicella immunizations should be given with instructions to avoid pregnancy for three months.

FAMILY HEALTH HISTORY

Pregnancy-related conditions and diseases that are familial are listed.

Preterm labour or delivery; hypertensive disorders of pregnancy; diethylstilbestrol (DES) exposure; multiple births in female relatives of patient's mother; chromosome abnormalities such as Down syndrome; genetic disorders such as Tay-Sachs or Gaucher's diseases or sickle cell disease; inheritable diseases, such as Huntington's chorea; congenital anomalies such as cleft lip or palate; neural tube defects; cardiac deformities; blood disorders; diabetes (gestational, Type 1 or 2 diabetes mellitus); neuromuscular diseases; psychiatric disorders; any history of abuse, neglect, or substance abuse

Family history of baby's father: genetic, hereditary, or chromosomal disorders, abuse or neglect, substance abuse

SOCIAL HISTORY

The components of the social history are linked to pregnancy factors and pathology.

Alcohol Use

Alcohol is a teratogen that can lead to fetal alcohol syndrome (FAS) or fetal alcohol effects (FHE). The absolute safe level of alcohol consumption is unknown. Problems have been documented with an average of 1–2 drinks of alcohol per day and with binge drinking (more than five drinks on one occasion).[11] Mothers over 35 are more likely to report alcohol use during pregnancy.[12]

Drug Use

Drug effects on the fetus vary according to the drug(s) used and the gestational age at time of use. The most common complications are spontaneous abortion, preterm delivery, congenital anomalies, and stillbirth. Some drugs, such as crack cocaine and heroin, lead to an addicted newborn who must then go through withdrawal after birth. Cocaine use is associated with a high incidence of abruptio placenta and preterm delivery.

Tobacco Use

Smoking can lead to a small-for-gestational-age (SGA) infant, preterm labour, spontaneous abortions, and lower Apgar scores (refer to Chapter 24). Pregnant women under 20 years of age are more likely to smoke.[13] The effects are dose related, and tobacco use during pregnancy should be discontinued. Referral to a smoking cessation program may be beneficial.

continues

Sexual Practice	Sexual expression or practice throughout pregnancy is not contraindicated unless there are high-risk restrictions. Sexual intercourse should be avoided after the membranes have ruptured.
Travel History	Travel more than two hours from home during the last month of pregnancy should be avoided. Air travel should be taken only in pressurized cabins.
Work Environment	Prolonged sitting or standing; heavy lifting; an extremely loud, cold, or wet environment; work with chemicals, lead, or mercury; or a one-way commute greater than one hour may put the pregnant woman at risk for preterm labour or congenital anomalies in the newborn.
Home Environment	Stairs may make domestic chores even more difficult for the pregnant woman and may be a significant factor for a high-risk patient who needs to maintain bed rest. The pregnant woman should avoid toxic chemicals; exposure to toxoplasmosis should be avoided by not cleaning cat litter boxes and by wearing gloves and washing hands after gardening. Household chores should be avoided if they either lead to excessive contractions or aggravate pregnancy discomforts.
Hobbies and Leisure Activities	May be continued during the pregnancy unless they present a physical risk such as certain high-risk sports, including skiing and horseback riding.
Stress	The patient's perception that she has more stress in her life than she comfortably can cope with should be addressed by practising relaxation techniques, seeking counselling if needed, and using family and social support systems. Excessive stress may be a risk factor for preterm labour.
HEALTH MAINTENANCE ACTIVITIES	*This information provides a bridge between the health maintenance activities and pregnancy.*
Sleep	Increased demand, complicated frequently by nocturia or difficulty in finding and maintaining a comfortable position
Diet	All meats should be well cooked and all dairy products should be pasteurized to prevent infections such as toxoplasmosis and listeria.
Exercise	Normal activities may be continued and exercise may help with some of the common complaints such as constipation. Pregnant women who engage in aerobic exercise for up to 1 hour, 3–4 times a week, maintain or improve their physical fitness and body image.[14] The patient should consider activities where the body is supported such as swimming and cycling but avoid activities involving physical contact or danger of falling. Exercise done in moderation is beneficial, but any exercise should be discontinued or modified if pain occurs; intensity and duration may need to be decreased from pre-pregnant exercise levels (e.g., heart rate should not exceed 150 beats per minute or moderate levels of perceived exertion).[15]
Use of Safety Devices	Pregnant women should always wear the lap and shoulder seat belt. The lap belt should be snug and low over the pelvic bones and not against the soft stomach area. The shoulder belt should be worn across the chest. If worn properly, the seat belt will not harm the baby.[16]
Health Check-ups	Gynecological evaluations; avoid X-rays.

Nursing Tip

Obstetric Abbreviations

You can classify pregnant patients according to their prior obstetric outcomes by using the following abbreviations. During the initial visit it is important to note all of the categories. In subsequent visits, every category may not be documented, just the number of pregnancies (gravida) and deliveries (para).

G = gravida
P = para
T = term
P = preterm
VP = very preterm
A = abortion (either therapeutic or spontaneous; may be listed separately)
E = ectopic pregnancy
LC = living children

Examples:

G 4, P 2, T 2, P 0, VP 0, A 1, E 1, LC 2 = 4 pregnancies, 2 births, 2 term births, 0 preterm or very preterm births, 1 abortion, 1 ectopic pregnancy, 2 living children

G 3, P 3, T 2, P 1, VP 0, A 0, E 0, LC 4 = 3 pregnancies, 3 births, 2 term births, 1 preterm birth, 0 very preterm, 0 abortions, 0 ectopic pregnancies, 4 living children (preterm birth = 1 set of twins)

G 3, P 3 = 3 pregnancies, 3 births

G 4, P 3, A 1 = 4 pregnancies, 3 births, 1 abortion

G 4, P 3, T 2, P 0, VP 1, A 1, E 0, LC 2 = 4 pregnancies, 3 births, 2 term births, 1 very preterm birth, 1 abortion, 0 ectopic pregnancies, 2 living children

TABLE 23-2 Obstetric History

PRESENT OBSTETRIC HISTORY

Last menstrual period (LMP)

History since LMP (e.g., fever, rashes, disease exposures, abnormal bleeding, nausea and vomiting, medication use, toxic exposures)

Signs and symptoms of pregnancy

Use of fertility drugs

Estimated date of delivery (EDD) or estimated date of confinement (EDC)*

Genetic predispositions

PAST OBSTETRIC HISTORY

Gravidity/gravida (number of pregnancies)

Parity/para (number of births 20 weeks or greater) usually listed as term (37–42 weeks gestational age), preterm (20–37 weeks gestational age), or postterm (>42 weeks gestational age)

Spontaneous abortion

Therapeutic abortion

Ectopic pregnancy

Multiples or multiple births (more than one fetus or baby)

Number of living children

Pregnancy history (Table 23-3 for high-risk factors):
- Complications during pregnancy
- Duration of gestation
- Date of delivery
- Type of delivery
  (vaginal versus cesarean)
  (if cesarean, reason)
  (forceps or vacuum extraction)
  (episiotomy or laceration, and degree)
- Length of labour
- Medications and anesthesia used
- Complications during labour and delivery
- Postpartum complications

Infant weight and sex, Apgar score

Type of feeding (breastfeeding versus bottle feeding)

Breastfeeding: difficulties

*Use Naegele's rule to determine EDD: subtract 3 months from the first day of the LMP, then add 7 days. This is based on a 28-day cycle and may have to be adjusted for shorter or longer cycles. For example, if the LMP is September 1, 9/1 – 3 months = 6/1
6/1 + 7 days = 6/8

The EDD for this patient is June 8.
A pregnancy wheel may also be used (Figure 23-6).

Figure 23-6   Gestation Calculation Wheel Used to Determine EDD. "First day of LMP" arrow is placed on that date. The other arrow labeled "expected delivery date" shows the expected date of delivery.

TABLE 23-3   Risk Factors for Pregnancy

There are many risk factor tools and scoring systems available with varying degress of sensitivity and specificity. Some prenatal forms include a risk screen in the history.

MATERNAL

Age less than 18 or older than 40

Single

Abusive relationship and other violence or family relationship stresses

Low socioeconomic status, poverty, or low educational level

Long work hours, long commute or long tiring trip; excessive fatigue

Stress or unusual anxiety, or both, per patient perception

Unplanned pregnancy or conflict about pregnancy, or both

Height less than 1.5 metres.

Weight less than 45 kgs.

Inadequate diet

Habits: smoking, excessive caffeine (greater than 400 mg caffeine per day – 4 to 5 cups of coffee), alcohol consumption, drug addiction

REPRODUCTIVE HISTORY

More than one prior abortion (some risk tools differentiate first and second trimester)

Uterine anomaly

Molar pregnancy/hydatidiform mole

Myomas (leiomyomas)

Sexually transmitted infections or diseases

Perinatal death

Preterm delivery or premature labour, or both

Delivery of infant less than 2500 g

Delivery of infant greater than 4000 g

Delivery of infant with congenital or perinatal disease

Delivery of infant with isoimmunization or ABO incompatibility

Gestational diabetes

Operative delivery

Cervical incompetence

Prior cerclage

MEDICAL PROBLEMS

Hypertension

Renal disease, pyelonephritis, asymptomatic bacteriuria

Diabetes mellitus

Heart disease

Sickle cell disease

Anemia

Pulmonary disease

Endocrine disorder

Neurological disorder

Autoimmune disorder

Hematological disorder

PRESENT PREGNANCY

Late, inadequate, or no prenatal care

Abdominal surgery

Bleeding

Placenta previa

Premature rupture of membranes

Anemia

Hypertension

Preeclampsia or eclampsia

Hydramnios

Multiple pregnancy

Abnormal glucose screen

Low or excessive weight gain

Rh-negative sensitization

Teratogenic exposure

Viral infections (especially fever-rash with first trimester)

Sexually transmitted infection(s) or disease(s)

Bacterial infections (bacterial vaginosis and group B streptococcus, in particular)

Protozoal infections

Abnormal presentation (i.e., breech, transverse) at approximately 36 weeks

Postdates

EQUIPMENT

- Stethoscope
- Doppler or **fetoscope**
- Centimetre tape measure
- Watch with a second hand
- Non-sterile gloves
- Speculum
- Genital culture supplies
- Pap smear supplies (see Chapter 20)
- Sphygmomanometer
- Urine cup
- Urine dipsticks

◄NURSING CHECKLIST►

General Approach to Assessment of the Pregnant Patient

1. Greet the patient and explain how the assessment will proceed.
2. Ensure that the examination room is ready and supplies are at hand.
3. Use a quiet room that will be free from interruptions.
4. Ensure that there is adequate lighting, including a light that is appropriate for the pelvic assessment.
5. Prior to the physical assessment, complete the health history and the nutritional and psychosocial assessments. (This is usually done in an office before proceeding to the examination room.)
6. Ask the patient to void prior to the examination, both for patient comfort and to facilitate uterine and adnexal evaluation (which can be impeded by a full bladder). The urine should be saved and checked for glucose and acetone.
7. For the physical assessment, instruct the patient to remove all street clothes, don an examination gown, and cover her lap with a sheet.
8. Perform the initial assessment in a head-to-toe manner. Try to minimize the patient's time in the supine position. Assist the patient in assuming the lithotomy position via verbal guidance and by assisting in placing her feet in the foot or leg stirrups. Always inform the patient before touching her of what you will be doing and what to expect. Special sensitivity should be given to adolescents and the patient who is having her first pelvic examination. The patient may be dizzy upon sitting up or upon standing. It may be beneficial to assist her to a sitting position or to brace her arm. She should be cautioned not to stand or sit up abruptly.

Life 360°

A Pregnant Woman with a History of Alcoholism

A woman who gave birth to a child with fetal alcohol syndrome two years ago visits your health clinic as she is pregnant. She states "I am so afraid that I might relapse with the stress and worry of being pregnant." How would you help this woman? How would you approach the situation if she arrived as the clinic with evidence of having used alcohol?

ASSESSMENT OF THE PREGNANT PATIENT

Assessment of the pregnant woman includes a complete initial assessment as well as subsequent specific follow-up prenatal visits. The initial assessment is done when the woman first seeks care. Encourage patients to seek prenatal care in the first trimester or as soon as pregnancy is suspected. Optimally, a health assessment should be conducted prior to conception, especially if there is a pre-existing medical problem such as diabetes mellitus or cardiac disease. Generally, the schedule for prenatal visits is as follows: every four weeks for weeks 6–28 of gestation, every two weeks for weeks 28–36 of gestation, and weekly from 36 weeks until delivery. Women who go beyond the 40th week of gestation (postdates) require additional evaluations. The following examination guidelines discuss how each system examination is different for the pregnant patient than for the non-pregnant patient. See the previous chapters for the specific assessment of each system. The goal of the assessment is not only to confirm pregnancy and gestational age but also to evaluate general health so that appropriate interventions and education can be implemented. See Table 23-4 for signs and symptoms of pregnancy.

TABLE 23-4	Signs and Symptoms of Pregnancy	
PRESUMPTIVE*	**PROBABLE†**	**POSITIVE‡**
Amenorrhea	Abdominal enlargement	Fetal heart beats
Breast tenderness and enlargement	Uterine changes	Fetal movement
Fatigue	Cervical changes	Fetal outline
Changes in skin pigmentation	Braxton Hicks contractions	
Nausea, vomiting, or both	Ballottement	Ultrasound
Urinary frequency	Quickening Hegar's sign Chadwick's sign Goodell's sign	
	Positive pregnancy test— HCG in blood or urine	

*Presumptive: Signs or symptoms that are associated with pregnancy but are not conclusive.

†Probable: Signs or symptoms that are more indicative of pregnancy, including physical assessment changes.

‡Positive: Signs or symptoms that confirm a definite pregnancy.

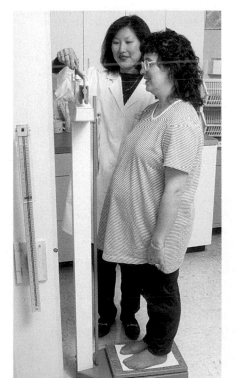

Figure 23-7 The patient's weight is determined at each prenatal visit.

General Assessment, Vital Signs, and Weight

E 1. Conduct a general assessment, including obtaining vital signs.
2. Obtain the patient's weight (Figure 23-7).

N See Chapter 9 for normal general assessment and page 830 for blood pressure changes that occur in pregnancy. See Chapter 7 for the recommended weight gain in pregnancy. See Table 23-5 for common complaints in pregnancy.

A Hypertension at any time in pregnancy is considered abnormal. In pregnancy, hypertension is defined as a systolic pressure greater than 140 and a diastolic pressure greater than 90. Another parameter is a systolic pressure increase of 30 mm Hg and a diastolic pressure increase of 15 mm Hg above pre-pregnancy pressures. This is assessed by taking the blood pressure twice, at least six hours apart. If a pre-pregnancy blood pressure is unknown, the greater than 140/90 criterion is used. Hypertension noted prior to 20 weeks is most likely chronic hypertension. After 20 weeks, hypertension is related to hypertensive disorders of pregnancy (PIH). See Table 23-6 for additional information on hypertensive disorders during pregnancy.

P The pathophysiology of PIH is still being researched. It is widely thought that vasospasms occurring throughout the vasculature contribute to PIH.

A A weight gain that is more than the recommended amount is abnormal.

P Excessive weight gain may be due to increased caloric intake, multiple pregnancies, polyhydramnios, and edema secondary to PIH.

A A weight gain that is less than the recommended amount is abnormal.

P Weight loss or insufficient weight gain in pregnancy can be due to hyperemesis gravidarum, decreased caloric intake, and malabsorption syndromes.

E Examination   N Normal Findings   A Abnormal Findings   P Pathophysiology

TABLE 23-5 Common Complaints in Pregnancy

COMPLAINT	RELIEF MEASURES
Backache, sciatic pain, femoral nerve pain	For posture, stand with abdomen pulled in and buttocks tucked in. Exercises that arch the back like a cat and stretching exercises for legs, gluteal muscles, and back can ease pain. Avoid bending at waist; bend at knees to pick up objects from floor. Wear flat, comfortable shoes. A maternity girdle or support can be helpful, as can local heat and massage.
Bleeding gums	Maintain good dental hygiene. Use a soft toothbrush.
Breast soreness, tenderness, or tingling	A well-fitting, supportive brassiere, worn as much as 24 hours a day.
Constipation	High-fibre diet and 8–10 glasses of water a day plus exercise.
Difficulty sleeping	Pillows for support, between legs, under abdomen, and shoulders. Exercise, a warm bath before bed. Avoid caffeine.
Dizziness	Avoid sudden position changes or prolonged standing, especially in heat or a closed room. Eat and drink frequently.
Edema	Left lateral position for rest to favour venous return. Elevate the feet while sitting, and sit for no longer than one hour at a time.
Fatigue	Increase rest and relaxation, which may necessitate a different division of duties at home or work and prioritization of projects and chores.
Headache	Frequent meals and increased rest. If severe, discuss with health care provider.
Heartburn	Small, frequent meals; avoid foods that aggravate heartburn, for example, spicy or fatty foods, carbonated drinks. Raise head and shoulders when lying down, eat slowly. If severe, discuss medication with provider.
Hemorrhoids	Avoid constipation. Local treatment with a witch hazel-type product may reduce burning and itching, at least temporarily. Rest in left lateral position.
Increased vaginal discharge	More frequent washing with plain tepid water, or a mild, non-irritating soap and water may be necessary. Avoid douching when pregnant. Panty liners may be necessary. Report any odour, itching, unusual colour, or any episode of bleeding.
Leg cramps	Stretching exercises, flexing calf muscle; avoid hyperextending calf muscle. Wear low-heeled shoes, avoid excessive milk intake (higher phosphorus content may cause muscle cramps) and discuss with the health team about the use of magnesium lactate or citrate (calcium intake has traditionally been recommended; however, the evidence that calcium reduces cramps is weak).[17]
Loss of balance	Wear flat shoes. Avoid activities where loss of balance could present a serious problem (e.g., bicycle riding). Use caution when changing position.

continues

TABLE 23-5 Common Complaints in Pregnancy (*continued*)

COMPLAINT	RELIEF MEASURES
Pelvic or abdominal discomfort or pressure	After ruling out a complication, increased rest, leg elevation, and maternity support devices may be beneficial.
Nausea or vomiting, or both	See Nursing Tip, page 830. If severe, associated with weight loss, or if nausea or vomiting persist, detailed assessment is required.
Shortness of breath	Extra pillows under head, shoulder, or upper back may help relieve pressure on the diaphragm, especially late in pregnancy.
Sweating/acne/melasma/ptyalism	Dress in layers. Fans may help at home or desk. Maintain hygiene, but avoid overcleaning, especially face so as not to irritate skin. Avoid prolonged sun exposure. Wear sunscreen when outside.
Urinary changes (increased frequency, urinary incontinence)	Maintain fluid intake. Arrange work and errands to allow for restroom break or stops. Dysuria must be reported.
Stuffy nose	Avoid allergens when possible. Saline nasal products may be helpful.
Varicose veins	Left lateral position for rest. Frequent movement of legs if work requires prolonged standing or sitting. Support hose or even antiembolism-type hose may be necessary.

TABLE 23-6 Hypertensive Disorders in Pregnancy

PREECLAMPSIA

A. Hypertension: ↑ of 30 mm Hg systolic or 15 mm Hg diastolic 2 times at least 6 hours apart. BP >140/90. ↑ MAP of 20 mm Hg or >105 mm Hg diastolic

B. Proteinuria: 0.1 g/L or > in at least 2 urine samples 6 hours apart, or >0.3 g/L in 24-hour urine sample.

C. Edema: generalized swelling or rapid weight gain

D. Severe preeclampsia:
   a. BP of at least 160/110 2 times at least 6 hours apart
   b. 5 g protein in 24-hour urine sample or persistent 3–4+ proteinuria on dipstick
   c. Oliguria: <400 ml for 24 hours
   d. Neurological symptoms: altered LOC, headache, blurred vision, or scotomata
   e. Pulmonary edema
   f. Epigastric or RUQ pain
   g. Impaired liver function
   h. Thrombocytopenia

ECLAMPSIA

A. Above signs or symptoms

B. Development of seizures

CHRONIC HYPERTENSION

A. Present prior to pregnancy or diagnosed <20 weeks

B. BP >140/90

C. Hypertension persists >42 days postpartum

continues

| TABLE 23-6 | Hypertensive Disorders in Pregnancy (*continued*) |

CHRONIC HYPERTENSION WITH SUPERIMPOSED PREECLAMPSIA

A. Chronic hypertension and showing signs of developing preeclampsia

B. BP ↑ >30 mm Hg systolic, >15 mm Hg diastolic, or >20 mm Hg MAP with appearance of edema or proteinuria

TRANSIENT HYPERTENSION

A. BP ↑ during the pregnancy or first 24 hours postpartum without other signs of preeclampsia or chronic hypertension

B. BP must return to normal within 10 days postpartum

Skin and Hair

E Examine the skin and hair.

N See Chapter 10 and pages 828 and 829.

A **Prurigo** of pregnancy presents as excoriated papules, which are highly pruritic and usually distributed on the hands and feet but in more severe cases may be noted on the upper trunk. They are most commonly found in mid- to late pregnancy and are abnormal.

P Etiology is poorly understood, but there is no increase in fetal mortality, and the eruptions fade after delivery.

A Papular dermatitis of pregnancy may manifest at any time during pregnancy as erythematous, pruritic, widespread, soft papules. These papules are typically 3 to 5 mm in size and are surmounted by smaller, firmer papules or small crusts. There tend to be several new eruptions daily, and those already present heal in seven to ten days, possibly with hyperpigmentation. Papular dermatitis is abnormal.

P The pathophysiology of these lesions is poorly understood. Papular dermatitis is associated with an increased risk for fetal loss, which may be significantly reduced by the use of oral prednisone.

A Erythematous plaques that develop into vesicular lesions that may become pustular are abnormal.

A Primary herpes (see Chapter 10) contracted in the first trimester places the fetus at risk for abnormalities. It is more virulent and likely to cross the placental barrier, leading to fetal abnormalities. Recurrent genital herpes lesions contain fewer viral particles and carry a less severe outcome throughout the pregnancy, most often leading to a cesarean delivery when lesions are noted in and around the vagina.

A Rashes are generally abnormal and should be further investigated.

P These should be evaluated for infectious, collagen, or other disease etiology as described in Chapter 10.

Head and Neck

E/N See Chapter 11 and page 829.

A The appearance of hyperthyroidism and hypothyroidism is abnormal in pregnancy.

P Neoplastic disorders such as choriocarcinoma, ovarian teratoma, and hydatidiform mole, as well as a single active thyroid nodule or multinodular goiter should be considered with the diagnosis of hyperthyroidism in the pregnant patient.

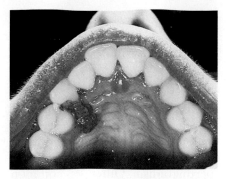

Figure 23-8 Pregnancy Tumour. *Courtesy of Dr. Joseph L. Konzelman, School of Dentistry, Medical College of Georgia.*

Press just behind areola

Normal nipple protraction

Pseudo-inverted

Inverted

Figure 23-9 Assessing for Protractivity of the Nipple.

Eyes, Ears, Nose, Mouth, and Throat

E/N See Chapters 12 and 13 and page 829.
A Arterial constriction of retinal vessels is abnormal. This may lead to blurred vision, scotomata, and rarely, a retinal detachment.
P This can occur in PIH.
A Any growth in the mouth is abnormal.
P Some women develop pregnancy tumours in their mouths (Figure 23-8). These growths are usually benign. The vascular proliferation occurs secondary to hormonal changes. They may not resolve at the end of pregnancy.

Breasts

E 1. Examine the breasts as described in Chapter 14.
   2. Don gloves.
   3. Assess the shape of each nipple by putting your thumb and index finger on the areola and pressing inward to express any discharge. Note whether the nipple protracts (becomes erect) or retracts (inverts) (Figure 23-9).
N Refer to Chapter 14 and page 830. Nipples normally protract when stimulated.
A Accessory breast tissue (supernumerary nipple), most commonly in the axilla, and secondary nipples on the nipple line are abnormal.
P This finding is a result of abnormal embryologic development, but does not present a problem in pregnancy. These areas may develop during the pregnancy along with the normal breast tissue.

Thorax and Lungs

E See Chapter 15.
N See Chapter 15 and page 830.
A/P Pathology noted in Chapter 15 would also be considered abnormal for the pregnant patient.

Heart and Peripheral Vasculature

E Assess the patient as described in Chapter 16.
N See Chapter 16 and pages 830.
A Generalized edema, in contrast to the dependent edema of pregnancy, is abnormal.
P The most common cause for this is PIH. This disease decreases the colloid osmotic pressure within the vasculature, therefore allowing fluid to leak into the tissues. Other potential causes to be considered are kidney disease and cardiovascular disease such as cardiomyopathy.

| E Examination | N Normal Findings | A Abnormal Findings | P Pathophysiology |

Abdomen

E Assess the patient as described in Chapter 17.

N See Chapter 17 and pages 830 and 831.

A Severe nausea and vomiting (**hyperemesis gravidarum**) leading to a weight loss > 5% of pre-pregnancy weight is abnormal.

P Hyperemesis gravidarum is a disease of unknown etiology. It usually presents in the first trimester and may continue throughout the pregnancy. This is more severe than morning sickness and may persist throughout the day, leading to nutritional deficiencies, electrolyte imbalance, and ketonuria. There often is associated hyperthyroidism. Other less common causes may include cholestasis, acute fatty liver disease, hepatitis, cirrhosis, appendicitis, and ulcers.

A Epigastric pain is abnormal.

P This symptom is usually a result of liver inflammation or necrosis from PIH. It must be differentiated from cholecystitis or other liver disorders. It may be confused with commonly experienced pregnancy heartburn, but epigastric pain resulting from liver pathology is over the liver itself, whereas heartburn is felt more midline.

Urinary System

E 1. Obtain a complete urinalysis at the initial prenatal visit.
2. Obtain a urine culture if indicated by urinalysis or patient history.
3. It is common to assess urine for protein, glucose, leukocytes, and nitrates at each subsequent prenatal visit.

N The urine may turn a brighter yellow as a result of prenatal vitamins. Trace amounts of protein may be noted. Glycosuria may be noted without pathology, but concern for diabetes mellitus cannot be ignored. Leukocytes and nitrates are normally absent.

A Nitrates or large amounts of leukocytes are abnormal.

P Nitrates, a breakdown product of bacteria, and large amounts of white blood cells (leukocytes) may indicate a urinary tract infection.

A Dysuria that presents as any of the following is abnormal: difficulty in initiating urinary flow, increased urinary frequency, a feeling of being unable to empty the bladder.

P Dysuria results most commonly from a bacterial infection, inflammation of the bladder (cystitis), or urinary tract infection.

A Pain in the flank area (costovertebral angle tenderness) is abnormal.

P The pregnant patient is more prone than the non-pregnant patient to develop pyelonephritis from a lower urinary tract infection secondary to the dilation of the ureters and renal pelvises, along with decreased tone and peristalsis, which lead to stasis. This results from the physiological changes that occur during pregnancy.

A Asymptomatic bacteriuria is abnormal.

P A clean-voided urine specimen containing more than 100,000 organisms of the same species per millilitre of urine is consistent with infection. Asymptomatic bacteriuria sometimes progresses to acute symptomatic infection unless treated. Through poorly understood mechanisms, bacteriuria is associated with an increased rate of preterm labour and birth.

A Proteinuria greater than trace as shown on a urine dipstick is abnormal.

P The most common cause is PIH. The vasospasms that occur also affect the kidneys and their ability to filter substances. Other possible causes are collagen disorders or kidney diseases.

| E | Examination | N | Normal Findings | A | Abnormal Findings | P | Pathophysiology |

Musculoskeletal System

E   Assess the patient as described in Chapter 18.
N   See Chapter 18 and page 831.
P   Abnormalities and pathology described in Chapter 18 are also considered abnormal for the pregnant patient.

Neurological System

E   Assess the patient as described in Chapter 19.
N   See Chapter 19 and page 832.
A   Seizures are abnormal.
P   Eclampsia is the most common cause of seizures in the pregnant patient. Other less common causes are stroke, tumours, or epilepsy. The coagulation and vascular changes associated with pregnancy may exacerbate pre-existing conditions.
A   Hyperreflexia and clonus are abnormal.
N   PIH can cause these findings.

Female Genitalia

E   1. For the initial prenatal visit, perform the assessment as described in Chapter 20.
    2. Perform cultures as indicated in Table 23-7.
    3. Postdate pregnancies and pregnancies complicated by preterm labour symptoms or preterm labour risk factors may require a cervical assessment at each visit.

TABLE 23-7   Laboratory Tests and Values in Pregnancy

TEST	REFERENCE RANGE (UNITS)*	TIMING
Prenatal Panel includes		
ABO and Rh (D) blood group antibody screening	A, B, O, AB, Rh(D) positive or negative	Initial visit; repeat antibody screening between 24 and 49 weeks if mother is Rh(D) negative; repeat if spontaneous or induced abortion, amniocentesis, CVS, or obstetrical complications. Repeat antibody screening within 72 hours of delivery of a Rh(D) positive baby.[18]
VDRL (Venereal disease research laboratory)	Negative for Treponema pallidum	Initial visit; may repeat at 36 weeks
Rubella (Canada has a very low incidence of rubella and congenital rubella syndrome [0–0.6/100,000 births] as a result of effective immunization programs. Immigrant women who have not had access to immunization programs are at higher risk)	Immune (non-immune patients should be cautioned to avoid contact with any possible exposure during the first trimester and will require a postpartum immunization)	Initial visit
Hepatitis B surface antigen	Negative	Initial visit; may repeat at 36 weeks
HIV (offered)	Negative	Initial visit; repeat based on history or exposure
Varicella	Immune	Initial visit if uncertain history

continues

TABLE 23-7 Laboratory Tests and Values in Pregnancy (*continued*)

TEST	REFERENCE RANGE (UNITS)*	TIMING
Human parvovirus B19 (fifth disease) IgG and IgM status	Positive IgG and negative IgM means immunity; negative IgG and IgM means precautions must be taken to avoid exposure; positive or negative IgG and positive IgM indicates possible recent infection.[19]	May be done on initial visit or as indicated by exposure
Hepatitis C antibody	Negative	Initial visit if indicated by history
CBC to include:		
HGB	100–140 g/L	Initial visit; repeat at 26–28 weeks and 36 weeks
HCT	0.32–0.42	
MCV	80–100 fL	
Platelets	$150–450 \times 10^9$	
Maternal serum alpha fetal protein (MSAFP) or triple marker screen	Both are maternal blood screening tests. MSAFP screens for neural tube defects and ventral wall defects, an elevation being a positive screen. As a screening test, there are false negatives (misses 20% of actual defects) and false positives, which may result from inaccurate dates, multiple fetus pregnancy, or bleeding with pregnancy. The MSAFP incidentally picks up 20% of Down-affected infants, as the alpha fetal protein will be diminished. Poorly understood is the association of an increased MSAFP with a normal fetus, but increased pregnancy complications such as preterm labour or delivery or PIH. The triple screen adds estradiol and HCG to the test and thus increases the detection of Down to approximately 60%.	15–20 weeks; 16–18 weeks is optimal
Cystic fibrosis screening	Non-carrier. Inherited as an autosomal recessive pattern and may not manifest with symptoms until later in childhood. Carried by 1 in 25 of Canadian Caucasians with 94–98.4% cases in Canada being in Caucasians.[20]	Ideally, prior to pregnancy, if not; at initial prenatal visit
Genital Cultures or Probes		
Chlamydia and gonorrhea by DNA probe or culture	Negative	Initial visit; may repeat at 36 weeks
Genital bacterial/group beta Streptococcus (GBS)	Normal flora or negative for pathogens	Initial visit; screening for GBS at 35–37 weeks gestation.[21] Intrapartum chemoprophylaxis of colonized women reduces colonization in neonate.
Urinalysis	Same as non-pregnant; glycosuria is a normal variant	Initial visit; as needed per symptoms and history
Urine culture	No notable pathogens	Screening once by culture method for asymptomatic bacteriuria at 12–16 weeks of pregnancy;[22] as needed per symptoms and history

continues

TABLE 23-7 Laboratory Tests and Values in Pregnancy (continued)

TEST	REFERENCE RANGE (UNITS)*	TIMING
Toxoplasma IgG	Negative; antibodies indicate past or current infection	As indicated by any history of exposures and symptoms
Glucose screen* for gestational diabetes mellitus (GDM): 1 hour post 50 gram glucose challenge test[23]	1 hour: < 7.8 mmol ; if ≥ 10.3 then gestational diabetes mellitus is diagnosed with no further testing	24–28 weeks for all pregnant women and an early test, preferably with initial prenatal panel, for a woman with a family history of diabetes or a prior macrosomic baby, or who is 34 years or older or obese

* A small but significant number of Canadian obstetricians and hospital centres have a "no screen" policy for GDM unless risk factors other than pregnancy as they believe there are insufficient RTCs to indicate benefit.

Oral glucose tolerance test (100 grams)	1 hour: < 10 mmol/L 2 hour: < 8.6 mmol/L 3 hour: < 7.8 mmol/L	If indicated by elevated screening glucose or with history of failure with screening in prior pregnancies

Nursing Tip

Women Who Are Rh-negative

Women whose blood group is Rh-negative sometimes form Rh-antibodies when carrying a Rh-positive baby. This is more likely during birth, but occasionally happens in late pregnancy. Sequelae include anemia, and possibly even death, for an Rh-positive baby in a subsequent pregnancy. Giving the mother anti-D after the first birth reduces risks and giving anti-D during pregnancy is likely to help as well.[24]

N See Chapter 20 for normal findings of the female genitalia assessment. The multiparous vulva and vagina may appear more relaxed in tone, with a shorter perineum. There is often a visible, white, milky discharge during pregnancy, and the cervix may show more ectropion (also called eversion and friability). Ectropion is the condition where the columnar epithelium extends from the os past the normal squamocolumnar junction, often producing a red, possibly inflamed appearance. See Table 23-1 on page 833 for additional changes in pelvic organs.

N Manual assessment should show uterine size appropriate for gestational age, and the uterus may be slightly more tender than in a non-pregnant woman. The retroverted and retroflexed uterus may be more difficult to assess. Palpation of the adnexa may demonstrate a slight tenderness and enlargement of the ovulatory ovary secondary to the corpus luteum of pregnancy.

A Persistent abdominal pain or tenderness is abnormal and should be evaluated.

P Either finding may indicate many underlying disorders related or unrelated to pregnancy. PIH and abruptio placenta are the most common causes of pain related to pregnancy. PIH pain is secondary to the hepatic involvement. Abruptio pain is from the retroplacental bleeding of the placental separation. Disorders unrelated to pregnancy include ulcers, cholecystitis, appendicitis, and pancreatitis.

A Painful adnexal masses are abnormal.

P In early pregnancy, these may indicate an **ectopic pregnancy** (pregnancy other than intrauterine, such as in the abdomen or fallopian tube), infection, or cancerous growth. Pain associated with an adnexal mass may be elicited via cervical motion during bimanual assessment.

Nursing Alert

Neural Tube Defects and Vitamin Supplementation

Increased use of vitamin supplements and of prenatal diagnosis has led to a marked decrease (more than 50%) in the number of Canadian children born with neural tube defects.[25] Folic acid (folate), one of the B vitamins, plays a role in the healthy development of the central nervous system. While mandatory folic

continues

E	Examination	N	Normal Findings	A	Abnormal Findings	P	Pathophysiology

acid fortification of flour, enriched pasta, and cornmeal commenced in 1998, the daily use of 0.4–1.0 mg of folic acid supplements is recommended for any woman who could become pregnant. Supplements should be taken at least three months before conception and continuing through the first three months of gestation. Higher doses of folic acid are recommended for women with a previous personal or family history of NTD or Type 2 diabetes mellitus, or who are prescribed valproic acid or carbamazapine.

Nursing Alert

Ectopic Pregnancy

A positive home pregnancy test, late menstruation followed by vaginal bleeding, an abnormal last period, and abdominal or pelvic soreness or pain that is typically one-sided are warning signs of an ectopic pregnancy. The pain is often perceived as a cramping sensation or intense localized pain. On physical examination, there may be cervical motion tenderness (CMT) and enlargement and tenderness in the affected area, although this is truer for a tubal pregnancy than for an abdominal pregnancy. There may or may not be blood on the cervix or in the vagina. In 2000–01, the ectopic pregnancy rate in Canada was 13.8/1,000 pregnancies; the range is from 9/1,000 in Prince Edward Island to 25.7/1,000 in Nunavut.[26]

Shock is a risk if a tubal pregnancy has ruptured. The woman should be told to call her health care provider immediately should any increased pain or bleeding occur. The woman and her family can experience much uncertainty as investigations such as serial quantitative serum HCGs or ultrasound, or both, are pending. Some tubal pregnancies can resolve on their own or with medical intervention such as methotrexate, but all require close supervision.

Uterine Size

Uterine size is determined by internal pelvic exam on the initial prenatal visit, by palpation if less than 18 weeks, and by fundal height in centimetres for subsequent visits. If the initial visit is late in pregnancy, it will include the internal pelvic exam and fundal height.

Fundal Height by Centimetres

E   1. Place the patient in a supine position.
     2. Place the zero centimetre mark of the tape measure at the symphysis pubis in the midline of the abdomen.
     3. Palpate the top of the fundus and pull tape measure to the top (Figure 23-10).
     4. Note the centimetre mark.

N   A 16-week uterus is between the symphysis pubis and umbilicus, a 20-week uterus is at the umbilicus, and from 18 to 32 weeks the size is equal to the centimetre height of the uterine fundus. After 32 weeks, although still used, this measurement is less accurate.

A   Uterine size larger than expected given LMP is abnormal.

P   This may indicate hydatidiform mole or molar pregnancy (especially in the absence of fetal heart tones), multiple gestation, inaccurate dating, uterine pathology (fibroid), polyhydramnios, or, in later pregnancy, **macrosomia** (newborn weighing greater than 4000 gm).

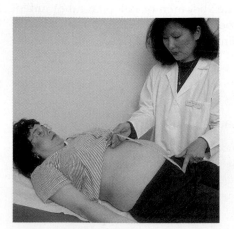

Figure 23-10 Measuring Fundal Height.

A   Uterine size smaller than expected given LMP is abnormal.

P   This may indicate a non-viable pregnancy, inaccurate dating, or, later in pregnancy, intrauterine growth restriction (IUGR) or transverse lie of the fetus.

Fetal Heart Rate

E   **1.** Place the patient in the supine position.

       2. Place Doppler or fetoscope (Figure 23-11) on abdomen and move it around until fetal heart tones (FHTs) are heard.

       3. Count the FHR for sufficient time to determine rate and absence of an irregularity (optimally one minute).

N   During early gestation, the fetal heart is generally heard in the midline area between the symphysis pubis and the umbilicus. It can be heard via Doppler by approximately 12 weeks (and maybe as early as nine weeks). Use Doppler to auscultate FHT prior to 20 weeks; a fetoscope can be used after 20 weeks. Doppler is commonly used throughout pregnancy, as it is more convenient and also allows the patient to hear FHTs. The normal rate is 110 to 160 bpm. If the FHT seems low, check the mother's pulse rate to verify it is the FHT that you are listening to and not the mother's heart rate. Near-term FHTs are generally heard at maximum intensity in the left or right lower quadrant. If FHTs are best heard above the umbilicus, one should suspect a breech presentation or placenta previa. The fetal heart is best heard through the fetal back, which can be located by performing Leopold's manoeuvre as described below.

A   FHR below 110 bpm indicates bradycardia, which is abnormal.

P   Bradycardia may be a sign of fetal distress or drug use. An FHR of 60 bpm or below may be indicative of a heart block. These conditions may be benign and convert to normal after delivery, but a consultation with a perinatologist is advised for consideration of intervention with the newborn.

A   Absence of fetal heart activity is abnormal.

P   Absence of fetal heart tones may indicate an ectopic pregnancy, a blighted ovum, fetal demise, or a molar pregnancy.

A   FHR above 160 bpm indicates tachycardia, which is abnormal.

P   Tachycardia may indicate a cardiac dysrhythmia, maternal fever, or drug use. Prior to approximately 28 weeks of gestation, tachycardia is a natural consequence of the immaturity of the fetal nervous system. In early gestation, the parasympathetic system exerts a greater influence. As the fetus matures, the sympathetic and parasympathetic systems mature and the FHR should remain within the normal range of 110 to 160 bpm.

Nursing Tip

Fetal Movement

At approximately 18 to 20 weeks, the first fetal movements felt in utero, known as **quickening**, are noticed by the pregnant woman as fluttering or kicking, and initially may be difficult to differentiate from other pregnancy symptoms such as gas and ligament stretching. Failure on the part of the pregnant woman to notice fetal movement by approximately 20 weeks should alert you to the possibility of either inaccurate dating or, in the absence of FHTs, non-viable pregnancy. Beginning at approximately 28 weeks for the at-risk pregnancy (e.g., maternal diabetes, previous fetal or newborn demise, multiple fetuses, and PIH) and at approximately 32 weeks for the low-risk pregnancy, fetal kick or movement self-monitoring should be introduced. The pregnant woman's sensation of fetal movement may change in the third trimester, going from "somersaults," to rolling from side to side, to kicks or subtle shifts; however, the actual number of fetal movements should not decrease dramatically. Any decrease in fetal movement requires rapid evaluation. See Table 23-8, page 854 for Cardiff and Sadovsky techniques of counting fetal movements.

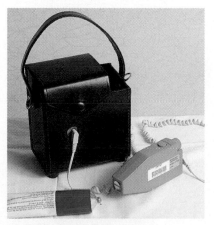

A. Doppler

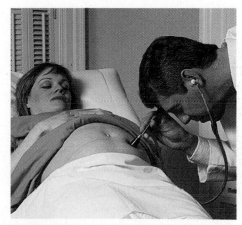

B. Fetoscope

Figure 23-11 Equipment Used for Fetal Heart Rate Determination.

| E | **Examination** | N | **Normal Findings** | A | **Abnormal Findings** | P | **Pathophysiology** |

Leopold's Manoeuvre

Beginning at 36 weeks, determine fetal presentation using Leopold's manoeuvre (Figure 23-12).

First Manoeuvre

E 1. Place the patient in a supine position with the knees bent.
2. Stand to the patient's right side facing her head.
3. Keeping the fingers of your hand together, palpate the uterine fundus.
4. Determine which fetal part presents at the fundus.

Second Manoeuvre

E 1. Move each of your hands to a side of the uterus.
2. Keep your left hand steady and palpate the patient's abdomen with the right hand.
3. Determine the positions of the fetus's back and small parts.
4. Keep your right hand steady and palpate the patient's abdomen with your left hand.

Third Manoeuvre

E 1. Place your right hand above the symphysis pubis with your thumb on one side of the fetus' presenting part and your fingers on the other side.
2. Gently palpate the fetus' presenting part.
3. Determine if the buttocks or the head is the presenting part in the pelvis. (This should confirm the findings of the first manoeuvre.)

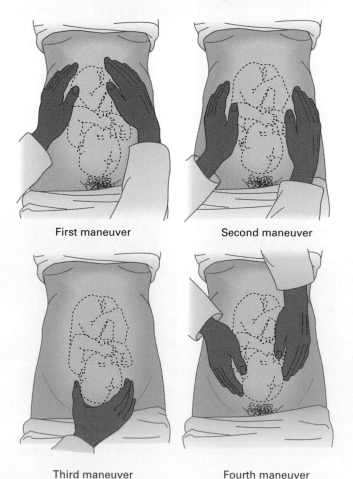

First maneuver   Second maneuver

Third maneuver   Fourth maneuver

Figure 23-12 Leopold's Manoeuvre.

Fourth Manoeuvre

E
1. Change your position so you are facing the patient's feet.
2. Place your hands on each side of the uterus above the symphysis pubis and attempt to palpate the cephalic prominence (forehead). This will assist you in determining the fetal lie (long axis of fetus in relationship to long axis of mother) and attitude (head flexed or extended).

N   The fetus' head is usually the presenting part. It feels firm, round, and smooth. The head can move freely when palpated. If the baby is in a breech position, the buttocks feel soft and irregular. With palpation, the fetus's whole body seems to move but not with as much ease as the head. The fetus's back is firm, smooth, and continuous. The limbs are bumpy and irregular. The long axis is vertical, and the fetal head is flexed. A fetus not in a vertex presentation can affect the type of delivery; for example, a fetus in a persistent transverse or oblique lie will need to be delivered by cesarean. A breech fetus may be delivered vaginally or by cesarean, depending on the health care provider's comfort and experience in doing a vaginal breech delivery. Breech presentation, if uncorrected (i.e., by external version [the manual turning of the fetus by the health care provider]), is associated with an increased rate of perinatal morbidity and mortality, prolapsed umbilical cord, placenta previa, fetal anomalies and abnormalities (which may not manifest immediately after birth), and uterine anomalies.

A   Inability to determine fetal outline is abnormal.

P   Polyhydramnios and maternal obesity can lead to an inability to outline the fetus.

Refer to a textbook on obstetrics for more specific information.

Hematological System

E/N   See Table 23-7.

Endocrine System

E   See Table 23-7 for information on the glucose screen.

N   See Table 23-7.

A   Glucose screen > 7.8 mmol/L one hour following 50 g glucose is abnormal.

P   Normal physiological changes that occur during pregnancy affect glucose metabolism. In some pregnant women, these changes accentuate and lead to gestational diabetes. These changes affect the known diabetic by altering her need for insulin throughout the pregnancy. The diabetic patient is at an increased risk for PIH, infection, macrosomia or intrauterine growth restriction (IUGR), fetal demise, polyhydramnios, and postpartum hemorrhage.

Nutritional Assessment

See Chapter 7.

Special Antepartum Tests and Evaluations

Table 23-8 lists special antepartum tests and evaluations that can be performed in pregnant women.

Psychosocial Assessment and Learning Needs

Learning that one is pregnant generally leads to a range of feelings. While many emotions can be positive, women may feel ambivalence, fear, uncertainty, depressed mood, and even anger. The meaning of the pregnancy to the woman and her family is important to assess as you begin to establish a therapeutic relationship. The planned versus unplanned nature of the pregnancy, reason for

TABLE 23-8 Special Antepartum Tests and Evaluations

TEST	DESCRIPTION
Ultrasound	Used only when the potential medical benefit outweighs any risk.[27] Not to be used for sex determination or keepsake photos/videos.[28] At any time for pregnancy dating, although more accurate for dates early in pregnancy. Confirm or rule out placenta previa, multiple pregnancy; confirm presenting fetal part. Evaluate amniotic fluid volume or fetal growth (especially to rule out intrauterine growth restriction or discordant growth with a multiple pregnancy). Evaluate for ectopic pregnancy or fetal demise.
Genetic testing: chorionic villi sampling (CVS), amniocentesis, chromosome studies[29]	• CVS for chromosome studies is usually performed between 10 and 13 weeks. There may be an approximately 1% increased risk of limb deformities associated with CVS, as well as a 1% increased risk of spontaneous abortion. • Amniocentesis is performed at mid-trimester between 15 to 16 weeks and has a 0.5–1% increased risk of spontaneous abortion. Early amniocentesis, performed between 11 to 12 weeks, carries increased risks. • Blood or tissue chromosome studies can be done at any time and are best done with a known family history prior to conception.
Non-stress test (NST) or contraction stress test (CST) (not common in Canada) for fetal well-being, e.g., with decreased fetal movement, known decreased fluid volume, history of certain maternal diseases (insulin dependent diabetes, collagen vascular disease) or obstetric complications, such as IUGR, postdates, pre-eclampsia, discordant twin, or multiples	For a non-stress test, an electrical fetal monitor is applied to the woman's abdomen, with a tocodynamometer to monitor and record uterine activity and fetal movement, and a Doppler to monitor and record FHR, looking at fetal heart response to fetal movement (and any spontaneous uterine contractions). Timing is typically 1 or 2 times per week, and may start as early as 32 weeks depending on the risk factor. With a contraction stress test, uterine activity is induced by timed breast nipple stimulation (which induces uterine contractions); failing adequate uterine stimulation from nipple stimulation, pitocin intravenously via a pump is used to induce uterine activity. (Relative contraindications for contraction stress test include any risk for uterine rupture, e.g., previous vertical cesarean section; premature delivery risk; any bleeding risk such as known placenta previa; or any unexplained vaginal bleeding.) Timing is typically once per week after 36 weeks.
Amniotic fluid volume (AFV), which may be described as amniotic fluid index (AFI), most commonly ordered with postdates pregnancies	Ultrasound measurement of AFV using an index to determine normal, increased, or decreased fluid levels.
Biophysical profile	A composite test that includes amniotic fluid volume, non-stress test, fetal breathing movements, fetal limb movements, and fetal tone; each rated on 0–2 score. This study is done most commonly for the same reasons as an NST or CST.
Fetal movement count	Can be done by all pregnant women, requires no equipment, and incurs no direct cost. There are many methods of doing fetal movement or kick counts, e.g., number of movements during the day, or at certain times of the day. *Cardiff technique*: starting at 09:00 women lie or sit and count how long it takes to experience 10 movements; if <10 have been felt by 10:00 then consultation should occur. *Sadovsky technique*: Women lie down for one hour after meals; if 4 movements have not been felt within 1 hour then monitoring continues for 1 more after which consultation should occur if 4 movements have not been felt.

becoming pregnant (to fulfill a maternal goal versus to lure a partner into a long-term relationship versus the result of rape), response of family and friends to the news of the pregnancy, woman's age and relative maturity, previous experience with pregnancy (personal or vicarious), socioeconomic status, presence of difficult symptoms of pregnancy, body image changes, presence of co-morbidities, and usual mood changes of pregnancy can all play a role in how the woman copes with the trajectory of pregnancy.

The nurse who is able to follow the family throughout the pregnancy is in an excellent position to assess the individual members and the family as a unit over time to determine strengths and risks as they plan for the arrival of the newborn. While the focus of the physical assessment is on the pregnant woman, the psychosocial assessment extends to the family. Maternal, paternal, sibling and extended family/friends' adjustment to pregnancy and the arrival of a new member should be assessed and monitored.

Early in pregnancy the woman may focus on herself and how the changes of pregnancy are affecting her physical state and her lifestyle. As pregnancy progresses, she will usually shift her focus from herself to the fetus as an individual and to the fetus's well-being. The mother's ability to "give of herself" as she promotes the health of the fetus can be difficult for some women as can "becoming a parent," which involves role clarification, becoming aware of explicit and implicit role expectations, and the development of specific knowledge and skills. You and the family can provide support during this process.

Many communities offer pregnancy-related classes that start with early pregnancy and progress through the childbirth process, breast-feeding, infant care, and sibling involvement. The first-trimester classes typically focus on the physiological changes occurring during pregnancy and what the woman can do to foster the growth of a healthy infant; for example, nutrition, rest, and behaviours to avoid. During the second trimester, emphasis shifts to information on danger signs and symptoms (Table 23-9). At 24 to 26 weeks, the patient should be provided verbal and written information on signs and symptoms of preterm labour.

TABLE 23-9 Danger Signs of Pregnancy

SIGN OR SYMPTOM	ACTION
Vaginal bleeding*	Call health care provider immediately. Small amounts of bleeding may require only rest and observation at home. More significant bleeding or significant cramping, pain, or fever may require intervention at a hospital. Concerns would be for abortion, preterm labour, and placenta previa.
Leaking or gush of watery fluid*	Call health care provider immediately. A sterile speculum must be used to evaluate for rupture of membranes. A sample of the fluid can be evaluated with the nitrazine test to evaluate whether it is amniotic fluid.
Abdominal or pelvic pain or cramping*	Call health care provider immediately after consideration of the normal discomforts of pregnancy (e.g., round or broad ligament pain). It is important to describe the quality of the pain, duration, and location. Concerns would be for premature labour, ectopic pregnancy, placenta abruptio, or urinary tract infection.
Severe headache or blurring of vision	Call health care provider immediately because of the concern for PIH. Evaluation would include BP and labs (blood chemistries, liver function tests, and platelet count).
Persistent chills or fever greater than 38.5°C	Call health care provider. Associated symptoms may be helpful in determining underlying cause and its significance (e.g., infection, dehydration). Acetaminophen may be used to decrease the actual fever.
Persistent vomiting	Call health care provider immediately. Necessary to determine underlying cause (e.g., gastritis, food poisoning) and treat symptoms before dehydration.
Decreased fetal movement or lack of fetal movement	Call health care provider immediately. At 20–24 weeks, lack of fetal movement will require an ultrasound to confirm dates and fetal viability. Decreased fetal movement or lack of movement later in pregnancy will require evaluation for fetal well-being.
Change in vaginal discharge or pelvic pressure before 36 to 37 weeks*	Call health care provider to evaluate for preterm labour.
Frequent (more than 4 per hour) uterine contractions or painless tightening between 20 and 37 weeks*	Call health care provider. Rest, fluids, or snack may be recommended if uterine activity is not excessive or for prolonged period of time. If either is true, evaluation for preterm labour is required.

Associated with preterm labour

Third-trimester classes focus on preparing for childbirth and the care of a newborn. The topic of breast-feeding should be introduced in the first trimester and discussed throughout the pregnancy.

Assess learning needs on an ongoing basis so that interventions can occur at the appropriate times. An interdisciplinary team approach is especially necessary for certain women and their families, such as those with a history of physical, emotional, or sexual abuse; those experiencing current drug and or alcohol abuse; and those requiring help with basic housing and food needs. Learning may require reinforcement, and educational needs should be reviewed and documented throughout the pregnancy. Appropriate written or visual information should be used to reinforce verbal discussions.

Intercourse is generally considered safe during pregnancy, although it may not always be easy or comfortable. During the first trimester, there may be no changes in libido for the woman, unless nausea and other physical changes leave her feeling excessively miserable. During the second trimester, the pregnant woman may experience increased libido, whereas the physical and psychological changes of the third trimester may decrease the woman's interest in sexual relations. As pregnancy advances, the woman may find she is most comfortable on her side, perhaps with a pillow under the abdomen, facing away from her partner. Male partners may express concern about injuring the fetus or the perceived discomfort of the pregnant partner.

Any couple who suffers fetal loss, whether intrauterine, stillborn, or newborn demise, should be offered supportive follow-up. Many communities have support groups, or couples may seek help from a range of health care or community agencies.

Subsequent or Return Prenatal Visits

Return prenatal visits include vital signs, FHR, fundal height, documentation of fetal movement appropriate for gestational age, weight, urine dipstick, assessment of any edema, assessment of uterine activity, assessment of any vaginal discharge or pelvic pain or pressure, and cervical exam, if done. Other issues discussed at return visits include concerns of the mother, weight gain, diet, childbirth preparation, breast-feeding, postpartum family planning, preparedness of the home, any family issues, and blood and other tests as appropriate to the gestational age.

Nursing Alert

Planning for Breast-Feeding

Nurses provide important antenatal counselling about the principles and practice of breast-feeding. The Canadian Pediatric Society, Dietitians of Canada, and Health Canada recommend exclusive breast-feeding for the first six months of life, as breast milk is the best food for optimal growth. Breast-feeding may continue for up to two years and beyond. The benefits of breast-feeding include reduced incidence of infection, prevention of SIDS (Sudden Infant Death Syndrome) and allergies, and even improved cognitive abilities. The few exceptions to breast-feeding include maternal cases of active tuberculosis and HIV antibody positive.[30, 31]

CASE STUDY   The Pregnant Client

Lindsey is a 24-year-old woman with a positive pregnancy test done in a local health clinic a week ago, January 22, after an incidence of irregular vaginal bleeding.

HEALTH HISTORY

PATIENT PROFILE	24 yo with partner who are "thrilled to be pregnant!"
REASON FOR SEEKING HEALTH CARE	⊕ pregnancy test during clinic visit for irregular vaginal bleeding
PRESENT HEALTH	"I was perfectly healthy until today"
OBSTETRICAL HISTORY	LMP: 12/14 (pt is sure of date), menstrual cycles: regular every 27–29 days, lasting 3–4 days, $\bar{c}$ menarche at age 10

History since LMP: No further bleeding, no cramping since 1/22 ER visit
Exposures since LMP: Denies fevers, rashes, or communicable diseases such as varicella or fifth's disease, or exposure to dangerous chemicals, heavy metals, or radiation. Has cats & sometimes changes the litter box, a task she shares $\bar{c}$ her partner. Primagravida, thus negative for history of hyperemesis, preterm labour or delivery, toxemia or pregnancy-induced hypertension, glucose intolerance, bleeding or postpartum hemorrhage, isoimmunization, or postpartum depression
S/S of Pregnancy: Amenorrhea ($\bar{x}^{\dagger}$ incidence of spotting); breast tenderness, & nausea controlled by small frequent meals
Use of Fertility Drugs: Ø
Contraception: contraceptive patch, but ran out in November
EDD: 9/22 by dates
Genetic Predisposition: Ø

Past Obstetric History	G: 1, P: 0, T: 0, P: 0, A: 0, E: 0, LC: 0
Gynecology	Hx of abnormal Pap smear age 18 (3 yrs p 1st intercourse) $\bar{c}$ HPV treated $\bar{c}$ cryotherapy following a colposcopy guided biopsy, ⊕ for CIN I, followed by normal Pap smears q yr. *Chlamydia* 7 yrs ago was treated, $\bar{c}$ a negative culture post tx. She has had 4 sexual partners in her life. No UTIs, urinary or genital infection $\bar{c}$ group B streptococcus. Denies any known reproductive organ abnormality
PAST HEALTH HISTORY	
Medical History	States no medical problems, $\bar{x}$ h/o recurrent tonsillitis & otitis media as a child
Surgical History	Tonsillectomy & adenoidectomy age 6, $\bar{s}$ surgical or anesthesia complications
Medications	Prenatal vitamins $\bar{c}$ folic acid daily (she was not planning this pregnancy thus was not taking folic acid at conception), ibuprofen prn for H/A
Communicable Diseases	⊕ h/o *chlamydia* & HPV; denies h/o TB, measles, mumps, fifth's disease (HPV B19), or exposure to ill children or viral illnesses. No h/o hepatitis, CMV, & toxoplasmosis. Denies risk factors for HIV, but she was unaware her hx of HPV & *chlamydia* put her at risk

continues

Allergies	PCN & sulfa
Injuries and Accidents	Denies
Special Needs	None
Blood Transfusion	None
Childhood Illnesses	Tonsillitis & otitis media
Immunizations	UTD including Hepatitis B vaccine series; last tetanus 5 yrs ago

FAMILY HEALTH HISTORY

LEGEND

 Living female

 Living male

Deceased female

Deceased male

Points to patient

A&W = Alive & well

BPH = Benign prostatic
      hypertrophy

CA = Cancer

DM = Diabetes mellitus

HTN = Hypertension

MR = Mental retardation

MVA = Motor vehicle
      accident

sz = Seizure

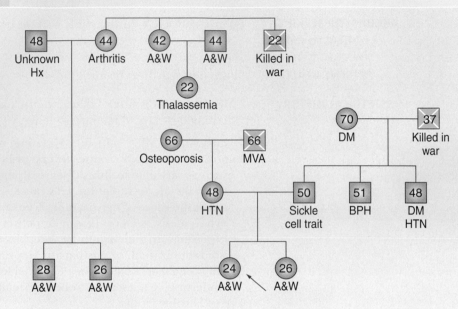

Denies mother or sister had problems c̄ pregnancies; denies mother took DES when pregnant c̄ LaTasha. Denies FHH of cerebral palsy, congenital anomalies, cystic fibrosis, Down syndrome, hemophilia, Huntington's chorea, MR, MD, neural tube defect, sickle cell dz or trait, Tay-Sachs, thalassemia A or B; FOB who is half Caucasian half Hmong denies FHH of above.

SOCIAL HISTORY

Alcohol Use	Occasional beer or drink c̄ friends; none since pregnancy; no binge or heavy drinking
Drug Use	She has occasionally smoked marijuana & states the baby's father used to smoke marijuana frequently, but stopped completely "a couple of years ago"
Tobacco Use	Denies ever using; father of baby does not smoke. No secondary-smoke exposure.
Domestic and Intimate Partner Violence	Denies hx of abuse or neglect in her family. Her partner's father was abusive.
Sexual Practice	Monogamous relationship; 3 prior relationships
Travel History	None out of Canada
Work Environment	Long hrs standing; salon well ventilated.
Home Environment	Secure & safe, comfortable. She has cats & sometimes changes the litter box, a task she shares c̄ her partner.
Hobbies and Leisure Activities	Dancing & clubbing, movies, hanging out c̄ friends

continues

Stress	She works long hrs as a hair stylist in an upscale salon; partner works in retail, managing the men's department in a lg department store
Education	Technical diploma in cosmetology
Economic Status	Getting by financially, but has no significant savings & is concerned about her loss of wages when she is off work on maternity leave
Religion/Spirituality	She is Christian, non-practising; husband's mother is Buddhist, but he has never been involved in any religion
Ethnicity	She is of Black descent and partner is from Southeast Asia.
Roles and Relationships	They have not yet thought about how they will manage work & parenting or the role expectations of each other; have not told respective families as there have been previous tensions in relation to the "interracial" nature of their relationship. L. worries that her family will "have a fit."
Characteristic Patterns of Daily Living	Rises at 07:30, showers, feeds cat, has breakfast; takes bus to work; arrives 09:00 and works until 18:00–19:00; brings her own lunch to work to save money; sometimes attends dance exercise class; takes turns with partner cooking dinner; may watch TV, do some chores, & goes to bed 23:30
HEALTH MAINTENANCE ACTIVITIES	
Sleep	6–8 hrs q night
Diet	Follows *Canada Food Guide.* Vegetables are well washed, & all meats are cooked to at least medium doneness to avoid toxoplasmosis
Exercise	She does dance exercise a few x per wk (45 min)
Stress Management	Exercise, friends, family support
Use of Safety Devices	Wears seat belt always; her car has front air bags only
Health Check-ups	GYN check c̄ Pap smear q yr since age 18
PHYSICAL ASSESSMENT	
General Assessment, Vital Signs and Weight	Young woman who looks healthy. Vital signs: 37.1°C (po), 84, 18, 118/82 Weight: 60 kg (prenatal wt: 56 kg)
Skin and Hair	Intact s̄ lesions, rashes, bruises
Head and Neck	Thyroid c̄ enlargement, Ø lymphadenopathy
Eyes, Ears, Nose, Throat	WNL
Breasts	Tender c̄ everted nipples, Ø nipple discharge; Ø masses
Thorax and Lungs	WNL, breath sounds clear
Heart and Peripheral Vasculature	Heart: Reg rhythm, Ø murmurs, no edema
Abdomen	⊕ bowel sounds, Ø mass, Ø HSM
Urinary System	Clean catch sent to lab; neg glycosuria, neg proteinuria
Musculoskeletal System	s̄ limitations in ROM, 5/5 strength all extremities
Neurological System	CN II XII grossly intact, mental status intact, cerebellar, motor & sensation WNL

continues

Female Genitalia	External genitalia: s̄ lesions, abnormalities, or tenderness; cx & vagina s̄ lesions or abnormalities, softening of the cx & cervical/uterine junction; uterus is 8 wks post LMP size. DNA probe for *chlamydia* & gonorrhea sent; HIV & hepatitis C antibodies sent
Hematological System	Prenatal panel drawn & sent to lab
Endocrine	No glucose test
Nutritional Assessment	Reports now eating balanced diet; s̄ physical s/s of malnutrition
Psychosocial Assessment and Learning Needs	Unplanned pregnancy but happy about it; encouraged to seek childbirth, infant care, & breast-feeding classes. Reticence over informing parents about pregnancy as worried re: tension over interracial issues.

◄NURSING CHECKLIST►

Assessment of the Pregnant Patient*

Fundal Height

Fetal Heart Rate

Leopold's Manoeuvres
- First manoeuvre
- Second manoeuvre
- Third manoeuvre
- Fourth manoeuvre

Only pregnancy-specific assessments are listed.

REVIEW QUESTIONS

1. In pregnancy the endocervical glands increase in number and size. This affects the cervix in what way?
   a. Softening of the cervical-uterine junction
   b. The formation of the mucous plug
   c. A softening of the cervix
   d. A thin, watery discharge
   The correct answer is (b).

2. Maria is pregnant for the fifth time. She has three children at home and had a spontaneous abortion. She also tells you that two of her children were preterm at 35 and 34 weeks. How would you most accurately write her obstetric history?
   a. Gravida 5, preterm 1, very preterm 1, abortion 1
   b. Gravida 5, para 3, living children 3
   c. Gravida 5, para 3, term 1, preterm 2, abortion 1
   d. Gravida 5, para 3, term 1, preterm 2, abortion 1, living children 3
   The correct answer is (d).

3. Rhonda comes to her first prenatal visit. Her home pregnancy test was positive. During her exam she complains of nausea. What can you tell her that might help?
   a. Drink lots of fluids.
   b. Do not eat between meals.
   c. Eat small, frequent meals of foods she finds appealing.
   d. Nothing can help nausea; it will pass.
   The correct answer is (c).

4. Stacia is a G4 P3 who recently had a 9-hour car trip. During a routine prenatal visit, she complains of swelling and pain in her left leg more than the right leg. On examination you find a warm, hard spot on her left calf. This is most likely:
   a. Deep vein thrombosis
   b. Normal, nothing to worry about
   c. Because she does not exercise enough
   d. Where she hit her leg on a chair at work
   The correct answer is (a).

5. The estimated date of delivery (EDD) for Sheila whose last LMP was December 12th is:
   a. September 5
   b. September 12
   c. September 19
   d. September 26
   The correct answer is (c).

6. Crystal is 30 weeks pregnant and seeing you for a routine prenatal visit. She complains of frequent urination with pain, flu-like symptoms, and backache. What would you do?
   a. Tell her that all pregnant women feel that way at 30 weeks.
   b. Ask her for more details regarding her symptoms and assess her for pyelonephritis and possibly preterm labour.
   c. Dipstick her urine for protein and take her blood pressure.
   d. Tell her it is because she does not rest enough and the uterus is pressing on the bladder.
   The correct answer is (b).

7. You are taking the initial history on Carol who is pregnant with her first child. Which answer to your questions will you need to counsel her about?
   a. Drinks 6–8 glasses of water a day
   b. Says she does not like milk but will eat cheese

   c. Smokes two packs of cigarettes a day
   d. Says she is allergic to nuts
   The correct answer is (c).

8. What information are you looking for when you do a triple marker screen on a pregnant patient?
   a. Neural tube defects and kidney disease
   b. Neural tube defects and genetic abnormalities
   c. Down syndrome or trisomy 18
   d. Down syndrome and neural tube defects
   The correct answer is (d).

9. Ann is of Black descent and is having her initial prenatal visit. Based on her ethnicity, what disease testing is essential for her?
   a. Sickle cell disease or trait
   b. Thalassemia
   c. Huntington's chorea
   d. Von Willebrand's disease
   The correct answer is (a).

10. Which of the following statements about physical abuse in pregnancy is false?
    a. Physical abuse rarely starts in pregnancy.
    b. Abuse may increase for some women.
    c. A woman who has a doting yet deprecating spouse may be a victim of abuse.
    d. Pregnant women experience an elevated severity of abuse compared to non-pregnant women.
    The correct answer is (a).

Visit the Estes online companion resource at
www.healthassessment.nelson.com for additional
content and study aids.

REFERENCES

1 Statistics Canada. (July 12, 2005). *The Daily—Births.* Retrieved May 29, 2006, from http://www.statcan.ca/Daily/English/050712/d050712a.htm

2 Ibid.

3 Health Canada. (2003). *Canadian perinatal health report.* Ottawa: Minister of Public Works and Government Services Canada. Retrieved November 9, 2006, from http://www.phac-aspc.gc.ca/publicat/cphr-rspc03/pdf/cphr-rspc03_e.pdf

4 Chalmers, B. & Wen, Shi Wu. (2004). Perinatal care in Canada. *BMC Women's Health* 2004, 4 (Suppl 1). Retrieved November 9, 2006, from http://bmc.ub.uni-potsdam.de/1472-6874-4-S1-S28

5 Statistics Canada. (2006). *Infant mortality rates, by province.* Retrieved November 9, 2006, from http://www40.statcan.ca/l01/cst01/health21a.htm

6 Arsenault, M.Y., for the Clinical Practice Obstetrics Committee (2002). The management of nausea and vomiting of pregnancy: SOGC clinical practice guidelines. *Journal of Obstetrics and Gynaecology Canada (JOGC),* 120, 1–7.

7 Canadian Perinatal Surveillance System. (2004, February). *Physical abuse during pregnancy.* Retrieved November 9, 2006, from http://www.phac-aspc.gc.ca/rhs-ssg/factshts/abuseprg_e.html

8 Public Health Agency of Canada. (2002). *Family-centered maternity and newborn care: National guidelines,* chap. 4. Retrieved November 9, 2006, from http://www.phac-aspc.gc.ca/dca-dea/publications/fcmc04_e.html

9 Health Canada. (2002). Congenital anomalies in Canada—A perinatal health report, 2002. Ottawa: Minister of Public Works and Government Services. Retrieved November 9, 2006, from http://www.phac-aspc.gc.ca/publicat/cac-acc02/pdf/cac2002_e.pdf

10 Health Canada. (2000). *Perinatal health indicators for Canada: A resource manual.* Ottawa: Minister of Public Works and Government Services Canada.

11 Canadian Pediatric Society with 17 other co-signatories (1997). Prevention of fetal alcohol syndrome (FAS) and fatal alcohol effect (FAE) in Canada. *Pediatric & Child Health,* 2(2), 143–145. [Reaffirmed March, 2004]

12 Health Canada. (2003). *Canadian perinatal health report.* Ottawa: Minister of Public Works and Government Services Canada. Retrieved November 9, 2006, from http://www.phac-aspc.gc.ca/publicat/cphr-rspc03/pdf/cphr-rspc03_e.pdf

[13]Canadian Pediatric Society with 17 other co-signatories (1997). *Prevention of fetal alcohol syndrome (FAS) and fetal alcohol effect (FAE) in Canada.*

[14]Kramer M.S. (2002). Aerobic exercise for women during pregnancy. *The Cochrane Database of Systematic Reviews,* Issue 2. Art. No.: CD000180.

[15]Canadian Fitness and Lifestyle Research Institute (2005). *Active living for expectant moms.* Retrieved November 18, 2006, from http://www.cflri.ca/eng/lifestyle/1991/expectant_mothers.php

[16]Transport Canada. (2006). *Road safety.* Retrieved November 18, 2006, from http://www.tc.gc.ca/roadsafety/menu.htm

[17]Young GL, Jewell D. Interventions for leg cramps in pregnancy. *The Cochrane Database of Systematic Reviews* 2002, Issue 1. Art. No.: CD000121.

[18]Beaulieu M.D. (1994). Screening for D (Rh) sensitization in pregnancy. Canadian Task Force on the Periodic Health Examination—Canadian Guide to Clinical Preventive Health Care. Ottawa: Health Canada, 1994; 116–24.

[19]Crane, J. for the Maternal Fetal Medicine Committee and Infectious Diseases Committee (2002). Parvovirus B19 infection in pregnancy: SOGC Clinical Practice Guidelines. *Journal of Obstetrics and Gynaecology Canada (JOGC), 119,* 1–8.

[20]Canadian Cystic Fibrosis Foundation (2002). *Report of the Canadian cystic fibrosis patient data registry.* Toronto, Ontario.

[21]Canadian Task Force on Preventive Health Care (2002). Prevention of group B streptococcal infection in newborns. *Canadian Medical Association Journal, 166* (7), 928–930.

[22]Nicolle L. E. (1994). Screening for asymptomatic bacteriuria in pregnancy. *Canadian Guide to Clinical Preventive Health Care.* Ottawa: Health Canada, 100–106.

[23]Berger, H., Crane, J., & Farine, D. for the Maternal-Fetal Medicine Committee (2002). Screening for gestational diabetes mellitus: SOGC clinical practice guidelines. *Journal of Obstetrics and Gynaecology Canada JOGN, 121,* 1–10.

[24]Crowther, C. A. & Middleton, P. (1999). Anti-D administration in pregnancy for preventing Rhesus alloimmunisation. *The Cochrane Database of Systematic Reviews,* Issue 2. Art. No.: CD000020.

[25]Wilson, R.D., for the Genetics Committee (2003). The use of folic acid for the prevention of neural tube defects and other congenital anomalies: SOGC clinical practice guidelines. *Journal of Obstetrics and Gynaecology Canada (JOGC), 138,* 1–7.

[26]Health Canada. (2000). *Perinatal health indicators for Canada: A resource manual.* Ottawa: Minister of Public Works and Government Services Canada.

[27]Bly, S., for the Diagnostic Imaging Committee. (2005). Obstetric ultrasound biological effects and safety: SOGC clinical practice guideline. *Journal of Obstetrics and Gynaecology Canada (JOGC), 27*(6), 572–575.

[28]Davies, G., for the Maternal-Fetal Medicine Committee and Medico-Legal Committee. (2000). Antenatal fetal assessment: SOGC clinical practice guidelines. *Journal of Obstetrics and Gynaecology Canada, 90* (1–7) June.

[29]Wilson, R.D., for the Genetics Committee. (2005). Amended Canadian guideline for prenatal diagnosis (2005). Techniques for prenatal diagnosis: SOGC clinical practice guidelines. *Journal of Obstetrics and Gynaecology Canada, 27*(11), 1048–1954.

[30]Canadian Paediatric Society, Dietitians of Canada and Health Canada. *Nutrition for Healthy Term Infants.* Minister of Public Works and Government Services, Ottawa, 2005.

[31]Health Canada (2005). Exclusive Breastfeeding Duration—2004 Health Canada Recommendation. Retrieved May 29, 2006, from http://www.hc-sc.gc.ca/fn-an/nutrition/child-enfant/infant-nourisson/excl_bf_dur-dur_am_excl_e.html

BIBLIOGRAPHY

Arnesen, S. J. (2006). Environmental health information resources: Healthy environments for healthy women and children. *Journal of Midwifery & Women's Health,* 51(1): 35–38, 65–66.

Blackburn, J. (2003). *Maternal, fetal and neonatal physiology: A clinical perspective* (2nd ed.). Philadelphia: W. B. Saunders.

Briggs, G. G., Freeman, R. K., & Yaffe, S. J. (2005). *Drugs in pregnancy and lactation: A reference guide to fetal and neonatal risk.* Philadelphia: Lippincott Williams & Wilkins.

Brown, H. C., & Smith, H. J. (2004). Giving women their own case notes to carry during pregnancy. *The Cochrane Database of Systematic Reviews,* Issue 2. Art. No.: CD002856.

Chaithongwongwatthana, S., Yamasmit, W., Limpongsanurak, S., Lumbiganon, P., DeSimone, J. A., Baxter, J. & Tolosa, J.E. (2006). Pneumococcal vaccination during pregnancy for preventing infant infection. *The Cochrane Database of Systematic Reviews,* Issue 1. Art. No.: CD004903.

Curry, M. A., Durham, L., Bullock, L., Bloom, T., & Davis, J. (2006). Nurse case management for pregnant women experiencing or at risk for abuse. *Journal of Obstetric, Gynecologic, & Neonatal Nursing,* 35, 181–186.

Doggett, C., Burrett, S. & Osborn, D. A. (2006). Home visits during pregnancy and after birth for women with an alcohol or drug problem. *The Cochrane Database of Systematic Reviews* 2005, Issue 4. Art. No.: CD004456.

Golden, J. (2005). *Message in a bottle: The making of fetal alcohol syndrome.* Cambridge, MA: Harvard University Press.

Hedrick J. (2005). The lived experience of pregnancy while carrying a child with a known, nonlethal congenital abnormality. *JOGNN: Journal of Obstetric, Gynecologic, and Neonatal Nursing,* 34(6): 732–740.

Martin, R. J., Fanaroff, A. A., & Walsh, M. C. (2006). *Fanaroff and Martin's neonatal-perinatal medicine: Diseases of the fetus and infant.* Philadelphia: Mosby Elsevier.

Mattson, S., & Smith, J. E. (Eds.). (2004). *Core curriculum for maternal newborn nursing* (3rd ed.). Philadelphia: W. B. Saunders.

McKinney, E. S., James, S. R., Murray, S. S., & Ashwill, J. W. (2005). *Maternal-child nursing* (2nd ed.). Philadelphia: W. B. Saunders.

McManus, A. J., Hunter, L. P., & Renn, H. (2006). Lesbian experiences and needs during childbirth: Guidance for health care providers. *Journal of Obstetric, Gynecologic, & Neonatal Nursing,* 35, 13–.

Moos, M. K. (2006). Prenatal care: Limitations and opportunities. *Journal of Obstetric, Gynecologic, & Neonatal Nursing,* 35, 278.

Palda, V. A., Guise, J. M., Wathen, C. N., and the Canadian Task Force on Preventive Health Care. (2003, October). *Interventions to promote breastfeeding: Updated recommendations from the Canadian Task Force on Preventive Health Care.* CTFPHC Technical Report #03-6. London, ON: Canadian Task Force.

Palmer, B. C. (2005). The childbearing experience of women who are childhood sexual abuse survivors. Doctoral Dissertation, The University of British Columbia.

WEB RESOURCES

Canadian Fitness and Lifestyle Research Institute: Active Living for Expectant Moms
http://www.cflri.ca/eng/lifestyle/1991/expectant_mothers.php

Canada Prenatal Nutrition Program (CPNP)
http://www.phac-aspc.gc.ca/dca-dea/programs-mes/cpnp_main_e.html

Canadian HIV/AIDS Legal Network: HIV testing and pregnancy
http://www.aidslaw.ca

Canadian Perinatal Surveillance System
http://www.phac-aspc.gc.ca/rhs-ssg/index.html

Maternity Experiences Survey—Statistics Canada (to be undertaken in fall 2006)
http://www.statcan.ca/english/survey/household/maternity/maternity.htm

Mother Risk (Sick Kids)—Treating the Mother: Protecting the Newborn
http://www.motherisk.org/women/index.jsp

Society of Obstetricians and Gynaecologists of Canada
http://www.sogc.org/

CHAPTER 24

Pediatric Patient

COMPETENCIES

1. Differentiate the structural and physiological variations of pediatric patients and adults.

2. Identify social, language, and fine and gross motor findings using approaches addressed in Chapter 4.

3. Elicit a complete health history from a patient or caregiver using standard components of a pediatric health history.

4. Identify various techniques of approaching patients at different developmental levels before initiating the physical assessment.

5. Perform inspection, palpation, percussion, and auscultation in a head-to-toe assessment of a pediatric patient.

Children are unique individuals who undergo rapid changes from birth through adolescence. Physical growth, motor skills, and cognitive and social development are evidence of the numerous changes family members, friends, and health care professionals observe throughout a child's maturing years. In the assessment of the pediatric patient, you must be aware of these changes to continually reassess what is considered within normal limits for the child.

PHYSICAL GROWTH

Physical growth parameters are required for pediatric health assessment. The parameters of weight, length or height, and head circumference (dependent on age) are essential in serial physical growth measurements. (Chest circumference is of less importance.) For example, by plotting a child's growth on a chart (Figure 24-2), the nurse is able to determine normal or abnormal growth curves according to the child's age.

Canada does not have a formal national pediatric surveillance system for collecting anthropometric data, so national growth charts do not exist for Canadian children. The Dietitians of Canada, The College of Family Physicians of Canada, Community Health Nurses Association of Canada, and the Canadian Paediatric Society have reviewed the evidence on the use of a range of growth charts and have concluded that the 2000 CDC (Centers for Disease Control) growth charts, containing the 3rd and 97th percentiles, should be used for assessing and monitoring the growth of Canadian infants and children. Previously, referral was established when growth was in the 5th and 95th percentiles; however, there was a high incidence of false-negative referrals at this cut-off. Now, the 3rd and 97th percentiles have been established as the cut-off points for referral.[1] The World Health Organization (WHO) is revising its growth standards. These international charts will be assessed within the Canadian context and, owing to the international representation in the WHO charts, may be more meaningful for measuring the relative growth patterns of Canadian children.

While special growth charts have been developed for children with specific health problems, such as the Cerebral Palsy Growth Chart (located at http://www.kennedykrieger.org/kki_misc.jsp?pid=2694), these charts have been developed from very small samples and relatively old data. As a result, disorder-specific charts may not reflect newer treatment protocols and may conceal an existing nutrition or growth problem.[2] Alternative anthropometric measurements (e.g., sitting height, segment lengths such as upper arm or lower leg) may be required when muscular contractures, spasms, or scoliosis make it difficult to obtain accurate measurement of weight or length/height in children with neuromuscular disabilities.

While the ideal frequency and timing of physical growth assessment has not been established, most Canadian health care agencies assess the child's growth in tandem with the schedule for immunizations, with additional visits in the first month of life. Visits are generally within one to two weeks after birth, at two, four, six, nine, 12, 18, and 24 months, and four to six years. Clinical judgment is used to determine if additional assessments are required. At any visit to a health care setting due to an illness or health concern, a physical growth assessment would be important.

Body Mass Index-for-Age Percentile charts are also available to determine if a child's weight is appropriate for his or her height. The BMI growth chart is available for use with children age two years and older. BMI = weight (kg)/height (m)2. Body Mass Index is correlated with certain medical risks based on whether the

Nursing Tip

Growth Patterns

- Breast-fed infants tend to be leaner after three to four months of life when compared with formula-fed infants. Parents may perceive this difference as "growth faltering" and be unnecessarily concerned about the adequacy of breast-feeding. Parents can be assured that this leaner growth pattern poses no risk and may, in fact, be a benefit.[3]

- The pattern of serial measurements of growth indicators is more important than the actual percentile on the growth curve. Some parents may erroneously interpret the percentile of growth as if it were a score on an examination; e.g., they view the 95th percentile of growth as "better" than the 40th, as the latter is "below average." Parents of a child who is always on the tenth percentile can be assured that the child is growing well; on the other hand, a child who falls from the 80th to the 60th to the 50th, or alternately goes from the 20th to the 60th to the 95th may be having health problems and should be assessed.

- The pictogram in Figure 24-1 can be useful as a teaching tool for parents.

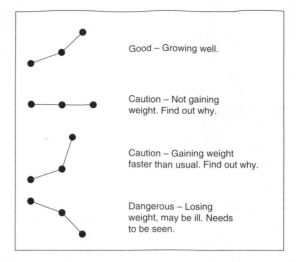

Good – Growing well.

Caution – Not gaining weight. Find out why.

Caution – Gaining weight faster than usual. Find out why.

Dangerous – Losing weight, may be ill. Needs to be seen.

Figure 24-1 Growth Patterns.

Source: Canadian Paediatric Society, Growth Patterns found at http://www.caringforkids.cps.ca/eating/Growth.htm. For more information, visit www.cps.ca/www.caringforkids.cps.ca

Nursing Tip

Adjustment for Prematurity

For the infant born prematurely, postnatal age should be corrected before plotting on the growth chart to ensure accurate interpretation of data. First, subtract the child's gestational age in weeks from 40 weeks (gestational age of term infant) to determine the adjustment for prematurity in weeks. Then subtract the adjustment for prematurity in weeks from the child's postnatal age in weeks to determine the child's gestation-adjusted age. For instance, a baby born prematurely on July 19 at 30 weeks gestation comes to the well-baby clinic on October 11, at a postnatal age of 12 weeks. This child is assessed as if he were a 2-week-old infant. (40 – 30 = 10 weeks adjustment for prematurity; 12 – 10 = 2 weeks gestation-adjusted age. The corrected age rule applies until the child is 24–36 months.[4]

Reflective Thinking

Routine Growth Monitoring: Help or Hindrance?

While nurses generally view regular growth monitoring as beneficial, a systematic review of literature has determined that there can be unanticipated and less favourable effects of such monitoring. In fact, the systematic review concluded that "at present, there is insufficient reliable information to be confident whether routine growth monitoring is of benefit to child health."[5] The authors note that it is not clear whether health professionals should actively pursue children to obtain measures of growth at arbitrarily defined intervals. While such monitoring may appear harmless, parents can become anxious about whether the baby is doing well, and may feel guilty if the clinic detects a loss of weight between visits. If the health worker appears to blame the parent, he or she may be reluctant to return to the clinic, and miss interventions known to be of benefit, such as vaccines. Parents may take their child's growth pattern personally and be shameful or fear being labelled as negligent if growth does not proceed as expected. Future research questions might include, What is the impact of growth monitoring on the parent? What types of nursing interventions support maternal competence when a child's growth is not progressing?

Nursing Tip

Ensuring Adequate Fluoride in Children[6]

- Children should use only a "pea-sized" amount of fluoridated toothpaste, and be encouraged not to swallow the excess.
- Because the action of fluoride is topical, no fluoride should be given before teeth have erupted.
- Supplemental fluoride should be administered (see Table 24-1) only from the age of six months, and only if the following conditions prevail:
  - The concentration of fluoride in drinking water is less than 0.3 ppm.
  - The child does not brush his or her teeth (or have them brushed by a parent or guardian) at least twice a day.
  - If, in the judgment of a dentist or other health professional, the child is susceptible to high caries activity (family history, or caries trends and patterns in communities or geographic areas).

TABLE 24-1 Recommended Supplemental Fluoride Concentrations for Children

AGE OF CHILD	FLUORIDE CONCENTRATION	
	<0.3 ppm	>0.3 ppm
0 to 6 months	None	None
>6 months to 3 years	0.25 mg/day	None
>3 to 6 years	0.5 mg/day	None
>6 years	1.00 mg/day	None

Source: Canadian Paediatric Society, Recommended supplemental fluoride concentrations for children found at http://www.cps.ca/english/statements/N/n02-01.htm. For more information, visit www.cps.ca/www.caringforkids.cps.ca

child is underweight, at risk of overweight or actually overweight (the term "obesity" is avoided because of the potential negative connotations). While there are no Canadian BMI references, the Dietitians of Canada, the Canadian Paediatric Society, the College of Family Physicians of Canada, and the Community Health Nurses Association of Canada recommend the CDC BMI-for-age charts containing the 5th, 85th, and 95th percentiles (see Figure 24-2, Charts G and H).[7]

Nursing Alert

The following cut-offs are recommended as guidance for further assessment, referral, or treatment, but not as diagnostic criteria for labelling children:[8]

- Length-for-age or height-for-age below 3rd percentile (shortness or stunting—the infant or child may be short because parents are short or he or she may be stunted because of malnutrition, delayed maturation, chronic illness, or a genetic disorder)
- BMI-for-age below 5th percentile or weight-for-length/-stature < 3rd percentile (underweight or wasting—may be indicative of recent malnutrition, dehydration, or a genetic disorder)
- Between 85th and < 95th percentile BMI-for-age (overweight)
- BMI-for-age (> 2 years old) at or above 95th percentile or weight-for-length (< 2 years old) at 97th percentile (obesity)

Nursing Alert

Obesity in Canada's Children–Worrisome Trends

The rate of obesity in Canadian children has doubled in the last 20 years. Adolescent obesity, which generally persists into adulthood, is a large concern as it has tripled between 1978 and 2004. The Atlantic provinces, especially New Brunswick and Manitoba, have the highest rates of obesity among the young. There is a strong correlation between obesity and time spent watching television, playing video games, and using the computer.[9] Some authors refer to this situation as a "ubiquitous epidemic" that crosses all regions of the country, both sexes, and all socioeconomic backgrounds. Several provinces and communities have increased hours of physical education in the school system, set limits on the type of foods children can have in their school lunches, and limited the sale of junk food in school cafeterias.

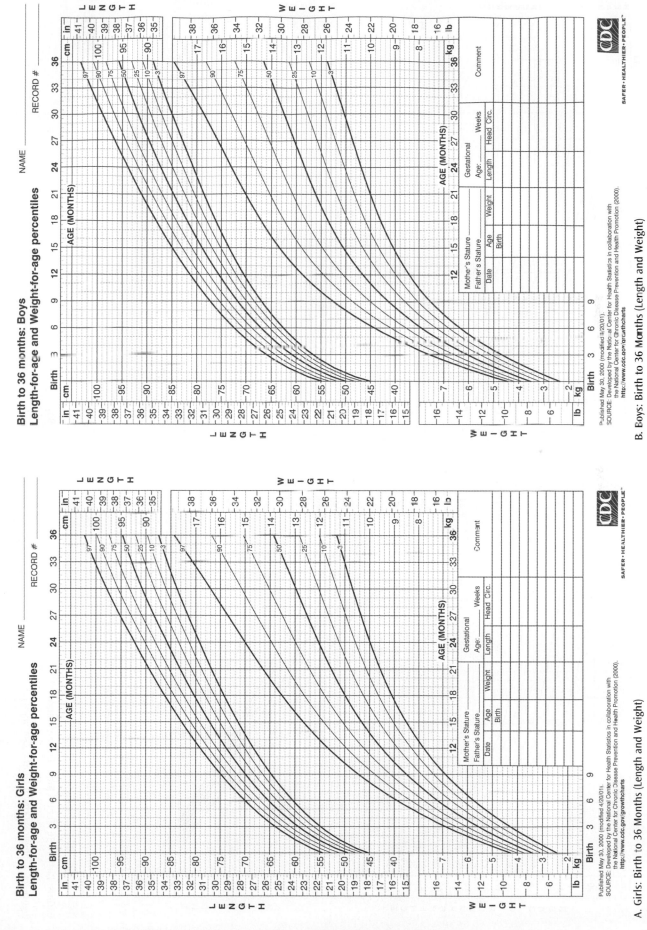

A. Girls: Birth to 36 Months (Length and Weight)

B. Boys: Birth to 36 Months (Length and Weight)

Figure 24-2 Physical Growth Charts.

Source: Courtesy of Centers for Disease Control and Prevention.

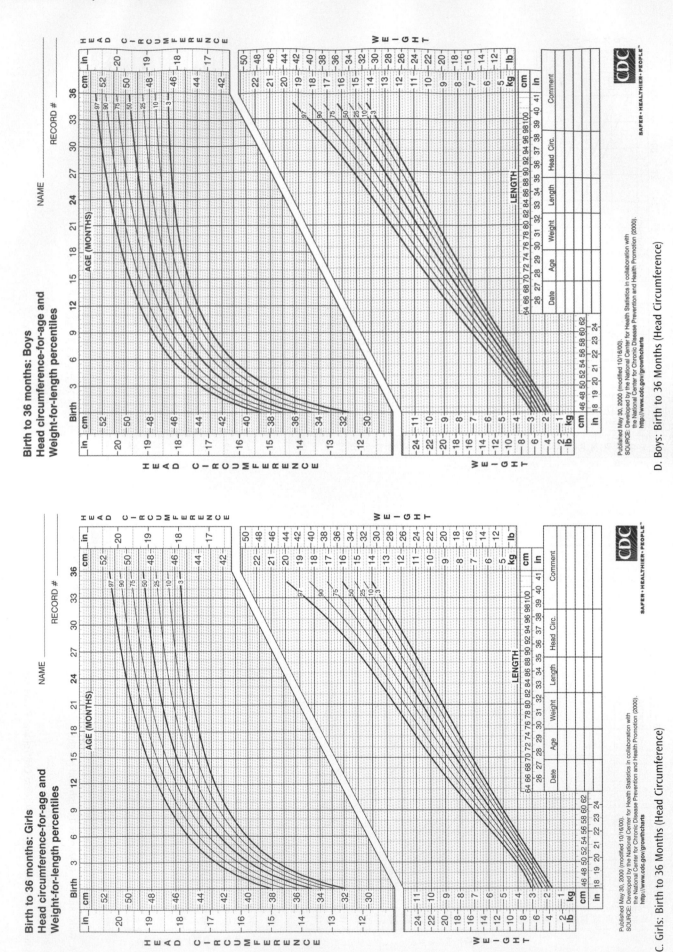

Birth to 36 months: Boys
Head circumference-for-age and
Weight-for-length percentiles

NAME _____

RECORD # _____

Published May 30, 2000 (modified 10/16/00).
SOURCE: Developed by the National Center for Health Statistics in collaboration with
the National Center for Chronic Disease Prevention and Health Promotion (2000).
http://www.cdc.gov/growthcharts

D. Boys: Birth to 36 Months (Head Circumference)

Birth to 36 months: Girls
Head circumference-for-age and
Weight-for-length percentiles

NAME _____

RECORD # _____

Published May 30, 2000 (modified 10/16/00).
SOURCE: Developed by the National Center for Health Statistics in collaboration with
the National Center for Chronic Disease Prevention and Health Promotion (2000).
http://www.cdc.gov/growthcharts

C. Girls: Birth to 36 Months (Head Circumference)

Figure 24-2 Physical Growth Charts. (*Continued*)

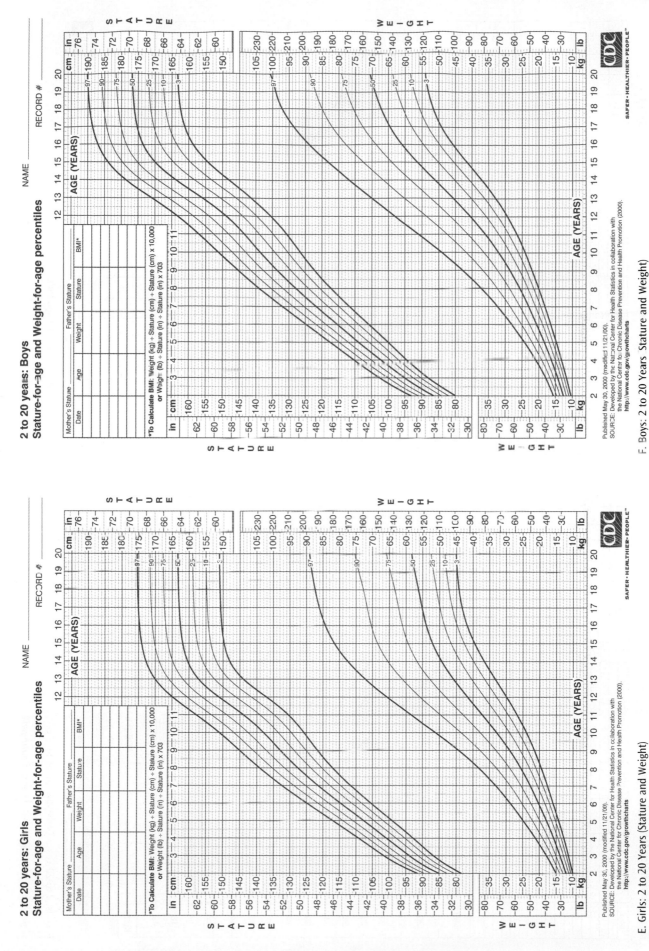

E. Girls: 2 to 20 Years (Stature and Weight)

F. Boys: 2 to 20 Years Stature and Weight

Figure 24-2 Physical Growth Charts. (*Continued*)

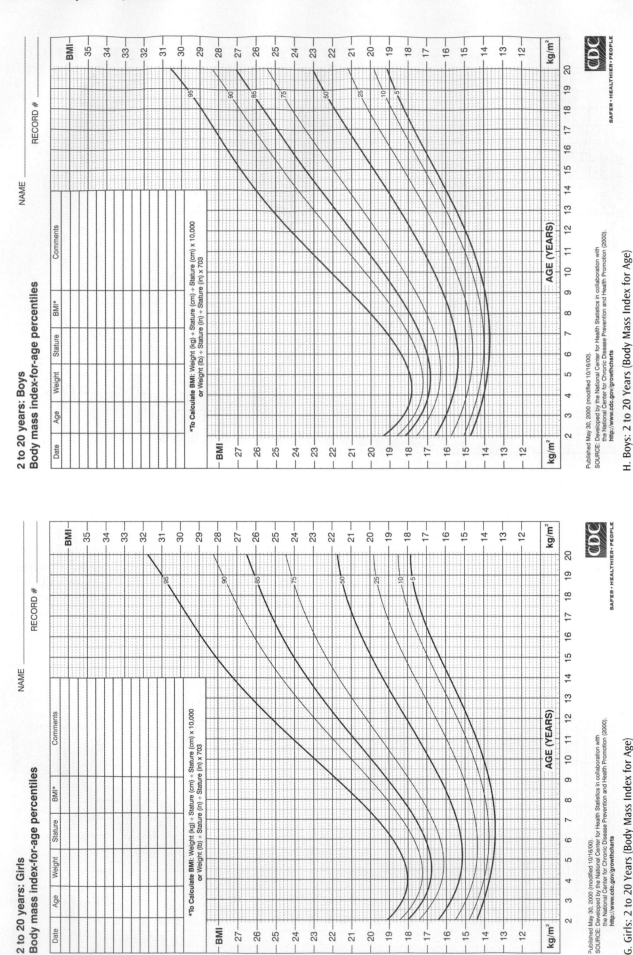

2 to 20 years: Girls
Body mass index-for-age percentiles

NAME _____   RECORD # _____

BMI

*To Calculate BMI: Weight (kg) ÷ Stature (cm) ÷ Stature (cm) x 10,000
or Weight (lb) ÷ Stature (in) ÷ Stature (in) x 703

95
90
85
75
50
25
10
5

AGE (YEARS)

kg/m²

Published May 30, 2000 (modified 10/16/00).
SOURCE: Developed by the National Center for Health Statistics in collaboration with
the National Center for Chronic Disease Prevention and Health Promotion (2000).
http://www.cdc.gov/growthcharts

G. Girls: 2 to 20 Years (Body Mass Index for Age)

2 to 20 years: Boys
Body mass index-for-age percentiles

NAME _____   RECORD # _____

BMI

*To Calculate BMI: Weight (kg) ÷ Stature (cm) ÷ Stature (cm) x 10,000
or Weight (lb) ÷ Stature (in) ÷ Stature (in) x 703

95
90
85
75
50
25
10
5

AGE (YEARS)

kg/m²

Published May 30, 2000 (modified 10/16/00).
SOURCE: Developed by the National Center for Health Statistics in collaboration with
the National Center for Chronic Disease Prevention and Health Promotion (2000).
http://www.cdc.gov/growthcharts

H. Boys: 2 to 20 Years (Body Mass Index for Age)

Figure 24-2 Physical Growth Charts. (*Continued*)

For infants the average birth weight is 3.5 kg, length is 48 to 53 cm, and head circumference is 33 to 35.5 cm. Infants should double birth weight at six months and triple birth weight by one year of age, although it is not uncommon for infants to double birth weight at four months. An infant's height increases about 2.5 cm per month for the first six months, and then slows to 1.3 cm per month until 12 months. Growth in the toddler period (12–24 months) begins to slow. The birth weight usually quadruples by 2.5 years of age, with an average weight gain during the toddler period of 1.8 to 2.7 kg per year. The toddler usually grows 7.6 cm.

Preschoolers (2–6 years) gain an average of 2.3 kg per year. Height increases 6.4 to 7.6 cm per year. The preschooler's birth length usually is doubled by four years of age. In contrast, the school-age child (6–12 years) grows 2.5 to 5 cm per year and gains 1.3 to 2.7 kg annually.

Infancy and adolescence (13–18 years) are two periods of rapid growth in children. Rapid growth in the adolescent is called the growth spurt. Females commonly experience this between ages 10 and 14, whereas in males it occurs somewhat later, between 12 and 16 years of age.

ANATOMY AND PHYSIOLOGY

Structural and Physiological Variations

Children differ from adults and among themselves at various stages of development in their structural and physiological makeups. Following is a list of important variations that occur from birth through a child's maturation.

Vital Signs

- A notable difference in the way children and adults regulate temperature is the inability of infants aged six months and younger to shiver in the face of lower ambient temperature. The absence of this important protective mechanism puts infants at risk for hypothermia, bradycardia, and acidosis.
- By age 4, temperature parameters are comparable to those seen in adults.
- Both pulse and respiratory rates in children tend to decline with advancing age and reach levels comparable to those found in adulthood by adolescence.
- In children one year of age and older, an easy rule of thumb for determining normal systolic blood pressure is:

$$\text{normal systolic BP (mm Hg)} = 80 + (2 \times \text{age in years}).$$

- Normal diastolic blood pressure is generally two-thirds of systolic blood pressure.

Skin and Hair

- **Lanugo**, a fine, downy hair, first appears at approximately 20 weeks gestation and while most of it disappears by 40 weeks gestation, there may still be some present in the newborn. The lanugo is most prominent over the temples of the forehead and on the upper arms, shoulders, back, and pinna of the ears. Dark-skinned newborns have an increased amount of lanugo, which is readily evident as very dark black hair.
- **Vernix caseosa**, a thick, cheesy, protective, integumentary deposit that consists of sebum and shed epithelial cells, is present on the newborn's skin.
- Relative to an adult, a child has a higher ratio of body surface area to body surface mass.

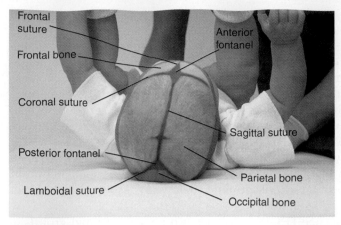

A. Superior View

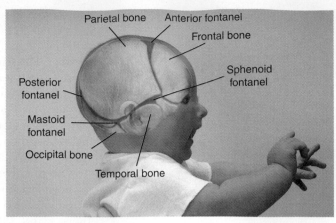

B. Lateral View

Figure 24-3 Infant Head Structures.

Head

- Suture ridges are palpable until approximately six months of age, at which time unionization occurs.
- The posterior fontanel, which is triangular in shape and is formed by the junction of the sagittal and lambdoidal sutures, usually closes by three months of age (Figure 24-3).
- The junction of the sagittal, coronal, and frontal sutures forms the anterior fontanel. It is diamond shaped. This fontanel should close by 19 months of age.

Eyes, Ears, Nose, Mouth, and Throat

- At birth, the newborn's peripheral vision is intact. Visual acuity is approximately 20/200. The child's visual acuity is usually 20/20 at 6–8 years.
- Newborns do not produce tears until their lacrimal ducts open, at around two to three months of age.
- The external auditory canal of a child is shorter than that of an adult, and it is positioned upward.
- The eustachian tube is more horizontal, wider, and shorter than that of an adult. These factors increase the likelihood of middle ear infections caused by migration of pathogens from the nasopharynx.
- Only the ethmoid and maxillary sinuses are present at birth. At approximately seven years of age, the frontal sinuses develop. The sphenoid sinuses do not develop until after puberty.
- Eruption of the first lower central incisors occurs between five and seven months of age. By 2.5 years of age, toddlers have 20 primary, or deciduous, teeth. Around puberty, permanent teeth and four molars have replaced the primary teeth. Wisdom teeth normally appear between 18 and 21 years of age (Figure 24-4).
- Salivation starts at about three months, and the infant drools until the swallowing reflex is more coordinated.

Breasts

- Breast tissue in the female starts to develop between eight and ten years of age. Mature adult breast tissue is achieved between 14 and 17 years of age. See Table 14-1, Sexual Maturity Rating for Female Breast Development, on page 436.

Nursing Tip

Sleep Environment

In an effort to reduce the risk of Sudden Infant Death Syndrome (SIDS), the Canadian Paediatric Society recommends that infants should sleep flat on their back, in cribs meeting Canadian safety standards, for the first year of life. Other risk factors to avoid include sleeping on soft bedding, maternal smoking, and use of pillows and stuffed animals in the infant's bed. Room-sharing, rather than bedsharing, is protective against SIDS.[10]

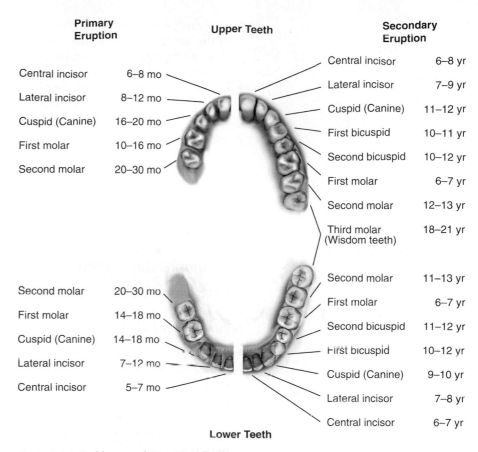

Primary Eruption		Upper Teeth	Secondary Eruption	
Central incisor	6–8 mo		Central incisor	6–8 yr
Lateral incisor	8–12 mo		Lateral incisor	7–9 yr
Cuspid (Canine)	16–20 mo		Cuspid (Canine)	11–12 yr
First molar	10–16 mo		First bicuspid	10–11 yr
Second molar	20–30 mo		Second bicuspid	10–12 yr
			First molar	6–7 yr
			Second molar	12–13 yr
			Third molar (Wisdom teeth)	18–21 yr
Second molar	20–30 mo		Second molar	11–13 yr
First molar	14–18 mo		First molar	6–7 yr
Cuspid (Canine)	14–18 mo		Second bicuspid	11–12 yr
Lateral incisor	7–12 mo		First bicuspid	10–12 yr
Central incisor	5–7 mo		Cuspid (Canine)	9–10 yr
			Lateral incisor	7–8 yr
		Lower Teeth	Central incisor	6–7 yr

Figure 24-4 Deciduous and Permanent Teeth.

Figure 24-5 Infant Chest Configuration.

Thorax and Lungs

- A newborn's chest is circular because the anteroposterior and transverse diameters are approximately equal (Figure 24-5). By six years of age, the ratio of anteroposterior to lateral diameters reaches adult values.
- Decreased muscularity is responsible for the thin chest wall in infants.
- Ribs are displaced horizontally in infants.
- The trachea is short in the newborn. By 18 months of age, it has grown from the newborn length of 5 cm to 7.6 cm. Toward the latter part of adolescence, the trachea has grown to the adult size, normally 10.2 to 12.7 cm.
- Until three to four months of age, infants are obligate nose breathers.
- During infancy and the toddler period, abdominal breathing is always prevalent over thoracic expansion.

Heart and Peripheral Vasculature

- The infant's, toddler's, and preschooler's heart lies more horizontally than an adult's heart; thus the apex is higher at about the left fourth intercostal space.
- The fetal circulation changes to a pulmonary circulation when the umbilical cord is separated from the maternal circulation. Normally, the three fetal shunts (ductus venosus, foramen ovale, and ductus arteriosus) close at birth or shortly thereafter. The ductus venosus allows blood to flow from the placenta into the right heart. Blood flows from the right side of the heart to the left through an opening called a foramen ovale. This opening is a flap valve located on the atrial septum between the septum secundum and septum primum. The ductus arteriosus, located between the left pulmonary artery and the descending aorta, allows blood to flow from the pulmonary artery to the aorta.

- The cardiac output of an infant is normally 1 litre/minute. Toward the end of the toddler period it increases to 1.5 litres/minute. At the age of four years it is 2.2 litres/minute. By 15 years of age cardiac output has reached the adult level of 5.5 litres/minute.
- Infants have a higher circulating blood volume (normally around 85 mL/kg) compared to that of an adult (65 mL/kg).

Abdomen

- At birth, the neonate's umbilical cord contains two arteries and one vein.
- The infant's liver is proportionately larger in the abdominal cavity than is the liver of an adult.
- Infants' and toddlers' abdomens are more protuberant but this does not necessarily indicate pathology.

Musculoskeletal System

- Bone growth ends at age 20, when the epiphyses close.

Neurological System

- The neurological system of the infant is incompletely developed. The autonomic nervous system helps maintain homeostasis as the cerebral cortex develops.
- In the first year, the neurons become myelinated, and primitive motor reflexes are replaced by purposeful movement. The myelinization occurs in a cephalocaudal and proximodistal manner (head and neck, trunk, and extremities).
- Mylenization in the bowel and bladder allows the child to control these functions.

Reflective Thinking

Overweight and Obesity in Children

A mother brings her 5-year-old to clinic for his immunization prior to commencing kindergarten. The child is noticeably obese. On being asked about dietary habits in general the mother responds, "I try to control what he eats but end up giving in when he cries for food. His father and I are divorced and when he spends every other weekend with his dad, he treats him to whatever he wants to eat. People tell me it is still baby fat but I am really worried." How would you approach this situation as the nurse working with this family? Would you start by reviewing the dietary requirements for a child this age, or would you focus on the dynamics of the family relationship? What beginning strategies could you offer this mother as she tries to promote her son's health?

Nursing Tip

Assessing for Attention Deficit Hyperactivity Disorder (ADHD)

Pose the following questions to the caregiver if the child is having periods of inattention, impulsiveness, and hyperactivity. If the caregiver answers yes to eight or more questions and the behaviours in question have been demonstrated for at least six months, a referral for a more comprehensive evaluation should be made to rule out ADHD.

- Does your child fidget with his hands or feet or squirm in his seat?
- Do you notice your child having difficulty remaining seated?
- Is your child easily distracted?
- Does your child have difficulty waiting in turn?
- Does your child blurt out answers prior to questions being completed?
- Do you have to repeatedly tell your child to do a task?
- Have you observed your child having difficulty staying focused on tasks or in play activities?
- Does your child go from one uncompleted activity to another?
- Do you notice your child having difficulty playing quietly?
- Does your child talk excessively?
- Do you notice your child interrupting others?
- Does your child have difficulty listening to what is said?
- Does your child lose items necessary for school activities or home tasks?
- Does your child take part in any activity that could be detrimental to his physical well-being, such as head banging?

> ## Nursing Alert
>
> **Risk Factors for Adolescent Suicide[11]**
>
> 1. Verbalizing about ways to commit suicide
> 2. Giving personal items away to friends and family
> 3. Withdrawing from friends and family
> 4. Demonstrating difficulty with accepting individual failures or disappointment
> 5. Exhibiting an attitude of disgust or discouragement with day-to-day living

Urinary System

In infancy, the urinary bladder is between the symphysis pubis and umbilicus.

Female Genitalia

- Development of pubic hair in girls begins at puberty, between 8 and 12 years of age. Within about one year, the pubic hair becomes dark, coarse, and curly but is not considered fully developed. Axillary hair follows six months later. After about age 13–15, pubic hair distribution approaches adult quantity and consistency. See Tanner's stages of pubic hair development in Table 20-1 on page 733.

Male Genitalia

- The testes usually descend by the age of one year.
- Puberty usually starts between the ages of 9½ and 13½ and can last two to five years. Testicular enlargement is usually the first area of sexual development to occur. Within about one year, the pubic hair becomes dark, coarse, and curly but is not fully developed. Axillary hair follows six months later. Facial hair follows approximately six months after the emergence of axillary hair. See Tanner's Sexual Maturity Rating in Table 21-1 on page 775 for additional information.

HEALTH HISTORY

The same principles that apply in obtaining an adult health history, such as questioning, listening, observing, and integrating, apply in the pediatric history. Because the historian in a pediatric history is less often the child and most likely the caregiver, it is important to document the historian's relationship to the child. The following serves only to expand on the adult health history by providing information not previously discussed but relevant to the child.

BIOGRAPHICAL DATA

Patient Name

In addition to the patient's name, obtain the full name of the legal guardian. Occasionally, the caregiver is not the legal guardian; for example, when the child is in foster care.

Address and Phone Number

Obtain the address and phone number of the caregiver if different from those of the patient.

continues

HEALTH ISSUE/CONCERN	The caregiver is often the individual who seeks health care for the child and provides a description of the perceived issues, especially for infants, toddlers, and young preschoolers whose verbal skills and cognitive abilities make it difficult for them to provide the health history. The caregiver is usually in tune to the changes in the child's "usual" pattern of behaviour and may even be aware of subtle signs of illness before any overt clinical indicators are noted. For instance, changes in sleeping patterns (difficulty falling asleep, reversion to night waking), regression to outgrown behaviours (bedwetting, finicky eating, thumb sucking), and unusual physical complaints in an otherwise healthy child (headaches, stomachaches) are important signs that the child may be experiencing stress or illness, and warrant further investigation. The older preschooler, school-age child, and adolescent are able to provide verbal descriptions of their complaints. Refer to Chapter 9 for pain rating scales that are used for children.
PAST HEALTH HISTORY	*Much of the information outlined in the past health history for an adult is applicable to a child. Additional pertinent information should be elicited regarding the birth history, including prenatal, labour and delivery, and postnatal history.*
Birth History	Obtaining the birth history is important as certain health issues can be linked to the health of the pregnancy, labour, and ultimate delivery of the child. Sensitivity is required throughout the data collection process, in particular around the birth history, because parents may feel guilty or under scrutiny.
Prenatal	The nature of the prenatal experience and care are important to assess intrauterine health and risks for any subsequent health issues that may arise from such situations as an unplanned pregnancy; use of alcohol, caffeine, or other drugs during pregnancy; smoking status of the mother during pregnancy; or physical abuse toward the mother. Other aspects of maternal health during the pregnancy that are important include any history of pregnancy-induced hypertension, preterm labour, gestational diabetes, group B streptococcus (GBS), TORCH infection (toxoplasmosis, rubella, cytomegalovirus, and herpes), or an abnormal finding on a prenatal ultrasound.
Labour and Delivery	*Labour*—length of the labour; spontaneous or induced; analgesia or anaesthetic agents used, including mode of delivery (e.g., epidural) are relevant to assess. *Delivery*—gestational age of the neonate at delivery; vaginal versus cesarean section delivery; if cesarean, why? Was the baby held or placed at the breast immediately after delivery? What were the baby's Apgar scores at one and five minutes? (See page 896 and 897.) What were the birth weight and length of the baby? Who was present at the birth, where did it take place (e.g., home, birthing centre, hospital)?
Postnatal	When were mother and baby discharged home? (Indicates overall health as extended stay generally indicates complications.) Did the baby have any breathing or feeding problems during the first week or require any medications or require special attention during the first weeks? Was there any jaundice? Were there any concerns about either maternal or neonatal health? Was the baby circumcised? What is the nature of feeding and were there any problems with the choice of feeding method?
Medical History	Inquire about the circumstances and outcomes of any hospitalizations or emergency department visits.
Injuries and Accidents	Determine if the child has a pattern of frequent injuries or accidents. Repeat trauma may indicate abuse.

continues

Childhood Illnesses	Document any past and current illness experiences the child may have had including any recent exposure to viral or bacterial infections.
Immunizations	Immunizations provide protection (active immunity) against many contagious diseases of childhood. Maternal antibodies pass through the placenta and breast milk, offering the baby limited protection from disease. See Table 3-1 on page 60 for the routine immunization schedule of infants, children, and youth. See Table 3-2 and Table 3-3, on pages 61 and 62, respectively for immunization schedules of children under seven years who were not immunized in early infancy, and for children ≥ 7 years who were not immunized in early infancy. See Table 3-5 on page 63 for a comparison of effects of diseases and vaccines.

FAMILY HEALTH HISTORY

See Family Health History in Chapter 3. In addition, be sure to also ask about a family history of sudden infant death syndrome (SIDS), attention deficit hyperactivity disorder (ADHD), congenital disorders or defects, or any situations of delayed cognitive, physical, or social growth in the family.

SOCIAL HISTORY

Work Environment	Daycare facilities and schools are the child's equivalent of a work environment. Inquire about the number of hours the child attends a day care facility per week. Inquire about the child's academic performance. In addition, ask if the child is home alone before or after school.
Home Environment	Many questions about the home environment relate to how it supports the health of the child. The Safety section (below and on page 880) identifies several questions on the home environment. Ask about location in relation to community services and resources, proximity to school or work, whether the child lives in the same home environment all the time or if he move from one caregiver's home to another? Is there adequate space for the family?
Child's Personal Habits	Determine what activities the child enjoys. Ask how the child self-regulates when experiencing stress, anger, or frustration; i.e., does he cry, retreat, use a security object (blanket, stuffed toy), have a tantrum?
Domestic and Intimate Partner Violence	Adolescents are not immune to intimate partner violence (IPV). Specific questions about IPV can be asked during the home environment section; e.g., do you have a boyfriend or girlfriend? What happens when the two of you disagree? Have you ever been hurt by someone you know?

HEALTH MAINTENANCE ACTIVITIES

Sleep	Determine if the child takes naps and if the child shares a bedroom, because children's different sleep habits may lead to interrupted sleep. Ask about night terrors or sleepwalking.
Diet	Questions concerning diet need to be tailored to the child's developmental level. See Chapter 7 for additional information.
Safety	Childproofing the environment, especially for young children, is essential. A thorough safety assessment includes such questions as: 1. How has the home been "childproofed"? 2. Are there safety gates on the top and bottom of the stairs?

continues

3. Do cribs, high chairs, play yards (play pens), changing tables, strollers, and infant carriers meet Health Canada recommendations (visit Childcare Equipment and Children's Furniture Fact Sheet at Health Canada (http://www.hc-sc.gc.ca/cps-spc/child-enfant/equip/index_e.html). Have baby walkers (banned in Canada) been destroyed?

4. Bumper pads should not be used in cribs because they pose an entanglement, entrapment, strangulation, and suffocation hazard to infants. Health Canada recommends that the Canadian public discontinue the use of these products.[12]

5. Have curtain and blind cords been secured out of reach of the child to avoid strangulation?

6. Is the hot water thermostat turned down to 49°C?

7. Have all sharp items such as razors and knives been placed out of reach of the child?

8. Is the child monitored constantly during bath time?

9. Is a non-skid bath mat in the tub?

10. Are there outlet covers on every outlet in the house? Are cords (power and telephone) secured?

11. When cooking, are pot or pan handles turned in?

12. Are plants out of reach?

13. If there is a pool in the yard, is it fenced in, or is a protective cover on the top? Is there a functional alarm system for the pool?

14. Are medications, cosmetics, pesticides, gasoline, cleaning solutions, paint thinner, and all other poisonous materials out of the child's reach?

15. Is the family aware of a local poison control telephone number?

16. Is there syrup of ipecac in the house, and do family members know why and when to use it?

17. Are smoke detectors in good order and close to or in the child's bedroom and on each floor of the house? Has the family practised a fire drill?

18. Is there a fire extinguisher on each floor?

19. Do family members know CPR or how to address choking?

20. Is there appropriate use of car seats based on age and height/weight recommendations for back seats, facing front or rear (see Nursing Tip below). Is a tether strap used to secure car seats when required? What happens when more than one car is used to transport the child; i.e., is the family able to install a permanent car seat in each car? If not, is the car seat secured in a consistently accurate manner?

21. Does the child use protective gear such as a helmet or knee or elbow pads if participating in an activity in which injuries may occur?

22. Are plastic dry cleaner overwraps, latex balloons (unattended by a caregiver), plastic garbage bags, and grocery bags out of the child's reach?

23. Have parents provided anticipatory guidance for streetproofing their child against "good" and "bad" touching, dealing with approaches by strangers, peer pressure to engage in risk-taking behaviours, etc.?

24. Any other question(s) that relate to the situation at hand.

Nursing Tip

Car Safety According to Transport Canada[13]

- Rear-facing seats used until the child is 1 year old.
- Forward-facing child seat from 10 kg (22 lb.) until 18 kg (40 lb.), generally from about age 1 to $4\frac{1}{2}$ years (some seats can be used longer up to 22 kg [48 lb.]).
- Booster seat from 18 kg (40 lb.), generally from about age $4\frac{1}{2}$ to 8 years.
- Vehicle rear seat and seat belt (ideally with a shoulder belt) from the time the child has outgrown the booster seat, from about age eight.

EQUIPMENT

- Equipment listed in Chapters 10–22
- Scale (infant or stand-up)
- Appropriate-sized blood pressure cuff
- Snellen E and Tumbling E charts
- Allen cards
- Ophthalmoscope
- Otoscope, speculum (2.5 to 4 mm), pneumatic attachment
- Pediatric stethoscope
- Growth chart, BMI chart
- Small bell
- Brightly coloured object
- Clean gloves
- Disposable centimetre tape measure

Growth and Development

Refer to Chapter 4 for a summary of normal cognitive, social, motor, language, and sensory development in children from infancy through adolescence.

PHYSICAL ASSESSMENT

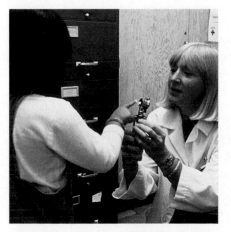

Figure 24-6 Allowing a child to manipulate assessment equipment may allay fears.

6. To promote the child's feeling of security, allow the infant who cannot sit up and the younger child to sit on the caregiver's lap for as much of the examination as possible.

7. Until the infant or toddler is comfortable, maintain eye contact with the caregiver while the assessment is taking place. Maintaining eye contact with the child who experiences anxiety in the presence of strangers can interfere with completing the examination. Maintain eye contact with caregiver if other means of alleviating the fears are not successful.

8. Interview the older school-age child or adolescent separately, without the caregiver. Talking to the individual without the caregiver present may yield important information not gained during a group interview (e.g., that the patient is using drugs).

9. Respect the patient's modesty.

10. Warm equipment (e.g., stethoscope).

11. Avoid making abrupt movements, which may startle a child.

12. If the child is sleeping, perform simple procedures (length, head circumference) and system assessments that require a quiet room (such as the cardiac and respiratory assessments) first.

13. Perform all invasive or uncomfortable procedures (ear inspection, hip palpation) last because they may cause discomfort, crying, fear, and increased heart rate.

14. Always provide comfort measures following pain. It is especially helpful to allow the caregiver the opportunity to provide supportive measures. This shows the child that you are genuinely concerned about his or her feelings.

15. To prevent falls, always keep one hand on any infant who is placed on the examination table.

16. Prior to completing the examination, ask the caregiver and patient if they have questions.

17. Use Figure 24-7 as a reference for age-specific components of the pediatric health visit.

Nursing Tip

Facilitating the Pediatric Assessment

- Use game playing and distraction to increase patient cooperativeness. It is important to have available different items of distraction that can be used when a patient is uncooperative or focusing on what will be done next. Distractions include safe small toys that easily hook onto a stethoscope, wind-up musical toys, and humming or whistling.
- Demonstrate procedures on a doll, stuffed toy, or even the caregiver prior to performing them on the child.

Nursing Tip

Obtaining Blood Pressure in Children

Never use the phrase "blood pressure" with a younger children because they may equate this with venipuncture. Say instead, "I am going to hug your arm with this cuff" or, to the older child, "I am going to measure your pressure."

Drs. Leslie Rourke, Denis Leduc and James Rourke
Revised May 2006
© Copyright *Canadian Family Physician*

Canadian Paediatric Society / Société canadienne de pédiatrie

The College of Family Physicians of Canada

Le Collège des médecins de famille du Canada

Rourke Baby Record: EVIDENCE-BASED INFANT/CHILD HEALTH MAINTENANCE GUIDE I

NAME: _____ Birth Date (d/m/yr): _____ M [ ] F [ ]

Birth Length: _____ cm Head Circ: _____ cm Birth Wt.: _____ g Discharge Wt.: _____ g

Birth remarks/Apgar:	Risk factors/Family history:

DATE OF VISIT	within 1 week			2 weeks (optional)			1 month (optional)		
GROWTH * Correct percentiles if < 36 weeks gestation	*Height*	*Weight*	*Head circ.* *av. 35 cm*	*Height*	*Weight*	*Head circ.*	*Height*	*Weight*	*Head circ.*
PARENTAL CONCERNS									

NUTRITION*	○ **Breastfeeding (exclusive)***
	   Vitamin D 10 µg = 400 IU/day*
	○ *Formula Feeding* (iron-fortified)
	   [150 mL = 5 oz/kg/day]
	○ Stool pattern and urine output
				○ **Breastfeeding (exclusive)***
				   Vitamin D 10 µg = 400 IU/day*
				○ *Formula Feeding* (iron-fortified)
				   [150 mL = 5 oz/kg/day]
				○ Stool pattern and urine output
							○ **Breastfeeding (exclusive)***
							   Vitamin D 10 µg = 400 IU/day*
							○ *Formula Feeding* (iron-fortified)
							○ Stool pattern and urine output		

EDUCATION AND ADVICE √ discussed and no concerns X if concerns	**Injury Prevention** ○ **Car seat (infant)*** ○ **Sleep position/bed sharing/co-sleeping*** ○ **Crib safety*** ○ **Firearm safety/removal*** ○ Carbon monoxide/*Smoke detectors** ○ *Hot water <49℃** ○ Choking/safe toys* Behaviour and family issues ○ Sleeping/crying** ○ Soothability/responsiveness ○ **Assess home visit need**** ○ Parenting/bonding ○ Parental fatigue/postpartum depression** ○ Family conflict/stress ○ Siblings Other Issues ○ **Second-hand smoke*** ○ *Inquiry on complementary/alternative medicine** ○ *Counsel on pacifier use** ○ Fever advice/thermometers* ○ *Temperature control and overdressing** ○ Sun exposure/sunscreens/insect repellent*								
DEVELOPMENT** *(Inquiry and observation of milestones)* Tasks are set **after** the time of normal milestone acquisition. **Absence of any item suggests the need for further assessment of development.** NB-Correct for age if < 36 weeks gestation √ if attained X if not attained							○ Focuses gaze ○ Startles to loud or sudden noise ○ Sucks well on nipple ○ No parent concerns		
PHYSICAL EXAMINATION Evidence-based screening for specific conditions is highlighted, but an appropriate age-specific focused physical examination is recommended at each visit.	○ *Skin (jaundice, dry)* ○ Fontanelles ○ *Eyes (red reflex)** ○ *Ears (TMs) Hearing inquiry/screening** ○ Heart/Lungs ○ Umbilicus ○ Femoral pulses ○ *Hips* ○ Muscle tone* ○ Testicles ○ Male urinary stream/foreskin care			○ *Skin (jaundice, dry)* ○ Fontanelles ○ *Eyes (red reflex)** ○ *Ears (TMs) Hearing inquiry/screening** ○ Heart/Lungs ○ Umbilicus ○ Femoral pulses ○ *Hips* ○ Muscle tone* ○ Testicles ○ Male urinary stream/foreskin care			○ Fontanelles ○ *Eyes (red reflex)** ○ *Corneal light reflex** ○ *Hearing inquiry/screening** ○ Heart ○ *Hips* ○ Muscle tone*		
PROBLEMS AND PLANS	○ **PKU, Thyroid** ○ **Hemoglobinopathy screen (if at risk)***								
IMMUNIZATION Provincial guidelines vary **Signature**	**Record on Guide V: Immunization Record** If HBsAg-positive parent or sibling: ○ **Hepatitis B vaccine**			**Record on Guide V: Immunization Record**			**Record on Guide V: Immunization Record** If HBsAg-positive parent or sibling: ○ **Hepatitis B vaccine**		

Grades of evidence: (A) **Bold type – Good evidence**   (B) *Italic – Fair evidence*   (C) Plain – Consensus with no definitive evidence
(*) see Infant/Child Health Maintenance: Selected Guidelines on reverse of Guide I   (**) see Healthy Child Development Selected Guidelines on reverse of Guide IV

Disclaimer: Given the constantly evolving nature of evidence and changing recommendations, the Rourke Baby Record: EB is meant to be used as a guide only.
Financial support for this revision is from the Strategic Initiatives Division of the Ontario Ministry of Children and Youth Services, with funds administered by the Ontario College of Family Physicians.

This form is reproduced by McNeil Consumer Healthcare. Printable versions are available at **www.cfpc.ca** and **www.cps.ca**
or by calling McNeil Consumer Healthcare at **1-800-265-7323**.

Figure 24-7 Rourke Baby Record from Canadian Paediatric Society.
Source: Reprinted from http://www.cfpc.ca/English/cfpc/programs/patient%20care/rourke%20baby/default.asp?s=1 with thanks to Drs. Leslie Rourke, Denis Leduc, and James Rourke. Funding for the 2006 RBR update was from the Strategic Initiatives Division of the Ontario Ministry of Children and Youth Services (MCYS) with fund administration by the Ontario College of Family Physicians.

ROURKE BABY RECORD INFANT/CHILD HEALTH MAINTENANCE SELECTED GUIDELINES/RESOURCES - May 2006

GROWTH

Measuring growth - Serial measurements of recumbent length (birth to ages 2 or 3) or height (≥ age 2), weight, and head circumference (birth to age 2) should be part of scheduled well-baby and well-child health visits in order to identify infants and children with disturbances in rates of weight gain or physical growth. Until internationally diverse growth charts are available and have been reviewed for use in Canada, the growth charts from the American Centers for Disease Control and Prevention (CDC) are recommended (set 2 with 3rd and 97th percentiles).

Important: Correct age if < 36 weeks gestation
- www.cdc.gov/nchs/about/major/nhanes/growthcharts/clinical_charts.htm#Clin%202
- Use of growth charts - www.cps.ca/english/statements/N/cps04-01.htm
- Guide to growth charts - www.cps.ca/english/statements/N/NutritionNoteGrowth.htm

NUTRITION

- Pediatric nutrition guidelines – Nutrition for Healthy Term Infants
  - www.hc-sc.gc.ca/fn-an/pubs/infant-nourrisson/nut_infant_nourrisson_term_e.html
- **Breastfeeding:** Exclusive breastfeeding is recommended for the first six months of life for healthy term infants. Breast milk is the optimal food for infants, and breastfeeding (with complementary foods) may continue for up to two years and beyond unless contraindicated. Breastfeeding reduces gastrointestinal and respiratory infections. Maternal support (both antepartum and postpartum) increases breastfeeding and prolongs its duration. Early and frequent mother-infant contact, rooming in, and banning handouts of free infant formula increase breastfeeding rates.
- Routine **Vitamin D supplementation** of 10 μg = 400 IU/day (20 μg = 800 IU/day in northern communities) is recommended for all breastfed full term infants until the diet provides a sufficient source of Vitamin D (about 1 year of age).
  Breastfeeding - www.cps.ca/english/statements/N/BreastfeedingMar05.htm
  Weaning - www.cps.ca/english/statements/CP/cp04-01.htm
  Vitamin D - www.cps.ca/english/statements/II/ii02-02.htm
  Colic - www.cps.ca/english/statements/N/NutritionNoteSept03.htm
  Ankyloglossia and breastfeeding - www.cps.ca/english/statements/CP/cp02-02.htm
  Maternal medications during breastfeeding – Medications and Mothers' Milk by T. Hale (2005).
  Motherisk - www.motherisk.org
- *Transition to lower fat diet:* A gradual transition from the high-fat infant diet to a lower-fat diet (max 30% fat / 10% saturated fat) begins after age 2 years.
  - www.cps.ca/english/statements/N/n94-01.htm
- Encourage a healthy diet as per Canada's Food Guide
  - www.hc-sc.gc.ca/fn-an/food-guide-aliment/index_e.html

INJURY PREVENTION

In Canada, unintentional injuries are the leading cause of death in children and youth. Most of these preventable injuries are caused by motor vehicle collisions, drowning, burns, choking, and falls.

Motor vehicle collisions
- Transport Canada 2002 recommendations for **Car seats:**
  Children < 13 years should sit in the rear seat. Keep kids away from all airbags.
  Use rear-facing infant seat until 10 kg (22 lb.) – birth to at least 1 year old
  Use forward-facing child seat from 10 kg (22 lb.) to 18-22 kg (40-48 lb.)
  – about 1-4½ years old – as per specific car seat model
  Use booster seat from 18-22 kg (40-48 lb.) to 27 kg (60 lb.) – about 4½ -8 years old
  Use lap and shoulder belt in the rear seat for older children
  - www.tc.gc.ca/roadsafety/childsafety/menu.htm, www.cmaj.ca/cgi/content/full/167/7/769
- **Bicycle:** wear bike helmets

Drowning
- **Bath safety:** Never leave a young child alone in the bath. Do not use infant bath rings or bath seats.
- Water safety: Encourage swimming lessons (after age 4 years). Encourage pool, diving, and boating safety to reduce the risk of drowning.
  - www.cps.ca/english/statements/IP/IP03-01.htm

Burns: *Install smoke detectors in the home on every level.*
    Keep hot water at a temperature < 49 °C.

Choking: Use safe toys and safe food (avoid hard, small and round, smooth and sticky solid foods until age 3 years).

Falls: Assess home for hazards, e.g. never leave baby alone on change table or other high surface; do not use baby walkers; use window guards and stair gates.

Poisons: Keep medicines and cleaners locked up and out of child's reach. Have Poison Control Centre number handy. *Use of ipecac is contraindicated in children.*

Safe sleeping environment: www.cps.ca/english/statements/CP/cp04-02.htm

- **Sleep position and SIDS/Positional plagiocephaly:** Healthy infants should be positioned on their backs for sleep. Their heads should be placed in different positions on alternate days. While awake, infants should have supervised tummy time. Counsel parents on the dangers of other contributory causes of SIDS such as overheating, maternal smoking or second-hand smoke.
- Positional plagiocephaly - www.cps.ca/english/statements/IP/cps01-02.htm
- **Bed sharing:** Advise against bed sharing.
- **Co-sleeping:** Encourage putting infant in a government-approved crib in parents' room for the first 6 months of life. Room sharing is protective against SIDS.

Firearm safety/removal: There is evidence-based association between a firearm in the home and increased risk of unintentional firearm injury, suicide, or homicide.

For more safety information: www.safekidscanada.ca
    www.cps.ca/english/publications/InjuryPrevention.htm

PROBLEMS AND PLANS (SCREENING)

Hemoglobin screening: All infants from high-risk groups for iron deficiency anemia require Hgb determination between 6 and 12 months of age, e.g. Lower SES; Asian; First Nations children; low-birth-weight infants, and infants fed whole cow's milk during their first year of life.

Hemoglobinopathy screening: Screen all neonates from high-risk groups, e.g. Asian, African, and Mediterranean.

OTHER

- **Second-hand smoke exposure:** contributes to childhood illnesses such as URTI, middle ear effusion, persistent cough, pneumonia, asthma, and SIDS.
- *Complementary and alternative medicine (CAM):* Questions should be routinely asked on the use of homeopathy and other complementary and alternative medicine therapy or products, especially for children with chronic conditions.
  - www.cps.ca/english/statements/DT/DT05-01.htm
  - Homeopathy - www.cps.ca/english/statements/CP/cp05-01.htm
- *Pacifier use:* is a parental choice. Pacifier use may decrease risk of SIDS, but may lead to breastfeeding difficulties, and should be restricted in children with chronic and recurrent otitis media. - www.cps.ca/english/statements/CP/cp03-01.htm
- Fever advice/thermometers: Rectal temperature is the method of choice in those < 5 years and oral temperature thereafter. Fever ≥ 38°C in an infant < 3 months needs urgent evaluation. Acetaminophen remains the first choice for antipyresis. Ibuprofen is off-label therapy for children < 2 years.
  - Temperature measurement - www.cps.ca/english/statements/CP/cp00-01.htm
- Footwear: Shoes are for protection, not correction. Walking barefoot develops good toe gripping and muscular strength - www.cps.ca/english/statements/CP/cp98-02.htm
- Healthy Active Living: Encourage increased physical activity and decreased sedentary pastimes with parents as role models.
  - www.cps.ca/english/statements/HAL/HAL02-01.htm
  - Media use - www.cps.ca/english/statements/PP/pp03-01.htm
- Sun exposure/sunscreens/insect repellents: Minimize sun exposure. Wear protective clothing, hats, properly applied sunscreen with SPF ≥ 30 for those > 6 months of age. No DEET in < 6 months; 6-12 months 10% apply maximum once daily.
- *Pesticides:* Avoid pesticide exposure. Encourage pesticide-free foods.
  - Pesticides/herbicides - www.ocfp.on.ca/english/ocfp/communications/publications/default.asp?s=1#EnvironmentHealth
- *Lead Screening* is recommended for children who:
  - in the last 6 months lived in a house or apartment built before 1950;
  - live in a home with recent or ongoing renovations or peeling or chipped paint.
  - have a sibling, housemate, or playmate with a prior history of lead poisoning;
  - have been seen eating paint chips.
- Websites about environmental issues:
  - Canadian Partnership for Children's Health & Environment (CPCHE) - www.healthyenvironmentforkids.ca/
  - Health and housing - www.cmhc-schl.gc.ca/
  - Environmental health section of CDC - www.cdc.gov/node.do/id/0900f3ec8000e044
  - Commission for Environmental Cooperation – www.cec.org/children
- **Dental Care:**
  - **Dental cleaning:** After the eruption of the first tooth, clean with only water using a washcloth or soft brush until age 2 years; thereafter using only a pea-sized amount of fluoridated dentifrice; independent brushing should occur under parental supervision.
  - **Fluoride** supplements are recommended where ingestion from all sources is low. Sources include fluoridated dentifrice and all home and child-care water sources. Fluoride is to be started only after the eruption of the first primary tooth. Dose for those at high risk for dental caries with water < 0.3 ppm fluoride is 0.25 mg for children 6 months to 3 years, 0.50 mg for age 3 to 6 years, and 1 mg for children > 6 years.
  - *To prevent dental caries:* avoid sweetened liquids and constant sipping of milk or natural juices in both bottle and cup.

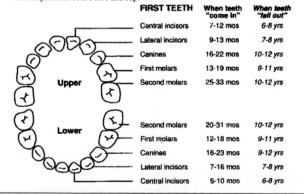

FIRST TEETH	When teeth "come in"	When teeth "fall out"
Upper		
Central incisors	7-12 mos	6-8 yrs
Lateral incisors	9-13 mos	7-8 yrs
Canines	16-22 mos	10-12 yrs
First molars	13-19 mos	9-11 yrs
Second molars	25-33 mos	10-12 yrs
Lower		
Second molars	20-31 mos	10-12 yrs
First molars	12-18 mos	9-11 yrs
Canines	16-23 mos	9-12 yrs
Lateral incisors	7-16 mos	7-8 yrs
Central incisors	6-10 mos	6-8 yrs

PHYSICAL EXAMINATION

- *Eyes – Corneal light reflex/Cover-uncover test and inquiry for strabismus:*
  With the child focusing on a light source, the light reflex on the cornea should be symmetrical. Each eye is then covered in turn, for 2-3 seconds, and then quickly uncovered. The test is abnormal if the covered eye "wanders" and when uncovered moves inward or outward to focus or "fix" on the light source.
- *Vision screening* – Children should be screened in their preschool years for amblyopia or its risk factors, as well as for serious ocular diseases, such as retinoblastoma and cataracts.
  - www.cps.ca/english/statements/CP/cp98-01.htm
- *Hearing screening/inquiry* – Questions on hearing acuity are recommended for all infants and children. In the absence of universal newborn screening, formal audiology testing should be performed in all high-risk infants. Older children should be screened if clinically indicated.
  - http://aappolicy.aappublications.org/cgi/content/full/pediatrics;111/2/436
- Muscle tone – Evaluation for spacticity, rigidity, and hypotonia should occur.
- Adenotonsillar hypertrophy and presence of sleep-disordered breathing warrants assessment re. obstructive sleep apnea.
  - http://aappolicy.aappublications.org/cgi/reprint/pediatrics;109/4/704.pdf

Figure 24-7 Rourke Baby Record from Canadian Paediatric Society. (*Continued*)

Drs. Leslie Rourke, Denis Leduc and James Rourke
Revised May 2006
© Copyright *Canadian Family Physician*

Rourke Baby Record: EVIDENCE-BASED INFANT/CHILD HEALTH MAINTENANCE GUIDE II

NAME: _____   Birth Date (d/m/yr): _____   M [ ]   F [ ]

Past problems/Risk factors:	Family history:

DATE OF VISIT	2 months			4 months			6 months		
GROWTH*	*Height*	*Weight*	*Head circ.*	*Height*	*Weight*	*Head circ.*	*Height*	*Weight (x2 BW)*	*Head circ.*
PARENTAL CONCERNS									
NUTRITION*	○ **Breastfeeding (exclusive)*** **Vitamin D 10 µg = 400 IU/day*** ○ *Formula Feeding* (iron-fortified)			○ **Breastfeeding (exclusive)*** **Vitamin D 10 µg = 400 IU/day*** ○ *Formula Feeding* (iron-fortified)			○ **Breastfeeding* - initial introduction of solids** **Vitamin D 10 µg = 400 IU/day*** ○ *Formula Feeding – iron-fortified follow-up* ○ No bottles in bed ○ No sweetened liquids, encourage water ○ Iron containing foods (cereals, meat, egg yolk, tofu) ○ Fruits and vegetables to follow ○ No egg white, nuts, or honey ○ Choking/safe food*		

EDUCATION AND ADVICE

√ discussed and no concerns
X if concerns

Injury Prevention
○ **Car seat (infant)***   ○ **Sleep position/bed sharing/co-sleeping/crib safety***   ○ **Poisons*; PCC#***   ○ **Firearm safety/removal***
○ *Electric plugs/cords*   ○ Carbon monoxide/*Smoke detectors**   ○ *Hot water <49 ℃/Bath safety**
○ *Falls (stairs, walkers, change table)**   ○ Choking/safe toys*

Behaviour and family issues
○ Sleeping/crying/**Night waking****   ○ Soothability/responsiveness   ○ **Assess home visit need****
○ Parenting/bonding   ○ Parental fatigue/postpartum depression**   ○ Family conflict/stress   ○ Siblings   ○ Child care/return to work

Other Issues
○ **Second-hand smoke***   ○ Teething/**Dental cleaning/Fluoride***   ○ *Complementary/alternative medicine**   ○ *Pacifier use**
○ *Temperature control and overdressing**   ○ *Fever advice/thermometers**   ○ *Sun exposure/sunscreens/insect repellent**   ○ *Pesticide exposure**

DEVELOPMENT** *(Inquiry and observation of milestones)* *Tasks are set **after** the time of normal milestone acquisition.* **Absence of any item suggests the need for further assessment of development.** NB-Correct for age if < 36 weeks gestation √ if attained X if not attained	○ Follows movement with eyes ○ Has a variety of sounds and cries ○ Holds head up when held at adult's shoulder ○ Enjoys being touched and cuddled ○ Smiles responsively ○ No parent concerns			○ Turns head toward sounds ○ Laughs/squeals at parent ○ Head steady ○ Grasps/reaches ○ No parent concerns			○ Follows a moving object ○ Looks in the direction of a new sound ○ Babbles ○ Rolls from back to stomach or stomach to back ○ Sits with support ○ Brings hands or toys to mouth ○ No parent concerns		
PHYSICAL EXAMINATION Evidence-based screening for specific conditions is highlighted, but an appropriate age-specific focused physical examination is recommended at each visit.	○ Fontanelles ○ *Eyes (red reflex)** ○ *Corneal light reflex** ○ *Hearing inquiry/screening** ○ Heart ○ *Hips* ○ Muscle tone*			○ *Eyes (red reflex)** ○ *Corneal light reflex** ○ *Hearing inquiry/screening** ○ *Hips* ○ Muscle tone*			○ Fontanelles ○ *Eyes (red reflex)** ○ *Corneal light reflex/Cover-uncover test and inquiry** ○ *Hearing inquiry/screening** ○ *Hips* ○ Muscle tone*		
PROBLEMS AND PLANS							○ Inquire about risk factors for TB		
IMMUNIZATION Provincial guidelines vary Signature	**Record on Guide V: Immunization Record**			**Record on Guide V: Immunization Record**			**Record on Guide V: Immunization Record** If HBsAg-positive parent or sibling: ○ Hepatitis B vaccine*		

Grades of evidence: (A) **Bold type – Good evidence** (B) *Italic – Fair evidence* (C) Plain – Consensus with no definitive evidence
(*) see Infant/Child Health Maintenance: Selected Guidelines on reverse of Guide I   (**) see Healthy Child Development Selected Guidelines on reverse of Guide IV

Disclaimer: Given the constantly evolving nature of evidence and changing recommendations, the Rourke Baby Record: EB is meant to be used as a guide only.
Financial support for this revision is from the Strategic Initiatives Division of the Ontario Ministry of Children and Youth Services, with funds administered by the Ontario College of Family Physicians.

This form is reproduced by McNeil Consumer Healthcare. Printable versions are available at **www.cfpc.ca** and **www.cps.ca**
or by calling McNeil Consumer Healthcare at **1-800-265-7323**.

Figure 24-7 Rourke Baby Record from Canadian Paediatric Society. (*Continued*)

Drs. Leslie Rourke, Denis Leduc and James Rourke
Revised May 2006
© Copyright *Canadian Family Physician*

Canadian Paediatric Society / Société canadienne de pédiatrie

The College of Family Physicians of Canada

Le Collège des médecins de famille du Canada

Rourke Baby Record: EVIDENCE-BASED INFANT/CHILD HEALTH MAINTENANCE GUIDE III

Past problems/Risk factors:	Family history:

NAME: _____ Birth Date (d/m/yr): _____ M [ ] F [ ]

DATE OF VISIT	9 months (optional)			12-13 months			15 months (optional)		
GROWTH*	*Height*	*Weight*	*Head circ.*	*Height*	*Weight (x3 BW)*	*Head circ. (av. 47cm)*	*Height*	*Weight*	*Head Circ.*
PARENTAL CONCERNS									

	9 months	12-13 months	15 months
NUTRITION*	○ **Breastfeeding*/** **Vitamin D 10 µg = 400 IU/day*** ○ *Formula Feeding – iron-fortified follow-up* ○ No bottles in bed ○ No sweetened liquids, encourage water ○ Cereal, meat/alternatives, fruits, vegetables ○ 1st introduction cow's milk products ○ No egg white, nuts, or honey ○ Choking/safe foods*	○ **Breastfeeding*** ○ Homogenized milk ○ Encourage cup instead of bottle ○ Appetite reduced ○ Choking/safe foods*	○ **Breastfeeding*** ○ Homogenized milk ○ Choking/safe foods* ○ Encourage cup instead of bottle
EDUCATION AND ADVICE √ discussed and no concerns X if concerns	**Injury Prevention** ○ **Car seat (infant/child)*** ○ Carbon monoxide/*Smoke detectors** Childproofing, including: ○ *Electric plugs/cords* **Behaviour and family issues** ○ Sleeping/crying/**Night waking**** ○ Parenting ○ *Parental fatigue/depression*** **Other Issues** ○ **Second-hand smoke*** ○ Teething/**Dental cleaning/Fluoride/Dentist*** ○ Fever advice/thermometers* ○ Active healthy living/media use* Environmental health including: ○ Sun exposure/sunscreens/insect repellent*	○ **Poisons*; PCC#*** ○ *Hot water < 49℃/Bath safety** ○ *Falls/stairs/walkers** ○ Soothability/responsiveness ○ Family conflict/stress ○ *Complementary/alternative medicine** ○ Encourage reading** ○ *Check serum lead if at risk**	○ **Firearm safety/removal*** ○ Choking/safe toys* ○ **Assess home visit need**** ○ Siblings ○ Child care/return to work ○ *Pacifier use** ○ Footwear ○ *Pesticide exposure**
DEVELOPMENT** *(Inquiry and observation of milestones)* Tasks are set **after** the time of normal milestone acquisition. **Absence of any item suggests the need for further assessment of development.** NB-Correct for age if < 36 weeks gestation √ if attained X if not attained	○ Looks for hidden toy ○ Babbles different sounds ○ Makes sounds to get attention ○ Sits without support ○ Stands with support ○ Opposes thumb and index finger ○ Reaches to be picked up and held ○ No parent concerns	○ Responds to own name ○ Understands simple requests, e.g. find your shoes ○ Chatters using 3 different sounds ○ Crawls or 'bum' shuffles ○ Pulls to stand/walks holding on ○ Shows many emotions ○ No parent concerns	○ Attempts to say 2 or more words (words do not have to be clear) ○ Tries to get something by making sounds, while reaching or pointing ○ Picks up and eats finger foods ○ Crawls up stairs/steps ○ Tries to squat to pick up toys from the floor ○ Removes socks and tries to untie shoes ○ Stacks 2 blocks ○ Looks at you to see how to react (when falls or with strangers) ○ No parent concerns
PHYSICAL EXAMINATION Evidence-based screening for specific conditions is highlighted, but an appropriate age-specific focused physical examination is recommended at each visit.	○ *Eyes (red reflex)** ○ *Corneal light reflex/Cover-uncover test and inquiry** ○ *Hearing inquiry/screening** ○ *Hips*	○ *Eyes (red reflex)** ○ *Corneal light reflex/Cover-uncover test and inquiry** ○ *Hearing inquiry/screening** ○ *Tonsil size/Teeth** ○ *Hips*	○ *Eyes (red reflex)** ○ *Corneal light reflex/Cover-uncover test and inquiry** ○ *Hearing inquiry/screening** ○ *Tonsil size/Teeth** ○ *Hips*
PROBLEMS AND PLANS	○ **Anti-HBs and HbsAG*** (If HbsAg positive mother) ○ *Hemoglobin (If at risk)**	○ *Hemoglobin (If at risk)**	
IMMUNIZATION Provincial guidelines vary Signature	Record on Guide V: Immunization Record	Record on Guide V: Immunization Record	Record on Guide V: Immunization Record

Grades of evidence: (A) **Bold type – Good evidence** (B) *Italic – Fair evidence* (C) Plain – Consensus with no definitive evidence
(*) see Infant/Child Health Maintenance: Selected Guidelines on reverse of Guide I (**) see Healthy Child Development Selected Guidelines on reverse of Guide IV

Disclaimer: Given the constantly evolving nature of evidence and changing recommendations, the Rourke Baby Record: EB is meant to be used as a guide only.
Financial support for this revision is from the Strategic Initiatives Division of the Ontario Ministry of Children and Youth Services, with funds administered by the Ontario College of Family Physicians.

This form is reproduced by McNeil Consumer Healthcare. Printable versions are available at **www.cfpc.ca** and **www.cps.ca**
or by calling McNeil Consumer Healthcare at **1-800-265-7323**.

Figure 24-7 Rourke Baby Record from Canadian Paediatric Society. (*Continued*)

Drs. Leslie Rourke, Denis Leduc and James Rourke
Revised May 2006
© Copyright *Canadian Family Physician*

Rourke Baby Record: EVIDENCE-BASED INFANT/CHILD HEALTH MAINTENANCE GUIDE IV

Birth Date (d/m/yr): _____

NAME: _____

M [ ] F [ ]

Past problems/Risk factors:	Family history:

	18 months			2-3 years			4-5 years	
DATE OF VISIT								
GROWTH*	*Height*	*Weight*	*Head circ.*	*Height.*	*Weight*	*Head circ.* -if prior abnormal	*Height*	*Weight*
PARENTAL CONCERNS								
NUTRITION*	O **Breastfeeding*** O Homogenized milk O No bottles			O Homogenized or 2% milk O *Gradual transition to lower fat diet** O Canada's Food Guide*			O 2% milk O Canada's Food Guide*	

EDUCATION AND ADVICE

	18 months	2-3 years	4-5 years
Injury Prevention	O **Car seat (child)*** O *Bath safety** O Choking/safe toys*	O **Car seat (child/booster)*** O *Bike Helmets** O Carbon monoxide/*Smoke detectors** O Matches	O **Firearm safety/removal*** O Water safety
Behaviour	O Parent/child interaction O *Discipline/Limit setting***	O Parent/child interaction O *Discipline/Limit setting*** O *High risk children*** O *Parental fatigue/depression*** O Family conflict/stress O Siblings	
Family	O *Parental fatigue/stress/depression*** O High-risk children**	O **Second-hand smoke*** O *Complementary/alternative medicine** O Active healthy living/media use* O Socializing opportunities O Encourage reading**	O **Dental cleaning/Fluoride/Dentist*** O Toilet learning**
Other √ discussed and no concerns X if concerns	O Socializing/peer play opportunities O **Dental Care/Dentist*** O Toilet learning**	O **Assess day care /preschool needs**/school readiness** Environmental health including: O Sun exposure/sunscreens/insect repellent* O *Pesticide exposure** O *Check serum lead if at risk**	

DEVELOPMENT^^ *(Inquiry and observation of milestones)* Tasks are set *after* the time of normal milestone acquisition. **Absence of any item suggests the need for further assessment of development.** NB-Correct for age if < 36 weeks gestation √ if attained X if not attained	Social/Emotional O Child's behaviour is usually manageable O Usually easy to soothe O Comes for comfort when distressed Communication Skills O Points to 3 different body parts O Tries to get your attention to see something of interest O Pretend play with toys and figures (e.g. feeds stuffed animal) O Turns when name is called O Imitates speech sounds regularly O Produces 3 consonants, e.g. P M B W H N Motor Skills O Walks backward 2 steps without support O Feeds self with spoon with little spilling Adaptive Skills O Removes hat/socks without help O No parent concerns	**2 years** O At least 1 new word/week O 2-word sentences O Tries to run O Puts objects into small container O Copies adult's actions O Continues to develop new skills O No parent concerns **3 years** O Understands 2 step direction O Twists lids off jars or turns knobs O Turns pages one at a time O Shares some of the time O Listens to music or stories for 5-10 minutes with adults O No parent concerns	**4 years** O Understands related 3-part directions O Asks lots of questions O Stands on 1 foot for 1-3 seconds O Draws a person with at least 3 body parts O Toilet trained during the day O Tries to comfort someone who is upset O No parent concerns **5 years** O Counts to 10 and knows common colours and shapes O Speaks clearly in sentences O Throws and catches a ball O Hops on 1 foot O Shares willingly O Works alone at an activity for 20-30 minutes O Separates easily from parents O No parent concerns
PHYSICAL EXAMINATION Evidence-based screening for specific conditions is highlighted, but an appropriate age-specific focused physical examination is recommended at each visit.	O *Eyes (red reflex)** O *Corneal light reflex/Cover-uncover test and inquiry** O Hearing inquiry O *Tonsil size/Teeth**	O *Blood pressure* O *Eyes (red reflex)/Visual acuity ** O *Corneal light reflex/Cover-uncover test and inquiry** O Hearing inquiry O *Tonsil size/Teeth**	O *Blood pressure* O *Eyes (red reflex)/Visual acuity** O *Corneal light reflex/Cover-uncover test and inquiry** O Hearing inquiry O *Tonsil size/Teeth**
PROBLEMS AND PLANS			
IMMUNIZATION Provincial guidelines vary **Signature**	Record on Guide V: Immunization Record	Record on Guide V: Immunization Record	Record on Guide V: Immunization Record

Grades of evidence: (A) **Bold type – Good evidence**   (B) *Italic – Fair evidence*   (C) Plain – Consensus with no definitive evidence
(*) see Infant/Child Health Maintenance: Selected Guidelines on reverse of Guide I   (**) see Healthy Child Development Selected Guidelines on reverse of Guide IV

Disclaimer: Given the constantly evolving nature of evidence and changing recommendations, the Rourke Baby Record: EB is meant to be used as a guide only.
Financial support for this revision is from the Strategic Initiatives Division of the Ontario Ministry of Children and Youth Services, with funds administered by the Ontario College of Family Physicians.

This form is reproduced by McNeil Consumer Healthcare. Printable versions are available at **www.cfpc.ca** and **www.cps.ca**
or by calling McNeil Consumer Healthcare at **1-800-265-7323**.

Figure 24-7   Rourke Baby Record from Canadian Paediatric Society. *(Continued)*

ROURKE BABY RECORD HEALTHY CHILD DEVELOPMENT SELECTED GUIDELINES/RESOURCES - May 2006

DEVELOPMENT
Maneuvers are based on the Nipissing District Development Screen (www.ndds.ca) and other developmental literature. They are not a developmental screen, but rather an aid to developmental surveillance. They are set **after** the time of normal milestone acquisition. Thus, absence of any one or more items is considered a high-risk marker and indicates the need for further developmental assessment, as does parental concern about development at any stage.
- "Best Start" website contains resources for maternal, newborn, and early child development
  - www.beststart.org/
- OCFP Healthy Child Development: Improving the Odds publication is a toolkit for primary healthcare providers
  - www.beststart.org/resources/hlthy_chld_dev/pdf/HCD_complete.pdf

BEHAVIOUR
Night waking/crying:
Night waking/crying occurs in 20% of infants and toddlers who do not require night feeding. Counselling around positive bedtime routines (including training the child to fall asleep alone), removing nighttime reinforcers, keeping morning awakening time consistent, and rewarding good sleep behaviour has been shown to reduce the prevalence of night waking/crying, especially when this counselling begins in the first 3 weeks of life.
- www.mja.com.au/public/issues/182_05_070305/sym10800_fm.html

PARENTING/**DISCIPLINE**
Promote effective discipline through evaluation, anticipatory guidance and counseling using the following principles: respect for parents, cultural sensitivity, improving social supports, increasing parental confidence, increasing parental pleasure in children, and supporting and improving parenting skills.
- www.cps.ca/english/statements/PP/pp04-01.htm
- OCFP Healthy Child Development
  www.beststart.org/resources/hlthy_chld_dev /pdf/HCD_complete.pdf (section 3)

TOILET LEARNING
The process of toilet learning has changed significantly over the years and within different cultures. In Western culture, a child-centred approach, where the timing and methodology of toilet learning is individualized as much as possible, is recommended.
- www.cps.ca/english/statements/CP/cp00-02.htm

LITERACY
Physicians can promote literacy and early childhood reading by facilitating reading in the office. Encourage parents to watch less television and read more to their children.
- www.cps.ca/english/statements/PP/pp02-01.htm

AUTISM SPECTRUM DISORDER
When developmental delay is suspected in an 18-month child, assess for autism spectrum disorder using the Checklist for Autism in Toddlers (CHAT) – Journal of Autism and Developmental Disorders 2001;31(2).
- www.beststart.org/resources/hlthy_chld_dev/pdf/HCD_complete.pdf (appendix L)

PARENTAL/FAMILY ISSUES AFFECTING DEVELOPMENT
- Maternal depression - Physicians should have a high awareness of maternal depression, which is a risk factor for the socioemotional and cognitive development of children. Although less studied, paternal factors may compound the maternal-infant issues.
  - www.cps.ca/english/statements/PP/pp04-03.htm
- Shaken baby syndrome - A high index of suspicion is suggested.
  - www.cps.ca/english/statements/PP/cps01-01.htm
- Fetal alcohol syndrome/effects (FAS/FAE) - Canadian Guidelines published in CMAJ supplement
  - Mar. 1/05 - www.cmaj.ca/cgi/content/full/172/5_suppl/S1

High-risk infants/children
- **Day Care:**
  Specialized day care or preschool is beneficial for children living in poverty (family income at or below Statistics Canada low-income cut-off). These disadvantaged children are at an increased risk of mortality and morbidity, including physical, emotional, social and education deficits.
- **Home Visits:**
  There is good evidence for home visiting by nurses during the perinatal period through infancy for first-time mothers of low socioeconomic status, single parents or teenaged parents to prevent physical abuse and/or neglect. Canadian Task Force on Preventative Health Care
  - www.cmaj.ca/cgi/content/full/163/11/1451

Risk factors for physical abuse:
- low SES
- young maternal age (< 19 years)
- single parent family
- parental experiences of own physical abuse in childhood
- spousal violence
- lack of social support
- unplanned pregnancy or negative parental attitude towards pregnancy

Risk factors for sexual abuse:
- living in a family without a natural parent
- growing up in a family with poor marital relations between parents
- presence of a stepfather
- poor child-parent relationships
- unhappy family life

EARLY CHILD DEVELOPMENT AND PARENTING RESOURCE SYSTEM

Figure 24-7 Rourke Baby Record from Canadian Paediatric Society. (*Continued*)

Drs. Leslie Rourke, Denis Leduc and James Rourke
Revised May 2006
© Copyright *Canadian Family Physician*

Rourke Baby Record: EVIDENCE-BASED INFANT/CHILD HEALTH MAINTENANCE GUIDE V
NAME: _____   Birth Date (d/m/yr): _____   M [ ]   F [ ]

Childhood Immunization Record as per NACI Recommendations (as of March 2006)
For additional information, refer to the National Advisory Committee on Immunization website: www.phac-aspc.gc.ca/naci-ccni/
Provincial guidelines are available online: www.phac-aspc.gc.ca/im/ptimprog-progimpt/table-1_e.html

Date given	NACI recommendations	Injection site	Lot number	Expiry date	Initials	Comments
DTaP/IPV/ Hib	4 doses (2, 4, 6, 18 months) dose #1 (2 months)					
	dose #2 (4 months)					
	dose #3 (6 months)					
	dose #4 (18 months)					
Pneu-Conj	4 doses (2, 4, 6, 12-15 months) dose #1 (2 months)					
	dose #2 (4 months)					
	dose #3 (6 months)					
	dose #4 (12-15 months)					
Men-Conj	3 doses (2, 4, 6 months) OR 1 dose (12 months OR 14-16 years)					
Hepatitis B	3 doses in infancy OR 2-3 doses preteen/teen dose #1					
	dose #2					
	± dose #3					
MMR	2 doses (12 months, 18 months OR 4 years) dose #1 (12 months)					
	dose #2 (18 months OR 4 years)					
Varicella	1 dose (12 months - 12 years) OR 2 doses ≥ 13 years dose #1					
	± dose #2					
DTaP/IPV	1 dose (4-6 years)					
dTap	1 dose (14-16 years)					
Influenza	1 dose annually (6-23 months and high risk > 2 years) First year only for < 9 years - give 2 doses one month apart					
Other						

Disclaimer: Given the constantly evolving nature of evidence and changing recommendations, the Rourke Baby Record: EB is meant to be used as a guide only.
Financial support for this revision is from the Strategic Initiatives Division of the Ontario Ministry of Children and Youth Services, with funds administered by the Ontario College of Family Physicians.

This form is reproduced by McNeil Consumer Healthcare. Printable versions are available at **www.cfpc.ca** and **www.cps.ca**
or by calling McNeil Consumer Healthcare at **1-800-265-7323**.

Figure 24-7   Rourke Baby Record from Canadian Paediatric Society. (*Continued*)

ROURKE BABY RECORD INFECTIOUS DISEASES AND IMMUNIZATION SELECTED GUIDELINES/RESOURCES - May 2006

ROUTINE IMMUNIZATION

National Advisory Committee on Immunization (NACI) recommended immunization schedules for infants, children and youth can be found at the following website: www.phac-aspc.gc.ca/naci-ccni/.

Provincial/territorial immunization schedules may differ based on funding differences. For provincial/territorial immunization schedules, see Canadian Nursing Coalition on Immunization chart on the website of the Public Health Agency of Canada: www.phac-aspc.gc.ca/im/ptimprog-progimpt/table-1_e.html.

For review, see "Immunization update 2005: Stepping forward" available on-line at www.cps.ca/english/statements/ID/PIDNoteImmunization2005.htm.

Vaccine Notes (Adapted from NACI):

Diphtheria, Tetanus, acellular Pertussis and inactivated Polio virus vaccine (DTaP-IPV): DTaP-IPV vaccine is the preferred vaccine for all doses in the vaccination series, including completion of the series in children < 7 years who have received ≥ 1 dose of DPT (whole cell) vaccine (e.g., recent immigrants).

Haemophilus influenzae type b conjugate vaccine (Hib): Hib schedule shown is for the Haemophilus b capsular polysaccharide – PRP conjugated to tetanus toxoid (Act-HIB™) or the Haemophilus b oligosaccharide conjugate - HbOC (HibTITER™) vaccines. This vaccine may be combined with DTaP in a single injection.

Measles, Mumps and Rubella vaccine (MMR): A second dose of MMR is recommended, at least 1 month after the first dose for the purpose of better measles protection. For convenience, options include giving it with the next scheduled vaccination at 18 months of age or at school entry (4-6 years) (depending on the provincial/territorial policy), or at any intervening age that is practical. The need for a second dose of mumps and rubella vaccine is not established but may benefit (given for convenience as MMR). The second dose of MMR should be given at the same visit as DTaP-IPV (± Hib) to ensure high uptake rates. MMR and varicella vaccines should be administered concurrently (at different sites) or separated by at least 4 weeks.

Varicella vaccine: Children aged 12 months to 12 years who have not had varicella should receive one dose of varicella vaccine. Unvaccinated individuals ≥ 13 years who have not had varicella should receive two doses at least 28 days apart. Varicella and MMR vaccines should be administered concurrently (at different sites) or separated by at least 4 weeks.

Hepatitis B vaccine (Hep B): Hepatitis B vaccine can be routinely given to infants or preadolescents, depending on the provincial/territorial policy. For infants born to chronic carrier mothers, the first dose should be given at birth (with Hepatitis B immune globulin), otherwise the first dose can be given at 2 months of age to fit more conveniently with other routine infant immunization visits. The second dose should be administered at least 1 month after the first dose, and the third at least 2 months after the second dose, but again may fit more conveniently into the 4- and 6-month immunization visits. A two-dose schedule for adolescents is an option. (See also SELECTED INFECTIOUS DISEASES RECOMMENDATIONS below.)

Pneumococcal conjugate vaccine - 7-valent (Pneu-Conj): Recommended schedule, number of doses and subsequent use of 23 valent polysaccharide pneumococcal vaccine depend on the age of the child, if at high risk for pneumococcal disease, and when vaccination is begun.

Meningococcal C conjugate vaccine (Men-Conj): Recommended schedule and number of doses of meningococcal vaccine depend on the age of the child. If the provincial/territorial policy is to give Men-Conj after 12 months of age, 1 dose is sufficient.

Diphtheria, Tetanus, acellular Pertussis vaccine - adult/adolescent formulation (dTap): a combined adsorbed "adult type" preparation for use in people ≥ 7 years of age, contains less diphtheria toxoid and pertussis antigens than preparations given to younger children and is less likely to cause reactions in older people. This vaccine should be used in individuals > 7 years receiving their primary series of vaccines.

Influenza vaccine (Flu): Recommended for all children between 6 and 23 months of age, and for older high-risk children. Previously unvaccinated children up to 9 years of age require 2 doses with an interval of at least 4 weeks. The second dose is not required if the child has received one or more doses of influenza vaccine during the previous immunization season.

SELECTED INFECTIOUS DISEASES RECOMMENDATIONS

See CPS position statements of the Infectious Diseases and Immunization Committee: www.cps.ca/english/publications/InfectiousDiseases.htm.

- **Hepatitis B immune globulin and immunization:**
  Infants with HBsAg-positive parents or siblings require Hepatitis B vaccine at birth, at 1 month, and 6 months of age.
  Infants of HBsAg-positive mothers also require Hepatitis B immune globulin at birth.

  Hepatitis B vaccine should also be given to all infants from high-risk groups, such as:
  - infants where at least one parent has emigrated from a country where Hepatitis B is endemic;
  - infants of mothers positive for Hepatitis C virus;
  - infants of substance-abusing mothers.

- **Human Immunodeficiency Virus type 1 (HIV-1) maternal infections:**
  Breastfeeding is contraindicated for an HIV-1 infected mother even if she is receiving antiretroviral therapy.

- **Hepatitis A or A/B combined (when Hepatitis B vaccine has not been previously given):**
  These vaccines should be considered when traveling to countries where Hepatitis A or B are endemic.

- **Tuberculosis - TB skin testing:**
  TB skin testing should be done if the infant is living with anyone being investigated or treated for TB. TB skin testing should also be considered in high-risk groups, including Aboriginal people, immigrants and long-term travellers from areas with a high prevalence of TB.

Figure 24-7 Rourke Baby Record from Canadian Paediatric Society. (*Continued*)

Many assessment techniques for the child are similar to those for the adult. Refer to the specific system chapters for detailed explanations of assessment techniques.

Techniques for approaching children vary from one age group to the next. A basic principle during any physical assessment is building a trusting relationship, which can be done in a variety of ways. First, always explain what will be done prior to each portion of the assessment and answer questions honestly. Second, praise the child for positive behaviours, for example, cooperating during assessment of the middle ear. Portraying a caring attitude will greatly influence both the patient's and the caregiver's sense of trust. Show respect for the patient as an individual and allow expression of feelings (whimpering, crying).

Vital Signs

General Approach

1. The act of measuring vital signs is often disturbing to a young patient. Past experiences influence the degree of cooperation you will encounter.
2. Vital signs may be obtained at the beginning of the assessment or during the assessment of a certain system. Blood pressure and rectal temperature measurements are more threatening and should be performed toward the end of the assessment, preferably before using the otoscope.
3. If the child is particularly anxious, it is best to integrate the assessment of vital signs into the overall assessment.

Temperature

The presence or absence of a fever is important in the assessment of a child. There has been significant debate as to the "most accurate" method of temperature measurement (see Chapter 9). Assessment in the pediatric client poses additional controversy in that rectal temperatures are generally not well received by children (and many parents), and oral temperature taking can be difficult if the child is too young to cooperate. Even if the child and parent are accepting of rectal temperature taking, it is not appropriate if the child has diarrhea, is immunocompromised, or is unable to remain still, thus posing a risk of perforation. Any child with a history of physical abuse could be traumatized by further crossing of physical boundaries. Axillary temperature, while quick and painless, is often less reliable than rectal or oral temperatures. See Table 24-2 for guidelines from the Canadian Paediatric Society.[14]

TABLE 24-2	Summary of Recommended Temperature Measurement Techniques
AGE	**RECOMMENDED TECHNIQUE**
Birth to 2 years	1. Rectal (definitive) 2. Axillary (screening low-risk children)
Over 2 years to 5 years	1. Rectal (definitive) 2. Axillary, tympanic (or temporal artery if in hospital) (screening)
Older than 5 years	1. Oral (definitive) 2. Axillary, tympanic (or temporal artery if in hospital) (screening)

Source: Canadian Paediatric Society, Summary of recommended temperature measurement techniques found at http://www.cps.ca/ english/statements/CP/cp00-01.htm. For more information, visit www .cps.ca/www.caringforkids.cps.ca

Axillary

E   1. When measuring axillary temperature, have the child sit or lie on the caregiver's lap to free your hands for other observations or to prepare for the next area of assessment.

2. Explain to the child that this type of temperature measurement does not hurt.

3. Place the thermometer into the middle of the axilla and fold the patient's arm across the chest to keep the thermometer in place. To pass time, ask the caregiver to read the child a story.

N/A/P   See Chapter 9.

Rectal

E   1. Children dislike having rectal temperature taken, so the approach to explanation should be matter of fact: "I need to measure your temperature in your bottom. You need to hold very still while I do this. Your mommy (or other appropriate person) will be right here with you."

2. Place the patient in either a side-lying or a prone position on the caregiver's lap or place the patient on the back on the examination table and firmly grasp the feet with your non-dominant hand (Figure 24-8).

3. After lubricating the stub-tipped thermometer, insert it gently into the patient's rectum: 1.25 cm for newborns, 1.9 cm for infants, and 2.5 cm for preschoolers and older patients. Hold the thermometer firmly between your fingers to avoid accidentally inserting it too far.

N/A/P   See Chapter 9.

A. Infant in Prone Position

B. Infant in Supine Position

Figure 24-8 Rectal Temperature Measurement.

Tympanic Thermometry

E   1. Though seen by adults as less invasive than rectal thermometer insertion, the child may feel that a physical boundary has been crossed when the probe is inserted into the ear. To help the child remain calm, the parent can hold the child on the lap or help the child lie comfortably in bed.

2. See Chapter 9, for full instructions. If the patient is under three years old, pull the pinna down, aiming the probe toward the opposite eye. If the patient is over three years old, grasp the pinna and pull gently up and back, aiming the probe toward the opposite ear.

N/A/P   See Chapter 9.

Temporal Artery Thermometry

E   1. This method is not invasive but still requires the child to remain still so the sensor will maintain contact.

2. See Chapter 9.

N/A/P   See Chapter 9.

Respiratory Rate

E   1. Try to obtain the rate early in the assessment, when the patient is most cooperative and not crying.

2. If the patient is crying, the measurement will not be accurate and should be retaken.

  3. Remember to observe the expansion of the abdomen in infants and toddlers.
N/A/P See Chapter 9.

Physical Growth

Weight

Use the same scale at each visit, if possible, to prevent variations in serial weight checks.

E 1. If using an infant scale, cover it with a paper protector.
  2. Balance or zero the scale.
  3. Place infants and young toddlers nude on the scale (Figure 24-9A). Always keep one hand on the child to prevent falls and lift your hand slightly when obtaining the actual weight reading.
  4. Preschoolers and young school-age children can wear street clothes to be weighed (Figure 24-9B). Have the older child undress, don a paper or cloth gown, and step on the standard platform scale.
  5. Note and record weight.

N Refer to growth charts, Figures 24-2A and B on page 869 and Figure 24-2E and F on page 871. Usually, neonates lose approximately 10% of birth weight by the third or fourth day after birth, then regain it by two weeks of age. This expected change in weight is called physiological weight loss, and it is due to a loss of extracellular fluid and meconium, a dark-green, sticky, stool-like substance excreted from the rectum within the first 24 hours after birth.

A A newborn weight less than the tenth gestational age percentile is considered abnormal.

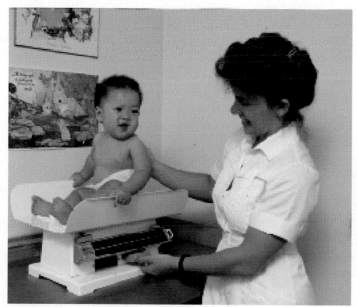

A. Infant

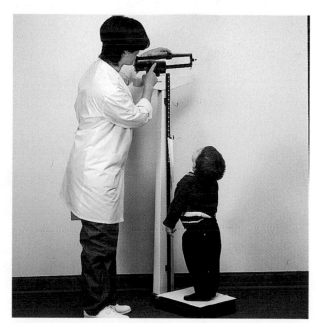

B. Preschooler

Figure 24-9 Measuring Weight in Children.

| E | **Examination** | N | **Normal Findings** | A | **Abnormal Findings** | P | **Pathophysiology** |

P   A newborn whose growth has been restricted in utero is referred to as small for gestational age (SGA). Potential causes include tobacco, alcohol, or drug abuse, or certain genetic syndromes. The overall rate of SGA in Canada is approximately 8%, ranging from 5% of live births in the Northwest Territories to 8.6% of live births in Alberta.[15]

A   A newborn weight greater than the 90th gestational age percentile is abnormal.

P   A diabetic mother or genetic predisposition may be responsible for producing a large for gestational age (LGA) newborn. Rates of LGA are increasing in Canada, with approximately 12% of live births falling in this category. The LGA range is from 10.4% of live births in Quebec to 18.1% of live births in the Northwest Territories.[16]

A   A weight below the 3rd or above the 97th percentiles warrants investigation, as does the patient who falls two standard deviations below his or her own established curve. Any such finding is abnormal.

P   Possible causes include organic or non-organic failure to thrive, congenital or cyanotic heart disease, cystic fibrosis (CF), fetal alcohol syndrome, and malabsorption diseases.

Nursing Alert

Fetal Alcohol Syndrome (FAS) and Fetal Alcohol Effects (FAE)

Alcohol is a teratogen that causes birth defects that can influence the newborn for life. FAS is a medical diagnosis that refers to a set of alcohol-related disabilities associated with the use of alcohol during pregnancy. Indicators include prenatal and/or postnatal growth restriction, CNS involvement such as neurological abnormalities, developmental delays, behavioural dysfunction, learning disabilities or other intellectual impairment, and skull and brain malformation. Characteristic facial features include short eye slits, thin upper lip, flattened cheekbones, and an indistinct groove between the upper lip and nose. When children have only some of these signs and alcohol use is being considered as a possible reason for growth delays then the term fetal alcohol effects is used.[17]

Nursing Tip

Obtaining Length and Height in Children under Two Years of Age

1. If measuring a recumbent length, always plot on the birth-to-36-month chart.
2. If measuring height, plot the measurement on a birth-to-36-month growth chart and subtract 1 centimetre.

Length and Height

Recumbent length is measured for children less than two years old.

E   1. Position the measuring board flat on the examination table.
     2. Place the child's head at the top of the board and the child's heels at the foot of the board, ensuring that the legs are fully extended.
     3. Measure and record the length.

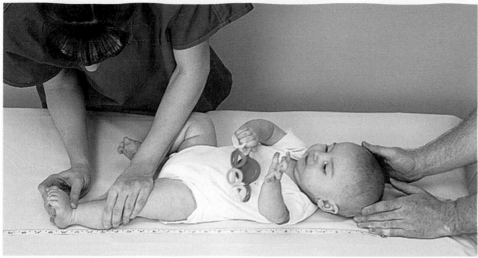

A. Recumbent Length in Infant

B. Height in Preschooler

Figure 24-10 Measuring Length and Height in Children.

    4. If a board is not available, place the child in a supine position and mark lines on the paper at the tip of the head and at the heel (Figure 24-10A), ensuring that the legs are fully extended.

    5. Measure between the lines and record.

    Height for all other age groups can be measured in the same fashion as for an adult. Figure 24-10B shows a preschooler's height being measured.

N   See growth charts in Figures 24-2A and B (on page 869) and Figures 24-2E and F (on page 871).

A   A height below the 3rd or above the 97th percentiles warrants investigation, as does the patient who falls two standard deviations below his or her own established curve. Any such finding is abnormal.

P   Possible causes include organic or non-organic failure to thrive, congenital or cyanotic heart disease, CF, fetal alcohol syndrome, and malabsorption diseases.

Head Circumference

Head circumference is measured in all children less than two years of age or serially in patients with known or suspected hydrocephalus. Measuring head circumference is an invaluable tool in the infant with suspected cessation of brain growth.

E   **1.** Place the patient in a sitting or supine position.

    2. Using a tape measure, measure anteriorly from above the eyebrows and around posteriorly to the occipital protuberance (Figure 24-11).

N   Refer to Figures 24-2C and D on page 870. Normal average head growth is 1 to 1.5 cm per month during the first year. Premature infants often have small head circumferences.

A   **Microcephaly**, a condition characterized by a small brain with a resultant small head, is an abnormal finding.

P   Microcephaly is a congenital finding associated with a mental deficit. Microcephaly can be caused by a variety of disorders including intrauterine

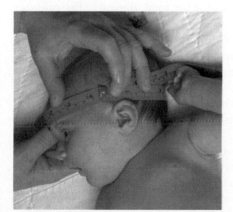

Figure 24-11 Measuring Head Circumference.

| E | Examination | N | Normal Findings | A | Abnormal Findings | P | Pathophysiology |

infections, drug or alcohol ingestion (fetal alcohol syndrome) during pregnancy, and genetic defects.

A **Hydrocephalus** (enlarged head) is indicated when an infant's or young child's head circumference is above the 97th percentile and crossing over the patient's established percentile lines from one serial measurement to the next. Hydrocephalus is abnormal. Note if the eyes are looking downward and the sclera is visible above the iris; this phenomenon is called the "setting sun" sign.

P Hydrocephalus is characterized by an imbalance in cerebrospinal fluid (CSF) production and reabsorption. Hydrocephalus may result from embryological malformations of the nervous system. Congenital hydrocephalus can also be caused by syphilis, rubella, toxoplasmosis, or cytomegalovirus. Bacterial meningitis or tumours are acquired causes of hydrocephalus. The setting sun sign results from progressive enlargement of the lateral and third ventricles related to excessive accumulation of CSF.

Chest Circumference

Chest circumference is measured up to one year of age. It is a measurement that by itself provides little information but is compared to head circumference to evaluate the child's overall growth.

E 1. Stand in front of the supine patient.
2. Measure the chest circumference by placing the tape measure around the chest at the nipple line (Figure 24-12).
3. Measure during exhalation.

N From birth to about one year, the head circumference is greater than the chest circumference. After age one, the chest circumference is greater than the head circumference.

A A measured chest circumference below normal limits is abnormal.

P A below-normal chest circumference for age may be attributed to prematurity.

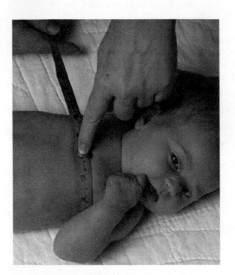

Figure 24-12 Measuring Chest Circumference.

Apgar Scoring

The **Apgar score** system provides a quick method to assess the need for newborn resuscitation in the delivery room. An Apgar score is given to a newborn at one and five minutes after birth. Perform steps 1 through 5 at one minute following birth; add the score in each category for the total. Repeat at five minutes following birth.

E 1. Auscultate the heart rate for one full minute.
2. Measure the degree of respiratory effort.
3. Evaluate muscle tone by attempting to straighten each extremity individually.
4. Evaluate the newborn's reflex irritability. Use a flicking motion of two fingers against the newborn's sole to rate reflex irritability.
5. Inspect the newborn's colour.

N A score of 8 to 10 demonstrates that the newborn is in good condition. Table 24-3 outlines the scoring system for each of the five areas assessed.

A A moderately depressed newborn earns a score of 4 to 7. A score of 0 to 3 indicates that the newborn is severely depressed and needs immediate resuscitation. Either finding is abnormal.

P A low score can be the result of one or numerous problems. Prematurity, central nervous system depression, blood or meconium in the trachea, maternal history of drug abuse, certain drugs that are given to the mother in preparation for delivery and that cross over and cause fetal depression, congenital complete heart block, and congenital heart disease are some of the potential etiologies for a low Apgar score.

TABLE 24-3	Apgar Scoring			
HEART RATE	**RESPIRATORY RATE**	**TONE**	**REFLEX IRRITABILITY**	**COLOUR**
Absent = 0	Apnea = 0	Flaccid = 0	No response = 0	Cyanosis = 0
< 100 = 1	Slow, irregular rate = 1	Some degree of flexion = 1	Grimace = 1	Body pink, extremities acrocyanotic = 1
> 100 = 2	Crying vigorously = 2	Full flexion = 2	Crying = 2	Completely pink = 2

Nursing Alert

Child Abuse

Child abuse refers to the violence, mistreatment, or neglect that a child or adolescent may experience while in the care of someone they either trust or depend on, such as a parent, sibling, other relative, or guardian.[18] Abuse can be physical, sexual, or psychological, and includes neglect. The annual incidence of child abuse in Canadian children is estimated at 38.33/1,000 children.[19] The majority of abuse, 30% of all cases, is in the form of neglect when physical, emotional, and psychological needs are not met. Exposure to family violence is the second most common cause of maltreatment (some classify this type of abuse as a form of emotional abuse), followed by physical (e.g., hitting, shaking, pushing, biting). Emotional abuse such as intimidation and verbal threats account for approximately 15% of abuse reports. Sexual abuse, such as being touched sexually, raped, or sodomized, occurs in an estimated 3% of all cases of maltreatment.

Unfortunately, the people most likely to abuse children are not strangers; rather they are their own family members or trusted adults. *If a child states that he or she is being abused, it is taken very seriously as children rarely lie about this experience; in fact, they are likely to deny any abuse for fear of negative repercussions.* As any form of abuse is unacceptable and because children are especially vulnerable, all provinces and territories require that any health professional who suspects maltreatment of a child must inform appropriate child protection agencies. See Table 24-4 for a summary of behavioural and physical indicators of abuse in children.

Skin

Inspection

Colour

E Observe the colour of the body, especially at the tip of the nose, the external ear, the lips, the hands, and the feet. These areas are prominent locations for detecting cyanosis or jaundice.

N The skin of a newborn is reddish in colour for the first 24 hours, then changes to varying shades of pale pink to pink to brown or black, depending on the child's race. It is normal for dark-skinned newborns to have a

E	**Examination**	N	**Normal Findings**	A	**Abnormal Findings**	P	**Pathophysiology**

TABLE 24-4 Behavioral and Physical Indicators of Various Types of Child Abuse

TYPE OF CHILD ABUSE	BEHAVIOURAL INDICATORS	PHYSICAL INDICATORS
Neglect: Failure to give due attention or care to a child resulting in serious emotional or physical harm	- pale, listless, unkempt - frequent absence from school - inappropriate clothing for the weather - dirty clothes - inappropriate acts or delinquent behaviour - abuse of alcohol/drugs - begging /stealing food - frequently tired - seeks inappropriate affection - mature for age - reports there is no caretaker	- poor hygiene - unattended physical or medical needs - consistent lack of supervision - underweight, poor growth, failure to thrive - constant hunger - undernourished
Emotional: Verbal attacks or demeaning actions that impact on a child's self esteem and self worth	- depression withdrawal or aggressive behaviour - overly compliant - too neat and clean - habit disorders (sucking, biting, rocking, etc.) - learning disorders - sleep disorders - unusual fearfulness - obsessive-compulsive behaviour - phobias - extreme behaviour - suicide attempts -developmental delays	- bed wetting - headaches - nausea - speech disorders - lags in physical development - disruptive behaviour
Physical Abuse: The intentional use of force against a child resulting in injury or causing bodily harm	- inconsistent explanation for injuries or cannot remember - wary of adults - flinch if touched unexpectedly - extremely aggressive or extremely withdrawn - feels deserving of punishment - apprehensive when others cry - frightened of parents - afraid to go home	- injuries not consistent with explanation - numerous injuries in varying stages of recovery or healing - presence of injuries over an extended period of time - facial injuries - injuries inconsistent with the child's age and developmental phase
Sexual Abuse: Any form of sexual conduct (touching, exploitation, intercourse) directed at a child	- sexual knowledge or play inappropriate to age - sophisticated or unusual sexual knowledge - prostitution - poor peer relationships - delinquent or runaway - reports sexual assault by caretaker - change in performance in school - sleeping disorders - aggressive behaviour - self-abusive behaviors - self mutilation	- unusual or excessive itching in the genital or anal area - stained or bloody underwear - pregnancy - injuries to the vaginal or anal areas - venereal disease - difficult in walking or sitting - pain when urinating - vaginal/penile discharge - excessive masturbation - urinary tract infections

Source: © (2006) HER MAJESTY THE QUEEN IN RIGHT OF CANADA as represented by the Royal Canadian Mounted Police (RCMP). Reproduced with the permission of the RCMP.

ruddy appearance and for light-skinned newborns to exhibit a bluish-purple colour of the hands and feet while the rest of the body remains pink. This is called acrocyanosis. It may disappear with warming. Mongolian spots, deep-blue pigmentation over the lumbar and sacral areas of the spine, over the buttocks, and sometimes over the upper back or shoulders in newborns of African, Latin American, or Asian descent, are extremely common and not to be confused with ecchymosis or signs of child abuse.

A A blue hue is abnormal.

P Cyanosis in the newborn is often associated with a congenital heart defect secondary to abnormal mixing of arterial and venous blood. In the older child with unrepaired heart disease, cyanosis may be a sign of decreasing levels of oxygen saturation.

A A yellowing of the skin or sclera is abnormal.

P Physiological jaundice of the newborn occurs on the second or third day of life. This type of jaundice results from increased levels of serum bilirubin. The newborn's body is unable to remove the bilirubin, thus producing a yellow cast or hue to the skin of light-skinned infants and to the sclera of both light- and dark-skinned newborns.

P Pathological jaundice of the newborn occurs within the first 24 hours of life. Possible causes of pathological jaundice include Rh/ABO incompatibility and maternal infections (rubella, herpes, syphilis, or toxoplasmosis). The pathophysiological response occurs because there is a deficiency or inactivity of bilirubin glucuronyl transferase in the newborn.

P Breast milk jaundice occurs within the first two weeks of life, with the onset being four to five days after birth. The etiology is not clear, but breast milk may contain an inhibitor of bilirubin conjugation.

A It is abnormal when the light-skinned newborn lies on a side and the dependent half becomes red or ruddy and the upper half turns pale in colour. In dark-skinned children, the dependent half becomes a ruddy colour and the upper half seems normal.

P **Harlequin colour change** is a benign condition thought to be a result of poor vasomotor control; it occurs between 48 and 96 hours after birth.

A Erythema of the palms or soles, edema of the hands or feet, or periungal desquamation is found in patients presenting with Kawasaki disease (mucocutaneous lymph node syndrome). In order for a practitioner to diagnose Kawasaki disease the child must present with fever for five days and with four of the five diagnostic criteria. Other than the previously mentioned signs above, other signs include bilateral, non-exudative conjunctival injection, at least one of the mucous membrane changes including injected or fissured lips, injected pharynx, or strawberry tongue; polymorphous exanthem, and acute nonsuppurative cervical lymphadenopathy.

P The cause of Kawasaki disease is unknown. Coronary artery vasculitis is a major concern as the disease progresses.

Lesions

E/N See Chapter 10.

A Lesions that are asymmetrical, scaly, erythematous patches or plaques with possible exudation and crusting are abnormal.

| E | Examination | N | Normal Findings | A | Abnormal Findings | P | Pathophysiology |

A   Eczema, or atopic dermatitis (AD), is a common abnormal skin disorder involving inflammation of the epidermis and superficial dermis. Inhaled allergens such as pollens, moulds, or dust mites, or food allergens are thought to induce mast-cell responses that cause AD.

A   Small, maculopapular lesions on an erythematous base, wheals, and vesicles that erupt on the newborn are abnormal.

P   Erythema toxicum is a benign rash. The cause is unknown.

A   Flat, deep, irregular, localized, pink areas in light-skinned children and deeper-red areas in dark-skinned children are abnormal.

P   **Telangiectatic nevi**, commonly known as **stork bites**, appear on the back of the neck, lower occiput, upper eyelids, and upper lip. The cause of telangiectatic nevi is capillary dilatation.

A   Diffuse redness, papules, vesicles, edema, scaling, and ulcerations on the area covered by a baby's diaper are abnormal.

P   Possible causes of diaper dermatitis include fecal enzymes, irritated skin, stool consistency and frequency, *Candida*, cleansing agents, sensitive skin, and poor nutrition.

A   Vesicles located on the palms of hands, soles of feet, and in the mouth are abnormal. A papular erythematous rash may also be on the buttocks.

P   Hand–foot–mouth disease is caused by coxsackievirus A16.

A   A dark black tuft of hair or a dimple over the lumbosacral area is abnormal.

P   The neural tube fails to fuse at about the fourth week of gestation and causes a vertebral defect known as spina bifida occulta.

Palpation

Texture

E   1. Use the finger pads to palpate the skin.
    2. The technique of palpating the skin of a younger child can be accomplished by playing games. For example, use the finger pads to walk up the abdomen and touch the nose.

N   Skin of the pediatric patient normally is smooth and soft. Milia, plugged sebaceous glands, present as small, white papules in the newborn. Milia occur mainly on the head, especially the cheeks and nose. Preterm infants have vernix caseosa.

A/P See Chapter 10.

Hair

Inspection

Lesions

E/N See Chapter 10.

A   Yellow, greasy-appearing scales on the scalp of a light-skinned infant are abnormal. In dark-skinned infants, the scaling is light grey.

P   Seborrheic dermatitis (**cradle cap**) is possibly related to increased epidermal tissue growth.

Head

Inspection

Shape and Symmetry

E   With the patient sitting upright either in the caregiver's arms or on the examination table, observe the symmetry of the frontal, parietal, and occipital prominences.

N   The shape of a child's head is symmetrical without depressions or protrusions. The anterior fontanel normally may pulsate with every heart beat.

The Asian infant generally has a flattened occiput, more so than infants of other races.

A   A flattened occipital bone with resultant hair loss over the same area is abnormal.

P   A prolonged supine position places pressure on the occipital bone.

Head Control

E   1. Assess head control while the patient is in the position used for assessing shape and symmetry.

2. With the head unsupported, observe the patient's ability to hold the head erect.

N   At three months of age, the infant is able to hold the head steady without lag.

A   Lack of head control is evidenced by the infant who is unable to hold the head steady while in a sitting position and is abnormal. Head lag beyond four to six months of age should be further investigated.

P   Documented prematurity, hydrocephalus, and illnesses causing developmental delays are possible causes of head lag.

Palpation

Fontanel

E   1. Place the child in an upright position.

2. Using the second or third finger pad, palpate the anterior fontanel at the junction of the sagittal, coronal, and frontal sutures.

3. Palpate the posterior fontanel at the junction of the sagittal and lambdoidal sutures.

4. Assess for bulging, pulsations, and size. To obtain accurate measurements, the patient should not be crying. Crying will produce a distorted, full, bulging appearance.

N   The anterior fontanel is soft and flat. Size ranges from 4 to 6 cm at birth. The fontanel gradually closes between 9 and 19 months of age. The posterior fontanel is also soft and flat. The size ranges from 0.5 to 1.5 centimetres at birth. The posterior fontanel gradually closes between one and three months of age. It is normal to feel pulsations related to the peripheral pulse.

A   Palpation reveals a bulging, tense fontanel, which is abnormal.

P   Signs of increased intracranial pressure are associated with meningitis and an increased amount of CSF.

A   A sunken, depressed fontanel is abnormal.

P   A sunken, depressed fontanel is a sign of dehydration.

A   A wide anterior fontanel in a child older than $2\frac{1}{2}$ years is an abnormal finding.

P   An anterior fontanel that remains open after $2\frac{1}{2}$ years of age may indicate disease such as rickets. In rickets, there is a low level of vitamin D relative to decreased phosphate levels. Other causes of enlarged fontanel include congenital hypothyroidism, Down syndrome, and hydrocephalus.

Suture Lines

E   1. With the finger pads, palpate the sagittal suture line. This runs from the anterior to the posterior portion of the skull in a midline position.

2. Palpate the coronal suture line. This runs along both sides of the head, starting at the anterior fontanel.

| E | Examination | N | Normal Findings | A | Abnormal Findings | P | Pathophysiology |

3. Palpate the lambdoidal suture. The lambdoidal suture runs along both sides of the head, starting at the posterior fontanel.

4. Ascertain if these suture lines are open, united, or overlapping.

N Grooves or ridges between sections of the skull are normally palpated up to six months of age.

A Suture lines that overlap or override one another, giving the head an unusual shape, warrant further investigation.

P **Craniosynostosis** is premature ossification of suture lines, whereby there is early formation and fusion of skull bones. Craniosynostosis may be caused by metabolic disorders or may be a secondary consequence of microcephaly.

Surface Characteristics

E 1. With the finger pads, palpate the skull in the same manner as the fontanels and suture lines.

2. Note surface edema and contour of the cranium.

N The skin covering the cranium is flush against the skull and without edema.

A A softening of the outer layer of the cranial bones behind and above the ears combined with a ping-pong ball sensation as the area is pressed in gently with the fingers is indicative of **craniotabes**, an abnormal finding.

P Craniotabes is associated with rickets, syphilis, hydrocephaly, or hypervitaminosis A.

P A resonant or "cracked pot" sound is produced upon percussion of the skull in an older infant.

P This is Macewen's sign. It is a normal finding in young infants when the cranial sutures are open. After early infancy, hydrocephalus and other pathologies that cause increased intracranial pressure cause cranial suture separation. This is when Macewen's sign may be elicited.

A A localized, subcutaneous swelling over one of the cranial bones of a newborn is referred to as a **cephalhematoma** and is abnormal. This abnormality differs from other surface characteristics in that edema does not cross suture lines with this condition. Varying degrees of swelling can persist up to three months.

P Cephalhematomas acquired during forceps deliveries are due to subperiosteal bleeding and usually resolve within a couple of weeks, but may persist longer.

A Swelling over the occipitoparietal region of the skull is abnormal.

P **Caput succedaneum** results from pressure over the occipitoparietal region during a prolonged delivery. It usually resolves within one to two weeks after birth.

A **Moulding** can occur in conjunction with caput succedaneum.

P The parietal bone overrides the frontal bone as a result of induced pressure during delivery. It should resolve within one week of delivery.

Advanced Technique

Assessing for Hydrocephalus and Anencephaly: Transillumination of the Skull

Transillumination of the infant's head to rule out hydrocephalus or anencephaly can be performed as a temporary alternative to magnetic resonance imaging (MRI) or computerized tomography (CT) scan if head circumference is not within normal limits.

E 1. Support the child in an elevated or sitting position.

2. Darken the room.

continues

3. Place a flashlight with a soft, flexible, rubber end directly against the frontal, parietal, and occipital areas of the skull.

4. Note the size of the light over the various areas.

N A normal finding over the frontal and parietal bones is a circle of light no larger than 2 cm around the flashlight. Over the occipital area, a circle of light no larger than 1 cm is considered within normal limits. Normal findings are the same for light- and dark-skinned children.

A is abnormal for the illuminated area to be more than 1 cm in the occipital area, and 2 cm elsewhere.

P **Anencephaly** is an abnormal finding whereby the cortex or cranium does not develop. The fetal nervous system fails to develop normally. Between the 18th and 24th day of gestation, the neural tube fails to close, resulting in anencephaly. These patients usually do not live more than 24 hours.

P Excess fluid in the cranial vault, as in hydrocephalus, may lead to positive transillumination.

Eyes

General Approach

1. From infancy through about eight to ten years, assess the eyes toward the end of the assessment, with the exception of testing vision, which should be done first. Remember that the child's attention span is short, and attentiveness decreases the longer you evaluate. Children generally are not cooperative for eyes, ears, and throat assessments.

2. Place the young infant, preschooler, school-age, or adolescent patient on the examination table. The older infant or the toddler can be held by the caregiver.

3. Become proficient at performing fundoscopic assessments on adults prior to assessing the pediatric patient.

Vision Screening

General Approach

1. The adult Snellen chart can be used on children as young as six years, provided they are able to read the alphabet. The E chart is used for a patient over three years of age or any child who cannot read the alphabet (Figure 24-13).

2. Newborn to three months and six to 12 months: complete eye exam including red reflex and corneal light reflex; three to five years: complete eye exam including E acuity card or Allen chart. Test every two years until ten; every three years thereafter.[20]

3. If the child resists wearing a cover patch over the eye, make a game out of wearing the patch. For example, the young child could pretend to be a pirate exploring new territory. Use your imagination to think of a fantasy situation.

4. The Allen test (a series of seven pictures on different cards) can be used with children as young as two years of age.

Figure 24-13 Tumbling E Chart.

Tumbling E Chart

E 1. Ask the child to point an arm in the direction the E is pointing.
2. Observe for squinting.

| E | **Examination** | N | **Normal Findings** | A | **Abnormal Findings** | P | **Pathophysiology** |

N Vision is 20/40 from two to approximately six years of age, when it approaches the normal 20/20 acuity. Refer the patient to an ophthalmologist if results are greater than 20/40 in a child two to six years of age or 20/30 or greater in a child six years or older, or if results vary by two or more lines between eyes even if in the passing range.

A/P Chapter 12.

Allen Test

E 1. With the child's eyes both open, show each card to the child and elicit a name for each picture. Do not use any pictures with which the child is not familiar. Usually, the only pictures children have difficulty with are the 1940s vintage telephone and the Christmas tree if they do not celebrate this holiday.

2. Place the 2- to 3-year-old child 4.5 m (15 feet) from where you will be standing. Place the 3- to 4-year-old child 6 m (20 feet) from you.

3. Ask the caregiver to help cover one of the child's eyes.

4. With the child's eye covered and the child standing at the appropriate distance listed, show the pictures one at a time, eliciting a response after each showing.

5. Show the same pictures in different sequence for the other eye.

6. To record findings, the denominator is always constant at 30, because a child with normal vision should see the picture on the card (target) at 9 m (30 feet). To document the numerator, determine the greatest distance at which three of the pictures are recognized by each eye, for example, right eye = 15/30, left eye = 20/30.

N The child should correctly identify three of the cards in three trials. Two- to three-year-old children should have 15/30 vision. Three- to four-year-old children should be able to achieve a score of 15/30 to 20/30. Each eye should have the same score.

A/P If the scores for the patient's right and left eyes differ by 1.5 m (5 feet) or more or either or both eyes score less than 15/30, refer the patient to an ophthalmologist.

Strabismus Screening

The Hirschberg test and the cover-uncover test screen for strabismus. The latter is the more definitive test.

Hirschberg Test

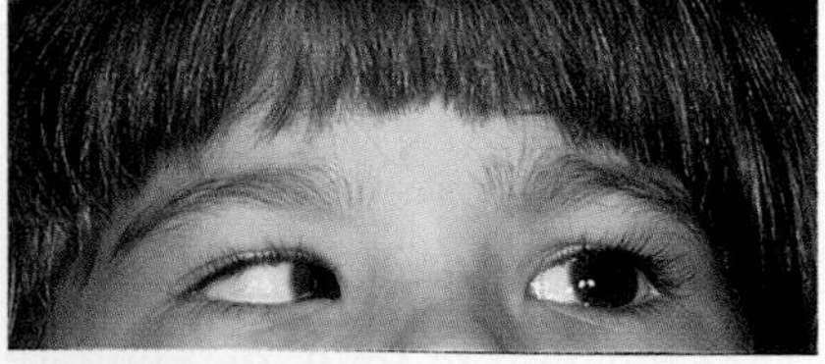

E/N See Chapter 12.

A It is abnormal for the light reflection to be displaced to the outer margin of the cornea as the eye deviates inward (Figure 24-14).

P Esotropia is thought to be congenital. Some theories suggest that neurological factors contribute to its development.

A It is abnormal for the light reflection to be displaced to the inner margin of the cornea as the eye deviates outward.

P Exotropia can result from eye muscle fatigue or can be congenital.

Figure 24-14 Infantile esotropia. *Courtesy of the Armed Forces Institute of Pathology.*

Cover-Uncover Test

E See Chapter 12.

N Neither eye moves when the occluder is being removed. Infants less than six months of age display strabismus due to poor neuromuscular control of eye muscles.

A It is abnormal for one or both eyes to move to focus on the penlight during assessment. Assume strabismus is present.

P Strabismus after six months of age is abnormal and indicates eye muscle weakness.

Inspection

Eyelids

E   1. Sit at the patient's eye level.
     2. Observe for symmetrical palpebral fissures and position of eyelids in relation to the iris.

N   The palpebral fissures of both eyes are positioned symmetrically. The upper eyelid normally covers a small portion of the iris, and the lower lid meets the iris. Epicanthal folds are normally present in children of Asian descent.

A   It is abnormal for a portion of the sclera to be seen above the iris.

P   The sclera is exposed above the iris in hydrocephalus. As the forehead becomes prominent, the eyebrows and eyelids are drawn up, creating a "setting sun" appearance of the child's eyes.

A   A fold of skin covering the inner canthus and lacrimal caruncle is abnormal.

P   During embryonic development, the fold of skin slants in a downward direction toward the nose. This is found in a child with Down syndrome. Epicanthal folds and short palpebral fissures are seen in a child with fetal alcohol syndrome.

Lacrimal Apparatus

E/N   See Chapter 12.

A   The patient's caregiver reports that the child is unable to produce tears, an abnormal finding.

P   The lacrimal ducts should be patent by three months of age. Dacryocystitis results when the distal end of the membranous lacrimal duct fails to open or a blockage occurs elsewhere.

Anterior Segment Structures

Sclera

E   See Chapter 12.

N   The newborn exhibits a bluish-tinged sclera related to thinness of the fibrous tissue. The sclera is white in light-skinned children and a slightly darker colour in some dark-skinned children.

A/P   See Chapter 12.

Iris

E   Conduct the examination in the same manner as for an adult.

N   Up to about six months of age, the colour of the iris is blue or slate grey in light-skinned infants and brownish in dark-skinned infants. Between six and 12 months of age, complete transition of iris colour has occurred.

A   Small white flecks, called **Brushfield's spots**, noted around the perimeter of the iris are abnormal.

P   Brushfield's spots are found on the iris of the patient with Down syndrome. The spots develop during embryonic maturation.

Pupils

E   See Chapter 12.

N   When the pupils' reaction to light is assessed, a newborn will normally blink and flex the head closer to the body. This is called the optical blink reflex.

A/P   See Chapter 12.

| E | Examination | N | Normal Findings | A | Abnormal Findings | P | Pathophysiology |

Posterior Segment Structures

General Approach
1. Observe the red reflex, retina, and optic disc.
2. The assessment is easier to accomplish if the infant or toddler is lying supine on an examination table. The assistance of another individual, such as the caregiver, to hold the patient in position is essential. The older patient may be allowed to sit, if cooperative.

Inspection

Red Reflex
E/N See Chapter 12.

A An absent red reflex is abnormal.

P Chromosomal disorders, intrauterine infections, and ocular trauma are possible causes of cataracts in newborns.

A A yellowish or white light reflex (cat's eye reflex) is abnormal.

P Retinoblastoma is a malignant glioma located in the posterior chamber of the eye.

Retina
E/N See Chapter 12.

A A red to dark-red colour is abnormal. Some areas may be rounded or flame shaped.

P Retinal hemorrhage is seen in trauma. Bleeding into the optic nerve sheath is found in children who have been physically shaken. This is called shaken-baby syndrome.

Optic Disc
E/N/A/P See Chapter 12.

Ears

Auditory Testing

General Approach
Hearing tests are available for children under three years of age. Referral to a local audiology department is made if the family or caretaker of the child responds with a "no" to any of the following indicators:

a. Does the child react to a loud noise?
b. Does the child react to the caregiver's voice by cooing, smiling, or turning eyes and head toward the voice?
c. Does the child try to imitate sounds?
d. Can the child imitate words and sounds?
e. Can the child follow directions?
f. Does the child respond to sounds not directed at him or her?

Perform auditory testing at about age three to four years of age or when the child can follow directions.

External Ear

Inspection of Pinna Position
E/N See Chapter 13.

A The top of the ear is below the imaginary line drawn from the outer canthus to the top of the ear.

P Kidneys and ears are formed at the same time in embryonic development. If a child's ears are low set, renal anomalies must be ruled out. Low-set ears can also occur in Down syndrome.

Internal Ear

Inspection

E 1. A cooperative patient may be allowed to sit for the assessment. A young child may be held as shown in Figure 24-15A.

2. Restrain the uncooperative young patient by placing him or her supine on a firm surface (Figure 24-15B). Instruct the caregiver or assistant to hold the patient's arms up near the head, embracing the elbow joints on both sides of either arm. Restrain the infant by having the caregiver hold the infant's hands down (see Figure 24-15C).

3. With your thumb and forefinger grasping the otoscope, use the lateral side of the hand to prevent the head from jerking. Your other hand can also be used to stabilize the patient's head.

4. Pull the lower auricle down and out to straighten the canal. This technique is used in children up to about three years of age. Use the adult technique after age 3.

5. Insert the speculum about 6–12 mm, depending on the patient's age.

6. Suspected otitis media must be evaluated with a pneumatic bulb attached to the side of the otoscope's light source.

7. Select a larger speculum to make a tight seal and prevent air from escaping from the canal.

8. Gently squeeze the bulb attachment to introduce air into the canal.

9. Observe the tympanic membrane for movement.

N/A/P See Chapter 13.

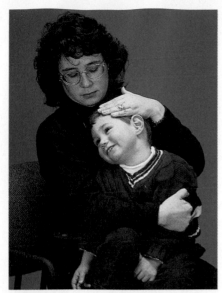

A. Preschooler in a Sitting Position

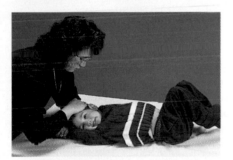

B. Preschooler in a Supine Position

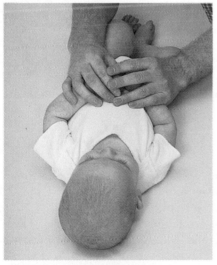

C. Infant in a Supine Position

Figure 24-15 Restraining the Child for the Otoscopic Examination.

Mouth and Throat

Inspection

Lips

E 1. Follow the same technique described in Chapter 13.

2. Observe if the lip edges meet.

N The lip edges should meet.

A It is abnormal if the lip edges do not meet.

P Cleft palates vary greatly in size and extent of malformation. They can be unilateral or bilateral relative to the midline of the palate. The cleft may involve the soft or hard palate, or both. If associated with cleft lip, the malformation may extend through the palates and into the nasal cavity. Cleft palates form between the sixth and tenth week of embryonic development, during fusion of the maxillary and premaxillary processes. Genetics plays a small role in etiology.

A A thin upper lip is abnormal.

P A child with fetal alcohol syndrome exhibits this finding, as well as a flat and elongated philtrum.

Buccal Mucosa

E Use the same technique as for an adult. If the patient is unable to open the mouth on command, use the edge of a tongue blade to lift the upper lip and move the lower lip down.

N See Chapter 13.

E	Examination	N	Normal Findings	A	Abnormal Findings	P	Pathophysiology

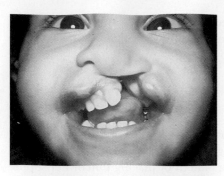

Figure 24-16 Cleft Lip. *Courtesy of Dr. Joseph Konzelman, School of Dentistry, Medical College of Georgia.*

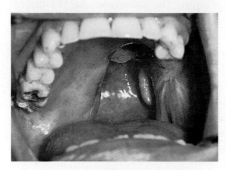

Figure 24-17 Cleft Palate. *Courtesy of Dr. Joseph Konzelman, School of Dentistry, Medical College of Georgia.*

A A thick, curdlike coating on the buccal mucosa or tongue is abnormal.

P Thrush can be acquired when a newborn passes through the vagina during delivery.

Teeth

E/N See Chapter 13.

A A lack of visible teeth coupled with roentgenographic findings revealing absence of tooth buds is abnormal.

P Absence of deciduous teeth beyond 16 months of age signifies an abnormality most commonly related to genetic causes.

A It is abnormal for the teeth to turn brownish black, possibly with indentations along the surfaces of the teeth.

P Carbohydrate-rich fluid (from milk or juice) causes severe caries when a child falls asleep with a bottle in the mouth.

Hard and Soft Palate

E 1. Observe the palate for continuity and shape.
   2. For infants, you will need to use a tongue depressor to push the tongue down. Infants usually cry in response to this action, which allows visualization of the palates.

N The roof of the mouth is continuous and has a slight arch.

A It is abnormal if the roof of the mouth is not continuous. This anomaly is called cleft palate (Figure 24-17).

P Cleft palates vary greatly in size and extent of malformation. They can be unilateral or bilateral relative to the midline of the palate. The cleft may involve the soft or hard palates or both. If associated with cleft lip, the malformation may extend through the palates and into the nasal cavity. Cleft palates form between the sixth and tenth week of embryonic development, during fusion of the maxillary and premaxillary processes. Genetics plays a small role in etiology.

A The roof of the mouth is abnormally arched. On inspection, the shape resembles an upside down letter V.

P High palates are usually associated with a particular syndrome. Examples include trisomy 21, trisomy 18, and Noonan syndrome.

A **Epstein's pearls** in the newborn appear on the hard palate and gum margins and are abnormal. The pearls are small, white cysts that feel hard when palpated.

P These cysts result from fragments of epithelial tissue trapped during palate formation.

Oropharynx

E See Chapter 13.

N Up to the age of 12 years, a tonsil grade of 2+ is considered normal. Around puberty, tonsillar tissue regresses. Tonsils should not interfere with the act of breathing.

A Excessive salivation is an early sign of a tracheoesophageal fistula (TEF). Drooling is accompanied by choking and coughing during the patient's feeding.

P The esophagus failed to develop as a continuous passage during embryonic formation.

A Exudative pharyngitis is present in infectious mononucleosis. Other symptoms include fever, sore throat, splenomegaly, petechiae on the palate, and cervical adenitis.

P Mononucleosis is caused by the Epstein-Barr virus.

A Hypertrophy of lymphoid tissue occurs in the posterior pharyngeal wall causing a condition known as enlarged or hypertrophied adenoids.

P Excessive lymphoid tissue interferes with passage of air through the nose, resulting in snoring and apnea. Obstruction of the eustachian tubes by enlarged lymphoid tissue can lead to otitis media. Sinusitis can occur when lymphoid tissue blocks the clearance of nasal mucous.

Neck

Inspection

General Appearance

E 1. Observe the neck in a midline position while the patient is sitting upright.
   2. Note shortening or thickness of the neck on both right and left sides.
   3. Note any swelling.

N There is a reasonable amount of skin tissue on the sides of the neck. There is no swelling.

A Additional weblike tissue found bilaterally from the ear to the shoulder is abnormal.

P Webbed necks are associated with congenital syndromes. One example is Turner syndrome, noted in female children.

A Unilateral or bilateral swelling of the neck below the angle of the jaw is abnormal (Figure 24-18).

P Enlargement of the parotid gland occurs in parotitis, or mumps, an inflammation of the parotid gland. There is pain and tenderness in the affected area.

A Torticollis is observed.

P Torticollis can be congenital and acquired. An infant who is always placed on the same side when supine can develop a lateral deviation at the neck with decreased range of motion.

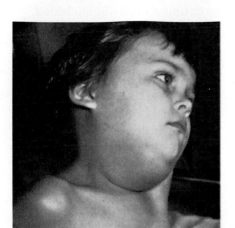

Figure 24-18 Parotitis (mumps). *Courtesy of Centers for Disease Control and Prevention (CDC).*

Palpation

Thyroid

E 1. Use the same technique as for an adult with the exception of using the first two finger pads on both hands.
   2. Have the younger child who is unable to swallow on command take a drink from a bottle or cup.

N/A/P The normal findings, abnormal findings, and pathophysiology are the same as for an adult.

Lymph Nodes

E 1. Because of the infant's short neck, extend the patient's chin upward with your hand before proceeding with palpation.
   2. With the finger pads, palpate the submental, submandibular, tonsillar, anterior cervical chain, posterior cervical chain, supraclavicular, preauricular, posterior auricular, and occipital lymph nodes.
   3. Use a circular motion. Note location, size, shape, tenderness, mobility, and associated skin inflammation of any swollen nodes palpated.

N Lymph nodes are generally not palpable. Children often have small, movable, cool, non-tender nodes referred to as "shotty" nodes. These benign nodes are related to environmental antigen exposure or residual effects of a prior illness and have no clinical significance.

A Enlargement of the anterior cervical chain is abnormal.

P This occurs in bacterial infections of the pharynx (strep throat) or viral infections (mononucleosis).

A Enlargement of the occipital nodes or posterior cervical chain nodes is abnormal.

P This can occur in infectious mononucleosis, tinea capitis, and acute otitis externa.

| E | Examination | N | Normal Findings | A | Abnormal Findings | P | Pathophysiology |

Breasts

Inspection of the breasts is performed throughout childhood. Palpation is not usually performed on the patient until puberty, unless otherwise indicated.

Sexual Maturity Rating (SMR)

E   1. Using the Tanner stages in Table 14-1 on page 436, assess the developmental stage of a female's breasts.

N   Breast development usually starts between the ages of eight and ten and is complete after 14 to 17 years of age.

A   A SMR that is less than expected for a female's age is abnormal.

P   Pituitary pathology needs to be considered, as well as familial predisposition.

Thorax and Lungs

General Approach

1. Remove the patient's clothes or gown.
2. Keep the infant warm during the assessment by placing a blanket over the chest until ready for this portion of assessment.

Inspection

Shape of Thorax

E   See Chapter 15.

N   The infant has a barrel chest; by age 6, the chest attains the adult configuration.

A   If a school-age child has an abnormal chest configuration, suspect pathology.

P   In addition to the conditions discussed in Chapter 15, cystic fibrosis can lead to an altered anteroposterior-transverse diameter.

Retractions

E   1. In children, it is important to evaluate intercostal muscles for signs of increased work of breathing.
       2. If at all possible, perform this examination when the patient is quiet because forceful crying will mimic retractions.

N   Retractions are not present.

A   In respiratory distress, retractions are seen as an inward collapse of the chest wall. Retractions can be seen in the suprasternal, supraclavicular, subcostal, and intercostal regions of the chest wall. Other signs of respiratory distress include but are not limited to nasal flaring, stridor, expiratory grunting, and wheezing.

P   Respiratory distress is a result of abnormal function or disruption of the respiratory pathway or within organs that control or influence respiration. Infants with respiratory syncytial virus (RSV) frequently present with retractions.

Palpation

Tactile Fremitus

Fremitus is easily felt when a child cries. If the infant or young patient is not crying, it is advisable to defer this procedure until later in the assessment, perhaps after the throat and ear examinations, which usually produce crying.

Percussion

E   See Chapter 15.

N   Normal diaphragmatic excursion in infants and young toddlers is one to two intercostal spaces.

A/P See Chapter 15.

Auscultation

Breath Sounds

E   Use the same assessment techniques as for an adult. Sometimes it is difficult to differentiate the various adventitious sounds because a child's respiratory rate is rapid; for example, differentiating expiratory wheezing from inspiratory wheezing can be difficult. Mastering the technique takes time and practice.

N   Of the three types of breath sounds—bronchial, bronchovesicular, and vesicular—the bronchovesicular are normally heard throughout the peripheral lung fields up to five to six years of age, because the chest wall is thin with decreased musculature. Lung fields are clear and equal bilaterally.

A   Crackles are abnormal.

P   Conditions such as bronchiolitis, CF, and bronchopulmonary dysplasia produce crackles.

A   Wheezing is abnormal.

P   Patients with CF and bronchiolitis may present with wheezing. Infants with RSV usually present with wheezing.

Heart and Peripheral Vasculature

General Approach

1. It is best to perform the cardiac assessment near the beginning of the examination, when the infant or young child is relatively calm.

2. Do not get discouraged during the assessment. The novice nurse is not expected to identify a murmur and location within the cardiac cycle. Be patient because skill will come only with practice.

3. During the assessment, note physical signs of a syndrome such as Down's facies in a child with trisomy 21 or Down syndrome. Many children with Down syndrome have associated atrioventricular (A-V) canal malformations. These defects each involve an atrial septal defect (ASD), ventricular septal defect (VSD), and a common A-V valve.

4. Cardiac landmarks change when a child has dextrocardia. In this condition, the apex of the heart points toward the right thoracic cavity, thus heart sounds are auscultated primarily on the right side of the chest.

Inspection

Apical Impulse

E   See Chapter 16.

N   In both infants and toddlers, the apical impulse is located at the fourth intercostal space and just left of the midclavicular line. The apical impulse of a child seven years or older is at the fifth intercostal space and to the right of the midclavicular line. The impulse may not be visible in all children, especially in those who have increased adipose tissue or muscle.

A/P See Chapter 16.

| E | Examination | N | Normal Findings | A | Abnormal Findings | P | Pathophysiology |

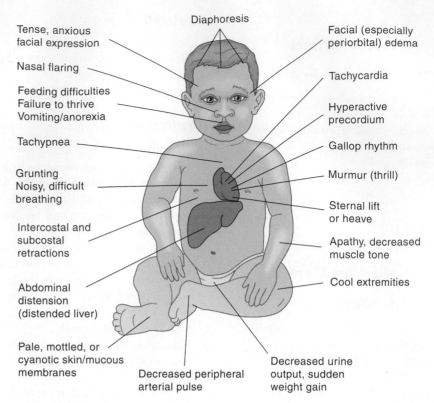

Figure 24-19 Infant with Congestive Heart Failure.

Diaphoresis

Tense, anxious facial expression

Nasal flaring

Feeding difficulties
Failure to thrive
Vomiting/anorexia

Tachypnea

Grunting
Noisy, difficult breathing

Intercostal and subcostal retractions

Abdominal distension (distended liver)

Pale, mottled, or cyanotic skin/mucous membranes

Facial (especially periorbital) edema

Tachycardia

Hyperactive precordium

Gallop rhythm

Murmur (thrill)

Sternal lift or heave

Apathy, decreased muscle tone

Cool extremities

Decreased peripheral arterial pulse

Decreased urine output, sudden weight gain

Precordium

E Observe the chest wall for any movements other than the apical impulse.

N Movements other than the apical impulse are abnormal.

A Lifting of the cardiac area is abnormal.

P Heaves are associated with volume overload. A child with congenital heart disease is at risk for developing congestive heart failure (CHF) with associated volume overload. Figure 24-19 depicts the manifestations of CHF in children. Large left-to-right shunt defects, such as a VSD, cause right ventricular volume overload.

Palpation

Thrill

E 1. Palpate as for an adult or use the proximal one-third of each finger and the areas over the metacarpophalangeal joints. Many nurses believe the latter method yields greater sensitivity to the presence of thrills.
  2. Place the hand vertically along the heart's apex and move the hand toward the sternum.
  3. Place the hand horizontally along the sternum, moving up the sternal border about 1.25 to 2.5 cm each time.
  4. When at the clavicular level, place the hand vertically and assess for a thrill at the heart's base.
  5. Use the finger pads to palpate a thrill at the suprasternal notch and along the carotid arteries.

N A thrill is not found in the healthy child.

A/P See Chapter 16.

Peripheral Pulses

E 1. Use the same finger to assess each peripheral pulse. The sensation of one finger pad versus another can be different.

2. Use the finger pads to palpate each pair of peripheral pulses simultaneously, except for the carotid pulse.

3. Palpate the brachial and femoral pulses simultaneously.

N Pulse qualities are the same in the adult and the child.

A A brachial-femoral lag, when femoral pulses are weaker than brachial pulses when palpated simultaneously, is abnormal.

P Coarctation is due to a narrowing of the aorta before, at, or just beyond the entrance of the ductus arteriosus. Thus, blood flow to the lower body is reduced.

Auscultation

Heart Sounds

Auscultating the infant's or the young pediatric patient's heart is difficult because the heart rate is rapid and breath sounds are easily transmitted through the chest wall.

E 1. Have the child lie down. If this position is not possible, the child should be held at a 45° angle in the caregiver's arms.

2. Use the Z pattern to auscultate the heart. Place the stethoscope in the apical area and gradually move it toward the right lower sternal border and up the sternal border in a right diagonal line. Move gradually from the patient's left to the right upper sternal borders (Figure 24-20).

3. Perform a second evaluation with the child in a sitting position.

N Fifty percent of all children develop an innocent murmur at some time in their lives. See Table 24-5. Innocent murmurs are accentuated in high cardiac output states such as fever, stress, or pregnancy. When the patient is sitting, murmurs are heard early in systole at the second or third intercostal space along the left sternal border and are softly musical in quality; they disappear when the patient lies down. Be aware of sinus arrhythmias during

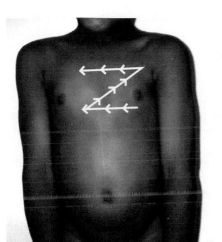

Figure 24-20 Z Auscultation Pattern for Young Children.

TABLE 24-5	Innocent Heart Murmurs			
TYPE	**AGE**	**INTENSITY/LOCATION**	**QUALITY**	**Other Characteristics**
Stills	>2 yrs	<III/VI midsystolic located at LMSB or between LLSB and apex	Twanging, squeaking, buzzing, musical, or vibratory sound	Low frequency heard with the bell with patient in supine position, softer when the patient is standing
Pulmonary ejection	8–14 yrs	<III/VI, early-midsystolic located at LUSB	Slightly grating, little radiation	Ejection-type murmur
Pulmonary flow murmur of the newborn	Low birthweight newborn	I-II/VI with wide transmission, audible at LUSB	Rough	Disappears at 3–6 months of age
Venous hum	3–6 yrs	<III/VI continuous murmur, audible in right or left infraclavicular and supraclavicular areas	Humming	Originates from turbulence in jugular venous system, heard in upright position, disappears in supine position, obliterated by rotating the head or gently occluding neck veins

| E | Examination | N | Normal Findings | A | Abnormal Findings | P | Pathophysiology |

auscultation of the heart's rhythm. On inspiration, the pulse rate speeds up, the pulse rate slows with expiration. To determine if the rhythm is normal, ask the child to hold his or her breath while you auscultate the heart. If the pulse stops varying with respirations, then a sinus arrhythmia is present. S_1 is best heard at the apex of the heart, left lower sternal border. S_2 is best heard at the heart base.

A A split S_2 sound is abnormal.

P If the S_2 split is fixed with the act of respiration, you can suspect an atrial septal defect. In children, S_2 physiologically splits with inspiration and becomes single with expiration. This phenomenon is due to a greater negative pressure in the thoracic cavity.

A In children, S_3 often sounds like the three syllables of the word "Kentucky," especially when accompanied by tachycardia.

P A loud third heart sound may be present in children with CHF or VSDs. S_3 is produced by rapid filling of the ventricle.

A With tachycardia, S_4 sounds like a gallop resembling the word "Tennessee."

P S_4 is not normally heard in children. If detected, aortic stenosis may be present. The left ventricle's ability to pump blood through the stenotic valve produces a dilation within the left ventricular muscle resulting in decreased ventricular compliance.

A A systolic ejection murmur is heard between the first and second heart sounds over the aortic or pulmonic areas.

P Ejection murmurs occur in aortic and pulmonic valvular stenosis. The murmur is the result of blood passing through stenotic valves.

A Holosystolic murmurs are heard maximally at the left lower sternal border. They begin with S_1 and continue until the second heart sound, S_2, is heard.

P Holosystolic or pansystolic murmurs are heard in children with VSDs, where blood flows from a chamber of higher pressure to one of lower pressure during systole.

A Diastolic murmurs are heard between S_2 and S_1.

P Diastolic murmurs are classified into early diastolic, mid-diastolic, and presystolic. Early diastolic murmurs are high pitched and blowing. They occur in aortic regurgitation and subaortic stenosis. A mid-diastolic murmur is a low-pitched rumble. These occur in mitral stenosis or VSDs with large left to right shunts. A presystolic murmur is heard in patients with mitral stenosis or tricuspid stenosis.

A Continuous murmurs heard throughout the cardiac cycle are abnormal.

P Collateral blood flow murmurs are heard radiating throughout the back, such as in pulmonary atresia.

P Continuous murmurs are present in coronary artery fistulas.

P Palliative shunt murmurs are normal and should be heard; if they are not heard, there is a possibility of a clotted shunt. These murmurs are heard over the right or left upper chest in the respective area where surgically placed. A palliative shunt is created temporarily until the patient is ready for corrective surgery. A palliative shunt may be needed in a small infant with a combination of Tetralogy of Fallot and pulmonary atresia or a hypoplastic pulmonary artery.

Advanced Technique

Assessing for Coarctation of the Aorta

If coarctation of the aorta is suspected (as when a brachial-femoral lag is present or with upper extremity hypertension or absent or decreased pedal pulses), obtain blood pressures and compare the right upper and left lower extremity readings.

continues

E 1. Take the upper extremity blood pressure in the right arm.

   2. Because weak or absent leg pulses accompany coarctation, measurements are difficult to obtain. Use a Doppler transducer to intensify the sound of the pulse. Until you feel proficient, the Doppler technique requires two people for accurate measurement; have the caregiver hold the child's leg still while you assess the pulse.

   3. Locate the right posterior tibial pulse with the Doppler transducer and make an "X" with a pen where the pulse is felt or heard.

   4. Obtain the blood pressure measurement in the left leg with the cuff 1.25 to 2.5 cm above the pulse location. Only the systolic number is obtained with this technique.

   5. Repeat the steps on the left side of body.

N Upper and lower extremity blood pressures are equal.

A If the systolic blood pressure in the leg is lower than that in the arm and femoral, popliteal, posterior tibial, or dorsalis pedis pulses are weak or absent, assume coarctation of the aorta is present. If undiagnosed, as the child becomes older, the upper extremity pulses become bounding.

P During the fifth or sixth week of embryonic development, the aorta may form abnormally.

Abdomen

General Approach

1. If possible, ask the caregiver to refrain from feeding the infant prior to the assessment because palpation of a full stomach may induce vomiting.
2. Children who are physically able should be encouraged to empty the bladder prior to the assessment.
3. The young infant, school-age child, or adolescent should lie on the examination table. Have the caregiver hold the toddler or preschooler supine on the lap, with the lower extremities bent at the knees and dangling.
4. If the child is crying, encourage the caregiver to help calm the child before you proceed with the assessment.
5. Observe non-verbal communication in children who are not able to verbally express feelings. During palpation, listen for a high-pitched cry and look for a change in facial expression or for sudden protective movements that may indicate a painful or tender area.

Inspection

Contour
E See Chapter 17.
N The young child may have a "potbelly."

Peristaltic Wave
E/N See Chapter 17.
A Visible peristaltic waves seen moving across the epigastrium from left to right are abnormal.
P Obstruction at the pyloric sphincter causes a condition called pyloric stenosis. The pyloric muscle hypertrophies, causing obstruction during embryonic development.

Auscultation

After performing auscultation of the lungs, it is helpful to proceed to auscultating the abdomen because doing so allows you to complete a good portion of

---

Nursing Tip

Assessing for Umbilical Hernias in Children

If the child is upset and crying, assess the umbilicus for an outward projection, which is indicative of an umbilical hernia. If an umbilical hernia is present, palpate the area to determine if the hernia reduces easily. Approximate the size of the inner ring (the diameter of the hernia).

E **Examination**   N **Normal Findings**   A **Abnormal Findings**   P **Pathophysiology**

auscultation all at once. If the child is not cooperating, a simple distracting phrase such as "I can hear your breakfast in there" can be helpful during auscultation.

Palpation

General Palpation

A/P See Chapter 17.

A On palpation, an olive-shaped mass felt in the epigastric area and to the upper right of the umbilicus is abnormal.

P This is indicative of pyloric stenosis.

A Abdominal distension coupled with palpable stool over the abdomen and the absence of stool in the rectum is abnormal.

P An aganglionic segment of the colon is responsible for Hirschsprung's disease, which produces abnormal gastrointestinal findings.

A A sausage-shaped mass that produces intermittent pain when palpated in the upper abdomen is abnormal.

P **Intussusception** occurs when the ileocecal region of the intestine prolapses down into the ileum itself (sometimes called telescoping). The telescoping proximal portion of bowel (e.g., intussusceptum) invaginates into the adjacent distal bowel (i.e., intussuscipiens). Classic symptoms are vomiting and stool mixed with blood and mucus.

A Bowel sounds heard in the thoracic cavity, a scaphoid abdomen, an upward displaced apical impulse, and signs of respiratory distress are abnormal findings in the newborn.

P In approximately the eighth week of embryonic development, the diaphragm fails to fuse, creating a **diaphragmatic hernia**. This condition results in protrusion of the intestines into the thoracic cavity.

Liver Palpation

E For infants and toddlers, use the outer edge of your right thumb to press down and scoop up at the right upper quadrant. For the remaining age groups, use the same technique as for an adult.

N **The liver is not normally palpated, although the liver edge can be found 1 cm below the right costal margin in a normal, healthy child. The liver edge is soft and regular.**

A It is abnormal for the liver edge to be palpated more than 1 cm below the right costal margin and be full with a firm, sharp border.

P Hepatomegaly occurs in several disease states such as viral or bacterial illnesses, tumours, congestive heart failure, and fat and glycogen storage diseases. Viral and bacterial illnesses and tumours cause liver cells to multiply in number, creating an enlarged liver. In heart failure, the hepatic veins and sinusoids enlarge from congestion, resulting in hemorrhage and fibrosis of the liver. In fat and glycogen storage diseases, fat and glycogen accumulate within the liver, and fibrosis ensues.

Musculoskeletal System

General Approach

1. The extent or degree of assessment depends greatly on the patient's or caregiver's complaints of musculoskeletal problems. Be aware that during periods of rapid growth, children complain of normal muscle aches.

2. Try to incorporate musculoskeletal assessment techniques into other system assessments. For instance, while inspecting the integument, inspect the muscles and joints.

3. Inspecting the musculoskeletal system in the ambulatory child is accomplished by allowing the child to move freely about and play in the examination room

while you inquire about the health history. Your observations of the child enable you to assess posture, muscle symmetry, and range of motion of muscles and joints.

4. Do not rush through the assessment. Throughout the assessment, incorporate game playing that facilitates evaluation of the musculoskeletal system.

5. Observe range of motion and joint flexibility as the child undresses.

Inspection

Muscles

E 1. Have the child disrobe down to a diaper or underwear.

2. To evaluate the small infant's shoulder muscles, place your hands under the axillae and pull the infant into a standing position. The infant should not slip through your hands. Be prepared to catch the infant if needed.

3. Evaluate the infant's leg strength in a semi-standing position. Lower the infant to the examination table so the infant's legs touch the table.

4. Place the infant older than four months in a prone position. Observe the infant's ability to lift the upper body off the examination table using the upper extremities.

N Degree of joint flexibility and range of motion are the same for the child as for the adult.

A Increased muscle tone (spasticity) is abnormal.

P Cerebral palsy (CP) results from a non-progressive abnormality in the pyramidal motor tract. One of the more common contributing factors, perinatal asphyxia, causes abnormal posture and gross motor development and varying degrees of abnormal muscle tone.

A The inability to rise from a sitting to a standing position is abnormal. In attempting to rise from a supine position, the child first turns over onto the abdomen and raises the trunk to a crawling position. Then, with the aid of the arms, the child places the feet firmly on the floor and gradually elevates the upper part of the body by climbing up the legs with the arms.

P This is called Gower's sign. Gower's sign occurs in Duchenne's muscular dystrophy (MD) early in childhood. Genetics is responsible for the abnormality in the short arm of the X chromosome.

Joints

E See Chapter 18.

N The infant's spine is C-shaped. Head control and standing create the normal S-shaped spine of the adult. Lordosis is normal as the child begins to walk. A toddler's protruding abdomen is counterbalanced by an inward deviation of the lumbar spine.

A Extra fingers or toes are abnormal.

P Supernumerary digits, or polydactyly, may be found in certain congenital syndromes such as Carpenter, fetal hydantoin, orofaciodigital, Smith-Lemli-Opitz, trisomy 13, and VATER.

A A fusion between two or more digits is abnormal.

P Syndactylism is also associated with certain congenital syndromes such as Aarskog, Apert, Carpenter, orofaciodigital, Russell-Silver, and acrocephalosyndactyly. Look for other physical signs of a syndrome if either syndactyly or polydactyly is present.

A It is abnormal for a young child usually two to 12 years old to present with a painless limp from the affected hip. The limp is accompanied by limited abduction and internal rotation, muscle spasm, and proximal thigh atrophy.

E	Examination	N	Normal Findings	A	Abnormal Findings	P	Pathophysiology

P Legg-Calvé-Perthes disease, also called coxa plana, is caused by an interruption in the blood supply to the capital femoral epiphysis. Avascular necrosis of the femoral head results.

A An exaggerated lumbar curvature of the spine is abnormal after six years of age.

P Lordosis can be attributed to bilateral developmental dislocation of the hip or postural factors such as progression of congenital kyphosis, or can occur secondary to contractures of hip flexors.

Tibiofemoral Bones

E 1. Instruct the child to stand on the examination table with the medial condyles together.
   2. Stand at eye level with the patient's knees.
   3. Measure the distance between the two medial malleoli.
   4. Measure the distance between the two medial condyles.

N **The distance between the medial malleoli is less than 5 cm. The distance between the medial condyles is less than 2.5 cm. Knock knees, or genu valgum, is common between two and four years of age. Bowleg, or genu varum, is normally present in many infants up to 12 months of age.**

A Genu valgum persisting after six years of age is abnormal. The distance between the medial condyles is less than 2.5 cm and the distance between the medial malleoli is more than 5 cm.

P The cause of genu valgum is usually physiological.

A The measured distance between the two medial condyles is greater than 2.5–5 cm.

P Genu varum persisting after two years of age is abnormal and may be caused by rickets.

Palpation

Joints

E/N See Chapter 18.

A Knee pain aggravated by any motion or activity that puts undue pressure on the joint is abnormal. Palpation of a slight elevation of the tibial tuberosity is abnormal.

P The deformed tubercle in Osgood-Schlatter disease is caused by repetitive stress on the area. A fibrocartilage microfracture may cause joint pain.

A Swollen, inflamed, painful joints are abnormal.

P Juvenile rheumatoid arthritis causes synovial inflammation and degeneration of the joint. Its cause is unknown.

Feet

E 1. Place the patient on the examination table or caregiver's lap.
   2. Stand in front of the child.
   3. Hold the right heel immobile with one hand while pushing the forefoot (medial base of great toe) toward a midline position with the other hand.
   4. Observe for toe and forefoot adduction and inversion.
   5. Repeat on the left foot.

N **The toes and forefoot are not deviated.**

A Toes or forefeet that are deviated are abnormal.

P **Metatarsus varus** is a medial forefoot malignment. In **talipes equinovarus** (clubfoot), there is heel inversion, forefoot adduction and plantar flexion of the foot. Heredity plays a role in the etiology as well as abnormal intrauterine position of the fetal foot.

Hip and Femur

Ortolani's manoeuvre is always performed at the very end of the assessment because it may produce crying. The test is performed on one hip at a time.

Nursing Tip

Palpating Muscle Strength in Children

Playing games will assist you if the child is resistant to formal examination. For example, you can test plantar flexion by asking the child to pretend that the feet are pushing the brake on a car while you bear the force with your hands.

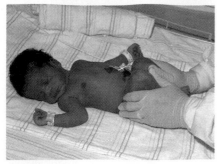

A. Hand Placement

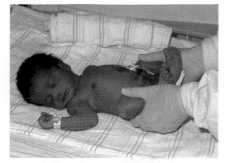

B. Hip Abduction

Figure 24-21 Ortolani Manoeuvre.

Evaluate the hips up until 18 months of age or until the child is an established walker.

E   1. Place the infant supine on an examination table with the feet facing you.
    2. Stand directly in front of the infant.
    3. With the thumb hold the inner thigh of the femur, and with the index and middle fingers hold the greater trochanter (Figure 24-21A). These two fingers should rest over the hip joint.
    4. Slowly press outward and abduct until the lateral aspects of the knees nearly touch the table (see Figure 24-21B). The tips of the fingers should palpate each femora's head as it rotates outward.
    5. Listen for an audible clunk (Ortolani's sign).
    6. With the fingers in the same locations, adduct the hips to elicit a palpable clunk (Ortolani's sign). As each hip is adducted, it is lifted anteriorly into the acetabulum.
    7. Place both of the infant's feet flat on the examination table with the knees together.
    8. Observe the height of the knees. This is called Allis sign.
    9. Turn the infant to a prone position and observe the levels of the gluteal folds.

N   A clunk is not audible or palpated. The knees should be at the same height with the feet on the examination table. The gluteal folds are approximately at the same level.

P   Abnormal findings include a positive Ortolani's sign, a sudden, painful cry during the test, asymmetrical thigh skin folds, uneven knee level, and limited hip abduction.

P   Epidemiology of **developmental dislocation of the hip** (DDII) is related to familial factors, maternal hormones associated with pelvic laxity, firstborn children, oligohydramnios, and breech presentations.

A   Knees that are not at the same level are abnormal.

P   This is another technique that can potentially detect DDH.

A   Unequal gluteal folds are abnormal.

P   This also can lead to a finding of DDH.

Neurological System

General Approach

1. Some aspects of the neurological assessment are different for the infant and the young child as compared to the adult. An infant functions mainly at the subcortical level. Memory and motor coordination are about three-quarters developed by two years of age, when cortical functioning is acquiring dominance.
2. Incorporate findings for fine and gross motor skills previously tested during the musculoskeletal assessment. Refer to normal developmental milestones (see Chapter 4) and extrapolate warning signs of neurological development lag.
3. Because the infant cannot verbally express level of consciousness, instead assess the newborn's ability to cry, level of activity, positioning, and general appearance.
4. Only reflex mechanisms and cranial nerve testing are described in this section. Refer to the adult neurological assessment for all other testing.

Reflex Mechanisms of the Infant

Neonatal reflexes must be lost before motor development can proceed.

| E | **Examination** | N | **Normal Findings** | A | **Abnormal Findings** | P | **Pathophysiology** |

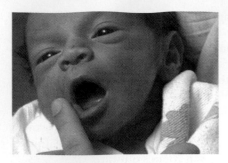

Figure 24-22 Rooting Reflex.

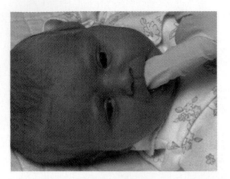

Figure 24-23 Sucking Reflex.

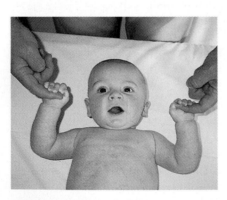

Figure 24-24 Palmar Reflex.

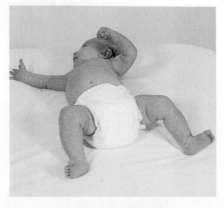

Figure 24-25 Tonic Neck Reflex.

Rooting Reflex

E **1.** Place the infant supine with the head in a midline position.
   2. With your forefinger, stroke the skin located at one corner of the mouth (Figure 24-22).
   3. Observe movement of the head.

N Up until three or four months of age, the infant will turn the head toward the side that was stroked. In the sleeping infant, the rooting reflex can be present normally until six months of age.

A An absent rooting reflex from birth through three to four months is abnormal.

P Central nervous system disease such as frontal lobe lesions accounts for an absent rooting reflex.

Sucking Reflex

E **1.** Place the infant in a supine position.
   2. With your forefinger, touch the infant's lips to stimulate a response (Figure 24-23).
   3. Observe for a sucking motion.

N The sucking reflex occurs up to approximately ten months.

A Absence of the sucking reflex is abnormal.

P A premature infant or a breast-fed infant of a mother who ingests barbiturates does not exhibit the reflex secondary to CNS depression.

Palmar Grasp Reflex

E **1.** Place the infant supine with the head in a midline position.
   2. Place the ulnar sides of both index fingers into the infant's hands while the infant's arms are in a semi-flexed position (Figure 24-24).
   3. Press your fingers into the infant's palmar surfaces.

N Normally, the infant grasps your fingers in flexion.

A Presence of the palmar grasp reflex after four months of age is abnormal.

P The etiology is attributed to frontal lobe lesions.

Tonic Neck Reflex

E **1.** Place the infant in a supine position on the examination table.
   2. Rotate the head to one side and hold the jaw area parallel to the shoulder.
   3. Observe for movement of the extremities.

N The upper and lower extremities on the side to which the jaw is turned extend, and the opposite arm and leg flex (Figure 24-25). Sometimes, this reflex does not show up until six to eight weeks of age.

A After six months of age, the tonic neck reflex is abnormal.

P Cerebral damage is suspected if the tonic neck reflex is seen after six months of age.

Stepping Reflex

E **1.** Stand behind the infant, grasp the infant under the axillae, and bring the body to a standing position on a flat surface. Use the thumbs to support the back of the head if needed.
   2. Push the infant's feet toward a flat surface and simultaneously lean the infant's body forward (Figure 24-26).
   3. Observe the legs and feet for stepping movements.

N Stepping movements are made by flexing one leg and moving the other leg forward. This reflex disappears at about three months of age.

A Presence of the stepping reflex beyond three months of age is abnormal.

P Patients with CP demonstrate a stepping reflex beyond three months of age.

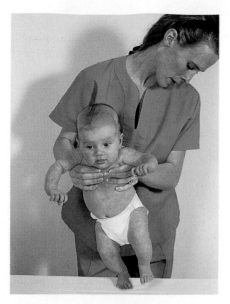
Figure 24-26 Stepping Reflex.

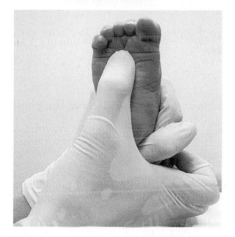
Figure 24-27 Plantar Grasp Reflex.

Plantar Grasp Reflex

E 1. Position the infant supine on the examination table.
2. Elevate the foot to be examined.
3. Touch the infant's foot on the plantar surface beneath the toes (Figure 24-27).
4. Repeat on the other side.

N The toes curl down until eight months of age.

A It is abnormal for the plantar grasp reflex to be absent on one or both feet.

P An obstructive lesion such as an abscess or tumour can cause the plantar grasp reflex to be absent on the affected side. Bilateral absence can occur in CP.

Babinski's Reflex

E 1. Position the infant supine on the examination table.
2. Elevate the foot to be examined.
3. Stroke the plantar surface of the foot from the lateral heel upward with the tip of the thumbnail.

N A child less than 15 to 18 months of age normally fans the toes outward and dorsiflexes the great toe (Figure 24-28).

A After the child masters walking, presence of Babinski's reflex is abnormal.

P Presence of Babinski's reflex after 18 months of age can be indicative of a perinatal insult such as cerebral palsy.

Moro (Startle) Reflex

E 1. Place the infant supine on the examination table.
2. Make a sudden loud noise such as hitting your hand on the examination table.
3. Another technique is to brace the infant's neck and back on the undersurface of your arm while holding the undersurface of the buttocks with the other hand and then mimicking a falling motion by quickly lowering the infant.

N The infant under four months of age quickly extends then flexes the arms and fingers while the manoeuvre is performed. The thumb and index fingers form a C shape (Figure 24-29).

A Presence of the startle reflex after four to six months of age is abnormal.

P Neurological disease such as CP can be a cause of a positive response after the normal age of disappearance.

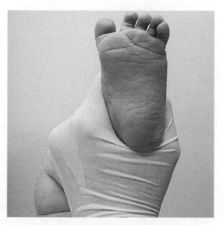
Figure 24-28 Babinksi's Reflex.

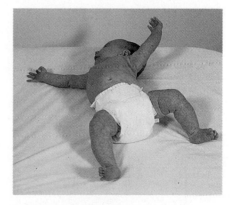
Figure 24-29 Moro Reflex.

E	Examination	N	Normal Findings	A	Abnormal Findings	P	Pathophysiology

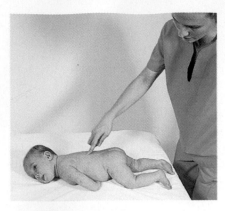

Figure 24-30 Galant Reflex.

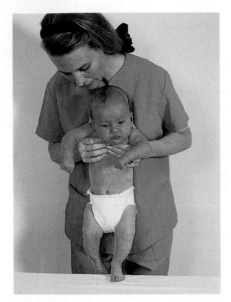

Figure 24-31 Placing Reflex.

Galant Reflex

E   1. Place the infant prone, with the infant's hands under the abdomen.
    2. Use your index finger to stroke the skin along the side of the spine (Figure 24-30).
    3. Observe the stimulated side for any movement.

N   An infant less than one to two months of age will turn the pelvis and shoulders toward the stimulated side.

A   Lack of response from an infant less than two months of age is abnormal.

P   A spinal cord lesion is suspected.

Placing Reflex

Do not test the placing and stepping reflexes at the same time because they are two different reflexes.

E   1. Grasp the infant under the axillae from behind and bring the body to a standing position. Use the thumbs to support the back of the head if needed.
    2. Touch the dorsum of one foot to the edge of the examination table (Figure 24-31).
    3. Observe the tested leg for movement.

N   The infant's tested leg will flex and lift onto the examination table.

A   Lack of response is abnormal.

A   It is difficult to elicit this reflex in breech-born babies and in those with paralysis or cerebral cortex abnormalities.

Landau Reflex

E   1. Carefully suspend the infant in a prone position, supporting the chest with your hand.
    2. Observe for extension of the head, trunk, and hips.

N   The arms and legs extend during the reflex. The reflex appears at about three months of age.

A   Presence of the Landau reflex beyond two years of age is abnormal. Also, it is abnormal for the infant to assume a limp position.

A   Mental retardation may account for an abnormality.

Cranial Nerve Function

A thorough assessment of cranial nerve function is difficult to perform on the infant less than one year old. Difficulty is also encountered with toddlers and preschoolers because they often cannot follow directions or are not willing to cooperate. Testing for the school-age child or the adolescent is carried out in the same manner as for an adult.

Infant (Birth to 12 Months)

E   1. To test cranial nerves (CNs) III, IV, and VI, move a brightly coloured toy along the infant's line of vision. An infant older than one month responds by following the object. Also evaluate the pupillary response to a bright light in each eye.
    2. CN V is tested by assessing the rooting or sucking reflexes.
    3. CN VII is tested up until two months by assessing the sucking reflex and by observing symmetrical sucking movements. After two months of age, an infant will smile, allowing assessment of symmetry of facial expressions.
    4. A positive Moro reflex in an infant less than six months old is evidence of normal functioning of CN VIII.
    5. CNs IX and X are examined by using a tongue blade to produce a gag reflex. Do not test if a positive response was already elicited by using a tongue blade to view the posterior pharynx.

6. To test CN XI, evaluate the infant's ability to lift the head while in a prone position.

7. CN XII is assessed by allowing the infant to suck on a pacifier or a bottle, abruptly removing the pacifier or bottle from the infant's mouth, and observing for lingering sucking movements.

N/A/P See Chapter 19.

Toddler and Preschooler (1–5 Years)

E 1. The older preschooler is able to identify familiar odours. Most children readily identify the smell of chocolate. Test CN I one side at a time by asking the child to close the eyes and to identify the smell of chocolate. Test each nostril with different substances while occluding the other nostril with your finger. *The use of peanut butter to test the olfactory nerve is discouraged because of the risk of allergic reaction in sensitive children.*

2. Test vision (CN II) using Allen cards.

3. CNs III, IV, and VI are tested in the same fashion as for the infant.

4. CN V is tested by giving the child something to eat and evaluating chewing movements. Sensory responses to light and sharp touch are still not easily interpreted in these age groups.

5. Observe facial weakness or paralysis (CN VII) by making the child smile or laugh. An older preschooler may cooperate by raising the eyebrows, frowning, puffing the cheeks out, and closing the eyes tightly on command.

6. To evaluate CN VIII, ring a small bell out of the child's vision and observe the response to unseen sounds.

7. Test CNs IX and X in the same manner as for the infant.

8. CN XII is difficult to assess in this particular age group.

N/A/P See Chapter 19.

Female Genitalia

General Approach

1. Place the up-to-preschool-age child on the caregiver's lap or examination table. Ask caregiver to assist by holding the legs in a froglike position. Place the child older than four years on the examination table in a semi-lithotomy position, without the feet in stirrups. Reserve the lithotomy position with the feet in stirrups for the older adolescent.

2. Explain the procedure prior to the assessment. Never ask the caregiver of the infant or young school-age child to leave the room during this portion of the examination because the caregiver is a source of comfort to the child.

3. The child should be told before the genitalia exam that the provider will touch the genitals only because it is necessary to perform the physical assessment.

4. Drape the older-than-preschool-age child.

5. A vaginal and pelvic exam is not routinely performed on young females. A vaginal assessment is warranted, however, when signs of possible sexual abuse are present. See Table 24-4 on page 898. The assessment is undertaken by a health care provider who is trained to perform pediatric vaginal examinations and can evaluate these problems.

6. Any female who has reached menarche needs to be evaluated for a pregnant uterus, when dictated by the health history.

> ### Nursing Tip
>
> **The Genital Examination**
>
> Conducting an assessment of either the female or male genitalia in children and adolescents requires sensitivity, discretion, and skill. Nurses conducting such assessments should be coached by those who have had experience to determine the extent of assessment that is needed and the approach to be used with the child or adolescent.

| E | **Examination** | N | **Normal Findings** | A | **Abnormal Findings** | P | **Pathophysiology** |

Inspection

Sexual Maturity Rating

E 1. Using the Tanner stages in Table 20-1 on page 733, assess the developmental stage of the pubic hair.
   2. Determine the SMR.

N Adolescents usually start developing pubic hair by 8–12 years of age. Females usually reach the adult stage by age 15.

A An SMR that is less than expected for a female's age is abnormal.

P Delayed puberty may be familial, genetic, or caused by chronic illnesses.

Nursing Alert

Sex Practices of Canadian Adolescents and Health Promotion

- The average age at first-time sexual intercourse is 16.5 years for both male and females.[21]
- 23% of boys and 19% of girls in grade 9 and 40% of boys and 46% of girls in grade 11 report having had sexual intercourse at least once.[22]

Worrisome is that knowledge about HIV/AIDS transmission and protection has declined. Two-thirds of grade 7 and half of grade 9 students are unaware that there is no cure for HIV/AIDS. Only one-quarter of students in grade 9 and one-third in grade 11 reported using condoms and birth control pills the last time they had sexual intercourse. Two-thirds of Grade 11 students believe vaginal sex is safer than anal sex with respect to HIV transmission.[23]

- While the proportion of youth having sex has decreased from previous studies, sexually active teens are more active. The earlier a teenager starts to have sex, the more likely he or she is to have multiple partners.[24]
- The following points may help in promoting dialogue about healthy sexual habits as you conduct the health assessment. While talking about sex may not be the first topic addressed, any health assessment should address the issues above.
  - If the adolescent is sexually active, discuss his or her feelings on the subject. Assess if he or she is being pressured into having sex or is doing it to fit in. Finding out if the teen is monogamous or has multiple partners will help identify risk but may be viewed with suspicion by the adolescent who fears the nurse will tell family or friends.
  - Discuss the topic of how to prevent pregnancy and avoid contracting STIs. If the teen is sexually active, a discussion of the pros and cons of having sex can be discussed. Blanket statements about abstinence with a teen who is sexually active by choice may not be received well so delicate discussion is required. Knowing the signs and symptoms of STIs will help the teenager know when to consult a health care professional.
  - Discuss facilities that offer confidential voluntary testing and counselling if the individual believes that he or she or a partner has contracted a sexually transmitted infection.

Perineal Area

E See Chapter 20.

N The infant's labia minora are sometimes larger than the labia majora. The hymen is sometimes intact up until the point of sexual activity.

A It is abnormal for the female infant to display a rudimentary penis in the clitoral area.

P   Genital ambiguity occurs during embryonic development as a consequence of genetic causes or androgens or androgen inhibitors that reverse genital characteristics.

A   A bloody discharge noted at the vaginal opening or on the diaper of a child over two weeks of age is abnormal.

P   It is not uncommon to note pseudomenstruation in an infant under two weeks of age due to circulating maternal hormones, however, discharge beyond two weeks requires further assessment.

Male Genitalia

General Approach

1. In case the infant or toddler urinates during the examination, have a diaper or disposable cloth available to catch the stream of urine.

2. The older school-age child and the adolescent should be draped in order to maintain modesty.

Inspection

Sexual Maturity Rating

E   1. Using the Tanner stages in Table 21-1 on page 775, assess the developmental stage of the pubic hair, penis, and scrotum.

2. Determine the SMR.

N   Males usually begin puberty between the ages of $9\frac{1}{2}$ and $13\frac{1}{2}$. The average male proceeds through puberty in about three years, with a possible range of two to five years.

A   An SMR that is less than expected for a male's age is abnormal.

P   Delayed puberty may be familial or caused by chronic illnesses.

A   A normally formed but diminutive penis is abnormal. There is a discrepancy between the penile size and the age of the individual.

P   A **microphallus** penis can result from a disorder in the hypothalamus or pituitary gland. It may be secondary to primary testicular failure due to partial androgen insensitivity. Maternal DES exposure has teratogenic effects caused by defects in nonandrogen-dependent regulatory agents. Microphallus can also be idiopathic in nature.

A   It is abnormal when the penis appears larger than what is generally expected for the stated age. This condition is usually evident only before the age of normal puberty.

P   Hormonal influence of tumours of the pineal gland or hypothalamus, tumours of the Leydig cells of the testes, tumours of the adrenal gland, or precocious genital maturity may cause penile hyperplasia.

A   A testicle that is smaller and softer than normal (less in the fully developed male) is abnormal.

P   An atrophic testicle may be the result of Klinefelter's syndrome (hypogonadism), hypopituitarism, estrogen therapy, or orchitis.

Penis

E   1. Note the appearance of the penis. If you are not able to determine circumcision status, ask the caregiver if the child was circumcised.

2. Note the position of the urethral meatus.

N   The meatus is normally found on the tip of the penis. A disappearing penis phenomenon occurs normally in infants with increased adipose tissue in the area surrounding the penis. Reassure the caregiver that this is normal and will resolve after adipose tissue is lost.

| E | Examination | N | Normal Findings | A | Abnormal Findings | P | Pathophysiology |

A It is abnormal for the urethral meatus to be located behind or along the ventral side of the penis.

P During the third month of fetal development, the urethral meatus fails to move toward the glans penis, creating a condition known as hypospadias. Children at greater risk for hypospadias are those whose mothers are on hydantoin for epilepsy.

A It is abnormal for the meatal opening to be on the dorsal surface of the penis.

P During the third month of fetal development, the urethral meatus fails to move toward the glans penis, causing an epispadias deformity.

Scrotum

E 1. Evaluate scrotal size and colour.
2. Note if the testes are seen in the scrotal sac.

N The scrotum appears proportionately large in size when compared to the penis. The sac colour is brown or black in dark-skinned children and pink in light-skinned children. Two testes should be present, but in infants they may retract into the inguinal canal or abdomen due to various stimuli, including cold and palpation.

A/P See Chapter 21.

Palpation

Scrotum

E 1. Place the infant in a supine position on the examination table. Instruct the young child to sit cross-legged to inhibit the cremasteric reflex from occurring. The older child may be allowed to stand for this portion of the exam.
2. Locate each testis within the scrotal sac by using the fingers of one hand in a milking motion to descend the testes.
3. Palpate and note the size, shape, and mobility of each testis.

N See Chapter 21.

A It is abnormal to be unable to palpate the testes.

P **Cryptorchidism** is a failure of the testis to descend into the scrotal sac. One or both testes failing to descend within the inguinal canal occurs during embryonic development.

A An enlargement of the scrotum is abnormal.

P A congenital hydrocele results from failure of the male reproductive tract to develop properly while the fetus is in utero. This mass will transilluminate.

Hernia

E 1. For the infant who is unable to stand, place the infant supine on the examination table. All other children should stand during the examination.
2. Use the little finger for the infant's and the index finger for the younger child's examination.
3. Follow the inguinal canal as is done on an adult male.
4. If possible, perform the assessment on a crying infant.
5. Have preschoolers and early school-age children attempt to blow up a balloon while you palpate the inguinal areas.
6. Palpate the inguinal areas while the older school-age child or adolescent coughs.

N/A/P See Chapter 21.

Anus

As a rule, rectal assessments are not performed on children unless you detect a problem or suspect abuse; in these cases, refer for further evaluation if not trained specifically for this procedure and follow your institution's guidelines.

Inspection

E 1. Ask the child to lie on the abdomen.
2. Gently separate the buttocks to allow direct visualization of the anal opening.
3. Observe for bleeding, fissures, prolapse, skin tags, hemorrhoids, lesions, and pinworms.
4. During separation of the buttocks, observe any movement of the anus.
5. Stroke the perianal area with your finger and note any movement. This is called the anal reflex or anal wink.

N No bleeding, fissures, prolapse, skin tags, hemorrhoids, lesions, or pinworms should be present. An anal reflex is observed.

A An absent anal reflex is abnormal.

P Conditions such as a spinal cord lesion, trauma, and tumours that interrupt nervous innervation to the anal sphincter cause this finding.

CASE STUDY

The Patient with Hypoplastic Left Heart Syndrome (HLHS)

The case study illustrates the application and objective documentation of the pediatric assessment.

Janie is a 2-day-old infant born with HLHS. Her parents are from a far northern village; her mother came to the urban centre to give birth as it was known that Janie would require immediate medical intervention at birth. Plans are for the family to return to their home village as soon as all is well. Janie is in the intensive care unit.

HEALTH HISTORY

LEGAL GUARDIAN	Mary and Mark Akulukjuk (biological parents)
SOURCE OF INFORMATION	Caregivers & chart from birth hospital
PATIENT PROFILE	2-day-old girl
HEALTH ISSUE/CONCERN	(Per mother) "Janie will need heart surgery to survive."
HISTORY OF ISSUE/CONCERN	Mrs. Akulukjuk states "I just want her heart to be ok—she is so fragile"
PAST HEALTH HISTORY	
Birth History	
Prenatal	No prior pregnancies, denies drug, ETOH, tobacco, caffeine, or ibuprofen use during pregnancy; fetal ultrasound done at 26 wks showed a small Ⓛ ventricle, referred to cardiologist for further studies, fetal echocardiogram done at 30 wks showed HLHS.
Labour and Delivery	38 wk gestation, delivered vaginally p̄ 12 hr labour, able to hold baby in delivery room for a short period of time, Apgar scores were 6 & 8, birth wt 3.5 kgs & length 53.3 cm.
Postnatal	Transferred into NICU shortly p̄ delivery & prostaglandin therapy begun (to maintain patency of ductus arteriosus), Ø adverse effects from the prostaglandin administration, Ø immunizations given; Mrs. Akulukjuk is using an electric breast pump q 3 hrs around the clock.

continues

Medical History	HLHS, pediatrician examined baby at birth hospital & did not find any other hl problems.
Surgical History	Nil
Medications	Prostaglandin infusion intravenously
Communicable Diseases	No known exposures
Allergies	NKA
Injuries and Accidents	Ø
Blood Transfusions	Ø
Immunizations	Ø

FAMILY HEALTH HISTORY

LEGEND

 Living female

 Living male

 Deceased female

 Deceased male

／ Points to patient

A&W = Alive & well

HLHS = Hypoplastic left
       heart syndrome

MVA = Motor vehicle
       accident

```
  65 ── 63        70 ── 69
  A&W    A&W       A&W    A&W

 33   36 ──── 35   33    22
A&W  A&W      A&W  A&W   MVA

          2
        days
        HLHS
```

Denies family hx of congenital heart dz, SIDS, ADHD, MR, thyroid dz.

SOCIAL HISTORY

Alcohol, Tobacco, Drug Use, Sexual Practice	N/A
Domestic and Intimate Partner Violence	Denies
Travel History	N/A
School Performance	N/A
Home Environment	Parents live in a bungalow, two dogs
Hobbies, Leisure Activities, Stress, Education	N/A
Economic Status	"We make do."

continues

Religion/Spirituality	"We have strong spiritual beliefs—I know they will help us get through this."
Ethnicity	Inuit
Roles and Relationships	Positive relationship described among all family members; some marital strain over the heart defect during pregnancy as Mrs. A. wanted to talk about it all the time and Mr. A. tried to avoid the subject as it made him too worried. Both Mr. and Mrs. Akulukjuk state they miss their family and friends since having to be away from home for the baby.
Child's Personal Habits	Likes to be wrapped tightly in receiving blanket
Characteristic Patterns of Daily Living	No set pattern yet
HEALTH MAINTENANCE ACTIVITIES	
Sleep	Pattern not identified by parents although they feel Janie sleeps "a lot."
Diet	NPO, mother is pumping q 3 hrs & freezing the milk for later use.
Exercise	N/A
Stress Management	Both parents very familiar $\bar{c}$ dx, continue to seek opportunities to increase knowledge about baby's condition; maternal and paternal grandparents live in same home town and will help when the A's return home.
Use of Safety Devices	No car
Safety	Smoke detectors in home, fire extinguisher in kitchen, parents both took a CPR course in the community, know number to dial in an emergency
Health Check-ups	N/A
DEVELOPMENT	
Gross and Fine Motor	Not assessed
Language	N/A
Personal-Social	Not assessed
PHYSICAL ASSESSMENT	
Vital Signs	T: 36.6°C rectally; apical HR: 136; RR: 72; B/P: 62/36
Physical Growth	wt: 3.5 kg (50th percentile); length: 53.3 cm (90th percentile); head circumference: 35.1 cm (50th percentile); chest circumference: 34 cm
Skin	
Inspection	No erythema, papules, vesicles, scaling or ulceration, mild periorbital edema, Mongolian spot 2 × 4 cm noted over lumbar-sacral area, generalized duskiness
Palpation	Soft, smooth $\bar{s}$ roughness, dryness, scaliness, or keratic areas; turgor WNL, no diaphoresis; arms & legs warm $\bar{c}$ 3-sec capillary refill in all 4 extremities

continues

Hair and Nails

Inspection and Palpation Scalp s̄ scaling, nails present

Head

Inspection Symmetrical, round, no bulges or prominence of forehead, no involuntary mvts, face symmetrical, unsteady head control

Palpation Anterior fontanel soft & flat (3 cm × 3.5 cm), posterior fontanel soft & flat (1 cm × 0.5 cm) suture lines not overriding

Eyes

Vision Screening N/A

Inspection No ptosis, sclera bluish-tinged in colour, positive optical blink response, conjunctiva dusky, cornea smooth & transparent, iris brown, PERRLA, positive red reflex, optic discs creamy pink, round, borders regular s̄ hemorrhages

Ears

Auditory Testing Reacts to loud noises

Inspection (External Ear) Top of pinna positioned at level of eyebrows bilaterally, pinna s̄ lesions or masses

Palpation (External Ear) No pain c̄ mvt

Inspection (Internal Ear) No erythema or cerumen in canal, vernix noted in canals bilaterally, bilateral TMs pearly s̄ retraction, bulging, perforation, fluid or air bubbles, TMs move well, landmarks intact, positive light reflex

Nose

Inspection Patent nares c̄ mild flaring, mucosa dusky, septum midline, no edema of turbinates

Mouth and Throat

Inspection Lips dusky, no fissures/cracking, edges meet, buccal mucosa dusky s̄ lesions, no teeth, tongue dusky & midline, nl positioned palate, both hard/soft palates intact s̄ lesions, tonsils not enlarged, no erythema or exudate, uvula midline

Neck

Inspection Symmetrical, short, & thin, no edema

Palpation Thyroid non-palpable, trachea midline, no lymphadenopathy

Breasts and Regional Lymphatics

Inspection Tanner stage I, no retractions, erythema, venous distention, edema; areolas circular & even bilaterally, negative masses & ulceration, nipples circular s̄ retractions/inversions, erythema, discharge, ulceration or supernumerary nipples

continues

Palpation	Breasts negative for nodes, glands, masses, or tenderness; axillary area: non-palpable nodes, negative tenderness or masses
Thorax and Lungs	
Inspection	Thorax round, mild intercostal retractions
Palpation	Positive tactile fremitus bilaterally
Percussion	Diaphragmatic excursion 1 ICS bilaterally
Auscultation	BS = bilaterally, bronchial sounds over trachea, bronchovesicular BS throughout peripheral lung fields, coarse rales throughout
Heart and Peripheral Vasculature	
Inspection	Apical impulse at 4th ICS to left of MCL, no heaves, lifts of precordium, no clubbing of fingers or toes, negative JVD
Palpation	Negative thrill, slight brachial-femoral lag, pulses 2+/4+ bilaterally
Auscultation	Apical HR even & regular, ① S_1, ① S_2, no S_3 or S_4, I/VI systolic ejection murmur along LSB
Abdomen	
Inspection	Rounded & symmetrical, umbilical stump drying, abdominal musculature continuous, no visible peristalsis
Auscultation	⊕ BS in all 4 quadrants, no venous hums, no bruits @ femoral, iliac, renal & aortic areas, no peritoneal friction rub
Percussion	Tympanic, negative fluid shift
Palpation	No pain or tenderness, no masses, liver edge down 1 cm below RCM, spleen not palpable, kidneys not palpable
Musculoskeletal	
Inspection	AROM in all 4 extremities, unable to hold head up, C-shaped spine
Palpation	Nl for age strength, negative Ortolani's manoeuvre
Neurological	
Inspection	Calms upon hearing mother's voice, ⊕ Babinski, ⊕ suck, ⊕ rooting reflex, ⊕ palmar grasp, ⊕ tonic neck reflex, stepping reflex deferred, ⊕ plantar grasp reflex, ⊕ Moro reflex, ⊕ Galant reflex, placing reflex & landau reflex deferred; CN V, VII, VIII, IX, X & XII grossly intact, DTR 2+/4+
Female Genitalia	
Inspection	Tanner stage I, labia dusky s̄ hypertrophy, excoriation, ulceration, small amount of bloody drainage noted on the diaper, perineum smooth s̄ laceration, hymen intact
Anus	
Inspection	Anal area s̄ lesions, bleeding, fissures, prolapse, or hemorrhoids; small dark black, sticky stool in diaper

◄NURSING CHECKLIST►

Pediatric Patient Assessment*

Physical Growth
- Weight
- Length and height
- Head circumference
- Chest circumference
- Body mass index

Physical Assessment
- Apgar scoring
- Head
  - Inspection of head control
  - Palpation of anterior fonta, posterior fonta, suture lines, surface characteristics
- Eyes
  - Vision screening through Allen test
- Musculoskeletal system
  - Inspection of tibiofemoral bones
  - Palpation of feet (metatarsus varus), hip and femur (Ortolani's manoeuvre)

*Only pediatric-specific tests are listed.

- Neurological System
  - Rooting
  - Sucking
  - Palmar grasp
  - Tonic neck
  - Stepping
  - Plantar grasp
  - Babinski
  - Moro (startle)
  - Galant
  - Placing
  - Landau

Advanced Techniques
- Assessing for hydrocephalus and anencephaly: Transillumination of the skull
- Assessing for coarctation of the aorta

REVIEW QUESTIONS

1. Jordan was born two months prematurely. She is at her 6-month well-child check and you are plotting her weight and length on the growth chart. Knowing that you should adjust her chronological age on the growth chart, where would you plot her corrected weight and height?
   a. 8 months
   b. 6 months
   c. 2 months
   d. 4 months
   The correct answer is (d).

2. The Canadian Paediatric Society recommends an infant be placed in which sleep position to decrease the risk of sudden infant death syndrome (SIDS)?
   a. On the abdomen.
   b. Side-lying position
   c. Flat on the back
   d. Rotating back to side to front lying
   The correct answer is (c).

3. It is important to auscultate the infant's heart during which portion of the examination?
   a. At the beginning of the examination
   b. After using an otoscope to observe an infant's tympanic membranes
   c. Immediately after checking for dysplasia of the hip
   d. At the end of the entire examination
   The correct answer is (a).

4. When measuring a recumbent length on a 23-month-old female child, which growth chart should be used to plot the measurements?
   a. Girls: 2 to 18 Years Physical Growth Chart
   b. Girls: Birth to 36 Months Physical Growth Chart
   c. Boys: 2 to 18 Years Physical Growth Chart
   d. Boys: Birth to 36 Months Physical Growth Chart
   The correct answer is (b).

5. An absent red reflex in the newborn is indicative of which condition?
   a. Shaken baby syndrome
   b. Osteogenesis imperfecta
   c. Cataract
   d. Glaucoma
   The correct answer is (c).

6. A newborn with weak to nearly absent pulses in the lower extremities reflects which cardiac condition?
   a. Ventricular septal defect
   b. Pulmonary atresia
   c. Subaortic stenosis
   d. Coarctation of the aorta
   The correct answer is (d).

7. Which series of cranial nerve function tests can be performed on an infant?
   a. CN V-XII
   b. CN I-XII
   c. CN III-XII

d. CN II-XII

The correct answer is (c).

8. Ortolani's manoeuvre is performed until which age?
   a. 18 months
   b. 3 years
   c. 2 years
   d. 6 months

   The correct answer is (a).

Questions 9 and 10 refer to the following situation:

Will is accompanied by his mother at his 6-month well-child check. Will had a lengthy hospitalization with the diagnosis of RSV (respiratory syncytial virus) at four months of age. His stay in the hospital included 1 month in the pediatric intensive care unit and two weeks on the floor for further observation.

9. Upon inspection of the head, you note Will's inability to hold his head steady. At what age would you refer a patient to physical therapy services for poor head control?
   a. 11–12 months
   b. 7–8 months
   c. 4–6 months
   d. 2–4 months

   The correct answer is (c).

10. Will's mother shares with you that Will cries when approached by health care professionals. Which measure may help him cope with an unfamiliar face?
    a. Allow him to stay on the examining table with his mother in the room.
    b. Allow the mother to hold Will on her lap.
    c. Ask another nurse to come into the room and hold Will.
    d. Use distraction techniques such as talking about a favourite television character.

    The correct answer is (b).

Visit the Estes online companion resource at **www.healthassessment.nelson.com** for additional content and study aids.

REFERENCES

[1] A collaborative statement from Dietitians of Canada, Canadian Paediatric Society, The College of Family Physicians of Canada, and Community Health Nurses Association of Canada. (2004, March). The use of growth charts for assessing and monitoring growth in Canadian infants and children. *Canadian Journal of Dietetic Practice and Research, 65,* 22–32.

[2] Ibid.

[3] Health Canada. (2005). Exclusive Breastfeeding Duration—2004 Health Canada Recommendation. Retrieved November 9, 2006, from http://www.hc-sc.gc.ca/fn-an/nutrition/child-enfant/infant-nourisson/excl_bf_dur-dur_am_ excl_e.html

[4] Wang, Z. & Sauve, R. S. (1998). Assessment of postneonatal growth in VLBW infants: Selection of growth references and age adjustment for prematurity. *Canadian Journal of Public Health, 89*(2), 109–114.

[5] Panpanich, R. & Garner, P. (1999). Growth monitoring in children. *The Cochrane Database of Systematic Reviews,* Issue 4. Art. No.: CD001443.

[6] Nutrition Committee, Canadian Paediatric Society (CPS). (2002). The use of fluoride in infants and children. *Paediatrics & Child Health, 7*(8):569–572. Reference No. N02-01 (Formerly N95-02) (revised 2003). Retrieved November 9, 2006, from http://www.cps.ca/english/statements/N/n02-01.htm

[7] A collaborative statement from Dietitians of Canada, Canadian Paediatric Society, The College of Family Physicians of Canada, and Community Health Nurses Association of Canada (2004, March).

[8] Ibid.

[9] Statistics Canada, (2004, July 6). Canadian community health survey: Obesity among children and adults. *The Daily.* Retrieved November 9, 2006, from http://www.statcan.ca/Daily/English/050706/d050706a.htm

[10] Community Paediatrics Committee, Canadian Paediatric Society (2004). Recommendations for safe sleeping environments for infants and children. *Paediatrics & Child Health, 9*(9), 659–663.

[11] Boynton, R. W., Dunn, E. S., Stephens, G. R. & Pulcini, J. (2003). *Manual of ambulatory pediatrics* (5th ed.). Philadelphia: Lippincott.

[12] Health Canada (2005). *Policy statement for bumper pads.* Retrieved November 9, 2006, from http://www.hc-sc.gc.ca/cps-spc/legislation/pol/bumper-bordure_e.html

[13] Transport Canada (2006). *Safety in the car.* Retrieved November 10, 2006, from http://www.tc.gc.ca/roadsafety/childsafety/menu.htm

[14] Community Paediatrics Committee: Canadian Paediatric Society. (2005). *Temperature measurement in paediatrics.* Retrieved November 9, 2006, from http://www.cps.ca/english/statements/CP/cp00-01.htm

[15] Health Canada (2003). *Canadian perinatal health report.* Ottawa: Minister of Public Works and Government Services Canada. Retrieved November 10, 2006, from http://www.phac-aspc.gc.ca/publicat/cphr-rspc03/pdf/cphr-rspc03_e.pdf

[16] Ibid.

[17] Canadian Paediatric Society and 17 other co-signatories. (1997; reaffirmed March 2004). Prevention of Fetal Alcohol Syndrome (FAS) and Fetal Alcohol Effects (FAE) in Canada. *Paediatrics & Child Health, 2*(2):143–145.

[18]Department of Justice Canada. (2006, July). *Child abuse: A fact sheet from the Department of Justice Canada.* Retrieved November 18, 2006, from http://www.justice.gc.ca/en/ps/fm/childafs.html#_edn3

[19]Trocme, N., Fallon, B., MacLaurin, B., Daciuk, J., Felstiner, T.B., Tonmyr, L., Blackstock, C., Barter, K., Turcotte, D. & Cloutier, R. (2005). *Canadian incidence study of reported child abuse and neglect—2003: Major findings.* Ottawa: Minister of Public Works and Government Services Canada.

[20]Community Paediatrics Committee: Canadian Paediatric Society (1998; reaffirmed January 2005). Visual screening in infants and children and youth. *Paediatrics & Child Health;* 3(4): 261–262.

[21]Rotermann, M. (2005). Sex, condoms and STDs among young people. *Health Reports,* volume 16, Number 3. Retrieved November 9, 2006, from http://www.statcan.ca/english/ads/82-003-XPE/pdf/16-3-04.pdf

[22]Boyce, W., Doherty, M., Fortin, C., & MacKinnon, D. (2003). The Canadian Youth, Sexual Health and HIV/AIDS Study (2003): Factors influencing knowledge, attitudes and behaviours. Toronto: Council of Ministers of Education. Retrieved November 9, 2006, from http://www.cmec.ca/ publications/aids

[23]Ibid.

[24]Ibid.

BIBLIOGRAPHY

Afifi, T. O., Enns, M. W., Cox, B. J., & Martens, P. J. (2005, November–December). Investigating health correlates of adolescent depression in Canada. *Canadian Journal of Public Health,* 96(6):427–31.

Bottorff, J. L., Johnson, J. L., Moffat, B., Grewal, J., Ratner, P. A. & Kalaw, C. (2006). Adolescent Constructions of Nicotine Addiction. Les perceptions des adolescents à l'égard de la dépendance à la nicotine. *CJNR (Canadian Journal of Nursing Research),* 36(1), 22–39.

Fleisher, G. R., Ludwig, S. & Baskin, M. N. (2004). *Textbook of pediatric emergency medicine* (2nd ed.). Philadelphia: Lippincott, Williams & Wilkins.

Flicker, S., Skinner, H., Read, S., Veinot, T. et al. (2005). Falling through the cracks of the big cities: Who is meeting the needs of HIV-positive youth? *Canadian Journal of Public Health,* 96(4), 308–312.

Gruskin, K. (Ed.) (2005). *Signs & symptoms in pediatrics: Urgent and emergent care.* Philadelphia: Elsevier Mosby.

Irwin, J., He, M., Sangster Bouck, L. M., Tucker, P. & Pollett, G.L. (2006). Preschoolers' physical activity behaviours: Parents' perspectives. *Canadian Journal of Public Health,* 96(4), 299–307.

Kleigman, R., Marcdante, K., Jenson, H., & Behrman, R. (2006). *Nelson essentials of pediatrics* (5th ed.). Philadelphia: W. B. Saunders.

Parker, S., Zuckerman, B., & Augustyn, M. (2005). *Developmental and behavioral pediatrics: A handbook for primary care.* Philadelphia: Lippincott Williams & Wilkins.

Walsh, A. E., Edwards, H. E., Courtney, M. D., Wilson, J. E., & Monaghan, S. J. (2006). Paediatric fever management: Continuing education for clinical nurses. *Nurse Education Today,* 26 (71–77).

WEB RESOURCES

Canadian Coalition for Immunization Awareness & Promotion
http://www.immunize.cpha.ca/english/hcprovd/provrese/provad.htm

Canadian Congenital Anomalies Surveillance Network (CCASN)
http://www.phac-aspc.gc.ca/ccasn-rcsac/index.html

Canadian Working Group on Childhood Hearing
http://www.phac-aspc.gc.ca/publicat/eh-dp/index.html

Caring for Kids (Canadian Paediatric Society)
http://www.caringforkids.cps.ca/index.htm

Sexuality and you (administered by the Society of Obstetricians and Gynecologists of Canada. This credible site has useful links for teens, parents, and health professionals.)
http://www.sexualityandu.ca/eng/index.cfm

Spina Bifida and Hydrocephalus Association of Canada
http://www.sbhac.ca/index.php?page=main

Putting It All Together

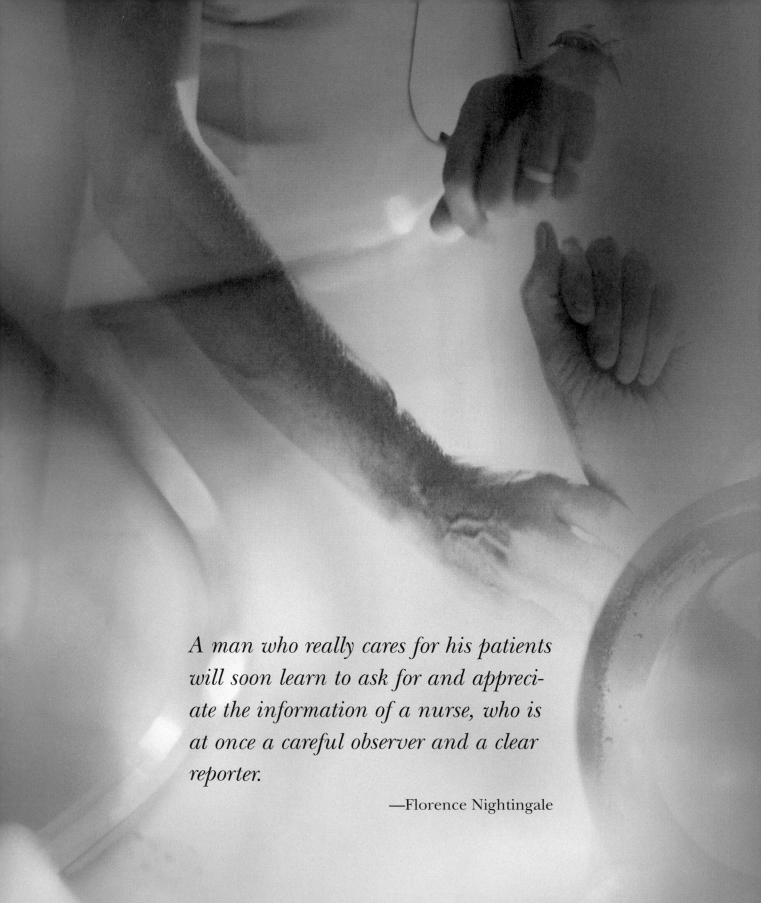

A man who really cares for his patients will soon learn to ask for and appreciate the information of a nurse, who is at once a careful observer and a clear reporter.

—Florence Nightingale

CHAPTER 25

The Complete Health History and Physical Examination

COMPETENCIES

1. Identify the components of the complete health history and physical examination.

2. Conduct a complete health history and physical examination on a patient.

3. Document a complete health history and physical examination.

*P*erforming a complete health history and physical examination is a skill that takes time and practice to develop. The reflective clinician will perfect interviewing techniques and assessment skills with ongoing purposeful practice. Use of a simulated learning laboratory to practise assessment skills with volunteer "patients" is a crucial step in skill mastery. Assessing a range of healthy patients ensures that the clinician can recognize normal findings in order to appreciate abnormal and pathological findings. Learning the assessment techniques system by system, as described in this text, helps to gradually build on previously developed skills.

As assessment skills are perfected, the amount of time it takes to perform them will decrease. It can take between 30 and 90 minutes to conduct a complete health history and physical examination. If the patient's health issue or concern is not of an urgent or critical nature, the patient's first visit to the health care facility is the ideal time to perform a comprehensive assessment. Interval or follow-up visits frequently require partial assessments that document changes from the initial database; these visits require substantially less time.

It is important to develop a routine that is comfortable so that steps in the assessment process will not be overlooked. However, the patient's physical, emotional, or mental state may necessitate a change in the usual progression of the assessment. Clinical judgment and experience will dictate when specific steps should be omitted, deferred, or repeated.

Once the content of Chapters 9 to 22 is learned and a comfort level in performing each assessment has been reached, it is time to integrate the entire health and physical assessment. This chapter provides a step-by-step approach to guide the clinician through the entire process for an adult patient.

Advanced techniques are normally inserted in the assessment process at different phases, depending on the techniques to be performed and the patient's condition. Experience will guide the nurse in determining when these advanced techniques are warranted. They are omitted in the following assessment sequence, which illustrates a "typical" head-to-toe assessment.

Nursing Tip

Fostering Patient Collaboration

The success of any health history and physical examination rests in part with obtaining and maintaining the patient's collaboration. Some guidelines include:

- Have the patient wait as short a time as possible prior to the examination; explain any delays that occur.
- Greet the patient first, shake hands, and put the patient at ease.
- Proceed in an efficient and organized manner.
- Encourage the patient to actively participate in the assessment process (e.g., provide information, ask questions, teach).
- Use terms the patient will understand.
- Ask the patient to repeat home care or self-examination instructions and to demonstrate learned skills when appropriate to verify patient understanding.
- Be honest; do not offer false reassurance or jump to conclusions.
- Discuss findings first without diagnosing; validate findings when indicated.
- Arrange for the presence of a third party if requested.

◄NURSING CHECKLIST►

General Assessment Reminders

- Understand illness in human terms, not just scientific terms.
- Approach the patient from a holistic viewpoint and try to understand the patient's perspective.
- Remember that nursing is both art and science.
- Follow your judgment; critical thinking incorporates the consideration of objective and subjective data. Always ask, "Why?"
- Act unhurried.
- Act in a professional manner at all times; remember that the patient is simultaneously examining you (mannerisms, facial expressions, hesitations in speech).
- Recognize both the patient's and your potential stressors (work, home environment, schedules) and try to account for them.
- Acknowledge emotional reactions to illness (anger, fear, anxiety, disbelief, confusion, guilt, shame, blame, hurt, and betrayal).
- Embrace sensitivity to cultural and spiritual issues.
- Show respect for the patient and his or her circumstances.
- Possess a sense of self-awareness to guide your actions.

Figure 25-1 Carefully document all interview responses and assessment findings.

HEALTH HISTORY

Conduct the health history. Depending on the patient's reason for the visit, this can be the complete, episodic, interval (follow-up), or emergency health history. The patient can be dressed in street clothes for this interview.

Components of the developmental, cultural, and spiritual assessments are continually evaluated during the course of the patient interaction. Thorough assessments of any or all of these special assessments can be completed as necessary based on the patient's situation. The inspection component of the nutrition assessment is noted during the health history. See Chapters 4–7.

PHYSICAL ASSESSMENT

This text has provided a head-to-toe assessment format in order to discuss body systems in their entirety. However, in practice, a head-to-toe assessment combines systems when assessing most body parts. For example, when assessing the hands, components of the skin, musculoskeletal, and neurological assessments are combined. For this reason, the complete physical examination, which demonstrates how to put it all together, reflects this clinical approach. The sample case study at the end of the chapter documents a standard format of the complete physical assessment.

General Survey

The patient's general appearance is assessed during the health history. Incorporate the following into this assessment:

1. Physical Presence
   - Age: stated age versus apparent age
   - General appearance
   - Body fat
   - Stature: posture, proportion of body limbs to trunk
   - Motor activity: gait, speed, and effort of movement; weight bearing; absence or presence of movement in different body areas
   - Body and breath odours
2. Psychological Presence
   - Dress, grooming, and personal hygiene
   - Mood and manner
   - Speech
   - Facial expressions
3. Distress
   - Physical
   - Psychological
   - Emotional
4. Pain

Neurological System

1. Assess mental status: facial expression, affect, level of consciousness, attention span, memory, judgment, insight, spatial perception, calculations, abstract reasoning, thought processes, and content.

After the mental status examination, ask the patient to undress and don an examination gown (underwear may be worn). The patient's bladder should be emptied prior to commencing the assessment process. The urine may be collected for a specimen. Ask the patient to sit on the examination table with the legs hanging over the front. A second drape can be provided to cover the lap and legs. Stand in front of the patient.

Measurements

Record the patient's:

1. Height
2. Weight
3. Temperature
4. Pulse (radial preferred site in adult)
5. Respirations
6. Blood pressure (both arms)
7. Anthropometric measurements (if indicated)

Skin

Throughout the entire head-to-toe assessment, inspect the skin for the following characteristics:

1. Colour
2. Bleeding
3. Ecchymosis
4. Vascularity
5. Lesions

Throughout the entire head-to-toe assessment, palpate the skin for:

1. Moisture
2. Temperature
3. Texture
4. Turgor
5. Edema

Head and Face

1. Inspect the shape of the head.
2. Inspect and palpate the head and scalp.
3. Inspect the colour and distribution of the hair. Note any infestations; palpate the hair.
4. Inspect the face for expression, shape, symmetry (CN VII), symmetry of eyes, eyebrows, ears, nose, and mouth.
5. Instruct the patient to raise the eyebrows, frown, smile, wrinkle the forehead, show the teeth, purse the lips, puff the cheeks, and whistle (CN VII).
6. Palpate the temporal pulses. Palpate the temporalis muscles (CN V).
7. Palpate and auscultate the temporomandibular joints.
8. Palpate the masseter muscles (CN V).

Eyes

1. Test distance vision and near vision (CN II).
2. Test colour vision.
3. Test visual fields via confrontation (CN II).
4. Assess extraocular muscle mobility: cover-uncover test, corneal light reflex, and six cardinal fields of gaze (CNs III, IV, VI).
5. Assess direct and consensual light reflexes and accommodation (CN III).
6. Inspect the eyelids, eyebrows, palpebral fissures, and position of eyes.
7. Inspect and palpate the lacrimal apparatus.
8. Inspect the conjunctiva, sclera, cornea, iris, pupils, and lens.
9. Assess the corneal reflex.
10. Conduct funduscopic assessment: retinal structures, macula.

Ears

1. Test gross hearing: voice-whisper test or watch-tick test (CN VIII).
2. Inspect and palpate the external ear.
3. Assess ear alignment.
4. Conduct otoscopic assessment: EAC and tympanic membrane.
5. Perform Weber and Rinne tests.

Nose and Sinuses

1. Inspect the external surface of the nose.
2. Assess nostril patency.
3. Test olfactory sense (CN I).
4. Conduct internal assessment with nasal speculum: mucosa, turbinates, and septum.
5. Inspect, percuss, and palpate frontal and maxillary sinuses.

Mouth and Throat

1. Note breath odour.
2. Inspect the lips, buccal mucosa, gums, and hard and soft palates.
3. Inspect the teeth; count the teeth.

4. Inspect the tongue; ask the patient to stick out the tongue (CN XII).
5. Inspect the uvula; note movement when the patient says "ah" (CNs IX, X).
6. Inspect the tonsils; note grade.
7. Inspect the oropharynx.
8. Test gag reflex (CNs IX, X).
9. Test taste (CN VII).
10. Palpate the lips and mouth if indicated.

Neck

1. Inspect the musculature of the neck.
2. Inspect range of motion, shoulder shrug, and strength of sternocleidomastoid and trapezius muscles (CN XI).
3. Palpate the musculature of the neck.
4. Inspect and palpate the trachea.
5. Palpate the carotid arteries (one at a time).
6. Inspect the jugular veins for distension; estimate jugular venous pressure (JVP) if indicated.
7. Inspect and palpate the thyroid (use only one approach, either anterior or posterior).
8. Auscultate the thyroid and carotid arteries.
9. Inspect and palpate the lymph nodes: preauricular, postauricular, occipital, submental, submandibular, tonsillar, anterior cervical chain, posterior cervical chain, supraclavicular, and infraclavicular.

Upper Extremities

1. Inspect nailbed colour, shape, and configuration; palpate nailbed texture.
2. Assess capillary refill on nailbed.
3. Inspect muscle size and palpate muscle tone of hands, arms, and shoulders.
4. Palpate the joints of fingers, wrists, elbows, and shoulders.
5. Assess range of motion and strength of fingers, wrists, elbows, and shoulders.
6. Test position sense.
7. Palpate radial and brachial pulses.
8. Palpate the epitrochlear node.

Move behind the patient. Untie the gown so that the entire back is exposed. The gown should cover the shoulders and the anterior chest.

Back, Posterior, and Lateral Thoraxes

1. Palpate the thyroid (posterior approach).
2. Inspect and palpate the spinous processes; inspect range of motion of the cervical spine.
3. Note thoracic configuration, symmetry of shoulders, and position of scapula.
4. Palpate the posterior thorax and lateral thorax.
5. Perform posterior thoracic expansion.
6. Perform tactile fremitus on the posterior thorax and lateral thorax.
7. Percuss the posterior thorax and lateral thorax.
8. Perform diaphragmatic excursion.
9. Palpate the costovertebral angle (CVA); percuss the CVA with your fist.
10. Auscultate the posterior thorax and lateral thorax, perform voice sounds if indicated.

Move in front of the patient. Drape the patient's gown at waist level (females may cover their breasts).

Anterior Thorax

1. Inspect shape of the thorax, symmetry of the chest wall, presence of superficial veins, costal angle, angle of ribs, intercostal spaces, muscles of respiration, respirations, and sputum.
2. Palpate the anterior thorax.
3. Perform anterior thoracic expansion.
4. Perform tactile fremitus.
5. Percuss the anterior thorax.
6. Auscultate the anterior thorax; perform voice sounds if indicated.

Heart

1. Auscultate cardiac landmarks: aortic, pulmonic, mitral, and tricuspid areas and Erb's point.

Ask the female patient to uncover her breasts.

Female Breasts

1. Inspect the breasts for colour, vascularity, thickening or edema, size, symmetry, contour, lesions or masses, and discharge with the patient in these positions: arms at side, arms raised over the head, hands pressed into hips, hands in front, and patient leaning forward.
2. Palpate the breasts with the patient's arms first at her side and then raised over her head.
3. Palpate the brachial, central axillary, pectoral, and subscapular lymph nodes.
4. Teach breast self-examination.

Male Breasts

1. Repeat the sequence used for female breasts. Having the patient lean forward is usually unnecessary unless gynecomastia is present.

Assist the patient into a supine position with the chest uncovered. Drape the abdomen and legs. Stand on the right side of the patient.

Jugular Veins

As the patient changes from a sitting to a supine position for the remainder of the breast assessment, observe the jugular veins when the patient is at a 45° angle. Assess again when the patient is supine.

1. Inspect the jugular veins for distension; estimate JVP if indicated.

Female and Male Breasts

1. Palpate each breast. The arm on the same side of the assessed breast should be raised over the head.
2. Compress the nipple to express any discharge.

Heart

1. Inspect cardiac landmarks for pulsations.
2. Palpate cardiac landmarks for pulsations, thrills, and heaves.
3. Palpate the apical impulse.

4. With the diaphragm of the stethoscope, auscultate the cardiac landmarks; count the apical pulse.
5. With the bell of the stethoscope, auscultate the cardiac landmarks.
6. Turn the patient on the left side and repeat auscultation of cardiac landmarks.

Return the patient to a supine position. Cover the patient's anterior thorax with the gown. Uncover the abdomen from the symphysis pubis to the costal margin.

Abdomen

1. Inspect contour, symmetry, pigmentation, and colour.
2. Note scars, striae, visible peristalsis, masses, and pulsations.
3. Inspect the rectus abdominis muscles (supine and with head raised) and respiratory movement of the abdomen.
4. Inspect the umbilicus.
5. Auscultate bowel sounds.
6. Auscultate for bruits, venous hum, and friction rub.
7. Percuss all four quadrants.
8. Percuss liver span and liver descent; percuss liver with fist if indicated.
9. Percuss the spleen, stomach, and bladder.
10. Lightly palpate all four quadrants.
11. Note any muscle guarding.
12. Deeply palpate all four quadrants.
13. Palpate the liver, spleen, kidney, aorta, and bladder.
14. Assess superficial abdominal reflexes.
15. Perform hepatojugular reflux if indicated.

Inguinal Area

1. Inspect and palpate the inguinal lymph nodes.
2. Inspect for inguinal hernias.
3. Palpate the femoral pulses.
4. Auscultate the femoral pulses for bruits.

Cover the exposed abdomen with the gown. Lift the drape from the bottom to expose the lower extremities.

Lower Extremities

1. Inspect for colour, capillary refill, edema, ulcerations, hair distribution, and varicose veins.
2. Palpate for temperature, edema, and texture.
3. Palpate the popliteal, dorsalis pedis, and posterior tibial pulses.
4. Inspect muscle size and palpate muscle tone of the legs and feet.
5. Palpate the joints of the hips, knees, ankles, and feet.
6. Assess range of motion and strength of the hips, knees, ankles, and feet.
7. Test position sense.
8. Assess for clonus.

Drape the lower extremities. Assist the patient to a sitting position and note the ease with which the patient sits up. Have the patient dangle the legs over the edge of the examination table.

Neurological System

1. Assess light touch: face (CN V), hands, lower arms, abdomen, feet, and legs.
2. Assess superficial pain (sharp and dull): face (CN V), hands, lower arms, abdomen, feet, and legs.

3. Assess two-point discrimination: tongue, lips, fingers, dorsum of hand, torso, and feet.
4. Assess vibration sense: fingers and toes.
5. Assess stereognosis, graphesthesia, and extinction.
6. Assess cerebellar function: finger to nose, rapid alternating hand movements, touching thumb to each finger, running heel down shin, and foot tapping.
7. Assess deep tendon reflexes: biceps, triceps, brachioradialis, patellar, and achilles.
8. Assess plantar reflex and Babinski's reflex.

Ask the patient to stand barefoot on the floor. If the patient is unsteady, use caution when performing these tests. Remain physically close to the patient at all times.

Musculoskeletal System

1. Assess mobility: casual walk, heel walk, toe walk, tandem walk, backward walk, stepping to the right and left, and deep knee bends (one knee at a time). Note any indications of discomfort.

Stand behind the patient.

2. Assess range of motion of the spine.

Open the patient's gown to expose the back. Ask the patient to bend forward at the waist.

3. Inspect the spine for scoliosis.

Close the patient's gown. Stand in front of the patient.

Neurological System

1. Perform the Romberg test; assess pronator drift.
2. Assess the ability to hop on one foot, run heel down shin, and draw a figure eight with foot.

Assist the female patient back to the examination table. Ask her to assume the lithotomy position. Drape the patient. Sit on a stool in front of the patient's legs.

Female Genitalia, Anus, and Rectum

1. Inspect pubic hair and skin colour and condition: mons pubis, vulva, clitoris, urethral meatus, vaginal introitus, sacrococcygeal area, perineum, and anal mucosa.
2. Palpate the labia, urethral meatus, Skene's glands, vaginal introitus, and perineum.
3. Insert the vaginal speculum.
4. Inspect the cervix: colour, position, size, surface characteristics, discharge, and shape of cervical os; inspect the vagina.
5. Collect specimens for cytological smears and cultures.

Stand in front of the patient's legs.

6. Perform bimanual assessment of the vagina, cervix, fornices, uterus, and adnexa.
7. Perform rectovaginal assessment.
8. Palpate the anus and rectum.
9. If stool is on the glove, save it to test for occult blood.

Assist the patient to a sitting position. Offer her some tissues to wipe the perineal area. Ask her to redress. You can answer her questions when she is dressed.

Ask the male patient to stand. Sit on a stool in front of the patient. Have the patient lift the gown to expose the genitalia.

Male Genitalia

1. Inspect hair distribution, penis, scrotum, and urethral meatus.
2. Palpate the penis, urethral meatus, and scrotum.
3. Palpate the inguinal area for hernias.
4. Auscultate the scrotum if indicated.
5. Teach testicular self-examination.

Ask the patient to bend over the examination table. If the patient is bedridden, the knee-chest or left lateral position may be used. Expose the buttocks. Stand behind the patient.

Male Anus, Rectum, and Prostate

1. Inspect the perineum, sacrococcygeal area, and anal mucosa.
2. Palpate the anus and rectum.
3. Palpate the prostate.
4. If stool is on the glove, save it to test for occult blood.

Re-cover the buttocks. Ask the patient to stand up and redress. Offer him tissues to wipe the rectal area. You can answer his questions when he is dressed.

The patient has the opportunity to regain composure and formulate questions about the assessment while getting redressed. It is often difficult for patients to discuss future plans when wearing an examination gown. For this reason, give the patient a few minutes to redress in privacy before proceeding with the assessment. Always thank the patient for his or her time and explain what can be expected next.

When completing the assessment, ensure that you return the patient to the state you found him or her in at the beginning of the assessment. For example, for the bedridden patient, ensure that the side rails are up (if appropriate) and that the call bell is readily accessible. Ask the patient if there is anything else that can be done to make him or her comfortable.

Now that you have all of this information, what do you do with it, and how do you make sense of it? Refer back to Chapter 1, which discussed how to make the leap from assessment data to formulating a nursing analysis and plan of care.

Nursing Tip

Communicating Bad News

Be sensitive when communicating bad or unexpected news to the patient, significant other(s), or caregiver. Talk to the patient in a quiet, private room. Speak in terms that will be understood. Give the patient time to process the information, alone if desired. Convey the same high level of respect that you have shown throughout the interview and assessment process. Finally, allow time for questions.

Nursing Tip

Assessing the Patient Who Is Comatose

For the comatose patient, the family and prior health care records can provide valuable information for the health history. Do not let the patient's condition deter you from conducting a thorough physical assessment. Omit components of the assessment that require volition and patient cooperation; complete the remainder of the assessment as indicated. Remember to assess neurological status thoroughly. Consider assessing: doll's eyes, corneal reflex, Babinski's reflex, clonus, and superficial and deep pain response.

Nursing Tip

Assessing the Patient Who Is Bedridden

The bedridden patient will likely be feeling unwell, possibly weak, and unable to move easily in bed as the various body parts are assessed. Components of the physical assessment that require the patient to be out of bed can be omitted. Cerebellar function of the lower extremities can still be assessed by having the patient run the heel of each foot down each shin and draw a figure 8 with each foot on the bed or in the air. It may be necessary to gain the assistance of another person to help during the assessment—both for the patient's and the nurse's ease and comfort. If the patient can tolerate a sitting position, the second person can help hold the patient in this position while an assessment of the head, face, neck, and anterior thorax is conducted.

LABORATORY AND DIAGNOSTIC DATA

The laboratory and diagnostic data that are obtained from the patient vary according to presenting symptoms and clinical assessment. Nurses play an important role in informing patients about how to prepare for specific tests and what to expect, which is particularly important if the test is invasive such as a lumbar puncture, or something the patient has never experienced such as a CT (computerized tomography) scan.

SUMMARY OF HEALTH ISSUES OR CONCERNS

The health history, physical examination, and laboratory and diagnostic data provide the database on which clinical action is taken. As described in Chapter 1, similar signs, symptoms, and findings are clustered together in a meaningful way. A list of the health issues and concerns is documented to provide a summary reference. Such lists help health care practitioners to be more efficient and accurate in follow-up visits. The summary list is modified as certain health issues or concerns are resolved, and new issues are added as they emerge. It is generally most helpful when the chronology of issues is noted by date of presentation and resolution. An example of a summary list of health issues or concerns is seen below:

ONSET DATE		HEALTH ISSUE/CONCERN	INACTIVE ISSUE/CONCERN
1970	1		Pneumonia
1971	2		ITP
1991	3	Bilat ovarian cysts	
1995	4	Allergic rhinitis	
1996	5	Reactive airway disease	
2003	6		Ⓛ plantar fasciitis
2007	7	Cystocele	

A plan of care is developed to address each active problem within this list and then the implementation and evaluation of the plan begin.

PREPARTICIPATION ATHLETIC EVALUATION

Nurses are often asked to assess if the client is able to participate in athletic activities. The purpose is to assess whether a particular activity can be taken on safely and, if that is not possible, to suggest other activities that better fit with the individual's abilities. The evaluation generally encompasses a thorough personal health history (especially cardiovascular and musculoskeletal) as well as physical examination (with emphasis on cardiovascular and musculoskeletal systems).

Conditions such as atlantoaxial instability, carditis, hypertrophic cardiomyopathy, uncontrolled severe hypertension, suspected coronary artery disease, specific ECG abnormalities (e.g., long QT interval), absence of a paired organ, poorly controlled seizure disorder, and hepatosplenomegaly may preclude activity in certain or all sports. The patient is evaluated on a case-by-case basis to assess fitness to participate in sports.

Nursing Tip

Physical Activity Readiness Questionnaire (PAR-Q)

Health Canada has developed the PAR-Q for people between 15 and 69 to determine if they need to consult a health care professional prior to commencing an activity. Those who answer **NO** to all of the questions noted below can be reasonably sure that they can start becoming more physically active without consultation. Those who answer **YES** to one or more questions are urged to consult a health care professional.

1. Has your doctor ever said that you have a heart condition and that you should do only physical activity recommended by a doctor?
2. Do you feel pain in your chest when you do physical activity?
3. In the past month, have you had chest pain when you were not doing physical activity?
4. Do you lose your balance because of dizziness, or do you ever lose consciousness?
5. Do you have a bone or joint problem that could be made worse by a change in your physical activity?
6. Is your doctor currently prescribing drugs (for example, water pills) for your blood pressure or heart condition?
7. Do you know of any other reason you should not do physical activity?

Source: www.phac-aspc.gc.ca/pau-uap/fitness/questionnaire.html, Public Health Agency of Canada & Canadian Society for Exercise Physiology, 2003. Reproduced with the permission of the Minister of Public Works and Government Services Canada, 2006.

Reflective Thinking

Evaluating Children for Sports Participation

A 12-year-old comes to the clinic because he needs a note from a health professional to say that he can play in the school's intramural basketball program. He is 157 cm tall and weighs 69 kg. His mother states that he has "exertional asthma." His blood pressure today was 152/85. What would you tell this child? What interventions would you plan?

CONCLUSION

Today's nurse is a sophisticated health professional prepared to meet the demands of the health care system. Whether nurses work in hospitals, outpatient clinics, home care, community or public health agencies, prisons, the military, public or private health care facilities, or rural or urban centres, or with any age group, they will need to be thorough and up to date on all aspects of the health history and physical examination. Because the entire plan of care is based on an accurate, relevant, and comprehensive patient assessment, all nurses must possess these assessment skills. This text has supplied the information to assist the novice and the experienced nurse in acquiring, refining, and perfecting health history and physical examination skills. The pathophysiological basis for the physical assessment findings empowers the nurse to fully understand the patient's clinical state and make appropriate clinical decisions in situations of illness. A health promotion and health maintenance approach enables our patients to achieve their life goals. Ultimately, the patients and their families are the benefactors of your knowledge, wisdom, and experience.

CASE STUDY	The Patient with Multisystem Problems

HEALTH HISTORY

TODAY'S DATE	*February 6, 2007*
BIOGRAPHICAL DATA	
Patient Name	Basma Assaf
Address	222 South Street, Apt. 1B Toronto, ON M0X 0l0
Phone Number	**(416) 555-0000**
Date of Birth	May 31, 1985
Birthplace	Vancouver, BC
Occupation	Fast-food employee
Usual Source of Health Care	None; parents used emergency room when young child
Source of Referral	Friend
Emergency Contact	Fakhria Assaf (sister)
Source and Reliability of Information	Pt doesn't always remember circumstances of events & dates; some info given contradicts info given earlier in interview
PATIENT PROFILE	*21 yo single woman who looks concerned and tired*
HEALTH ISSUE/CONCERN	*"I have a fever. I feel so bad. My throat hurts. My back hurts. It hurts when I pass urine. Please help me."*
HISTORY OF ISSUE/CONCERN	In usual state of hl until 5 d ago when started to have a sore throat; difficult to swallow; took acetaminophen $\times$ 2 (dose?) $\bar{s}$ much relief; felt feverish the next day; urinary frequency (q 20–30 min) developed 3 d ago; $\neq$ feel her bladder is being emptied completely; noted hematuria next day along $\bar{c}$ shaking chills, LBP, flank pain, malaise, nausea, $\oplus$ H/A; has not been active sexually; no vomiting, diarrhea, constipation, vaginal discharge; LMP 10 d ago; unable to sleep 2 hr to sx; pt remembers having dysuria every few yrs (2–3 $\times$) but sx went away $\bar{s}$ tx $\bar{p}$ a few days; pt has missed work $\times$ 4d & needs to get well so she can get back to work
PAST HEALTH HISTORY	
Medical History	Seasonal allergies; in fall gets pruritic ears/eyes $\bar{c}$ clear rhinorrhea & sneezing Recalls having frequent ear infections as a child with "tubes" inserted; no current problems
Surgical History	Bilateral tubal myringotomy as child; $\neq$ know where inserted/when

continues

Medications	Acetaminophen 1–2 tabs po prn (≠ sure which strength); usually 2–3 × wk Diphenhydramine 1–2 pills bid 2 mos ago for 3 wks (≠ sure dose) for allergies
Communicable Diseases	Recalls mother having TB last yr; ≠ living c̄ her at that time, but visited her wkly; was never tested Denies HSV, STIs, hepatitis, ⊕ HIV
Allergies	NKDA; no allergies to foods, insect bites/bee stings
Injuries and Accidents	None
Special Needs	States none
Blood Transfusions	None
Childhood Illnesses	Frequent sore throats that her mother treated c̄ cold fluids as she was growing up
Immunizations	Not sure

FAMILY HEALTH HISTORY

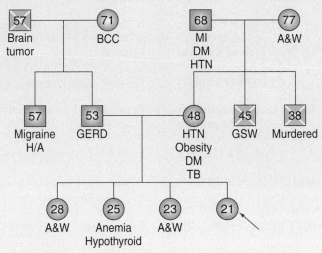

LEGEND

- ⬤ Living female
- ◼ Living male
- ⊗ Deceased female
- ⊠ Deceased male
- ╱ Points to patient

A&W = Alive & well
BCC = Basal cell carcinoma
DM = Diabetes mellitus
GERD = Gastroesophageal reflux disease
GSW = Gunshot wound
H/A = Headache
HTN = Hypertension
MI = Myocardial infarction
TB = Tuberculosis

57 Brain tumor — 71 BCC

68 MI DM HTN — 77 A&W

57 Migraine H/A

53 GERD

48 HTN Obesity DM TB

45 GSW

38 Murdered

28 A&W

25 Anemia Hypothyroid

23 A&W

21

Denies FHH of CVA, kidney dz, epilepsy, gout, liver dz, asthma, allergic disorders, alcoholism, mental illness, drug addiction, AIDS, HIV dz, violent rx.

SOCIAL HISTORY

Alcohol Use	Denies ever using/trying
Drug Use	Denies
Domestic and Intimate Partner Violence	Denies
Tobacco Use	Denies
Sexual Practice	Never been sexually active
Travel History	Never been out of the country

continues

Work Environment	Works in fast-food burger restaurant 40–50 hrs/wk; usually takes orders & fills orders; rarely cooks; rotates shifts ranging from 04:00–MN; schedule constantly Δ; frequently feels tired from being on feet all day
Home Environment	Lives in basement, 1 bedroom apt c̄ 3 older sisters in low-income housing; they pool salaries to pay rent & utilities; smoke detector—usually s̄ batteries; on bus line
Hobbies and Leisure Activities	Watches TV, window shops
Stress	Current hl status; mother is pressuring her & older sisters to get married; feels like she is "not going anywhere"; "I feel like I have no direction I don't know what I want to do with the rest of my life."
Education	Finished HS; describes self as "mediocre" student
Economic Status	Lives paycheque to paycheque; she & her sisters equally share living expenses of food, housing; little money left over for socializing
Religion	Muslim; fasts during Ramadan; avoids pork & pork products; reads the Koran regularly
Ethnicity	"My parents are from Egypt and I was born in Canada."
Roles and Relationships	Turns to older sisters for advice & support; they are her friends & she values them greatly; sees parents wkly; enjoys friends at work but ≠ socialize c̄ them outside of work
Characteristic Patterns of Daily Living	Varies due to work schedule but usually wakes at 04:30 & leaves for work by 05:00; catches bus to work & starts at 05:30; has breakfast at work ā she starts shift; break from 10:00–10:30 & eats lunch at this time; works until 14:00–17:00; catches bus & goes home; she & sisters rotate cooking, grocery shopping, & cleaning of apt duties; roster in kitchen is updated wkly c̄ chores; eats dinner c̄ sisters, watches TV & goes to bed by 22:00–23:00
HEALTH MAINTENANCE ACTIVITIES	
Sleep	$5\frac{1}{2}$–$6\frac{1}{2}$ hrs q PM; feels tired much of the day; has difficulty falling asleep; ≠ employ any strategies to promote sleep
Diet	Breakfast & lunch at fast-food restaurant; dinner usually rice & fish c̄ vegetables
Exercise	Currently no exercise but would like to start walking
Stress Management	Usually cries until she feels better
Use of Safety Devices	Seat belt used regularly
Health Check-Ups	Does not know date of last physical examination/dentist; never had eyes examined; never had a gyn exam Usually very healthy
REVIEW OF SYSTEMS	
Skin	Denies rashes, itching, Δ in skin pigmentation, ecchymoses, Δ in skin texture, sores, lumps, odours, sweating, acne, denies sunbathing, ≠ use sunblock
Hair	Occasional dandruff & itchy scalp—uses dandruff shampoo wkly; denies alopecia/hirsutism

continues

Nails	Denies use of chemicals; ≠ use false nails/polish; denies splitting/breaking or △ in texture
Eyes	No photophobia, ↑ tearing, diplopia, eye drainage, bloodshot eyes, eye pain, blind spots, flashing lights, halos around objects, glaucoma, cataracts; never been examined by specialist
Ears	No hearing deficits, hearing assistive device, ear pain, discharge, vertigo, earaches, tinnitus, infection
Nose and Sinuses	Allergies per PHH; denies frequent URIs, discharge, itching, postnasal drip, stuffiness, sinus pain, nasal polyps, obstruction, △ in sense of smell, nosebleeds pain/stiffness, goiter
Mouth	Brushes teeth bid–tid, floss; denies toothache, tooth abscess, bleeding/swollen gums, difficulty chewing, sore tongue, △ in taste, lesions, △ in salivation, bad breath; last check-up >5 yrs ago
Throat/Neck	Sore throat per health history; denies hoarseness, △ in voice, difficulty swallowing.
Breasts	No pain, tenderness, discharge, lumps, dimpling; doesn't perform BSE
Respiratory	⊕ exposure to mother's TB last year; mother has completed med course; denies having PPD, CX-ray or screening for TB; denies SOB, DOE, cough, sputum, wheezing, hemoptysis, asthma
Cardiovascular	Denies PND, CP, orthopnea, heart murmur, palpitations, syncope, edema, cold hands/feet, leg cramps, MI, valvular dz, thrombophlebitis, anemia.
Gastrointestinal	Soft brown stool every other day; denies △ in appetite, N, V, D, constipation, melena, hematemesis, △ in stool colour, flatulence, belching, regurgitation, heartburn, dysphagia, abd pain, jaundice, hemorrhoids, hepatitis, PUD, gallstones
Muskuloskeletal	Denies back pain, redness, swelling, bone deformity, weakness, broken bones, dislocations, sprains, gout, arthritis, herniated disc
Neurological	Denies △ in balance, incoordination, loss of mvt, △ in sensory/perception, △ in speech, △ in smell, loss of memory, tremors, involuntary mvt, Ø LOC, sz, weakness
Psychological	Denies irritability, nervousness, tension, ↑ stress, difficulty concentrating, mood changes, suicidal thoughts, depression
Urinary	Dysuria per health history; no △ in urine colour, hesitancy, reduced force of stream, bedwetting, incontinence, suprapubic pain, kidney stones, UTI
Female Reproductive	Menarche age 12; reg menses q 27–29 d lasting 5 d; heaviest flow days 2–3; menses accompanied by mild cramping relieved by acetaminophen; ≠ sexually active; denies vaginal discharge, intermenstrual bleeding
Nutrition	Not sure of usual/current wt; thinks she has gained wt recently b/c some of her clothes are getting tight; likes hamburgers & fries—gets 2 meals free daily & c̄ limited income she eats fried food at work; prefers fish & vegetables; c/o indigestion p̄ eating onions
Endocrine	Denies bulging eyes, fatigue, △ in size of head/hands/feet, heat/cold intolerance, ↑ sweating, ↑ thirst, ↑ hunger, △ in body hair distribution, swelling in ant neck, DM
Lymph Nodes	Tenderness on Ⓡ side of neck; denies enlargement
Hematological	No bleeding tendency, no bruising, doesn't know blood type.

continues

PHYSICAL EXAMINATION

General Survey and Vital Signs	BP: 115/72 (Ⓛ arm sitting), 118/74 (Ⓛ arm lying), 112/70 (Ⓡarm sitting) Looks stated age, worried, well groomed HT: 163.6 cm WT: 63 kg T: 38.5°C po P: 92 R: 16
Skin, Hair, and Nails	s̄ lesions, rashes, ecchymoses, edema, bleeding; very warm to touch c̄ diaphoresis, smooth texture, ↓ turgor; hair shiny black c̄ even distribution, s̄ infestations; patches of scattered seborrhea; nailbeds pink, firm c̄ T̄ sec cap refill, no clubbing
Head	Normocephalic s̄ lesions, masses, depressions, or tenderness; face symmetrical s̄ involuntary mvt or swelling; scalp shiny & intact s̄ lesions or masses; TMJ articulates smoothly s̄ clicking or crepitus
Eyes	Acuity by Snellen chart: OD 20/30, OS 20/25, able to read newspaper s̄ difficulty, colour vision intact, visual fields by confrontation intact, eyebrows full & symmetrical, eyelashes evenly distributed & s̄ inflammation, Ø ptosis or lid lag, lacrimal apparatus s̄ inflammation or discharge, corneal light reflex symmetrical s̄ strabismus, cover-uncover test s̄ deviation, EOM mvt intact, Ø nystagmus, conjunctiva pink, Ø foreign bodies, Ø tearing, sclera white s̄ exudate, PERRLA (3 mm)
Ears	Funduscopic: ⊕ red reflex, discs flat c̄ sharp margins, vessels in A-V ratio of 2:3, background uniformly pink s̄ hemorrhages or exudate Gross hearing intact by watch tick test; pinna s̄ masses, lesions, nodules, inflammation, or tenderness, EAC clear s inflammation; TMs shiny c̄ myringotomy tubes placed inferiorly to malleus bilaterally; Weber midline; Rinne AC > BC
Nose and Sinuses, Throat	Ø deformities, bleeding, lesions, masses, swelling; nares patent, non-tender; septum midline s̄ perforation; mucosa pale & boggy; sinuses non-tender, resonant Halitosis; lips pink s̄ swelling or lesions; gums & mucosa pink & moist; 30 teeth in good repair; tongue midline, well papillated, & s̄ fasciculations, lesions, swelling, or bleeding; hard & soft palates intact s̄ lesions or masses; pharynx erythematous; uvula midline & rises c̄ phonation; 2+/4+ tonsils; ⊕ gag reflex; white exudate patches on Ⓡ
Neck	Supple s̄ masses or spasms & c̄ full ROM, neck symmetrical s̄ masses or tenderness, lymph nodes tender Ⓡ ant cervical chain & tonsillar lymphadenopathy, trachea midline, thyroid non-tender s̄ enlargement, Ø bruits, Ø JVD at 90°, 45°, & supine
Breasts	Ø thickening, edema, vascularity, erosion, fissures, lesions, masses, retraction, discharge; areola & nipples dark in pigmentation; non-palpable lymph nodes
Thorax and Lungs	AP: transverse diameter = 1:2, chest wall symmetrical, costal angle <90°, angle of the ribs c̄ sternum = 45°, Ø bulging of ICS or retractions, no use of accessory muscles, resp reg, thoracic expansion 4 cm ant & 4 cm post, tactile fremitus = bilaterally, lungs resonant, diaphragmatic excursion 3 cm bilat, clear breath sounds; Ø adventitious breath sounds

continues

Heart	Precordium $\bar{s}$ pulsations/heaves/thrills, apical pulse 90, apical impulse 1 cm at 5th ICS 2 cm to Ⓛ of MCL, S_1 & S_2 present $\bar{c}$ II/VI SEM heard best LSB; Ø JVD
Abdomen	Flat $\bar{s}$ striae, dilated veins, scars, incisions; ⊕ bowel sounds in 4 quads, Ø bruits, venous hum, friction rub; tympanic x immediately superior to symphysis pubis for 3 cm; abd soft, Ø masses/tenderness to light/deep palpation; liver span 8 cm in Ⓡ MCL; ⊕ bilateral CVA tenderness
Peripheral Vasculature	Ø edema or ulcerations, ⊖ Homan's sign, pulse reg & strong, Ø pulsus paradoxus, Ø bruits

	Carotid	Brachial	Radial	Femoral	Popliteal	Dorsalis Pedis	Posterior Tibial
R	2+	2+	2+	2+	2+	2+	2+
L	2+	2+	2+	2+	2+	2+	2+

Scale: 0–3+

Musculoskeletal	Posture/gait/mobility WNL; joints $\bar{s}$ erythema, edema, deformity, crepitus; muscles $\bar{s}$ atrophy, = in size $\bar{c}$ adequate tone; 5/5 muscle strength UE & LE; Ø involuntary mvt; UE & LE $\bar{c}$ full ROM
Neurological	Mental status: appropriate affect, mood, & behaviour, A, A & O × 3, thought processes & memory intact CN II–XII: intact, CN I deferred. Sensory: light touch, pain, position & vibration senses intact; stereognosis, graphesthesia, & 2-point discrimination intact Motor: ⊖ pronator drift Cerebellar: ⊖ Romberg, gait smooth & steady, tandem walk steady, draws figure 8 $\bar{c}$ each foot, finger-to-nose & rapid alternating hand movements intact Reflexes:

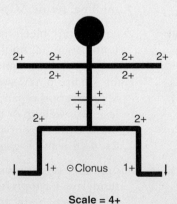

Scale = 4+

Genitalia and Rectum	Pt refused $\bar{p}$ repeated explanations of importance
LABORATORY DATA	
Strep Screen	⊕ (nl = neg) (only abnormal results are shown)
Blood Work	
Urinalysis	

Eosinophils	0.23	(nl = 0–0.08%)
BUN	15.7	(nl = 2.9–8.9 mmol/L)
Creatinine	186	(nl = 53–133 μmol/L)

continues

Urine Culture

Clarity	hazy	(nl = clear)
Protein	100	(nl = 0 mg/dl)
Blood	large	(nl = neg)
Leukocyte	small	(nl = neg)
RBC/HPF	25–50	(0–3/hpf)
WBC/HPF	25–50	(0–5/hpf)
WBC clumps	many	(nl = none/hpf)
Bacteria	moderate	(nl = few/hpf)

> 100,000 organisms (*E. coli*)

SUMMARY HEALTH ISSUES/CONCERNS

1. Seborrhea
2. Allergic rhinitis
3. Streptococcal pharyngitis
4. Myringotomy of extended duration
5. New systolic heart murmur
6. Urinary tract infection
7. Renal dysfunction
8. TB exposure
9. Symptom management
10. Identifying developmental goals

Visit the Estes online companion resource at www.healthassessment.nelson.com for additional content and study aids.

Appendix A
Public Health Agency of Canada Notifiable Diseases

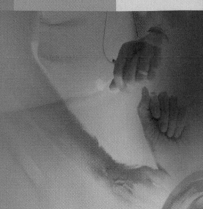

TABLE A-1 Public Health Agency of Canada Notifiable Diseases

DISEASES	ICD-9*
Acute Flaccid Paralysis	045
AIDS	042-044
Botulism	005.1
Brucellosis	023
Campylobacteriosis	008.41
Chickenpox	052
Chlamydia Genital	099.81
Cholera	001
Creutzfeld Jakob Disease	0461
Cryptosporidiosis	136.8
Cyclospora	
Diphtheria	032
Giardiasis	007.1
Gonococcal Infections	098
Group B Streptococcal Disease in Neonates	038.0
Haemophilus Influenza B (all-invasive)	3200.0,038.41
Hantavirus Pulmonary Syndrome	480.8
Hepatitis A	070.0,070.1
Hepatitis B	070.2,070.3
Hepatitis C	
Human Immunodeficiency Virus	
Invasive Group A Streptococcal Disease	034,035,670
Invasive Pricumococcal Disease	481
Laboratory-Confirmed Influenza	
Legionellosis	482.41
Leprosy	030
Malaria	084
Measles	055
Meningococcal Infections	036
Mumps	072

continues

TABLE A-1 Public Health Agency of Canada Notifiable Diseases (*continued*)

DISEASES	ICD-9
Pertussis	033
Plague	020
Poliomyelitis	045
Rabies	071
Rubella	056
Congenital Rubella	771.0
Salmonellosis	003
Shigellosis	004
Syphilis (all types)	090
Tetanus	037
Tuberculosis	010–018
Tularemia	
Typhoid	002.0
Verotoxigenic E. coli	008.01
Yellow Fever	060

ICD = International Classification of Diseases

Source: Public Health Agency Notifiable Diseases Summary (Preliminary) New Cases Report from 1st January to 31 March 2005, www.phac-aspc.gc.ca/publicat/ccdr-rmtc/06pdf/cdr3202. pdf. Reproduced with the permission of the Minister of Public Works and Government Services Canada, 2006.

Appendix B
Partner Notification Reference Chart

TABLE B-1 Partner Notification Reference Chart

INFECTION/SYNDROME	REPORTABLE DISEASE	TRACE-BACK PERIOD	WHO TO NOTIFY/EVALUATE	SPECIAL CONSIDERATIONS
Chlamydia (LGV and non LGV serovars)	Yes	60 days	SP/NB	• If no sexual partner(s) in the last 60 days, trace back to last sexual partner
Gonorrhea	Yes	60 days	SP/NB	• Partner notification is not required in most provinces and territories as a public health measure but is highly recommended for NGU, MPC, PID, and epididymitis
Chancroid	Yes	14 days	SP	
Non-gonococcal urethritis	No	60 days	SP	
Mucopurulent cervicitis	No	60 days	SP	
Pelvic inflammatory disease	No	60 days	SP	
Epididymitis	No	60 days	SP	
Primary syphilis	Yes	3 months	SP/NB	
Secondary syphilis	Yes	6 months	SP/NB	
Early latent syphilis	Yes	1 year	SP/NB	
Late latent syphilis/stage undetermined	Yes	Variable	SP/NB/CMC	
Genital herpes	In some jurisdictions	Current/future	SP/NB	Partner notification is not required as a public health measure but is highly recommended
Trichomoniasis	In some jurisdictions	Current	SP	No need to test partners; treat as for index case
Human papilloma virus	No	Current/future	SP	Partner notification is not required as a public health measure; patients should be encouraged to notify their sexual partners, but there is no proof that this will lower the risk to the partner
Acute hepatitis B	Yes	Variable	SP/NSP/HC/NB/CMC	• All unvaccinated/non-immune contacts should be notified; may benefit from PEP • Newborns must receive HBIG and vaccine postnatally
Chronic hepatitis B	Yes	Variable	SP/NSP/HC/NB/CMC	• All unvaccinated/non-immune contacts should be notified; may benefit from PEP • Newborns must receive HBIG and vaccine postnatally

continues

TABLE B-1   Partner Notification Reference Chart (*continued*)

INFECTION/SYNDROME	REPORTABLE DISEASE	TRACE-BACK PERIOD	WHO TO NOTIFY/EVALUATE	SPECIAL CONSIDERATIONS
HIV/AIDS	Yes	Variable	SP/NSP/NB/CMC	• Start with recent sexual and needle-sharing partners; outer limit is onset of risk behaviour or to last known negative test • Post-exposure prophylaxis may be considered by health care providers for individuals who have been in contact with HIV, and appropriately timed initiation of antiretroviral therapy is associated with a better prognosis and is a prerequisite to prevention of further transmission of disease; please consult with an expert in HIV

CMC = children of maternal case; HBIG = hepatitis B immunoglobulin; HC = household contacts; LGV = lymphogranuloma venereum; MPC = mucupurulent cervicitis; NB = newborns of infected mothers; NGU = non-gonococcal urethritis; NSP = needle-sharing partners; PEP = post-exposure prophylaxsis; PID = pelvic inflammatory disease; SP = sexual partners

Source: "Partner Notification Reference Chart," www.phac-aspc.gc.ca/std-mts/sti_2006/pdf/primary_care-soins_primaires_e%20.pdf. Reproduced with the permission of the Minister of Public Works and Government Services Canada, 2006.

Appendix C
The Denver II

The Denver II is composed of four sections: personal–social, fine motor–adaptive, language, and gross motor, and can be used to assess children from birth to 6 years. A total of 125 items are described on the test; some items can be accomplished easily by observing the child without commands from the observer. For instance, the child may be smiling spontaneously, saying words other than "mama" or "dada," or sitting with the head held steady. Certain items can be given an automatic pass mark if the caregiver indicates that the child is able to accomplish the corresponding item, such as drinking from a cup, washing and drying hands, or dressing without help.

Before administering the test, determine the child's chronological age and draw a straight line through the four sections intersecting the age intervals on the top and bottom of the sheet. This line indicates which items are to be tested for the child's chronological age. Begin testing by assessing the item that is three items to the left of the age line. Documentation is reflected by using a "P" for pass, "F" for fail, "R" for refuses, and "NO" for no opportunity. Give up to three trials before documenting the particular item's score on the Denver II. At the end, complete the five Test Behaviour questions. A normal test consists of no delays and a maximum of one caution. A caution is failure of the patient to perform an item that has been achieved by 75% to 90% of children the same age. A delay is a failure of any item to the left of the age line. A suspect test is one with 1 or more delays or 2 or more cautions; in these instances, retest the child in 1 to 2 weeks.

Keep in mind that current illness, lack of sleep, fear and anxiety, deafness, or blindness can affect a child's performance. If these or other logical rationale can explain a child's failure to successfully complete a series of Denver II items during a session, readminister the test in 1 month, providing resolution of the pre-existing condition is accomplished, where appropriate. If the child does in fact have a developmental disability, early detection can lead to appropriate intervention and assistance.

DIRECTIONS FOR ADMINISTRATION

1. Try to get child to smile by smiling, talking, or waving. Do not touch him or her.
2. Child must stare at hand for several seconds.
3. Parent may help guide toothbrush and put toothpaste on brush.
4. Child does not have to be able to tie shoes or button/zip in the back.
5. Move yarn slowly in an arc from one side to the other, about 20 cm above child's face.
6. Pass if child grasps rattle when it is touched to the backs or tips of fingers.
7. Pass if child tries to see where yarn went. Yarn should be dropped quickly from sight from tester's hand without arm movement.
8. Child must transfer cube from hand to hand without help of body, mouth, or table.
9. Pass if child picks up raisin with any part of thumb and finger.
10. Line can vary only 30° or less from tester's line.
11. Make a fist with thumb pointing upward and wiggle only the thumb. Pass if child imitates and does not move any fingers other than the thumb.
12. Pass any enclosed form. Fail continuous round motions.
13. Which line is longer? (Not bigger.) Turn paper upside down and repeat. (Pass 3 of 3 or 5 of 6.)
14. Pass any lines crossing near midpoint.
15. Have child copy first. If failed, demonstrate. When giving items 12, 14, and 15, do not name the forms. Do not demonstrate 12 and 14.
16. When scoring, each pair (2 arms, 2 legs, etc.) counts as one part.
17. Place one cube in cup and shake gently near the child's ear, but out of sight. Repeat for other ear.
18. Point to picture and have child name it. (No credit is given for sounds only.) If fewer than 4 pictures are named correctly, have child point to picture as each is named by tester.
19. Using doll, tell child: Show me the nose, eyes, ears, mouth, hands, feet, tummy, hair. Pass 6 of 8.

20. Using pictures, ask child: Which one flies? . . . says meow? . . . talks? . . . barks? . . . gallops? Pass 2 of 5, 4 of 5.

21. Ask child: What do you do when you are cold? . . . tired? . . . hungry? Pass 2 of 3, 3 of 3.

22. Ask child: What do you do with a cup? What is a chair used for? What is a pencil used for? Action words must be included in answers.

23. Pass if child correctly placed and says how many blocks are on paper. (1, 5)

24. Tell child: Put block **on** table; **under** table; **in front of** me, **behind** me. Pass 4 of 4. (Do not help child by pointing or moving head or eyes.)

25. Ask child: What is a ball? . . . lake? . . . desk? . . . house? . . . banana? . . . curtain? . . . fence? . . . ceiling? Pass if defined in terms of use, shape, what it is made of, or general category (such as banana is fruit, not just yellow). Pass 5 of 8, 7 of 8.

26. Ask child: If a horse is big, a mouse is __? If fire is hot, ice is __? If the sun shines during the day, the moon shines during the __? Pass 2 of 3.

27. Child may use wall or rail only, not person. May not crawl.

28. Child must throw ball overhand 3 feet to within arm's reach of tester.

29. Child must perform standing broad jump over width of test sheet ($8\frac{1}{2}$ inches).

30. Tell child to walk forward, heel within 2.5 cm of toe. Tester may demonstrate. Child must walk 4 consecutive steps.

31. In the second year, half of normal children are noncompliant.

OBSERVATIONS:

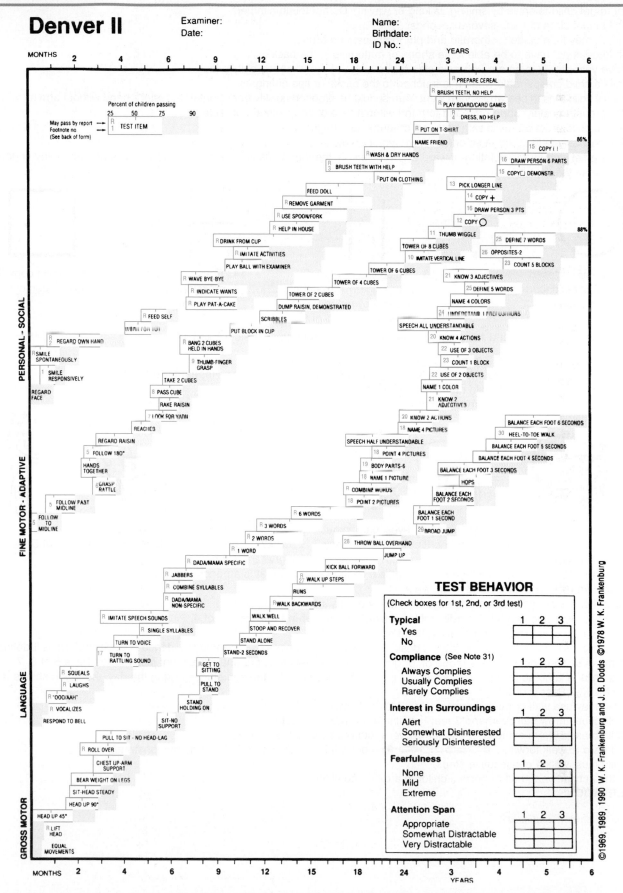

Figure C-1 Denver II. *Reprinted with permission of Denver Developmental Materials, Denver, CO*

continues

DIRECTIONS FOR ADMINISTRATION

1. Try to get child to smile by smiling, talking or waving. Do not touch him/her.
2. Child must stare at hand several seconds.
3. Parent may help guide toothbrush and put toothpaste on brush.
4. Child does not have to be able to tie shoes or button/zip in the back.
5. Move yarn slowly in an arc from one side to the other, about 8" above child's face.
6. Pass if child grasps rattle when it is touched to the backs or tips of fingers.
7. Pass if child tries to see where yarn went. Yarn should be dropped quickly from sight from tester's hand without arm movement.
8. Child must transfer cube from hand to hand without help of body, mouth, or table.
9. Pass if child picks up raisin with any part of thumb and finger.
10. Line can vary only 30 degrees or less from tester's line.
11. Make a fist with thumb pointing upward and wiggle only the thumb. Pass if child imitates and does not move any fingers other than the thumb.

12. Pass any enclosed form. Fail continuous round motions.
13. Which line is longer? (Not bigger.) Turn paper upside down and repeat. (Pass 3 of 3 or 5 of 6.)
14. Pass any lines crossing near midpoint.
15. Have child copy first. If failed, demonstrate.

When giving items 12, 14, and 15, do not name the forms. Do not demonstrate 12 and 14.

16. When scoring, each pair (2 arms, 2 legs, etc.) counts as one part.
17. Place one cube in cup and shake gently near the child's ear, but out of sight. Repeat for other ear.
18. Point to picture and have child name it. (No credit is given for sounds only.)
    If less than 4 pictures are named correctly, have child point to picture as each is named by tester.

19. Using doll, tell child: Show me the nose, eyes, ears, mouth, hands, feet, tummy, hair. Pass 6 of 8.
20. Using pictures, ask child: Which one flies? . . . says meow? . . . talks? . . . barks? . . . gallops? Pass 2 of 5, 4 of 5.
21. Ask child: What do you do when you are cold? . . . tired? . . . hungry? Pass 2 of 3, 3 of 3.
22. Ask child: What do you do with a cup? What is a chair used for? What is a pencil used for?
    Action words must be included in answers.
23. Pass if child correctly placed <u>and</u> says how many blocks are on paper. (1, 5)
24. Tell child: Put block **on** table; **under** table; **in front of** me, **behind** me. Pass 4 of 4.
    (Do not help child by pointing, moving head or eyes.)
25. Ask child: What is a ball? . . . lake? . . . desk? . . . house? . . . banana? . . . curtain? . . . fence? . . . ceiling? Pass if defined in terms of use, shape, what it is made of, or general category (such as banana is fruit, not just yellow). Pass 5 of 8, 7 of 8.
26. Ask child: If a horse is big, a mouse is __? If fire is hot, ice is __? If the sun shines during the day, the moon shines during the __? Pass 2 of 3.
27. Child may use wall or rail only, not person. May not crawl.
28. Child must throw ball overhand 3 feet to within arm's reach of tester.
29. Child must perform standing broad jump over width of test sheet (8½ inches).
30. Tell child to walk forward, ⚭⚭⚭⚭➡ heel within 1 inch of toe. Tester may demonstrate.
    Child must walk 4 consecutive steps.
31. In the second year, half of normal children are non-compliant.

OBSERVATIONS:

Figure C-1 Denver II *continued*

Appendix D
Functional Assessments:
Instrumental Activities of Daily Living (IADLs) and Physical Self-Maintenance Activities

I. **Instrumental Activities of Daily Living**

A. Ability to use telephone
1. Operates telephone independently—looks up and dials numbers
2. Dials a few well-known numbers
3. Answers phone but does not dial or use touch tone
4. Does not use telephone at all

B. Housekeeping
1. Maintains house independently or with occasional assistance for "heavy work"
2. Performs light tasks such as bedmaking and dishwashing
3. Performs light daily tasks but cannot maintain adequate level of cleanliness
4. Needs assistance with all home maintenance tasks
5. Does not participate in any tasks

C. Laundry
1. Does personal laundry completely
2. Launders small items such as socks and stockings
3. All laundry must be done by others

D. Mode of transportation
1. Independently drives own car or uses public transportation
2. Arranges own travel via taxi or special transportation services, but does not use public transportation and does not drive
3. Travels on public transportation when assisted or with others
4. Travel limited to taxi or auto with assistance
5. Does not travel at all

E. Responsibility for medications
1. Takes medication in correct dosages at correct time independently
2. Takes medication if medication is prepared in advance in separate doses
3. Not capable of dispensing own medications

F. Ability to handle finances
1. Independently manages finances—writes cheques, pays bills, keeps track of income
2. Manages own finances with assistance
3. Not capable of managing own finances

G. Shopping
1. Does all of the shopping independently
2. Shops for small purchases independently
3. Not able to go shopping without assistance
4. Unable to shop for any purchase

H. Food preparation
1. Able to prepare and serve food without assistance
2. Prepares adequate meals if supplied with food
3. Able to heat and serve prepared meals
4. Unable to prepare and serve meals

Adapted from "Assessment of Older People: Self-Maintaining and Instrumental Activities of Daily Living" by M. Lawton and E. Brody, 1969, The Gerontologist, 9, *179–186.*

II. **Physical Self-Maintenance Activities**

A. Feeding
1. Eats without assistance
2. Eats with minor assistance at mealtimes and helps in cleaning up
3. Feeds self with moderate assistance
4. Requires extensive assistance—all meals
5. Does not feed self at all and resists efforts of others to feed him or her

B. Toilet
1. Cares for self completely, no incontinence
2. Needs to be reminded or needs help in cleaning self
3. Soils the bed while asleep—more than once a week
4. Soils clothing while awake—more than once a week
5. No control of bladder or bowel

C. Grooming (hairs, nails, hands, face)
1. Able to care for self
2. Occasional minor assistance needed (e.g., with shaving)
3. Moderate and regular assistance needed
4. Needs total grooming care, but accepts some
5. Actively negates efforts of others to maintain grooming

D. Bathing
 1. Bathes self without help
 2. Bathes self with help into and out of tub or shower
 3. Can wash face and hands only
 4. Does not wash self but is cooperative
 5. Does not try to wash self and resists efforts of others to help

E. Dressing
 1. Dresses, undresses, and selects clothes from wardrobe
 2. Dresses and undresses with minor assistance
 3. Needs moderate assistance in dressing or selection of clothes
 4. Needs major assistance

 5. Completely unable to dress self and resists efforts of others to help

F. Ambulation
 1. Ambulates about grounds or city without assistance
 2. Ambulates within residence or nearby
 3. Ambulates with assistance of
    a. another person
    b. a railing
    c. cane
    d. walker
    e. wheelchair
 4. Sits unsupported in chair or wheelchair but cannot propel self
 5. Bedridden more than half the time

Appendix E
ISMP List of Error-Prone Abbreviations, Symbols, and Dose Designations

Abbreviations	Intended Meaning	Misinterpretation	Correction
μg	Microgram	Mistaken as "mg"	Use "mcg"
AD, AS, AU	Right ear, left ear, each ear	Mistaken as OD, OS, OU (right eye, left eye, each eye)	Use "right ear," "left ear," or "each ear"
OD, OS, OU	Right eye, left eye, each eye	Mistaken as AD, AS, AU (right ear, left ear, each ear)	Use "right eye," "left eye," or "each eye"
BT	Bedtime	Mistaken as "BID" (twice daily)	Use "bedtime"
cc	Cubic centimeters	Mistaken as "u" (units)	Use "mL"
D/C	Discharge or discontinue	Premature discontinuation of medications if D/C (intended to mean "discharge") has been misinterpreted as "discontinued" when followed by a list of discharge medications	Use "discharge" and "discontinue"
IJ	Injection	Mistaken as "IV" or "intrajugular"	Use "injection"
IN	Intranasal	Mistaken as "IM" or "IV"	Use "intranasal" or "NAS"
HS	Half-strength	Mistaken as bedtime	Use "half-strength" or "bedtime"
hs	At bedtime, hours of sleep	Mistaken as half-strength	
IU**	International unit	Mistaken as IV (intravenous) or 10 (ten)	Use "units"
o.d. or OD	Once daily	Mistaken as "right eye" (OD-oculus dexter), leading to oral liquid medications administered in the eye	Use "daily"
OJ	Orange juice	Mistaken as OD or OS (right or left eye); drugs meant to be diluted in orange juice may be given in the eye	Use "orange juice"
Per os	By mouth, orally	The "os" can be mistaken as "left eye" (OS-oculus sinister)	Use "PO," "by mouth," or "orally"
q.d. or QD**	Every day	Mistaken as q.i.d., especially if the period after the "q" or the tail of the "q" is misunderstood as an "I"	Use "daily"
qhs	At bedtime	Mistaken as "qhr" or every hour	Use "at bedtime"
qn	Nightly	Mistaken as "qh" (every hour)	Use "nightly"
q.o.d. or QOD**	Every other day	Mistaken as "q.d." (daily) or "q.i.d." (four times daily) if the "o" is poorly written	Use "every other day"
q1d	Daily	Mistaken as q.i.d. (four times daily)	Use "daily"
q6PM, etc.	Every evening at 6 PM	Mistaken as every 6 hours	Use "6 PM nightly" or "6 PM daily"
SC, SQ, sub q	Subcutaneous	SC mistaken as SL (sublingual); SQ mistaken as "5 every;" the "q" in "sub q" has been mistaken as "every" (e.g., a heparin dose ordered "sub q 2 hours before surgery" misunderstood as every 2 hours before surgery)	Use "subcut" or "subcutaneously"
ss	Sliding scale (insulin) or ½ (apothecary)	Mistaken as "55"	Spell out "sliding scale;" use "one-half" or "½"
SSRI	Sliding scale regular insulin	Mistaken as selective-serotonin reuptake inhibitor	Spell out "sliding scale (insulin)"
SSI	Sliding scale insulin	Mistaken as Strong Solution of Iodine (Lugol's)	
1/d	One daily	Mistaken as "tid"	Use "1 daily"
TIW or tiw	3 times a week	Mistaken as "3 times a day" or "twice in a week"	Use "3 times weekly"
U or u**	Unit	Mistaken as the number 0 or 4, causing a 10-fold overdose or greater (e.g., 4U seen as "40" or 4u seen as "44"); mistaken as "cc" so dose given in volume instead of units (e.g., 4u seen as 4cc)	Use "unit"

Dose Designations and Other Information	Intended Meaning	Misinterpretation	Correction
Trailing zero after decimal point (e.g., 1.0 mg)**	1 mg	Mistaken as 10 mg if the decimal point is not seen	Do not use trailing zeros for doses expressed in whole numbers
No leading zero before a decimal dose (e.g., .5 mg)**	0.5 mg	Mistaken as 5 mg if the decimal point is not seen	Use zero before a decimal point when the dose is less than a whole unit

Dose Designations and Other Information	Intended Meaning	Misinterpretation	Correction
Drug name and dose run together (especially problematic for drug names that end in "L" such as Inderal40 mg; Tegretol300 mg)	Inderal 40 mg Tegretol 300 mg	Mistaken as Inderal 140 mg Mistaken as Tegretol 1300 mg	Place adequate space between the drug name, dose, and unit of measure
Numerical dose and unit of measure run together (e.g., 10mg, 100mL)	10 mg 100 mL	The "m" is sometimes mistaken as a zero or two zeros, risking a 10- to 100-fold overdose	Place adequate space between the dose and unit of measure
Abbreviations such as mg. or mL. with a period following the abbreviation	mg mL	The period is unnecessary and could be mistaken as the number 1 if written poorly	Use mg, mL, etc. without a terminal period
Large doses without properly placed commas (e.g., 100000 units; 1000000 units)	100,000 units 1,000,000 units	100000 has been mistaken as 10,000 or 1,000,000; 1000000 has been mistaken as 100,000	Use commas for dosing units at or above 1,000, or use words such as 100 "thousand" or 1 "million" to improve readability

Drug Name Abbreviations	Intended Meaning	Misinterpretation	Correction
ARA A	vidarabine	Mistaken as cytarabine (ARA C)	Use complete drug name
AZT	zidovudine (Retrovir)	Mistaken as azathioprine or aztreonam	Use complete drug name
CPZ	Compazine (prochlorperazine)	Mistaken as chlorpromazine	Use complete drug name
DPT	Demerol-Phenergan-Thorazine	Mistaken as diphtheria-pertussis-tetanus (vaccine)	Use complete drug name
DTO	Diluted tincture of opium, or deodorized tincture of opium (Paregoric)	Mistaken as tincture of opium	Use complete drug name
HCl	hydrochloric acid or hydrochloride	Mistaken as potassium chloride (The "H" is misinterpreted as "K")	Use complete drug name unless expressed as a salt of a drug
HCT	hydrocortisone	Mistaken as hydrochlorothiazide	Use complete drug name
HCTZ	hydrochlorothiazide	Mistaken as hydrocortisone (seen as HCT250 mg)	Use complete drug name
MgSO4**	magnesium sulfate	Mistaken as morphine sulfate	Use complete drug name
MS, MSO4**	morphine sulfate	Mistaken as magnesium sulfate	Use complete drug name
MTX	methotrexate	Mistaken as mitoxantrone	Use complete drug name
PCA	procainamide	Mistaken as Patient Controlled Analgesia	Use complete drug name
PTU	propylthiouracil	Mistaken as mercaptopurine	Use complete drug name
T3	Tylenol with codeine No. 3	Mistaken as liothyronine	Use complete drug name
TAC	triamcinolone	Mistaken as tetracaine, Adrenalin, cocaine	Use complete drug name
TNK	TNKase	Mistaken as "TPA"	Use complete drug name
ZnSO4	zinc sulfate	Mistaken as morphine sulfate	Use complete drug name

Stemmed Drug Names	Intended Meaning	Misinterpretation	Correction
"Nitro" drip	nitroglycerin infusion	Mistaken as sodium nitroprusside infusion	Use complete drug name
"Norflox"	norfloxacin	Mistaken as Norflex	Use complete drug name
"IV Vanc"	intravenous vancomycin	Mistaken as Invanz	Use complete drug name

Symbols	Intended Meaning	Misinterpretation	Correction
ʒ ♏	Dram Minim	Symbol for dram mistaken as "3" Symbol for minim mistaken as "mL"	Use the metric system
x3d	For three days	Mistaken as "3 doses"	Use "for three days"
> and <	Greater than and less than	Mistaken as opposite of intended; mistakenly use incorrect symbol; "< 10" mistaken as "40"	Use "greater than" or "less than"
/ (slash mark)	Separates two doses or indicates "per"	Mistaken as the number 1 (e.g., "25 units/10 units" misread as "25 units and 110" units)	Use "per" rather than a slash mark to separate doses
@	At	Mistaken as "2"	Use "at"
&	And	Mistaken as "2"	Use "and"
+	Plus or and	Mistaken as "4"	Use "and"
°	Hour	Mistaken as a zero (e.g., q2° seen as q 20)	Use "hr," "h," or "hour"

**Abbreviations with a double asterisk are also included on the Joint Commission on Accreditation of Healthcare Organizations' "minimum list" of dangerous abbreviations, acronyms, and symbols that must be included on an organization's "do not use" list effective January 1, 2004. An updated list of frequently asked questions about this JCAHO requirement can be found at www.jcaho.org.*

Appendix F
Woman Abuse Screening Tool (WAST)

TABLE F-1 Woman Abuse Screening Tool (WAST)

1. In general, how would you describe your relationship?

   ☐ a lot of tension   ☐ some tension   ☐ no tension

2. Do you and your partner work out arguments with:

   ☐ great difficulty   ☐ some difficulty   ☐ no difficulty

3. Do arguments ever result in you feeling down or bad about yourself?

   ☐ often   ☐ sometimes   ☐ never

4. Do arguments ever result in hitting, kicking, or pushing?

   ☐ often   ☐ sometimes   ☐ never

5. Do you ever feel frightened by what your partner says or does?

   ☐ often   ☐ sometimes   ☐ never

6. Has your partner ever abused you physically?

   ☐ often   ☐ sometimes   ☐ never

7. Has your partner ever abused you emotionally?

   ☐ often   ☐ sometimes   ☐ never

8. Has your partner ever abused you sexually?

   ☐ often   ☐ sometimes   ☐ never

Scoring of the WAST: for the first question, "a lot of tension" gets a score of 1 and the other 2 get a 0. For the second question, "great difficulty" gets a score of 1 and the other 2 get 0. For the remaining questions, "often" gets a score of 1, "sometimes" gets a score of 2, and "never" gets a score of 3.

Source: Brown, J. B., Lent, B., Schmidt, G., & Sas. G. (2000). Application of the woman abuse screening tool WAST and WAST-short in the family practice setting. *Journal of Family Practice, 49(10)*, 896–903.

Glossary

A

Abruptio Placenta Separation of the placenta from the uterine wall, which may cause significant internal (and perhaps external) bleeding, pain, and fetal compromise.

Accommodation Visual focusing from far to near as pupils constrict and eyes converge.

Acculturation Informal process of adaptation through which the beliefs, values, norms, and practices of a dominant culture are learned by a new member born into a different culture.

Acini *See* **Alveoli (of the Breast)**.

Acrocyanosis Normal phenomenon in light-skinned newborns whereby the hands and feet are blue and the rest of the body is pink.

Acromegaly Abnormal enlargement of the skull and bony facial structures caused by excessive secretion of growth hormone.

Action Response An interview technique that stimulates patients to make some change in their thinking and behaviour.

Active Listening Act of perceiving what is said both verbally and nonverbally.

Adnexa Fallopian tubes, ovaries, and their supporting ligaments.

Advance Directive Document (living will or power of attorney) outlining what should be done if a patient is too ill to self-direct medical care.

Adventitious Breath Sound Breath sound that is superimposed on normal breath sounds.

Afterload Initial resistance the ventricles must overcome in order to open the semilunar valves to propel the blood into both the systemic and the pulmonary circulation.

Ages and Stages Developmental Theory Belief that individuals experience similar sequential physical, cognitive, socioemotional, and moral changes during the same age periods, each of which is termed a developmental stage.

Ageusia Loss of the sense of taste.

Aggravating Factors Factors that worsen the severity of the patient's principal sign or symptom.

Agnosia Inability to recognize the form and nature of objects or persons.

Agnostic Person who is unsure if God exists.

Agonal Respirations Irregularly irregular respirations that signal impending death or compression of the respiratory centre.

Agoraphobia Fear and avoidance of being in places or situations from which escape might be difficult or in which help may not be available.

Agraphia Loss of the ability to write.

Air Trapping Abnormal respiratory pattern with rapid, shallow respirations and forced expirations; the lungs have insufficient time to fully exhale and air becomes trapped, leading to overexpansion of the lungs.

Albinism A congenital inability to form melanin resulting in a generalized lack of pigment of the skin, hair, and eyebrow.

Albumin Substance that transports nutrients, blood, and hormones and helps maintain osmotic pressure.

Alexia Loss of the ability to grasp the meaning of written words and sentences; also known as word blindness.

Allen Test Test used to assess for the patency of the radial and ulnar arteries.

Alleviating Factors Factors that decrease the severity of the patient's principal sign or symptom.

Alogia Inability to express oneself through speech.

Alopecia Sparse or absent distribution of hair; male or female pattern baldness.

Alveoli (of the Breast) Milk-producing glands located in the lobules; also called acini.

Alveoli (of the Lung) Smallest functional unit of the respiratory system; where gas exchange occurs.

Amblyopia Permanent loss of visual acuity resulting from uncorrected strabismus or certain other medical conditions.

Amenorrhea Absence of menses.

Anal Canal Terminal 3 to 4 cm of the large intestine.

Anal Columns Longitudinal folds of mucosa in the superior portion of the anal canal.

Anal Fissure   Linear tear in the epidermis of the anal canal.

Anal Incontinence   Involuntary release of rectal contents.

Anal Orifice   Exit to the gastrointestinal tract; located at the seam of the gluteal folds.

Anal Sinuses   Pockets in the anal canal that lie superior to the anal valves; secrete mucous when compressed by feces.

Anal Valves   Folds in the anal canal formed by joining anal columns.

Analgesia   Insensitivity to pain.

Anemia   Reduced number of red blood cells.

Anencephaly   Condition where the cerebral cortex or cranium does not develop.

Anergy   Diminished reaction to antigens.

Aneroid Manometer   Blood pressure measurement equipment with a calibrated dial and indicator that points to numbers representing air pressure within the blood pressure cuff.

Anesthesia   Absence of touch sensation.

Angina Pectoris   Myocardial ischemia that manifests as chest, neck, or arm pain.

Angle of Louis (Manubriosternal Junction or Sternal Angle)   Junction of the manubrium and the sternum.

Animism   Belief that all things in nature have souls.

Anisocoria   Condition of small difference in pupil sizes.

Annular   Lesions arranged in a circular pattern.

Anoderm   A thin, pale, stratified, squamus epithelium that lines the lower 2 cm of the anal canal.

Anorectal Abscess   Undrained collection of perianal pus of the tissue spaces in and adjacent to the anorectum.

Anorectal Fistula   Hollow, fibrous tract lined by granulation tissue and filled with purulent or serosanguineous discharge; has an opening inside the anal canal or rectum and one or more orifices in the perianal skin.

Anorectum   Area where the anal canal fuses with the rectum.

Anosmia   Loss of the sense of smell.

Anterior Axillary Line   Vertical line drawn from the origin of the anterior axillary fold along the anterolateral aspect of the thorax.

Anterior Chamber   Space anterior to the pupil and iris.

Anterior Triangle   Area of the neck formed by the mandible, the trachea, and the sternocleidomastoid muscle; contains the anterior cervical lymph nodes, the trachea, and the thyroid gland.

Anthropometric Measurements   Measurements of the human body, including height, weight, and body proportions.

Anticipatory Guidance   Approach covering health promotion and education; designed to inform at-risk individuals of physical, cognitive, psychological, and social changes that occur and what their nutritional needs are.

Antigen Skin Testing   Test of immune function.

Apex (of the Heart)   Lower portion of the heart.

Apex (of the Lung)   Top of the lung.

Apgar Score   A system for evaluating the newborn at one and five minutes of age, giving 0–2 points each for heart rate, respiratory effort, muscle tone, reflex irritability, and colour.

Aphasia   Impairment or absence of language function.

Aphonia   Total loss of voice.

Apnea   Lack of spontaneous respirations for 10 or more seconds.

Apneustic Respirations   Prolonged gasping during inspiration followed by a very short, inefficient expiration; pauses can last 30 to 60 seconds.

Apocrine Glands   Sweat glands that are associated with hair follicles.

Appendicular Skeleton   Peripheral skeleton including the limbs, pelvis, scapula, and clavicle.

Apraxia   Inability to convert intended speech into the motor act of speech; inability to perform purposeful acts or to manipulate objects.

Arcus Senilis   Benign degeneration of the peripheral cornea; a hazy, grey ring about 2 mm in size and located just inside the limbus; most commonly found in older individuals.

Areola   Pigmented area approximately 2.5 to 10 cm in diameter that surrounds the nipple.

Arrector Pili Muscle   Muscle that causes contraction of the skin and hair, resulting in "goose bumps."

Arrhythmia   Irregular heart rhythm; also known as dysrhythmia.

Ascites   Excess accumulation of fluid in the abdominal cavity.

Assessment   First step of the nursing process; the orderly collection of objective and subjective data on the patient's health status.

Associated Manifestations   Signs and symptoms that accompany a patient's principal sign or symptom.

Astereognosis   Inability to recognize the nature of objects by touch.

Asystole   Absence of cardia activity; flat line on EKG.

Ataxic Respirations   *See* **Biot's Respirations**.

Atheist   Person who does not believe in the existence of God.

Atherosclerosis   Development of lipid plaques along the coronary arteries.

Atlas   First cervical vertebra.

Atrial Kick   Final phase of diastole, when the atria contract to complete the final 20% to 30% of ventricular filling.

Atrioventricular (A-V) Node   One of the heart's pacemakers with an inherent rate of 40 to 60 beats per minute; receives the cardiac impulse from the sinoatrial node and conducts it to the atrioventricular bundle of His and thence to the walls of the ventricles.

Atrioventricular (A-V) Valves   Valves that prevent blood from entering the ventricles until diastole and prevent retrograde blood flow during systole; composed of the tricuspid and mitral valves.

Atrophy   Reduction in muscle size.

Augmentation Mammoplasty   Surgical breast enlargement.

Auricle   External ear; also called the pinna.

Auscultation   Process of active listening to sounds within the body to gather information on a patient's health status.

Auscultatory Gap   A silent interval that may be heard between the systolic and diastolic blood pressures that can occur in hypertensive patients or because the blood pressure cuff was deflated too rapidly.

Avolition   Lack of motivation for work or other goal-directed activity.

Axial Skeleton   Central skeleton, including the facial bones, skull, auditory ossicles, hyoid bone, ribs, sternum, and vertebrae.

Axillary Nodes   Lymphoid organs composed of four groups: central axillary, pectoral (anterior), subscapular (posterior), and brachial (lateral).

Axis Second cervical vertebra.

B

Balanitis   Inflammation of the glans penis.

Ballottement   Palpation technique to identify an organ or fluid.

Baroreceptors   Receptors located in the walls of most of the great arteries that sense hypotension and initiate reflex vasoconstriction and tachycardia to bring the blood pressure back to normal.

Barrel Chest   Abnormal thorax configuration where the ratio of the anteroposterior diameter to the transverse diameter of the chest is approximately 1:1.

Bartholin's Glands (Greater Vestibular Glands)   Located in the cleft between the labia minora and the hymenal ring; small, pea-shaped glands deep in the perineal structures that secrete a clear, viscid, odorless, alkaline mucous that improves the viability and motility of sperm along the female reproductive tract.

Base (of the Heart)   Uppermost portion of the heart.

Base (of the Lung)   Bottom of the lung.

Bell's Palsy   Idiopathic facial palsy of CN VII resulting in asymmetry of the palpebral fissures, nasolabial folds, mouth, and facial expression on the affected side.

Bilingualism   Habitual use of two different languages, particularly when speaking.

Biot's (or Ataxic) Respirations   Irregularly irregular respiratory pattern caused by damage to the medulla.

Blepharitis   Inflamed, scaly, red-rimmed eyelids, sometimes with loss of the eyelashes.

Blood Pressure   Vital sign collected to assess cardiac output and vascular resistance; it measures the force exerted by the flow of blood pumped into the large arteries.

Body Mass Index (BMI)   Measurement that indicates body composition based on a person's height and weight; an increased BMI indicates obesity and a decreased BMI indicates possible malnutrition.

Borborygmi   Normal hyperactive bowel sounds.

Bouchard's Node   Bony enlargement of the proximal interphalangeal joint of the finger.

Bow Legs *See* **Genu Varum**.

Bradycardia   Pulse rate under 60 beats per minute in a resting adult.

Bradypnea   Respiratory rate under 12 breaths per minute.

Braxton Hicks Contractions   Irregular, painless uterine contractions; false labour.

Breasts   Pair of mammary glands located on the anterior chest wall and extending vertically from the second to the sixth rib and laterally from the sternal border to the axillae.

Bregma   Junction of the coronal and sagittal sutures.

Bronchial (or Tubular) Breath Sound   Breath sound that is high in pitch and loud in intensity and that is heard best over the trachea; has a blowing or hollow quality; heard longer on expiration than inspiration.

Bronchophony   Voice sound test in which the lungs are auscultated while the patient says the words "ninety-nine" or "one, two, three."

Bronchovesicular Breath Sound   Breath sound that is moderate in pitch and intensity and that is heard best between the scapula and the first and second intercostal spaces lateral to the sternum; its quality is a combination of bronchial and vesicular breath sounds; heard equally in inspiration and expiration.

Bruit   Blowing sound heard when blood flow becomes turbulent as it rushes past an obstruction.

Brushfield's Spots   Small, white flecks located around the perimeter of the iris; associated with Down syndrome.

Bulbar Conjunctiva   Covering of the anterior surface of the sclera.

Bulbourethral (Cowper's) Glands   Pea-sized glands located below the prostate; secrete an alkaline substance at ejaculation that protects sperm by neutralizing the acidity of the vagina.

Bullae Elevated mass in the epidermis, greater than 0.5 cm. diameter, containing serous fluid.

Bunion *See* **Hallux Valgus**.

Bursae Sacs filled with fluid.

C

Cachexia Extreme malnutrition in which the patient exhibits wasting.

Callus Thickening of the skin caused by prolonged pressure.

Canthus Nasal or temporal angle where the eyelids meet.

Caput Medusae Appearance of engorged or congested veins around the umbilicus; attributed to circulatory obstruction of the portal vein or the superior or inferior vena cava.

Caput Succedaneum Swelling over the occipitoparietal region of the skull that occurs during delivery of the newborn.

Carbohydrate Major source of energy for various functions of the body; supplies fibre and assists in the utilization of fat.

Cardiomegaly Enlargement of the heart.

Carotenemia A condition of elevated levels of serum carotene resulting from excessive ingestion of carotene-rich foods such as carrots.

Carpal Tunnel Syndrome Pressure on the median nerve at the carpal tunnel of the wrist, causing numbness, tingling, weakness, and pain.

Caruncle Round, red structure in the inner canthus; contains sebaceous glands.

Castration Anxiety Young boys' fear of having the penis cut off or mutilated.

Cataract Opacity in the lens of the eye that gives the pupil a pearly grey appearance.

Cephalhematoma Localized subcutaneous swelling over one cranial bone of the newborn.

Cephalocaudal Head-to-toe approach.

Cerumen Waxlike substance produced in the ear canal.

Cervix Inferior aspect of the uterus.

Chadwick's Sign A blue, soft cervix, normally during pregnancy.

Chalazion Chronic inflammation of the meibomian gland in the upper or lower eyelid.

Chancre Reddish, round ulcer or small papular lesion with a depressed centre and raised, indurated edges.

Chancroid Tender, ulcerated, exudative, papular lesion with an erythematous halo, surrounding edema, and a friable base.

Chandelier's Sign Pain or mobility of the cervix on palpation.

Characteristic Patterns of Daily Living Patient's normal daily routines; includes meal, work, sleeping schedules and patterns of social interactions.

Chemosis Swelling of the palpebral conjunctiva.

Cherry Angioma Bright-red, circumscribed area that may be flat or raised and that darkens with age.

Cheyne-Stokes Respirations Crescendo/decrescendo respiratory pattern interspersed between periods of apnea.

Chloasma *See* **Melasma**.

Cholelithiasis Presence or formation of bile stone or calculi in the gallbladder or duct.

Cholestasis Arrest of bile excretion.

Cholesterol Lipid found only in animal products; it is transported in the body by high-density lipoproteins (HDLs) and low-density lipoproteins (LDLs).

Choroid Vascular tissue that lines the inner surface of the eye just beneath the retina; provides nutrition to the retinal pigment epithelium and helps absorb excess light.

Chorionic Villi Sampling (CVS) Intracervical (or less commonly, intra-abdominal) sampling of the chorionic villi for chromosome analysis. It is an alternative to traditional or early amniocentesis and is typically performed at approximately 9–10 weeks.

Ciliary Body Anterior extension of the uveal tract that produces aqueous humour.

Circadian Rhythm Normal fluctuation of body temperature, pulse, and blood pressure during a 24-hour period.

Click Abnormal systolic heart sound that is high pitched and can radiate in the chest wall.

Clinical Reasoning A disciplined, creative, and reflective approach used together with critical thinking; its purpose is to establish potential strategies for patients to reach their desired health goals.

Clitoris Cylindrical, erectile body located at the superior aspect of the vulva, between the labia minora; contains erectile tissue and has a significant supply of nerve endings.

Clonus Rhythmic oscillation of involuntary muscle contraction.

Clostridial myonecrosis A gram-positive infection that affects skeletal muscles that have decreased oxygenation; more commonly reffered to as gas gangrene.

Clustering Placing similar or related data into meaningful groups.

Coarse Crackle Discontinuous adventitious breath sound caused by air passing through moisture in large airways that suddenly reinflate; a low-pitched crackling or gurgling sound.

Cochlea Snail-shaped structure in the bony labyrinth of the inner ear.

Code of Ethics Codified beliefs and lists of mandatory or prohibited acts.

Collaborative Problem   Patient problem for which the nurse works jointly with the physician and other health care workers to monitor, plan, and implement treatment.

Coloboma   Congenital defect of the choroid and retina.

Colostrum   A thin, milky secretion expressed by the breast during pregnancy and for a few days after parturition; it is rich in antibodies and colostrum corpuscles.

Complete Health History   Comprehensive history of the patient's past and present health status; includes physical, emotional, psychological, developmental, cultural, and spiritual data.

Condyloma Acuminatum   Genital wart.

Cones   Retinal structures found in the macular region; responsible for colour vision and fine visual discrimination.

Confabulation   Fabrication of answers, experiences, or situations unrelated to facts.

Confluent   Lesions merge and run together.

Conservation   The understanding that altering the physical state of an object does not change the basic properties of that object.

Constructional Apraxia   Inability to reproduce figures on paper.

Cooper's Ligaments   Connective tissue fibres that extend vertically from the deep fascia through the breast to the inner layer of the skin and provide support for the breast tissue.

Corn   Conical area of thickened skin.

Cornea   Nonvascular, transparent covering of the iris.

Costal Angle   Angle formed by the intersection of the costal margins at the sternum.

Costal Margin   Medial border created by the articulation of the false ribs.

Cradle Cap   Seborrheic dermatitis manifesting as greasy-appearing scales on an infant's scalp.

Craniotabes   Softening of the skull.

Creatinine   Substance found in muscle and excreted in the urine.

Crepitus   Subcutaneous emphysema; beads of air escape from the lungs and create a crackling sound when palpated.

Crescendo   Heart murmur configuration that proceeds from soft to loud.

Critical Thinking   A purposeful, goal-directed thinking process that uses clinical reasoning to resolve patient care issues.

Cryptorchidism   Condition in which a testicle has not descended into the scrotum.

Cullen's Sign   Blue discoloration encircling the umbilicus, suggestive of blood in the peritoneal cavity.

Cult   Organized group centred around religious devotion to a set of beliefs or to a person.

Cultural Beliefs   Explanatory ideas and knowledge about various aspects of the world in which members of a given culture place their faith and confidence.

Cultural Competence   the application of knowledge, skill, attitudes, and personal attributes required by nurses to provide appropriate care and services in relation to cultural characteristics of their clients (individuals, families, groups, and the population at large).

Cultural Diversity   State of different combinations of cultural and subcultural minorities (e.g., ethnic, racial, national, religious, generational, marital status, socioeconomic, occupational, health status, and preference in life partner orientations) coexisting in a given location.

Cultural Identity   Subjective sense of cultural definition or cultural orientation with which an individual self-identifies.

Cultural Norms   Often unwritten but generally understood prescriptions for acceptable behaviour by members of a cultural group.

Cultural Relativism   Belief that no culture is either inferior or superior to another; that behaviour must be evaluated in relation to the cultural context in which it occurs; and that respect, equality, and justice are basic rights for all racial, ethnic, subcultural, and cultural groups.

Cultural Rituals   Highly structured and prescribed patterns of behaviour used by a cultural group to respond to or in anticipation of specific life events such as birth, death, illness, healing, marriage, and worship.

Cultural Safety   Care that is based on recognition and respect rather than on power inequities, or individual or institutional discrimination.

Cultural Values   Fundamental, often unshakable and unchanging set of principles on which the cultural beliefs, behaviours, and customs of all members of the culture are based.

Culturally Competent Nursing Care   Nursing care that is provided by nurses who use cross-cultural nursing models and research to identify health care needs and to plan and evaluate the care provided within the cultural context of their patients.

Culture   Learned and socially transmitted orientation and way of life of a group of people that is based on shared values, beliefs, customs, and norms of behaviour, and that determines how members of the group think, act, and relate to and with others as well as how they perceive and respond to all aspects of their life.

Culture Shock   Disorientation and uncertainty that results from the expenditure of mental, emotional, and physical energy during the process of adjusting to a new cultural group; it can lead to frustration, anger, alienation, or depression.

Custom   Frequent or common practice carried out by tradition; culturally learned behaviours associated with a specific culture, including communication patterns, family and kinship relations, work patterns, dietary and religious practices, and health behaviours and practices.

Cutaneous Hypersensitivity Stimulus detecting specific zones of peritoneal irritation.

Cyanosis Blue coloration of the skin or nails that occurs when more than 50 g/L of hemoglobin is deoxygenated in the blood.

Cyst Encapsulated fluid-filled or a semi-solid mass in the subcutaneous tissue or dermis.

Cystocele Bulging of the anterior vaginal wall.

Cystourethrocele Bulging of the anterior vaginal wall, bladder, and urethra into the vaginal introitus.

D

Dacryoadenitis Acute inflammation of the lacrimal gland.

Dacryocystitis Inflammation of the lacrimal duct.

Decerebrate Rigidity Rigidity and sustained contraction of the extensor muscle.

Decorticate Rigidity Hyperflexion of the arms, hyperextension and internal rotation of the legs, and plantar flexion.

Decrescendo Heart murmur configuration that proceeds from loud to soft.

Deep Palpation Palpating the body's internal structures to a depth of 4 to 5 cm to elicit information on organs and masses, including position, size, shape, mobility, consistency, and areas of discomfort.

Defecation Expulsion of feces from the rectum.

Dehydration Lack of fluid in the tissues.

Delerium A temporary disordered mental state, characterized by acute and sudden onset of cognitive impairment, disorientation, disturbances in attention, decline in level of consciousness and/or perceptual disturbances such as hallucinations.

Dementia Progressive deterioration of all cognitive function with little or no disturbance of consciousness or perception.

Dermatome Skin area innervated by afferent spinal nerves from a specific nerve root.

Dermis Corium, or the second layer of the skin.

Desquamation Shedding of old skin cells as new cells are pushed up from the lower layers of the epidermis.

Determinants of Health A range of proximal and distal variables that can influence the patient's health such as lifestyle, environment, human biology, and health services.

Development Patterned and predictable increases in the physical, cognitive, socioemotional, and moral capacities of individuals that enable them to successfully adapt to their environments.

Developmental Dislocation of the Hip Dislocated hip found in newborns and young infants; related to familial factors, maternal hormones, firstborn children, oligohydramnios, and breech presentations.

Developmental Stage One of multiple sequential age periods during which individuals experience the same physical, cognitive, socioemotional, and moral changes.

Developmental Task Specific physical or psychosocial skill that must be acquired during a developmental stage.

Diaphoresis Profuse production of perspiration.

Diaphragmatic Excursion Distance the diaphragm moves during inspiration and expiration; used to assess the patient's depth of ventilation.

Diaphragmatic Hernia Protrusion of intestines into the thoracic cavity.

Diaphysis Central shaft of the long bone.

Diastasis Recti Separation of the rectus muscle of the abdominal wall.

Diastole Period of relaxation in the cardiac cycle; reflects the pressure remaining in the arteries after the heart has pumped.

Dietary Reference Intakes Nutrient reference values developed by the Institute of Medicine that are used to assess a person's diet; comprises three components: adequate intake, tolerable upper intake level, and recommended dietary allowances.

Direct Fist Percussion Using the ulnar aspect of a closed fist to strike the patient's body to elicit tenderness over specific body areas.

Direct Inguinal Hernia Protrusion of the bowel and/or omentum directly through the external inguinal ring.

Direct (or Immediate) Auscultation Active listening to body sounds via the unaided ear.

Direct (or Immediate) Percussion Striking of an area of the body directly with the index or middle finger pad or fist to elicit sound.

Discrete Lesions arranged as individual, separate, and distinct.

Dislocation Complete dislodgement of a bone from its joint cavity.

Distress Negative stress that is harmful and unpleasant.

Disuse Atrophy Decrease in muscle mass and strength as a result of immobility.

Dogma Beliefs that are essential to the identity of a religion.

Doppler Device that emits ultrasound waves and senses shifts in frequency as the ultrasound waves are reflected from fetal heart valves.

Down Syndrome Congenital chromosomal aberration marked by slanted eyes with inner epicanthal folds; a short, flat nose; a protruding, thick tongue, and mental retardation.

Ductus (Vas) Deferens   Duct that ascends from the scrotum and permits sperm to exit from the scrotal sac upward into the abdominal cavity.

Dullness   Descriptor for a percussable sound that is moderate in intensity, moderate in duration, of high pitch, thudlike, and normally located over organs.

Dysarthria   Disturbance in muscular control of speech.

Dyscalculia   Inability to perform mathematical calculations.

Dysdiadochokinesia   Inability to perform rapid, alternating movements.

Dysesthesia   Abnormal interpretation of a stimulus (e.g., a stimulus such as touch or superficial pain is interpreted as burning or tingling).

Dysmenorrhea   Pain or cramping during menses.

Dysmetria   Impairment of judgment of distance, range, speed, and force of movement.

Dyspareunia   Painful sexual intercourse.

Dysphagia   Difficulty swallowing.

Dysphonia   Difficulty in making laryngeal speech sounds.

Dyspnea   Subjective feeling of shortness of breath.

Dysrhythmia   *See* **Arrhythmia**.

Dyssynergy   Lack of coordinated action of the muscle groups.

Dysuria   Difficult or painful urination.

E

Ecchymosis   A red-purple discoloration of varying size caused by extravasation of blood into the skin; a black-and-blue mark.

Eccrine glands   Sweat glands that are not associated with hair follicles.

Echolalia   Involuntary repetition of a word or sentence that was uttered by another person.

Eclampsia   Seizure associated with pregnancy-induced hypertension.

Ecomap   A diagram depicting a person's relationship with his or her family, as well as significant friends, peers, neighbours, and work associates.

Ectodermal Galactic Band   *See* **Milk Line**.

Ectopic pregnancy   Pregnancy other than intrauterine.

Ectropion (of the Eye)   A turning outward, or eversion, of the eyelid, usually the lower.

Ectropion (or Eversion, of the Cervix)   Reddish circle around the cervical os as the columnar epithelium extends from the os past the normal squamocolumnar junction.

Edema   Accumulation of fluid in the intercellular spaces.

Ego   Personality component that is conscious and rational; emerges during the first year of life, and seeks realistic and acceptable ways to meet needs.

Egocentrism   Viewing the world in terms of only the self and interpreting one's own actions and all other events in terms of the consequences for the self.

Egophony   Voice sound test in which the lungs are auscultated while the patient says "ee."

Ejaculatory Ducts   Two short tubes located posterior to the urinary bladder; they eject sperm into the prostatic urethra prior to ejaculation.

Electrocardiogram (ECG)   Record of the electrical activity of the heart.

Emergency Health History   History taken from the patient or other sources when the patient is experiencing a life-threatening state.

Enculturation   Informal process through which the beliefs, values, norms, and practices of a culture are learned by members born into that culture.

Enophthalmos   Backward displacement of the globe of the eye.

Entropion   Turning inward or inversion of the eyelid, usually the lower.

Epidermis   Multilayered outer covering of the skin, consisting of four layers throughout the body, except for the palms of the hands and soles of the feet, where there are five layers.

Epididymis   Comma-shaped tightly coiled tube located on the top and behind the testis and inside the scrotum; where sperm maturation occurs.

Epimysium   Strong, connective tissue sheath covering the muscle belly.

Epiphyses   Ends of the long bone.

Episodic Health History   History taken from the patient specific to the current reason for seeking health care.

Epispadias   Congenital abnormality in which the urethral meatus lies on the dorsal surface of the penis.

Epistaxis   Nosebleed.

Epstein's Pearls   Small, hard, white cysts found on a newborn's hard palate and gum margins.

Erosion   Lesion involving loss of epidermis.

Eructation   Belching.

Erythema   An inflammatory redness of the skin.

Escutcheon   Characteristic triangular pattern of coarse, curly hair that develops over the mons pubis at puberty.

Esophoria   Latent misalignment of the eye; nasal, or inward, drift.

Esotropia   Inward deviation of the eye.

Ethnic Group   Classification of individuals based on their unique national or regional origin and social, cultural, and linguistic heritage.

Ethnic Identity   Subjective sense of ethnic definition or social orientation with which an individual self-identifies.

Ethnocentrism   Condition that occurs when individuals or groups of people perceive their own cultural group and cultural values, beliefs, norms, and customs to be superior to all others and have disdain for the expression of any way of life but their own.

Eupnea   Normal breathing; respirations are 12 to 20 per minute for the resting adult.

Eustachian Tube   Auditory tube that serves as an air channel connecting the middle ear to the nasopharynx to allow equalization between the air pressure in the ear and in the atmosphere.

Eustress   Positive stress that challenges, provides motivation, and prevents stagnation.

Evaluation   Last step of the nursing process; the patient's progress in achieving the goal(s) is determined.

Evidence-Based Practice   Uses the outcomes of well-designed and executed scientific studies to guide clinical decision making and clinical care.

Exophoria   Latent misalignment of the eye; temporal, or outward, drift.

Exophthalmos   Abnormal protrusion of the globe of the eye.

Exotropia   Outward deviation of the eye.

F

Faith   Orientation to a belief structure.

Fallopian Tubes   Site of fertilization; extend from the cornu of the uterus to the ovaries and are supported by the broad ligaments.

False Ribs   Rib pairs 8–10.

Fat-Soluble Vitamins   Vitamins stored in dietary fat and absorbed in the fat portions of the body's cells.

Fats   Substances that supply essential fatty acids, which form a part of the structure of all cells.

Femoral Hernia   Protrusion of the omentum or bowel through the femoral wall.

Fetal Alcohol Syndrome (FAS)   A pattern of craniofacial, cardiovascular, and limb defects, with prenatal and postnatal growth retardation associated with maternal alcohol use.

Fetoscope   Special stethoscope for auscultating fetal heart beats.

Fibroma   Fibrous, encapsulated, tumour of connective tissue, often called fibroid or myoma.

Fine Crackle   Discontinuous adventitious breath sound caused by air passing through moisture in small airways that suddenly reinflate; a high-pitched crackling sound.

Fissure   Groove separating the different lobes of the lungs.

Fissure   Linear crack in the epidermis that can extend into the dermis.

Flatness   Descriptor for a percussable sound that is soft in intensity, short in duration, of high pitch, and normally located over muscle or bone.

Flatulence   Passage of excess gas via the rectum.

Floating Ribs   Rib pairs 11 and 12; they do not articulate at their anterior ends.

Folk Illness   Illness believed to be caused by disharmony, an imbalance, or as a punishment.

Folk Practitioner   Healer or other individual who is not part of the scientific care system but is believed to have special knowledge or power to prevent, treat, or provide resources needed to heal folk illnesses.

Follow-Up Health History   *See* **Interval Health History**.

Fornices   Pouchlike recesses around the cervix.

Fourchette   Transverse fold of skin of the posterior aspect of the labia minora; also known as frenulum.

Fovea Centralis   Centre of the macula; the area of sharpest vision.

Frenulum (of the Mouth)   Tissue that connects the tongue to the floor of the mouth.

Friability   Susceptibility to bleeding from the cervix.

Functional Health Assessment   Documents a person's ability to perform instrumental activities of daily living and physical self-maintenance activities.

Fundus   Superior aspect of the uterus.

G

Gallop   Extra heart sound; an S_3 is a ventricular gallop, whereas an S_4 is an atrial gallop.

Ganglion   Benign growth that is usually nontender.

Genogram   Pictorial representation of the patient's family health history.

Genomics   The study of the genetic makeup of the human cell.

Genu Valgum   Inward deviation toward the midline at the level of the knees; also known as knock knees.

Genu Varum   Outward deviation away from the midline at the level of the knees; also known as bowlegs.

Glans Penis   Bulbous end of the penis.

Glasgow Coma Scale   International scale used in grading neurological response.

Glaucoma   Disease in which intraocular pressure is elevated.

Glycosuria   Glucose in the urine.

God   Concept of a deity or personal, present being.

Goiter   Enlargement of the thyroid gland.

Goniometer   Device used to measure the angle of the skeletal joint during range of motion; protractor with two movable arms.

Granulomatous Reaction (in the Breast)   Development of small, nodular, inflammatory lesions and capsular membranes over the breasts.

Graphanesthesia   Inability to identify numbers, letters, or shapes drawn on the skin.

Graphesthesia   Ability to identify numbers, letters, or shapes drawn on the skin.

Growth   Increase in body size and function to the point of optimum maturity.

Gynecomastia   Enlargement of male breast tissue; may occur normally in adolescent and elderly males.

H

Hallux Valgus   Lateral deviation of the big toe and medial deviation of the first metatarsal; also known as bunion.

Hammer Toe   Flexion of the proximal interphalangeal joint and hyperextension of the distal metatarsophalangeal joint.

Harlequin Colour Change   Condition in which one-half of a newborn's body is red or ruddy and the other half appears pale.

Health Maintenance Activities   Practices that a person incorporates into a lifestyle that can promote healthy living.

Heave   Lifting of the cardiac area secondary to an increased workload and force of left ventricular contraction; also known as a lift.

Heaven   Blissful resting place for souls after death, according to Christianity.

Heberden's Node   Bony enlargement of the distal interphalangeal joint of the finger.

HELLP Syndrome   Complication of pregnancy-induced hypertension; the acronym represents hemolysis, elevated liver enzymes, and low platelets.

Hematemesis   Vomiting of blood.

Hematochezia   Passage of bright red blood from the rectum, with or without feces.

Hematocrit   Measurement to determine the percentage of red blood cells to the volume of whole blood.

Hemiparesis   Unilateral weakness or paralysis; also known as hemiplegia.

Hemiplegia   *See* **Hemiparesis**.

Hemoglobin   Measurement of the iron component that transports oxygen in the blood.

Hemorrhoids   Dilatation of hemorrhoidal veins in the anorectum.

High-Density Lipoprotein   Substance that carries cholesterol away from the heart and arteries and toward the liver.

Hirsutism   Condition of excessive body hair.

History of the Health Issue or Concern   Chronological account of the patient's health issue or concern and the events surrounding it.

Holistic Nursing   A form of nursing that addresses all aspects of a patient's health and well-being, including spirituality and religion.

Holosystolic   Murmur that is heard throughout all of systole; also known as pansystolic.

Homan's Sign   Pain in the calf when the foot is dorsiflexed; sign of venous thrombosis or thrombophlebitis of the deep veins of the calf.

Hordeolum   Infection of a sebaceous gland in the eyelid.

Hydatidiform Mole   Molar or trophoblastic pregnancy. Often requires careful monitoring of HCG after dilation and curettage of the uterus. If HCG remains elevated, chemotherapy may be indicated.

Hydrocele   Fluid collection within the tunica vaginalis of the testis.

Hydrocephalus   Enlargement of the head without enlargement of the facial structures; due to increased accumulation of cerebrospinal fluid within the ventricles of the brain.

Hymen   Avascular, thin fold of connective tissue surrounding the vaginal introitus; may be annular or crescentic in shape.

Hypalgesia   Diminished sensitivity to pain.

Hyperalgesia   Increased sensitivity to pain.

Hyperemesis Gravidarum   Severe nausea and vomiting during pregnancy.

Hyperesthesia   Abnormal acuteness to the sensitivity of touch.

Hyperglycemia   Increase in serum glucose.

Hyperhidrosis   Abnormally increased axillary, plantar, facial, and/or truncal perspiration, in excess of that required for regulation of body temperature.

Hyperkinetic   Condition of increased movement.

Hyperopia   Farsightedness.

Hyperpnea   Breath that is greater in volume than the resting tidal volume.

Hyperresonance   Descriptor for a percussable sound that is very loud in intensity, long in duration, of very low pitch, boomlike, and normally not found in the healthy adult.

Hypertension Blood pressure remaining consistently above 140 mm Hg systolic or 90 mm Hg diastolic in an adult.

Hyperthermia Condition in which the body temperature exceeds 38.5°C; excessive warming of the skin that may be generalized or localized.

Hypertrophy Increase in muscle size and shape due to an increase in the muscle fibres.

Hypesthesia Diminished sense of touch; also known as hypoesthesia.

Hyphema Condition in which there is bleeding from vessels in the iris.

Hypoesthesia *See* **Hypesthesia**.

Hypogeusia Diminution of taste.

Hypoglycemia Decrease in serum glucose.

Hypokinetic Condition of decreased movement.

Hypospadias Congenital abnormality in which the urethral meatus opens on the ventral surface of the penis.

Hypotension Blood pressure that is lower than what is needed to maintain adequate tissue perfusion and oxygenation.

Hypothermia Condition in which the body temperature is below 34°C; cooling of the skin that may be generalized or localized.

Hypotonicity Decrease in normal muscle tone (flaccidity).

I

Id Personality component that is inborn, unconscious, and driven by biological instincts and urges to seek immediate gratification of needs such as hunger, thirst, and physical comfort.

Iliopsoas Muscle Test Technique used to assess for an inflamed or perforated appendix.

Immediate Auscultation *See* **Direct (or Immediate) Auscultation**.

Immediate Percussion *See* **Direct (or Immediate) Percussion**.

Implementation Fifth step of the nursing process; the execution of the nursing interventions that were devised during the planning stage to help the patient meet predetermined outcomes.

Impotence Inability to achieve or maintain an erection.

Indirect Fist Percussion Using the closed ulnar aspect of the fist of the dominant hand to strike the nondominant hand to elicit tenderness over specific body areas.

Indirect Inguinal Hernia Portions of the bowel or omentum that enter the inguinal canal through the internal inguinal ring and exit at the external inguinal ring.

Indirect (or Mediate) Auscultation Active listening to body sounds via some amplification or mechanical device, such as a stethoscope or Doppler transducer.

Indirect (or Mediate) Percussion Using the plexor to strike the pleximeter to elicit sound.

Infarction (Myocardial) Necrosis of cardiac muscle due to decreased blood supply.

Injection Redness around the cornea.

Inspection Use of one's senses to consciously observe the patient; in physical assessment, vision, hearing, smell, and touch are used.

Insufficiency *See* **Regurgitation**.

Integumentary System Skin, or cutaneous tissue.

Intensity (of Percussion) Relative loudness or softness of sound; amplitude.

Intercostal Space Area between the ribs.

Intermediary Individual who serves to assist with communication between the patient and another individual, usually a member of the health care team.

Interpleural Space *See* **Mediastinum**.

Intertriginous Between folds or juxtaposed surfaces of the skin.

Interval (or Follow-Up) Health History History that builds on the patient's last health care visit and documents resolution or nonresolution of a problem or health care need.

Intervention Planned strategy, based on scientific rationale, to assist the patient in meeting health outcomes.

Intussusception Formation of a sausage-shaped mass in the upper abdomen resulting when the ileocecal region of the intestine telescopes into the ileum.

Iris Most anterior portion of the uveal tract; provides a distinctive colour for the eye.

Ischemia (Myocardial) Local and temporary lack of blood supply to the heart; may progress to an infarction if left untreated.

Isoelectric Line A flat line after the T-wave on the electrocardiogram indicating an electrical resting period.

Iso-immunization Most common Rh hemolytic disease, now almost completely eliminated by the antepartum administration of Rh gamma globulin to Rh negative mothers, and readministration after delivery if newborn is Rh positive.

Isthmus (of the Thyroid) Narrow portion of the thyroid gland that connects the two lobes and rests on top of the trachea, inferior to the cricoid cartilage.

Isthmus (of the Uterus) Constricted area between the body of the uterus and the cervix.

J

Jaundice Yellow-green to orange cast or coloration of skin, sclera, or mucous membranes; caused by an elevated bilirubin level.

Joining Stage Introduction or first stage of the interview process, during which the nurse and patient establish trust and rapport.

Joint Union between two bones.

K

Keratosis Lesions on the epidermis characterized by overgrowth of the horny layer.

Kilocalorie Amount of heat required to raise 1 g of water 1°C; also called calorie.

Knock Knees *See* **Genu Valgum**.

Korotkoff Sounds Sounds generated when the flow of blood through an artery is altered by the inflation of a blood pressure cuff around the extremity.

Kussmaul's Respirations Extreme increased rate and depth of respiration, as in diabetic ketoacidosis.

Kwashiorkor Severe deficiency of protein.

Kyphosis Excessive convexity of the thoracic spine; also known as "humpback."

L

Labia Majora Two longitudinal folds of adipose and connective tissue that extend from the clitoris anteriorly and gradually narrow to merge and form the posterior commissure of the perineum.

Labia Minora Two thin folds of skin that enclose the vulval vestibule and extend anteriorly to form the prepuce, or hood, of the clitoris and posteriorly to form a transverse fold of skin forming the fourchette.

Labyrinth Complex, closed system of interconnecting tubes in the inner ear that is essential for hearing and equilibrium; has bony and membranous portions.

Lacrimal Apparatus Lacrimal gland and ducts.

Lactiferous Ducts Openings at the nipple through which milk and colostrum are excreted.

Lagophthalmos Condition in which the patient is unable to completely close the eyelid.

Lanugo Fine, downy hair present during gestational life that gradually disappears toward the end of pregnancy; remains in smaller quantities over the temples, back, shoulders, and upper arms after birth.

Lens Crystalline structure of the eye that changes shape to refract light from various focusing distances.

Lentigo Areas of hyperpigmentation resulting from the inability of melanocytes to produce even pigmentation of the skin; known as "liver spots."

Lesion Circumscribed, pathological change in tissue.

Lichenification Localized thickening, hardening, and roughness of the skin.

Life Event or Transitional Developmental Theory Belief that development occurs in response to specific events, such as new roles (e.g., parenthood), and life transitions (e.g., career changes).

Life Review Reflection on the experiences, relationships, and events of one's life as a whole, viewing successes and failures from the perspective of age, and accepting one's life and accompanying life choices and outcomes in their entirety.

Lift *See* **Heave**.

Ligament Strong, fibrous connective tissue that connects bones to each other at a joint.

Light Palpation Superficial palpation; depressing the skin 1 cm to elicit information on skin texture and moisture, masses, fluid, muscle guarding, and tenderness.

Lightening Descent of the presenting fetal part into the pelvis.

Limbus Junction of the sclera and cornea.

Linea Alba Tendinous tissue that extends from the sternum to the symphysis pubis in the middle of the abdomen.

Linear Lesions That form a line.

Linea Nigra Darkening of the abdominal linea alba during pregnancy.

Linear Raphe Linear ridge in the middle of the hard palate.

Lipoma Nonmobile, fatty mass with a smooth, circular edge.

List Leaning of the spine.

Listening Response Attempt made by the nurse to accurately receive, process, and respond to the patient's messages.

Lobes (of the Breast) Glandular breast tissue arranged radially in the form of 12 to 20 spokes.

Lobules (of the Breast) Grapelike bunches that are clustered around several lactiferous ducts; each lobe is composed of 20 to 40 lobules that contain milk-producing glands called alveoli or acini.

Lordosis Excessive concavity of the lumbar spine.

Low-Density Lipoprotein Substance that carries cholesterol toward the heart.

Lunula White, crescent-shaped area at the proximal end of each nail.

Lymphatic Drainage Yellow, alkaline drainage originating in the lymph vessels and composed primarily of lymphocytes.

M

Macromineral Major mineral needed by the body in large amounts.

Macrosomia Newborn weighing more than 4000 g.

Mania Exaggerated feelings of well-being, energy, and confidence in which a person can lose touch with reality. Symptoms of mania include flight of ideas or racing thoughts; inflated self-esteem; decreased need for sleep; talkativeness; and irritability.

Macula Tiny, darker area in the temporal area of the retina.

Macule A nonpalpable skin lesion; localized changes in skin colour of less than 1 cm in diameter.

Major Defining Characteristics Signs and symptoms that must be present in the patient to use a specific NANDA-approved diagnostic label.

Manubriosternal Junction *See* **Angle of Louis**.

Manubrium Upper bone of the sternum; articulates with the clavicles and the first pair of ribs.

Marasmus Form of protein calorie malnutrition.

Mastectomy Excision, or surgical removal, of the breast.

Maternal Serum Alpha-Fetal Protein (MSAFP) A blood test to screen for certain fetal abnormalities.

Matrix Undifferentiated epithelial tissue from which keratinized cells arise to form the nail plate.

McBurney's Point Anatomic location that is approximately at the normal location of the appendix in the right lower quadrant; point of increased tenderness in appendicitis.

Meconium Dark-green, sticky, stool-like material excreted from the rectum of the newborn within the first 24 hours after birth.

Mediastinum (Interpleural Space) Area between the lungs.

Mediate Auscultation *See* **Indirect Auscultation**.

Mediate Percussion *See* **Indirect Percussion**.

Medullary Cavity Interior of the diaphysis; contains the bone marrow.

Melanocytes Cells that produce pigmented substances that provide colour to the hair, skin, and choroid of the eye.

Melasma Irregular pigmentation on the face due to pregnancy; also known as chloasma.

Melena Black, tarry stool.

Menarche Onset of menstruation.

Menopause Cessation of menstruation.

Menorrhagia Heavy menses.

Mercury Manometer Blood pressure measurement device that uses a calibrated column of mercury that indicates blood pressure values.

Metatarsus Varus Medial forefoot malignment.

Microcephaly Condition characterized by a small brain with a resultant small head.

Micromineral Trace mineral needed by the body in small amounts.

Microphallus Small penis for developmental stage.

Mid-Arm Circumference (MAC) Anthropometric measurement that provides information on skeletal muscle mass and adipose tissue.

Mid-Arm Muscle Circumference (MMAC) Anthropometric measurement derived from mid-arm circumference; provides information on skeletal muscle mass and adipose tissue.

Midaxillary Line Vertical line drawn from the apex of the axilla; lies midway between the anterior and the posterior axillary lines.

Midclavicular Line Vertical line drawn from the midpoint of the clavicle.

Midspinal (or Vertebral) Line Vertical line drawn from the midpoint of the spinous processes.

Midsternal Line Vertical line drawn from the midpoint of the sternum.

Milia Plugged sebaceous glands manifesting as small, white papules and appearing on the infant's head, especially on the cheeks and nose.

Milk Line Ectodermal galactic band that develops from the axilla to the groin during the fifth week of fetal development.

Mineral Inorganic element that regulates body processes and builds body tissue; classified into macrominerals and microminerals.

Minority Group Members Individuals who are considered by themselves and others to be members of a minority because they have a different racial, ethnic, cultural, gender, socioeconomic, or sexual orientation than the members of the dominant cultural group.

Mole A small congenital growth on the human skin, usually slightly raised and dark and sometimes hairy, especially a pigmented nevus.

Molding Condition in which the newborn's parietal bone overrides the frontal bone as a result of increased pressure during delivery.

Mongolian Spots Deep blue areas of pigmentation on the lumbar and sacral areas of the spine, over the buttocks, and sometimes over the upper back or shoulders in newborns of African, Latino, or Asian descent.

Monotheism Belief in one all-powerful, omnipresent, and omnipotent god.

Monounsaturated Fats Fatty acids found in olive and canola oils that lower LDL and but do not lower HDL.

Mons Pubis Pad of subcutaneous fatty tissue lying over the anterior symphysis pubis.

Montgomery's Tubercles Sebaceous glands present on the surface of the areola.

Mucopurulent Wound drainage that contains mucus and pus.

Multicultural Identity Unique combination of cultural influences that result from membership in a variety of subcultures within the primary culture.

Multiparous Any number of prior deliveries.

Multiculturalism The act of living and functioning in two or more cultures simultaneously.

Murphy's Sign Abnormal finding elicited during abdominal palpation in the right upper quadrant, revealing gallbladder inflammation; characteristically, the patient will abruptly stop inspiration and complain of sharp pain with palpation.

Muscle belly The wide central aspect of a muscle.

Myopia Nearsightedness.

N

Nabothian Cysts Small, round, yellow lesions on the cervical surface.

Nailbed Vascular area located beneath the nail plate.

Nail Plate Tissue that covers and protects the distal portion of the digits.

Nail Root Nail portion that is posterior to the cuticle and attached to the matrix.

NANDA North American Nursing Diagnosis Association; the professional nursing organization that sets the standards for the development, clinical testing, and approval of nursing diagnoses.

Naturalistic Illness Illness believed to be caused by an imbalance or disequilibrium between essentially impersonal factors, for example, hot and cold.

Necrosis Tissue death.

Neologism Word coined by a patient that is meaningful only to the patient.

Nevi Pigmented moles that may be flat or elevated.

Nevus Flammeus A nevus composed of mature but thin-walled capillaries; a port-wine stain.

New Age A popular, heterogeneous, free-flowing spiritual movement that has no holy book, organization, membership, clergy, geographic centre, dogma, or creed, but includes a cluster of common beliefs that may be grafted onto an existing religion.

Nipple A round, hairless, pigmented protrusion of erectile tissue approximately 0.5 to 1.5 cm in diameter located in the centre of the breast.

Nirvana Buddhist belief of the perfect blessedness and peace of the soul.

Nitrogen A compound of amino acids; incorporated into protein and excreted in urine and feces.

Nociception Pain perception; a multistep process that involves the nervous system and other body systems.

Nociceptors Receptive neurons of pain sensation located in the skin and various viscera.

Nocturia Night arousal to void.

Nodule Palpable, solid, and elevated lesion, 0.5-2.0 cm in diameter, that extends deeper than papules into the dermis or subcutaneous tissues.

Nonverbal Communication Conveying a message without speaking.

Nulliparous Descriptor for a woman who has not given birth.

Nursing Care Plan A plan of care developed by the nurse to assist the patient in meeting short-term and long-term outcomes. The nursing care plan uses the nursing process as its framework and serves as a means of communicating patient progress to other health care professionals.

Nursing Diagnosis "A clinical judgment about individual, family, or community responses to actual or potential health problems/life processes" (NANDA, 2005, p. 277).

Nursing Process Dynamic, five-step process that uses information in a meaningful way through the use of problem-solving strategies to place the patient, family, or community in an optimal health state; includes assessment, diagnosis, planning, implementation, and evaluation.

Nutrient Substance found in food that is nourishing or useful to the body.

Nutrition Processes of the human body that metabolize and utilize nutrients.

Nystagmus Involuntary oscillation of the eye.

O

Obesity Condition when BMI is >30 kg/m^2; weight greater than 120% of ideal body weight.

Object Permanence Ability to form a mental image of an object and to recognize that, although removed from view, the object still exists.

Objective Data Information that is observable and measurable and can be verified by more than one person.

Obturator Sign Differential technique for assessing appendicitis, indicative of an irritated obturator internus muscle.

Oedipus Complex Boys' sexual attraction toward their mothers and feelings of rivalry toward their fathers.

Oogenesis Development and formation of an ovum.

Optic Disc Round or oval area with distinct margins on the nasal side of the retina; retinal fibres join at the optic disk to form the optic nerve.

Orchitis   Acute inflammation of the testis.

Orthopnea   Difficulty breathing in positions other than upright.

Orthostatic Hypotension   A drop in blood pressure that occurs when changing from a supine to an upright position.

Ossicles   Three tiny bones in the middle ear—the malleus, the incus, and the stapes—that play a crucial role in the transmission of sound.

Osteoporosis   Disease characterized by reduced bone mass.

Otitis Media   Inflammation or infection of the middle ear.

Outcome Identification   The fourth step of the nursing process.

Ovaries   Pair of almond-shaped glands, approximately 3 to 4 cm in length, in the upper pelvic cavity; oogenesis and hormonal production are the ovaries' principal function.

P

Pack/Year History   The number of packs of cigarettes smoked on a daily basis multiplied by the number of years that the patient has smoked.

Pagan   A person who does not belong to a monotheistic religion, or a person whose principles reflect an animistic and usually polytheistic, spirit-filled belief system.

Paget's Disease   Malignant neoplasm, usually unilateral in its involvement, that presents as persistent eczematous dermatitis of the areola and nipple.

Pain   An unpleasant sensory or emotional experience associated with actual or potential tissue damage, or described in terms of such damage.

Pallor   Lack of colour.

Palpation   Touching the patient in a diagnostic manner to elicit specific information.

Palpebral Conjunctiva   Mucous membrane covering the interior surface of the eyelid muscle.

Palpebral Fissure   Opening between the eyelids.

Palpitation   Irregular and rapid heart beat, or sensation of fluttering of the heart.

Pansystolic   *See* **Holosystolic**.

Pantheism   A religion in which god is believed to be in everything that exists; followers believe in reincarnation, auras, energy fields, ecology, personal transformation, and evolution toward a "new age" in which wars and discrimination will not exist, and all will be peace and harmony.

Papilla   Small projection on the dorsal surface of the tongue and containing opening to taste buds.

Papillary Layer   Upper layer of the dermis; composed primarily of loose connective tissue, small elastic fibres, and an extensive network of capillaries that serve to nourish the epidermis.

Papule   Red, solid, circumscribed, elevated area of the skin.

Papule   Red, solid, circumscribed, elevated area of the skin less than 0.5 cm in diameter.

Paranasal Sinuses   Air-filled cavities in the cranial bones; lined with mucous membranes.

Paraphimosis   Condition in which the retracted foreskin develops a fixed constriction proximal to the glans penis.

Paresthesia   An abnormal sensation, such as numbness, pricking, or tingling.

Parietal Pericardium   Layer of the pericardium that lies close to the fibrous tissues.

Parietal Pleura   Lining of the chest wall and the superior surface of the lung.

Parous   Descriptor for a woman who has given birth to one or more neonates.

Past Health History   History that covers the patient's health from birth to the present.

Pastoral Care   Care and response needed when a person is in spiritual crisis.

Patch   Nonpalpable lesion; localized changes in skin colour of greater than 1 cm in diameter.

Patient Profile   Demographics that may be linked to health status.

Peau d'Orange   Thickening or edema of the breast tissue or nipple; may present itself as enlarged skin pores that give the appearance of an orange rind.

Pectus Carinatum   Abnormal thorax configuration in which there is a marked protrusion of the sternum; known as "pigeon chest."

Pectus Excavatum   Abnormal thorax configuration in which there is a depression in the lower body of the sternum; known as "funnel chest."

Penis   Cylindrical male organ of copulation and urination.

Penis Envy   Young girls' desire to have a penis.

Percussion   Striking one object against another to cause vibrations that produce sound.

Pericarditis   Inflammation of the pericardium.

Perineum   External surface located between the fourchette and the anus.

Peripheral Vasculature Resistance   Opposing force against which the left ventricle must contract to pump blood into the aorta.

Periungual Tissue   Tissue that surrounds the nail plate and the free edge of the nail.

Personalistic Illness Illness that is believed to occur either because an individual committed some offense and is being punished, or as a result of acts of aggression (sometimes unintentional) by other individuals.

Pertinent Negatives Manifestations that are expected in the patient with a suspected pathology but that are denied or absent.

Pes Cavus Foot with an exaggerated height to the arch.

PES Method Acronym for problem, etiology, and signs or symptoms; the nursing diagnosis comprises these elements.

Pes Planus Foot with a low longitudinal arch; also known as "flatfoot."

Pes Valgus Foot that is turned laterally away from the midline.

Pes Varus Foot that is turned inward toward the midline.

Petechiae Violaceous (red-purple) skin discoloration that is less than 0.5 cm in diameter and does not blanch.

Phimosis Constriction of the distal penile foreskin that prevents normal retraction over the glans.

Phoria Latent misalignment of an eye.

Physiologic Cup Pale, central area of the optic disc.

Physiological Weight Loss Tendency of a neonate to lose approximately 10% of birth weight within a few days after birth, regaining it by two weeks of age.

Pica Craving for substances other than food (e.g., dirt, clay, starch, ice cubes).

Pinguecula Yellow nodule on the nasal, or temporal, side of the bulbar conjunctiva.

Pinna *See* **Auricle**.

Pitch (of Percussion) Highness or lowness of a sound.

Placenta Previa Placenta implantation partially (partial previa) or totally (complete previa) covering the cervical os.

Planning Third step of the nursing process; involves the prioritization of nursing diagnoses, formulation of patient goals, and selection of nursing interventions.

Plaque Palpable, solid, elevated lesion greater than 0.5 cm. in diameter.

Pleura Serous sac that encases the lung.

Pleural Friction Fremitus Palpable grating that feels more pronounced on inspiration when there is an inflammatory process between the visceral and parietal pleurae.

Pleural Friction Rub Continuous adventitious breath sound caused by inflamed parietal and visceral pleurae; resembles a creaking or grating sound.

Pleximeter Stationary finger of the nondominant hand used in indirect percussion.

Plexor Middle finger of the dominant hand; used to strike the pleximeter to elicit sound in indirect percussion.

Polycyclic Lesions arranged in concentric circles.

Polycythemia Condition of elevated number of red blood cells.

Polydactyly Congenital presence of extra digits on the hand or foot.

Polytheism Belief in many gods of different levels of power and status.

Posterior Axillary Line Vertical line drawn from the posterior axillary fold.

Posterior Chamber Space immediately posterior to the iris.

Posterior Triangle Area of the neck between the sternocleidomastoid and the trapezius muscles, with the clavicle at the base; contains the posterior cervical lymph nodes.

Prayer Communication with a higher, spiritual power.

Prealbumin (also called thyroxine-binding prealbumin) The transport protein for thyroxine and retinol-binding protein.

Precordium Area on the anterior surface of the body that lies over the heart, its great vessels, the pericardium, and some pulmonary tissue.

Preload Resting force on the myocardium as determined by the pressure in the ventricles at the end of diastole.

Prepuce Foreskin covering the glans penis.

Presbycusis Hearing loss commonly found in older individuals.

Presbyopia Condition in which the lens cortex becomes more dense, compromising its ability to change shape and focus; impaired near vision.

Priapism Abnormal prolonged penile erection unrelated to sexual desire.

Proprioception Position sense.

Prostate Glandular organ that lies below the bladder and encircles the urethra; an accessory male sex organ.

Protein Nutrient that is needed to supply nine essential amino acids and used to form the basis of all cell structures in the body.

Proteinuria Presence of protein in the urine.

Prurigo Itchy skin eruptions of unknown cause.

Pruritus Severe itching.

Pterygium Triangular, yellow thickening of the bulbar conjunctiva, extending from the nasal side of the cornea to the pupil.

Ptosis Drooping of the eyelid.

Ptyalism Excessive secretion of saliva.

Puddle Sign Percussion technique that indicates excess accumulation of fluid in the abdominal cavity.

Pulse Palpable expansion of an artery in response to cardiac functioning; used to determine heart rate, rhythm, and estimated volume of blood being pumped by the heart.

Pulse Deficit   Apical pulse rate greater than radial pulse rate; occurs when some heart contractions are too weak to produce a palpable pulse at the radial site.

Pulse Pressure   Difference between systolic and diastolic blood pressures.

Pulsus Paradoxus   Pathological decrease in systolic blood pressure by 10 mm Hg or more on inspiration.

Puncta   Opening at the inner canthus of the eye through which tears drain.

Pupil   Opening in the centre of the iris; regulates the amount of light entering the eye.

Purpura   Condition characterized by the presence of confluent petechiae or confluent ecchymosis over any part of the body.

Purulent   Containing or forming pus.

Pus: A protein-rich liquid inflammation product made up of leukocytes, serum, and cellular debris.

Pustule   Vesicles or bullae that become filled with pus, usually less than 0.5 cm. in diameter.

Pyelonephritis   Kidney infection or inflammation.

Q

Quality (of Percussion)   Timbre; how a sound is perceived musically.

Quickening   First fetal movements felt by the pregnant woman.

R

Race   Classification of individuals based on shared inherited biological traits such as skin colour, facial features, and body build.

Rash   Cutaneous skin eruption that may be localized or generalized.

Rebound Tenderness   Pain elicited during deep palpation, frequently associated with peritoneal inflammation or appendicitis.

Rectal Prolapse   Protrusion of the rectum through the anal orifice.

Rectocele   Bulging of the posterior vaginal wall with a portion of the rectum.

Rectouterine Pouch   Deep recess formed by the outer layer of the peritoneum; the lowest point in the pelvic cavity, encompassing the lower posterior wall of the uterus, the upper portion of the vagina, and the intestinal surface of the rectum.

Rectovaginal Septum   Surface that separates the rectum from the posterior aspect of the vagina.

Rectum   Lower portion of the large intestine; passes downward in front of the sacrum.

Reepithelialization   Reformation of epithelium over denuded skin.

Regurgitation   Backward flow of blood through a heart valve; also known as insufficiency.

Reincarnation   Belief that after death, a person lives another life on earth in another body.

Related Factors   "Factors that appear to show some type of patterned relationship with the nursing diagnosis" (NANDA, 2005, p. 278).

Religion   Organized system of beliefs that is usually centred around the worship of a supernatural force or being and that, in turn, defines the self and the self's purpose in life.

Resonance   Descriptor for a percussable sound that is loud in intensity, moderate to long in duration, low in pitch, hollow, and normally located in healthy lungs.

Respiration   Act of breathing that supplies oxygen to the body and occurs in response to changes in the concentration of oxygen, carbon dioxide, and hydrogen in the arterial blood.

Reticular Layer   Lower layer of the dermis that is formed by a dense bed of vascular connective tissue; it also includes nerves and lymphatic tissue.

Retina   Innermost layer of the eye.

Retroflexed Uterus   A condition in which the main body of the uterus is tipped back at the cervix.

Retromammary Adipose Tissue   Tissue that composes the bulk of the breast.

Retroverted Uterus   A uterus that is displaced backward, with the cervix pointing upward toward the symphysis pubis.

Reversibility   The understanding that an action does not need to be experienced before one can anticipate the results or consequences of the action.

Review of Systems   The patient's subjective response to a series of body-system–related questions; serves as a double-check that vital information is not overlooked.

Rhonchal Fremitus   Coarse, palpable vibration produced by the passage of air through thick exudate in the large bronchi or the trachea.

Rinne Test   Method of evaluating hearing loss by comparing air and bone conduction of tuning fork vibrations.

Risk Nursing Diagnosis   "Describes human responses to health conditions/life processes that may develop in a vulnerable individual, family, or community" (NANDA, 2005, p. 277).

Ritual   Solemn, ceremonial act that reinforces faith.

Rod   Retinal structure responsible for peripheral vision and dark or light discrimination.

Routine practices   Practices health care providers use to prevent the exchange of blood and body fluids when coming into contact with a patient; developed by Health Canada's Laboratory Centre for Disease Control.

S

Rovsing's Sign Technique to elicit referred pain indicative of peritoneal inflammation.

S

Sanguinous Wound exudate containing blood.

Saturated Fats Lipids derived from animal or vegetable sources.

Scapular Line Vertical line drawn from the inferior angle of the scapula.

Schismatic Person who shares the essential beliefs or dogma of a religion but who is separated from the group because of political or other disagreements.

Scientific Illness Illness in which the presence of pathology is the defining characteristic.

Sclera Opaque covering of the eye; appears white.

Scoliosis Lateral curvature of the thoracic or lumbar vertebrae.

Scrotum Pouchlike supporting structure of the testes.

Sebaceous Glands Sebum-producing glands that are found almost everywhere in the dermis except for the palmar and plantar surfaces.

Seborrhea Dandruff.

Sebum Oily secretion that is thought to stop evaporation and water loss from the epidermal surface.

Seizure Transient disturbance of cerebral function caused by an excessive discharge of neurons.

Semicircular Canals Anterior, lateral, and posterior canals in the body labyrinth of the inner ear that provide balance and equilibrium.

Seminal Vesicles Two pouches located posteriorly to and at the base of the bladder; contribute about 60% of the volume of semen.

Septum (of the Heart) Wall that divides the left side of the heart from the right side.

Sequelae Complications, aftereffects.

Serosanguinous Containing both serum and blood.

Serous Wound exudate containing serum.

Serum Iron Amount of transferrin-bound iron.

Shifting Dullness Abnormal finding elicited during percussion; indicates ascites.

Short-Term Outcome Goal that a patient strives to achieve in a relatively brief time frame (hour, day, or week).

Sibilant Wheeze Continuous adventitious breath sound caused by the narrowing of large airways or obstruction of a bronchus; a musical sound.

Sighing Normal respiration interrupted by a deep inspiration and followed by a deep expiration.

Sign Objective finding.

Sin Deliberate and conscious act against the teachings of a belief system.

Sinoatrial (S-A) Node Normal pacemaker of the heart; initiates a rhythmic impulse approximately 70 times per minute.

Skene's Glands (Paraurethral Glands) Glands that open in a posterolateral position to the urethral meatus and provide lubrication to protect the skin.

Skinfold Thickness Anthropometric measurement to determine body fat stores and nutritional status.

Smegma White, cottage cheese-like substance sometimes found under the female labia minora or the male foreskin.

Snap Abnormal high-pitched sound that is heard in early diastole; usually occurs in mitral stenosis.

Snellen Chart Instrument used for testing distance vision; contains letters of various sizes with standardized visual acuity numbers at the end of each line of letters.

Social History Information that is related to the patient's lifestyle that can affect health.

Sonorous Wheeze Continuous adventitious breath sound caused by the narrowing of large airways or obstruction of a bronchus; a snoring sound.

Soul Essential, spiritual part of a person; thought to continue after physical death.

Spasticity Increase in muscle tension on passive stretching, especially rapid or forced stretching of a muscle.

Spermatic Cord Connective tissue sheath made up of arteries, autonomic nerves, veins, lymphatic vessels, and the cremaster muscle.

Spermatocele Well-defined cystic mass on the superior testes.

Spermatogenesis Production of sperm.

Sphygmomanometer Gauge used to measure blood pressure; consists of a blood pressure cuff with an inflatable bladder, connecting tubes, bulb air pump, and a manometer.

Spider Angioma Bright-red, star-shaped vascular marking that often has a central pulsation; blanches in the extensions when pressure is applied.

Spinnbarkeit Elasticity of cervical mucous during ovulation.

Spirit Soul, being, or supernatural force.

Spiritual Distress State in which a person feels that the belief system, or her or his place within it, is threatened.

Spirituality A person's concern for the meaning and purpose of life.

Sputum Substance that is produced by the respiratory tract and can be expectorated or swallowed; it is composed of mucous, blood, purulent material, microorganisms, cellular debris, and, occasionally, foreign objects.

Squamocolumnar Junction Cervical area between the squamous epithelial surface and the columnar epithelial surface.

Steatorrhea Pale-yellow, greasy, fatty stool.

Stellate Star shaped.

Stenosis Narrowing or constriction (e.g., diseased heart valve).

Stensen's Ducts Ducts through which the parotid glands secrete amylase-rich fluid; located just opposite the upper second molars.

Stereognosis Ability to identify objects by manipulating and touching them.

Sternal Angle *See* **Angle of Louis**.

Stork Bites *See* **Telangiectatic Nevi**.

Strabismus True deviation of gaze due to extraocular muscle dysfunction.

Stratum Corneum Horny layer, or outer layer of the epidermis.

Stratum Germinativum Basal cell layer, or deepest layer of the epidermis.

Stratum Granulosum Epidermal layer where skin cell death occurs; it overlays the stratum spinosum.

Stratum Lucidum Additional layer of skin found exclusively on the palmar and plantar surfaces.

Stratum Spinosum Epidermal layer that overlays the stratum germinativum and consists of layers of polyhedral cells.

Stress Physiologically defined response to changes that disrupt the resting equilibrium of an individual.

Striae Atrophic lines or scars, commonly found on the abdomen, breasts, thighs, or buttocks.

Striae Gravidarum Stretch marks that occur in pregnancy.

Stridor Continuous adventitious breath sound that is caused by a partial airway obstruction in the larynx or trachea; a crowing sound.

Subculture Within a larger cultural group, a smaller group whose members share most of the beliefs and ways of life of the larger cultural group but differ on others.

Subcutaneous Tissue Superficial fascia, composed of loose areolar connective tissue or adipose tissue, depending on its location in the body; it lies below the dermis.

Subjective Data Information, usually gathered from the patient, that cannot always be verified by an independent observer.

Subluxation Partial dislodgement of a bone from its place in the joint cavity.

Sulcus Terminalis Midline depression separating the anterior two-thirds from the posterior one-third of the tongue.

Superego Personality component that represents the internalization of the moral values formed as children interact with their parents and significant others.

Supernumerary Nipples Extra nipples or breast tissue along the milk line resulting from incomplete atrophy of the ectodermal galactic band.

Suprasternal Notch Visible and palpable depression in the midsternal line superior to the manubrium.

Sutures Immovable joints connecting the cranial bones.

Sweat Glands Glands that produce perspiration; composed of two types: eccrine and apocrine glands.

Symptom Subjective finding.

Syncope Fainting; transient loss of consciousness due to decreased oxygen or glucose supply to the brain.

Syndactyly Congenital webbing or fusion of two or more digits on the hand or foot.

Synovial Effusion Excessive synovial joint fluid.

Systole First phase in the cardiac cycle; the myocardial fibres contract and tighten to eject blood from the ventricles.

T

Tachycardia Pulse rate greater than 100 beats per minute in an adult.

Tachypnea Respiratory rate greater than 20 breaths per minute in an adult.

Tactile (or Vocal) Fremitus Palpable vibration of the chest wall that is produced by the spoken word.

Tail of Spence Upper outer quadrant of the breast that extends into the axilla.

Talipes Equinovarus (**Clubfoot**) Medially adducted and inverted toes and forefoot.

Tangential Lighting Light that is shone at an angle on the patient to accentuate shadows and highlight subtle findings.

Tarsal Plates Connective tissue that gives shape to the upper eyelid.

Taxonomy Classification system.

Telangiectatic Nevi Marks appearing on the back of the neck, lower occiput, upper eyelids, and upper lip of the newborn that are flat, deep, irregular, and pink in light-skinned children and deep-red in dark-skinned children; also known as "stork bites."

Temperature Vital sign collected to assess core body heat.

Tendons Ends of the epimysium that attach the muscle to a bone.

Terminal Hair Coarse body hair in the eyebrows, eyelashes, scalp, and the axillary and pubic areas; also found on the chest and face in men.

Termination Stage Last segment of the interview process, during which information is summarized and validated.

Testes Pair of oval glands, located in the scrotum, that produce sperm.

Thenar Eminence Rounded prominence at the base of the thumb.

Thoracic Expansion The extent and symmetry of chest wall expansion.

Thrill Vibration related to turbulent blood flow that feels similar to what one feels when a hand is placed on a purring cat.

Tilts Set of blood pressures taken in supine, sitting, and standing positions.

Torticollis Lateral deviation of the neck; intermittent or sustained dystonic contraction of the muscles on one side of the neck.

Total Iron-Binding Capacity (TIBC) Amount of iron with which transferrin can bind.

Transferrin Protein that regulates iron absorption.

Transmission-Based Precautions Infection control practices involving contact, droplet, and airborne transmission of microorganisms that are known to exist in a patient or are suspected in a patient. They are practiced in conjunction with Routine Practices.

Triceps Skinfold Anthropometric measurement used to determine body fat stores and nutritional status.

Triglyceride Substance that accounts for most of the fat stored in the body's tissues.

True Ribs *See* **Vertebrosternal Ribs**.

Tubular Breath Sound *See* **Bronchial Breath Sound**.

Tumour Palpable, solid, and elevated lesion, greater than 2.0 cm in diameter, that extends deeper than papules into the dermis or subcutaneous tissues.

Turbinate (or Concha) Projection from the lateral wall of the nose; covered with mucous membranes that greatly increase the surface area within the nose.

Turgor Elasticity of the skin; reflects the skin's state of hydration.

Tussive Fremitus Palpable vibration produced by coughing.

Tympany Descriptor for a percussable sound that is loud in intensity, long in duration, of high pitch, drumlike, and normally located over a gastric air bubble.

U

Ulcer A depressed lesion of the epidermis and upper papillary layer of the dermis.

Urethra Duct from the urinary bladder to the urethral meatus; carries urine and, in the male, semen.

Uterus Inverted pear-shaped, hollow, muscular organ in which the impregnated ovum develops into a fetus.

Uvula Fingerlike projection hanging down from the centre of the soft palate.

V

Vagina Pink, hollow, muscular tube extending from the cervix to the vulva; located posterior to the bladder and anterior to the rectum.

Vaginal Introitus Entrance to the vagina, situated at the inferior aspect of the vulval vestibule.

Value Orientation Patterned principles (about time, human nature, activity, relations, and people-to-nature) that provide order and give direction to an individual's thoughts and behaviours related to the solution of commonly occurring human problems.

Varicocele Bluish mass resulting from abnormal dilatation of the veins of the pampiniform plexus of the spermatic cord.

Vellus Hair Fine, faint hair that covers most of the body.

Venous Hum Continuous, medium pitched sound originating in the inferior vena cava and associated with obstructed portal circulation.

Venous Star Linear or irregularly shaped blue vascular pattern on the skin; does not blanch when pressure is applied.

Vernix Caseosa Thick, cheesy, protective, integumentary deposit that consists of sebum and shed epithelial cells; present on the newborn's skin.

Vertebra Prominens The long spinous process of the seventh cervical vertebra.

Vertebrosternal (or True) Ribs Rib pairs 1–7; articulated to the sternum via the costal cartilage.

Vertigo Dizziness or lightheadedness.

Vesicle Elevated mass in the epidermis, less than 0.5 cm. diameter, containing serous fluid.

Vesicular Breath Sound Breath sound that is low in pitch and soft in intensity and is heard best over the peripheral lung; has a breezy, gentle rustling quality; heard longer on inspiration than expiration.

Vestibule Boat-shaped area between the two folds of the labia minora that contains the urethral meatus, openings of the Skene's glands, hymen, openings of the Bartholin's glands, and vaginal introitus.

Vestibule (of the Ear) Part of the inner ear located between the cochlea and the semicircular canals; important in hearing and balance.

Visceral Pericardium Layer of the pericardium that lies against the actual heart muscle.

Visceral Pleura Lining of the external surface of the lungs.

Visual Analog Scale Numerical scale of 0 to 10 used to rate pain.

Vital Signs Measurements, including temperature, pulse, respirations, blood pressure, and level of pain that provide an index of the patient's physiological status.

Vitamin Organic substance needed to maintain the function of the body.

Vitiligo Condition of patchy, symmetrical areas of white on the skin.

Vitreous Humour Clear, gelatinous material that fills the centre cavity of the eye and helps maintain the shape of the eye and the position of the internal structures.

Vocal Fremitus *See* **Tactile Fremitus**.

Voice Sounds Sounds that are assessed to determine whether the lungs are filled with air or fluid, or are solid.

W

Water-Soluble Vitamin Vitamin soluble in water; is not stored in the body and is excreted in the urine.

Weber Test Tuning fork test to evaluate hearing loss and determine whether the loss is conductive or sensorineural.

Wharton's Ducts Ducts through which submaxillary glands secrete fluid in the mouth.

Wheal Localized edema in the epidermis causing irregular elevation that may be red or pale.

Whispered Pectoriloquy Voice sound where the patient whispers the words "ninety-nine" or "one, two, three" to determine if the lungs are filled with air, fluid, or a solid.

Working Stage That segment of the interview process during which the majority of data are collected.

X

Xanthelasma Raised, yellow, nonpainful plaque on the upper and lower eyelids, often secondary to hypercholesterolemia.

Xerosis Excessive dryness of the skin.

Xiphoid Process Cartilaginous protrusion at the base of the sternum; does not articulate with the ribs.

Z

Zosteriform Linear arrangement of lesions along a nerve root.

Contributors

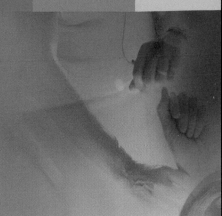

Caroline E. Marchionni RN, MSc Admin, MSc (A.)
Chapter 7, Nutrition

Mitzi Boilanger, RNC, MS
Clinical Nurse Specialist
Clarian Health Partners, Inc.
Indianapolis, Indiana
Chapter 23: Pregnant Patient

Tamera D. Cauthorne-Burnette, RN, MSN, FNP, CS
Family Nurse Practitioner
Montpelier Family Practice
Montpelier, Virginia
and
Family Nurse Practitioner
James E. Jones, Jr., MD and Associates
Obstetrics and Gynecology
Richmond, Virginia
and
Graduate Clinical Faculty
Medical College of Virginia
Virginia Commonwealth University
School of Nursing
Richmond, Virginia
Chapter 10: Skin, Hair, and Nails
Chapter 14: Breasts and Regional Nodes
Chapter 20: Female Genitalia

Catherine Wilson Cox, RN, PhD, CCRN, CEN, CCNS
Assistant Professor
School of Nursing & Health Studies
Georgetown University
Washington, DC
Chapter 16: Heart and Peripheral Vasculature

Jane L. Echols, RN, PhD
Professor of Nursing
School of Health Professions
Marymount University
Arlington, Virginia
Chapter 4: Developmental Assessment
Chapter 5: Cultural Assessment

Barbara Springer Edwards, RN, BSN, MTS
Former Director
Cardiac Surgical Unit
Alexandria Hospital
Alexandria, Virginia
Chapter 6: Spiritual Assessment

Joseph Haymore, RN, MS, CNRN, CCRN, ACNP
Nurse Practitioner
Montgomery Neurosurgery-P.A.
Silver Spring, Maryland
and
Adjunct Clinical Faculty
School of Nursing & Health Studies
Georgetown University
Washington, DC
Chapter 19: Mental Status and Neurological Techniques

Randie R. McLaughlin, MS, CRNP
Certified Adult and Geriatric Nurse Practitioner
Urology Private Practice
Frederick, Maryland
Chapter 21: Male Genitalia
Chapter 22: Anus, Rectum, and Prostate

Kathy Murphy, RN, MSN, CS
Clinical Nurse Specialist
Children's Healthcare of Atlanta
Sibley Heart Center
Atlanta, Georgia
Chapter 24: Pediatric Patient

JoAnne Peach, RN, MSN, FNP
Family Nurse Practitioner
Forest Lakes Family Medicine
Charlottesville, Virginia
Chapter 11: Head, Neck, and Regional Lymphatics
Chapter 12: Eyes
Chapter 13: Ears, Nose, Mouth, and Throat

Susan Abbott Rogge, RN, NP
Department of Obstetrics and Gynecology
University of California, Davis
Sacramento, California
and
Private Practice
Sacramento, California
Chapter 23: Pregnant Patient

Bonnie R. Sakallaris, RN, MSN
Director, Cardiac Services
Washington Hospital Center
Washington, DC
Chapter 19: Mental Status and Neurological Techniques

Index

Assessment in Brief

Heart and Peripheral Vasculature Assessment

Assessment of the Precordium
- Inspection
  - Aortic area
  - Pulmonic area
  - Midprecordial area
  - Tricuspid area
  - Mitral area
- Palpation
  - Aortic area
  - Pulmonic area
  - Midprecordial area
  - Tricuspid area
  - Mitral area
- Auscultation
  - Aortic area
  - Pulmonic area
  - Midprecordial area
  - Tricuspid area
  - Mitral area
  - Mitral and tricuspid areas (S_3)
  - Mitral and tricuspid areas (S_4)
  - Murmurs
  - Pericardial friction rub
  - Prosthetic heart valves

continues

Assessment in Brief

Abdominal Assessment

Inspection
- Contour
- Symmetry
- Rectus abdominis muscles
- Pigmentation and colour
- Scars
- Striae
- Respiratory movement
- Masses or nodules
- Visible peristalsis
- Pulsation
- Umbilicus

Auscultation
- Bowel sounds
- Vascular sounds
- Venous hum
- Friction rubs

Percussion
- General percussion
- Liver span
- Liver descent
- Spleen
- Stomach
- Fist percussion
  - Kidney
  - Liver
- Bladder

Palpation
- Light palpation
- Deep palpation
- Liver
  - Bimanual method
  - Hook method
- Spleen
- Kidneys
- Aorta
- Bladder
- Inguinal lymph nodes

continues

Assessment in Brief

Musculoskeletal Assessment

General Assessment
- Overall appearance
- Posture
- Gait and mobility

Inspection
- Muscle size and shape
- Joint contour and periarticular tissue

Palpation
- Muscle tone
- Joints

Range of Motion

Muscle Strength

Examination of Joints
- Temporomandibular joint
- Cervical spine
- Shoulders
- Elbows
- Wrists and hands
- Hips
- Knees
- Ankles and feet
- Spine

Advanced Techniques
- Measuring limb circumference
- Using a goniometer
- Chvostek's sign (assessing for neuroexcitability)
- Trousseau's sign (assessing for neuroexcitability)
- Drop arm test (assessing for rotator cuff damage)

continues

Assessment in Brief

Mental Status Assessment and Neurological Techniques

Mental Status Assessment
- Physical appearance and behaviour
  - Posture and movements
  - Dress, grooming, and personal hygiene
  - Facial expression
  - Affect
- Communication
- Level of consciousness
- Cognitive abilities and mentation
  - Attention
  - Memory
  - Judgment
  - Insight
  - Spatial perception
  - Calculation
  - Abstract reasoning
  - Thought process and content
  - Suicidal ideation

Sensory Assessment
- Exteroceptive sensation
  - Light touch
  - Superficial pain
  - Temperature
- Proprioceptive sensation
  - Motion and position
  - Vibration sense
- Cortical sensation
  - Stereognosis
  - Graphesthesia
  - Two-point discrimination
  - Extinction

continues

Advanced Techniques

- Assessing for ascites
  - Shifting dullness
  - Puddle sign
- Fluid wave
- Murphy's sign

- Rebound tenderness
- Rovsing's sign
- Cutaneous hypersensitivity
- Iliopsoas muscle test
- Obturator muscle test

Abdominal Tubes and Drains

- Tubes
  - Enteral tube
  - Nasogastric suction tube
  - Intestinal tube
  - Gastrostomy
- Drains
  - Abdominal cavity drain
  - Biliary drain

- Intestinal diversions
  - Colostomy
  - Ileostomy
- Urinary diversions
  - Ileal conduit
  - Ureteral stent
  - Indwelling catheter

Assessment of the Peripheral Vasculature

- Inspection of the jugular venous pressure
- Inspection of the hepatojugular reflux
- Palpation and auscultation of arterial pulses
- Inspection and palpation of peripheral perfusion
  - Peripheral pulse
  - Colour
  - Clubbing
  - Capillary refill
  - Skin temperature
  - Edema
  - Ulcerations
  - Skin texture
  - Hair distribution
- Palpation of the epitrochlear node

Advanced Techniques

- Orthostatic hypotension assessment
- Assessing for pulsus paradoxus
- Assessing the venous system
  - Homan's sign
  - Manual compression
- Assessing the arterial system
  - Pallor
  - Colour return and venous filling time
  - Allen test

Cranial Nerves Assessment

- Olfactory nerve (CN I)
- Optic nerve (CN II)
  - Visual acuity
  - Visual fields
  - Funduscopic examination
- Oculomotor nerve (CN III)
  - Cardinal fields of gaze
  - Eyelid elevation
  - Pupil reactions
- Trochlear nerve (CN IV)
  - Cardinal fields of gaze
- Trigeminal nerve (CN V)
  - Motor component
  - Sensory component
- Abducens nerve (CN VI)
  - Cardinal fields of gaze

- Facial nerve (CN VII)
  - Motor component
  - Sensory component
- Acoustic nerve (CN VIII)
  - Cochlear division
    Hearing
    Weber test
    Rinne test
  - Vestibular division
- Glossopharyngeal nerve (CN IX)
- Vagus nerve (CN X)
- Spinal accessory nerve (CN XI)
- Hypoglossal nerve (CN XII)

Motor System Assessment

- Muscle size
- Muscle tone
- Muscle strength
- Involuntary movements
- Pronator drift

Cerebellar Function

- Coordination
- Gait

- Assessing grip strength using a blood pressure cuff
- Tinel's sign (assessing for carpal tunnel syndrome)
- Phalen's sign (assessing for carpal tunnel syndrome)
- Trendelenburg test (assessing for hip dislocation)
- Measuring limb length
- Bulge sign (assessing for small effusions)
- Patellar ballottement (assessing for large effusions)
- McMurray's sign (assessing for meniscal tears)
- Anterior drawer test (assessing for ankle sprain)
- Talar tilt test (assessing for ankle sprain)
- Assessing neurovascular status of distal limbs and digits
- Adams forward bend test (assessing for scoliosis) and use of the scoliometer
- Straight leg-raising test (Lasègue's test) (assessing for herniated disc)

Assistive Devices

- Crutches
- Cane
- Walker
- Brace, splint, immobilizer
- Cast

continues

Reflexes

- Deep tendon reflexes
  - Brachioradialis
  - Biceps
  - Triceps
  - Patellar
  - Achilles
- Superficial reflexes
  - Abdominal
  - Plantar
  - Cremasteric
  - Bulbocavernosus
- Pathological reflexes
  - Glabellar
  - Clonus
  - Babinski

Advanced Techniques

- Doll's eyes phenomenon
- Romberg test
- Meningeal irritation
  - Nuchal rigidity
  - Kernig's sign
  - Brudzinski's sign

Assessment in Brief

Female Genitalia Assessment

Inspection of the External Genitalia

- Pubic hair
- Skin colour and condition
  - Mons pubis and vulva
  - Clitoris
  - Urethral meatus
  - Vaginal introitus
  - Perineum and anus

Palpation of the External Genitalia

- Labia
- Urethral meatus and Skene's glands
- Vaginal introitus
- Perineum

Speculum Examination of the Internal Genitalia

- Cervix
  - Colour
  - Position
  - Size
  - Surface characteristics
  - Discharge
  - Shape of the cervical os

continues

Assessment in Brief

Male Genitalia Assessment

Inspection

- Sexual maturity rating
- Hair distribution
- Penis
- Scrotum
- Urethral meatus
- Inguinal area

Palpation

- Penis
- Urethral meatus
- Scrotum
- Inguinal area

Auscultation

- Scrotum

Advanced Techniques

- Urethral culture: Identifying penile pathogens
- Prehn's sign: Assessing for testicular torsion
- Transillumination of the scrotum: Assessing for a scrotal mass

Assessment in Brief

Anus, Rectum, and Prostate Assessment

Inspection

- Perineum and sacrococcygeal area
- Anal mucosa

Palpation

- Anus and rectum
- Prostate

Collecting Specimens for Cytological Smears and Cultures
- Pap smear
  - Endocervical smear
  - Cervical smear
  - Vaginal pool smear
- Chlamydia culture specimen
- Gonococcal culture specimen
- Saline mount or "wet prep"
- KOH prep
- Five percent acetic acid wash
- Anal culture

Inspection of the Vaginal Wall

Bimanual Examination
- Vagina
- Cervix
- Fornices
- Uterus
- Adnexa

Rectovaginal Examination

Assessment in Brief

Assessment of the Pregnant Patient*

Fundal Height

Fetal Heart Rate

Leopold's Manoeuvre
- First manoeuvre
- Second manoeuvre
- Third manoeuvre
- Fourth manoeuvre

Only pregnancy-specific assessments are listed.

Assessment in Brief

Pediatric Patient Assessment*

Physical Growth
- Weight
- Length or height
- Head circumference
- Average weight gain
- Growth patterns
- Body mass index

Physical Assessment
- Apgar scoring
- Head
  - Inspection
    Head control
  - Palpation
    Anterior fontanel
    Posterior fontanel
    Suture lines
    Surface characteristics
- Eyes
  - Vision screening
    Allen test

Only pediatric-specific tests are listed.

 continues

Assessment in Brief

Family Health History

The family health history records the health status of the patient as well as immediate blood relatives. At a minimum, the history needs to contain the age and health status of the patient, spouse, children, siblings, and the patient's parents. Ideally, the patient's grandparents, aunts, and uncles should be incorporated into the history as well. Documentation of this information is done in two parts: the genogram, or family tree, and a list of familial diseases.

The second component of the family health history is the report of occurrences of familial or genetic diseases. Such information is crucial to the patient's health and may not have been revealed previously because some familial illnesses do not occur in every generation. The pertinent negative findings are documented in the family health history below the genogram.

 continues

Assessment in Brief

Review of Systems

General
- Patient's perception of general state of health at the present, difference from usual state, vitality and energy levels, body odours, fever, chills, night sweats

Skin
- Rashes, itching, changes in skin pigmentation, ecchymoses, change in colour or size of mole, sores, lumps, dry or moist skin, pruritus, change in skin texture, odours, excessive sweating, acne, warts, eczema, psoriasis, amount of time spent in the sun, use of sunscreen, skin cancer

Hair
- Alopecia, excessive growth of hair or growth of hair in unusual locations (hirsutism), use of chemicals on hair, dandruff, pediculosis, scalp lesions

Nails
- Change in nails, splitting, breaking, thickened, texture change, onychomycosis, use of chemicals, false nails

Eyes
- Blurred vision, visual acuity, glasses, contacts, photophobia, excessive tearing, night blindness, diplopia, drainage, bloodshot eyes, pain, blind spots, flashing lights, halos around objects, floaters, glaucoma, cataracts, use of sunglasses, use of protective eyewear

 continues

- Musculoskeletal system
  - Inspection
    Tibiofemoral bones
  - Palpation
    Feet (metatarsus varus)
    Hip and femur (Ortolani's manoeuvre)
- Neurological System
  - Rooting
  - Sucking
  - Palmar grasp
  - Tonic neck
  - Stepping
  - Plantar grasp
  - Babinski
  - Moro (startle)
  - Galant
  - Placing
  - Landau

Advanced Techniques
- Assessing for hydrocephalus and anencephaly:
  Transillumination of the skull
- Assessing for coarctation of the aorta

Ears
- Cleaning method, hearing deficits, hearing aid, pain, phonophobia, discharge, lightheadedness (vertigo), ringing in the ears (tinnitus), usual noise level, earaches, infection, piercings, use of ear protection, amount of cerumen

Nose and Sinuses
- Number of colds per year, discharge, itching, hay fever, postnasal drip, stuffiness, sinus pain, sinusitis, polyps, obstruction, epistaxis, change in sense of smell, allergies, snoring

Mouth
- Dental habits (brushing, flossing, mouth rinses), toothache, tooth abscess, dentures, bleeding or swollen gums, difficulty chewing, sore tongue, change in taste, lesions, change in salivation, bad breath, caries, teeth extractions, orthodontics

Throat and Neck
- Hoarseness, change in voice, frequent sore throats, dysphagia, pain or stiffness, enlarged thyroid (goiter), lymphadenopathy, tonsillectomy, adenoidectomy

Breasts and Axilla
- Pain, tenderness, discharge, lumps, change in size, dimpling, rash, benign breast disease, breast cancer, results of recent mammogram, breast self-examination.

Respiratory
- Dyspnea on exertion, shortness of breath, sputum, cough, sneezing, wheezing, hemoptysis, frequent upper respiratory tract infections, pneumonia, emphysema, asthma, tuberculosis, tuberculosis exposure, result of last chest X-ray or PPD

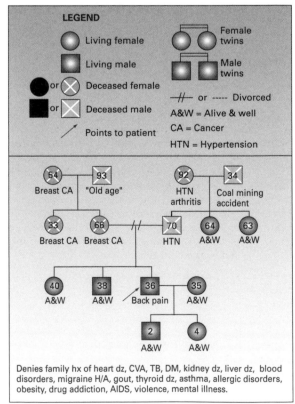

Family Health History and Genogram

Cardiovascular and Peripheral Vasculature

- Paroxysmal nocturnal dyspnea, chest pain, cyanosis, heart murmur, palpitations, syncope, orthopnea (state number of pillows used), edema, cold or discoloured hands or feet, leg cramps, myocardial infarction, hypertension, valvular disease, intermittent claudication, varicose veins, thrombophlebitis, deep vein thrombosis, use of support hose, anemia, result of last ECG

Gastrointestinal

- Change in appetite, nausea, vomiting, diarrhea, constipation, usual bowel habits, melena, rectal bleeding, hematemesis, change in stool colour, flatulence, belching, regurgitation, heartburn, dysphagia, abdominal pain, jaundice, ascites, hemorrhoids, hepatitis, peptic ulcers, gallstones, gastro-esophageal reflux disease, appendicitis, ulcerative colitis, Crohn's disease, diverticulitis, hernia

Urinary

- Change in urine colour, voiding habits, dysuria, hesitancy, urgency, frequency, nocturia, polyuria, dribbling, loss in force of stream, bedwetting, change in urine volume, incontinence, urinary retention, suprapubic pain, flank pain, kidney stones, urinary tract infections

Musculoskeletal

- Joint stiffness, muscle pain, cramps, back pain, limitation of movement, redness, swelling, weakness, bony deformity, broken bones, dislocations, sprains, crepitus, gout, arthritis, osteoporosis, herniated disc

continues

Assessment in Brief

Complete Health History

- Today's date

Biographical Data

- Patient's name
- Address
- Phone number
- Date of birth
- Birth place
- Health Care Number
- Occupation
- Work address and phone number
- Usual source of health care
- Source of referral
- Emergency contact
- Source and Reliability of Information

Patient Profile

- Age
- Gender
- Ethnicity
- Brief summary of appearance

Health issue or concern

Present health and history of health issue or concern

Past Health History

- Medical history
- Surgical history
- Medications

continues

Health Maintenance Activities

- Sleep
- Diet
- Exercise
- Stress management
- Use of safety devices
- Health check-ups

Review of Systems

- General
- Skin
- Hair
- Nails
- Eyes
- Ears
- Nose and sinuses
- Mouth
- Throat and neck
- Respiratory
- Cardiovascular and peripheral vasculature
- Breasts and axilla
- Gastrointestinal
- Urinary
- Musculoskeletal
- Neurological
- Psychological
- Reproductive
- Nutrition
- Endocrine
- Lymph nodes
- Hematological

Endocrine

- Exophthalmos, fatigue, change in size of head, hands, or feet, weight change, heat and cold intolerances, excessive sweating, polydipsia, polyphagia, polyuria, increased hunger, change in body hair distribution, goiter, diabetes mellitus

Lymph Nodes

- Enlargement, tenderness

Hematological

- Easy bruising or bleeding, anemia, sickle cell anemia, blood type, exposure to radiation

   – Prescriptions
   – OTC
- Communicable diseases
- Allergies
- Injuries and accidents
- Special needs
- Blood transfusions
- Childhood illnesses
- Immunizations

Family Health History

Social History

- Alcohol use
- Drug use
- Tobacco use
- Domestic and intimate partner violence
- Sexual practice
- Travel history
- Work environment
- Home environment
   – Physical environment
   – Psychosocial environment
- Hobbies and leisure activities
- Stress
- Education
- Economic status
- Religion and spirituality
- Ethnicity
- Roles and relationships
- Characteristic patterns of daily living

Neurological
- Headache, change in balance, incoordination, loss of movement, change in sensory perception or feeling in an extremity, change in speech, change in smell, syncope, loss of memory, tremors, involuntary movement, loss of consciousness, seizures, weakness, head injury, vertigo, tic, paralysis, stroke, spasm

Psychological
- Irritability, nervousness, tension, increased stress, difficulty concentrating, mood changes, suicidal thoughts, depression, anxiety, sleep disturbances

Female Reproductive
- Vaginal discharge, change in libido, infertility, sterility, pelvic pain, pain during intercourse, postcoital bleeding; menses: last menstrual period (LMP), menarche, regularity, duration, amount of bleeding, premenstrual symptoms, intramenstrual bleeding, dysmenorrhea, menorrhagia, fibroids; menopause: age of onset, duration, symptoms, bleeding; obstetrical: number of pregnancies, number of miscarriages or abortions, number of children, type of delivery, complications; type of birth control, hormone replacement therapy

Male Reproductive
- Change in libido, infertility, sterility, impotence, pain during intercourse, age at onset of puberty, testicular or penile pain, penile discharge, erections, emissions, hernias, enlarged prostate, type of birth control, testicular self-examination

Nutrition
- Present weight, usual weight, desired weight, food intolerances, food likes and dislikes, where meals are eaten, caffeine intake, vitamin supplements

continues

continues

Assessment in Brief

Effective Interviewing

- Be aware of your personal beliefs and how they were acquired. Avoid imposing your beliefs on those you interview.
- Listen and observe. Attend to verbal and affective content as well as to nonverbal cues.
- Focus your attention on the patient. Do not listen with "half an ear." Do not think about other things when you are interviewing.
- Maintain eye contact with the patient as is appropriate for the patient's culture.
- Notice the patient's speech patterns and any recurring themes. Note any extra emphasis that the patient places on certain words or topics.
- Do not assume that you understand the meaning of all patient communications. Clarify frequently.
- Paraphrase and summarize occasionally to help patients organize their thinking, clarify issues, and begin to explore specific concerns more deeply.
- Allow for periods of silence.
- Remember that attitudes and feelings may be conveyed nonverbally.
- Consistently monitor your reactions to the patient's verbal and nonverbal messages.
- Do not judge, criticize, or preach.
- Avoid the use of nontherapeutic interviewing techniques.

Assessment in Brief

General Approach to the Health History

- Present with a professional appearance. Avoid extremes in dress so that your appearance does not hinder information gathering.
- Ensure an appropriate environment, e.g., adequate privacy, good lighting, comfortable temperature, and ensure there are no noise or distractions.
- Sit facing the patient at eye level, with the patient in a chair or on a bed. Ensure that the patient is as comfortable as possible because obtaining the health history can be a lengthy process.
- Ask the patient whether he or she has any questions about the interview before it is started.
- Avoid the use of medical jargon. Use terms the patient can understand.
- Ask intimate and personal questions only when rapport has been established.
- Remain flexible in obtaining the health history. It does not have to be obtained in the exact order it is presented in this chapter or on institutional forms.
- Remind the patient that all information will be treated confidentially.

Assessment in Brief

Developmental Assessment

- Note the patient's stated chronological age.
- Tailor your questions to the patient's expected level of ability according to developmental parameters until you can accurately assess the actual developmental level.
- When assessing small children, verify information with the caregiver.
- If a third party is assisting in the interview (for an elderly or handicapped patient), address all questions to the patient, not the intermediary.

Assessment in Brief

Fundamental Cultural Values

- What are the values and beliefs that most characterize each culture and subculture to which you belong, and with which do you agree?
- Do any of your values and beliefs that are derived from membership in one culture or subculture conflict with those from any other?
- If there is any conflict between the values of two or more of the cultures or subcultures with which you identify (e.g., health care professional subculture, religious subculture, socioeconomic subculture, political party subculture), have you resolved these conflicts, and if so, how have you done this and what helped you to reconcile these conflicts?
- What is your time orientation?
- What do you believe about the basic nature of human beings?
- What do you believe is your basic nature?
- What do you believe is your primary purpose in life?
- What do you believe about the purpose of human relations?
- What do you believe your relation is to nature and the supernatural?

Assessment in Brief

General Approach to Spiritual Assessment

- Conduct this assessment as part of the history-taking portion of a general patient assessment once trust has been established, rather than as a stand-alone interview.
- Choose a quiet, private room that will be free from interruptions.
- Ensure that the room's light is sufficiently bright to observe the patient's verbal and nonverbal reactions.
- Greet the patient, introduce yourself, and explain that you will be taking a health history.
- Position yourself at eye level with the patient.
- Portray an interested, nonjudgmental manner throughout the interview. Respect silence and diversity.

Assessment in Brief

Nutritional Assessment

Nutritional History

Physical Assessment

Anthropometric Measurements
- Height
- Weight
- Body mass index (BMI)
- Waist-to-hip ratio
- Skinfold thickness
- Mid-arm and mid-arm muscle circumference

Laboratory Data
- Hematocrit/hemoglobin
- Lipids
- Transferrin, total iron-binding capacity, and iron
- Total lymphocyte count
- Antigen skin testing
- Prealbumin
- Albumin
- Glucose
- Creatinine height index
- Nitrogen balance

Diagnostic Data
- X-rays
- DEXA scan

Assessment in Brief

Comprehensive Nutritional Assessment

Nutritional History

Physical Assessment
- General appearance
- Skin
- Nails
- Hair
- Eyes
- Mouth
- Head and neck
- Heart and peripheral vasculature
- Abdomen
- Musculoskeletal system
- Neurological system
- Female genitalia

Anthropometric Measurements
- Height: _____ cm
- Weight: _____ kg
- % Usual body weight: _____
- % Weight change: _____
- Body Mass Index (BMI): _____
- Waist-to-hip ratio: _____
- Triceps skinfold: _____ mm
- Mid-arm circumference: _____ cm
- Mid-arm muscle circumference: _____ cm

 continues

Assessment in Brief

Diet History

Part 1: General Diet Information
- Do you follow a particular diet?
- What are your food likes and dislikes?
- Do you have any especially strong cravings?
- How often do you eat fast foods?
- How often do you eat at restaurants?
- Do you have adequate financial resources to purchase your food?
- How do you obtain, store, and prepare your food?
- Do you eat alone or with a family member or other person?
- In the last 12 months have you
  - Experienced any change in weight?
  - Had a change in your appetite?
  - Had a change in your diet?
  - Experienced nausea, vomiting, or diarrhea from your diet?
  - Changed your diet because of difficulty in feeding yourself, eating, chewing, or swallowing?

 continues

Questions for Ascertaining a Patient's Spiritual Beliefs

- What kind of faith do you have?
- Are you a person of faith?
- Do you attend worship services regularly?
- What is the most important thing in your life?
- What do you depend on when things go wrong?
- Do you pray?
- What do you believe in?
- Why do you think you have become ill now?
- Is there anything more important to you than regaining your health?

Diet History continued (2 of 2)

Part 2: Food Intake History
(24-hour recall, three-day diary, direct observation)

Time	Food/Drink	Amount	Method of Preparation	Eating Location

Comprehensive Nutritional Assessment continued (2 of 2)

Laboratory Data

- Hematocrit (Hct): _____
- Hemoglobin (Hgb): _____ g/L
- Cholesterol: _____ mmol/L
- HDL–C: _____ mmol/L
- LDL–C: _____ mmol/L
- Total cholesterol: HDL–C:_____ ratio
- Triglycerides: _____ mmol/L
- Transferrin: _____ g/L
- TIBC: _____ μmol/L
- Iron: _____ μmol/L
- Total lymphocyte count: _____ 10^9cells/L
- Antigen skin testing: _____
- Prealbumin: _____ mg/L
- Albumin: _____ g/L
- Glucose: _____ mmol/L
- CHI: _____ %
- Nitrogen balance: _____ g

Diagnostic Data

- X-rays _____
- DEXA Scan _____

Assessment in Brief

Physical Assessment Techniques

Inspection
- Vision
- Smell

Palpation
- Light palpation
- Deep palpation

Percussion
- Immediate, or direct, percussion
- Mediate, or indirect, percussion
- Direct fist percussion
- Indirect fist percussion

Auscultation
- Immediate, or direct, auscultation
- Mediate, or indirect, auscultation

Assessment in Brief

General Survey, Vital Signs, and Pain

General Survey
- Physical presence
  - Stated age versus apparent age
  - General appearance
  - Body fat
  - Stature
  - Motor activity
  - Body and breath odours
- Psychological presence
  - Dress, grooming, and personal hygiene
  - Mood and manner
  - Speech
  - Facial expression
- Distress

Vital Signs
- Respiration
- Pulse
- Temperature
- Blood pressure

Pain
- Location
- Radiation
- Quality
- Quantity
- Associated manifestations
- Aggravating and alleviating factors
- Setting
- Timing
- Meaning and impact

Assessment in Brief

Skin, Hair, and Nails Assessment

Inspection of the Skin
- Colour
- Bleeding, ecchymosis, and vascularity
- Lesions

Palpation of the Skin
- Moisture
- Temperature
- Tenderness
- Texture
- Turgor
- Edema

Inspection of the Hair
- Colour
- Distribution
- Lesions

Palpation of the Hair
- Texture

Inspection of the Nails
- Colour
- Shape and configuration

Palpation of the Nails
- Texture

Advanced Technique
- Skin scraping for scabies

Assessment in Brief

Head, Neck, and Regional Lymphatics Assessment

Inspection
- Shape of the head
- Scalp
- Face
  - Symmetry
  - Shape and features
- Neck
- Thyroid gland
- Lymph nodes

Palpation
- Head
- Scalp
- Mandible
- Neck
- Thyroid gland
  - Posterior approach
  - Anterior approach
- Lymph nodes

Auscultation
- Mandible
- Thyroid gland

Assessment in Brief

Eye Assessment

Visual Acuity
• Distance vision
• Near vision
• Colour vision

Visual Fields

External Eye and Lacrimal Apparatus
• Eyelids
• Lacrimal apparatus
  – Inspection
  – Palpation

Extraocular Muscle Function
• Corneal light reflex
• Cover/uncover test
• Cardinal fields of gaze

Anterior Segment Structures
• Conjunctiva
• Sclera
• Cornea
• Anterior chamber
• Iris
• Pupil
• Lens

Posterior Segment Structures
• Retinal structures
• Macula

Assessment in Brief

Ears, Nose, Mouth, and Throat Assessment

Ears
• Auditory screening
  – Voice-whisper test
  – Tuning fork tests
    Weber test
    Rinne test
• External ear
  – Inspection
  – Palpation
• Otoscopic Assessment

Nose
• External inspection
• Patency
• Internal inspection

Sinuses
• Inspection
• Palpation and percussion

Mouth and Throat
• Mouth
  – Breath
  – Lips
    Inspection
    Palpation
  – Tongue
  – Buccal mucosa
  – Gums
  – Teeth
  – Palate
• Throat

Advanced Technique
• Transillumination of the sinuses

Assessment in Brief

Breasts and Regional Nodes Assessment

Inspection
• Colour
• Vascularity
• Thickening or edema
• Size and symmetry
• Contour
• Lesions or masses
• Discharge

Palpation
• Supraclavicular and infraclavicular lymph nodes
• Breasts: Patient in sitting position
• Axillary lymph node region
• Breasts: Patient in supine position

Assessment in Brief

Thorax and Lung Assessment

Inspection
• Shape of thorax
• Symmetry of chest wall
• Presence of superficial veins
• Costal angle
• Angle of the ribs
• Intercostal spaces
• Muscles of respiration
• Respirations
  – Rate
  – Pattern
  – Depth
  – Symmetry
  – Audibility
  – Patient position
  – Mode of breathing
• Sputum

Palpation
• General palpation
  – Pulsations
  – Masses
  – Thoracic tenderness
  – Crepitus
• Thoracic expansion
• Tactile fremitus
• Tracheal position

continues

Percussion
- General percussion
- Diaphragmatic excursion

Auscultation
- General auscultation
- Breath sounds
- Voice sounds

Advanced Techniques
- Forced expiratory time

Assistive Devices
- Oxygen
- Incentive spirometer
- Endotracheal tube
- Tracheostomy tube
- Mechanical ventilation
- Pulse oximeter
- Peak flow meter

Abbreviations

A, A, & O × 3	awake, alert, & oriented times three (to person, place & time)
$\overline{a}$	before
AB	abortion
abd	abdomen; abdominal
ABG	arterial blood gas
Abx	antibiotic
$\overline{ac}$	before meals
AC>BC	air conduction is greater than bone conduction
AC<BC	air conduction is less than bone conduction
ACL	anterior cruciate ligament
AD*	right ear
ADL	activities of daily living
AEB	as evidenced by
AFI	amniotic fluid index
AGA	appropriate for gestational age
AIDS	acquired immunodeficiency syndrome
AKA	above the knee amputation
ALS	amyotrophic lateral sclerosis
ant	anterior
AOM	acute otitis media
AP	apical pulse; anteroposterior
A&P	anterior & posterior; auscultation & percussion
AROM	active range of motion; artificial rupture of membranes
AS	aortic stenosis
AS*	left ear
ASA	acetylsalicylic acid
ASD	atrial septal defect
Atb	antibiotic
AU*	both ears
AV	arteriovenous
A-V	atrioventricular
A&W	alive & well
AWMI	anterior wall myocardial infarction
ax	axillary
bid	twice a day
bil	bilateral
BKA	below the knee amputation
BP	blood pressure
BPH	benign prostatic hypertrophy
BPM	beats per minute
BS	bowel sounds; breath sounds
b/t	between
BSE	breast self-examination
BUN	blood urea nitrogen
bx	biopsy
C	Celsius, centigrade
$\overline{c}$	with
CA	cancer
CABG	coronary artery bypass graft
CAD	coronary artery disease
CBS	capillary blood sugar
CC	chief complaint
cc*	cubic centimeter
CCD	congenital cardiovascular defect
CHD	childhood diseases; congenital heart disease
CHF	congestive heart failure
CHI	closed head injury; creatinine height index
CI	chloride
cm	centimeter
CMT	cervical motion tenderness
CMV	cytomegalovirus
CN I–XII	cranial nerves I–XII
CNS	central nervous system
c/o	complaining of; complaints of
CO_2	carbon dioxide
COA	coarctation of the aorta
COPD	chronic obstructive pulmonary disease
CP	chest pain; cerebral palsy
CPD	cephalopelvic disproportion
creat	creatinine
CRC	colorectal cancer
C/S	cesarean section delivery
CT	computerized tomography
CV	cardiovascular
CVA	costovertebral angle; cerebrovascular accident
CVP	central venous pressure
CVS	chorionic villi sampling
CXray	chest X ray
cx	cervix
d	day(s)
DBP	diastolic blood pressure
d/c*	discontinue; discharge
D&C	dilation & curettage
DDST II	Denver Developmental Screening Test II
DES	diethylstilbestrol
DM	diabetes mellitus
DOA	dead on arrival
DOB	date of birth
DOE	dyspnea on exertion
DRE	digital rectal examination
DTR	deep tendon reflex
DUB	dysfunctional uterine bleeding
DVT	deep vein thrombosis
dx	diagnosis
dz	disease
EAC	external auricular canal
EDC	expected date of confinement (delivery date)
EDD	estimated date of delivery
EEG	electroencephalogram
EENT	eyes, ears, nose, throat
EFM	electronic fetal monitoring
EKG	electrocardiogram
ENAP	examination, normal findings, abnormal findings, pathophysiology
EOM	extraocular muscle
ESR	erythrocyte sedimentation rate
ETOH	ethyl alcohol
FAS	fetal alcohol syndrome
Fe	iron
FHH	family health history
FHR	fetal heart rate
FHT	fetal heart tone
FLM	fetal lung maturity
FM	fetal movement
FOB	father of baby
FOBT	fecal occult blood test
FROM	full range of motion
FSH	follicle-stimulating hormone
FTT	failure to thrive
fx	fracture
Ⓖ	gallop
GC	gonorrhea and Chlamydia
GCS	Glasgow Coma Scale
GDM	gestational diabetes mellitus
GERD	gastroesophageal reflux disease
GI	gastrointestinal
GU	genitourinary
GYN	gynecologic
H/A	headache
HCG	human chorionic gonadotropin
HDL	high-density lipoprotein
HEENT	head, eyes, ears, nose, throat
HELLP	hemolysis, elevated liver enzymes, low platelets
H/H	hemoglobin & hematocrit
Hib	Haemophilus influenzae b
HIV	human immunodeficiency virus
hl	health
HNP	herniated nucleus pulposus
h/o	history of
HOB	head of bed
HPI	history of present illness
HPV	human papillomavirus
HR	heart rate
hs*	at bedtime
HSV	herpes simplex virus
HT	height
HTN	hypertension
hx	history
IADL	instrumental activities of daily living
IBW	ideal body weight
ICP	intracranial pressure
ICS	intercostal space
IDM	infant of diabetic mother
IICP	increased intracranial pressure
I&O	intake & output
IOP	intraocular pressure
IPPA	inspection, palpation, percussion, auscultation
IUD	intrauterine device
IUGR	intrauterine growth retardation
IUP	intrauterine pregnancy
IUPC	intrauterine pressure catheter
IV	intravenous
IWMI	inferior wall myocardial infarction
JVD	jugular venous distension
JVP	jugular venous pressure
K^+	potassium
kg	kilogram
KOH	potassium hydroxide
KUB	kidneys, ureters, bladder
L	liter
Ⓛ	left
LAD	left anterior descending (coronary artery)
lat	lateral
LBP	low back pain
LCM	left costal margin
LDL	low-density lipoprotein
LE	lower extremity
lg	large
LGA	large for gestational age
LH	leutinizing hormone
LLE	left lower extremity
LLL	left lower lobe (of lung)
LLQ	left lower quadrant (of abdomen)
LLSB	left lower sternal border
LMD	local medical doctor
LMP	last menstrual period
LOC	level of/loss of consciousness
LSB	left sternal border
LUE	left upper extremity
LUL	left upper lobe (of lung)
LUQ	left upper quadrant (of abdomen)
Ⓜ	murmur
MAC	mid-arm circumference
MAL	midaxillary line
MAMC	mid-arm muscle circumference
MCL	midclavicular line
MD	muscular dystrophy, doctor
Mec	meconium
MF	milk fat
MGR	murmur, gallop, rub
MI	myocardial infarction
MMR	measles, mumps, rubella
MMSE	Mini Mental State Exam
MN	midnight
MRI	magnetic resonance imaging
MS	multiple sclerosis

*The Institute for Safe Medication Practices (ISMP) considers these abbreviations dangerous because of possible misinterpretation. For additional information, see Appendix E: ISMP List of Error-Prone Abbreviations, Symbols, and Dose Designations.